CENTRAL NIGERIA UNMASKED

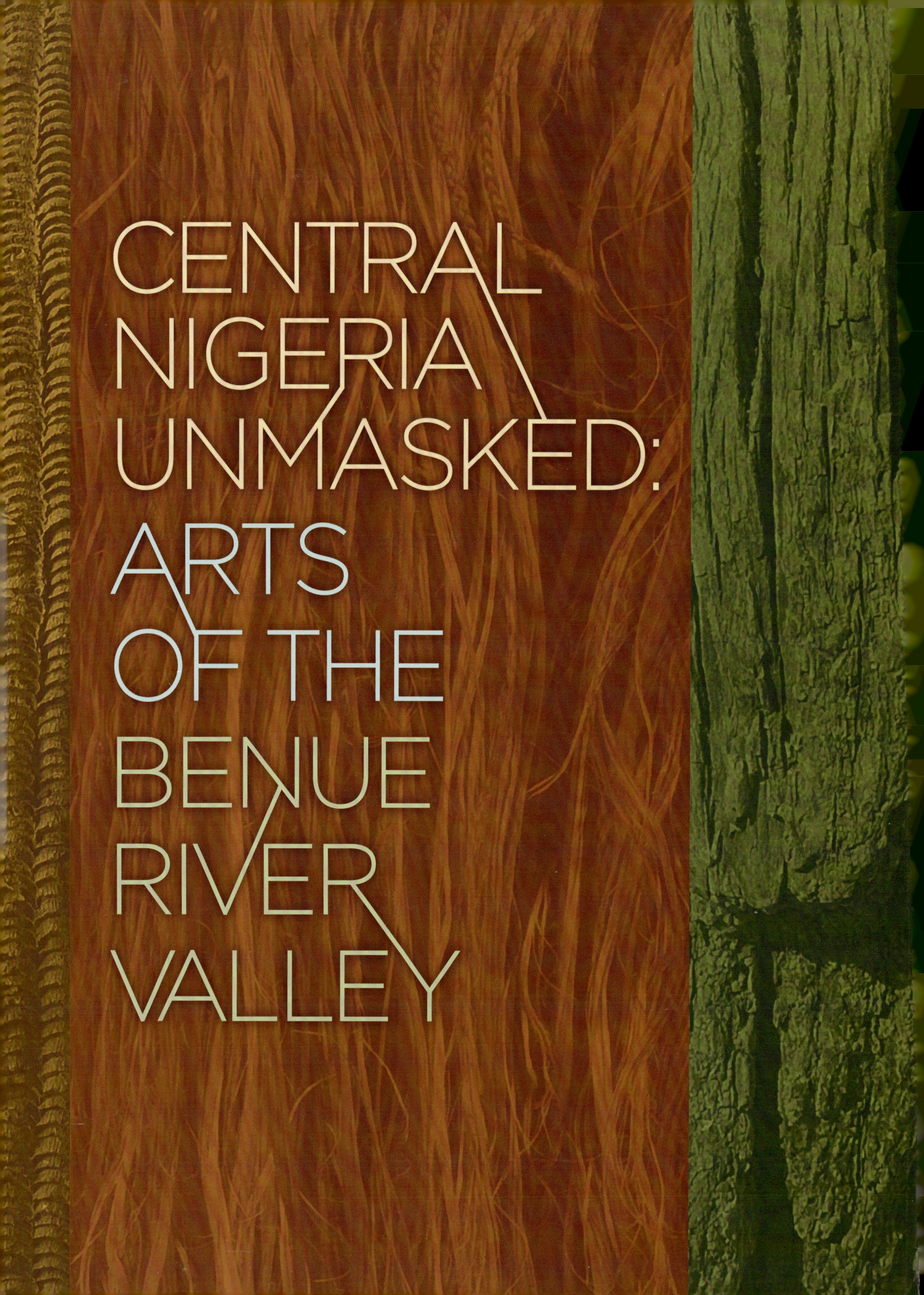

CENTRAL NIGERIA UNMASKED: ARTS OF THE BENUE RIVER VALLEY

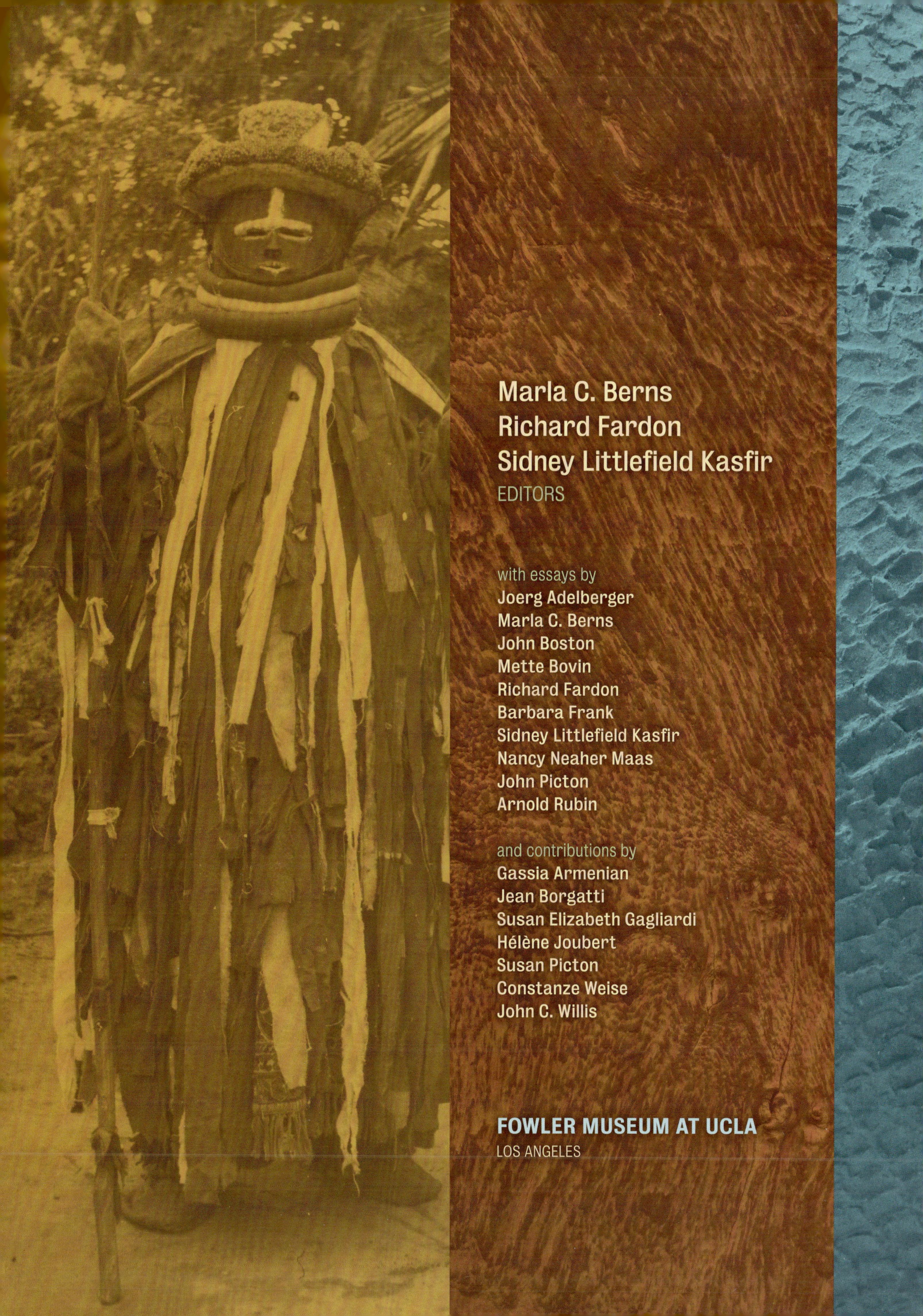

Marla C. Berns
Richard Fardon
Sidney Littlefield Kasfir

EDITORS

with essays by
Joerg Adelberger
Marla C. Berns
John Boston
Mette Bovin
Richard Fardon
Barbara Frank
Sidney Littlefield Kasfir
Nancy Neaher Maas
John Picton
Arnold Rubin

and contributions by
Gassia Armenian
Jean Borgatti
Susan Elizabeth Gagliardi
Hélène Joubert
Susan Picton
Constanze Weise
John C. Willis

FOWLER MUSEUM AT UCLA
LOS ANGELES

PROJECT FUNDING

Major support for *Central Nigeria Unmasked: Arts of the Benue River Valley* is provided by the National Endowment for the Arts, the Shirley and Ralph Shapiro Director's Discretionary Fund, Jay and Deborah Last, Ceil and Michael Pulitzer, the Joseph and Barbara Goldenberg Estate, the Robert T. Wall Family, and Jill and Barry Kitnick.

This publication is made possible by The Ahmanson Foundation with additional support from the Ethnic Arts Council of Los Angeles.

Central Nigeria Unmasked was presented at the Fowler Museum by American Express.

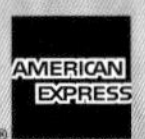

Additional funding for the exhibition is provided by Udo and Wally Horstmann, Edwin and Cherie K. Silver, and Helen Kuhn. Educational outreach programs at the Fowler Museum were made possible by the Wallace Family, the Jerome L. Joss Fund, the Yvonne Lenart Public Programs Fund, and Manus, the support group of the Fowler Museum. The planning phase of the project was funded by a grant from the National Endowment for the Humanities.

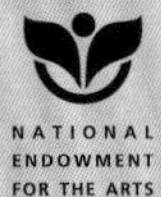 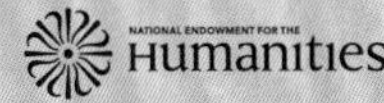

EXHIBITION VENUES

Fowler Museum at UCLA
Los Angeles, California
February 13–July 24, 2011

National Museum of African Art
Smithsonian Institution
Washington, D.C.
September 14, 2011–February 12, 2012

Cantor Arts Center at Stanford University
Stanford, California
May 16–September 2, 2012

Musée du quai Branly
Paris
November 12, 2012–January 27, 2013

LENDERS TO THE EXHIBITION

Individuals

Keith Achepohl

Richard and Jan Baum

Samir and Mina Borro

Mark Clayton

Sidney and Bernice Clyman

Pierre Dartevelle

Alain and Rosemarie Dufour

Michel and Liliane Durand-Dessert

Mark Groudine and Cynthia Putnam

Bernard de Grunne

Barry and Toby Hecht

Udo and Wally Horstmann

Max Itzikovitz

Barry and Jill Kitnick

Aimery Langlois-Meurinne

Jay T. and Deborah Last

Alain and Claudie Lebas

Hélène and Philippe Leloup

Jean-Claude and Nicole Marian

Bruce and Michelle Moore

James and Laura Ross

Richard Scheller

Sieber Collection

Bill and Gale Simmons

Robert Wall and Margaret Rinkevich

Jean-Claude and Josette Weill

James and Lin Willis

Ziff Family

Institutions

Art Institute of Chicago

Barbier-Mueller Museum, Geneva

The British Museum, London

Fine Arts Museums of San Francisco, de Young Museum

Fowler Museum at UCLA

High Museum of Art, Atlanta

The Horniman Museum, London

Indiana University Art Museum, Bloomington

Indianapolis Museum of Art

The Menil Collection, Houston

Metropolitan Museum of Art, New York

Musée du quai Branly, Paris

Museum for African Art, New York

Museum der Kulturen Basel

National Museum of African Art, Smithsonian Institution, Washington, D.C.

New Orleans Museum of Art

Seattle Art Museum

Staatliche Museen zu Berlin, Ethnologisches Museum

Virginia Museum of Fine Arts, Richmond

Yale University Art Gallery, New Haven

Dedication

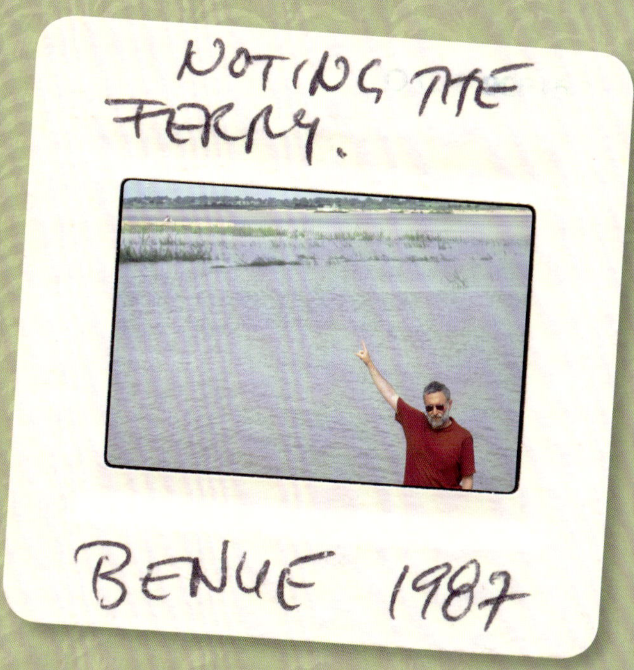

Central Nigeria Unmasked: Arts of the Benue River Valley
is dedicated to the memory of Arnold Rubin, the UCLA art historian
and Benue River Valley scholar who launched this project in the 1980s.

Contents

Forewords

Central Nigeria Unmasked: Arts of the Benue River Valley continues the Fowler Museum's long-standing commitment to investigating the arts of sub-Saharan Africa with a major focus on Nigeria, the most populous and ethnically diverse of its countries. The Museum's exploration of Nigerian arts through exhibitions accompanied by scholarly publications dates to 1971 with the presentation of *Black Gods and Kings: Yoruba Art at UCLA*. This was the first of several endeavors featuring our collections and their connections to new field research on the arts of the Yoruba peoples who occupy Nigeria's southwest and beyond. *Beads, Body, and Soul: Art and Light in the Yoruba Universe* (1998) extended the discussion of Yoruba beadwork in Africa to its rich representation in the Americas. Moving to Nigeria's southeast and its dominant population, the Fowler presented the first comprehensive view of Igbo-speaking peoples in *Igbo Arts: Community and Cosmos* (1984). Alongside such concentrations on single ethnic groups (and we can add to the list the Bini and other Edo-speakers) are projects with a more regional, cross-cultural point of view. *Ways of the Rivers: Arts and Environment of the Niger Delta* (2002) covered an enormous area and took as its subject the complexities of intercultural relationships in this watery zone. *The Essential Gourd: Art and History in Northeastern Nigeria* (1986), also regional in its scope, focused on a single genre whose uses and decoration are as various as the twenty-five ethnic groups who create it. All of these projects drew heavily on the Fowler's own extensive collections of Nigerian art, often engendering new gifts and acquisitions, and always engaging the contributions of key scholars and specialists.

Central Nigeria Unmasked extends this lineage by turning to Nigeria's "Middle Belt" and offering a penetrating account of the many peoples living across the Benue River Valley. Like the Nigerian exhibitions listed above, it too qualifies as a "first": the first to focus on the peoples of this "in-between zone"; the first to feature sculptural traditions never before seen in public exhibitions; and the first to present unpublished field research, field photographs, and films by many important international scholars. This ambitious undertaking adds to the Fowler's history of breaking new ground in terms of scope, subject, and approach.

The near thirty-year-long history of this project at UCLA began with a proposal made by the late art historian Arnold Rubin, as detailed in the preface that follows. The visit to the Fowler of Hélène Joubert, the curator for African collections at the Musée du quai Branly, Paris, in 2005 was the impetus for reinvigorating the endeavor after a long hiatus. I extend my very sincere thanks to Stéphane Martin, President of the Musée du quai Branly, for supporting our curatorial partnership and for sharing my delight in exploring and investigating the intensely inventive arts of the Benue Valley region. Both the Fowler Museum and the Musée du quai Branly have large and diverse Nigerian collections and a shared commitment to their dynamic presentation and thoughtful interpretation. In closing, we would jointly like to acknowledge the support of our colleague, Nath Mayo Adediran, Director of Nigerian Museums, and thank him for applauding our effort to "unmask" the arts of the Benue River Valley and to ensure their place in the pantheon of Nigeria's celebrated artistic traditions.

Marla C. Berns
SHIRLEY & RALPH SHAPIRO DIRECTOR, FOWLER MUSEUM

Central Nigeria Unmasked illuminates the remarkable creativity of peoples occupying the region proximate to the Benue River, a principal tributary of the great Niger. A vast region, the Benue River Valley extends from the very heart of present-day Nigeria eastward to its border with Cameroon, and it is home to a very large number of ethnic and linguistic groups. Among the best known are perhaps the Tiv, Idoma, Jukun, Wurkun, and Mumuye peoples. These groups have all produced sculptures that are remarkable for their variety—some with a startling presence in their abstract forms and tension inherent in their articulations, and others with a grace and equilibrium in their proportions.

The works of art represented in this volume and displayed in the exhibition that accompanies it were selected with great care and precision by a small group of eminent specialists, who benefited from a lengthy period of intense dialogue and deliberation followed by exhaustive efforts to secure appropriate works of art and to provide documentation and contextual illustrations. Drawn from public and private collections in Europe and the United States, these artworks exemplify important formal typologies within the region. At the same time, however, the authors of the present volume have taken great care to demonstrate that the stylistic tendencies visible in these pieces were constantly evolving due to cultural exchanges, mutual influences, and other points of contact in an area that like the Benue River itself was historically in a state of flux. These objects thus speak to us not only through their superb formal qualities but also through the circumstances of their being rooted in a turbulent past, one situated between war and colonization. The end result is, moreover, perhaps the most accurate reflection possible of the history of a very large number of peoples who have yet to reveal to us all the secrets of their creative genius.

I would like to express my sincere gratitude to the director of the Fowler Museum, Marla C. Berns, for being the driving force behind this complicated and ambitious project and bringing together this exceptional group of objects for the book—many heretofore unpublished—and the traveling exhibition that it accompanies. The collaboration of the Musée du quai Branly with the Fowler Museum bears witness to the close cooperative ties that exist between two institutions that are very much a part of an intercultural dialogue and a commitment to the circulation of works of art and of a shared universal patrimony.

I offer thanks as well to Hélène Joubert of the Musée du quai Branly who served as a co-curator of this exhibition. In 2005 Joubert paid a visit to Marla Berns (who is herself a renowned specialist in the arts and traditions of the Benue region and a former student of Arnold Rubin), expressing interest in a project on the arts of the Benue River Valley and in the Arnold Rubin Archive. This fruitful encounter led to the collaboration, spurring Berns to undertake this endeavor, which was initially envisioned many years before.

Finally, my thanks are due to the National Endowment for the Arts for its generous support, as well as to the various lenders, without whom this exhibition would have been impossible.

Stéphane Martin
PRESIDENT, MUSÉE DU QUAI BRANLY, PARIS

A Note from the Director of Museums, National Commission for Museums and Monuments, Nigeria

From the border of the Republic of Cameroon to the Niger-Benue confluence in the center of Nigeria, the Benue River Valley in Nigeria stretches for over 650 miles. It is home to myriad peoples in what is often referred to as Nigeria's "Middle Belt." Its central position is reflected in a history of outside influences that came from both north and south. These resulted in immense complexity and pervasive movement of people, objects, and ideas. Intensive studies of the arts of the region began only in the early twentieth century and had to contend with colonial stereotypes and inadequate knowledge of the complex history of the Benue Valley.

Central Nigeria Unmasked: Arts of the Benue River Valley presents a collection of essays by authors who have studied and documented the arts of the region for decades. It is the most comprehensive revelation of the complicated relationships among the many groups populating the Benue River Valley and their ritual arts. While presenting a vast array of relatively little-known artistic treasures of the region, this book attempts to reconstruct the lost histories of the peoples who created them—their identities, their interactions, and their influences. The exhibition that accompanies the volume is the first of its magnitude ever mounted on the region.

In the year following Nigeria's celebration of its Golden Jubilee, *Central Nigeria Unmasked: Arts of the Benue River Valley* is a welcome development put together by seasoned researchers, anthropologists, art historians, and ethnographers. It is a great delight for me to be associated with this presentation. I thank all the contributors to the book, as well as the coordinators of the wonderful exhibition that accompanies it. Both shed much light on the history, the dynamic relationships, and the sociopolitical interplay of the diverse peoples of the Benue Valley. I congratulate you all and wish all the readers of this volume and viewers of the exhibition enjoyment and the great depth of appreciation and understanding that will accompany it.

Nath Mayo Adediran
DIRECTOR OF MUSEUMS

Preface

Central Nigeria Unmasked presents two remarkable legacies, the full significance of which has begun to be appreciated only with the passage of time. The first is that of the artists of the Benue River Valley, whose works are presented here in their most comprehensive and detailed survey to date. The second is that of the art historian Arnold Rubin (1937–1988), who between October 1964 and January 1966, as a doctoral student, carried out fieldwork extensively throughout the Benue River Valley and intensively on the people called the Jukun, whose history has usually been seen to hold a key to that of the region as a whole. Gaining his doctorate in 1969, Rubin returned to deepen and broaden his survey of the region's arts between September 1969 and March 1971. While also pursuing other interests, he continued to write about the arts of Central Nigeria throughout the 1970s, and by the 1980s he was planning a major project, *Sculpture of the Benue River Valley*, intended to show how the art forms and styles of the region's peoples provided evidence for their history. As he saw it (and wrote in the draft introduction to his manuscript), looking at similarities and differences in the forms, functions, and meanings of objects contributed to building a history of art where "written documents, sequences of monuments, and other conventional art historical resources are unavailable" (1988, 9).

Arnold Rubin first brought the idea for this project to the Fowler Museum (then the UCLA Museum of Cultural History) in the early 1980s, when it was under the leadership of Christopher Donnan, Director, and Doran H. Ross, Associate Director. Drawing on his own extensive fieldwork across the Benue River Valley, Rubin proposed to curate a major exhibition and act as lead author and editor of an accompanying scholarly publication, which would summarize his research. By the time of his untimely death in 1988, Rubin had amassed a large but incomplete inventory of potential objects for the exhibition, identified field photographs for his essays, and completed a draft manuscript for the book. The many boxes of materials accumulated for the Benue River Valley project became a part of Rubin's scholarly archive, which is now housed in the Fowler Museum.

As Rubin's literary executor, I had always intended that the project be completed, both as a tribute to him and his groundbreaking scholarship and observations and because I believed, as he did, that the region's arts were deserving of such comprehensive treatment. As his doctoral student I had done fieldwork in the upper reaches of the Benue centered on its major tributary, the Gongola River, which Rubin had previously visited, determining that its peoples and its arts would be a fruitful subject for study. Not only had Rubin's non-Western courses in the art history department at UCLA completely changed the course of my studies, his unconventional approaches and open-ended definition of what constituted "art" influenced the direction and focus of my field research.

Rubin returned to Nigeria twice in the 1980s, once during my field stay in 1982 when we traveled to a number of Middle Benue towns where he had worked, including the Jukun capital of Wukari (fig. A). In 1987 he made a second, and final, trip with the express purpose of identifying potential objects for the Benue exhibition in Nigerian museums. Now, almost a quarter of a century later, the project he begun has been completed. It encompasses the work of many colleagues and friends, who have all lent

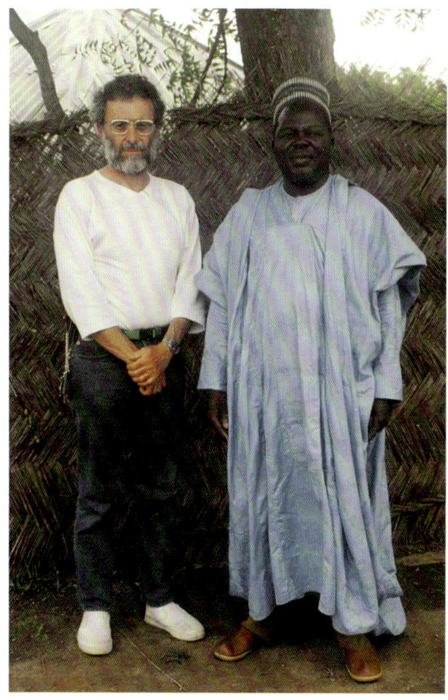

A

Arnold Rubin with the Aku Uka (chief) of Wukari, named Shekarau Angyu Masa Ibi Kuvyon II.
PHOTOGRAPH BY MARLA C. BERNS, WUKARI, 1982.

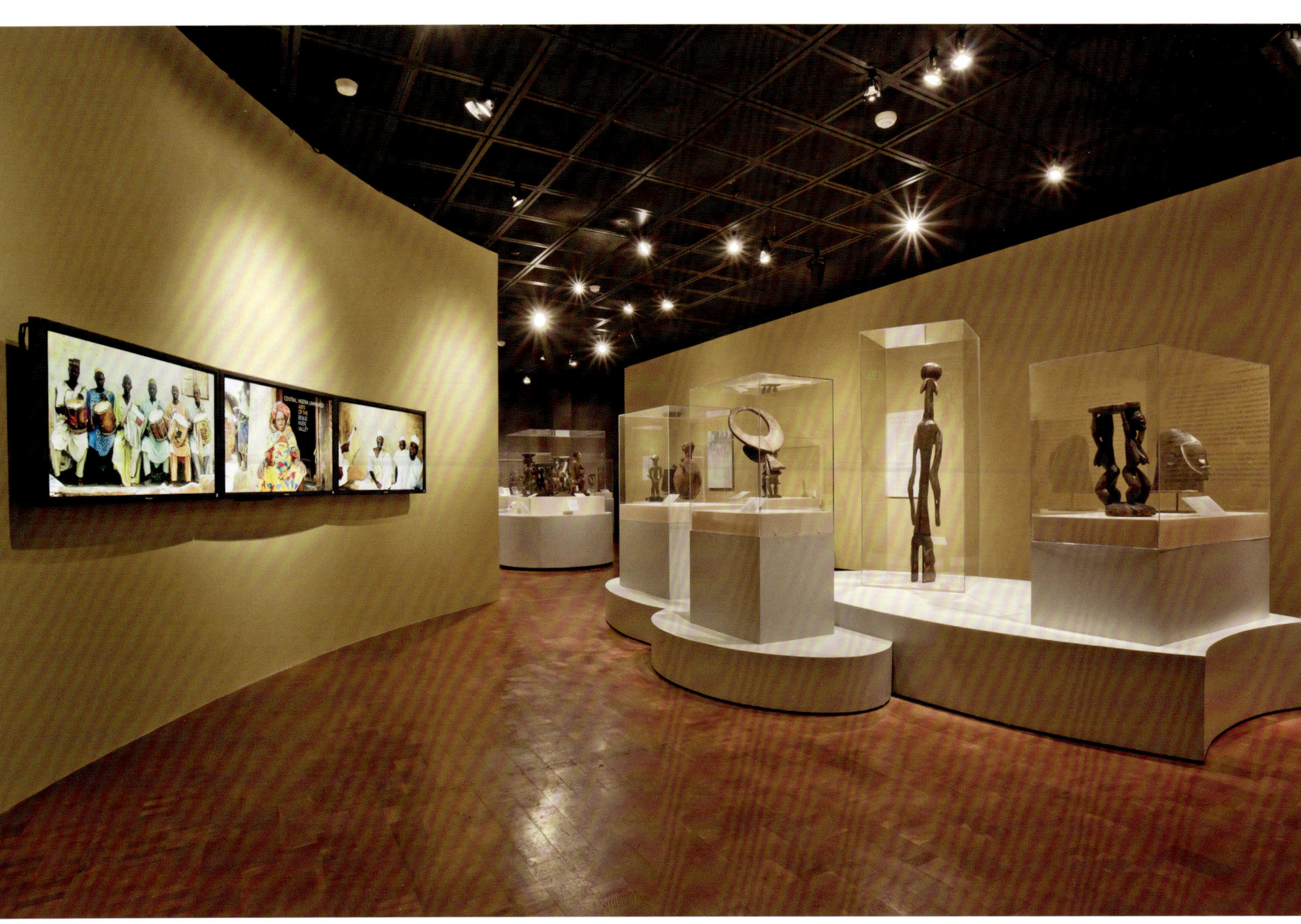

B

Installation view of the introductory section
of *Central Nigeria Unmasked: Arts of the Benue
River Valley* at the Fowler Museum at UCLA.
PHOTOGRAPH © JOSHUA WHITE, 2011.

the enterprise a seriousness of purpose, a grand ambition, and an attention to detail
that Arnold would have praised. That it has taken those of us who inherited it so long
to complete is a reflection of how much we have had to learn and just how complicated
the effort was—becoming even more complex as artworks surfaced in international
collections and changed hands over this period. For me, it brings the satisfaction of
knowing that the promise made to Arnold in 1988 has been fulfilled. The project's
completion also has special meaning for Zena Pearlstone, Arnold's partner during the
final years of his life (who as my friend has also been a constant source of encouragement), and for his children, Hannele and Gabriel.

From the outset, Arnold had envisioned the project to be collaborative and had
identified a list of consultants. Funds provided by a 1987 NEH planning grant, which
also supported Rubin's travel to collections, underwrote a consultants planning meeting
in 1989, held during the ACASA Triennial Symposium in Washington, D.C. Convened
by Doran H. Ross (then Associate Director and Curator of Africa, Southeast Asia, and
Oceania at the Museum), who has been a great champion of the effort, the meeting
brought together several key scholars of Benue Valley arts: Sidney Kasfir (Idoma),
Richard Fardon (Chamba), and the late Roy Sieber (generalist on Benue arts). Representing Upper Benue arts, I also served as the meeting's chair. The team reviewed
Rubin's object selections and proposed a restructuring of his manuscript to include
a greater role for the consultants. A second planning meeting was held in 1993 at the
African Studies Association meeting in Boston, and by then, most of the essays for the

original book had been submitted. Although the key consultants on the project kept in touch over the years, for a variety of reasons the project was put on hold until 2005.

The present volume aims to realize at least some of Arnold Rubin's ambitions, and it does so in large part by leaning heavily on his research, especially on the Middle Benue region and most specifically on the Jukun-speaking peoples. We have relied on the draft manuscript he completed for *Sculpture of the Benue River Valley* (1988) as well as his previous publications. The chapter he wrote on the Jukun is reproduced here as a "memoir" (see chapter 9) and includes the field photographs he had selected to illustrate it. Other chapters draw upon his legacy in a variety of ways—for information, insights, and images. His copious fieldnotes, photographs, film recordings, and field-collected objects remain an invaluable resource. Rubin collected two sets of comparable objects in the field, one deposited in Nigerian museums, especially the Jos Museum, and one that was eventually donated in large part to the Fowler Museum in 1986 (and which complements a number of pieces he donated earlier). Many of the chapters in this volume were written by scholars Rubin himself had invited to contribute, two of whom, John Boston and Barbara Frank, did not live to see the project reach completion. The editors of this volume also asked other specialists to write, including several whose fieldwork was accomplished after Rubin's death, in order to provide a comprehensive account of the research on and reconsiderations of Benue arts and culture.

It is to the artists of the Benue River Valley and to Arnold Rubin's inspiring investigation of their work that we dedicate this volume, which accompanies an exhibition that opened at the Fowler Museum in February 2011 (fig. B) and will travel to venues in Washington, D.C., Stanford, and Paris. Although much remains to be unmasked in our study of the peoples, arts, and cultures of Central Nigeria, it is our hope that our efforts to expose new audiences to the artistic wealth of this region will arouse a wider interest and provoke further scholarly investigation.

A project of this scope and ambition has reached fruition only with the contributions and generosity of a vast number of people over three decades. Many were instrumental during the first phase of the project, providing contacts, photographs, and information to Rubin in his development of a master plan. Because many of the same people aided us during the second, and final, phase of development, we will list everyone together below. Rubin did note, however, in the draft preface to his manuscript that he owed a special debt to Roy Sieber, his mentor and dissertation advisor, whose own art historical fieldwork in Central Nigeria paved the way for Arnold's intensive research in the Middle Benue Valley. Sieber was the first to do survey work, albeit briefly, in the area in 1958, under the auspices of the Ford Foundation. This became a crucial baseline of information about peoples we still know so little about. His slim catalog *Sculpture of Northern Nigeria* (1961), which accompanied an exhibition of the same name held at the Museum of Primitive Art in New York, remains a primary resource for identifying objects made by the eastern Igala, Idoma, Goemai, Montol, and Jaba. It is also remarkable for its rare contextual photographs, several of which are reproduced in the present volume. Despite the brevity of his Nigerian experience, Sieber remained a connoisseur of Benue arts throughout his lifetime (see Sieber and Vevers 1974; Sieber and Hecht 2002). It was to Roy Sieber and Kenneth Murray (the first director of the British colonial Department of Antiquities) that Rubin had dedicated his manuscript in 1988.

I begin by acknowledging the crucial role played by Richard Fardon (Professor of West African Anthropology, School of Oriental and African Studies, University of London) and Sidney Kasfir (Professor of Art History, Emory University, Atlanta, Georgia), specialists on the Middle Benue and Lower Benue subregions, respectively. I invited them to join me as co-editors and co-curators and to provide expertise concerning their areas of specialization as well as sharing in the complex process of conceptualizing the exhibition and selecting the objects that would best narrate its stories. With my own focus on Upper Benue arts, we became a scholarly trio, and met on several occasions over a three-year period to develop the exhibition, mine Rubin's archives, and finalize an outline for this publication, which represents our rethinking and recasting of Rubin's original organization of the manuscript.

I cannot thank Richard and Sidney enough. They have been responsive to the flurries of e-mails and phone calls that have sustained our joint endeavor despite the many miles separating us. The demands of the newly conceptualized project meant that we all have rewritten and expanded our original essays to encompass its goals. Richard, in particular, is to be acknowledged for thoughtfully plumbing the depths of Arnold's original fieldnotes and photographs to write more extensively about the Mumuye and other groups with whom he has not done direct field research. We have all stretched beyond our comfort zones to restore to the objects selected for the exhibition something of their original meanings and purposes, even when provenance is missing or documentation sparse. That we all have other professional commitments may explain, in part, the duration of our effort. But, a shared dedication to its completion has made *Central Nigeria Unmasked* as much a labor of love as anything else, acknowledging our shared intellectual and personal debt to Arnold Rubin and his visionary ideas.

My sincere thanks also go to the fourth member of our curatorial team, Hélène Joubert, Curator for African Collections, Musée du quai Branly, Paris, who has participated actively in the development of the exhibition since 2005 when our two institutions forged a partnership. I thank her especially for her generosity in introducing me to, and often accompanying me to visit, European private collectors and for sharing the extensive inventory she had amassed of Benue objects. Hélène traveled to UCLA many times over the past five years to collaborate on developing the exhibition's themes, determining the objects to illustrate them, and outlining the narrative flow. She also took on the important task of interviewing many European collectors of Benue Valley arts, documenting their activities during the intensive period of collecting following the Nigerian Civil War (1967–1970). Her synopsis of these interviews is presented as an epilogue to this publication.

From the moment I began to re-embark on this effort in 2005, I have relied heavily upon Gassia Armenian, the Fowler's Curatorial and Research Associate, whose competence, tenacity, and diligence are unparalleled. Her sustained curatorial contribution includes researching objects and their provenance, uncovering bibliographic source materials, mastering the contents of the Rubin Archive, tracking the progress of the exhibition's checklist, and maintaining files of all incoming photographic materials. The project's co-curators join me in acknowledging Gassia's invaluable and steadfast assistance.

Our collective gratitude goes to the many authors who have written essays for this volume, both long and short, assuring its status as the most extensive and detailed scholarly resource to date on Benue arts. The original research of nearly every specialist on the region's arts and cultures over the past fifty years is represented. All the authors have shared their insights and knowledge, written thoughtfully about objects selected for the exhibition, and granted us permission to publish their important field photographs: Joerg Adelberger, Jean Borgatti, the late John Boston, Mette Bovin, the late Barbara Frank, Susan Elizabeth Gagliardi, Nancy Neaher Maas, John Picton, Susan Picton, Constanze Weise, and John Willis. Many of these authors revisited fieldnotes and photographs associated with their early Benue Valley research, which had been long eclipsed by other projects. We thank them all for their contributions to this collective enterprise. Joerg Adelberger has been exceptionally generous in sharing newly discovered information, combing archives, and identifying obscure bibliographic sources and illustrations.

The list of individuals who have helped us over the past years is vast—providing contacts, directing us to objects in collections, sourcing photographs and providing permission for the use of field or object photographs, or sharing precious bits of information. We list them here in alphabetical order and apologize if there is anyone we may have inadvertently overlooked: Ayo Arowoshegbe, Valentina Bandelloni, Lowell Bassett, Harold Bergsma, Corinne Besançon, Yaëlle Biro, Jacques Blazy, Anne-Cécile Bobin, the late Laura Bohannan, Sally Boston, Carol Braide, Federica Brivio, Martial Bronsin, Timothy Burns, Brigitte Cavanagh, Amy Chien, Frederic Cloth, Oliver and Pamela Cobb, Herbert S. Cole, Jeremy Coote, Douglas Dawson, Bernard de Grunne, Louis de Strycker, John and Nicole Dintenfass, Hughes Dubois, Frantz Dufour, Kevin Dumouchelle, Kim Dziurman, Jennifer Elliot, Christophe Evers, Marc Felix, Hermann Forkl, Jean Fritts, Patrik Fröhlich, Tad Fruits, Stacey Gannon-Wright, Bernhard Gardi, Colette Ghysels, Emmanuel Godine, Susan Grinols, Mark Groudine, Philippe Guimiot, Barry Hecht, Robert Hensleigh, Rev. Fr. Edmund M. Hogan, Lorenz Homberger, Jean-Michel Huguenin, Jennifer Ickes, Ruth Janson, Kathie Jenkins, Mike Jensen, Ryan Jensen, Peter David Joralemon, Audrey Jouany, Randy Kahn, Michael Kan, Anne Kerchache-Douaoui, Franko Khoury, Zachary Kingdon, Brian Krecik, Kristen Lefevre, Hélène Leloup, Johann Levy, Iva Lisikewycz, Albert Lutz, Daniel and Marian Malcolm, Jackie Maman, Amanda Maples, Aldo Mauro, Jean-Willy Mestach, Amyas Naegele, Tanja Narr, Julia Nicholson, Robert Nooter, Michael O'Hanlon, Bjarke Paarup-Laursen, Howell Perkins, Sajid Rizvi, Carolyn Routledge, Agata Rutkowska, Markus Schindlbeck, Heinrich Schweitzer, Gary Seaman, Christine Seige, Amy Seymour, Ellen Sieber, Matthew Sieber, Elizabeth Solak, Michael Sorafine, Greg Staley, Amy Staples, Christine Stelzig, Jessica Stephenson, Kathy Ann Taylor, Frank Treml, Don Tuttle, Kristina Van Dyke, Guy van Rijn, Anne and René Vanderstraete, Benjamin Watkins, Adam L. Weintraub, David Whaples, Deborah Wythe, Anja Zenner, Ben Zilber, and Elisabeth Zindler-Frank.

Keeping track of the myriad details associated with such a comprehensive and long-term effort has been no easy task. Paulette Parker, Rubin's graduate student and research assistant at the Fowler starting in 1986, was responsible for superbly handling the organization of his collections research, correspondence, and photographic records. His archived lists and files, which Paulette kept current until 1993 when she left the Museum, have provided a crucial blueprint for my subsequent efforts, especially the resumption of locating and identifying objects in private and museum collections in the United States and Europe.

The comprehensive research effort that underpins this project has also benefited from the input of several key scholars and specialists who have reviewed aspects of this manuscript: Roger Blench, Theodore Celenko, Herbert M. Cole, Nicholas David, Russell Schuh, Richard Shain, Judy Sterner, James Wade, and David Zeitlyn. To this list, I add the names of others who directly assisted Arnold Rubin or provided original field materials: Philip Allison, Robert Armstrong, Frank Conant, Eberhard Fischer, Jacqueline and Philip Fry, Heinz Jockers, Hans Joachim Koloss, Rob Koops, Elsie Leuzinger, Wulf Lohse, Roxana Ma, Frank McEwen, Robert Netting, Paul Newman, Angelika Rumpf, Thurstan Shaw, Phillips Stevens Jr., and Jurgen Zwernemann.

Very special thanks are also due my colleagues at UCLA, who participated in several planning sessions and assisted in the formulation of the exhibition's content and narrative flow: Andrew Apter (Professor, History Department), Mary (Polly) Nooter Roberts (Professor, World Arts and Cultures; formerly, Deputy Director and Chief Curator, Fowler Museum), Allen Roberts (Professor, World Arts and Cultures), and Doran H. Ross (Independent Scholar; Director Emeritus, Fowler Museum). My work has benefited greatly from their collegiality and friendship over the years.

The Fowler Museum is very grateful to many individuals and organizations who have provided generous financial support for this ambitious undertaking. The early planning phase was funded by a grant from the National Endowment for the Humanities. To support the research and implementation phase from 2005 to 2011, we received major support from the National Endowment for the Arts, the Shirley and Ralph Shapiro Director's Discretionary Fund, Jay and Deborah Last, Ceil and Michael Pulitzer, the Joseph and Barbara Goldenberg Estate, the Robert T. Wall Family, and Jill and Barry Kitnick. Additional funding was provided by Udo and Wally Horstmann, Edwin and Cherie K. Silver, and Helen Kuhn. The Ahmanson Foundation awarded us a major grant to help underwrite this publication along with additional support from the Ethnic Arts Council of Los Angeles. American Express was the presenting corporate sponsor of *Central Nigeria Unmasked* at the Fowler. Educational outreach programs were made possible by the Wallace Family, the Jerome L. Joss Fund, the Yvonne Lenart Public Programs Fund, and Manus, the support group of the Fowler Museum.

The international traveling exhibition this volume accompanies has depended on the magnanimity of forty-seven private and institutional lenders in the United States and Europe. They have made available to us a stellar group of over 150 objects selected from the hundreds of Benue Valley arts in global collections. We would like to thank all of the lenders (and their staffs) for making these crucial loans possible: (1) *private lenders in the United States*: Keith Achepohl, Richard and Jan Baum, Mark Clayton, Sidney and Bernice Clyman, Mark Groudine and Cynthia Putnam, Barry and Toby Hecht, Barry and Jill Kitnick, Jay T. and Deborah Last, Bruce and Michelle Moore, James and Laura Ross, Richard Scheller, Sieber Collection, Bill and Gale Simmons, Robert Wall and Margaret Rinkevich, James and Lin Willis, Ziff Family; (2) *private lenders in Europe*: Samir and Mina Borro, Pierre Dartevelle, Alain and Rosemarie Dufour, Michel and Liliane Durand-Dessert, Bernard de Grunne, Udo and Wally Horstmann, Max Itzikovitz, Aimery Langlois-Meurinne, Alain and Claudie Lebas, Hélène and Philippe Leloup, Jean-Claude and Nicole Marian, Jean-Claude and Josette Weill; (3) *institutional lenders in the United States*: Art Institute of Chicago (James Cuno, Kathleen Bickford Berzock, Elizabeth Pope), Fine Arts Museums of San Francisco, de Young Museum (John Buchanan, Kathleen Berrin, Maria Reilly), High Museum of Art (Michael E. Shapiro, Carol Thompson, Paula Haymon), Indiana University Art Museum (Heidi Gealt, Diane Pelrine, Anita Bracalente, Kathy Taylor), Indianapolis Museum of Art (Maxwell Anderson, Theodore Celenko, Kristen Krause, Sherry Peglow), the Menil Collection (Josèf Helfenstein, Kristina Van Dyke, Judy Kwon), Metropolitan Museum of Art (Thomas P. Campbell, Alisa LaGamma, Emily Foss, Yaëlle Biro), Museum for African Art (Elsie McCabe Thompson, Enid Schildkrout, Amanda Thompson, Donna Ghelerter), National Museum of African Art, Smithsonian Institution (Johnnetta Betsch Cole, Christine M. Kreamer, Julie Link Haifley), New Orleans Museum of Art (E. John Bullard, William A. Fagaly, Paul Tarver, Jennifer Ickes), Seattle Art Museum (Derrick Cartwright, Pamela McClusky, Lauren Mellon, Lauren Tucker), Virginia Museum of Fine Arts (Alex Nyerges, Richard Woodward, Mary L. Sullivan), Yale University Art Gallery (Jock Reynolds, Frederick Lamp, Lynne Addison); (4) *institutional lenders in Europe*: Barbier-Mueller Museum (Jean Paul Barbier-Mueller, Laurence Mattet, Audrey Jouany), the British Museum (Neil MacGregor, the late Claude Ardouin, Fiona Grisdale, Heidi Cutts), Ethnologisches Museum Berlin (Viola König, Peter Junge, Maria Gaida, Anja Zenner), the Horniman Museum & Gardens (Janet Vitmayer, Wayne Modest, Bill Curtis, Louise Bacon), Musée du quai Branly (Stéphane Martin, Sylvie Camile, Valérie Eyéné, Yves Le Fur, Hélène Joubert, Hélène Fulgence, Corinne Pignon, Delphine Davenier, Candice Rogers), Museum der Kulturen, Basel (Anna Schmid, Samuel Bachmann, Bernhard Gardi, Corinne Besançon).

The international tour of *Central Nigeria Unmasked* has assured that the exhibition will reach a large and diverse audience. We acknowledge with gratitude the participation, cooperation, and assistance of the three venues and their staffs that have partnered in this venture: National Museum of African Art, Smithsonian Institution, Washington, D.C. (Johnnetta Betsch Cole, Christine Kreamer, Karen Milbourne); Iris & B. Gerald Cantor Center for the Visual Arts, Stanford University (Thomas K. Seligman, Alison Roth, Katie Clifford, Sara Cabot), and Musée du quai Branly, Paris (Stéphane Martin, Hélène Joubert, Hélène Fulgence, Corinne Pignon, Delphine Davenier, Candice Rogers, Muriel Rausch).

The authors of this volume owe a huge collective debt to our Nigerian hosts and informants. The list of individuals who have assisted us with our research since the 1960s, whether living in the villages and towns where fieldwork was conducted or working in the museums, universities, and libraries that provided assistance or access to resources, is too long to present here. Suffice it to say, none of us could have completed our research or advanced our careers without significant help from our Nigerian friends and colleagues. In the context of this volume, I offer Nath Mayo Adediran, Director of Museums, National Commission for Museums and Monuments, Abuja, Nigeria, our profound gratitude for his support and the generous permission to reproduce many images held in the Photographic Archives of the National Museum, Lagos.

A project of this scope and magnitude is necessarily the work of many hands. I would like to extend my deepest thanks to the many staff members of the Fowler Museum who have been tireless in their efforts to complete this ambitious project (a full staff list is provided at the end of this volume). Several have labored intensively since the exhibition development process was revived in 2005, and they deserve special recognition. In addition to Gassia Armenian, whose unstinting dedication has been detailed above, David Blair, Deputy Director, has overseen all of the complex details of the project's budgeting, contract negotiations, institutional partnerships, and registration of loans with astute judgment and unwavering commitment. Betsy D. Quick, Director of Education and Curatorial Affairs, and Agnes Stauber, Media Analyst, have participated actively in the development of interpretive strategies to contextualize the many genres of Benue Valley arts. With her many years of experience and finely tuned insights, Betsy helped shape a cogent organizational schema for unfolding the exhibition's themes. Agnes thoughtfully conceived and produced the various media components for the installation, including a compelling and concise three-screen video introduction to the Benue Valley and its history. She also edited and produced two sequences of rare and exhilarating archival masquerade footage to enliven the objects on view. Polly Roberts, former Deputy Director and Chief Curator until 2009, provided creative insights and incisive suggestions during the project's conceptual development. Sebastian Clough, Director of Exhibitions, who began working at the Fowler in 2008, immediately joined our planning process, envisioning a design for the installation that would mirror the "flow" of the Benue River and the path visitors would take to discover its peoples, histories, and arts.

Susan Elizabeth Gagliardi, who worked at the Fowler as a curatorial assistant during her final year in the doctoral program in UCLA's Department of Art History, carried out meticulous research, plumbing the depths of the Rubin Archive to facilitate our publication of more of his original field photographs and notes, including her own precise exposition of two Mumuye masquerades that Rubin had documented. Leah Niederstadt, an intern at the Fowler in 2006–2007 from the University of Michigan, assisted with important early bibliographic work on several ethnic groups.

In the final intense year of preparations, Sheryl Nakano, contract registrar, managed the elaborate negotiations with lenders, as well as all of the complex packing, shipping, and courier arrangements with precision and professionalism. Sheryl worked closely with Rachel Raynor, Director of Registration and Collections Management (and her staff), as well as with Jo Hill, Director of Conservation, and Christian de Brer,

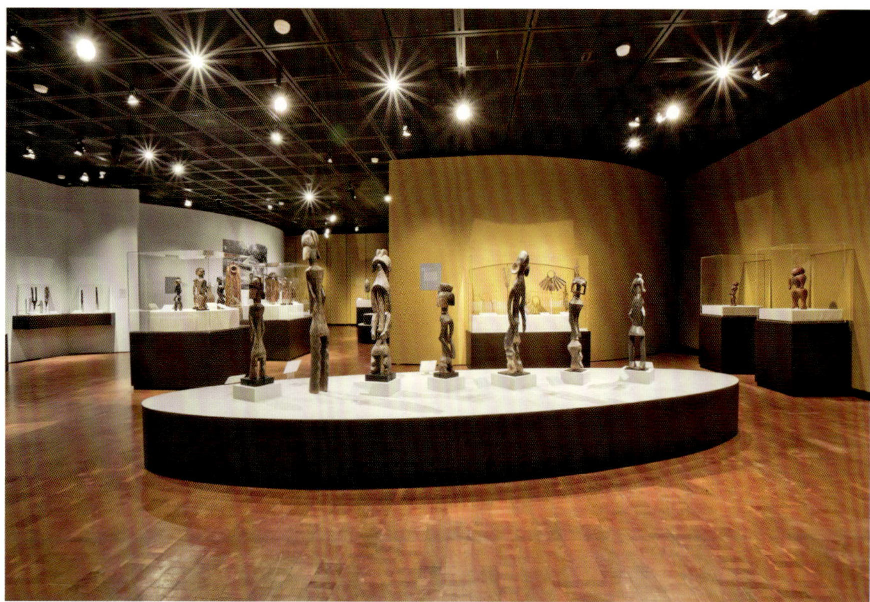

C, D

Installation views of the Middle Benue section
of *Central Nigeria Unmasked: Arts of the Benue
River Valley* at the Fowler Museum at UCLA.
PHOTOGRAPH © JOSHUA WHITE, 2011.

Assistant Conservator (and their interns and volunteers), to transact the high-pressure
tasks of receiving, unpacking, condition reporting, and overseeing the making of
mounts and installation of objects by our exhibition crew. All the members of this
team are to be congratulated for their excellent work.

The installation at the Fowler was superbly and sympathetically designed by
Sebastian Clough, who understood our curatorial objectives and the interpretive
strategies we developed to meet them. His crew, led by Seth Augustine, did a tremendous job of building the "set," making mounts, and installing the objects in the gallery,
demonstrating their care and attention to detail. The handsome exhibition graphics
and custom maps (also included in this volume) were finely executed by Jenna Kush,
Joe Bodwin, and Scott Kepford. We could not have hoped for a more stunning backdrop for the remarkable artworks of the Benue River Valley (figs. C, D).

There are a number of Fowler staff who work behind the scenes to ensure that
our exhibitions are well publicized in the media and promoted through educational
programming and outreach. Recognition goes to Stacey Abarbanel, Director of External Affairs, for her leadership in this domain and for her strategic and effective use of
limited resources to ensure strong media coverage. Bonnie Poon, Manager of Public
Programs, arranged a series of stimulating lectures, panels, and films, all designed
to enhance an understanding of Nigeria's rich cultural arts. Gina Hall, Manager of
School and Family Services, developed a menu of creative activities as well as teacher
training and exhibition tours for K–12 students. A curriculum resource guide to accompany the exhibition was produced by Lyn Avins, our indefatigable volunteer, and Betsy
D. Quick. They have applied their combined wisdom and imagination to make the
exhibition's themes comprehensible and relevant for our young visitors.

Others in the Fowler's administrative arena have made significant contributions
over the years of the exhibition's development. Lynne Brodhead Clark and Nicole
Dunn, former Development officers for the Fowler, were instrumental to our receipt
of initial funding, including a critical grant from the National Endowment for the Arts.
Betsy Escandor, my former Executive Assistant, did yeoman's work in planning my
many trips and visits to museums and collectors' homes, helping to organize documentation files, and assisting with the preparation of my essays. Sophia Livsey, my current
Executive Assistant, has continued Betsy's fine work and has been enormously helpful
throughout the final stages of preparing final chapter copy and the lengthy bibliography
for publication. Sarah Charleton, student assistant in the front office, was endlessly
helpful to anyone who needed her. Pablo Dominguez, Financial Services Coordinator,

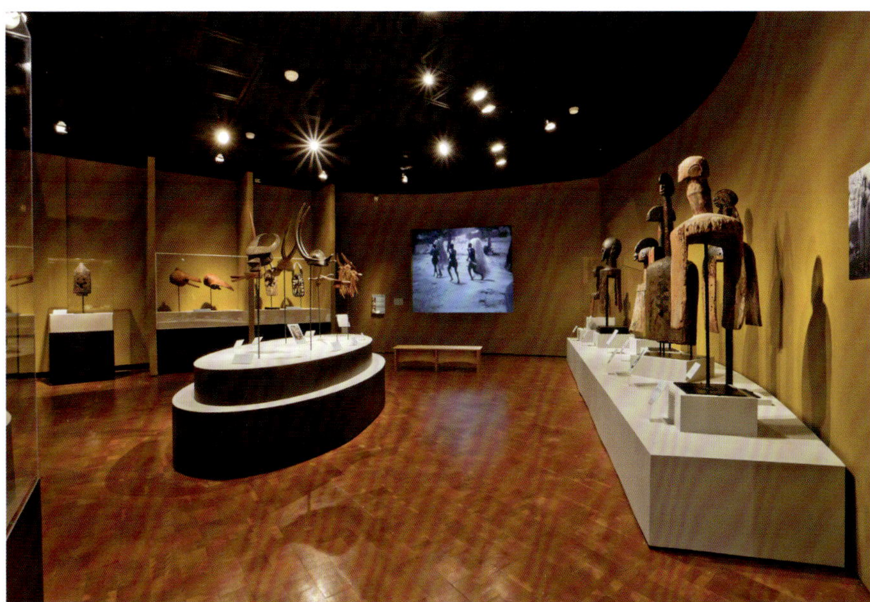

makes sure vendors are paid and consultants reimbursed, navigating UCLA's complicated accounting system. Roberto Salazar, Human Resources Coordinator, makes sure staff get hired and compensated. Others who labor, often at the margins, to make the Fowler both an intimate and inviting place for visitors of all ages include our Operations and Security supervisors, Manuel Baltodano, Emry Thomas, and Luis Figueroa (and their terrific security staff); Bridget DuLong, Events and Visitor Services Manager; Jennifer Leitch, Development Coordinator; Lori Lavelle, Membership Coordinator; and Stella Krieger, Museum Store Manager. Although not directly involved, I thank our Fowler curators, Roy Hamilton, Gemma Rodrigues, and Patrick Polk, for their ideas, observations, and moral support along the way.

A publication of this length, scope, and depth, and with a long list of international contributors, has required the concentrated efforts of the Fowler's stellar publication team. Lynne Kostman, Managing Editor, is to be congratulated for editing an array of highly specialized and heavily illustrated essays and bringing them all into conformity. She has managed the long and highly complex editing process with her usual brilliance, clarity, and good humor. Gassia Armenian has been a constant support, performing the critical task of organizing all the photographic source materials for publication. Don Cole, the Fowler's photographer, has taken his typically beautiful studio images of objects from the Museum's collections and those of our Los Angeles lenders. Lastly, but never least, I acknowledge the remarkable work of Danny Brauer, Director of Publications, who designed this book with certainty, elegance, and flair born of substantial talent and experience. Everyone deserves high praise for producing a tome that is rich in content and lavish in beauty.

Central Nigeria Unmasked has taken me on a long and arduous but ultimately highly satisfying journey. I offer my heartfelt thanks to everyone who has indulged my near-obsession with this project over the past few years. I am grateful to my colleagues at the Fowler for understanding my curatorial preoccupation, which refocused my energies especially over the last year. To my family and friends, with whom I have been less than fully present, I am indebted to you for comprehending my priorities and supporting my efforts in so many nourishing ways. And, to Arnold Rubin, my mentor and inspiration, thank you for igniting the fire that has fueled this and so many of my professional endeavors.

Marla C. Berns

Introduction:
Central Nigeria Unmasked

MARLA C. BERNS AND RICHARD FARDON

In the draft introduction to his manuscript of 1988, Arnold Rubin characterized the arts of the peoples of Nigeria, taken as a whole, as among the best known and most thoroughly studied in all of sub-Saharan Africa.[1] Archaeological investigations had been carried out in Benin, Ife, and Igbo Ukwu, as well as detailed field research on the celebrated artistic traditions of the majority populations of southwestern and southeastern Nigeria, which included Yoruba, Igbo, Edo, and Ijaw speakers. The Hausa and Fulani who dominated the north of the country had also been studied, albeit less intensively. Within Nigeria, however, as Rubin noted, "There remain large areas and sizable numbers of smaller-scale ethnic groups whose arts are inadequately reported. Perhaps the largest concentration of such little-known groups is located in the Benue River Valley" (1988, 1).

This imbalance of attention had its roots in history, since the Benue River Valley (figs. 1, 2) was too far south for Sudanic Arab chroniclers to have visited and too far north for coastal European traders and explorers to have penetrated before the mid-nineteenth century. Hence it remained relatively remote from the view of outsiders before the colonial period. Even in the twentieth century, the central region of Nigeria attracted fewer researchers than did the south, particularly the southwest. The plethora of Benue Valley peoples, living for the most part in small communities, was largely, though not wholly, as we shall see, overlooked. While it remains the case that our knowledge is richest in relation to only a modest number (mostly the larger) of the more than two hundred ethnolinguistic groups living in Central Nigeria,[2] we know more than enough to grasp the main features of one of the major artistic legacies of sub-Saharan Africa and to place it within its wider geographic and historical contexts.

THE NIGERIAN "MIDDLE BELT"

The region lying to the east of the confluence of the great Niger and Benue rivers is the heartland of the Nigerian Middle Belt, located in the country's vast geographic center. The phrase "Middle Belt" has interlinked political, spatial, and cultural connotations. In a country most simply typified as having a North and a South (and the capitalization is not accidental), the middle is contextually an in-between place. Its distinctive character is owed in part to the tensions between its history and identity, and those of the northern and southern societies through which outside influences had to pass in order to reach it. Nigeria is not unique in possessing such a region. The geography of West Africa is such that a similar space could be mapped across it. Nonetheless, the Nigerian situation has a unique symmetry; the Middle Belt really does sit between northern and southern sections of the country that are roughly equivalent both in extent and in population.

Like all regions, West Africa is itself the result of human imaginings—and hence might conceivably be delineated differently from the way it conventionally is—but in this case, geography and, in part as a consequence, history have lent imagination a substantial helping hand. West Africa is geographically bounded, but its boundaries are the porous membrane through which West Africa has been felt in the wider world. To the north, West Africa opens upon the Sahara, historically crossed by trade routes to the markets of North Africa and the Middle East, as well as to the Mediterranean world. People, products, and ideas moved across the vast desert in and out of the region over recorded history, and it was from North Africa that the influence of Islam came first.

The Atlantic Ocean breaks on the southern and western shores of the West African region, linking it via sea routes to Europe and the Americas. As well as trade in people and products, this was the route of Christian missionary endeavor and European colonization. It has been the predominant route of West African dispersion both in terms of population and of culture. The eastern border of the region comprises the forests of Central Africa, stretching from eastern Cameroon. People leaving the area around what is now the Cameroon-Nigeria border headed predominantly east and south from West Africa and populated Central and Southern Africa with speakers of Bantu languages.

Leaving aside local micro-ecologies, within the West African region delineated by these boundaries climatic bands run laterally. It becomes dryer going north to the Sahel and Sahara and wetter going south until reaching the coastal forest belt. Tree cover increases from north to south, and animals that are not tsetse resistant (like Arab horses and humped zebu cattle) cannot live in forested areas where tsetse is endemic.

The more northerly part of West Africa has looked toward the Sahara for its trade and the cultural and religious influences that have interacted with the legacies of sub-Saharan Africa. This has been the world of ancient Muslim-ruled empires, controlled by the cavalries of their ruling dynasties, a countryside through which pastoralists have migrated seasonally with their herds of cattle and goats. Southerly West Africa has, by contrast, looked toward the coast for the past half a millennium. Kingdoms rose and fell according to their access to the Atlantic trade and to the firearms and other goods it brought. Neither horses nor cattle thrived. Increasingly, the peoples of the coast were Christianized by missionaries, many of whom were themselves African by origin.

It is in this broad context that the distinctiveness of the Nigerian Middle Belt becomes apparent. Peoples there were not directly exposed to either early Islam or early Christianity to the same degree as their forest and Sahelian neighbors. Trade routes crossed the Middle Belt taking goods and people into both the desert and ocean trade circuits, but Middle Belt experience of the trade termini was indirect. More generally, situated in the center of its region, the Middle Belt felt external influences secondhand and often much later than the North or South. Kingdoms of some thousands in population flourished alongside social forms that were much less hierarchical. Before the colonial period, these societies for the most part did not adhere to the world religions (although the leaders of some might be nominally Muslim) but practiced the historic religions of West Africa. The betweenness of the societies of the Middle Belt meant that they retained some cultural autonomy from both the Saharan and Atlantic worlds, but they became increasingly subject to the influence of both as trade, particularly the slave trade, grew in extent, and the world religions pressed more insistently on them from North and South.

APPROACHING BENUE VALLEY ART FORMS, STYLES, AND SUBREGIONS

Living at the very center of Nigeria's Middle Belt, the people of the Benue River Valley created works of art in a variety of forms, which in many ways reflect their geographic and historical position (fig. 3). The Idoma and Igala of the Lower Benue, toward the confluence with the Niger River, were demonstrably influenced artistically by contact with the peoples of southeastern Nigeria and the Cross River. As we ascend

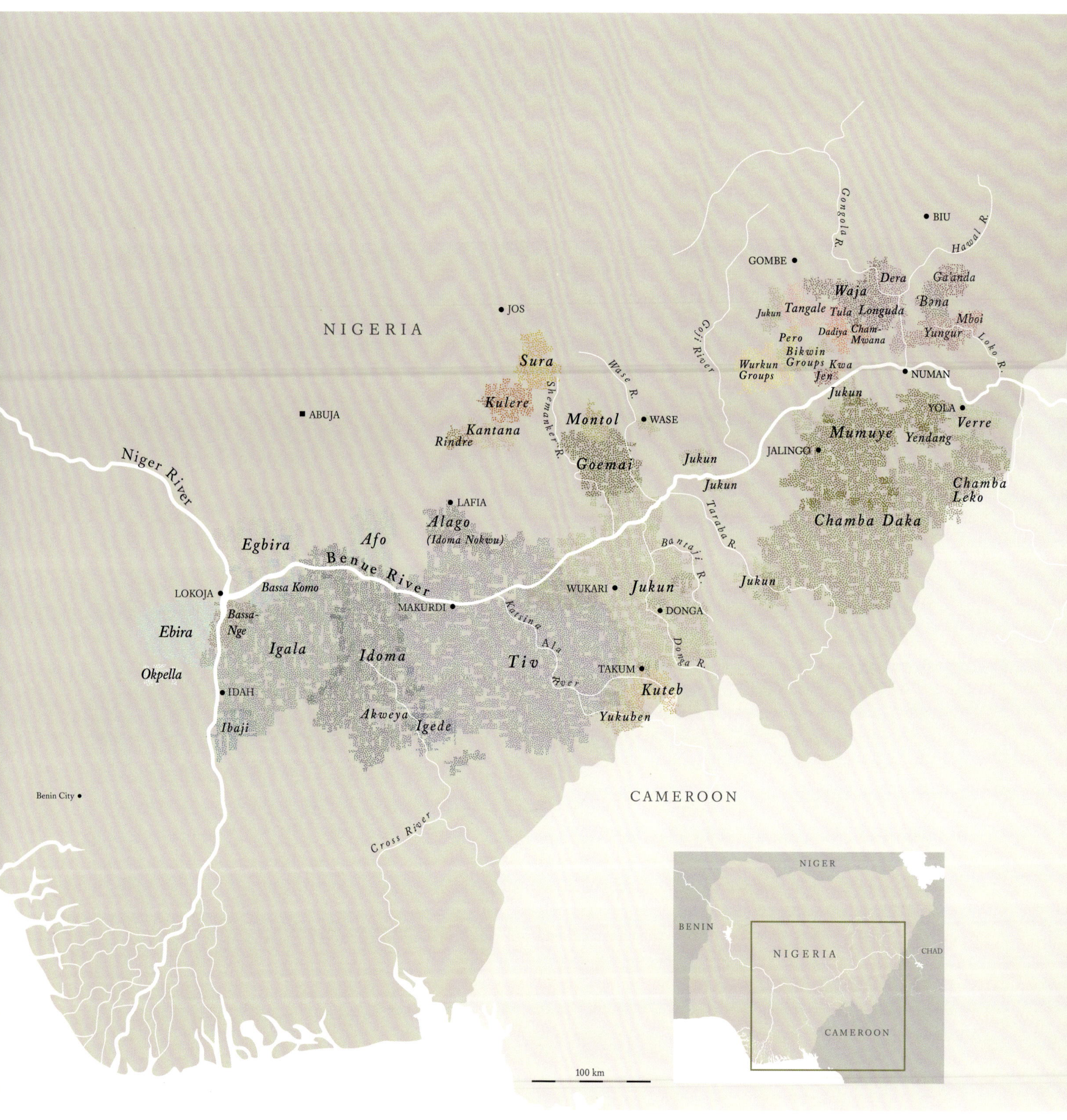

1

This map locates many Benue River Valley peoples whose arts are represented in this volume. It does not include all the ethnic groups who live in Nigeria or even Central Nigeria. Most peoples live in dispersed villages and towns, and the boundaries between them are not hard-edged. Our intent is to suggest that there were and continue to be population movements within and among groups. This map is based on a compilation of late twentieth-century language maps, road atlases, and the expertise of project consultants, and it is accurate to the best of our abilities.

© 2011 FOWLER MUSEUM AT UCLA.

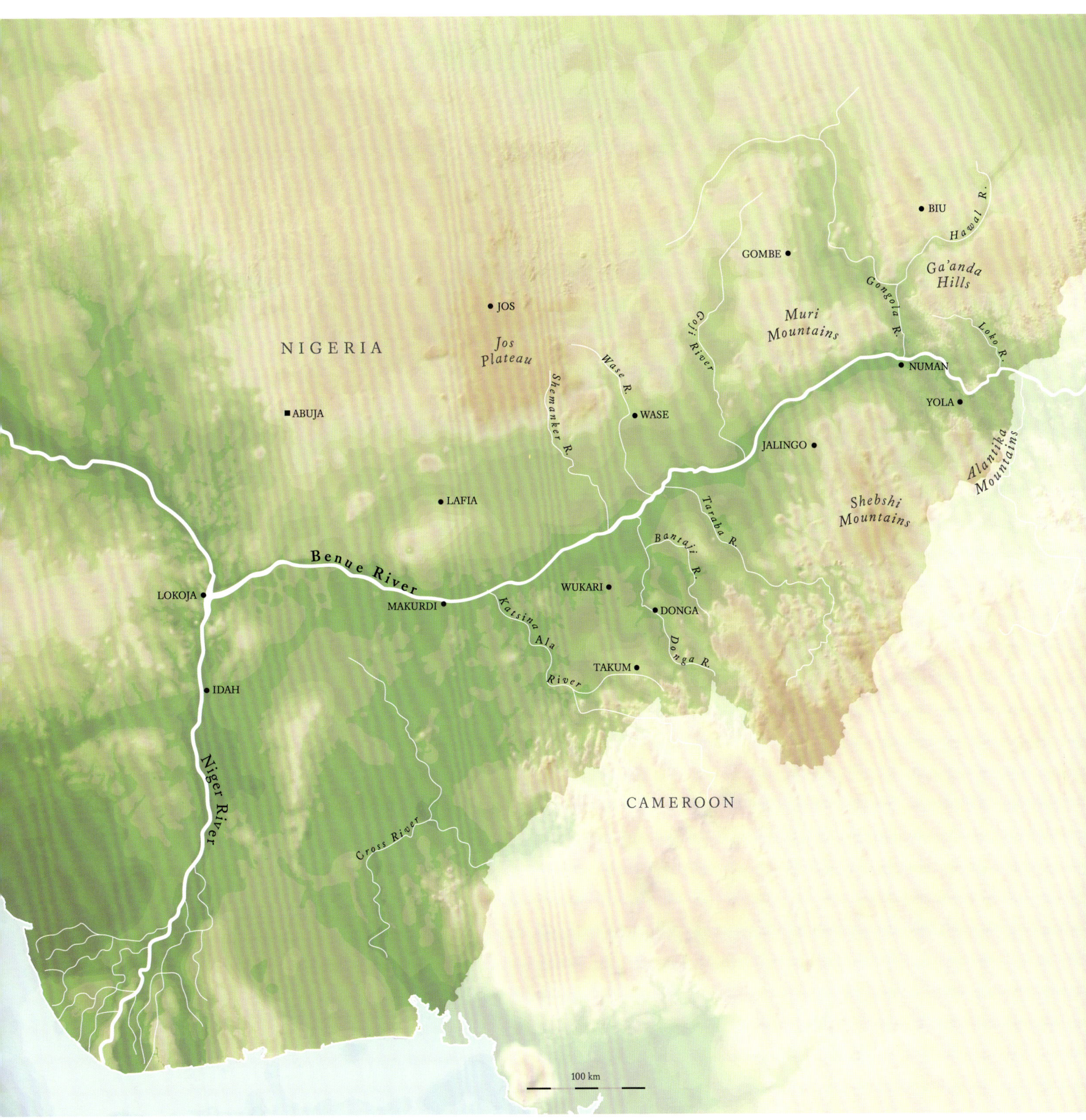

2

This topographic map represents the same area as shown in figure 1.

BASED UPON A MAP DESIGNED BY INTERCARTO.
© INTERCARTO, FRANCE.

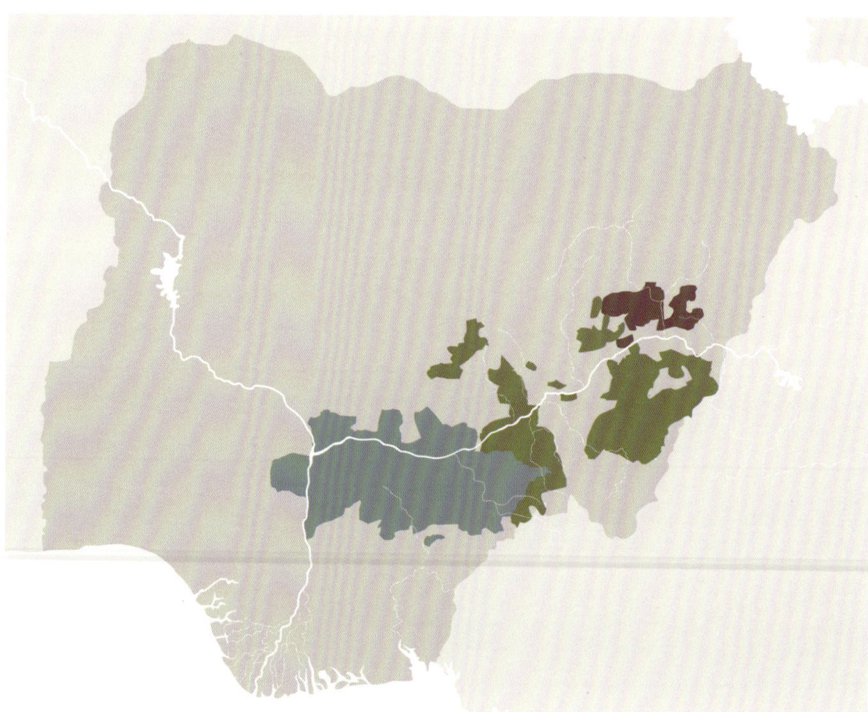

3
The subregions of the Benue River Valley
(Lower, Middle, and Upper) appear from left
to right and are designated by different colors.
© 2011 FOWLER MUSEUM AT UCLA.

from the Niger-Benue confluence toward the Middle Benue, we find that artworks, particularly figures and masquerades, become increasingly distinctive from those of neighboring peoples, whether to the north or the south. It is here and in the Upper Benue that the ethnic composition of groups is at its most complex, and resemblances in art forms and styles suggest intensive exchange alongside the emergence of idiosyncratic traditions that speak of local innovations. In the Upper Benue, the most isolated of the Benue Valley regions, wood sculpture is nearly absent, and distinctive sculptural ceramic vessels predominate as the focus of religious practices.

As the reader will by now have gathered, the heterogeneity of the Benue River Valley both contributes to its richness and poses challenges to its study. Details of local geography, language, ethnography, and history threaten to become so overwhelming as to obscure appreciation of the regional distributions of art forms. Hence, we have needed to simplify, even at the risk of initially oversimplifying. Division into Lower, Middle, and Upper Benue subregions is intended only to be understood in relative terms and not to suggest that they were hard-edged and impermeable. Yet, these divisions are not arbitrary either: each was, and is, home to peoples with more or less shared characteristics who produced artworks that complemented their particular ways of living in and trying to control their world. The density of resemblances, and we would argue of historical interactions, was greater within each of the subregions than it was between them. Our division of the region into three subregions represents a considerable simplification of Arnold Rubin's original schema of five "Style Regions," which he separated further into "Sub-Regions" and "Sectors" (the rationale for which we quote in full below). In part this is because, for practical reasons, we have defined the Benue Valley more narrowly than he did. Although we have simplified his schema, we have retained his emphasis on "style" as an important indication of communication and exchange having taken place between peoples. This was an insight he stressed. Rubin used the term *tribal* in the quotation below in two ways that we might not today: when in quotation marks, "tribal" refers to the erroneous analytic essentializing of identities at the heart of an already outmoded museological practice of classification; without the quotation marks, Rubin uses *tribal* to describe the terms of identity that come along with objects and narrow their provenance. He argued that we need to work with these latter tribal labels. Scholars after him, especially today, would probably feel more comfortable substituting the adjective *ethnic* for *tribal*. The underlying problem, irrespective of our terms, however, remains much as Rubin stated it: when dealing with object attributions, we are typically trying to extract sense from tribal labels rather than from sophisticated applications of a sociological understanding of ethnicity. Indeed, to work our way from a tribal label to an ethnic appreciation of an object involves a sea change in understandings of identity, something that is part of our purpose here. Rubin reasoned that a focus on style, and delineation of "style regions," allowed tribal labeling of objects to be transcended (1988,7):

> The concepts of Regions and Sub-regions developed here are offered...as a provisional alternative to the "tribal" rubrics according to which most studies of African art and, indeed other aspects of African culture, are still being organized. Tribal designations are undeniably useful in museological contexts. In the absence of information regarding precise origins for particular objects— all too frequently the case—they make possible attributions slightly finer than "West Africa" or "Mali" or "Southeastern Nigeria." It seems a curious atavism, however, that assignment of particular objects to such makeshift categories should still represent a primary concern for specialists in African art studies. This exercise has tended to become something of an end in itself rather than a way to move ahead to art-historical reconstruction or other synthetic enterprise. Tribal designations of the sort being discussed convey implications, on the one hand, of homogeneity in artistic form and meaning within a group, and, on the other, of clear distinctions between the arts of neighboring groups. The data presented here explicitly contradict both of these assumptions: first, particular forms, styles, meanings, and functions consistently cut across tribal lines—within and beyond the Benue Valley; and second, in several cases, traditions are not uniformly or continuously distributed within a single group.
>
> The regions, sub-regions and sectors that form the basis for this study should not be understood as partaking of the qualities of abruptly demarcated "tribal" enclaves; a more accurate model would entail a series of nodes shading off into one another at their margins. Further, the variable—indeed, highly personal—weighting of factors used in defining the regions, sub-regions and sectors must be acknowledged: having evaluated the evidence, I have concluded that land, life, and art within these hypothetical boundaries are more consistent than divergent, the people having more in common with each other than with adjacent populations. As Kasfir (1984: 168, 184) points out, "The concept of style-region, like those of culture and ethnicity, appears to require a definition which is both fluid and situational."

Practically, then, we find ourselves juggling a number of perspectives in an effort to create plausible narratives about artworks: the "tribal" labels that come attached to objects, our understanding (more or less refined according to the accounts at our disposal) of what a "tribal" label might mean in the light of a sociological grasp of the complexity of identities (including ethnicity), and our broader sense of resemblances between the artworks of regional or subregional clusters of peoples as a result of direct or indirect intercourse among them, either recent or in the past. Making arguments from these kinds of materials is a challenge familiar to art historians and archaeologists, and it involves practical compromises with frustratingly incomplete and partial records. These are, however, the records we have, and work with them we must.

Rubin's thinking, which we try to develop here, was encouraged by his reading of René Bravmann's essay for the exhibition catalog *Open Frontiers: The Mobility of Art in Black Africa* (1973). Instead of "tribes" as hermetically sealed entities with monolithic styles impervious to outside stimuli (a notion, it has to be added, thoroughly superseded in African anthropology by that time), Bravmann's foregrounding of "open frontiers" emphasized the forces that bring peoples *into* contact, the mobility of artists and specialists, and the movement of: shrines, the forces thought to inhere within them, and their custodians. Sidney Kasfir's essay, "One Tribe, One Style? Paradigms in the Historiography of African Art" (1984), which overturned the simple association of tribe with style in its title, also supported Rubin's approach. Looking to such records as we have of objects and their uses in the Benue River Valley, we need to be attentive both to locality and to movement, particularly in the nineteenth and twentieth centuries (beyond which detailed reconstruction is difficult).

A BRIEF HISTORY OF THE BENUE VALLEY REGION

Archaeological investigations undertaken on the Jos Plateau have revealed evidence of human habitation extending back nearly forty thousand years with most of the known sites of the so-called Nok culture (500 BCE–500 CE) located within the Benue region (Willett 2002, 65). Speakers of Africa's major language families (Niger-Congo and Afroasiatic) are found in the region, and as previously noted, the ancestral forms of the modern Bantu languages (belonging to the Benue-Congo branch of Niger-Congo) used throughout central, eastern, and southern Africa may have originally been spoken in the Benue Valley.

While the Benue Valley has certainly not been marginal to the history of Africa—which is to say, human history—little is known about it with any certainty prior to the eighteenth century. The Kano and Bornu chronicles do, however, provide documentary evidence of a powerful confederacy called Kwararafa (Kororofa) by the peoples to the north and Apá by its own members. It is thought to have existed from the fourteenth century in the Middle Benue region and was latterly centered near present-day Wukari, now a site of Jukun occupation. After waging three centuries of periodic attacks against Hausa cities such as Kano, the Kwararafa federation fragmented in the seventeenth and eighteenth centuries. Arnold Rubin devoted much of his doctoral dissertation to the study of Kwararafa without reaching conclusions that he found satisfying. Which people made up the federation, what form it took, and who were its leaders remain unresolved and contentious issues.[3]

Further obscuring the region's distant past are dramatic and disruptive events that occurred in the nineteenth century, shaking the Benue River Valley and in the process decreasing its isolation. From the northwest came a Fulani jihad, declared in 1804 by the militant reformer Usman dan Fodio. The effects of this holy war would continue to resonate throughout the century, and they echo down to the present. Fulani cavalry attacked and burned towns on the north bank of the Benue near its confluence with the Niger forcing entire villages to flee across the river. Once there, people scattered and gradually established new communities and relationships with neighboring groups. Further upriver, in the Middle Benue, communities living on the open plains were forced to take refuge in hills and rough terrain in order to resist the Fulani who had established several powerful local emirates. Only to the far east in the Upper Benue/Gongola River Valley, where settlements had long been established in the rugged and hilly landscape, were people able to maintain their independence in the face of mounted Fulani warriors. Meanwhile, Chamba peoples, in alliance with or in emulation of the Fulani, set themselves up as slave raiders in the early nineteenth century, terrorizing local populations at the southeastern end of the Middle Benue Valley.

Yet another incursion was felt from the south in the form of European ambitions to explore, trade, and missionize eastward from the Niger-Benue confluence. This was to intensify during the second half of the nineteenth century, and by the end of the century, most of the Benue Valley had fallen within the British sphere of influence. British Colonial rule was formally established in 1900. The eastern Benue Valley and the headwaters of the Benue River were, however, absorbed into the new German colony of Kamerun.

Before the advent of colonialism many peoples of the Middle Belt—unlike the conquering Fulani—had lived in small-scale, mostly decentralized, communities. The exceptions to this generalization were several modest-sized kingdoms and chiefdoms found among the Chamba, Igala, Idoma, and Jukun, most of which had been thoroughly disrupted by the Fulani invasion. This paucity of centralized political structures in the Benue region posed a challenge to the preferred British strategy of indirect colonial rule mediated through local rulers. Episodes of violent confrontation, occurring both before the colonial period—notably involving the Royal Niger Company and its Royal Niger Constabulary—and during the imposition of colonial rule, gave the peoples of the region a reputation for lawless backwardness when compared to the Yoruba, Igbo, Hausa, and other larger groups (see chapters 1 and 2 in Falola 2009). The implications of a pax Britannica differed, however, from what was experienced elsewhere in Nigeria because the Benue region had already experienced and resisted an attempt at external conquest directed from the Caliphate of Sokoto (the Islamic state founded by Usman dan Fodio in 1809). Although ruthless in the early stages of its establishment, British rule restrained the Fulani and other local aggressors sufficiently to encourage the movement of many Benue populations down from their mountain and hilltop refuges and back to the plains. In order to control these populations, the British created administrative units using a variety of ethnic and territorial bases, often naming "native authorities" after "tribal" identities. This is too complicated a subject to explore in detail here, except to note that institutionalizing the association between ethnic identities and demarcated territorial units was to have an enduring impact on ethnic politics, reinforcing particular senses of belonging to a people and place and thereby exacerbating the potential for conflicts with other groups.

The colonial period also marked a watershed in relation to the arts of the region. A great majority of Benue Valley artworks, as in most other parts of the world until recently, were of religious significance, forming part of the efforts people made to represent and control the forces that affected their well-being, both for good and bad. Changes in life circumstances entailed changes in religious practices. The twentieth century witnessed an overall erosion of historic religious practices in the face of Christianity and Islam. Seen in its entirety the process was slow and unidirectional. There were, nonetheless, moments of wholesale conversion and rejection of the past, as well as instances where historic religions persisted well into the second half of the twentieth century.

Understandably, changes of this sort could prove a source of generational friction as sons and daughters turned their backs on the religious practices of their parents. After 1960, when Nigeria achieved independence, and 1961, when the eastern end of the Benue Valley was incorporated after the end of the United Nations Cameroons Trusteeship, successive delineations of states and local government areas and the adoption of policies of modernization, alongside the intensified work of Christian missionaries and Muslim reformers, increased the pressures on Middle Belt populations to abandon their historic religions and the local systems of political and social organization that corresponded to them. Much of the religious art of the region came to be viewed as "pagan," and by the end of the twentieth century, many of the types of objects described in this volume had disappeared from local usage; others had shifted in form, purpose, or intention; and yet others had been destroyed, sold, or stolen. For the most part, the tradition-based arts of the Benue Valley have become objects of historical inquiry, including an emerging interest on the part of the peoples whose ancestors created these works, even though they are now more likely to encounter most of them in international art collections or in Nigerian museums than in local practice. Figurative shrine sculpture seems to have been especially vulnerable to these late twentieth-century impacts, while masquerades, since they are also a form of rural entertainment, have been more resilient, especially in the Lower Benue Valley.

EUROPEAN ENCOUNTERS WITH BENUE ARTS AND PEOPLES

What to Europeans appeared as the "exploration" of the Benue occurred largely during the second half of the nineteenth century. We pass over it briefly because it has little bearing for the most part on our grasp of the arts of the Benue Valley, which were virtually unknown before the twentieth century. On his second trip to West Africa, Richard Lander, along with his brother John, followed the course of the Niger downstream by canoe from Bussa, passing the confluence with the Benue (or Tchadda) River on October 25, 1830, and witnessed that the Benue indeed flowed into the Niger. Merchants on the coast did not attempt to ascend the River Niger, and before the switch from sail to steam power, and to shallow draft, would have struggled to do so. The trader John Whitford, in an account of 1877 that drew on his experience from the 1860s onward, describes the long-standing practice (1877, 27).

> Inside several mouths of the river Niger, for a century and a-half, sailing-vessels have been in the habit of anchoring for longer or shorter period, sometimes extended to many months. These ships were carefully housed over with palm-thatch, to exclude the sun, and also to afford shelter during the rains. The masters or supercargoes traded with important chiefs and other clever natives, formerly for slaves, but latterly principally for palm-oil. Strange to say, the trading agents remained in ignorance that they were living at the entrance to the puzzling Niger [that is to the same river described by Mungo Park].

In 1833, the Scottish merchant MacGregor Laird and surgeon R. A. K. Oldfield had been among the few survivors of a party that reached the Benue upriver from the Niger and ascended it a little more than a hundred miles in an iron sternwheeler. It seemed likely that this river was the same as the one Heinrich Barth subsequently reached from the north in 1851 on his ill-starred trip to Yola where the Emir had no wish to receive him. Macgregor Laird was contracted to organize the Pleiad expedition of 1854 that gained the upper reaches of the river and confirmed that the rivers known from the south and north were indeed one and the same (Crowther 1855; Hutchison 1855; Baikie 1856). That no lives were lost during this expedition was due largely to the use of quinine as an anti-malarial and to the diplomatic skills of Samuel Crowther. Soon, European merchants were routinely circumventing the monopolies of African coastal traders by turning the Niger and Benue rivers into thoroughfares, as Whitford describes.

> At the present time six or seven steamers of light draught run for nine months of the year, making as many trips as they can to and from the factories as far as the Confluence, and during the height of the rainy season they are enabled to proceed to factories established above the Confluence. They deliver goods and receive produce; but they are obliged to be well armed, for the savages in the Delta frequently fire upon them as they pass to and fro. [1877, 130–31]

The subsequent history of the river from the perspective of European proto-colonization revolved around the activities of successive British trading companies directed by George Goldie (the United Africa Company 1877, National Africa Company 1881, Royal Niger Company 1886 until revocation of its charter in 1900). These staved off French and German competition until spheres of interest were agreed at the Berlin Conference (1884–1885). Its main significance from the point of view of the Benue River was agreement to the broad principles to be used in subsequent border demarcation between Nigeria and German Kamerun. Very few artworks were collected or documented during this "exploratory," or more strictly "commercializing," period, although some expeditions left behind useful records of their forays into the Benue Valley (for instance those of the Germans Eduard Flegel, 1890, and Siegfried Passarge,

1895; the Frenchman Louis Mizon, 1892; or the Belgian Adolphe Burdo, 1880). It is
to the twentieth century that we must look for more intensive documentation.

The formal colonization of Nigeria and Kamerun inaugurated a qualitatively different documentation and collection of artworks, upon which this volume draws heavily. Many of the most important early acquisitions were made before the First World
War by colonial officers in the course of their duties rather than by specialists. German
officers were particularly active at the eastern end of the Valley in what was then
Kamerun. Their collections, which often mixed "Völkerkunde" with natural specimens,
were sent via the Berlin museums, which took first pick of items with the remainder
reaching the museums of other great cities (notably the Linden-Museum in Stuttgart
[see fig. 10.39, this volume], and collections in Dresden, Leipzig etc.). The most significant of the professional collectors from Germany, the indefatigable and rapacious Leo
Frobenius, traversed both British and German territories during 1911–1912, making the
most extensive single collection of the period, parts of which were acquired by all the
major German museums (see figs. 10.6, 16.40, 16.41).

A British woman, Olive Macleod (who would soon become Olive Temple),
ascended the River Benue with a surveying expedition of 1910 in search of the resting
place of her intended husband, Boyd Alexander, who had been killed earlier that year.
Her collection of objects was serendipitous compared to the systematic scouring of
a Frobenius, mostly "curios" to use her own term (MacLeod 1912, 6)—small items
of slight value acquired at markets or as gifts from British officials—but her journey
nonetheless resulted in accessions to the collections of the British Museum in London
(see figs 15.8; 16.13) and the Liverpool Museum. Missionaries and colonial officers in
pre–World War I Nigeria made occasional contributions both to written records and
collections that are particularly significant for often being our earliest in the archive
of artworks and their documentation.

The partition of German Kamerun after the First World War put another eastern
slice of the Benue Valley under British administration and meant that documentation
of its art between the two World Wars became a predominantly British affair. This is
the period when colonial officers with anthropological interests completed substantial
work (from senior officials such as H. R. Palmer, at the time Lieutenant Governor of the
Northern Provinces, and C. L. Temple, to R. C. Abraham, R. M. Downes, E. S. Lilley,
among others). The Department of Anthropology in the Nigerian Colonial Service was
established in 1924 (Kasfir 2007, 86). The most significant researcher for the Benue River
Valley, and the one most often cited in this volume, was C. K. Meek, appointed a government anthropologist in 1925, who at the behest of H. R. Palmer authored a substantial
monograph on the Jukun (Meek 1931a), as well as a series of extensive studies on many of
the peoples of the Benue Valley (largely anthologized in two volumes; see Meek 1931b).

By the Second World War more professional expertise was brought to bear on the
study of arts. A survey of Nigerian art commissioned from the artist and art teacher
Kenneth Murray in 1943 led to the establishment of a Department of Antiquities of
which he became the first director (Willett 2002, 38; Kasfir 1999, 144; Jegede 1996,
129). The National Museum at Lagos was supplemented by an active branch in Jos,
which collected objects particularly from the Benue Valley. Professional anthropological
research in the region also intensified during this period, notably with the Tiv researches
between 1949 and 1953 of Laura and Paul Bohannan. They were to be followed by
numerous researchers during the later 1950s and early 1960s (some of the pioneers,
like the late John Boston, as well as Mette Bovin, are represented in this volume).

A second major wave of collecting occurred in the late 1960s and 1970s when
an exodus of objects, mainly through Cameroon, followed the disturbances caused
by the Nigerian Civil War (1967–1970), fought in the country's southeastern region
over the attempted secession of Biafra. Emerging onto the international art market,
most of these works entered private collections, and today a substantial number have

been acquired by museums in the United States and Europe. We have a good overall grasp of this trade through which predominantly African "runners" (as dealers called those who went into the field)[4] prospected the Benue Valley either directly on behalf of French, and secondarily Belgian, dealers based in Cameroon, or occasionally for Cameroonian dealers who in turn dealt with Europeans (see Joubert, pp. 561–67; also Geary and Xatart 2007, 14, for insight into the Cameroonian organization). Shipped to Europe, these pieces entered private collections (sometimes those of the dealers themselves) and quickly found their way to galleries in the United States (some of them managed by European dealers).

It is more difficult to reconstruct the circumstances under which these objects entered the hands of African "runners" in local communities. While there is no doubt that they were usually bought or bartered, quite who had the right to sell such religious objects remains contentious. The broader political, religious, and economic contexts of these Civil War years, which occurred during a period of coercive action against "heathenism," provided ample license for abuses of property rights. These were, in many cases, more complex than issues of individual ownership. The entry of Benue Valley objects onto the international art market through these mediations tended to reinforce the already-existing inclination to associate genres of objects with "tribal" labels because of the identifications provided to dealers by the "runners" who had collected them. The terms used by art dealers and gallery owners to identify objects then current in the art market were hence out of step with, and considerably less sophisticated than, the discourse by scholars on Benue Valley arts, one notably begun by Roy Sieber in the late 1950s and continued by Arnold Rubin in the 1960s.

The 1970s and 1980s saw several social anthropologists, historians, and art historians—including some represented in this volume—undertake studies of particular peoples that were either centrally concerned with their arts or, at the least, curious about them. This pattern continued in the last decade of the twentieth century and into the twenty-first, though perhaps with reduced intensity. How much scope remains for research into the historic art forms of the region, especially those associated with local religious practices, varies in different parts of the Benue Valley, but in some places must be considered very limited indeed (by exception, see Weise and Willis in this volume, whose doctoral research concerns the more resilient Niger-Benue confluence masquerades). Despite at least a half-century of intensive field research, the documentation of artistic genres *in situ* is uneven. Yet, when it is allied to the record of collecting, and given the correspondences between many of the peoples occupying the Benue River Valley subregions, it provides the basis for a more detailed reconstruction of the region's arts than has previously been attempted or indeed thought possible.

ISSUES OF COLLECTING, PROVENANCE, AND PATRIMONY

Without doubt, the history of collecting strongly colors our knowledge of Benue arts. As indicated already, much of the corpus of Benue River Valley collections derives from two sources: from the early colonial period, which provided predominantly documented pieces to museum collections, and from the period of the Nigerian Civil War and its aftermath, which produced many more pieces but much less information. The upshot is that we find ourselves going back to the colonial collections to assist in restoring context to objects that exited Nigeria later, mostly without information and before intensive fieldwork was accomplished. Because Arnold Rubin's earliest fieldwork pre-dated the Civil War, the value of the extensive documentation he left us is readily apparent.

In several ways, we need to repair the loss of context most objects have undergone. This can be a physical loss: in the course of being removed from their former contexts to new owners, both private and public in the West, many of the objects shown here have lost accretions of use or accoutrements of display, which were thought to disguise the "pure" sculptural forms preferred by collectors. Some of these transformations are striking (cf. figs. 4.1, 4.4). More often the loss involves the origins and purposes of art-works (fig. 4). Photographs taken in situ by researchers help us narrow the provenance of works entering collections without documentation. In some instances we can match the very objects photographed in context with those now in collections. Ascertaining provenance, however, does not suffice to reconstruct the lifeways of objects; for this we need the evidence of ethnographic investigation.

Many objects featured here were sold or stolen during and in the aftermath of the Biafran War, when traders (both runners and dealers) took advantage of Nigeria's porous eastern border and the calamitous poverty of a war-ravaged country. We can only speculate on the local circumstances. The same era witnessed the increasing aban-donment of local religious practices and of the objects that served them, so the cash or goods offered by runners who serviced the growing market in Benue Valley sculpture must have seemed enticing to the local sellers, whoever they were. These sellers, in their turn, may have convinced themselves that such things were no longer needed, or were even actively unwanted.[5] It is unlikely they would have been aware that the sale of things owned within their communities required licenses for their ultimate export from Nigeria.[6] This begs the question about the rights and wrongs of chains of actions instigated forty or more years ago that involved many actors who have exited the stage. Nonetheless their consequences persist. What, then, do we do in the present? We cannot resolve all the issues of proprietorship, but as scholars we are conscious of a responsibility to the historic record. John Picton (2010, 6) has written that,

> The fact that a work of art, once in a shrine or temple, is now in a museum, wherever that museum might be, cannot automatically imply that the process of its disposal was necessarily illegal. More research is the only answer to that question. Meanwhile, at least let us agree that the material should be seen and published, otherwise we remain in ignorance fired by stereotype and misinformation.

In this spirit, we include objects here that offer testimony to the Benue River Valley's artistic and cultural legacy. They are published with our best efforts to reconstruct their provenance, whether from direct evidence or by comparison and argument, and without any attempt to conceal their arduous and conflicted journeys. A principal aim of this effort is to unite Benue Valley objects, labeled by us as works of art, with the field obser-vations that restore their former significance, so that they can be understood not simply through Western eyes but also through the purposes of those who made and used them.

Sometimes, as a recent case demonstrates, the theft of a material container may involve the loss of its contents. The spirit vessels made by the Ga'anda peoples of the Upper Benue region are among the more recent exports from Nigeria into Western col-lections (see figs. 17.14a, 17.15a; also Kren 2010, figs. 2–6). According to e-mail exchanges Marla Berns has had with several Ga'anda men who are writing their own history (see Ayuba Chifartawa 2009; also chapter 15, 472–73), these ceramic vessels were taken from shrines under circumstances where few elders remain to protect them or to maintain the long-held traditions in which they once held important religious currency. Many are abandoned in remote locations a long distance from communities where relatives of former custodians live. In a video interview conducted by Ga'anda historian Felix Theman with several elders in Ga'anda Town in 2010 (fig. 5), he asked them to describe the current efficacy of such spirit pots and the situation surrounding their removal from shrines. A summary of their responses is telling: "Theft is becoming a worrisome issue. But there is little you can do about a thief who is determined to take away your property, especially if the item is isolated.…These pots are containers. The spirit in them never dies, so when a new pot is provided the spirit occupies it.… It was only the pot that was stolen, leaving the spirit behind. The performance of the spirit does not change because

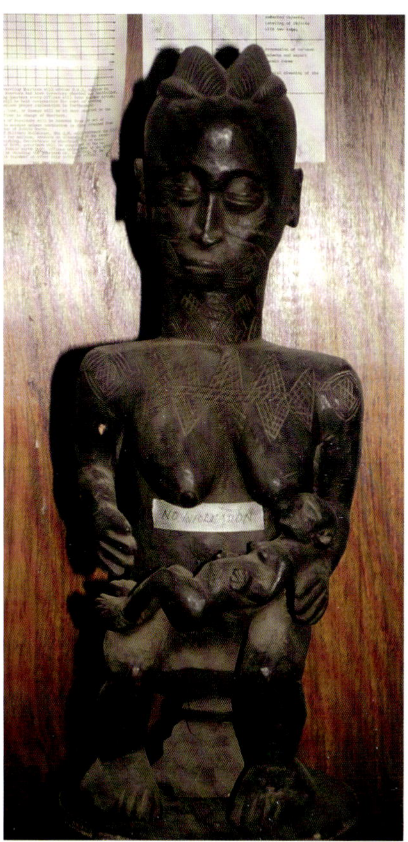

4
This amusing, and unfortunately all too accurate, image confirms that many sculp-tures found their way into the storerooms of Nigerian museums accompanied by little or no information. Arnold Rubin took this pic-ture in 1982 when he visited the Jos Museum where the figure was labeled as "Kaduna-Eloi" (JM.51.35.4). Based on similar figures, it may have come from an Afo village (Eloi being an alternate name for the Afo people).

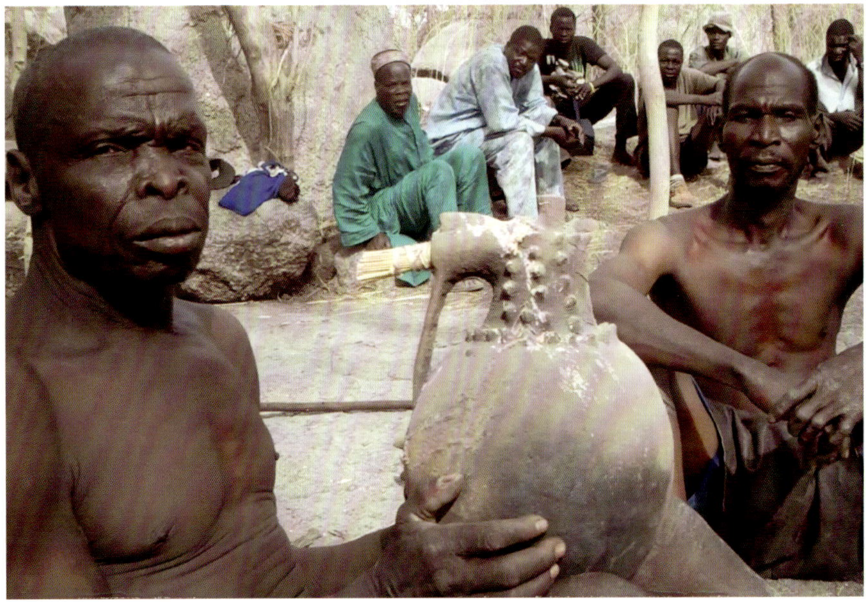

it is in a new pot." The objects we venerate as art and value for their physical properties
are thus emptied of their former power, which stays behind and can be refocused into
newly made containers (figs. 6, 7; see also fig. 17.10). This malleability does not excuse
the removal of once spirit-charged objects under unwanted circumstances nor ignore
their shifts in meaning as they enter new public arenas. When Felix Theman and his
fellow historians were informed that we wanted to publish (and display) several Ga'anda
vessels now residing in Western collections, they and their elders embraced the proposal
as a source of pride as well as a way to preserve their fast-retreating cultural heritage.

We carry the burden that some of our own fieldwork and publications (particularly
those that are illustrated) have provided treasure maps. As Arnold Rubin (1988, 9) wrote
in response to learning that Jukun sculptures from the village of Gwana had emerged in
collections only years after he had photographed them in 1966 and reproduced them in
his dissertation of 1969 (see figs 8.52–8.54): "there exists an obligation to the priests and
elders who provided information and access, believing in the value of their heritage but
feeling themselves without heirs, and thus with no alternative to placing their heritage
in the public domain as the only hope for preservation."[7] It is with respect for the identities and purposes these objects once held, and in the hope of correcting misconcep-
tions and misattributions, that we have included them here. Even those with uncertain
or illegitimate ownership are included in an effort to promote knowledge about them
and to make them accessible for additional study. We do not yet possess the wider "ethnography of loss" for the Benue Valley that might help us understand the significance
of these formerly powerful ritual objects to new generations of Nigerians seeking to
comprehend their past. Ethnic self-consciousness, we would venture, will inevitably lead
new actors, like the Ga'anda historians mentioned above, to explore their patrimonies
and write more chapters about the "meanings" of the artworks of the Benue Valley.

Taking the course of the Benue River from its source in Cameroon down to its confluence with the Niger as both a geographical actuality and a concrete metaphor, the essays
in *Central Nigeria Unmasked* highlight the ways that artworks—their movements and
malleability—bear witness to histories of exchange and interaction between local communities, concentrating on the nineteenth and twentieth century. Artistic genres were
rarely confined to particular peoples, places, or even contexts of use. Artworks might
be made by one group and used by another; the meanings and purposes of the same
artworks might change within a locality; newly adopted objects might be reinvented

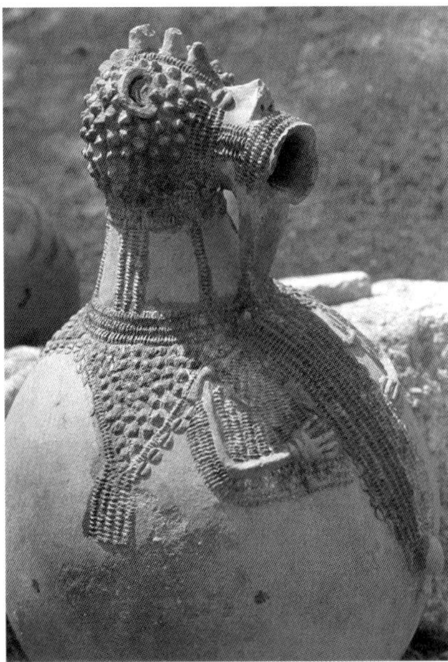

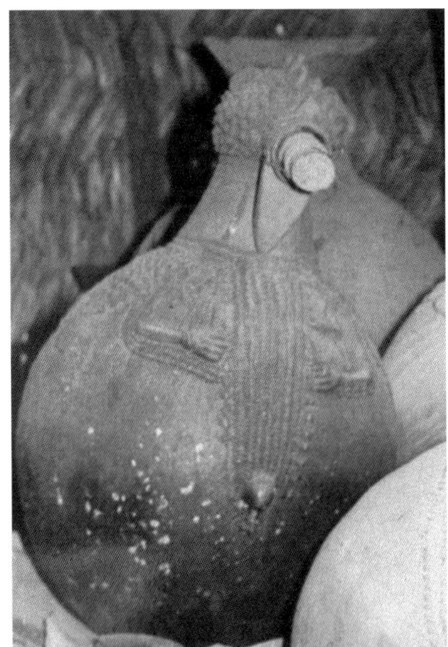

6
The now-missing Mbir'thleng'nda was removed from its enclosure on Makwar Hill during annual propitiation rituals in 1980. Its whereabouts today are unknown, but it was stolen sometime after this photograph was taken (see also fig. 17.10).
PHOTOGRAPH BY MARLA C. BERNS, 1980.

7
This is a rare photograph of the Mbir'thleng'nda pot seen in figure 6 situated within its shrine enclosure on Makwar Hill, taken by the Danish missionary Erna Lindgaard of the Sudan United Mission, who was stationed in Ga'anda from at least 1957–1960 (Nissen 1968, 225). Arnold Rubin copied Miss Lindgaard's photo on March 24, 1970, during his visit to Ga'anda.
RUBIN ARCHIVE, FOWLER MUSEUM AT UCLA, NEG. NO. 2546.

in particular ways; stylistic traits or approaches, rather than specific objects, might be shared; and objects may have been collected from places they were neither originally created or used. As Kasfir notes in chapter 2 of this volume, valuable or sacred objects do not stay put. From the evidence of numerous examples documented in this volume, the "life histories" of artworks were seldom simple. Their complex itineraries, extending from Nigeria to museums, galleries, and private collections in the West, frequently involved multiple actors who have influenced how we have come to understand them (creators, practitioners, initiates, traders, collectors, and scholars). This is an open-ended list of cautions about the historical complexity of our area of study, from which the main conclusion to draw is the need for investigators to counter the "tribal style" thinking of older sources in two regards: with sociologically subtle understandings of ethnicity and identity and with an aesthetically informed grasp of regionally distributed forms.

This volume unfolds in three main sections following the course of the Benue River through its valley upriver, between its confluences with the Niger and Gongola rivers. The editors of the three sections, Sidney Littlefield. Kasfir (Lower Benue), Richard Fardon (Middle Benue), and Marla C. Berns (Upper Benue), introduce the geography and history of each subregion and follow with one or more major essays on the distinctive artistic genres made by its varied and interconnected peoples, concentrating on the issues and applying the approaches discussed above. Chapters follow in each section written by contributing authors focusing on the arts of specific groups, on particular genres whose stylistic resemblances reveal shared histories, or on local areas where ethnic and artistic identities are complex and fluid. Full chapters are interspersed with shorter "interleaves," which spotlight the work of particular artists or constellations of objects. Throughout, this account is heavily illustrated with field photographs—many never before published—and with studio photographs, most of them depicting objects included in the traveling exhibition this volume accompanies.

The comparative, cross-cultural, and geographical approach that underlies *Central Nigeria Unmasked* is designed to go beyond revelations of style in order to examine the extent to which complex formal and functional correspondences, or even partial connections, can be considered by-products of history. In so doing, this project "unmasks" the dynamic and fluid nature of art and reveals local spheres of interaction, adaptation, and transformation in which objects have moved. Over the centuries, the Benue River Valley witnessed a confluence of peoples, institutions, and ideas that on the occasion of this exhibition and accompanying publication can now be understood as having resulted in one of the major artistic heritages of sub-Saharan Africa.

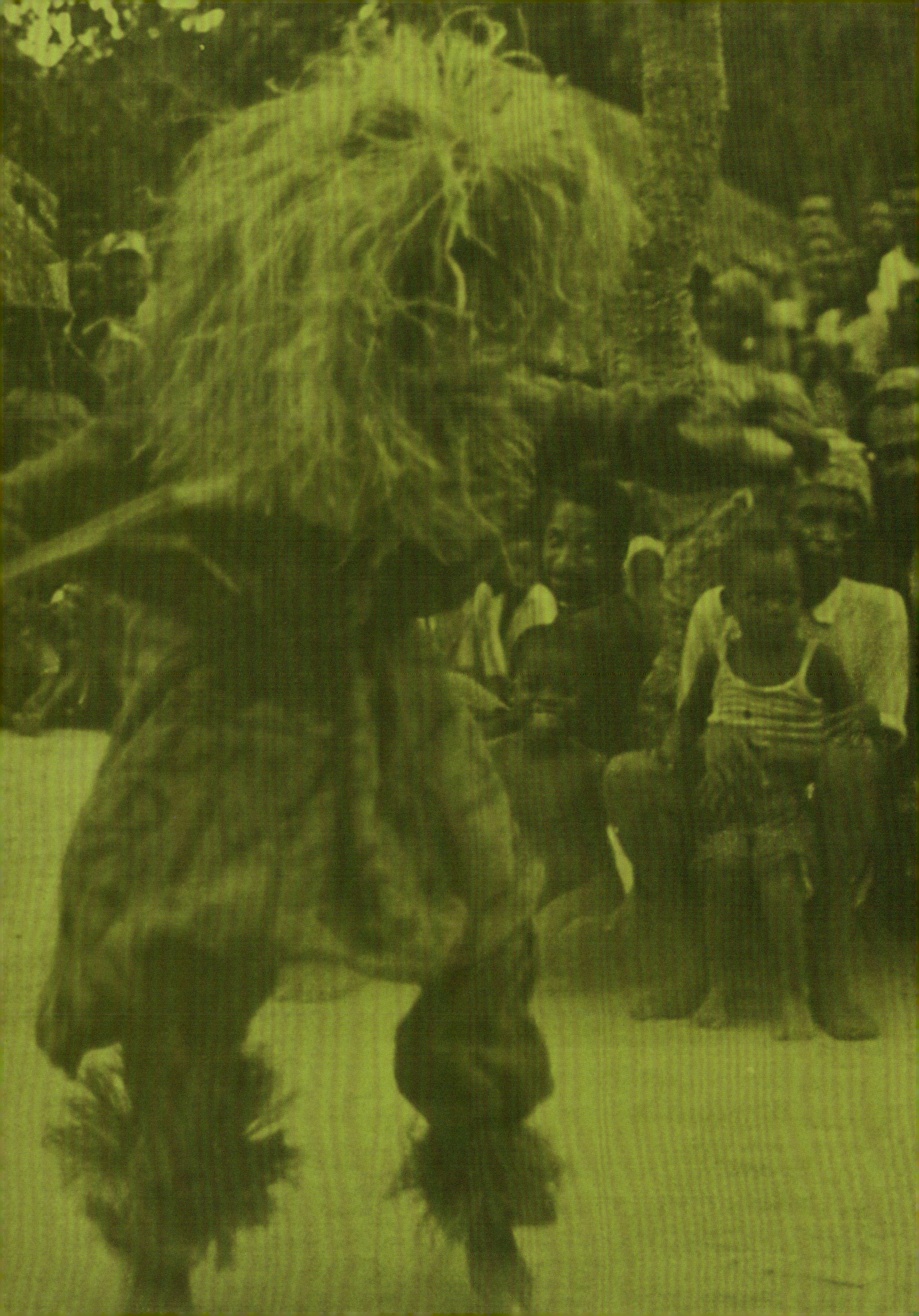

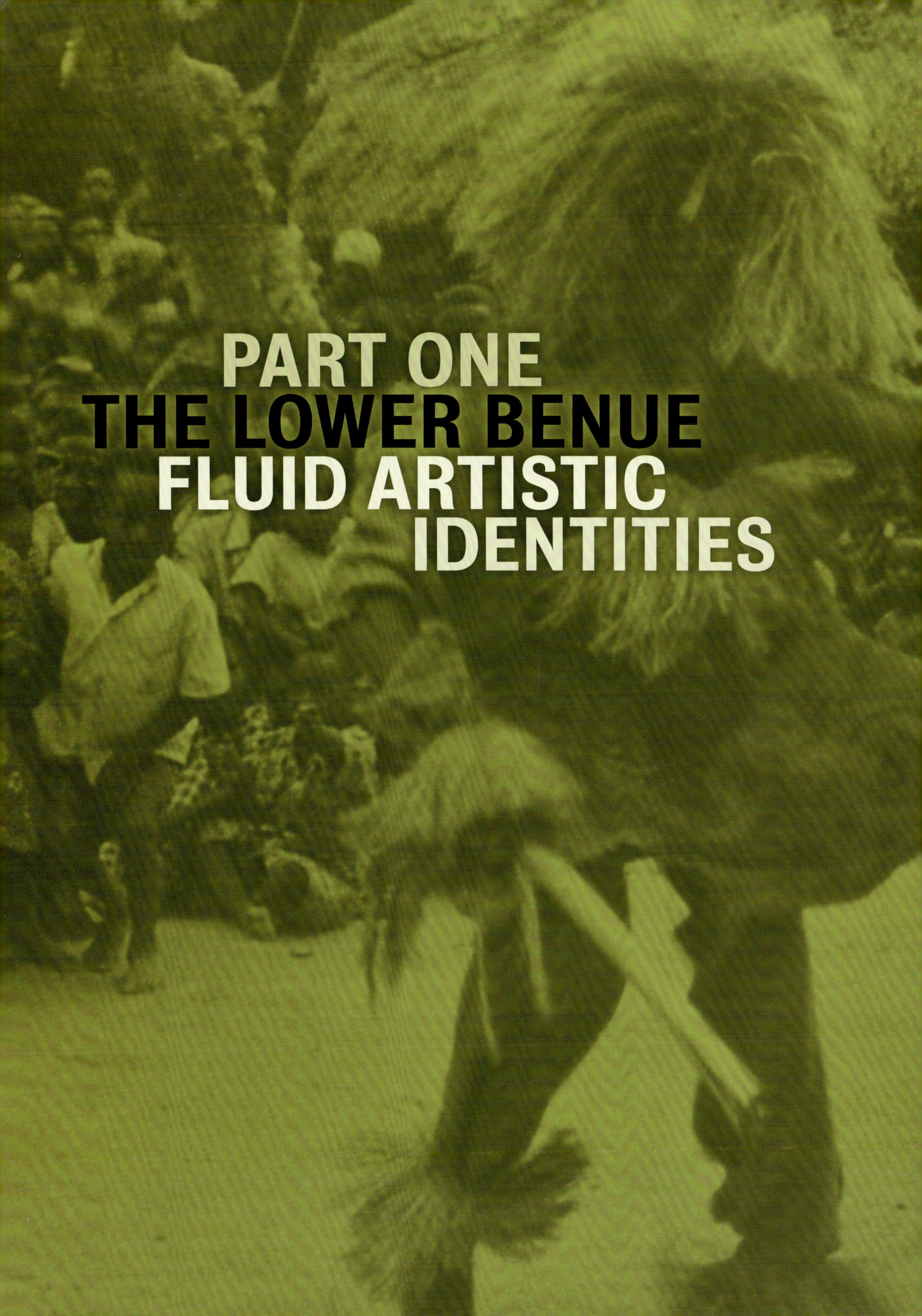
PART ONE
THE LOWER BENUE
FLUID ARTISTIC
IDENTITIES

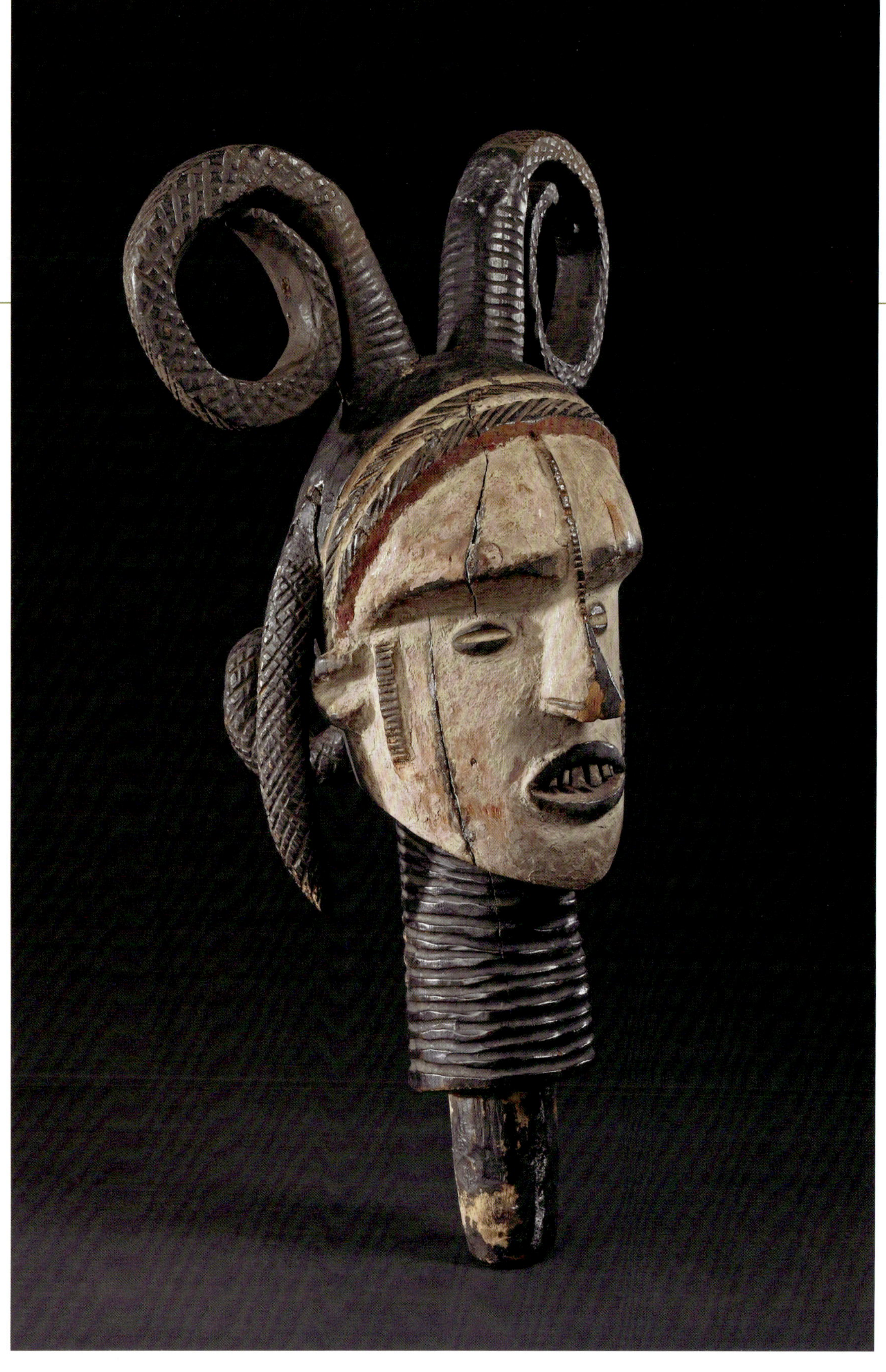

CHAPTER 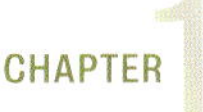

Introduction: Reimagining Lower Benue Art History

SIDNEY LITTLEFIELD KASFIR

The Lower Benue region lies within the Niger-Benue trough. Its surface has been cut by centuries of erosion into table-like hills and gorges, and it is humid most of the year, relief coming only during the harmattan season of December to February when dry winds blow from the Sahara (fig. 1.2). Long savanna grasses dotted by trees occupy both banks of the Benue, giving way to a forest-savanna mosaic in the more southern districts. Within this region the principal ethnolinguistic groups are Igala, Idoma, and Tiv on the south bank; Afo, Alago (Idoma Nokwu), and Egbira on the north bank; and Ebira across the Niger-Benue confluence. Also at or near the confluence are Nupe, Yoruba, Okpella, Bassa Nge, and Bassa Komo.

The combination of adequate rainfall (127–190 cm per year) and relatively open orchard bush alternating with stands of high forest (figs. 1.3, 1.4) makes possible the cultivation of both savanna grains (millet, guinea corn, maize) and forest root crops (yam, cassava), giving rise to the term "Middle Belt." These crops not only form the basis of subsistence farming but are also important in the ritual cycle. While yams are ritualized in the more southern districts, it is millet and guinea corn that are sung of in the ancestral chants of central and northern Idoma and Igala. This is a key point in the traditions of origin of certain masquerades. The most important feature of the region, however, both historically and in the landscape, has been the Benue River itself. The Benue rises in the highlands of Cameroon and flows west into Nigeria toward its confluence with the Niger. In the rainy season, it is easily navigable and is more than a mile wide in places. Historically, this has made it both path and barrier, depending on the circumstances: a path of escape, trade, or migration by canoe, but a barrier for the cavalry of the nineteenth-century Fulani jihad and earlier conflicts. My broad subject is the role of the Benue River as a corridor for the movement of art styles, forms, and ideas over a period of several centuries of change, roughly from 1600 to 1900.

THE BRITISH ENCOUNTER

Prior to British colonization, several exploring voyages up the Lower Niger and Benue rivers provide the first maps and written accounts of the region. The diaries of these nineteenth-century travelers (Laird and Oldfield 1837; Crowther 1855; Hutchison 1855; Baikie 1856) do not distinguish between Idoma and central and eastern Igala, referring to both regions as "Akpoto." The term "Igara" (Igala) at that time described only a narrow strip along the Niger (Kwara) River from the confluence to Ibaji (fig. 1.5), which included the capital town of Idah (Idda). The multiple features that Igala and Idoma culture have in common, especially ancestral masquerades and kingship rituals, may

Masks of this type are derived from the former practice of warriors who, during dances among their groups, wore human crania atop their own heads. This was common in the Cross River region, southeastern Idoma, and Ogoja during the late nineteenth and early twentieth centuries.

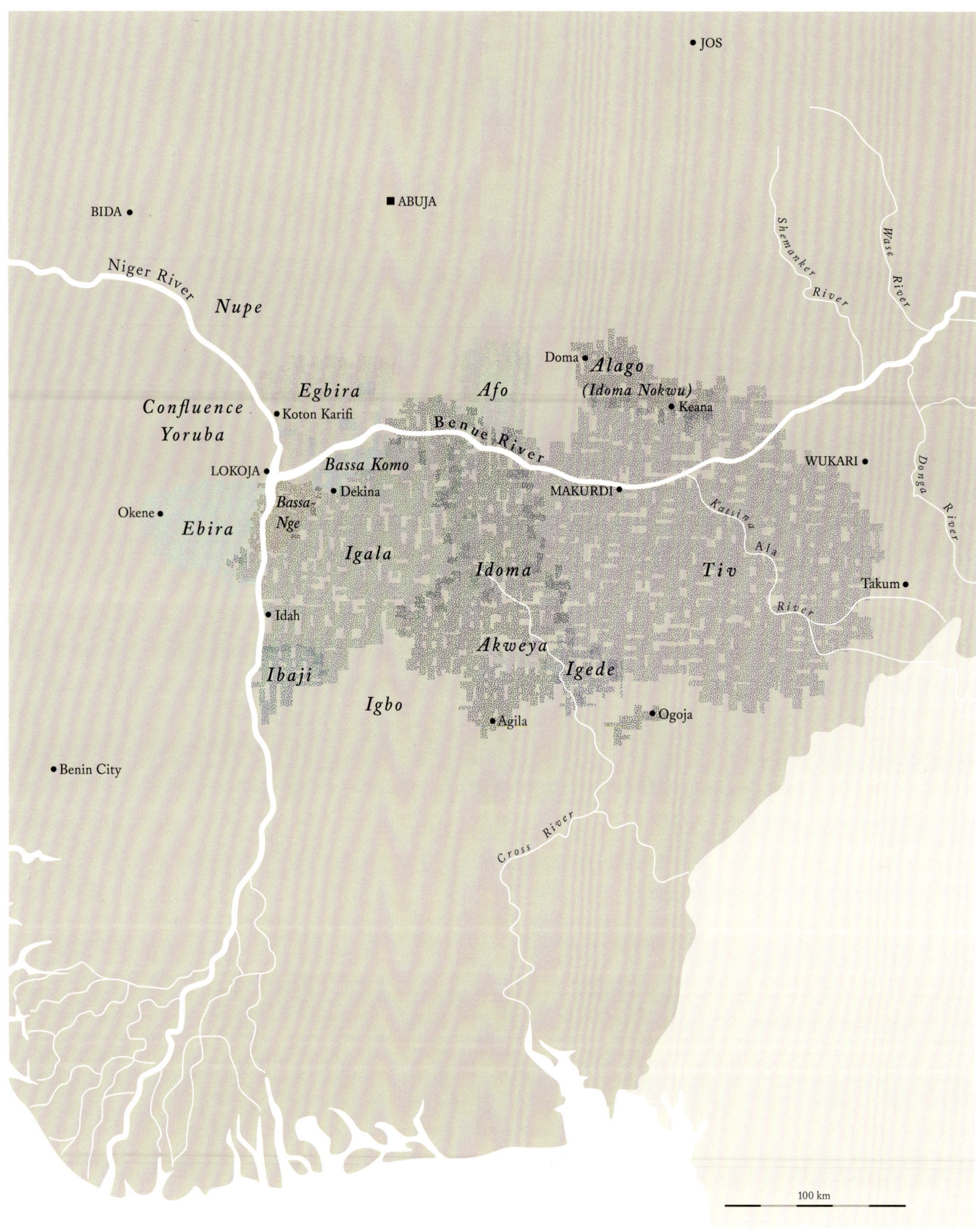

1.2

Map showing the peoples of the Lower Benue
region discussed in part 1.

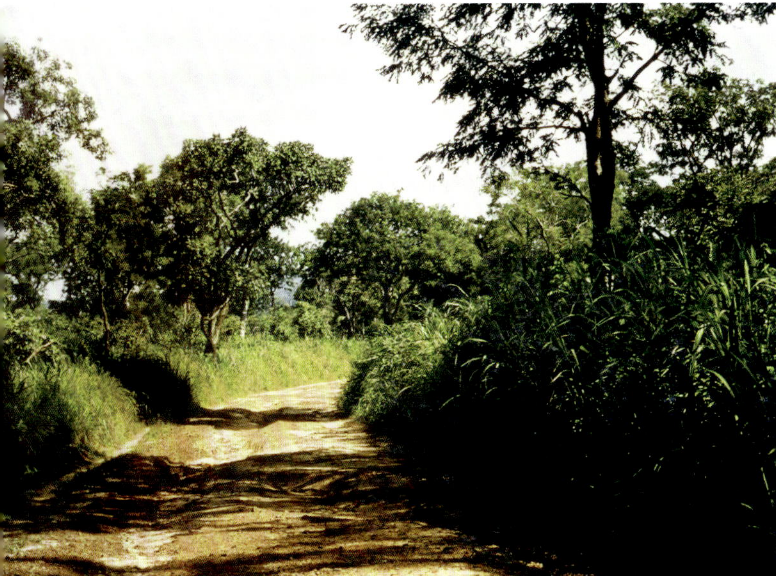

1.3

A road meanders through trees and tall grasses in central Idomaland.

PHOTOGRAPH BY SIDNEY LITTLEFIELD KASFIR, 1976.

1.4

A woman stands outside her compound.

PHOTOGRAPH BY SIDNEY LITTLEFIELD KASFIR, CENTRAL IDOMALAND, 1976.

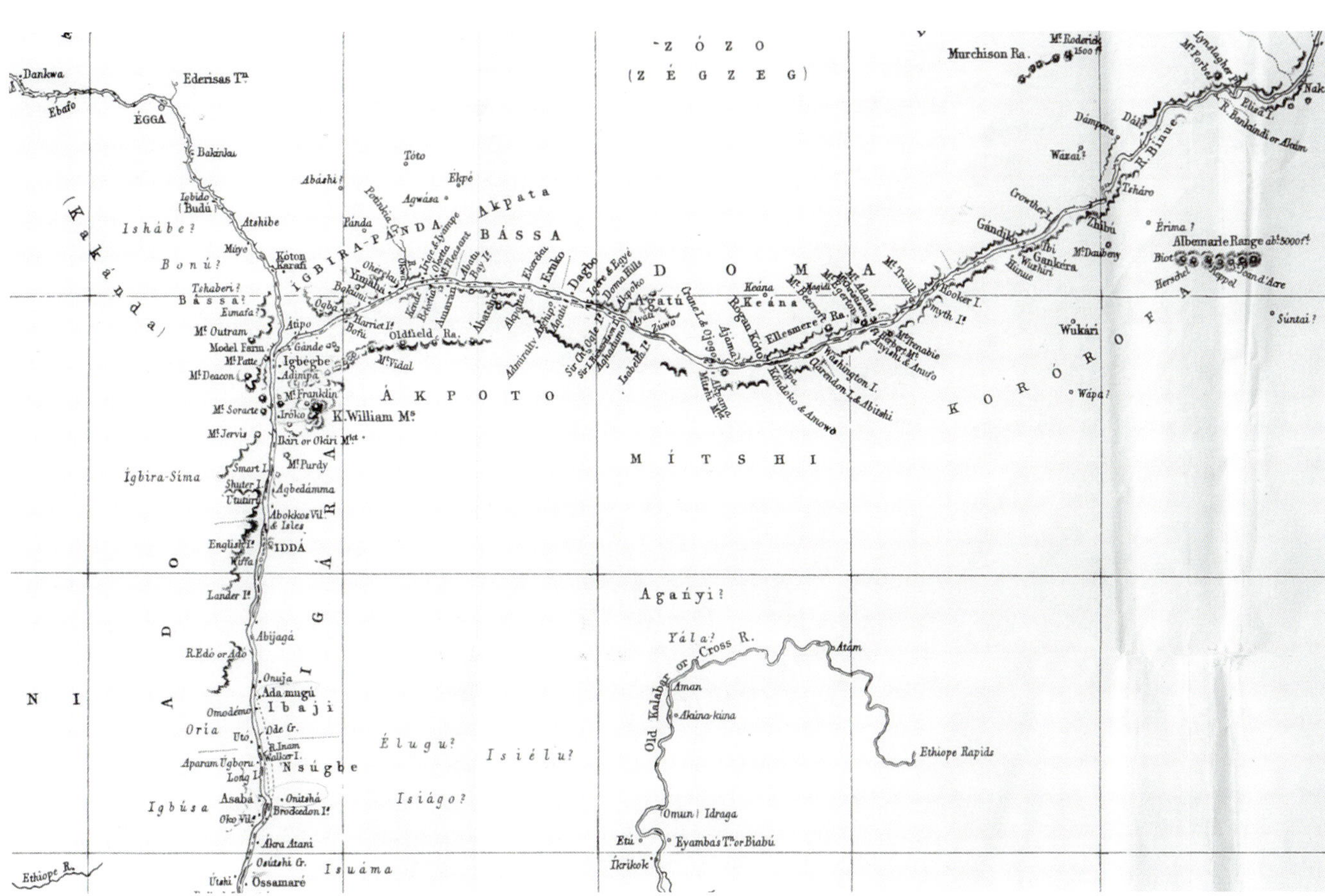

1.5

This map is reproduced from William Baikie's *Narrative of an Exploring Voyage up the Rivers Kwóra and Bínue, Commonly Known as the Niger and Tsádda in 1854* (1856). The name "Akpoto" is used to designate the area occupied by the Igala and Idoma.

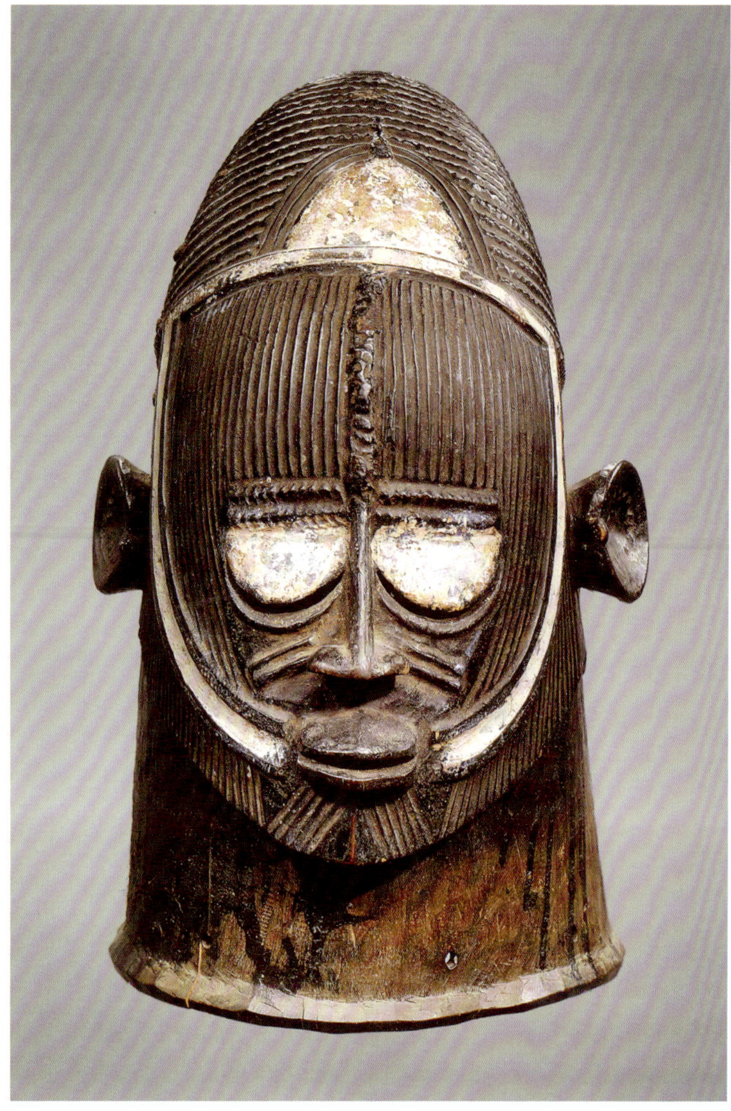

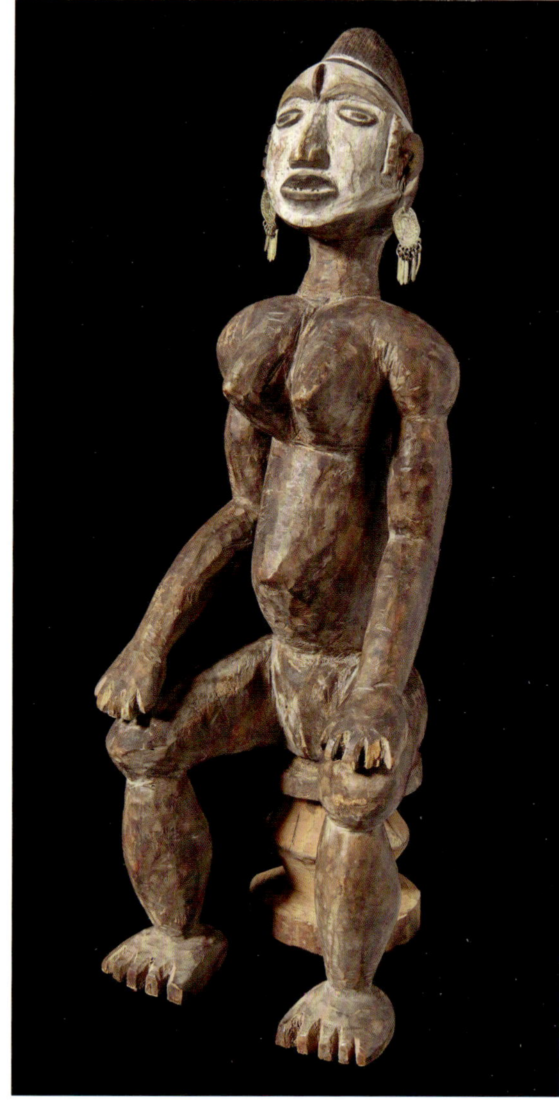

1.6

Helmet mask (Agba)
Igala peoples, nineteenth–early twentieth century
Wood, polychrome
H: 34 cm

COLLECTION OF LILIANE AND MICHEL DURAND-DESSERT
IMAGE: COURTESY PRIVATE COLLECTOR. PHOTOGRAPH © HUGHES DUBOIS
PROVENANCE: COLLECTED BY JEAN-MICHEL HUGUENIN, NIGERIA, 1967

This mask found in the Ibaji area of southern Igala generically resembles the royal Odumado mask (see fig. 5.7) in the Egwu Ata set of masquerades in the capital city of Idah. In Ibaji, however, Agba comes out at funerals and festivals to commemorate the founders of local lineage groups. The faces of both types have vertical striations, two parallel scars originating at the sides of the nose, and whitened ridges running from mouth to temple. They also share prominent downcast eyes, a vertical forehead ridge, and a small beard.

well be evidence of a deep shared past, partly obscured by the imposition of an alien Igala kingship and Igala language.[1] The greatest problem in accepting "Akpoto" identity as a key unlocking a common origin for the proto-Idoma and proto-Igala peoples is language: Idoma and Igala are distinctly different Eastern Kwa languages, and there is no evidence whatever of a separate "Akpoto" language. Yet the early colonial district records are full of references to Akpoto or Okpoto, usually in the western districts of Idoma near eastern Igala.[2]

If nineteenth-century explorers created one map of the Benue, the colonization process that followed produced another. The British administration after 1900 created divisional boundaries, and as a technique of Indirect Rule, local rulers were used to enforce colonial authority. Inevitably, the ruler's lineage was elevated in power and importance, and the immigrant groups within the newly created Idoma Division gradually adopted an Idoma identity, even while maintaining their own masking traditions and other signs of difference.[3]

The first researchers[4] to arrive in what was Benue Province (referred to as the "Lower Benue" in the present book) in the late colonial period found three modern administrative divisions corresponding to the south bank's ethnic boundaries: Igala, Idoma, and Tiv. While the centralized Igala kingship had been in existence for centuries, precolonial Idoma-speaking peoples south of the Benue had been divided into many small independent kingdoms and chiefdoms over whom the British had appointed an Och'Idoma for administrative convenience within their system of Indirect Rule. Seeing themselves at a political disadvantage, the traditionally egalitarian and acephalous Tiv pressed the British for a parallel authority whom they named the Tor Tiv.

After Nigerian Independence in 1960, several successive military regimes appointed military governors as secular heads of the new states including Benue State. So-called traditional rulers like the Och'Idoma have continued to handle local affairs such as land disputes. But these late colonial and postcolonial political arrangements have occluded the history that lies behind them, which is crucial to understanding Lower Benue art in its regional setting. A major objective of this essay and others that follow is to show how unique histories and geographies have affected the major genres of this art: masks (fig. 1.6) and figure sculpture (fig. 1.7).

COMPETING SCENARIOS OF BENUE VALLEY ART HISTORY BEFORE 1800

The Benue River Valley is too far south for the Arab geographers to have visited and too far north for the European coastal traders to have penetrated before the mid-nineteenth century, so it remains something of a historical puzzle in which fundamental questions have not yet been settled. Even such a basic issue as the existence of Kororofa (Kwararafa, Apá) as a precolonial state has not been accepted by some scholars. For the past forty years, there have been two competing models of Lower and Middle Benue Valley history prior to 1800, one favored by functionalist anthropologists writing in the tradition of Bronislaw Malinowski, the other by oral historians who were students of J. B. Webster.

In the first model, using mainly the evidence of linguistic distributions and discounting the face value of oral traditions, all the cultures of the Lower and Middle Benue, with the exception of the Tiv, have "always" occupied substantially the same territory that they do now. In this view, the elaborate accounts of migration from the Jukun homeland of Apá—claimed by Idoma, Igala, Alago, Ebira, Goemai, and others—are strategies designed to lend legitimacy to present politics by conferring an ancient pedigree upon them. This view implicitly casts doubt on a Kororofa "state," which later broke apart, ever existing in the Benue region.

The second model, by contrast, accepts the truth of systematically collected oral traditions at face value whenever cross-checking reveals congruence (e.g., Erim 1981). In this interpretation the Idoma, the present Igala ruling lineages, the Alago, Ebira, Goemai, Akweya, and others lived "near Okali" (Wukari) in close proximity to the Jukun and Abakwariga (non-Muslim Hausa) in a federation of small states known in Hausa traditions as Kororofa and among themselves as Apá. The Kano Chronicle records that Kororofa attacked Kano in the sixteenth century.[5] The Bornu Chronicle contains similar accounts, both suggesting that Kororofa not only existed but was a formidable military expansionist state or federation of states between the fourteenth and sixteenth centuries. The Jukun (who call themselves Apá or Apajuku) gradually gained dominance in the confederacy, causing its capital to be moved from the Gongola Valley to Puje south of the Benue River.

A "horse war," according to the Idoma, forced them to move out of this area, eventually to settle further west in their present location where the British military patrols first encountered them early in the twentieth century. While Robert G. Armstrong (1955, 97) had assumed that this horse war referred to the Fulani jihad against the Benue in the nineteenth century, Erim O. Erim's (1981, 23) informants claimed that it happened two or three hundred years earlier, which caused him to link it to the defeat of Kororofa by the armies of Bornu.

More dramatically, the history of the Igala Kingdom contains three separate periods of dominance according to its oral traditions, in contrast to the "has always been there" linguistic mapping in which, like Yoruba to the west and Idoma to the east, Igala is an Eastern Kwa language. John Boston, the principal ethnographer of the Igala who conducted his research in the late fifties and early sixties (see chapter 5), bridged

1.7 (OPPOSITE, RIGHT)
Water spirit figure (Anjenu)
Idoma peoples, circa 1932
Wood, pigment, metal
H: 39.5 cm
PITT RIVERS MUSEUM, UNIVERSITY OF OXFORD, 1932.33.1
IMAGE: © PITT RIVERS MUSEUM, UNIVERSITY OF OXFORD
PROVENANCE: COLLECTED BY CAPTAIN BEAVER, 1932 (NOT IN EXHIBITON)

This is one of two similar figures that were probably commissioned by Captain Beaver from an Akweya artist, possibly Ochai (see interleaf A). The two figures show no signs of use.

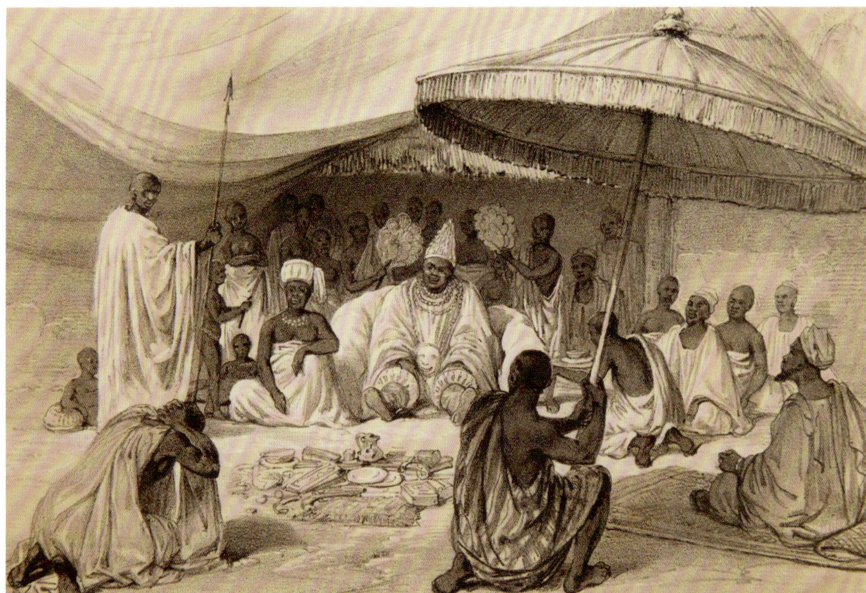

1.8
This nineteenth-century engraving shows
the Ata of Idah wearing the Ejube-jailo brass
pectoral mask.
REPRODUCED FROM WILLIAM ALLEN, *PICTURESQUE
VIEWS ON THE RIVER NIGER: SKETCHED DURING
LANDER'S LAST VISIT IN 1832–33* (LONDON: MURRAY,
1840).

these two models by collecting detailed oral traditions but then subjecting them to
the caveats of the functionalist approach: "oral traditions perform a political as well
as a historical function—in Malinowski's phrase, they provide charters of institutions.
And when we look at them as supposedly objective records of the past, we are perhaps
distorting their perspective and failing to grasp something of the essential function of
oral tradition" (Boston 1969, 29–30).

Nonetheless, Boston went on to affirm that the ruling dynasty in Igala has been an
immigrant one for many centuries and to sketch three probable periods of foreign influence. The most ancient connection, he argued, was to the Yoruba, based on the structure
of the Igala kingship—which is very similar to that of the Yoruba—and on the close
linguistic affinity of Igala to Yoruba; the second period, according to Boston, was one of
dominance of the kingship by Benin following the Igala-Benin War of 1517. Here there
is material evidence in addition to oral traditions: a famous brass pectoral mask called
Ejube-jailo said to be the most important item of regalia of the Ata, or king, of Idah in
Igalaland, which has been attributed by both William Fagg (1960, 33) and Kenneth Murray (1949, 86, 92) to Benin and dates from the early sixteenth century (fig. 1.8).

But the most complicated question in Igala art and history is what happened
after the sixteenth century? Here oral tradition openly contradicts the language map
of the Lower and Middle Benue: according to Igala oral history (Boston 1969, 40),
they were paying an annual tribute to the Jukun king at Wukari, and their refusal to
continue paying this tribute led to an attack by the Jukun army, which resulted in the
Jukun abandoning certain masquerades on the battleground as they retreated. Is this
a novel post hoc explanation for the resemblance between a certain type of Jukun and
Igala helmet mask, or has it a basis in actual events (see figs. 1.6, 2.38a,b)? There is
broad evidence from Idoma, Igala, and Yoruba oral traditions that powerful masquerades did lead troops into battle prior to British colonization. It is, however, only one
kind of evidence of a Jukun connection and has to be assessed against the fact that the
Igala kingship bears very little resemblance to that of the Jukun, nor is there a close
relationship between the Igala and Jukun languages.

ACCEPTING AMBIGUITY

Whether one sees oral traditions as "raw data" to be shaped into coherent narratives
(Webster; Erim; Sargent) or as already-mediated histories (Vansina 1985), the actual
details of such population movements are less crucial for purposes of art history than
the perceived historical interactions of the Idoma, Jukun, Abakwariga, Tiv, Igala,

Ebira, northern Igbo, and others. Whether wholly or only partly true, they form a "coherent cosmology" (Vansina 1985, 22) of belief, which is crucial for an understanding of Lower Benue art forms. The Idoma, Alago, Igala, Ebira, and Jukun see themselves as "People of Apá" and have adopted those institutions that emphasize this connection—particularly rituals surrounding kingship and ancestral masquerades.

Running counter to this, there is also an important "southern component" in Idoma and Igala art and ritual, which bespeaks connections to Igbo or Ogoja-Cross River institutions. Foremost among these are the whiteface masks and mask headdresses of the Idoma (see fig. 1.1) and the Okegga figures of the Ibaji in southern Igala. Unlike the kingship rituals and ancestral masquerades, however, these art forms are not embedded in a political narrative connecting them with Apá.

The other piece of the historical puzzle that is significant for Benue Valley art history is the expansion of the Tiv into the Benue from southwestern Cameroon. Linguistically and culturally, the Tiv are relative strangers to the Benue Valley. While the dates for this expansion are vague, the Tiv were certainly in the Benue region in the mid-nineteenth century (Baikie 1856, 102) and possibly as early as 1700 (Erim 1981, 39). Based on the ethnographies of Laura and Paul Bohannan (1953) and on Akighirga Sai's *Akiga's Story* (1939), Elizabeth Isichei (1983, 227) has placed the initial Tiv migration in the second half of the eighteenth century. Whichever date one assumes, it is clear that the Tiv now live between the Idoma and Jukun, but prior to their arrival the Idoma and Jukun were neighbors. It is only necessary to hypothesize that the Idoma were "squeezed" westward by Tiv expansion in order to explain their present location, even if not a single migration account had been collected.[6] By accepting the Tiv and Fulani historical interventions as forcing fundamental realignments—and the other events as plausible but speculative—the art history can be given a firmer base.

To summarize, the Fulani incursion from the north shook loose a great many mask and figure traditions on the north side of the Benue, which were then scattered and regrouped on the south side, but it also stimulated their adoption by local communities who had not used them before. The Tiv on the other hand expanded peacefully from the south, creating a wedge between the Jukun and Idoma south (and by the twentieth century, north) of the Benue River. Unlike the jihadists who were cleansing Muslim backsliders of their "pagan" ways and making forced conversions in the process, the Tiv were, and still are, great aggrandizers of other people's material culture. They didn't have their own carved masks, so in the 1950s they created the Kwaghir puppet performances instead—perhaps modeled after Annang Ekon puppet dramas (see Messenger 1973, 119)—using Idoma and Annang masks, which Tiv artists later copied. Tiv figure sculpture, originally limited to Akombo and Ihambe figures (figs. 2.12–2.14), underwent a creative expansion through contact with neighboring Idoma sculptural forms. For example, the Idoma carver Okati of Adoka was successfully emulated by the Tiv artist Aba of Nagi; both men resided close to the Tiv-Idoma borderland (Kasfir 2000; see also interleaf A, this volume).

The stream of migrant movement from Apá in the 1600s and of refugees fleeing the Fulani jihad two hundred years later ran along the southern banks and through the Middle and Lower Benue River itself as far as the confluence with the Niger. Idomaland, in the middle of this two hundred mile stretch forms the nexus of this continual remapping since it borders Igala in the west and Tiv (but formerly Jukun) on the east, the Igbo to the south, and the Benue, which bisects the Afo and the Idoma kingdoms to the north (Doma and Keana) from the others south of the river.

As a result, the connections that matter most in Idoma art and ritual are with the Igala—a fact that surfaces immediately in the investigations of Ekwuafia ancestral masks (see chapter 3), sculpture for the Anjenu water spirits (see chapter 2), and the regalia of sacred kingship and the earth cult. After Igala, the Ebira have the closest ritual links to Idoma within the ancestral mask complex (Kasfir 1985). In the southern

Idoma kingdoms, there are important political connections with the Igbo, some of whom were absorbed as commoner lineages and brought with them their own powerful Enkpe masquerade (Kasfir 1984). In southeastern Idoma (Igede), Cross River Janus-faced mask complexes appear (see figs. 2.52, 2.53), and in northern Idoma, there are important correspondences with Afo chameleon headdresses and seated female figures (Kasfir 1980). Interestingly, there seem to be very few direct connections between Idoma and Jukun masks. This apparent anomaly has an explanation however: there *are* numerous historical tie-ins to the Abakwariga, or non-Muslim Hausa, called Abakpa by the Idoma (Kasfir 1985). It seems clear from C. K. Meek's (1931a) account that the Abakwariga were ritual specialists to the Jukun and subsequent research by J. B. Webster in a 1975 paper has argued that many of the masquerades in Wukari were in fact Abakwariga.

Narratives such as the Alago migration myth, in which they journey all the way west from Apá to Idah and the Niger before turning back eastward to settle in their present location north of the Benue, are unlikely as mass population movements. Yet one is still left with the awkward fact that the Alago Kingdom of Keana possesses a helmet masquerade known as Okpatonu, which resembles nothing local but is very close in style to one of the Igala royal masks (see figs. 1.6, 5.7). I take up these helmet masks in a later chapter. What might have been a single individual, a carver, a trader, or the mask's owner, who traveled this route, could have expanded in successive narrations into a family group and eventually a whole lineage or group of lineages. The extreme portability of ritual objects makes their use as historical evidence both tantalizing and highly conditional. Their histories are best thought of as texts to be approached critically.

THE LOWER BENUE AFTER 1800

The two most disruptive events occurring in the nineteenth century were the Fulani jihad led by the reformer Usman dan Fodio, beginning in 1804 and continuing into mid-century, and the coming of the British, first to explore, trade, and missionize beginning in the 1840s and then to conquer militarily and pacify in the early twentieth century.[7] Yet much of the art historical scholarship on Central Nigeria has been written as if neither of these ruptures, despite the changes they wrought, had major consequences for the understanding of ritual objects, which have come to be known as "African art" in the West. This essay is therefore an attempt to link a local and regional art history, that of the Lower Benue region of Central and Southeastern Nigeria, to a larger political, but also cultural, scenario of conquest and colonization unfolding at the same time that the first collecting of African material for European museums was taking place.

Understanding the various genres of sculpture from this region first requires the recognition of how these two incursions caused the scattering and, a few decades later, the collection and the description of these objects for mainly German and British ethnographic museums. At the very least, one must acknowledge how ideological forces (both Fulani and British), which categorized these masks and figures as heathen idols, hastened either their destruction or their movement into Western collections, first as specimens of idolatry and later, with the development of a taste for "the primitive," as valued art market commodities. In writings that framed the African art canon (e.g., Fagg 1965), these objects were assumed to exist in a hypothetical tradition that had been in place from time immemorial to the colonial incursion. In this early cultural script (which was generated as much by influential dealers and collectors as by scholars), strongly localized identities such as Idoma, Igala, and Tiv were tied to particular genres, obscuring the fact that many of them, such as the Benue Valley maternity figures, were actually pan-regional. The famous Horniman maternity figures, successively attributed to the Yoruba, Idoma, and Afo, are paradigmatic of this colonial confusion (see chapter 2). In fact the whole ethnoscape of African art up to about the 1970s was given shape in this fashion, leaving the present generation with the job of deconstructing and reimagining it.

THE BENUE AS CONTACT ZONE AFTER 1800

Around the year 1800, the territory that today constitutes the modern state of Nigeria consisted of a hugely diverse group of polities ranging from shifting federations of centralized states scattered through the north and southwest, to much smaller chiefdoms and village groups, especially in the central regions—the so-called Middle Belt—defined geographically by the Benue River and its northern and southern banks. This area became first a contact zone, and then later a shatter zone for Benue north bank populations fleeing the Fulani jihad.

The Hausa states in the north had become Islamized through a gradual process of accommodation between the new religion and the much older set of beliefs and practices that constituted a Hausa worldview. All the former Hausa kingdoms had been established by the fifteenth century, but it is uncertain as to exactly when Islam became widely adopted in them. H. R. Palmer (1928, 3: 104) dated its introduction to the fourteenth century, others as late as the seventeenth (Adamu 1978, 18, n. 42). Before the nineteenth-century jihad, Hausa rulers, though nominally Muslims, typically tolerated practices such as masquerading and the Bori spirit possession cult, as well as such worldly pleasures as music, dancing, and the wearing of silk cloth (*tsamiya*) and cosmetics. The resulting hybridity, however attractive it might seem today, was deeply offensive to the true spirit of Islam in the eyes of reformers, and in 1804, Shaikh Usman dan Fodio began his challenge to these laxities in Sokoto and Gobir.

The jihad was at first an intellectual reform movement led by a community of preachers from the Shaikh's Qadirriya brotherhood, but eventually the scholars' lack of impact on the Hausa and Kanuri backsliders required that they be supplanted by a military force recruited by the Shaikh from rural Fulbe (Fulani) pastoralists he had converted. Over the next half century, his followers and then successors consolidated their control of the Hausa states and then moved southward toward the Niger and Benue. Nupe, on the Niger, fell in the 1830s (though it was was not consolidated until 1859), and MacGregor Laird visited the Egbira (Igbira) town of Koton Karifi in 1833, a year after it had been sacked by the Fulani invaders. Panda, the Egbira capital located closer to the Niger-Benue confluence, was overrun in 1853. Both Samuel Crowther (1855, 152–59) and William Baikie (1856, 83–84) described the smoldering ruins of Panda, which had fallen only nine months before their arrival. Between mid-century and about 1880, several other European explorers (e.g., Heinrich Barth, Gustav Nachtigal,and Adolphe Burdo) saw north-bank towns in ruins as well as refugee communities on the south side of the Benue.[8]

Newly reformed emirates such as Zaria (Zazzau) in turn formed relationships with smaller non-Islamic states that lay between them and the Benue, such as Doma (Idoma Nokwu) and offered them protection in exchange for yearly tribute. The scenarios were many and complex: a common one was the conversion of the ruler and his councilors, while the general population, especially outside the capital, remained unconverted. Another was the creation of a new emirate within the bounds of an older and larger state, as when the new Yoruba emirate of Ilorin was carved out of the Old Oyo Empire after its fall in 1830.

The two surest ways to escape the jihadists' cavalry attacks were to move high into the hills and escarpments, as certain Afo villages did, or to cross the Benue River in canoes, as did Egbira, Bassa Komo, and riverain Afo. The northern Idoma district of Agatu, directly across the river from the Afo villages, was described in the earliest colonial reports as the most ethnically diverse of all the Idoma chiefdoms—a direct result of these forced population movements in the previous century. Under these conditions, ethnic identities were fluid and situational, and the objects associated with them equally so. It will be our task here to use these objects to elicit Benue Valley art history in those turbulent times and to place them within the broader narrative of conquest and migration. ●

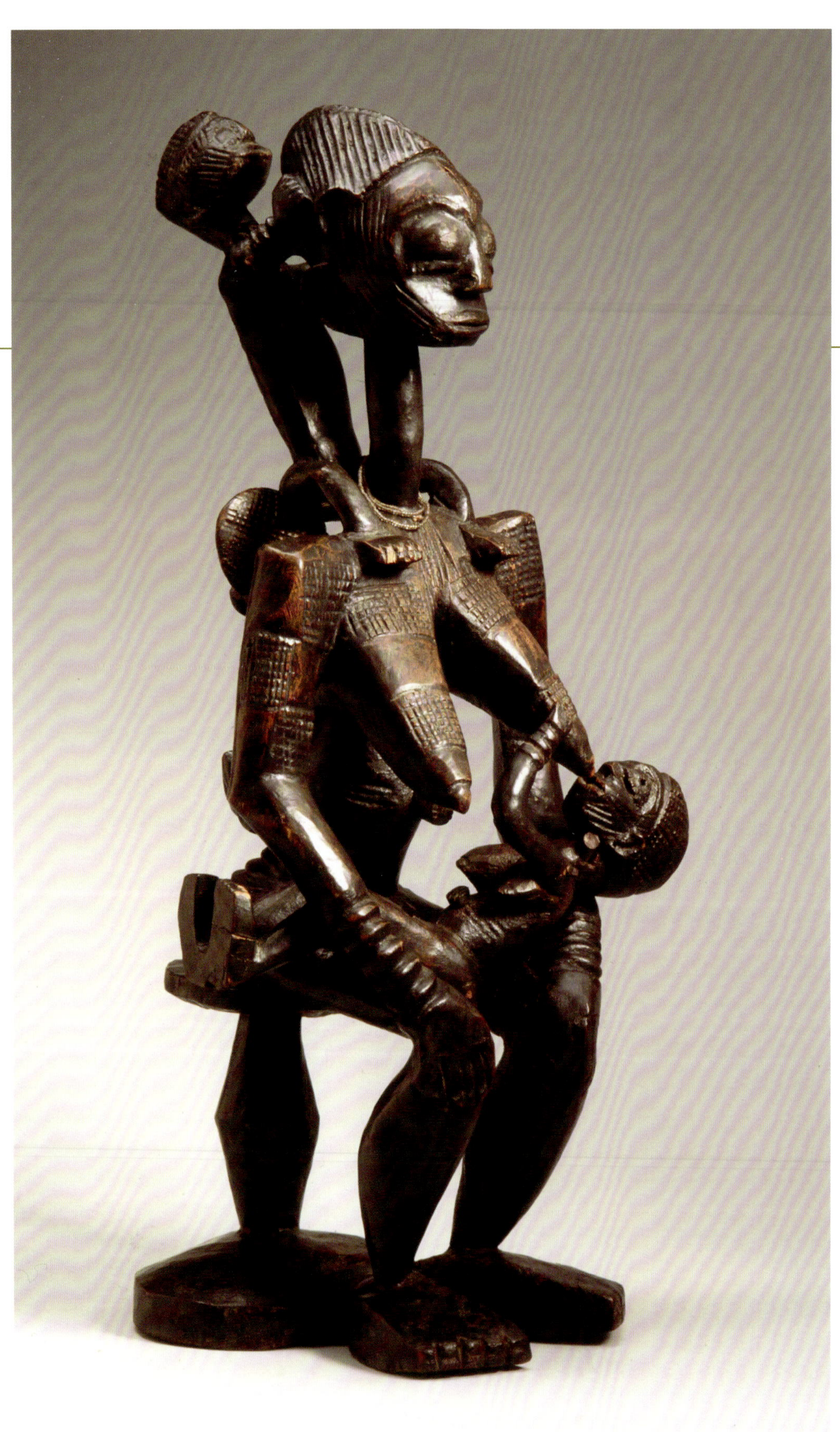

Idoma Art and the Intersection of Benue Histories and Geographies

SIDNEY LITTLEFIELD KASFIR

Modern Idomaland lies directly south of the Benue River about eighty miles east of its confluence with the great Niger. Its shape is that of an irregular corridor, about ninety-six miles long, narrowest in the northern portion and gradually widening out to a maximum of seventy-five miles in the south. It is probable that in the precolonial past, Idoma-speaking people occupied a substantially larger area than this. Even today, all Idoma do not live in Idomaland. The Etulo (Tiv: "Utur") are a small enclave of Idoma culture surrounded and modified by Tivland. North of the Benue are the old Idoma kingdoms of Doma and Keana. The inhabitants are known by the Hausa name Alago (Arago), but they refer to their land as Idoma Nokwu (greater Idoma). Their language and Idoma are virtually 100 percent cognate, while Idoma and Etulo are about 66 percent cognate (Robert G. Armstrong, personal communication, 1986).

Erim O. Erim (1981), the only historian to have completed a book-length study of Idoma precolonial history thus far, distinguishes the former types of political organization among the various Idoma lands (Aje), from small chieflets and chiefdoms to the centralized southern states of Agila and Igumale. The latter are comparable in size to the smaller Cameroon Grassfields kingdoms. A major variable in these lands is the power of the Oche (Otse), or sacred king, who in most cases "reigns but does not rule." It is the ruling lineages themselves, usually descended from the first settlers, who control affairs through the Igabo, or council of titled elders. The Oche is usually the senior ranking member of his lineage, therefore the spokesman for it, and at the same time the "owner" of the earth shrine (Olaaje) and mediator with the ancestors (Adaalekwu); he is literally "father of the dead." It follows that he is often too old to play any active role in governance (fig. 2.2). In Agila and Igumale there is also a kingmaker (*achadu* in Igumale; *ochonu* in Agila) who, along with the titled elders, represents the nonroyal lineages and balances the authority of the king.

Counterpoised against this gerontocracy is the Aiuta (sons of the law), composed of hamlet heads and members of secret societies (*aiekwu*) and dance groups (*aiije*). According to Roy Abraham (1935, 14; 1967, 195–98), this system arose as a strategy on the part of the elders to control the youthful excesses of the warrior associations. By giving younger men the responsibility for law enforcement and the imposition of fines, potential law breakers became instead a part of the constabulary. The best-known examples were the Oglinye (Ogrinye) and Ichahoho societies, which both began as warriors' dance groups and became masquerade societies after the cessation of internal warfare by the 1920s (fig. 2.3). As will be seen, the impact of colonialism changed the

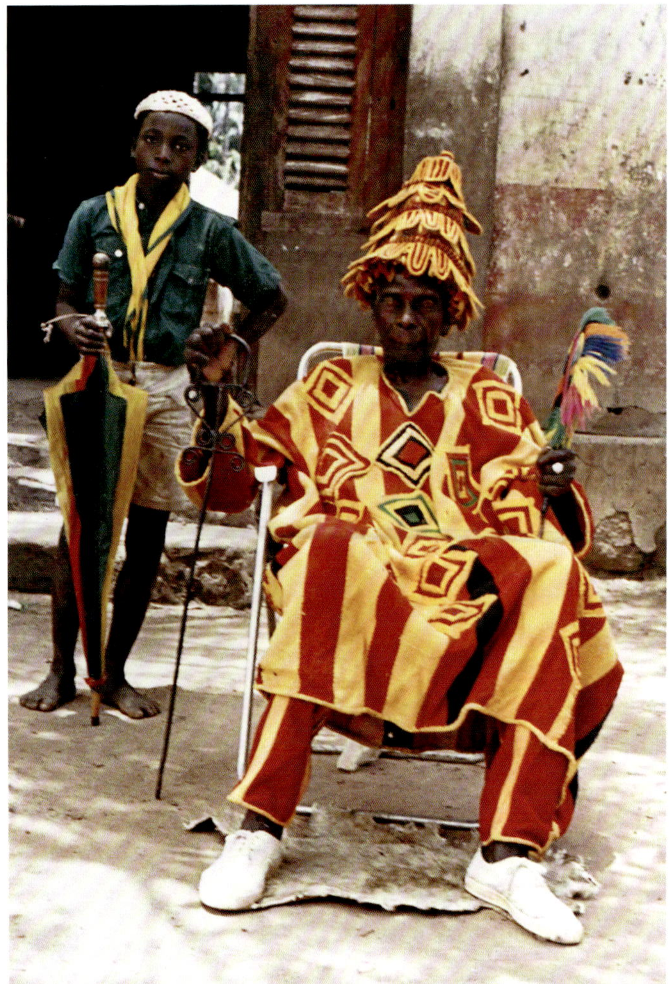

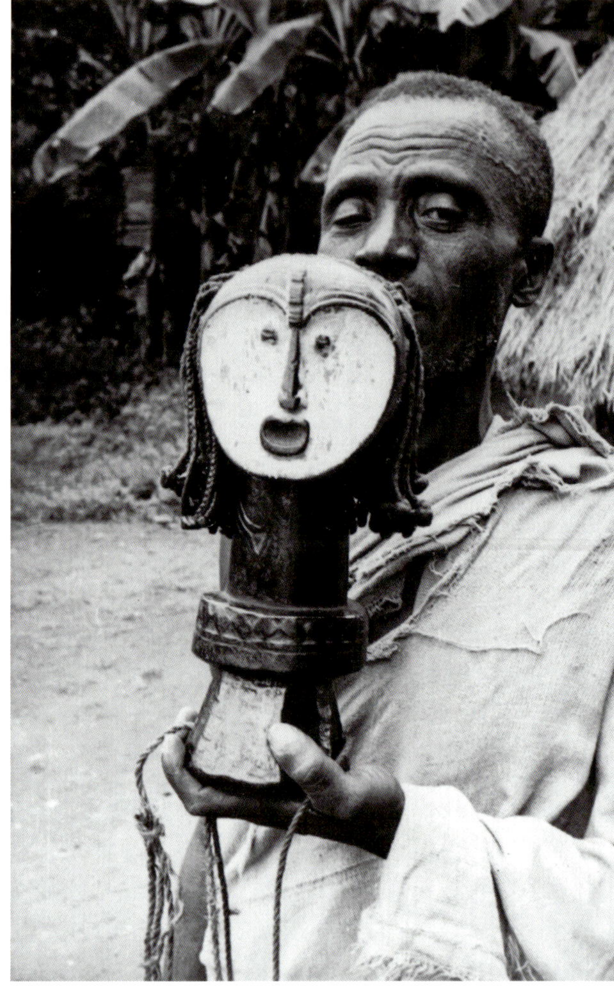

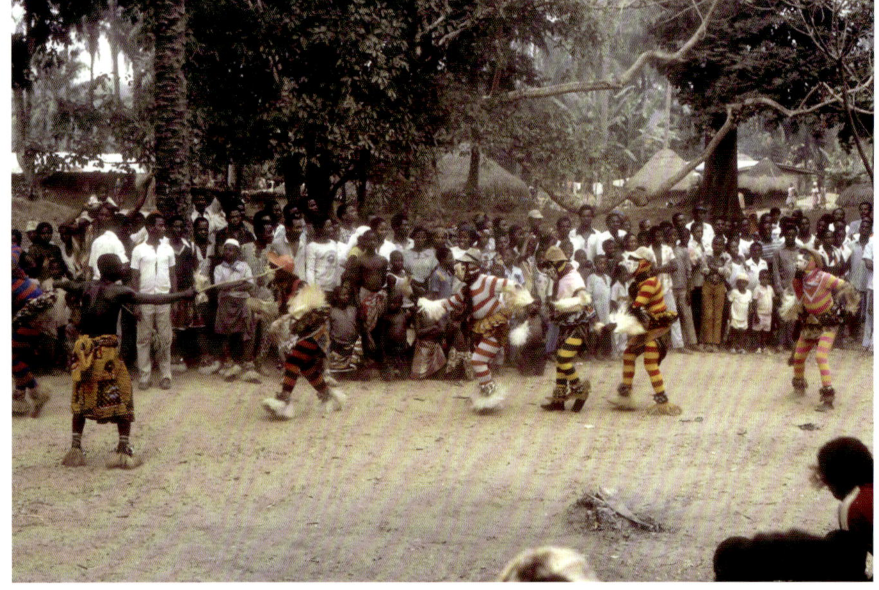

2.2
When Igumale was overrun by Biafran soldiers during the Nigerian Civil War (1967–1970), only the aging Ogaba, or king, remained to face them. His personal bravery inspired his people to return and resettle the town.
PHOTOGRAPH BY SIDNEY LITTLEFIELD KASFIR, 1974.

2.3
Roy Sieber was told that this "Ogrinya" (Oglinye, Ogrinye) head (see fig. 2.40) was carved by Ochai, who was active from about 1910 to 1950, but it displays the square mouth and jaw seen in several Boki pieces. It was owned by Ahola.
PHOTOGRAPH BY ROY SIEBER, OTOBI VILLAGE, SEPTEMBER 11, 1958. COPYRIGHT: ROY AND SOPHIA SIEBER FAMILY TRUST.

2.4
This masquerade materialized sometime after my departure from Nigeria in 1978 and my return in 1986. It was called "Eighteen" based on the number of performers usually involved (only five are visible in this photograph). It follows the same general style of Ichahoho and other whiteface masks worn with knitted body suits and brightly colored peplums.
PHOTOGRAPH BY SIDNEY LITTLEFIELD KASFIR, EJOR VILLAGE, 1986.

Aiuta irrevocably, though the masquerades that they controlled were still performed at second burials for their members as recently as the 1980s.

Following Nigerian Independence in 1960, increased labor migration and schooling outside Idoma spheres of influence turned younger Idoma men into more cosmopolitan citizens of Nigeria even as they remained "sons of the soil." This is reflected in the styles of their age-set masquerades since the 1980s with non-Idoma names such as "Foknopay" (pidgin: "free sex") and "Eighteen" (fig. 2.4). The old way to express youthful hubris was to be a warrior, while now it is to be brashly modern. Both ways are calculated to challenge the authority of the elders.

Not only the style but the periodicity of these performances has changed. The old ritual cycle of dry-season mask appearances linked to the annual pause in the agricultural calendar has not disappeared, but it has been overlaid with a new template of school terms and national holidays such as Christmas and New Year's Day. North of the Benue in Doma and Keana the major Islamic feasts are also factored into the calendar. At the same time, people in Nigeria are poorer than they were a generation ago, despite the country's oil wealth. This has meant that the lavish feasting at three-day second burial ceremonies (commemorative funerals), where many masquerades performed and which used to occur nearly every weekend during each dry season, is much more difficult for families to afford. The result has been a move toward group commemorations of several deceased relatives at once, often years after their deaths and burials have taken place.

PAN-REGIONAL SHRINE SCULPTURE

Contemporary refugees in African conflicts often carry paper documents such as cards of identity and school certificates. For the Idoma and many other Benue Valley peoples in the nineteenth century, however, any form of uprooting such as political unrest required moving the contents of the community's earth shrine. This is in fact the Idoma definition of the fundamental sociopolitical unit: those who worship at the same earth shrine (*ikpaaje*). Shrine sculpture, where it existed, was therefore implicated in these moves.[1] Typically this sculpture took the form of a female figure, often with one child or several on her back or lap and usually seated on a stool (though there are several variants of this including the reverse in which the figure supports the stool in caryatid fashion). I argue here that these sculptures need to be approached as a pan-regional genre and not simply given ethnic labels, which often conceal more than they reveal.

The most famous of the genre are certainly the two figures in the Horniman Museum, London (fig. 2.1) and one in the Berlin Museum of Ethnology, formerly the Museum für Völkerkunde (fig. 2.5). One or both of the Horniman figures were collected somewhere in the Middle Benue region by Major F. H. Ruxton, the Assistant Resident and later Resident of Muri Province between 1901 and 1914. The Berlin figure was collected at Wukari by Captain Glauning in 1904 (Fagg 1965, 42). An extraordinarily similar example to the Berlin double-caryatid figure, quite possibly by the same artist, was photographed by Theodore Celenko in 1975 east of the Niger-Benue confluence in northern Egbira territory (fig. 2.6), almost two hundred miles west of Wukari where Captain Glauning collected the Berlin piece in 1904. Celenko was told it was not carved by the Egbira. This is a peerless example of the argument we are advancing in this volume, that such scattering and recontextualizing of shrine sculpture celebrating maternity is a historical fact across the whole Lower Benue region and not just art historical speculation.

The Berlin and one of the Horniman figures are very similar in style. All three have been given an Afo origin since the late 1950s on the authority of William Fagg (1958,192; 1965, 42), although in earlier books and articles they were attributed to the northern Yoruba or the Idoma (e.g., Sadler 1935; Underwood 1947). Elsy Leuzinger (1960; 1966), the Swiss ethnographer who conducted fieldwork among the Afo in the

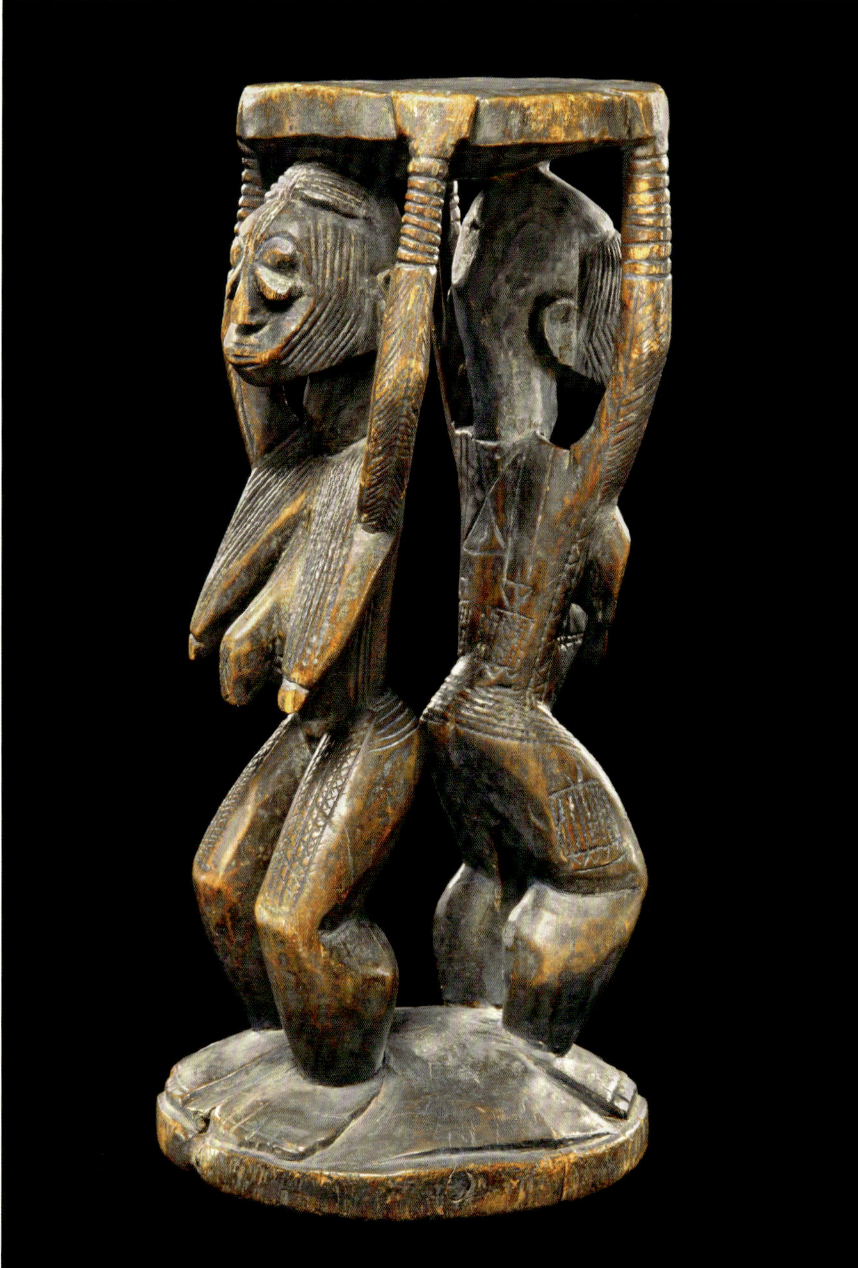

2.5
Double caryatid figure
Lower Benue peoples, nineteenth century
Wood
H: 57 cm
STAATLICHE MUSEEN ZU BERLIN, ETHNOLOGIS-
CHES MUSEUM, III C 18455
IMAGE: © STAATLICHE MUSEEN ZU BERLIN,
PREUSSISCHER KULTURBESITZ, ETHNOLO-
GISCHES MUSEUM. PHOTOGRAPH BY MARTIN
FRANKEN, 2010
PROVENANCE: COLLECTED BY CAPTAIN GLAUNING,
WUKARI, 1904

Calling figures 2.1 and 2.5 Afo was an inspired
guess on the part of William and Bernard
Fagg as neither sculpture was found in an
Afo shrine. Arguments can be made for and
against such an attribution, and many closely
related figures are referred to here as simply
coming from the "Lower Benue Valley."

1950s, was more cautious and referred to these objects as "Afo-Jukun" in order to give
due weight to the fact that none were actually collected in an Afo village. Moreover,
she saw nothing in the same style during her fieldwork.

This uncertain set of identities (Yoruba, Idoma, Afo, Jukun) is directly related
to the scattered and minimally documented sites and contexts where the figures were
found, all in the Benue River region, as well as their overlapping styles and genres.
It also rests, however, upon attempts at classification by scholars conducting fieldwork
and collecting in the late colonial period. William Fagg's brother, Bernard, Government Archaeologist and Director of the Jos Museum, had begun to excavate sites north
of the Benue in the vicinity of the Nok village finds nearby the Afo villages.

In a brief note in 1948 he reported a seated female figure "of unrecorded style,"
which was collected by a district officer, W. H. Mellor, and presented to the Jos
Museum in 1945. It had been in use for some years at Onda, an Afo village near
Nasarawa. Fagg noted in the article his brother William's opinion that the figure bore
specific resemblances to "two fine Northern Yoruba carvings of this kind in the Horniman Museum" (B. Fagg 1948, 125, pl. A). With the advantage of hindsight, one can

see that it is in precisely the same style later field documented by Leuzinger, which is similar to the Horniman and Berlin figures in its body scarification but emphatically not in the same style. A second figure seen later by Anna Craven while collecting for the Jos Museum falls somewhere between the Onda figure and the Horniman example that is not illustrated in the present volume in terms of the handling of the figure, though its head is very rounded, unlike the wedge-shaped Horniman and Berlin heads that inspired the original northern Yoruba attribution by William Fagg. It was brought to the Jos Museum and placed with the group of Afo figures seen in the 1940s and 1950s by W. H. Mellor and Elsy Leuzinger (fig. 2.7).

This piece is pivotal in understanding the interrelation of the early figures collected by Glauning and Ruxton around the beginning of the twentieth century and the much less accomplished Afo figures seen and collected fifty years later. It is the only piece I know that shares attributes of both. In a "space-clearing gesture," one might minimize the differences, call all the pieces Afo, and be done with it; however, stubborn questions surrounding agency would persist. For example, how much variation was there in the work of different artists in the very small Afo community (about six villages with a total population of a few thousand at most)? In a workshop apprenticeship system, any such variation would be extremely unlikely, but this was not a large population with specialist workshops. Just as will be seen in Tiv and Idoma cases, anomalous styles are possible wherever artists are not rigorously trained to a specific canon. As the artist Ojiji (see interleaf A) observed of the Idoma artists' personal styles, it only has to be "recognizable" as part of a genre to be acceptable to the community of patrons.

The whole series of figures—Horniman, Berlin, and Jos Museums—could have been made by as few as four sculptors over a fifty-year period. In neighboring Idoma it took a population of roughly one thousand people to support one part-time specialist wood-carver, so it is just barely possible that all four were Afo, but it is much more likely that half of them were not. Instead, the prevalence of the maternity genre (seated and standing) is strong evidence of pre-Jihad and precolonial networks of production and exchange across both sides of the Lower to Middle Benue from Lokoja all the way to Wukari.

In a second, unrelated find, Roy Sieber documented a stylistically distinct version of the maternity figure genre called Ekotame in Otukp'icho, a village in central Idomaland close to the Tiv border, during his 1958 field trip to the Lower Benue. The field photograph was subsequently published in Sieber's *Sculpture of Northern Nigeria* (1961). I discovered this figure to be still in Otukp'icho in the late 1970s when I was in my first phase of Idoma fieldwork (figs. 2.8–2.10), and just as the supposedly Afo figures do not provide a stylistic match to those Leuzinger later found in Afo village shrines, neither does the Ekotame figure resemble the female figures found in other Idoma shrines. I shall discuss these in greater detail momentarily, but first there is the larger issue: how might these well-known works of art relate to each other if at all, and what is to be learned from connecting them in a single narrative of displacement and dispersion—or simply trade in highly valued objects—within the Benue Valley?

I bring the brothers Fagg and Roy Sieber into the discussion because the work of scholars connected with Western museums and universities is really the final stage in a three-part narrative of jihad and slave raiding, followed by colonization and collecting, and finally canon formation. While the second stage—the collecting of the earliest pieces by colonial officials or sponsored expeditions and their subsequent journeys to museums in London, Oxford, and Berlin—was the single most dramatic step in propelling them onto a world stage, this project remained incomplete until they could be assigned a place in the emerging canon of Nigerian art. Smoothing out the rough edges of artistic geographies, then drawing the boundaries of styles and genre distributions was a comparativist project that could only be accomplished through a combination of fieldwork, exercises in classification, and the practiced eye

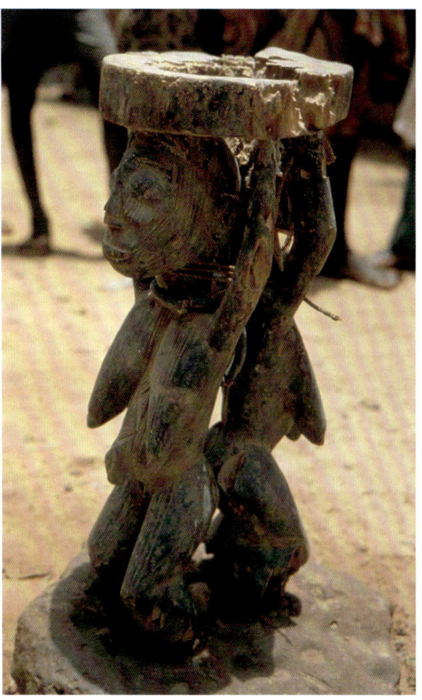

2.6
This double-caryatid figure was documented at Gebu-Beki village among the Egbira-Igu peoples, but it was almost certainly carved by the same artist as the double-caryatid sculpture in figure 2.5.
PHOTOGRAPH BY THEODORE CELENKO, 1975.

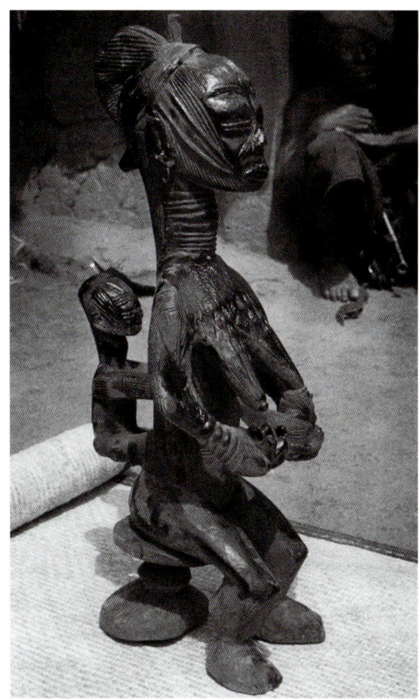

2.7
This maternity figure was reportedly seen in a shrine near Lafia in the 1940s and was later collected for the Jos Museum. The photograph appears in Bernard Fagg's personal archive and may have been taken by him (Angela Fagg Rackham and John Picton, personal communication, July 2010).
REPRODUCED WITH PERMISSION OF ANGELA FAGG RACKHAM.

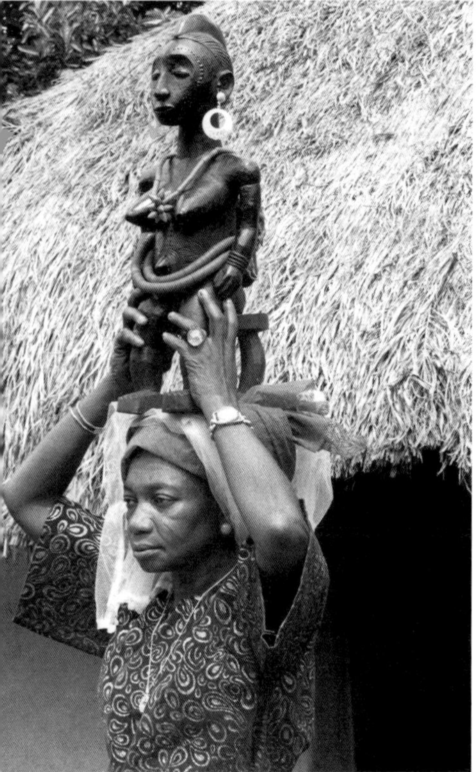

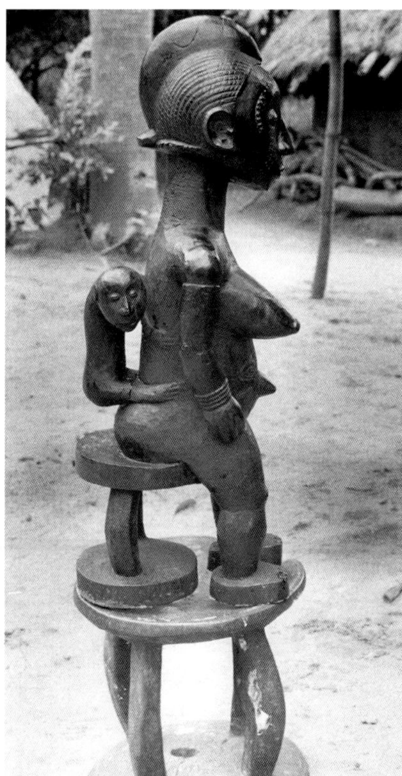

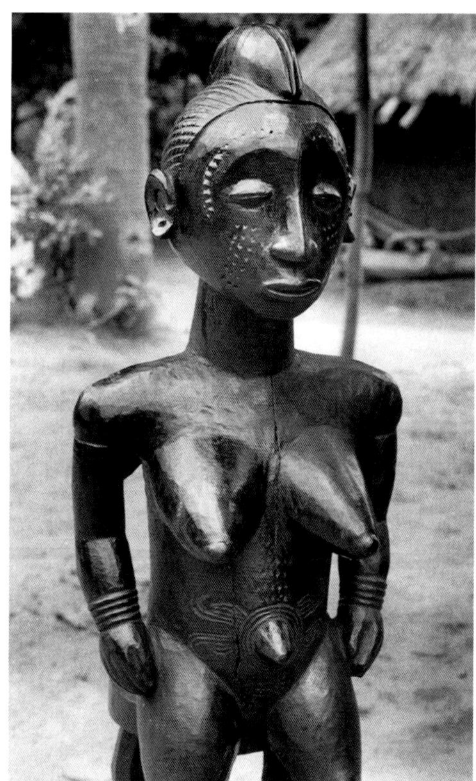

2.8
A senior woman in the family of the owner of this Ekotame figure demonstrates how the sculpture would be displayed and carried during special events.
PHOTOGRAPH BY SIDNEY LITTLEFIELD KASFIR, OTUKP'ICHO VILLAGE, 1977.

2.9
Like the Horniman maternity figures, the Ekotame (see also figs. 2.8, 2.10) is seated on a platform stool, in this case with a child at her back whose face is turned sideways.
PHOTOGRAPH BY SIDNEY LITTLEFIELD KASFIR, OTUKP'ICHO VILLAGE, 1977.

2.10
The scarification around the navel of the Otukp'icho Ekotame figure (see also figs. 2.8, 2.9) is unmistakably a Tiv mudfish pattern.
PHOTOGRAPH BY SIDNEY LITTLEFIELD KASFIR, OTUKP'ICHO VILLAGE, 1977.

of connoisseurship. Unfortunately, the expectation of clearly defined cultural boundaries, an idea that undergirded William Fagg's most basic assumptions about so-called traditional societies, and which in his writings he termed "tribality," contained a self-defeating limitation: it made no allowance for history's effect on such cultural mapping, particularly the destabilizing influence of historical conflict such as jihad. History tends to drop out of the discussion because it would require a constant state of revision, based on hard-to-acquire local knowledge.

Thus, although the actual porousness of these boundaries began to be acknowledged early in the 1970s beginning with René Bravmann's groundbreaking *Open Frontiers* (1973), it was a culture's spatial frontiers, its defining "edge," but not its temporality, that began to be rethought. Even today, a generation later, most art museums still retain this spatialized and ahistorical display principle in their African installations, the Yoruba over here, the Dogon over there, regardless of which century or even which millenium, while European art in the same museum is exhibited by both cultural region and historical period.

The result, in the Benue Valley case, was a cultural mapping that was a far more crystalline version of the contested real-life territory, so that the map, not the territory came to be accepted as reality (cf. Baudrillard 1983, 2). This meant that sometimes figures or masks, which may have had very complicated genealogies, when they ended up in Berlin, London, and New York and were incorporated into the existing canon or map, underwent a clarification process based on authoritative opinion from scholars practiced in the art of connoisseurship, such as William Fagg, whose diagnoses of style were considered oracular. The Horniman "Afo" figures are one example.

To understand how far apart the cultural map sometimes was from the real territory, consider that first the communities to which many of the objects belonged were deterritorialized as a result of the jihad, scattered into remote hills and across the Benue. Ironically, considering the purpose of the jihad, the reach or trajectory of a community's ritual complex was suddenly much more spatially extended, and with it, its ritual sculpture. Genres that had previously been enclaved in certain localities spread into wider circles of patronage and exchange.

Jihad-related dispersions also brought about major changes in longevity, duration, and the breaking apart of ritual sets and sequences of genres. An object is embedded with a history of its meanings and encounters, and these were sometimes lost, forgotten, or intentionally suppressed and had to be reinvented. This reinvention began in earnest in the late nineteenth century and continued well into the twentieth when the British Colonial Office created a Department of Anthropology in the Nigerian Colonial Service in 1925 in order to better implement Lord Lugard's policy of Indirect Rule. District officers assigned to Benue Province (most of them freshly schooled in classics at Oxford or Cambridge) dutifully filled notebooks and annual reports with the "customs of the X tribe," while employing Hausa interpreters who only rarely had a full grasp of the local language. In the Idoma case, everyone was happy with this arrangement: the officer was able to demonstrate to his superiors that he really understood the rather troublesome people he was administering, the interpreter was praised for his enthusiastic help, and the Idoma were able to keep their secrets to themselves (Smith 1968).

PAN-REGIONAL SHRINE SCULPTURE
Ekotame

As noted above, in 1958 Roy Sieber photographed a very well-kept female figure seated on a stool in the Idoma village of Otukp'icho. He was told by its owners that its name was Ekotame (or Ekwotame), which simply means "spirit with breasts," or female spirit. If the reputedly "Afo" Horniman and Berlin female figures collected in the Benue region are part of a pan-regional genre and may not actually be Afo in origin at all, the supposedly Idoma Ekotame is also suspect. Two features of the Otukp'icho Ekotame (figs. 2.9, 2.10) are immediately very arresting: one is the general similarity of posture, pose, and iconographic details (though not style) to those of the Horniman figures; the other is the unmistakable use of not Idoma but Tiv mudfish scarification patterns around the navel (see fig. 2.15). These heavy weals raised in concentric circles and further accentuated by the umbilical hernia are quite unlike Idoma abdominal scars. Besides this, the arc of raised lumps, or *abaji* scars (see fig. A.18), at the outer edge of the eye are also a well-known Tiv characteristic seen on people born before 1915 or so (Bohannan 1956).

The crested hairstyle, known as *agbada*, was formerly observed on both Tiv and Idoma women. The genealogical evidence surrounding the acquisition and ownership of the figure gives a probable origin date of about 1870 somewhere in the Tiv-Idoma borderland. The figure was purchased by the brother of the grandfather of the 1970s owner, who purportedly saw it in a Tiv village. The carver was said to have been one Aka of Ikanga, who was compensated with one slave, one dane gun, and a brass bracelet. On the other hand, the figure simply does not resemble any carving known to be Tiv.

A third example strongly resembling both the Berlin "Afo" caryatid and the Ekotame in genre, as well as in its handling of compressed sculptural masses and bent legs, is a female caryatid shrine figure photographed in 1965 by Arnold Rubin in the village of Gidan Yaku in western Jukunland a few miles downstream from Ibi (fig. 2.11). Instead of a Tiv mudfish pattern, the Gidan Yaku figure has a large umbilical hernia and stands holding a winnowing basket on its head, the tubular arms covered in bracelets in a convention also seen in the Ebira caryatid stool (see fig. 4.20).[2]

At a further remove, both in style and in purpose, are a group of figures identified as Tiv based on their group resemblance to Tiv Ihambe figures published by Akiga Sai and Rupert East (1939) and R. M. Downes (1971, pl. ix). The Ihambe-icigh figures (figs. 2.12–2.14)—sometimes called Twel after the circular mound they stand upon—form one part of a large class of protective objects known as Akombo. Prior to the onset of colonial administration, these figures stood guard outside the entrances to houses in which the wife had been taken in exchange marriage. A female Ihambe actually represents not the bride herself but the spirit of her husband's deceased mother,

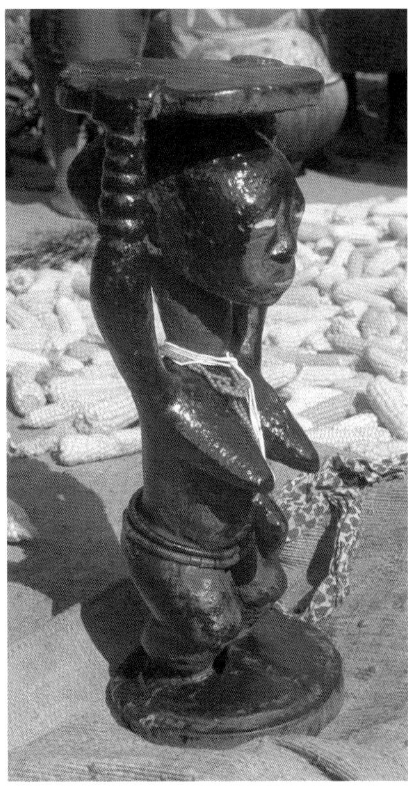

2.11
This caryatid figure was found by Arnold Rubin in western Jukunland. She holds a winnowing tray aloft rather than supporting a stool.
PHOTOGRAPH BY ARNOLD RUBIN, GIDAN YAKU, 1965, RUBIN ARCHIVE, FOWLER MUSEUM AT UCLA, NEG. NO. 789.

2.12
Male figure (Ihambe)
Tiv peoples, before 1930s
Wood
H: 110 cm
MUSÉE DU QUAI BRANLY, PARIS, 73.1997.4.55
IMAGE: © 2010 MUSÉE DU QUAI BRANLY. PHOTO-
GRAPH BY THIERRY OLLIVIER/MICHEL URTADO/
SCALA, FLORENCE
PROVENANCE: BARBIER-MUELLER, GENEVA; JOHN
HEWETT

2.13
Female figure (Ihambe)
Tiv peoples, before 1930s
Wood, pigment
H: 76.2 cm
HIGH MUSEUM OF ART, ATLANTA, GEORGIA;
FRED AND RITA RICHMAN COLLECTION, 72.40.234
PHOTOGRAPH © MIKE JENSEN, 2010

2.14
Female figure (Ihambe)
Tiv peoples, before 1930s
Wood
H: 167 cm
PRIVATE COLLECTION, PARIS
IMAGE: COURTESY PRIVATE COLLECTOR. PHOTO-
GRAPH © JACQUES BLAZY, 2010
PROVENANCE: LELOUP COLLECTION

Ihambe figures guarded the entrances of the
houses of women who had been married
through an exchange of daughters by two
families. Figure 2.13 displays the Tiv pattern
of navel scarification also seen in a field
photograph of a young Tiv woman (fig. 2.15).
All three Ihambe possess the concave face
observed on many Tiv figures, though the
treatment of the body differs in each case.

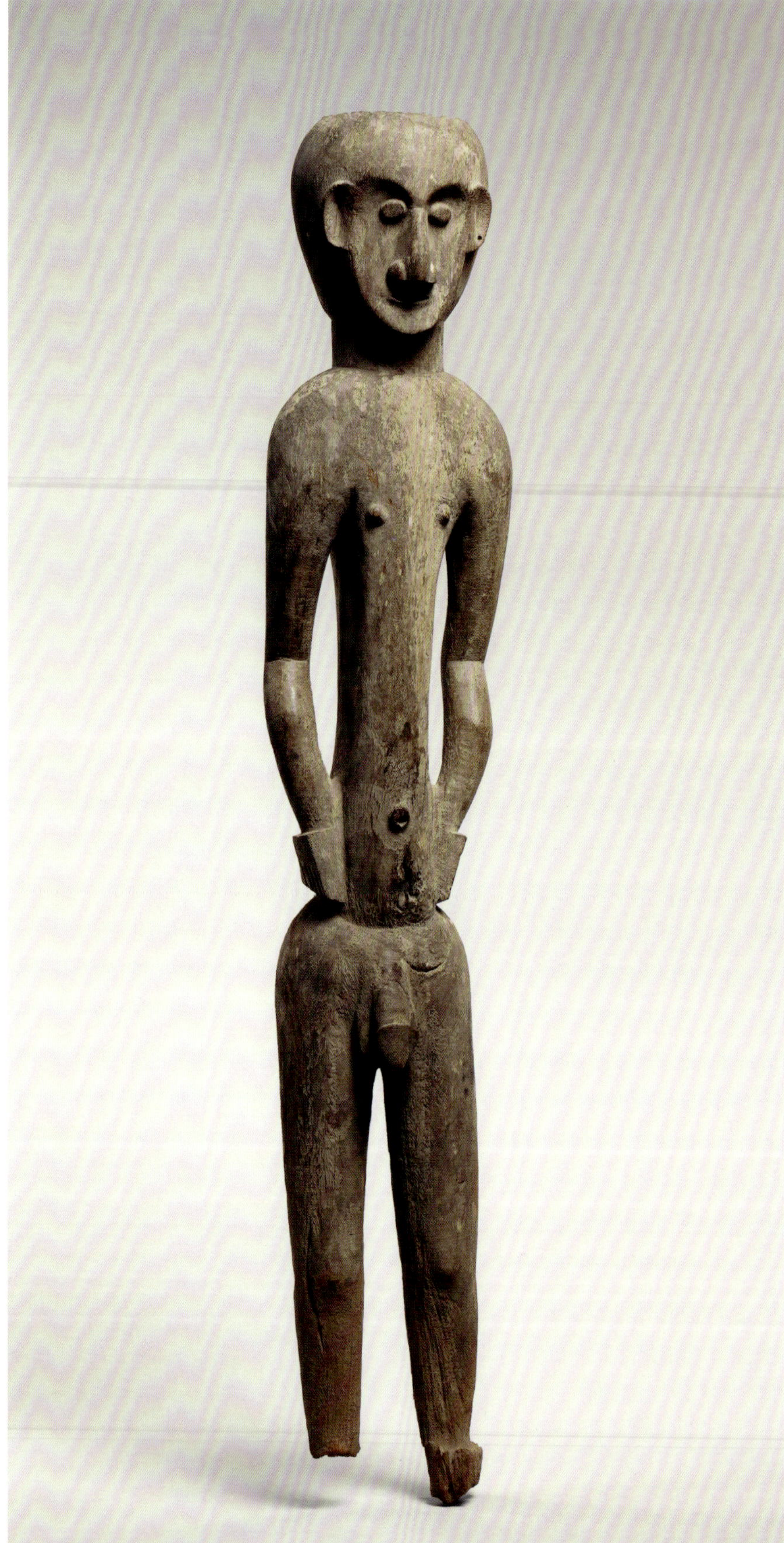

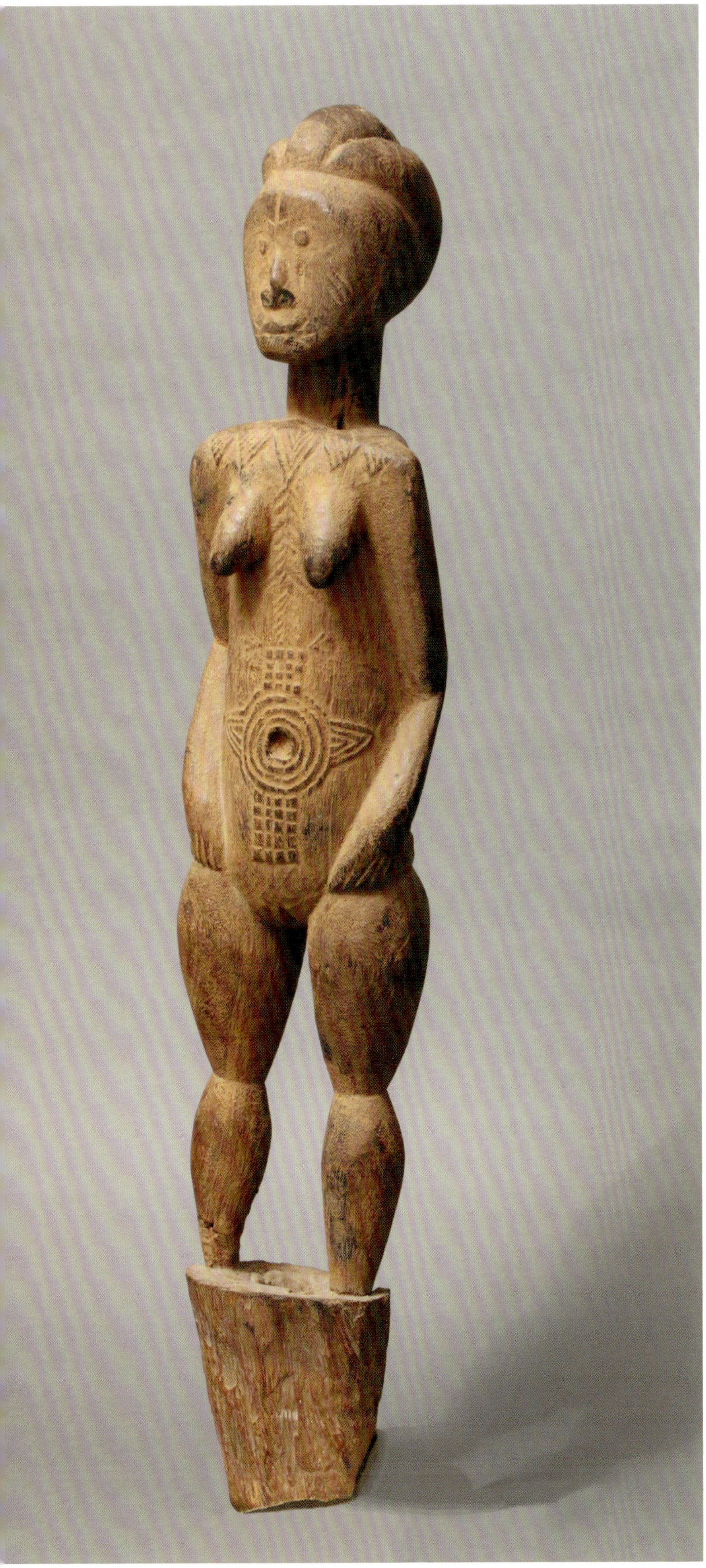

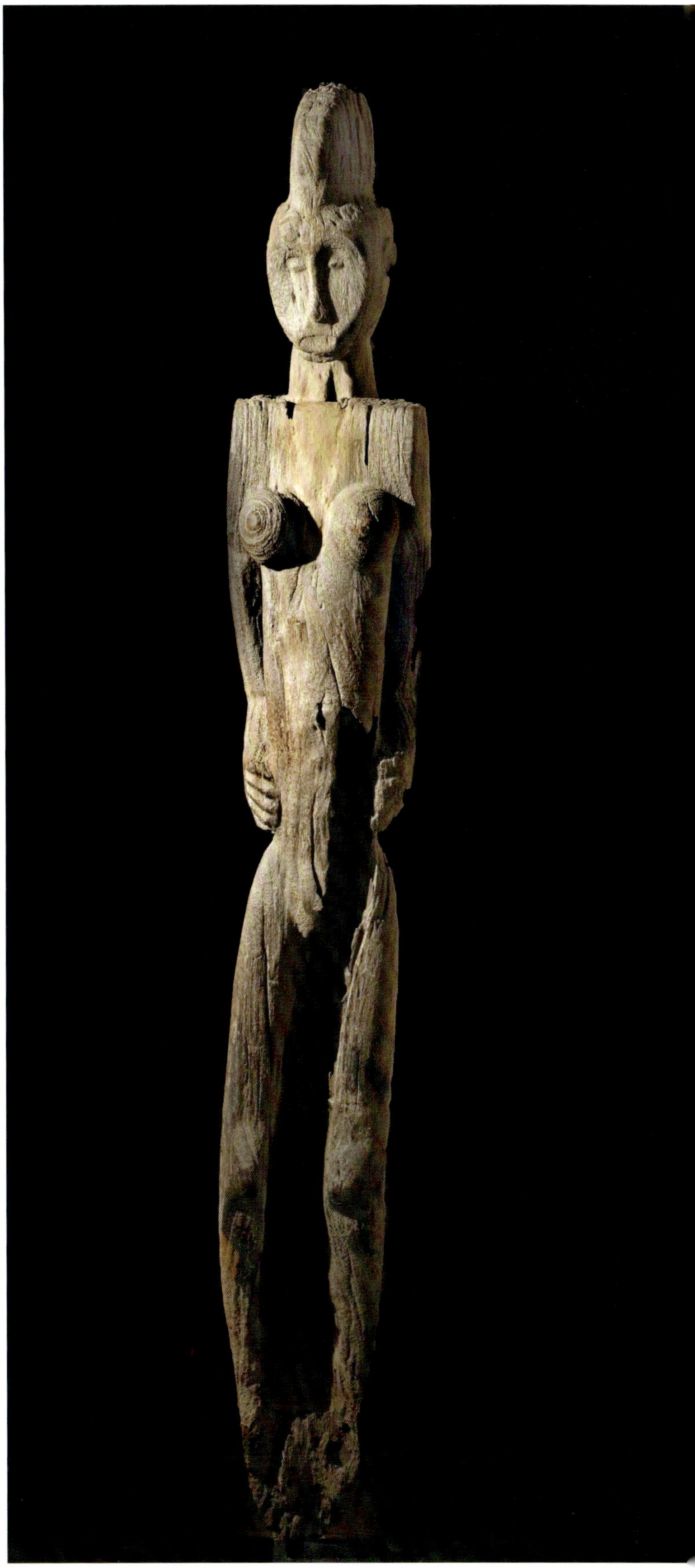

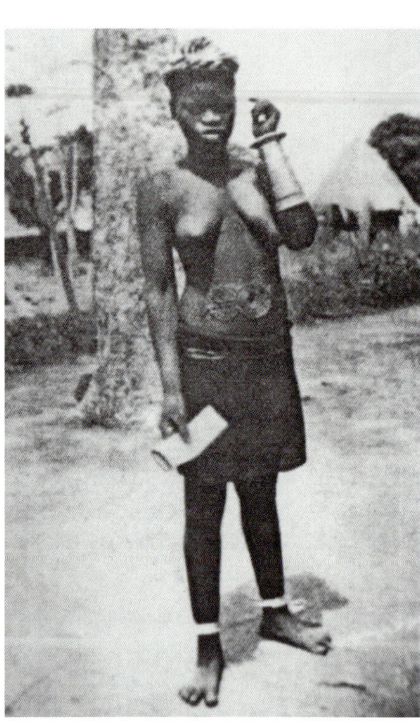

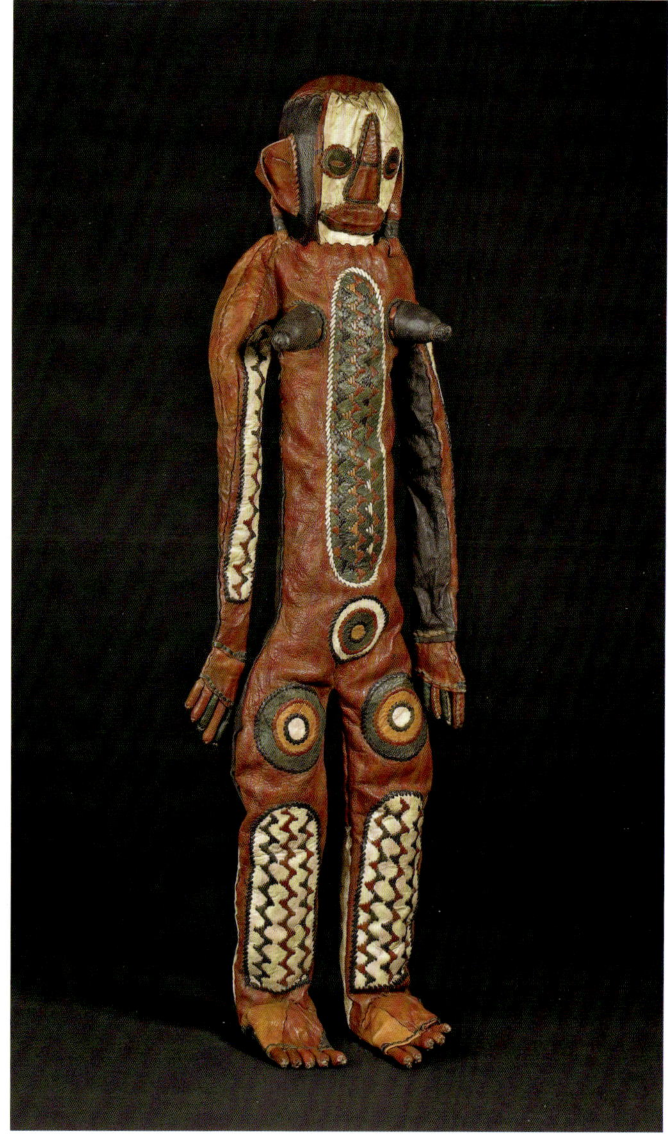

2.15
This photograph taken in the 1930s shows keloid mudfish patterns circumscribing a young Tiv woman's navel.

REPRODUCED FROM SAI AND EAST (1939).

2.16
Doll-like figure
Tiv peoples, before 1931
Leather, pigment
H: 73 cm
THE TRUSTEES OF THE BRITISH MUSEUM,
AF9132,0516.32
IMAGE: © TRUSTEES OF THE BRITISH MUSEUM.
PHOTOGRAPH BY MICHAEL ROW, 2010
PROVENANCE: COLLECTED BY R. C. ABRAHAM, 1931

The Tiv are skilled at leatherwork, a practice they probably learned from the Hausa. This doll-like figure was apparently used in connection with Biamegh ceremonies concerning ancestral relics, though what it represented is unclear.

who was thought able to transmit her own fertility to the bride, to domestic animals, and to crops (Downes 1971, 82). British disapproval of exchange marriage caused the practice to fade, and the figures ceased to be made in this form. They were replaced by much more abstract male and female symbols, the former pointed at the top and the latter more rounded, resembling the end of a baseball bat.

As guardians these sculptures permanently stood on display in one place, unlike the Ekotame, Gidan Yaku, and other seated or caryatid figures from the Benue, which were kept inside shrines and then carried on the head in public during festivals. In keeping with their more architectonic purpose, Twel and Ihambe body proportions are usually elongated, while the Ekotame is full and compressed. Their only shared iconographic feature is the elaborately cicatrized navel and in a few cases the raised *abaji* scars on the temples. This suggests that, regardless of its originator, the Ekotame represents a Tiv woman as they are known to have worn these intricate navel cicatrices (fig. 2.15).

A leather doll-like figure was collected by R. C. Abraham, who, like Downes, had been a District Officer among the Tiv people. It was illustrated in his ethnography of the Tiv and sent to the British Museum (fig. 2.16). Its use, though not explained by Abraham, was apparently connected to Biamegh ceremonies.[3] These are associated with funerary observances and relics, and the "doll-like figure" could have been an innovative substitute for the more usual clay image of the deceased. The figure displays the well-known Tiv skill in leatherwork, very much in the general style of the Hausa. The

Tiv undoubtedly acquired this ability after their migration north from the Cross River region—yet another example of their creative adoption of new artisanal practices.

Returning now to the cultural identity of the artist who made the Ekotame figure, we can surmise that he (1) possessed a full understanding of both the plastic and surface possibilities of wood as a medium, (2) was intimately familiar with a tradition tending toward naturalism, and (3) both knew and admired a Tiv aesthetic as expressed in Tiv body scarification. Does this mean he was Tiv? A few of the Ihambe and Twel figures are very sophisticated, and they remind us that in the absence of any apprenticeship system, Tiv sculpture can not be easily summarized in stylistic terms. The majority of Tiv guardian figures, however, are extremely simple and nonfigural, resembling a baseball bat with eye and mouth slits, and this, combined with the lack of any mask-carving tradition before the introduction of Kwaghir puppets in the 1950s, undercuts the argument for a Tiv sculptor.

It is just as likely that the artist was an Idoma working in the Tiv-Idoma borderland. In this area today one finds Tiv artifacts in Idoma villages and vice-versa. The Idoma have adopted a Tiv style of roof thatching and frequently use Tiv pottery in addition to their own. Idoma weavers use Tiv cotton thread, while the Tiv use Idoma masks and figure sculpture in their Kwaghir plays (see fig. A.20). Intermarriage is common, and the owners of Ekotame have even evolved a legitimizing myth to prove that the Tiv and Idoma are genealogically related. The possibility that Ekotame is an Idoma-adopted genre of Tiv female figure is certainly not impossible, but it requires us to unthink canon- and collection-driven judgments, which all begin with the assumption that ritual objects are made and used in the same culturally homogeneous environment. Instead it is more accurate to understand them as what Arjun Appadurai (1986) calls "enclaved commodities," valuable or sacred things, which normally do stay put but which on occasion (especially in times of radical change) can become highly valued objects with a negotiated exchange value—in this case, the slave, dane gun, and brass bracelet. With the depredations of both the Fulani and the British, the late nineteenth century easily qualifies as a time of radical changes.

I've come back repeatedly to the Ekotame, because it is paradigmatic of the fluid interactions and dense networks that governed both cross-currents of influence and actual movements of ritual objects in the Lower Benue and confluence region. One is still left with the puzzle of a sculpture in a decidedly un-Tiv style and genre but apparently representing a Tiv woman, which formerly resided in an Idoma lineage and was considered a very powerful emblem by Idoma near and far: form and function, uncoupled; space extended; time recycled in a new trajectory. And with its disappearance (undoubtedly into a private collection) sometime in the 1980s, culturally remapped onto new territory.[4]

One other Idoma figure besides the Ekotame seems to transcend the usual genres (fig. 2.17). This exquisite seated figure appears to be Idoma or Akweya based on its facial structure and features, particularly the nose and mouth, but its large size (72 cm) all but precludes its former identification as an Anjenu figure (Neyt 1985, 3: 28; Sieber in Schmalenbach 1988, 163). All the Anjenu figures I have seen in shrines were less than half this size (25–40 cm). Based on its size and elaboration, I take this to be a singular piece. The body designs seem to represent *ena* body painting rather than scarification, which might lead one to assume it comes from Agila, the southern district where *ena* is practiced. However, no seated female figures were in evidence in my many trips there. On the other hand, the "coat hanger" shoulders, two hands resting on thighs or knees, the prominent umbilical hernia used as a design element, the stout muscular legs, and the tense seated posture leaning slightly forward are strongly reminiscent of a style seen on Anjenu figures by Ochai (see figs. A.2, A.7). In the absence of field collection data, it should tentatively be assigned to an Akweya artist, possibly a predecessor of Ochai or even Ochai himself.

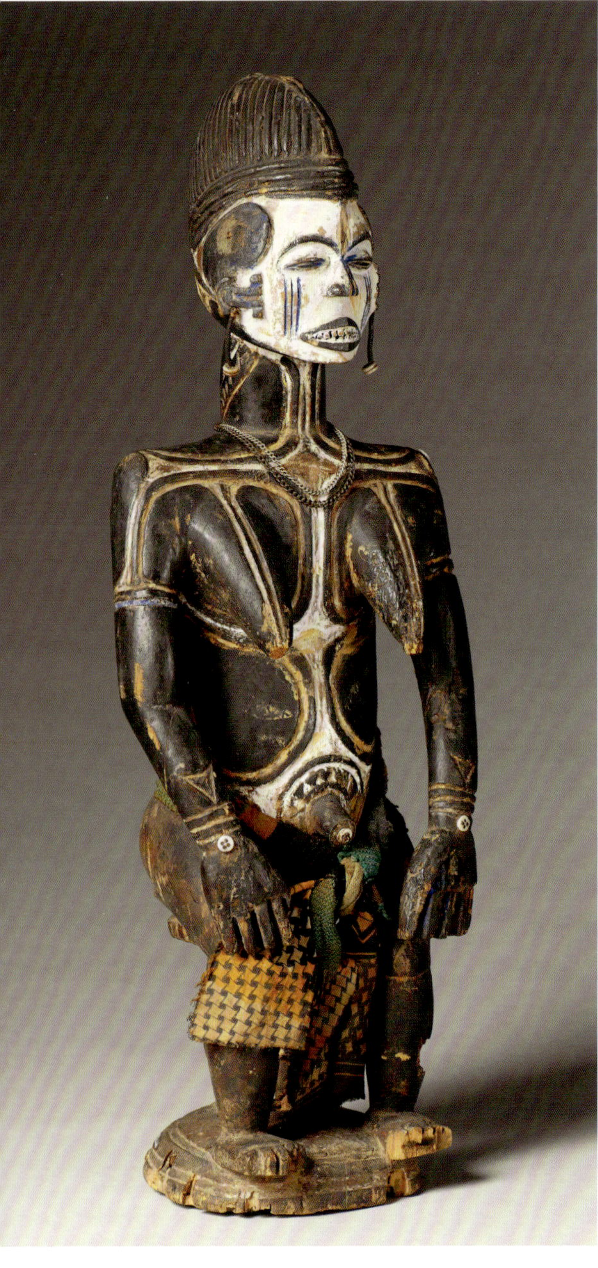

2.17
Seated female figure (Anjenu?)
Idoma peoples, Akweya subgroup (?),
early twentieth century
Wood, pigment, fabric, buttons (mother-
of-pearl), metal
H: 72 cm
MUSÉE DU QUAI BRANLY, PARIS, 73.1996.1.46
IMAGE: © 2010, MUSÉE DU QUAI BRANLY. PHOTO-
GRAPH BY PATRICK GRIES/SCALA, FLORENCE
PROVENANCE: JOHN KLEJMAN, NEW YORK;
BARBIER-MUELLER, GENEVA

In its sharp black and white contrasts, this
finely carved figure has affinities with the
doll-like Tiv figure (fig. 2.16), though in a
completely different style and medium. While
the body designs are unusual for Idoma and
Akweya sculpture, the posture and proportions are similar to those of the Ekotame
figure, and the face closely resembles the
Akweya style made familiar in the work of
Ochai (see figs. 2.40, 2.41, and interleaf A).

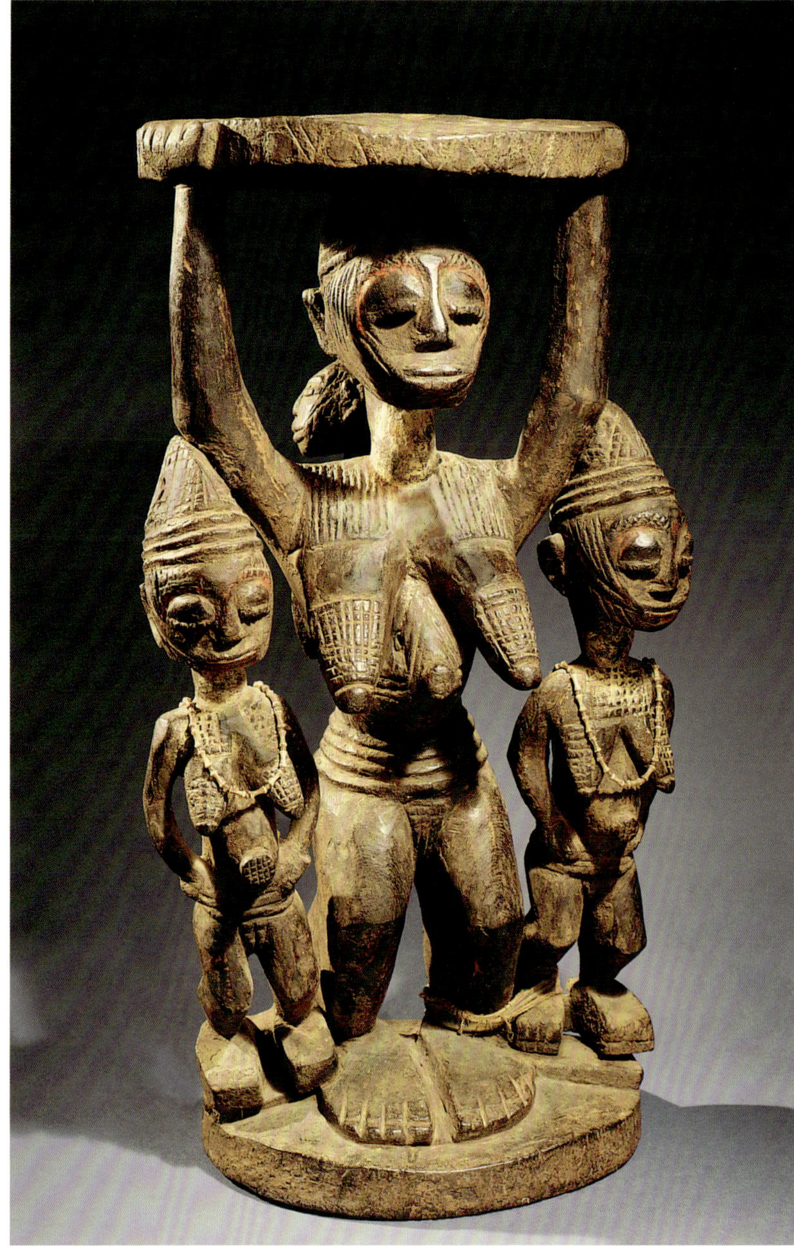

2.18
Maternity figure
Lower Benue peoples (Afo?), before 1977
Wood
H: 59 cm
PRIVATE COLLECTION, PARIS
IMAGE: COURTESY PRIVATE COLLECTOR. PHOTO-
GRAPH BY FLORIN DRAGU
PROVENANCE: PURCHASED IN AFRICA, 1970S

This rendering of the caryatid figure with two
smaller devotees in conical caps displays a
hybridization of attributes from as far west as
the Ekiti Yoruba and as far east as the Afo.

Afo Okeshi

The other important link to Idoma female figures in this regional, pan-ethnic perspective—quite apart from the Horniman, Berlin, and Gidan Yaku figures with their ambiguous provenances—consists of the well-documented Afo maternity figures known as Okeshi, owned by the Alanya Beshi (or Ngorongoro) society (Tschudi 1956; Kasfir 1981,163) and used in the annual Aya fertility rituals. Both seated and standing Okeshi figures display prominent body scarification, a crested hairstyle, and a child on the back or the lap. With the high incidence of interaction between Idoma and Afo in their adjacent villages on the north bank of the Benue, it is possible to see the Okeshi as prototypes for the Ekotame, or vice-versa.

There are other finely sculpted maternity figures illustrated in this volume whose attributes point toward a Benue origin but for which there are no reliable field data. Here one is on precarious ground in assigning origins, since the connoisseurship arguments used by experienced dealers and collectors are often at odds with the narrower but deeper knowledge of field researchers, and each tends to downplay the credibility of the other. A caryatid in the heavily cicatrized style of the "Afo" Berlin double caryatid figure, but with maternity attributes and a shorter, more compressed body, has a Yoruba-like pair of small figures wearing conical headdresses, making it easy to see the attribution puzzle such figures posed in the early literature. Yoruba-Idoma-Jukun-Afo: all seem possibilities based on one feature or another (fig. 2.18), but in fact this underscores the argument that looking for ethnically distinct styles is a misguided project in this part of Nigeria (figs. 2.20, 2.21).

Idoma Anyanmole

Figures such as Okeshi, which women on the Afo side of the Benue had appealed to annually for their own fertility, reemerged in north central Idoma (Adoka) in new forms such as Anyanmole, which literally means "women spoil the compound," a social commentary on the breakdown of traditional female comportment (see figs. A.16, A.17).[5] Anyanmole came into special prominence in the 1940s as part of a strategy for controlling socially deviant women. The World War II years saw a new interest in cash crops—rubber, palm produce, soya beans, cotton—which the British needed for their own ends. This resulted in a corresponding rise in the economic status of women, who were the main producers. In this new climate, women asserted themselves in ways men found threatening to the traditional status quo (Ochonu 2010).

The balance was restored by the introduction of a dance called *osobo* (a name for the Urhobo people of the Niger Delta) in which the Anyanmole figure was carried aloft. Songs of social derision were directed at the young women, while the aggressive, seductive aspects of their appearance were represented in the Anyanmole figure, now transformed into a metaphor for shameless sexuality by the addition of cloth and cheap trinkets and the removal of the customary infant from the figure's lap (Paul Anyebe, personal communication, 1979).

Idoma Anjenu

By far the most widespread form of figure sculpture in Idomaland (as well as in museums) is that of the Anjenu water spirits (Kasfir 1982). While similar in style to Anyanmole and Ekotame, Anjenu figures represent something quite different (see fig. 1.7). They are vessels for receiving those nature spirits that dwell in the Benue River, the Okpokwu River, and smaller local streams (*alenyi*, "people of the water") or for other spirits that emanate from termite hills or the atmosphere (*echekwu*, "world spirits"; see figs. A.2, A.5, A.7, A.14). Anjenu spirits often make themselves known to people by causing physical symptoms such as headaches, dreams, infertility, or the death of young chidren. The afflicted person visits an Anjenu priestess (or more rarely a priest) who addresses the symptoms by arranging for the sufferer to undergo a session of

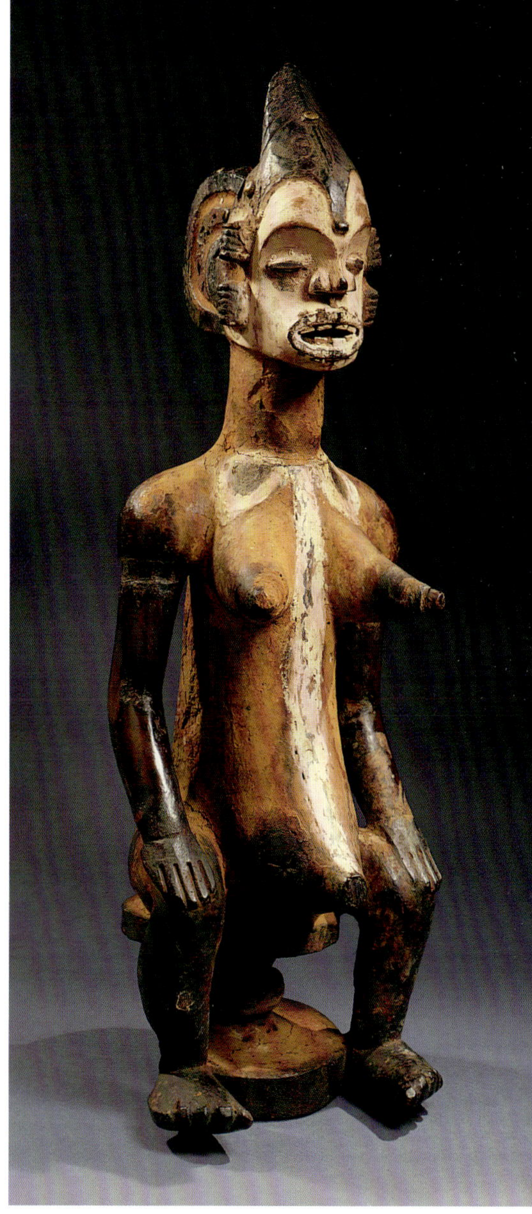

2.19
Seated female figure (Anjenu)
Idoma peoples (?), before 1977
Wood, pigment
H: 77 cm
PRIVATE COLLECTION, PARIS
IMAGE: COURTESY PRIVATE COLLECTOR. PHOTOGRAPH BY FLORIN DRAGU
PROVENANCE: PURCHASED IN AFRICA, 1970S

The identification of this type of seated female figure (there are several examples in collections) has been elusive, as none of them has been documented in a shrine. Purely on the basis of style, I have suggested an origin in Igede or Ogoja, an area where Cross River cultural features intersect with those of the Idoma.

2.20 (RIGHT)
Maternity figure
Lower Benue peoples, before 1970s
Wood
H: 56 cm
PRIVATE COLLECTION, PARIS
IMAGE: COURTESY PRIVATE COLLECTOR.
PHOTOGRAPH © HUGHES DUBOIS
PROVENANCE: PURCHASED IN THE 1970S

This maternity figure reverses the usual
emphasis on the breasts, drawing attention
instead to prominently rounded buttocks
and a large umbilical hernia. The hair is also
unusual, protruding from the back of the head
in an upturned narrow coil. Like figure 2.21,
this figure was photographed in 1976 in situ in
a Ganagana village, in this case called Adiho.
The area is located in northern Egbira and
also shares cultural ties with Nupe.

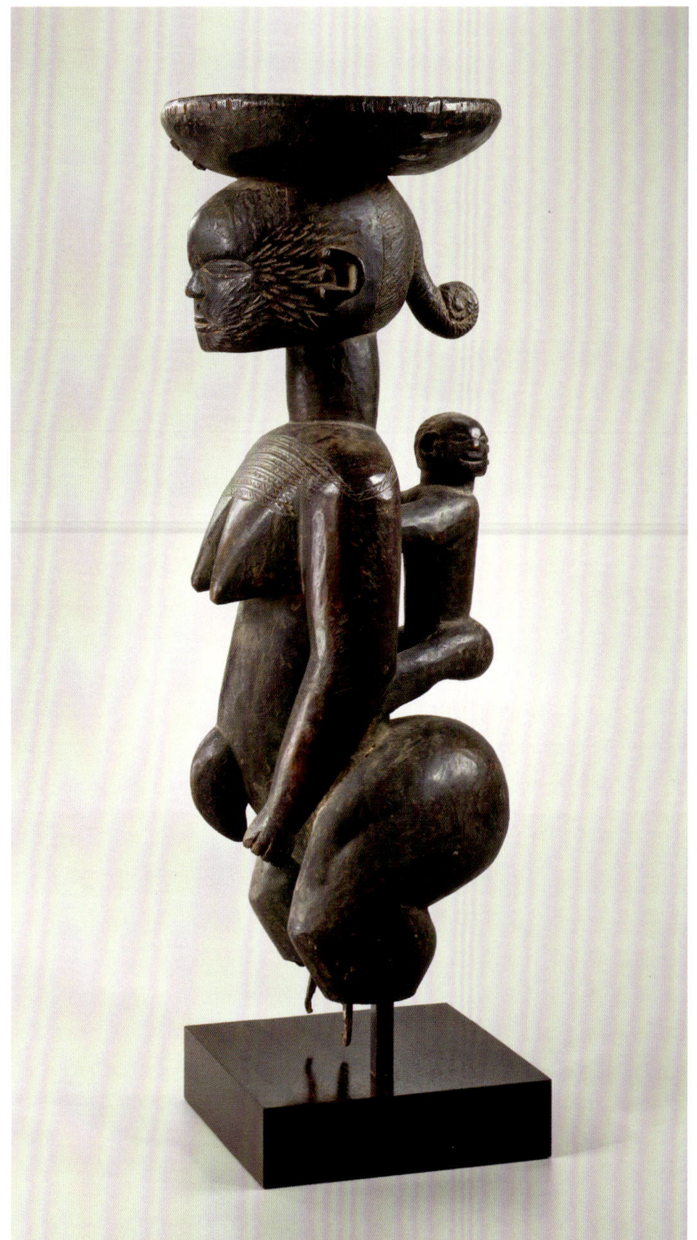

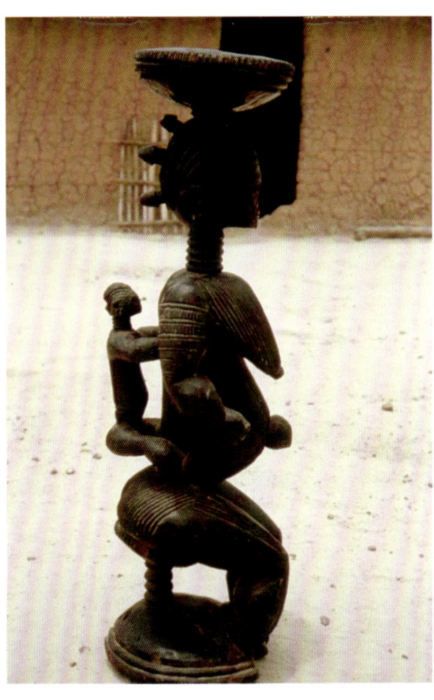

2.21 (ABOVE)
This seated maternity figure features a baby
at the back, large umbilical hernia, and unusual
striations on the face, torso, and short arms. It
sits on a stool that echoes in inverted form the
shape of the bowl on its head. In like manner
the ringed neck of the figure is repeated on
the column of the stool, reflecting the artist's
strong commitment to symmetry.
PHOTOGRAPH BY TED CELENKO, NYABA, A GANA-
GANA VILLAGE, 1975–1976.

therapy in which the spirits are called from rivers or streams to possess their adepts
and to receive offerings of food and drink.

The belief in nature spirits who "seize" or temporarily possess their followers is
well documented in Nigeria. In Igboland (Cole 1982; Jell-Bahlsen 1982; Jenkins in Cole
and Aniakor 1984; Drewal 1988, 2008) and in the Cross River (Salmons 1977), they
are often manifested as Mami Wata, a spirit dwelling beneath the water who calls her
disciples to join her while they are dreaming or in a trance state. In exchange for their
loyalty, she promises her followers riches. In Northern Nigeria, they appear as jinn
or Bori spirits (Tremearne 1914; Greenberg 1946; Onwuegeogwu 1969) who inhabit a
parallel spirit city in the bush and are summoned by mediums (as with Mami Wata,
usually women) to enter the bodies of their disciples. The resulting performances, with
their special songs, costumes, props, and musical instruments, give women some of
the ritual roles that are reserved for men in Nigerian masquerades. Within the Benue
region, Anjenu exhibits aspects of both Mami Wata and Bori.

The Idoma say Anjenu is not an old ritual complex,[6] but one that arrived in Idoma
country at about the same time as the white man (around the turn of the twentieth
century). It is said to come from Igala, and in fact many of the songs are sung in that

language. Furthermore the Idoma, Igala, Hausa, and Yoruba terms are closely cognate (Igala: "Alijenu" and "Anjenu"; Yoruba: "Anjanun"; Hausa: "Aljanu"). One explanation is that the particular set of ritual practices filtered into Igala and northern Yoruba country with Hausa who migrated southward and from there into Idomaland. The belief in water spirits who dwell in certain rivers and streams is, however, very ancient and a part of a wider set of beliefs concerning the sacrality of nature.

While there are a few male priests, Anjenu is spoken of as "women's juju" related to healing and fertility. The usual route to discipleship is through the advice of a diviner who is consulted when a woman fails to conceive or gives birth to a stillborn child. This misfortune is diagnosed as the intervention of Anjenu spirits, who must be fed with sacrifices and appeased with rituals in their honor. Anjenu is profoundly concerned not only with the well-being of women who would conceive but also with the mortality of the child and the ever-present closeness of death itself. Anjenu songs, sung in the early dawn hours when the spirits are close at hand, attest to this:

> The people-that-live-inside-the-water
> > [*alenyi*] are beating their drum;
> The dance is theirs.
> When grass is being burnt
> Vultures are not deterred.
> Eagles take chickens from a known place, not an unknown place.
> Death is like a hawk
>
> [*refrain*] That child, that child.
> A mother sends her child
> > That child, that child.
> A fence doesn't keep out death.
> > That child, that child.
> Death travels in the air
> > That child, that child.
> Who can fight with death?
> > That child, that child.

As the song suggests, the drum to call the spirits is another crucial object associated with Anjenu. Sometimes it is replaced with *ugbadu,* a calabash turned upside down on the water and beaten with a stick. This is a technique learned from the Hausa Bori performances. Not only that, Ojiji, the Anjenu priest with whom I spoke in Oko village in 1977 (see interleaf A), used the term "Mami Wata" synonymously with Anjenu:

> You go and fetch water from the stream and cover it with the calabash. Then beat the calabash. That would let the Mami Wata know you are calling it. Because it is in the water, once you touch the *ugbadu* with stick, the water will tremble and it will know you are calling it.... "My mother, come home, I want to give you some food." Just like they telephone people. That means you've phoned her. She should come and eat. If you do not do that she cannot come and eat the [sacrificial] food.

Idoma Anjenu figures are of two types: animal representations made of mud or wood and anthropomorphic carved figures, many of which are in museum collections (fig. A.5b). Similar mud shrine figures of animals are common among both the Afo and Alago within the Idoma cluster, as well as among other Benue cultures further east. In Afo country the most common representation is the buffalo or bushcow (Temple 1919,

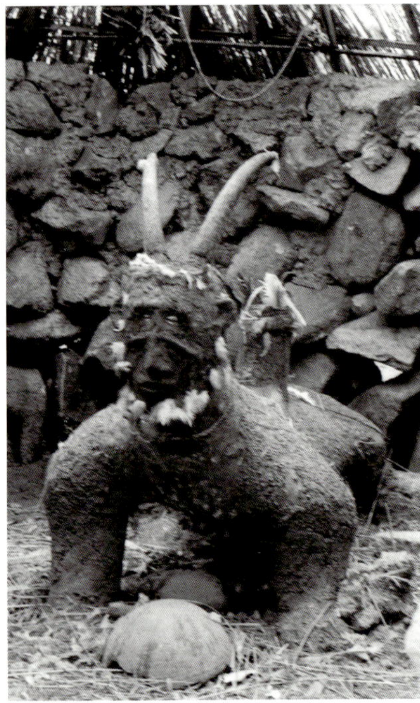

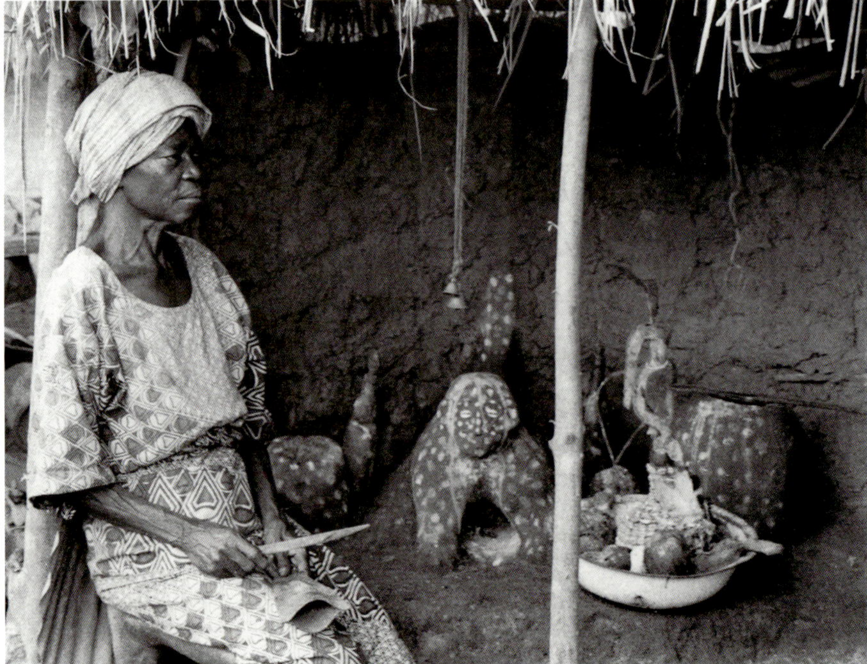

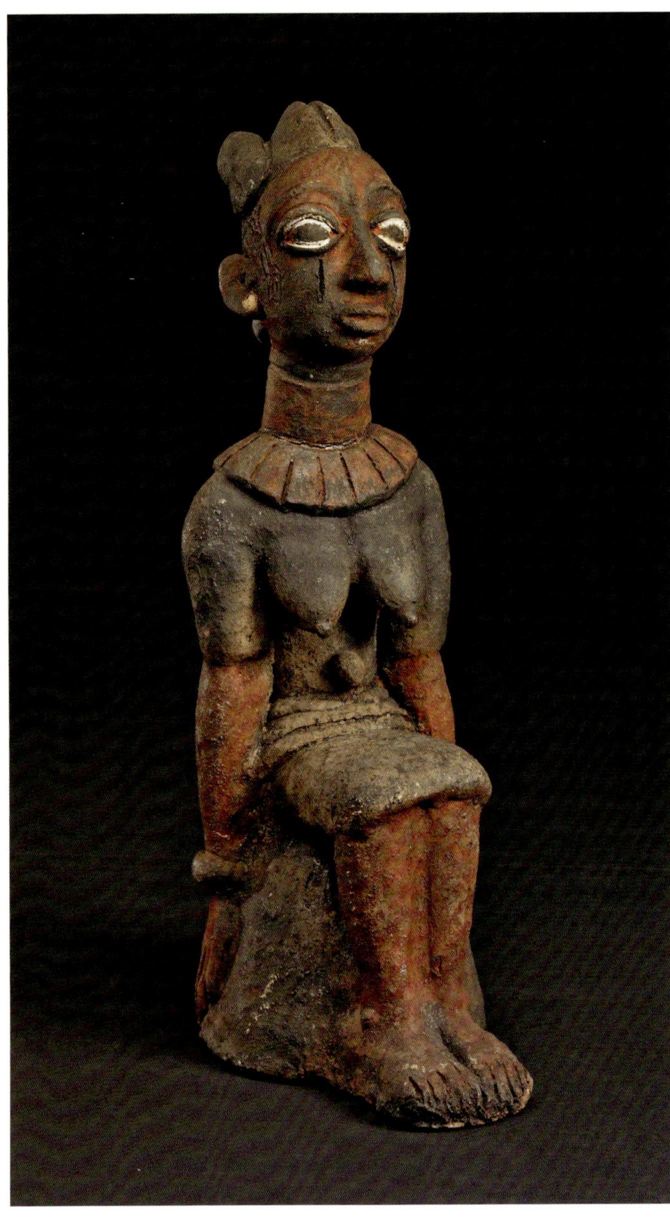

2.22

This Afo power figure, described as a lion despite its horns, was made by the artist Egba around 1940 and used during times of war to make enemies thirsty or hungry. Although bushcow and buffalo forms are more common among the Afo, the lion is seen in Idoma Anjenu shrine assemblages, though on a smaller scale than this example, since it must vie for attention with spirits in human form and sacred water vessels and medicines.

PHOTOGRAPH BY SIDNEY LITTLEFIELD KASFIR, ONDA VILLAGE, 1974.

2.23

A woman sits at her Anjenu shrine next to a mud sculpture of a lion, which she made herself. To the far right sitting in a basin is a medicine calabash with an *oklakla* (stork) stopper.

PHOTOGRAPH BY SIDNEY LITTLEFIELD KASFIR, OTUKP'ICHO VILLAGE, 1978.

2.24

Azume (d. 1951)
Seated female figure
Goemai peoples, before 1951
Ceramic
H: 30 cm
THE TRUSTEES OF THE BRITISH MUSEUM, AF1950.03.1
IMAGE: © TRUSTEES OF THE BRITISH MUSEUM.
PHOTOGRAPH BY MICHAEL ROW, 2010
PROVENANCE: PURCHASED FROM G. H. TUCKER, 1950

Azume was a well-known artist, and her works, chiefly ceramic sculptures depicting women, were highly sought after and made principally for other women and the local elite. It remains unclear whether they were used in ritual contexts. Her work is notewor-thy for its naturalistic approach (cf. fig. 2.27).

27; Tschudi 1970, 93), which Tschudi associated with Afo beliefs about conception but which is also propitiated because it is powerful and dangerous. In one Afo village, however, I found a massive lion image with human face and antelope horns, and it is the lion (*agaba*) that also appears in most Idoma Anjenu shrines as a metaphor for power. The salutation for a king in Idoma is *agabaidu,* or "lion-cobra" (fig. 2.22).

The second important animal is the stork ("*oklakla*" or "*okrakra*") in the form of a carved stopper and fertility emblem that fits into the neck of the *eka* medicine calabash, the most important power emblem of the Anjenu cult. Additional carved stoppers in the shape of human heads fit into bottles of sacred water from the Benue and occasionally from as far away as Bar Beach, Lagos. These are *ahana*, little people of the water. Finally there are often small, carved images of the leopard (*eje),* placed among the anthropomorphic figures. The metaphor, as with the lion, relates to the power of the wild.

The human Anjenu figures represent social categories as diverse as mother and child, soldier, policeman (see fig. A.14), "lady doctor," and "information officer"—these last two seen only in the shrine of a rather innovative carver and Anjenu priest, Onu Agbo (Kasfir 1987). The incursions of modern social categories are only proof that the spirits and their disciples, like everything else, must move with the times.

My discussion has thus far centered on Anjenu found in the central Idoma districts, particularly Akpa, where Otobi village is located and the artists Ochai and Oba lived, and Okwoga, where Onu of Okpudu turned out so many Anjenu figures for his own shrine. Anjenu was, however, much more widespread than this in the 1970s and 1980s, and it was particularly strong in southern Idoma districts (see fig. 2.19). Identifying these figures in southeastern Idoma (Igede District), Ogoja, and adjacent areas just north of the Middle Cross River often means identifying the faces by comparing them with masks from the area, since my visits to Igede and Ogoja lasted only a few days in 1986 and 1989. Like the Niger-Benue confluence, which John Picton writes about in this volume, the Ogoja area is a "shatter zone" between Idomaland and the Cross River, where it is impossible to classify styles and genres on the basis of ethnicity, a point made many years ago by G. I. Jones (1984) for southeast Nigeria as a whole.

In fact, an Anjenu shrine did not need to have images to be effective, and whether or not they were part of the ritual paraphernalia depended on both the local presence of a sculptor able to make them and the ability of the devotee to commission and pay for them. Since a large majority of the followers were women, they frequently were unable to afford anything except the requisite water from the Benue, kept in stoppered bottles, and the *eka* medicine calabash used in healing afflictions.

Goemai

Roy Sieber also spent a few days with the Goemai (in Hausa, Ankwe) in 1958. They are a small ethnic group who live about 100 miles north of the Benue and the Jukun capital of Wukari and south of the Jos Plateau. Their sculpture appeared at first to follow two quite contradictory aesthetic leanings, the stylized but descriptive naturalism of the pan-ethnic maternity genre that I have already discussed (attributed variously to Afo, Yoruba, and Idoma), and the much more rigid and anatomically schematic figuration of the Middle Benue region. The Paramount Chief of the Goemai, known as the Long Goemai, was questioned by the then head of the Department of Antiquities in Jos, Bernard Fagg, who in turn told Sieber (1961, 12) that the more naturalistic style was only found in terracotta and was the work of a talented woman named Azume (fig. 2.24), who had died in 1951, and a second woman, less accomplished, working in the same style.[7]

The carved wooden figures, however, were the work of male artists and were used primarily in a men's society called Kwompten (fig. 2.25), which performed curing rituals for its members. A photograph taken by Sieber in September 1958 in the Goemai village of Tenzet shows nine figures used in Kwompten. He identified eight of these as Goemai

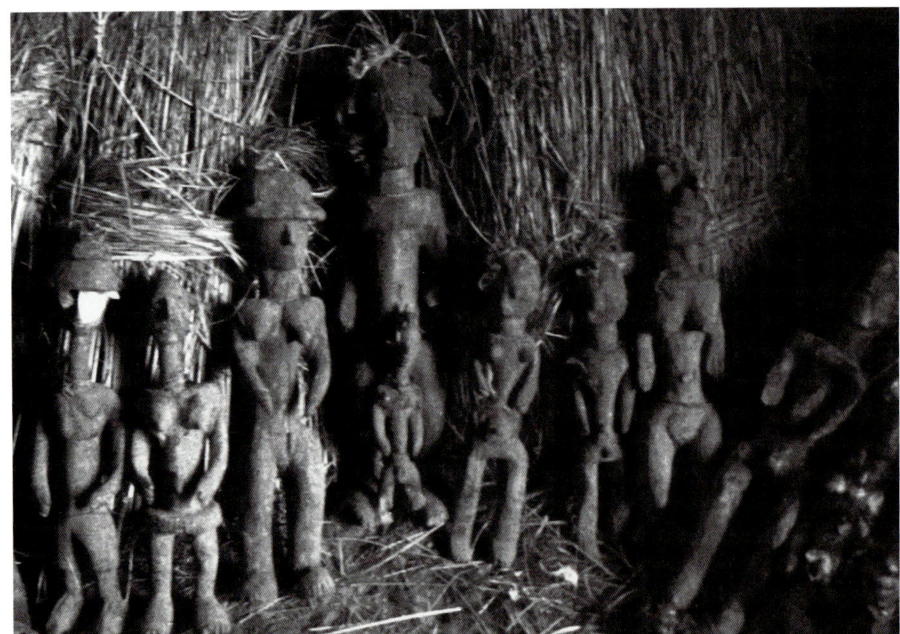

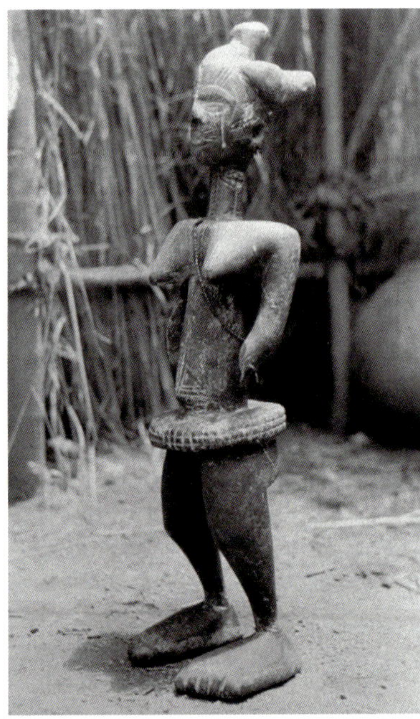

2.25

These nine wooden figures were used in the men's society called Kwompten by the Goemai as part of its curing rituals. The eight figures to the left were made by Worwon, a Goemai carver who was also their owner. The one on the right was made by a Montol carver whose name could no longer be recalled.

PHOTOGRAPH BY ROY SIEBER, TENZET VILLAGE, SEPTEMBER 1, 1958. COPYRIGHT: ROY AND SOPHIA SIEBER FAMILY TRUST.

2.26

This Goemai standing figure was photographed while still in the possession of its carver, Longte. It later entered the collection of the Jos Museum.

PHOTOGRAPH BY ROY SIEBER, JUNE 18, 1958, KURGWI VILLAGE. COPYRIGHT: ROY AND SOPHIA SIEBER FAMILY TRUST.

2.27

Maternity figure
Goemai peoples, nineteenth to twentieth century
Wood
H: 50.8 cm

THE METROPOLITAN MUSEUM OF ART, THE MICHAEL C. ROCKEFELLER MEMORIAL COLLECTION, PURCHASE, NELSON A. ROCKEFELLER GIFT, 1971, 1978.412.629

IMAGE: © THE METROPOLITAN MUSEUM OF ART/ ART RESOURCE, NY

PROVENANCE: ALAN BRANDT, NEW YORK, 1971

Male and female figures were used by the Goemai men's society known as Kwompten during curing rituals. The form of this maternity figure is transitional between the columnar figurative sculpture of Middle Benue peoples and the descriptive naturalism of Lower Benue maternity figures.

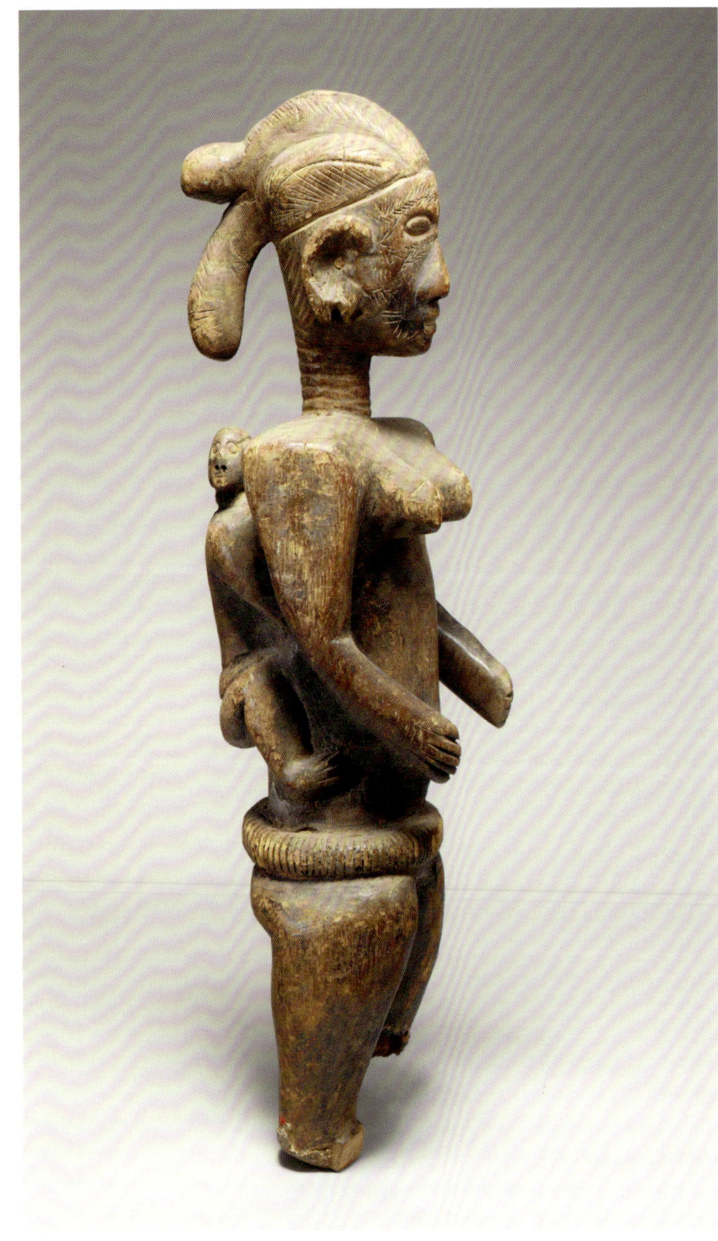

(all by Goemai woodcarver Worwon) and one as Montol. They are carved in the more columnar style associated with the neighboring Montol (see fig. 8.2), who sometimes supplied figures to the Goemai. Related to these field-documented sculptures are two others, a Goemai maternity figure in the collection of the Metropolitan Museum of Art (fig. 2.27) and a standing figure (fig. 2.26) in the collection of the Jos Museum.[8] Both pieces appear transitional in form between the more columnar approach of the Montol and the descriptive naturalism of the Lower Benue maternity genre. Both have bodies with an elongated and narrow torso, legs and arms with a slight outward curvature, and a distinctive ring or "belt" around the waist. The multi-lobed hairstyle of these wood figures is also present on Azume's ceramic sculpture, suggesting it may have been a style worn by Goemai women in the mid-twentieth century.

What is most intriguing here is the gender-based style distinction, or perhaps more accurately the way in which the work of a single artist, in this case Azume, can be totally unlike the work of others producing in the same small cultural space (see fig. 2.24). It is not clear whether her female figures were used in specific rituals or were simply prestige objects made for other women or the local elite. It demonstrates that what an earlier generation of collectors and scholars perceived as a "tribal style" could actually be a much narrower type of artistic production determined by factors such as the artist's gender (and therefore space of interaction), material, and technique, and finally the purpose for which it was intended and the conceptual space it was to inhabit.

THE IDOMA MASK SCENARIO: A CHANGING CULTURAL SCRIPT

In retrospect it seems astonishing that early British colonial documents reported that the Idoma "have no art." British notions of "art," however, did not include masquerades, and even less so did they consider weaving, resist dyeing, pottery, and brass casting. While figure sculpture might have qualified, it was hidden away from public view in shrine houses. Applying the traditional Western "art-craft" distinction was, moreover, not limited to colonial officers. It has framed the practice of collecting as well. While "masks" were accepted by early modernist collectors and dealers such as Picasso and Henri Kahnweiler, this meant objects sculpted in wood or very occasionally cast in metal, and without their costumes—in other words, as "pure sculpture." Many of the most elaborate Idoma masquerades surveyed here are made from textiles or from plant fibers, and they don't appear in collections outside Nigeria.

If one speaks of masking throughout the continent, as well as in the Benue region specifically, the oldest and most widespread are acoustic masks. These are conceptualized as "invisible spirits" and usually have powerful sanctions and taboos associated with breaking that envelope of invisibility, provided either by the darkness of night or, if heard during daylight hours, by being hidden from view. Examples in Idomaland would be Ifim and Owarika (Akpa District), Achukwu (central Idoma), and Arekweeka (Agila). Next oldest after acoustic masks are masks made of leaves, tree bark (such as the "Mumbo Jumbo" seen by Francis Moore in 1738 on the Gambia River and identified with the modern Kankurang mask made from the bark of the *fara* tree). In Idomaland such masks were constructed of millet and guinea corn stalks or raffia palm fibers. The most widespread of these fiber masks in Idoma are Akatakpa and Ikpokwu. Textile masquerades can be assumed to have developed after the introduction of the portable double-heddle loom through the trans-Saharan trade. For the Benue region this would have been no earlier than the tenth century. Ancestral masquerades that employ these textiles as burial shrouds are dated independently in Idoma, Igala, and Yoruba oral traditions to approximately the sixteenth century. The introduction of carved wooden masks seems to have developed in several ways. Some, such as the Oglinye mask described below, were the outgrowth of an earlier use of enemy skulls in warriors' dances. When I asked Idoma elders, however, I was consistently told that fiber masks and a few carved examples originated "on the farm," made by slaves or children

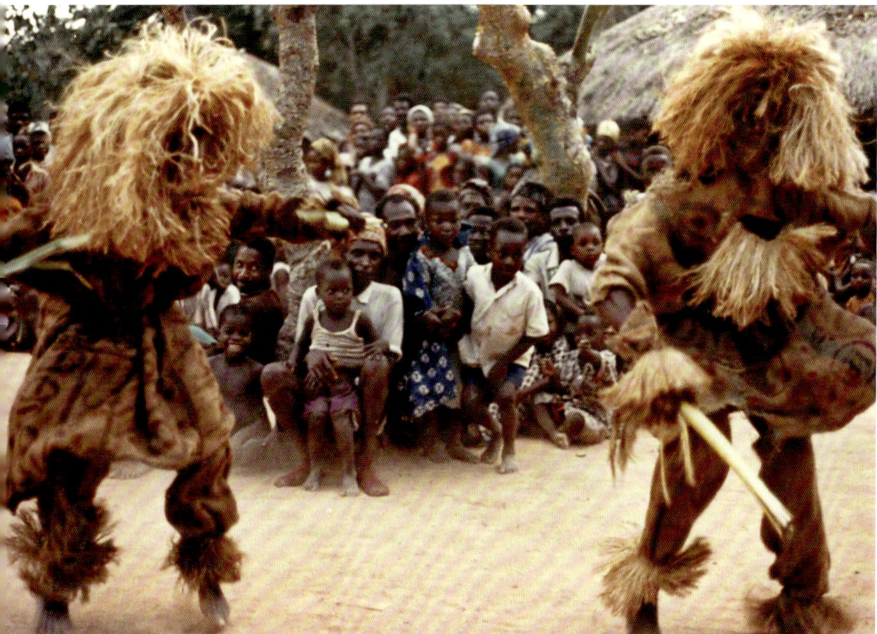

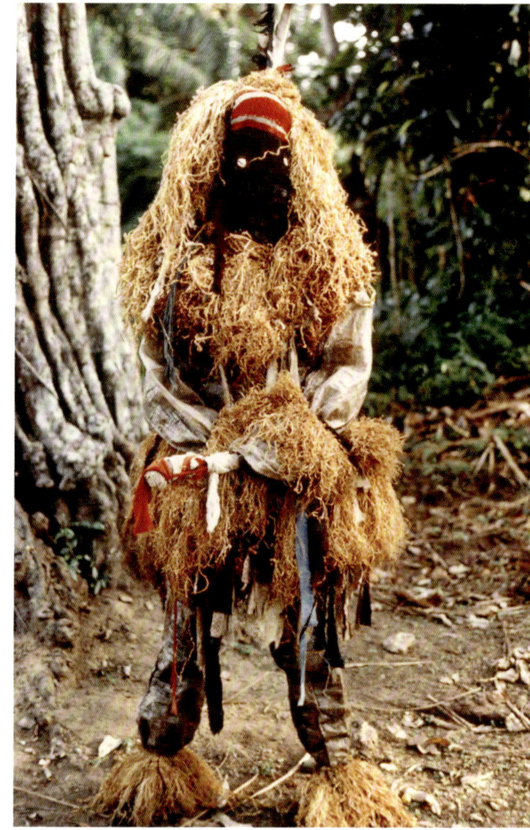

2.28

Ikpokwu (Ikpekwu) mask costumes were originally made from barkcloth, examples of which are held in the British Museum. Today, however, barkcloth is no longer produced locally, and instead, burlap (hessian) sacks are cut apart, painted, and sewn into loose-fitting costumes that are worn with raffia palm fiber ruffs.

PHOTOGRAPH BY SIDNEY LITTLEFIELD KASFIR, OTOBI VILLAGE, 1976.

2.29

Like Ikpokwu in Akpa District (see fig. 2.28), Akatakpa wears a combination of raffia and burlap. His primary performance mode is as a runner, appearing out of nowhere and chasing women and girls on market days in a ritual inversion of his supposed slave status.

PHOTOGRAPH BY SIDNEY LITTLEFIELD KASFIR, AGILA, 1978.

2.30

Boys in the group known as Anyuwowo practice the Idoma warrior dance style with its rapid foot movements executed while bending forward from the waist.

PHOTOGRAPH BY SIDNEY LITTLEFIELD KASFIR, OTOBI VILLAGE, 1978.

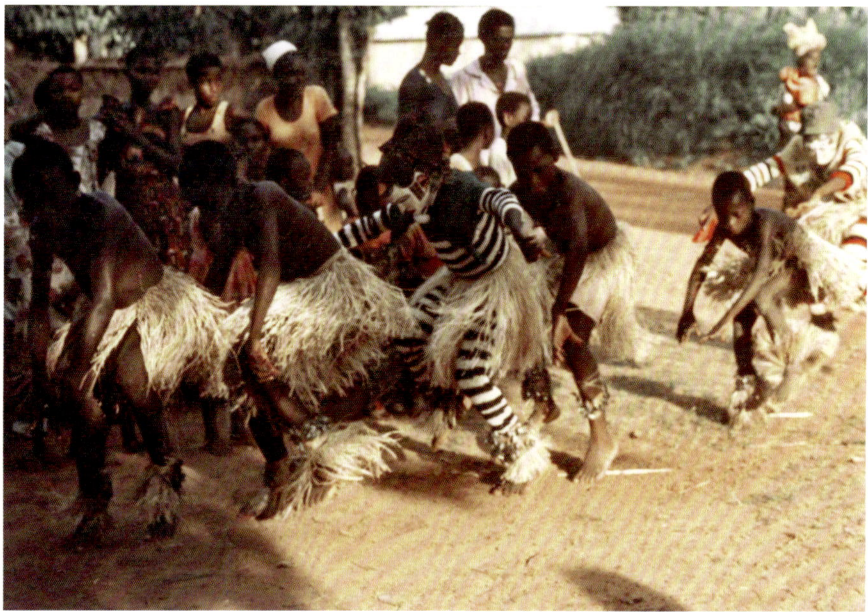

assigned to guard the millet or guinea corn harvest from birds—in other words, as scarecrows. Eventually these were brought back to the settlements and performed there. While probably an apocryphal story, it nonetheless conveys part of the Idoma cosmology of belief concerning masking and its common association with the bush.

Older generations of Idoma men typically belonged to four or five masquerade and dance societies, whose main performances were at the commemorative funerals (second burials) of their members. Not all Idoma lands (Aje, politico-religious units) have handled this practice in the same way, since there are cross-cutting loyalties between age-set or community-wide regulatory society masquerades and lineage-owned masquerades, such as Alekwuafia, which raise up dead fathers. In some places there are no "second burials," just the raising of Alekwuafia. In others, Alekwuafia is incorporated into second burials along with the society masquerade performances. Further, in mainly immigrant districts, there would be society masks but no Alekwuafia. I can illustrate this with the example of Akpa District where I lived, a cultural enclave of Akweya speakers with their own clan masks as well as the regulatory society masks found in many Idoma districts. There a second burial (*owyi onyonyi*) is a three-day celebration occurring during the dry season at some time (months or even years) after an actual burial (*okowyi*) takes place, normally on the day after a person's death.

The second-burial celebration usually begins with drumming and the sounds of Ifim on the first night. The second day is given over to feasting and the gathering of male and female age-sets to dance, drink, and socialize. The food and drink are supplied by the deceased's family, which is why it may take a substantial period of time to accumulate the resources to hold the event. Late in the afternoon, regulatory society masquerades such as Oglinye and Ichahoho perform, including some who may be invited from other villages. On the final day, society masquerades continue to appear, and at the end of the day, amidst a great deal of commotion, the Akweya clan masks Akpnmobe, Okpnma, and Igllo make brief appearances. This is the high point of the celebration, the Akweya equivalent to an appearance by Alekwuafia. Because some relatives of the deceased will have to travel from outside Idomaland, modern second burials usually take place from Friday through Sunday.

Masks of Slaves and Children's Masking

A large group of raffia fiber masks in Central and Southern Nigeria are designated as guardians, "policemen," or heralds, who precede the more important masks into the dance arena and who have the responsibility of crowd control during mask performances (fig. 2.28). So for example, I was once slapped across the face with a branch by an Agboogbo mask for being where he thought I shouldn't be. In terms of their status, they are far below the masquerades they herald, rather like the police motorcyclists who precede the car of a head of state. In Idoma, however, raffia-fiber masquerades have another role, which is that of a trickster character who is allowed through a process of ritual inversion to break normal social rules (fig. 2.29). For example, the Akatakpa masquerades in Agila are permitted to chase and "beat" women and girls on one day of the five-day week. These social trespassers are described as mask spirits of slaves, "whose only home is the bush." Again the connection between slaves and the bush is the farms that are often several miles outside nucleated settlements where most people live. It was on these farms that slaves were once used to guard the harvest.

Children learn to masquerade when they are very young, both in their own unsupervised play and while watching with their mothers on the ritual periphery of mask performances (see. figs. 2.28, 2.46). By the time they are six or seven years old, both boys and girls are taught to dance. On moonlit nights girls stay out late to practice their dances, and boys organize themselves as age-set masquerade groups. The boys' masking and dance group in Otobi is called Anyuwowo, and they perform with white-face masks that they have commissioned themselves and raffia skirts (figs. 2.30). At Christmastime, informal groups of boys wearing inexpensive masks entertain anyone who will watch in exchange for "small money" (fig 2.31).

The Migration of Masquerades

Masquerades in Central and Southern Nigeria were and are highly mobile. They could be taken as war booty, bought and sold, adopted with or without an accompanying set of rituals, and subsequently altered to suit the aesthetic and social requirements of the adopting community. Unlike shrine sculpture, their meanings are primarily constructed through performance so their former associations could quite easily be detached when they traveled.

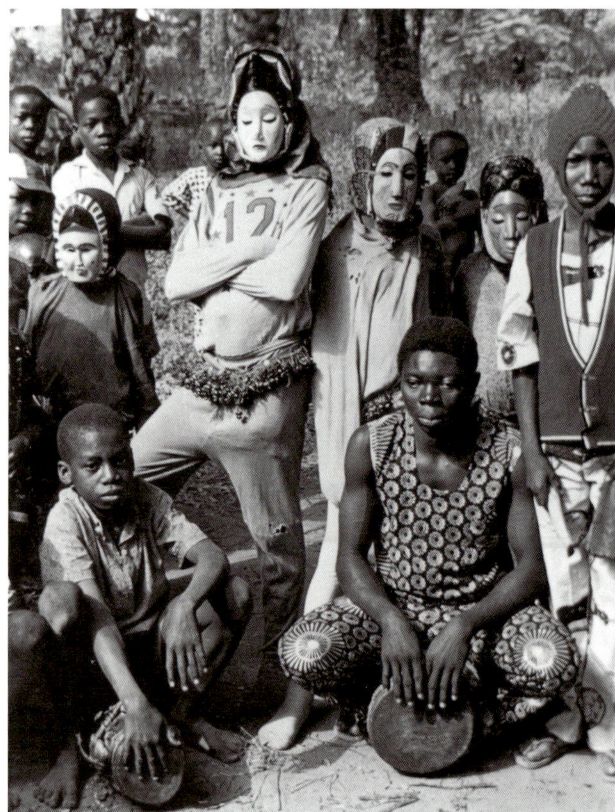

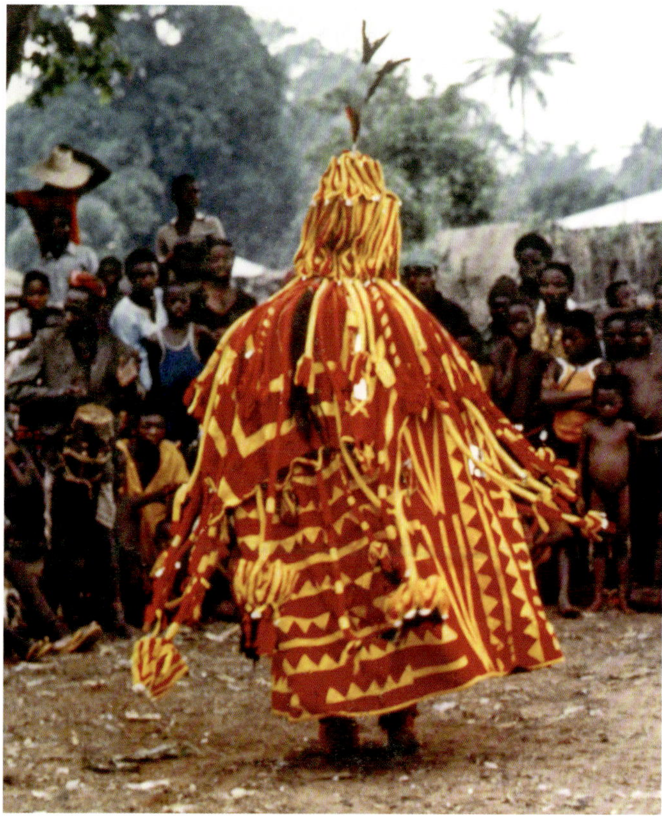

2.31
Youthful Idoma masqueraders wear Annang
masks from Ikot-Ekpene at Christmas.
PHOTOGRAPH BY SIDNEY LITTLEFIELD KASFIR,
IGUMALE, 1975.

2.32
The dress of the Agila Unaaloko masquerade
is less massive than that of Igumale, but it has
the added detail of the breeding plumes of the
standard-winged nightjar atop the head, which
have nocturnal associations.
PHOTOGRAPH BY SIDNEY LITTLEFIELD KASFIR,
AGILA, 1978.

At the same time that masks migrate—and are therefore inveterate boundary
crossers—they also retain telltale traces of where they have been. It may be a name,
an origin story, an accompanying weapon or musical instrument, an idiosyncratic
dance step, a special textile or feather or animal pelt. The mixture of elements tends
to fragment, absorb local scenarios, and undergo constant revision. Masquerades rarely
move completely intact, and their paths are there to be traced.

Idoma masking, located at the interface of Lower and Middle Benue regions
and on both sides of the river, is a historical nexus of many such paths. One points
westward to Igala, a second east to Apá, a third north toward the Hausa, and finally,
a fourth points south and east to northern Igbo country and Ogoja, the interface with
the Middle Cross River. The politically powerful ancestral masquerades are treated
here in a separate essay (see chapter 3), since they involve several groups in addition
to the Idoma. Known locally by names such as "tall ghost," "hooded cobra," and even
"horse," they form a distinct genre not seen outside Nigeria, which is characterized
by the resurrected ancestor wearing a burial shroud and capable of being increased in
height by various devices. Although rarely observed in art collections, both because
they are primarily textiles, not sculpture, and because they are hedged about with
taboos that would prevent their being sold, they are nonetheless the most deeply
revered in the mask repertories where they appear.

MASKS WITH IGALA CONNECTIONS: UNAALOKO AND EKWAJA

In the two southernmost Idoma kingdoms, Igumale and Agila, several lineages own
spectacular red and yellow appliqué masquerades known as Unaaloko (see fig. 2.32),
and in Agila alone, they possess an equally prominent carved mask called Ekwaja (see
fig. 2.34). Both masks are unique in the Idoma mask repertory, as they claim to commemorate Igala women, a queen and a slave. Agila's connections to Igala are couched
in oral narratives, which claim a sojourn there en route from Apá (which if true would
constitute a kind of large-scale U-turn). As I discussed in chapter 1, this is accepted
cosmology, not necessarily an actual historical route. Agila is actually contiguous with

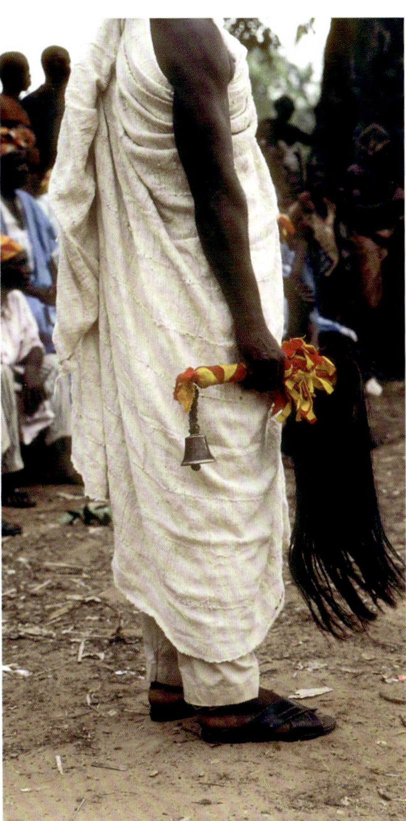

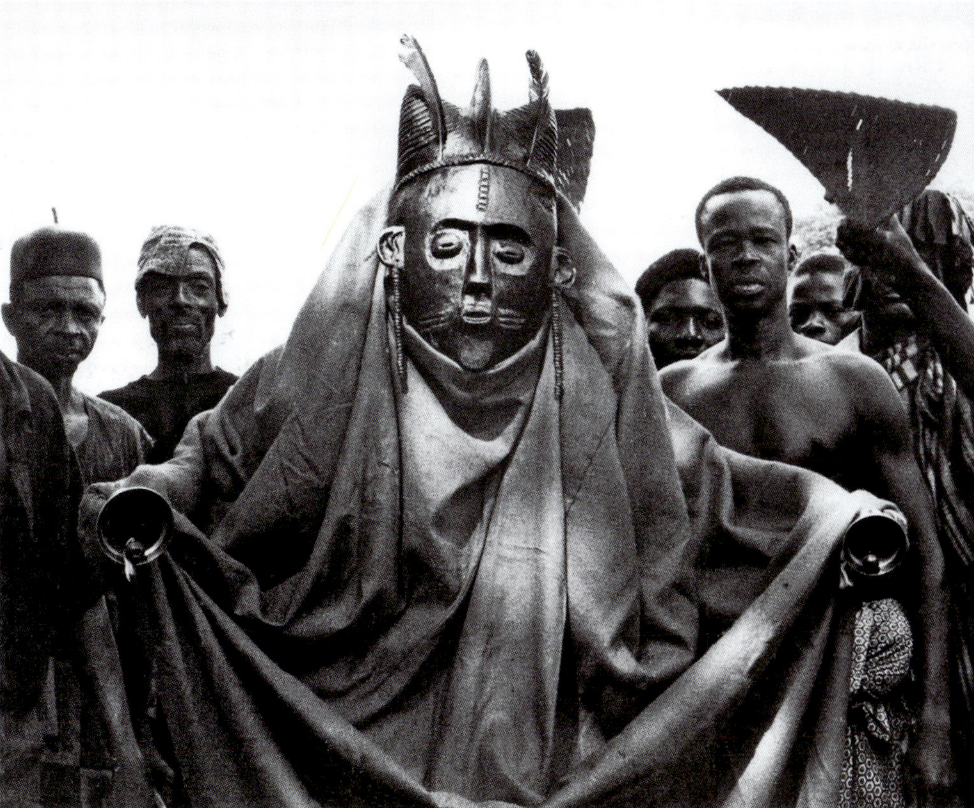

northern Igboland and has absorbed many Igbo settlers with their own ancestral masquerade known as Enkpe (Igbo: "Emukpe"), yet another "tall ghost."

Agila town is the best remaining example of the large nucleated settlements that were once more common throughout Idomaland. It is subdivided into a number of lineage-based wards, or quarters, each of which is comparable in size and structure to the hamlets or small villages found in the other Idoma districts south of the Benue. Important masquerades are owned by the different wards in Agila, each of which has its own village playground for mask performances. In the smaller settlements there is usually a single village playground (*ojira, ojila*), which serves this purpose. In Idoma, lineages are territorially based corporate bodies and can wield a great deal of power. Masquerades owned by lineages therefore have this same territorial base and symbolize this corporate power by embodying the lineage ancestors.

Unaaloko

Like the Yoruba *paka* Egungun, Unaaloko is an assemblage of sumptuous cloth over a large frame (fig. 2.32), its panels meant to be seen whirling centrifugally as the masker turns slowly, accompanied by an attendant carrying its horsetail whisk and bell (fig. 2.33). Its distinctive features are its massive size; the red *ododo* and yellow *ongazi* cloth appliqué resembling that worn by the king, title-holders, and ancestral masqueraders; numerous mirrors and bells; and (in Agila) atop the whole ensemble, the breeding plumes of the standard-winged nightjar (*opiempiekwu,* or Macrodypteryx longipennis; see chapter 3, p. 122). The Igumale version instead wears the red *uloko* feather of the scarlet lovebird, a sign of bravery worn by former warriors.

The two versions also have distinct myths of origin. In Igumale the Unaaloko mask is said to have been discovered by women who were fishing with traps when the water suddenly turned red. Unaaloko emerged from the water and followed them home, asking to be taken to the chief. In Agila it is said to impersonate a female slave who was so loyal that she gave up her life for the King of Idah—a myth that has more direct political ramifications. Such references are to be understood as legitimating the

Agila-Idah connection. Interestingly, both Agila and Igumale versions involve interventions by women and both are seen as benevolent spirits. In performance, Unaaloko displays the grace associated with a feminine aesthetic, turning slowly and delicately, as befits a royal mask of great age. If one looks for an existing Igala masquerade with any formal similarities, it would have to be Ekwe, the only royal mask with an appliqué costume (though with quite different designs), which is also hemmed with small brass bells (see fig. 5.3). Ekwe, according to Robert Sargent (1988) is the only royal mask in Igala to represent all lineages.

Ekwaja

In the Agila Kingdom, there is only one carved mask amidst a plethora of textile, raffia, and "invisible" (auditory) masquerades. This is Ekwaja (Ekwu-Aja, the "mask of Aja"; Kasfir 1986). A historical masquerade, Ekwaja commemorates the first Queen of Idah and is owned by the Efopfu and Osiroko founding lineages (fig. 2.34). Her title, Ekwataida (Ekwu-Ata-Ida, "mask of the King of Idah") makes clear her royal associations. Such an important object seems to create authority for the claim of the founding Agila settlers that they came from the Igala royal house. Yet no royal mask in Idah, the Igala capital, resembles Ekwaja in stylistic or iconographic terms. The face is also distinctly different from that of Idoma masks of the neighboring central and western districts. While other Idoma anthropomorphic masks are whiteface with black outlines, Ekwaja is all black. The typical eyes of Idoma masks are narrow slits turned slightly downward at the outer edge, but Ekwaja has eyes of a shape resembling cowrie shells and a much broader face. The coiffure of twin cones contrasts with the flat, undifferentiated hairstyle of whiteface masks, and the corners of the small open mouth are marked by cat's whisker scars, seen in both Idoma and Igala masks. The ears, noticeably large, are pierced by pendant earrings of brown glass beads worn by all royals in Agila and also identified there with Idah. These beads, probably of Nupe manufacture, are also seen in northern Igboland.

Ekwaja, dressed in red cloth and carrying two brass bells, dances in stately, measured fashion to a drumming pattern that, again, is very different from others heard in Idoma. Is Ekwaja then a historical remnant, an Idah mask no longer found in Idah but living on in Agila? Or is it a surviving example of an indigenous Agila mask style now supplanted by textile masquerades? The kings of Agila and Igumale both go to Idah to receive their beads of office, so they have seen the Egwu Ata royal masquerades, which then form part of the Agila cultural landscape, however distant.

ALAGO (IDOMA NOKWU) MASKING: JUKUN INFLUENCE AND THE HAUSA FACTOR

Arnold Rubin's pioneering survey research in the Middle Benue in the 1960s, indispensable to the work of anyone studying the region, was centered on the Jukun. In the course of his fieldwork, however, he concluded that the Jukun-centric view of the Benue—the portrait of Jukun dominance promoted by H. R. (Sir Richmond) Palmer, influential Arabist scholar and Lieutenant Governor of the Northern Provinces in the 1920s—was greatly overplayed.[9] Taking a cue from Mahdi Adamu's equally important study, *The Hausa Factor in West African History* (1978), I suggest that the Hausa factor has been underplayed mainly because the Hausa are not part of the "known world" of African art. Many Hausa itinerants lived outside the established Hausa states. They took up residence throughout the Benue region, which they referred to as Kasashen Bauchi, and before the nineteenth-century jihad, they were often not Muslim. They were long-distance traders, elephant hunters, skilled craftsmen (such as weavers), and ritual specialists. Although the Hausa Bori spirit possession complex is well known, Nigerian art history has typically left the Hausa out of discussions of masquerades. They were, nonetheless, major actors in Benue

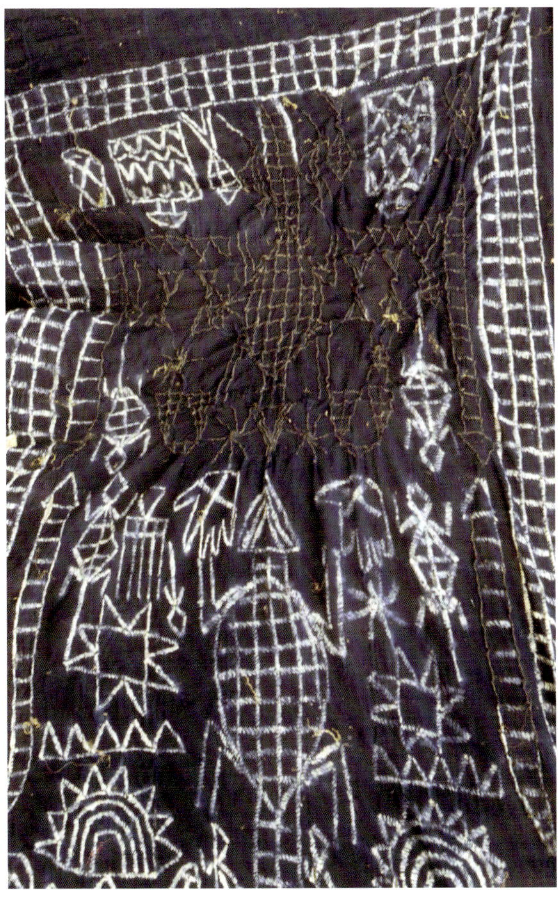

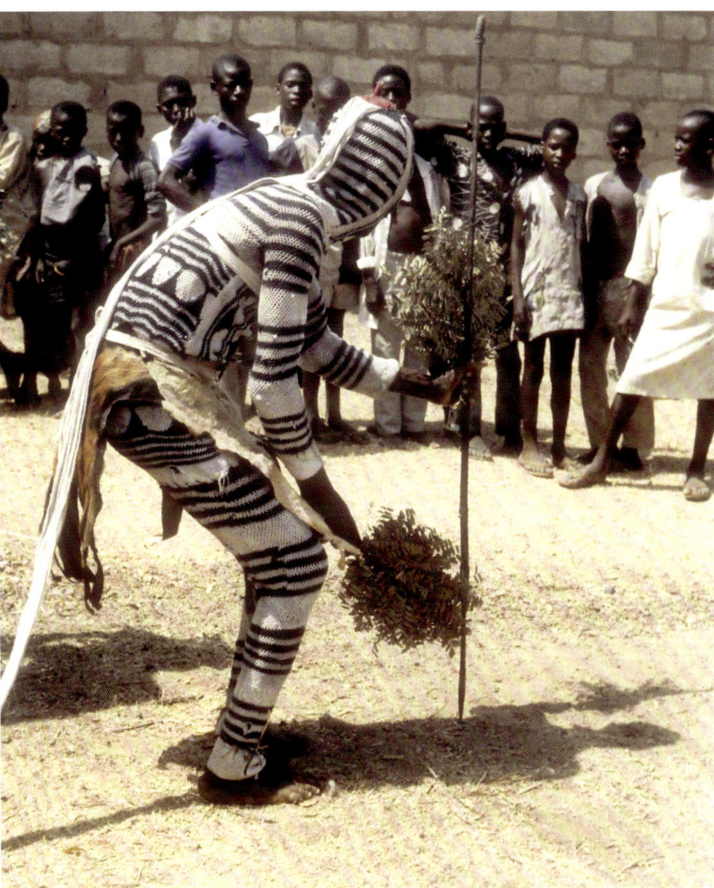

Valley ritual systems, and any discussion of Idoma masking north of the Benue has to acknowledge their influence.

The problem is how to assess origins of particular forms, such as the "tall ghost" ancestral masquerade. A simple "donor-recipient" model of transmission makes little sense since a number of different cultures were closely interdigitated in and around the various Benue Valley centers of power between 1500 and 1800. Instead, it is more productive to think of an ethnoscape of shared mask forms, similar to the pan-regional genre of shrine figures but much older than the jihad. And the dominant culture in this ethnoscape was at times Jukun and at other times Alago (Idoma Nokwu) or Igala with each drawing upon specialized Hausa knowledge of medicines and magic as well as the Hausa veneration of ancestors.[10]

As one crosses the Benue southward into what I will call "British Idomaland," i.e., colonial Idoma Division, Hausa influence recedes into a few well-defined pockets, but north of the Benue River in the Alago kingdoms of Doma and Keana (Idoma Nokwu, "greater Idoma"), it is palpably felt. The Andoma (king) of Doma has a royal orchestra with Hausa trumpets and *bata* drums, and principal officeholders have both Alago and Hausa titles, the latter including Dan Galadima (town chief) and Sarkin Dawaki (king's chief of horses). Doma itself is also an exporter of cultural forms: the pattern-dyed cloth of the Iwagu and Ashama masquerade is of *odu mele*, or "Doma cloth," made in the town by Alago craftsmen such as Yakubu Jikan Maikudi (fig. 2.35). This important ritual cloth, used in both masquerades and as a burial wrapper for elites, is also made in Wukari by Abakwariga (non-Muslim Hausa), but from its name it is obvious that Doma probably lays claim to its first production. It has a regional distribution through middlemen who trade it southward and into the Cameroon Grassfields. A type of men's trouser called *wondondoma* was also made in Doma and exported to Hausaland. In addition, Doma weavers, both men and women produced a variety of prestige cloths as well as *opa*, the plain (but also sacred) burial cloth used for ordinary people. In the past,

2.35
This pattern-dyed, indigo, Doma *odu mele* cloth is first painted with a stick, then the painted lines are covered over with raffia stitching, and the whole is resist dyed in local indigo dye pits. When the stitching is removed, the drawn lines, which have not absorbed the dye, appear in white. In this example, the stitching has been removed in the lower section of the cloth; whereas it still remains in the upper half.
PHOTOGRAPH BY SIDNEY LITTLEFIELD KASFIR, DOMA TOWN, 1986.

2.36
The Ikashi is a bush spirit masquerade. When performing, it is accompanied by older women playing water pot drums.
PHOTOGRAPH BY SIDNEY LITTLEFIELD KASFIR, KEANA, 1989.

in order to purchase horses for the cavalry (*ayonya*), they exported both cloth and salt (from Keana), as well as poisoned arrows.

Not surprisingly, given both woven and pattern-dyed indigo cloth production, the preponderance of masquerades have been textile, knit, or raffia. Iwagu, the ancestral mask most closely connected to Idoma south of the Benue, is also known as Osumoku, or "one's forefather" (see fig. 3.9). But whereas in central Idoma its counterpart, the Alekwuafia masquerade, recites the genealogies of past kings and migrations, this role is played not by Iwagu but by the Okwe masquerade in Doma, who recites not only kinglists but elaborate town histories.

In most parts of Africa, bush spirits are embodied as either masquerades or as the tutelary patrons of spirit possession complexes. Here in the northern Benue region close to Hausaland, there are instances of both. Early colonial reports by British officers using Hausa interpreters called all northern masquerades "*dodo*," but it is generally the non-ancestral masks that are associated with bush spirits, which the Hausa call Iskoki or Aljanun and the Idoma, Anjenu. Alago masks of bush spirits include Ekukashi (in Doma) or Ikashi (in Keana; fig. 2.36), both cognate with Jukun Agashi in Wukari. These masks dress in the faceless, tightly fitted bodysuit seen as far south as the Cross River. In Doma and Keana, however, instead of the animal pelt (usually that of a civet cat), the mask wears a long, woven cloth streamer and performs in slow catlike movements very distinct from the aggressive dances of warrior masquerades from the south.

ALAGO, AFO, IGALA, AND JUKUN INTERSECTIONS: GENRE-CROSSING STYLES AND STYLE-CROSSING GENRES

There are occasional close similarities between the Alago and Jukun masks reported by Rubin (chapter 9) for at least two reasons. Before the Jukun moved their capital south of the Benue, the Jukun and Alago kingdoms, especially Keana, were geographically contiguous, and in addition both interacted with and absorbed certain Hausa (Abakwariga) forms of masquerade. Keana's version of Doma's Okwe mask is Okwakpa, or "Okwe of the Akpa (Jukun)," and it is a carved wooden mask nearly identical to the Jukun Aku-Wunu (see figs. 9.20–9.22). Keana also owns Adashan, which sings in Jukun, a fiber mask with tubular cylinder eyes that is topped with feathers. Keana is also the only place in Idoma, either north or south of the river, where I have observed men wearing the Jukun-style ritual hair braid.

Finally, Rubin documented an Alago helmet mask called Okpatonu in Keana (fig. 2.37), a crude version of a type associated with both Jukun and Igala, offering more confirmation of the existence of Middle Benue versions of masks better known much further west among the Ata of Igala's royal masquerades (figs. 2.38a,b; see also figs. 9.27a,b). Not only do there appear to be variations of the same mask type appearing at both ends of a two-hundred-mile stretch from the Middle Benue to the confluence, there are also instances of maternity figures assumed to come from the Afo-Idoma region sharing very detailed likenesses with some of the Igala royal masks, particularly facial contours and scarification (see Vogel and Thompson 1981, 163–64, cat. No. 96). This similarity, at times very close, has caused decades of confusion about possible connections.

Using scarification patterns as a form of iconographic system, i.e., as marks of identity, Cornelius Adepegba (circa 1985) compared in detail the facial scars on the Igala royal masks known as Jamadeka and Odumado with those on certain Afo and Jukun or Kororofa (Kwararafa) masks and figures. He concluded that since none of the neighboring groups surrounding Igala owned such masks, nor were they found in nonroyal Igala masquerades, the style must have followed the westward course of the Benue River from Jukun and Afo territory more than 250 miles to the Igala Kingdom. This sounds like an easy solution to the question of provenance, but it raises three rather large issues: (1) Is scarification represented on a piece of sculpture a reliable way of tracing provenance?

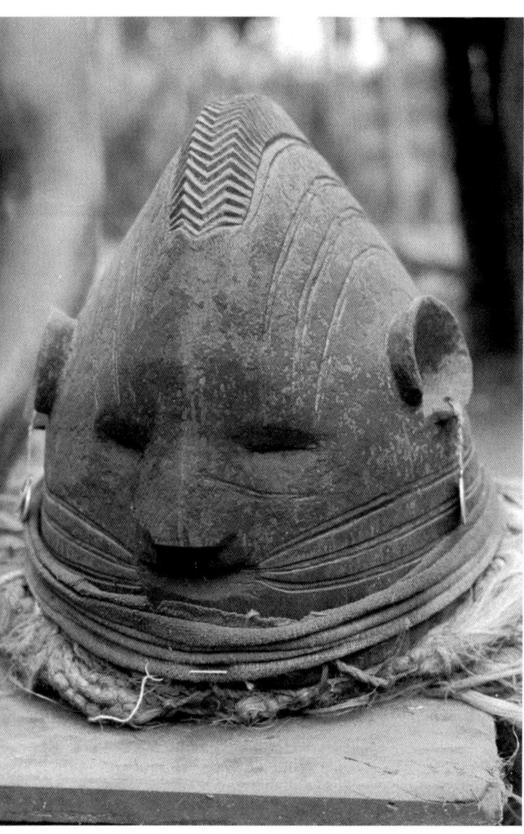

2.37
Photographed in Keana this Okpatonu mask is related to masks associated with both Jukun and Igala.
PHOTOGRAPH BY ARNOLD RUBIN, JANUARY 10, 1971, RUBIN ARCHIVE, FOWLER MUSEUM AT UCLA, NEG. NO. 2986.

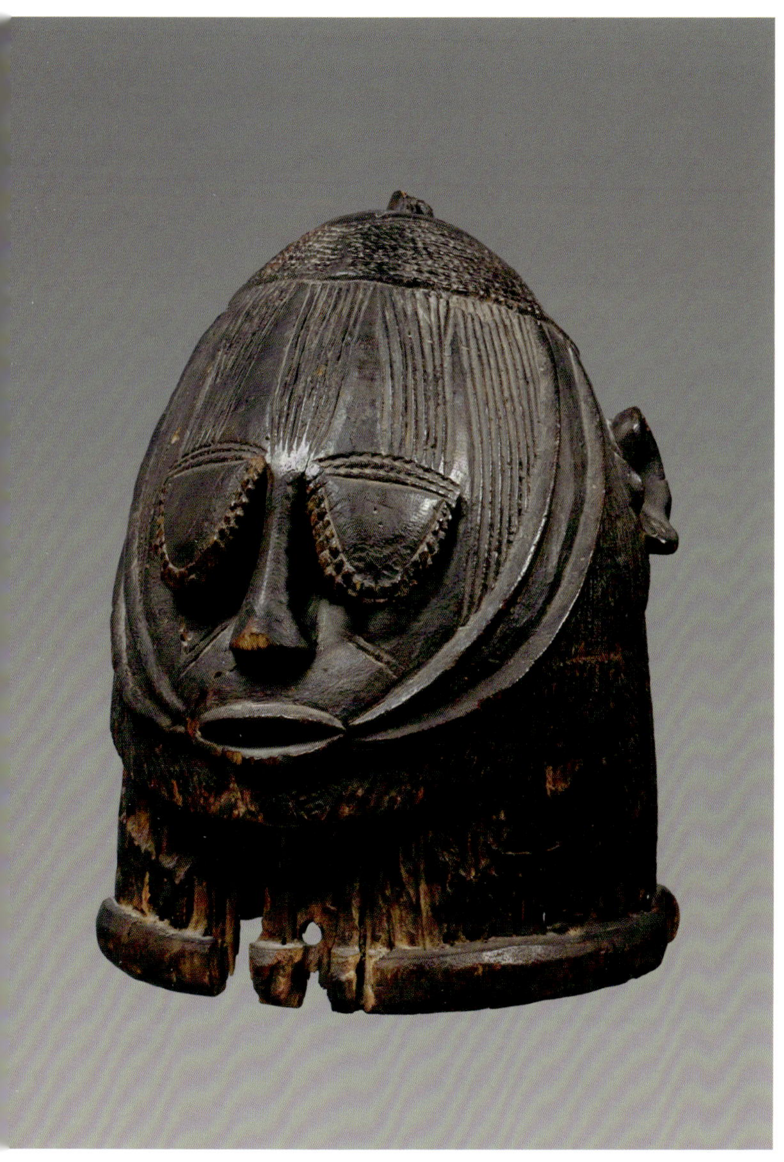
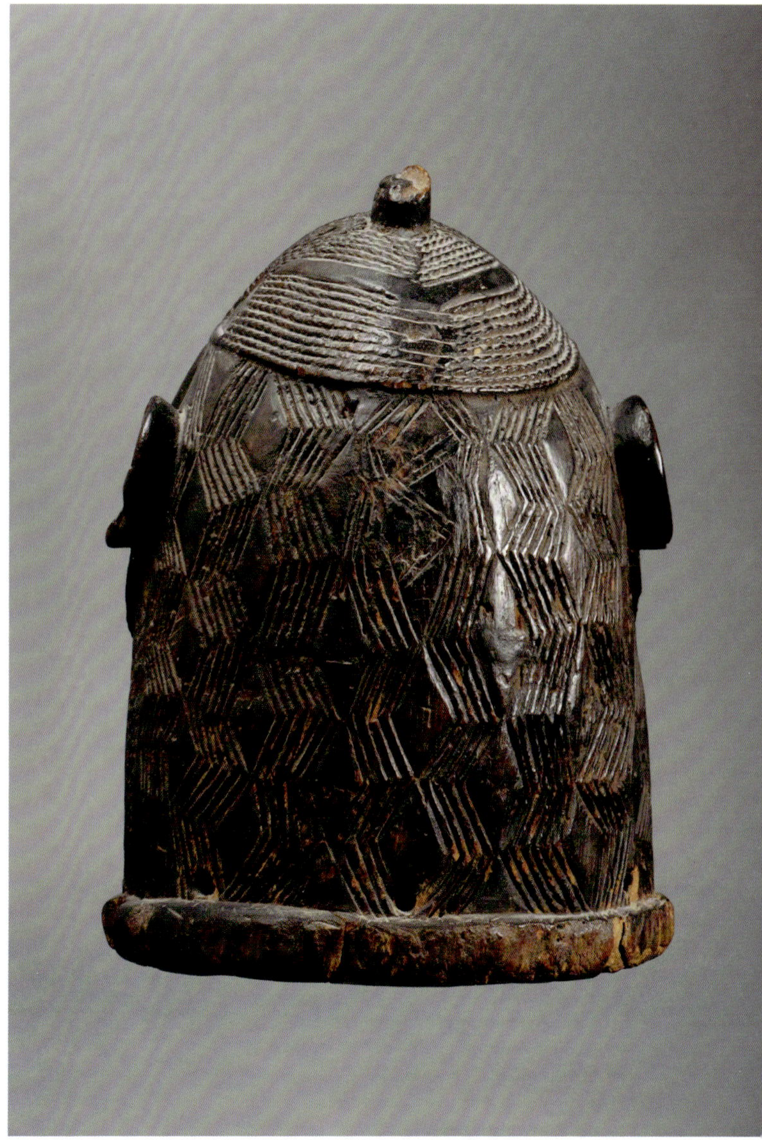

(2) What oral history evidence is there to back the river theory? (3) Are we speaking of a population movement, or the movement of objects, or maybe both?

C. K. Meek, a prominent Nigerian government ethnographer in the 1920s and 1930s, rejected the idea that so-called tribal marks were reliable as forms of identity. In his ethnography of the Northern Provinces, he argued that the scars were on the one hand, marks of ethnic identity, but on the other, they could also be abandoned or changed in situations of slavery, migration, war, or even a change in fashion (1925, 1: 44–49). Meek's text contains an illustration of the marks Adepegba identified as Afo or Jukun (which Meek called Kakanda, a group related to the Afo).

I saw evidence of such a shift in practice in my own Nigerian fieldwork. The Idoma people had abandoned facial scarification during the colonial period, but when the Nigerian Civil War erupted in 1967, the Idoma found themselves living on the border of the Biafran secessionist movement and readopted scarification to differentiate themselves from their Biafran neighbors in conflict situations. If Meek's observations were correct, Adepegba's premise may be slightly slippery.

Wars and Migration

So what about the other form of proof through oral traditions of wars and population movements? As already described in chapter 1, oral traditions claim three immigrant dynasties have ruled the Igala Kingdom after its mythical founding by the son of a

2.38a,b

Helmet mask (Aku Washenki)
Jukun peoples, before 1965
Wood
H: 30 cm
PRIVATE COLLECTION, PARIS
PHOTOGRAPH BY PRIVATE COLLECTOR
PROVENANCE: PURCHASED IN THE 1970S

Arnold Rubin photographed this mask in the western Jukun village of Arufu in 1965. It was used there as the female of the husband-wife pair in the Aku masquerade, which has connections to chieftaincy (see fig. 9.27a,b).

2.40 (RIGHT)
Ochai? (active circa 1910–1950)
Crest mask (Oglinye)
Idoma peoples, Akweya subgroup, early to
mid-twentieth century
Wood, pigment, vegetable fiber, beads (?)
H: 32 cm
PRIVATE COLLECTION, PARIS
IMAGE: COURTESY PRIVATE COLLECTOR. PHOTO-
GRAPH © HUGHES DUBOIS, 2010
PROVENANCE: PURCHASED IN AFRICA, PRIOR TO 1977

I photographed this head in Otobi village in
1977 (see fig. A.8; also fig. 2.3 for a photograph
of the head by Roy Sieber). It displays facial
features that resemble Boki masks more than
Ochai's usual style.

2.41 (OPPOSITE, LEFT)
Ochai (active circa 1910–1950)
Ichahoho mask
Idoma peoples, Akweya subgroup, early to
mid-twentieth century
Wood, pigment, fiber
H: 34 cm
COLLECTION OF TOBY AND BARRY HECHT
PHOTOGRAPH © 2010, GREG STALEY
PROVENANCE: PRIVATE COLLECTION, PARIS; CHRIS-
TIAN DUPONCHEEL

This mask, unquestionably by Ochai (see
interleaf A), could have been carved anytime
between 1900 and 1950, but its relative lack of
signs of wear and tear suggests the end of that
period.

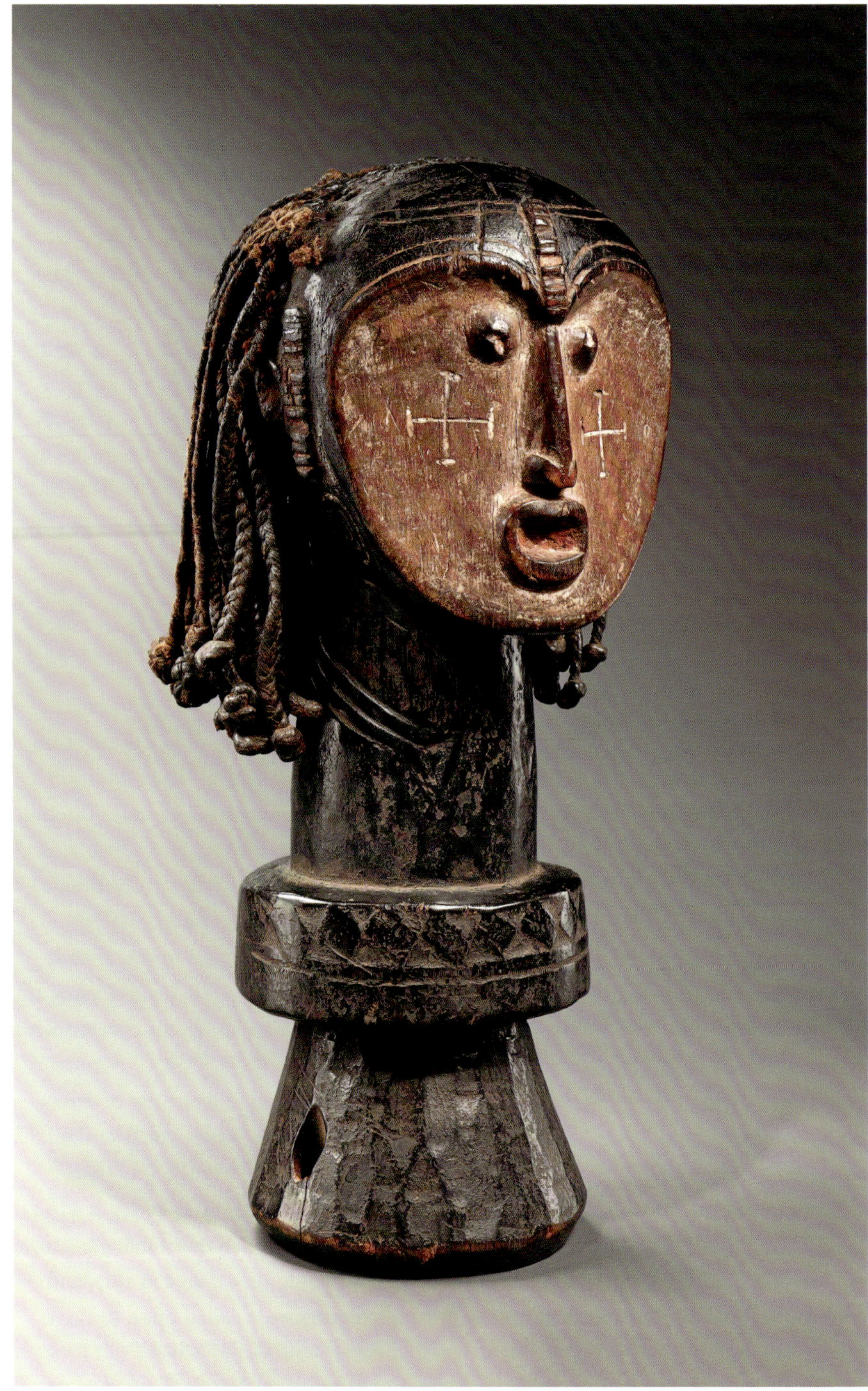

collected an account of its entry into Idomaland, suggesting that it occurred in the
previous generation. The popularity of warriors' dances was a major source of concern
to the Idoma elders, who tried to co-opt their members by incorporating them into
the Aiuta constabulary. This was done, but the Oglinye, and later Ichahoho, members seemed to retain a large degree of autonomy from the traditional councils. This
allowed them to sometimes steal with impunity and constitute themselves into illegal
tribunals to judge other wrongdoers.

   At the onset of colonial administration, the British did not understand or even
suspect the law-enforcement functions of the Aiuta (Abraham 1951, 196–97), and they
regarded the dance groups and their masquerades as a major obstacle to the British
"civilizing mission," due to their close associations with warriorhood (Magid 1976, 43).
They therefore did everything possible to destroy their power. Oglinye was proscribed
in 1917, and during the next fifteen years, warriors who were caught with trophy heads in

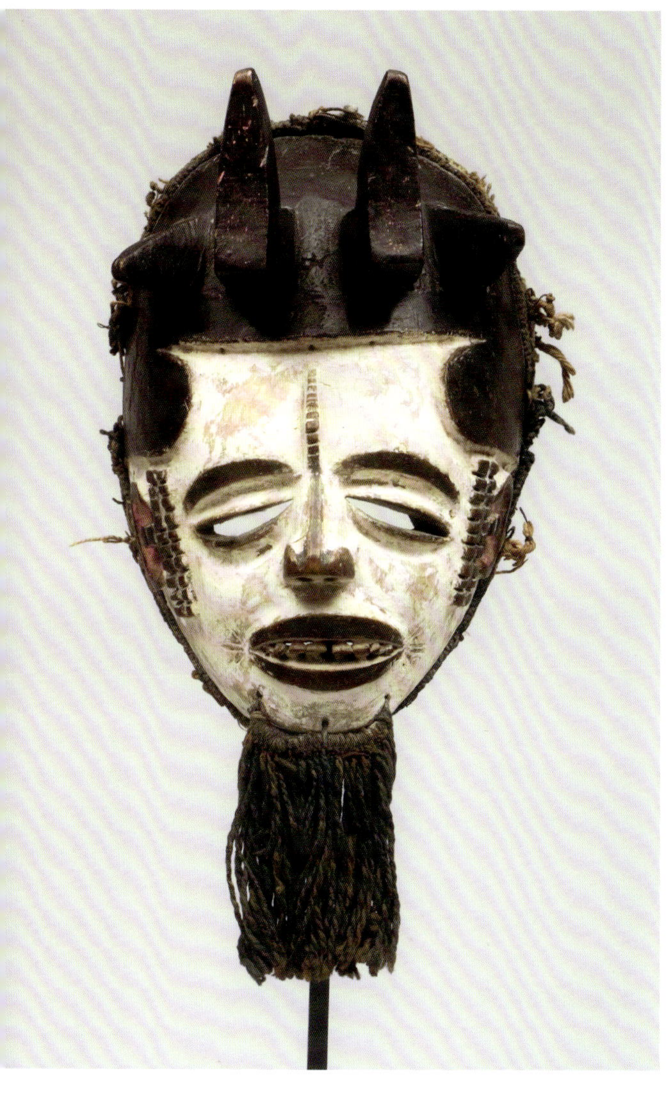

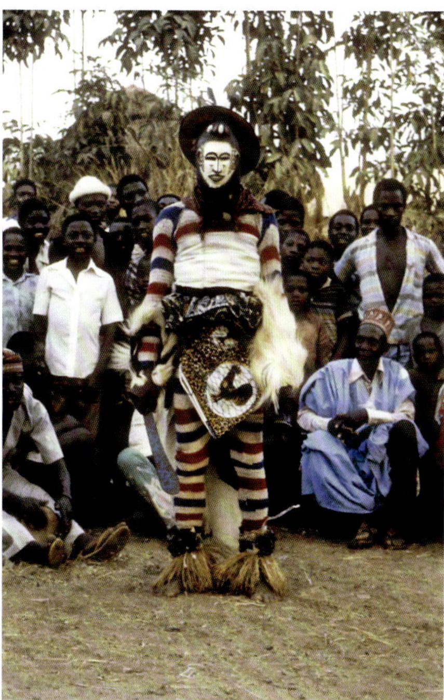

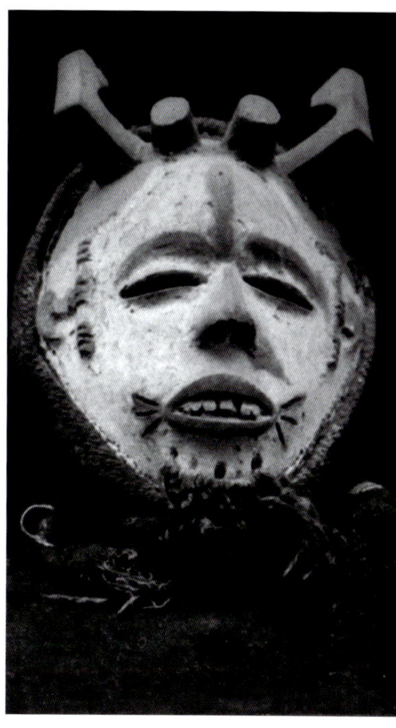

their possession were hung. From the 1940s onward, the British reversed themselves and made intermittent attempts to use the secret societies and dance groups (which had survived as underground or "bush" organizations) to help collect taxes and enforce orders, but with questionable success. The groups continued, however, to be an important political and cultural force in postcolonial Idoma with many adult men as members.

In contrast to Oglinye, Ichahoho appears to have been an indigenous masquerade that arose sometime after Oglinye and in some places eclipsed it (Abraham 1967, 196–97). A district officer described "Chafofo" thus in the 1920s, "A masked figure appears covered head to foot in a tight fitting costume rather reminiscent of a suit of knitted combinations and the head winners each bearing a machete dance round the figure with stiff movements" (Macleod 1925, 19). Macleod was writing about the western districts. In Akpa, both Oglinye and Ichahoho dress in this fashion, and both carry machetes and challenge older men with the warrior title *obgu* to mock battle during their performances. The major difference in the two masquerades is that Ichahoho is a horned but otherwise anthropomorphic face mask, while Oglinye is a sculpted head (figs. 2.41, 2.42; see fig. A.3) In Akpa District, there is a third mask associated with headwinners called Ikpa, which closely resembles Ichahoho. Both are whiteface masks displaying horns sprouting above the forehead, but they otherwise exhibit a high degree of realism, which may have had its stylistic genesis in the earlier trophy heads. Where Oglinye can be tracked entering Idomaland from the Cross River and Ogoja, Ikpa was an indigenous Idoma headwinners' dance, demonstrating that it was the Oglinye mask and not the custom of taking enemy heads that was imported (fig. 2.43).

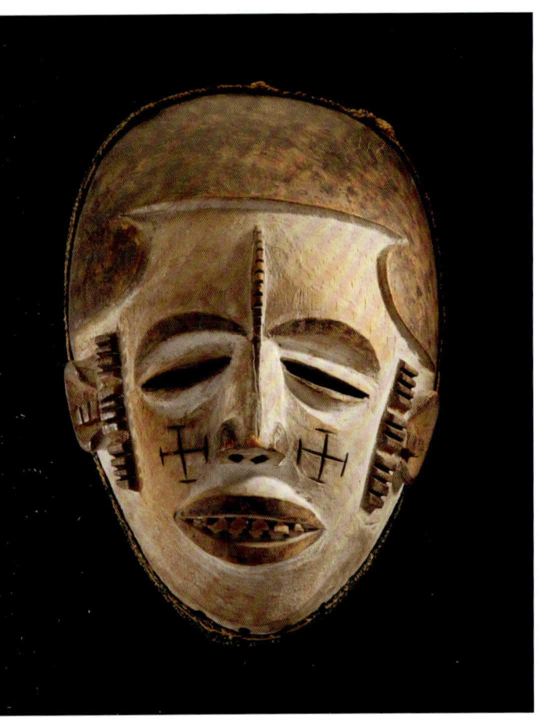

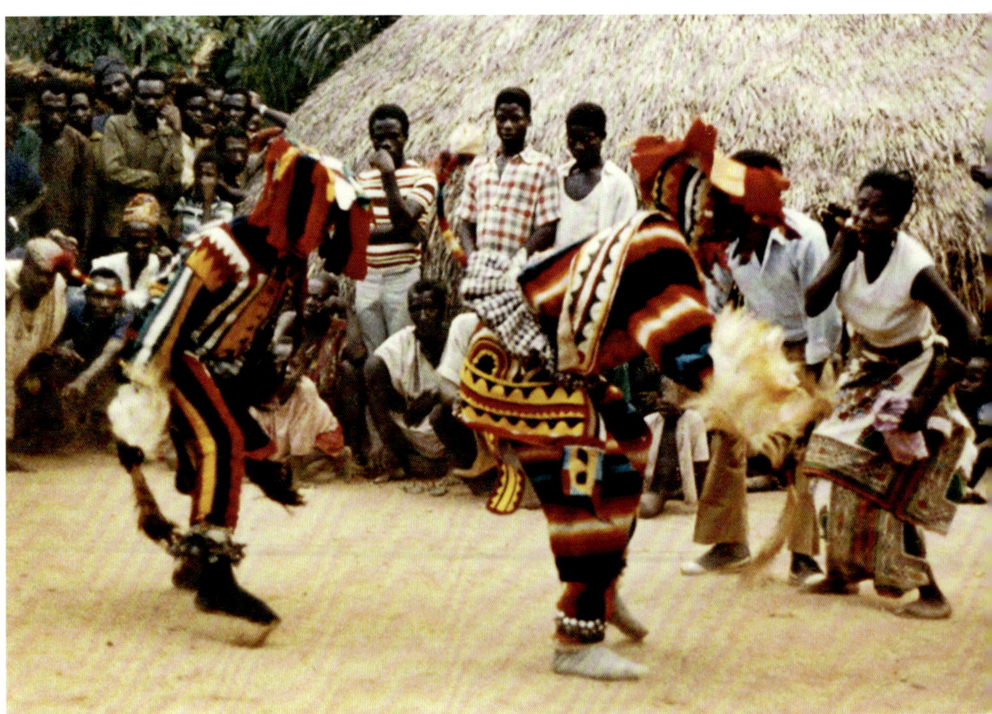

2.44
Ochai? (active circa 1910–1950)
Whiteface mask (Ikpobi?)
Idoma peoples, Akweya subgroup, 1930s
Wood, pigment
H: 22.5 cm
FOWLER MUSEUM AT UCLA X2009.16.1; GIFT OF
BERNICE BARTH
IMAGE: © 2010 FOWLER MUSEUM AT UCLA.
PHOTOGRAPH BY DON COLE
PROVENANCE: SOTHEBY'S AUCTION, NEW YORK, 1967

Although not used in the same social context,
this Ikpobi-type mask resembles warrior
masks such as Ichahoho but without the
horns. The form with its vertical forehead scar,
scalloped hairline, downturned half-closed
eyes, and keloid scars at the temples, plus the
slightly open mouth with visible teeth, has all
the standard hallmarks of Idoma origin.

2.45
Like Oglinye, Odumu (hyena) is another
example of a masquerade whose social purpose changed from the instrumental to the
symbolic realm under colonialism. Its original
purpose was to dispose of children born with
serious abnormalities that would render their
survival highly unlikely.
PHOTOGRAPH BY SIDNEY LITTLEFIELD KASFIR,
OTOBI VILLAGE, 1977.

Several other whiteface masks, identical to Ichahoho except for the absence of
horns, are used in second burial performances. A common one in Akweya villages is
the mask called Ikpobi, which sometimes appears as one of a "husband and wife" pair.
The example shown here (fig. 2.44) was probably made in the 1930s, as it seems to
be by the same hand as several pieces commissioned by a British colonial officer and
presented to the Pitt Rivers Museum in Oxford at that time. It is carved in the style
of Ochai, though not as finely detailed as his pieces generally are (see fig. A.3).

Odumu (Akweya: "Odom")

The Odumu (Idoma: "hyena") masquerade is owned by a regulatory society that was
active through a wide swatch of Idoma country in the precolonization period as an element of social control. The work of the society was to euthanize babies born with serious physical defects that would render them unable to survive in a harsh environment.
Parents could call upon Odumu for this service, which was provided anonymously by a
masked figure and its assistants (figs. 2.45). Odumu is a textile masquerade but in the
bodysuit form, with a large mirror, surrounded by red and yellow felt streamers, worn
in place of a face. Its "slave," Ofi-Odom, on the other hand is a carved mask headdress consisting of two female figures back to back (see fig. A.4). I have only seen the
Odumu masquerade perform in Otobi but was told that it had a wider distribution.

Ekpe Masquerades

Much less is known about the Ekpe masquerade in Idoma and Akweya, though it
seems to be imported from Igboland and is conceptually distinct from the well-known
Leopard society (Ngbe) of the Cross River.[14] Ekpe as it was performed in the Akweya
village of Otobi in 1976 had four masked figures: a hooded whipping mask, dressed
in a men's wrapper tied at the waist and carrying branches; a pair of nearly identical
dancers in appliqué cloth suits that also covered the head; and Ogongo, a carved face
mask worn, like Oglinye and Ichahoho, with a knitted white bodysuit (figs. 2.46, 2.47).
While Idoma men do knit masquerade costumes (and were quite incredulous when
I told them that women knit in Western countries), the appliqué suits were probably
imported from the Anambra River region of Igbo country where their production has
been documented by Boston (1960) and Cole (Cole and Aniakor 1984, pl. 39). The

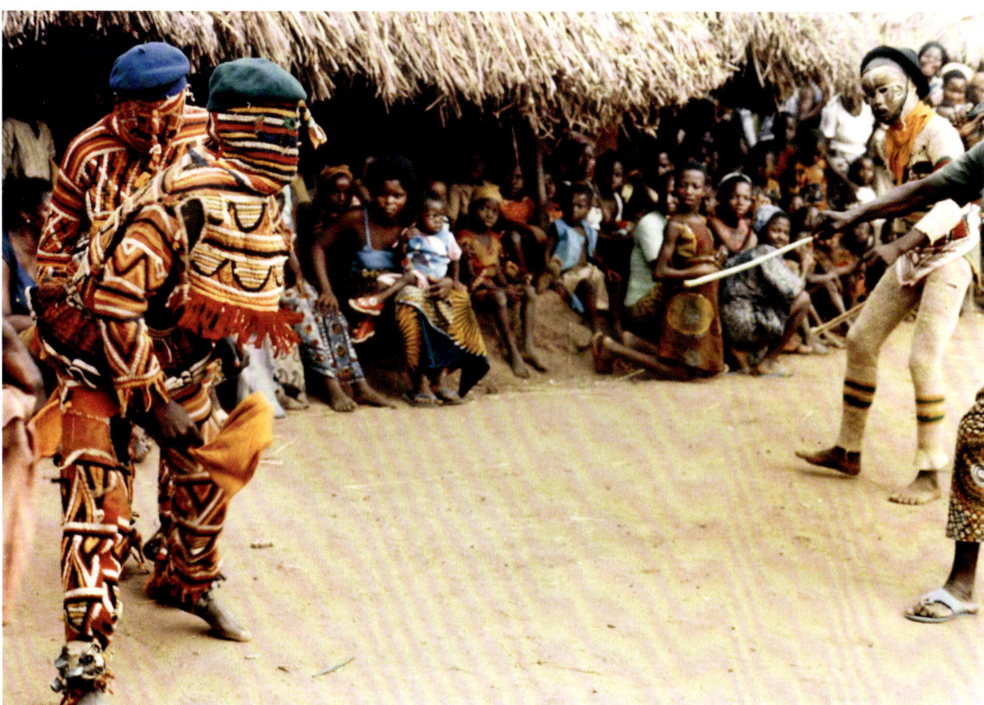

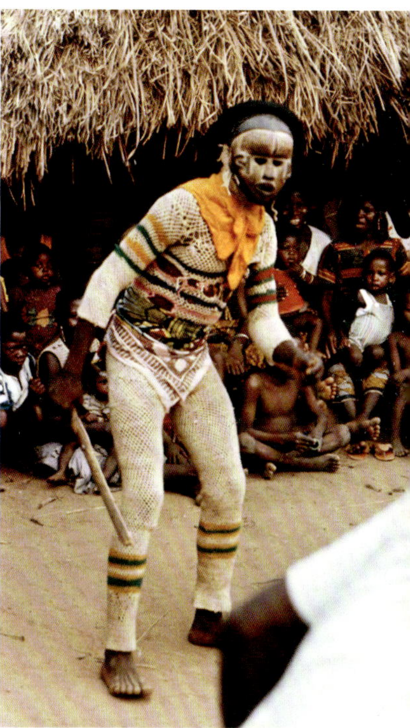

carved Ogongo mask bears a strong resemblance to a very fine mask in the British Museum (1949.Af.46.224) with the dubious attribution "Munchi" (Tiv), collected originally in 1929, presumably in Tivland.

The Akweya version of Ekpe could have come either through Utonkon, the district bordering Akpa on the south, which was settled by Orri-speaking Ufia people from former Abakaliki Division, or through the close connections between the Akweya and their kinfolk residing in Ogoja. Interestingly, Ogongo is cognate with Okonko (Cole and Aniakor 1984, 178), a graded secret society similar to the Cross River Ekpe, which was powerful in Ngwa and other eastern Igbo areas. Cole and Aniakor comment that Okonko and Ekpe are nowadays difficult to disentangle—perhaps a possible explanation of Ogongo's appearance in Ekpe at Otobi.

In yet another variant, three masks called Efu-Ekpe were collected by Anita Glaze in Owukpa, a western Idoma district, in 1965 (Jos Museum 667.4.84, 66J.4.91, and 667.4.84.92), of which two were imported from Igboland and the third was made by Ainyi Ugwo, a local Idoma carver. All three were carved in the Nsukka Igbo style used for maiden masks, with a small narrow white face and high crested hairstyle. The degree of creative synthesis displayed here can be more fully appreciated when one learns that the masks were used in the performance of the Igede war dance, originating in the southeastern Idoma region of that name, at the burials of important old men!

Akweya Masks: The Ogoja-Cross River Connection

More than any other local grouping, the masks and figures of the Akweya-speaking people of Akpa District have come to represent the "Idoma style" to the collecting world. The reasons for this go back to Roy Sieber's two-week visit in 1958, when he documented pieces he was told were by the carver Ochai in Otobi, the chief lineage village of the Akweya-speaking group of late eighteenth- or early nineteenth-century settlers. He then published work attributed to Ochai in *Sculpture from Northern Nigeria*, which was subsequently cited by William Fagg (1965), and the rest is history. While the Akweya, like their Idoma neighbors, adhere to an Apá cosmology ("we are people of Apa"), their closest relatives both linguistically and culturally are the Yachi of Ogoja District, north of the Middle Cross River. The Ekpari, Mbo, and Ifu-Akpa lineages own several highly powerful clan masks that are functionally, though not visually or

2.46
Ekpe is popular in southeastern Nigeria and has been described as an Igbo masquerade by Cole and Aniakor (1984). While Idoma masquerades typically appear in pairs or alone, Ekpe in Akpa District has at least four characters including the whipping mask.
PHOTOGRAPH BY SIDNEY LITTLEFIELD KASFIR, OTOBI VILLAGE, 1976.

2.47
Ogongo, the face mask that appears with Ekpe, is clearly cognate with the Igbo Okonko.
PHOTOGRAPH BY SIDNEY LITTLEFIELD KASFIR, OTOBI VILLAGE, 1976.

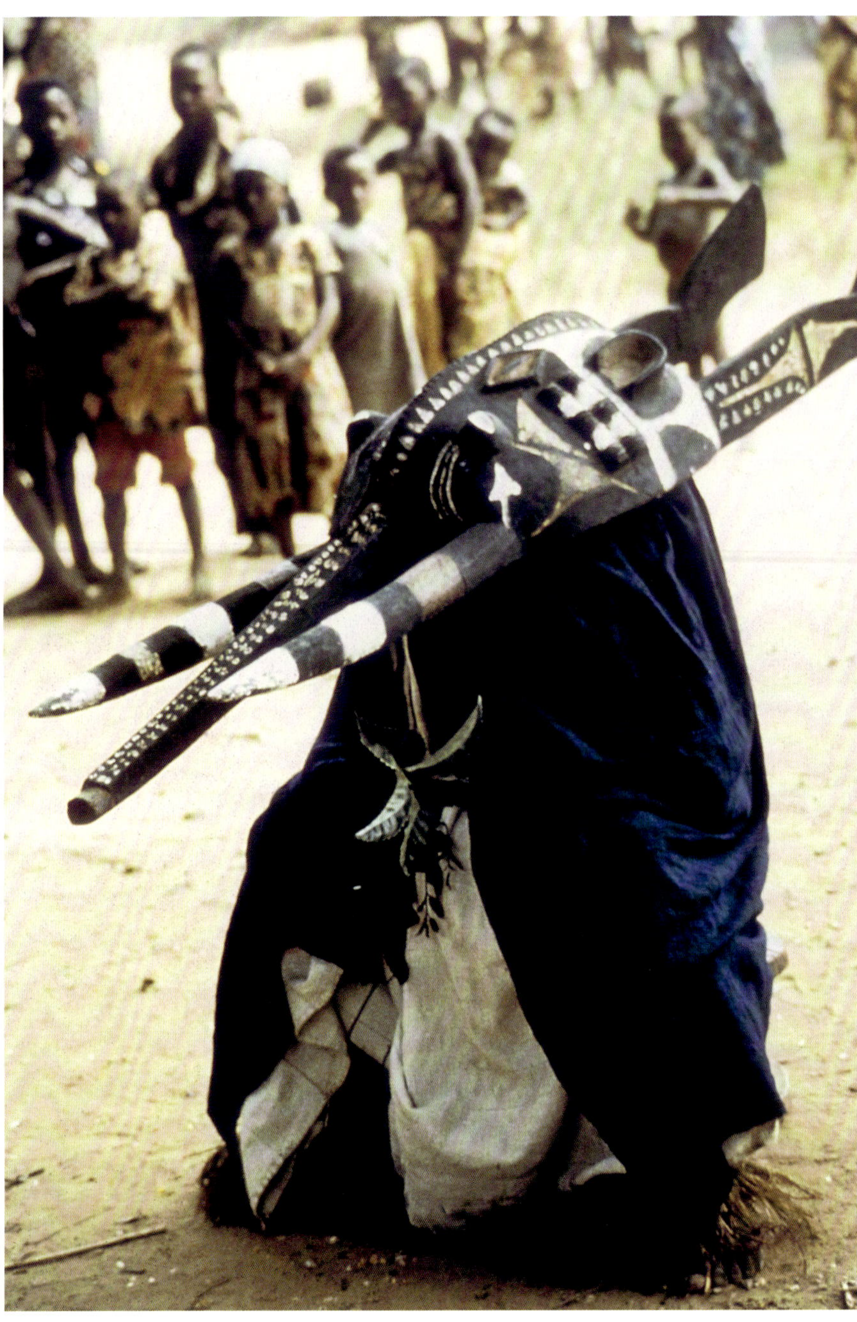

2.48
The Itrokwu mask seen here performing in
Otobi village, has moved on to a "second
career" as a sought-after artworld possession
(see fig. A.1).
PHOTOGRAPH BY SIDNEY LITTLEFIELD KASFIR, 1986.

2.49
This Jukun mask resembles the elephant-like
Itrokwu. Arnold Rubin was told that it was
named "Akuma Ataji."
PHOTOGRAPH BY ARNOLD RUBIN, WUKARI, JANU-
ARY 14, 1965, RUBIN ARCHIVE, FOWLER MUSEUM
AT UCLA, NEG. NO. 28.

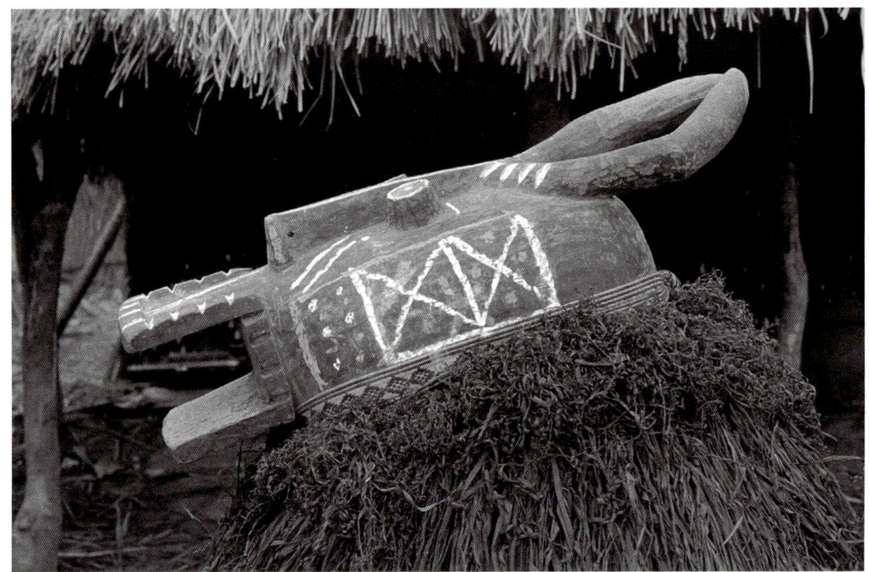

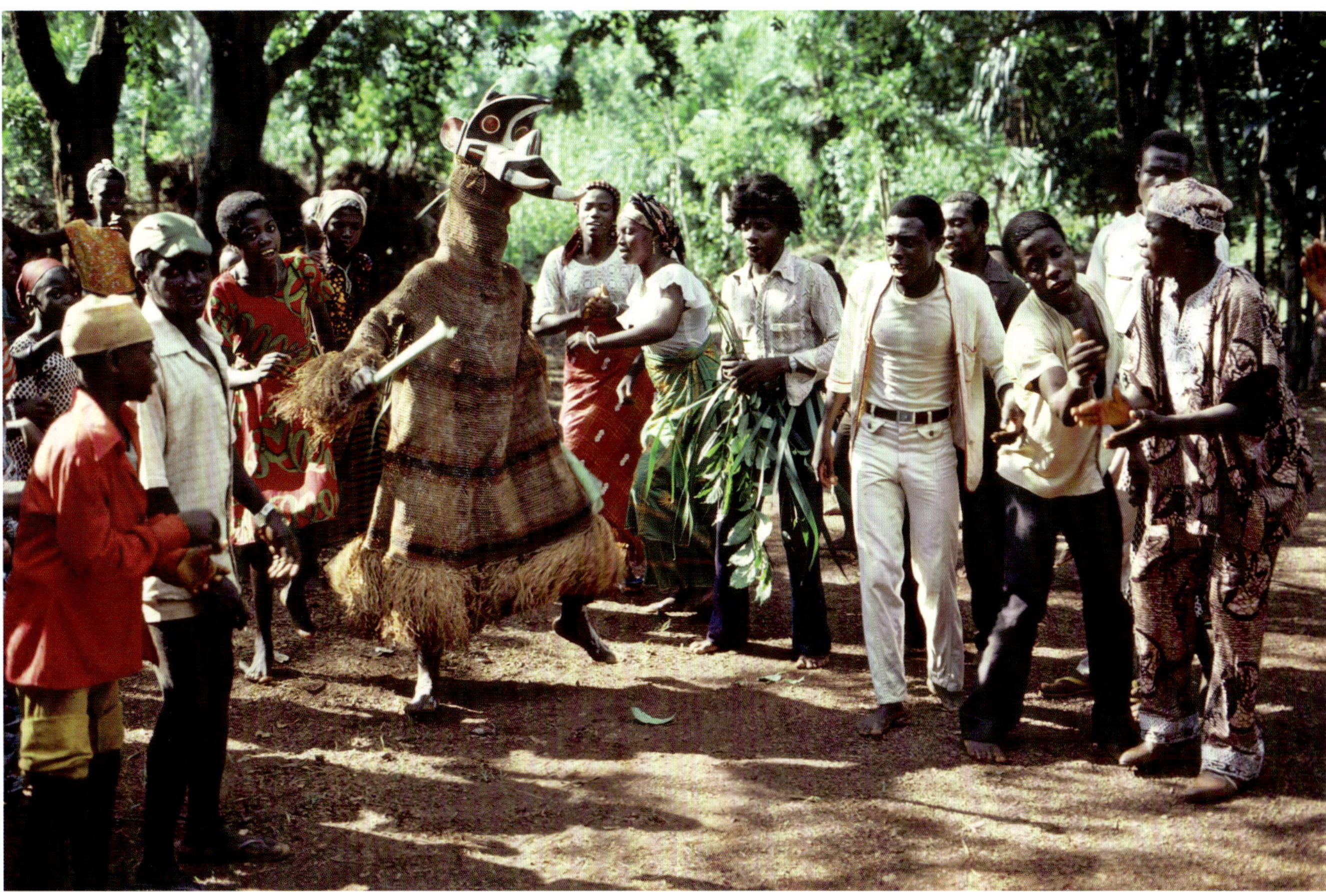

ritually, similar to Alekwuafia in the rest of Idomaland and are seen only in this district. Before two were stolen in 1988, they did not exist in any museum or private collection.

The colonial and early independence periods were politically assimilationist, with officials encouraging an expansive definition of Idoma ethnicity, but the new generation of Akweya now have their own Web site and are promoting the uniqueness of their culture on the Internet. To bridge this conceptual ambiguity, I have grouped them here as a special category of Idoma masks, but unlike Itrokwu and Ungulali, the ancestral clan masks Okpnma and Akpnmobe described below should be understood as wholly Akweya, since they have no connection to other Idoma mask traditions. In March 1986, I accompanied the Och'Akpa, Ekereke Odaba, and several of his councilors on a two-day journey through the bush to their Yachi kinsmen in Ogoja, where I was able to confirm for myself many of the connections in masking and ritual that I had heard about in Otobi.

Itrokwu

Itrokwu is a spectacular elephant-like horizontal mask local to Akpa District and the nearby Otukpo village of Asa, which has been strongly influenced by masking four miles away in Otobi (fig. 2.48 and see fig. A.1) First described by Roy Sieber (1961, ills. 20, 20a) as "Utro Eku" (Akweya: "Itrokwu"; Idoma: "Akatakpurapura"), this chiefly mask is a metaphor of enormous size and destructive power.[15] It is the only Akweya mask that bears resemblance to a Jukun counterpart (fig. 2.49) called "Akuma Ataji" (Rubin 1969, 69, pls. 68–72). Itrokwu performs in an indigo burial cloth (*ochicidi*), worn as a kind of cloak over other layers of cloth to enhance its size, and is closely followed by an attendant with a stool for it to sit on. Its dance is "hot," bursting into the compound aggressively, knocking over food-drying platforms, scattering cooking pots and audience members, who remain at a respectful distance. Its footwork is very rapid, unlike that of other chiefly masquerades who move in

2.50
The Ogbodo Enyi masquerade of the northeast Igbo dances for an appreciative crowd. Although there is a superficial resemblance between it and the Itrokwu mask, the meaning and significance of the two are quite different.
PHOTOGRAPH BY HERBERT M. COLE, ENYIGBA IZZI, 1983.

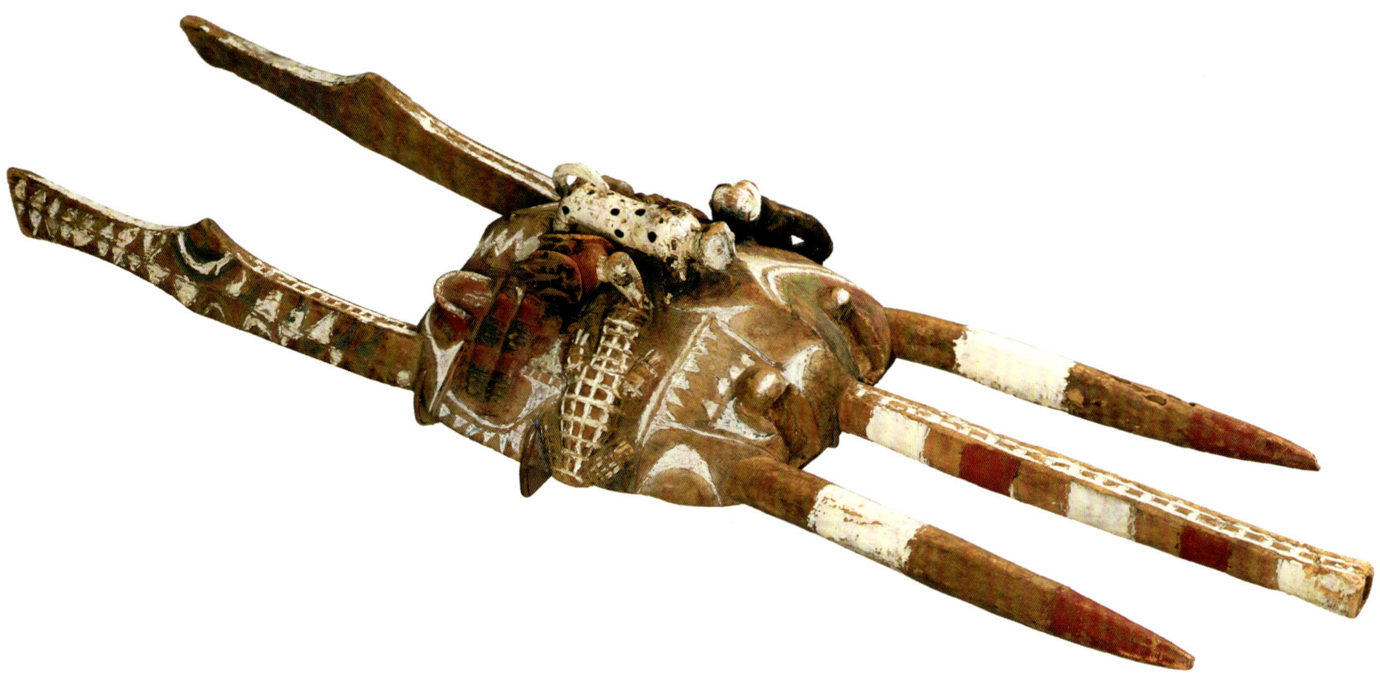

2.51
Oba (active circa 1930s–1950)
Itrokwu mask
Idoma peoples, Akweya subgroup, early to
mid-twentieth century
Wood, pigment, paint
L: 157.5 cm

This Itrokwu mask by Oba features a small
leopard and a bird near its crest.

stately fashion, and the masker is fanned by attendants with boughs of green leaves
in an effort to cool its power and avert danger. While its appearance and movement
suggest initial comparison to the northeast Igbo Ogbodo Enyi masquerade (Weston
in Cole and Aniakor 1984, 157–59), its chiefly status and accoutrements—the burial
cloth and the stool—make it clear that the masks are unrelated in meaning (fig. 2.50).
Nor is there any evidence of similarity in meaning to the Jukun Aku-Ma-Wunu. The
horizontal animal mask is a genre so widespread in Central and Southern Nigeria that
stylistics alone cannot establish links.

Sieber was told in 1958 that Ochai had carved the Itrokwu mask in 1944 that he
had seen in Otobi, but figure A.1, which I first saw in Otobi in 1976, was almost certainly carved by Oba, Ochai's follower, after Ochai's mask was destroyed. This mask
has had several "careers." I was told by the Akpa District Head that in about 1988,
Otobi elders sold to an Igbo trader the Itrokwu that I had seen and photographed
there in 1976, 1978, and 1986. The quid pro quo, as is usual in these situations, was
that the buyer also paid to have a replacement carved. Oba's mask eventually found
its way (probably via Fumban) to Paris, then to the Barbier-Mueller collection in
Geneva in 1991, and finally to the Musée du quai Branly in Paris where it now resides.
Ojiji, a fellow carver, told me in 1976 that Oba carved three Itrokwu masks in the
1950s, which differ only slightly from one another: a large python is attached to the
head, parallel to the "elephant ears," on the second example, found in Asa village and
collected by Sieber in 1958 for the Jos Museum. A third has a leopard and bird on top
and was gifted by Washington, D.C., collectors Toby and Barry Hecht to the Michael
C. Carlos Museum in 2005 (fig. 2.51).

Ungulali

Ungulali (flute), a multifaced mask headdress(figs. 2.52, 2.53), is invariably described
as Idoma, based on the acquisition of one example by Sieber for the Lagos Museum
and its publication by William Fagg (1980, 94). While the first Ungulali was purchased
from Ochai's family and was said to be carved by him, Sieber later stated (Schmalenbach 1988, 162) that neither the Barbier-Mueller mask now in the Musée du quai
Branly, nor the similar one he collected for the Nigerian museum in 1958 had any
resemblance to the personal style of Ochai or any other known Idoma artist. When

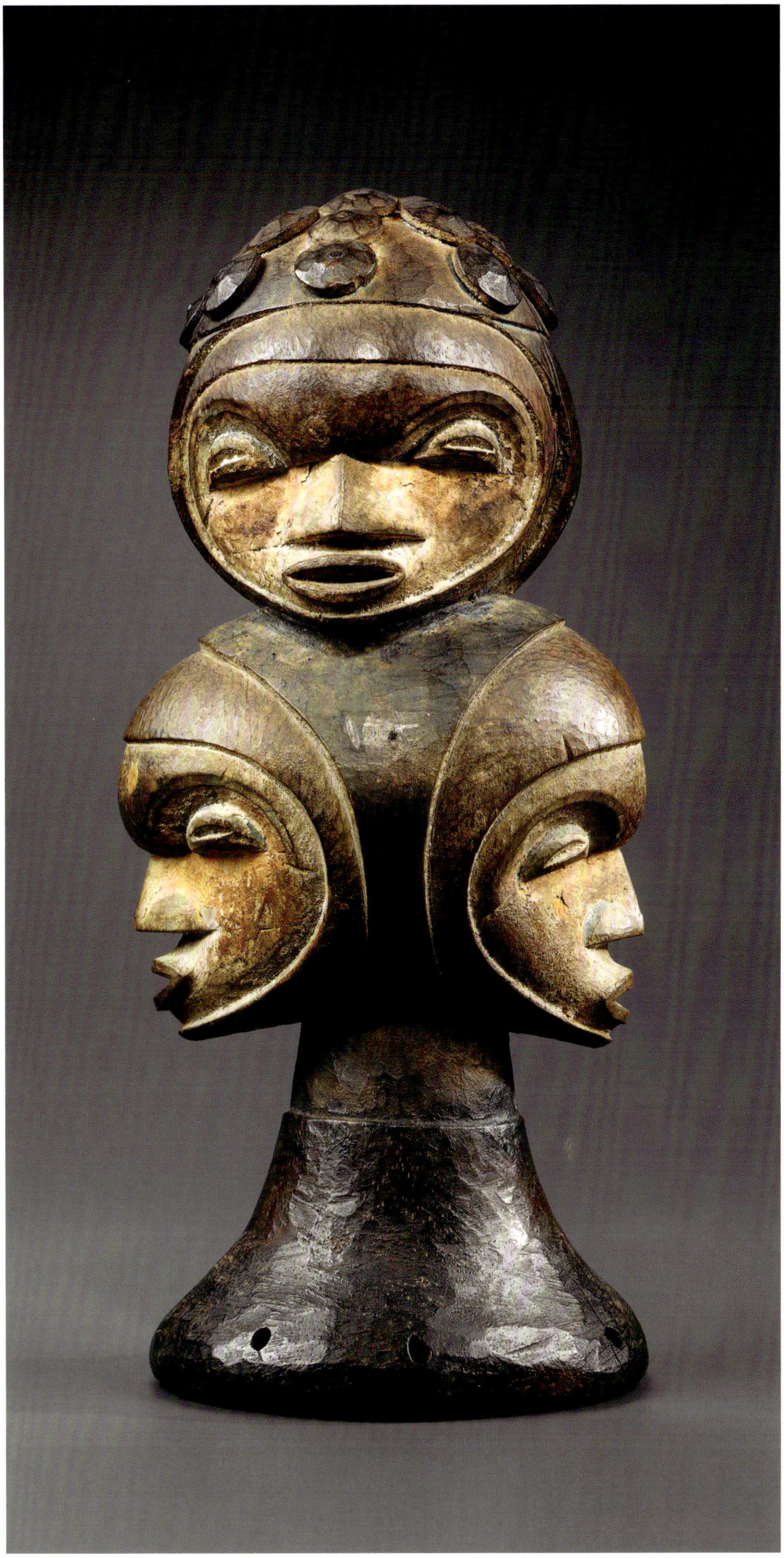

2.52
Mask headdress (Ungulali)
Probably Cross River peoples, early twentieth century
Wood
H: 40 cm
PRIVATE COLLECTION, PARIS
IMAGE: COURTESY PRIVATE COLLECTOR PARIS.
PHOTOGRAPH © HUGHES DUBOIS, 2010

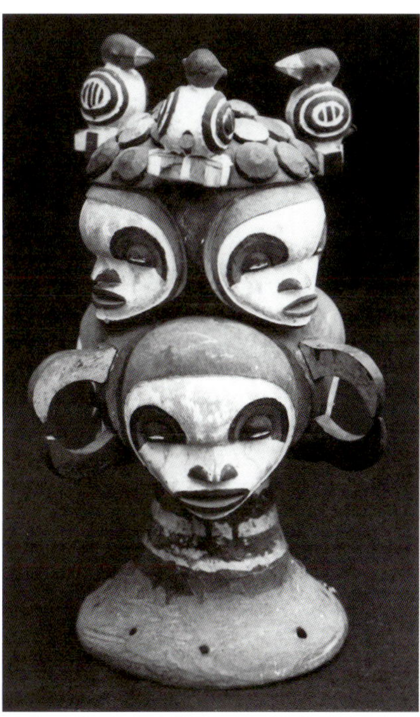

2.53
The deep-set eyes and spheroid-shaped faces in a symmetrical arrangement that are characteristic of this headdress and of that illustrated in figure 2.52 have been admired by collectors and museums alike, though they are very unlikely to be Idoma. These crest masks, known as Ungulali (flute) exist in several variations. Birds pecking at the disk-like shapes add greatly to the charm and complexity of this example from the National Museum, Lagos, originally collected by Roy Sieber in 1958. He acquired it from the family of the artist Ochai (see interleaf A). Sieber was later to note, however, that the mask did not resemble the style of Ochai or of any other Idoma artist with whom he was familiar.
REPRODUCED COURTESY OF THE NATIONAL COMMISSION FOR MUSEUMS AND MONUMENTS, NIGERIA.

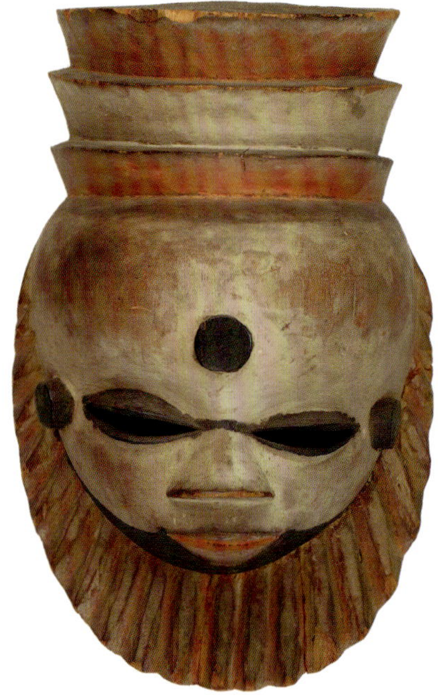

2.54
Ekpo society mask
Annang Ibibio peoples, twentieth century
Wood, pigment
H: 27.9 cm

FINE ARTS MUSEUMS OF SAN FRANCISCO; GIFT
OF THE ERLE LORAN FAMILY COLLECTION,
2008.38.61

IMAGE: © FINE ARTS MUSEUMS OF SAN FRAN-
CISCO. PHOTOGRAPH BY JOSEPH MCDONALD, 2010
(NOT IN EXHIBITION)

The very strong resemblance of this mask to
the Ungulali (see figs. 2.52, 2.53) is the basis
for the latter's Cross River reattribution.

I conducted fieldwork twenty years later, no one in Otobi had heard of Ungulali or recognized the photographs I showed them.

On the other hand, both the multifaced design and the bulbous forehead have been seen in Ibibio masks such as the example in the De Young Museum shown here (fig. 2.54). The fact that Ungulali was described to Sieber by its Idoma owners as a harvest and Christmas "play" mask, rather than one appearing at funerals, further strengthens the likelihood of a non-local origin. Janiform masks, found as both helmets and as crests, are especially common in Igede, Ogoja, and the Cross River. I conclude on the basis of both form and function that this mask type either originated in the Igede-Ogoja-Cross River region or else with an immigrant Ogoja-Cross River artist who settled somewhere in Idomaland. None of these attempts to discern the origin of the form diminishes in any way the stunning visual effect of the individual faces: the very deep and wide-set closed eyes with their semicircular eyebrows are repeated perfectly in the oblate spheroid shape of each face. In the Lagos Museum example, small detachable birds perch on the upper tier decorated by flat disks, which suggested to Sieber that they were pecking at fruits or berries.

Akpnmobe

Of the many other Akweya masks, one stands out in both form and meaning: Akpn-mobe, a carved warrior mask about eight feet high that carries a spear and shield and accompanied warriors into battle in precolonial days. To see this mask from a distance, proceeding along a bush path, high above the elephant grass, gives some inkling of the fear it must have inspired in enemies. Its sheer size, as well as its part-human, part-animal countenance with the wide-open, gaping mouth is intended to frighten and rout adversaries. The long black feather at the back of the head signifies the fierceness associated with warriors and other great men.

The massive cylinder-shaped body of the masquerade, covering the head and upper torso of the mask carrier, is carved from dense hardwood to withstand the enemies' arrows. There were two Akpnmobe masks, owned by the Ekpari and Ifu-Akpa clans, but they were seen nowhere in Idoma outside Akpa District.[16] The one illustrated here was carved by Oba of Otobi (fig. 2.55). After the imposition of the pax Britannica on internecine warfare early in the twentieth century, it was seen mainly at funerals, as the guardian mask to the highly secret and even more powerful Okpnma. These masks, while foreign to the rest of Idoma, are closely cognate with clan masks of the Yachi of Ogoja. They are the strongest statement of a Cross River-Ogoja component in Idoma masking.

Okpnma

Akpnmobe acts as a warrior guarding Okpnma, who appears for a brief and elec-trifying moment amid ululations and shouts, as the culminating masquerade in the three-day funeral of a clan elder. Okpnma is not a carved mask, which means it has escaped the notice of collectors as far as I know, but as in many other cases in the Benue region, the textile masquerade is more ritually significant than its carved, and more visually arresting, partner. Okpnma is a hunchback, covered by a voluminous strip-woven cloth over which an abstract cloth and cowrie-shell face mask is worn (fig. 2.56). Like the Itrokwu masquerade, Okpnma is closely followed by an attendant with a stool, since his performance is very "hot," leaving the audience filled with excitement and tension as he runs at top speed around the dance arena twice.[17]

Okerekwu

The most unusual mask I found in an Akweya-speaking community was Okerekwu in 1978 (figs. 2.57a–c). It consists of a large face mask mounted on top of a cap base, with a standing figure on the opposite side, two small masquettes filling in the sides, and

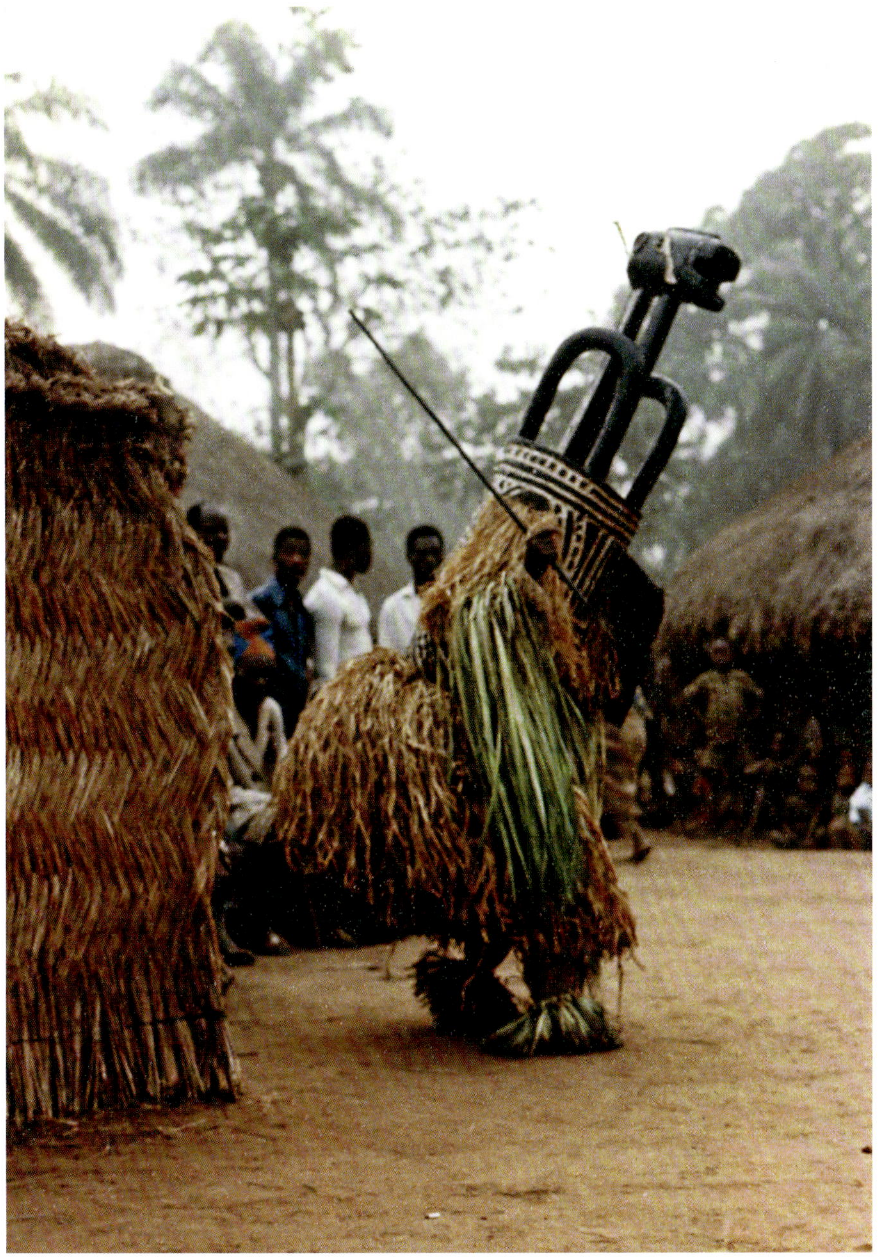

2.55
This Akpnmobe masquerade was carved by
Oba of Otobi (see interleaf A) and appeared
at a second burial held in 1977. It was stolen
eleven years after this photograph was taken
and reappeared on the international art market.
PHOTOGRAPH BY SIDNEY LITTLEFIELD KASFIR,
OTOBI, 1977.

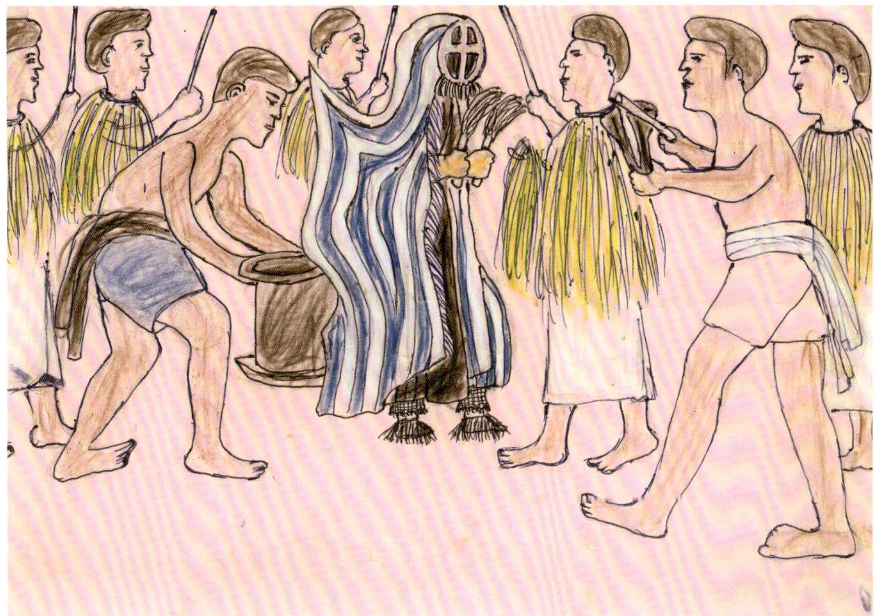

2.56
This sketch of Okpnma was made from
memory by a local twelve-year-old school boy.
It is very similar to what I witnessed in Otobi
in 1977 except that the version I saw had
cowrie shells sewn on the face.

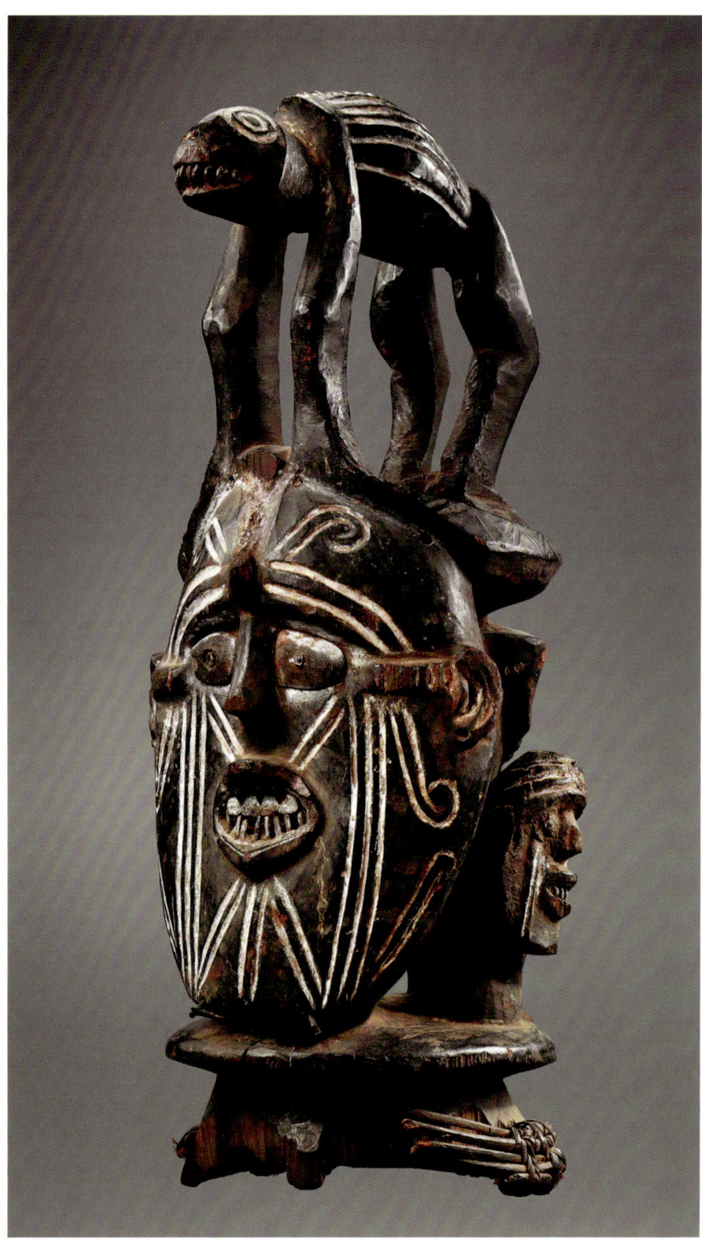

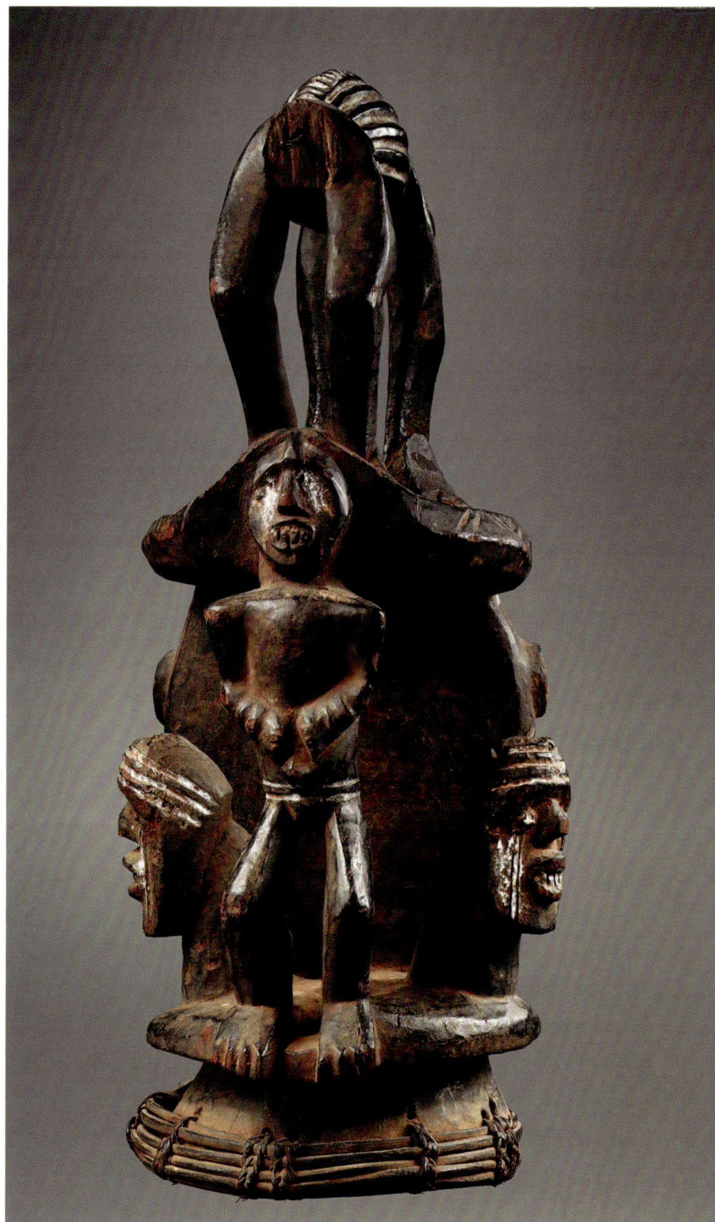

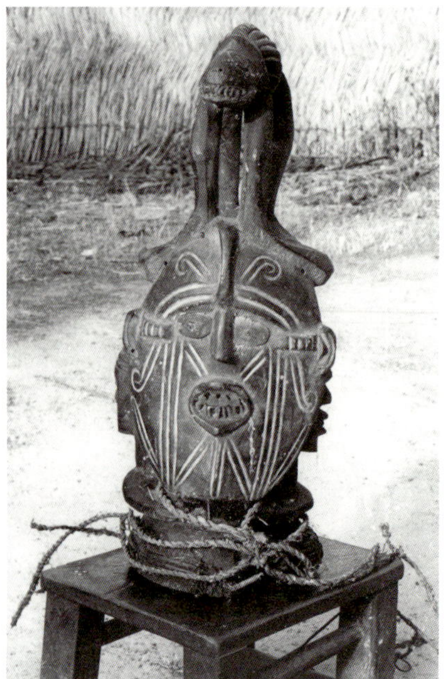

2.57a (BELOW)

I was shown this Okerekwu head crest (also illustrated in fig. 2.57b,c) in a small hamlet in Akpa District but was unable to meet its owner. It is unlike most Idoma and Akweya masks in its facial proportions and scarification patterns, as well as its use of a reptilian figure atop the head and small masquettes on the sides. These features strongly suggest that it came from elsewhere.

PHOTOGRAPH BY SIDNEY LITTLEFIELD KASFIR, ONYUWEI VILLAGE, 1978.

2.57b,c (ABOVE)

Mask (Okerekwu)
Idoma peoples (?), before 1977
Wood, pigment
H: 47 cm
PRIVATE COLLECTION, PARIS
IMAGE: COURTESY PRIVATE COLLECTOR, PARIS.
PHOTOGRAPH © HUGHES DUBOIS, 2010
PROVENANCE: PURCHASED IN AFRICA, AFTER 1978

Front and back views of the Okerekwu mask (see. fig. 2.57a), now in a private collection in Paris, reveal in detail the side masquettes and the standing figure.

atop the whole grouping an animal looking vaguely like a tortoise or large lizard. It is also the mask about which I know the least, other than that it was used in Christmas masquerades and bears no resemblance to other masks from Akpa District. Both of these facts suggest that it originated elsewhere, but where? Combing the storage in the Jos Museum, I found a possible resemblance in a mask called Efu-ibo collected in Owukpa District and used in children's stilt dances. In Idoma, "Ibo" is generic for any stilt dance, but the tones are different from those used for the ethnic group of that name (fig. 2.58). The rectangular eyes and small straight nose suggest a match, as do the exaggerated distance from mouth to chin. On the other hand I also saw a Boki mask in the British Museum that had Janus faces of identical profile to Oker-ekwu's small masquettes. The Boki live south of the Yachi in the Ogoja region just north of the Middle Cross River, and they have been a source for warrior and other masquerades in southern Idomaland. Whichever direction the Okerekwu mask came from originally, it was swept up in the wave of thefts (several) and sales (occasional) of masks and figures within Akpa District in 1988, and it appears here as figure 2.57b,c on loan from a private collection in Paris, another case of an object's multiple careers described by Igor Kopytoff in *The Social Life of Things* (1986).

Adagba: A Borderland Mask Summation

Little has been said until now about masking in the western districts of Otukpa and Owukpa. There is very little overlap with other areas so far discussed, aside from ubiquitous Akatakpa "policemen," who in this case wear carved bushcow and abstract masks with their raffia costumes. Oglinye was once danced here, too, but most of the masks are closer to eastern Igala and northern Igbo prototypes. The most spectacular of these is the Adagba mask documented by Sieber in 1958 (Cole 1970, 41, pl.85) and still in use when I saw it in 1978 (see figs. A.9, A.10). Adagba (elephant), a massive multifaced platform mask, is crowded with figures of human celebrants with upraised arms, hornbills, a hunter killing a leopard, and beer cans, which are filled with palm oil and ignited during a performance. As Cole noted, the multiplication of faces is in some sense a multiplication of the mask's power. The word "Olabochai" painted promi-nently on the front refers to the Otukpa village of the same name where the mask is owned by the Egbu-Ata age-group. The artist was Oklenyi of Okungaga, a nearby village very close to the Idoma-Igala border (see fig. A.11). Heralded by Akatakpa, the Adagba appears in August at the time of the yam harvest, as well as at funerals of age-set members. Its general resemblance to Igala Ajamalede masks, as well as numerous Nsukka Igbo masks, stems from its location in the borderland, where people witness masquerades of Igbo, Idoma, and Igala origin. This absorptive tendency can be seen in all the Idoma borderlands, north, south, east and west. It is proof of the vitality of Idoma masking that there are actually more masquerades now than there were a half-century ago when Armstrong (1955) began his fieldwork, while virtually every mask he mentioned was still being performed at the end of the twentieth century. ●

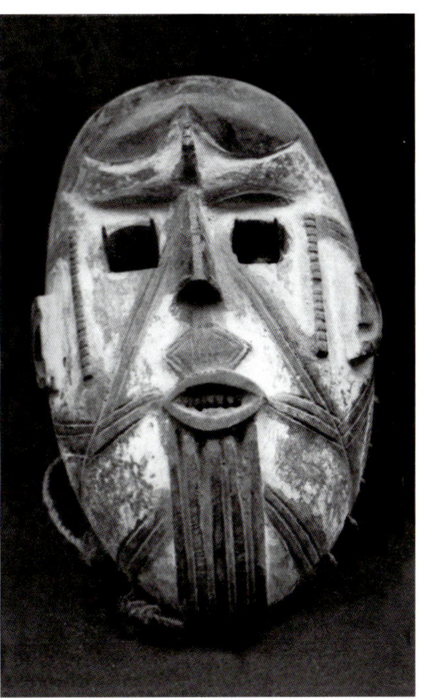

2.58
A mask labeled Idoma and named Efu-ibo is in the collection of the Jos Museum and matches a few of the features of Okerekwu (see figs. 2.57a–c), but so does a mask labeled as Boki in the British Museum, leaving its provenance a puzzle.
REPRODUCED COURTESY OF THE NATIONAL COMMISSION FOR MUSEUMS AND MONUMENTS, NIGERIA, JOS MUSEUM.

INTERLEAF a

Idoma and Tiv Artists

SIDNEY LITTLEFIELD KASFIR

In this brief essay I sketch informal and fleeting portraits of artists whom I met or learned of over thirty years ago (1974–1978) when I first began to do fieldwork in Idomaland. With one exception, all of these artists were born close to 1900, a time before British military patrols penetrated the Idoma lands lying south of the Benue River, and all have since moved on to become ancestors. (One artist, Ochai, was perhaps twenty years older than the others I will discuss.) Aside from being members of the first generation to grow up under British colonialism, these artists for the most part shared the experience of being part-time specialist wood-carvers and full-time yam farmers in rural Idoma villages that were reachable only by footpaths or dry-season roads. None had traveled outside Idomaland, gone to school, spoken on the telephone, or learned how to read and write; yet they were experts at many now-forgotten skills such as lion hunting and brass casting, as well as being repositories of extensive knowledge concerning every tree, plant, and bush animal. They were also excellent storytellers and, if not exactly philosophers in the Ogotemmeli mode,[1] certainly incisive philosophizers.

The first academically trained researcher to visit Idoma districts and the Akweya-speaking enclave therein was C. K. (Charles Kingsley) Meek, appointed as government anthropologist to the Northern Provinces in 1925. At that time, however, masks and shrine sculpture that today would be considered "art" (or in Nigerian popular speech, "antiquities") were treated simply as ethnographic data. It goes without saying then that there was no attempt to identify individual artists. Robert Gelton Armstrong began studying Idoma language and music in the early 1950s, and while he generously shared his photographs of masquerades with me twenty-five years later, he had not collected any consistent information about the artists who carved or fashioned them. In 1958, Roy Sieber became the first

art historian to visit Idomaland, and while his trip was very short (about two weeks) and intended to be only a preliminary survey, he was the first to mention three of the artists discussed here: Ochai, Oba, and Oklenyi (Sieber 1961).

OCHAI OF OTOBI

When Sieber visited Otobi, the large lineage village of the Ekpari clan in Akweya-speaking Akpa District, he was told that Ochai, who had died around 1950, had carved almost every significant mask or figure that he documented or collected there. If that had been the case, Ochai would have had a versatility that was truly unique and an output that defied all probability. In retrospect, the artist does seem to have been very productive, though not superhuman (see Kasfir 1982). He made several of the whiteface dance society masks (e.g., Ichahoho, Ikpobi) in Otobi and elsewhere in the district, a significant number of Anjenu figure sculptures, two large Itrokwu masks, and an Ifi-Odom mask, as well as the semisecret Ekpari clan masks (figs. A.2–A.4). Two Anjenu figures in the Pitt Rivers Museum, collected in the 1930s by Captain Beaver, may have been made by him but appear never to have been used (see fig. 1.7). Attributions to Ochai made by Sieber (1961) and later repeated by Fagg (1965; 1970), include an Oglinye (Ogrinya) head and various Ungulali masks, none of which I am fully able to accept due to their very different styles. Unlike most other artists, Ochai was a full-time sculptor and had commissions from a wide range of villages beyond Otobi. His style is bold and expressive, and his figurative sculpture has a tense energy, the legs muscular and bent, the body leaning forward, and the chin usually slightly lifted. In the Ichahoho masks that he carved, the face displays what David Napier (1986) has termed an "expression of arrest," as if capturing a frozen moment, perhaps the instant when the head is being separated from the body by the warrior's machete.

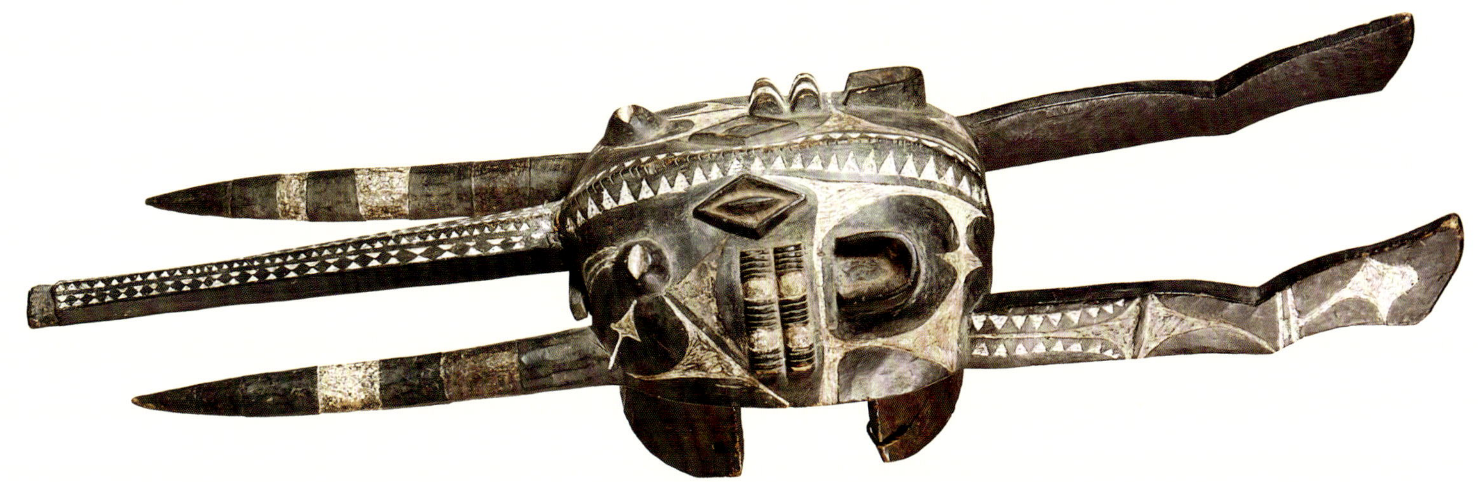

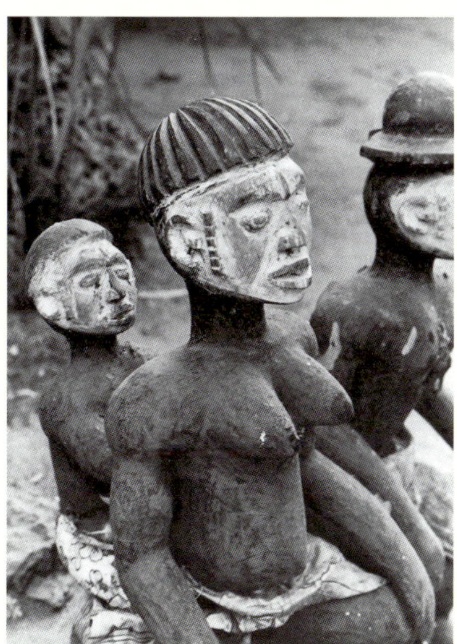

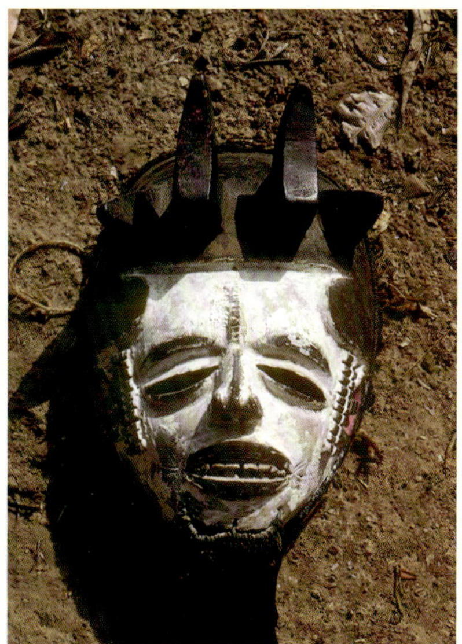

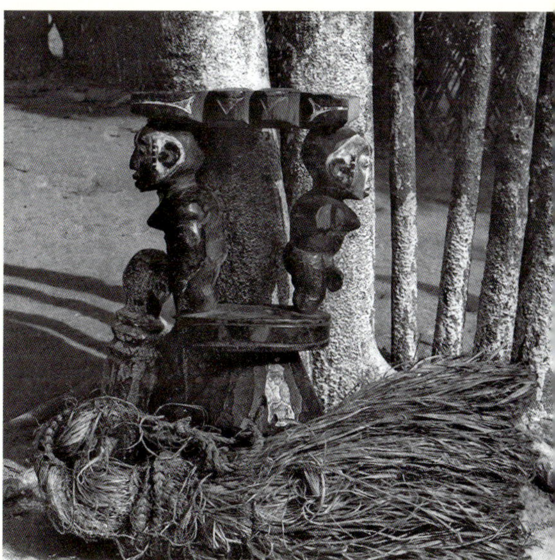

A.1 (TOP)
Oba (active circa 1930s–1950)
Itrokwu mask
Idoma peoples, Akweya subgroup, early to mid-twentieth century
Wood, pigment
L: 170 cm
MUSÉE DU QUAI BRANLY, PARIS, 73.1996.1.75
IMAGE: © 2010 MUSÉE DU QUAI BRANLY. PHOTOGRAPH BY SANDRINE EXPILLY/
SCALA, FLORENCE
PROVENANCE: SOLD TO A TRADER, CIRCA 1988; BARBIER-MUELLER COLLECTION,
GENEVA, 1991

This Itrokwu mask by Oba (for further discussion of its attribution, see
chapter 2, p. 82), depicting an elephant with a trunk, tusks, and two sets
of ears—one tiny and one in the form of long horn-like extensions—was
photographed by Roy Sieber in 1958 in Otobi village and seen and photographed by me in 1976, 1978, and 1986. It was sold to a trader around
1988, and I next saw it in the Barbier-Mueller collection in Geneva in
1991. It is presently in the collection of the Musée du quai Branly, Paris.

A.2 (ABOVE LEFT)
These Anjenu shrine figures were carved by the artist Ochai. The male
figure wears a narrow-brimmed European hat. Both he and his spirit
wife lean forward, displaying a tense energy. At some point after Ochai's
death around 1950, these figures came into the possession of the artist
Ojiji, who in turn kept them at his Anjenu shrine (see fig. A.7). The male
and female figure disappeared from Ojiji's shrine after his own death in
the early 1980s.
PHOTOGRAPH BY SIDNEY LITTLEFIELD KASFIR, OKO VILLAGE, 1974.

A.3 (ABOVE CENTER)
The Ichahoho society was formerly very active in Akpa District. As a
result, there were several Ichahoho masks made by Ochai in Otobi as
well as surrounding hamlets. The peg-like protrusions at the top of this
mask, which suggest the horns of a young animal, are what distinguish
Ichahoho from other very similar Idoma and Akweya whiteface masks
(see fig. 2.41).
PHOTOGRAPH BY SIDNEY LITTLEFIELD KASFIR, ONYUWEI VILLAGE, 1977.

A.4 (ABOVE RIGHT)
Hyena society masks (Idoma: "Odumu"; Akweya: "Odom") appear in
pairs. This mask, carved by Ochai, with double, whiteface female figures
is the "wife" of Odom (see p. 78). It is the only mask like it that I have
ever seen and possibly represents a unique interpretation by the artist.
PHOTOGRAPH BY SIDNEY LITTLEFIED KASFIR, OTOBI VILLAGE, 1977.

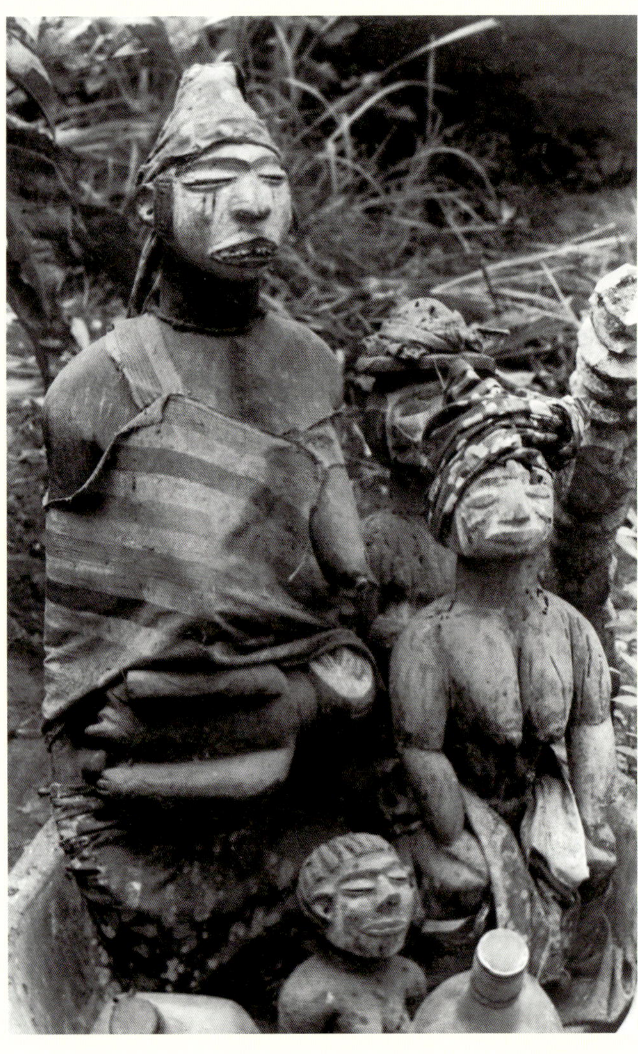

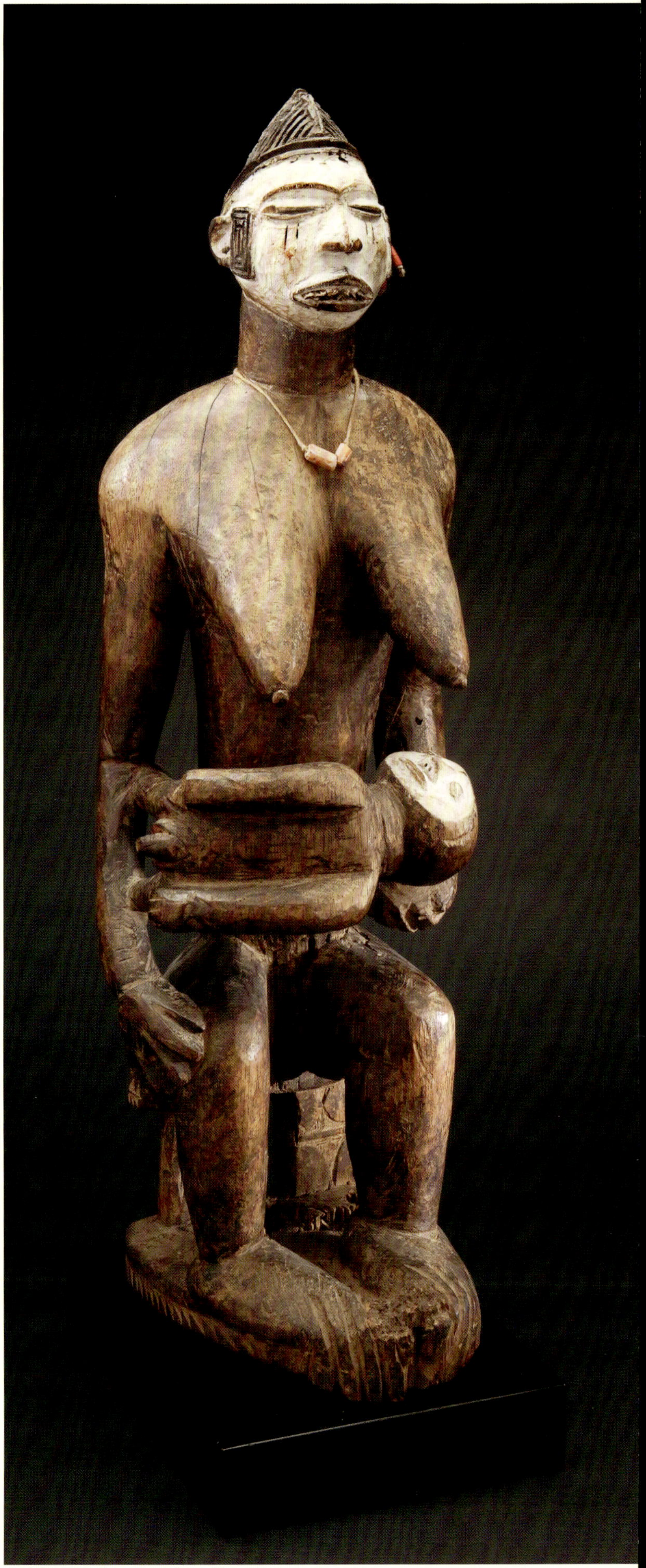

A.5a
Oba carved many shrine figures in and around Otobi village. This one,
is shown as it was when dressed and in its shrine. It is now in the collection of the Fowler Museum and in its current state demonstrates how
such sculptures frequently "lose" their clothing when they enter the art
market (see A.5b).
PHOTOGRAPH BY SIDNEY LITTLEFIELD KASFIR, ONYUWEI VILLAGE, 1978.

A.5b
Oba (active 1930s–circa 1950)
Anjenu figure
Idoma peoples, Akweya subgroup, early to mid-twentieth century
Wood, String, beads, pigment
H: 71 cm
FOWLER MUSEUM AT UCLA X95.36.4; GIFT OF MR. AND MRS. JEFFREY KUHN
IMAGE: © 2010 FOWLER MUSEUM AT UCLA. PHOTOGRAPH BY DON COLE
PROVENANCE: PACE GALLERY, NEW YORK; KUHN COLLECTION, LOS ANGELES

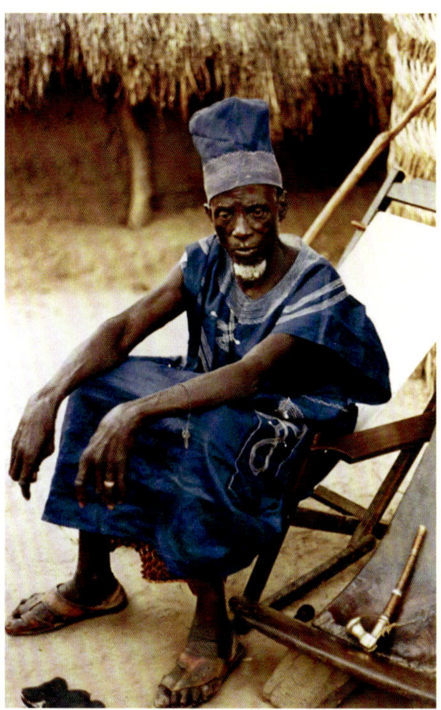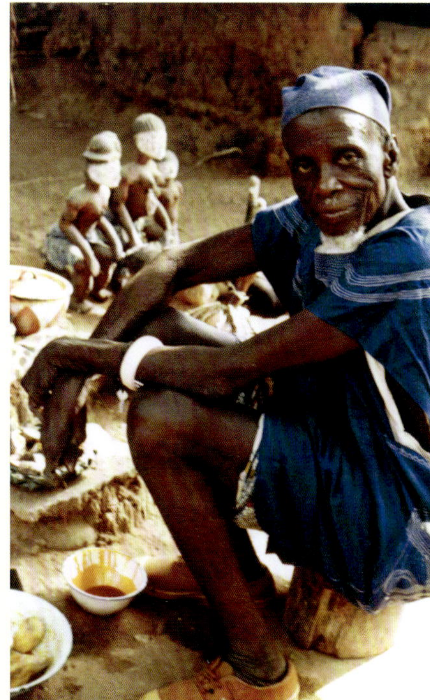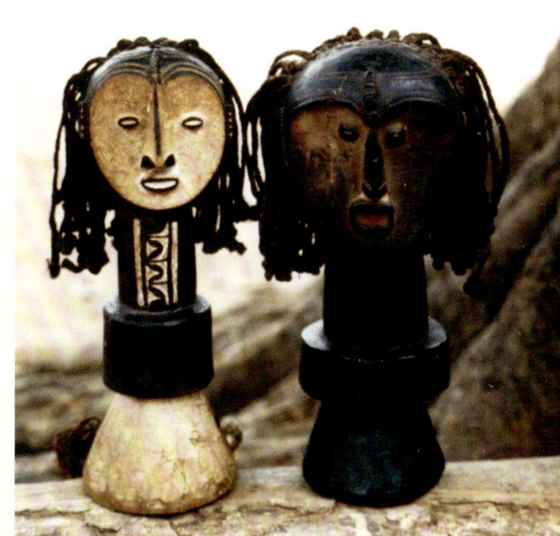

OBA OF OCHOBO AND OTOBI

Oba, who died sometime between Sieber's visit (1961, 9) and my arrival about twenty years later, was younger than Ochai but carved many of the same subjects (figs. A.1, A.5a,b), especially Anjenu shrine figures, the Itrokwu mask, and other large zoomorphic fusion masks such as an Eku, which Sieber collected in 1958 and was later donated to the Museum of Primitive Art in New York (entering the Metropolitan Museum of Art in 1978, 1978.412.462). Oba's work lacks the finesse of Ochai's, but in its roughness it is sometimes even more expressive. If there were any oral evidence of it, I would have assumed Oba to have been Ochai's disciple, but no apprenticeship system exists in Idoma or Idoma-Akweya wood carving. That said, cultural rules are rarely watertight. There have been a few exceptions to the "no apprenticeship" rule, and perhaps this was one. Some of Oba's work was collected in Ochobo, a village in Oglewu District, where he either lived at one time or had siblings.[2]

OJIJI IGUMALE

Ojiji Igumale, who like Ochai before him lived in Otobi village, was not only a sculptor but also a well-known diviner, a dancer (during his youth), a raconteur, and an Anjenu priest (Kasfir 1989). Unlike Ochai, Ojiji was not Akweya-speaking but belonged to a lineage that originally came from Ijaha in Idomaland. While young, he watched Ochai at work, but he evolved a style of his own that was distinctly more abstract. At the same time it had to be, as he put it, "recognizable" as falling within the accepted parameters of an Otobi style, in order for people to accept it (figs. A.6–A.8). The one segment of the local carving repertory from which he, as a member of a "stranger" lineage, was excluded was the creation of Ekpari clan masks.

A.6
Ojiji poses for his portrait. The brass pipe next to him was one of his favorite possessions.
PHOTOGRAPH BY SIDNEY LITTLEFIELD KASFIR, OTOBI VILLAGE, 1974.

A.7
Ojiji made regular food sacrifices at his Anjenu shrine, usually boiled yam and a chicken, which was roasted afterward and eaten by everyone present. The food had to be offered in a traditional receptacle, which, if lacking, Ojiji would weave on the spot from palm leaves. In the background are three Ajenu figures carved by Ochai (see fig. A.2).
PHOTOGRAPH SIDNEY LITTLEFIELD KASFIR, OKO VILLAGE, 1976.

A.8
Ojiji's work as a wood-carver was secondary to his roles as a diviner and an Anjenu priest. His Oglinye heads were more abstract than others, but in his opinion an artist's work in a known genre had only to be "recognizable" as such, and beyond that, it could vary according to the artist's personal taste. An example of this would be the abstract curvilinear designs on the neck of the figure on the viewer's left. To the right is an Oglinye head that was first photographed by Roy Sieber in 1958. Sieber attributed this head to Ochai; however, based on stylistic grounds, I am unable to fully accept this attribution.
PHOTOGRAPH BY SIDNEY LITTLEFIELD KASFIR, OTOBI VILLAGE, 1976.

Since they personify ancestors, they could only be sculpted by clan members in secrecy in the bush.

The other lesson I learned from Ojiji's life and death was the local conviction that life is a zero-sum game: one person's success comes at the expense of another's ill fortune. A few years after my departure from Nigeria in 1978, I was told that Ojiji had died in an accidental house fire. When I investigated on my return in 1986, I learned that the fire had actually been set. One of Ojiji's middle-aged sons had died suddenly while in apparent good health, and certain people had suspected that Ojiji, a priest and diviner as well as maker of powerful images, had exercised supernatural sanctions to bring about the death of his son.

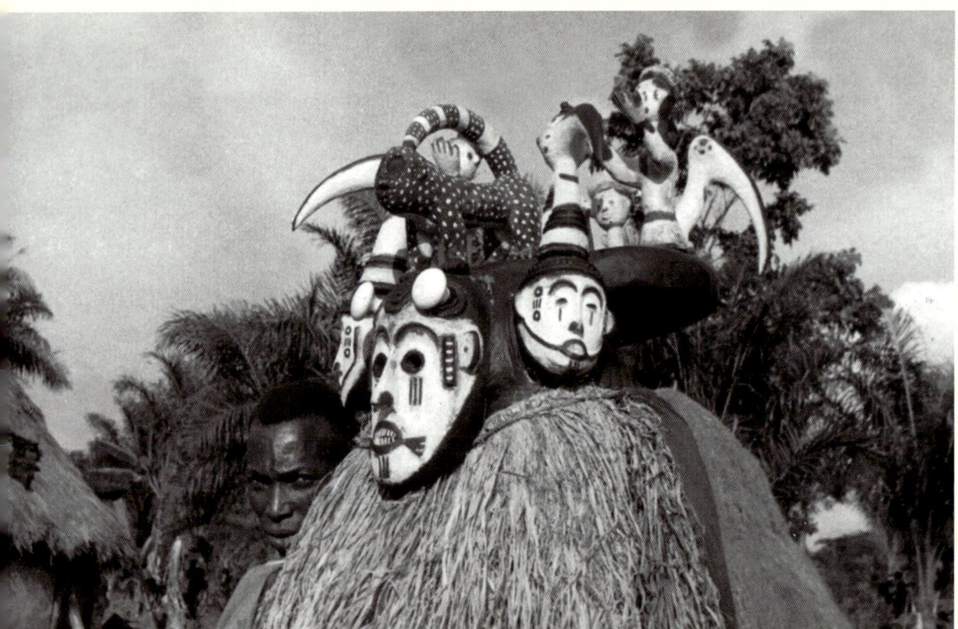

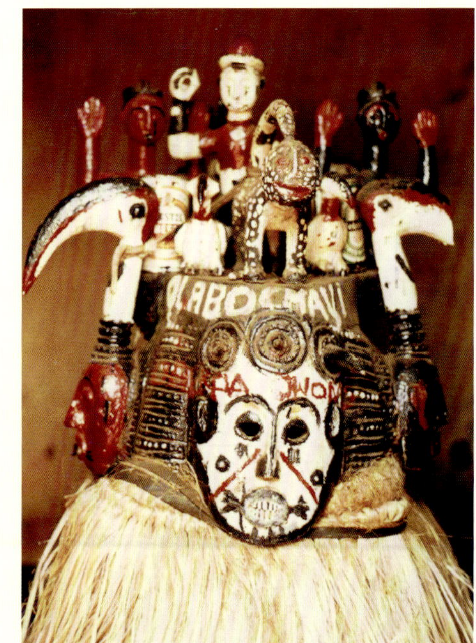

A.9

Oklenyi carved this large and complex platform mask some time in the 1950s. Roy Sieber saw and photographed it in 1958 and also purchased from the artist one of the mask's figures, the woman with upraised arms ("lady praying in church"), which went to the Rockefeller collection at the Metropolitan Museum of Art.

PHOTOGRAPH ROY SIEBER, OLABOCHAI VILLAGE, 1958.

A.10

Twenty years after Roy Sieber took the photograph reproduced here as figure A.9, the same Adagba mask by Oklenyi was still being used. It had been repainted in red with the name of the village, "Olobochai," emblazoned across the front.

PHOTOGRAPH SIDNEY LITTLEFIELD KASFIR, OLABOCHAI VILLAGE, 1978.

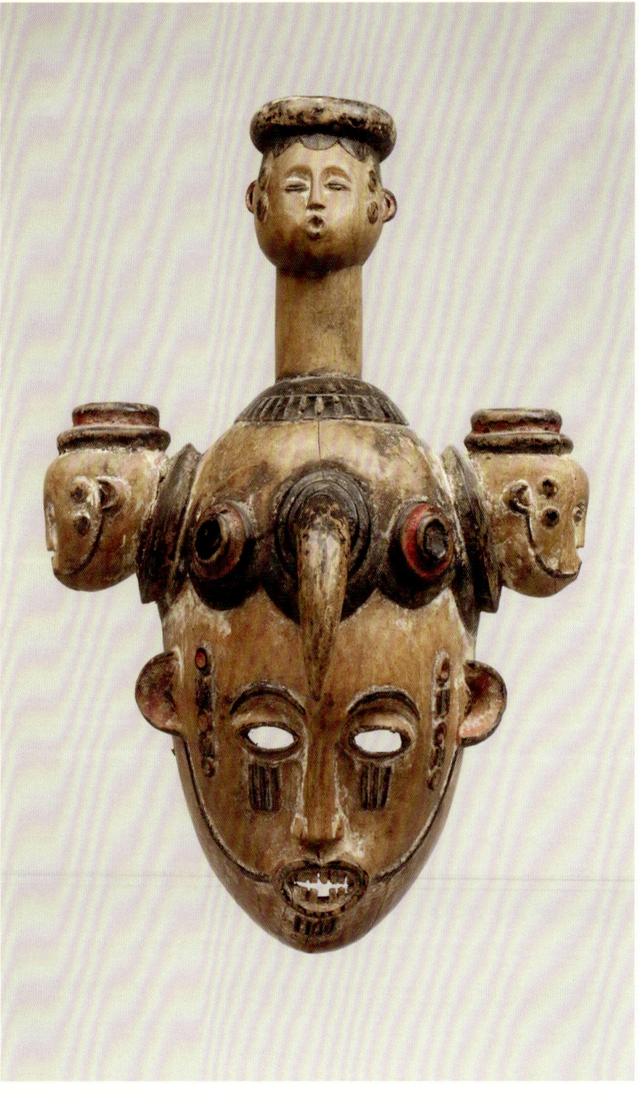

A.11

Oklenyi (active 1930s–1970s)
Multiple-face mask
Idoma peoples, early to mid-twentieth century
Wood, pigment
H: 35 cm

COLLECTION OF TOBY AND BARRY HECHT
PHOTOGRAPH © 2010, GREG STALEY
PROVENANCE: CHARLES JONES

Oklenyi's personal face mask style with its "painted doll" symmetry and prettiness was unmistakable and seemingly not imitated by any other sculptor.

OKLENYI OF OKUNGAGA

Okungaga, the home of the Idoma sculptor Oklenyi (figs. A.9–A.11), is a tiny Idoma village, located in Otukpa District, on the border of eastern Igala, that was first documented by Roy Sieber in 1958. One of Oklenyi's distinctive whiteface masks appears in Sieber's *Sculpture of Northern Nigeria* (1961, fig. 41), and a large superstructure mask by the artist is reproduced from a Sieber photograph in Herbert Cole's *African Arts of Transformation* (1970, 41, fig. 85). This latter mask, known as Adagba (elephant), was still in use in Olabochai, an Otukpa District village, in 1978 when I visited, though no one recalled who had made it. In the interim, however, it had come to sport extra splashes of red paint and beer cans on its platform, which were filled with kerosene and lit for its nighttime performances.

At Oklenyi's village, I found the artist, old but still sprightly, engaged in carving replacement figures for another version of the same Adagba—including a new woman with raised arms ("lady praying in church") for its platform, similar to the figure collected in 1958 by Sieber (1961, 31, cat. no. 17) and now in the Metropolitan Museum of Art. Oklenyi's face masks are unmistakable with their unusual round mouths and neat rows of upper and lower teeth, which are often set off by upward curving scars originating at the edges of the mouth. The eyes and eyebrows repeat this same ovoid shape in reverse. His work demonstrates the high degree of individual agency encouraged in Idoma artists, who lack workshops and apprenticeship systems. In Oklenyi's case, it is important to remember that the location of his home, Okungaga, also exposed him to the eastern Igala mask complex and at the same time distanced him from the work of other Idoma artists.

ONU OF OKPUDU

Onu was, like Ojiji, a man of many callings: a sculptor, a blacksmith, and an Anjenu priest who carved his own shrine figures (figs. A.12–A.15). He lived in Okpudu, Okwoga District. His dwelling was next to a path that people took to the village market, and as a consequence, unlike any other Idoma artist I had met, he advertised. His marketing efforts consisted of a display rack stuck into the ground beside the path with one or two masks hanging from it "in case someone wanted to place an order." As an elder and a priest, he was highly respected, but despite his dignity, he was extremely inventive and displayed a whimsical and sometimes sly sense of humor. What little he knew of modernity, he loved. His Anjenu figures demonstrated this, and while they were supposedly water spirits, they took the form of a lady doctor, a policeman, an "information officer," and "Sergeant Augustine Idoma" of the Nigerian Army, along with "his beautiful wife, Elizabeth." Okpoga, the main village in the district, had been a British colonial administrative headquarters in Onu's youth, and this experience had provided him with a lifetime's worth of material and inspiration. In addition, the village was the site of a missionary hospital, and he received an occasional commission from the Irish doctor there.

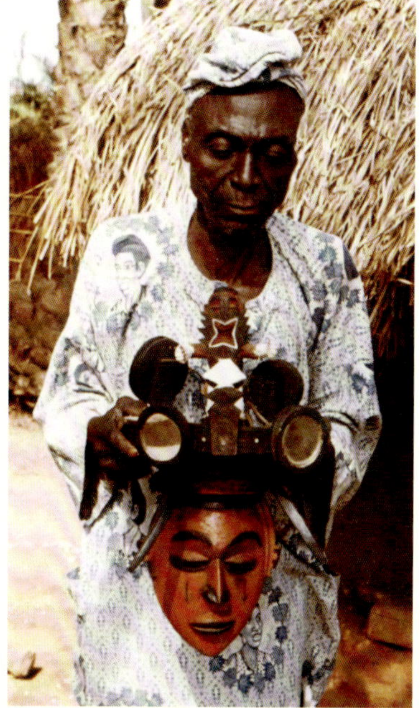

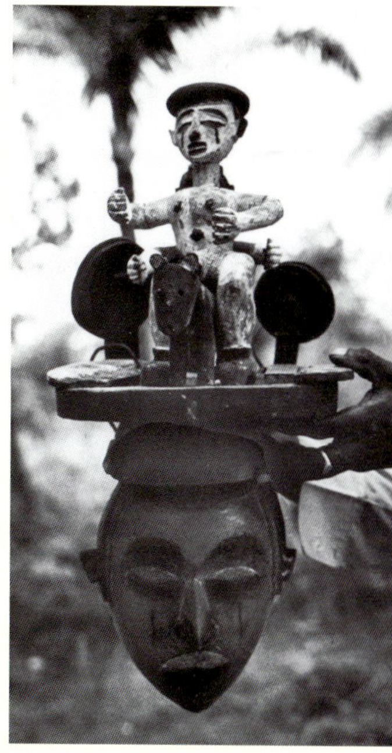

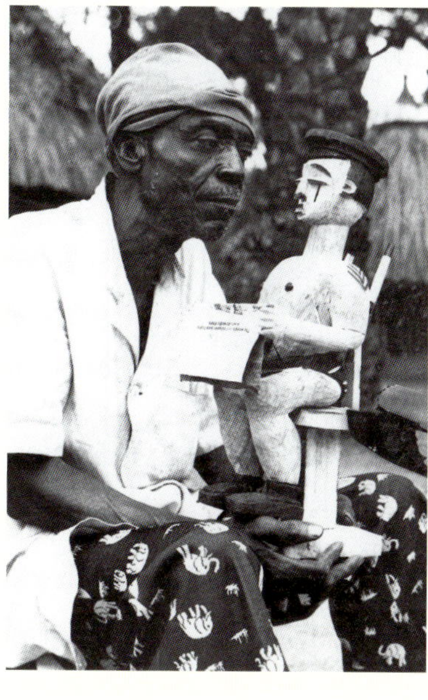

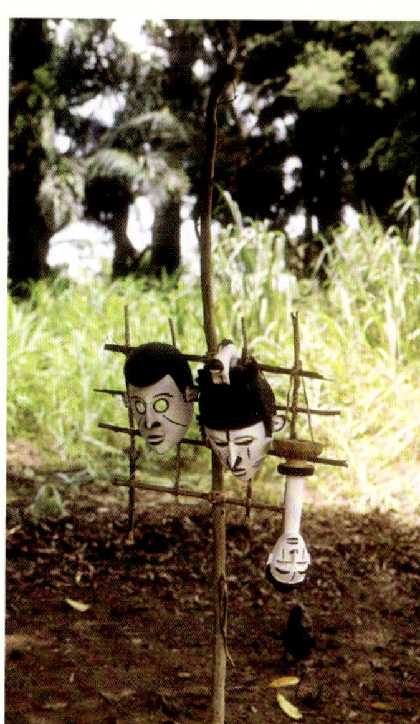

A.12 (TOP LEFT)
There is a strong element of self-portraiture in Onu's Alewu mask despite its supposed feminine representation.
PHOTOGRAPH BY SIDNEY LITTLEFIELD KASFIR, OKPUDU VILLAGE, 1976.

A.13 (TOP RIGHT)
The rider depicted in this Obekwu equestrian mask by Onu is called "Al-Haji" and the soldier is named "Godwin," an ecumenical arrangement. Obekwu and Alewu (see fig. A.12) are "husband" and "wife," and together they perform the Idoga masquerade owned by an age group who call themselves "Church."
PHOTOGRAPH BY SIDNEY LITTLEFIELD KASFIR, OKPUDU VILLAGE, 1978.

A.14 (BOTTOM LEFT)
Onu contemplates his Anjenu shrine figure called "policeman." The policeman appears among Anjenu spirits as a modern authority figure.
PHOTOGRAPH BY SIDNEY LITTLEFIELD KASFIR, OKPUDU VILLAGE, 1976.

A.15 (BOTTOM RIGHT)
To market his works, Onu would display semi-finished masks near a path leading to the local market.
PHOTOGRAPH BY SIDNEY LITTLEFIELD KASFIR, OKPUDU VILLAGE, 1977.

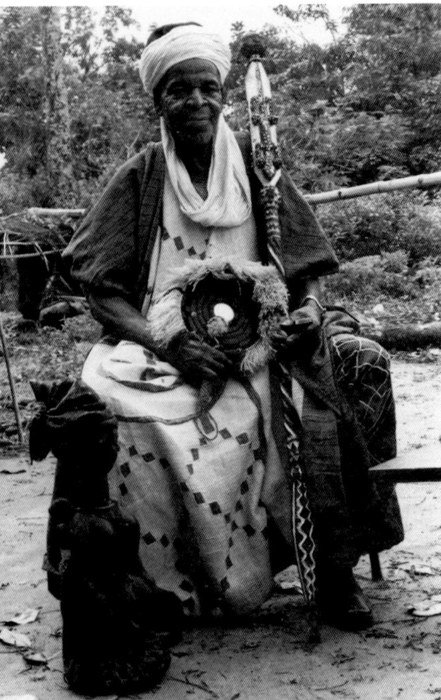 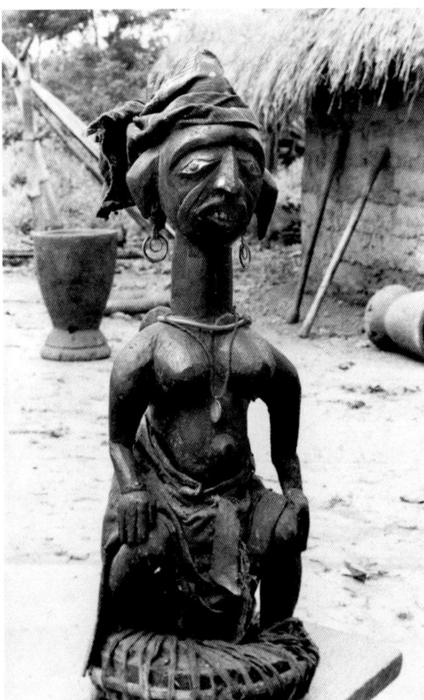 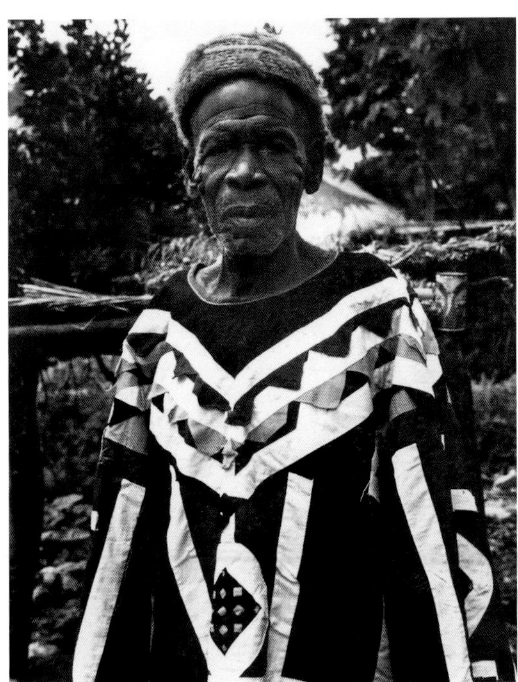

A.16
Okati appears with one of his walking sticks. The figure on the stick takes the form of a schematic crocodile that is often found on carvings and textiles in the Idoma-Alago region. The handle of the stick, however, is a bulbous human head. On the ground at the left is the Anyanmole carving seen in figure A.17. Here the child on her back is more visible.
PHOTOGRAPH SIDNEY LITTLEFIELD KASFIR, OJAKPAMA VILLAGE, 1978.

A.17
This Anyanmole (women spoil the compound) figure was carved by Okati. Such figures were very much a late-colonial, post–World War II phenomenon. Leaving aside their attempt to subvert modernity in the form of female independence, they must have had a more traditional antecedent that occupied a place within the Lower Benue Valley maternity genre (see fig. A.16, where the child is clearly visible on the figure's back).
PHOTOGRAPH BY SIDNEY LITTLEFIELD KASFIR, OJAKPAMA VILLAGE 1978.

A.18
The Tiv have a song with the verse "Everywhere, everywhere is my country." Here, Aba poses in his best clothing, a gown that was made by an Igala tailor.
PHOTOGRAPH BY SIDNEY LITTLEFIELD KASFIR, NAGI CAMP, 1978.

OKATI OF OJAKPAMA

I encountered the work of Okati in the Jos Museum well before I met him in person (figs. A.16, A.17). I was attracted to a playful mask called *Ije Honda* (*Like a Honda*), which I had identified as made by the same artist as an equally whimsical throne with articulated puppets that had been tucked away in a storeroom of the Och'Idoma's palace. As is the case with the sculpture of several other artists described here, Okati's work could be found in more than one Idoma district because he had spent time in both his mother's and his wife's natal villages. He had nonetheless lived in Adoka District, near the Benue, most of his life. Okati also shared another quality with the artists I already knew: he was at once a dignified elder and an innovative artist. For example, his contribution to the maternity figure genre found widely in Afo, Idoma, and Igala districts was given a modern twist as Anyanmole (women spoil the compound), a male social critique of independent women who left their villages to migrate to northern cities during the 1940s and 1950s. His figures wear costume jewelry and are paraded aloft while songs of social derision are sung aimed at these "delinquent" women with jutting breasts.

Another of Okati's innovations was a "respect stick" carved with an elaborate portrait of its owner. All older Idoma men covet these walking sticks, but they are almost never anthropomorphic in design, making Okati's versions highly desirable (Kasfir 2000).

ABA OF AGAGBE

It is not possible to speak of Okati without considering the Tiv artist Aba of Agagbe who lived in a Tiv settlement only fifteen miles away through bush paths (figs. A.18–A.21). Although Okati and Aba claimed they had no knowledge of each other, they were about the same age (in their seventies) and both had

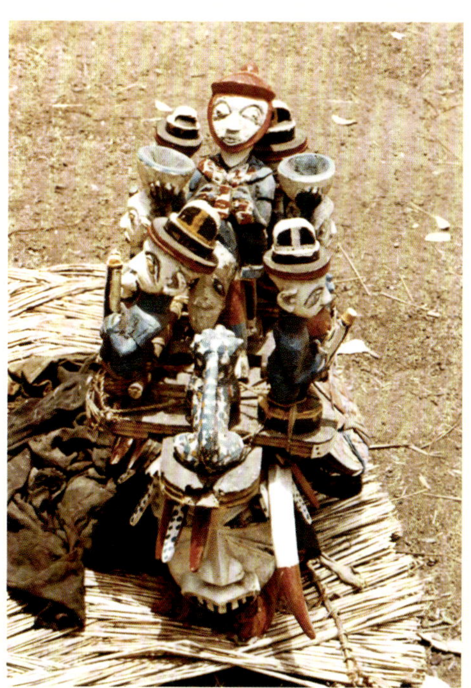

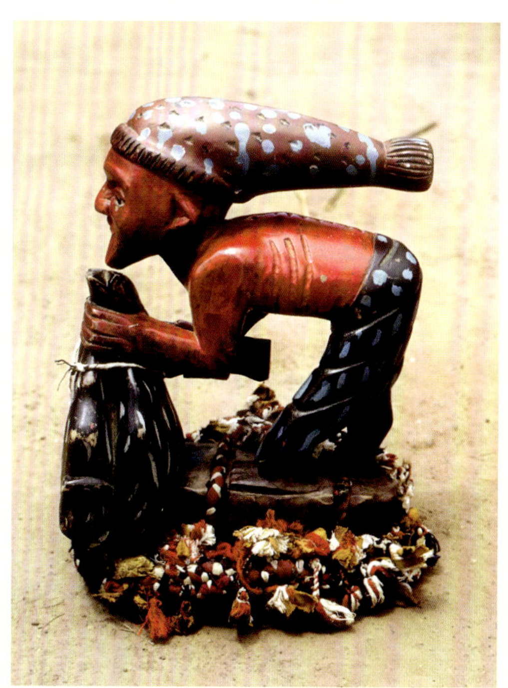

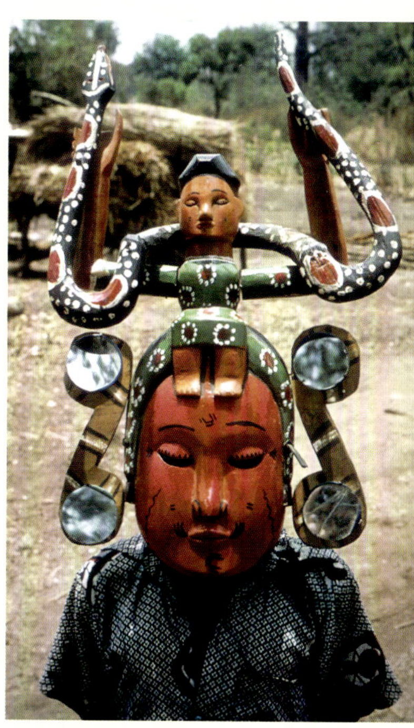

keloid *abaji* scars on their faces, which were fashionable among young men around 1915. I had heard vague references to Aba for years but his home, like Okati's, could be reached only on a dry-season track followed by a walk on bush paths. After two failed attempts, I finally visited him in 1977 and 1978. He showed me a motley array of carvings in different styles, one of which, a large platform, equestrian mask he called Gowon,[3] was executed in the exact style of Okati, right down to the droopy eyes. Despite my questioning, Aba insisted he had carved it, and he had never met or heard of any carver called Okati (though he admitted that he had got the idea for Gowon from another Idoma platform mask he had seen in Onyagedde). He claimed to have carved a Mami Wata mask, which was plainly in the Annang style of Ikot Ekpene,[4] and (more plausibly) that he had made the various Kwaghir puppet figures that he showed me.

When I visited Okati some months later he professed to not recall the Gowon mask (though he admitted it "looked familiar") and never to have heard of Aba. At that moment I realized that I was completely thwarted. Did Okati carve the mask and not remember it? Did Aba carve it copying Okati's style? Did Aba buy, beg, borrow, or steal this mask and the Annang-style Mami Wata? I think I will argue for "borrow" in the broad sense of passing something from one person to another, remembering that the Tiv are enthusiastic aggrandizers of other people's culture.

We might also recall here Paul Bohannan's (1966) classic essay on Tiv artistic criticism in which the designs on a single walking stick are carved by four men passing it around during an evening of conversation, ignoring any sense of artistic ownership. There are important lessons here about the relationship of a style to an artist's personal agency that could be fed back into one of the larger questions raised in this volume: why do

A.19

This Gowon mask was owned by Aba. The Gowon military group, like the Anyanmole figure (see fig. A.17), is at once modern and couched in premodern antecedents such as the culture hero, a stock figure in many sculptural traditions. Gowon was clearly a heroic figure to many Benue and Plateau people.

PHOTOGRAPH BY SIDNEY LITTLEFIELD KASFIR, NAGI CAMP, 1978.

A.20

Tiv Kwaghir figures typically perform on a box-like stage under which the hidden puppeteer manipulates their movement. This Kwaghir figure was carved by Aba.

PHOTOGRAPH BY SIDNEY LITTLEFIELD KASFIR, NAGI CAMP, 1978.

A.21

Although the water spirit Mami Wata does not figure in the Tiv belief system, she does appear in the repertoire of Kwaghir characters and may have been borrowed from Annang puppet plays.

PHOTOGRAPH BY SIDNEY LITTLEFIELD KASFIR, NAGI CAMP, 1978.

we have to assume that styles and genres are always specific to particular artists or workshops? History and geography both suggest otherwise in the Benue region. Later in Bohannan's essay, he watches a man stitching raffia designs very haphazardly onto a length of cloth he is about to resist-dye, while listening intently to a political discussion. When the anthropologist inquires why he does not pay more attention to what he is doing, the man replies that one does not look at a pattern until it is finished, in order to see how it has come out (pp. 251–52): "If this one does not come out well…I will sell it to the Ibo; if it does, I shall keep it. And if it comes out extraordinarily well, I shall give it to my mother-in-law." The point is that Western notions of artistic agency, or even of artisanship itself, don't always apply. Nor, in the case of Okati and Aba, does it appear that a style is thought to be the exclusive property of one person or one ethnic group. ●

INTERLEAF b

Umale Oganegi, Igala Artist

SUSAN PICTON

I met Umale Oganegi twice in 1969 while visiting villages around Dekina, a northern Igala-speaking community southeast of the Niger-Benue confluence (fig. B.2). He lived and worked in the village of Ukuaja, via Iyale, near Dekina. My two short visits were part of a brief survey of the area undertaken for the Nigerian Government's Department of Antiquities (now the National Commission for Museums and Monuments), and I had no opportunity to return and follow up on them. By the time I met him, Umale had developed an easily recognizable style of sculpture and wood carving, and unidentified examples of his work had already been collected for the Nigerian Museum, Lagos (now the National Museum, Lagos) by Philip Allison seven or eight years previously.

At the time of our meeting, Umale was reckoned to be around forty years of age; and as a result of a fall from a tree some thirty years previously, he had suffered extensive damage to his spine and legs. He had therefore been unable to work in the usual way for a young man in a rural area and had taken up wood carving as his means of earning a living. He told me he had never traveled and claimed to be self-taught. He first started carving as a "small boy," drawing his ideas from the things around him, whether locally made or traded from further afield. He related, for example, that "women would go out and buy stools and bring them back." He must, however, have had some instruction in the uses of the many adzes and knives that were scattered around him. He told me that his junior brother would go out to collect and cut the wood for him and bring it to a glade in the bush, just outside the village, where he worked. At the time of our meetings, he was such a well-known and popular artist in the area that people sometimes attributed work to him that was clearly carved by others.

Umale's work was characterized by a bold simplicity: flat planes with protruding elements (e.g., noses, hair crests, breasts) and incised markings; and these contrasts were heightened by the use of a red-hot blade or poker to darken some

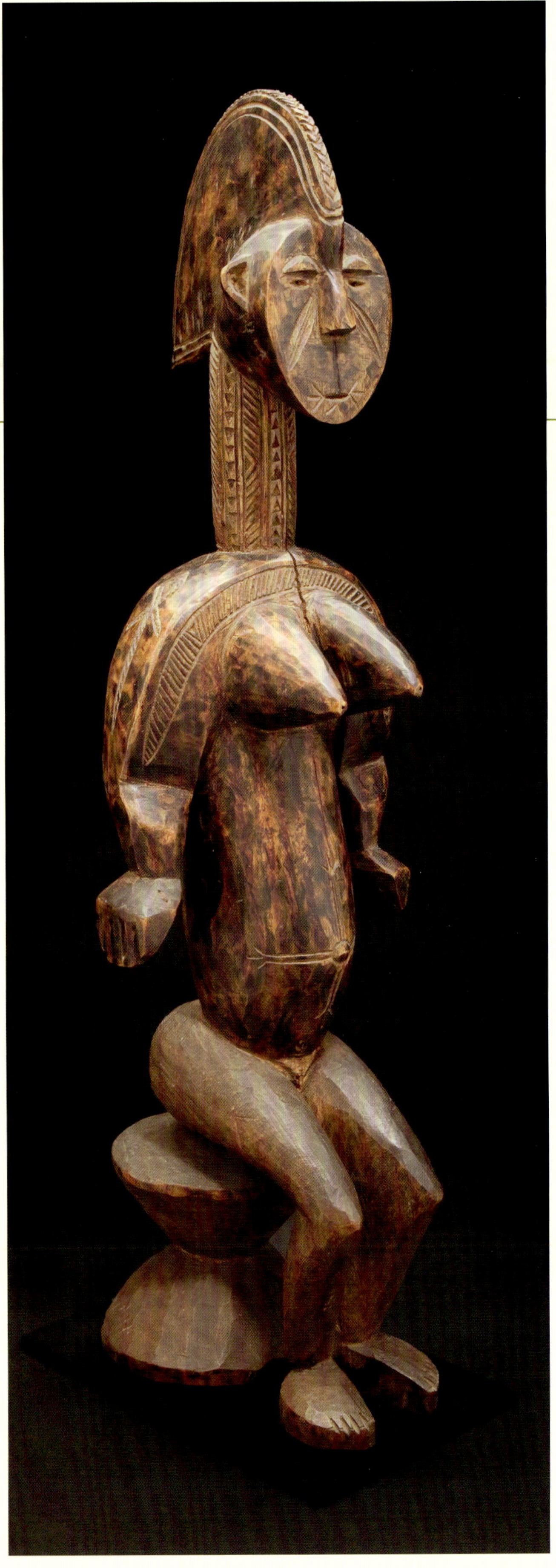

surfaces. His output, in my experience, included figure sculptures, mostly female and for display or shrine purposes (figs. B.1, B3–B.6), animal-headed helmet masks, cosmetic boxes (fig. B.7), mirror frames (see fig. B.2), and stools. The latter were typically nonfigurative, while the mirror frames (always with a cover, as glass attracts lightning) sometimes had head and legs with the frame forming the torso of the figure. Shortly before my visits, Umale had been patronized by a Voluntary Service Overseas (VSO, the United Kingdom's equivalent of the Peace Corps) volunteer working in the area who had shown him pictures of diverse African art objects and had encouraged him to copy them. Thus, in addition to the female figure and the mirror frame in figure B.2, I also collected a small figure based on an Asante *akuaba*, carved by Umale. I myself showed him a Yoruba *ibeji* figure that I had with me at that time, which he liked, particularly the face and the hands on the waist! He told me that he was planning to work on a sculpture of Yakubu Gowon, then Nigerian head of state, defeating Colonel Chukwuemeka Ojukwu, leader of the Republic of Biafra (my visits took place at the height of the Nigerian Civil War). I have had no contact with Umale since 1969 and have no idea if he is still alive or how his work might have developed since I last saw him. ●

B.1
Umale Oganegi (active 1940s–1970s)
Female figure
Igala peoples, mid-twentieth century
Wood
H: 60 cm
DR. RICHARD AND JAN BAUM
IMAGE: © 2010 FOWLER MUSEUM AT UCLA. PHOTOGRAPH BY DON COLE
PROVENANCE: COMTESSE DU CHASTEL, BRUSSELS

B.2
Igala artist Umale Oganegi is shown seated among fellow villagers at home in Ukuaja. He displays two examples of his work: a mirror case (*ojijo*), which he holds in front of him, and a seated female figure (*ojibo*).
PHOTOGRAPH BY SUSAN PICTON, APRIL 1969.

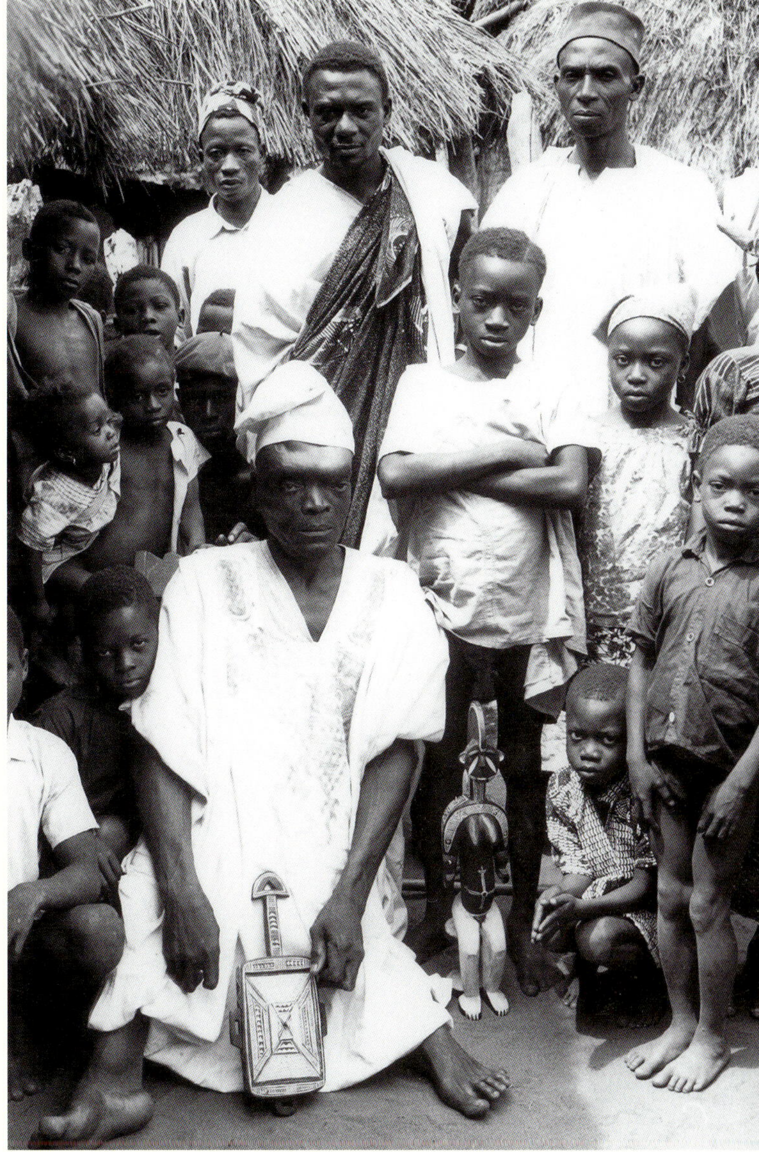

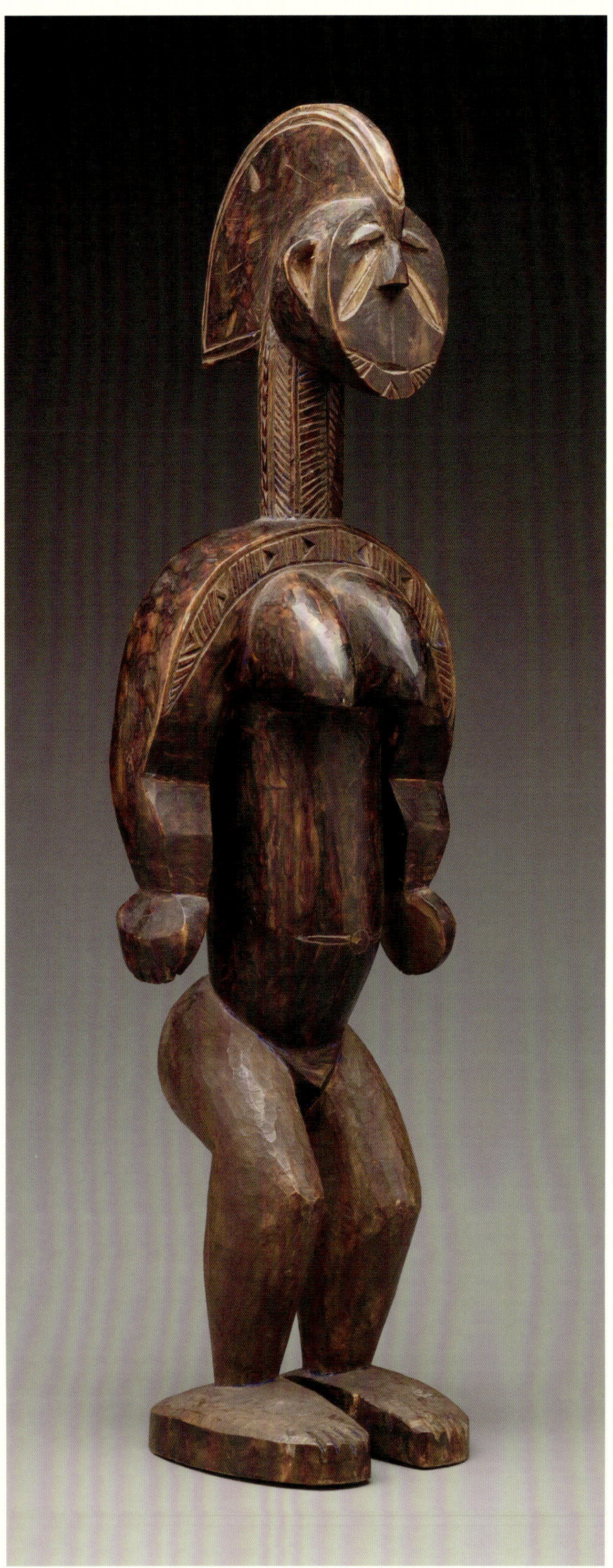

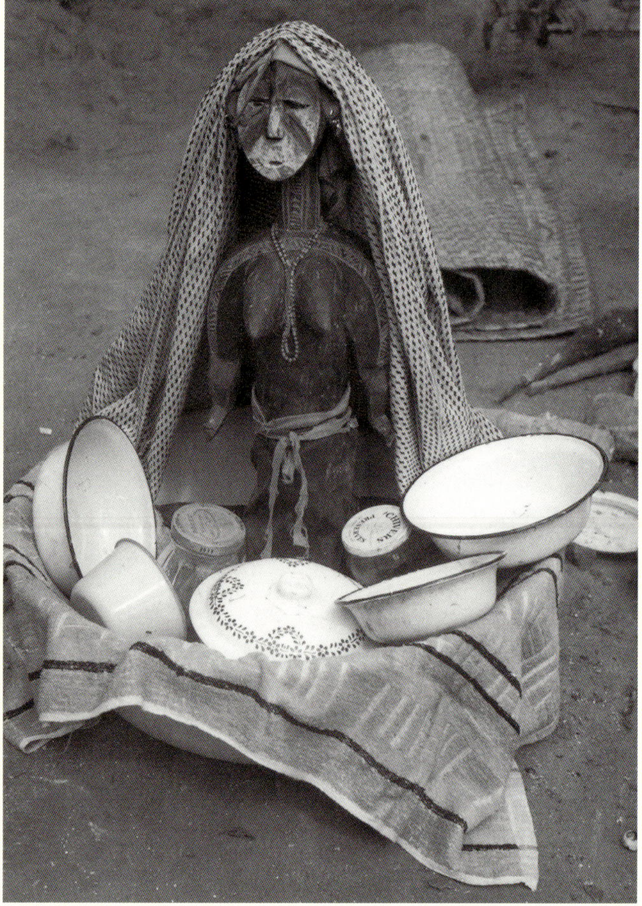

B.4 (ABOVE)

This wooden female figure carved by Umale was called Mamiwater and was used in an Anjenu shrine for purposes of protection. The figure wears earrings and the face is colored with bluing and chalk. The figure was owned by Amanyi in Iyale.

PHOTOGRAPH BY SUSAN PICTON, JUNE 1969.

B.5 (OPPOSITE, TOP LEFT)

Within an Anjenu shrine, this female figure (*ojibo*), carved by Umale, was set in mud in a calabash decorated with strands of cowries. Behind a layer of feathers, the figure appears with a mirror propped in front of it. To the right is a small bottle.

PHOTOGRAPH BY SUSAN PICTON, IYALE, JUNE 1969.

B.6 (OPPOSITE, BOTTOM LEFT)

This Ibaji Igala female *okegga* figure was carved by Umale. Sidney Kasfir has remarked that the use of this female figure as an *okegga* suggests that the Igala are less exclusive than the Igbo in associating this cult with the male sex.

PHOTOGRAPH BY JOHN BOSTON, IDAH, 1961.

B.3

Umale Oganegi (active 1940s–1970s)
Female figure
Igala peoples, circa 1950
Wood, pigment
H: 60 cm

INDIANAPOLIS MUSEUM OF ART; GIFT OF MR. AND MRS. HARRISON EITELJORG, 1989.3

IMAGE: © COURTESY OF INDIANAPOLIS MUSEUM OF ART. PHOTOGRAPH BY MIKE RIPPY

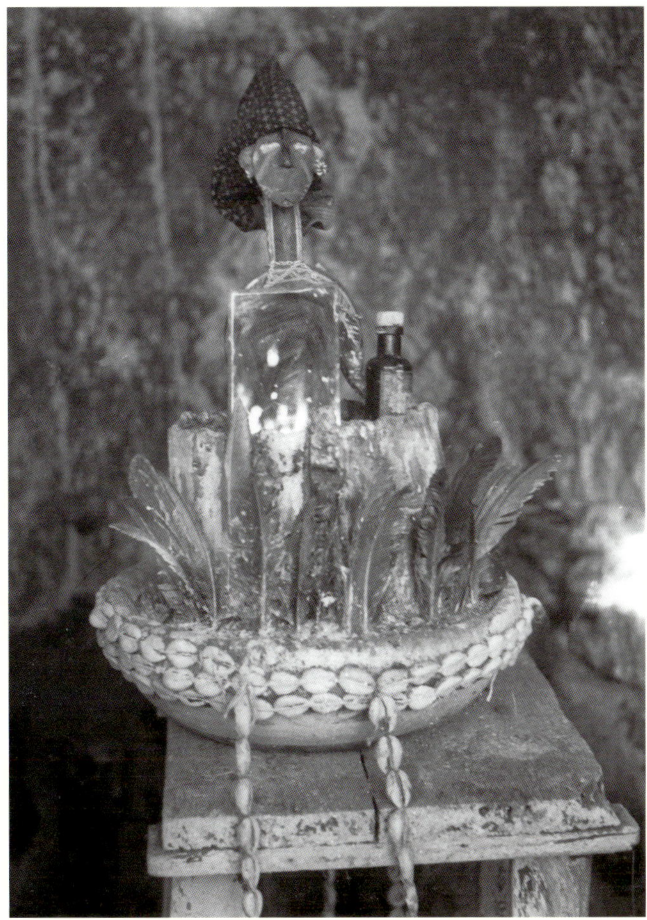

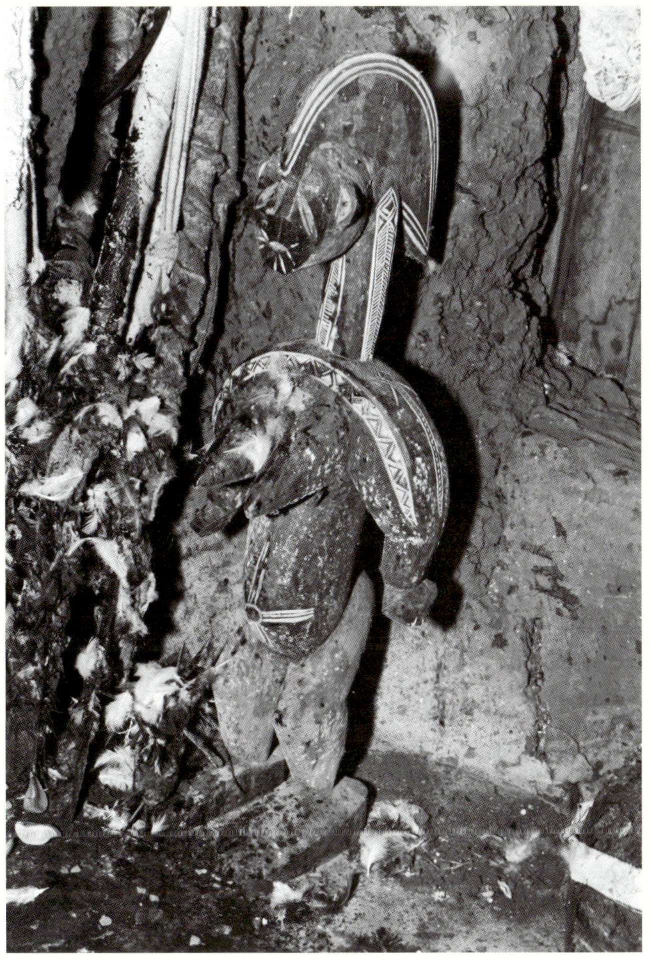

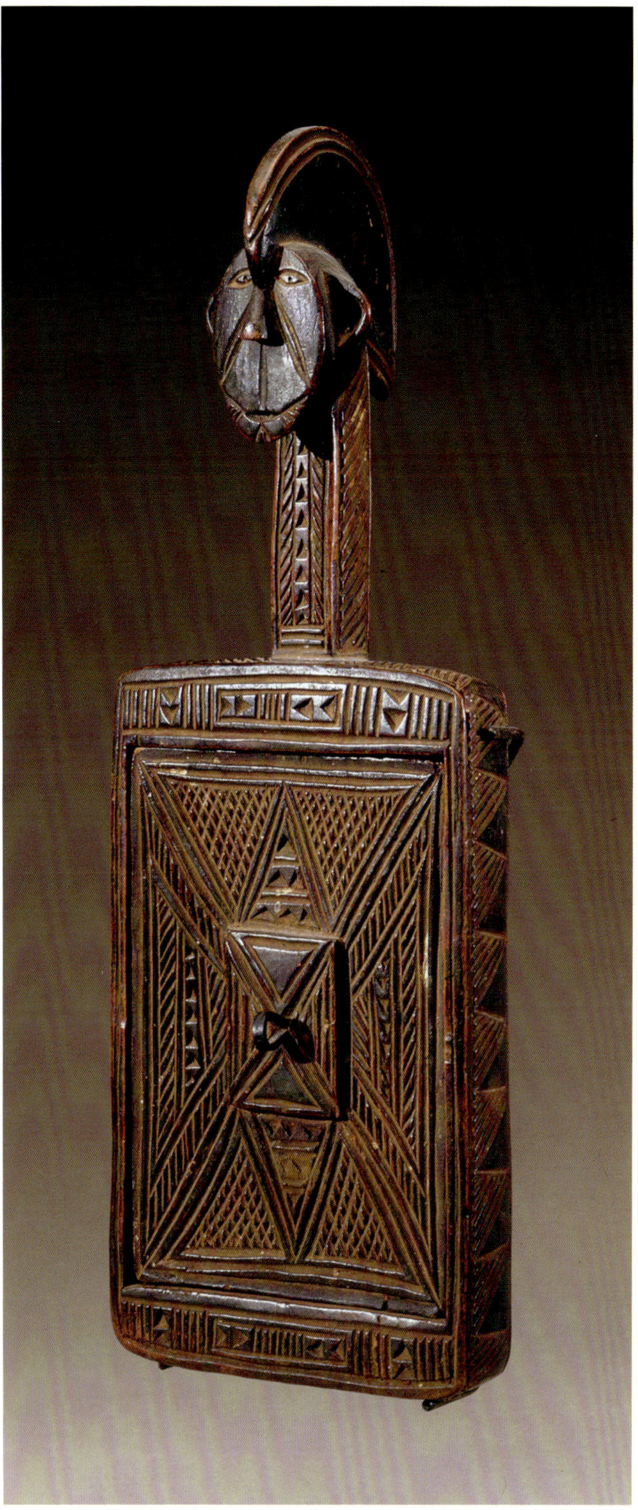

B.7
Umale Oganegi (active 1940s–1970s)
Cosmetic box
Igala peoples, mid-twentieth century
Wood, metal, ocher
H: 35 cm
NEW ORLEANS MUSEUM OF ART; MUSEUM PURCHASE, ROBERT P. GORDY FUND,
92.379A,B
IMAGE: © COURTESY OF NEW ORLEANS MUSEUM OF ART
PROVENANCE: DAVIS GALLERY, NEW ORLEANS

Umale was known for his "figurative" boxes with lids, which were made
to hold cosmetics or as frames for mirrors. This elaborately carved
example was a container for ocher or camwood, which was mixed with oil
and applied to the skin as a cosmetic.

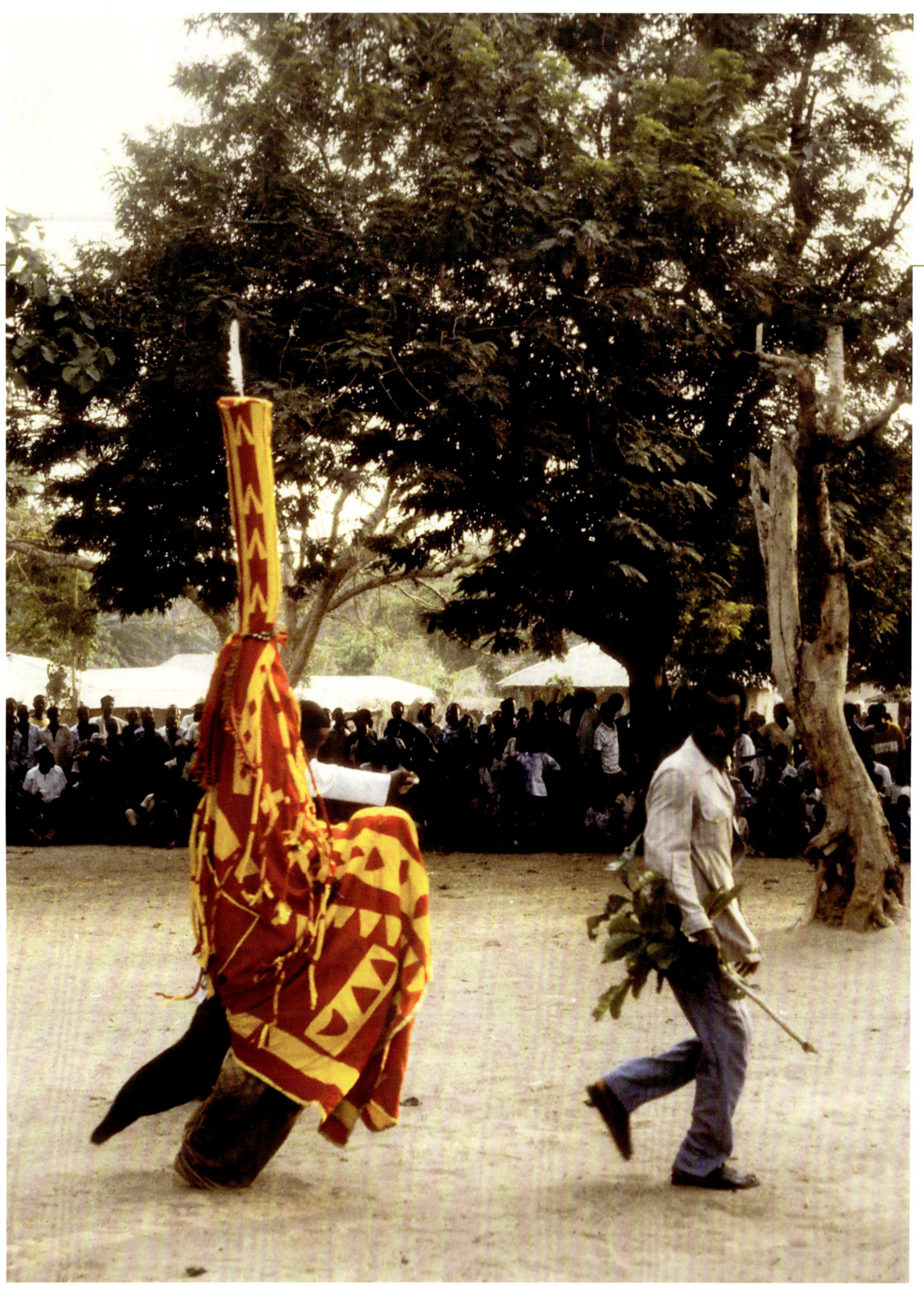

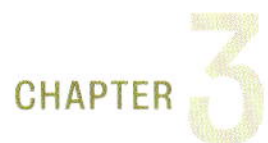

CHAPTER 3

The Ancestral Masquerade:
A Paradigm of Benue Valley Art History

SIDNEY LITTLEFIELD KASFIR
with contributions by JOHN BOSTON, JOHN PICTON,
CONSTANZE WEISE, JOHN C. WILLIS, and JEAN BORGATTI

Certain masks are politically as well as spiritually powerful, especially those owned by lineages that have the ability to control corporately held land and to support political rivalries. When ownership and control are represented through the incarnation of important lineage ancestors, such as kings or other powerful figures, real-life politics as well as religion frequently enter into their deployment. The most famous example of this is the reputed adoption of the Egungun masquerade by the Oyo Yoruba—following a war with the Nupe—in order to expand Oyo hegemony over other Yoruba rivals (see Willis, this chapter). This, however, is only one of many examples in a very broad distribution along the Benue Valley and in the Niger-Benue confluence region. At least a dozen different Nigerian cultures including Yoruba, Igala, Ebira ("Igbira" in the colonial-period literature), Idoma, Idoma Nokwu (Alago), Gwari, Onitsha Igbo, Afo, Gade, Koro, and Abakwariga own some version of the ancestral masquerade in its basic form as a resurrected ancestor concealed in a textile meant to suggest a burial shroud, which is usually elongated by means of a structure of some type hidden beneath the cloth (hence such praise names as "tall ghost," "hooded cobra," or "the mask that leans").

While all represent "our forefathers," at least collectively, certain of these masquerades such as the Idoma Alekwuafia (fig. 3.3) and Ebira Ekuoba (fig. 3.4, and see figs. 4.24, 4.25), are identified as individual, named ancestors, resurrected by their oldest surviving sons. This means that on important ritual occasions, dozens of Idoma ancestral masquerades participate simultaneously in a type of mass outing, making, in the words of Idoma writer A. P. Anyebe (n.d.), "a physical appearance in their spiritual structures."[1] An important historical function of the ancestral mask in several of these communities has been the dispensation of justice, which could include everything from settling family disputes to the trial and execution of criminals, using such methods as the sasswood poison ordeal, wherein survival indicated innocence. This last duty of trying criminals sometimes included the ferreting out of covert antisocial practices, an important link between the Oyo Yoruba Egungun and the Nupe Ndako Gboya. The Nupe mask was embedded in a different set of ritual practices from most of the other forms considered here, but nonetheless it is an elongated shape-changing masquerade (see fig. 3.34; Nadel 1954, 188; also see Willis and Weise in this chapter) and so shares morphological similarities as well as an ancestral (Ndako, "father") spirit identity with the tall ghost masquerades of the Niger-Benue confluence.[2]

There is also a great variation in the degree of elaboration in these masks, from a conical basketry infrastructure—held in place by the masquerader's arm—which is

Enkpe (Igbo: "Emukpe") visits Agila when dead fathers are being raised. It is said to come from Ogbodo Aba, the nearby Igbo "town of the dead."
PHOTOGRAPH BY SIDNEY LITTLEFIELD KASFIR, AGILA, 1989.

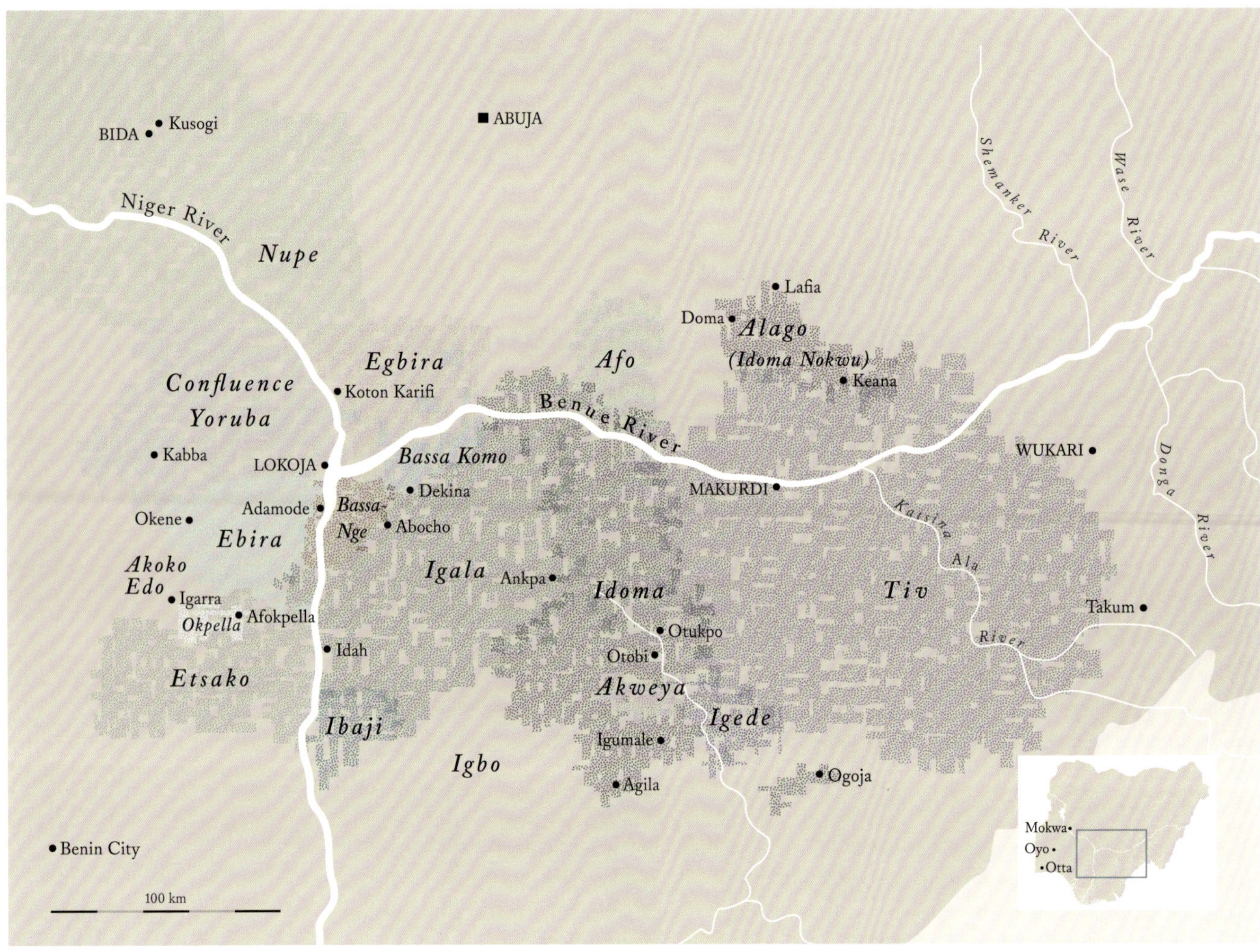

concealed inside the Idoma version, to a simple gathered closure effected by pinning together two sides of a cloth tube for the Ebira, which is then raised up or lowered with one hand. The textile representing the burial shroud is typically made of *opa*, a white strip-woven cloth widely traded along the Benue prior to British colonization and used for wrapping the dead. This may be alternated with strips of an indigo cloth also used for burial (fig. 3.5). The Idoma masquerade costume, however, is rarely left at that: opulence in the form of layered, red-wool felt *ododo* and yellow *ongazi* grace the southern Idoma version (fig. 3.6, and see fig. 3.3). The Yoruba Egungun is of many types, including the version often photographed, with appliquéd panels that fly outward as it twirls. Red *ododo* cloth also figures in Egungun's capacious mythology, which links its adoption to Sango, the putative fourth Alafin of Oyo, whose mother was supposedly from Nupe (Thompson 1974, 221). The version of Egungun that corresponds to the burial shroud is not this type, however, but the Egungun Alago masquerade, which wears a long train trailing behind it.[3]

Although Egungun is the best known of all Nigerian ancestral masquerades, it is probably not the oldest or even the most influential historically. This essay considers the backstory, which, I argue, is the spread of the ancestral masquerade along the Benue to the confluence including Igala and Nupe, from its origins among proto-Idoma and Abakwariga communities in Apá. It also considers more briefly the reverse path, from the Nupe-Oyo Yoruba nexus southward through the Niger-Benue confluence and eastward along the Benue. Both historical hypotheses are weighed here, and both are plausible in differing degrees, though I will argue for the former and its founding within the federation of small states known collectively as Apá (Kororofa, Kwararafa) on the Middle Benue.

3.3

In southern Idoma the Alekwuafia masquerade is known as Ekwula or Ekwila. The mask projection in the Idoma case is not vertical but extends from the left arm and leans on the shoulder of the masquerader. From the tip of the projection the large tassel-like *afia* hang down. This elaborate version with red and yellow appliquéd wool felt suggests the wealth and royalty of the ancestor's lineage.

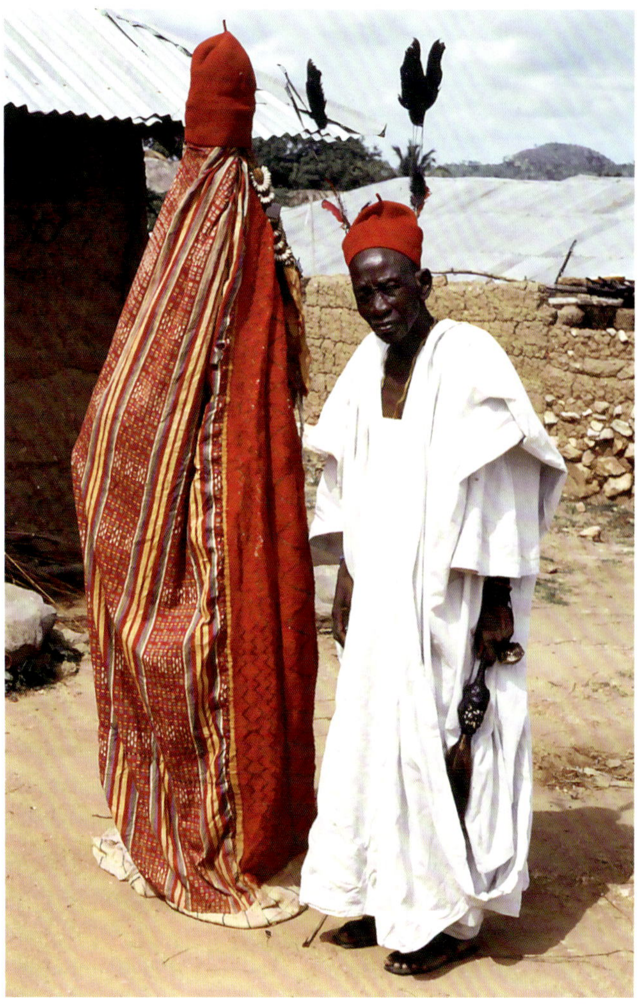

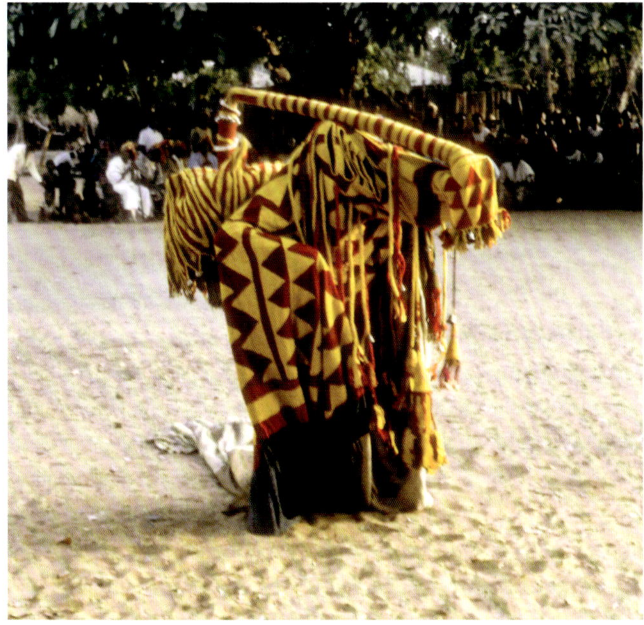

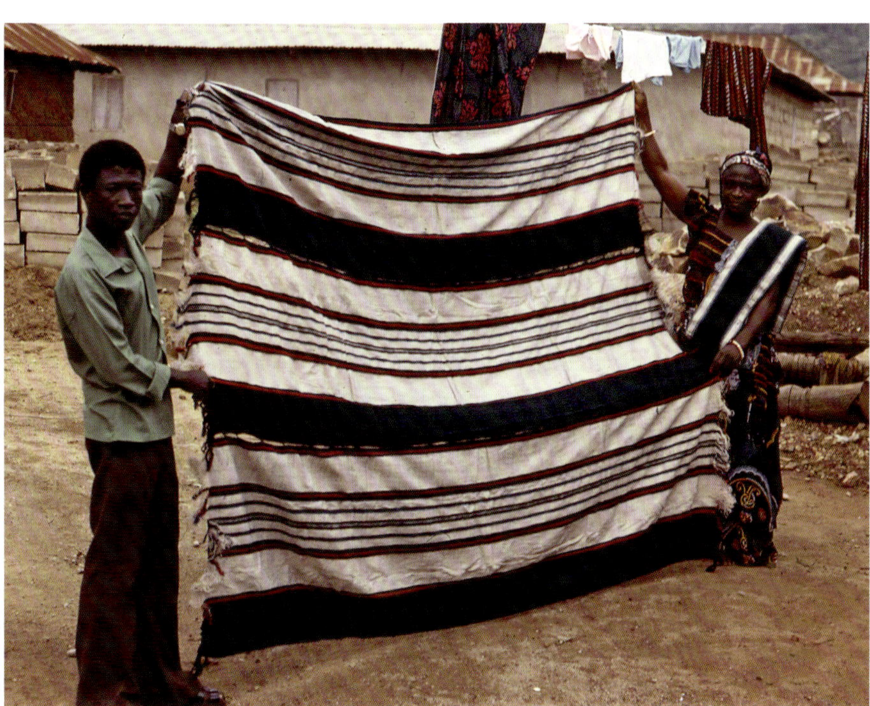

3.4

In May 1967, Yusuf Onoko, diviner and singer (see also figs. 4.5, 4.6, 4.9), took the title of Adeika, in Kuroko, Adavi District, Ebira. Here he wears the feathers signifying his new status, breeding plumes of the standard-winged nightjar and wing feathers from the violet plaintain eater. At his side is the Ekuoba that installed him in his title. The masquerader has stretched himself up at the photographer's request. Hanging down the back of the Ekuoba, decorated with cowrie shells, is a length of cloth with relics from the deceased sewn into it. The front panel of the costume, through which the performer sees, is a length of printed cotton cloth, sewn to heavily brocaded Abinu fabric.

3.5

The handspun cotton cloth displayed here shows the pattern of indigo and white stripes appropriate for wrapping the corpse of a man ready for burial. It is also used in masquerade costuming. The cloth used for wrapping the corpse of a woman is marked by a very different pattern of indigo and white stripes.

> The Alekwu came to Ajitata,[8]
> Ajitata the home of the dead.
> When the Alekwu came to the Land of Ajitata
> The Alekwu was trying to get to Otiya, home of Odu,
> home of the father that begot both of us.
>
> They quit the Land of Ajitata
> Then they came to the Land of Okene.
> A stream overflowed its banks in the Land of Okene
>
> Since the stream had so overflowed
> The Alekwu-of-the-Litany could not pass,
> Then the Alekwu slept at Okene.
> The Alekwu understood Okene:
> That is why the Alekwu speaks Igbira.

In the verses that follow these, the Alekwu, having seemingly crossed the Niger to the Ebira settlement of Okene reverses direction and returns to Ankpa in eastern Igalaland, then tries again to reach Ajitata in nearby Idomaland, but at every attempt, rain and floods prevent the Alekwu's passage. This long, circular, and historically implausible path can be made much more logical if Okene, an Ebira settlement west of the Niger founded only in the nineteenth century, is replaced by Igu or Panda, the earlier Egbira polities north of the Benue. Panda was destroyed during the Fulani jihad about 1850; Igu, in 1892. From Ajitata to Umaisha, the Panda town on the north bank of the Benue, would have been a short distance across the river and downstream. But in the 1970s when this chant was recorded, Okene was the only major Ebira town left. This is one of the instances where a chant singer must "correct" the narrative to have it make sense to an audience of contemporaries.

But even if one can reduce the path of transmission to a tight circle from Apá to Idoma, Ebira, Igala, and back to Idoma, the most intriguing yet puzzling revelation in this chant is not this route but the statement which follows:

> Then they went to pass Akono.
> That Akono is the land of Apakpando who made
> the costume for the Alekwu.

This passage, which is repeated several times in different forms, states that the Abakpa (Hausa) or Abakpando ("those who wander," e.g., itinerant Hausa craftsmen or traders) made the costume of the Alekwu. It is a clear acknowledgment that the text is speaking about the physical masquerade and not just the Alekwu, or ancestral spirit, that it embodies. But like the "Okene" passage, it is misleading and does not mean what it says literally. Its real meaning, I argue, will become clear in the following section.

THE REGIONAL PICTURE: MAKING SENSE OUT OF COMPLEXITY
The Argument for Apá Origin

Apá is an actual place in the Middle Benue region, but it is equally a mythopoeic place of origin, as Ile-Ife is for the Yoruba. The historical Apá (Hausa: "Kororofa" or "Kwararafa") was a loose confederation of small states appearing in Hausa chronicles of wars from the thirteenth to the seventeenth century. With its multiple ethnicities (Jukun, Idoma, Igala, Ebira, Afo, etc.) and intersecting oral histories, it was probably the crucible for the genre of masquerade unique to this part of Africa: the incarnated ancestor clad in an indigo and/or white strip-woven *opa* burial cloth, to which many

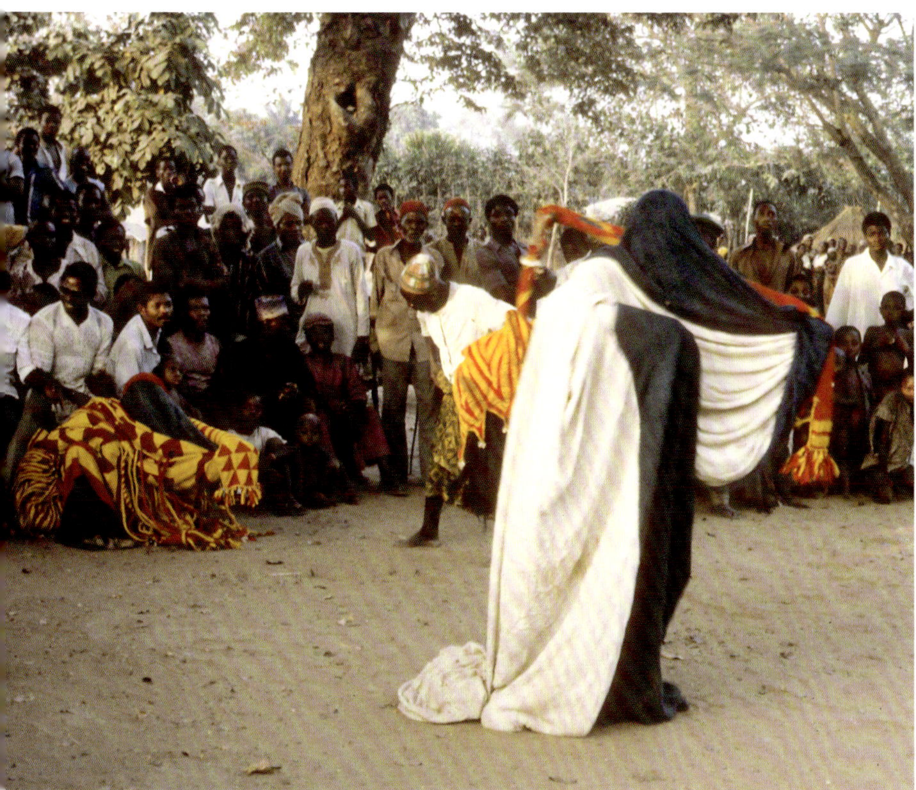

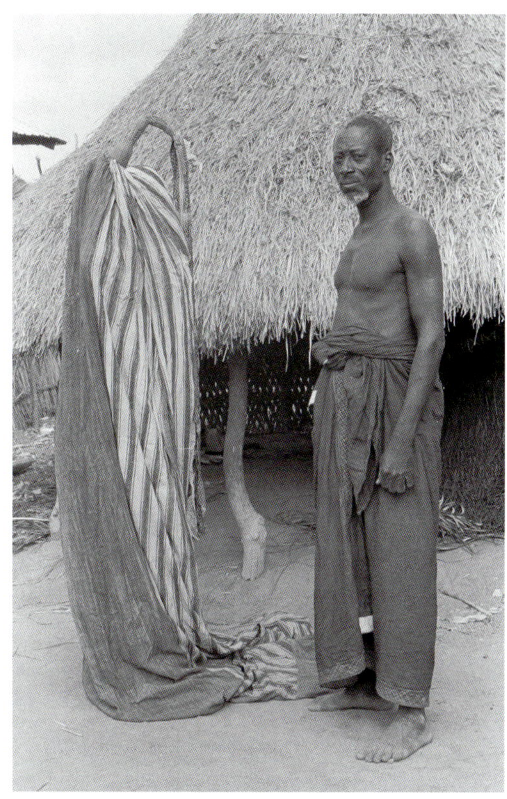

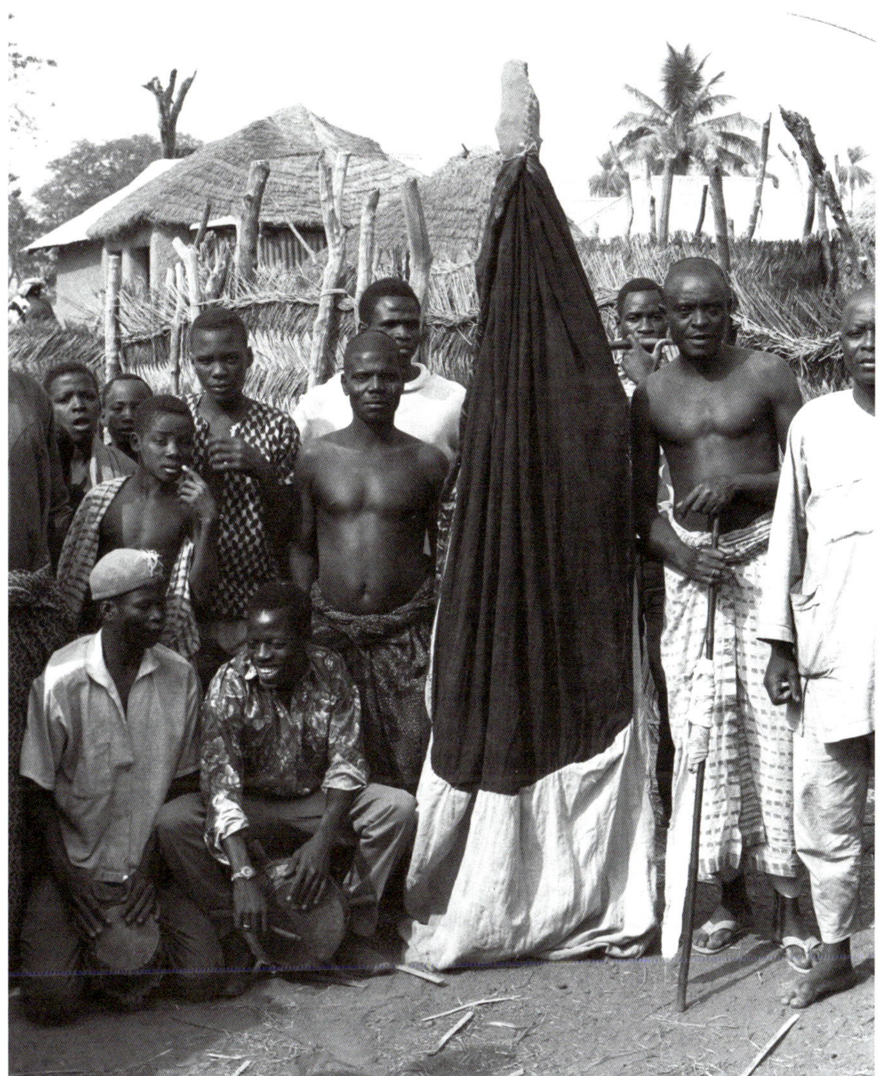

3.7
This is the basic Ekwula as it appears before embellishments are added. It wears only an indigo and white, handspun and handwoven burial cloth.
PHOTOGRAPH BY SIDNEY LITTLEFIELD KASFIR, AGILA, 1986.

3.8
 The Abakwariga Ashama masquerade embodies a risen forefather and forms a part of pre-Islamic Hausa religious practice.
PHOTOGRAPH BY ARNOLD RUBIN, WUKARI, 1965, RUBIN ARCHIVE, FOWLER MUSEUM AT UCLA, NEG. NO. 25.

3.9
Iwagu is owned by the Ashama lineage in Doma, who are not Abakwariga but Alago, making the two masquerades very close cognates. In addition to appearing at the funerals of important men, Iwagu also ensures good crops and community health.
PHOTOGRAPH BY ARNOLD RUBIN, ASSAIKIO VILLAGE, JANUARY 11, 1971, RUBIN ARCHIVE, FOWLER MUSEUM AT UCLA, NEG. NO. 2993.

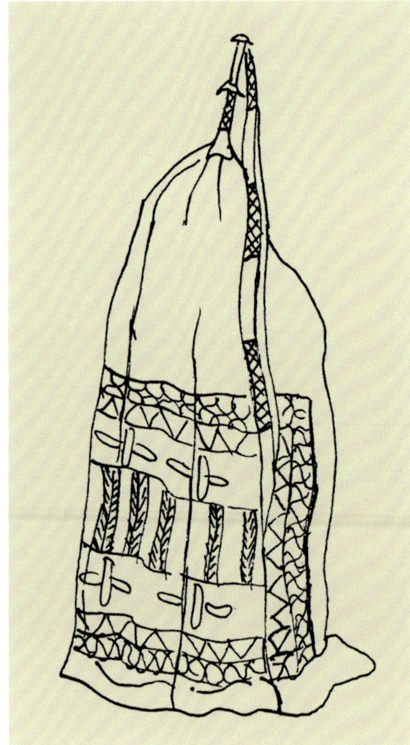

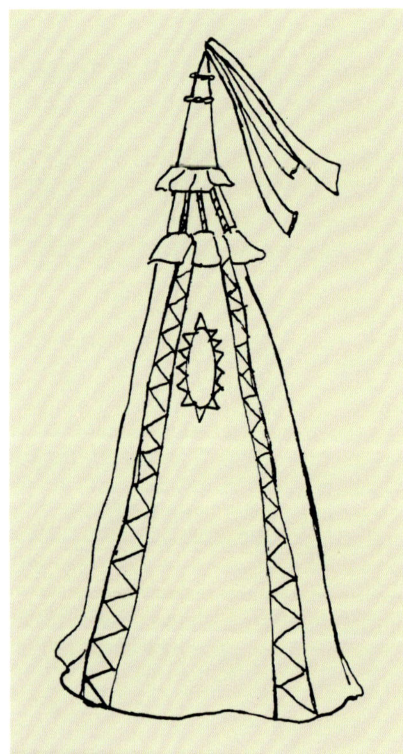

3.10
This drawing illustrates an Ashama masquerade collected by C. K. Meek circa 1931 and presently in the collection of the Pitt Rivers Museum.
DRAWING BY SIDNEY LITTLEFIELD KASFIR.

3.11
This schematic drawing illustrates the Otukpo Alekwuafia masquerade.
DRAWING BY SIDNEY LITTLEFIELD KASFIR, 1978.

sumptuous extensions may be added (fig. 3.7).[9] Today the most highly elaborated of these masquerades occur in the southernmost Idoma kingdoms of Igumale and Agila where they are known as Ekwila, Ekwula, or Ekpila. As a concept, political strategy, and performance, I argue that this textile masquerade probably spread, between about 1500 and 1800, from the Idoma (of Doma Kingdom) or Abakwariga (non-Muslim Hausa) in the Apá region of the Middle Benue westward into Gwari, Ebira, Nupe, Oyo Yoruba, Igala, and certain Niger Igbo communities such as Onitsha. Since the Tiv and Akweya do not have either the masquerade or the ritual complex to support it, it probably predates their arrival in the Lower Benue from the Cross River region some time after the breakup and dispersal of the Apá cluster of small states.

The prototypical Doma example is Iwagu, found in the Idoma Nokwu (Hausa: "Arago" or "Alago") kingdoms of Doma[10] and Keana north of the Benue. It features the same conical cloth structure called Ashama by Abakwariga at Okali (Wukari), the most recent Apá-Jukun capital. The so-called Abakwariga, Hausa immigrants in the Benue region who moved south to resist conversion to Islam from the fifteenth century onward, were traders, craftsmen, and elephant hunters, but they were also famous as ritual specialists to the dominant Jukun (Meek 1931a). The focus of Abakwariga ancestral religion[11] was the belief system embodied by the Ashama masquerade as a risen forefather (Adamu 1978). For the Jukun themselves, virtually all masquerades had ancestral connotations, but none resembled the Ashama. Meek collected an Ashama masquerade costume for the Pitt Rivers Museum in Oxford, and Rubin (1969) photographed and described both an Ashama and an Iwagu in his unpublished dissertation (figs. 3.8, 3.9). There are no examples of Idoma ancestral masquerades in museum collections because, at least in Idomaland south of the Benue, each mask is buried with the last surviving son of the person being resurrected. Yet such masquerades are much more powerful than the carved Idoma masks that grace museums and private collections.

An unresolved (and probably unresolvable) question is which came first, the Doma Iwagu masquerade or the Abakwariga Ashama? Rubin (1982) assumed that the somewhat simpler Iwagu costume must have derived from the Ashama, in keeping with his assumption that Doma and Keana kingdoms were founded from Apá. This is the Jukun oral history version. A map in the *Description of Africa* by the traveler Leo Africanus, written before 1526, however, includes Doma but not Apá,[12] and present-day Doma court historians insist that the Iwagu masquerade is as old as Doma itself.[13] They also point out that "*ashama*" is an Alago word of eulogy and that the so-named Ashama lineage of Alago who own the Iwagu masquerade are among the original Doma settlers.

Both the Ashama and Iwagu versions have cloth streamers at the top, and hidden inside are relics of the deceased such as hair or nail parings, which make this part of the mask both numinous and dangerous. In the Ashama masquerade costume, which Meek was able to collect for the Pitt Rivers Museum, plain strip-woven burial cloth used widely along the Benue is sewn to indigo resist-dyed cloth (fig. 3.10). This stitched and indigo resist-dyed cloth was (and still is) made by both Doma (as *odu mele*) and Abakwariga (as *akya*) and exported along a precolonial trade route into the nearby Cameroon Grassfields where it was known simply as "Doma" or "Wukari" cloth. The cloth streamers on the Pitt Rivers Ashama are of tightly woven Jukun *kyadze* cloth with an indigo weft-inlay design. A translation of this form into Alekwuafia was witnessed by the author in 1978 in a village near Otukpo in central Idomaland south of the Benue. The overall shape was similar, but the Doma/Abakwariga elements had been replaced: the projection from the top was now a cone and the streamers were red *ododo* cloth. The resist-dyed Doma cloth had become an appliquéd lozenge-shaped *ododo* panel similar to those worn by Idoma sacred kings (fig. 3.11; and see fig. 2.2).

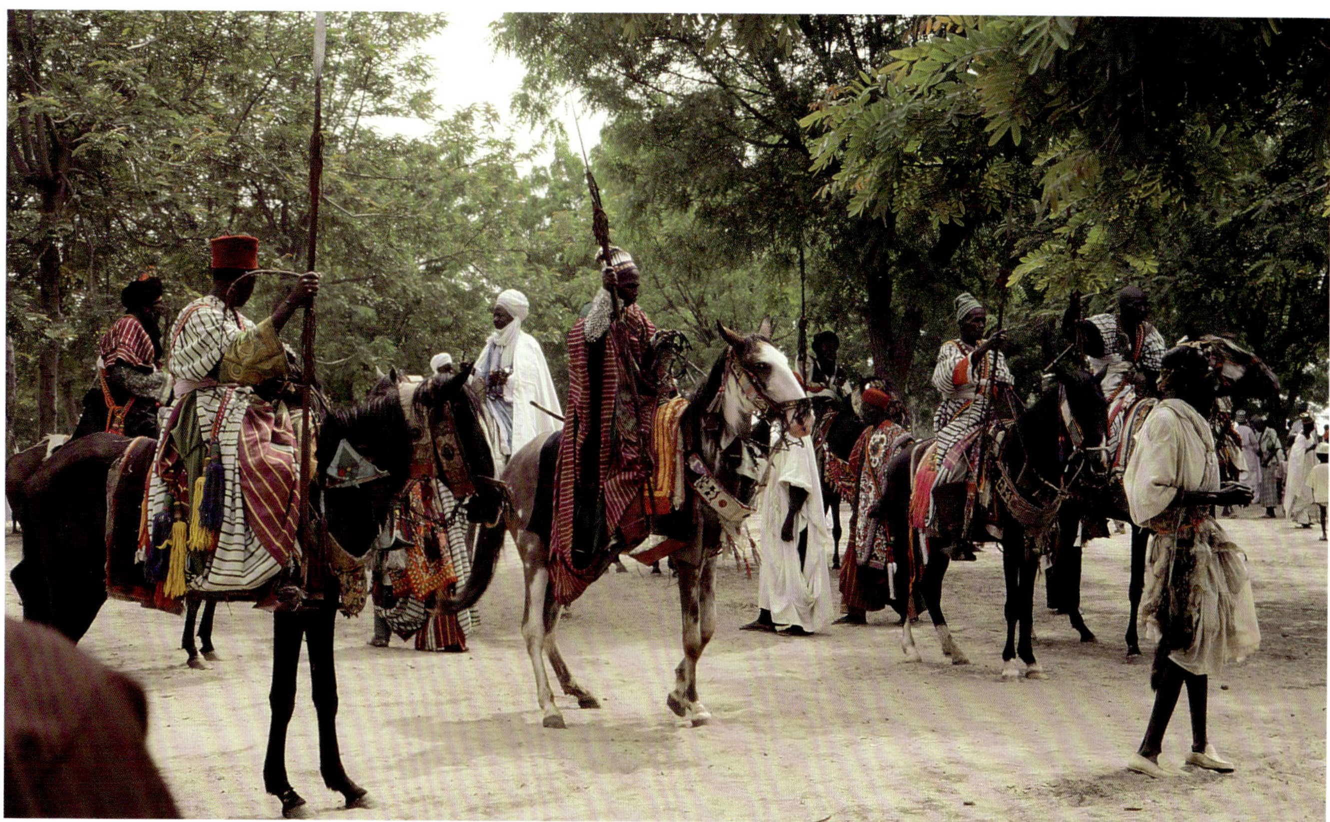

3.12
There are no descriptions of the trappings formerly worn by the cavalries of Doma and Keana or the armies of the Kororofa federation. It is likely, however, that they resembled those of the Hausa and other northern armies. This photograph shows a local Emir and his entourage in the Northern Nigerian town of Gombe at the annual celebration of Id al-Adha, which marks the end of the pilgrimage to Mecca. Both men and horses wear their most elaborate regalia.
PHOTOGRAPH BY MARLA C. BERNS, GOMBE, NORTHERN NIGERIA, 1982.

Double-heddle loom weaving technology reached the Benue Valley with Hausa craftsmen as they migrated further southward into the vast region known to them as Kasashen Bauchi.[14] The adoption of the burial cloth made from parallel strips of narrow-band weaving provided the prototype for the characteristic form of the ancestral masquerade. This is corroborated by the fact that the ritual tailor who sews the masquerade cloth is known as *abakpa,* the Idoma term for Hausa (and also for "those who wander," i.e., itinerant traders and craftsmen). While its tailor is not literally a Hausa, the lexical term suggests that Hausa artisanship is somehow connected to its history.

In the rituals surrounding the making of the masquerade costume, the maker is framed as someone totally unrelated to the real-world tailoring profession despite the intricacy of the artisanship required. In Okwoga District, Allan Bassing (1973) was told that the maker is chosen through revelation in a dream, in which he is told he must find a needle stuck in the bark of a certain tree. In Otukpo District, a virgin is led blindfolded in the middle of the night to the men's meeting house (*itakpa*) to help bring forth the new Alekwuafia. She is given a needle and the *abakpa* hands her a black thread, which, despite the darkness, she passes through the eye of the needle (Anyebe 1980). In Agila District I was told that such powerful things are not made by human hands at all but by a "chief of masquerades" spirit. All these explanations seem bent on divorcing the making of the masquerade costume from any form of trained artisanship and instead placing it in the realm of spiritual intervention.

The other aspect of the ancestral masquerade ensemble that relates it to the Apá-Kororofa period of Idoma history is its metaphoric identity as a "horse" (*onya*) with full trappings (figs. 3.1, 3.12). Horses were traded into the Benue region from Kano in exchange for salt and slaves (Fischer 1972; Adamu 1978; Kasfir 1989). The military power of Kororofa has been in part attributed to its cavalry, which in turn provided a powerful visual metaphor for the repertoire of its ritual specialists. South of the Benue, however, horses have been rare due to tsetse fly infestation in the stands of high forest and riverbanks. Partly because of this rarity, they endure as a symbol of political power and influence, one that is strongly associated with the savanna and Apá.

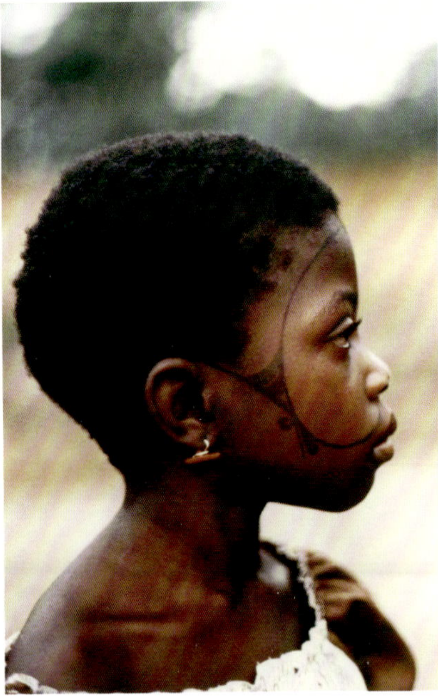

3.13
The *ena* body painting practiced in Agila is similar to the *uli* painting of the northern Igbo area. *Ena* is an art used by women to adorn the skin of women and children, the walls of shrine houses, the membrane of the pottery *esoba* drum, and the large drum membrane of the king's royal orchestra.
PHOTOGRAPH BY SIDNEY LITTLEFIELD KASFIR, AGILA, 1978.

3.14
This black and white image of Enkpe taken by a local photographer in Agila dates from a generation before the image reproduced in figure 3.1, but it features the same vertical projection and voluminous robes.
PHOTOGRAPHER UNKNOWN.

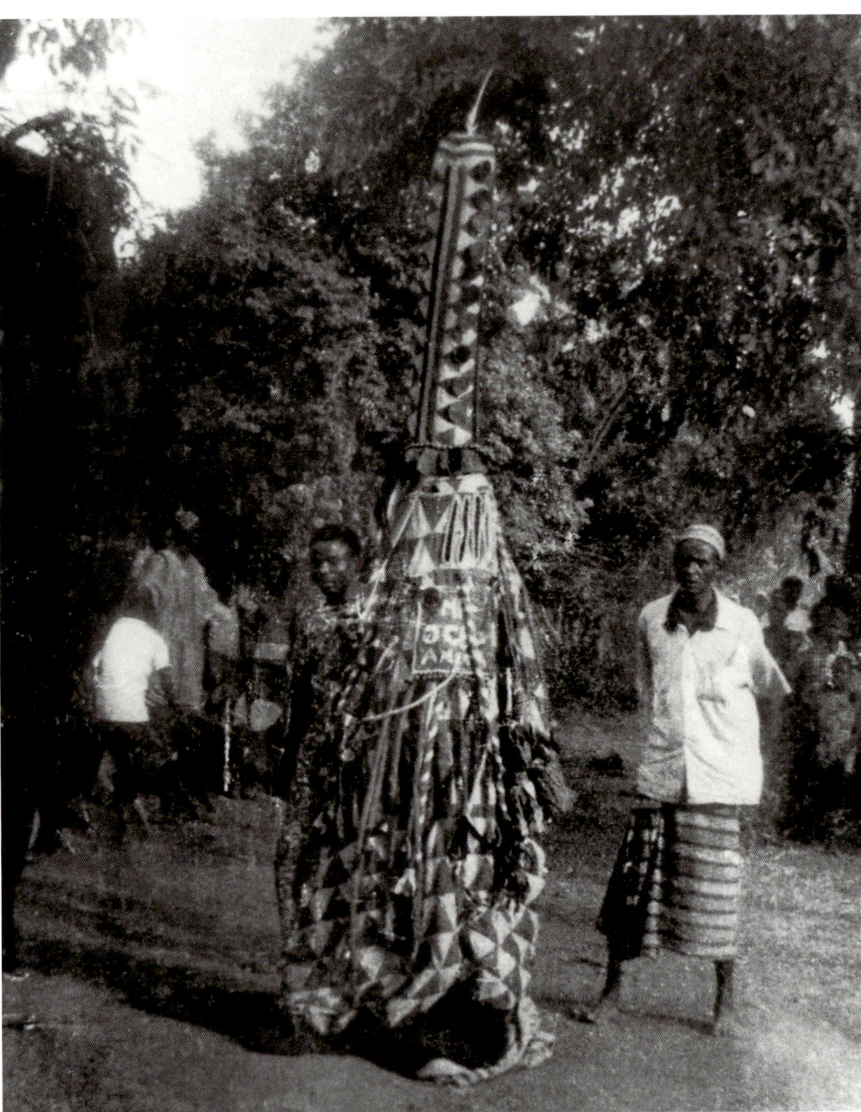

In ideological terms, Alekwuafia confirms the power of the ancestors over the land and its people. In precolonial times, these re-embodied spirits were the ultimate source of moral authority, above chiefs or kings. This authority was vested in the "collective elder dead" (cf. Henderson 1972), for whom the masquerades, as resurrected ancestors, are the concrete manifestations. Like the Yoruba Egungun, they were called in both to settle disputes and conduct investigations including accusations of witchcraft. Their ruling was law and was never abrogated. In central Idomaland, they passed judgment on those accused of serious crimes. The sacred cloth streamers (*afia*) attached to the projection at the top of the masquerade would be dipped in water, which the accused then was made to drink. If the person were guilty, death would follow soon afterward (Kasfir 1979). After 1914 the British introduced a court system to try criminals, but it was ineffective in comparison since people feared the justice of the ancestors much more than the courts.

Southern Idomaland: The Nexus of Idoma, Igbo, and Igala Ancestral Masquerades

Before colonialism, Idomaland south of the Benue was comprised of twenty-two independent polities of varying size and complexity. The southernmost kingdoms of Igumale and Agila were in effect small states,[15] whose kingship and political organization closely resembled neighboring Igala's and who claimed to be founded from Idah after their earlier residence in Apá.[16] Several Agila or Igumale masquerades such as Ekwaja and Unaaloko, which I discuss in chapter 2, are given an Idah backstory (though I have found no Igala counterparts for any of them).

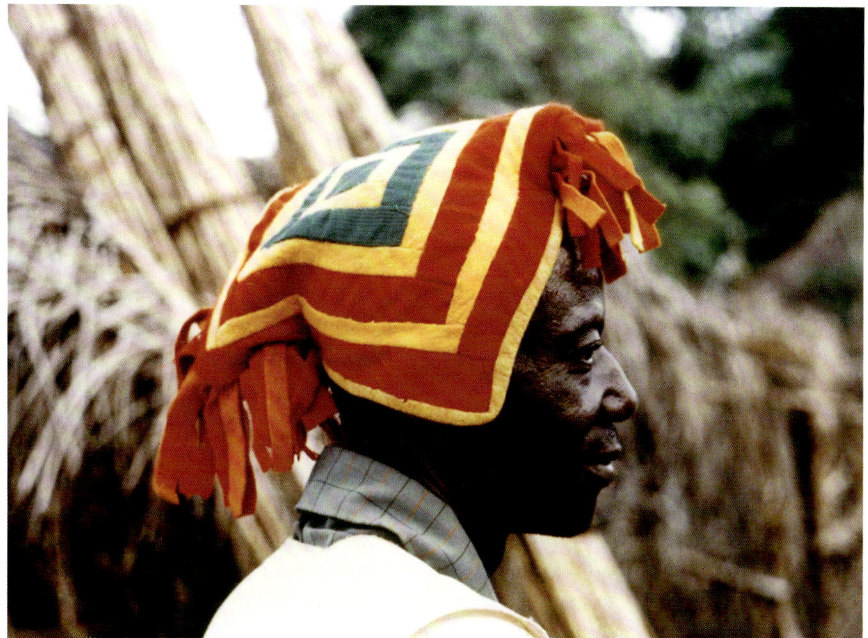

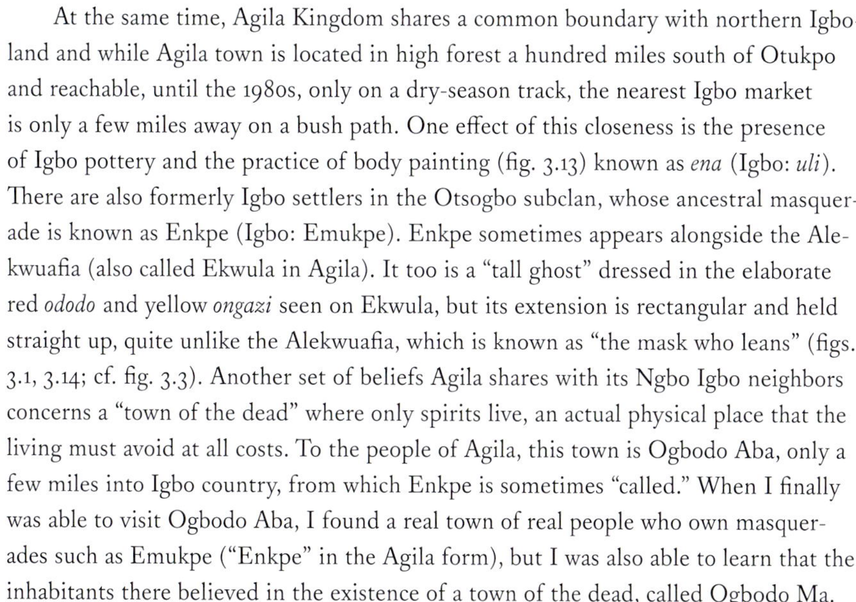

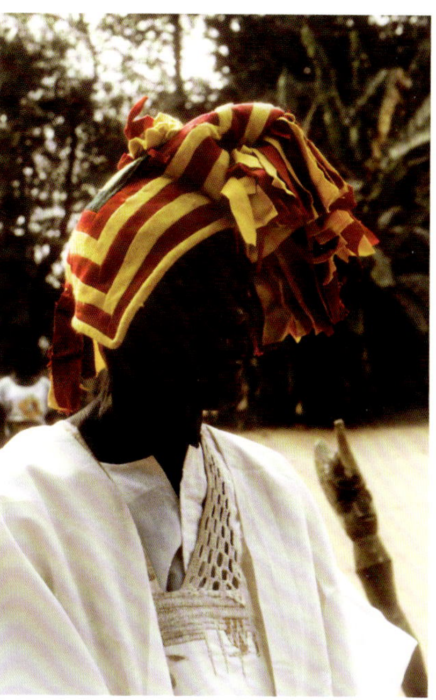

3.15
The Ochonu (prime minister) of Agila, wearing *akpalewo* (dogs' ears) signifying his office as the highest-ranked commoner.
PHOTOGRAPH BY SIDNEY LITTLEFIELD KASFIR, 1978

3.16
Emeje Ogbu, titled elder and primary schoolmaster, wearing *akpalewo*.
PHOTOGRAPH BY SIDNEY LITTLEFIELD KASFIR, AGILA, 1986.

At the same time, Agila Kingdom shares a common boundary with northern Igboland and while Agila town is located in high forest a hundred miles south of Otukpo and reachable, until the 1980s, only on a dry-season track, the nearest Igbo market is only a few miles away on a bush path. One effect of this closeness is the presence of Igbo pottery and the practice of body painting (fig. 3.13) known as *ena* (Igbo: *uli*). There are also formerly Igbo settlers in the Otsogbo subclan, whose ancestral masquerade is known as Enkpe (Igbo: Emukpe). Enkpe sometimes appears alongside the Alekwuafia (also called Ekwula in Agila). It too is a "tall ghost" dressed in the elaborate red *ododo* and yellow *ongazi* seen on Ekwula, but its extension is rectangular and held straight up, quite unlike the Alekwuafia, which is known as "the mask who leans" (figs. 3.1, 3.14; cf. fig. 3.3). Another set of beliefs Agila shares with its Ngbo Igbo neighbors concerns a "town of the dead" where only spirits live, an actual physical place that the living must avoid at all costs. To the people of Agila, this town is Ogbodo Aba, only a few miles into Igbo country, from which Enkpe is sometimes "called." When I finally was able to visit Ogbodo Aba, I found a real town of real people who own masquerades such as Emukpe ("Enkpe" in the Agila form), but I was also able to learn that the inhabitants there believed in the existence of a town of the dead, called Ogbodo Ma.

A strong visual theme runs through all the royal and ancestral masks in Agila and Igumale, as well as the robes of the king and prime minister, and it extends even further to the hats worn by titled elders, known by their shape as *akpalewo* (dogs' ears). All repeat the predominantly red and yellow triangle and lozenge pattern in a wool felt called *ododo* (red) and *ongazi* (yellow), which was formerly acquired from the large Hausa slave market in the Idoma town of Yangedde[17] (figs. 3.15, 3.16). To the best of my knowledge, the *akpalewo* are unique in Nigeria. To find the same preponderance of these colors and designs, one has to look eastward to the Cameroon Grassfields (Northern 1975). Interestingly, both Idoma and Grassfields informants identify the triangular red-yellow pattern as "spots of the leopard," which in the Idoma ritual system is equated with the king. (When an Idoma king dies, it is said that "the leopard has gone to the forest.")[18] While colonial and postcolonial history have separated Grassfields and Benue Valley scholarship into categories circumscribed by national boundaries, it is worth remembering that the former Apá/Kororofa confederacy, which included Idoma, was located midway between the Niger-Benue confluence and the Grassfields. Furthermore there was an active cloth trade, as described earlier, from both Doma and Wukari to Bamenda (Kasfir, fieldnotes, 1989).

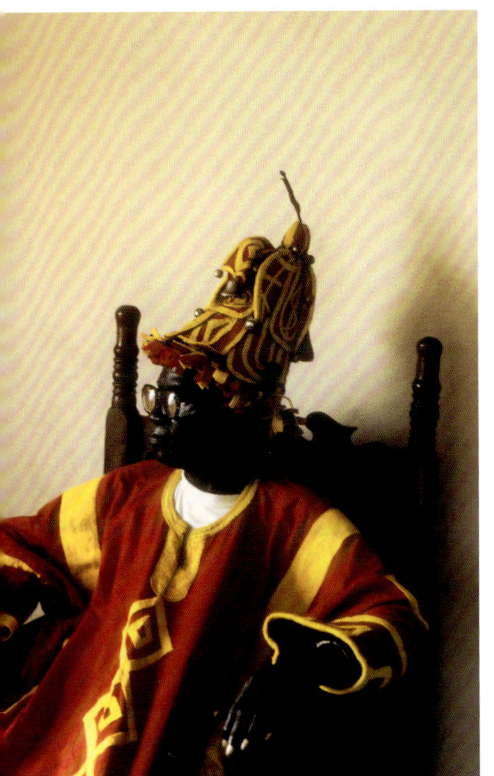

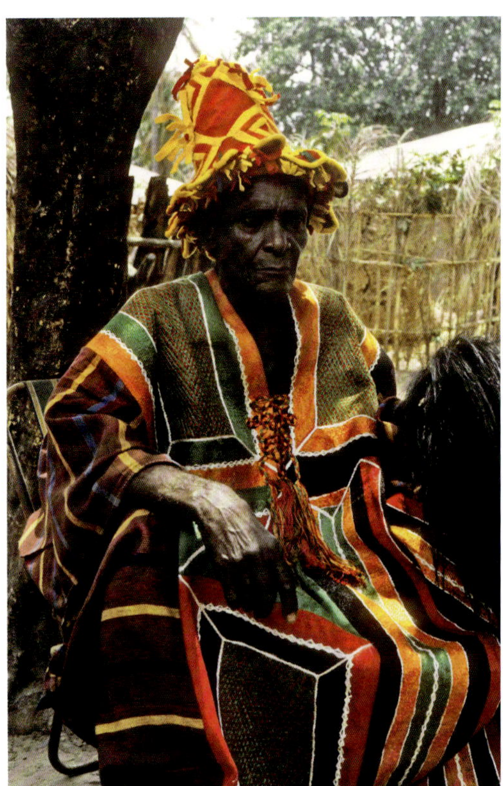

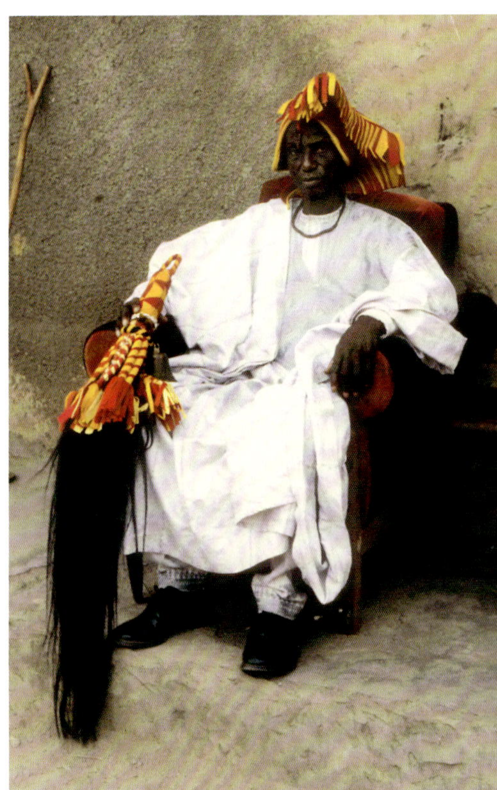

3.17
Each new Ogaba (king) of Igumale designs his own hat while in the period of ritual seclusion prior to being installed, and it is made by a special tailor (cf. fig. 2.2, which shows the dress of an earlier Ogaba.)
PHOTOGRAPH BY SIDNEY LITTLEFIELD KASFIR, IGUMALE, 1986.

3.18
The Achadu (prime minister) of Igumale wears a conical headdress of different design but the same overall "pagoda" shape as that worn by the Ogaba, or king, (cf. figs. 2.2, 3.17).
PHOTOGRAPH BY SIDNEY LITTLEFIELD KASFIR, 1986.

3.19
The Ots'Agila (king of Agila), unlike his equivalent in neighboring Igumale, wears *akpalewo* similar to those worn by his title-holders. The large horsetail whisk (representing a horse sacrifice performed at his installation) is, however, his most important symbol of office.
PHOTOGRAPH BY SIDNEY LITTLEFIELD KASFIR, 1978.

The King as Mask

The final aspect of the Idoma Alekwuafia, which would be worthy of a more detailed study, is the close parallelism between the symbolism and regalia of Idoma sacred kingship and that of the fully elaborated ancestral masquerade as it is found in the southern Idoma kingdoms. The underlying logic is seemingly clear: the king "dies" prior to his installation and is then resurrected as a sacred being, no longer subject to human laws and frailties. Likewise the dead elder is resurrected from the grave and makes his appearance in the form of a masquerade. Sacred kings are secluded, so like masquerades, they are normally hidden from view and seen only under special circumstances (figs. 3.17, 3.19). In visual terms, they wear the same red/yellow sawtooth, triangle or lozenge designs. When I commented to the Ots'Agila (king of Agila) on the similarities, he simply said, "the king is also a mask." To complete the circle, when the king physically dies, his regalia is displayed on the roof of the palace above the main entrance. What an explanation based wholly on symbolism leaves out, however, is the aesthetics of display and the obvious prestige attached to making one's father appear king-like in his finery. So is the king a kind of mask, or is the mask taking on the attributes of the king? Today, with all the changes that have taken place due to the opening up of Agila and Igumale with a tarmac road, it may be difficult to find out.

COMPARATIVE PERSPECTIVES FROM IGALA, EBIRA, NUPE, YORUBA, AND OKPELLA

To conclude this chapter, five regional specialists will describe variants of the masquerade in different parts of the Lower Benue and the Niger-Benue confluence. We hope to make two important points in adopting this approach: (1) wars, political fortunes, and subsequent population movements (colonizers, refugees, returned captives, or simply migrants) were vital to constructing the regional variations of this central concept of the embodiment of a risen ancestor in the form of a masquerade; (2) a straightforward donor-recipient model works in only a few cases, while most of the time the evidence suggests instead a dense network of relationships born out of intersecting religious, artistic, and political practice. In both respects, the ancestral "tall ghost" is the paradigmatic example of Benue Valley art history.

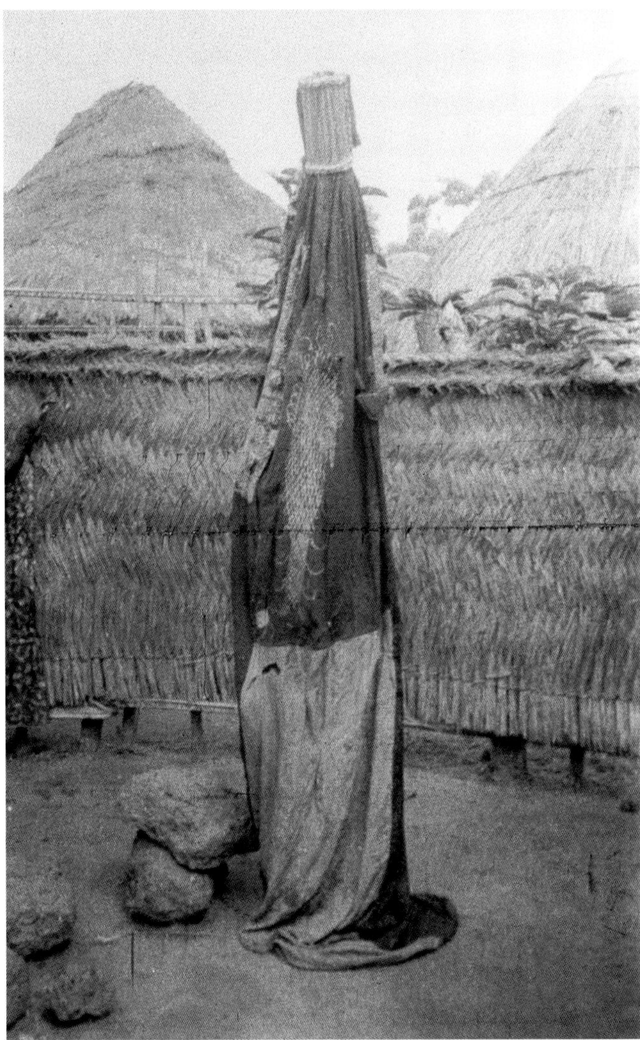

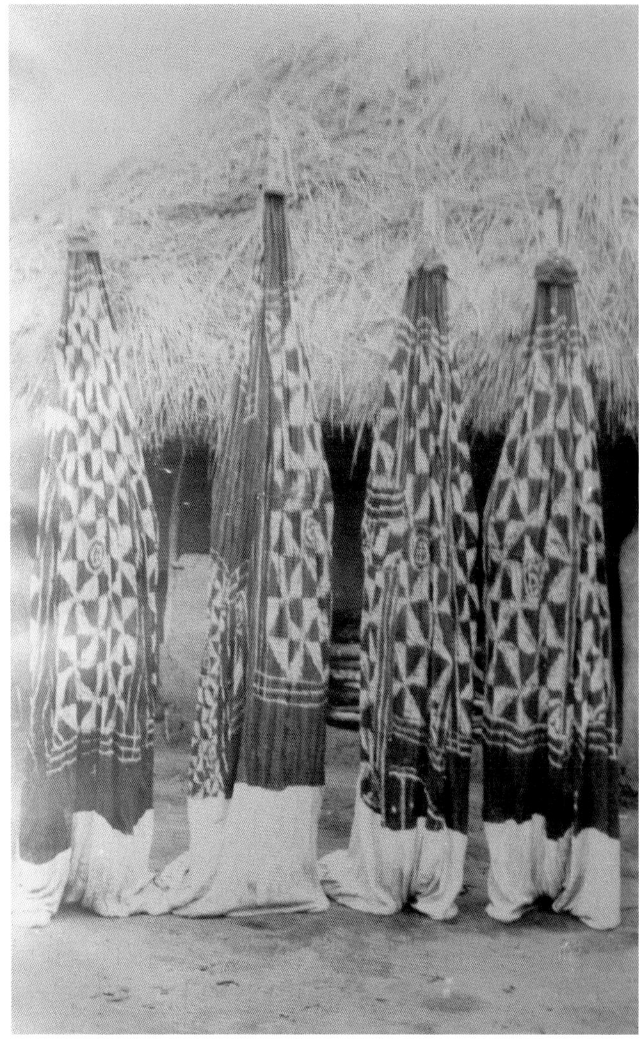

A. THE IGALA EGWU AFIA—JOHN BOSTON

The function of impersonating the dead is performed by the Egwu Afia masquerades throughout Igalaland.[19] Egwu Afia costumes are tall and tapering, reaching a narrow and pointed apex at a height of some eight feet. They are usually made of cloth dyed indigo blue with white panels or triangles, and I have seen some colored red and white and other costumes in multiple colors (figs. 3.20, 3.21). The crest may be embroidered with cowries or ornamental stitching, or it may support a red hat if the dead man being impersonated was a title-holder during his lifetime. On some costumes the dried skin of a genet (*ewolo*) hangs from the crest down the masquerade's back. This is an allusion to the elusive and mysterious nature of the genet, for, say the Igala, "no one knows where the genet deposits its droppings."

The identification of this masquerade with the dead takes a number of different forms. Within the crest is a small packet called *ajibo,* made from a short narrow strip of white cloth, *okpe,* which is split apart and knotted at each end to represent the arms and legs of a man. The *ajibo* may also contain nail and hair clippings from the dead man, and in some cases dry earth from his grave. The presence of these relics of the dead in the crest of the costume explains the prohibition that the wearer of the costume observes against looking up into the apex of his masquerade. Igala maintain that to look upward within the costume will result in madness or death for the wearer. The tall point of the costume is supported from within by a stick held in the right hand.

At the annual ancestor festival called Òkula, the dead are reunited with the living. The costumes are taken in the box-stool in which they are stored to a sacred grove (*an'okuta*) and are then laid out on a mat in the grove. Sacrifices of cocks are made over

This Igala Egwu Afia masquerade from Abocho District appeared at burial ceremonies and at the Ibegwu festival. Local handwoven cloth was dyed blue and used in combination with imported red cloth that was embroidered in silver thread.
PHOTOGRAPH BY JOHN BOSTON.

These Egwu Afia masquerades—seen at Odochalla village in Ibaji District—were made of handwoven cloth that was obtained from Igbo and resist-dyed blue. Cowries and small bells were tied to the crests. Each of these masquerades had a personal name (from left to right): Ejogwanu (the snake leaves his skin behind); Ako, which is the name of the village founder; Ikpeami (he does wonderful things); and Afobibipaulokonya (the bad wind who cuts down the branches of the Iroko).
PHOTOGRAPH BY JOHN BOSTON.

the costumes, and part of the offerings is roasted and eaten by the men present in a communal meal. One of the men speaks through a voice disguiser (*akpa*), to represent the voice of the most recently dead ancestor, and he initiates any young boys present who do not already know the secrets of masquerading. Those who are to be initiated are led into the grove blindfolded and are tested with a few questions before being allowed to see the voice disguiser and the costumes laid out on the mat.

Toward early evening the Afia costumes are put on, and the masquerades process from the grove into the hamlet adjoining, with each masquerader attended by a small group of close male relatives. The women and children rejoice as they crowd round to welcome their ancestors. And they sing songs in praise of marriage and of the begetting of children, as in the following examples:

> *agaji ki lagigo oma e*
> Barren woman, come and look at children.
> *okpete abioma ichebutu kpana*
> The stool of a woman who has children is cracked and dirty.
> *atami nalio koli makere*
> My father go carefully and don't stumble.
> *okomi chemi ologbo uchologwo, okomi chemi obaja omi chobaja*
> My husband do well by me and I will do well, neglect me and I will neglect [you].

Each masquerader pauses to touch the roof of the entrance house with its crest before entering the homestead of the senior elder in the hamlet, thus imparting blessings to the whole family. The procession ends with the masqueraders and male supporters crowding into the elder's reception house (*atakpa*), where the costumes are removed and the men eat, drink beer, and relax while waiting for darkness to fall. Later that night the expert with the voice disguiser impersonates the dead founder of the homestead and gives advice to the women assembled outside and to the men sitting around him inside the *atakpa*. He reviews any issues that may have divided the men and women of the family during the preceding year and tries to settle their quarrels. He advises what sacrifices need to be made for good health, prosperity, and fertility, and he includes in his admonitions support for the head of the family as leader of the group. The masquerader's words are repeated by an interpreter (*agbolaka*). And from time to time the masker leads singing in which all the men join. Examples of these songs are as follows:

> *idenekwu idaregwu yo yo yo*
> Worms abound masquerade, very many.
> *abo mi li mi li one no*
> I can see a costume (*abo*) but I don't see a living person.
> *ejo gwano i the fioo*
> The snake changes its skin so smoothly.

One of the main functions of the Egwu Afia play in Igala is to support the authority of the elders, who organize the Okula festival as the living descendants and representatives of the ancestors commemorated by the masqueraders. Authority and social control, however, are not the only principles at work within this festival. Okula is a joyous occasion, a celebration of the well-being and prosperity of the whole family concerned. The descent group responsible may be a complex patrilineage as at Ibochi, where I saw ninety masquerades in one Okula procession; or it may, more typically, be a minor lineage within an extended family, celebrating the return of some five or six ancestors to the hamlet where they formerly dwelt. In either case the unity of the group is renewed in this annual celebration, bringing joy, happiness, and blessings to all who take part in it.

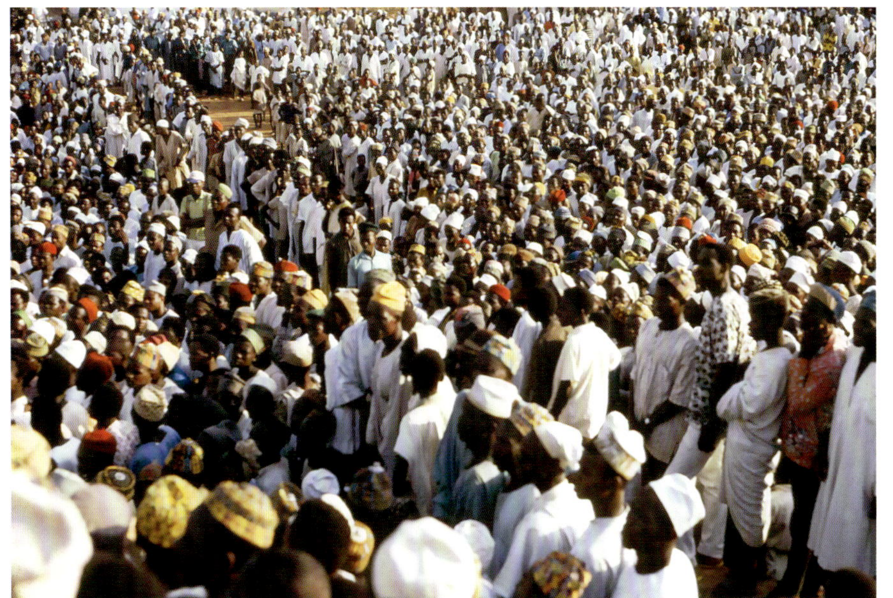

3.22
By 7:00 a.m., an immense crowd of men had gathered in Okene marketplace to listen to the final performance of Ovasaraki, one of the most popular Ebira masquerades singing at the Ekueci festival, December 1968. Each of his songs was taken up by the audience. Later that afternoon, the festivities marking the end of the period when one year overlaps with the next concluded with performances by Ekuecici. In other communities this was also the final appearance of the Ekuoba chosen for that year.
PHOTOGRAPH BY JOHN PICTON.
REPRODUCED BY PERMISSION OF THE NATIONAL COMMISSION FOR MUSEUMS AND MONUMENTS, NIGERIA.

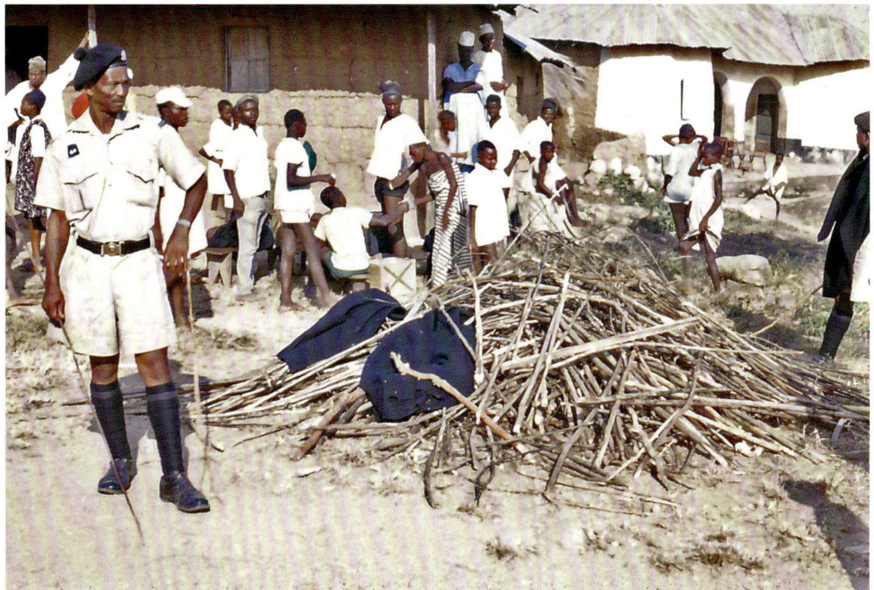

3.23
Early in the morning, a local policeman stands near a pile of sticks confiscated from gangs of young men supporting the most popular masquerades at the night festival of Ekueci in Kuroko, Adavi District, November 1966.
PHOTOGRAPH BY JOHN PICTON.
REPRODUCED BY PERMISSION OF THE NATIONAL COMMISSION FOR MUSEUMS AND MONUMENTS, NIGERIA.

B. EBIRA MASQUERADE AND ITS HISTORIES—JOHN PICTON

Through the cycle of festivals, masquerade imparted a sense of being Ebira that was unifying but also distinctive in regard to different districts and lineages, as well as surrounding peoples (fig. 3.22). It entailed collaboration by lineage elders in any given location, thereby reiterating their authority; it presupposed and reenacted male difference from and dependence upon women in domestic, economic, and ritual domains; it provided public performances that entertained even as they replayed values taken for granted; it enabled the healing of affliction, most especially the barrenness of women; it presupposed the authority of deceased elders, the ancestors; and it proved itself capable of incorporating, and thereby interpreting and domesticating, the novelties of colonial and postcolonial change.

Masquerade also allowed for the release of pent-up male energies, with inter-masquerade rivalries based on lineage and/or political party identities. These sometimes provoked a measure of violence, and this had been accepted as part of the political and aesthetic context of performance, but only within the still relatively small-scale environment of the village and within the control provided by the negative sanctions available to the elders.

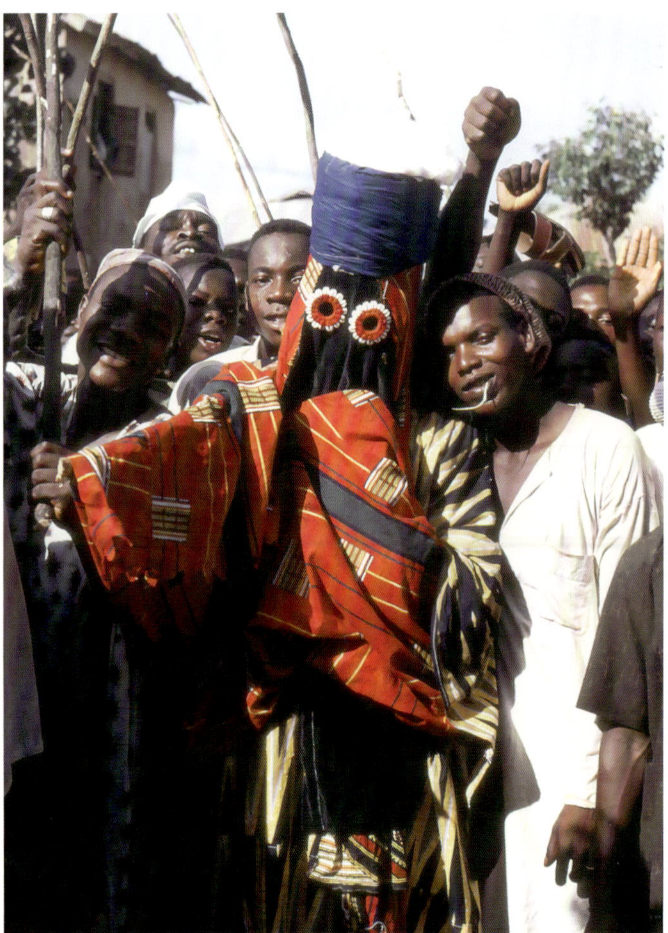

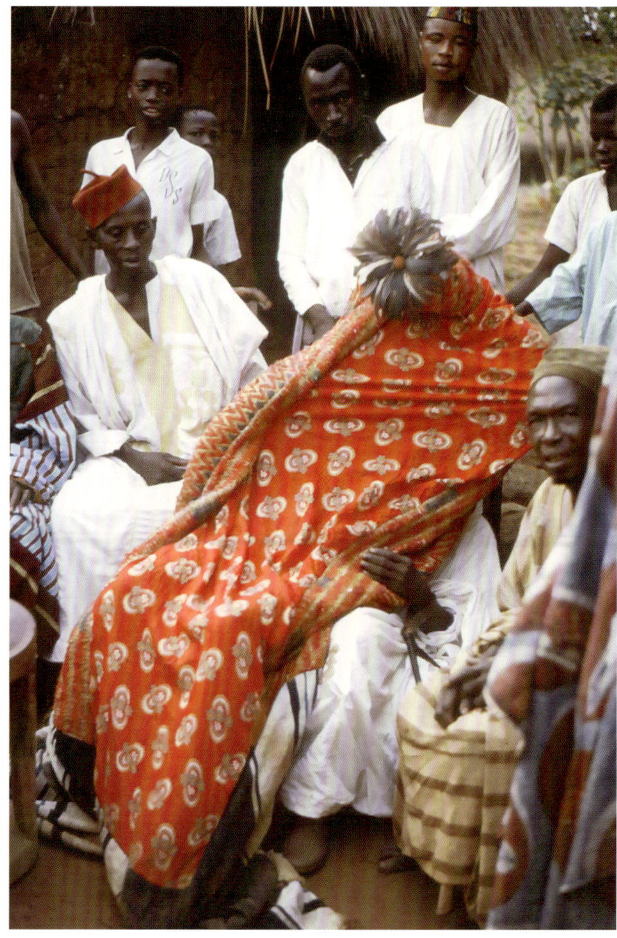

Interlineage rivalry actually entailed recognition of the necessity for the collaboration among lineages. Modern political party rivalries, however, ultimately led
to disputes incapable of resolution. In Okene through the 1970s and 1980s, episodes
of violence at the major feasts escalated to such a degree that they could no longer be
controlled through the authority of lineage elders and the ritual sanctions at their disposal. Rival, sometimes armed, gangs frequently took to the streets under the pretext
of supporting popular masked performances (fig. 3.23). Proscription was inevitable.
Too many people had been killed, and by the late 1980s, in the interests of public order
and safety, the police had little choice but to insist upon it.[20]

To that extent, the process of "handing on" that constitutes tradition and at the
same time enables, as in all traditions, a particular context of change and development, had failed. So too had the structural-functional model, which continued to rule
my imagination as I began my Ebira research (see below): in a self-regulating coherent system, things were not supposed to break down! Nevertheless, there had been
plentiful evidence of ongoing change, past as well as present: the use of a wide range
of textiles in costuming (figs. 3.24–3.26), as well as masks from all over Nigeria for
the Ekuecici, the servant class of masquerade; the creation of these masquerade forms
independent of the re-embodied ancestors, which according to my interpretation gave
them a place and a purpose; the adoption of mask names that incorporated aspects of
local change or novelty; the addition of topical subject matter to stories and songs;
the possibility that night-singing performances might be an early twentieth-century
innovation within Ebira tradition; the decline, and in some districts disappearance of,
some masquerade forms, especially those more concerned with ancestral ritual, and the
adaptations in performance to take account thereof; the increased popularity of other
forms, especially the Ekuecici and the night singers, which encouraged a competitive
individuality in performance (figs. 3.27, 3.28); the manner in which that competitive

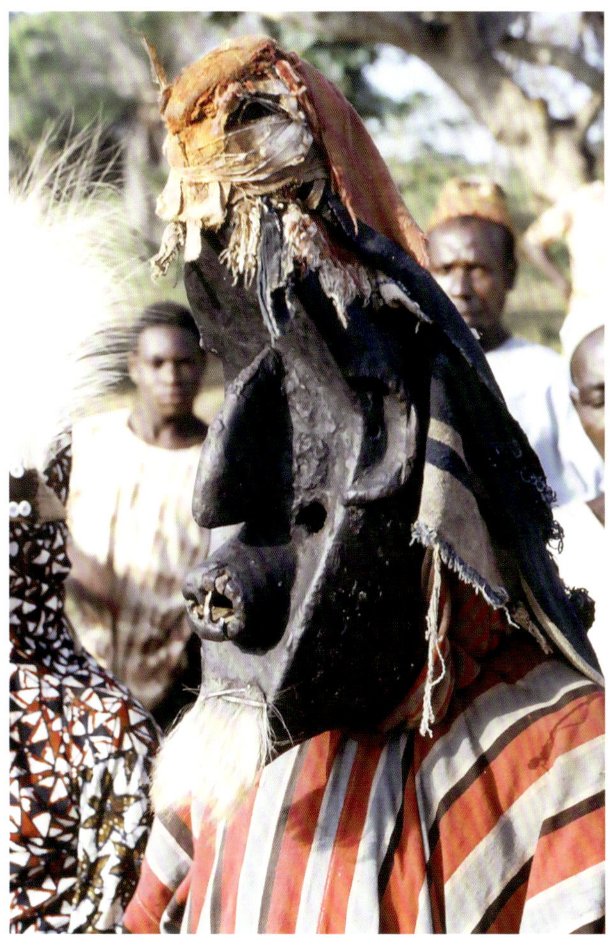

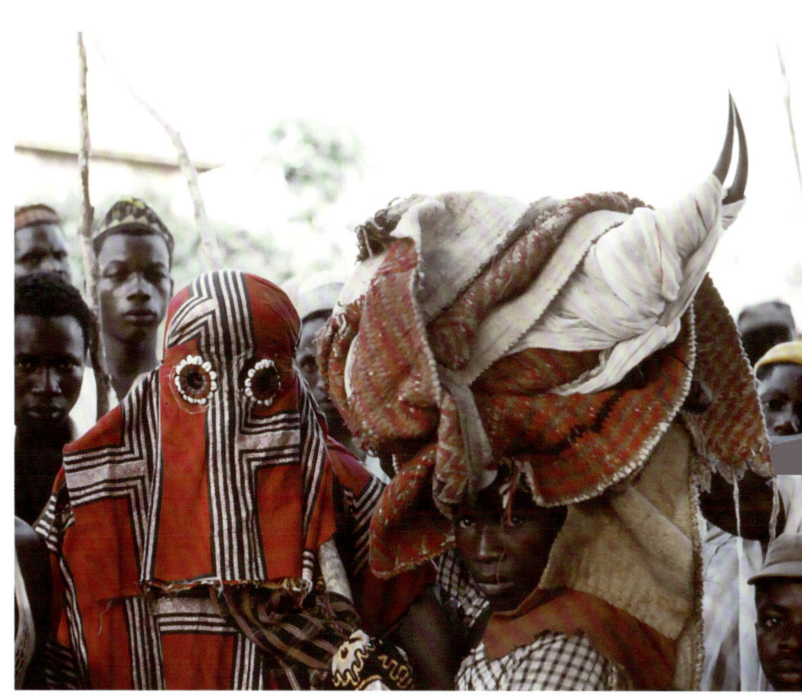

3.26

This mask, carved in the eastern Ebira form typical of Eganyi District by an unknown, early twentieth-century sculptor, was photographed at Adogu, Ajaokuta District, an Igala village on the west bank of the Niger three hours by canoe south of Ajaokuta. Magical medicines have been placed at the top, indigo and white shroud cloth hangs from the back of the mask, and locally woven cloth using machine-spun cotton, probably Ebira, has been used for the tunic. Masks of this form are also found in Edo-speaking villages to the south. The entire ensemble demonstrates the impossibility of ethnic certainties throughout the confluence region. The significance of the mask in an Igala ritual context is not known.

PHOTOGRAPH BY JOHN PICTON, NOVEMBER 1968.

REPRODUCED BY PERMISSION OF THE NATIONAL COMMISSION FOR MUSEUMS AND MONUMENTS, NIGERIA.

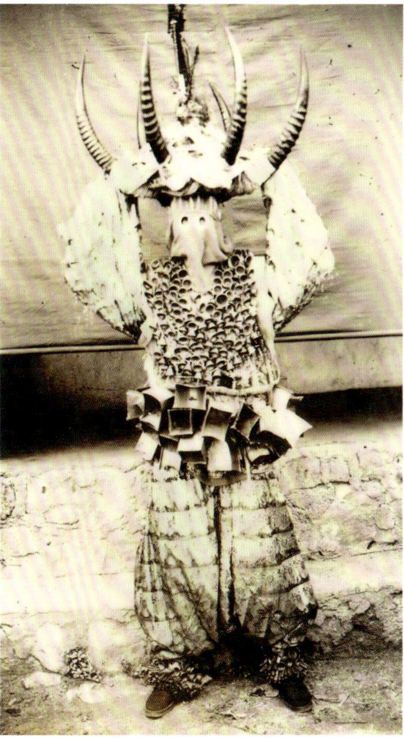

3.27

In order to enhance the vigorous individuality of his performance, this masked performer replaced the heavy wooden mask with a hood sewn of factory-printed cotton cloth. The mask itself, wrapped in Abinu brocaded cloth hangings, was carried by a young assistant.

PHOTOGRAPH BY JOHN PICTON, ECANE, IHIMA DISTRICT, APRIL 1967.

REPRODUCED BY PERMISSION OF THE NATIONAL COMMISSION FOR MUSEUMS AND MONUMENTS, NIGERIA.

3.28

This tinted photograph of Avereho, a popular performer at one of the night festivals in Okene, was commissioned by the masquerader himself, circa 1960, from an unknown photographer and given to John Picton. The costume was typical of night masqueraders at that time: shiny clothing, bells at the chest, waist, and ankles. The cloth hood, however, is worn only for the photograph so that women will not recognize the performer. The horned dish he holds on his head would be carried by one of his assistants: it is a magical medicine intended to enhance performance and to restrain his enemies and rivals.

nature became adapted, whether deliberately or coincidentally, to local party political identities, sometimes reinforcing, sometimes transgressing lineage identities.

In retrospect (at last taking note of the criticisms of structural-functionalism by my teachers a decade before), it became possible to see the cycle of festivals as a developing process, a series of events, each event necessarily with its history, whether "real time" or mythic, and to see that what I had perceived as an integrated series of events was merely the forms as they had evolved within a given social milieu and continued to evolve during the period of my research (1965–1990). The use of African-print cloth for costuming in place of burial shroud cloth or a polished ebony mask in place of a rough-hewn example made locally was no longer a seemingly regrettable departure from tradition, it *was* the tradition.

Another kind of history was entailed in points of likeness and difference between the masquerades of Ebira and other communities. There are traces of all this in terminology, in the ritual point of contact between the domains of living and dead, in the sewing of the Ekuoba (the re-embodied elder), in the structure of its costume, in the manner of its appearance, and in the status of two birds, the violet plantain eater and the standard-winged nightjar.

In regard to terminology, I was fortunate that as my Ebira research developed I had the benefit of a comparative context provided by discussions with John Boston and Robert Armstrong, both members of the academic faculty of Ibadan University in the 1960s, a context reinforced in the 1970s by Sidney Kasfir's Idoma research. The comparative terminology, admittedly incomplete, of death and masquerade is especially revealing:

	TO DIE	CORPSE	MASQUERADE
IDOMA	*kwu*	*okwu*	*ekwu*
EBIRA	*su*	*oku*	*eku*
YORUBA	*ku*	*oku*	*egun*

I think the tonal patterns of these words match each other (and if they do not, the comparison is obviously faulty); and although I do not know the Igala terms (apart from the generic term *egwu*, though there were other points of likeness), even this brief comparison suggests that for the region and peoples covered by these three languages there is the kind of "common ground" that suggests a historical relationship in regard to at least some aspects of the connection between death and masked performance with its origin located in the Middle Benue area. Obviously, the Ebira verb for "to die" bears no relationship to the corpse/masquerade terminology, and the conceptual relationship between the two categories is made primarily through the fact that cloth-masked performers dress in burial cloth (see Picton 2009).

As to the point of contact between living and dead, in every Ebira community (or a group of related communities), somewhere at the conceptual margin between "home" and "farm" (see Picton 1989), there was a place called *ireba*—perhaps a rock shelter or a tree—with a heap of stones marking the site. This is where a deceased elder, already chosen by divination and re-embodied in the person of his performer reestablished contact with the world of the dead (Eku) and thereby initiated the annual cycle of festivals. The stones were said to cover a place at which the performer, not dressed in costume, would hear and answer the voice of the dead within the earth. It was perhaps the most hallowed place in an Ebira community, but it was not enclosed in any way. Rather, the "path to *ireba*" was known to the community and avoided by all women and by those men who had no business going there. In eastern Ebira districts, the *ireba* was also known as *okura*, which is also the Igala word for this location, *okula* (Ebira lacks the letter "l"). In confluence Yoruba districts *okura/okula* was also the term used for this location, though in my experience it was an enclosed area and to that extent unlike its Ebira equivalent.

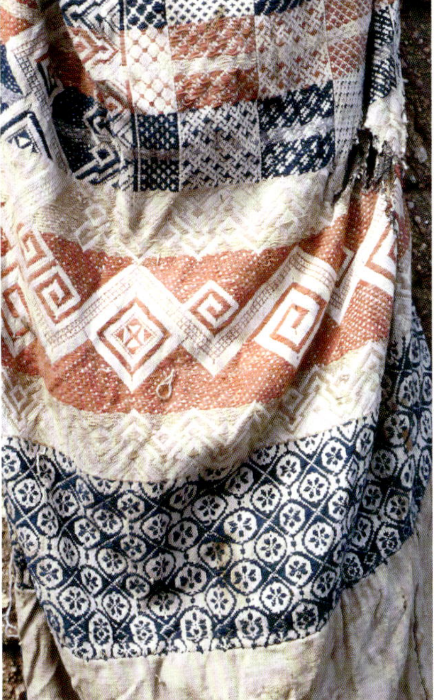

3.29

This is a detail of the cloth used for Izigagu (see fig. 3.30). Any suggestions as to the date and origin of this cloth would be gladly received.

PHOTOGRAPH BY JOHN PICTON, MAY 1967.
REPRODUCED BY PERMISSION OF THE NATIONAL COMMISSION FOR MUSEUMS AND MONUMENTS, NIGERIA.

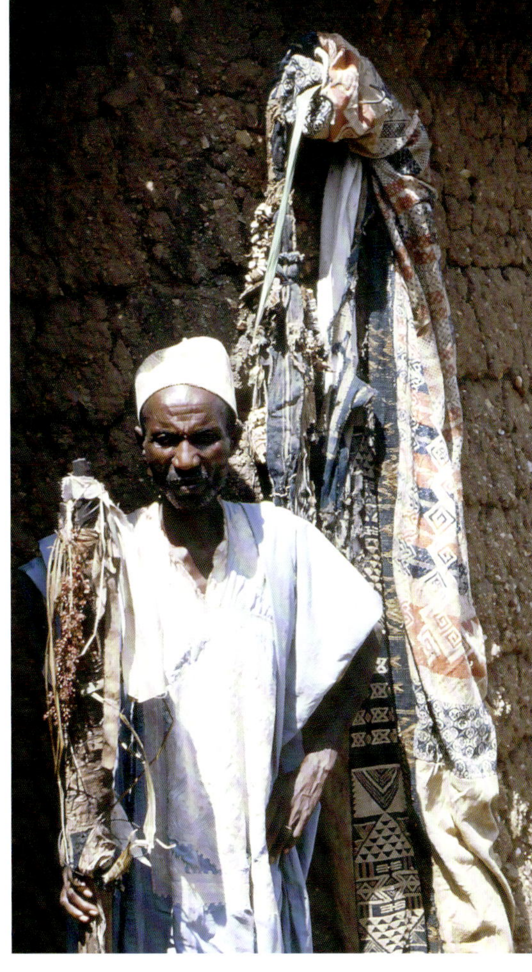

3.30

Hanging on the wall of a house is Izigagu, the Ekuoba that re-embodied the deceased elder who had introduced masquerade performance to Kuroko, Adavi District, possibly in the mid-nineteenth century. To the left of the Izigagu is the elder's grandson Belo Ataa who was also the Ohi'reba (master of the *ireba*), the official charged with regulating all aspects of masked performance in Kuroko.

PHOTOGRAPH BY JOHN PICTON, MAY 1967.
REPRODUCED BY PERMISSION OF THE NATIONAL COMMISSION FOR MUSEUMS AND MONUMENTS, NIGERIA.

The Ebira word for the person who sewed the cloths together to make the costume for Ekuoba, was *ovopa*. This term had no etymological significance within the Ebira language, whereas its likeness to *abakpa* (a component of the word "Abakpariga,"[21] the Hausa-related Abakwariga who were the artisans within the Jukun-speaking area) is obvious: in the translation of foreign words into Ebira phonology, "b" always becomes a bilabial fricative "v"; while the "kp" becomes "p." The Ebira term *ovopa* is clearly of Middle Benue derivation.

The costume of the re-embodied elder was a simple tube sewn of two kinds of cloth, one being the more costly red, brocaded cloth woven in Abinu (also Bunu; see Renne 1995, ch. 6). The performer would put his left arm through the tube, and, holding it bunched together at the top, where the relics from the deceased were sewn, he used his right hand to pull the red cap of an elder over it (see fig. 3.4), then thrusting an iron poker through the cap and bunched-up cloth to hold it all together. (Red caps were also worn by some Igala Egwu Afia: see Boston 1968, pl. 6). By standing up and lifting up his left arm, the costume would slip down over his body leaving his right hand free inside the costume to manipulate a kazoo and thereby disguise his voice. The costume would thus be held by the performer's left arm and rested upon his head, though it could be raised up as he danced. In this it could be seen as a "primitive" version of the single left arm of the Idoma version of this masquerade (see, for example, fig. 3.3). On the other hand, in eastern Ebira, as in confluence Yoruba and Igala, the cloth appeared to be tied around a short stick, as also seen in the Jukun costume in the Pitt Rivers Museum, Oxford, made from Abakpariga resist-dyed cloth. If the Ebira form can be considered a "primitive" survival elaborated upon in Idoma, is it also possible to argue, on the basis of Constanze Weise's research (see below) that the short-stick variant might be the "primitive" basis for the more elaborate middle Niger development of the Ndako Gboya? Or should it be argued the other way around, that the more complex forms are the older, the very complexity as evidence of the longer time needed for their development?

As to the cloth used in Ebira, I was shown only one Ekuoba that was not made of Abinu burial cloth. This was the costume for Izigagu, the re-embodiment of the lineage elder in Kuroko village who had brought masquerade there, and established the *ireba* (figs. 3.29, 3.30). There may well have been others, but the circumstances of their appearance were so rare and ritually circumscribed that I did not see them.

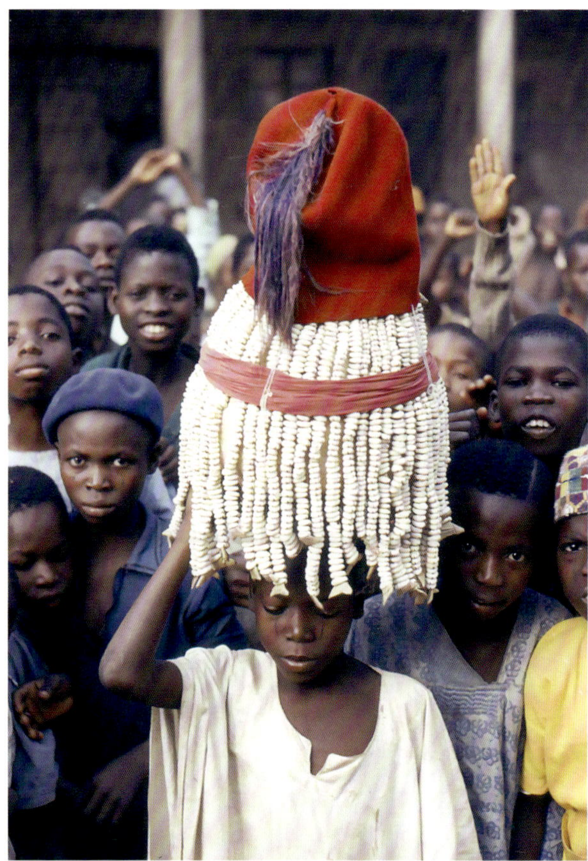

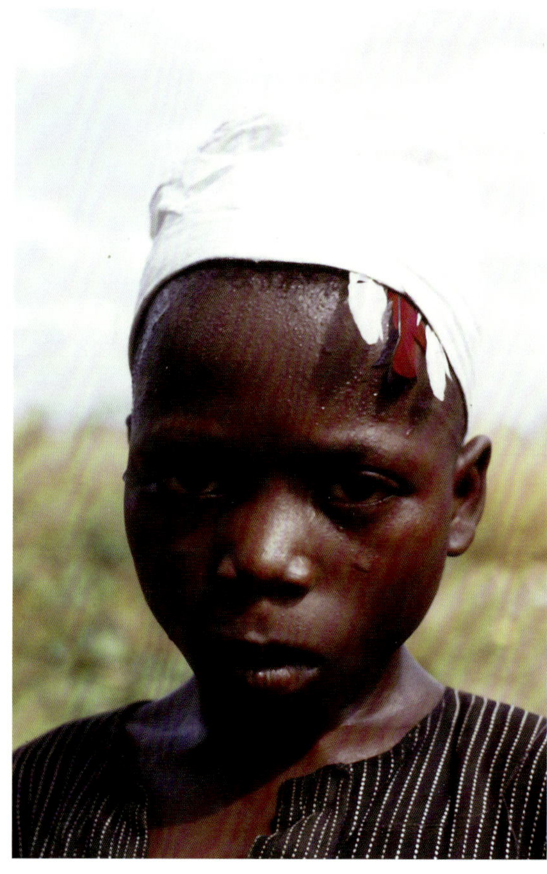

3.31

Eny'ohu (things of the market) is a display piece put together for a procession commemorating a wealthy and powerful woman. It is made up of a wide calabash plate bearing a woman's stool, over which are draped cowrie shells, signifying the wealth that comes from trading, and an elder's red cap, red being the color associated with achievement. This particular example commemorated the mother of Sule Otu, a popular Okene singer (but not in masquerade).

PHOTOGRAPH BY JOHN PICTON, DECEMBER 1969, OKENE.

REPRODUCED BY PERMISSION OF THE NATIONAL COMMISSION FOR MUSEUMS AND MONUMENTS, NIGERIA.

3.32

This boy, the reincarnation of a deceased ancestor, was about to meet that ancestor, re-embodied as the Ekuoba chosen to perform during the period when one year overlaps with the next. The red (violet plantain eater) and white (chicken) feathers in the boy's cap mark his status.

PHOTOGRAPH BY JOHN PICTON, OZIOKUTU VILLAGE, EIKA DISTRICT, DECEMBER 1968.

REPRODUCED BY PERMISSION OF THE NATIONAL COMMISSION FOR MUSEUMS AND MONUMENTS, NIGERIA.

Izigagu, however, was a richly patterned cloth, brocaded (or possibly embroidered) in red and blue on a white ground, perhaps of Scandinavian origin. Nevertheless, the hospital-blanket red of the Abinu textiles fitted well with Ebira ideas of red as a color denoting achievement and therein providing for its ritual value (fig. 3.31), as also seen in other contexts: the camwood smeared on the body of a woman following the successful delivery of a child; the felt hats worn by elders, titled men, and Ekuoba; the red flowers of certain trees and grasses in late September/early October, thereby a sign of the season in which "two years meet" (see below); and wing feathers of *oroko*, the violet plantain eater, worn (together with nightjar feathers, see below) by lineage titled men. *Oroko* was sometimes called the "chief of birds," but this seemed to me to be a feeding back on to the bird of ideas about redness, ritual, and achievement, rather than anything coming from poetry or myth associated with the bird itself. To the west and south of Ebira, the bright red tail feathers of the African gray parrot had ritual value (e.g., see Gore 2007, ch. 7) but not in Ebira, where the slightly purplish, but no less bright, wing feathers of the violet plantain eater were worn, sometimes juxtaposed with white feathers (fig. 3.32), by titled men and others in particular ritual circumstances (e.g., Picton 2009, 310). Elisha Renne (1995, 220–21, n. 8) cites various possibilities for procuring red yarn prior to the ready availability of colonial hospital blankets, but the rarity of a suitable yarn may well have made the Abinu cloths too expensive for regular Ebira consumption. Thus it would only have been in the hospital-blanket era that their utility in confirming Ebira notions of redness could be capitalized upon. For the moment, however, this remains entirely speculative; but the evidence, such as it is, of Izigagu and the equivalent masquerades east of the lower Niger and along the Benue Valley region (where I have no evidence for the use of Abinu textiles) could suggest that a greater variety of textiles had once been used in making Ekuoba.

In Ebira the re-embodied elder only appeared in costume on three occasions. The first was in the rites of the period "when two years meet," from the new moon of late September/early October to the new moon of late November/early December. The

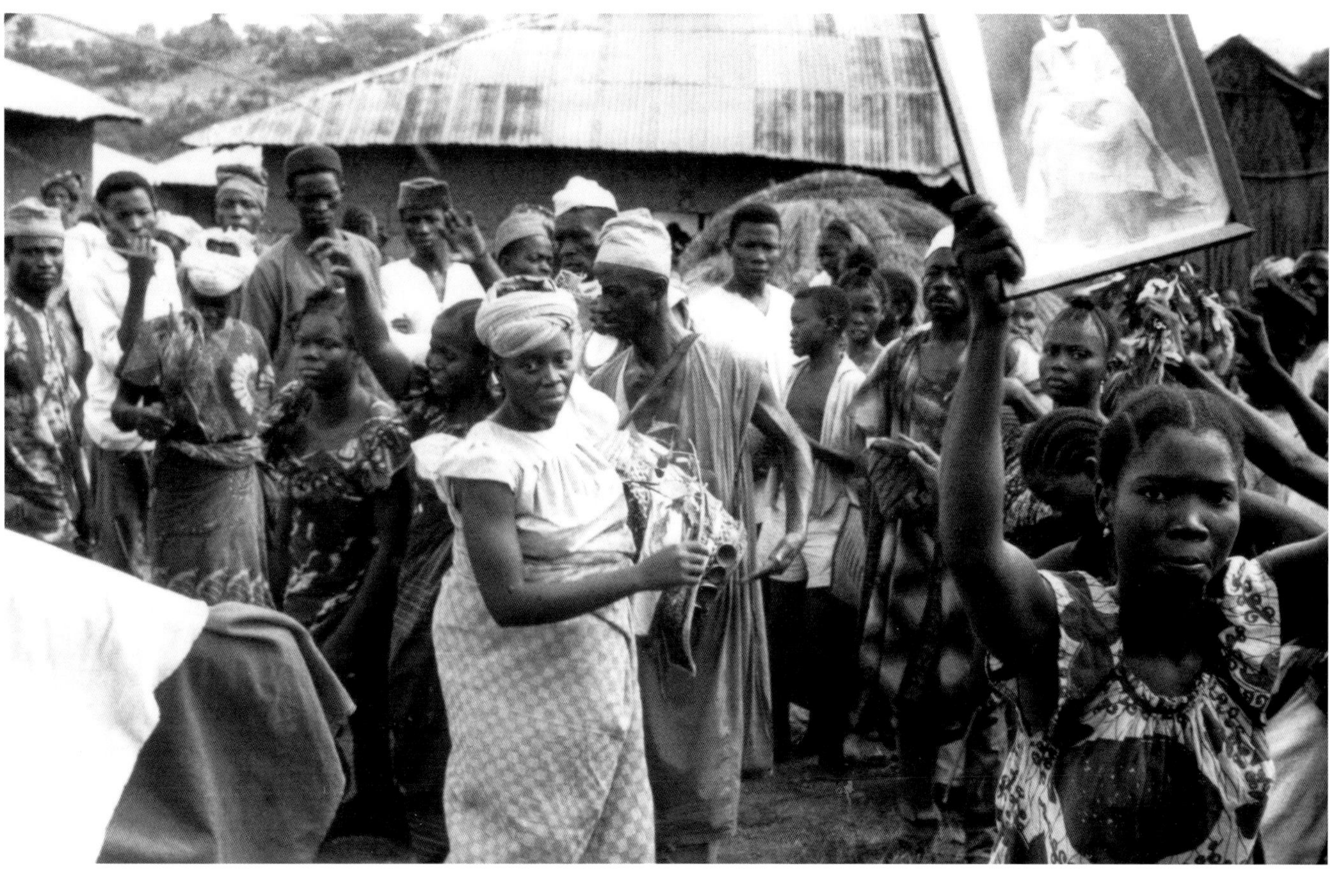

3.33
A daughter dances with a photograph of her deceased father during the procession immediately before the burial of his corpse.
PHOTOGRAPH BY JOHN PICTON, 1968.
REPRODUCED BY PERMISSION OF THE NATIONAL COMMISSION FOR MUSEUMS AND MONUMENTS, NIGERIA.

second was at the rites initiating a new lineage titled man. The would-be title-holder would disappear into seclusion at a secret location, to be found and led through his installation by the Ekuoba re-embodying the deceased elder selected via divination for this purpose. There had formerly been a third occasion for the appearance of Ekuoba, at a rite regarded as parallel to the installation of a titled man, when an existing Ekuoba led a newly made Ekuoba through its rites of entry into the social community of the living. The fact that the re-embodied elders appeared only one at a time—and two at a time only in the latter case—is perhaps the most obvious difference in practice between Ebira on the one hand, and Igala, Idoma, and Okpella, on the other.

By the 1960s the Ebira preparation of new Ekuoba had long since been abandoned, though existing costumes continued to be buried with the last surviving son of the deceased, who thus took it into Eku to present his father with the evidence of how well they had celebrated his passing. There was just one exception: the Ekuoba that permitted the re-embodiment of the elder who had initially instituted masquerade and prepared the *ireba* in a given place was preserved, a hallowed presence of considerable negative force, as in the example of Izigagu. Overall, therefore, the Ekuoba costume was a diminishing resource. Because of this, some communities had prepared a generic costume that served to re-embody whomsoever had been selected by divination for this or that event. Other communities had transferred the daytime appearance of Ekuoba to the night, when in an unlit village the performer was effectively hidden by darkness and by those processing around him. Moreover, the funerary role of Ekuoba, in which the deceased revisited his household, had found something of a substitute in the display of photographs of the deceased carried in funerary processions (fig. 3.33; see also Picton 2002).

One last subject of interest in this context is the use of the breeding plumes of the standard-winged nightjar (see fig. 3.4). The nightjar is not a large bird (approximately 27 cm), and the male of the standard-winged species has a pair of long plumes, one on each wing, during the breeding season. Each plume takes the form of a long stem

The Nupe in central Nupeland share with those in the diaspora[25] the use of ancestral[26] masks belonging to a "tall ghost" masquerade genre (figs. 3.34, 3.35), which in the past performed a number of functions in Nupe society (Nadel [1954] 1970, 163–206; 1935c, 423–47; 1937, 91–130; 1949, 177–86; 1942). These included a judicial role, involvement in policing, and the detection of witches. These masquerades are known in central Nupeland as Ndako Gboya,[27] among the Bassa Nge as Egbunu (Habi 2006, 16), and among the Yoruba as Igunnu (Nadel [1954] 1970, 189)[28] Another name for the masquerade is Gunnuko (the great Gunnu), which may have been more commonly used in the nineteenth and early twentieth centuries as it appears in missionary and anthropological accounts of that time period (Crowther and Taylor [1859] 1968, 215). The masquerade is the property of the Nupe king (Etsu) and, as noted, served as an important judicial control mechanism. Hence it was characterized as *kuti'tsu* (*kútí etsu*), or "the ritual force of the king."[29]

Some oral traditions that refer to the foundation of the Nupe Kingdom recount that the Ndako Gboya was one of several magical objects that the founding hero Tsoede (Tsoèdè), who was also the first Nupe king, brought with him to Nupeland in a bronze canoe when he left Idah, the capital of the Igala Kingdom, where his father, the Igala king (Ata), is said to have reigned.[30] Other oral accounts indicate that Tsoede met the Ndako Gboya in Nupeland when he arrived.[31] Today, most Ndako Gboya centers remain firm in the belief that Tsoede brought the masquerades with him, along with an iron chain and iron fetters. Upon his arrival in Nupeland, he distributed pieces of this magical chain among priests and chiefs, entering into a politico-religious contract with them and bestowing upon them judicial and executive power in the kingdom.[32] The Egbunu masquerade of the Bassa Nge has retained judicial and "witch hunting" functions. Ndako Gboya of central Nupeland has, however, lost these functions in public, although the masquerade still has the potential to exercise performative authority.[33] Increasing Islamization and decreasing religious authority of the Ndako Gboya cult centers,[34] since the prohibition of the cult by the British colonial administration in 1921, have led to a loss of the masquerade's legitimacy as a public "witch-finding" institution in central Nupeland (Nadel 1935c, 442).[35] As a consequence, Ndako Gboya masquerade performances have become increasingly secularized and today tend to be associated with cultural displays on stage, radio, and television. The great masks of Kusogi, for example, are invited to perform regularly for the Nupe king of Bida and during the celebrations of the major Islamic festivals Id al-Fitr and Id al–Kabir. In addition, they are often invited to "greet" important guests and visitors of the Emir of Bida (Kohnert 2007, 68).

Because of their spectacular appearance and performance (fig. 3.36), the Ndako Gboya masquerades have also become well-known tourist attractions beyond Nupeland. The masquerade figures can move in all directions, roll, and change height suddenly and dramatically, shooting up to fifteen feet and then dropping to appear almost flat. An internal, collapsible bamboo frame supporting a long tube of cloth allows the mask carrier to manipulate the movement of the structure with a stick, elongating and compacting the cylindrical form, as well as causing it to sway back and forth. Though the design of the form may have remained constant, the cloth used for the masquerade costumes has not, reflecting clearly the dynamics of change in the Nupe ritual landscape. In the past, the Nupe used strip-woven burial cloth, white in color and fringed, to create these masquerades, which collectively represent the departed ancestors (Perani and Wolff 1999, 42). The masquerade costumes were regarded as sacred, epitomizing a spirit that had to be invoked (Nadel [1954] 1970, 198). Today, most of the masquerade figures that are performed in public are made from brightly colored factory cloth. The material transformation of the masquerade is just one consequence of its secularization. Performance and public reaction appear to be different as well. Certainly, the joyful and playful dance of these beautiful forms in their colorful fringed fabrics (fig. 3.37) seems

3.34

Two Ndako Gboya masquerades tower above villagers. The masquerades are dressed in predominantly white, handwoven shroud cloth. The attendant at the right keeps the audience at a safe distance from the masqueraders, whose power could negatively affect those who come too close.

Photograph by Leo Frobenius, Mokwa, 1911. Copyright Frobenius-Institut, Frankfurt am Main, EBA-B 00654-C.

3.35

Assembled cult members observe and dance with the Ndako Gboya masquerade.

Photograph by Leo Frobenius, Mokwa 1911. Copyright Frobenius-Institut, Frankfurt am Main, KBA 10730-A.

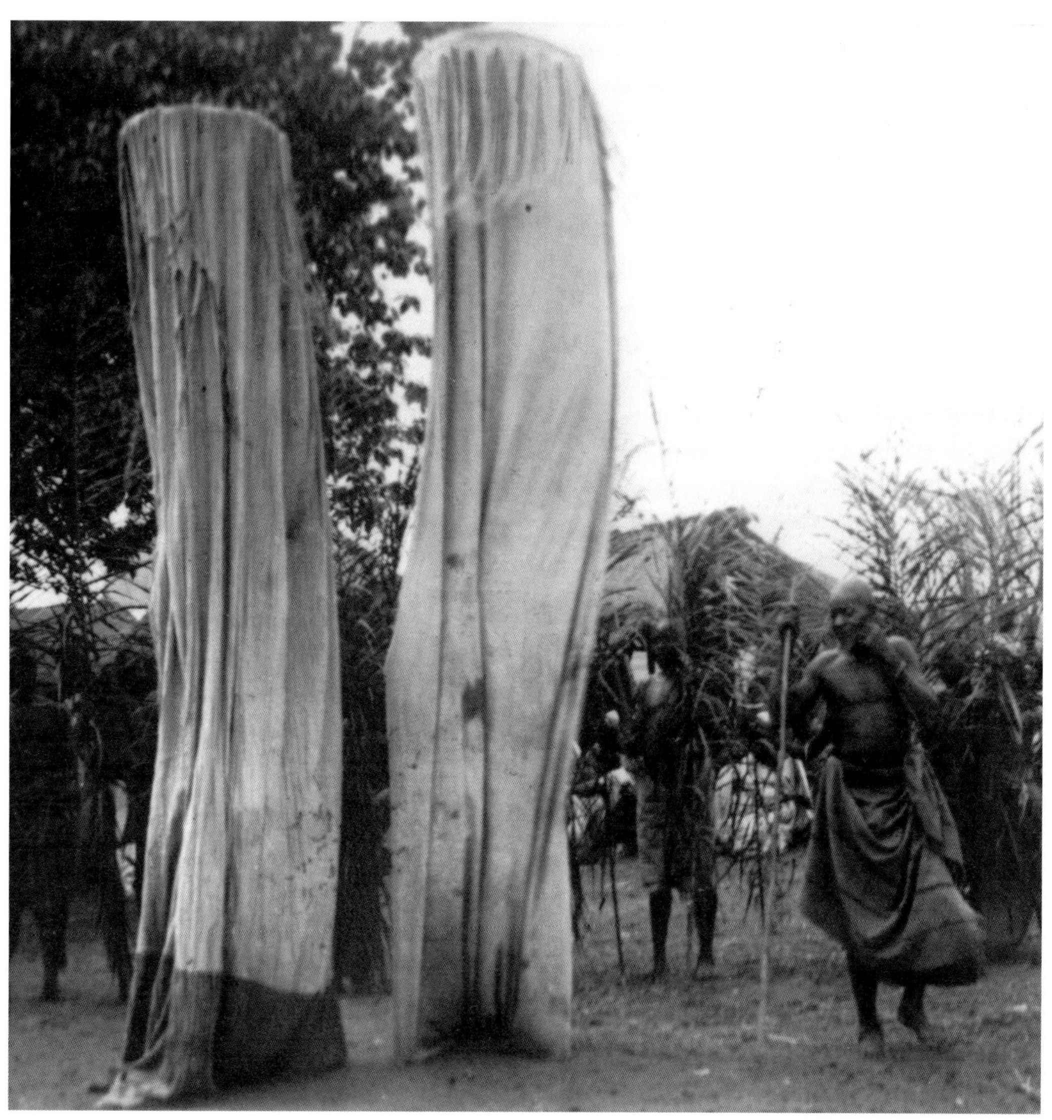

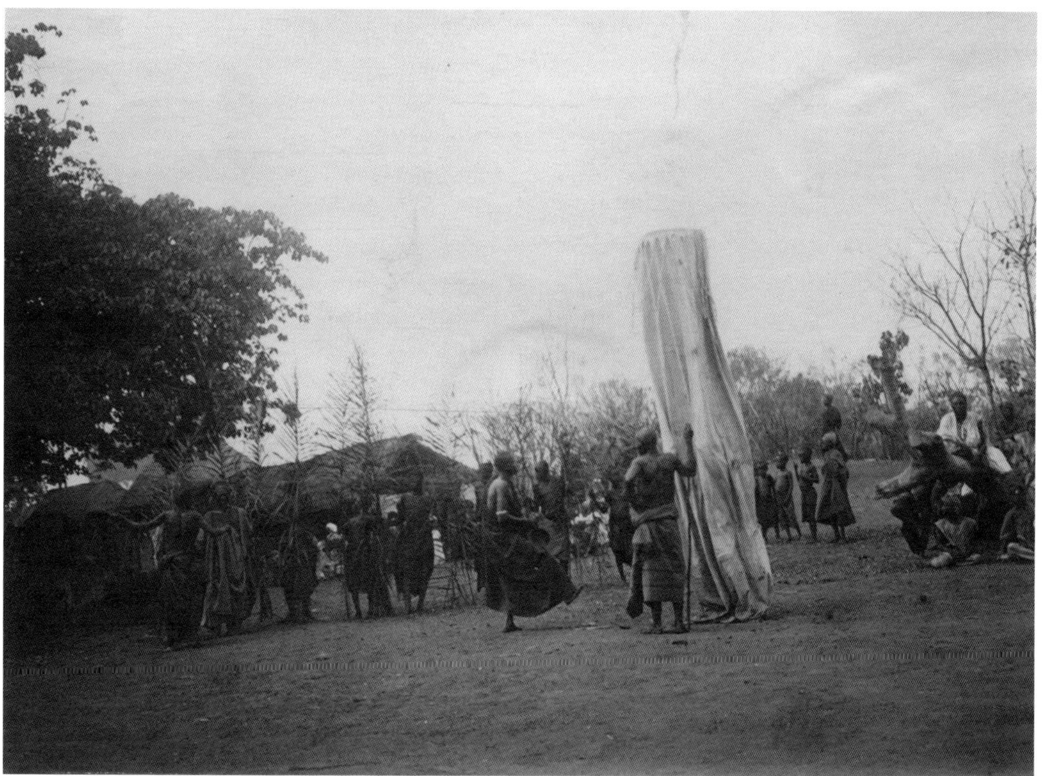

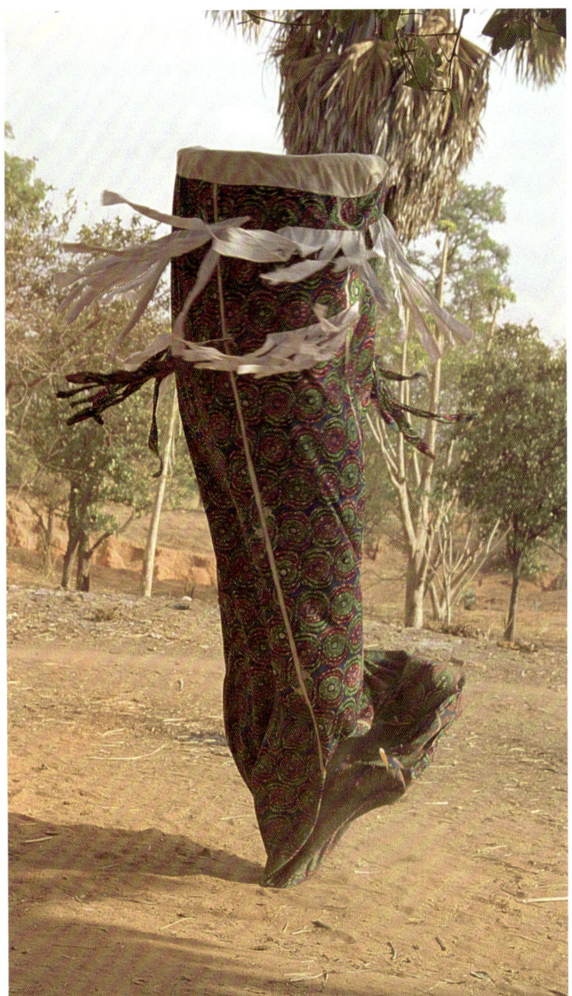

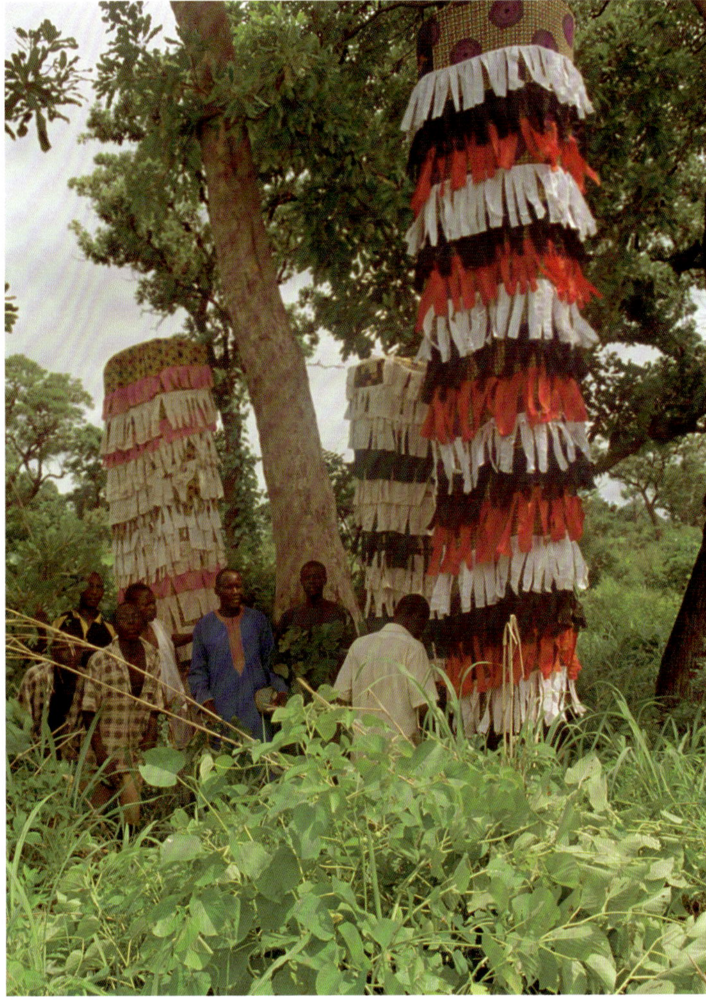

3.36

This Ndako Gboya is clothed in colorful factory-made fabric. The masquerader, a newly initiated boy, leaps while performing for the first time. Only initiated association members can perform the masquerade. This boy was the son of the late head of the Ndako Gboya association in Kusogi.

PHOTOGRAPH BY CONSTANZE WEISE, KUSOGI, 2000.

3.37

These Ndako Gboya masquerades are unusual for their bright colors and many layers of fringe. They emerge from the woods in the company of members of the local Ndako Gboya association.

PHOTOGRAPH BY CONSTANZE WEISE, 2000.

to have little in common with the redoubtable masquerades described at the end of the nineteenth and the beginning of the twentieth century by elderly eyewitnesses from Nupeland as well as missionaries and anthropologists.

In 1859 Samuel Crowther and John Christopher Taylor, two CMS (Church Missionary Society) representatives, described the Ndako Gboya (referred to in their account as Gunnuko), encountered in the Raba-Mokwa region, as dancing from village to village and receiving cowries by exercising "some tyrannical influence over the people during the time of their appearance" (Crowther and Taylor [1859] 1968, 215). Missionaries and British colonial administrators alike condemned Nupe traditional religious practices as pagan and representations of an evil that had to be destroyed.[36] The German anthropologist, Leo Frobenius, who visited Nupeland during his fourth research expedition to Nigeria and Cameroon in 1910–1912, was told that missionaries from the CMS station at Mokwa (established in 1906) had burned the Ndako Gboya masks (Frobenius 1912, 1: 39). Nonetheless, in 1911 Frobenius was able to locate and photograph some masquerades at Mokwa and became the first anthropologist to do so (see figs. 3.34, 3.35). Among Frobenius's published collections of Nupe myths, legends, proverbs, and tales are some that refer to the Ndako Gboya as well as to the Gunnu ritual (Frobenius 1924; 1925).[37] The painter Carl Arriens who accompanied the Frobenius expedition made drawings of some of the masquerades.

The most profound, and as yet unsurpassed, anthropological work on the Nupe, however, was carried out by Siegfried Nadel in 1934 and 1935–1936 (fig. 3.38). Nadel, an Austrian-born British anthropologist, studied at the London School of Economics under Bronislaw Malinowski. Nadel described Ndako Gboya as an "anti-witchcraft cult" and a secret society (Nadel 1935c, 435).[38] He recounted a legend according to

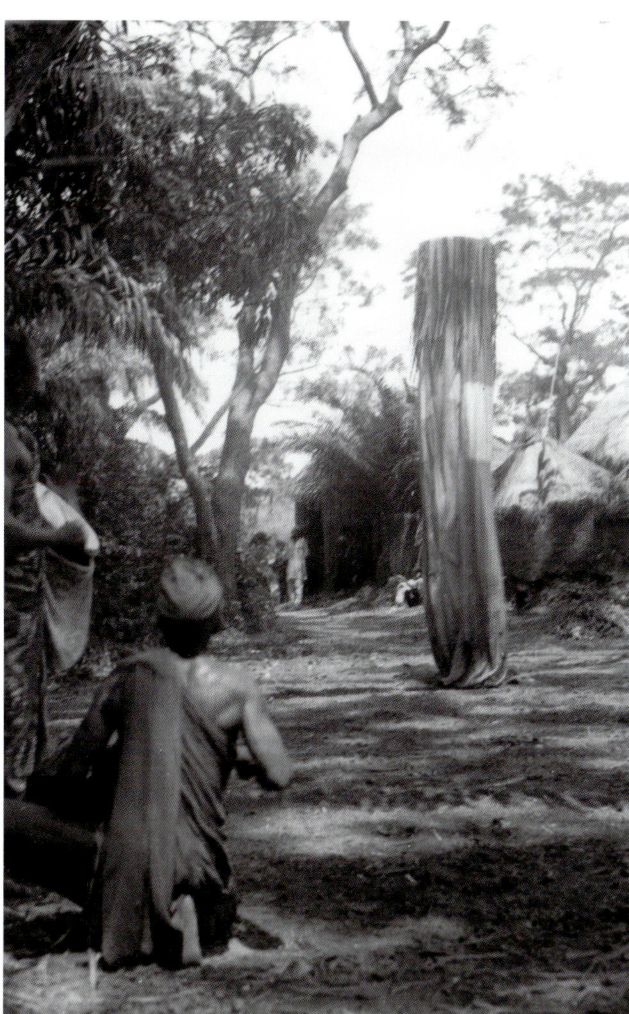

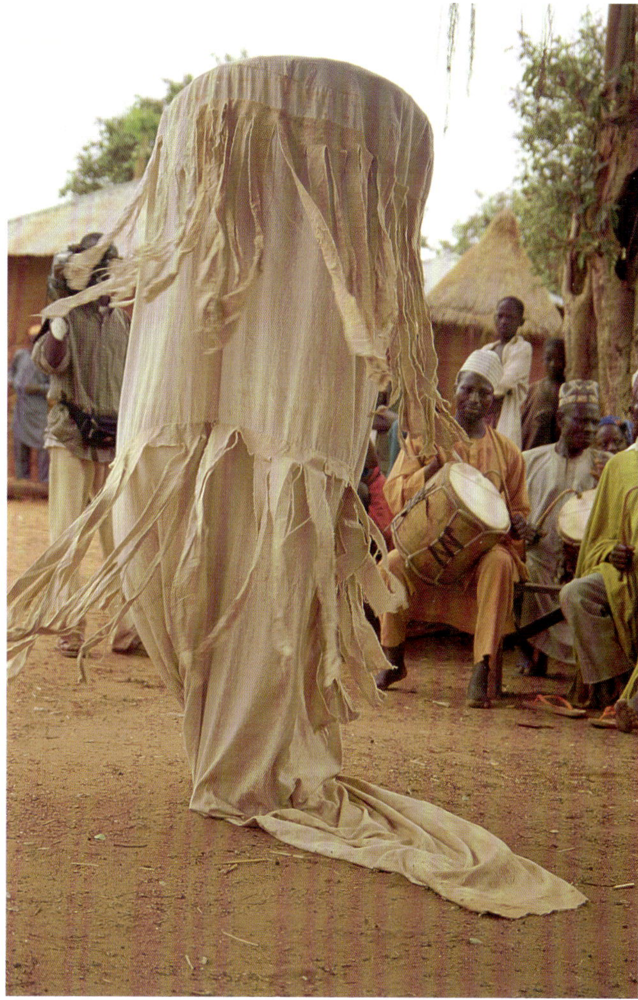

which the masquerades became the "anti-witchcraft" instrument of the kings. In this account a Nupe king had been rendered powerless by his mother. He consulted a diviner, who, according to Nadel,

> instructed the king to procure ten lengths of cloth. The diviner then sewed the pieces together, in the form of a tall, hollow tube, and used a "secret" on it. The cloth rose up, flew through the air, and dropped upon the king's mother, covering her. It carried her up into the sky, and she was never seen again. From this day on the "secret" remained a *kuti* ([*kútí*] ritual, magic) of the kings. Whenever a woman is guilty of witchcraft, the king will employ the *kuti*, which is *ndako gboya*.

The Ndako Gboya "anti-witchcraft" association still exists today in Nupeland, generally in smaller villages. The cult centers, however, record decreasing membership due to the loss of the masquerade's public function as an institution for finding witches; increasing Islamization; the migration of the youth to urban centers; and the high cost of initiation.[39] Membership in the society requires initiation, as does the actual dancing of the masquerade.[40] Nadel learned that the dancer of the masquerades (in Nupe society the dancing of masquerades is the exclusive province of men) must drink and wash himself with *cigbe* ([*cigbè*] an "anti-witchcraft" medicine) before entering the masquerade. He must sacrifice beer and fowl over the *cigbe* shrine and the cloth mask (Nadel [1954] 1970, 190). The medicine would make him "like a witch." Nadel observed that "once the performer is inside the mask he is inseparable from the thing he 'represents,' he is *ndako gboya*" (fig. 3.39). Nadel further relates that "any person

3.38
The man in the foreground keeps an appropriate distance from a masquerade and pays reverence to it by kneeling. Given its height, the mask is thought to have the ability to observe all.
PHOTOGRAPH BY SIEGFRIED NADEL, SHEBE.
COPYRIGHT ARCHIVES DIVISION OF THE LONDON SCHOOL OF ECONOMICS AND POLITICAL SCIENCE, NADEL/16/4/193.

3.39
This masquerade is clothed in white factory-made cloth that has been given a double layer of fringe. The extra fabric "train" trailing on the ground will be taken up when the masquerade is extended to its full height by means of an inner framework. Drummers in the background accompany the masquerade during its appearance.
PHOTOGRAPH BY CONSTANZE WEISE, KUSOGI, 2000.

who has not been initiated into the *ndako gboya* society or has omitted the preparatory rites would be killed by the mask as soon as he entered it" (Nadel [1954] 1970, 191). Although the majority of the Ndako Gboya cult members are initiated men, both noninitiated men and women also participate in the public masquerade performances, notably the drummers and the men who use a cane to direct the masquerade during its dance and who simultaneously keep the crowd away, as well as female singers (the spouses of initiated members) and the Sagi, a woman considered the most powerful "witch" in the village, as well as leader of the women in the cult center. As such a powerful "witch," the Sagi [Sagì], or Lelu [Lelú], possessed secret knowledge that could be used to benefit the community when channeled into an organ of village administration. She was, and still is, perceived as having the power to check and control the subversive activities of other witches (Nadel 1942, 147–49; Constanze Weise, fieldnotes, Gbado, June 29 and 30, 2000). The Sagi thus has a role in the cult, and she dances during public performances opposite the masquerade.

The question of exactly what the Ndako Gboya represents is not easy to answer. Nadel called it a "spirit'" and denied that the masquerade had any ancestral connotation (Nadel [1954] 1970, 190). The priest of the Ndako Gboya lodge with whom he worked in 1935 described the Ndako Gboya to him as a "strong secret" (*àsiri gbóká*) and a "mystical force, capable of being invoked and manipulated by man" (Nadel [1954] 1970, 191). Nadel, however, seems to have overlooked the fact that these masquerades epitomize the governing cosmological law established by the ancestors and the creator god Soko, whose mediators are the Nupe kings and Ndako Gboya priests. Today most scholars agree that the Ndako Gboya masks belong to the genre of ancestral masquerades and represent the ancestors in their collectivity. This is underscored by empirical data. My own field research confirms that these masquerades are ancestral. I witnessed the initiation of the son of the late head of the Ndako Gboya cult in Kusogi in 2000. During this initiation references to the ancestors were constantly made, with special mention of the founding ancestor Tsoede. Furthermore, toward the end of the seven-day initiation period, the initiate has to visit the ancestors in the other world, which is divided into two parts separated by a sacred crossroad. The world of the ancestors is the world of the dead, which men should not enter, but the second part may be entered by the masquerade dancers so they can greet the ancestors, and obtain their approval. On the day of initiations, the young boy had to enter the other world and greet the ancestors at the sacred crossroad. If he had not returned to this world, he would have stayed in the other world and crossed into the land of the dead. It would also have meant the ancestors would not have given the approval to the dancer to represent them. After his return from the other world the young initiate was able to enter the masquerade and dance it. When I asked who the masquerade represented, I was answered with: "It represents the ancestors in their collectivity."[41]

Though the Ndako Gboya masquerades in central Nupeland are no longer associated with mystical force and public policing functions, the Bassa Nge masquerade, Egbunu, has retained these features. According to the Egbunu priest Nomba of Bassaland, Egbunu would appear to warn the public if a "witch" endangered the society and reveal the name of that witch (personal communication, June 28, 2009). The witch would then be tried in a court (*kutímbà*), consisting of the priest, other members of the Egbunu secret society, Egbunu, and the ancestors. The trial would take place at a shrine (also known as *kutimba*) in the forest where the ancestors reside. "Egbunu does not dance," I was told. "Those who dance its dance steps are the Egbunu children," boys organized into age-grades who are guarded by the Egbunu. They are disguised by white- and red-colored dots painted on their bare skin when they perform the dance steps of the Egbunu. Today, the occasion for this would be the so-called Bassa Day, December 26, in Bassaland.

In central Nupeland this performance was linked to the annual Gunnu festival that would be celebrated during the dry season to ask for renewed fertility of the land. During this festival, boys would undergo a rite of passage in the forest. Nadel describes this rite of passage in his seminal essay "Gunnu, a Fertility Cult of the Nupe in Northern Nigeria" (1937). This festival is no longer performed in central Nupeland. We learn from Nadel's description, however, that the festival required that young men dress as women during their initiation ceremony. This ritual transvestism signified that boys admitted to the Gunnu were on the threshold of manhood a point at which they could no longer be confused with girls (Nadel [1954] 1970, 133). One Ndako Gboya masquerade used to appear during the vigil in the bush in order to "warn the youths to obey their elders, and whip offenders" (Nadel [1954] 1970, 189). In this regard Ndako Gboya was called "the policeman of the *gunnu*." The masqueraders would reappear during the public part of the initiation ceremony "to frighten all women, to discourage would-be witches, and to weaken, by their very presence, the evil powers of witchcraft" (Nadel [1954] 1970, 189).[42]

Although the Ndako Gboya centers in central Nupeland no longer perform judicial functions, their priests are still consulted for divination and medicine by the Nupe population. Witchcraft protection still ranks the highest among the many reasons they are consulted. In an incantation recorded in 2000, Maji Dodo, the late head of the Ndako Gboya cult center in Kusogi, invoked this image of the Ndako Gboya centers today:

> By the time we were empowered
> When we were disarming the witches and wizards
> The Etsu [king] gave us the knife
> Which stood like a symbol
> The knife we sharpened
> What the Etsus gave to our forefathers is that
> We have the permission to punish
> Anybody that is wicked
> Any wicked person who is warned or asked to stop but refuses
> People will come and inform us
> ....
> Ndako Gboya masquerade is the lord of witches and wizards
> But now that the situation has come
> Under the control of changes, we have suspended our actions
> In the time of our forefathers we were able to stop the witches and wizards
> That power was with our forefathers
> And it is still with us—today.[43]

D. POWER AND GENDER IN THE HISTORY OF EGUNGUN—JOHN C. WILLIS

Egungun is the name of an Oyo Yoruba masquerade and masking society that honors ancestors and their living descendants. The masquerade is a performance by a masked figure, whom devotees assume to be a man embodying a resurrected ancestor. It is accompanied by drummers, singers, ritual specialists, and a crowd of followers. The Egungun society comprises a council of chiefs, which includes men and a few nominally powerful women. The female chiefs do not enjoy the same privileges as the men, however, and they are generally prohibited from entering the grove or shrine where the men meet to perform their most sacred rituals. Scholars of African history, art history, and anthropology have often described Egungun as a male-centered practice and institution that men use to control women (Johnson 1921, 29–31, 160, 172, 329–30; Bascom 1944, 50–59; Morton-Williams 1954, 1960; Beier 1956, 1964; Adedeji 1969; Drewal and Drewal 1978, 30). The presence of women in existing accounts of the origin of Egungun at Oyo, however, suggests a more complex relationship of gender to Egungun.

The origin of Egungun at Oyo is a matter of speculation, as written evidence on Egungun prior to the nineteenth century is virtually nonexistent (Johnson 1921, 29–31; Law 1995, 209–10; Shields 1997, 249–52, 280–85). Investigators have therefore had to rely on missionary texts, along with ritual performances and oral traditions, to reconstruct this history. Oral traditions exist in the form of historical narratives, praise poems, and songs that have long served as indigenous historical records and are recognized by scholars as such (Vansina 1965, 1985; Barber 1991). Samuel Johnson, a nineteenth-century Yoruba missionary and historian, collected many oral traditions from Oyo's royal court historians and documented them in the form of written narratives. One tradition that Johnson collected attributes the origins of the Egungun masquerade to a (possibly mythological) Alafin (king) of Oyo; another tradition links the creation of the Egungun society to a political alliance between Oyo's rulers and Nupe immigrants (Johnson 1921, 43–44).

The first of the traditions collected by Samuel Johnson attributes the creation of the Egungun masquerade to the Alafin Shango. According to this tradition, Shango wished to legitimize his authority by honoring his father, Oranyan, the former ruler of Oyo, with an elaborate funeral. Shango requested that the remains of his late father be brought from Ile-Ife to Oyo. When he was unable to obtain Oranyan's corpse, Shango developed an alternate plan: he ordered the creation of a masquerade to represent the spirit of his departed father and the construction of a mausoleum, known as the Bara, to house the mask within the palace. Shango's next move is central to the argument of this essay, as he then placed a palace priestess, an old woman known as the Iyamode, and a group of old women, the Baba Bara (fathers in Bara), in charge of performing rituals for this royal ancestral masquerade.[44] It is interesting to note the ambiguous gender role of the Baba Bara. According to Johnson, they are celibate females who live in convent-like conditions and whose sole responsibility is to guard the remains and serve as the mouthpiece of deceased kings. Their title, which as noted above, means "father," suggests that they are regarded as being masculine in gender. This tradition clearly makes a distinction between sex and gender, but the reasons for the distinction and for its omission from the literature on Egungun are obscure.

Devotees of Egungun often refer to the Shango tradition when discussing the origins of Egungun and the relationship of women to its practice and organization.[45] By entrusting a group of women with introducing (or birthing) a new ritual for honoring deceased kings, Shango made women central to his ability to legitimize his status as the successor to Oranyan, the founder of the Oyo Kingdom (Adedeji 1969. 71). He also set a precedent for subsequent generations of his followers to entrust women with important ritual functions and offices in the arena of Egungun.[46]

Shango's mother, who, according to other traditions associated with Shango, was Nupe, should also be considered with respect to the role of women in the early history of Egungun. Although she is absent from the Shango tradition involving the creation of Egungun, she may have been part of her son's inspiration for entrusting women with overseeing the royal masquerade. In a related tradition that is associated with the creation of the Egungun society at Oyo in order to address a particular crisis, the mother of an Alafin inspired important ritual innovations at a moment when new ideas about masquerades were being appropriated. It is in this latter tradition that the Nupe contribution to the emergence of the Egungun society at Oyo is most evident.

Many scholars attribute the origin of Egungun to the adoption by the Oyo of a masking tradition from the Nupe people who lived to the north (Johnson 1921, 160–61; Morton-Williams 1954, 91). Johnson, recounts that when Onigbogi ascended to the throne around 1500, his mother, a Yoruba woman from Otta, named Aruigba-Ifa, traveled to Oyo and advised the leadership of Oyo to adopt Ifa as the sacred oracle for the kingdom. The Oyo leaders rejected her recommendation, and shortly thereafter the Alafin's mother departed from Oyo (Johnson 1921, 159–60). Soon after Aruigba-Ifa's departure, a minor rebellion against Alafin Onigbogi began in a nearby town. The Alafin sent the Bashorun (war minister) to suppress the rebellion. The rulers of neighboring communities soon learned of the Bashorun's temporary absence from Oyo, and the Nupe king swiftly attacked Oyo-Ile. A Nupe masquerader reportedly led the invading army. Yoruba theater historian Joel Adedeji (1969, 73–75) speculates that the Nupe masquerade was grotesque and nonhuman in appearance, designed to inspire fear in those who beheld it (Harley 1950; Jedrej 1980; Kramer 1993). The use of terrifying masks may have represented an attempt to appropriate the power of violent spirits, a practice that was widespread in sub-Saharan African communities where masquerades exist (Alagoa 1980, 4; Ellis 1999, ch. 6). Adedeji believes that the Oyo people viewed the Nupe masquerader as a spirit or ancestor of the invading Nupe army and that they may have perceived it as arriving to punish them for immoral behavior (1969, 75).

In order to further explain the Oyo people's reaction to the Nupe masquerade, Adedeji also calls attention to an event that, according to the oral traditions at Ile-Ife, predated the Nupe invasion of Oyo. According to this tradition, a group of Igbo people used a masquerader during an attack on the inhabitants of Ife. The story of this Igbo attack was incorporated into the lore of the Oyo people.[47] Adedeji (1969, 74–75) speculates that when the Nupe masquerader led the attack on Oyo, its inhabitants may have recalled the story of the earlier attack on Ile-Ife by the Igbo masquerade. This association between the Nupe invaders and the Igbo may have heightened the Oyo people's fear of the Nupe masked warrior as it advanced on the battlefield. Adedeji concludes that two distinct masquerade concepts converged during the Nupe invasion: the masquerade as a "reincarnation" of ancestors and the masquerade as a disguise technique utilized by a secret society for political purposes—a technique of intimidation. What is most interesting about the Ife tradition is that a woman, who had been enslaved by the Igbo invaders, supposedly learned the secrets of the Igbo masquerade and later disclosed them to the Ife, who in turn used this knowledge against their attackers. While in this instance it is a woman who is credited with having introduced a new ritual practice, in the case of the Nupe tradition, it was the rejection of the wisdom of the king's mother that led to a chain of events culminating in the kingdom adopting a new masquerade society, as well as a new ritual knowledge, Ifa.

According to this tradition, a Nupe army overthrew the Alafin, causing him and his supporters to flee from Oyo-Ile into exile (Johnson 1921, 159–60). In the aftermath of the Nupe attack, Oyo's rulers and their followers relocated in Igboho, where four consecutive kings of Oyo sought refuge from the attacks of their Nupe and Borgu neighbors. In the process of restructuring their government and military in exile, they adopted the Nupe tradition of masquerading, creating a powerful masking society known as Egungun. A number of lineage histories and praise poems indicate that the first Egungun society of chiefs was formed while Alafin Ofinran, the first of the four kings to rule after the Nupe invasion, and his supporters were in exile at Kusu. Johnson claims that the mysteries behind the Nupe masquerade were revealed to Saha, the head slave of the Alafin, who subsequently shared this knowledge with the king. Then a group of Nupe migrants, along with others from the Bariba region, joined forces with the Alafin's supporters and further instructed them in the secrets of the Nupe masquerade. Among the Nupe contingent was the Alapinni, who became the political head of the Egungun society and its representative on the Oyo Mesi, the council of chiefs that co-ruled Oyo alongside the Alafin. The Alagba became the first ritual head of the Egungun society and its representative in the royal court. The creation of the Egungun society was one of the reforms instituted at Kusu to reorganize the political and military structure of Oyo (Johnson 1921, 160).[48]

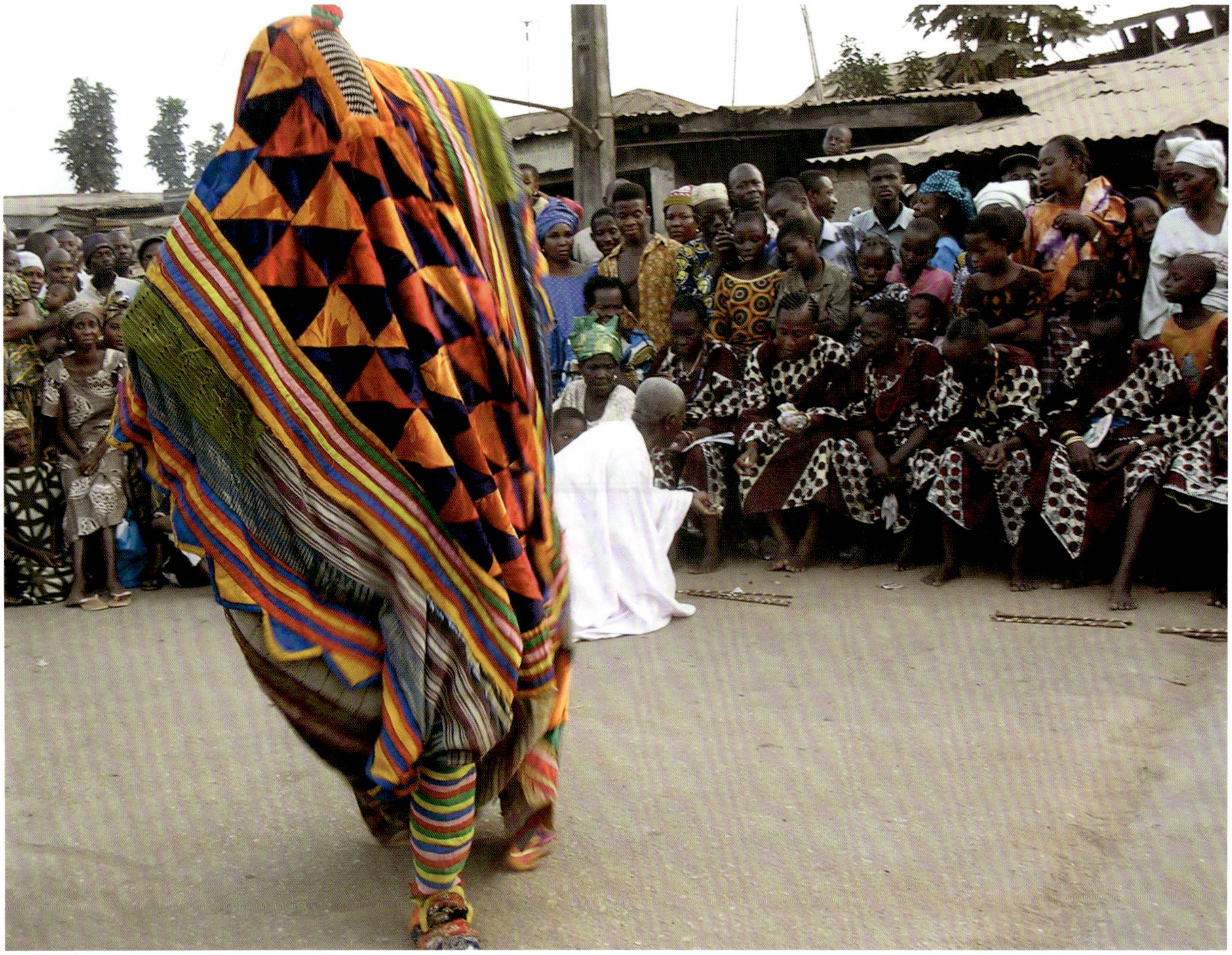

3.40

An Alabala Egungun masquerader performs at the Egungun festival in the Awori-Yoruba town of Otta. His brilliantly colored costume is made of panels of cotton, velvet, and *aso-oke* cloth. As he dances, an elderly man in white kneels before the Iya Agba Oje (the elderly women chiefs of Egungun) requesting gifts of money from them.

PHOTOGRAPH BY JOHN WILLIS, 2004.

3.41

An Alabala Egungun masquerader prostrates himself before the women chiefs of Egungun. The Atokun, dressed in white, uses a stick to direct the masquerader here and throughout the performance.

PHOTOGRAPH BY JOHN WILLIS, AWORI-YORUBA, OTTA, 2004.

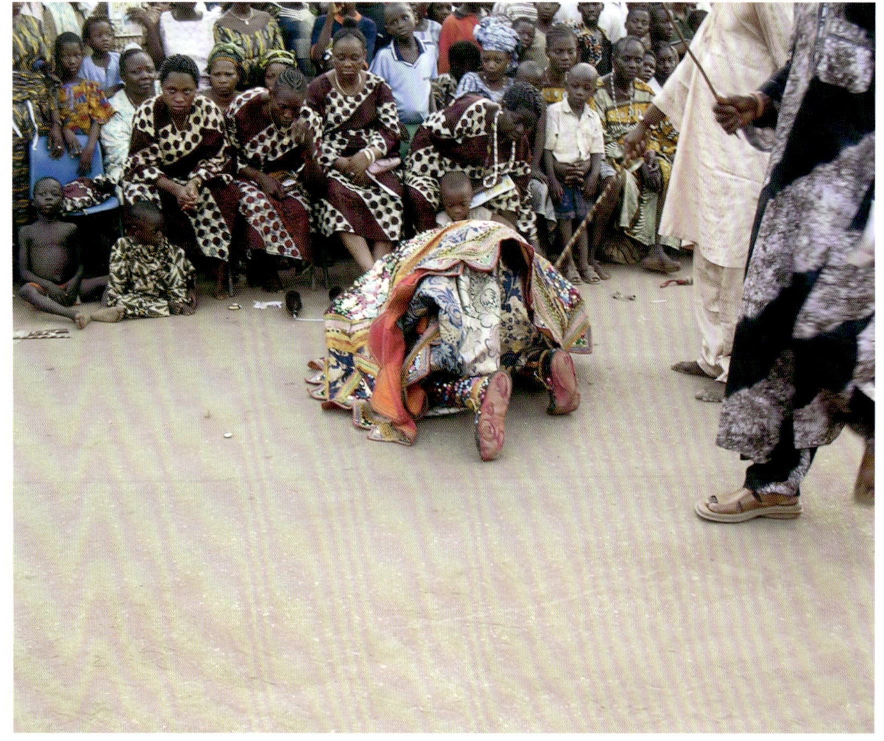

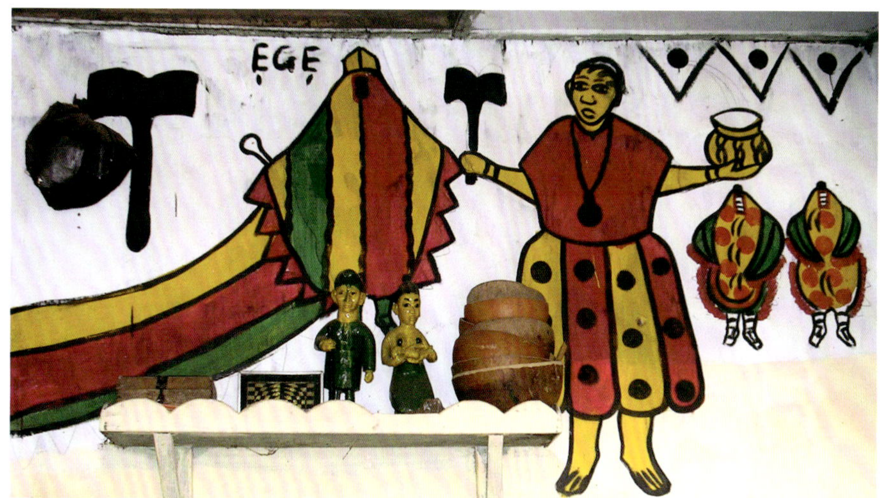

3.42
An Awori-Yoruba mural features an Egungun masquerader bearing the name "Ege" and wearing a striped costume. To the right is a Shango devotee who holds the Oshe Shango (the double-headed ax that is a symbol of the deity). Another such ax appears at the far left of the mural. At the far right are two more Egungun masqueraders belonging to the Alabala category.
PHOTOGRAPH BY JOHN WILLIS, OTTA, 2005.

Contrary to the Shango tradition, in which women appear prominently, the "Nupe invasion" tradition is silent in terms of the place of women within it. The only woman mentioned in the Nupe invasion tradition is the mother of the Alafin, whose recommendations were initially rejected. It was only after the kingdom experienced near destruction and its inhabitants were displaced that the leaders of Oyo embraced the Ifa oracle that she had offered. While this tradition tends to be read as a warning against neglecting the ancestors, it also offers a warning against neglecting women's power and authority, a recurring theme in many of the oral traditions that describe the origins and early development of Egungun (Verger 1965, 151–53; Abiodun 1989, 3–6, 2001; Abimbola 2001, 144).

Whether we consider the implications of the two traditions examined here in the context of a gendered history of Egungun, it appears that the creation of the Egungun society at Kusu may have reflected a moment in which women's influence on Egungun was challenged. It at least points to a moment in which royal power, which depended on the labor of and was represented through the bodies of women, had to contend with new challenges from the Alapinni and his Nupe followers. These challengers gained new prominence among the council of nonroyal chiefs who co-ruled Oyo with the king and among the members of the newly formed Egungun society.

The presence of women among the most senior Egungun chiefs in many contemporary Yoruba towns, e.g., Otta, Ilaro, and Iragbiji, serves as a reminder that women are at least visible and in some cases wield tremendous power over the affairs of Egungun. At Otta, a group of female Egungun chiefs, known as the Iya Agba Oje, who work alongside the male Egungun chiefs, are revered by elder men and by Egungun masqueraders themselves. One image taken at Otta during an Egungun festival shows a colorfully, adorned Egungun dancing; in the background, an elder male wearing white kneels and appears to request money from a group of female Egungun chiefs, who all wear the same red and white fabric and sit on the first row of spectators (fig. 3.40). A second image taken on the same day features another Egungun prostrating himself before the same chiefs (fig. 3.41). Contemporary devotees often invoke the Shango tradition described above or other traditions in which women were among the first to adorn or serve as the custodians of Egungun masqueraders. Another image on the mural inside the sacred grove of the female Egungun officials shows a female Shango devotee on the right next to a senior Egungun mask at Otta. The images in the mural corroborate oral testimony that reveals an overlap in the ritual spaces and devotees of Shango and Egungun at Otta (fig. 3.42). More research is needed on the history of women with respect to Egungun in other Yoruba towns in order to better evaluate the validity of the assumed maleness or pervasiveness of masculinity in the arena of Egungun.

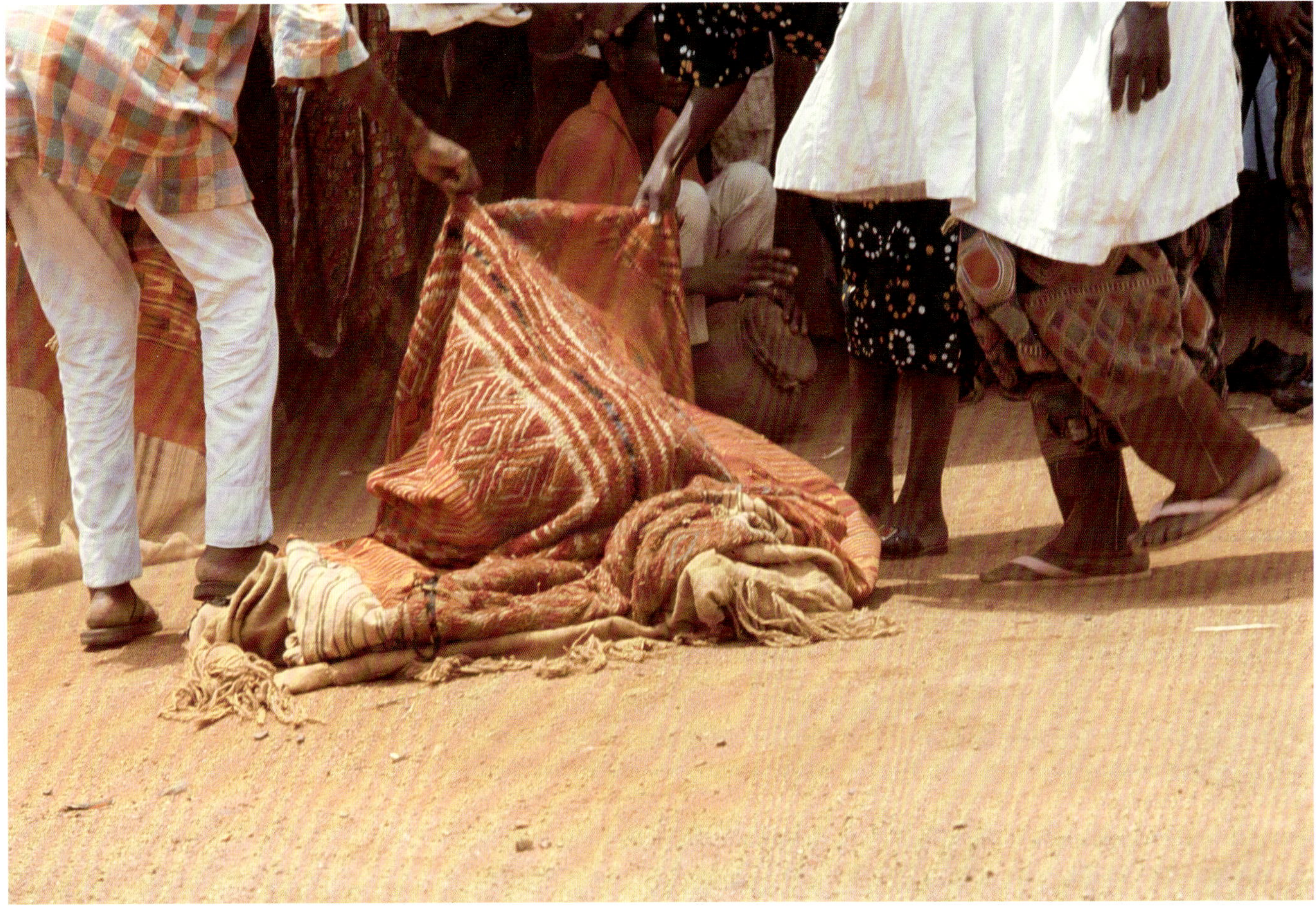

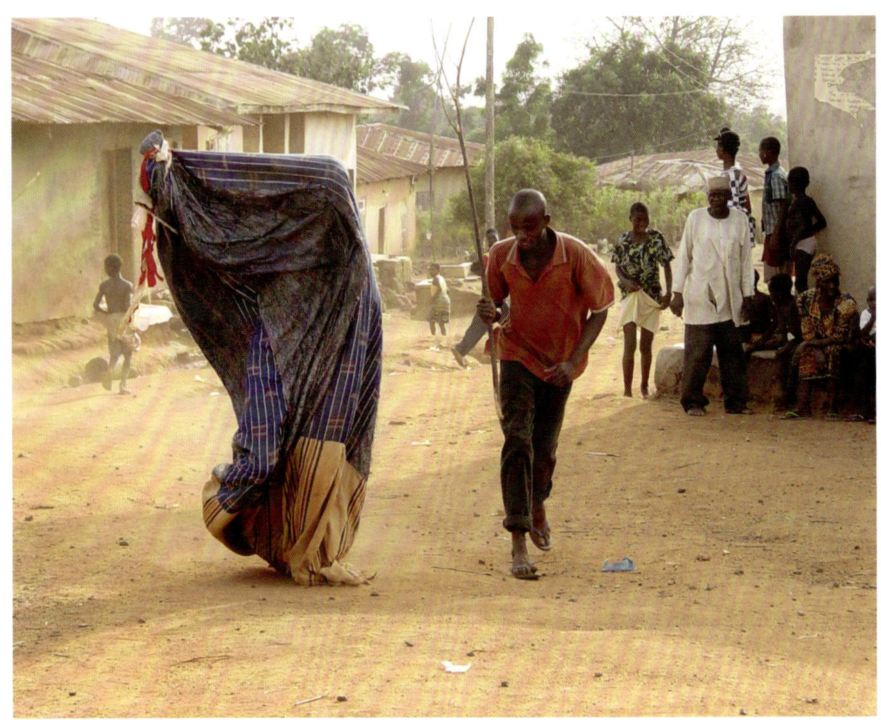

3.48

The commemorative masquerade Omeshe Sado rests and is fanned by attendants following a vigorous performance during the ancestral festival of Olimi.

PHOTOGRAPH BY JEAN BORGATTI, AFOKPELLA TOWN, IMIAMUNE QUARTER, MARCH 18, 1973.

3.49

The commemorative masquerade Omeshe Ogene runs with his handler during the ancestral festival of Olimi. This masquerade was created circa 1983 to honor the late Ogene.

PHOTOGRAPH BY JEAN BORGATTI, AFOKPELLA TOWN, IMIAMUNE QUARTER, MARCH 31, 2003.

prayer. They may execute the rapid sequences of half-twists that make their performances so impressive. After exerting themselves, they retire to seats of honor next to the musicians where attendants fan them by plucking at their cloth and letting it fall (fig. 3.48). As the afternoon progresses, the pulsating figure(s) flank the orchestra, watching the other masquerades perform.

Omeshe requires special training of the performer, the only masquerade in Okpella that does. The costume, sewn like a large sack, presents the dancer with particular problems. He must be physically strong (*ototo*) and well practiced in order to manage the cloth effectively, raising and lowering its level without tripping. Falling would lessen the dance's dramatic impact as well as undermine popular belief in the inherent superiority of personified spirits. The performer is a man in his forties—older than those who dance the commemorative Dead Mother and various entertainment masquerades (*olimi nikeke*, lit., "minor spirits") or those who dance the messenger Anogiri. He appears enclosed in the sack, which is fastened at the top around the stem of the topknot. He grasps the stem with his right hand and holds it over his head; his left arm is outstretched to fan the cloth laterally, a common pose.

The dance is "hard" (*dua dua*)[63] and "hot"—displaying the highest energy level of any of the daylight dances—and carries the praise name *onokaka* (something arduous). The dancer changes the shape of the image, its direction, and its level while maintaining a constant rhythm pattern and a tempo measured at 240 beats per minute.[64] Unlike other Olimi festival masquerades, Omeshe is not anthropomorphic. It is "the thing that walks leaving no footprints on the ground" (*Emi ni e kia eke ni ai me owe o.*)[65] Descriptions liken it to a cloth carried by the wind[66] or to spirals of wind-blown dust, so-called dust devils.[67] Observers marvel that "It has no eyes, no hand or foot, yet leaps about when dancing.[68] It never falls."[69]

The Okpella exploit the symbolic potential of Omeshe to several ends. Rigorous performance and visual reference to title status combine to make it a metaphor that expresses notions of masculinity and individual achievement, an image even more compelling when contrasted with that of the women's commemorative mask (see Borgatti 1979b). Powerful and uncanny movement serves the ends of the senior night society, who embody the terrifying protective power of the collective dead as enforcers of moral law.[70] The Alukpekpe, their visual symbol, reinforces the idea of invincibility which they seek to project. The Okpella further use the mystery of Omeshe to create "the Aja," the masquerade that closes the annual ancestral festival. After intoning the last prayers on behalf of the community, the Aja skips about, brushing all footprints from the playing ground (*Aja o fuomi olele*) to assure that the spirits depart leaving no trace (see Borgatti 1976a, 172). ●

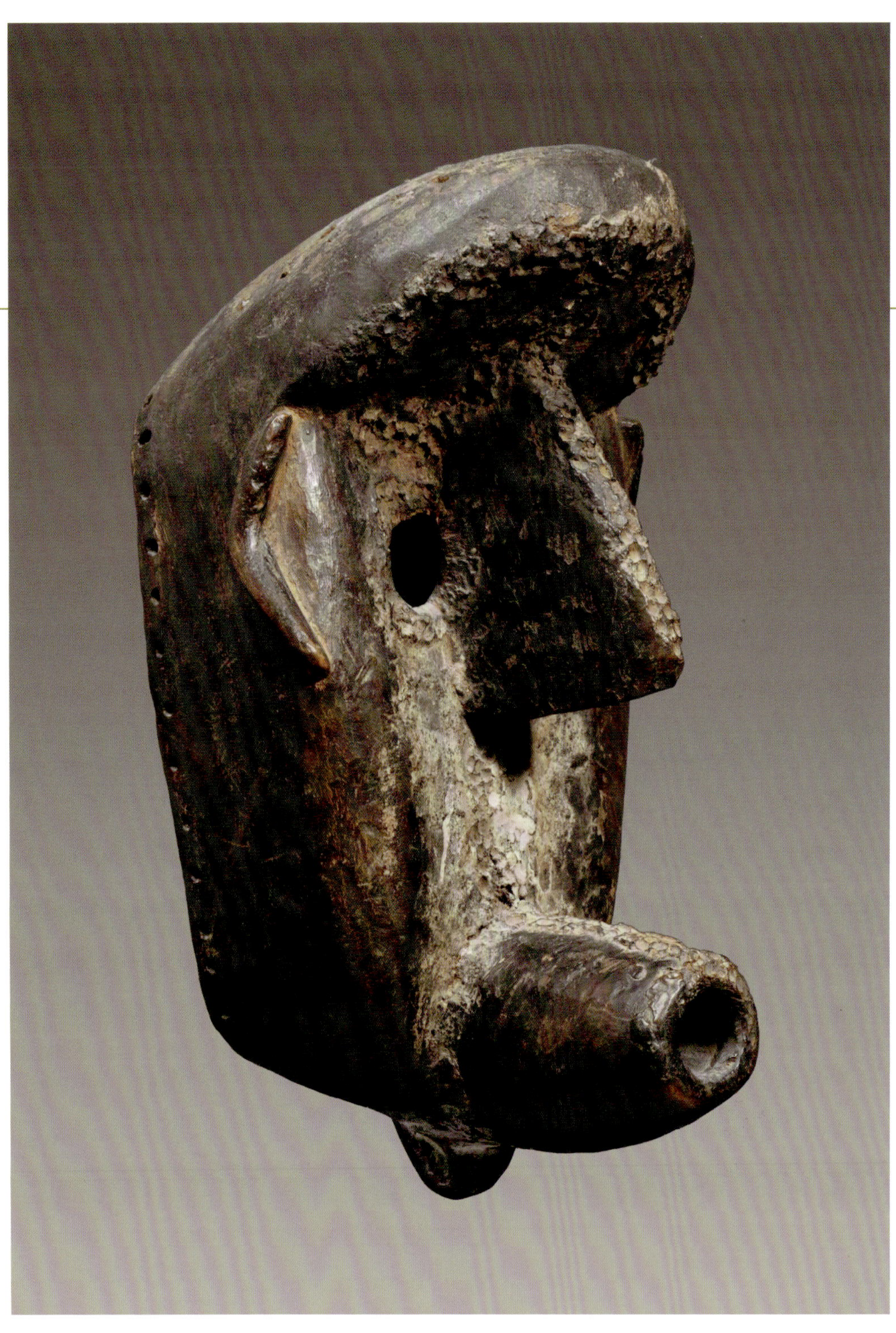

 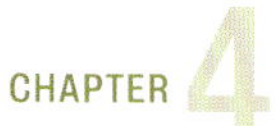

Ebira and the Niger–Benue Confluence: Material Culture and Masquerade; Artifact and Identity Revisited

JOHN PICTON

The region within the vicinity of the confluence of the Niger and Benue rivers defies any attempt at simple circumscription (see map, fig. 3.2). Neither history, nor geography, nor ethnicity, nor language, nor social structure, nor material culture, nor masquerade, nor trade, nor myth, nor warfare and conquest or defeat provides on its own the complete basis for understanding the region, though each contributes. So how do I conceptualize all this in writing a brief essay? Are there alternatives to the conventional yet problematic privileging of supposedly ethnic labels in the literature of African art? After all, words such as "Ebira," "Yoruba," and "Akoko-Edo" do not describe equivalent categories, while another, "Bassa Nge" (pronounced: basa ŋge), is Nupe for "we are not Bassa" (Gunn and Conant 1960, 72).

This is not a new problem, of course, as anyone familiar with the second chapter of Siegfried Nadel's *A Black Byzantium* (1942) will be well aware. Ethnicity is just one among many forms of identity and difference; and the distribution of the forms and works of social, visual, or performance practice may or may not be determined by ethnicity. Particular ethnicities come into being in specific circumstances, sometimes more or less deliberately constructed (e.g., see Peel 2000), and they evolve; and they can disappear. They are not the only things that have histories, and the convenience of ethnic categorization must be balanced against its paradigmatic inadequacy as the basis for writing a history of art in Africa. The question of how one maps all this through space and time is given particular emphasis toward the end of this essay, for there are aspects of the visual and performance practices of the region that were initiated in processes of cultural reinvention marking the period following the late nineteenth-century conflict of empires.

I write in memory of Arnold Rubin, whose research in the Benue Valley, carried out over more than twenty years until his death in 1988, lies at the basis of the present volume and the accompanying exhibition. In a previous paper written in Arnold's memory in 1991[1] and revisited here, I explored something of the relationship between aesthetic and social categories in the confluence region of Nigeria.[2] I noted then, in regard to the notion of a "border-crossing" artifact (the border being that of ethnicity), that "if the distribution of a particular kind of artifact is not constrained by the boundaries of language or political affiliation, then it is more precise to note that such boundaries do not exist for that artifact" (1991, 35–36). I take this a little further here, encouraged by Richard Fardon who, fifteen years ago remarked: "To continue to write as if societies and cultures were stable spatializations risks irrelevance in the form of perverse attachment to conventions that fly in the face of the way the world now

This mask was carved for use by an Ekuecici, probably in Ihima, the westernmost district of Ebira, either by a smith of Akoko-Edo origin or a local freeborn Ebira. It would have had red abrus seeds embedded in the dried beeswax across the face. The holes around the edge were for the attachment of cloth, and magical medicines may have once been placed in the top.

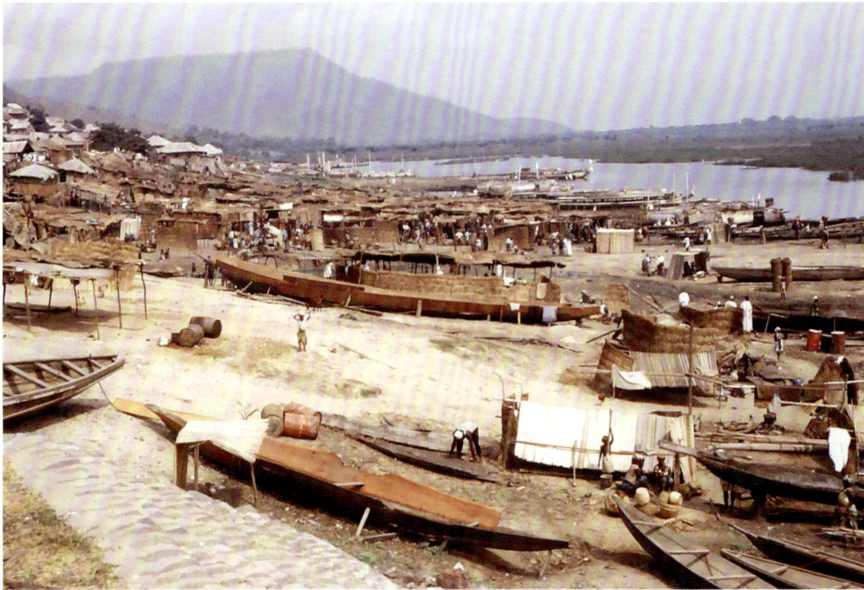

4.2

Canoes used in fishing, river transport, and trading are carved, moored, and repaired at Lokoja on the west bank of the confluence. Larger trading canoes, often housing families and livestock, reach along the navigable parts of the Niger and Benue rivers all the way to the Niger Delta and the Atlantic coast. This photograph shows the river at its lowest point in the dry season.

PHOTOGRAPH BY SUSAN PICTON, DECEMBER 1969. REPRODUCED BY PERMISSION OF THE NATIONAL COMMISSION FOR MUSEUMS AND MONUMENTS, NIGERIA.

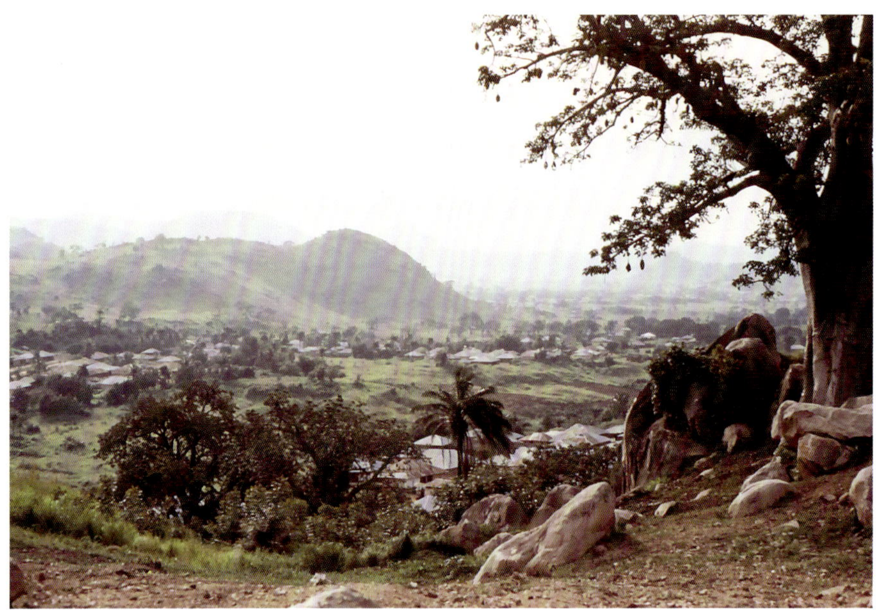

4.3

The view from Osisi, Adavi District, looking northward across the Ebira countryside some 40–50 miles southwest of the confluence, shows an essentially level, wooded savanna plain punctuated by steep hills. These once provided safety from warfare and feuding. Some villages, such as Osisi, still occupy hilltop sites, though most have moved down to the plain below.

PHOTOGRAPH BY JOHN PICTON, SEPTEMBER 1971.

seems to be pictured credibly" (Fardon 1995, 4).[3] My intention is, therefore, where possible, to draw attention to the engagements between "things"[4] that are local to a given place and things from further away (not necessarily "global"). Such engagements are much more characteristic of social practice in Africa than we have been habituated to admit.[5] In any case, it is only reasonable to expect that the confluence of two rivers would entail movement of, and engagements among, peoples, artifacts, skills, names, and ideas (fig. 4.2).

This essay takes Ebira, a people dominating the area to the immediate southwest of Lokoja, as its major theme in discussing the confluence area (fig. 4.3) The reason for this choice is masquerade.[6] Ebira people know themselves as Anebira (people or inhabitants of Ebira), a word denoting their language, social practices, cultural values, textiles, and masquerades and thus imparting a distinctive ethnic identity forged in opposition to surrounding peoples as they moved into and expanded within their present area, a hilly tract of land between the extreme Yoruba northeast and the Edo-speaking peoples. Any consideration of Ebira must therefore take account of some of the Yoruba- and Edo-related communities to their north and south[7] as the study of the material and performance culture of the region reveals interdependence:

(1) these neighboring communities adopted masked forms mediated by Ebira people; (2) at least one of these forms has a distribution as far to the northeast as Jukun and/ or Abakwariga (or Abakpariga), their craftspeople of Hausa origin; (3) artists in these Edo- and Yoruba-related communities have been the sources of many of the artifacts incorporated into confluence institutions and practices.

In contrast to Ebira/Anebira, Akoko-Edo to the southwest was a government division, one of the four local administrations to the north of the Edo (or Benin) Kingdom. To the east of Akoko-Edo, and also bordering with Ebira, is Etsako; and some of the differences in masking practice between Ososo peoples in Akoko-Edo and Okpella peoples in Etsako can be attributed to differing sources within Ebira. Whereas Etsako is mostly comprised of speakers of a single language, however, Akoko-Edo encompasses several Edo-related languages, some Yoruba-related languages, and some as yet unclassified.[8] Igarra, the administrative center of Akoko-Edo, is a town of Ebira origin founded from Okene (see Picton 1991 for maps based on Susan Picton's research). The network of markets for the sale of ironwork, pottery, and textiles, among other things, gave Akoko-Edo a greater appearance of unity than was actually the case.

However, whereas Ebira is an ethnic group, and Akoko-Edo a government administrative area, "Yoruba" is an altogether more problematic category. It is an identity based upon the Empire of Oyo, and it evolved in its present form more or less at the same time as the emergence of a Nigerian national identity. Both processes were initiated in the mid-nineteenth century through the efforts of highly educated freed slaves, some of them ministers of the Church of England, who were repatriated from Sierra Leone. They began the intellectual work of describing what would soon become known as Yoruba culture and of producing a modern language for education, publishing, and the translation of the Bible. The inhabitants of Ijumu, Igbede, Owe (Kabba), Abinu (Bunu), and Aworo, the groups to the north of Ebira, would only have come to know themselves as "Yoruba" beginning in the mid-twentieth century because of the research initiated just a century earlier; and while their languages are distant dialects of Yoruba, the pattern of their social organization is more closely related to Edo and Igbo than to the Yoruba kingdoms to their west or to the "Yoruba"-related Igala to the east.[9] The masking practices of these groups take on a more monumental Ekiti-Yoruba appearance as one proceeds westward, and a more schematic Ebira-like appearance as one proceeds eastward, at least to Abinu. The Aworo group is directly adjacent to the confluence and the sources of their masquerades are diverse. I shall refer to these groups collectively as "confluence Yoruba" for the remainder of this essay.[10]

The region to the immediate north of the confluence was dominated by people known as Egbira (or Egbura). Clearly "Ebira" and "Egbira" are dialect variations of each other suggesting a historical link between them, but precisely what that link might be is very unclear. There is no practical relationship at the present time. We have no detailed descriptions of Egbira masquerades, and the published literature on their political and social institutions, such as it is, does not suggest a close likeness to anything southwest of the confluence. The Egbira communities of Igu and Opanda are, for example, described as kingdoms (Husaini 1986; Ibrahim 2000), whereas "kingship" in Ebira was imposed by the British colonial administration because of its preference for Indirect Rule (see Sani 1993, 71–72). There are two more elements in this mosaic of forms, names, and practices that must be noted: the contrast between "Bassa Nge" and Bassa Komo, and Ebira-Igala relationships, both discussed below.[11]

ETHNICITIES AND EMPIRES

Although I have placed Ebira masquerade at the center of my discussion of the confluence, in May 1990, the last time I visited Ebira, it was disconcerting to find that it had been abolished two years previously by the local authorities at police insistence. Understanding how this came to pass is an essential part of understanding the character of Ebira masquerade, and for this we must begin by reckoning with the complex local politics of Ebira. In the 1960s I found at least four political systems existing simultaneously, and each of these agencies had become entailed, at some level, in masked performance.

Before the inception of military rule in 1966, there was a process for electing members to regional and national parliaments. The party affiliations engendered thereby affected all aspects of Ebira life, including masquerade. Masks, like the households that owned them, had party loyalties. Even during military rule when party politics had no place—and thereafter when new parties were formed—loyalties established in the 1950s were translated into ongoing circumstances and remained part of Ebira life. Standing outside the party system was the Divisional Officer (the DO), representing the regional government, with the police at his side. The DO's partner in local government was the Native Authority (the NA; and no matter how "colonial" that may sound, this remained the terminology in use in the 1960s—it was later renamed). The local government system that had emerged through the British policy of Indirect Rule was led by a Paramount Ruler, a position established by the colonial administration. Throughout my research this was Alhaji Sani Omolori, who had succeeded his controversial predecessor, Alhaji Ibrahim, in 1956 (see below). However, while both the DO and the NA were expected to stand outside the party system, the NA was said, by the DO and his superiors, to be deeply involved in it, and this led to tensions between the two. Nevertheless, the NA issued permits to the individual masked performers for the two popular festivals of Ekueci and Ecane (see below).[12] Last but not least, effective governance also depended on a negotiation between the NA and lineage elders, whose authority was based upon the inheritance of a tradition that extended back to a mythic past located in the settlement of the various Ebira communities. Land rights, chiefly titles, and most aspects of masquerade, were among the many domains of local government that were still their responsibility. Masked performances were habitually marked by household and lineage rivalries, and although a certain measure of violence was inevitable and accepted, the elders remained in control with the support of the police.

By the 1980s, however, fueled by political party and other interests that neither the elders nor the police could any longer constrain, masquerade performances at the major festivals had become caught up in a lethal cycle of violence. Local government and the police, with fundamentalist Islamic support, attempted to bring masquerade to an end.[13] Nevertheless, discussion began almost immediately about the possibility of reviving it in a less violent form, and such was the force of Ebira attachment to these performances that some twenty years later the ban was lifted and the festivals were revived, albeit with a heavy police presence. I only know this, however, through the generosity of Constanze Weise and Adinoyi-Ojo Onukaba in sharing their more recent research data with me. (For an account of the often tortuous politics of Ebira see Sani 1993, 55–77, 93–115; and for and account of research in Ebira masquerade subsequent to my own but prior to the 1988 ban see Onukaba 1996.)

The authority of elders subsisted within a political tradition that was defined by the absence of centralized rule and by the possibilities of settling disputes by feuding between individuals and lineages if the mediating role of elders failed. Moreover, the settlement of their present region had been marked by conflict, as already noted, and prior to British colonial rule[14] other empires had left their traces across the confluence region. In Ebira, politics was always traumatic, whether practiced in feuding and warfare or represented and celebrated in masquerade! Through the latter half of the nineteenth century, Nupe armies raided the area around the confluence, the northern Edo-related peoples, and into the Edo Kingdom. They took captives, some of whom ended up in the trans-Saharan slave trade, while others, once freed, became Christian missionaries. Here and there, as in Auchi (which in due course became the administrative center of Etsako),

Nupe warlords set up new dynasties of vassal-kings. Nupe raids, together with the local feuding within and between groups and communities, encouraged the location of Ebira and Akoko-Edo communities at the tops of hills, sometimes protected by almost impenetrable walls of cactus.

It was only with the establishment of British authority at the beginning of the twentieth century that communities felt safe in coming down to the plains, a process even now not entirely completed. Nupe success was often restricted to catching people at work on the lowland farms, and in 1874 Ebira hunters defending the hilltop settlement of Okene, armed with poisoned arrows (still an Ebira speciality), drove off the combined armies of Nupe, Ilorin, and Ibadan.[15] A century later, the defeat of these attackers was still commemorated in masquerade (fig. 4.4), for example by masks called Anivado (the Ibadan man) and Anibaba (the Bariba man). Bariba mercenaries fought in the Nupe armies; while the armies of Ibadan had also raided the confluence region independently of Nupe. It should be noted that these were masks of servile status, Ekuecici (masks of rubbish), made to accompany the masked re-embodiment of a deceased elder (the walking shroud) and thereby to commemorate his successful exploits. The continued popularity of such masks traces and celebrates Ebira military success.

Another empire of relevance to the confluence is Edo/Benin. Although Edo political authority even at its fullest extent did not incorporate all of the peoples to its north, the relationship of some of these peoples to Edo can be traced through language and social patterning. This patterning and linguistic diversification, especially in Akoko-Edo, must, however, have been well established prior to the rise of the Edo state.[16] Ebira people were not in the region at the height of the Edo Empire in the sixteenth century, and as relative newcomers, their social and political institutions are very different. Almost the only signs of Edo influence in Ebira were a handful of arcane words in the ritual vocabulary and, very occasionally, Edo artifacts that had found their way into Ebira ritual apparatus. The Igala Kingdom, in contrast, had been incorporated into the Edo Empire by conquest in the early sixteenth century, and the new king provided with a brass mask. This supposedly represented the severed head of his predecessor, as evidence of vassal status. In the following century, however, Igala threw off Edo hegemony but retained the mask, now known as "The Eye That Surpasses All Other Eyes," as evidence of a political independence that lasted until the arrival of the British. In colonial and postcolonial Nigeria, the mask has continued to be worn hanging around the neck of the Igala King (see fig. 1.8).[17]

LINEAGES, AGE-GRADES, TITLES

If we consider the social patterning of the region to the south of the confluence, it is evident that on both sides of the lower Niger there was, broadly speaking, a common system and structure of authority and access thereto. There were, of course, local variations[18] and, more significantly, two exceptions. The first exception was Igala, structured by landholding lineages within which titles are inherited as part of Igala political order. The second was Ebira, also structured by landholding lineages, but with authority vested in elders whose status as such was determined by absolute age. Otherwise, from the confluence Yoruba peoples (and unlike both Yoruba further to the west and Igala), through the great variety of Edo-speaking peoples, as well as the Igbo-speaking peoples to the east of the lower Niger, communities were structured by means of age-grades. These provided a social definition of age and authority and led to title-taking associations, membership in which was based not on lineage ascription and inheritance but personal achievement. There might also be landholding lineages (though not in the Edo Kingdom as described by Bradbury [1957; 1973], where land was village property), and the patterns of descent could be patrilineal and/or matrilineal (in some Akoko-Edo communities, e.g., Ososo, there were complex double-descent systems), but lineages alone did not provide for the overt authority structure of a community.

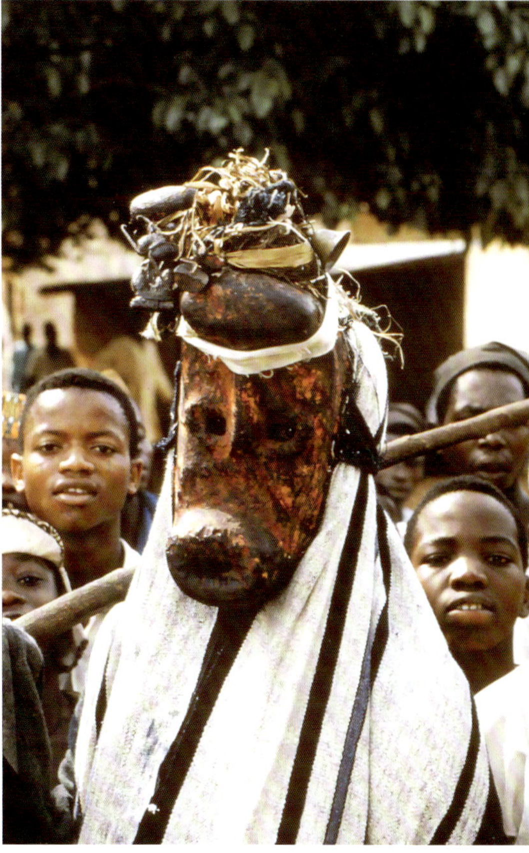

4.4

Anibaba (the Bariba man) performs at the midyear festival of Ecane in Oboroke, Ihima, the westernmost Ebira district. The name "Anibaba" commemorates the Ebira defeat of Bariba mercenaries fighting in the Nupe army in the late nineteenth century. The masquerade wears a male burial cloth. An assortment of magical medicines and sacrificial remains appear atop the mask. The red color smeared on the soot- and blood-blackened face is camwood—offered by a woman in thanks for a successful childbirth.

PHOTOGRAPH BY JOHN PICTON, APRIL 1967.

REPRODUCED BY PERMISSION OF THE NATIONAL COMMISSION FOR MUSEUMS AND MONUMENTS, NIGERIA.

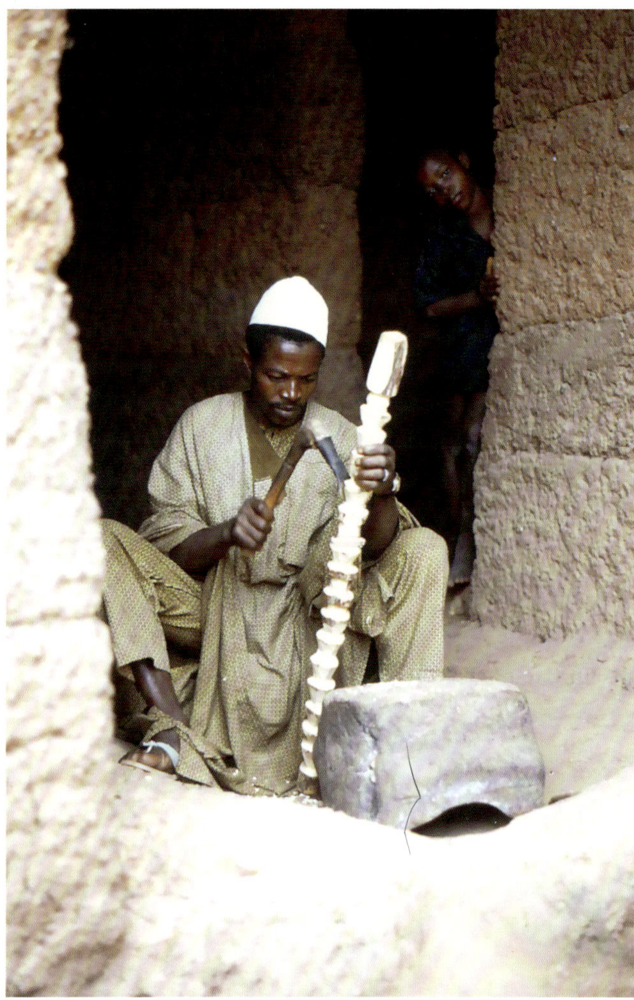

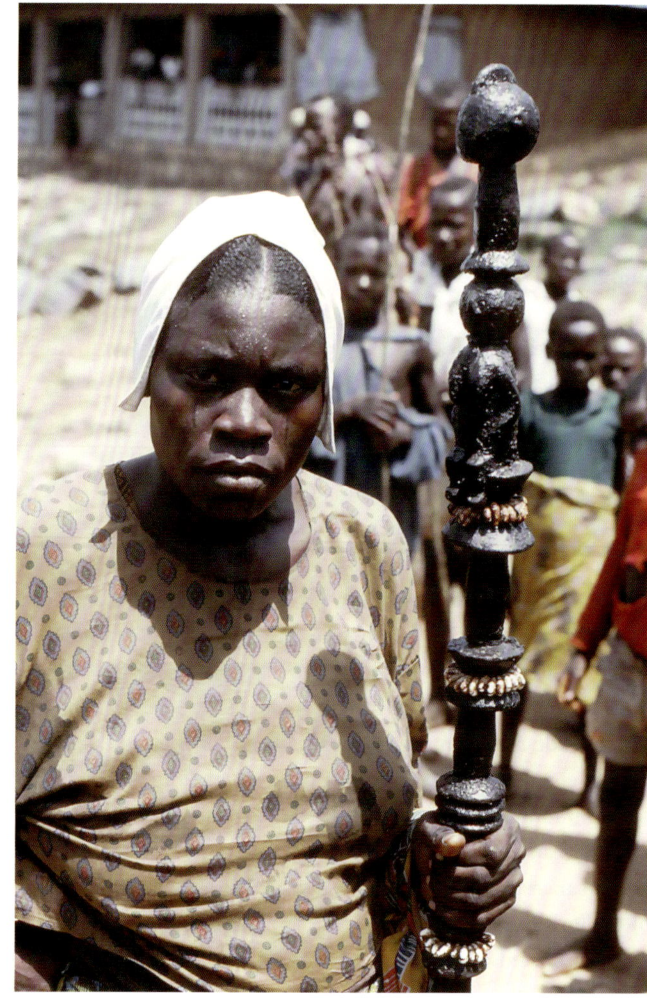

4.8

Karimu, the youngest son of Ihiovi, the elder of Opopoco village in Oboroke, Ihima District, carves an old man's staff. (The finished work is now in the collection of the British Museum.)

PHOTOGRAPH BY JOHN PICTON, JUNE 1966.
REPRODUCED BY PERMISSION OF THE NATIONAL COMMISSION FOR MUSEUMS AND MONUMENTS, NIGERIA.

4.9

The eldest daughter of Yusuf Onoko is dressed for a procession celebrating her father's taking the title of Adeika in Kuroko, Adavi District. She wears a man's cap and holds the staff that her father inherited from a previous title-holder within the same lineage. It would usually be considered very dangerous for a woman to even touch this staff or to wear male attire. Male success was, however, considered dependent upon the energies of women, and within the liminal circumstances of title-taking, a woman can be recognized.

PHOTOGRAPH BY JOHN PICTON, MAY 1967.
REPRODUCED BY PERMISSION OF THE NATIONAL COMMISSION FOR MUSEUMS AND MONUMENTS, NIGERIA.

Uneme smiths were also wood-carvers, although they were not the only ones in the region. There was a demand for hafts for iron tools (fig. 4.8), domestic stools (every woman has her own), larger commissioned stools (figs. 4.10–4.12), and staffs (figs. 4.9, 4.13, 4.14) required by elders and titled men (sometimes embellished with schematic figuration), flutes (fig. 4.15), hollow-log bells (always carved and played in pairs; fig. 4.16), masks often of highly schematic form (fig. 4.1), and very occasionally freestanding figure sculptures (fig. 4.17), used for display at chiefly installations, funerals, and other celebrations. Throughout Akoko-Edo, there were well-established local traditions of wood sculpture, also seen in age-grade masks, door panels, and offering bowls with figure sculpture. All of this work was characteristically schematic in ways that suggest the possibility of identifying individual artists. The schematization of Akoko-Edo sculptors was not as rough-hewn as that of the Uneme smiths, but it is not always possible to be sure which is which. Moreover, due to patterns of contact across the region and for a variety of reasons, sculptures originating in Akoko-Edo, whether carved by smith or nonsmith, can be found in Ebira households. Meanwhile, in Ebira, the Uneme smiths were a dependent caste, enjoying a status little better than slaves. They could make all the artifacts associated with elder status and masquerade and could be hired to perform in masquerade, but they could not personally own any of these things. Metalworking set the smiths apart, and while no Ebira man worked metal, he might well take up wood carving so as not to have to patronize a smith more than was necessary.

Among the confluence Yoruba communities, as in Akoko-Edo, there were both local and smith wood-carvers, and the work of at least some of the local carvers was distinguished by a smoothly finished schematization unlike anything made in Ebira or Akoko-Edo. The work of Akoko-Edo and Kabba area sculptors often found its way to Ebira,

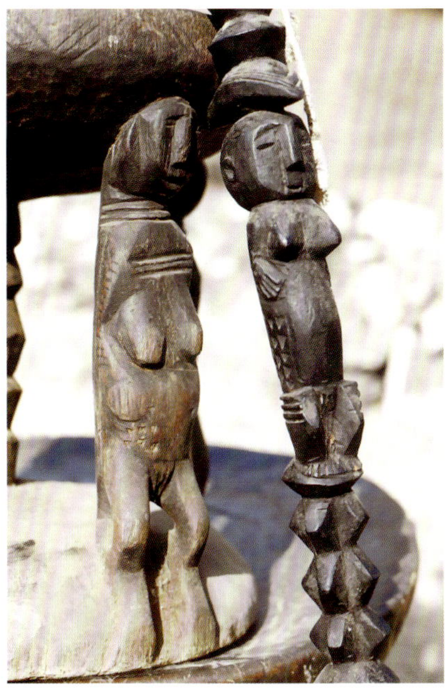

4.10
This stool and the staff leaning against it were carved by Aceuri of Iruvojo, a now-deserted village in Eganyi, the easternmost Ebira district, for Una, a titled man.
PHOTOGRAPH BY JOHN PICTON, JANUARY 1966.
REPRODUCED BY PERMISSION OF THE NATIONAL COMMISSION FOR MUSEUMS AND MONUMENTS, NIGERIA.

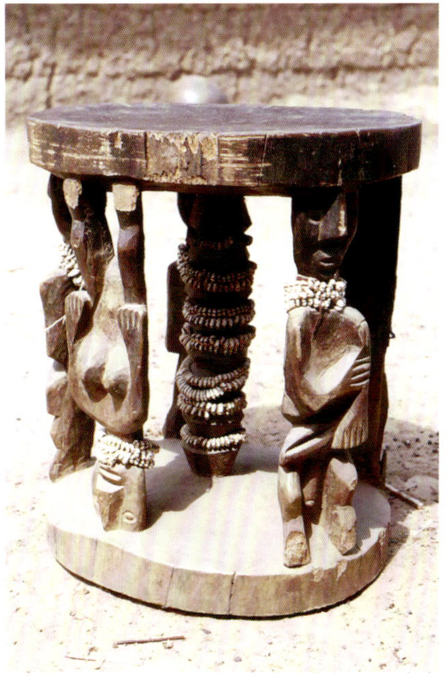

4.11
This stool was commissioned by Amehwami of Oziokutu ward, Ogaminana, Adavi District, in preparation for taking a lineage title, perhaps in the 1920s. The carver, whose name was not remembered, was from Ihima in western Ebira.
PHOTOGRAPH BY JOHN PICTON, DECEMBER 1965.
REPRODUCED BY PERMISSION OF THE NATIONAL COMMISSION FOR MUSEUMS AND MONUMENTS, NIGERIA.

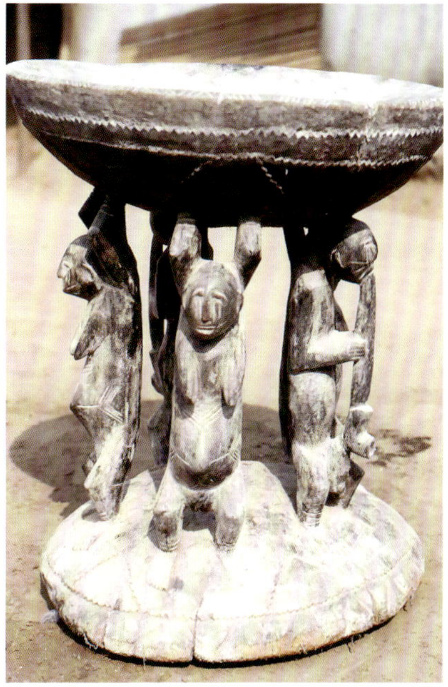

4.12
This wooden stool was carved for Uye, an elder who died in the 1920s, grandfather of Raji Ohweyi, Adogo village, Eganyi District. The name of the sculptor was not remembered though he was said to have been Ebira (i.e., not a smith). Nevertheless, the highly schematic images of women with their arms raised recalls young Akoko-Edo women dancing at their coming-of-age rites, a form that has no basis in Ebira practice.
PHOTOGRAPH BY JOHN PICTON, JANUARY 1966.
REPRODUCED BY PERMISSION OF THE NATIONAL COMMISSION FOR MUSEUMS AND MONUMENTS, NIGERIA.

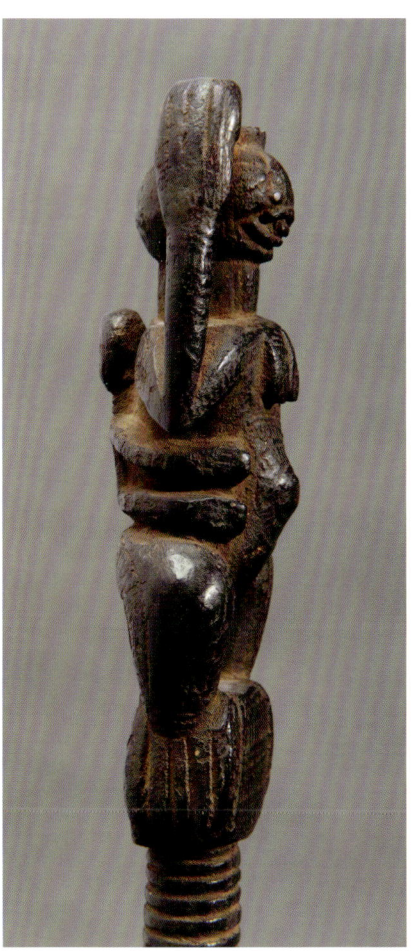

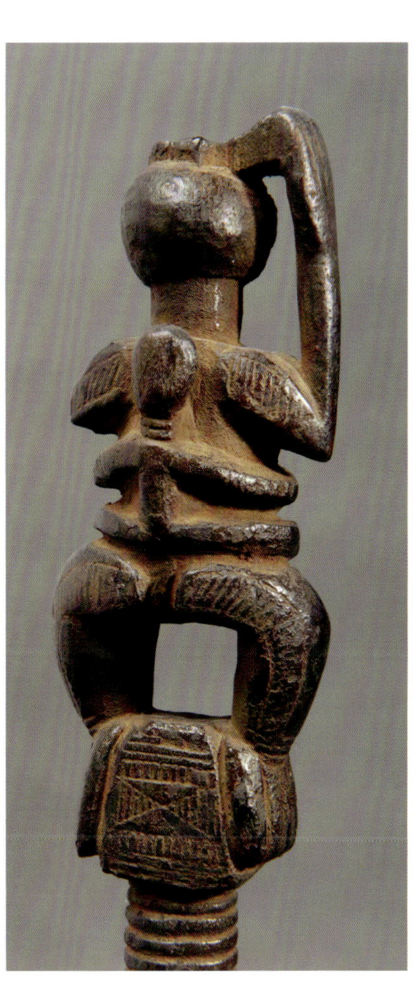

4.13a,b
Staff with maternity figure
Niger-Benue confluence, early twentieth century (?)
Wood
H: 108 cm
PRIVATE COLLECTION, PARIS
IMAGE: © PRIVATE COLLECTOR.
PHOTOGRAPH BY PRIVATE COLLECTOR
PROVENANCE: PURCHASED IN THE 1970s

This staff would have been commissioned by an elder or titled man probably somewhere in the region southwest of the confluence. The carver was almost certainly neither Ebira nor Akoko Edo, nor does the staff come from the area around Kabba. It might originate from one of the confluence Yoruba villages in the Abinu or, more likely, Aworo districts northeast of Kabba.

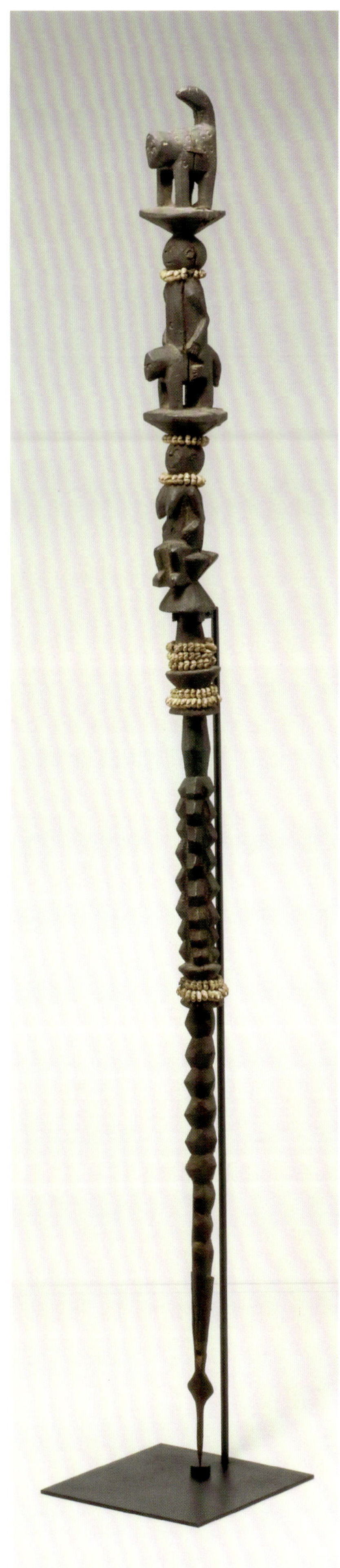

4.14

Staff

Ebira peoples, circa 1900

Wood, cowries, metal, thread

H: 165.74 cm

This staff would have been commissioned by an
elder or titled man, probably in Ebira. It shows
a leopard on the head of a man on horseback.
Several staffs with this form and imagery are
known in Ebira and in museum collections, but
the carver remains as yet unidentified.

as did the occasional work from Ekiti to the west. Most of the Ekuecici masks in Ebira
were locally carved, however, whether by smith or Ebira, whereas the staffs and stools
for elders and titled men tended to show a greater diversity of likely origin. Sometimes
the imagery on a stool might indicate an Akoko-Edo origin, most especially the image
of the unmarried virgin dressed for her coming-of-age celebrations, her hands and arms
held high to give relief to the sheer weight of the brass bracelets encasing them, an
image of absolutely no relevance in Ebira (figs. 4.18–4.20). Any wood sculpture in Ebira
thus had the possibility of several origins: Uneme smith—whether domiciled in Ebira,
Akoko-Edo, or Yoruba—or freeborn carver—whether from Ebira, Akoko-Edo, or the
Kabba region. Given these choices, it is not always possible to be certain about origin or
artist, either because the data are incomplete or because the corpus of certainly attributable work is insufficient for the purpose. I have also come across masks, display figures,
and staffs said to have been carved by "Bassa Nge" sculptors,[20] but they exhibit no consistency of style such as to permit identification on that basis alone. Masks from further
afield also very occasionally found their way into Ebira, whether made by carvers from
Ikot Ekpene in southeast Nigeria, Gelede masks from southwest Yoruba, or ebony masks
made for domestic ornamental use by tourists. This eclectic attitude was best understood
in the context of the competitive performances of Ekuecici as a tradition that while
insisting upon precedent was nonetheless open to novelty.

Throughout the region southwest of the confluence, women engaged in spinning
and weaving. They indigo-dyed cotton yarn and used an upright single-heddle broad
loom (fig. 4.22). There were local variants of pattern and form within commonplace
technologies that are, or were, broadly shared among diverse peoples. Textiles collected
in the late 1930s show that two developments within this tradition were already in place:
the weavers' access to machine-spun cotton yarn as well as "silk" (i.e., rayon and, in due
course, viscose fibers) and their use of a supplementary shed-stick system (fig. 4.23) to
facilitate float-weave patterns (Picton 1980; and for the technical vocabulary, see Picton
and Mack 1989). They also had access to industrially produced dyes available in local
markets, if their yarn was not already dyed to the required colors. The initiative for
these developments is usually credited to Alhaji Ibrahim who had been appointed by the
British as Native Authority in 1917.[21] By the 1960s women were creating a vast array of
patterned textiles, mostly for sale in the local markets for distribution throughout Nigeria. In the 1970s, as in every other Nigerian weaving tradition, Lurex (a laminated plastic
fiber with a glittering metal insert) became the decorative yard of fashion. Ten years
later Yoruba women weaving masters had begun introducing young women to the narrow-strip weaving technology associated historically with the Empire of Oyo, signaling
the probable demise of the broad-loom technology. Ebira, Akoko-Edo, and the Kabba
region also each had a center of pottery manufacture, employing diverse techniques suggesting, in contrast to broad-loom weaving, the absence of a common tradition.

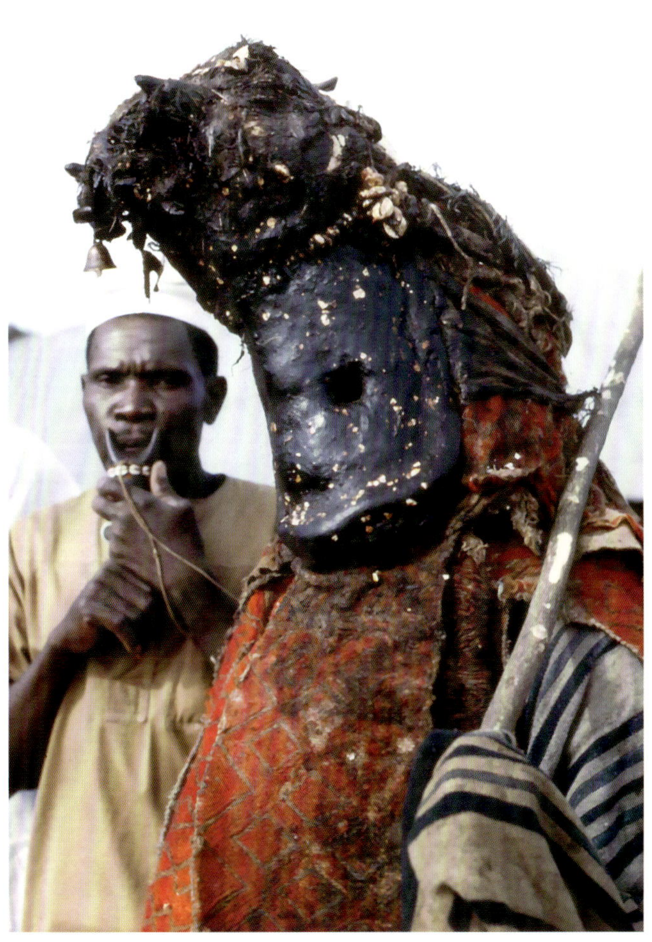

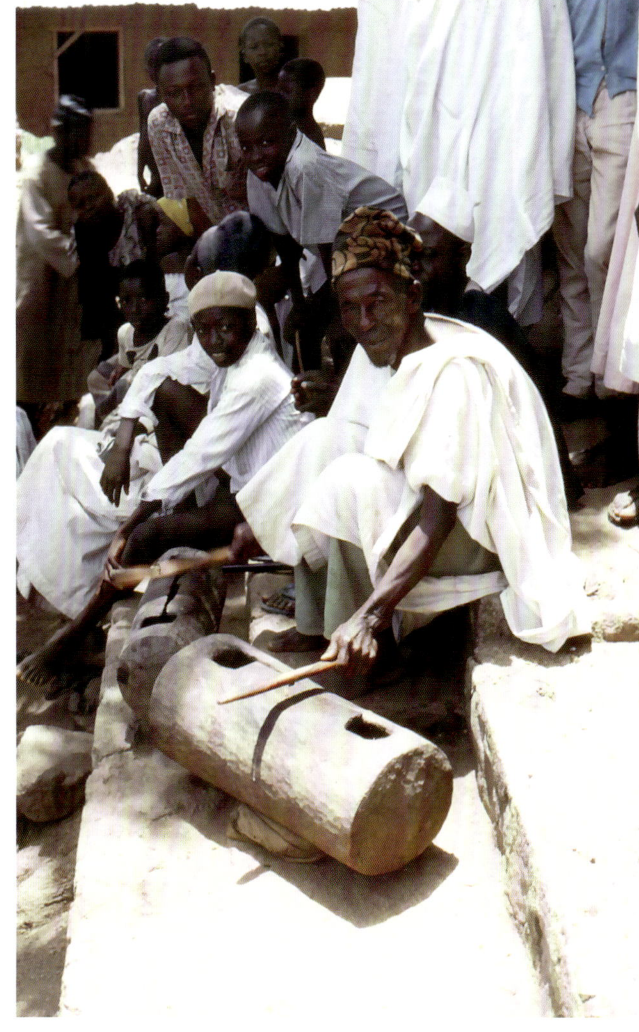

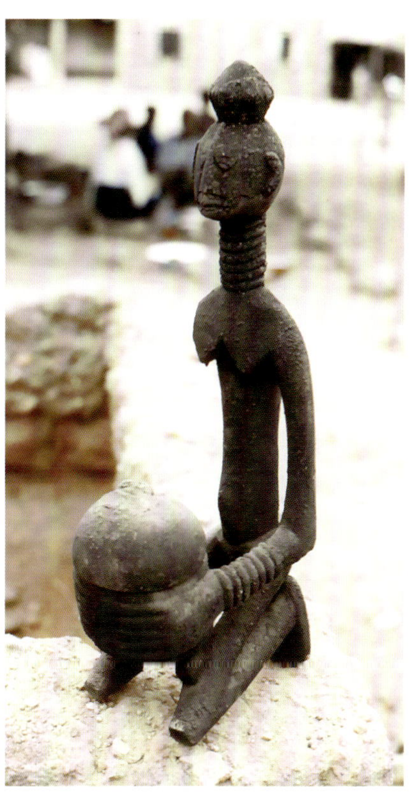

4.15

Onogidi (the Ogidi man) was the most power-ful masquerade at the Ecane festival in Kuroko, Adavi District. The flute player at his side "sings" his praises. The grandfathers of those who were the elders in the Anuhwami lineage in the 1960s had raided Ogidi, a confluence Yoruba village north of Ebira, and stolen a medicine that protected the farmland. This medicine was used to make this masquerade. By the time I saw Onogidi it had grown in status well beyond a mere Ekuecici, and at Ecane all the other masquerades in Kuroko acknowledged its greater age.

PHOTOGRAPH BY JOHN PICTON JUNE 1967.

REPRODUCED BY PERMISSION OF THE NATIONAL COMMISSION FOR MUSEUMS AND MONUMENTS, NIGERIA.

4.16

A pair of log bells (*agidibo*) is beaten at all ritual occasions, and by reproducing the tonal pattern of Ebira language, the musician presents a commentary through proverbs and praises. They are played here at the annual sacrifice to the stool of Okino (see fig. 4.19), a warrior celebrated for his leadership in the defeat of the Nupe and Ibadan forces in 1874.

PHOTOGRAPH BY JOHN PICTON, OKEN'EBA, APRIL 1967.

REPRODUCED BY PERMISSION OF THE NATIONAL COMMISSION FOR MUSEUMS AND MONUMENTS, NIGERIA.

4.17

Ebira figure sculptures, generally known as *onyonokumi* (someone weak or disabled), are rare. Ogido of Adavi-Eba, the original settlement within Adavi District, inherited this example from his father and used it in the same manner: as a receptacle for kola nuts when offering sacrifice. Such figures must go back to an early phase of contact with Akoko-Edo, where they would show young women presenting gifts to a prospective father-in-law.

PHOTOGRAPH BY JOHN PICTON, JANUARY 1966.

REPRODUCED BY PERMISSION OF THE NATIONAL COMMISSION FOR MUSEUMS AND MONUMENTS, NIGERIA.

4.18 (TOP LEFT)

This stool belonged to Umece of Upogoro, near Okene, Ebira. He was the son of Adangara, a heroic warrior; but the stool is said to have been carved even before the time of Adangara. If this is true, it could have been carved well back into the nineteenth century. It can be attributed to an Akoko-Edo carver, though his name and location were not remembered. The figure shown is a young Akoko-Edo woman dancing at her coming-of-age ceremony with her arms raised to better support the weight of all her bracelets.

PHOTOGRAPH BY JOHN PICTON, AUGUST 1966. REPRODUCED BY PERMISSION OF THE NATIONAL COMMISSION FOR MUSEUMS AND MONUMENTS, NIGERIA.

4.19 (TOP RIGHT)

This is the stool of Okino, a skilled hunter and warrior at Oken'eba—the original hilltop settlement of Okene—who employed poison arrows with deadly accuracy. Okino died in 1935, and following his instructions, the stool became the shrine to his continued presence among his descendants, sacrifices taking place annually during the Ecane festival (see fig. 4.16). Hunting trophies and the bones of sacrificed animals are left on the stool. Okino's great-grandfather was said to have been the first person to settle in Oken'eba. The stool was acquired perhaps in the late nineteenth century from an Akoko-Edo sculptor, given the image of a young woman at her coming-of-age ceremony.

PHOTOGRAPH BY JOHN PICTON, MARCH 1967. REPRODUCED BY PERMISSION OF THE NATIONAL COMMISSION FOR MUSEUMS AND MONUMENTS, NIGERIA.

4.20 (RIGHT)

Stool
Ebira peoples, early to mid-twentieth century
Wood
H: 56 cm
COLLECTION OF TOBY AND BARRY HECHT
PHOTOGRAPH © 2010, GREG STALEY
PROVENANCE: GEORGE UWECHUE, NIGERIA

This stool was certainly carved in Akoko-Edo, though the precise location is uncertain. Two of the figures are young women dressed and dancing during their coming-of-age rites, while the other two figures are young men during one of a series of age-grade rites, both are aspects of Akoko-Edo practice. Formal age-grades are unknown in Ebira. Stools of this sort, however, are commonplace there.

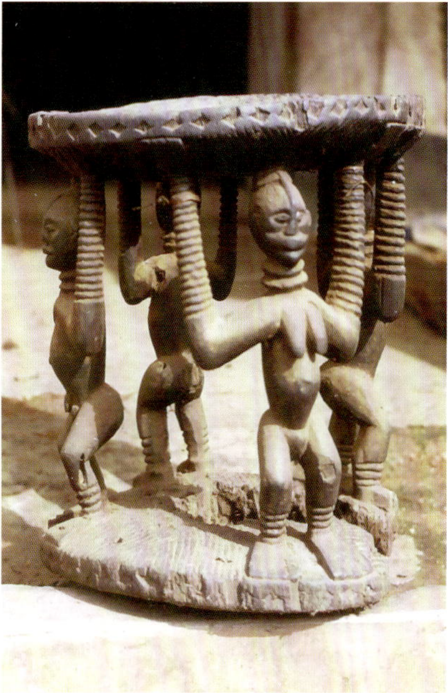

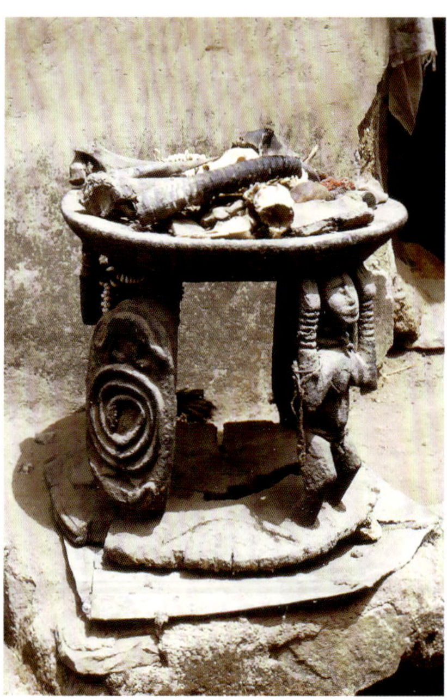

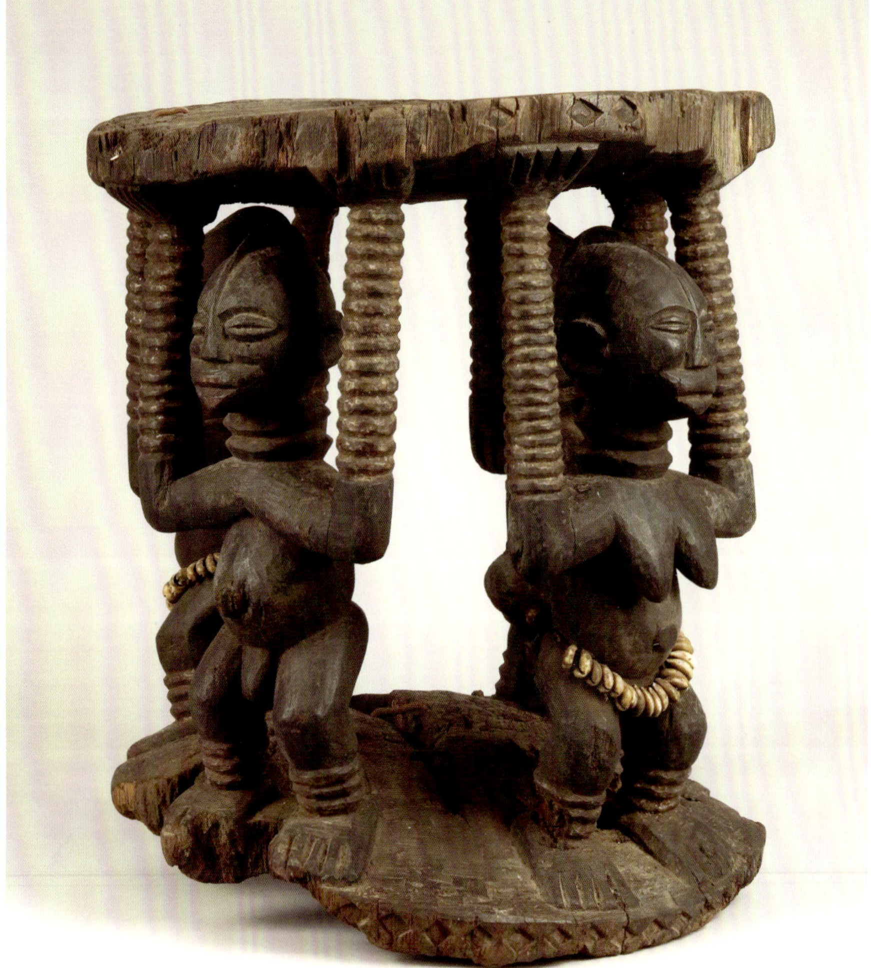

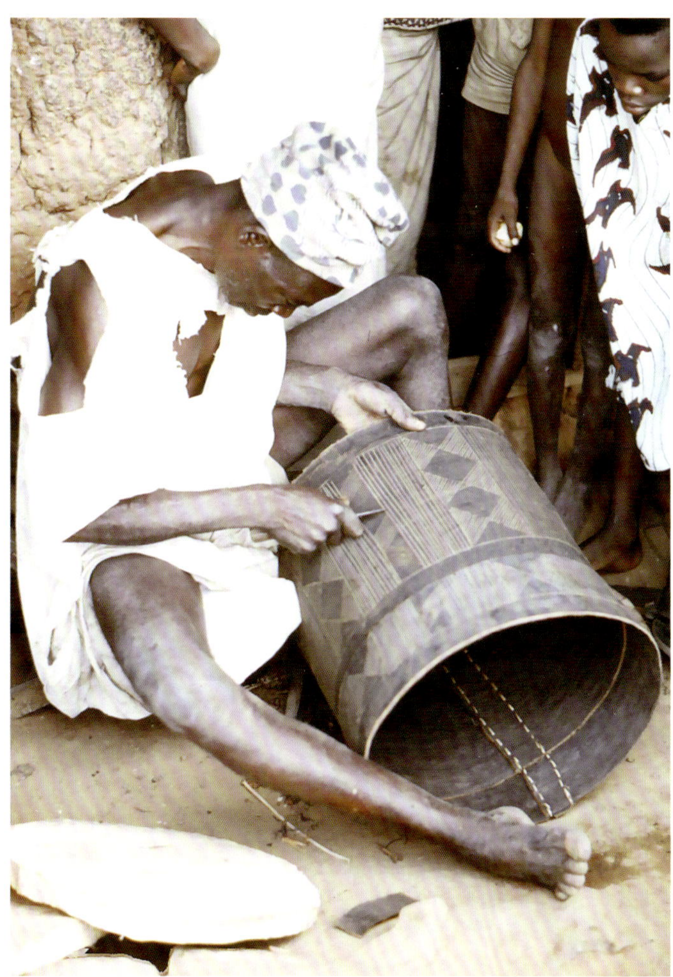

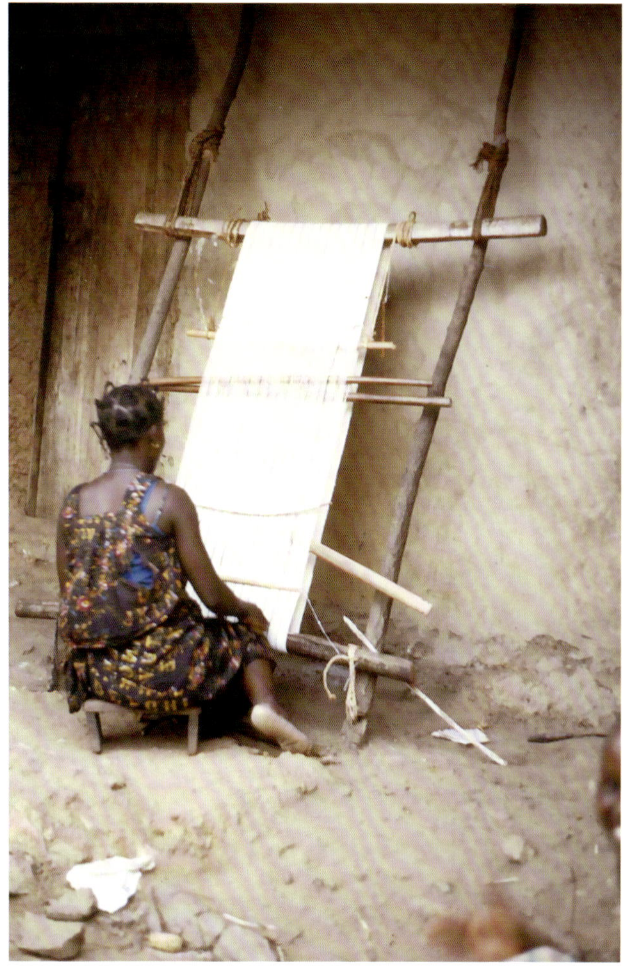

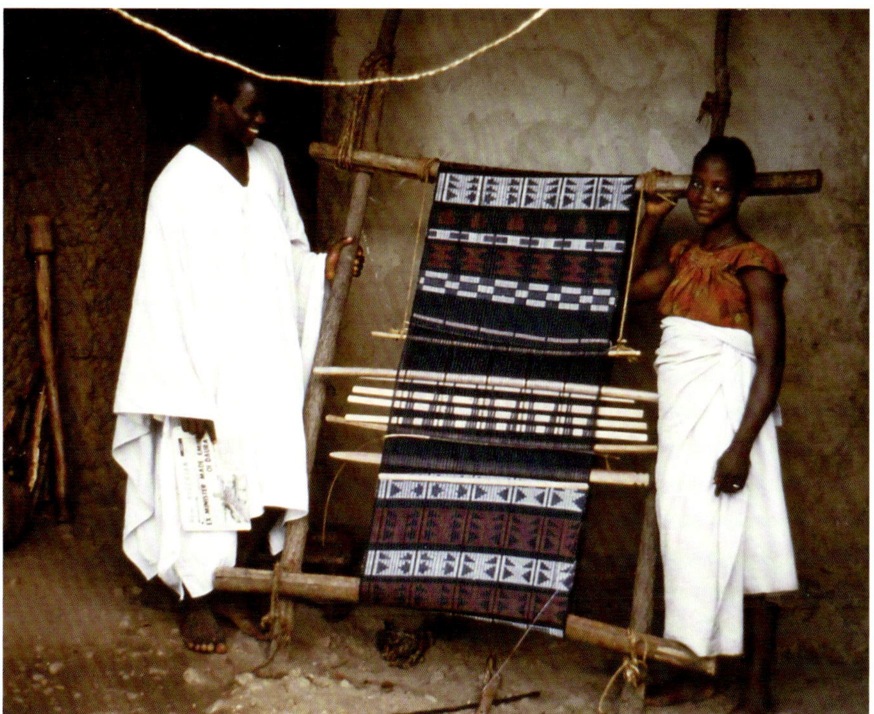

4.21 (TOP LEFT)

Alao of the Anemani lineage, Obeiba, Ihima District, makes an *irapa*, the bark box used for storing masquerade dress. The patterns he incises are named according to their geometric forms, and they have no significance beyond presenting a patterned surface. The ends of the box can be seen on the ground next to Alao. Only men in Anemani lineage made *irapa*, and Alao and his brother Iraka were the only ones still doing so.

PHOTOGRAPH BY JOHN PICTON, APRIL 1967.

REPRODUCED BY PERMISSION OF THE NATIONAL COMMISSION FOR MUSEUMS AND MONUMENTS, NIGERIA.

4.22 (TOP RIGHT)

Agnes Omaku sits at her loom weaving hand-spun cotton cloth in Karaworo, Adavi District. The cloth is for sale in Okene market.

PHOTOGRAPH BY JOHN PICTON, JUNE 1966.

REPRODUCED BY PERMISSION OF THE NATIONAL COMMISSION FOR MUSEUMS AND MONUMENTS, NIGERIA.

4.23 (LEFT)

Agnes Omaku and her husband, Edward, stand with a loom she has set up with machine-spun cotton and viscose fibers. Five supplementary shed sticks permit float-weave patterning.

PHOTOGRAPH BY JOHN PICTON, JUNE 1966.

REPRODUCED BY PERMISSION OF THE NATIONAL COMMISSION FOR MUSEUMS AND MONUMENTS, NIGERIA.

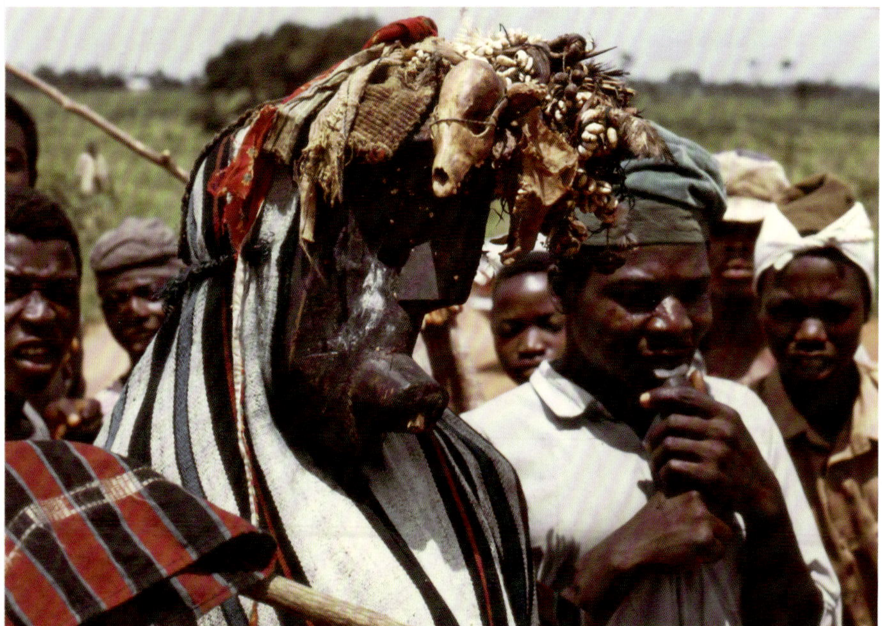

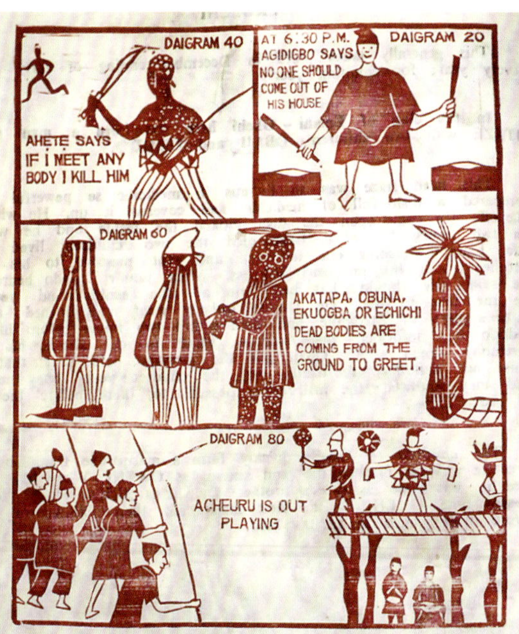

4.28

Ojova, a masquerade at Ecane in Oboroke, Ihima District, is named after a popular local market because his performance—like the market—draws people together (cf. fig. 4.15). Magical medicines and sacrificial remains, including a dog's skull, are attached to the head of the mask. Shroud cloth woven of hand-spun cotton is stitched to the mask, while a tunic of some other locally woven fabric covers the arms and hands. No part of the performer's body is left exposed. The heavy stick is used to chase and beat people, and the entourage includes a flute-player singing Ojova's praises.

4.29

A local illustration of the New Year Ekueci festival is included in an anonymous booklet about Ebira tradition, *Ohindase the Great: Facts about Ohindase Chieftaincy in Igbirra Land* (Okene: Alafia-Tayo Press, late 1970s?). Aceru (bottom right) was one of the two most popular night-singing masquerades in Okene. The illustration has to be read from right to left, and it also displays the Ebira habit of counting in pairs.

4.30

Adebira, an Eku'rahu (night masquerade), performs on his platform in the early hours of the morning before the close of the night feast of Ekueci in Kuroko, Adavi District. Although created around the identity of a son who has predeceased his mother, each Eku'rahu takes a praise name as his public persona. In this case it is Ad'ebira (father of Ebira).

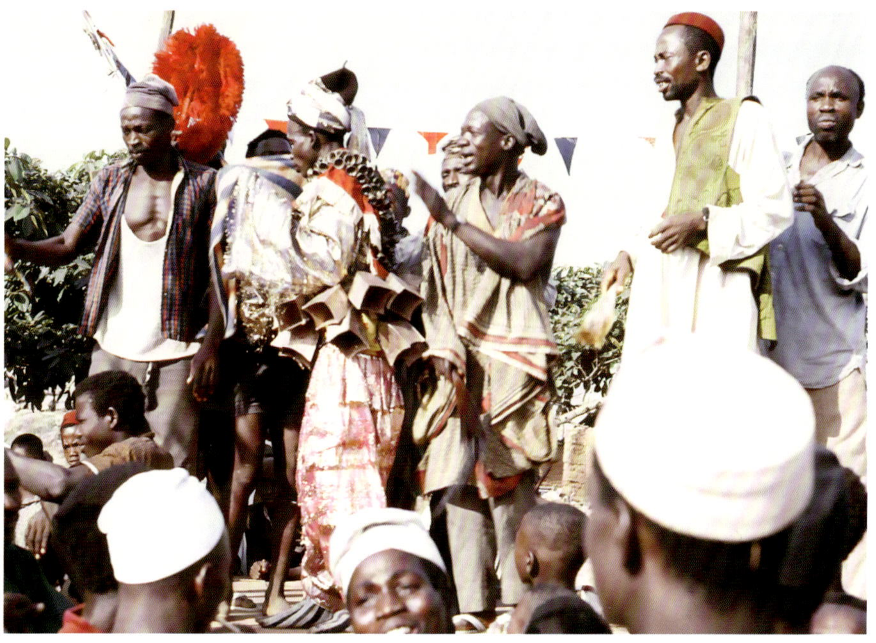

in warfare or hunting, by means of a name that denoted some event or quality in his life history. The basis of the costume for Ekuecici was *itokueta*, the indigo and white cotton cloth woven for the initial wrapping of the corpse of a dead man, which was tailored with distinct arms, legs, and a face sometimes covered by a wooden mask. The costume was almost invariably embellished with all manner of textiles and colors (figs. 4.27, 4.28). These masks, once created (and there were ways of making them independently of the post-burial rites for deceased elders) had their own festival, the midyear Ecane (feast of women), a daytime celebration that women are permitted to watch.

By the time of my research in the 1960s, the most popular Ebira masquerades were the Eku'rahu (masquerades of the night), a form that may well have developed only in the early years of the twentieth century within the context of the night feast marking the end of the transition period from one year to the next. Each performer was identified—through the divination that preceded the inception of a new identity within the corpus of Eku'rahu in any community—with a son who had predeceased his mother. The feast was called Ekueci (meaning: *eku* [masquerade/world of the dead] descends), a highly imploded phrase that denotes the deceased coming to enjoy the hospitality of the living.[23] This is the night when all the dead return home, a celebration from which women were excluded and required to remain in their rooms from dusk till daylight (fig. 4.29). The performers were dressed in glittery textiles, hung with bells, but they did not cover their faces, as masks were only necessary in the presence of women (fig. 4.30). While the celebration was of unknown antiquity and marked by the appearance of many different categories of mask,[24] it was evident from the memories of elders that it was only within the period of their youth that sons who had predeceased their mothers began to sing on this night alone for the entertainment of the community.[25] Ekueci was preceded by the appearance through the previous month of the re-embodied elder chosen to offer healing and prescribe the sacrifices to be made house by house for the benefit of the coming year (fig. 4.31).

Ebira masquerade represents a tradition shared, at least in some respects, with other peoples east of the Niger-Benue confluence,[26] an inheritance that has also changed and developed in the period since Ebira arrival in the hilly marches of Edo- and Yoruba-speaking peoples. It is also clear that in some Akoko-Edo, Etsako, and confluence Yoruba communities, there are mask forms of Ebira derivation. In and around Kabba there was a mythic account of a raid on an Ebira village during which a box was taken that turned out to contain masquerade costumes. Ebira advice had to be sought as to their use and performance. In Abinu, Elisha Renne (1995, esp. ch. 5 and 6) found that there are two different sets of masquerade, one of which includes the equivalent of Ebira Ekuoba, said to have been given to a hunter by a local deity. In many Akoko-Edo communities there are masks associated with age-grade ceremonial. In a few places, these include wooden helmets with figurative superstructures that, when worn, produce a figure some ten feet in height (Picton 1991). Elsewhere, age-grade masks were rather less-dramatic figures made of basketry and fiber; and it was in these instances that Ebira forms had sometimes been adopted as a better kind of public entertainment, with the added attraction of the representation of overt male dominance over women. Ososo was such a case, where the cycle of night and day feasts had been developed but without the ancestral re-embodiments, and the night singers even performed in the Ebira language. Such was their popularity that several interest groups (including Uneme smiths who could thereby achieve an authority denied them in Ebira) claimed responsibility for their introduction with such enthusiasm that the question could not be resolved. By 1990, however, a predominantly Christian elite had successfully encouraged the abandonment of Ebira-style masquerade on the grounds that it was not a local thing. In Etsako communities it seems that a process of cultural reinvention took place in the face of colonial rule, drawing upon several traditions, including Ebira and Igbo in addition to those local to the area. Jean Borgatti's study of Okpella (1976b; 1979b; 1982) is the authoritative account of a series of direct and indirect borrowings. The fact that some confluence Yoruba and Edo-related communities had taken up Ebira masquerade reinforced the sense of Ebira cultural and ethnic identity, but it is worth adding that even in Ebira there is (or was) a completely separate tradition of masking associated with the night feasts of Ramadan, masking that has simply not yet been investigated.

SCULPTURE AND MASQUERADE, OTHER TRADITIONS

In the mid- to late nineteenth century, communities of Nupe-speaking fishermen settled along both sides of the Niger (though mostly along the eastern banks), south of Lokoja. There they became known as Bassa Nge (in Nupe: "we are not Bassa"). This differentiates them from the Bassa Komo (also Kwomu or Ukuomu), or the "true" Bassa, who were scattered through the area to the north of the confluence and often lived under Nupe or Egbira overlords. In the nineteenth century, the Bassa Komo also moved south of the Benue east of Lokoja. The Nupe-speaking Bassa Nge

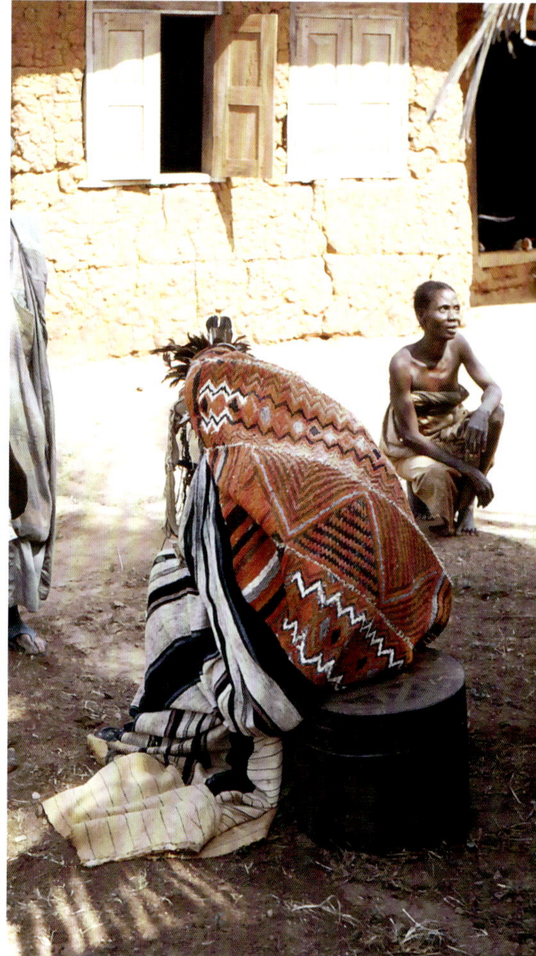

4.31
A woman consults the Ekuoba chosen through divination to visit the community of his descendants in the weeks prior to the New Year festival of Ekueci. He sits on the bark box in which the masquerade dress is kept.

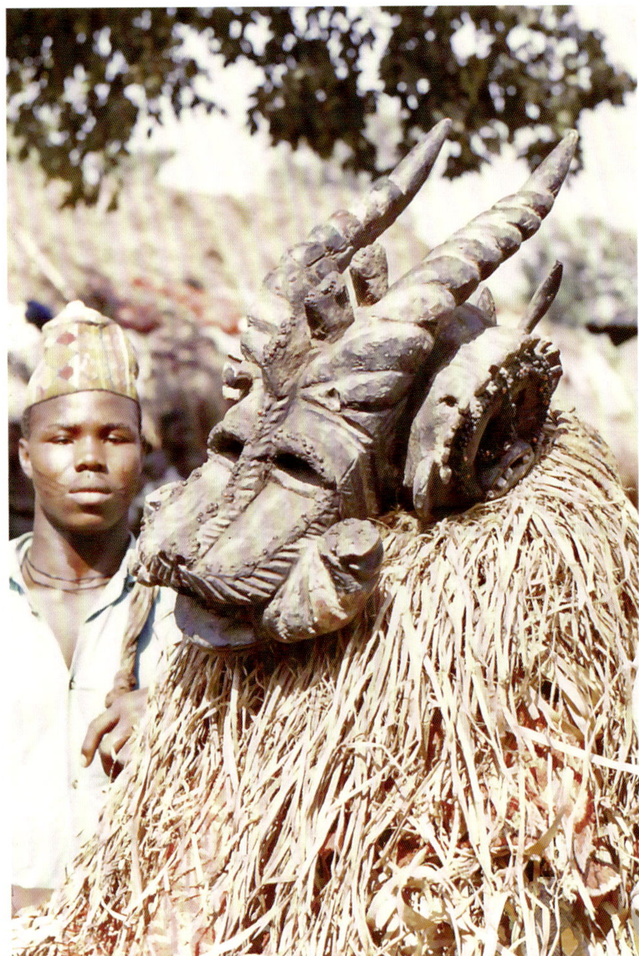

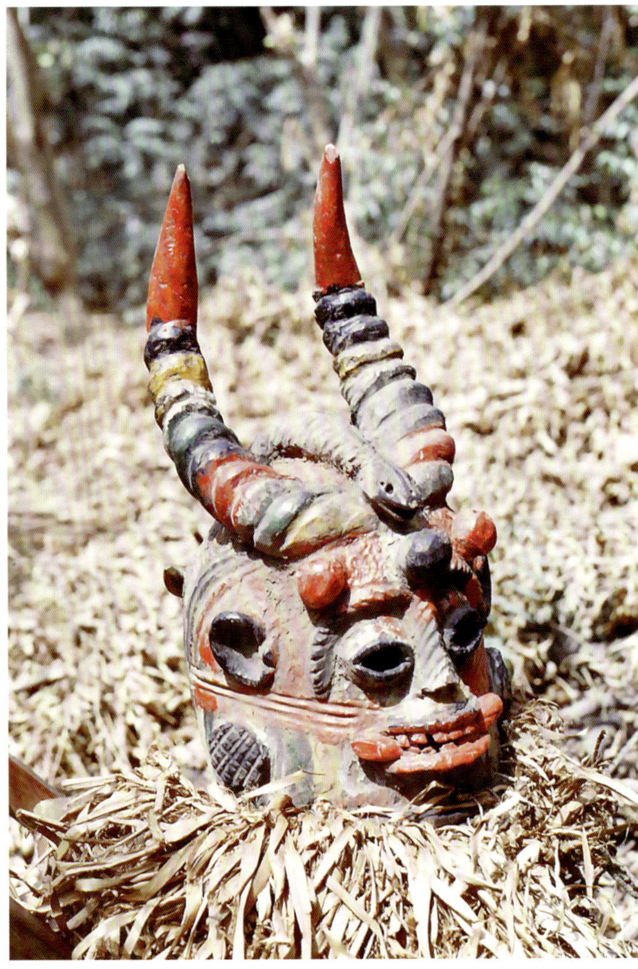

4.32

This helmet mask at Gbagana, a Bassa Nge village north of Ajaokuta on the west bank of the lower Niger, was said to perform in a ferocious manner at funerary and other celebrations, including (by the 1960s) Muslim festivals. It combines the features of buffalo and warthog. It was commissioned from a Bassa Nge sculptor (whose name was not remembered), perhaps around 1900, by its owner's grandfather when he was living in Agbaja (Aworo, confluence Yoruba) before moving southward.

Photograph by John Picton, January 1967.
Reproduced by permission of the National Commission for Museums and Monuments, Nigeria.

4.33

This helmet mask was probably commissioned in the 1920s by the elders of Ododobaji, a Bassa Nge village on the east bank of the lower Niger opposite Ajaokuta. The sculptor was local to the village, but his name was not remembered. Though originally made for funerary rites and local festivals, by the 1960s the villagers had all become Muslim, and the masquerade performed at the Muslim festivals.

Photograph by John Picton, February 1967.
Reproduced by permission of the National Commission for Museums and Monuments, Nigeria.

are Muslim, and I saw some of their sculpturally powerful masks in 1969 and was told that they performed at Islamic feasts. The forms of these masks, however, clearly derive from central and southern Igala prototypes (figs. 4.32, 4.33). The use of masks at Muslim festivals elsewhere in the Nupe-speaking area has also been documented (Stevens 1973). In contrast, the witch-hunting Ndako Gboya of the Nupe might be thought of as related to the Ebira Ekuoba because of its capacity to extend its great height and because of the anti-witchcraft policing role it once had. The latter suggests a measure of common purpose with Ebira where masked performers might sometimes speak as oracles with the capacity to heal afflictions caused by witchcraft. The square internal construction of the Ndako Gboya mask, over which the costume is sewn, together with the mechanism for raising and lowering it, are, however, completely different from the Ebira Ekuoba. Furthermore, Nadel's account of the Ndako Gboya (1954) does not portray it as an ancestral re-embodiment. For these reasons I had been rather dismissive of the idea that the Ndako Gboya might be part of the same complex as Ekuoba and the others. On the other hand, in reading Nadel one rather gained the impression that making sense of Ndako Gboya eluded him, whereas its ancestral connotations were made very clear to Constanze Weise in her recent research (see chapter 3, pp. 123–29). I have, in consequence, revised my opinion on this matter. For further data regarding Ebira Ekuoba, see "Ebira Masquerade and Its Histories" (this volume, chapter 3, pp. 115–23).

There is, of course, a good deal of Nupe sculpture, some of it of architectural dimensions: veranda posts and doors in addition to an array of more domestic artifacts. Examples are figurative and schematic. Yet it is a schematization out of character with confluence and Benue Valley work. Art historically, Nupe sculpture (see Stevens 1966) is probably better understood as a more schematic variant of central Yoruba work.

As for the Bassa Komo to the east of Lokoja, we still know little about them, though for what it is worth, their language is classed in the Benue-Congo group (as is Jukun) rather than Kwa (to which Yoruba, Edo, Ebira, Nupe, Igala, and Idoma belong). Most of the few sculptures known from Bassa Komo territory are masks and headpieces, so schematic and utterly rudimentary in their display of sculptural ability that it is impossible to say much else about them (fig. 4.34). Indeed, I would think that anything of any sculptural ability with a Bassa Komo label on it was almost certainly carved by non-Bassa.

EBIRA-IGALA RELATIONSHIPS AND CONFLUENCE HISTORY

The mythic aura of Jukun origin, authority, influence, or whatever seems to have acquired much the same kind of "taken-for-granted" status along the Benue Valley as has the mythic origin of modern Yoruba culture in ancient Ife. In neither case is there any firm archaeological or historical evidence, but at least Ife is a source of local ideas about kingship, whereas presumptions of Jukun origins seem to stem largely from British colonial wishful thinking. There are interconnections, of course, that we perceive in words, material forms, and social practices, most obviously in the context of ancestral masquerades—from Jukun/Abakwariga to the Niger-Benue confluence—but the borrowing of something does not necessitate a common political authority or the dominance of one group by another. After all, confluence Yoruba and Akoko-Edo borrowings of Ebira masquerade took place in spite of local rivalries and the endemic feuding and warfare that was only brought to an end by British colonial rule. Nor does borrowing demand a common or closely related linguistic basis. Ebira is a Kwa language in common with Idoma, Igala, Nupe, Edo, Igbo, Yoruba, and so forth; whereas Jukun is a Benue-Congo language, as are Tiv, Bassa Komo, and the languages of the Cross River region and the whole of Bantu-speaking central, eastern, and southern Africa.

Yakubu Ibrahim (2000, 2) writes about Egbira traders and settlements throughout the region east of the confluence, and perhaps at some early stage there was the recognition of Jukun authority in the payment of tribute. This is feasible, but when he describes the Igala royal dynasty founded by Ayagba om Idoko (Ayagba son of Idoko) probably in the late seventeenth century as an "Ebira-Jukun" dynasty (because a Jukun prince had migrated to Igala with his Egbira supporters [Ibrahim 2000, 3]), he is relying upon merely one of a range of mythic options, as Boston (1968, 6–27) had already made clear. For Ayagba om Idoko was also, and more forcefully, identified as descended from the impregnation of an Igala woman by a leopard and as the heroic figure who throws off Jukun (and Edo?) authority in his refusal to pay tribute.

The commonplace assumptions of recent Ebira scholarship (Ibrahim 2000; Husaini 1986) are indeed that Egbira people migrated into Igala with the Jukun founders of its royal dynasty in the late seventeenth century and then during the following century moved on in three directions. One was northward to found the kingdoms of Igu, based at Koton Karifi, and Opanda, a major trading center destroyed by the Fulani-led jihad in the mid-nineteenth century. Boston (1968, 51), however, records a myth in which Ayagba om Idoko relies on the assistance of Agaidoko, an Egbira riverain lineage founded *from* Opanda (see below) in the preparation of a magical medicine to protect newborn children. A second migration from Igala led to the settlement we now know (via dialect changes) as Ebira. People crossed the river and moved westward from the area known as Ebir'opete, because that is where Ebira people supposedly first "sat down" after passing through Igala (*opete* is one of the words for the large stool of an elder). A third migration led to the foundation of the Akoko-Edo town of Igarra, also known in Ebira as Etuno ("the land of Uno," who was the king of the original inhabitants of the place; Husaini 1986, 133). There are two variant myths here, one that the founders passed through the Okene area but moved south, the other that Etuno was founded from Okene, which was itself only of mid-nineteenth-century

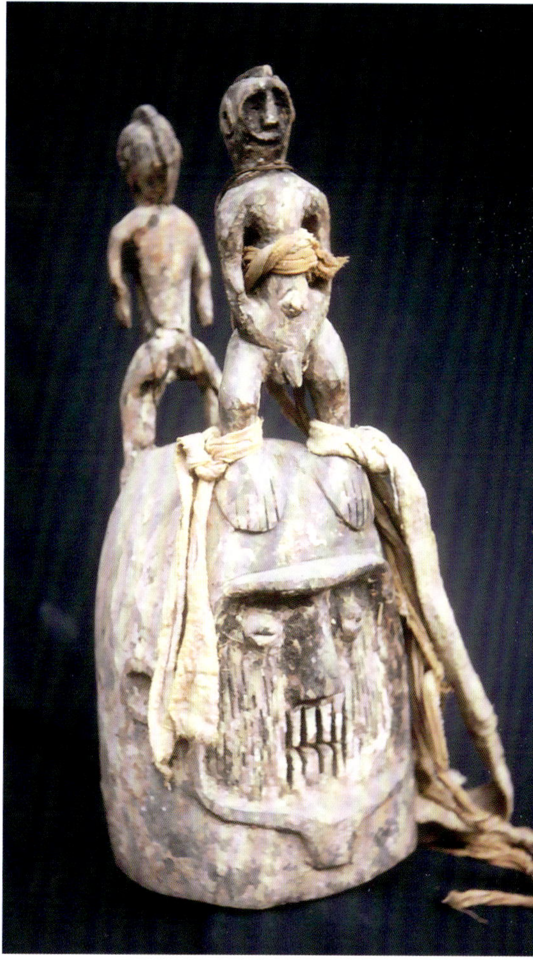

4.34
This Bassa Komo helmet mask was collected by John Boston for the National Museum, Lagos.
PHOTOGRAPH BY CHRISTOPHER AWE, 1969.
REPRODUCED BY PERMISSION OF THE NATIONAL COMMISSION FOR MUSEUMS AND MONUMENTS, NIGERIA.

foundation. Igarra was the preferred name in order to trace their mythic journey (there is no "l" in Ebira).

My own research, though not concerned primarily with oral histories, suggested a rather different scenario. Firstly, different lineages in Ebira seemed to have different routes into the region we now call Et'Ebira (Ebiraland), some crossing the Niger at Ebir'opete and heading westward, others crossing perhaps further south and moving northward through the Edo-speaking region. Bearing in mind the foundation of Igarra, this suggests a rather more confusing picture of small groups of hunters and their families criss-crossing the same region in different directions from the late eighteenth century, but mostly ending up in the hilly region between Akoko-Edo and confluence Yoruba, from where other small groups moved on, southward to Igarra in the mid-nineteenth century, southwest to the region around the Yoruba city of Owo, as well as northeast toward Lokoja to found the farming villages of Atami and Osara in the mid-twentieth century. This notion of groups of hunters continually moving on and opening up new farmlands and settlements is a dominant cultural theme in Ebira tradition.

In support of this we have to remember that the entire riverain area of the Igala state was under the authority of three lineages of Egbira origin (Boston 1968, 110), which had a history of feuding over the rights to profitable riverain markets that could have provided the impetus for the migrations leading to Ebira and Etuno settlements. So, what about Igu and Opanda? Boston tells us (1968, 102) that most of the lineages that are Igala by assimilation rather than by origin claim Egbira ancestry, mostly from Opanda or Igu, although "the points of origin mentioned in the legends cannot always be identified and in some cases the reference is simply to Ojukpali, the hilly north." This could mean anywhere!

Indeed, Alhaji Isa Husaini (1986, 86) says that Opanda had been settled long before the mid-eighteenth-century establishment of the ruling lineage that was in place at the time of the Fulani-led Jihad. Elsewhere, Husaini (1986, 15–16) says that Igu was founded from a migration from Idah after the unsuccessful bid by an Egbira "blood relation" of Ayagba om Idoko to succeed Ayagba after his death. The disappointed relative, his household, and his sons traveled via Opanda and eventually settled in Koton Karifi. On the other hand, in November 1969, when I was working with village elders in the Ebir'opete region, I was told two versions of the migration into that area, both suggesting that the Egbira settlement of Igu and Opanda was prior to their sojourn in Igala. The elders who told me all this were, however, quick to emphasize that these were "mere stories," for Ebira people are not habitually given to myth. In Ebira the kinds of narrative regarded elsewhere as "myth" are found in the stories told by masked performers at nighttime festivals. In other words, they may be amusing, but one should not take them too seriously! Nevertheless, taken together with what we know of Egbira-derived Igala lineages, they do suggest that we should not date the Egbira inhabitance of the region north of the confluence from any supposed dates associated with ruling lineages. They further suggest that there was a back and forth movement between Igala, riverain Egbira, Igu, and Opanda of rather greater antiquity. The obvious point is that we get nowhere by collapsing the histories of peoples into the myths of ruling lineages.

There were movements of people around the confluence, largely in search of new hunting, fishing, and farming opportunities that we can date: the Ebira movement westward across the Niger as from the late eighteenth century (there is no incontrovertible certainty about that estimate, but the longest lineage ancestry I found in Ebira only went back six generations from the 1960s), and the Nupe and Bassa movements in the nineteenth century that give us the Bassa Nge and Bassa Komo. Leaving these to one side, together with myths accounting for the formation of royal dynasties, I can only conclude that the peoples we now call Egbira, Akoko-Edo, and confluence Yoruba, together with the Akpoto basis of the Igala state (assuming Akpoto has anything other than a mythic existence, perhaps with a common ancestry with what we now call "Yoruba"), have all been more or less just where they now are for a very long time, and almost certainly (in my view) long before the upheavals caused by the collapse of the Jukun empire of Kororofa (Kwararafa), the sixteenth-century Edo conquest of the protodynastic Igala state, the late seventeenth-century foundation of the present Igala royal dynasty by Ayagba om Idoko, or the Fulani-led Jihad that fizzled its way through much of the nineteenth century.

At this point I have two more comments. First, once Ebira people had begun to settle the region from the lower Niger to the hills between Akoko-Edo and confluence Yoruba they had no reason to go back to Igala or anywhere else. Ebira hunters, farmers, and traders looked north, south, and west; and the distribution of Ebira-derived masked performance corresponds to that pattern. The Ebira-Egbira-Igala linkages were known but irrelevant to the practical work of living and moving on. Second, there were histories to be traced in the inevitably composite nature of masked performances in particular locations. Ebira masquerade comprised elements of local dramatic innovation long after the settlement of their present area together with elements that must have a common ancestry with things done elsewhere: the Igala Egwu Afia are masks conceptually and materially related to Ebira Ekuoba, for example. Yet Igala masquerade is equally composite, including, for example, the metropolitan set of royal masks that are neither part of nor derived from the ancestral system. One of these is the early sixteenth-century brass mask cast in Benin City, "The Eye That Surpasses All Other Eyes," created to denote Igala subservience to the Edo Empire but later reenvisaged as emblematic of freedom from Edo and Jukun (and in due course Nupe-Fulani?) domination, perhaps the most magnificent work of art in the confluence region (see fig. 1.8).

MAPPING CONFLUENCE ART HISTORY

Each element of confluence practice has a distribution that traces a history, a particular trajectory that entails a network of forms, practices, and relationships that are distinct even when overlapping, yet interdependent or otherwise related to other elements. The very fact that the age-grade/title-taking system is common to much of the lower Niger region (except for Ebira and Igala) suggests something about the early history of the region, though it is impossible to tell whether or not these practices were established prior to the evolution of the differences of language, material culture, and ethnicity. We can at least be fairly certain that the age-grade/title-talking system dates prior to the inception of the Edo state, which evidently draws upon it in the relationship between palace associations and chiefly titles. The very absence of these institutions in Ebira defines them as relative newcomers. Meanwhile, one imagines that the contrasting social order (landholding lineages within which chiefly titles were inherited) evident in Igala to the east, and in Ekiti, Oyo, and so forth, to the west presents us with an alternative patterning also of considerable antiquity. No remnant of these patterns would appear archaeologically, even assuming that we knew the sites or had the data. Indeed, the evidence from ironworking (see below) would confuse rather than explain.

The single-heddle loom technology of woven textiles presents a different but overlapping trajectory. It spread through the lower Niger region, as did the age-grade/title-taking system, but with two significant differences. First, this technology was once widespread throughout the entire Yoruba-speaking region—though by the 1960s it had largely been discarded except in Ekiti and eastward—a distribution that suggests an antiquity at least as great perhaps as the contrast between the social systems just discussed. Second, whereas Ebira people did not adopt age-grades, except in Igarra, Ebira women did take up the single-heddle loom as they settled in the borderland between confluence Yoruba and Edo-related peoples. Then, during the second quarter of the twentieth century, with the availability of new yarns and dye colors, Ebira women developed a distinctive range of patterns and forms, using warp striping and the supplementary-weft technique to imitate narrow-strip patterning from

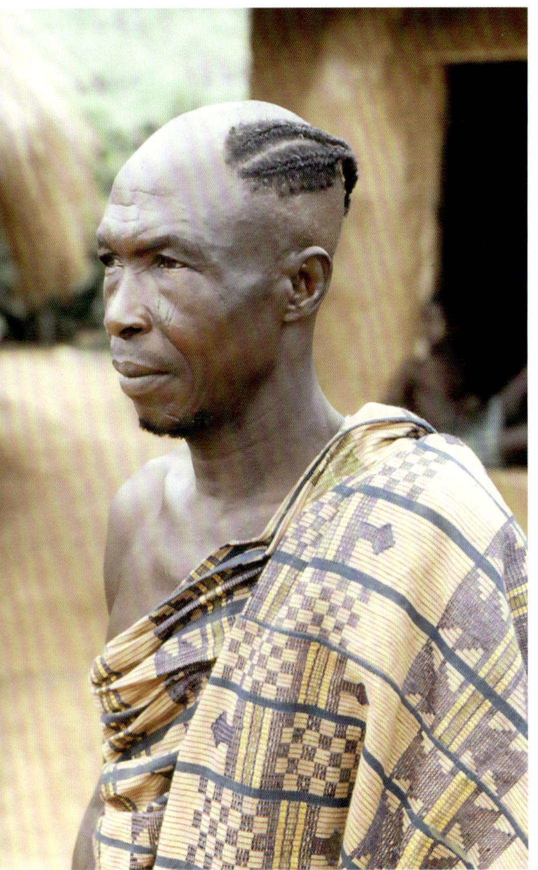

4.35

Audu Idoko of Ozuri, Adavi District, wears a textile woven in Ebira on the broad loom in imitation of Yoruba *aso oke*. It was an unusually expensive cloth for lounging around at home: to go out he would wear a wide-sleeved gown. The unshaved area above his left ear marks the place where magical medicine has been embedded. His face is marked with scarification, a practice that rapidly disappeared during the early twentieth century.

Photograph by John Picton, May 1967. Reproduced by permission of the National Commission for Museums and Monuments, Nigeria.

the region of the Oyo Empire (fig. 4.35) and the distinctive broad-loom traditions of Nupe and the southern Igbo town of Akwete. They also developed uniquely Ebira patterns that make their textiles distinctive within an array of local pattern-making traditions. None of this would survive archaeologically, but a collection of looms and other equipment, unless thoroughly documented, would suggest a unity across a wide region that is denied by other aspects of social and visual practice.

The distribution of ironworking technology, however, through all the communities of the region southwest of the confluence traces the migration of the Edo-related Uneme people away from their homeland. Ironworking today remains in the hands of the Uneme, an occupational caste defined by its ethnic origins. Among the smiths living in Ebira in the 1960s, the knowledge and use of the Uneme language had been lost, but the manner of their integration into Ebira society was still contingent upon their origin. A distinct ethnic identity as Uneme was maintained in the remembrance of the relationships of smith households to ancestral Ebira patronage, and certain practices remained prohibited to the Uneme, including the ownership of masquerade.

When we turn to masquerade, it is evident that once Ebira people became established in their present location, the performance styles characteristic of their masquerades proved so attractive to some nearby Yoruba- and Edo-related communities that they adopted parts of them as their own. In and around Kabba and in the Etsako communities of Okpella, these borrowings included the walking shrouds that enable the re-embodiment of deceased elders. In the Akoko-Edo village of Ososo, however, the pattern of alternating night and day festivals was adopted together with the night singers and the daytime servants of the world of the dead, but not the walking shrouds. This places the Ososo borrowing no earlier than the opening decades of the twentieth century, which is, I am reasonably certain, when this form of masquerade was initiated in Ebira. In Kabba the origins of masquerade were attributed to the theft of boxes containing Ebira costumes during a feud, whereas in Abinu there were two distinct sets of masquerades, some of local inception and the walking shroud form, which in this case could have had its origins in direct contact with Igala. Beyond the general association of masquerade and the dead, the Abinu explanation of the walking shroud bears little relationship to Ebira ideas (Renne 1995, ch. 5, 6). Another Abinu masquerade, Ouna, was once included among the Ebira repertoire of forms, but had disappeared before the 1960s, while the Abinu Naroko clearly relates to the Idoma Unaaloko, a mask form not found as a distinct category in Ebira. Confluence art history is evidently far more complex that even this essay has so far suggested.

In regard to wood carving, the distribution of the stools and staffs that mark a man's age and authority was not limited to the particular system and structure that gave them definition. Whether the status of an elder was determined socially via an age-grade system or absolutely as in Ebira, staffs and stools were still required, and one cannot determine which system they were used in from their forms. The same applies to the differing methods of title-taking, with the additional point that one cannot tell from the form whether it was for an elder or a titled man. Rather, what we seem to be presented with is a series of idiosyncratic schematizations associated with individual sculptors whose identities may still only be known from the forms and imagery of the works themselves. The ideas of the staff and the stool must be of considerable antiquity, given previous comments, though the extant works of art themselves were mostly of the recent past and rarely as old as the late nineteenth century. Staffs and stools clearly traveled, perhaps along with their owners. Stools and staffs from Akoko-Edo and Kabba-Yoruba (fig. 4.36), as well as the occasional Bassa Nge mask, were to be found in Ebira. Some of these had formal attributes that enabled identification. Otherwise, in my experience, it was only possible to be certain that a work in Ebira was by a smith, a freeborn Ebira, or whomever else, if one knew the artist personally and could recognize his hand.

I have often thought that for some works and/or sites of material, visual, and performance practice, the idea of an "artworld" (i.e., the functional interrelationship between the institutions and practices of training, making and/or performing, patronage, display, criticism) is the appropriate paradigm, more revealing of social and historical realities than ethnicity; yet the "artworld" appropriate to Ebira masquerade was a social configuration completely unlike the distribution, for example, of walking-shroud masquerades. Indeed, for the history of art sketched out in this essay, the "artworld" has little relevance. This confirms my view that different explanations are needed for different things, even within a given locality—feuding here, trade there, and so forth, each element with a history that might or might not be entailed in a local definition of social identity and that, in turn, might or might not be "phrased" in terms of ethnicity. After all, ethnicities, as with all the elements of form and practice discussed in this essay, have histories that are necessarily contingent upon other elements and their histories, as the relationships between Ebira and Uneme indicate. In other words, in these engagements between technology, social structure, and ethnicity, there were alternative outcomes. As Ebira people expanded within their present area, they ignored the prevailing social system, borrowed the weaving technology, maintained their difference from the smiths, made do with local carving styles and forms, and introduced new masquerades. Yet this is only one possible interpretation of the data, and it is no more than a choice facilitated by the tradition of writing about African art. For the boundaries of these forms cannot be equated with the geographical limits of Ebira ethnicity, and it would be just as possible to write a history that privileges the walking shroud masquerade form, or the loom, or the hands of wood-carvers. Each element has its own distribution through time and space, and if that seems to entail an almost impossibly complicated mapping process, I can only return to Arnold Rubin, who once said, "the messier it is, the more likely it is to be true."[27]

There is just one more thing to think about. I have suggested that the popular Ebira night masquerade was an early twentieth-century innovation within Ebira tradition. Its inception followed the demise of the Nupe and Ibadan empires and coincided more or less with the rise of British imperial control. Jean Borgatti has suggested the same sort of period for the putting together of the cycle of masking festivals she documented in Okpella (1976b; 1979b; 1982). William Rea (2000; 2008), researching the town of Ikole-Ekiti, has suggested that much of the masking there has a similar date of inception and that at least one element of current practice indicates an Ebira source: while the generic term *egun* is used of masquerade, there are some Ikole forms known as Eku, which surely is the Ebira word.[28] There are more or less substantial elements in the histories of Ebira, Ikole, and Okpella masquerade that can be seen as comparable examples of what has finally emerged in this essay as the twin themes of: (1) the complexities of art historical mapping; and (2) the social necessities of cultural reinvention in the face of novel circumstances. Is it too much to suggest that in the face of the effective inception of British colonial administration and all that came with it, we find processes of cultural reinvention within communities, distant from better-documented places such as Benin City,[29] Ibadan,[30] and Lagos[31] that were informed by practices, forms, words, and traditions that can be traced along the Benue Valley? ●

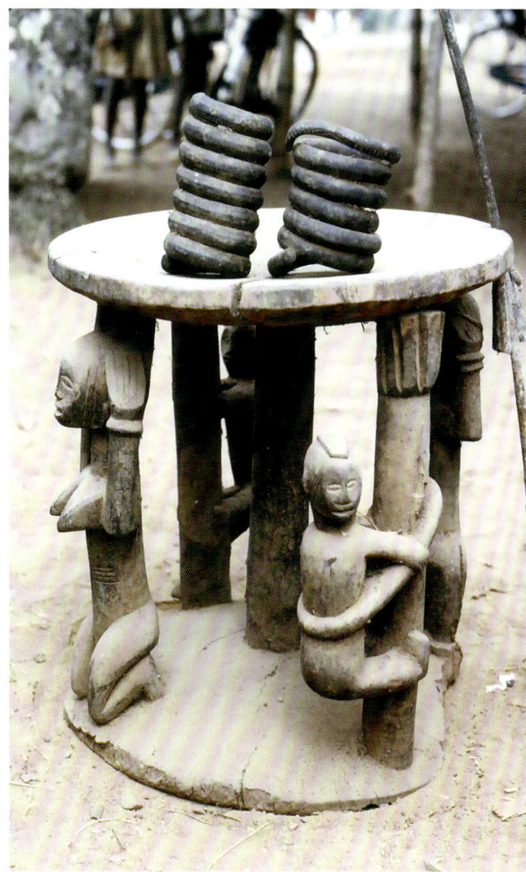

4.36
This stool was carved in the region of Kabba (i.e., confluence Yoruba). It was inherited by Damisa of the Ezuka lineage, Adavi-Eba, Ebira, from his father. The coiled brassware was said once to have been worn by girls to indicate betrothal (somewhat in the manner of Akoko-Edo), but if this was once an Ebira practice, it was long since forgotten.
PHOTOGRAPH BY JOHN PICTON, JANUARY 1966.
REPRODUCED BY PERMISSION OF THE NATIONAL COMMISSION FOR MUSEUMS AND MONUMENTS, NIGERIA.

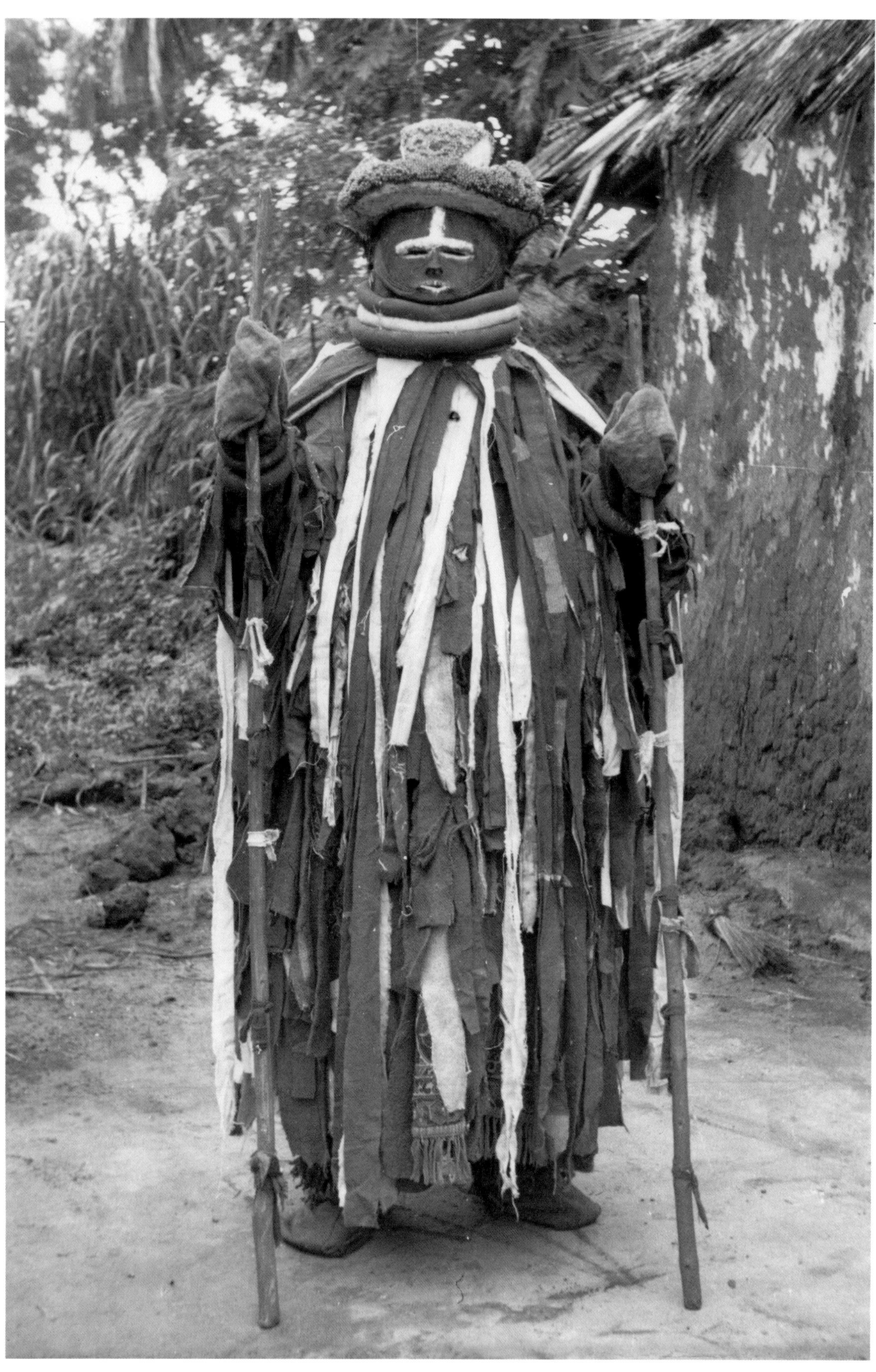

CHAPTER 5

Igala Masquerades and Figure Sculpture

JOHN BOSTON[1]

The Igala-speaking peoples live to the southeast of the confluence of the Niger and Benue rivers, and they share a common boundary with the Igbo to the south and the Idoma to the east. Their strategic position has brought them into contact with many other peoples, and they have specific traditions of conflict in the past with Benin and with the Jukun Kingdom. Linguistically and culturally, however, they have more in common with the Yoruba, though this underlying similarity does not extend to sharing the Yoruba preference for urban living. The Igala live by farming, hunting, fishing, and trading. They practice shifting cultivation and grow typical forest crops such as yams and maize, together with savanna crops such as millet, guinea corn, and benne seed. Tree fruits form an important part of the economy

Formerly, the Igala were united politically by respect for their king, the Ata, whose office was regarded as sacred. Effective authority was divided between landowning clans of indigenous origin—which controlled a network of traditional districts— and an immigrant royal group. The latter dominated the capital, Idah, and various other royal subclan centers, such as Ankpa. This dual system of administration was integrated by a complex system of descent, kinship, and marriage ties, with the many spreading branches of the royal clan articulating links with the smaller nonroyal clans. Descent, inheritance, and succession were traced through male links, but ties through females were important politically, socially, and in ancestor ritual.

The traditional Igala belief system recognized Ojo, a supreme being and creator, who ultimately maintained justice in the world. Igala also regarded the earth as sacred and maintained a correct relationship with it through cults at the district and the national level. Ancestral rituals kept alive the memory of forebears, and their presence was dramatized through masquerading. Anti-witchcraft spirits were important, and medicines and power objects were also employed by individuals and groups. Divination, using the Ifa oracle, brought order and predictability into the religious system.

IGALA RELIGION: THE CONTEXT FOR IGALA ART

In an earlier publication, I prefaced a comparison of carved horned figures found among the Igbo and the Igala with the remark that the Igala are less rich in art than the Igbo in terms of quantity and variety of output. Nevertheless, I pointed out that it has to be recognized that many individual Igala pieces are of high quality aesthetically and that Igala carvers and other artists are no less able and creative than their Igbo counterparts. The present study tries to justify and illustrate this by bringing together material from Igala that was collected either in 1957, while I was working for the

5.1
Ugbodu Achadu masquerade. [The Achadu is the representative of the Igbo nonroyal settlers in Igala and is the highest ranking commoner. All Egwu Ata masquerades represent the historically diverse ethnicities that have made up the Igala Kingdom.—Eds.].
PHOTOGRAPH BY JOHN BOSTON, IDAH, 1957.

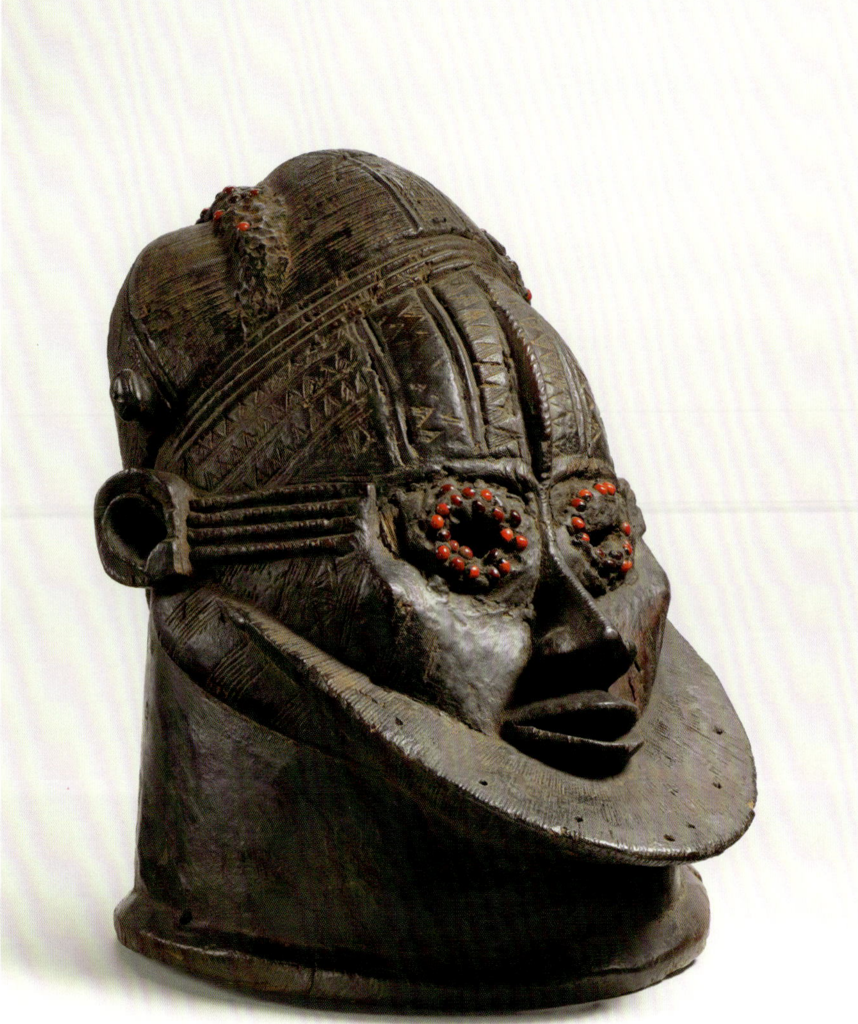

5.2
Helmet mask (Epe)
Igala peoples, twentieth century
Wood, pigment, abrus seeds
H: 36 cm
MUSÉE DU QUAI BRANLY, PARIS, 73.1996.1.81

IMAGE: © 2010 MUSÉE DU QUAI BRANLY. PHOTO-
GRAPH BY THIERRY OLLIVIER/MICHEL URTADO/
SCALA, FLORENCE

PROVENANCE: BARBIER-MUELLER COLLECTION,
GENEVA

Epe, one of the most powerful royal masks
owned by the Ata, or king, of Igala, can
be identified by the four parallel rows of
scarification extending from the eyes to the
ears and by a disc-shaped beard. This version
is unusually naturalistic in its proportions.
The full presentation, missing here, would
have included an *uloko* feather from the scarlet
lovebird, which would have been attached at
the forehead, and an abrus seed head covering.
The *uloko* feather, worn by warriors throughout the Lower and Middle Benue, suggests a
possible Kwororofan (Kwararafan)—that is,
post-1700—historical connection of the mask
to the present ruling dynasty in Idah.

Nigerian Antiquities Department (as it was then called), or in 1960–1962, when I was
Research Fellow of the Nigerian Institute of Social and Economic Research.

Igala art is characterized by considerable variety in form and style, ranging from
the brooding helmet masks of the Idah and Ibaji areas in the south (fig. 5.2) to the
Idoma-like whiteface masks of the Igala-Idoma border area to the northeast. At first
sight it seems that a great deal of borrowing from neighboring peoples has taken place
and also that there has been full scope in the art forms for individual invention and
creation. To explain, and at the same time to understand, this diversity, it is important
to stress that there are certain underlying uniformities in Igala culture, particularly at
the level of belief and ritual. It seems appropriate therefore to begin this analysis with
a description of Igala religious and magical beliefs and their associated rituals.

Ojo

The aforementioned supreme being, Ojo, is the creator of mankind and the final arbi-
ter in human relationships. Ojo has no shrines or other associated material forms, nor
is there any ritual in Igala of which he is the immediate object. This does not mean,
however, that he is remote or indifferent. Everyday speech in Igala contains frequent
references to Ojo and conveys the idea that he is the source of justice and morality
in human affairs. Common greetings incorporate references to him and relate the
vagaries of experience and fortune to his will. He does not need ritual since relations

with him are perfect in themselves and not subject to mischance and entropy. God is the one who creates and controls mankind; he owns "both the ax and the man who fells the tree."

A second usage of the term "Ojo" is an expression of belief in the relationship that exists between each individual and his or her guardian ancestral spirit or spirit of destiny. In principle this relationship becomes manifest on the fourteenth day after the birth of a baby when diviners consult the Ifa oracle (see below) to discover which individual, among a range of ancestors whose names are submitted by the baby's parents, is the one appointed by Ojo to watch over the child throughout its life. Igala share the common belief that the unborn choose their destiny while still in the spirit world, and the personal guardian spirit ensures that this choice is fulfilled in due course during the person's lifetime. Igala distinguish between the two meanings of the name "Ojo" through qualification. To refer to the supreme being, they use either Ojo Odobogagu (God the Almighty) or Ojochamachala (God in the heavens). For the personal guardian spirit, they refer to Ojo ki done wa (God that brings a person) or Ojo one (God of person).

Ane (Earth)

Igala believe that the earth is sacred and must not be polluted by behavior or occurrences regarded as unnatural and disruptive. Polluting actions are called *enwelifo* (lit., "things forbidden") and demand special sacrifices to remove the abomination. Bloodshed falls into this category. So do certain forms of death that are classed as *ukwu bibi* (bad deaths). Underlying this concept of pollution runs the assumption that the local community must maintain its solidarity and integrity through any stress on normalcy that occurs in the course of everyday life. This assumption has political as well as ritual aspects, as I have tried to show elsewhere (Boston 1968).

Egwu: Ritual for the Dead

Igala have few important rites of passage. Their birth and puberty rituals, for example, are carried out on a small scale and make relatively little impact on the life of the community. Transition rites at the end of the life cycle are, however, elaborate and involve much expenditure of time and effort. For the funeral ceremonies of important people, exchanges of gifts of cloth and food are made and sacrifices are also carried out. Masquerades appear, and the translation of the dead to ancestral status is dramatized in two major series of rituals, called respectively Oji and Aku (Akwu) or Ubi. The first series centers on interment of the body, the vacation of statuses, and the honoring of the deceased by his or her social contacts, friends, and relatives. In the second and final series of the obsequies—which may, according to the resources of the family, be held at an interval after the death and burial—masquerades appear to symbolize the welcoming of the dead into the ancestral world.

Funeral ritual involving masquerades is one of the major focal points of Igala art and symbolic activity, and I discuss this in detail below. In addition to their involvement in funeral rites, the ancestors (sing.: Egwu; pl.: Abegwu) also return annually to the community during the performance of the Egwu ceremonies by royal groups in Igala or for the Okula festival in the case of nonroyal descent groups.

Ebo

In Igala eyes, spirits in the *ebo* category play an important role in providing protection from witchcraft (*ochu*) and ill wishing or malice (*inacha*). Igala believe strongly in witchcraft and are preoccupied with the connection between it and illness and death. Until its use was banned by the colonial authorities, Igala employed the sasswood ordeal (*orachi*) in cases of suspected witchcraft. The suspect was forced to drink a poison derived from the sasswood tree; if vomiting resulted, the suspect was presumed innocent, but if death ensued the person was guilty. In more modern times people had recourse to *ebo* shrines for protection. The *ebo* receives an offering and is invoked to make the suspected witch ill and to force the witch to confess openly to the crimes in question. At the time of my fieldwork, and within a radius of some thirty miles from Idah, the Igala capital, the most important anti-witchcraft spirit was Iye, the goddess of smallpox. Shrines for this *ebo* were widely diffused in villages and homesteads throughout the metropolitan area. One particularly important shrine for Iye, situated at Orunu near Ajaka, attracted supplicants from a wide area. This *ebo* was not restricted to the infliction of smallpox as punishment for witchcraft but could take the form of any illness.

Other important *ebo* spirits in the central districts of Igala were Ichekpa, Ukpak-achi, and Alijenu. The last two of these were said to have been introduced into Igala comparatively recently. Other spirits that appear to have gone out of fashion in the recent past include Adalo, Ebi, Egbunu, Okpabili, Icheku, and several others.[2]

Ogwu (Medicines) and *Ode* (Power Objects)

Igala medicines are compounds of vegetables substances (*oli ogwu*) and magical ingre-dients (*ayibo*). The mixture is usually prepared when it is needed, and after the medi-cine has done its work, a small offering of kola nuts or food may be placed at the foot of the tree or bush from which the ingredients were taken. Power objects [known in older literature as "fetishes."—Eds.] are prepared from the same kinds of ingredients as medicines but are preserved by roasting or being ground into powder before they are enclosed in a pot or bundle. Such power objects, unlike medicines, receive blood sacrifices and are associated with individual success and achievement.

Ifa Divination

The Ifa oracle advises individual Igala where they stand in relation to the spirits at any given moment and also reveals the reaction of the spirits to ritual and sacrifice. The oracle thus has a two-way relationship encompassing both the petitioner and the spir-its. Ifa is said to seek to reveal (Ifa *ena*) information about the supernatural that will affect the well-being and the response of the individual. The Ifa diviner utilizes either four chains (Ifa *anwa*) or sand patterns (Ifa *ebutu*) to interpret meanings in the divina-tion process. Every consultation of Ifa is a dialogue between diviner and client carried on in symbolic language, which recites the names of the principal oracular patterns as they appear in the chains or sand patterns and explains their application to the matter at hand. Ifa catalyses the fluid elements in a situation and gives practical advice about what sacrifices and other ritual and practical steps should be taken to solve a problem. Such help is available whenever needed. For instance, if a ritual appears to have failed or a major undertaking such as a court case is pressing, Ifa is used to clarify the pos-sibilities and to discover the best way forward.

THE ART FORMS ASSOCIATED WITH SPECIFIC RITUALS

The majority of the religious elements and beliefs discussed above are not associated with art forms. For instance, Ojo, the creator god, has no cult objects and no ritual, nor does he receive offerings or sacrifices. The second Ojo, the guardian or tutelary spirit, is the object of both annual and occasional ritual, which includes sacrifice. This ritual, however, is performed either at the ancestor shrine of the ward of the adept or some other central point of the compound, such as the doorsill (*alugbona*) of the ward's main house. Earth shrines in the bush are marked by the shoots of quick-growing trees, while in the homestead the site of the earth shrine is marked by a few large stones placed in a central spot by the Chief of the Land or District Head (Onu Ane).

Ebo spirits may in some cases be represented by rather crudely modeled clay figures, but this is rare. More typically their shrines center on a clay pot supported on

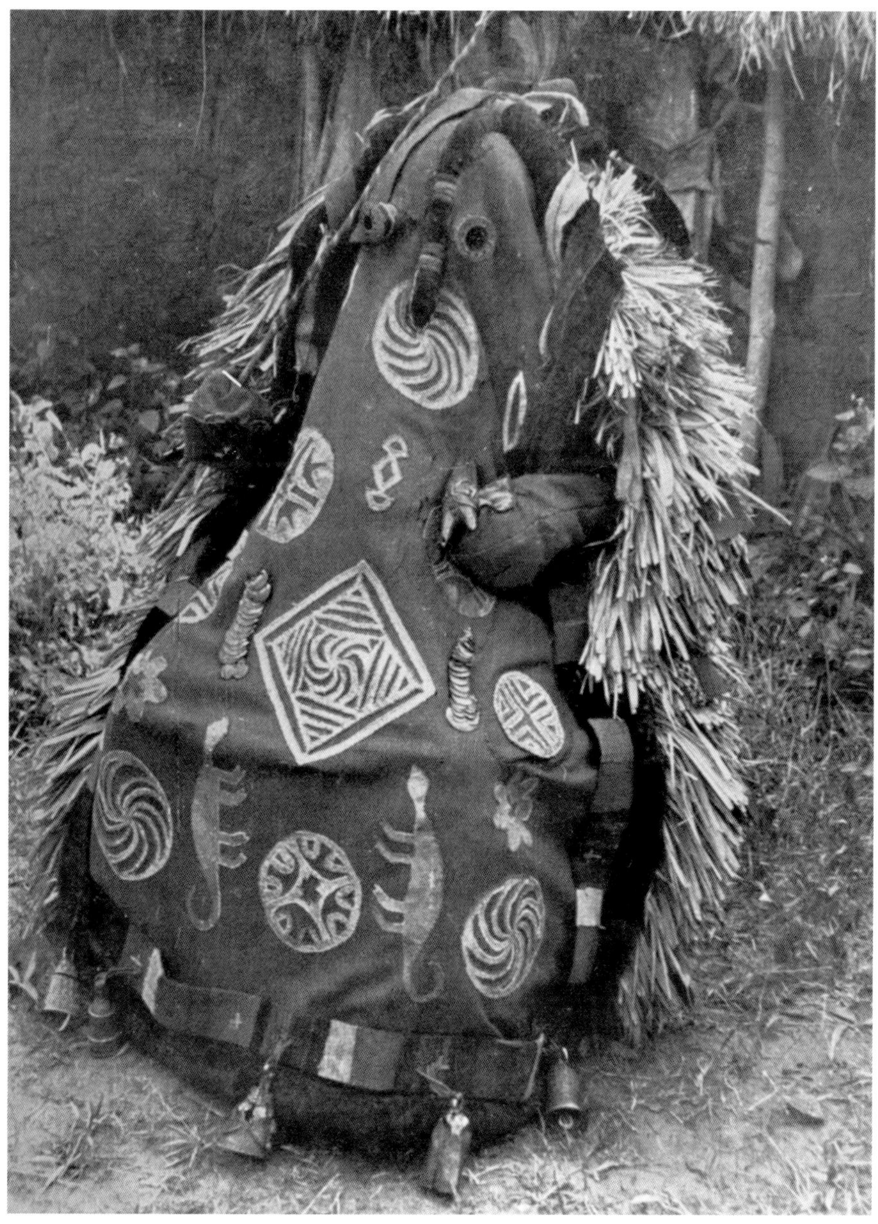

5.3
Igala Ekwe royal masquerade.
PHOTOGRAPH BY KENNETH MURRAY, IDAH, 1949.
REPRODUCED FROM MURRAY (1949A, 87).

a forked stick or mud pillar and sheltered by a small hut. Ukpakachi spirit shrines take
the form of a covered calabash decorated around the rim with a narrow strip of white
cloth to which cowrie shells are attached in a line. Sticks of white chalk are kept in the
calabash, and its outer surface may also be whitened. Alijenu spirits are represented
by bottles filled with water, which are embedded vertically in the ground alongside
the entrance path (*ojikpologu*) that leads into the homestead. The Ichekpa bush spirits
have small huts built for them and are thought to use small toadstool-shaped termite
mounds placed in the huts as stools.

The only spirits consistently associated with art forms in all parts of Igalaland
are Abegwu (ancestors). Before conversion to Islam or Christianity became common,
most Igala homesteads included houses for the ancestors in their domestic layout.
Typically, the compound of the head of an extended family was fronted by an *atakpa,
a* rectangular house used for receiving visitors and transacting other public business.
This led into an inner area called the *anuku,* bordered by smaller houses (*unyi aje*)
and still-smaller constructions that often included a house for the ancestors (*unyi
ibegwu*). The presence of the dead was symbolized in these shrines by collections of
spears (*okwo*) or staffs (*okwute*) standing in a corner or rested against one wall. Okegga
figures, which are associated with individual or family success, might be kept in the

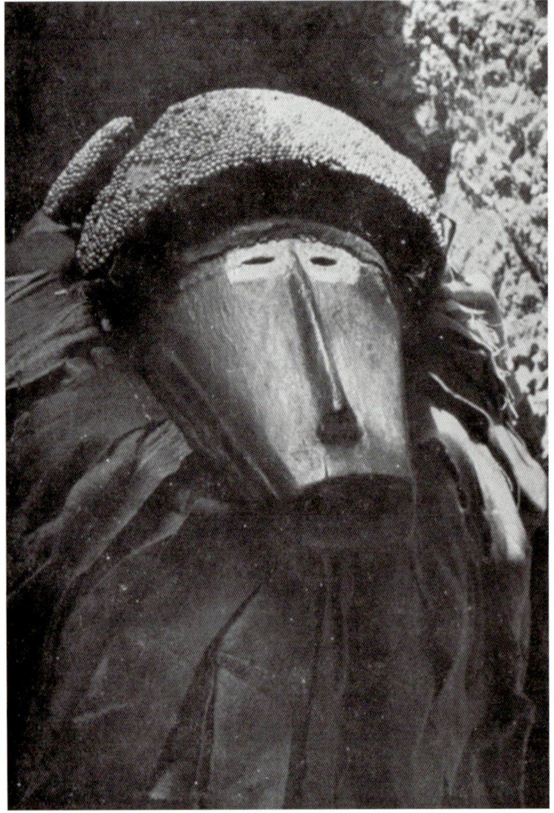

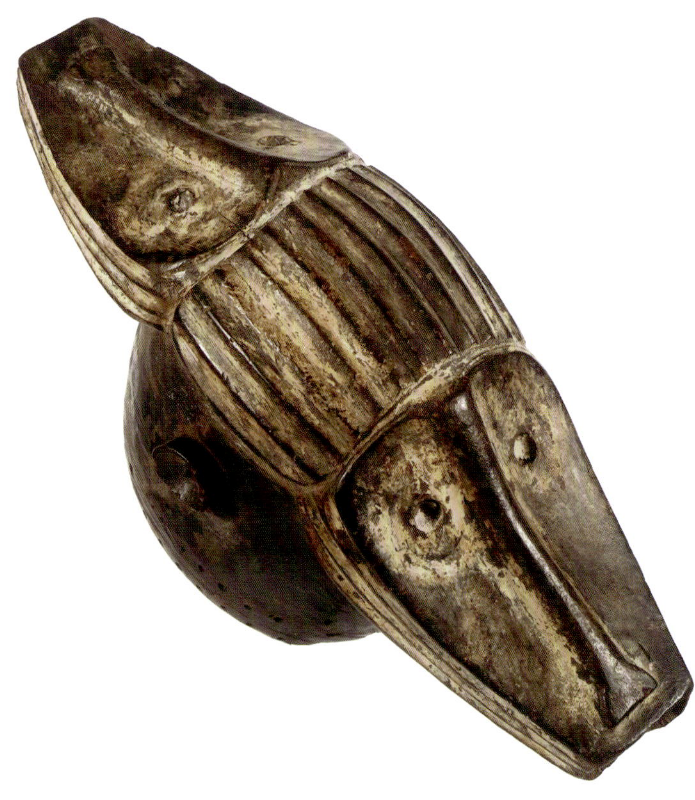

5.4
Igala Agbanabo royal masquerade.
PHOTOGRAPH BY KENNETH MURRAY, IDAH, 1949.
REPRODUCED FROM MURRAY (1949A, 88).

5.5
Janus-faced helmet mask (Agbanabo?)
Igala peoples, before 1978
Wood, pigment
L: 70 cm
SAMIR AND MINA BORRO, BRUSSELS
PHOTOGRAPH COURTESY SAMIR AND MINA BORRO
PROVENANCE: PURCHASED IN PARIS, 1970

This Janus-faced zoomorphic mask has a long
snout and bears a partial resemblance to the
Agbanabo, a masquerade described by scholars
as an enforcer of law and order that is feared
for its violent outbursts.

shrine in addition to an *ofo*, or medicine, bundle and the owner's *ode* (power objects).
Reminders of sacrifices performed in the past also made up part of the furnishings,
usually in the form of skulls of sacrificial offerings or bundles of feathers suspended
from the rafters. Ancestor shrines are often built over a grave but not invariably so.

The principal art form in Igala is, however, the art of masquerading, which
employs headdresses and costumes in a great variety of forms and materials (fig. 5.1).
Masquerades, known as Egwu, come from the land of the dead and in some cases
impersonate dead individuals by taking on their names and some of their roles. The
most ancient of these Egwu is Egwu Afia, owned by the nonroyal clans in Igala who
control the ritual of the earth. (see chapter 3, pp. 113–14). The royal clan, however, does
not have Egwu Afia, nor does it celebrate the annual Okula festival as do nonroyal
clans. The royal group commemorates its ancestors at an annual festival called Egwu,
held in the sixth month, around August. And instead of Egwu Afia, the royal clan has
its own masquerades, known collectively as Egwu Ata, the Ata being the Igala king, as
previously noted.

The most senior of the Ata's masquerades is Ekwe (fig. 5.3), whose fabric costume
is decorated with appliqué work in designs said to resemble Jukun motifs (Murray
1949, 85–92). This masquerade performs certain rituals for the king in addition to
accompanying him at the royal Egwu and Ocho festivals. Ekwe purifies the royal
palace if anyone dies within its precincts, and a similar purification is carried out if any
person is found guilty of having abused the king. To perform this duty Ekwe walks
three times around the palace, following the path outside its outer wall.

If the Ata wished to divorce one of his wives, she was taken to *okete* Ekwe (Ekwe's
compound), and the Ekwe then pronounced the following formula:

> Forever the Ata does not want you
> again. Your mother did not sell you
> to me. Your father did not sell you
> to me. The Ata will never touch you again.

Igala also claim that in the past Ekwe's compound offered sanctuary to any offender, no matter what the offense. The guilty party would become a slave of Ekwe, helping to repair the compound under the direction of Enefola, the palace eunuch, who was responsible for this masquerade and its compound.

Ekwe has his own praise names and songs, as follows:

Ide abikeke ki d'olopu Enefola	Horned caterpillar from Enefola's family.
Kwutu kwugu adagba joka ki ma gbo okaga	Elephant eating corn that takes no notice of the drum [beaten to drive it away].

Ekwe also ritually purifies the Ata himself at the Ocho and Ogaingain festivals by touching him lightly with the whip (*itali*) that he carries.

The second royal masquerade in order of seniority is Agbanabo (figs. 5.4, 5.5), whose headdress incorporates a long snout. It is said of this figure that he once came out for a royal festival carrying two spears (*okwo*). He stood on the small earth mound outside his house and then noticed one of the Ata's wives, a woman called Ebi, who was standing nearby and looking at him. Agbanabo ran toward her, but she still stood there, unafraid. Agbanabo went back to his earth mound and stood there, thinking. The woman stood unmoved and chewed some tobacco. Agbanabo's followers chanted his praise names, until the masquerade suddenly rushed at the woman and stabbed her through the body with his spears so that she fell dead. When the Ata heard about this, he at first ruled that Agbanabo should never appear again, but his people pleaded for the masquerade. Finally, it was decided that the masquerade could continue, but with Agbanabo carrying two sticks in place of the two spears.

It was explained to me that every royal masquerade has an *igbudu,* a small mound of earth, in front of the house from which it appears. It is the throne or couch belonging to that masquerade, and the masquerade stands on the mound before it makes its appearance in public. When one masquerader passes another's *igbudu*, it can, if it is senior, stand on the mound or even break it down deliberately. A junior masquerader would not stand upon the *igbudu* of a senior masquerade but would salute it by swinging and then stamping its right foot while waving the stick or sticks that it carries.

For Odumado (figs. 5.6, 5.7), another of the royal masquerades at Idah, I was given the following praise names:

Odumado mado alu gbonyen	What a freeborn man can do without trouble would cause offense if done by a stranger.
Egwujio kpama	Ancestor is buried O, keep to one side.
Ino nata ino nanyo	The bee that stings its honey has sweetness.
Ojali ma ka, ma Ii ma ma	Perfectly clear they say, if they see they will know.
Odumado kanyofe chunuchunu	Odumado let us go softly to the palace.
Ejumudekpa nyi koko, aja imomenegen	Eyes become red and round, the *aja* bird no longer knows its own children.
Ogada mejejio ogada, oga idiba am one mejin	Strong man takes no heed of two people, he is stronger than they.

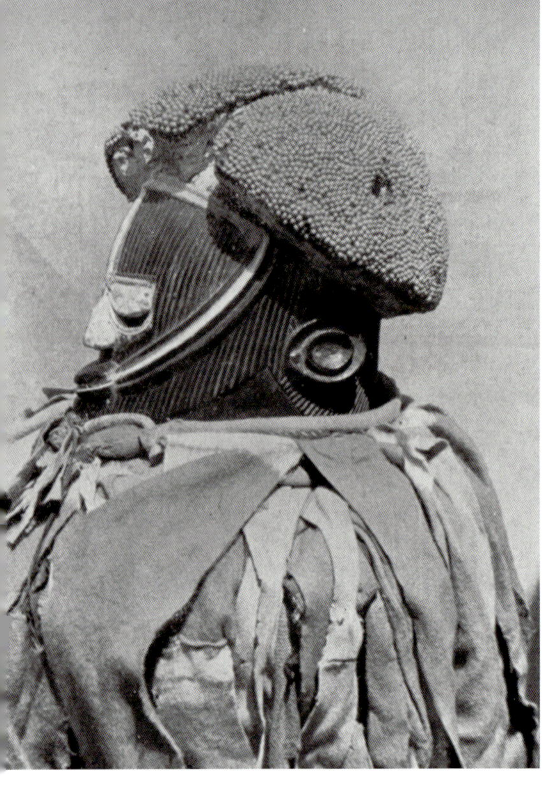

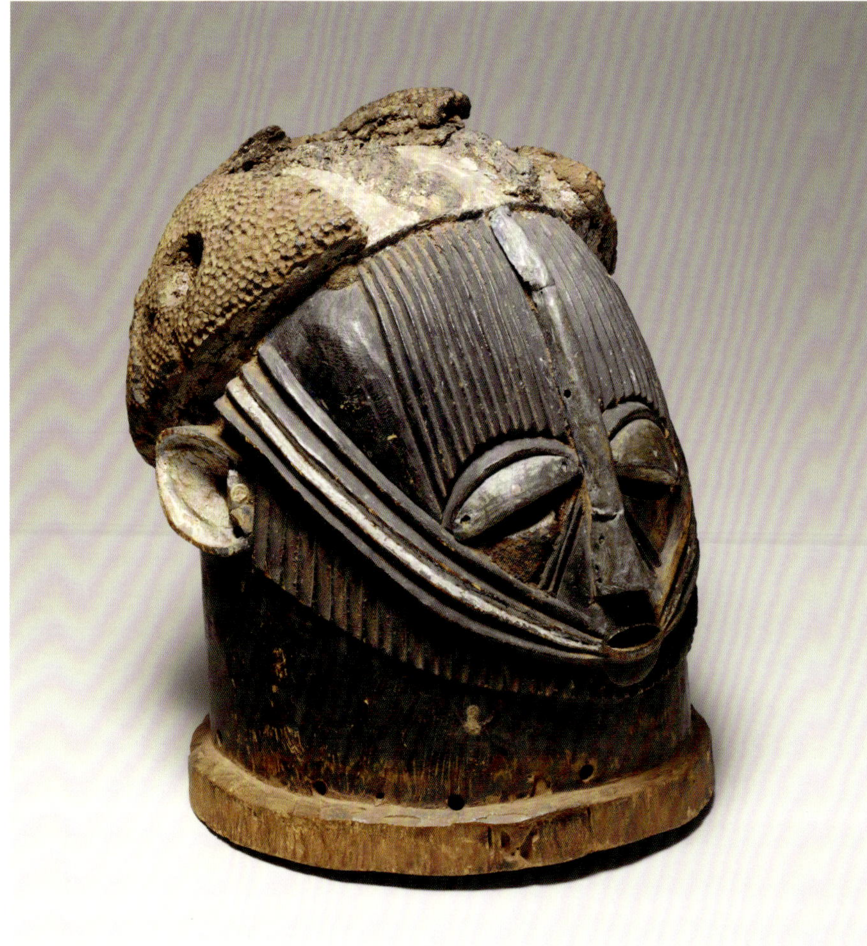

5.6
Igala Odumado masquerade.

5.7
Helmet mask (Odumado)
Igala peoples, nineteenth to twentieth century
Wood, pigment
H: 29.2 cm

Odumado is one of the Egwu Ata masquerades
owned by the royal clan in the Igala Kingdom. It is said to have originated among the
Akpoto indigenous population, who were later
overthrown in a war with Benin around 1520.
The heavy facial scarification, especially the
cat's whisker pattern observed running from
the sides of the mouth to the ears, is found on
many Igala masks. The top of the mask was
originally covered with red abrus seeds.

The Egwu Ata royal masquerades at Idah do not represent or impersonate the
dead, although whenever Ekwe comes out he is accompanied by a young man bearing a staff wrapped in cloth called *okwute* Ayagba (Ayagba's ancestor staff). On some
royal occasions Ekwe comes out without the other eight or nine royal masquerades.
For instance, he appears by himself on the day that the Ata performs rituals for his
own Ojo, or personal guardian spirit. One of the other Egwu Ata, called Ichawula
(fig. 5.8) makes a solo appearance on the night before the Ogbadu festival. One of the
royal chiefs with the title Omakoji Ata goes to keep watch on the northern approach
to Idah, the Igala capital, and when he returns from his vigil to report that there is no
threat to the town, Ichawula comes out to greet him and lead him home with rejoicing.

In discussions about the Egwu Ata and their possible connection with the royal
dead, it was explained to me that the masquerades come from the world of the dead
(Oja Egwu) but that they do not represent actual dead members of the royal house.
This was forcefully expressed by one informant who claimed that Ekwe is an *ebo,* an
anti-witchcraft spirit with responsibility for the care of the war medicines employed
by the founder of the royal house, Ayagba om Idoko. Ekwe is also described as the
spouse of Obajadaka, an *ebo* of fearsome reputation who makes occasional appearances at Idah in the form of a tall, collapsible masquerade. Ekwe carries a whip (*itali*)
in one hand, in the form of a peeled wand of *inoli*. In the other hand he grasps a small
Janus-headed staff made of brass. Ekwe, like the other royal masquerades, has his own
box stool, which in this case is decorated with beaten brass and rows of small cast-brass
figures (*ojibo*).

In addition to appearing at the Egwu and Ocho festivals and for lesser celebrations, the Egwu Ata perform for the second and final funeral ceremonies known as
Aku or Ubi. This final set of obsequies centers on an assemblage (*ihi*) of spears, arrows,

and cooking spoons, which is set up outside the dead person's house and decorated with strings of cowrie shells and strips of white cloth (*okpe*). The spot chosen for the *ihi* is in the center of the yard or a clearing outside the house where the entrance path (*ojikpologu*) debouches into the compound. Here, each evening for the seven days of the Aku period, men, women, and children gather to dance and sing (*etogba*) in honor of the dead. The crowd arranges itself in two lines flanking the entrance path, and the dancers stamp and swirl their way up the path left clear between the lines of mourners and then dance around the *ihi* at the apex of the crowd, in the center of the compound.

Music for the dancing is provided by singing and drumming. Many of the songs are obscene comments relating to genitalia and relations between the sexes. Some examples of these songs follow:

1. *Abobule me kalinamime*   Women let us see this thing yours.
    Inamime de folo gaaji   This thing yours is there hollow and erect.
    Abokele me kalinamime   Men let us see this thing yours.
    Inamime de woho wahia   Your thing is there hanging bulging.

2. *Ikpao i to o, agadama chofo*   It is ripe o it is soft o; their loins are open.
    Ikpao i Io o, agadama chofo   It is ripe o, it is soft o; their loins are empty.
    [This implies that the husband is cheated when he finds that his wife is not a virgin, while the wife is cheated when her husband turns out to be impotent.]

3. *Abu chekeli Iyegwi,*   How do I see you Iyegwi, lying spread out.
    datsi ajinga
    Mahi cha chaka   They have intercourse with her, every one.

For the final night of the Aku celebrations, which brings the whole funeral cycle to a climax, the dancing around the *ihi* is performed by masqueraders, who are brought out for the occasion by the in-laws (*ana*) of the dead person's family. The in-laws build temporary shelters (*ala*) out of palm fronds, so that they can sleep in the compound of the dead. And they also bring oil drums, water pots, grain, and firewood for brewing beer to celebrate the occasion. All the preparations culminate in a night of masked dancing along the *ojikpologu*, or entrance path, leading into the compound. In addition to drumming and singing, a staccato rhythm (*ogba*) is beaten out with heavy sticks on a wooden mortar placed on its side. The dancing does not commence until the night is well advanced, and kerosene pressure lamps are used to illuminate the scene. One by one, the masquerades take their turn performing with keen competition between the different dancers whose displays are carefully appraised by the spectators. The dancing continues at least to the small hours of the night and often until daybreak.

Igala say that the display of dancing represents the rejoicing in the world of the dead with which the newly deceased spirit is welcomed by the ancestors. And the whole festival is described as an *icholo* (essential rite or ritual). Aku is the most lavish of all ordinary Igala celebrations. And it is the chief occasion on which masquerades appear. The principal dancing Egwu for *ogba* are Inyelikpi (fig. 5.9), Owuna (fig. 5.10), Olagenyi (figs. 5.11, 5.12), and Ikpalikpa (fig. 5.13). The first of these (fig. 5.9) wears a whiteface, sloping cap mask that recalls the angled features of the Yoruba Gelede, while at the same time incorporating the whitened face of the typical Igbo or Idoma female dancing masquerade. Its costume is a rich brocade in vivid colors. Owuna (fig. 5.10), the second dancing type, is in many cases a juvenile masquerade with a fabric costume and cloth headpiece crowned with the white feathers of a bird called *icha-kolo*. Its features are marked by an oval or circular inset piece of net, sometimes sewn around with a string of white cowries. Olagenyi is a large bulky figure, portraying

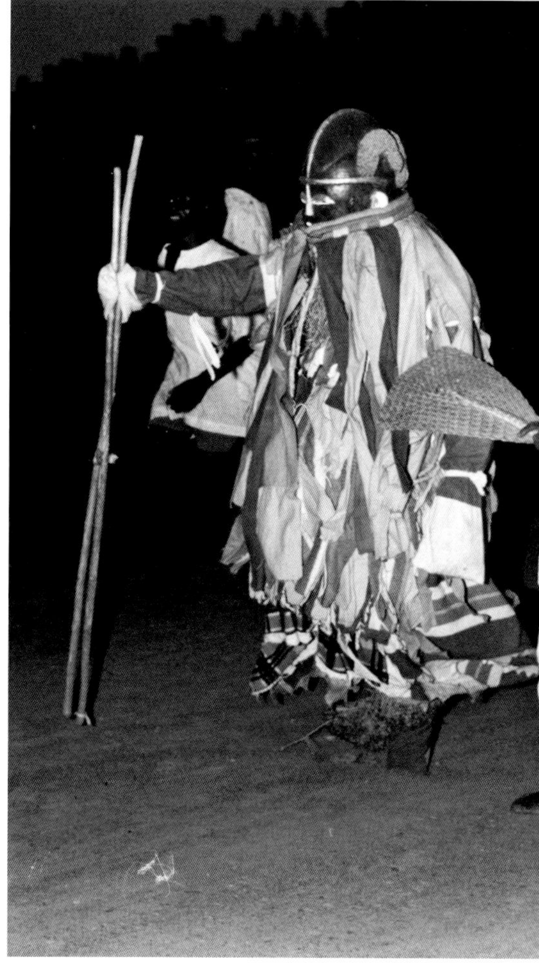

5.8
Igala Ichawula royal masquerade appearing at night during the Ogbadu festival.
PHOTOGRAPH BY JOHN BOSTON, IDAH, 1961.

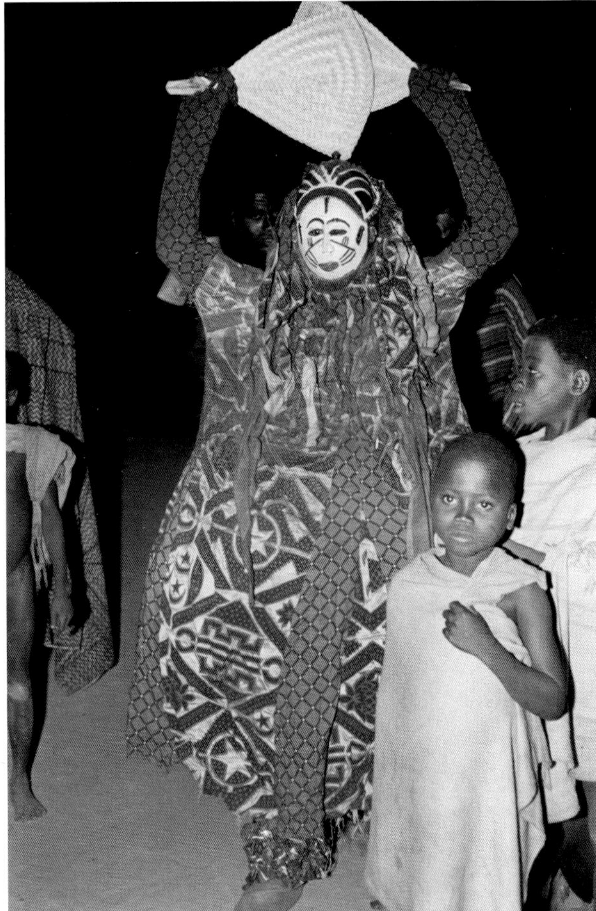

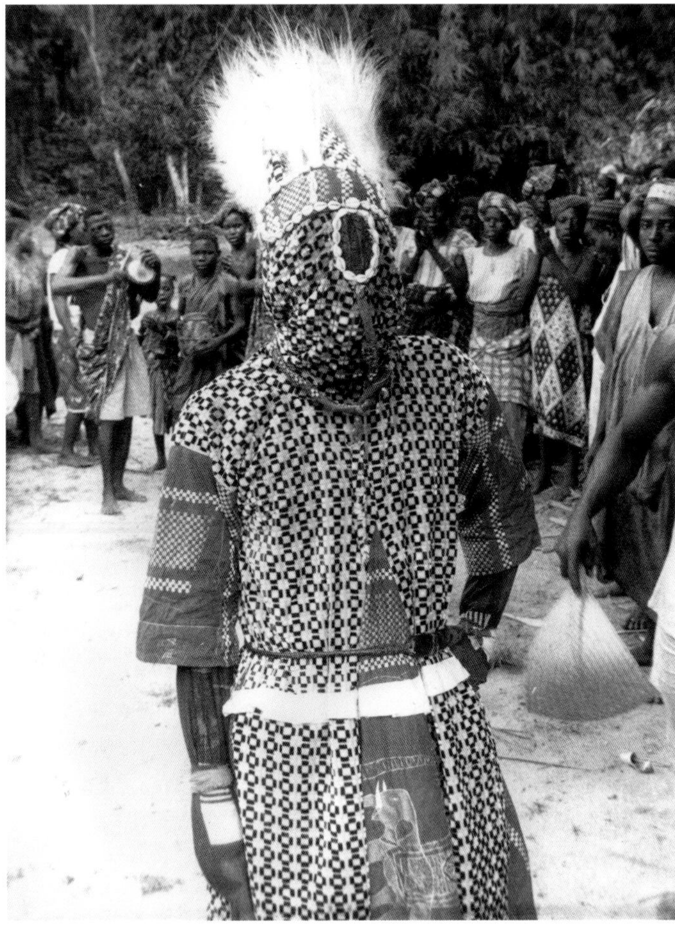

5.9
Igala Inyelikpi masquerade dancing at an
Aku ceremony.
PHOTOGRAPH BY JOHN BOSTON, 1961.

5.10
Igala Owuna, a juvenile dancing masquerade.
PHOTOGRAPH BY JOHN BOSTON, ALADE, 1957.

5.11 (OPPOSITE, TOP LEFT)
Igala Olagenyi masquerade dancing at an
Aku ceremony.
PHOTOGRAPH BY JOHN BOSTON, 1961.

5.12 (OPPOSITE, TOP RIGHT)
Igala Olagenyi, a senior masquerade.
PHOTOGRAPH BY JOHN BOSTON, ALADE, 1957.

5.13 (OPPOSITE, BOTTOM LEFT)
Igala Ikpalikpa, an aggressive masquerade.
PHOTOGRAPH BY JOHN BOSTON, ALADE, 1957.

5.14 (OPPOSITE, BOTTOM RIGHT)
Iga, an aggressive masquerade purchased from
Awka in Igbo country.
PHOTOGRAPH BY JOHN BOSTON, ALADE, 1957.

seniority and authority. The examples in figures 5.11 and 5.12 should be compared with
Ajadu (fig. 5.21), which has the same role. Ikpalikpa (fig. 5.13) is a vigorous, aggressive
character with a baboon-like face and prominent teeth. Another aggressive masquerade
is the horned figure called Iga (fig. 5.14).

In some of the communities of Ibaji (the region of Igalaland south of Idah and
north of Igboland, which is recognized for its own hybrid art styles and ritual practices), the Aku ceremony is an annual festival and is performed by an entire village
on a particular day. The men in each village who have died during the year leading
up to the festival are each commemorated by a Bogodo masker if they have taken the
Amanwulu or Ibena title during their lifetime. This is the first of the four title grades
in Unale, where I witnessed the festival. A shelter made of palm fronds and sticks is
set up in the center of the village, and the widows of the dead males spend part of
each day there for the seven days of the festival. The shelter is called *unyi do* or *unyieku*
(house of mourning). Each morning and evening, when all the widows are assembled,
the Bogodo masqueraders, representing the dead men dance round the shelter and are
greeted by outbursts of wailing from the widows within. On the seventh day other
masqueraders appear, and the widows' mourning ends with the Bogodo demolishing
the *unyi do* while the widows are still inside. During the week of their performance,
the Bogodo stay in the house of one of the oldest men in the village who is known in
this capacity as *okolo ibena*. They are given food by the sons and other close relatives
of the dead and continue to represent the dead until the moment when they scatter to
their own homes after demolishing the house of mourning.

More than half of the masquerades that I saw in Ibaji represented the dead and
could thus be said to play a part in the cult of ancestors. Egwu Afia occur in this
southern border area to keep alive the names and memory of the immediate forebears.
In addition the founders of extended families or of lineage segments are represented

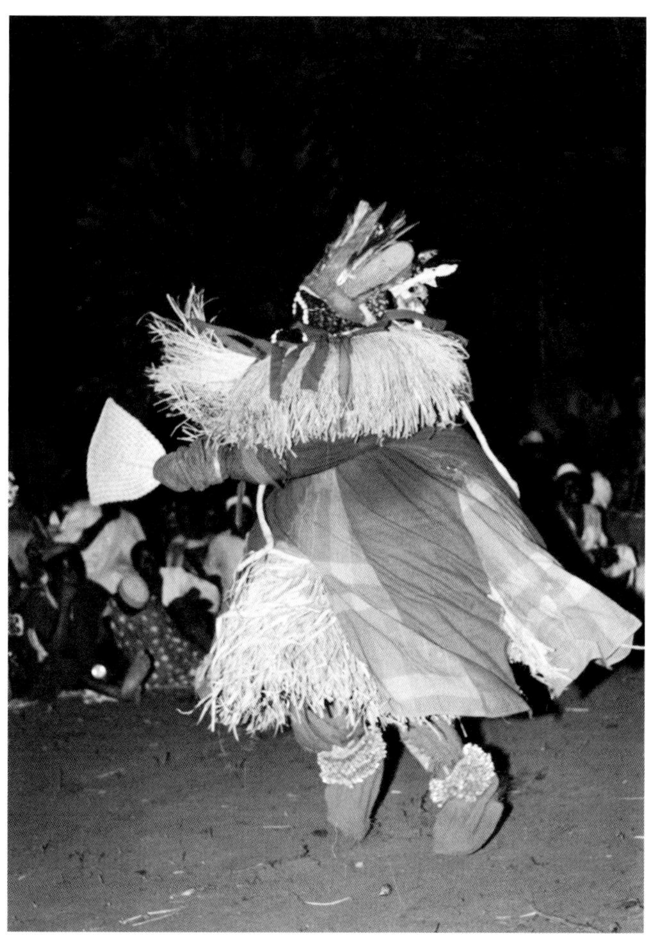

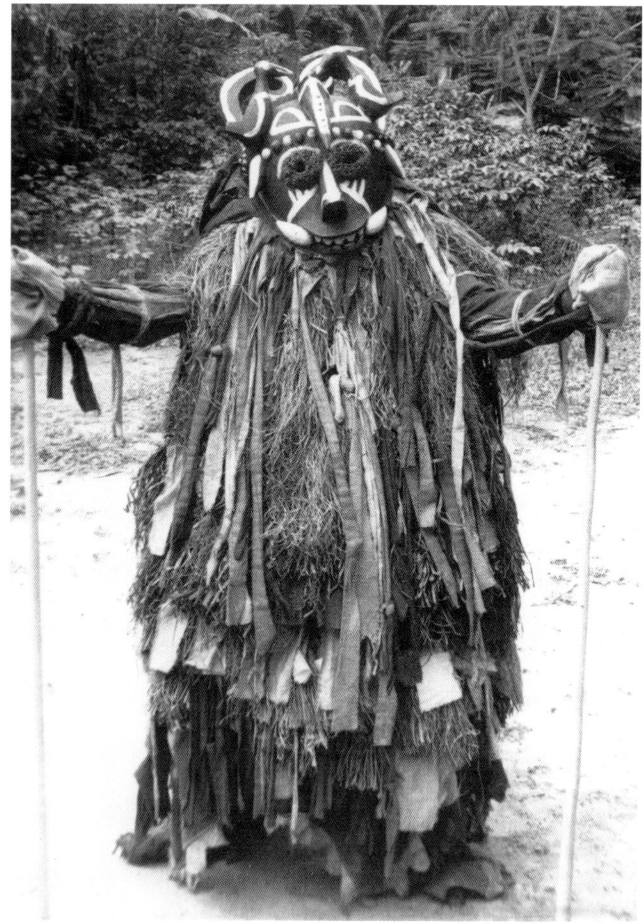

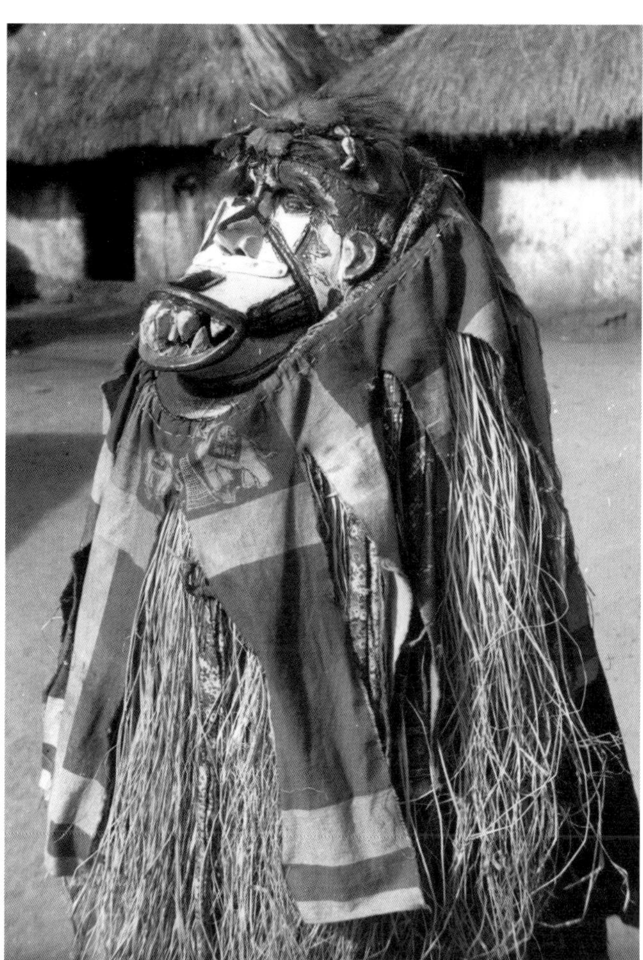

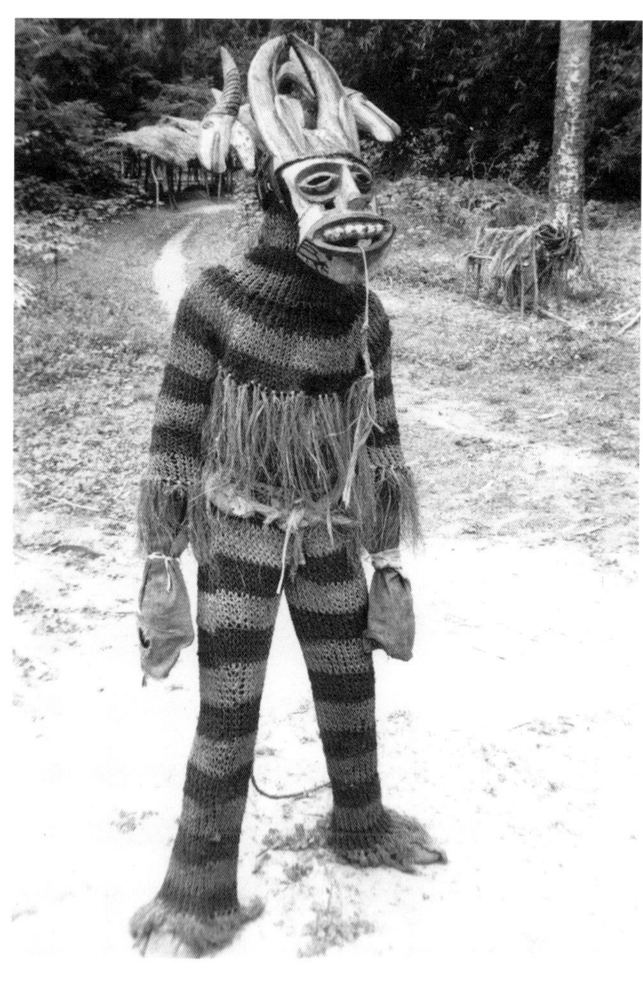

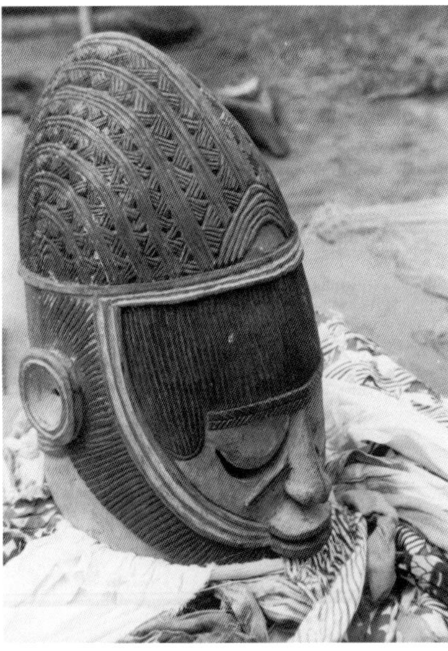

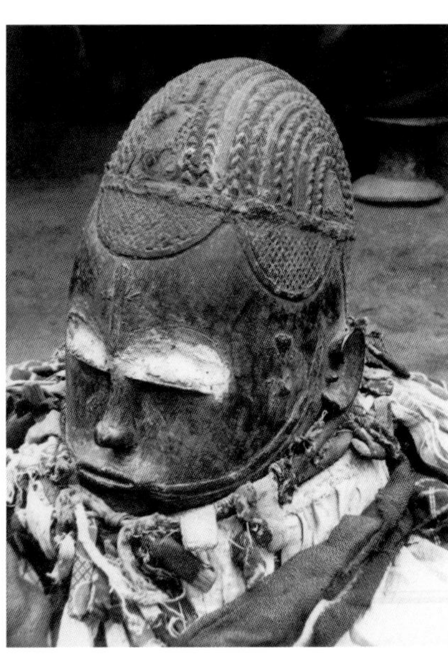

5.15
Ibaji Agba helmet mask.
PHOTOGRAPH BY JOHN BOSTON, UNALE, 1957

5.16
Ibaji Agba (Inyelikpi) helmet for a dancing masquerade.
PHOTOGRAPH BY JOHN BOSTON, ONYEDEGA, 1957.

5.17
Ibaji Agba, a dancing masquerade.
PHOTOGRAPH BY JOHN BOSTON, AYA, 1957.

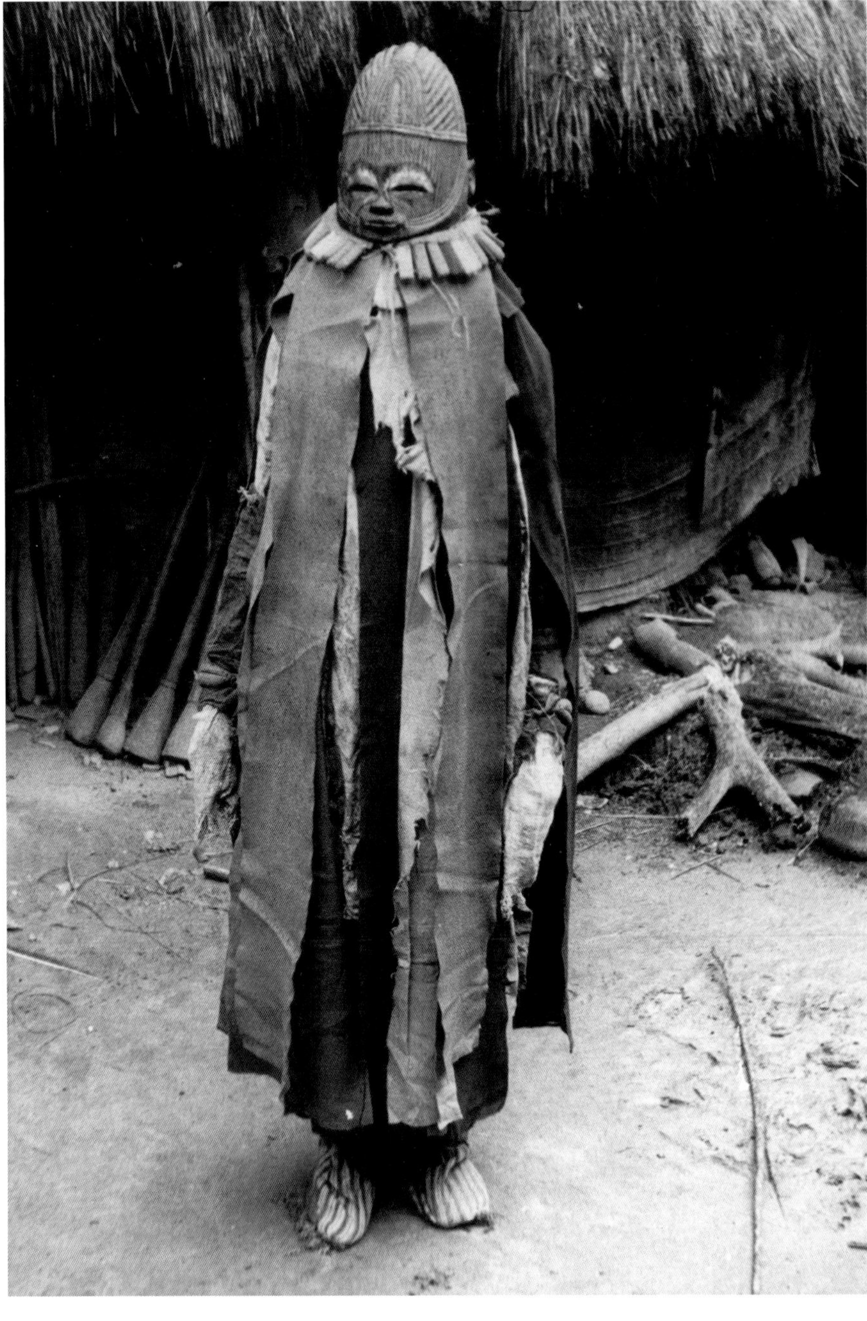

by other masquerade types, which appear at second funeral ceremonies and at other major festivals. The Ibaji equivalent of the principal dancing masquerade, Inyelikpi, is Agba, which is costumed like the royal masqueraders. The most striking feature of the Agba dress is the black helmet encasing the head of the dancer (figs. 5.15, 5.16, and see fig. 1.6). On these helmets hairstyles are represented by rows of chevrons or of oblique lines with a central ridge indicating a sagittal crest in some cases. The visages give prominence to heavy drooping eyes and to elaborate facial scarification covering the forehead in some instances. Igala scarification marks that extend from the corners of the mouth to the base of the ears are also invariably accentuated. The resemblance of these Ibaji helmets to those of the royal masquerades at Idah does not include the addition of abrus seeds, but it extends to the costume, which is founded upon a raffia or cloth base concealed by strips of orange, red, and green cloth hanging full length from the base of the helmet (fig. 5.17).

The Ibaji Agba masqueraders do not control and discipline the crowds of spectators at festivals in the manner of the royal masks in the capital. Instead they compete in dancing and display their art at the Aku festival in any convenient corner of the village when the main drama centering on the Bogodo and the house of mourning is over. Agba is a typically Ibaji form of masquerade and is limited in its distribution to the villages south of Idah where it extends as far as Inoma, an Igala village incorporated in the Igbo state of Anambra.

A second distinctive Ibaji type with the same geographic distribution as Agba is a whipping masquerade called variously, Egwu Ane, Ummanwu, Olabiene, or Otimoku. For this masquerade a cap mask (fig. 5.18) is worn that takes the form of a platform on which the face is scooped out in low relief at the front while a triple set of open-arched horns springs from behind the facial features. The platform is thin and is pointed at the front where it terminates in a mouth. The edge of the platform, forming a narrow rim, is decorated with incised lines, possibly representing facial scarification. The costume has either a raffia or cloth base with strips of cloth hanging down to form an outer layer.

A third masquerade type with Ibaji associations centers on a character called Ulaga (fig. 5.19). In name only this masquerader can be linked with the northwest Igbo masquerade called Ulaga. Whereas the Igbo type employs a cap mask combining bird-like characteristics with human features, however, the Ibaji Ulaga wears a simple, oval

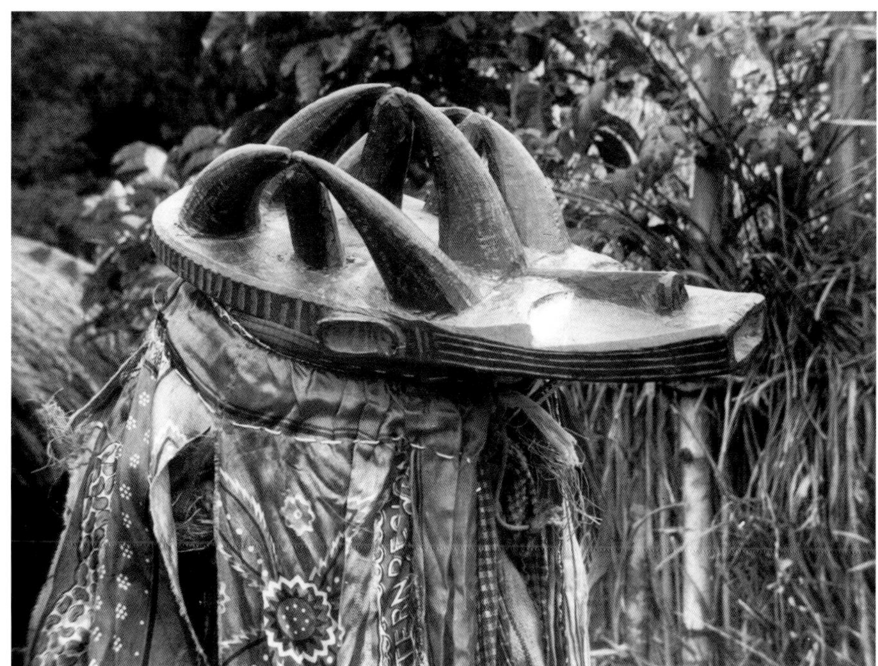

5.18
Ibaji Olabiene masquerade.
PHOTOGRAPH BY JOHN BOSTON, UNALE, 1957.

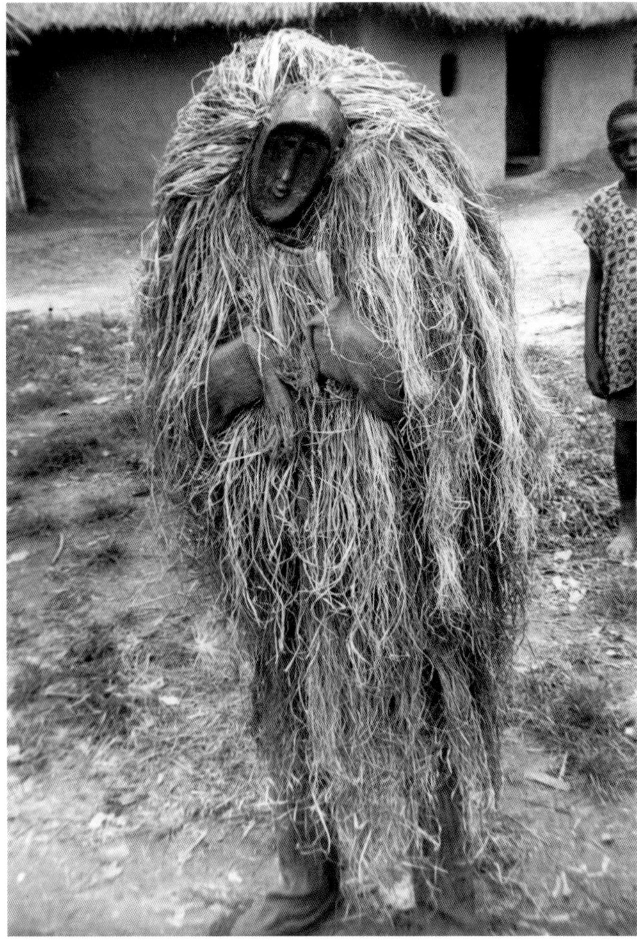

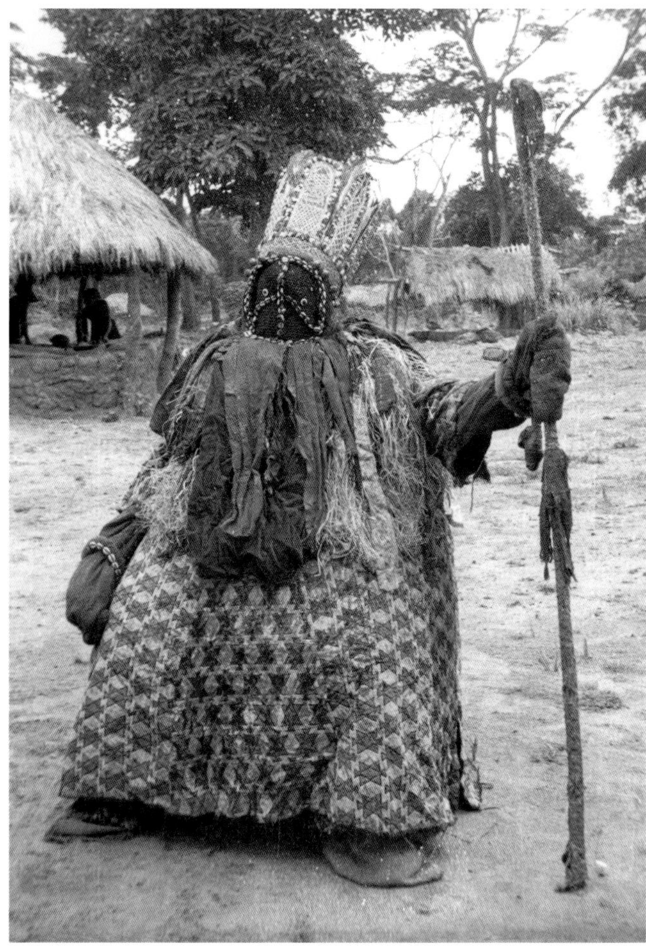

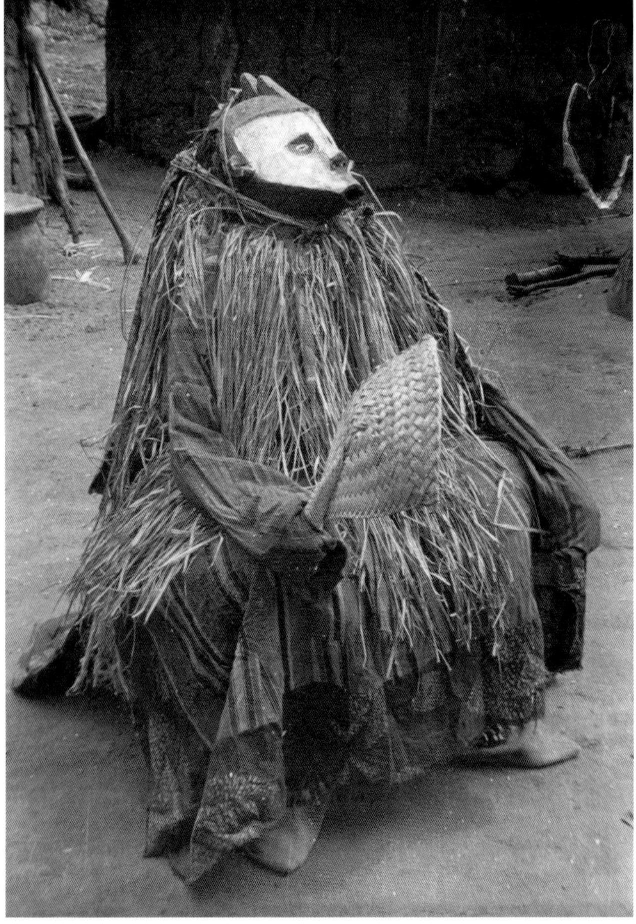

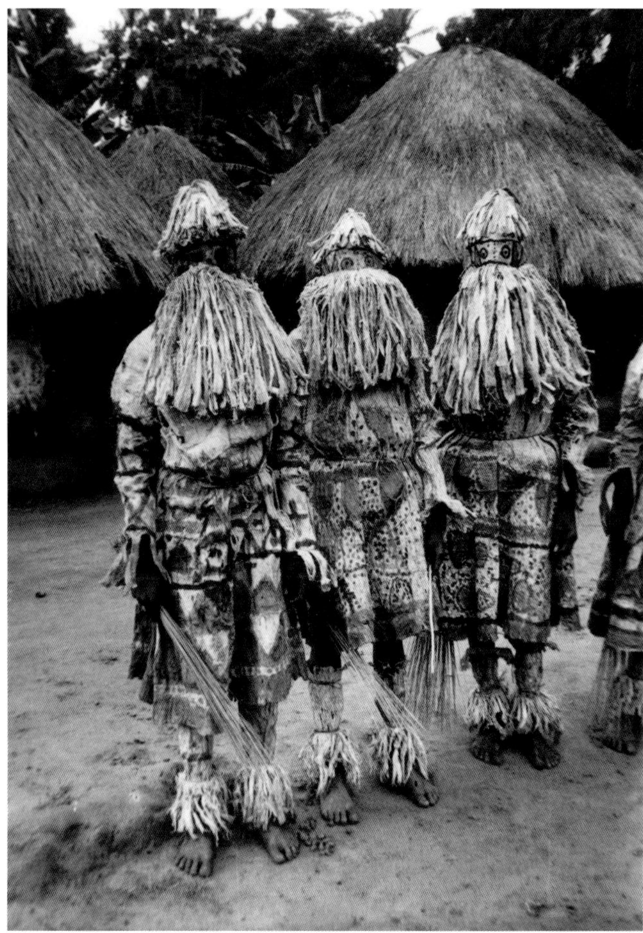

face mask with a raffia costume. The Ibaji play is based on chasing after spectators and running a lot.

I witnessed only two examples of the last distinctively Ibaji masquerade type, which is called Ofogili (the foolish or worthless one; fig. 5.20). The helmets worn for this play are animal in character without specific associations. Once again the triple Igala face marks are a prominent feature, and the whitening of the eyes is reminiscent of a practice associated with title-taking in the Igbo area to the south. Ofogili appears mainly for funeral ceremonies and seems to be a comic rather than a tragic figure. Both of the headdresses I saw were said to be more than fifty years old and to have been carved by an Ibaji artist.

In some of the other kinds of masquerades that occur in the Ibaji area, Igbo influence is strong, and in some cases the costumes and headdresses employed were in fact the work of itinerant Igbo artists. One such instance involved a pair of brightly colored maiden spirit maskers whose costumes were decorated with appliqué and embroidery and whose headdresses were made of cane and cloth. I saw four examples of homed masquerades of the type that the northern Igbo call Odugu Mmanwu. Two of their horned helmets were of the composition type, while the other two were carved, one by an Igbo carver. The horned figures are called Iga, Ogbodo, or Ugbaja by the Igala in this area, and they appear to portray fierce, aggressive characters in much the same way as this type of masquerade does among the northern Igbo.

To the north of the Idah metropolitan area, brief visits were made to the Abocho area and to villages around Ankpa. In the former area the most senior masquerade was Olagenyi, massive figure in a bulky raffia and cloth costume with a crowning headpiece simulating a circlet of feathers (cf. fig. 5.11). These pseudo-feathers are made of stiff felt embroidered with abstract designs: on one example the decoration was of silver paper cutouts stuck onto the feathers. Olagenyi is a chief among masks and radiates authority and power. In one village the figure was said to discipline any absentees from collective voluntary labor. It also comes out for second funeral ceremonies and the for the Egwu (Ibegwu) festival.

Also in the Abocho area a talkative figure called Ojamelede was observed wearing a helmet that supported a tableau of figures. The headdress seen at Abocho was carved by a Bassa Nge carver, but other examples seen elsewhere were carved in a similar style by Igala artists. Finally in these Abocho villages I saw a whiteface masquerade called Ajadu (the savior), which combined animal and human features (fig. 5.21).

In the Ankpa region the most senior masquerades are those whose costumes are made from barkcloth (*abu*). These are of two kinds, including one called Ukpoku, which is costumed entirely in this material including the headdress (fig. 5.22). The costumes are painted with patterns in orange, indigo, and mauve, the colors being obtained from *otoli* roots, a leaf called *ugbogbo*, and a fruit called *oro elo*, respectively. Ukpoku masqueraders appear in groups and chase bystanders as their main activity. They can also visit sick men in the village to drive away any suspected witchcraft. The second senior barkcloth masker wears a horned wooden helmet, cylindrical in form with an elongated mouth and features. The figure is called Ikonyi and comes out alone at funeral ceremonies and for the Egwu festival (fig. 5.23). Its form and the use of abrus seeds around its mouth and eyebrows link it to other Benue styles. Costumes of fabric, sewn with black cotton to represent hair, are worn by dancing masqueraders in the Ankpa region in a juvenile masquerade generically called Jegeje (Sieber 1961, 6). This masquerade like Owuna, its equivalent in the Idah area, is not considered sufficiently important to represent the dead but dances instead to provide entertainment.

In Ojoku District, near the border with Idoma, two whiteface masks were seen that were said to have been carved by Idoma artists (see chapter 2). One, called Odum, wore a costume that came from Igumale in Idoma country, as did its face mask. The exact provenance of the other mask was unknown, apart from its being of Idoma

5.19 (OPPOSITE, TOP LEFT)
Ibaji Ulaga juvenile masquerade.
PHOTOGRAPH BY JOHN BOSTON, UNALE, 1957.

5.20 (OPPOSITE, TOP RIGHT)
Ibaji Ofogili (the foolish one).
PHOTOGRAPH BY JOHN BOSTON, OCHUCHU, 1957.

5.21 (OPPOSITE, BOTTOM LEFT)
Igala Ajadu masquerade.
PHOTOGRAPH BY JOHN BOSTON, EMEWE, 1957.

5.22 (OPPOSITE, BOTTOM RIGHT)
Igala Ukpoku barkcloth masquerades.
PHOTOGRAPH BY JOHN BOSTON, EJEGBO, 1957.

5.23
Igala Ikonyi barkcloth masquerade.
PHOTOGRAPH BY JOHN BOSTON, OKABA, 1957.

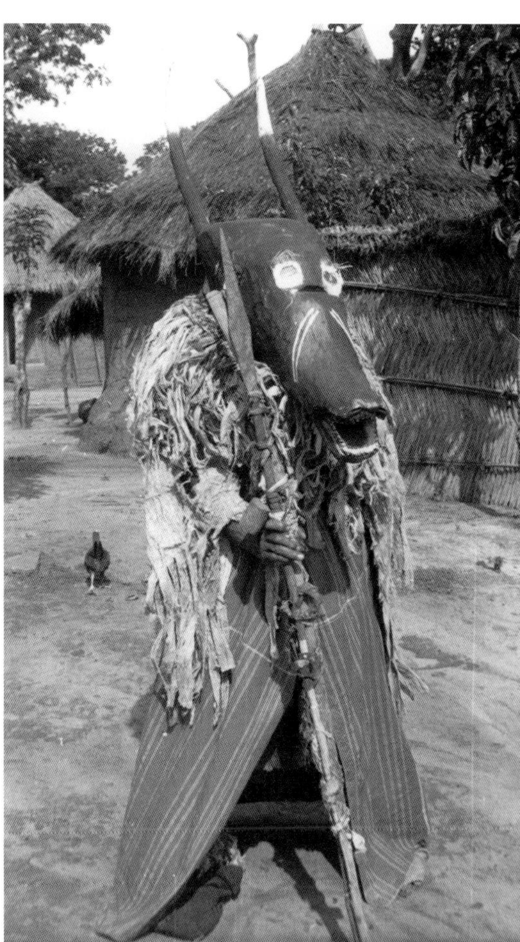

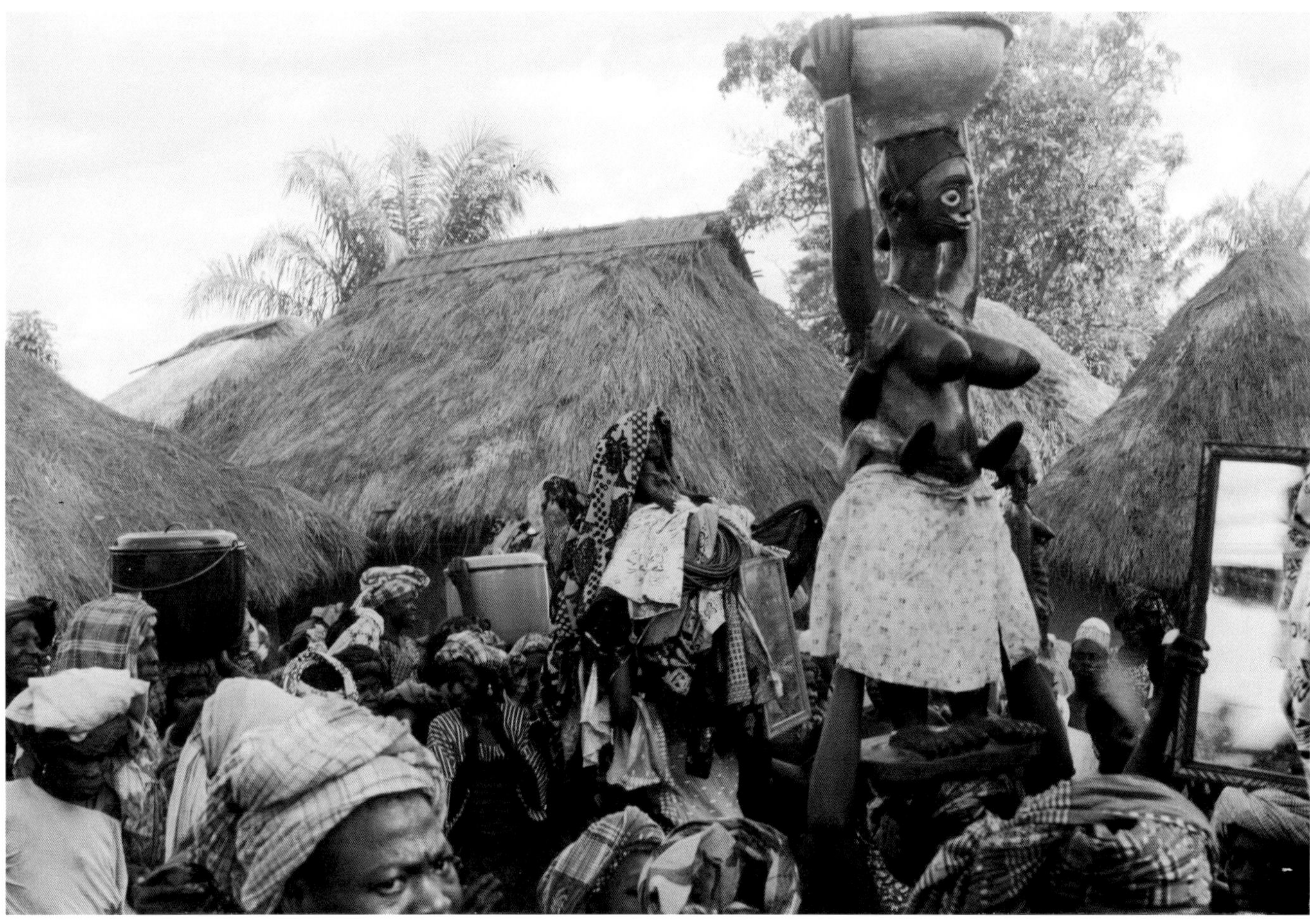

5.24

Ibaji *etecha*, a display of wealth by the grand-children of a dead man at his Aku ceremony.
PHOTOGRAPH BY JOHN BOSTON, IGEBIJE, 1962.

manufacture. Its name, Ogelinya, relates it to the former Idoma head-hunting associations called Oglinye.

Through this survey of Igala masquerades, we have seen that there is great variety of form and a number of different local styles. The only uniform masquerade throughout Igala is Egwu Afia, but there are otherwise several variations on the themes of ritualized authority and power, ranging from the unchallenged supremacy of Ekwe in the capital to the judicial role of the Orumamu masquerade described by Roy Sieber (1961, fig. 2) in the northeastern villages of Igala. Art forms other than masquerades show the same lack of uniformity. Figure carving in northern Igala, for instance, is represented mainly by the output of one carver, Umale, living near Iyale (see interleaf B). His figures and anthropomorphic mirror frames have no exact counterpart in any other part of Igala. Similarly, the figures photographed by Sieber in Etetekpe and Abachi are individual creations. Sieber and François Neyt have also published pictures of zoomorphic calabash stoppers for Alijenu *ebo* around Ankpa (see chapter 2, pp. 59–63). But this art form does not occur in the central or southern areas.

Ibaji has its own styles of figure carving, for images that are in some cases of social rather than ritual significance. The pair of female figures called *ojibo* belong to all the women of Unale and are kept in the house of the oldest woman (fig. 5.25). They are paraded through the village in much the same way that display figures (*ugonachamma*) are brought out for festivals by the Igbo to the south of Ibaji. The *ojibo* are used mainly in the Ibaji area for display at funeral ceremonies when they are decked out with cloth, waist beads (*jigida*), and other signs of wealth, including coins. Such displays are called *etecha,* and are arranged by the grandchildren of the dead person to express the continuity and prosperity of the family responsible for the funeral (fig. 5.24).

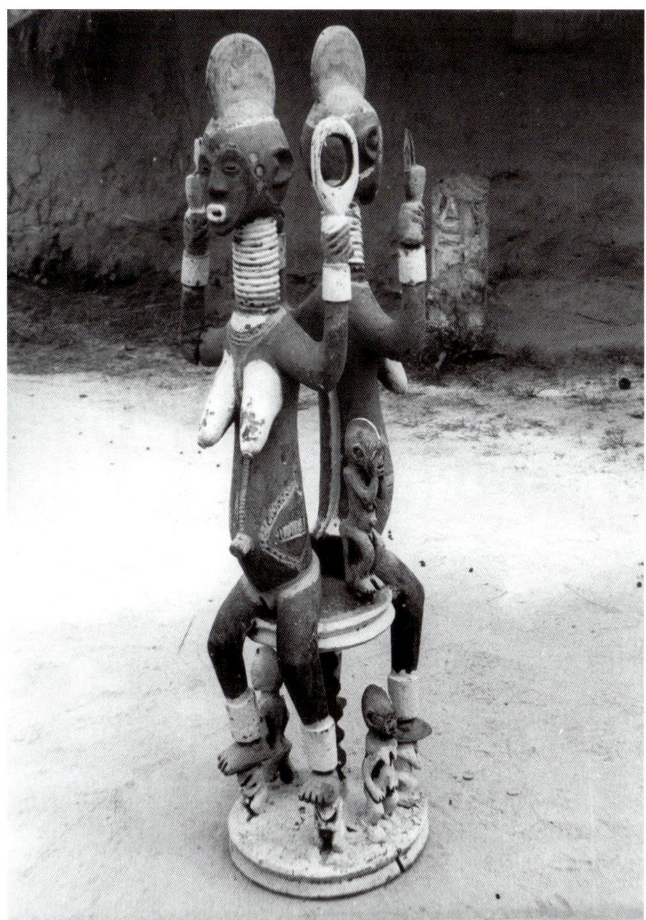

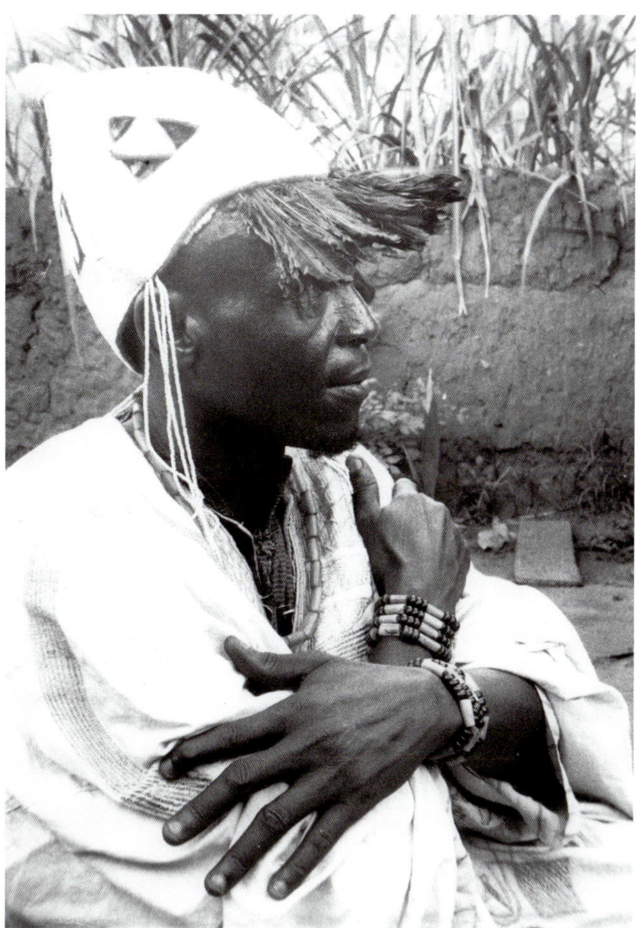

Ibaji men often possess carved horned images (*okegga*) showing the influence of the Igbo cult of Ikenga, which is associated by both the Igbo and the Ibaji Igala with success in men's activities such as hunting, farming, title-taking, and warfare (see fig. B.6). The Igala contribution to this genre, as I have shown elsewhere (Boston 1977) is a tall, tiered arrangement of figures that is associated with the well-being of the male and female members of a family group. These tiered *okegga* are often described as belonging to a local chief whose title is hereditary within a clan. *Okegga* occur infrequently in the central or Idah metropolitan area.

Other art forms that are now comparatively rare in Igala include carved doors in the northern villages and mud figures in Ibaji. Carved stools (*okpete*) and wooden bowls and spoons were still in use in Ibaji and the central area until recently. I conclude this survey with a photograph of a titled chief, the Ochijenu, at Idah, in full regalia (fig. 5.26). He is wearing a white beaded hat (*otajia ofe*) with a fringe of red feathers (*okebetsi*). Around his neck is a string of blue beads (*oku*), and on his wrists are wristlets of red and blue glass beads (*oka*). Igala claim that the craft of making these glass beads was practiced at Idah until the skill was lost. ●

5.25
Ibaji *ojibo* figure pair owned by the women of Unale.
PHOTOGRAPH BY JOHN BOSTON, 1957.

5.26
Igala Ochijenu, hereditary titled chief.
PHOTOGRAPH BY JOHN BOSTON, IDAH, 1957.

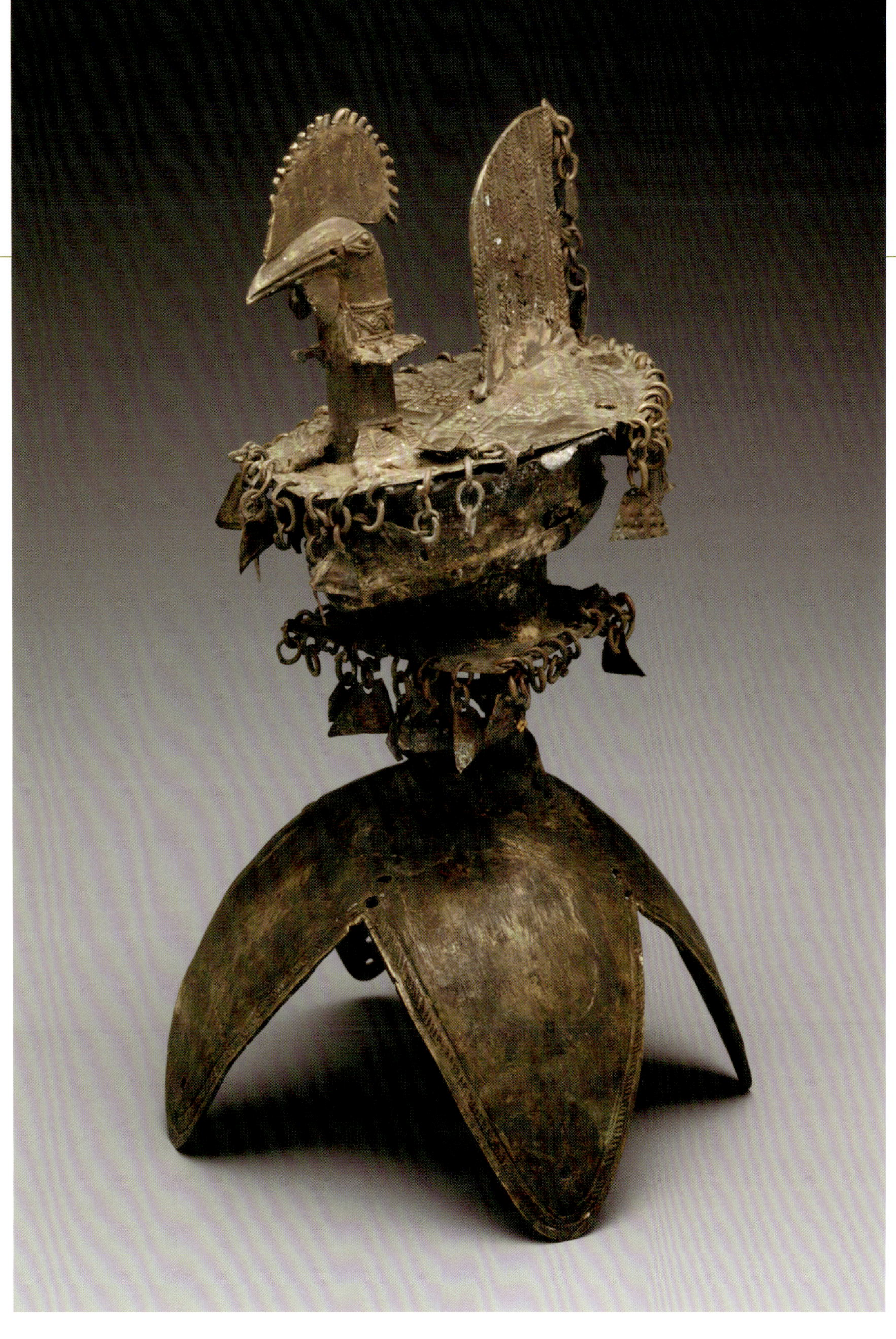

CHAPTER 6

Lost-Wax Casting along the Benue

NANCY NEAHER MAAS

The Benue is home to an array of fascinating and little-known objects cast in copper alloys, commonly known as either brass or bronze.[1] Because the Benue corridor embraces a wide expanse of Central Nigeria, the copper-alley objects thought to be from the region reflect a variety of aesthetic and technical approaches. At first glance the multiplicity of forms can be bewildering, especially if one is aware of Nigeria's other famous metalworking legacies. The ancient Yoruba finds linked to Ife, the monumental royal arts of Benin, and the archaeological treasures excavated at Igbo-Ukwu have all enjoyed worldwide exposure in major museum collections and exhibitions, as well as a wide range of publications. As such, they provide a formidable backdrop for understanding these less-known works from the Benue region.

CHALLENGES

The Benue and its connecting waterways provided veritable highways for the movement of people, goods, and ideas. Visitors to the region were struck by the intensity of traffic, as well as by its cosmopolitan composition. Typical comments from the mid-nineteenth century include this observation made at the confluence of the Niger and Benue rivers: "The scene showed the disposition of the people to trade…. The languages spoken here are Igara, Igbira, Nupe, Kakanda, Hausa and Yoruba…. People speaking Doma or Djuku, the language of Kororofa, also visit the market at Igbebe at the Confluence, and the Ibo traders come up as far as this from the Delta" (Crowther 1855, 167). In the early twentieth century, on his way to Lake Chad, Frederick Migeod noted that "three big canoes from Onitsha had been keeping pace with us for several days. It was a Hausa party, men and women, who had been down to Onitsha to buy kerosene, kola, salt…to sell at Yola" (1924, 38). Travelers also took a special interest in the worldly goods of riverain communities. For example, the dress of women included "armlets or wristlets, either fine brass ones bought at the Confluence, or smaller ones from the Hausa markets or from Wukari (Baikie 1856, 113). Around the same time, Thomas Hutchinson remarked that "Some of the females here (at "Anoofo", Benue River) wear brass wire wound round the arm, in the same cylindrical form as it is worn in Old Calabar, and I have no doubt of this wire being brought up from the oil rivers" (1855, 146). Migeod stated that items he collected in Wukari were made by the Bamun of the then-French Cameroons (1923, 183). As a matter of fact, "brass work" was thought to originate from many different locales—at both ends of the Benue, to the north, the south, and far beyond. It could reasonably be said to be moving in all directions!

6.1
Head crest with rooster
Egbira peoples, mid- to late nineteenth century
Copper alloy
H: 28 cm
INDIANAPOLIS MUSEUM OF ART, RUSSELL AND BECKY CURTIS ART PURCHASE ENDOWMENT FUND, 1999.21
IMAGE: © COURTESY OF INDIANAPOLIS MUSEUM OF ART. PHOTOGRAPH BY TAD FRUITS.

This elaborate tiered headdress relates to the copper-alloy crests associated with the Afo, Goemai, and others (see figs. 6.3, 6.4). It was worn during funerals by a performer who would have been completely concealed with cloth and netting. In the 1850s the Egbira kingdoms were overtaken by the expansion of Islamic forces from the north. After Egbira rulers adopted Islam, the production of non-Islamic ritual objects, such as these head crests, was eventually eliminated.

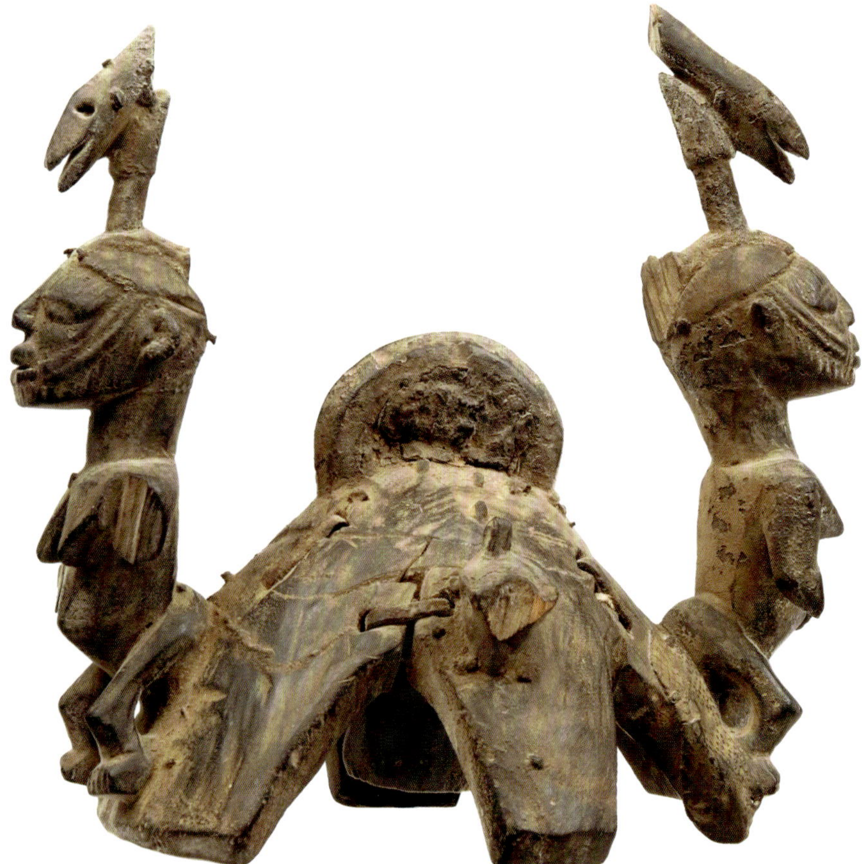

6.5
Head crest
Afo peoples, early to mid-twentieth century
Wood, metal, abrus seeds
H: 26.4 cm
COLLECTION OF TOBY AND BARRY HECHT
PHOTOGRAPH © 2010, GREG STALEY
PROVENANCE: CHRISTIAN DUPONCHEEL

The two small figures on this crest wear
representations of "hunting decoys" on their
heads. Actual hunting decoys found throughout the region are made with the beaks of
birds. The linear striations on the faces of
the figures link them to other kinds of Afo
sculpture and to figurative styles found across
the Lower Benue.

in the Lower Benue. Traces of metal are evident on the cap, suggesting that it may
once have been partially covered in a copper alloy, which may help explain why this
distinctive genre of funerary regalia would exist in two such different materials. The
use of metal surely elevated prestige value.

Tiv

Residing on the eastern edges of the Lower Benue, the Tiv pose another challenge
to defining metalworking within the region. The product of historic migrations from
the south, Tiv-speaking peoples drove a wedge between the Jukun on the east and the
Igala, Egbira, and, most directly, the Idoma to the west, all of whom are believed to
have shared strong cultural traditions (see chapter 7). As a result, Tiv material culture
diverges from its neighbors in singular ways. These include the presence of unique
object types, as well as generic items like tobacco pipes, staffs, swords, sheaths, and
daggers. A short discussion of selected examples will be followed by conjectures on
the nature of a Tiv metalworking industry.

A unique object attributed to the Tiv is an ax with a crowned head (fig. 6.6), from
the mouth of which an iron blade projects. Chiefs of Tiv clans possessed metal regalia of iron and brass, indicating their status and power (Rubin 1973, 229). According
to Arnold Rubin (1982, 45), the "militantly egalitarian and democratic" Tiv may have
adopted this type of ceremonial regalia from the highly centralized Jukun as they moved
northward in the nineteenth century into the Jukun orbit (see fig. 6.12).[6] Axes have been
collected at least since the late nineteenth century and are located in various museums
in Nigeria and Europe.[7] While the ax blade can vary in shape, the head conforms to a
strict formula: a finely decorated sagittal crest; an egg-shaped head featuring circular
eyes, ears, and mouth; and a yellow-gold "brass" color. A flanged brass collar caps the
lower end of the staff with the iron shaft exposed at midsection. Revealingly close in
appearance is the tall intact Tiv staff (fig. 6.7), its "head" displaying a crest covered with

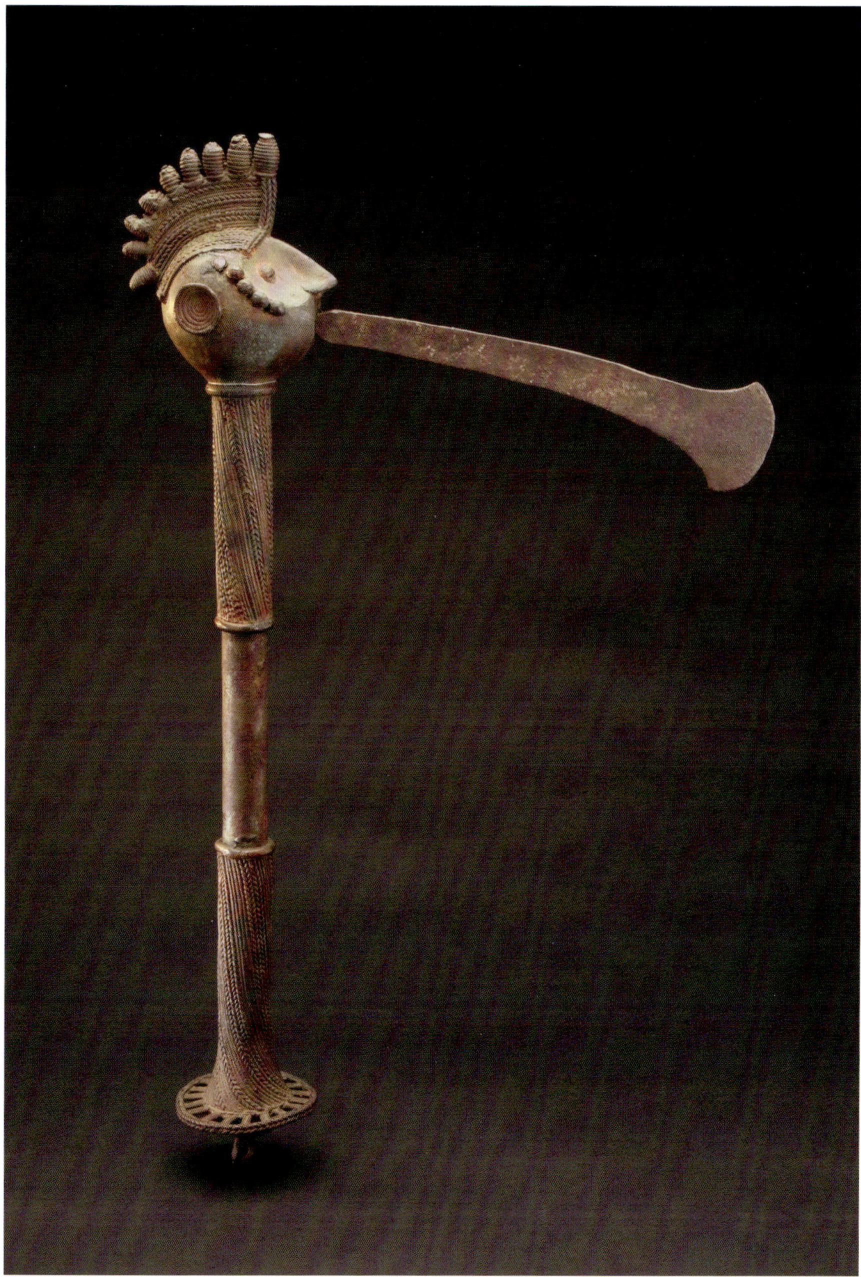

6.6
Figurative ax
Tiv peoples, early twentieth century
Copper alloy, iron
H: 40.5 cm
FOWLER MUSEUM AT UCLA X79.827; ANONYMOUS
GIFT
IMAGE: © 2010 FOWLER MUSEUM AT UCLA.
PHOTOGRAPH BY DON COLE
PROVENANCE: PRIVATE COLLECTION, LOS ANGELES

Tiv clan leaders possessed regalia made of
iron and copper alloys that indicated their
status and power. The head of this ax is recognizably "Tiv." These regalia were not limited
to the Tiv, however, and the axes in particular
were documented among their eastern Jukun
and Abakwariga neighbors, whose sophisticated metalworking may have been adopted
by Tiv immigrants to the Benue River valley
(see fig. 6.12).

6.7
Staff with human head
Tiv peoples, nineteenth century
Copper alloy
H: 110 cm
YALE UNIVERSITY ART GALLERY, PROMISED
GIFT OF DWIGHT B. AND ANNA COOPER HEATH,
2009.6.89
IMAGE: © COURTESY YALE UNIVERSITY ART GALLERY

The head on this staff is unmistakably similar
to those seen on Tiv axes (see fig. 6.6).

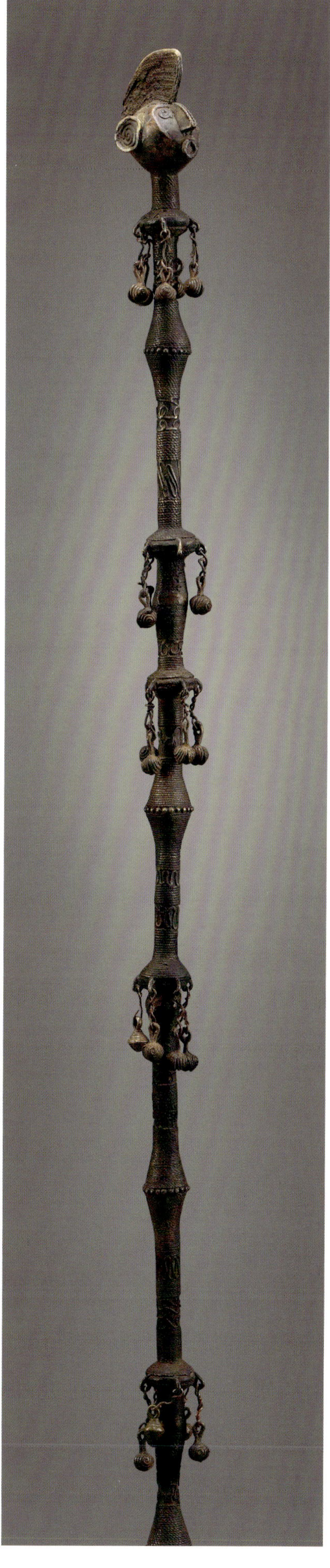

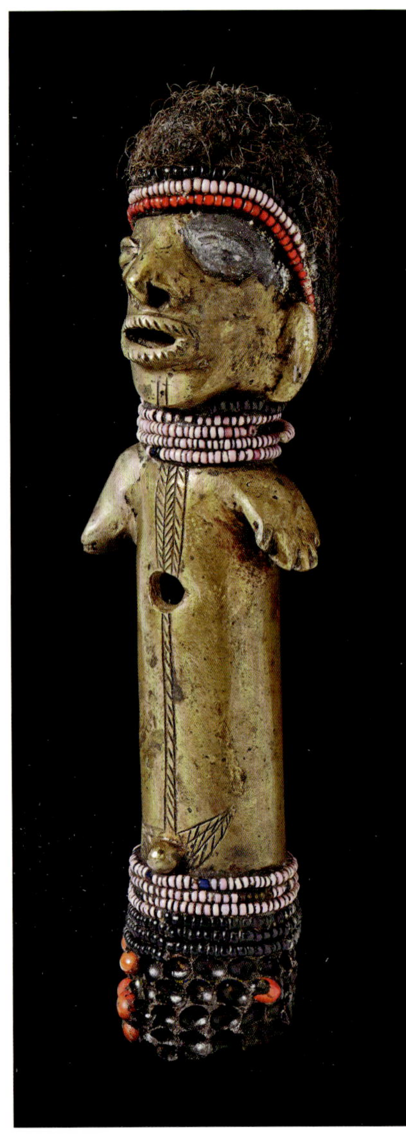

6.8
Voice disguiser (*imborivungu*)
Tiv peoples, before 1932
Brass, metal, human hair
H: 18.5 cm
PITT RIVERS MUSEUM, UNIVERSITY OF OXFORD,
1932.18.17
IMAGE: © PITT RIVERS MUSEUM, UNIVERSITY OF
OXFORD
PROVENANCE: FIELD COLLECTED BY 1932 BY THE
WUKARI NATIVE ADMINISTRATION, BENUE PROV-
INCE, N. NIGERIA
(NOT IN EXHIBITION)

This small brass figurative object belongs
to a class of religious emblems called *akombo*.
The open bottom of the figure was covered
with spider web material. When a ritual
leader spoke into the opening in the figure's
chest, it would cause the web material to
vibrate, producing an eerie sound.

delicate braiding in horizontal tiers and ears modeled in concentric circles. The shaft is
also decorated with fine striations, small globular projections, and other linear motifs.
Considered together, the axes and staff reflect a standardization of form and detail that
suggests a tradition emphasizing uniformity and quality control. The restraint in form
also contrasts with the Lower Benue metalworks discussed earlier, which tend to be
much more densely ornamental in nature.

Other objects associated with a Tiv corpus reflect parallels in intent and execution, demonstrating an assured and relatively sophisticated approach to creating
objects in brass or bronze. For example, numerous brass snuff takers conceived as
elaborate rings, bracelets, swords, and pipe bowls credited to Tiv craftsmanship are
elegantly formed with decorative accents including spirals, striations, chevrons, and
other relief designs applied in impressively diminutive scale (see Brincard 1982, 118,
H2). Such fine work is often associated with modeling in latex. The Tiv are also known
for small figurative works in brass (*akombo*), which were believed to be imbued with
deep powers critical to survival (Rubin 1973, 44). Perhaps the most striking are the
voice disguisers (*imborivungu;* fig. 6.8), which were utilized in secrecy by clan elders
and linked to powerful ancestral rites. While similar voice disguisers have been
documented for other parts of Nigeria, the Tiv version in cast copper-alloy takes the
concept to a higher level of interpretation.[8] The adoption of brass voice disguisers
is thought to have originated with British fiat (Downes 1971, 56; Abraham 1940, ch.
3), which banned the earlier use of human leg bones in *imborivungu* construction.
Examples can be found in several museum and private collections, and while they
display slight variations in style, they nonetheless adhere to a fairly set pattern. Most
are about 18 centimeters in height, with brass head and "torso," limbs, and indications
of gender. Despite their small size, each is individualized with a specific hairstyle and
facial features, something like the Igala/Egbira *okute*. Crotal bells are often attached.
Liberal use is made of the tiny decorative rope-like or chevron patterns observed
on snuff takers, weaponry, and other objects attributed to the Tiv. The *imborivungu*
illustrated in figure 6.8 is relatively rudimentary, with undersized arms and no legs. Its
face is elongated, as opposed to circular, with cowrie-shell eyes and carefully modeled
nose and nostrils. It was cast with a head crest, although this one is enveloped in real
hair. Beads ring the head, neck, and lower torso. The designs appear cursory: a simple
chevron strip from neck to the hole used for producing sound and striation patterns in
a mudfish pattern at the navel (see figs. 2.13, 2.15).

It is difficult to know whether cast copper-alloy *imborivungu*, likely introduced
as a result of colonialist impact on Tiv lifeways, were in the early stages of a stylistic
development or whether their variety merely reflects the hands of different artists in
isolated workshops. Diversity would be appropriate considering the fact that the Tiv,
while numerous, did not have a tradition of centralized political organization. Unlike
the Igala or the Egbira, for instance, social control was maintained by familial clans
and by the secret men's societies that were patrons of this particular genre. Idiosyn-
cratically styled sacred objects would not seem out of place in such a cultural context.
Thus formal looseness contrasts with the axes and other paraphernalia credited to Tiv
material culture, which bear witness to a more tightly controlled mode of production.

Published accounts point to the existence of a metalworking tradition among
the Tiv, but one of undetermined longevity and scale. Although the famous German
explorer Leo Frobenius described their brass hairpins as of "ancient Ethiopian craftsmanship" (1913, 2: 650), dismissing the likelihood of local manufacture, other sources
clearly contradict him. Not only was a respectable industry noted by various observers, but in several cases actual metalsmiths are mentioned by name. These accounts
include recognition of competent skills, the use of rubber latex in achieving fine detail,
the manufacture of large numbers of brass pipe bowls in a specific area of Tiv country,
and the persistence of brass casting into at least the middle of the twentieth century.[9]

Contributions could also have been made by others who plied Tiv country in search of clients. In the first half of the twentieth century, Igbo smiths were reported in several locations in Tiv country (Migeod 1925, 244; Bohannan 1954, 81; Neaher 1975). The presence of Igbo metalworkers has been amply documented for various regions of South and Central Nigeria; their activities in Igala country are noted in interleaf C of this volume. Yet according to a firsthand account, they by no means supplanted local enterprise, for the Tiv were "good metal workers themselves" (Migeod 1925, 244). The Abakwariga, members of the Jukun community with a distinctive Hausa heritage, have been cited by scholars as the putative creators of bronze arts found not only among the Tiv but also throughout the Middle Benue and possibly beyond. William Fagg, one of the founders of Nigerian art and archaeological studies, was convinced that the Abakwariga made the famous Tiv axes (1965). Rubin, too, argues that the Abakwariga might be the group responsible for so much otherwise unattributed and unexplained metalworking along the Benue (1973, 223, 230), a possibility we will return to later.

From the current record, the Tiv have at least as much claim to a copper-alloy casting industry as any other people located in the environs of the Benue. Witnesses reported a variety of activities involving metal casting and, most valuably, saw smiths in action. Whether there was a two-tier system of production with small-scale manufacturies responsible for Tiv-centric objects like *akombo*, while others created the axes and other fine works attributed to the Tiv, we do not know.

MIDDLE BENUE

As one proceeds eastward along the Benue corridor, metal arts ebb and flow, sometimes hinting at strong traditions with cohesive standards of production, other times dissolving into full-fledged mysteries, electric with possibilities but without any definitive answers at this time. Arnold Rubin's research in the Middle and Upper Benue still serves as a benchmark for this section. His findings in Jukun country suggest links with metalworking traditions, both along the Benue corridor and beyond.

As was noted earlier in this volume, the Jukun were significant players in the history and culture of the Middle Benue, sharing affinities with their former neighbors the Idoma, Igala, Egbira, and others. Commonalities included the role of metal arts as affirmations of regal status and power. Rubin illustrates numerous items located at the capital, Wukari, or nearby in Jukun country. A number of these objects evince similar formal features. Characterizing swords, scabbards, anklets, gauntlets or bracelets, and "crowns," often with tiers of small crotal bells, is the frequent use of delicate, generously proportioned openwork, suggesting that they were made by accomplished metalsmiths exercising great control in releasing a modeling paste on a preexisting armature (fig. 6.9). While not as handsome as the openwork types, other objects show considerable skill at casting metal in planar form with strategically placed tiers of small bells. Rubin was hesitant to identify any of these examples as expressly Jukun, tentatively positing that they may belong either to a tradition emanating from the Adamawa region, where the Verre of the Upper Benue live, or that they reflect resident Abakwariga worksmanship (1973, 229–30).

Prominent in Rubin's article of 1973 on the Middle Benue are several swords with significance for the Aku, or ruler, at Wukari, for subgroups of the Jukun, and for neighboring Chamba leaders. An arresting example consists of a T-shaped "grip" with projections that have tiny heads atop them, accompanied by crotals and openwork shafts (fig. 6.10). Rubin identified these with Verre weapons, again highlighting the possibility that metal arts circulated freely in the Middle and Upper Benue regions (1973, 225).

The dynamism of artistic interaction reflected in Rubin's research among the Jukun plays out in further ways. In his essay of 1973 on the bronzes of the Middle Benue, Rubin alludes to metalworks that may derive from other traditions or localities. Relevant here are a series of "road creatures," four-legged animals cast in bronze, some

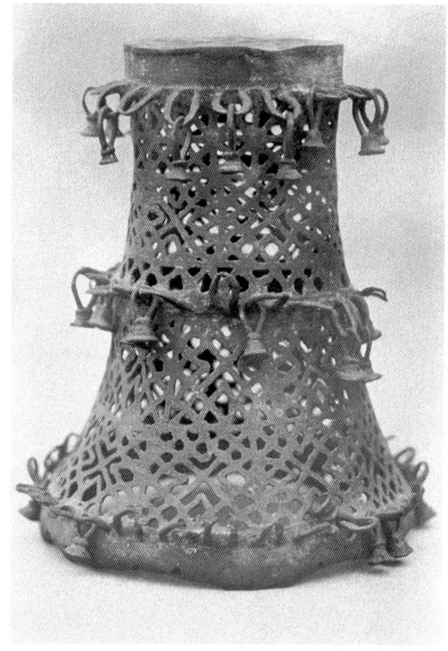

6.9

This tour de force of openwork copper-alloy casting was found in Wukari and acquired by the Nigerian Museum, Lagos, in 1944 (NML-54.L.1). Arnold Rubin later identified it as "probably a crown" (*ataba*).

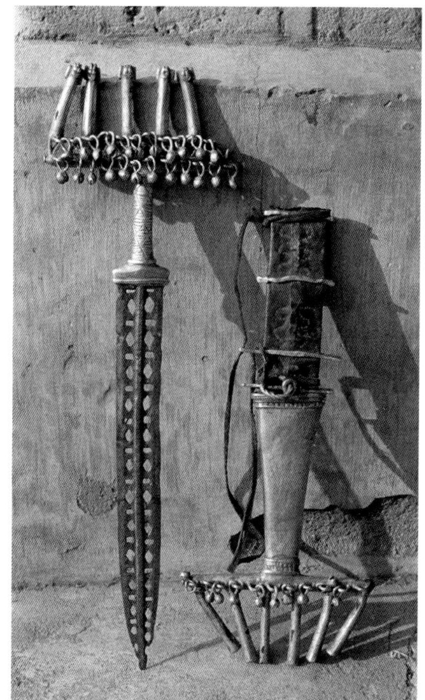

6.10

The copper-alloy "sword of Kimbi" formed part of the regalia of the Kimbi of Donga in Jukun country.

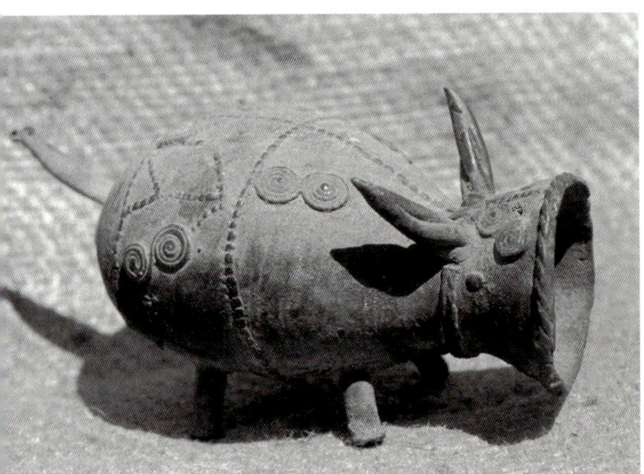

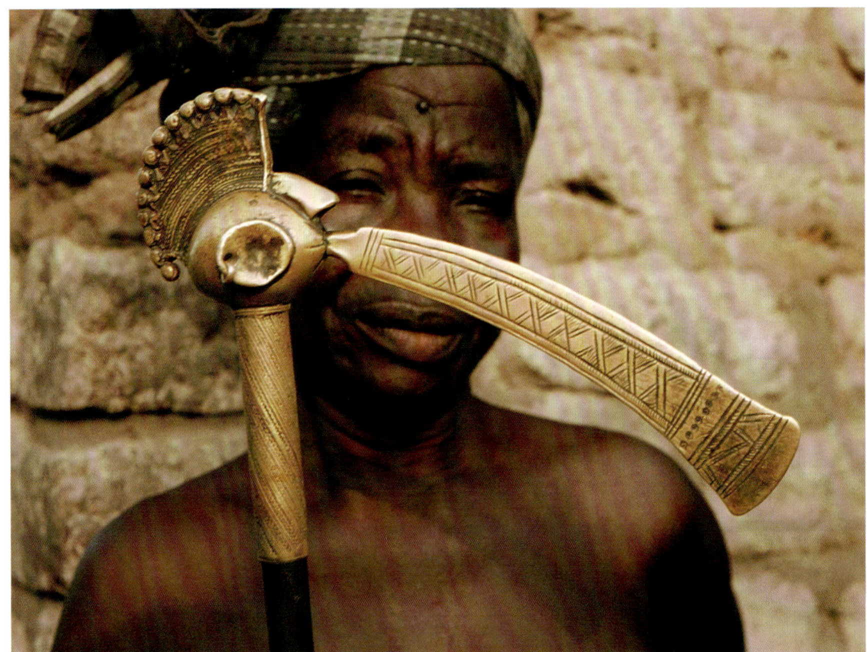

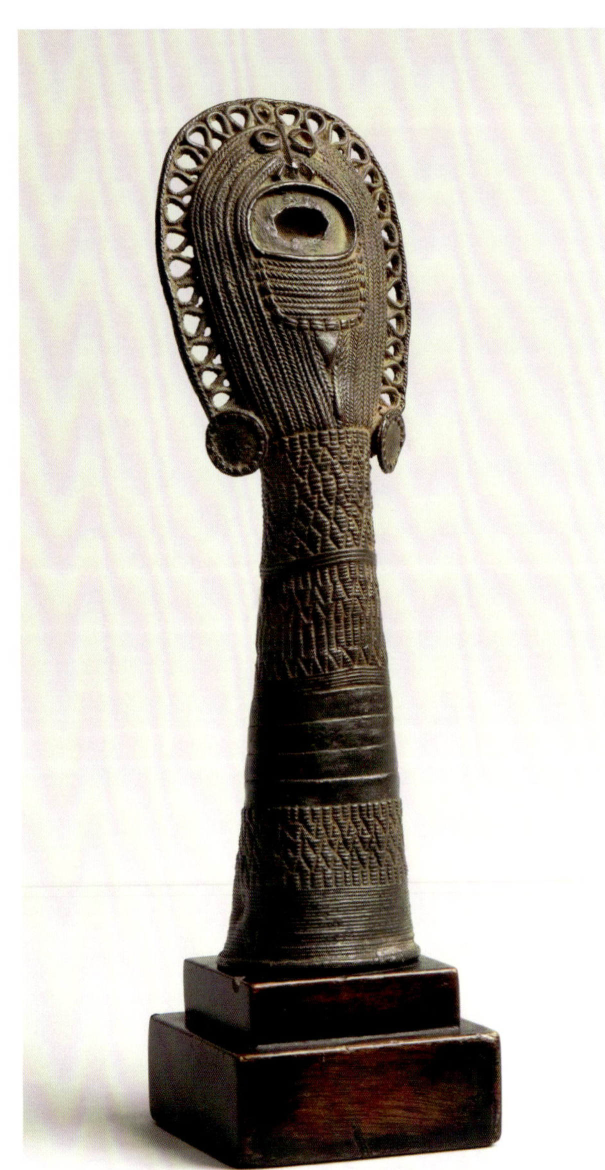

6.11
This small cast copper-alloy creature (possibly representing a hippopotamus) was one of six discovered in the early 1950s near Wukari. It is presently in the collection of the National Museum, Lagos.

PHOTOGRAPH BY ARNOLD RUBIN, RUBIN ARCHIVE, FOWLER MUSEUM AT UCLA, NEG. NO. 1721. REPRODUCED COURTESY OF THE NATIONAL COMMISSION FOR MUSEUMS AND MONUMENTS, NIGERIA.

6.12
This ax was used by women in Jonkpa rites, which were practiced among the Jukun and neighboring groups. Its resemblance to the Tiv ax (see fig. 6.6) is striking.

PHOTOGRAPH BY ARNOLD RUBIN, WUKARI, 1965, RUBIN ARCHIVE, FOWLER MUSEUM AT UCLA, SLIDE NO. A1.12.5.6.

6.13
Figurative wand
Jukun peoples (?), early twentieth century
Copper alloy
H: 20.3 cm
COLLECTION OF TOBY AND BARRY HECHT
IMAGE: PHOTOGRAPH © BY GREG STALEY, 2010
PROVENANCE: CHRISTIAN DUPONCHEEL, LATE 1960S; AULD AND PHILLIPS, LONDON (PUBLISHED IN 1979); MERTON SIMPSON, 1994

This wand may have been associated with a Jukun spirit possession association called Yaku. Female devotees took part in Yaku rituals to secure the good will of spirits. The large open mouth on this wand is unusually expressive and may refer to the devotee's ecstatic state during possession. This piece echoes the high standards of workmanship associated with other Middle Benue cast objects.

with openwork hides (1973, pls. XXII, XXIII), which point to a contribution from south of the Benue, an idea that we will return to later (fig. 6.11).

Adding further richness to the Middle Benue repertory, the distinctive "Tiv ax" surfaces within the context of a Jukun religious tradition (fig. 6.12), along with a unique bronze "wand" (fig. 6.13).[10] Rubin (1973, 228–29; 1982, 45) and Meek before him (1931a, 276ff.) describe Aljanu, Jonkpa, or Kuspa rites among the Jukun and neighboring groups. These involved ecstatic, trance-like behaviors similar to the Hausa Bori. Participants were mainly Abakwariga women who operated with the authority of the Aku (chief) of Wukari or of local chiefs in neighboring villages, who carried these axes as part of the ritual. Meek writes that after a succession of challenges, one woman might be singled out by the presiding deity to become its oracle (*aga*), serving as a conduit for communication between community members and the divinity itself. As the "local Sibyl," the chosen one exercised considerable power, receiving pilgrims petitioning the deity.

Meek includes a drawing made by a "Jukun artist" of the symbol of office of the "*aga*," or oracle, which resembles the figurated wand (fig. 6.14). No information is included with the sketch, suggesting that Meek may not have seen the object himself. Nonetheless, the slightly tapered grip and the inverted U-shaped head with projecting elements resemble the wand's shape. Despite its modest size, the wand is powerfully expressive. The facial features, dominated by an enormous open mouth, convey raw emotion, diverging from the more restrained human representations from the area. Technically, the object appears to be a forceful and superior example of workmanship. The precision of detailing on "body" and "face," as well as the openwork running loops along the top, echo standards of craftsmanship associated with the tier of very fine objects seen by Rubin in the Middle Benue. The braid work on the face resembles that found on other Tiv axes, while the low-relief patterns on the "grip" could conceivably emulate textile designs, like the resist patterns on sacred cloths made in Nigeria for peoples of the Cameroon highlands (Rubin 1982, 45; Sidney Kasfir, personal communication, 2009; Akinwumi 1998, 99). Other conjectures as to its provenance include "Lower Niger," Goemai, and Tiv (specifically as an *imborivungu*).[11] A similar but poorly crafted figure is attributed to the Cross River region (see Brincard 1982, 126, H 21, 156). Although the legs in that example are splayed, the head and decorative elements suggest affinities with this handsome specimen.

Jukun Metalsmithing, the Abakwariga Factor

In his articles on Middle and Upper Benue metalworking, Arnold Rubin is supremely thorough in determining possible sources and locales for the manufacture of the various cast objects under discussion. Had the Jukun maintained a tradition of casting in the mid-1960s, Rubin would surely have discovered it. As he noted, however, even the axes in active use in Wukari were not manufactured during his tenure there (1973, 229): "little trace of a former large-scale bronzeworking industry was evident in the Jukun area in 1964.... [M]ass-produced imports and the products of the metropolitan Hausa and Nupe workshops have swept away whatever local manufactories had existed earlier" (Rubin 1973, 224).

As noted previously, however, both Rubin and William Fagg advanced the idea that Hausa (Abakpa or Abakwariga) were important metalworkers in the Middle Benue region. Rubin discusses a people who may have inhabited the Wukari area from ancient times, predating the Jukun. His description coalesces with earlier observations of an "almost autonomous Hausa colony" in Wukari, whose members, despite their independence, were known to be "respectful and loyal" to the Jukun king. The term "Abakwa" is said to be Jukun for Hausa (Ruxton 1907, 381). Over time, they lost their "faith, language and most of their original characteristics," thus earning the nomenclature "pagan" among Rubin's informants (Ruxton 1907, 381; Rubin 1973, 223). During the course of his own fieldwork in Wukari, he interviewed both an Abakwariga brass

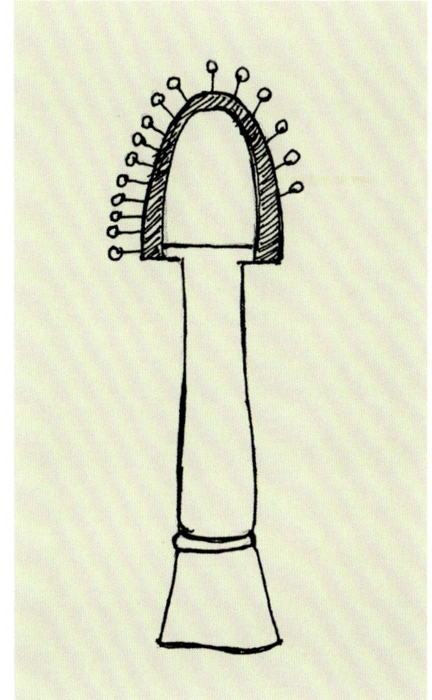

6.14
This symbol of office was used by a woman chosen to serve as the oracle (*aga*) of the Yaku spirit possession association. In shape it resembles the wand illustrated in figure 6.13. The original drawing, which was illustrated by C. K. Meek was purportedly by a "Jukun artist."
DRAWING BY NANCY NEAHER MAAS, AFTER MEEK (1931A, 280).

caster and blacksmith, which at the very minimum gives credence to separate established skill sets among this group (1985). Rubin adds that they also excelled at textile production and were long-distance traders "in a wide variety of commodities, sustaining a network of trade which originated in the emporia of the far north, permeated the Benue Valley, and terminated in Bamenda and southern Idoma" (Rubin 1982, 45; Akinwumi 1998, 99; Shain 2005).

From the earliest reports, Abakwariga were associated with a Jukun identity, as rivals or subordinates of the Jukun kingship or as purely Hausa migrants from the north.[12] Recent scholarship defines the Jukun, or Apá, as the product of an enduring alliance of three groups: local salt producers, Jukun-speaking "owners" of important rainmaking cults, and Hausa-speaking Abakwariga salt merchants (Shain 2005). While affirming the Abakwariga as a critical component of Jukun identity, their historic association with craft industries remains unclear. According to Richard Shain, reports of their involvement in craft production may actually postdate the Islamic reformist invasions of the nineteenth century. According to his interpretation, reformist Hausa migrants took control of long-standing trade roles of the Abakwariga in the 1820s and 1830s, as punishment for practicing a syncretic Islamic faith unacceptable to metropolitan Hausa. Some Abakwariga retreated into crafts production—such as textiles and blacksmithing—to avoid total displacement, while others "re-converted to Islam and joined the interlopers" (2005, 253). On the other hand, based on his study of traditions of origin of the Abakwariga community, Olayemi Akinwumi credits the Abakwariga with introducing and practicing blacksmithing for several hundred years (1998, 99).

Northern Hausa dominance in eastern Central Nigeria in the nineteenth century certainly must have had an impact on the manufacture and trade in metal along the Benue, as Rubin noted. These invaders brought with them an imposing arsenal of talents, not the least of which was their expertise in war, the production of weaponry, and their equestrian skills, all of which likely required a retinue of metalsmiths. Their imposing urban communities to the north at Kano and elsewhere, elaborate leadership categories, artisan and long-distance trade activities, distinctive dress and military acumen surely contributed to an overriding impression of power and achievement, not only among observant outsider-travelers but also among indigenous local groups of subjugated populations.

Thus, it is difficult to isolate a precise Abakwariga contribution in the literature, as it may be obfuscated by so-called Hausa accomplishments. Thomas Hutchinson's comment on Hausa superiority in working brass into "fanciful ornament" like horse bells (1855, 68–69) is typical. Meek credits the "Hausa" with teaching the Jukun how to cast bronze pipe bowls, using the same casting techniques they employed for the manufacture of swords (1931a, 435). P. L. Jaggar published a survey of Kano Hausa smiths and mentions occasional forays into the hinterland, both in search of iron and to sell various metal products, without differentiating between the various subgroups (1973, 24, see also Tremearne 1912, 186). Other sources also speak of the itinerant dimensions of their industry.[13] Hausa traders surely dealt in metalwork as they moved through other areas (Temple 1919, 318), in the same way the Awka Igbo smiths imported bells back to their home territory (see interleaf C). It is possible that the Abakwariga were celebrated producers and traders but that after the middle of the nineteenth century, Wukari and other Benue areas were likely swamped with "new" Hausa from the north, whose enterprises were to be celebrated by so many observers from the mid-nineteenth century onward (Shain 2005; Akinwumi 1998, 101).[14]

In sum, a broad distribution of fairly homogeneous metal types—embracing sophisticated form and openwork decorative treatments—suggests that highly competent and organized artisans might have been behind their creation. Until further research is conducted, however, a Hausa and/or specifically Abakwariga provenience evades us, remaining in the realm of speculation.

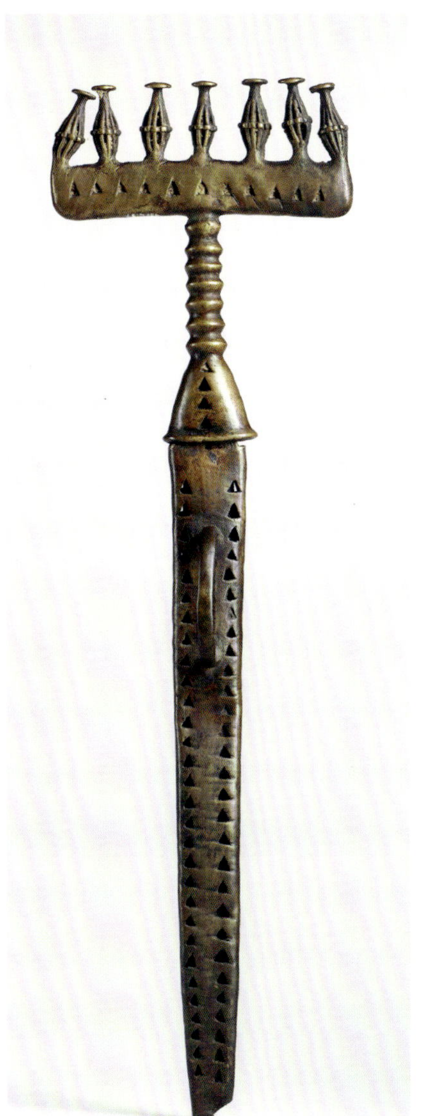

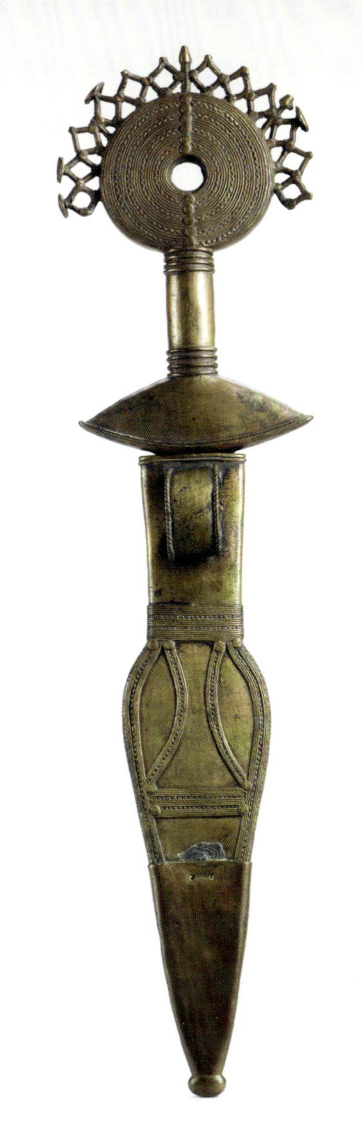

6.15, 6.16
Short sword and sheath (*wek suktunkak*)
Verre peoples, early twentieth century
Copper alloy, iron
H: 45 cm
MUSÉE DU QUAI BRANLY, PARIS, 73.1997.4.57
IMAGE: © 2010 MUSÉE DU QUAI BRANLY. PHOTO-
GRAPH BY THIERRY OLLIVIER/MICHEL URTADO/
SCALA, FLORENCE
PROVENANCE: JOSEF MUELLER

Short sword and sheath (*wek suktunkak*)
Verre peoples, early twentieth century
Copper alloy, iron
H: 41 cm
MUSÉE DU QUAI BRANLY, PARIS, 73.1997.4.58
IMAGE: © 2010 MUSÉE DU QUAI BRANLY. PHOTO-
GRAPH BY THIERRY OLLIVIER/MICHEL URTADO/
SCALA, FLORENCE
PROVENANCE: JOSEF MUELLER

The best-known Verre metal objects are
elaborately decorated short swords and
sheaths, worn primarily by boys at their
initiation ceremonies. Because the Verre lived
close to the city of Yola, where the Fulani
established an emirate in 1841, it is possible
that such swords were influenced by Islamic
forms of decoration.

UPPER BENUE

Evidence of brass casting surfaces frequently among the small, relatively isolated communities of the Upper Benue. Smithing is often associated with endogamous groups
or clans like the Killa of Bura and various villages among the Verre (Meek 1931b, 1:
23; Neher 1964; Rubin 1974, 173, 1985, 6–7; Chappel 1982, 1997; and see Jos Museum
acquisitions 1966, e.g., 66J.230, 663). In addition, not only the Chamba but also the
Mumuye may well have engaged in smithing (Schädler 1997, 264). Other candidates
include the Kyibaku, Pabir, and Bura north of the Gongola-Hawal confluence (Meek
1931b, 1: 23; Neher 1964, 17, 20; Rubin 1974, 173) and the Ga'anda, Tula, and Longuda
of the Lower Gongola, who are spread across a daunting stretch of territory along the
upper reaches of the Benue. There is even tentative evidence of copper ore on the
Verre plateau, although Thurstan Shaw, the archaeologist responsible for documenting
the Igbo-Ukwu corpus, expresses skepticism (Jos Museum, 66J.11.749). Nonetheless,
ample supplies of copper alloy must have been available since the generous proportions and quantities of cast objects attributed to some Upper Benue traditions predi-
cated abundant resources. Whether these derived from intense trade or from local
extraction, we cannot know at this time.

Daggers and sheaths have already come under scrutiny in regard to a type
observed by Arnold Rubin among the Jukun (see fig. 6.10). Similar objects have been
collected in northeastern Nigeria from the time of Frobenius onward (figs. 6.15, 6.16).

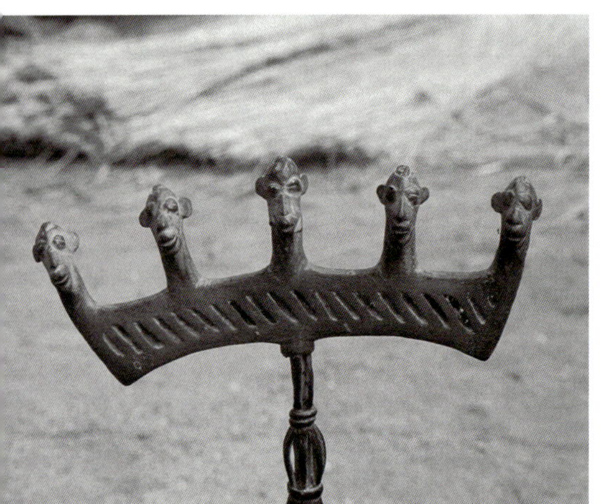

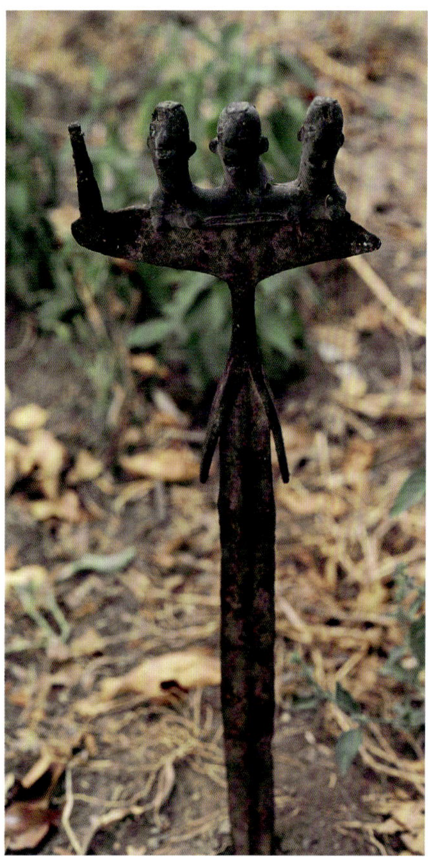

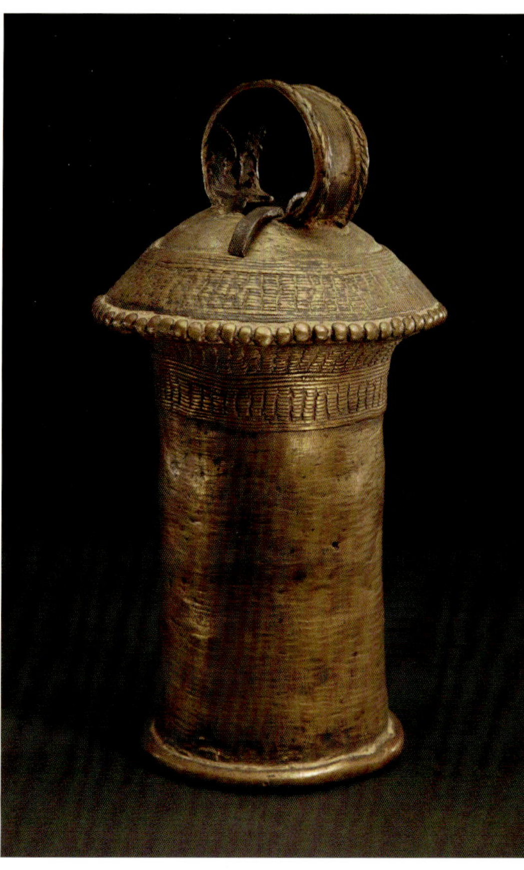

6.17
This detail illustrates the T-shaped grip of a dagger from the Ga'anda district of Gabun. The five human heads mounted on protrusions represent the chief (Kutira), occupying the central position, and his assistants. Similar protrusions, although lacking heads, appear on the Verre dagger illustrated as figure 6.15.
PHOTOGRAPH BY ARNOLD RUBIN, GABUN TOWN, MARCH 23, 1970, RUBIN ARCHIVE, FOWLER MUSEUM AT UCLA, NEG. NO. 2529.

6.18
This dagger (*sakumwang*) from the Longuda peoples is made of copper alloy and iron. It is related in form to the Ga'anda dagger (fig. 6.17), as well as to the Verre example illustrated as fig. 6.15.
PHOTOGRAPH BY MARLA C. BERNS, WALU VILLAGE, 1982.

6.19
Bell
Verre peoples, before 1969
Copper alloy
H: 17.5 cm
FOWLER MUSEUM MUSEUM AT UCLA X88.155; PURCHASE IN MEMORY OF DR. ARNOLD RUBIN
IMAGE: © 2010 FOWLER MUSEUM AT UCLA. PHOTOGRAPH BY DON COLE
PROVENANCE: FIELD COLLECTED BY ARNOLD RUBIN, NIGERIA, 1969
(NOT IN EXHIBITON)

In addition to weaponry (see figs. 6.15, 6.16), the Verre also created numerous other cast copper-alloy objects, including bells such as this one.

Whether they were inspired by Hausa/Islamic precedents from Northern Nigeria or by as yet unexamined sources to the northeast is not known at this time.[15] While the Verre daggers often retain the cross-shaped pommel characteristic of northern-based weaponry, the transverse element has been transformed into a platform for diminutive projections, many of which feature individually modeled human heads. A number also feature openwork designs; small triangular cut-outs adorn the sheath and/or elements of the dagger itself.

Among the Verre these were known as *wek suktunkak* (sing.) and were used during the boys' initiation ceremony (*gangni*; see Martin 1997, 296, figs. 308–12). Taking place every seven years, the ceremony involved circumcision rites marking entrance into manhood. A sword owned by a senior man was suspended from the initiate's neck and hung down the boy's back, resting against the buttocks.

This distinctive dagger associated with the Verre has also been documented north of the Benue River in the Lower Gongola Valley. Rubin (fieldnotes, March 23, 1970) and Marla Berns (1986, 99) recorded three of these daggers among the Ga'anda peoples, who live east of the Gongola River, where they were called *thluuti kuturcha* (knives of chieftaincy; see fig. 17.23). According to Berns, all were considered heirlooms and were said to have been brought with the Ga'anda from the "east" in the Mandara Mountains when they migrated to their present location. They were displayed on the bodies of deceased chiefs during pre-burial rites. The horizontal crossbar of the hilt carries the same fully modeled heads representing the Kutira (chief) in the center surrounded by four assistants (fig. 6.17). The central head wears the distinctive coiffure of an initiated man, called *topro*, with tufts of hair along the transverse crest. The historical significance of this dagger form is suggested by its representation on the surface of the Ga'anda spirit vessel, known as Ngum-Ngumi, which is said to have led the Ga'anda in their westward migration (see fig. 17.22).

Another related dagger (*sakumwang*) was documented among the Longuda, who live to the west of the Gongola River. It, too, was said to have been brought from a sacred homeland, Wanda, located in the hills to their north (fig. 6.18; Marla Berns, personal communication, 2010). The three remaining heads on the fragmentary example in figure 6.18 are similar to those on the Ga'anda versions. One head has plaits of hair along its crest with a single topknot, likely representing a coiffure once associated with leadership.

The Verre, populating the hills, valleys, and flatlands near the main community at Yola, are credited with the creation of many object types in cast copper-alloy. Aside from weaponry, these include a series of handsome bells, some with projections terminating in tiny faces as found on weaponry described earlier (fig. 6.19); equestrian fittings; snuff containers; bowls; body ornaments, such as the distinctive top-shaped pendants worn by women; and brass crooks, which may be skeuomorphs of a traditional type of leadership baton. In every case, the Verre material evinces a formal homogeneity—generously scaled with repeated designs and relief work and a pronounced brassy color. To a limited degree, the Verre corpus resembles metalwork emanating from the Cameroon highlands further to the east. That these traditions might show similarities shouldn't come as a surprise, given the energetic exchange of concepts and goods along the Benue. As a matter of fact, shared roots are reported for some Cameroon groups with links to Chamba smithing (Jeffreys 1962, 193; Harter 1973, 37–39). Yola, the original capital of the Fulani sultanate of Adamawa, was known as "the gateway to the so far unoccupied area around Lake Chad" (Passarge 1893, cited in Kirk-Greene 1957, 92), but specifics are needed before generalities of this scope can be reliably advanced.[16]

As to a recognized tradition of smithing, Temple called the Verre "superior blacksmiths…work[ing] in brass as well as iron" but emphasized that they were best at farming (1919, 359). Meek refers to villagers at Soli, a name that crops up in museum archives, stating that blacksmiths were endogamous, only intermarrying with other smiths in neighboring hamlets (1931b, 1: 415). Tim Chappel, who collected artifacts for the Nigerian museums in the 1960s, claims that the Verre had a vibrant metalworking tradition, eclipsing that of their neighbors, the Bata (1982, 79; 1997). Before the advent of the Fulani, Verre smiths (*tibia*) as members of an endogamous "caste," enjoyed high status in the community. Smiths also possessed more prestigious and physically large objects made of "brass" than were commissioned by nonsmiths (*gazabi*; Chappel 1997, 223). Of particular note, a bell and an iron hoe donated to the Nigerian Museum, Lagos, by the Catholic Mission at Yola document their maker as a "Verre smith at Laindai Boi" (Father Cullen's gift, 1946: 46.29.8 and 17), providing us with specific, if anonymous, information on a working artisan who was conversant both in ironsmithing and casting. The bell is a classic Verre type, featuring a sloped "roof" ornamented with fine crotal-like projections (National Museum, Lagos 46.29.8). What is lacking is an understanding of time depth and of Verre relationships with neighboring traditions, including those of western Cameroon. Undoubtedly the eastern regions of the Benue constituted a realm of intense exchange oblivious to national boundaries.[17]

Field research conducted by Arnold Rubin in the 1970s and Marla Berns in the 1980s revealed that a range of other cast cuprous objects were made and used as regalia by the Ga'anda and Longuda peoples of the Upper Benue region and their neighbors. For example, distinctive gauntlets were worn by young Longuda girls to signify their status (fig. 6.21). Some of these had elaborate openwork designs. The Longuda also kept cast clapper-bells with a sloped roof (*gilaungla*) so that when a hunter killed a leopard or a lion, such a bell could be hung around his neck in a dance celebrating his prowess. Longuda informants claimed that these items came from elsewhere (mentioning the Dera people of Shellen town to their west), but they also maintained that in the distant past the Longuda had their own casting traditions.[18]

Centered in the village of Tula Wange and situated west of the Longuda in the Muri Mountains, the Tula peoples' cast clapper bells (*hweli*), which were strung

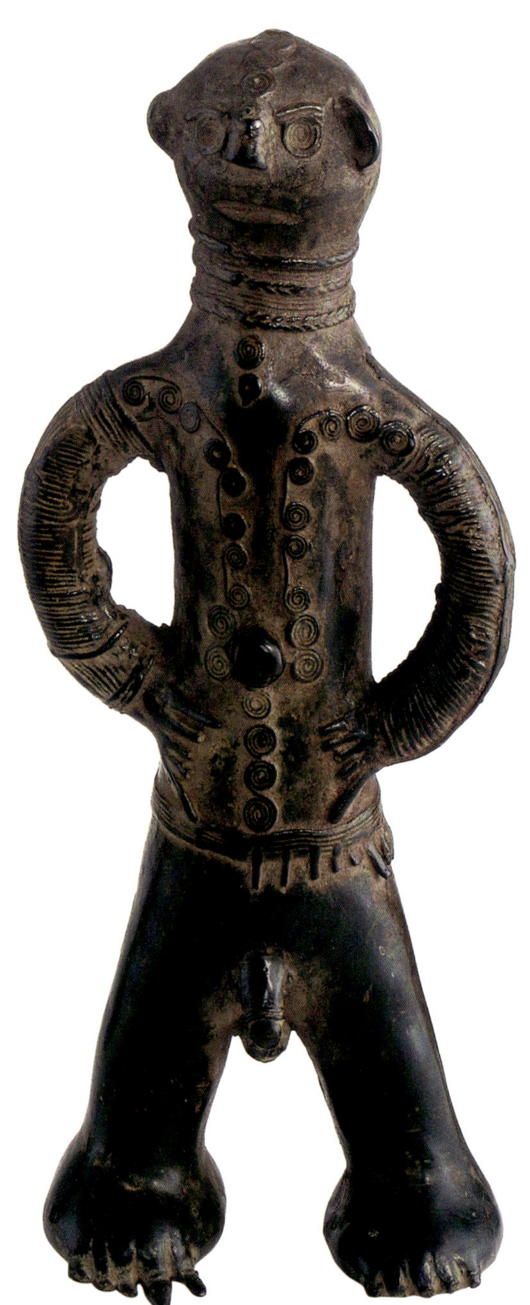

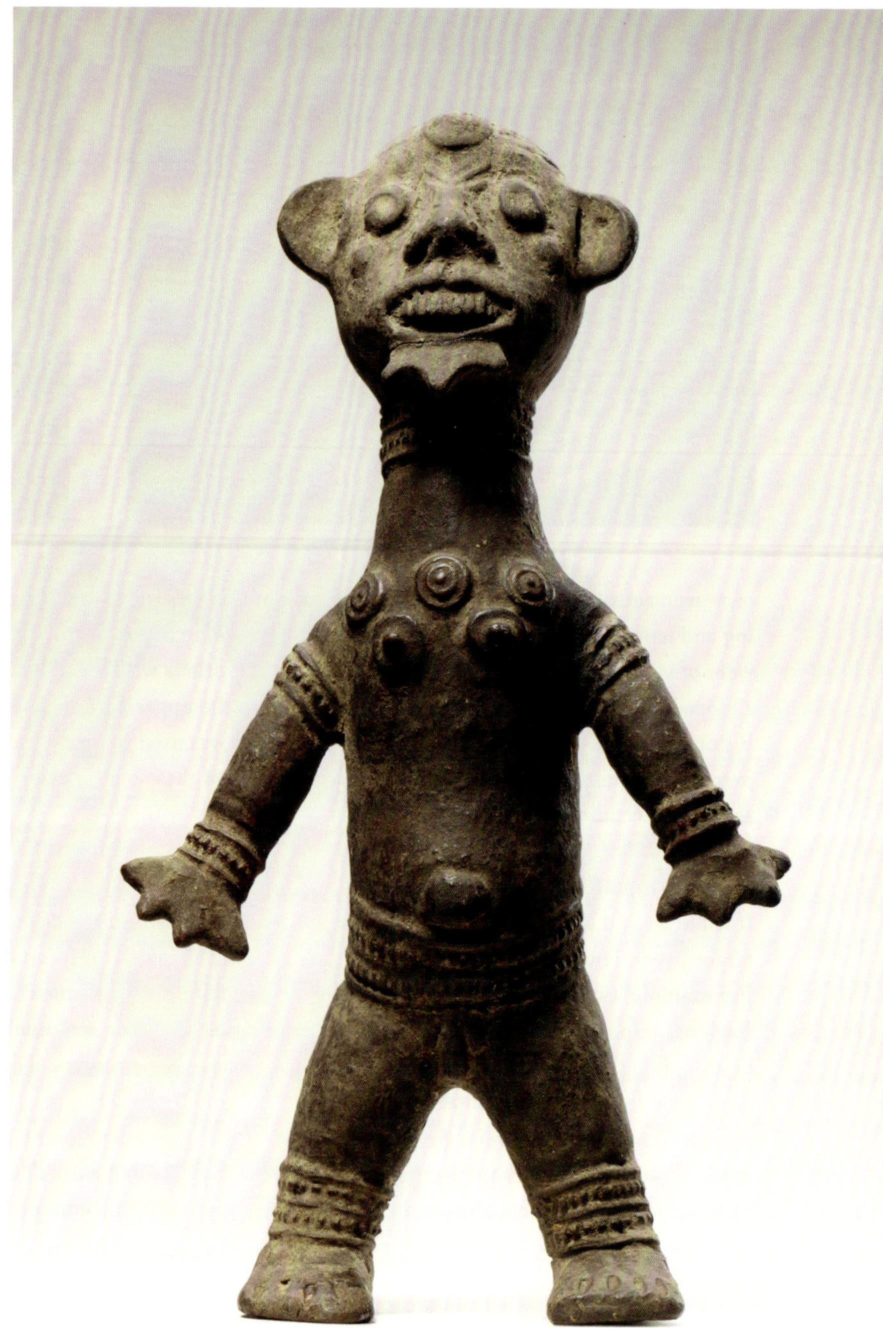

6.23, 6.24

Male figure
Benue River Valley peoples (?), mid-
nineteenth century
Copper alloy
H: 27 cm
THE MENIL COLLECTION, HOUSTON, Y805
IMAGE: © THE MENIL COLLECTION, HOUSTON.
PHOTOGRAPH BY HICKEY-ROBERTSON, 2010
PROVENANCE: MERTON D. SIMPSON, NEW YORK;
DOMINIQUE DE MENIL, 1977; MENIL FOUNDATION,
INC., 1998

Male figure
Benue River Valley peoples (?), late nine-
teenth to early twentieth century
Ceramic
H: 23.5 cm
MUSÉE DU QUAI BRANLY, PARIS, 73.1996.1.9
IMAGE: © 2010 MUSÉE DU QUAI BRANLY. PHOTO-
GRAPH BY THIERRY OLLIVIER/MICHEL URTADO/
SCALA, FLORENCE
PROVENANCE: BARBIER-MUELLER COLLECTION,
GENEVA

Small cast bronze or brass figures standing in
a wide-legged stance and covered in elaborate
spiral decoration, like figure 6.23, have been
identified with cultures of the Benue and the
Cross River regions. Their production seems
to have ended in the nineteenth century, and
we have few clues as to the peoples or casting
industries that produced them. Intriguing
stylistic similarities exist between such metal
figures and the ceramic figure illustrated as
figure 6.24.

adorned with rings and bell-like objects. The arms of the example in figure 6.23 create an arc, detached from the trunk; others of this genre integrate the arms into the trunk either partially or entirely. Like those discovered to the southeast, this figure features decorative designs of coiled spirals and thread work, although it lacks the refinement of some of the other examples. One possibly significant element is the presence of unique banding on the arms. Leon Siroto considers this "addition" to indicate a northern connection in terms of an iconographic contribution. The Hausa apparently wrap the arms in such a manner prior to boxing matches (Menil Archives, n.d.). A small ceramic figure (fig. 6.24) reveals a resemblance to this cast-copper figure. The ceramic figure was modeled with very finely applied clay decoration, which emulates the process used to build a decorative surface with latex or beeswax before casting. This decorative approach is less typical of ceramic than it is of metal. A systematic exploration of similar figures in clay and other media might yield fruitful insights in ascertaining the identity of the metal figure.

Despite the evidence, however, southeast Nigerian points of origin are hard to eliminate. A number of cast animals associated with the region bear the coiled spiral markings found on some of these figures. Such markings have a long history in southeastern Nigeria, going back to the finds at Igbo-Ukwu dated to the ninth century CE. Rubin's "road creatures," illustrated in his article on the Middle Benue, also evince similarities in surface treatments with Southern Nigeria (1973, 228). To give just one example, a long-eared, chubby quadruped (Rubin 1973, pl. XXIIIa) bears virtually identical markings to a bell associated with the Bende region (National Museum, Lagos, 73.1.738). The slender bell, shaped like an inverted lotus, numbers among many of this kind found in Igbo country. Keith Nicklin provides primary material on "companion" figures and was able to subject one to thermoluminescence dating, yielding a mid-nineteenth-century date. While local manufacture cannot be discounted, other groups like itinerant Awka and/or Abiriba smiths may also have played a role in the production, movement, and possible emulation of these intriguing figures.[19]

In short, a growing body of evidence reveals strong connections between the Middle/Upper Benue and the Cross River area of southeastern Nigeria. Regardless of original provenance, small portable cast objects easily could have made their way along these corridors as they have so frequently elsewhere, replicating a pattern of behavior that characterizes the life of Benue metal arts as a whole. ●

INTERLEAF C

A Note on the "Igala" Bell

NANCY NEAHER MAAS

Clapper that is inside the bell…
—AN INVOCATION TO ROYAL ANCESTORS (BOSTON 1968, 202)

The story of a distinctive bell type reflects in microcosm the reality of copper-alloy and iron studies along the Benue.[1] The bell type in question is relatively simple in form: an elliptically shaped body, broad of shoulder, and approximately 15–20 centimeters in height (figs. C.1, C.2). Some examples flare slightly at the bottom, while others are tubular in profile. Each has a small looped handle on top and usually an iron clapper attached within it. Of special interest are the various designs decorating the shoulder of the bell: striations, circular nubs, whorls, and defining bands. Most are in relief, although some bells feature incised repeats of triangles or running loops. A band at the base of the bell carries similar patterns. Made using the lost-wax casting process, these bells can vary in color from a deep bronze to an almost chocolate hue. A few are thin cast with delicate surface treatment, yet most are bulkier and appear less refined in their execution and detail.

Multitudes of bells have been found in various parts of Nigeria, many with clear visual references to the culture within which they were created. Certainly the Benin bells fit this description, as do the numerous face bells of the Ijebu-Ode Yoruba. The Igbo-Ukwu corpus includes bells that conform to the elaborately ornamented bronze style of that tradition. Within this context, the bell under consideration also possesses a singular "look," as though it were made in conformity with an established aesthetic. And, while we can entertain some possibilities, at present any originating cultural matrix or matrices remain a mystery.

Based on historical references and oral testimony, the bell type in question is popularly known as the "Igala" bell, referring to the Igala Kingdom, which extends across a section of the Lower Benue. Charles Partridge, a British officer who served several tours of duty in the Nigerian colony was

stationed in the Igala capital of Idah at the turn of the twentieth century. He collected several of these bells and donated them to the Ipswich Museum, apparently believing they were made at Benin across the Niger River to the west (figs. C.3, C.4). They were taken from what Patridge referred to as a "ruinous burial hut," possibly during his visit to royal grave sites near Idah (Ipswich Museum, 1928 15-B; Partridge 1904, 335; Boston 1968, 11). John Boston also reported seeing brass bells in ancestor shrines of titled clan heads, identifying them as *okpogo ilo*, a specific Igala nomenclature that distinguished them from smaller types and examples associated with the Kingdom of Benin (1974). According to Boston, the Igala practiced "structural amnesia," maintaining burial shrines of the last nine deceased who had held the position of Ata, or king, while memorials to more ancient rulers were abandoned (1968,11, 53). These older shrines were allowed to fall into disrepair, explaining the circumstances under which Partridge most likely obtained his bells.

The elliptical bell was associated with royalty and high status. It was often employed to "call" the ancestors and petition their aid for some human need (Boston 1968, 242). Today the regalia of the Ata of Idah includes bells, at least two of which typify the "Igala" bell, although in smaller scale (8.9 and 10.2 cm). The absence of a "classic" elliptical bell is notable, lending weight to reports that ancient Igala bells disappeared into the crucibles of contemporary smiths (Allison 1968, 8).

The "Igala" bell was, however, by no means restricted to the Igala. On the contrary, it has been identified and collected at the Niger-Benue confluence, eastward up the Benue River, and into the interior of southeast Nigeria, sometimes bearing designations including Bassa, Egbira,[2] Afo, and Idoma. Dating from the 1940s, several museum specimens surfaced

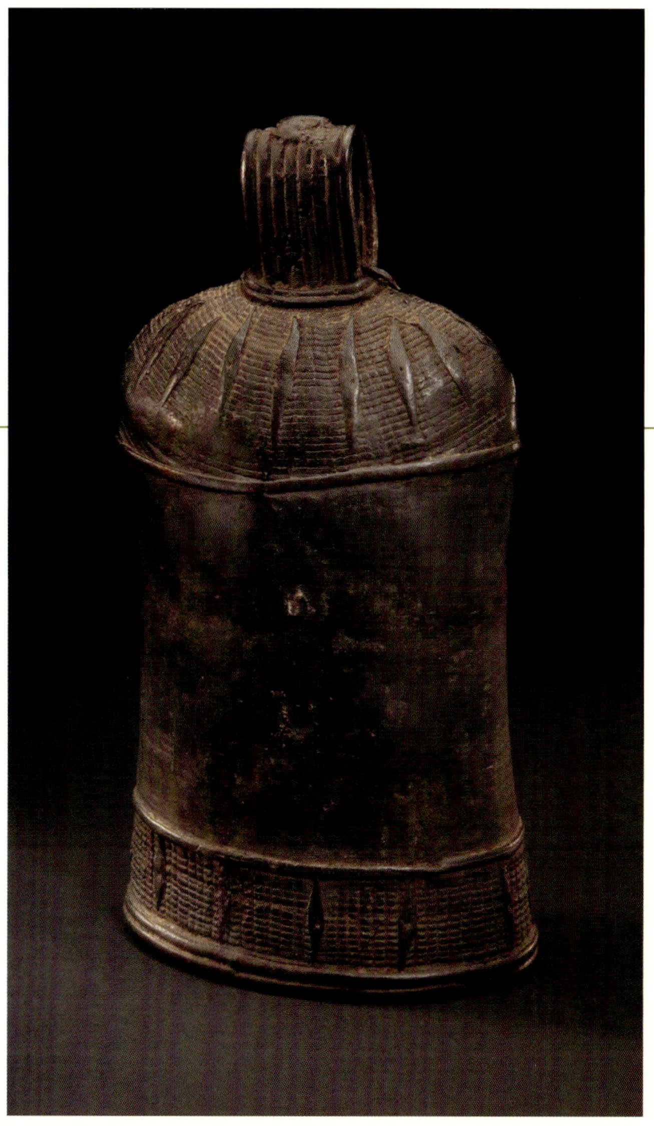

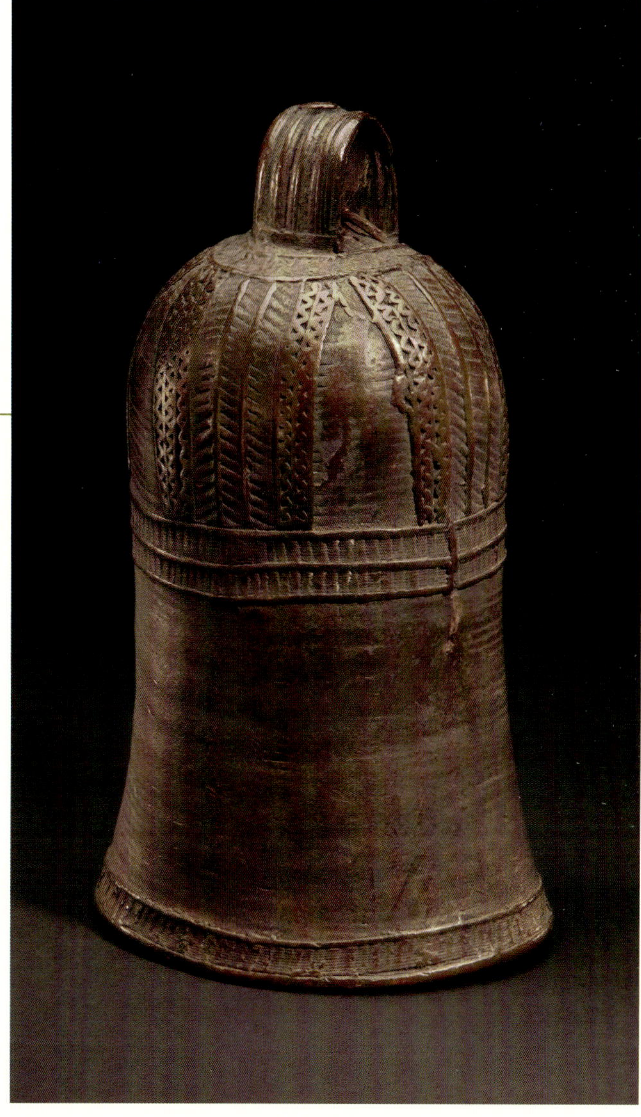

from Egbira country where they functioned as attributes of royal or chiefly status, similar to stated roles among the Igala. Additionally, the bell enjoyed a more egalitarian context among some Egbira communities and others of the Lower Benue (e.g., National Museum, Lagos [NML], 66.1.19; de Rachewitz 1964, 276–78; Byng-Hall 1908, 19; Temple 1919, 47). Some bells were retrieved from locations further east along the Middle Benue corridor. For example, one was collected in the 1940s in Jukun country from a member of the Abakwariga, a distinct group of Hausa lineage (NML LG549). "Igala" bells also traveled south into Igbo country and to the southeast to the Cross River (NML 61.1.150 and 153). By pursuing the peregrinations of this deceptively simple form, we can gain a more nuanced picture of metal arts along the Benue. Beginning with the Igala, we will consider their metalworking heritage, followed by observations on the Egbira, the Igbo, and the Abakwariga.

C.1, C.2
Bells
Igala peoples, early twentieth century (?)
Copper alloy
H: 22.5 cm
COLLECTION OF MARK CLAYTON
IMAGE: © 2010 FOWLER MUSEUM AT UCLA. PHOTOGRAPH BY DON COLE
PROVENANCE: FIELD COLLECTED, NIGERIA, 2005

Elliptically shaped bells with looped handles were associated with Igala royalty and men of high status. The bells were kept in ancestor shrines belonging to titled clan leaders, where they could be used to "call" the ancestors and petition their aid. They were also kept in the treasury of the Igala king (Ata). Beyond the Igala, this particular kind of bell has been documented among a number of Lower and Middle Benue peoples and others in southeastern Nigeria. Its "celebrity" must have had something to do with its powerful political and ritual connotations as well as with the status afforded Igala smiths, whose products were found well beyond the royal Igala court at Idah.

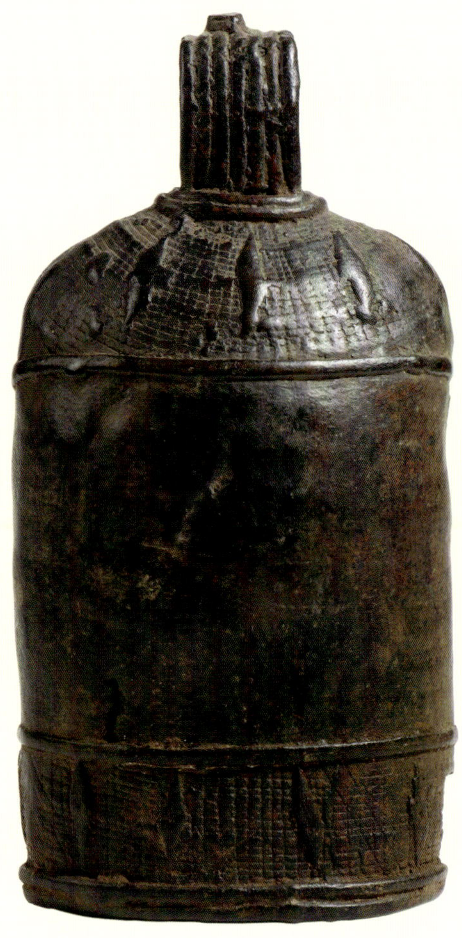

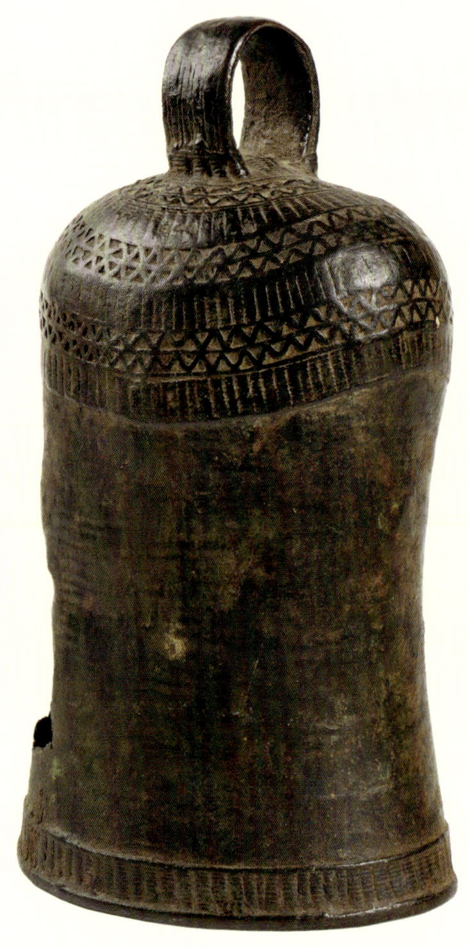

IGALA

The Igala Kingdom has figured prominently in the history of the Lower Benue. The kingdom reached its apex in the eighteenth century, but still maintained its influence to a lesser degree into the nineteenth and twentieth centuries. At a crossroads in Nigerian geography, Igala enjoyed close ties with other peoples, notably the kingdom of Benin to the west and the peoples of the Niger-Benue confluence, including the northen Edo, the Nupe, and Egbira. Their influence and connections also extended further east to the Idoma and to the Jukun, who may at one time have exercised hegemony over the Igala. Shared social and cultural ties among these peoples reflect the possible fracturing of a regional confederacy, followed by the movement of the Igala, Idoma, and Egbira westward along the Benue.

Of particular interest to this study are Igala relations with the Egbira. Their respective oral traditions recount shared origins, the Egbira originating three of the nine founding clans of Igala royalty, while the Igala were said to have founded the Egbira lineage at Panda (Laird 1837, 2: 123–24, 129, n. 46; Lander 1837, 7: 26). During the epoch of Igala primacy, the Egbira became clients of the Igala Kingdom (Baikie 1856, 88–89; Boston 1968, 3–4, 124) with rulers engaging in reciprocal gift giving (Wilson-Haffenden 1927, 381; Boston 1968, 102; Rubin 1983, 46, n. 8). Even today both the Igala ruler and the chief of Egbira Panda possess ceremonial items reflective of this custom.

C.3, C.4
Clapperless bell
Igala peoples, before 1928
Copper alloy
H: 21.2 cm
IPSWICH MUSEUM, R.1928-75.8A
IMAGE: COURTESY OF THE COLCHESTER AND IPSWICH MUSEUM SERVICE
PROVENANCE: COLLECTED BY CHARLES PARTRIDGE, IGALA
(NOT IN EXHIBITION)

Clapperless bell
Igala peoples, before 1928
Copper alloy
H: 21.2 cm
IPSWICH MUSEUM, R.1928-75.8E.
IMAGE: COURTESY OF THE COLCHESTER AND IPSWICH MUSEUM SERVICE
PROVENANCE: COLLECTED BY CHARLES PARTRIDGE, IGALA
(NOT IN EXHIBITION)

These bells, along with others, were collected by British colonial officer Charles Partridge who reportedly found them in a burial shrine.

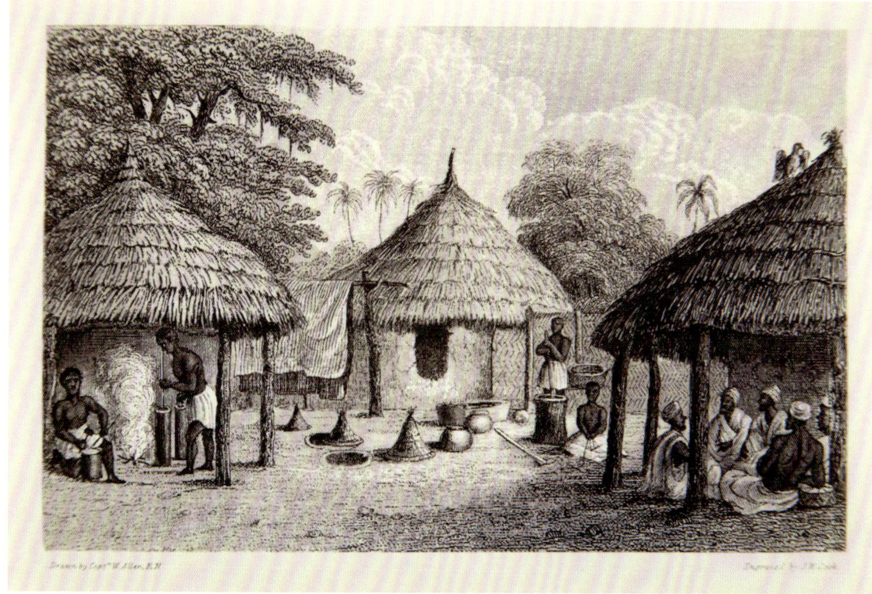

C.5
William Allen's illustration "Native Manufacturing at Idah" shows men actively engaged in metalworking at the left.
REPRODUCED FROM ALLEN AND THOMPSON (1848, 1: 323, FIG. 48).

IGALA METALWORKING

Evidence of an active metalworking legacy lacks dedicated inquiries among the Igala, so it is difficult to sort out the scale and relative sophistication of an indigenous industry. Prior to the mid-nineteenth century, William Allen's journals from an expedition led by the British Royal Navy stressed the importance of an Igala smithing profession (fig. c.5), second only to cloth manufacture and dyeing (1848, 1: 323, fig. 48). Slightly more than a half-century later, Charles Partridge witnessed the "royal" blacksmiths at work preparing the coffin of a newly deceased Ata. He noted two distinct specialties: the "hereditary maker of brass plates for the coffin" and "the maker of the iron trestles" upon which it would rest (1904, 333). The coffin pictured in his publication was clearly created from cold-hammered elements, although it is possible the "maker of brass plates" might also have been adept at lost-wax casting. The acknowledgment of separate skills fits comfortably with the idea that the Igala maintained an established smithing tradition devoted to a kingly patron. The members of the Igala clan responsible for smithing traced their origin to the Egbira (Boston 1968, 83, 117); they were also credited with making bells (*okpogo ilo*), which were given to new chiefs as an affirmation of authority (Boston 1974; Neaher 1975). Brass rods traded along the Niger and Benue likely provided raw material (Temple 1919, 153; Monckton 1927, 21; Seton 1928, 259, 261). Significantly, the Igala credited the great Benin workshops on the other side of the Niger with some of the important brass arts associated with the Ata of Idah's regalia, but they insisted on an Igala origin for the bells (Boston 1974).

Other sources attest to the activities of Igala smiths, namely the testimony of itinerant Igbo metalsmiths who plied Igala country during the remembered past. Their recollections fully support earlier findings. They went further to say that while they worked iron, the Igala cast brass and bells for the Ata. By the 1920s, the demand for these bells was notably in decline, leading to their demise in the smith's crucible (Allison 1968, 8; Neaher 1975).

THE EGBIRA

Before the tidal wave of Fulani incursions in the nineteenth century, the Egbira were recognized as significant producers of metal and other artisanal goods, as well as important players in long-distance trade. For example, the community of Panda was described as a "weaving and smithing centre of 30,000 inhabitants north of the Benue" prior to 1800 (Northrop 1972, 222). The Egbira traded up the "dark water [the Benue]" (Allen 1837, 1: 375ff.), possibly for "ore" that came from the east down the river for use in making pipes, vessels, and iron products such as spears, bows, and arrows (Laird 1837, 1: 231). Intriguingly, the name of the other principal Egbira community, Koton Karifi, was said to derive from a Hausa designation for either iron or brass, referring to its location near iron reserves and/or to its important commercial role in the import of brass rods brought up the Niger River (Mockler-Ferryman 1892, 7). Reported, too, were commercial exchanges with "Arabs and Felatahs" (Laird 1837, 1: 232), implying a broad network extending well beyond the Benue.

With the onset of Fulani attacks north of the Benue, Egbira were forced to flee, sometimes settling on the south banks of the Benue in Igala territory. The Igala ruler apparently welcomed their presence, and at one point, he planned an attack on the Fulani with the help of the King of Panda (Laird 1837, 2: 123–24). How long the Egbira remained subject to the Igala is not clear. When Baikie wrote his report in the 1850s, he claimed that they were independent, albeit residing within Igala dominions (1856, 89). Nonetheless, strong bonds with the Igala persisted.

EGBIRA METALWORKING

*[T]he profession of the blacksmith is held in high estima-
tion, and the Vulcans of Fundah [Panda] are no exception…they rank next to the king in importance and are
quite consequential.*

—LAIRD (1837, 1: 232)

MacGregor Laird, one of the earliest nineteenth-century travelers along the Benue, describes the manufacture from native
iron of "hatchets, chisels, nails and clamps (with) copper…used
in…the manufacture of bowls for their tobacco pipes" (1837, 1:
230; Hutchinson 1855, 149, 98). Pipe bowls are cast products,
suggesting that Egbira not only worked iron but also engaged
in lost-wax casting. Allen also reported seeing a "great deal of
dross (copper) lying about" being used to make pipe bowls at
Panda (1848, 1: 404). Another locality, Rogan-Koto, was noted
for its fine textiles and "manufactury of brass work" (Hutchinson 1855, 98). Hutchinson commended the locals thus: "Manu-
factures…show evidence of the people's industry; and were
they not in daily dread of another attack from the Beriberi
Filatahs…I have very little doubt that their town would soon
present an aspect of thriving industry" (1855, 149).

Whether copper rods "came up the Niger" or "down the
Benue," it is clear that metalworking was alive and well prior
to the turbulence of Fulani incursions. Travelers lamented the
destruction the Egbira federation and the loss of its extensive smithing industry (Laird 1837, 1: 232; Hutchinson 1855,
98). In the twentieth century, however, we learn that some
brass casting survived. Philip Allison, who collected artifacts
on behalf of the Nigerian Department of Antiquities, stated
that the last of the brass casters worked at Iji, a mile south of
Koton Karifi, recycling old cast bells to mend cooking pots
(1974). Another bell was documented as created by a brass-
working family from Egbira-Panda (NML 61.1.105). As noted
previously, numerous bells of the "Igala" type in the collection
of the Nigerian museums identify an Egbira purchase point,
and museum archives are rich with local nomenclature and
itemized uses in either community ceremonies or as regalia of
Egbira chiefs.

THE BELL AND THE IGBO

M. D. W. Jeffreys, a British administrator who served in the
Igbo Awka area south of the Igala homeland, offers more data
on "Igala" bells collected in 1930. Among many artifacts given
by him to the British Museum are "Igala" elliptical bells. These
were obtained in the environs of Awka/Nri (1968, figs. 53, 54).
Bells have a rich and storied history among the Igbo, so it is
not surprising that they would be among the items he accumulated. For example, the highest-ranking members of the western Igbo men's societies (*ozo*) possessed bells as an attribute of
office. Although active usage of bells has declined, a representative collection can be viewed at the town museum of Nri.

Bells very similar to the "Igala" type enjoy an antiquity
among the Igbo not documented elsewhere. Several were discovered in the burial of a "prominent person" dated to the late
fifteenth century (1495+/-95) by the archaeologist Donald Hartle
(Shaw 1968). He excavated them at Ezira, an oracle center in the
heart of Igbo country (fig. C.6). This discovery lends the bell an
impressive time depth and might ordinarily pivot research on a
different trajectory. Unfortunately, the finds disappeared during
the Biafran War (1967–1970), leaving us once again in the realm
of speculation as to the antiquity of this bell type. At the very
least, it is likely that the bell, known as *odu*, is a very old concept.

The contributions made by Jeffreys might well be interpreted as contradictory evidence, placing the bells in the
homeland of the well-known itinerant Igbo smiths of Awka who
were famous for their metalworking arts (figs. C.7a,b). The seven
subdivisions of the community routinely traversed far and wide
in Southern and Central Nigeria, establishing temporary homesteads and providing needed goods to clients of differing ethnic
backgrounds. For instance, the smiths of Umubele and Umuzo-
cha subdivisions traveled regularly to Igala country and resided
there, spending intervals at Awka to fulfill religious responsibilities (Neaher 1979). Field interviews conducted among
these proud and confident smiths revealed that while they were
familiar with the elliptical bell, they emphatically denied making
it, crediting the Igala instead. As noted earlier, these elderly
informants claimed to have witnessed the modeling of such bells
by Igala smiths. They also stated that the Igala smiths used a
type of latex, rather than beeswax, for modeling, underscoring a
difference in technique noteworthy to a fellow artisan. The Awka
smiths took a special interest in these bells, given the wide array
of possible uses bells enjoyed in Igbo culture. Sometimes they
imported them into Igbo country on their travels home. One
informant claimed the Igala brass workers not only made bells
for the Ata of Idah but also secretly sold some to willing buyers.
Another reported seeing the bells on sale in Aguleri in northern
Igbo country. Lastly, the Awka smiths admitted that they not
only traded in the genuine article but also copied the bell for
local use from time to time (Neaher 1975; 1976, 123, 140.).

The involvement of the Awka smiths in the distribution
and emulation of the "Igala" bell goes a long way to explaining its dispersion across areas far removed from Igala country.
Once back in Awka, smiths could swap or sell accumulated
goods from their respective work stations, enhancing the
movement of desired items far and wide. The possibilities of
diffusion, if not limitless, were certainly extensive. If the rivers
themselves served as conduits for goods, the interior was also
punctuated with a network of trading nodes. For example, a
series of markets fanned out from Idah, whose principal articles
of trade were "ivory, locally woven cloth, swords, knives, spears
and metal wares of local manufacture and other imported
goods" (Ukpabi 1971, 107). Obviously, the vitality and density
of patterns of exchange determined the destinies of individual
bells, moving them far beyond their place of origin.

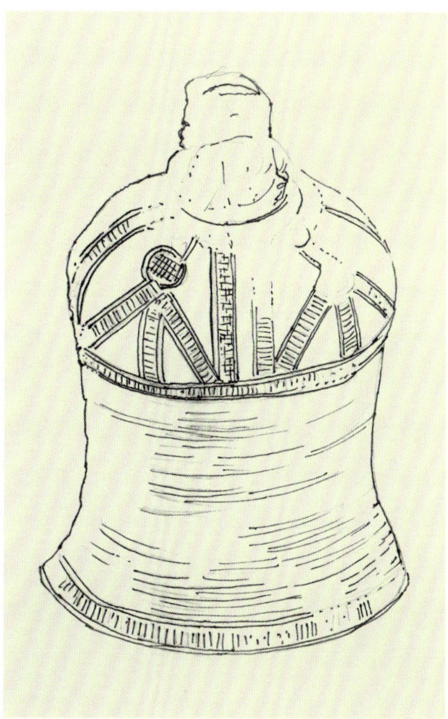

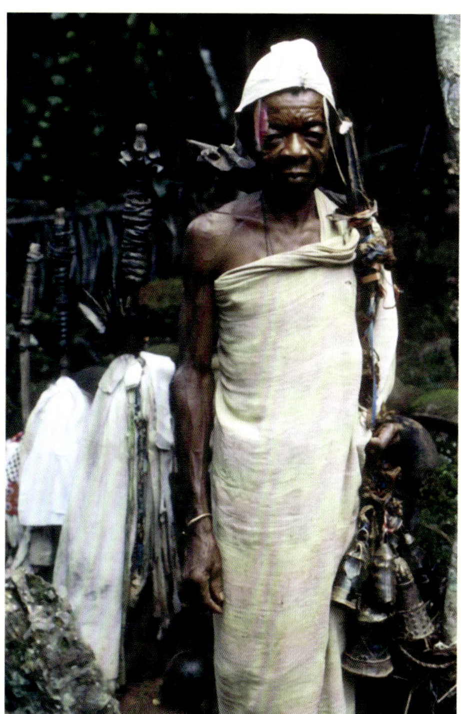

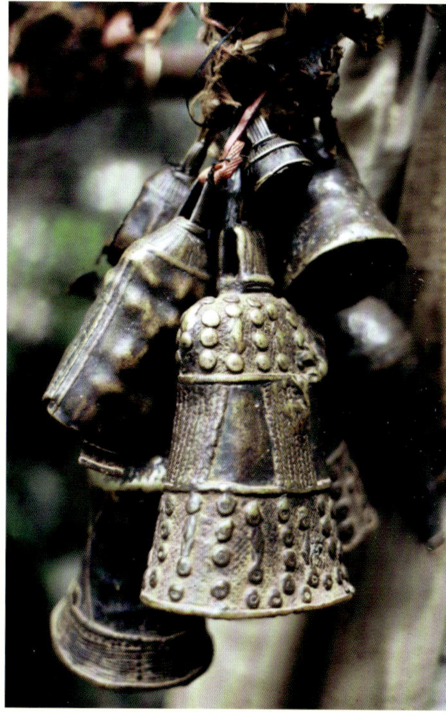

C.6
This "Igala" bell was excavated by archaeologist Donald Hartle at the Ifeka Garden Site in Ezira in Igboland. It may date as early as the late fifteenth century.
DRAWING BY NANCY NEAHER AFTER ISICHEI (1976, PL. 2B).

C.7a,b
The Atama (priest) holds a cluster of bells from the Ide shrine in Ugbene Ovoro (near Nsukka). Figure C.7b is a detail of the seven old copper-alloy bells, which were reported as having been cast in Awka.
PHOTOGRAPH BY HERBERT M. COLE, NORTHERN IGBOLAND, 1983.

ABAKWARIGA

To add to this mosaic, we must briefly consider a group who inhabited the Middle Benue region around Wukari in Jukun country. A more detailed consideration of Abakwariga contributions to metalworking can be found in chapter 6, yet they deserve brief comment here in regard to the "Igala" bell. The head Abaka of the Abakwariga community sold an "Igala" bell to Kenneth Murray of the Nigerian Department of Antiquities in 1944, claiming it was the property of his grandfather (National Museum, Lagos 549). What might be the history of this particular specimen? Was it shipped eastward from a Lower Benue source? Was it made locally by Abakwariga smiths? One thing is certain: the bell is crafted on an "Igala" model; it bears the classic imprint in form and surface treatment, yet its somewhat rough-hewn character suggests it was a copy rather than an original. It does not resemble the Verre or Cameroonian bells found in profusion along eastern reaches of the Benue (see chapter 6), eliminating these areas as an alternative source for its manufacture.

"IGALA BELLS" AND THE BENUE

The "Igala" bell presents us with a shifting landscape of production, transfer, reproduction, and emulation. The anthropological and historical record identifies Igala smiths servicing the court at Idah and selling metalwork for profit on the side. Egbira artisans undoubtedly made a substantial contribution as well, considering their repeated identification in museum records. Awka Igbo itinerants facilitated the movement of the bells—either originals or copies—to their Igbo homeland and beyond. Moreover, other Igbo smiths from Nsukka and Enugu may also have copied the *odu* (Murray 1949, 86). Its occasional appearance at the extremes of its sphere of distribution suggests that artisans like the Abakwariga may also have been involved in the bell's manufacture and trade, although to a lesser degree. A mold-made specimen in the collection of the American Museum of Natural History (VI, 63, 90.0/1984) suggests the importation of mass-produced "Igala" bells from a non-Nigerian source. It wouldn't be the first time that imports made for the African trade were inspired by indigenous models (Neaher 1976, 154). We may never know why the "Igala" bell enjoyed such celebrity. Perhaps it had something to do with its relatively generous size or its sound when rung or struck. Perhaps the elliptical concept, enhanced by delicate design treatments, was especially appealing to a broad range of communities. Its likely manufacture at the hands of these distinct groups hints at the possibility that the bell might have had a far wider appeal than we can estimate now, given finite evidence. Complicating this picture is the fact that numerous bells of this shape and decorative treatment are surfacing in private art collections today. With the application of scholarly and scientific analyses, this newly emerging corpus might help to shed further light on a shadowy corner in the larger drama of the arts of the Benue. ●

INTERLEAF d

A Note on Idoma Bells and Smoking Pipes

SIDNEY LITTLEFIELD KASFIR

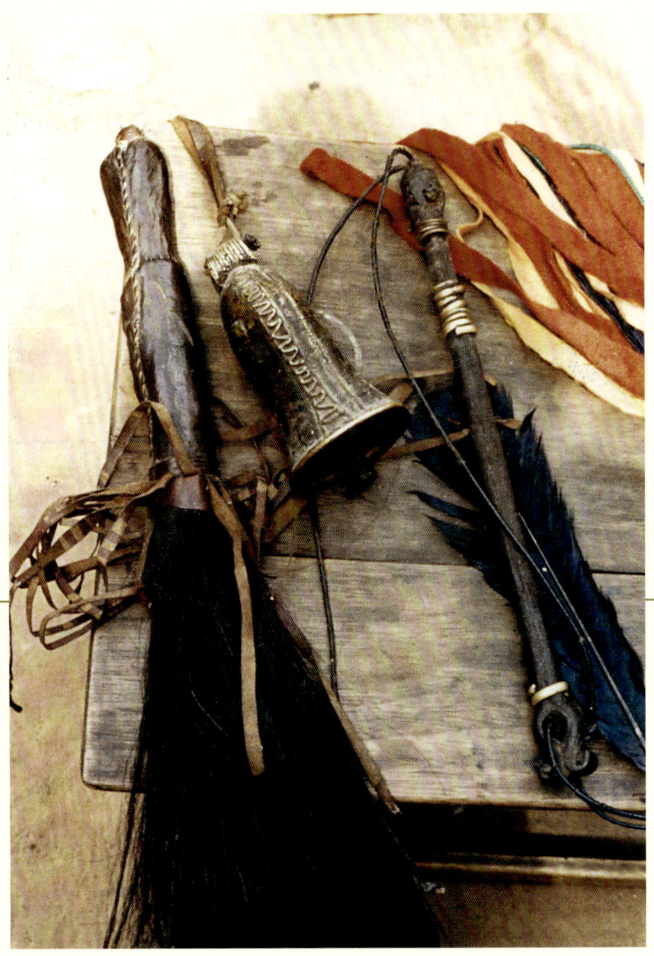

The subject of copper-alloy bells—treated by Nancy Neaher Maas in interleaf C of this volume—has never been adequately studied among the Idoma. Here I offer a glimpse into their usage and style, but the question of their origin remains open, depending on how much weight is given to which oral traditions. The royal bell of the Och'Akpa (chief of the Akweya clans) was used to summon subjects for important ceremonies (figs. D.1, D.2). Several bells of similar shape and decoration were shown to me (usually after much prognostication) in different Idoma districts, but I was very rarely allowed to photograph them.

An exception was made in Otobi, where I was resident for several seasons. The bell kept there in the Agbo shrine of Omaga An'ne (figs. D.3a,b) was said to have been passed down by Ekpa, the ancestor of the Ekpari clan. While this belongs in the category of mythic history, it does indicate a direction of origin that points mythically to Apá (i.e., east) but linguistically south to the middle Cross River and Ogoja. To add to the confusion, all Idoma kings have historically gone west to Idah to receive their beads of office from the Ata of Igala, so oral history in this case occludes more than it reveals. Metallurgical analyses have never been performed, but the same overall shape can be found in Igala bells and, according to Maas, in Bende as well. Both the southern Idoma Unaaloko masquerade and the Igala royal Ekwe masquerade (see fig. 5.3) wear small bells at the hems of their costumes, and the Unaaloko's ritual attendant also carries a bell attached to a horsetail whisk (see fig. 2.33).

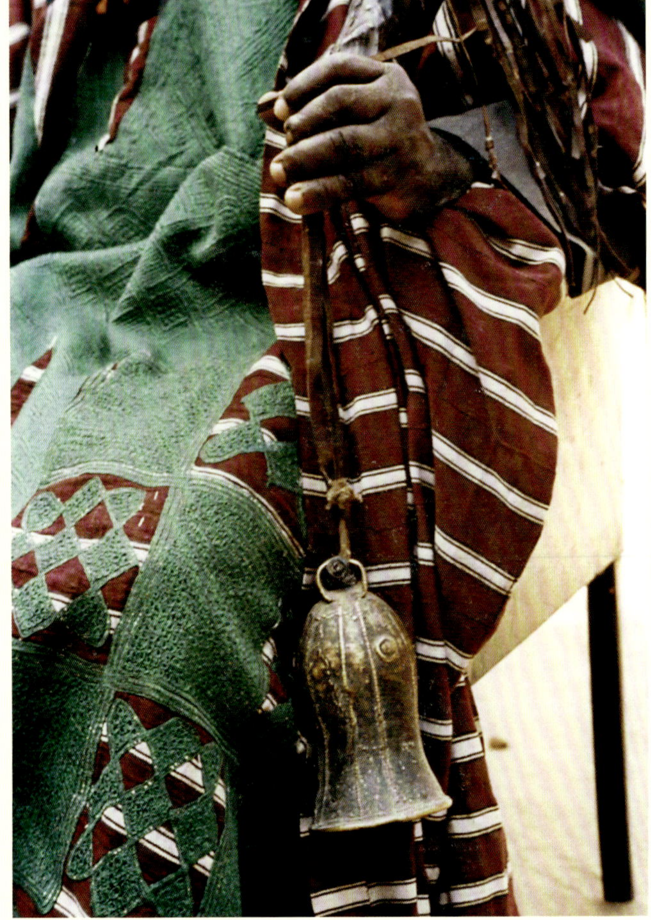

D.1

The regalia of the Och'Akpa (chief of the Akweya clans) reflects the Akweya saying, "Apá was our father and Yachi our mother." The hybrid dress and accoutrements include a Cross River type feathered cap, worn with a Hausa gown, an Apá-Kwararafa horsetail whisk, and a copper-alloy bell (*ingblinya*) said to be "from Apá" but having the same shape as those seen in Igala and also Bende Igbo (Nancy Neaher Maas, personal communication). The other side of the same bell is shown in figure D.2.

PHOTOGRAPH BY SIDNEY LITTLEFIELD KASFIR, OTOBI, 1974.

D.2

The designs on Akweya bells are created using a latex rather than a beeswax modeling technique for the surface. The two sides of a single bell bear contrasting designs. This photograph shows the obverse of the bell pictured in figure D.1.

PHOTOGRAPH BY SIDNEY LITTLEFIELD KASFIR, OTOBI, 1974.

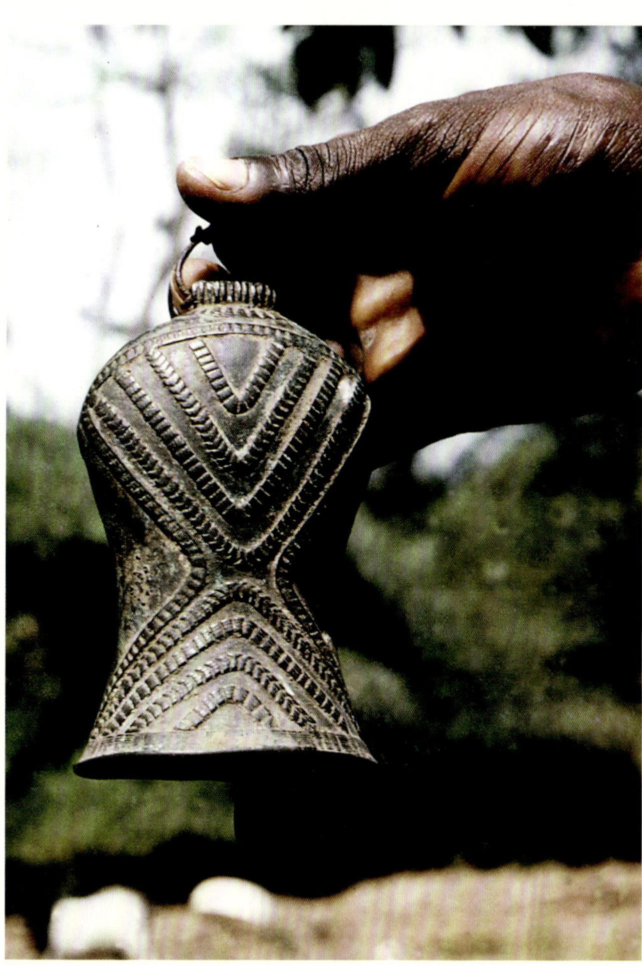

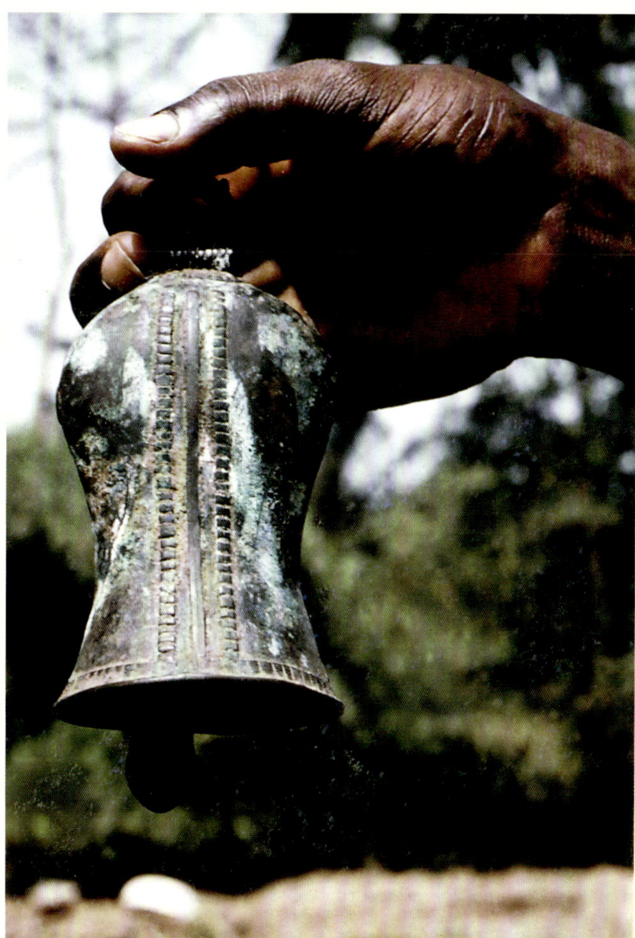

D.3a,b

This shrine bell (both sides of which are illustrated), is of the same shape as the Och'Akpa's bell (see figs. D.1, D.2) despite the fact that its surface design differs. Bells kept in Akweya shrines are closely protected, and I was allowed to photograph this example only because the shrine owner knew me well.

PHOTOGRAPH BY SIDNEY LITTLEFIELD KASFIR, OTOBI, 1978.

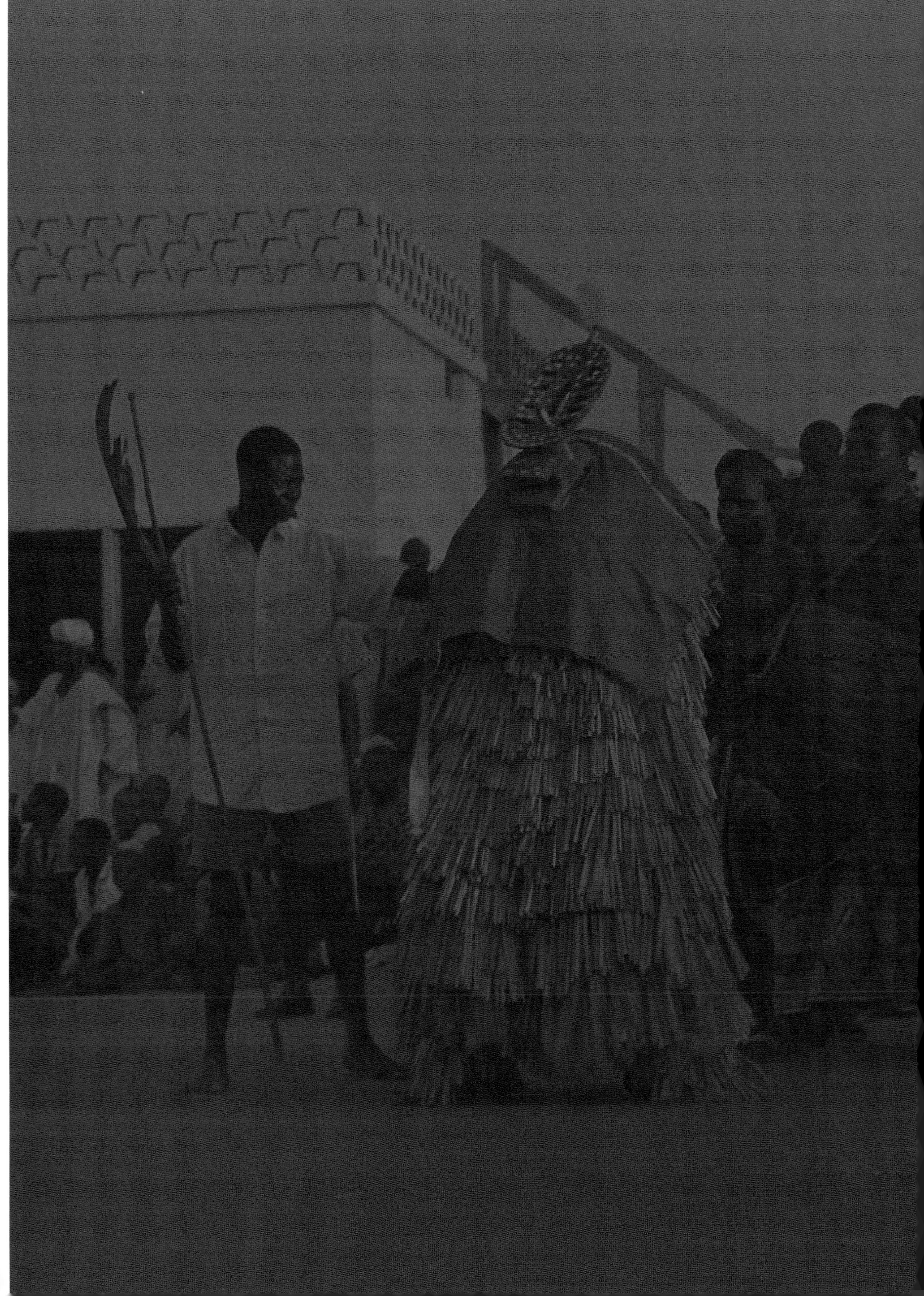

PART TWO
THE MIDDLE BENUE
VISUAL RESEMBLANCES, CONNECTED HISTORIES

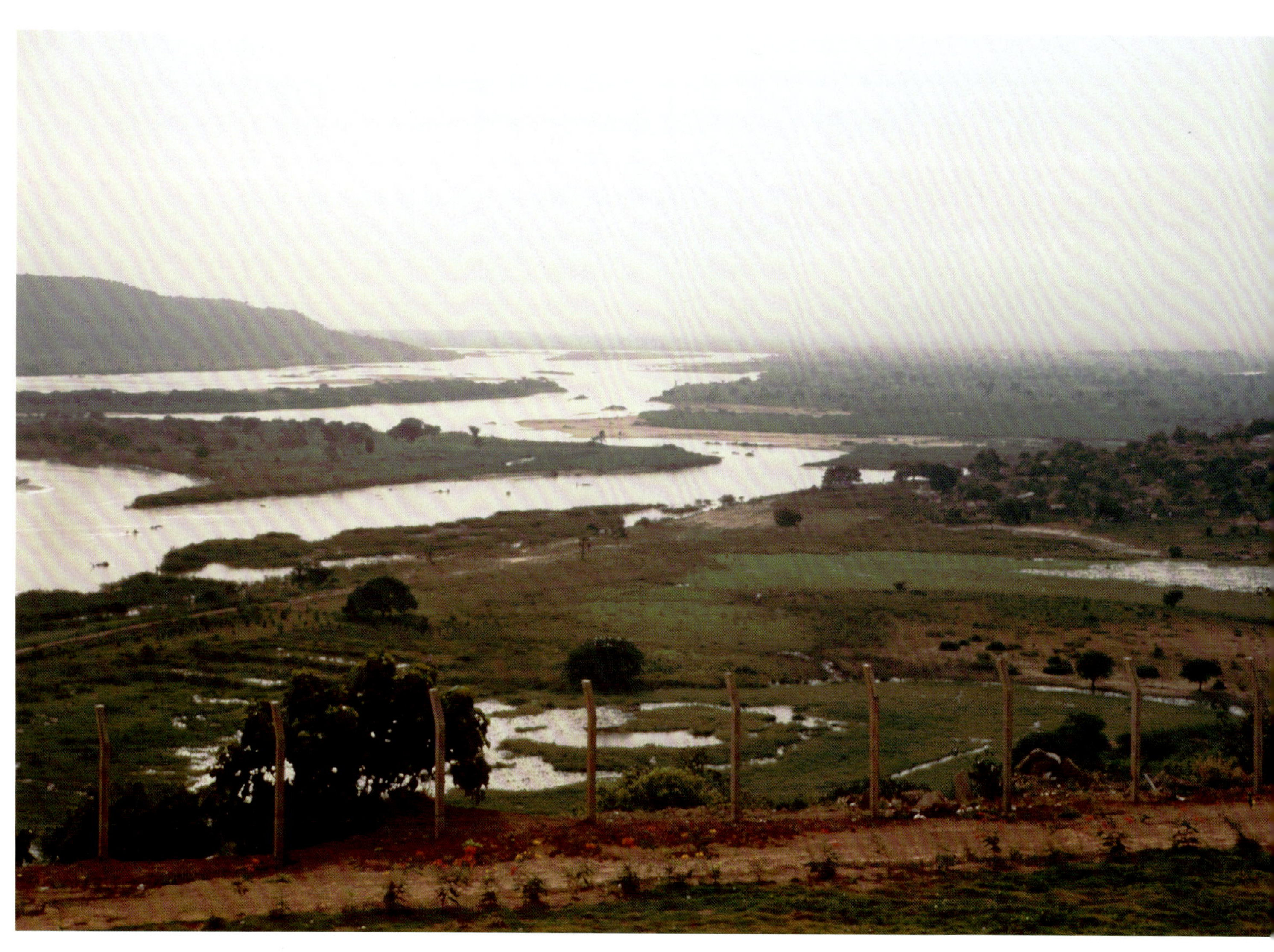

CHAPTER 7

Introduction:
The Middle Benue

RICHARD FARDON

Like other parts of the West African Middle Belt, looked at closely the Middle Benue has its own specific characteristics (fig. 7.2). The plains north and south of the middle reaches of the Benue River are remarkably flat. Extending, lightly wooded, as far as the eye can see, and for the most part lying 150 to 300 meters above sea level, they would have made good cavalry country (figs. 7.1, 7.3). Aside from its open skies, the countryside gains drama from the numerous larger and smaller tributaries of the Benue River and from the boulder-strewn mountain ranges and isolated hills that rear out of its general flatness (figs. 7.4, 7.5). The Jos Plateau and Muri Mountains north of the Benue, as well as the Shebshi and Alantika Mountains to its south, have always been inhabited by populations that found the plains dangerous, or the heights conducive, or both (fig. 7.6). Mounted warriors were able to exploit the flatlands better than they could mount escarpments, but the highlands had attractions other than defense: they offered specialized animal and plant environments, as well as coolness, spring water, and relative freedom from mosquitoes and similar annoyances.

In the eighteenth century, the Middle Benue lay at the southern margin of the ancient Empire of Bornu, and east of the numerous Hausa city-states, both of which were in principle Muslim. The political scale of Middle Benue societies varied between relatively uncentralized settlements and kingdoms with populations of a few thousand. A variety of ritual relations and alliances recognized among localities and between clans gave life a regional rather than wholly local texture, and these ties left their traces in shared genres of artwork and styles of artistic expression. As the eighteenth century drew on, slave raiding must have intensified as the epicenter of the European transatlantic trade moved eastward along the West African coast. Droughts apparently occurred during the same period, and duress turned to calamity when the Fulani declared jihad under their leader Usman dan Fodio at the onset of the nineteenth century. After the Hausa states were overrun, the eastern end of the Middle Benue fell prey to the two rather peripheral emirates of Muri and Adamawa. The latter especially, most of it in territorial terms now in Cameroon—though its capital at Yola is in Nigeria—remained a cluster of squabbling Fulani aspirant princes each based in his own fortified, and periodically shifting, settlement. Warfare was hardly constrained by the niceties of jihad, rather it was a scramble for wealth and slaves in which non-Fulani were enlisted to fight one another, and Fulani princes sought to expand away from their neighbors and colonize fresh resources of people and wealth. The processes set in train by the jihads during the nineteenth century were controlled but not reversed by Indirect Rule after colonization, leaving a pervasive legacy of

7.1
The Benue River at Numan as it appeared at the end of rainy season.
PHOTOGRAPH BY JOERG ADELBERGER, 1990.

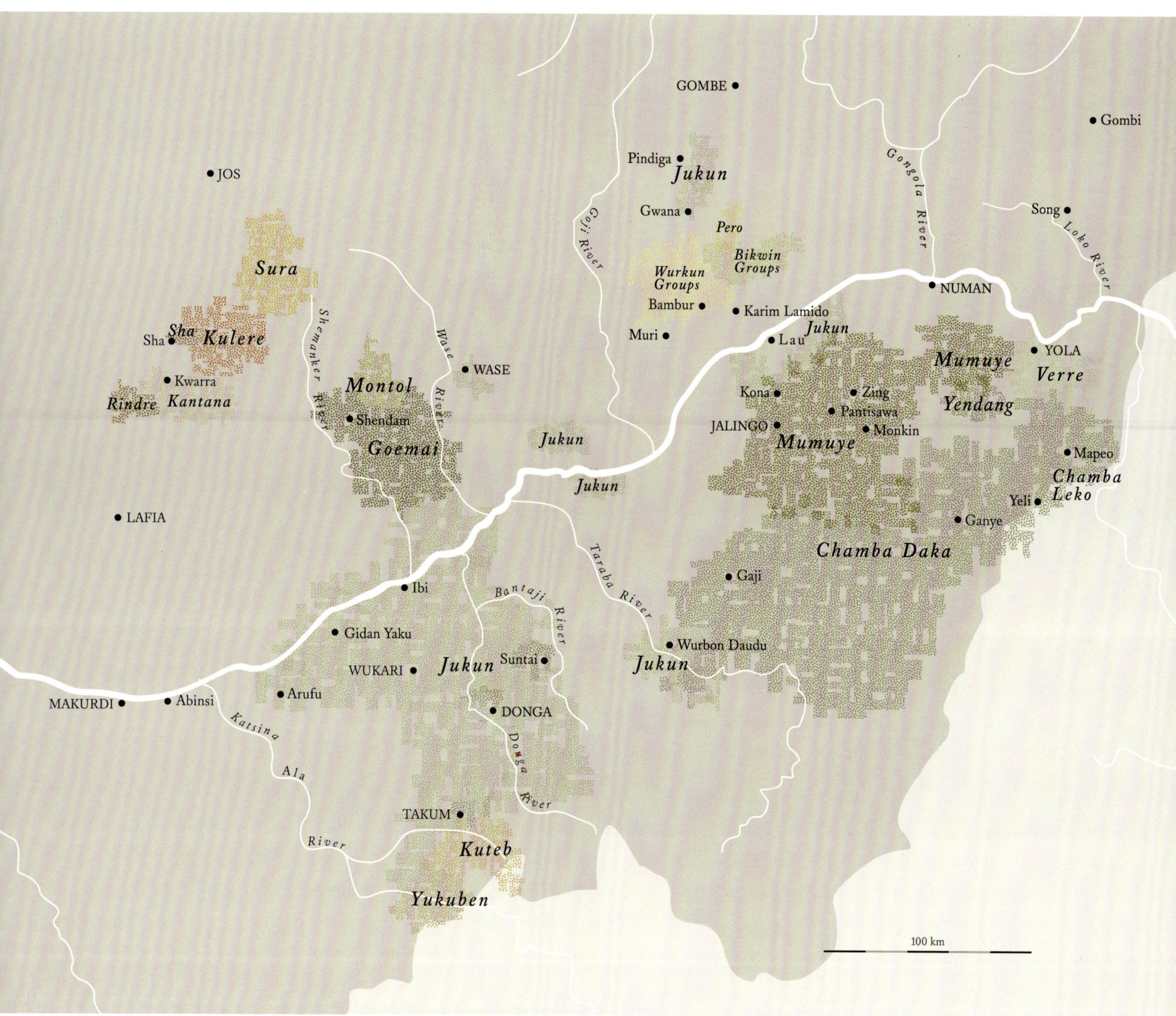

7.2
Map showing the peoples of the Middle
Benue region discussed in part 2.
© 2011 FOWLER MUSEUM AT UCLA.

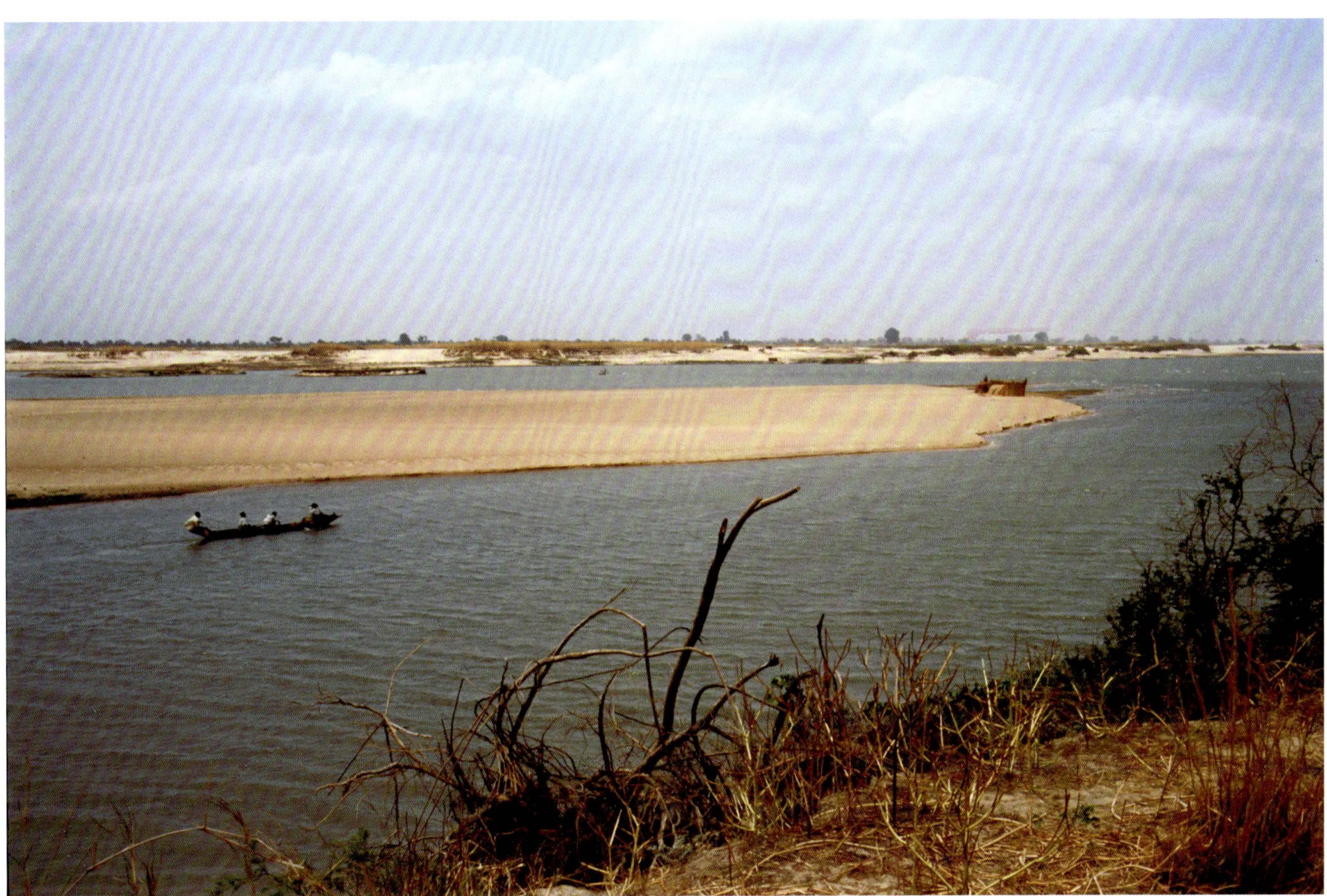

7.3
Fisherman ply their trade on the Benue River at Jen.

Hausa-Fulani domination, or accusations of such. In presenting the arts of the non-Hausa-Fulani Middle Benue, we are forced to do so in terms of a series of subaltern identities, and as we shall see, there are necessary uncertainties in deciding quite what the precursors of these identities might have been in earlier periods.

Like the Lower Benue around the Niger-Benue confluence, described by Sidney Kasfir, John Picton, and John Boston (see chapters 2, 4, 5, respectively, this volume), the Middle Benue was a mosaic of contextually relevant identities. A broad and simplifying account is needed to give the reader unfamiliar with the area some grasp of it. This account, however, serves also to highlight the problems over which simplification has to skate.

The geographical distinction we are making in this exhibition between the peoples of the Lower Benue—located around the Niger-Benue confluence and including, for example, Igala, Idoma, and Ebira—and those of the Middle Benue is not entirely arbitrary in cultural terms. Two centuries earlier, the cultural transition from Lower to Middle Benue would have been smoother than it had become by the beginning of the twentieth century. From west to east, the Igala, Idoma, and Jukun would have been neighbors, and there must have been more significant populations of peoples who were to become small enclaves, like the Etulo. Even before the main impact of the jihad had been felt, however, movements of people from the eastern side of the Middle Benue, and in all likelihood wider adoption of the identities they brought with them, had produced a more marked transition between Lower and Middle Benue.

The most extensive of these movements was under way during the eighteenth century and had begun earlier. Members of lineages claiming common descent in the male line from a founder they called Tiv entered the plains south of the Benue River from the southeast. Culturally and, as speakers of a Southern Bantoid language, also linguistically, they shared more with people living in the uplands along the current Cameroon-Nigeria border than they did with the then inhabitants of the plains. They

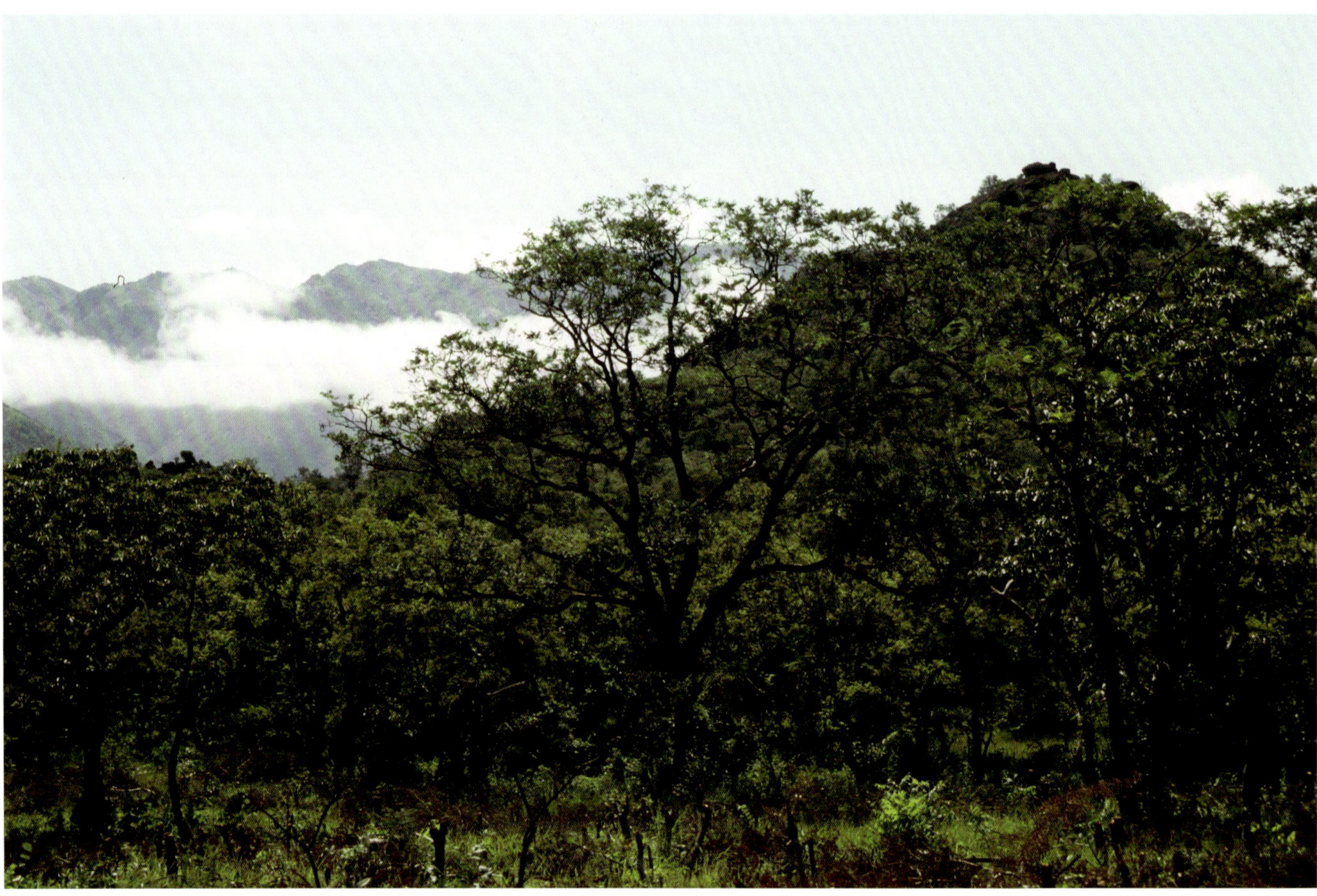

7.4
The clouds can hang low over the Alantika
Mountains during the wet season.
PHOTOGRAPH BY RICHARD FARDON, 1987.

expanded at an extraordinary rate, pushing northwestward and not only occupied the
plains south of the Benue but crossed the river to continue their expansion on its north
bank. As might be anticipated, this land-hungry expansion brought the descendants
of Tiv into competition with their neighbors, inaugurating conflicts that continue to
the present. How might so dramatic a population shift be explained? While we do not
have direct evidence, it seems likely that, prior to the intensification of slaving from the
north attendant on the early nineteenth-century jihads, societies south of the Benue
River would have been weakened by the expansion of the Atlantic slave trade that was
being sourced from what is now coastal Nigeria and Cameroon. Tiv traditions claim the
areas into which they expanded were not heavily populated; if this was so, it is unlikely
always to have been the case. The Tiv practiced yam cultivation and expanded among
people who were predominantly cereal cultivators. The technique of yam cultivation
by mounding topsoil requires frequent displacements to new land, and the Tiv lineage
system is described as facilitating the mobilization of large groups of patrilineally
related men against their most distant neighbors (Bohannan 1954; Bohannan and
Bohannan 1968; Sahlins 1961). Simultaneously, the form of marriage by exchange practiced amongst Tiv put a premium on importing women from their neighbors, either by
payment of brideprice or else as slaves traveling along the trade routes that crossed the
area into which they moved (Akiga 1939; discussed in Fardon 1984). The overall effect
was a snowballing migration as Tiv displaced, absorbed, or intermarried with Benue
plains people, both recruiting population and growing rapidly through reproduction
(perhaps thanks to their marriage strategies and any nutritional advantages bestowed
by yams). While these factors are individually speculative, the fact that Tiv achieved
domination of large swaths of the southern Benue plains suggests that several factors
acted in their favor and that these factors reinforced one another.

Tiv collided with another intrusive westward movement that had first been set in
motion some distance to their north. Speakers of Chamba Leko, an Adamawa-Ubangi

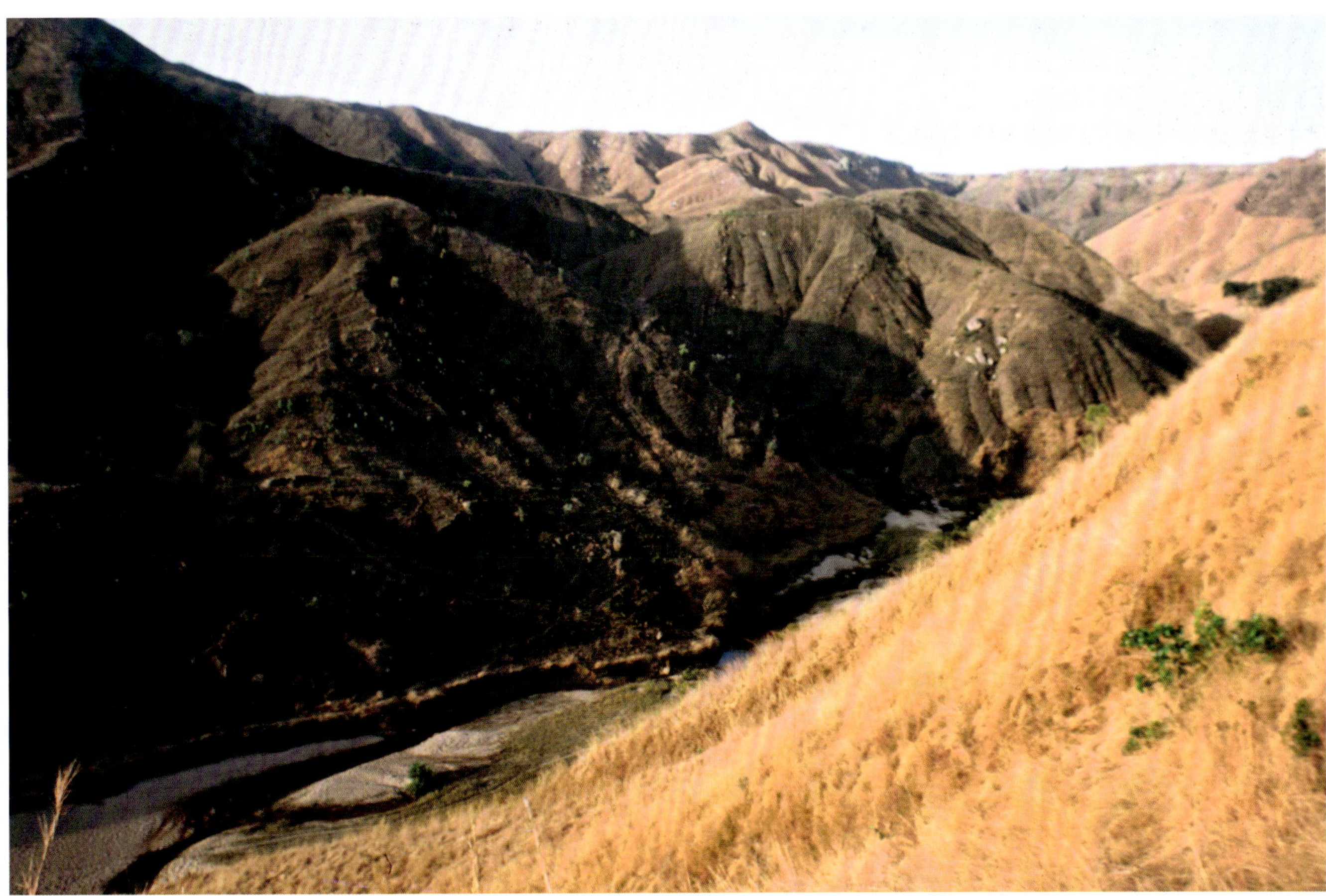

7.5
The dry season during the 1977–1978 year was particularly harsh, as can be seen from this view of the interior of the Shebshi Mountains.
PHOTOGRAPH BY RICHARD FARDON, 1977.

language, had been displaced from chiefdoms east of the Alantika Mountains by the early Fulani jihad in Adamawa. Some had sought refuge in the Alantika and Shebshi Mountains, while others set off southwestward at the head of numerous raiding parties, several of which crossed through the gaps between the mountain ranges to, almost literally, erupt into the plains beneath the Benue River. Unlike the Tiv, Chamba did not initially assimilate the peoples they picked up en route but instead incorporated them as clans that were recalled to have ethnically distinctive origins. As had been the case with the Tiv, speakers of Jukunoid languages felt the brunt of the Chamba pressure, but there were also areas, particularly in the valley of the Taraba River, where the two newcomers, Tiv and Chamba, clashed with one another.

Together the Tiv and Chamba brought cultures and language from the eastern Middle Benue westward, and in so doing, they displaced and submerged what would probably have been striking cultural continuities between peoples previously living there. The Jukun were particularly disrupted, and this was to provoke a good deal of speculation about their earlier organization.

The Fulani subsequently redrew the political map of the Middle Benue even more drastically than had the Tiv and Chamba Leko. Several Fulani chiefdoms affiliated with the emirates of Muri, Bauchi, and Adamawa were implanted, and wherever they settled, Fulani radically changed the conditions of life for the previous inhabitants. Extensive nucleated Fulani towns incorporated large numbers of subordinated local people and might also control surrounding villages that were effectively enslaved. Hence, many non-Fulani took themselves wherever the reach of the Fulani did not extend or could be resisted. Mountainous refuges became heavily populated, as did other less-penetrable spots. Inaccessibility to cavalry might be allied to violent resistance where that was possible and to the occasional payment of tithes, effectively protection money, when that seemed judicious. The lasting legacy of Fulani oppression has been rancor between them and others in the Middle Benue.

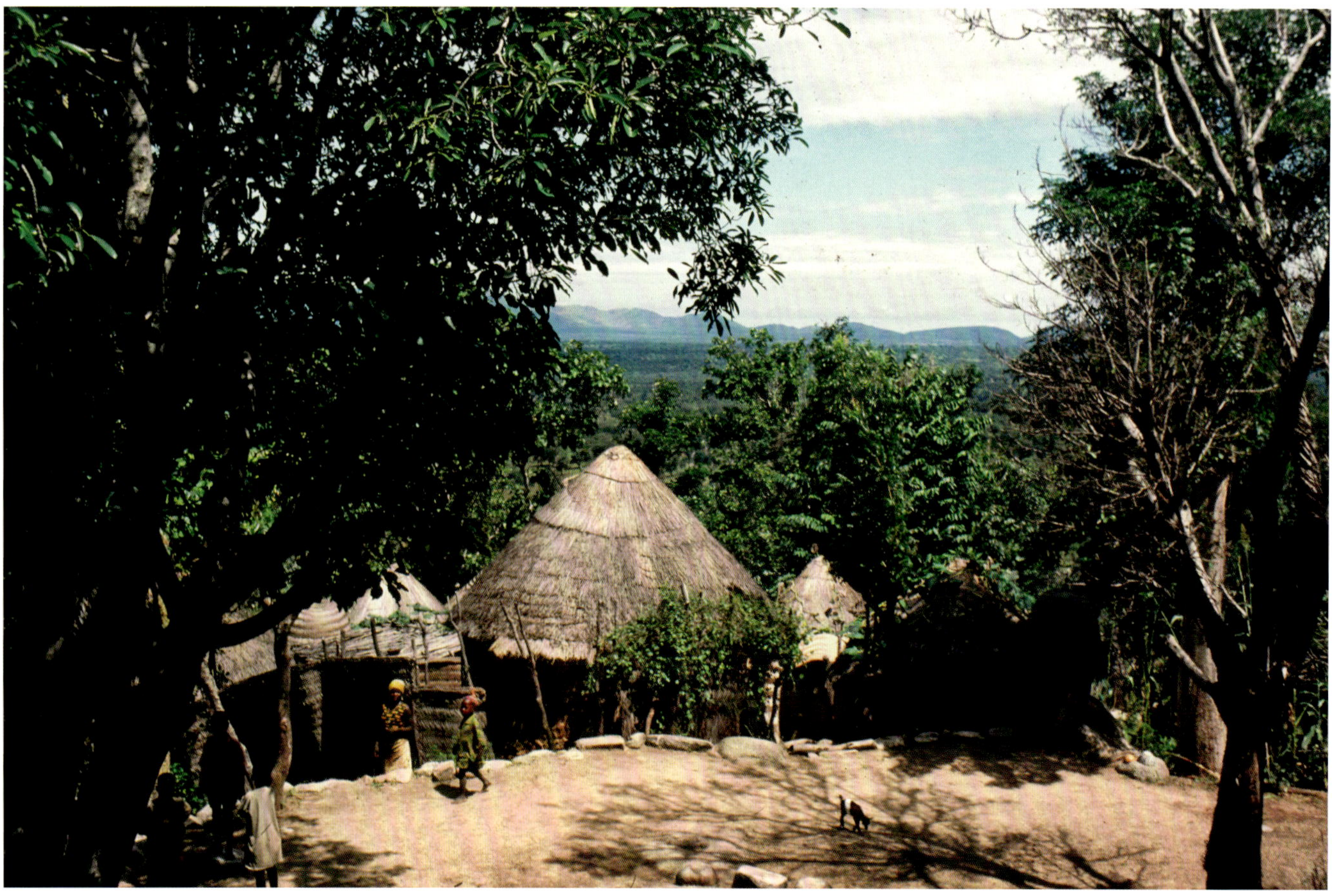

7.6

In 1976 not all of the hamlets of Mapeo had left the Alantika Mountains to move alongside the road, as evidenced by this hill village. PHOTOGRAPH BY RICHARD FARDON.

By the time that colonization added to the disruption of the Middle Benue, the area had undergone a tumultuous two centuries (fig. 7.7). This makes it difficult to re-create adequate cultural, social, and historical contexts for the often enigmatic artworks that have entered collections from hereabouts. Without knowing what people thought about these striking objects, as well as how and when they used them, the material culture created by Middle Belt peoples can be, and has been, subjected to all kinds of fanciful interpretations. Precisely because records of provenance and use are thin, uncertainties will remain in our understanding of the things that have been collected, but careful use of collection records and ethnographic descriptions where these exist get us a long way before resorting to outright conjecture. Many of these objects have now spent longer outside Nigeria than they ever did within it, and this circulation also belongs to their biographies as artefacts.

ARTEFACTUAL ETHNICITY: CULTWORLDS TO ARTWORLDS— THE PUBLIC LIVES OF PRIVATE OBJECTS

The comparative survey chapters, case studies, and interleaves that make up this part of the present volume predominantly describe statuary and masks in wood collected from peoples in the Middle Benue. Collecting circuits have isolated these things from their contexts and turned them into art objects. Other materials were, however, just as or even more essential than wood to ritual contexts. These included not only pottery and iron, though they were pervasive, but also the fibers needed to make the costumes that allow wooden mask heads to perform as masquerades and the leaves and other plant matter, as well as the stones, beer, water, and other liquids used in rituals, some of which took place to the accompaniment of wind and percussion instruments made from calabashes, animal horns, and skins. In suggesting how Middle Benue peoples used the artefacts they had created or bought during their ceremonies and rituals, I draw heavily on the ethnographic researches I have carried out among predominantly

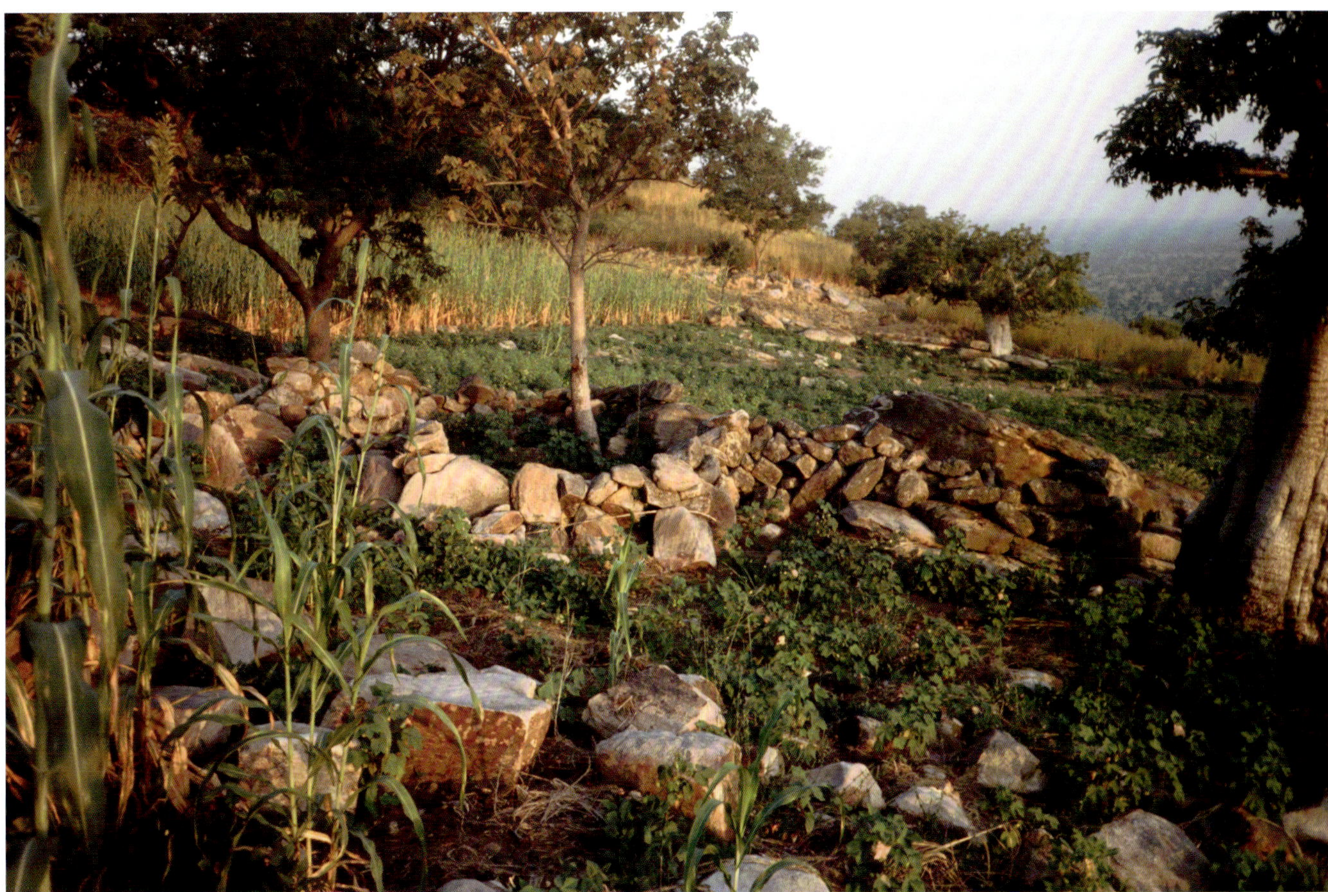

7.7
These are remnants of a Kulung hamlet in the Bambur area. With the advent of British colonialism, many hill settlements were abandoned, and their inhabitants moved to the foothills.
PHOTOGRAPH BY JOERG ADELBERGER, 1990.

Chamba-speaking peoples intermittently for over thirty years, especially those I undertook during the earlier years when historic Chamba religion still provided the thought style of many older men and women (see particularly Fardon 1988; 1991; 2007; Fardon and Stelzig 2005). This research demonstrated to me that earlier writers on Chamba material culture, including some who had visited Chambaland, often got their interpretations badly wrong. This was not only a matter of the translational problems that would arise wherever inquirers tried to resolve questions of belief and ritual action through interpreters, exacerbated by the distance between the concepts in play in African and European languages. Chamba religion posed the particular challenge of being almost entirely set within initiatory frameworks. Knowledge was acquired in the course of successive initiations, and it was acquired by witnessing as much as it was by instruction. Neither in principle nor in practice were Chamba religious thought and action susceptible to the question-and-answer routines that might illuminate aspects of the catechisms and canonical beliefs of some world religions.

Chamba were not unusual in this respect. The peoples of the Middle Benue shared many of their religious ideas and practices, so we could say that they made up a cultural and confessional ecumene (Kopytoff 1987, 10), where similar supernatural powers held sway and were approached in similar ways. Everywhere religious practices were learned through initiatory processes, so it is sensible to extend to early writers on other Middle Benue peoples the same caution I came to feel toward their counterparts writing on Chamba. Many of their questions were likely to have been inappropriate either because they assumed the religious knowledge they sought would consist of propositions that could be elicited from informants, or else because they did not understand that knowledge of some elements of religious thought was secretive and answers could be designed to mislead rather than inform the interlocutor. Because neighboring Middle Benue peoples shared many traits of culture and social organization (though not always the same ones), Chamba culture potentially offers us clues that are as helpful to understanding artworks collected from their neighbors as are inappropriate and superficial inquiries made amongst them.

We can go further in questioning the coincidence between the "tribal" terms that have become familiar labels for artworks from the region and the significance these objects had in their original contexts. Most ethnic identities in the Middle Benue did not crystallize in their current form until the twentieth century, so we should not feel disinclined on the grounds of supposed ethnic differences to extrapolate understanding of one group in terms derived from another. Rather than a series of distinct cultures, we face instead interlaced skeins of ritual institutions that involved particular bodily dramatizations and material props. Hence a particular cult might enjoy a performative culture that extended across several contemporary ethnic groups. As John Picton notes for the Lower Benue, cultural traits and ethnic attributions frequently fail to coincide.

Even taken in their entirety, the artworks now in museums and private collections cannot be assumed representative of the region as a whole. The intensity of collecting varied both over time and between places. German and British colonial ethnographic collecting, particularly during its earlier years, was largely confined to "subject" peoples on the grounds that the Fulani had little to tickle the ethnologically attuned curiosities either of travelers and curators—associated in one way or another with museums—or of touring colonial officers. By and large collection was undertaken by men (meant, with a notable exception, exclusively of women) on the move, and the records they left us have to be read in the knowledge that their grasp of the lifeworlds of the communities through which they passed was at best superficial. Such is the paucity of early documentation of material culture that the investigator has to attempt to profit from understanding whatever records survive for these early collected pieces.

Until the First World War, the eastern end of the Middle Benue, located in present-day Nigeria, fell within the German colony of Kamerun. Compared to their British counterparts, German colonial officers were relatively active in seeking out pieces for German metropolitan museums in such cities as Berlin, Dresden, Leipzig, and Stuttgart. The most extensive collecting expedition in the Middle Benue, which also traversed Nigeria in 1911–1912, took place under the direction of the German ethnologist Leo Frobenius, and its haul was later divided among German museums. Frobenius elicited copious documentation from his informants, often with startling insights into matters that were supposed to be secret (for this region, see Frobenius 1913; 1924; [1925] 1987). The British record of collecting was more haphazard, but significant acquisitions reached the British Museum, Liverpool Museum (now the World Museum Liverpool), and the Pitt Rivers Museum in Oxford. French collection during their Cameroonian mandate and trusteeship in this area was relatively insignificant, although holdings in French museums have grown since the end of the colonial era (see Joubert, this volume, pp. 561–67).

Both the acquisition and the accession of artworks, as well as everyday objects, took place in terms of the ethnic (what would then have been called "tribal") identities that were sedimenting and solidifying alongside the weakening of a more flexible regional interlacing of local institutions that had existed earlier. Often this occurred through the intermediation of Hausa and Fulani colonial auxiliaries (translators, guides, local administrators, and so forth), who applied their own terms of classification to the peoples they had sought to subject in precolonial times, and among whom they now assisted in constructing the governmental mechanisms of the colonial state. The labels applied to the people were also attached to the items of material culture collected from them in what were parallel aspects of a process of ethnicization: as they were sorted and subjected to control, so peoples and their things were subjected to similar classification. On occasions we find these "tribal" labels supplemented by indication of the area of collection or sometimes even the precise villages from which pieces were taken. This reveals that the style of stock items (e.g., statues, masks, spears) in the material repertoire of the larger region varied from place to place, but it did not do so simply on ethnic lines. Stylistic variations might be more numerous than a simple listing of ethnic groups suggests: smiths, carvers, and potters speaking the same language might nonetheless produce recognizably different objects in different places. Conversely, specialists in one place might make items that were exported to wherever else they were in demand. No contemporary account of material culture would now argue that there were "tribal styles" in all West African art. But accepting this is not to deny that some style features clustered geographically in ways that corresponded (albeit not neatly or one-to-one) with ethnic distinctions. Moreover, the ethnonyms, or "tribal names," people themselves adopted added an element of self-consciousness to identities that might come to be reflected in their own expectations of what "their" artwork should look like. A photograph taken by Arnold Rubin neatly exemplifies the horns of this dilemma: it shows a Jukun Aku-Ma mask one horn of which has been emblazoned with "Wukari," the contemporary Jukun capital, and the other with "Kororofa" (Kwararafa), the historically contentious "empire" of the Middle Benue to which the Jukun claim to be heirs (fig. 7.8). The relationship between material culture and ethnicity is not simple, but neither is it null—a nonrelationship. On those occasions when the record of acquisition and contextualization is thin, an ethnic designation may be the only way we have to map an object at all.

If the collection record of the colonial period requires careful appraisal, at least there is a record to appraise. The documentation of artworks exported in the postcolonial period is thin or, more commonly, nonexistent. Very large quantities of materials were exported around the years of the Biafran Civil War in Nigeria (1967–1970), emerging onto the international art market in the early 1970s. Often collected in villages or small administrative towns by African "runners," who sold directly or indirectly to a few European dealers, objects were identified by the ethnic names applied to them by these field collectors. Corroboration was sought by dealers in the far from extensive documentation of colonial collections, and it was supported by a good deal of guesswork on the basis of perceived stylistic similarities. Styles attributed to specific ethnic groups emerged from this process to serve, among other things, as retail labels for marketable objects. These styles might or might not be immediately recognizable to the people who shared their ethnic name with these artworks, as the following anecdote illustrates.

In 2006, I took with me copies of a book on Chamba figure sculptures that I had co-authored with Christine Stelzig (2005) to show to friends in Ganye, a town at the eastern end of the Middle Belt. Ganye, a Hausa name, is the capital of what was for a time during the colonial period called the Chamba Native Authority. Now, as a result of a struggle over ethnic ownership of the area, to the displeasure of most Chamba it is more neutrally called Ganye Chieftaincy. Those I gave or showed copies of the book included middle-aged men, all of whom told me that they were seeing this "Chamba" art for the first time in their lives. From the evidence of museum and private collections, I knew the statues illustrated were "Chamba," but my Chamba friends had no sense of how to distinguish a Chamba piece from any other. A palace museum was being mooted, but the one statue collected for it that I was shown bore, to my mind, no resemblance to anything that might historically have been used by Chamba. In short the artefacts that the artworld considered "Chamba" were not recognizable to the people who recognized themselves as "Chamba."

There was no particular mystery to this: my friends in Ganye had for the most part not been initiated to historic Chamba religion, and even if they had, most statuary would have left their country before they reached the age to witness cults. The actual objects illustrated in the book I co-wrote with Christine Stelzig, or others similar to them, would have been familiar to the practitioners of Chamba historic religion whom I had known in the mid-1970s, but that generation had since died out and were unbookish in any case. As a young man, I had seen only a few examples of Chamba statues in

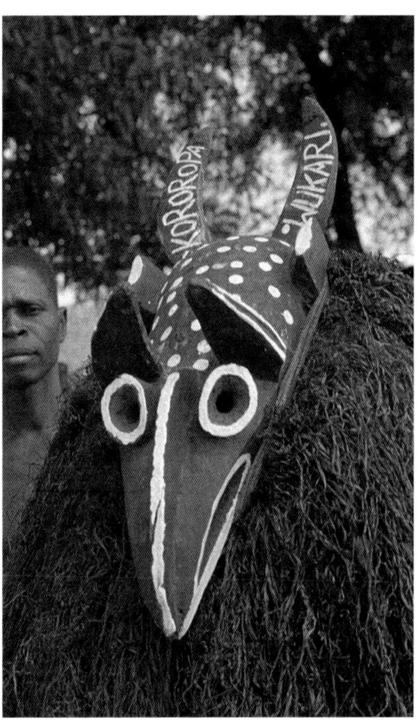

7.8
One of the horns of this Aku-Ma mask is labeled "Wukari" and the other "Kororofa." Thus the connection is made between the contemporary Jukun capital of Wukari and Kororofa, believed by some to be the ancient empire from which the Jukun descend.
PHOTOGRAPH BY ARNOLD RUBIN, WUKARI, JANUARY 14, 1965, RUBIN ARCHIVE, FOWLER MUSEUM AT UCLA, NEG. NO. 23.

situ, having first arrived a half-dozen years after the objects were exported (as best as I can reconstruct the circumstances) by runners operating across an effectively open border with Cameroon between 1967 and 1970. Few of the statues that were sold (not always by their owners it was alleged) were replaced; the religious practices they served were in decline as the rising generation turned their backs on the cults.

Had my book on Chamba masks been published earlier that year, I could have taken that with me when I next returned in 2007, and I know the reaction would have been quite different. The masquerade is markedly and distinctively Chamba, and it has functioned in public spaces at least since the traditional art jamborees of 1970s Nigeria (including FESTAC, the Second World Black and African Festival of Arts and Culture). Unlike the wooden figures, the masquerade performed a public function, and it had been to a degree unlinked from its specific functions in historic Chamba religion. Like Chamba statuary, Chamba masks were exported in large numbers from the late 1960s onward. They can be differentiated stylistically (and I have spent what seems even to me an undue amount of my time doing so on the basis of examples in museum collections that were collected early on). The international art market, however, does not (yet) distinguish subtypes of Chamba masks, as reflected in either price or presentation, other than by perceived quality of carving and perhaps condition. Chamba masquerades continue to perform, and there must be twenty-first-century carvers able to make wooden mask heads. (I had no difficulty commissioning a mask for a planned museum in Garoua, northern Cameroon, in the mid-1980s.) There even seems to have been a degree of innovation in the genre, since the trio of male, female, and infant masquerades featuring on souvenirs from a recent paramount chiefly installation was new to me and without any long-standing precedent (fig. 7.9). Masks have become increasingly ethnic possessions in Chamba eyes, and their presence at a ceremonial event virtually mandatory (compare Bovin's comments on the presentation of Mumuye culture in this volume, p. 375).

So it might appear that there is a continuity to Chamba masquerade that Chamba figure carving lacks. Even that would be too simple a conclusion to draw: neither masks nor figures were historically carved to be "Chamba," rather they were acquired

7.9

This "nuclear family" of Chamba masquer-aders—consisting of a female and infant (both without horns) and a male—is an innovation. They are pictured here at the elevation of the Gangwari of Ganye to a first-class paramountcy.

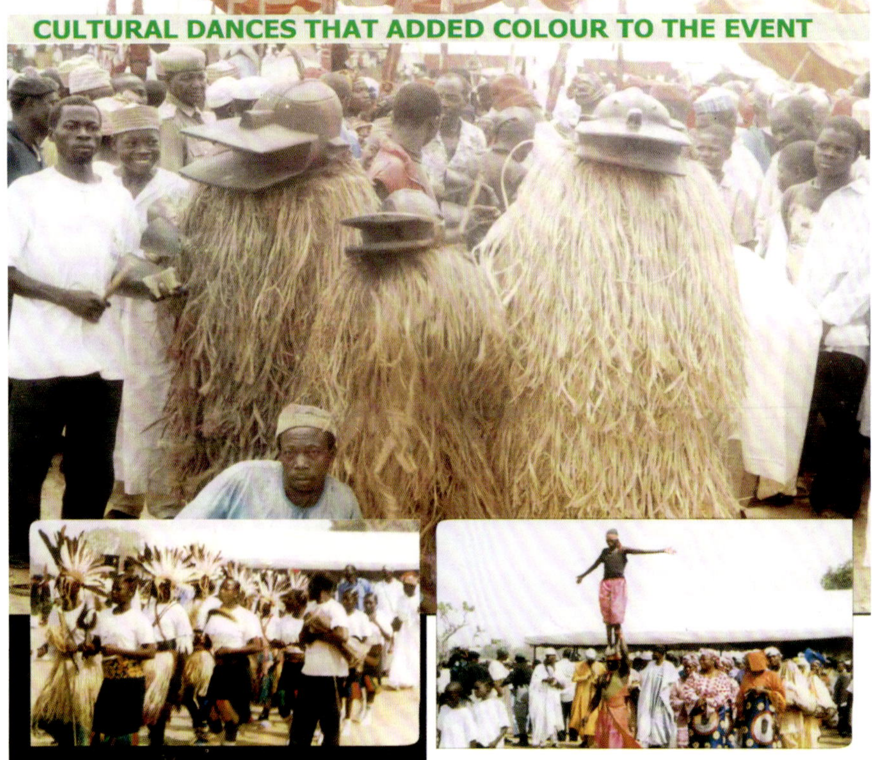

by particular users (chiefs, clans, or cults) to be used in particular and often named performances. Counterparts to our terms such as "masquerade" and "statue" typically do not exist in the languages of those who used these things, and the term for an object used in a particular context has been written into accession records and then repeated as if it referred to a formal category of things (as my discussion of Mumuye artworks later illustrates, pp. 247–50). The classificatory matrix (as much in Nigerian as in other collections) has wanted to identify an object as belonging to an exclusive class of things (mask, statue, pot, etc.), coming from a named people (Chamba, Jukun, Mumuye, etc.), and preferably, for the sake of "authenticity," identifiable by a name in a local language (despite local language being otherwise disregarded).

I refer to the making of these interlaced identifications among types of artwork, ethnic labels, and local names for things, as "artefactual ethnicity." The foregrounded sense of the phrase is meant to underline the oddness of things acquiring narrow and specific ethnicity (including the ability to be named in local languages). I am, however, also keen to retain a broader sense that ethnicity itself is an artefact, something fashioned according to aesthetic criteria of rightness and not something given in the nature of human sociality. The artefactual ethnicity of Chamba statues within the artworld depended on attributions by runners and dealers, on the literature of the art market, including auction catalogs, on acquisitions and accessions by museums and private collectors and the further circulation of their knowledge, and on subsequent literature, including the volume you are now reading. Artefactual ethnicity is not produced once and for all but is reproduced and circulated. Their ethnic identity has become an attribute of the agency of Chamba statues, an aspect of what they do as objects ensnared in unprecedented relations of connoisseurship and market value. In all this they resemble Chamba masks, but the masks have an additional agency so far missing from the statues, they can stand for Chamba ethnicity in the eyes of Chamba themselves. In order to produce a dynamic and historical understanding of Middle Benue objects (and of course others), we need to comprehend the artefactual ethnicity with which they have been imbued since their first creation.

I am not suggesting that the significance of artworks has been exhausted by what I am calling artefactual ethnicity. Within the Western artworld, Middle Benue carved works in wood have acquired attributes additional to their ethnicity that derive from expert aesthetic appreciation of them as African artworks, which can be made to contribute to broader art narratives, for instance that of Western modernism. But it is notable that this accretion of aesthetic value or plenitude cannot occur unless the object has already had conferred upon it the artefactual ethnicity that bestows authenticity, and the other values accrued supplement but do not displace the work's ethnicity (while this is not the place to make an extended argument, something similar occurs in relation to national identity where African modern artists' works are concerned). These qualities are so significant because they appear to suture the relationship between the economy of the artworld and that of the erstwhile African ritual economy. The agencies of objects are redefined in transition between these contexts: they lose capacities in transition (like the ability to divine the occult causes of suffering or the capacity to mediate sacrifices to ancestors or to the dead), but they also acquire agency (the general aura of the capacities they have lost, as well as defined ethnicity and transcendent properties derived from comparative aesthetics). While these frames can be seen contrastively, even polemically, in tracing the histories of objects it is more constructive to think of their involvement in the translation of values with particular attention to what their capacity to move between worlds tells us about them.

Even treated simply as material phenomena, the objects themselves do not stay the same as they transit between their place in African cults and in museum and artworld collections. Depending on their assessment of the market, runners and dealers have often removed the patina built up by handling, decoration, sacrificial offerings, and weathering. Conversely, on occasions, patina has been added deliberately to misrepresent objects in a variety of ways, including the disguise of extensive restoration. Chamba statues in Western collections have miraculously "regrown" missing arms and legs while passing through the hands of European dealers (one of whom confided that American clients in the 1970s were particularly averse to damaged goods). More straightforwardly, patination can also be used to age objects falsely or to disguise complete fakes. Even here, there is some interest in asking why some objects and not others are aged or faked, by whom, and for whom.

MIDDLE BENUE ARTWORKS IN THE CONTEXTS FOR WHICH THEY WERE DESTINED

Only a small minority of the carved objects collected from the Middle Benue during the early twentieth century is likely to predate the late nineteenth century. This is not to deny that there are some, even considerably, earlier pieces; but a century of disruption, allied to the way wooden objects were used and stored, suggests they are exceptional. Nonetheless, the geographic distribution of artistic forms is largely continuous, which implies that the overall terms of artistic endeavor, if not the spread of particular artefacts, were relatively stable and probably long-standing. This commensurability of artistic forms reflects the compatibility of institutions among neighboring peoples. Societies varied in their organizations of kinship and clanship, as well as in their degree of hierarchy, but they all regulated their environment through cult institutions (known under different generic and specific names). Who owned the cults, and how far they were under royal control, varied; the existence of cults did not.

Cults were transacted between peoples as commodities and in order to cement alliances. Particular cults were concerned with inflicting and curing a specialized range of maladies, most of them diseases, but also including drought, locusts, lightning strikes, and accidents. The group that owned the cult, usually kin-defined in some way, was able to initiate members upon their payment of dues, which allowed them to see stages of the cult. The cult also accrued wealth when it "caught" people who breached its rules and had to pay reparation in order to seek well-being. These rules commonly concerned misdemeanors sanctioned by the cult (theft, adultery, insult, witchcraft, violence, and so on), as well as violation of the cult's taboos by its own members. The happy combination of opportunities for wealth creation, occasions for (predominantly but not exclusively) male conviviality, access to a hierarchy of esoteric knowledge, and the fear and respect that cult membership inspired in the rest of the community (notably women and younger men) sufficiently explain the attractiveness of cults. Judging by the Chamba example (as well as the detailed ethnography that exists on peoples such as Tiv), adult men committed very substantial resources to competitively mastering the cults.

Each of these cults had its own intimate culture, including some or all of: a roster of occasions to meet, musical instruments and performance, ritual routines, masquerade, a story of origin, medicines, and an assemblage of powerful objects. This last concerns us most here, since it might include in addition to stones, shells, and other found objects, man-made artefacts in brass, iron, pottery, and wood. The assemblage of objects in cults was the focus of practices designed to harness powers that came from the wilderness or bush, and from the dead or ancestors, however these were locally conceived in more exact terms. Cults set up fields of powers amenable to a degree of human control, but this control was not complete, so practitioners potentially put themselves at risk from the very dangers they sought to master. In more centralized societies, some of the cults attracted to themselves the additional power and prestige of belonging to kings or priests; or, to put it the other way around, the power of certain cults made them attractive to control by the upper echelons of a hierarchy. Under these circumstances we find reports of cults extending their powers beyond their immediate localities to become regional in character. Frequently, traditions of origin are traced by clans, particularly the clans of chiefs and priests, from the centers of regional cults. The preeminence recalled for the Jukun before and during the jihadic wars of the nineteenth century probably had something of the character of a regional cult.

Almost all the artefacts surveyed here belonged in some way and degree to the cults. They were made throughout the nineteenth century because, unlike their owners, cults thrived during the Fulani jihad, which exacerbated the misfortunes people faced, and which the cults addressed. After the Second World War, when conversions to the world religions accelerated, the material culture of the cults gradually ceased to be replaced. Cults and their accoutrements became associated with paganism by both Christians and Muslims, and locally this might lead to relatively rapid abandonment. The process overall was slow and uneven, nonetheless, as was the progress of the world religions in this geographically central yet culturally and politically rather peripheral area of the modern state. A few items of material culture were able to be redefined as elements of ethnic culture (like the Chamba and Jukun masquerades discussed above), but for the most part, cults were passing entirely into history during the first postcolonial decade and nowadays seem to persist only in deep rural areas. They have not been subject to revival either on their own terms or by syncretism with elements of world religions. Cultural revival following decline does, however, often involve a three- to four-generation process, so it would be hasty to conclude that the cults will not be revived.

The decline in general adherence to cults meant that when a second intensive phase of collection in the Middle Benue occurred around the time of the Biafran War, a majority of the objects that left the region were probably not replaced, and in many areas, the skills to replace them with artworks of similar quality no longer existed. This generalization, like most, needs tempering in relation to particular places, and I do so below. It was only in a very few areas, however, that intensive collection of artefacts actually stimulated production for sale during the 1970s, as seems to be the case for Mumuye given the extraordinary numbers of seemingly new Mumuye statues appearing around this time.

One result of the outflow of Middle Benue objects in the early postcolonial period was an intensification of interest in the artworks of the region among European and American collectors from about the 1970s. Because a high proportion of works passed through the hands of a few well-connected French, Belgian, and Dutch dealers in the first instance, a broad provenance and collection history can be established for many of them. They were sold, some of them several times over, according to ethnic classification, often with inflated claims for their antiquity. Research into private collections, carried out by Arnold Rubin and Marla Berns in connection with the current project, has revealed the global collection of Middle Benue artworks to be more extensive than anyone, at least to my knowledge, had previously guessed. There have been some remarkable identifications in particular collections, including several pieces known from field photographs taken in the 1960s by Arnold Rubin, and in one case what appears to be the (or a) male forming a pair with a female figure collected by a British colonial officer in 1921. Inevitably, the collectors' curiosity, whetted by sales of the artworks exported by the early 1970s, provoked a demand that could not be satisfied by the quantity of objects transferred between the ritual economy and that of the artworld. Various kinds of faking have come to light: ranging from "improvement" of objects with good provenance to local copying for the market and outright attempts to mislead the market with objects likely to have been made elsewhere in Africa to meet demand for Middle Benue art.

The chapters following this introduction largely use the ethnic labeling of objects current in the artworld, with the reservations noted earlier, and commit a major anachronism by not being written consistently in the past tense, instead reserving this use of tense for those instances when historical questions are particularly placed in the foreground. Most attention is paid to the "currents of resemblance" apparent in three major types of object in wood: anthropomorphic figures, theranthropic (animal-human

8.2

Female (?) statue
Montol peoples, 1950
Wood, pigment, mastic
H: 38.1 cm
INDIANA UNIVERSITY ART MUSEUM, BLOOM-
INGTON, INDIANA; GIFT OF THE RAYMOND AND
LAURA WIELGUS COLLECTION IN MEMORY OF ROY
SIEBER, 2005.13
IMAGE: © 2010 INDIANA UNIVERSITY ART
MUSEUM. PHOTOGRAPH BY MICHAEL CAVANAGH
AND KEVIN MONTAGUE
PROVENANCE: ROY SIEBER, LALIN VILLAGE,
NIGERIA, 1958

This powerful, probably female, figure is
carved in the more slender of two styles
favored by the Montol of the southern escarpments of the Jos Plateau (for the more fully
embodied form, see figs. 8.61 and 8.62). It was
commissioned by a healer in Baltip village in
1950 and was collected in 1958 by Roy Sieber
from its then owner, Gunuze, who lived in
Lalin village, a nearby settlement (Sieber and
Walker 1987, 77, fig. 34). Sieber also photographed the piece in situ.

8.3

Double-figure columnar statue
Chamba peoples, before 1903
Wood, cordage
H: 45 cm
STAATLICHE MUSEEN ZU BERLIN, ETHNOLOGIS-
CHES MUSEUM, III C19023
IMAGE: © STAATLICHE MUSEEN ZU BERLIN,
PREUSSISCHER KULTURBESITZ, ETHNOLO-
GISCHES MUSEUM. PHOTOGRAPH BY MARTIN
FRANKEN, 2010
PROVENANCE: COLLECTED BY HANS GLAUNING,
TIM DƏSI, 1903

Five double-figure columnar Chamba statues
were collected by the German colonial officer
Hans Glauning (as is the case with this example) or by Leo Frobenius between 1903 and
1911. Remarkably, no similar statues emerged
in the following century. This particularly
slender example was collected from a village
called Tim Dəsi, near Dalami, in the plain
between the Alantika and Shebshi mountains.
It was designed to be fixed into an iron shoe
but apparently never completed (since it lacks
the hole through which the buckle of the iron
shoe would have passed to lock it in place). To
judge by the preponderant, but not invariant,
convention: the figure on the proper right
(the viewer's left) with a sagittal crest is male,
while the one on the proper left, with a tall,
flat-topped coiffure is female. The complete
absence of anatomical detail, however, makes
definite identification impossible.

Readers may be familiar with the experience of standing before display cases
of African statues, looking at the wooden figures individually, from various angles,
comparing them, in the silence (or mood-setting acoustic envelope) typical of galleries, and reading the labels thoughtfully supplied by curators to explain the significance of unfamiliar objects. The ambience encourages self-possession, concentration
in tranquility, freedom to gaze or move on, perhaps a quiet word exchanged with a
companion. None of this would apply in the contexts where young male initiates saw
figure sculptures for the first time. They would in all likelihood be afraid, scared by
threats, and hazed by beatings from older men; their eyes might be covered or averted
throughout much of the ceremony in which the statues took part. The statues themselves would be placed among an initially bewildering variety of apparatus that might
include: leaves and other plant products, pots of unusual construction, colored stones,
terra-cotta animal figurines, iron rattles, staffs, animal skulls, musical instruments, in
short all manner of things. The event would likely be hot and noisy and occur outside,
or on the margins of the village. The statues would be a focal point for sacrifice and
invocations, not all (or even much) of which would make immediate sense. Exegesis
by the older men would be minimal, but the absolute injunction not to speak of what
they had seen would be impressed repeatedly upon the initiates. Beyond that, they
may have been left to their own devices to make what sense they could of the small
parts of initiatory knowledge shown to them, and to await a time when a little more
might be revealed. Initiation, in short, was not an inquisitive and explanatory exercise
in the way gallery display usually is.

This was the world of Chamba historic religion in the village of Mapeo into which
I became absorbed on undertaking my first field research in the mid-1970s. I heard
about anthropomorphic figures in both wood and metal, which informants told me
wonderfully resembled live people. Yet when I saw these figures for myself (more
often in European and American collections and publications than I had in the field),
I was struck by how "abstract" they seemed: sketches of human features that left the
viewer's glance to provide completion, as awestruck initiates might. The men with
whom I spent my time were in the main around thirty years my senior, born by the
early to mid-1920s, though the oldest among them remembered German colonialism
before the First World War. The younger members belonged to the cohort that had
been split by the impact of the Catholic mission in the 1940s and the simultaneously
deepening reach of conversion to Islam. Other members of their generation had been
to school, perhaps become catechists, or even gone on to further education, to be
teachers; or they had opted for conversion to Islam, achieving greater or lesser competence in Koranic study, and perhaps becoming local tax collectors.

The senior cult followers (*jub-tu-bu*) held on to a vision of life that was evidently,
even to them, being superseded by the world religions, and they lived with relatively
few images. I don't recall them having photographs, although these were not uncom-
mon in other circles, and they were not literate. They were not, I suspect, particularly
familiar with their own images. Rather than shaving themselves in a mirror, they were
shaved by the barber (their faces, apart from the goatee signifying elderhood, being
shaved when it was time for their heads to be shaved too). They were the last members
of a generation for whom sculptures were the only familiar human-like images. Even
the diminishing numbers of younger men they managed to press into joining the cults
lived in a different world of images. Similar transitions from African historic to world
religions were underway throughout the Middle Benue. In generational terms some
were ahead of the Chamba, while others changed more slowly, but the process was
essentially similar and has continued during the more than three decades I have now
visited the region. The relative ease with which statuary (but not masks) was stripped
from cult settings and not replaced is explicable only in terms of this broad process
and its wider economic and political setting. What of the figures themselves?

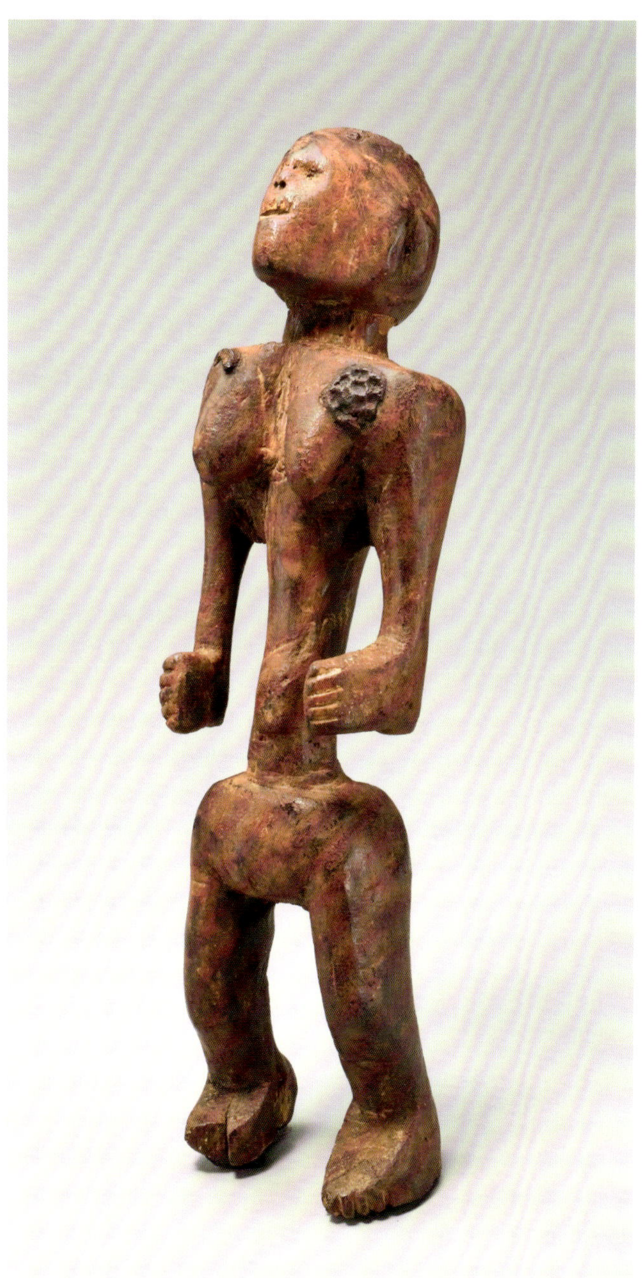

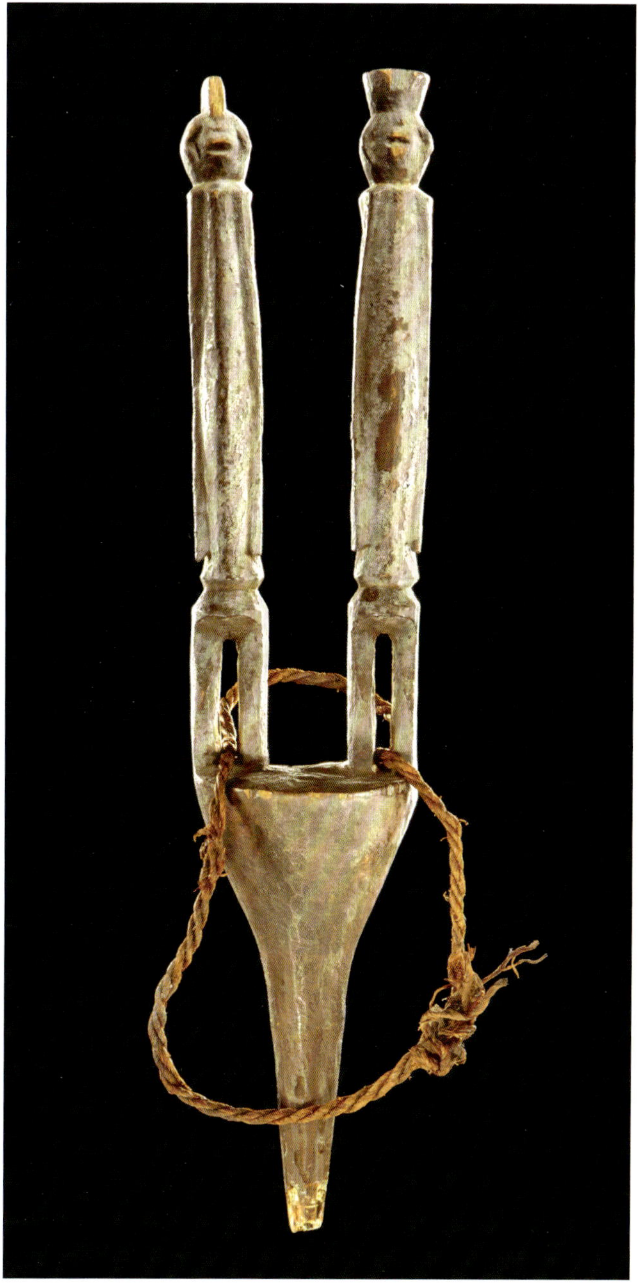

ANTHROPOMORPHIC STATUES[1]

A striking change in artistic concern is evident in figurative sculptures from the Lower and Middle Benue. The favored subject of Lower Benue sculptors was the woman as mother, often with a child on her back or at her breast (see fig. 2.1). Women without children are nonetheless shown as solid maternal images: seated, hands on knees supporting torsos weighed down by jutting, angular breasts (see fig. 2.19). Beyond the edges of the region, such as Goemai (see chapter 2, pp. 63–65), this maternal image disappears from the corpus of wooden figures from the Middle and Upper Benue. Aside from occasional, slight differences in size, Middle Benue male and female sculptures are similar, differentiated by features of the head (particularly coiffure, earrings, or headgear, which are treated as secondary gendered characteristics) and by additions to otherwise identical, predominantly columnar, torsos and legs (fig. 8.3). Where breasts are indicated, they are small schematic features, so that it is difficult to be sure a figure is supposed to be female unless the male of the pair, which might also have prominent nipples, is available for comparison. The dimorphism of paired figures may or may not be indicated by outline genitalia, but these are rarely exaggerated

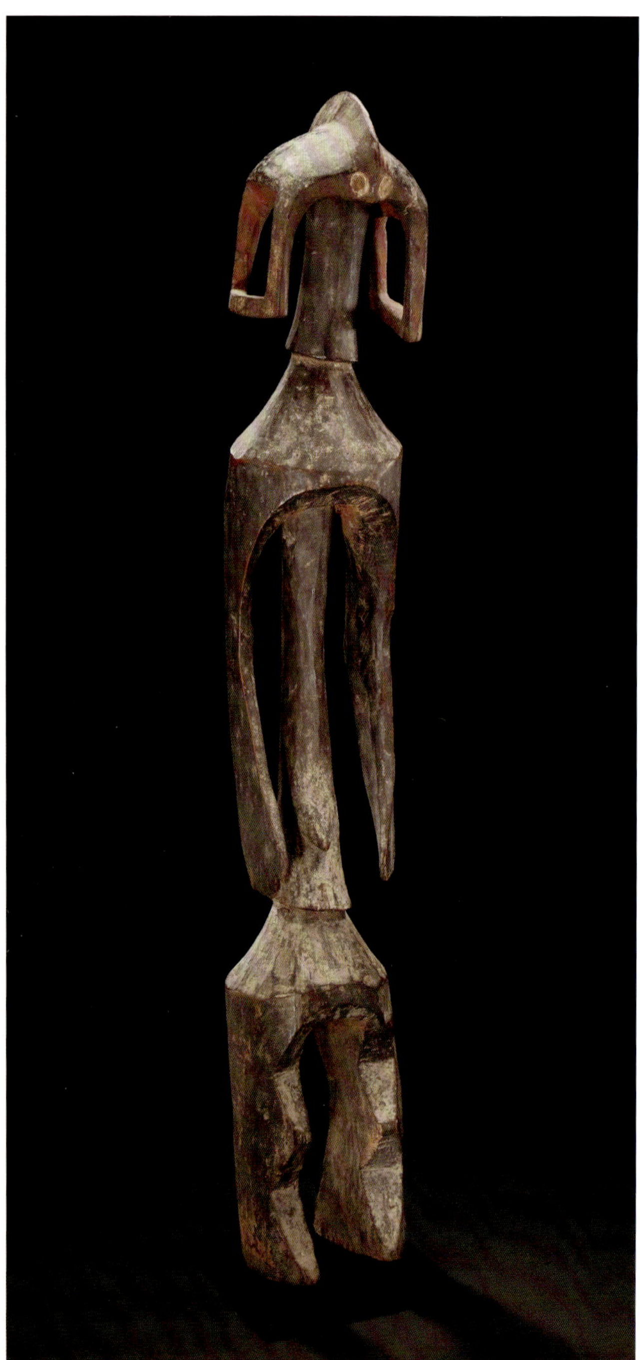

8.4 (LEFT)
Columnar statue
Mumuye peoples, mid-twentieth century
or earlier
Wood, pigment
H: 84 cm
PRIVATE COLLECTION, LOS ANGELES
IMAGE: © 2010 FOWLER MUSEUM AT UCLA.
PHOTOGRAPH BY DON COLE
PROVENANCE: AARON FURMAN GALLERY, NEW
YORK, 1969

Devoid of gendered anatomical detail, this tall
columnar Mumuye figure is probably female
(the sculptor has indicated a protruding navel,
but this is typical of such figures whether
female or male). The features of the head are
highly stylized, merging the eyes, perforated
pendant earlobes, and hair crest if a female
(or possibly eyes and cap with earflaps if a
male) into a single shape. The internal mass
(torso and neck) and external surfaces of the
figure are clearly distinguished. This figure
would have been among the earliest Mumuye
statues exported from Nigeria in the second
half of the 1960s.

8.5 (OPPOSITE)
Female columnar statue
Chamba peoples, mid-twentieth century
or earlier
Wood, metal
H: 39.5 cm
STAATLICHE MUSEEN ZU BERLIN, ETHNOLOGIS-
CHES MUSEUM, III C43418
IMAGE: © STAATLICHE MUSEEN ZU BERLIN,
PREUSSISCHER KULTURBESITZ, ETHNOLOGISCHES
MUSEUM. PHOTOGRAPH BY MARTIN FRANKEN, 2010
PROVENANCE: BERND MUHLACK, CAMEROON,
1962–1963

This female, iron-shod figure has a conical
headdress (perhaps representing a tall, flat-
topped hairstyle, more commonly found on
female figures than male) and small facial
features. Breasts and genitalia are indicated
but are evidently not the carver's focus of
interest. This piece was added to the collection of the Ethnologisches Museum in Berlin
in 1975, having apparently been bought in
Cameroon by Bernd Muhlack in 1962–1963.
Similar figures have appeared on the art
market in numbers subsequently.

or prominent in the way that bodily decorations or modifications (coiffure or headdress, piercings or scarification, nose or earplugs) often are. Some ethnic styles, like
Mumuye, scarcely differentiate paired male and female figure sculptures at all (fig.
8.4); and within other traditions, like Chamba, gendered differentiation is less obvious
the more that statues are pole-like in form (see below).

Although considerable stylistic variation is evident from examples collected from
the Middle Benue, ethnographic reports suggest peoples of the region used anthropomorphic statues for similar purposes. They were invariably gendered, although as
noted it is not always easy to grasp the conventions that should tell us which figure
is which. The overwhelming majority of statues have been collected singly, though
they were often used in, not necessarily matching, opposite-sex pairs. Much rarer are
double-figure statues, composed of joined male and female figures, used by Chamba
and Verre. Figures evoked human-like capacities and characteristics, whether of ancestors, the dead, or spirits. Commonly, they were parts of the paraphernalia of cults, and

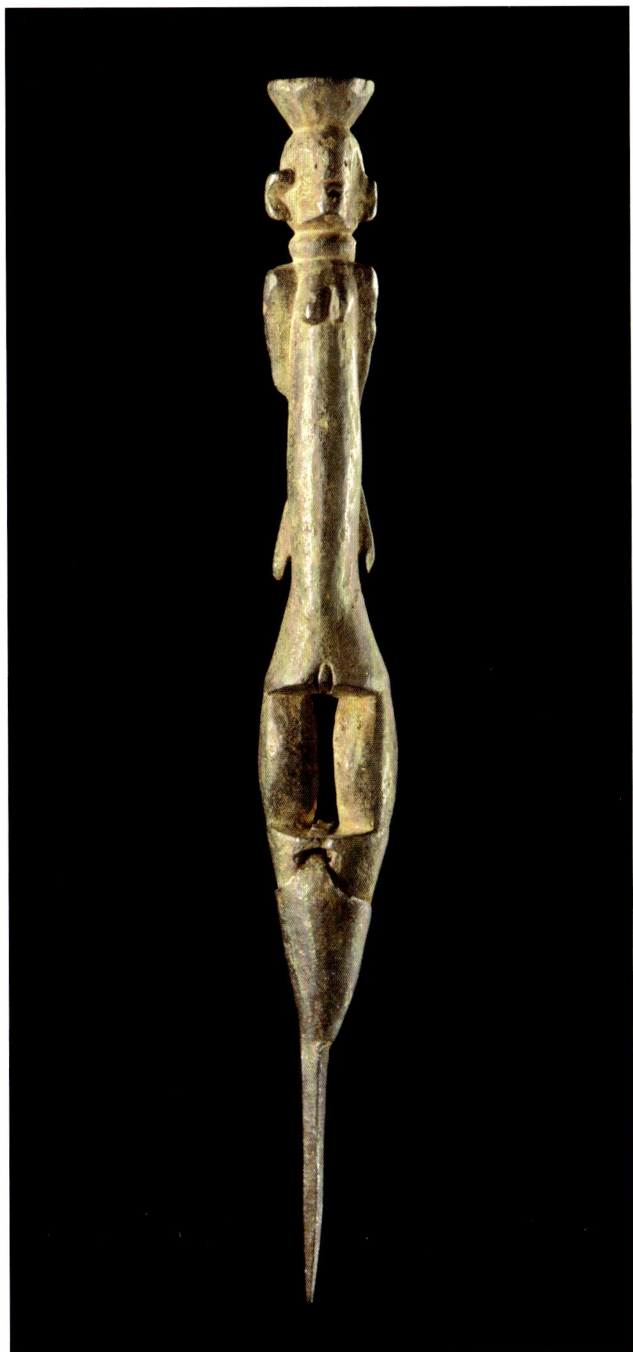
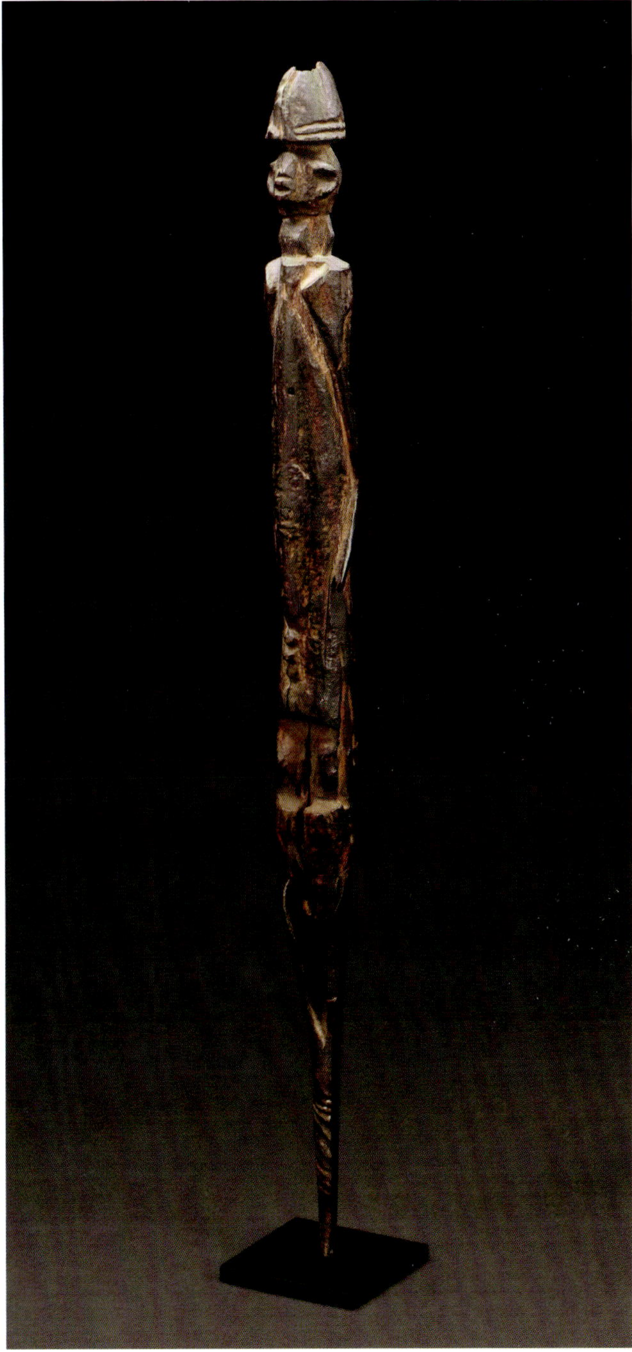

8.6
Columnar statue
Chamba peoples, mid-twentieth century
or earlier
Wood, metal
H: 49 cm
FOWLER MUSEUM AT UCLA X2006.18.7A,B; MUSEUM
PURCHASE WITH FUNDS PROVIDED BY J. T. LAST
IMAGE: © 2010 FOWLER MUSEUM AT UCLA.
PHOTOGRAPH BY DON COLE
PROVENANCE: PACE PRIMITIVE, NEW YORK; LEE
LORENZ COLLECTION, NEW YORK; AMYAS NAE-
GELE COLLECTION, NEW YORK

This iron-shod, columnar figure acquired in
2006 by the Fowler Museum is probably male.
In its extreme columnar form it is similar to
many that have appeared on the art market.

these in turn might mediate forces that were predominantly associated with (more
or less ancestralized) dead, or with (more or less naturalized) forces of the wild, or,
indeed, with entities that had something of both of these types of characteristics about
them. Rather than standing for something specific other than themselves, figures
provided cult practitioners with a point of address, so that cultic power (in the final
analysis mysterious even to its adepts) might be disposed to react favorably to entreat-
ies accompanied by offerings made with appropriate ritual formalism. In different
styles and executed with varying degrees of expertise (including homemade versions
created by nonspecialists where nothing more skillfully carved was needed or could
be afforded), statues were all capable of playing this role.

If not placed in cults, then figures were found in ancestral shrines of one kind
or another. There have been suggestions that statues in some of these ancestral collections might represent particular chiefs, but such identification is likely to have been
post hoc, since there is no evidence for attempts to achieve likeness, however that is

8.7 (OPPOSITE, LEFT)
Soompa (active 1920s–1940s)
Volumetric female statue
Chamba peoples, 1920s–1940s
Wood
H: 45 cm
PRIVATE COLLECTION, STANFORD
IMAGE: COURTESY OF PRIVATE COLLECTOR.
PHOTOGRAPH BY ROBERT KATO, 2010
PROVENANCE: PIERRE DARTEVELLE, BRUSSELS
(ACQUIRED IN JALINGO, 1968)

This female figure is the most complete of
only five single-figure statues attributed to
the Chamba carver Soompa. Its swelling form
contrasts strongly with the uniform thickness
of Chamba columnar figures. To judge by
less-used examples, the statue's facial features
would originally have included eyes and scarification which have largely disappeared under
a patina of oil and red powder. The stylized,
narrow sagittal crest is typical of Soompa's
female statues. This figure was bought in 1968
in Jalingo, Nigeria, an important administrative town that had a busy regional art market
at the time.

understood (Stevens 1976). We might call these "generic" portraits, following Jean
Borgatti (1980; Borgatti and Brilliant 1990), but to my mind this stretches the idea
of portraiture in a way that makes sense if one is primarily interested cross-culturally
in the notion of the portrait but is less persuasive when one's goal is translation of the
significance of figures. Having been acquired, a statue might perhaps be associated
with a particular ancestor, but the impression from the literature (and from Chamba
fieldwork) is that statues carried diffuse, rather than individual, ancestral reference
and that this readily shaded into a generic class of spirit entities thanks to the way in
which the dead and the underworld tended to be elided. This status, rather than the
particular identity of the deceased, seems to be what the statue represented. By and
large there was not a great development of palace or chiefly art, when compared with
great centers of palace building like, for instance, the Bamenda Grassfields of Cameroon into which some Chamba migrated during the mid-nineteenth century, adopting
the local emphases on ornamentation and display (Fardon 2006).

In a previous publication, Christine Stelzig and I suggested a gross distinction
between two forms of statue among Chamba: columnar and volumetric (Fardon and
Stelzig 2005). Single Chamba columnar statues are fashioned by the subtraction of
wood from a block or branch to excavate the main features of a human figure—head,
torso, arms, legs (fig. 8.5). Some examples of the form remain little more than poles:
with arms indicated in raised relief, rather than being separated from the body. The
most rudimentary form recorded by Father Malachy Cullen in his notes on Mapeo
Chamba was a carved forked stick used to substitute for a statue where none could
be afforded (Cullen 1944). Most columnar statues are more elaborate than this, but
in either case the aesthetic is subtractive, so the mind's eye readily reconstructs the
symmetrical piece of wood with which the carver began. Unlike some Mumuye figures,
Chamba columnar statues were rigidly upright rather than flexed or twisted. Most of
them were designed to be iron shod for insertion into the ground or into a piece of
wood, and the dimensions of the standard socketed iron shoe (which is far more common than the alternative of a simple spike inserted into statue's base or foot) limited
the range of variation in the diameter of statues since their lower ends needed to be
pared down to fit into it (fig. 8.6). Volumetric statues, by contrast, have a swelling sense
of internal space and demand greater plasticity in the use of wood (as if preparing a
wax model for brass casting or molding clay were inspirations). The finest volumetric
figures are animated by a sense that their substance grows outward from its core into a
modeled form (fig. 8.7). It is noticeable that the dimorphic gendered features of figures
are more prominent in volumetric forms than they are in columnar types. In short,
volumetric figures are more embodied than are columnar.

Shod columnar statues were in all likelihood carved predominantly by the smiths
who forged the iron fixtures for them. Conversely, it is conceivable that carving larger,
freestanding, columnar statuary, and even more so volumetric statuary, was less the
preserve of a particular occupational grouping. This consideration, along with the
limitations on overall form imposed by the almost invariant iron shoe, goes some way
to explaining the fact that these types of figures varied more among themselves than
did iron-shod columnar figures. Volumetric statues are far less common than columnar
statues among Chamba, and their production seems to have been restricted to Chamba
neighboring the Verre, among whom such statues predominated in recent times. That
no iron-shod statues have been attributed to Verre is striking given the local renown of
their smiths and smelters. Those that have been collected are volumetric and notably
"naturalistic" relative to Chamba. For instance, in their long-leggedness, Verre figures
are closer to human proportions than the predominantly short-legged Chamba and
Mumuye figures. The faces and braided hair of recent examples are also—by the
standards of their neighbors—naturalistic (Fardon and Stelzig 2005, 123, pls. 20a–e,
illustrating five examples that may be by the same artist or workshop).

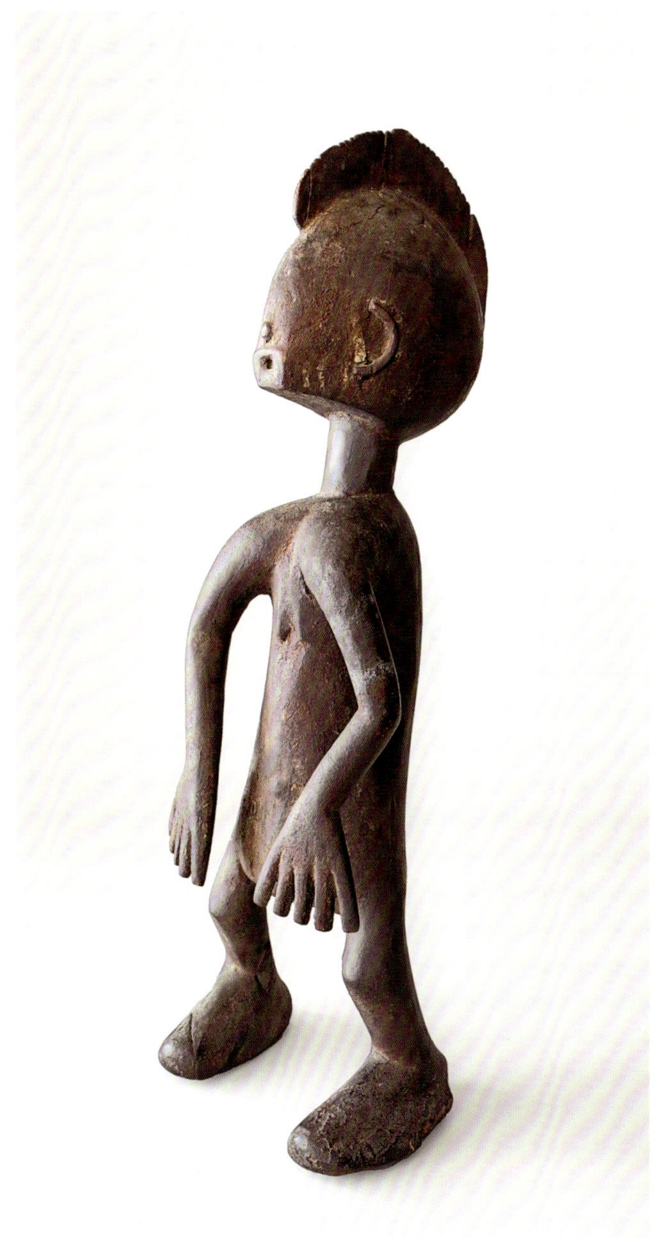

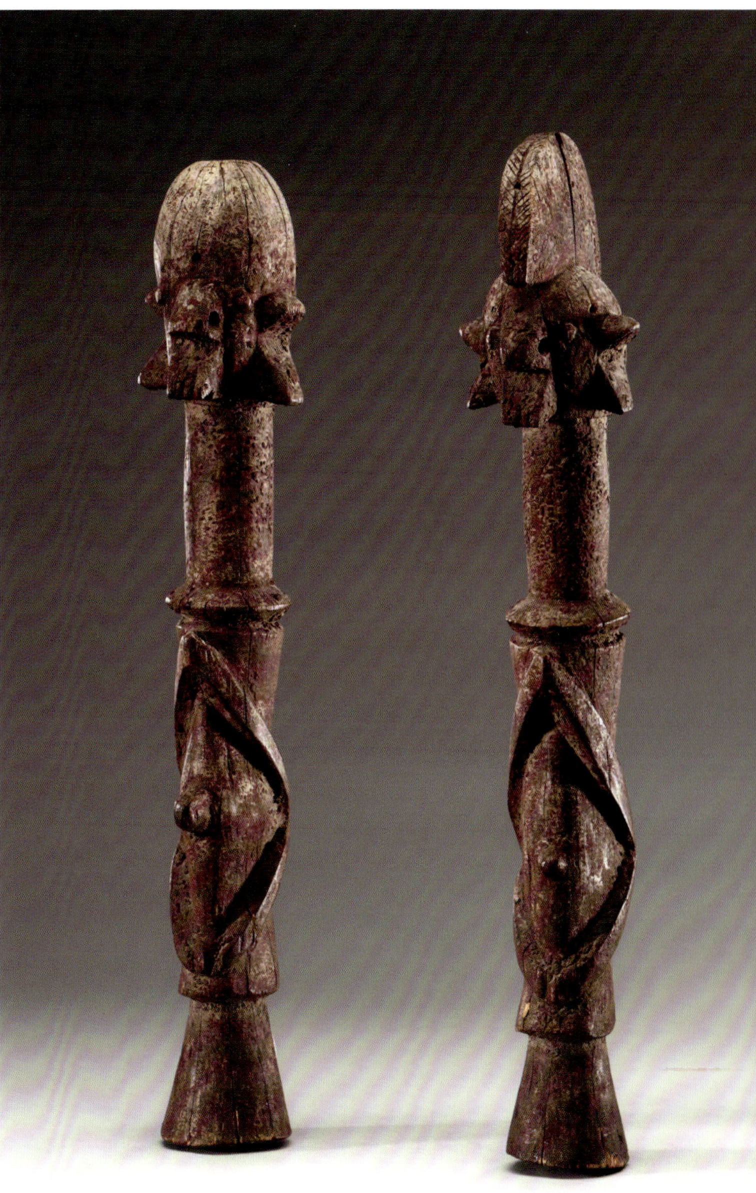

8.8
Two columnar statues (*kundul*)
Wurkun peoples, mid-twentieth century
Wood
H: 41.5 cm
PRIVATE COLLECTION
IMAGE: COURTESY PRIVATE COLLECTOR. © STU-
DIO PHILIPPE DE FORMANOIR, BRUSSELS, 2010
PROVENANCE: LANCE ENTWISTLE; ATLANTIC ART
PARTNERS, NEW YORK, 1990

These distinctive Wurkun *kundul* figures
represent the most columnar style found in
the Benue River Valley. The figure with the
rounded head and two small protrusions on its
torso would seem to be female. The sculptor
has been particularly attentive to the sagittal
hair ridge on the other figure, as well as to
what may be a goatee on its chin. This figure
has a single protrusion on its torso, probably
a navel. Arms in raised relief are sculpted
almost as a closed oval shape on both figures.

Western Chamba statues, both shod and freestanding, tend to be strongly columnar, as are the more strikingly varied statues of the Mumuye who neighbor them
further west. The most purely columnar figurative sculpture of the Middle Benue,
however, must be that of the peoples classified together as Wurkun (see chapter 13).
The most characteristic forms of Wurkun figure sculpture are almost wand-like:
entirely carved in raised relief and lacking either legs or feet (fig. 8.8; see also chapter
13).[2] Many of their characteristics, particularly the representation of arms as a lozenge
outlined in raised relief on the body, are shared by Chamba columnar statues (and
apparently also by some peoples on the eastern side of the Middle Benue subregion,
including the Pere). The most radically columnar statues collected from Chamba were
among the earliest to enter a public collection. They formed a pair that was picked up
by the missionary C. L. Whitman in Donga, and he donated them to the then Commercial Museum in Philadelphia (illustrated in Gunn 1960, who quotes the accession
note in which the two statues are described as field guardians; Rubin 1969, 96).[3] It
may not be coincidental that the Donga Chamba passed through and also incorporated some peoples with minimalist columnar sculptural traditions. Rather than being

iron shod, these Donga figures have iron rods simply inserted into their bases, presumably to hold them upright when stuck into the ground. The distinction between types of statue among Chamba seems applicable to the statues of their neighbors as well, so I use it here of the region as a whole. While some statues fall squarely into the types, for others it is more helpful to think of these descriptors as relative terms rather than distinct categories, some statues being "more columnar" or "more volumetric" than others.

CHAMBA (LEKO AND DAKA); PERE

In describing Chamba statues, I am drawing on the results of research carried out collaboratively for which Christine Stelzig and I (2005) created a database of more than a hundred statues attributed to Chamba, along with their characteristics and collection histories (when these were available). With the exception of the "Wurkun" and Wurbo, about whom Joerg Adelberger and Marla Berns write in this volume, comparable exercises have not as yet been undertaken for other peoples. The Mumuye particularly invite a similar project, although the sheer size of the corpus would make it a formidable challenge.

Acquisition of Chamba objects in Africa peaked in two periods: the first, which I call "Kamerunian" for short, occurred during the early twentieth century when most Chamba lived in the German colony of Kamerun. Partition of the German colony into British and French League of Nations' Mandates after the First World War, placed a majority of these erstwhile Kamerunian Chamba under British administration; they eventually joined Nigeria a year after Nigerian Independence in 1961. The second period of intensive collection took place shortly after independence when Biafran secession (1967–1970) plunged Nigeria into civil war (see, for example Coppens n.d.; Fardon and Stelzig 2005, appendix). From a scholarly perspective, the fruits of these two periods of collecting could hardly be more different. Artefacts from colonial Kamerun typically found their way to German museums from field collection in situ; most, therefore, had accompanying notes specifying who collected them, where and when they did so, and some indication (often rough and ready) of what the local name and significance of these things might be (see fig. 8.3). Objects collected in the post-independence period directly entered the art market rather than museums. Through the intermediation of African "runners," most were bought by European dealers, predominantly based across the border from Nigeria in Cameroon. Typically, the runners applied to their wares only an ethnic designation of origin. A minority of these objects subsequently found their way into public collections, and more are doing so all the time, particularly in the United States, but they lack records of acquisition. Even in these cases, however, provenance records, which develop as the objects pass between owners, are important because they may allow us to date when objects left West Africa and through which of the main dealers they passed. This in turn may provide clues as to where they were collected, since particular regions appear to have been "worked out" by prospecting runners, and knowing when this happened helps distinguish objects exported during the immediate post-independence period of collection from outright faked objects made later.

As explained in the previous chapter, from the mid-twentieth century on, the ritual contexts requiring the mediation of statues were being eroded in the face of world religions. This process accelerated during the early decades of the post-independence period in Nigeria, given an extra push by political support for campaigns against "heathenism," and by the sale and theft of ritual paraphernalia, which local chiefs as political clients on occasions facilitated. As a result the majority of the statues leaving Chambaland during the second period of collecting would not have been replaced; there was no longer a demand for them. This, however, did not stem the tide of "Chamba" artefacts reaching the art market. The unwitting copying of demonstrable

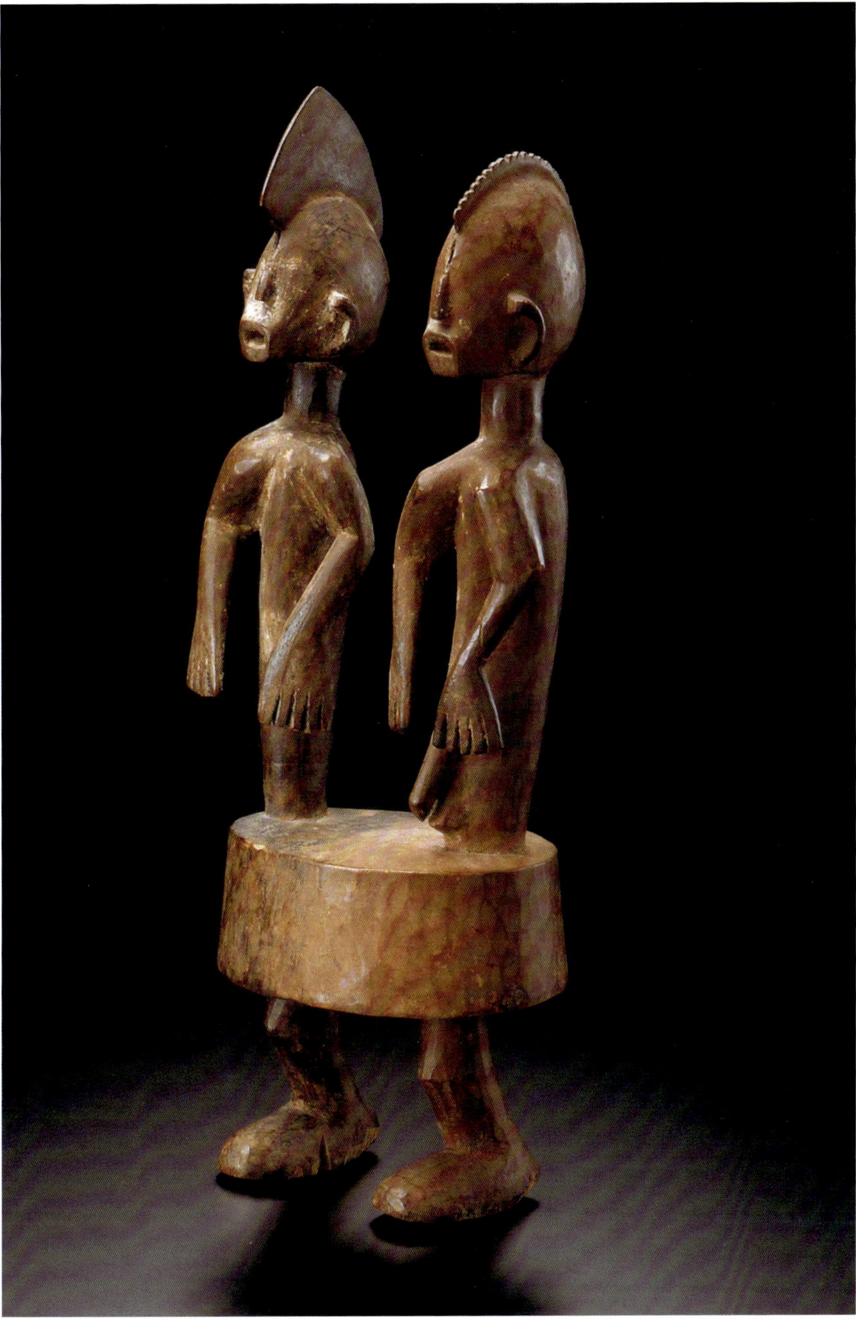

8.9
Soompa (active 1920s–1940s)
Double-figure statue
Chamba peoples, 1920s–1940s
Wood
H: 48 cm
COLLECTION OF JEAN WILLY MESTACH, BRUSSELS
IMAGE: © JEAN WILLY MESTACH. PHOTOGRAPH BY
ALAIN SPELTDOORN, 2003
PROVENANCE: PIERRE DARTEVELLE, CAMEROON,
LATE 1960S
(NOT IN EXHIBITION)

Like the Virginia statue (fig. 8.1), this double-figure volumetric statue by Soompa entered the international art world by purchase in Cameroon during the late 1960s. Jean Willy Mestach graciously consented to having the statue CAT scanned, which revealed that the lower left arm of the male figure had been replaced and the crest of the female figure repaired with a pin. Such repairs to Soompa's figures are so common that an absence of restoration begs explanation. This example is characteristic of the genre in all respects: the male figure stands on the proper left (the right when viewed frontally), and only the male figure has schematic genitalia.

features of restoration rather than original design provides clear evidence for the outright faking of some "Chamba" statues. Less unambiguous, but suspicious nonetheless, is the appearance of very similar, iron-shod statues in apparently good condition in the last years of the twentieth century when no evidence suggests that Chamba smiths still produced iron mounts. Despite these doubts about parts of the "Chamba" corpus, Christine Stelzig and I were able to draw significant conclusions from looking at that collection in as much as we were able to assemble of its entirety. Where the corpus is manageable, we feel that entering it into a database is both methodologically helpful and, given a combination of e-mail inquiry and digital photography, practically feasible if time-consuming. Marla Berns's account of vertical masks in this volume further demonstrates the dividends that this kind of spadework can yield (see chapter 14).

Our most pleasing discovery was that a group of statues in volumetric style, showing every indication of being by the same hand, had been carved during the mid-colonial period by an identifiable artist. These had entered the market virtually at a single moment around the end of the Biafran War. The statues were usually considered, for instance in auction and exhibition catalogs, to be of nineteenth-century origin; however, Father Malachy Cullen, a Roman Catholic priest in the Chamba villages of Mapeo, documented the activities of their carver, Soompa, in 1944 and donated a newly made, pristine statue by Soompa to the Nigerian National Museum in Lagos, which was accessioned in 1946 (Cullen 1944). These indications allowed us to state categorically that all such statues must be datable to the first half of the twentieth century, a dating that is corroborated and further narrowed by the negative evidence that no example of a Chamba statue in this style was acquired during the Kamerunian period of collection, despite the extensive touring undertaken by German colonial officers and ethnologists before the First World War, when their expeditions visited the very settlements in which Soompa worked. The likeliest conclusion to draw from this is that some at least of Soompa's statues replaced older statues similar to those collected by German visitors during this first phase.

The corpus of Soompa's statues that survived into the 1970s consisted of at least fourteen or fifteen works. Of these, eight or nine (depending whether all nine are accepted as authentic) are particularly distinctive double-figure statues formed from the torsos of male and female figures, joined around the hips, and sharing a single pair of legs (figs. 8.1, 8.9). Five single statues (two female figures and three male figures; see fig. 8.7)[4] may originally have been displayed in opposite-sex pairs. What may be a unique entire surviving example of a forked pole carved into a double-figure statue seems also to be by Soompa (fig. 8.10).[5] This group has to be considered closed unless more statues with the same characteristics emerge that were demonstrably collected around the time of the Biafran War.

The volumetric statues attributed to Soompa have not only been considered by far the finest of Chamba statues (and this by some margin to judge from six-figure art-market valuations) but also typical of Chamba statuary in some respects. The latter assumption, however, is far from the case. Soompa's statues are exceptionally fine examples of the less-common, volumetric form of Chamba statues, but by far the majority of Chamba statues were columnar. Father Cullen's notes indicate that Soompa was a Chamba Leko (that is a speaker of the eastern Chamba language) who lived around the Cameroon/Nigeria border during the first half of the twentieth century. He supplied carvings to the Chamba Leko-speaking chiefdom of Yeli (Cameroon) and subsequently to the large Chamba Daka-speaking refuge settlements of Mapeo (Nigeria). Cullen was told that Soompa had been forbidden to sell his statues in Yeli where instead he was obliged to donate them to the shrines controlled by the Priest-Chief. If Soompa really was distancing himself from Yeli, then his move may have coincided with the Anglo-French division on paper of German Kamerun becoming a more practical reality in the mid-1920s. Numerous Chamba Leko settlements are recorded in the colonial archives as moving into Nigeria around this time. Assuming Soompa was active for at least a decade preceding his move and continued working until sometime after 1944, then we might date his carvings between 1915 and 1950 in the most approximate terms, though the period of his most intensive activity is likely to have been shorter than this (perhaps 1920s to 1940s).

It is not clear whether Soompa innovated the form of the figures he carved or if he worked in a previous genre. None of the statues we can identify as Soompa's is iron shod. With the exception of the forked double figure that is apparently designed to be stuck into the ground, both his single- and double-figure statues stand upon a pair of slightly flexed legs with doll-like feet. The double-figure statues are particularly distinctive in this respect and may be original to him. Cullen's notes suggest that Soompa had emulators in his own time; and double-figure statues that are joined at the hip and stand on a single pair of legs, executed in various styles, came onto the market around the same time as Soompa's and have continued to do so subsequently. None of these statues appears as weathered as Soompa's, and several of them were made by

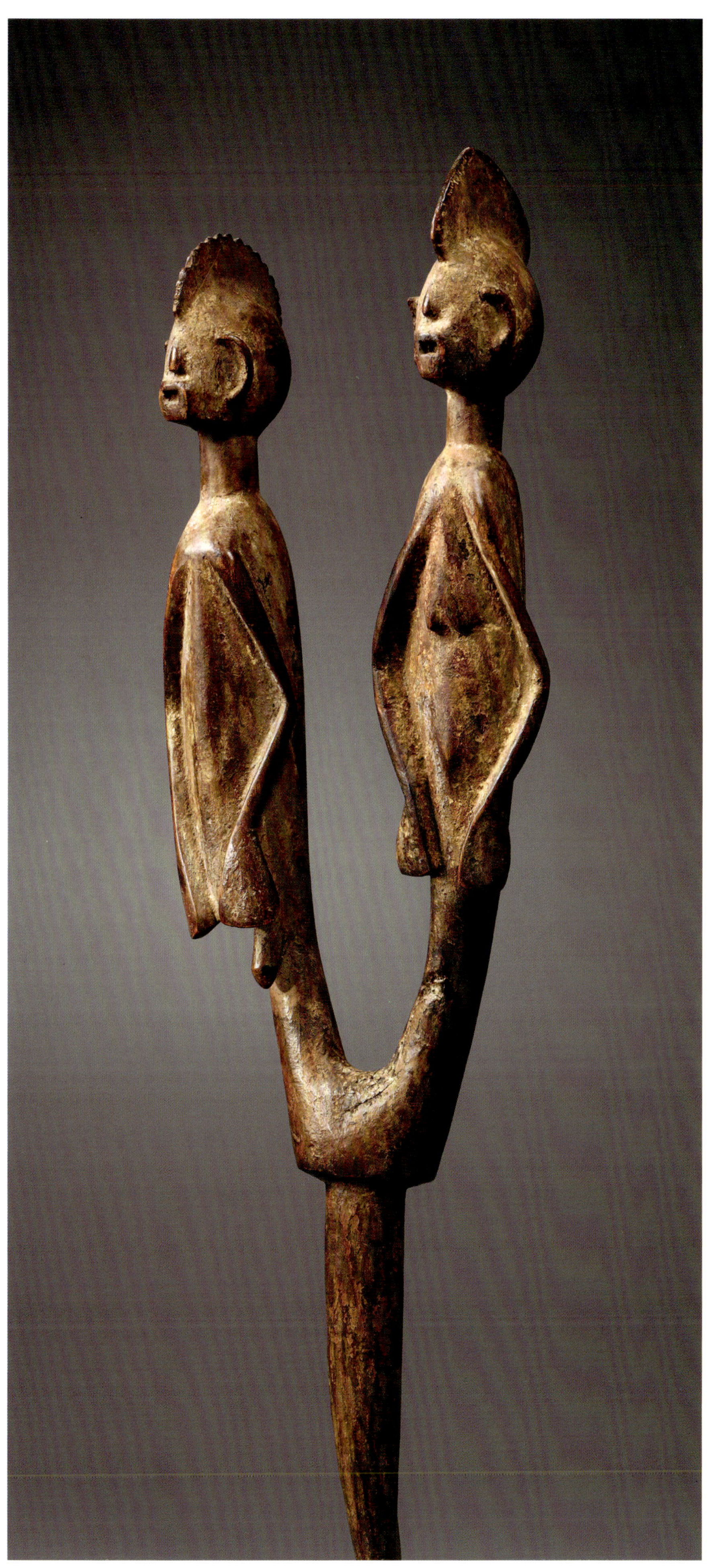

8.10
Soompa (active 1920s–1940s)
Double-figure statue carved from a forked branch
Chamba peoples, 1920s–1940s
Wood
H: 60 cm
PRIVATE COLLECTION, PARIS
IMAGE: COURTESY PRIVATE COLLECTOR.
© HUGHES DUBOIS, 2010
PROVENANCE: PHILIPPE GUIMIOT, CAMEROON, 1968; JACQUES BLANKAERT, 1970S

This beautifully carved forked double-figure statue by Soompa was previously thought to be unique as a complete example, although another example has since been proposed but not yet authenticated. Like the standing double-figure statues, pieces of this sort were made to be part of a cult apparatus, particularly in Mapeo.

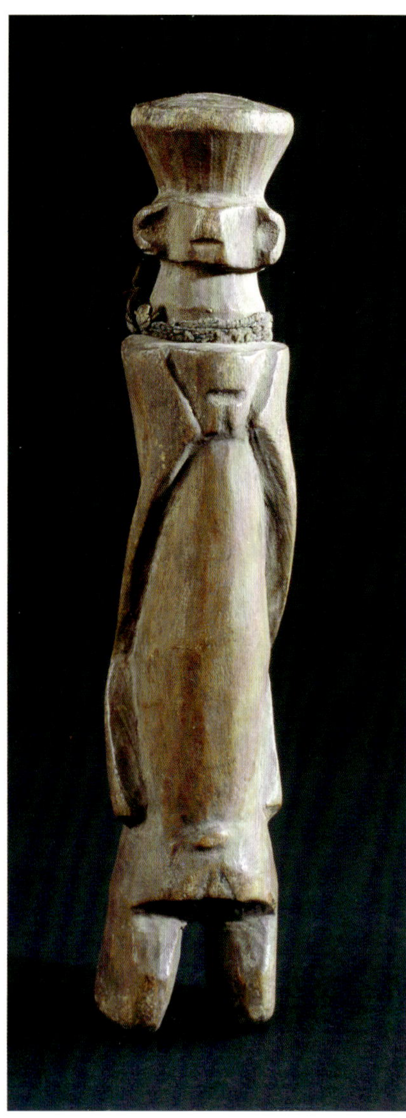

8.13
Single freestanding columnar statue
Chamba peoples, before 1907
Wood
H: 22 cm
MUSEUM FÜR VÖLKERKUNDE DRESDEN,
STAATLICHE ETHNOGRAPHISCHE SAMMLUNGEN
SACHSEN, 24065
PROVENANCE: COLLECTED BY JOHANNES ROTHE, 1907
(NOT IN EXHIBITION)

A sturdy, markedly columnar figure, probably
female, with a flat headdress and elongated
torso on which arms are outlined in raised
relief, this statue stands on short legs rather
than a visible metal spike. It was collected on
tour by a German colonial officer, Oberleut-
nant H. F. Johannes Rothe, probably from
the southern margins of Gurumpawo, one of
the largest Daka-speaking chiefdoms on the
eastern side of the Shebshi Mountains.

in German collections (*Heiliges Gerät der Dakka*, sketched by Carl Arriens, Frobenius [1913], reproduced in this volume as fig. G.8; the 1911 Dalami figure once in Berlin, now lost, may have been number 4 in this diagram).

A British Assistant District Officer, E. S. Lilley, collected four statues from the Chamba Daka-speaking chiefdom of Binyeri. Two of these figures are now generally considered to be Mumuye in style, so I discuss them later in that context. The other two form a male-female matching pair collected in unused condition. Respectively colored red and black, the male and female are most obviously distinguished by the female figure's tall headdress. Each figure has a metal spike in the sole of its foot, presumably to assist their remaining upright. This is an unusual feature in extant examples (though only a systematic check of Chamba figures would confirm whether they also had holes indicating the earlier presence of spikes).

Freestanding statuary predominated among the pieces reaching the art market during the last quarter of the twentieth century. This trend might have something to do with the demise of local smithing, given that carvers were often smiths and that statues were predominantly iron shod in the past, as well as with a shift in the epicenter of collecting toward the Shebshi Mountains, the eastern slopes of which had been on the boundary of German Kamerun. Some recent freestanding statues, although likely to come from the region, are crudely executed by comparison with those collected earlier and have been carved from particularly lightweight wood (Stevens 1976). Freestanding columnar statues show a greater degree of stylistic variation than either volumetric or iron-shod states. Some part of this seems attributable to the rather different stylistic preferences of the Verre (to the east) and the Mumuye (to the west) who sold pieces to Chamba users and may also have influenced the products of Chamba carvers.

VERRE

That the wooden statuary of the Verre, living to the north and northeast of the eastern Chamba, has attracted little scholarly attention is readily explained by the paucity of examples. Verre smelters and smiths, working in both iron and bronze, made a variety of ceremonial and mundane wares that to my knowledge were highly prized by their Chamba neighbors. Eastern Chamba also bought Verre carved figures, but it is difficult to know whether this trade was long-standing or a surrogate for the demise of local Chamba carving. The Verre carvings I saw in Mapeo Chamba cults were all recent acquisitions, and my impression is that these, and other pieces entering collections around the same time, derived from a small number of carvers or workshops.

The earliest collected examples, three Verre figures, all female, entered the British Museum in 1913 (BM 1913 10-13.11/12/13) donated by Mr. and Mrs. C. L. Temple. Like the Wurkun figure in the World Museum Liverpool, they belonged to the somewhat haphazard collection assembled by Miss MacLeod, soon to be Mrs. Temple, during her journey to Late Chad and back in 1910–1911 (MacLeod 1912). All three figures are colored black and retain some of what had been a general encrustation of abrus seeds. Their carving is highly schematic, even crude, and in that respect differs from the remarkably fine finish of more recently collected Verre figures. Where the later figures do resemble these early examples is in their relatively naturalistic proportions and the separated legs with doll-like feet on which they can stand by themselves (a feature shared with Soompa's statues, which must have been carved slightly later). So far as I am aware, no other example of Verre sculpture in wood surfaced during the colonial period.

Verre wooden figures were next collected and accessioned from the second half of the 1960s. Examples would include three single figures in the Jos Museum Nigeria[7] (Fardon and Stelzig 2005, 123, nos. 20a–c) and an influx to private collections. Fardon and Stelzig illustrate two figures that passed through the hands of Karl-Ferdinand

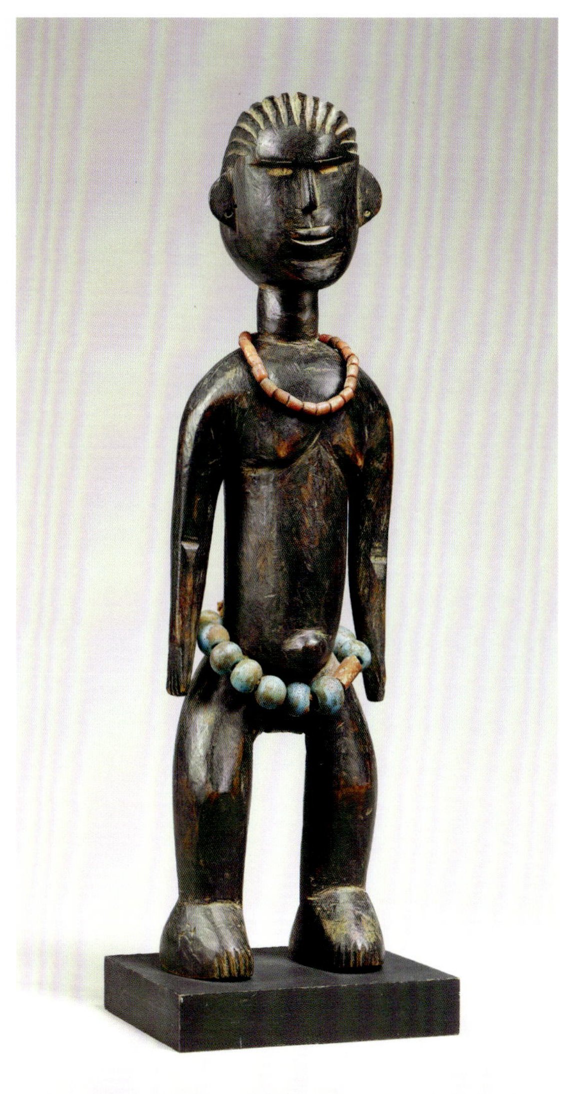

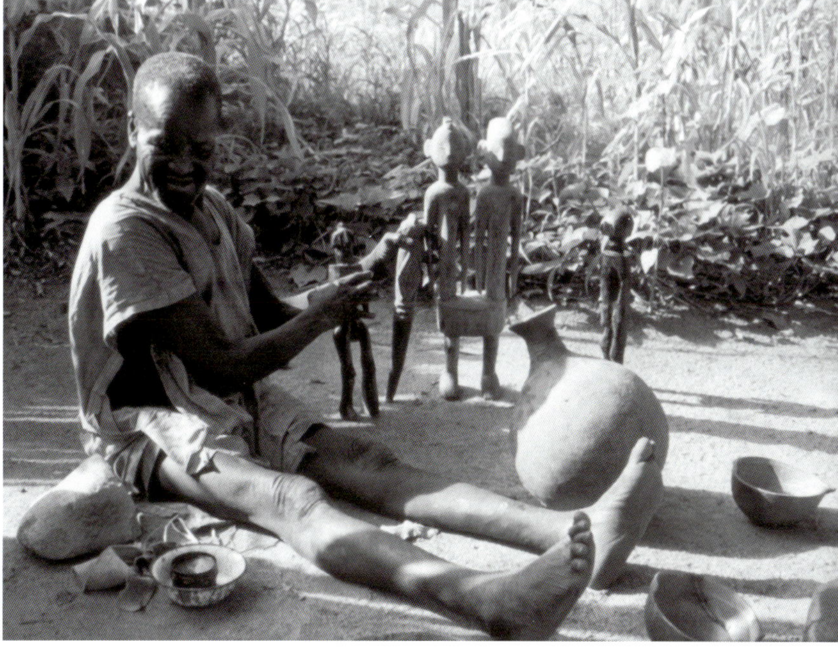

Schaedler to private buyers (2005, 123, nos. 20d–e), and these bear close similarities to two statues (fig. 8.14) donated to Paris museums by the art dealer Alain Dufour in 1969 and 1970, which are now in the Musée du quai Branly (Musée national des arts d'Afrique et d'Oceanie 73.1970.1.1; Musée de l'Homme 71.1969.131.1, illustrated in Fry 1970, 6, fig. 3). The Verre statues collected for the Jos Museum in 1966 are recorded to have been carved in Karlahi, a village that hosts one in the seven-day cycle of markets frequented by people from the Chamba settlements of Mapeo. The figures emerging at this period are sufficiently similar to be from the same workshop and predominantly by the same hand. To these I think we can add double-figure statues such as I photographed in Mapeo—and which circulate in the international art market (Fardon and Stelzig 2005, 43 in collections, 112 in Mapeo; fig. 8.15). These pieces all share the proportions and lower limbs of Soompa's volumetric figures, but they lack their suppleness.[8] Typically the heads and torsos are unflexed, and their eyes stare straight ahead with arms held at their sides. The figures are stained deepest black or perhaps carbonized. Particular care has been taken to carve braids on the female figures, which predominate (perhaps to the exclusion of males), and several are supplied with belts or necklaces or small beads, as well as ear ornaments.

Speculation on the relationship between Verre statuary and Chamba volumetric statues in Soompa's style is inviting but finally inconclusive. As we saw, the record of provenanced Chamba statues suggests that Soompa's statues may have replaced columnar figures in the Mapeo area; it seems possible that insofar as Soompa's figures

8.14
Single female statue
Verre peoples, before 1969
Wood, beads
H: 49 cm
MUSÉE DU QUAI BRANLY (EX-MUSÉE DE L'HOMME 71.1969.131.1, ILLUSTRATED IN FRY 1970, 6, FIG. 3)
IMAGE: © 2010 MUSÉE DU QUAI BRANLY. PHOTO-GRAPH BY CLAUDE GERMAIN/SCALA, FLORENCE
PROVENANCE: PRIVATE COLLECTION, PARIS (NOT IN EXHIBITION)

A number of similar, deep black, highly finished female figures attributed to the Verre came onto the art market from the 1960s in relatively new condition. They were probably the work of a single sculptor or workshop in the village of Toza, just north of the market town of Karlahi in Nigeria, close to the border with Cameroon

8.15
Sandami prepares new statues for addition to cults in Mapeo in 1987. The double-figure statue was bought from Verre carvers and seems to represent a local copy of Soompa's distinctive style, though it is much more rigid and upright, losing the fluidity and implied motion of the original.
PHOTOGRAPH BY RICHARD FARDON.

8.16
Single-figure statue
Mumuye peoples, before 1970
Wood, pigment, leather
H: 78.4 cm
PRIVATE COLLECTION
IMAGE: © PRIVATE COLLECTION. PHOTOGRAPH BY
BENJAMIN WATKINS
PROVENANCE: PATRICIA WITHOFS, LONDON; PHILIP
GOLDMAN, LONDON, LATE 1970S

Mumuye figures vary too widely for any
to be considered typical, however many,
including this example, display some common characteristics. These include the clear
distinction between a central core (consisting
of torso and neck) and outer surfaces that
draw together shoulders and hips; notched
legs and flexed arms; a prominent navel
(which suggests connection between core and
surface); and a stylized head, which has been
the subject of the most intensive carving. The
crest and flaps on the head of this figure are
more likely to evoke a warrior's helmet than
a combination of coiffure and extended ears.
Lack of anatomical detail makes definite gender attribution of Mumuye figures difficult.
This figure does not appear to be flexed or
asymmetric, which are common characteristics of the earliest collected Mumuye pieces.

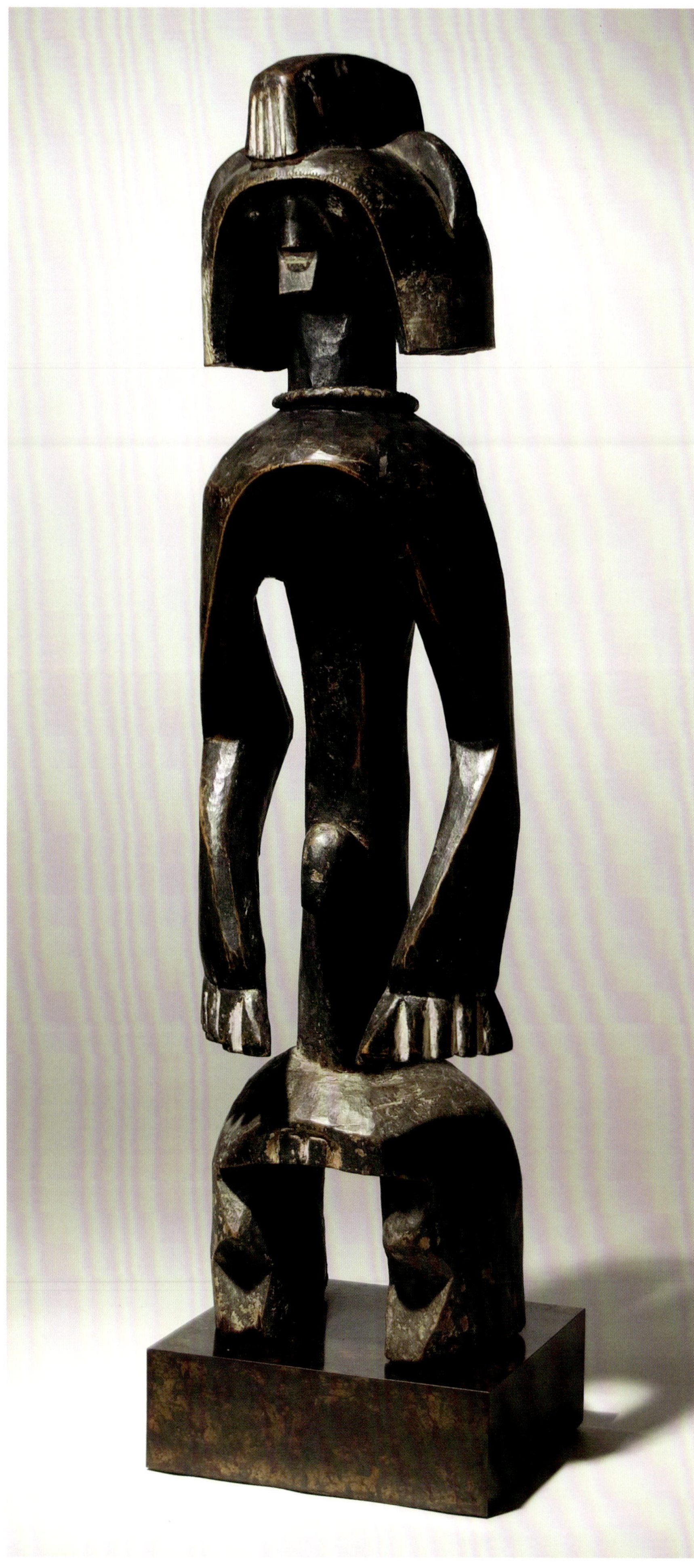

were subsequently replaced at all, their replacements were predominantly Verre figures from a workshop north of Mapeo. The only precedent in the Mapeo area for statues with the proportions, feet, and legs favored by Soompa, however, are the Verre figures collected by Olive MacLeod in 1910 and now in the British Museum. All this seems to suggest not "ethnic" styles, to revert to an earlier discussion, but rather a micro-regional hotspot of interactions among speakers of Verre, Chamba Daka (like the inhabitants of Mapeo), and Chamba Leko (like Soompa). Even in this instance, however, we are reliant upon a speculative overinterpretation of slight evidence to suggest how works of figure sculptors might have been caught up in a local eddy of influences. The scenario is plausible, but the evidence for it well short of conclusive.

Moving from Verre west to Mumuye takes us from famine to feast. The Mumuye are the most prolific figure sculptors of the Middle Benue, which makes one wonder again whether the paucity of wooden sculpture among Verre expresses a preference deriving from their expertise in metal working rather than simply being an accident of the collection record.

MUMUYE
Context

Once the bold forms of their human figures forcibly struck mid-twentieth-century curators and modern artists (fig. 8.16), the Mumuye, immediate western and north-western neighbors of the Chamba, became the most celebrated figure sculptors of the Middle Benue (see epilogue, pp. 561–67).[9] Several hundred statues have subsequently been attributed to them,[10] a figure likely to represent a modest proportion of a total running into thousands. Ethnographic documentation of both the Mumuye and their figures is, however, thin, and detail, context, and accuracy have been casualties in the frequent repetition of what has been recorded.

To begin then: who are the Mumuye? Given its phonic shape (a doubled and extended "moo"), Mumuye probably originated as a derogatory ethnic term applied by outsiders to speakers of related dialects who looked and sounded similar to their neighbors, though not to one another. Two inquiries of the colonial period, that of the government anthropologist C. K. Meek, based on brief firsthand experience, and the Temples' collation of administrative officers' reports, record a belief current that the name had been bestowed on Mumuye by the Fulani (Meek 1931b, 1: 446; Temple and Temple 1922, 287). If only because of the usefulness of such generalizing terms for neighbors, I suspect—as Meek does, though not on the grounds of his speculative etymology—that the name was of longer standing. Meek reported both that Mumuye had no general term for themselves and that Mumuye was accepted in self-description by people around the edges of the seven main Mumuye dialect groups who were not, in the "strictest" sense, Mumuye on grounds of language, "physical appearance," or "culture" (1931b, 1: 447). These only apparently contradictory statements can be recon-ciled if they are interpreted in terms of a process that involved the gradual adoption by Mumuye of an externally given ethnonym that through repeated use was becoming institutionalized within the wider colonial context of which they were increasingly part. Hence core Mumuye could afford to resist a general label, while periph-eral potential members gravitated toward it. Like *the* "Chamba" or *the* "Wurkun," "Mumuye" were coming into being as a designated people. Being Mumuye was becoming an element of personal identity, and this entailed reining in some ancient antagonisms (for instance the antipathy between the people of particular places, like Zing and Yakoko, which Mette Bovin describes in chapter 11). Criteria of inclusion and exclusion had to be negotiated around the edges of the identity, as people assessed the attractions that belonging to it offered (including not just political opportunities but the intellectual question of whether adoption of this identity was plausible to them-selves and to others).

Harking back to the earlier discussion of "artefactual ethnicity" (see pp. 220–36), the viability of an identity for Mumuye people has an obvious implication in the possibility of there being Mumuye sculpture. The sculptural traditions, however, predated the ethnic term, hence older "Mumuye" sculpture could not have been created with a view to this identity. This bears upon the likelihood of uniformity in sculptures because, whatever it was artists in the precolonial period thought they were creating, it could not by definition have been "Mumuye sculpture" but had to be sculpture for some particular use or in some locally appreciated style appropriate to a variety of purposes. Unlike most other sculptural traditions of the Middle Benue, there is evidence for a vigorous continuation of Mumuye figure carving into the postcolonial period, by which time it probably was the case that artists created self-consciously "Mumuye" artworks for purchasers who wanted just that. In short, although we have to speak of "Mumuye sculpture," not only is this category recent, its invention has probably affected the body of work we shall be examining. This alone should make us reread cautiously, and perhaps even skeptically, accounts that aspire to offer a definitive description of Mumuye stylistics, past or present or both.

Questions of scale further complicate our sense of what "Mumuye" might mean and how it became a designation for the culture of both people and things. Speakers of the related dialects who would come to be called Mumuye were one of the most numerous populations of the Middle Benue, probably the largest indigenous group after the Tiv. The Temples' estimate of more than 25,000 Mumuye[11] at the beginning of the 1920s seems to have been thought on the low side by later authors. British administration had divided the Mumuye between the two Fulani emirates of Yola and Muri. Jan Strybol quotes an estimate of 15,000 Mumuye in Yola alone by 1906–1907, and, according to the Temples, the bulk of the Mumuye, some two-thirds of them, lived in Muri Emirate (Strybol 1998, 19; Temple and Temple 1922, 287). Supposing some broad validity to a population estimate of 60,000–70,000 by the late 1920s, as Meek suggested, by the twenty-first century there should be well in excess of 400,000 Mumuye and perhaps a half million. At Meek's time, hamlets would consist of at most a few hundred inhabitants, and a group of neighboring hamlets would cooperate (1931b, 1: 450). Migration from the hills into the plains had been occurring since the colonial regime had imposed at least some restraint on the slave-raiding activities of the Fulani emirates, so villages would have been larger in the period before this need for defensive confinement lessened.

Without kings or chiefs, the widest powers that Mumuye recognized were those of their rainmakers, but even they might not travel unmolested outside their local areas (as Bovin confirms here, see p. 368). Otherwise, the government of individual and communal affairs rested at the levels of clan, cult, and locality. If sculpted figures were involved at these levels of religious observance, then it stands to reason that they must have been numerous. This plenty and the fact that conversion to world religions occurred without the skills of sculptors being wholly lost helped to make possible the phenomenal exodus of Mumuye sculpture that has occurred since the late 1960s.

In most places, Mumuye had resisted unfamiliar outside forces until shortly before the end of the colonial period; however, they mingled more freely with their long-term neighbors. Western Mumuye acknowledged the power of shrines under the control of the Jukun of Kona and shared with them the ways of making and performing with tall vertical masks (see chapter 14). They assisted the walled settlement of Kona to hold out against the Fulani until 1892 when its walls were finally breached by the canon of the French adventurer Lieutenant Louis Antoine Mizon, leading to its destruction and the massacre, enslavement, or dispersion of its population (Adelberger and Storch 2009). For their part, northeastern Mumuye had been subject to other influences, and some of them had become incorporated into the

Chamba conquest kingdoms of the area, but for the rest, and particularly for those to the south, Mumuye retained independence thanks to the formidable obstacle that mountains posed to cavalry.

Understanding the Flight of Mumuye Sculptures

It was as late as 1970 that a pioneering article by Philip Fry identified the Mumuye as the authors of a number of statues that had entered Parisian collections and galleries in the late 1960s. A first exhibition of Mumuye arts, organized in Denmark by Mette Bovin in 1965 at the Moesgård Museum affiliated with the University of Aarhus, is unlikely to have attracted more than a local audience. As Bernard de Grunne notes, however, the first French show of eighteen figures, organized in 1968 by the dealers Jean-Michel Huguenin and Edouard Klejman at the Galerie Majestic in Paris, made a significant splash, all the pieces being sold on the opening day to Henri Kamer and John J. Klejman (de Grunne 2001, 84, n. 11).[12] The timing was not accidental: the exodus of statuary from Mumuye country took place at the height of the Biafran War in Nigeria when border control over the export of antiquities virtually collapsed, particularly in the Benue Valley whence objects could be removed via the lightly policed Cameroonian border with the assistance of border chiefs.[13] The scale of the exodus was extraordinary.

The immediate stimulus to Fry's curiosity had been the acquisition by the Musée de l'Homme of a female figure that had at first been attributed to Jukun and then to Chamba before final reassignment to Mumuye (Fry 1970, 5, fig. 2; see fig 8.17). Intrigued, he assembled a corpus of fifty-three examples as a basis for formal analysis. Less than a decade later, Arnold Rubin would contribute a catalog note on a Mumuye statue purchased in Paris in 1970 for the Canadian National Museum of Man (B.4.99), which was included in an Ottawa exhibition of twenty-five African sculptures organized by Jacqueline Delange Fry (first wife of Philip Fry). Having briefly described the common stylistic features of Mumuye figurative sculptures, Rubin continued,

> An astonishing range of variations on these fairly modest parameters has come to light in the past decade, probably numbering several thousand examples. Unfortunately, only an infinitesimal proportion of these sculptures appears to have been documented in the field before the unsettled conditions of Nigeria during and immediately after the Biafran conflict saw their illegal exportation on a massive scale. If time and resources had been sufficient for determining local and regional variations in form and style, and correlating such variations with functional differences, some progress in disentangling the ethnic composition of what now emerges as a dauntingly complex cultural and artistic region might have been possible, and the place of these traditions in the constellation of the Benue Valley styles elucidated. [A. Rubin 1978, 108]

The passage of three decades since he wrote has improved the situation Rubin described little. What Philip Fry had intended as a provisional account of a newly recognized sculptural tradition has been developed (for instance by Neyt 2006) but not surpassed in any fundamental respect, a situation made possible by a very specific conjuncture of factors. I will list only a few of them. Late incorporation into colonial and missionary projects meant general participation in Mumuye historic religion persisted longer than was the case for the neighboring Jukun or Chamba. As a result of this, figurative sculpting in wood continued in response to a demand for ritual use alongside a developing external market. The gelling of a Mumuye identity in the late colonial and early postcolonial periods encompassed a large population and an entire regional production, making the category of "Mumuye figures" particularly numerous

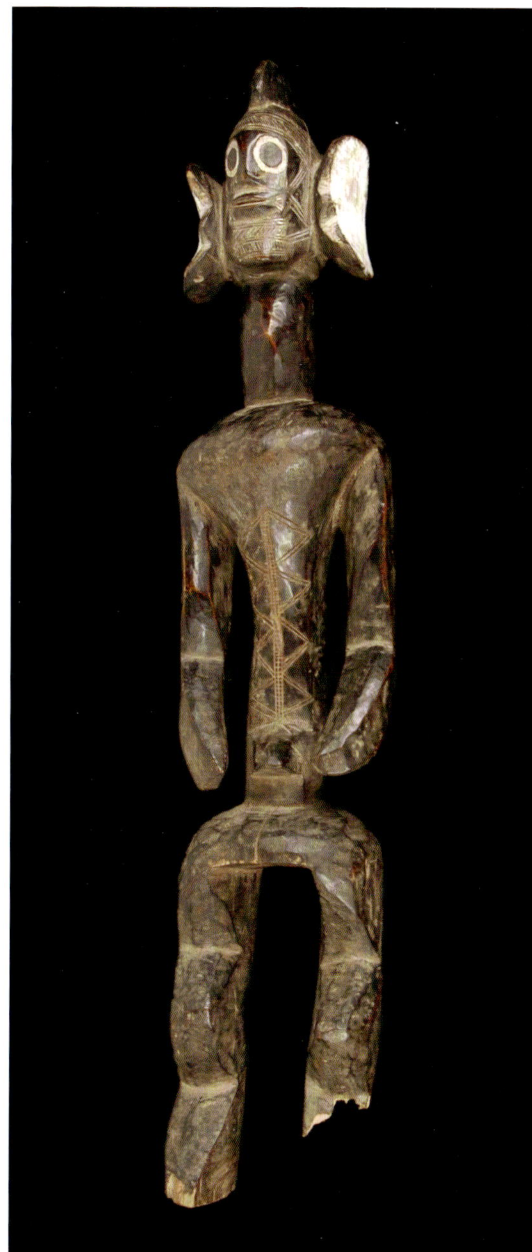

8.17
Single-figure statue
Mumuye peoples, 1960s or earlier
Wood, kaolin
H: 100 cm
MUSÉE DU QUAI BRANLY (EX-MUSÉE DE L'HOMME,
 ILLUSTRATED IN FRY 1970, 5, FIG. 2) 71.69.21.1
IMAGE: © 2010 MUSÉE DU QUAI BRANLY. PHOTO-
GRAPH BY SCALA/FLORENCE
(NOT IN EXHIBITON)

The acquisition of this Mumuye figure in 1969 by the Musée de l'Homme was one of the spurs to Philip Fry writing an important essay that defined Mumuye figure sculpture as a genre. Fry identifies the figure as female (1970, fig. 2 caption), but gendered anatomical detail appears absent (and a doubter might point to an Adam's apple as a possible indication of male gender). The facial features: sagittal crest, white circles for eyes, trumpet-shaped ears, lateral mouth and prominent chin are shared with some other Mumuye figures coming onto the market around the same time.

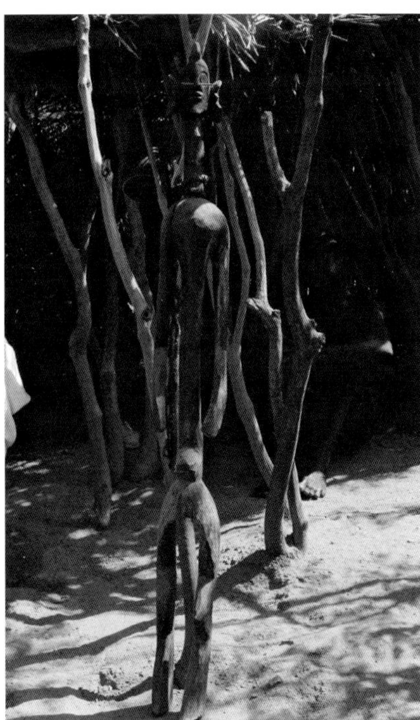

8.18
Philip Fry suggested that this elongated
figure, documented on the ground as the work
of the Mumuye sculptor Nyavo of Pantisawa,
resembled that acquired by the Musée de
l'Homme in 1969 (see fig. 8.17).
PHOTOGRAPH BY ARNOLD RUBIN, PANTISAWA,
OCTOBER 17, 1965, RUBIN ARCHIVE, FOWLER
MUSEUM AT UCLA, NEG. NO. 967.

and diverse. The expansion by predominantly African "runners" and European dealers of collecting circuits into the Middle Benue fed already-established art-trading
networks leading via Cameroon to Paris and Brussels and onward to New York. The
Biafran War loosened the Nigerian regulative framework, which might otherwise have
constrained the exodus of objects. Local Fulani emirs were already participants in
the effort to Islamize the Middle Belt as part of Northern Nigeria, so they supported
attempts to extirpate "paganism" and encouraged their District and Village Heads to
do the same. The monetary incentives with which "runners" were able to reward whoever either offered them artworks (whether or not they were their owners) or provided
them with opportunities to acquire artworks, added a further ingredient
to an already-rich brew.

In an attempt to stem the tide, the Nigerian Federal Department of Antiquities
(later the Nigerian National Commission for Museums and Monuments) in the Jos
Museum licensed selected dealers to supply the museum directly with sculptures.
It was too late, however, to bolt this proverbial stable door, the finest figures had
already fled. In the event, the museum probably received only those sculptures that
were of less appeal to European dealers, and the policy to halt the outflow of antiquities almost certainly had the effect of stimulating local artisanal activity oriented
toward this market. The surviving accession ledgers of the Jos Museum for 1972 give
some indication of the likely form that the trade had taken in the preceding years,
as the museum's capacity to process objects was overwhelmed by the productivity
of the dealers it licensed. A period between June and September 1972 is particularly
striking; several groups of objects (accessioned as 72J 39/41/45/46/47/48, each number referencing such a group), mostly statues, were acquired in batches of up to fifty
at a time from traders (presumably Hausa to judge by such names as Rabiu Garda,
Kawo Kano, Tanko Mohammed, and Abdul Wahabi Umaru). Individual statues
are recorded to have been bought from the traders for between £3 and £12 (£1 was
worth around US$2.50 at the time), depending apparently on size and condition
(the amounts paid by the traders to Mumuye would have been considerably less).
Ledger entries are repetitive, describing the acquisitions as *gunki* (i.e., "statue" in
Hausa) and claiming an age of fifty or more years for them (presumably to satisfy
one criterion for antiquities, since many show little sign of wear and tear). Where
collection details are provided at all, it appears that they were bought in or around
the regional capital of Jalingo, which had become a center of brokerage for antiquities more widely.

Rather than attempting mass comparison allied to rapid local surveys, which
might or might not have produced interesting results, later writers attempting to
reconstruct something of the contexts for Mumuye sculpture have relied on research
already carried out by the time Fry wrote his analysis in 1970. This is why, despite the
enormous increase in examples, it has proven difficult to improve on that analysis,
indeed the vast number of purported Mumuye artworks in circulation has become part
of the problem, because statues emerging since the 1970s have been unprovenanced
and of dubious authenticity even in the broadest sense (that is, of definitely having
been made by Mumuye carvers, whether contemporary or not). Two observations
about the early research on Mumuye art are telling. First, Mumuye statues were strikingly fugitive in situ. Given the extent of investigation and the scale of later outflow,
remarkably few were documented in the field before about 1968. Second, the statues
that were seen in the field during the mid-1960s largely lacked the overall artistic
quality that had made the earliest examples to arrive in Europe such a sensation, albeit
most of those photographed by Rubin in the field possessed the individual characteristics that identified figures as Mumuye for collectors. As we shall see later, these problems are compounded by the paucity of Mumuye statuary in European and American
collections before the late 1960s.

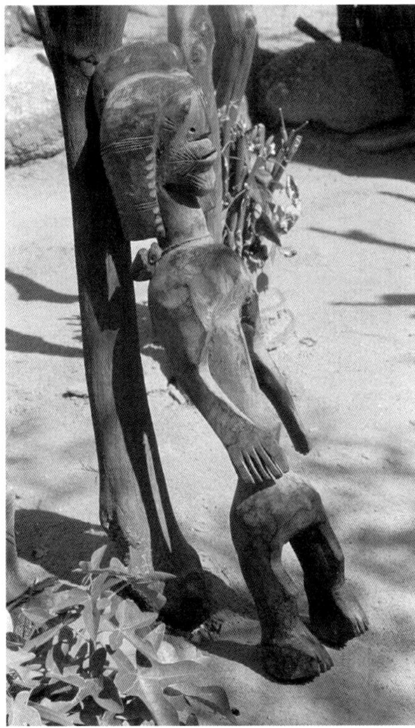

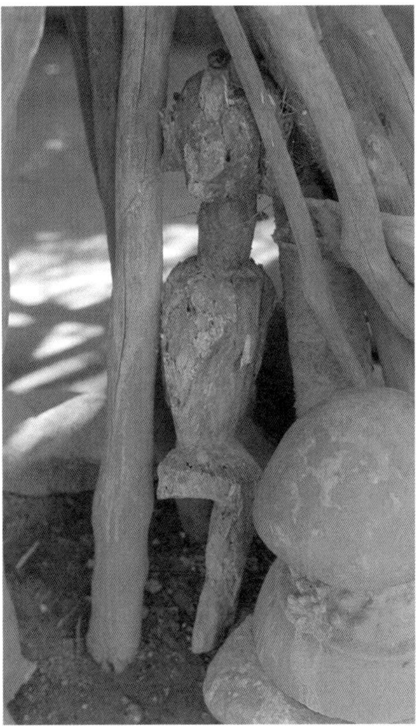

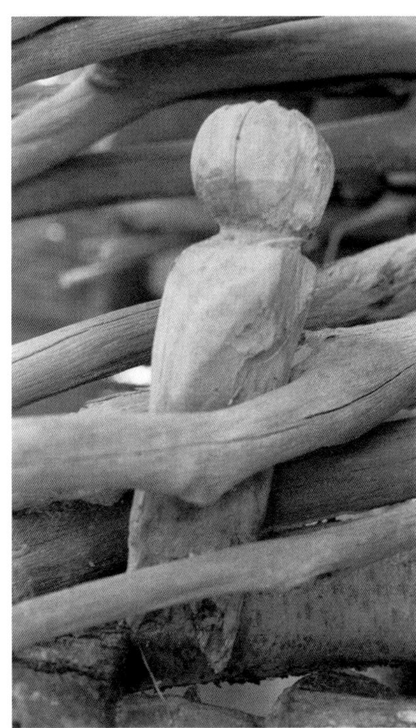

The Field Reports

Two investigators left us field records of Mumuye from the mid-1960s. Arnold Rubin[14] carried out the fieldwork on which his doctorate was based between 1964 and 1966, visiting Mumuye in October 1965, and he revisited Mumuye for short periods in 1970 and 1971, yet he writes that he saw fewer than a dozen figurative sculptures in all this time (of which at least five from the later period of research were donated to the Jos Museum: 70.J.88: 13, 48, 58, 59, 62, in a collection of altogether 191 objects). His field-notes suggest that Rubin saw and photographed slightly more examples than his later comment recalled, twenty statues (some in pairs), although he might have considered some of these too damaged to count. Quibbling aside, a figure between twelve and twenty remains remarkably low given his estimate (quoted above) that several thousand figures were circulating in the artworld. Rubin's field researches, like those of Mette Bovin around the same time, serve to heighten rather than resolve the mystery surrounding the most celebrated of the Mumuye figurative artworks.

Writing at the end of the 1960s, Philip Fry was able to draw only upon the earlier of Rubin's two periods of Mumuye fieldwork, which Rubin had described in a letter written to Fry's wife, Jacqueline Delange Fry, early in 1968. On this basis, Philip Fry suggested resemblance between the Mumuye statue that entered the Musée de l'Homme in 1969 (fig. 8.17) and another that Rubin had photographed in a village near Jalingo, and attributed to a carver called Nyavo (1970, 8, fig.5; fig. 8.18). He ventured that the two were probably by the same hand.[15] Rubin had met Nyavo in October 1965, and in interview it transpired that Nyavo had begun to carve only four years previously, after observing his father at work for three years. The four figures Rubin documented on this occasion remained in the possession of the carver for his own use. Six years later Rubin came across another of Nyavo's figures in a village a little distance from Pantisawa (Popoli), suggesting that his reputation had consolidated in the intervening years (see fig. 8.22). The four of his own works that remained in Nyavo's possession in 1965 were quite diverse, ranging from a sturdy figure with pendant earflaps (fig. 8.19) to the taller, slimmer figure with elongated neck and ears shaped like flaring horns, which Fry was to find similar to that in Paris (see fig. 8.18). The other two figures (figs. 8.20, 8.21) are equally diverse, so that Nyavo's figures seem to share little beyond symmetrically sloping shoulders and hips, and legs carved with

8.19
Nyavo's figure sculptures differed quite widely from one another, as this example, also documented by Arnold Rubin, demonstrates. All those Rubin saw in 1965, however, were identified as "Jagana." Several similar figures have reached the international art market.
PHOTOGRAPH BY ARNOLD RUBIN, PANTISAWA, OCTOBER 17, 1965, RUBIN ARCHIVE, FOWLER MUSEUM AT UCLA, NEG. NO. 965.

8.20
Extreme weathering does not always mean great age. Although this figure looked old in 1965, Nyavo told Rubin that he had carved it only two years earlier but discovered that the wood was not good.
PHOTOGRAPH BY ARNOLD RUBIN, PANTISAWA, OCTOBER 17, 1965, RUBIN ARCHIVE, FOWLER MUSEUM AT UCLA, NEG. NO. 970.

8.21
Nyavo told Rubin that this was his earliest attempt at figure sculpture carved in 1961. It is very rudimentary in form compared to the subtlety he was soon to achieve.
PHOTOGRAPH BY ARNOLD RUBIN, PANTISAWA, OCTOBER 17, 1965, RUBIN ARCHIVE, FOWLER MUSEUM AT UCLA, NEG. NO. 971.

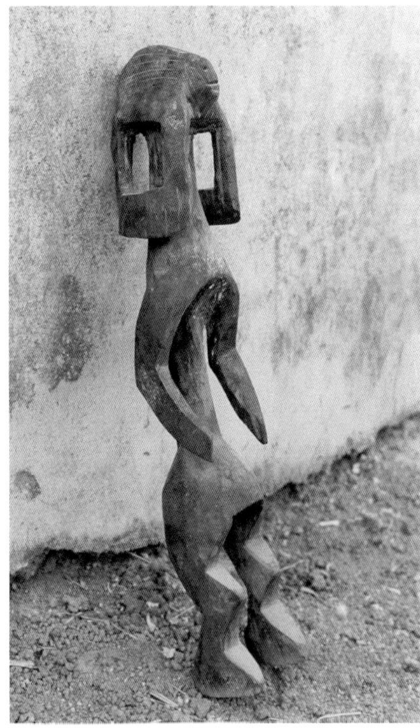 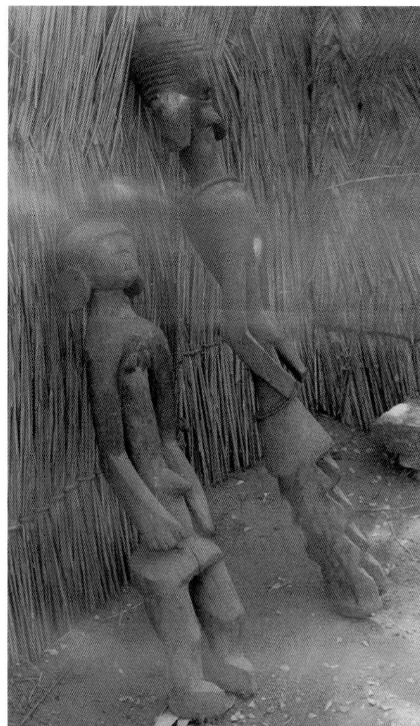 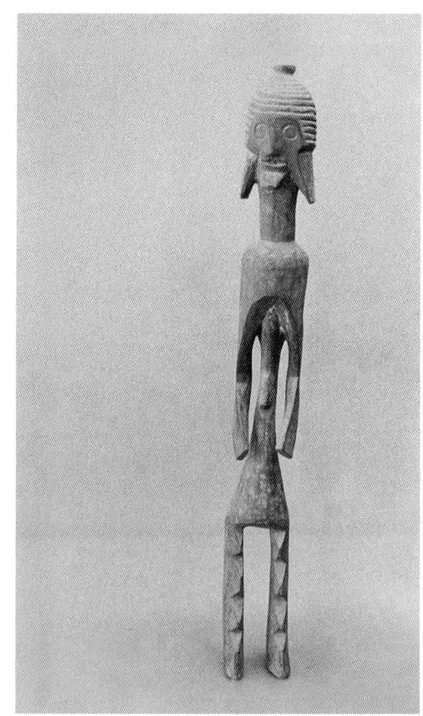

8.22

Another figure attributed to Nyavo of Panti-sawa that had been carved around 1968 was photographed by Arnold Rubin in 1971, where it had been bought as a divination figure and was called Tsovon (chicken pox.) The overall body shape remains similar to some of Nyavo's earlier work (figs 8.18, 8.19), however, the head has been simplified, and the openwork ears designate a female subject.

PHOTOGRAPH BY ARNOLD RUBIN, POPOLI, FEBRU-ARY 19, 1971, RUBIN ARCHIVE, FOWLER MUSEUM AT UCLA, NEG. NO. 3138.

8.23a,b

Arnold Rubin photographed a pair of *jagana* figures in Pantisawa in 1965 that were attrib-uted by their elderly owner to a deceased carver he identified as Kubwen of Dila (fig. 8.23a). This negative seems to have been partly exposed before developing, but sufficient detail remains to recognize the taller male fig-ure in the background, or one identical to it, as a figure that entered a private collection soon afterward and was published by Fry (1970, 16, fig. 11; fig. 8.23b). Two figures now in public collections in the United States are similar and may also be the work of Kubwen (cf. figs. 11.21, 11.22)

PHOTOGRAPHS BY ARNOLD RUBIN, PANTISAWA, OCTOBER 17, 1965, RUBIN ARCHIVE, FOWLER MUSEUM AT UCLA. FIGURE 8.23A: NEG. NO. 962. FIGURE 8.23B: NEG. NO. 1918.

a single notch at their knees. We might interpret this diversity in the work of one carver either as a counsel of caution about claims to detect the hand of any particular Mumuye artist at work, or else as an indication that Nyavo was experimenting before settling on his own style or styles.

Figures Documented by Rubin as Carved by Nyavo (1965, 1971)

RUBIN'S FIELD PHOTOGRAPH REFERENCE, *NON-FIELD PHOTOGRAPH REFERENCE*	DATE	PLACE	OBJECT	OWNER/ CURRENT OWNER	CARVER/ APPROX. DATE	SEE FIG.
964-5-6, *1901*	17 Oct 1965	Pantisawa	figure	Nyavo, Probably in Jos Museum	Nyavo, 1963	8.19
967-8-9	17 Oct 1965	Pantisawa	figure	Nyavo	Nyavo, 1963	8.18
970-1	17 Oct 1965	Pantisawa	2 figures	Nyavo	Nyavo, 1961-63	8.20, 8.21
3137-8	18 Feb 1971	Popoli	figure	Mwochuku	Nyavo, 1968	8.22

Aside from Nyavo, Rubin documented the work of only two other figure carvers during his 1965 investigations among Mumuye, though neither appeared in Fry's account. In Pantisawa he saw a pair of figures attributed by their elderly owner to a deceased carver he identified as Kubwen of Dila from whom he had bought them as a younger man (fig. 8.23a,b); another pair of figures in the possession of the Panti Lapo, eponymous head of Pantilapo, had been bought eighteen years previously from a village he called Gulum, although the name of their carver was unknown to him (fig. 8.24).

Figures Documented by Rubin as Carved by Kubwen of Dila and an Anonymous Artist (1965)

RUBIN'S FIELD PHOTOGRAPH REFERENCE, *NON-FIELD PHOTOGRAPH REFERENCE*	DATE	PLACE	OBJECT	OWNER/ CURRENT OWNER	CARVER/ APPROXIMATE DATE	SEE FIG.
961-2-3, *1918* of male figure only	17 Oct 1965	Pantisawa	Male (larger) and female figures	Mashi Male figure in private collection?	Kubwen of Dila, 1950	8.23a,b
983, 984-6, 994-5	17 Oct 1965	Pantilapo	Female of paired figures	Panti Lapo	unknown (bought in Gulum, 1947)	8.24
983, 987-9, 990-3	17 Oct 1965	Pantilapo	Male of paired figures	Panti Lapo	unknown (bought in Gulum, 1947)	8.24

Although they did not meet, the anthropologist Mette Bovin, who was another of Fry's correspondents, undertook field researches among Mumuye at the same time as Arnold Rubin (for some months in 1964 and 1968). She saw very few statues, or indeed masks, something we might have attributed entirely to her status as a young woman, as Bovin herself suggests (see p. 375), had the same not been the case for Rubin. As she relates in her memoir (chapter 11, pp. 379, 382), in 1964 Bovin bought figures (see fig. 11.18) via an intermediary that had been carved by a blacksmith called Musa Dafe (Musa from the small village of Dafe, near Monkin, which is well to the east of Zinna, present-day Zing). A male and female couple of these is illustrated by Philip Fry (1970, 25, fig. 21). The male, crested, figure had subsequently been donated to the Jos Museum in Nigeria (64J.179). Bovin allowed her field photograph of this same figure to be published by Rubin (1978, 107, fig. 29), which showed it displayed by the intermediary who delivered it, Dikko Barau Zinna (presumably Dikko Barau of Zinna). The female pair to this figure, which lacks a sagittal crest, seems to be that given to the collection of the Moesgård Museum. Such figures were used to swear oaths in the district court of Zinna, for which purpose a similar pair had been acquired by the Wakili (Muslim judge). The Jos accession note applies the term *janari* to this figure. A second figure that Bovin donated to the Jos Museum (64J.1.180) was much more crudely carved. It is described as a "talking" statue called Langanang in the possession of Abdullahi Wali

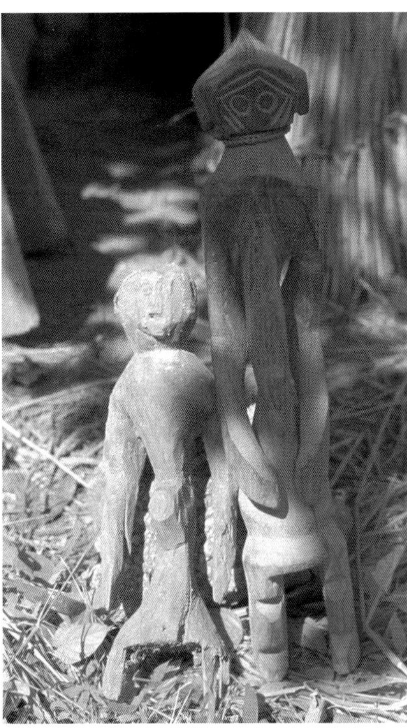

8.24
These figures, the "children" of the Vaa-Bong cult, were photographed in 1965 when in the possession of the Panti Lapo, the head of Pantilapo village. He had bought the pair around 1947 to replace "spoiled" figures. He did not know the name of the sculptor, since the figures had been taken from the place where masks were kept in the village of Gulum and sold to him. The taller male figure has incisions on its face in the shape of a pentagram (missing its lower side). The smaller, female, of the two figures is reminiscent of a figure Bovin documented from Yoro (see fig. 11.19).
PHOTOGRAPH BY ARNOLD RUBIN, PANTILAPO, OCTOBER 19, 1965, RUBIN ARCHIVE, FOWLER MUSEUM AT UCLA, NEG. NO. 983.

8.25 (TOP LEFT)

This non-matching pair of *janari* divination figures was said to be a mother and daughter. The larger statue was attributed by their owner, Zin Tanru of Zinna, to the carver Kwenza, who lived at Kpmezan on the mountain near Pantisawa. It had been carved about three months previously. In some respects, it is similar in style to that attributed to Nyavo (see fig. 8.18) who also lived in Pantisawa. The smaller figure was bought a year earlier but no information on its provenance is given. Rubin field collected both examples, giving the larger to the Nigerian Federal Department of Antiquities.

PHOTOGRAPH BY ARNOLD RUBIN, ZINNA, APRIL 4, 1970, RUBIN ARCHIVE, FOWLER MUSEUM AT UCLA, NEG. NO. 2570.

8.26 (TOP RIGHT)

This small and roughly carved female figure, photographed in the village of Kasa in 1970, had been made three years earlier by its owner, Mako, for his own use. Called *lagana* it was held capable of afflicting enemies with smallpox and also assisting in childbirth. Mako claimed this was the only figure he had carved.

PHOTOGRAPH BY ARNOLD RUBIN, KASA, APRIL 9, 1970, RUBIN ARCHIVE, FOWLER MUSEUM AT UCLA, NEG. NO. 2595.

8.27 (BOTTOM LEFT)

The larger of these two male figures, called Suyoro, was claimed by its owner Vabun to have been carved around 1930 by a sculptor named Dashi. The smaller figure, called Gwalun Yoro, belonged to Salifu, and was the work of Malika. It had been acquired around the same time as the larger figure. In some respects, this smaller figure is similar to the trumpet-eared figure attributed to Nyavo. Both figures were claimed to come from Yoro, where Rubin was assured both women and men inserted ornaments into pierced nasal septa.

PHOTOGRAPH BY ARNOLD RUBIN, KASA, APRIL 9, 1970, RUBIN ARCHIVE, FOWLER MUSEUM AT UCLA, NEG. NO. 2597.

8.28 (BOTTOM RIGHT)

This male figure identified as Supa was in the possession of Gantome of Monkin. It had been carved by Majeladinki of Zaro, near Pantisawa, around 1955. The most remarkable feature of this figure is its "scarification" both on the face and torso. Rubin acquired it for the Federal Department of Antiquities.

PHOTOGRAPH BY ARNOLD RUBIN APRIL 11, 1970, MONKIN, RUBIN ARCHIVE, FOWLER MUSEUM AT UCLA, NEG. NO. 2600.

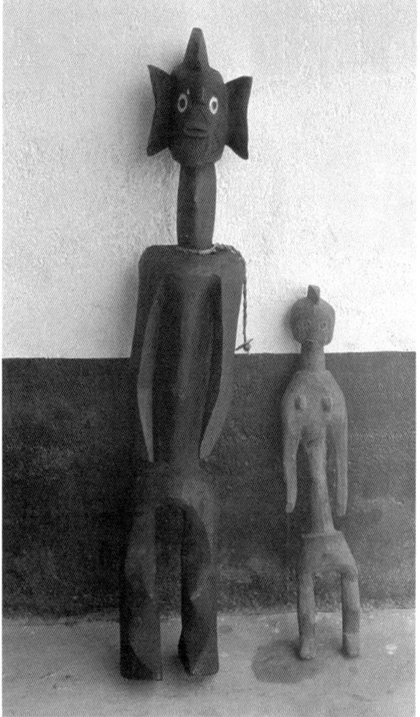

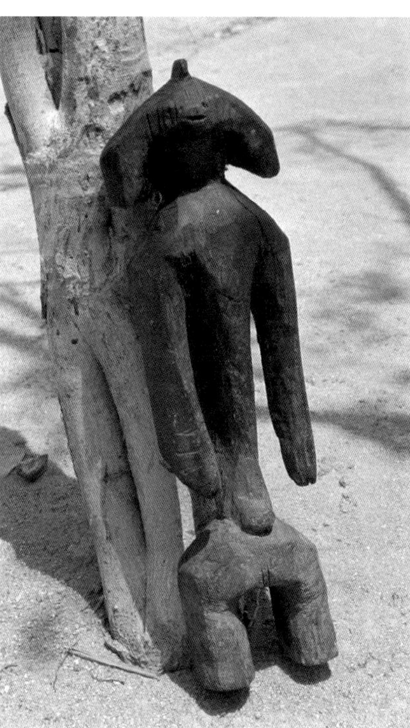

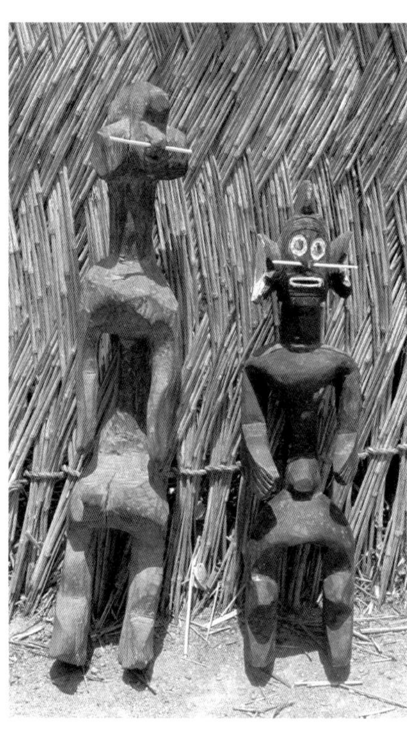

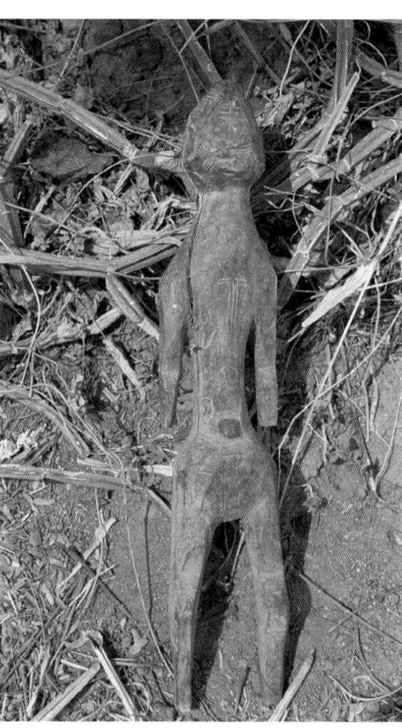

of Yoro (a place discussed below). Along with its owner, it was also illustrated by Fry (1970, 26, fig. 22; this photograph is from the same series as fig. 11.19).

Five years after his initial researches, Arnold Rubin returned to continue fieldwork in the Middle Benue visiting Mumuye in April 1970 and February 1971. The first occasion found him around Monkin and Zinna, east and northeast of Jalingo, where he documented another ten figures that might have been the work of as many as eight carvers (figs. 8.25–8.32). In 1971 he added two more figures and perhaps another couple of carvers. In total, that is eleven named figure sculptors in the three visits, plus perhaps another three unnamed. Add those identified by Bovin, and a considerable number of sculptors were at work, certainly sufficient to fulfill the ritual needs of this cash-poor region.

Figures Documented by Rubin (1970–1971)

RUBIN'S FIELD PHOTOGRAPH REFERENCE, *NON-FIELD PHOTOGRAPH REFERENCE*	DATE	PLACE	OBJECT	OWNER/ CURRENT OWNER OR JOS MUSEUM ACCESSSION	CARVER/ APPROX. DATE	SEE FIG.
2570, *3308 WF4 (mother)* *3310 WF8 (daughter)*	4 April 1970	Zinna	Mother (taller) and daughter	Zin Tanru 70.J.88.62 Zin Tanru Private collection?	Kwenza of Kpmezan, near Pantisawa, 1970 Unknown, 1969	8.25
2595	9 April 1970	Kasa	Female figure	Mako	Mako, 1967	8.26
2597-8	9 April 1970	Kasa	2 male figures	Vabun (larger) Salifu	Dashi of Yoro, 1930 Malika of Yoro, 1930	8.27
2600 *3310 WF9*	11 April 1970	Monkin	Male figure	Gantome 70J.88.48	Majeladinki of Zaro, near Pantisawa, 1955	8.28
2567-8, *3308 WF5*	4 April 1970	Monkin	Male figure	Jauro Konko Private collecton?	Da'inyauware, 1960	8.29a,b
3310 WF6 *3312 WFO*	21 April 1970	Pantisawa	Male and female figures	Panti Sawa 70J.88.58 70J.88.59	Unknown, inherited by owner	8.30
3096-7 *3324 WF32*	16 Feb 1971	Garin Kachella	figure	Kuzo 70J.88.13	Unknown, from Monkin market, 1966	8.31
3113-4	17 Feb 1971	Pantibelli	figure	Aga	Madin, bought at Pantisawa, 1951	8.32

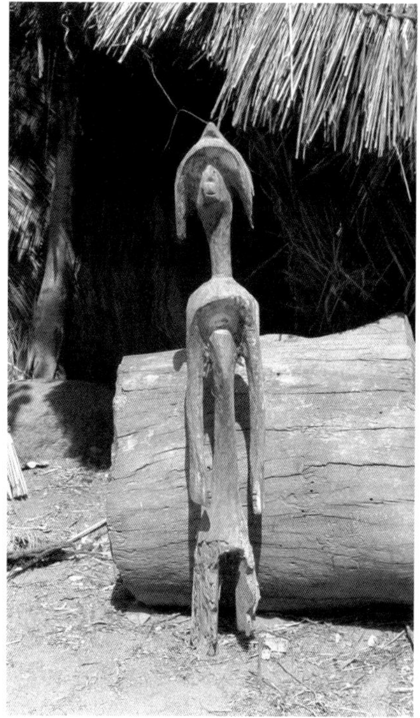

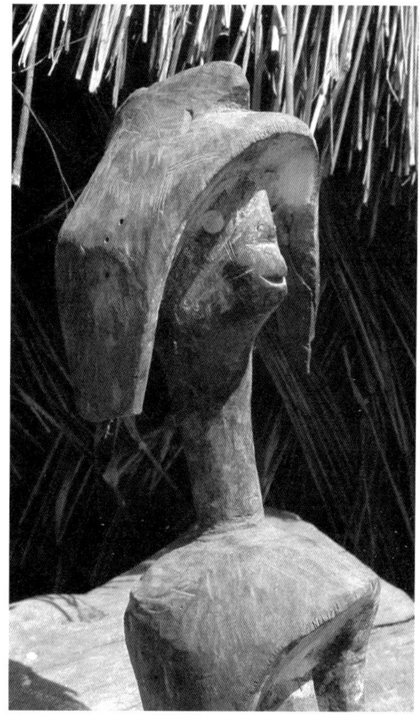

8.29a,b

This male figure called Supa, collected in the field by Arnold Rubin, is the only example of a sculpture attributed to Da'inyauware. It was said to have been carved around 1960. In overall conception—a hooded face, with long arms, hands angled toward the horizontal, short notched legs, and a formal resonance between the hood, shoulders, and hips—it resembles many of the most famous Mumuye figures (see figs 8.33 and 8.34).

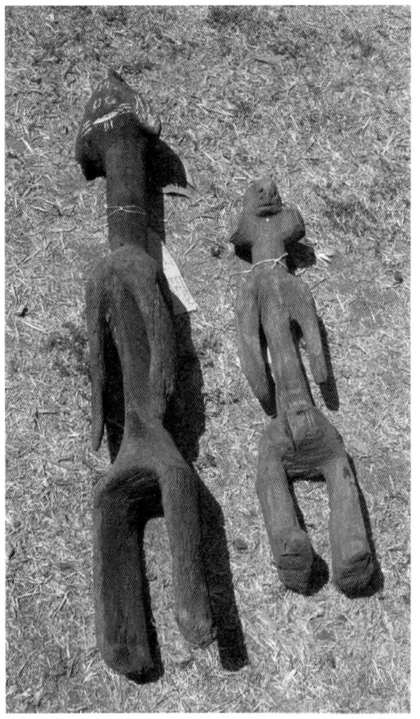

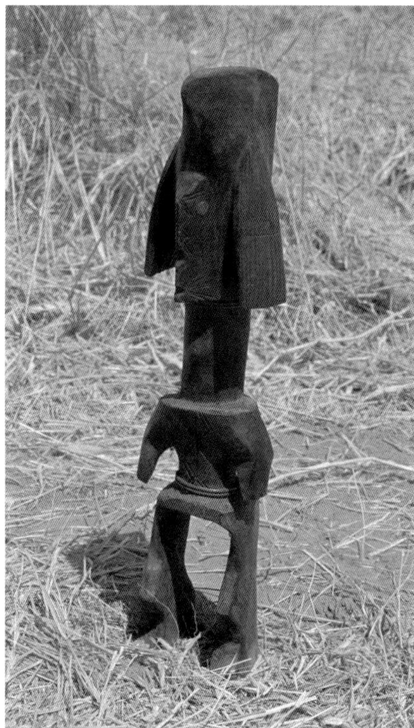

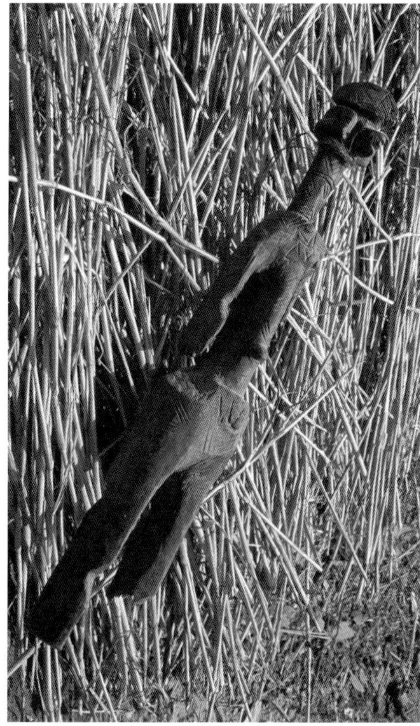

8.30

A pair of male and female *lagana* divination figures photographed in the compound of the Panti Sawa and acquired by Rubin for the Federal Department of Antiquities.

PHOTOGRAPH BY ARNOLD RUBIN APRIL 21, 1970, RUBIN ARCHIVE, FOWLER MUSEUM AT UCLA, NEG. NO. 3312.

8.31

This squat, square *lagana* divination figure was bought by Kuzo of the village of Garin Kachella from Monkin market around 1965. It was acquired by Rubin for the Federal Department of Antiquities.

PHOTOGRAPH BY ARNOLD RUBIN, GARIN KACHELLA, FEBRUARY 16, 1971, RUBIN ARCHIVE, FOWLER MUSEUM AT UCLA, NEG. NO. 3096.

8.32

Owned by Aga of Pantibelli, this *lagana* divination figure was purchased around 1950 in Pantisawa. It had been carved by Madin.

PHOTOGRAPH BY ARNOLD RUBIN FEBRUARY 17, 1971, RUBIN ARCHIVE, FOWLER MUSEUM AT UCLA, NEG. NO. 3113.

From the Field to the Gallery

Can connections be drawn between the ethnographic record of texts and examples provided by Bovin and Rubin and the acknowledged masterpieces of Mumuye sculpture that entered the artworld in the late 1960s? The most ambitious attempt made in this direction to date has been the identification of an artist whom Bernard de Grunne (2001, 85–86) has dubbed the "Master of the Pantisawa workshops." While the ambition is laudable, the claim merits careful attention, because some of the steps in de Grunne's reasoning toward it strike me as difficult to defend.

The strongest part of de Grunne's argument starts from observation of the close resemblance between two imposing Mumuye figures: one in the Metropolitan Museum of Art in New York (1983.189, Tishman Gift; fig. 8.33), the other in the Fondation Beyeler in Basel (de Grunne 2001, 87; fig. 8.34). Both are heavily hooded (see below) and have legs only a third of the height of their torsos, a feature of what de Grunne calls *"style trapu"* (a thickset or stocky style) and claims to be the most classical of Mumuye sculptural styles, though quite what *"classique"* means here, other than particularly appreciated by European connoisseurs, is unclear. De Grunne also claims to discover anthropo-zoomorphic ambiguity in the faces of these figures, a proposition that strikes me as unlikely both on general and particular grounds. The general argument against it is that Middle Benue figures seem almost invariably to be anthropomorphic except where they are clearly composed of a human body and mask-like head in an almost telltale relation to masquerade. The more particular argument concerns the conventions for indicating the features of the heads of Mumuye figures (on which more below). The heads of these two pieces are surmounted by pointed helmets, like those documented as worn by Mumuye men, particularly warriors. The headdresses obscure most of the figures' faces, and this causes some displacement of their features. De Grunne bolsters his argument for anthropo-zoomorphic ambiguity by reference to a third figure in an unnamed private collection, which he claims to be by the same hand as those in New York and Basel (2001, 89, cat. 21). While I agree with de Grunne that the Metropolitan Museum and Beyeler Mumuye figures are almost certainly by the same master carver, I do not believe this of the third figure he adduces. One small detail is particularly telling: the Metropolitan Museum and Beyeler Mumuye figures share a distinctive rendering of their wrists and hands, which is entirely absent from

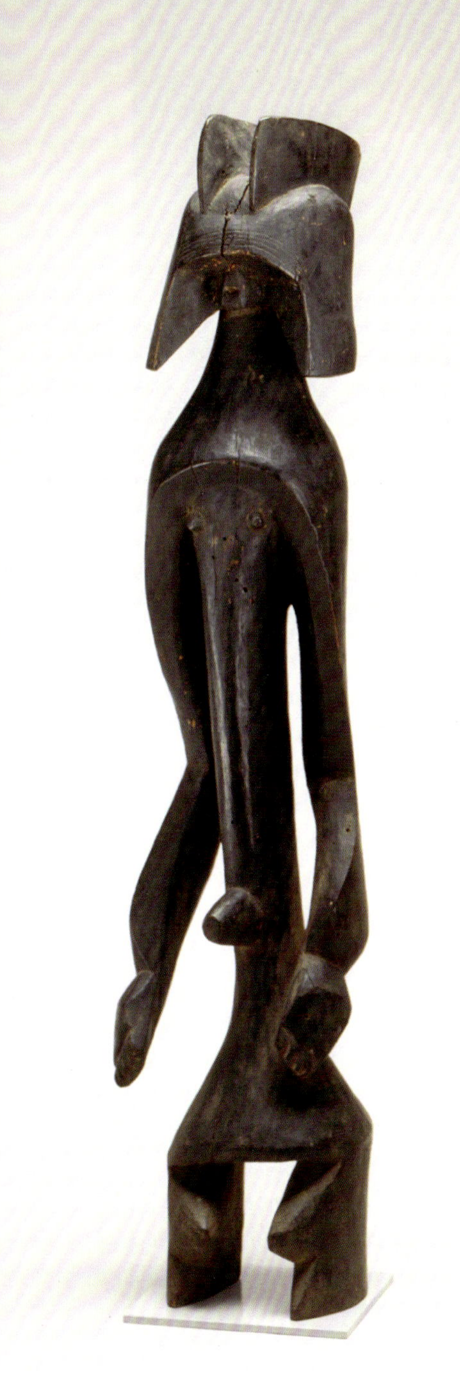

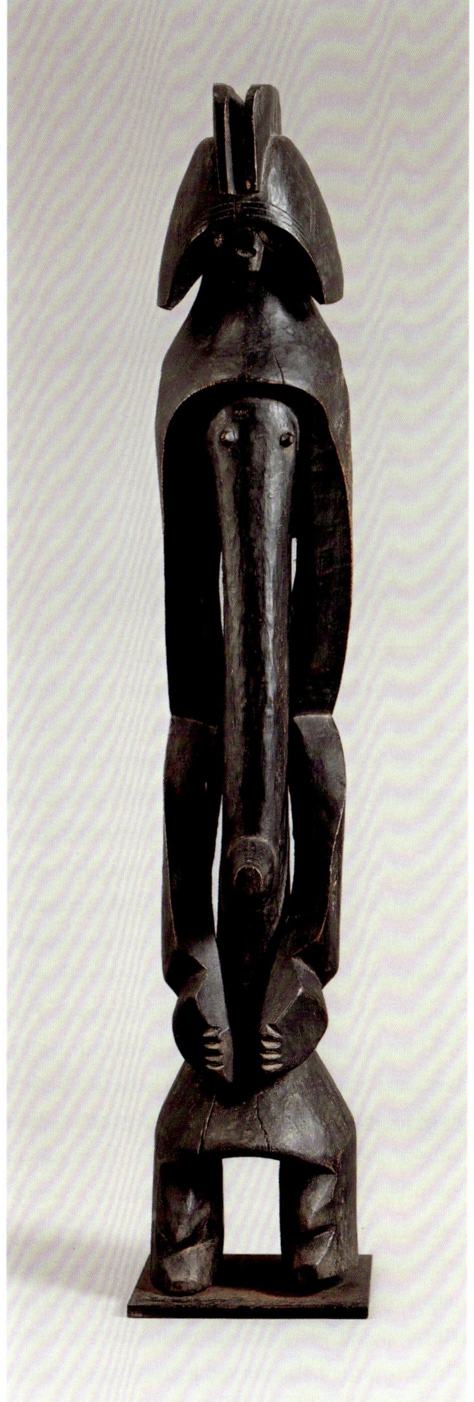

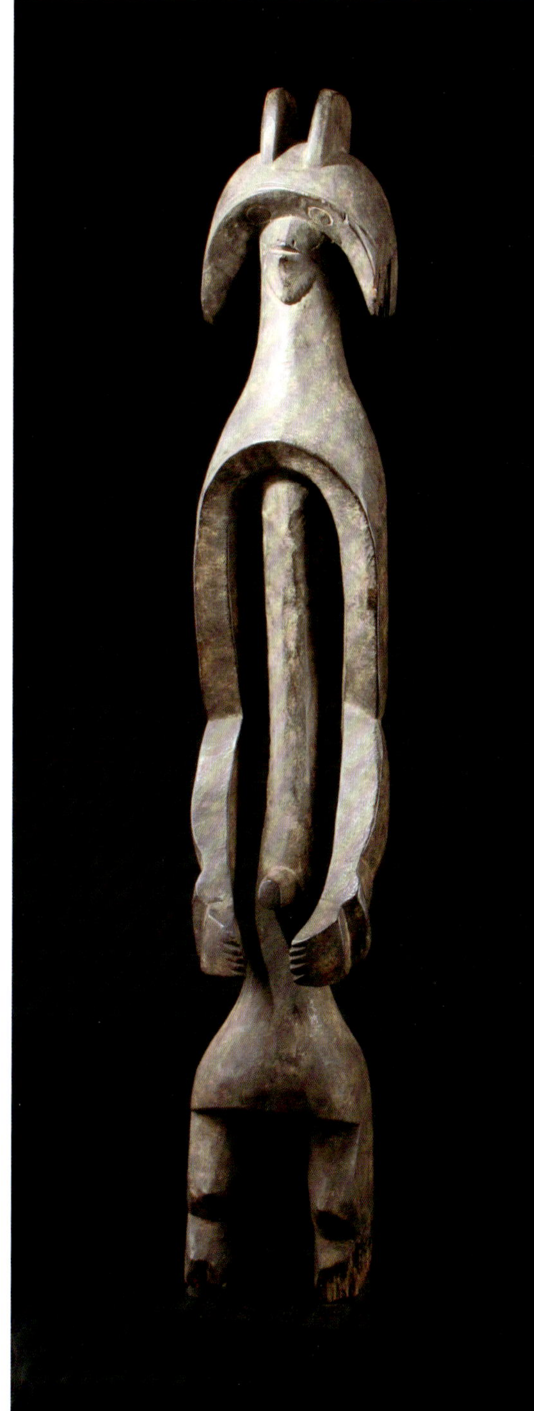

8.33
Freestanding statue
Mumuye peoples, nineteenth to twentieth century
Wood
H: 93.3 cm
METROPOLITAN MUSEUM OF ART 1983.189; GIFT OF PAUL AND RUTH W. TISHMAN, 1983
IMAGE: © THE METROPOLITAN MUSEUM OF ART/ ART RESOURCE, N.Y. PHOTOGRAPH BY SCHECTER LEE
(NOT IN EXHIBITION)

Among the most celebrated of Mumuye statues, this tall figure has a deep patina, elegant headdress with double crests, long arms with well-delineated wrists and hands, and very short notched legs. The entire figure is flexed.

8.34
Freestanding statue
Mumuye peoples, nineteenth to twentieth century
Wood
H: 99 cm
FONDATION BEYELER, RIEHEN/BASEL
PHOTOGRAPH BY PETER SCHIBLI, BASEL
(NOT IN EXHIBITION)

This figure is almost certainly by the carver of the Mumuye statue in the Metropolitan Museum of Art (fig. 8.33). Its arms are held slightly closer to its body, but it has the same wrists and hands. Again, the headdress obscures most of the face and may impart an overall phallic form to the statue.

8.35
Freestanding statue
Mumuye peoples, nineteenth to twentieth century
Wood
H: 98 cm
UDO AND WALLY HORSTMANN, ZUG
PHOTOGRAPH BY UDO HORSTMANN
PROVENANCE: GALERIE DUPERRIER, PARIS, 1980

This figure seems to be closely related to those in the Metropolitan Museum of Art (fig. 8.33) and the Fondation Beyeler (fig. 8.34). In addition to an overall similarity in conception, the modeling of the hands is unlikely to be independent.

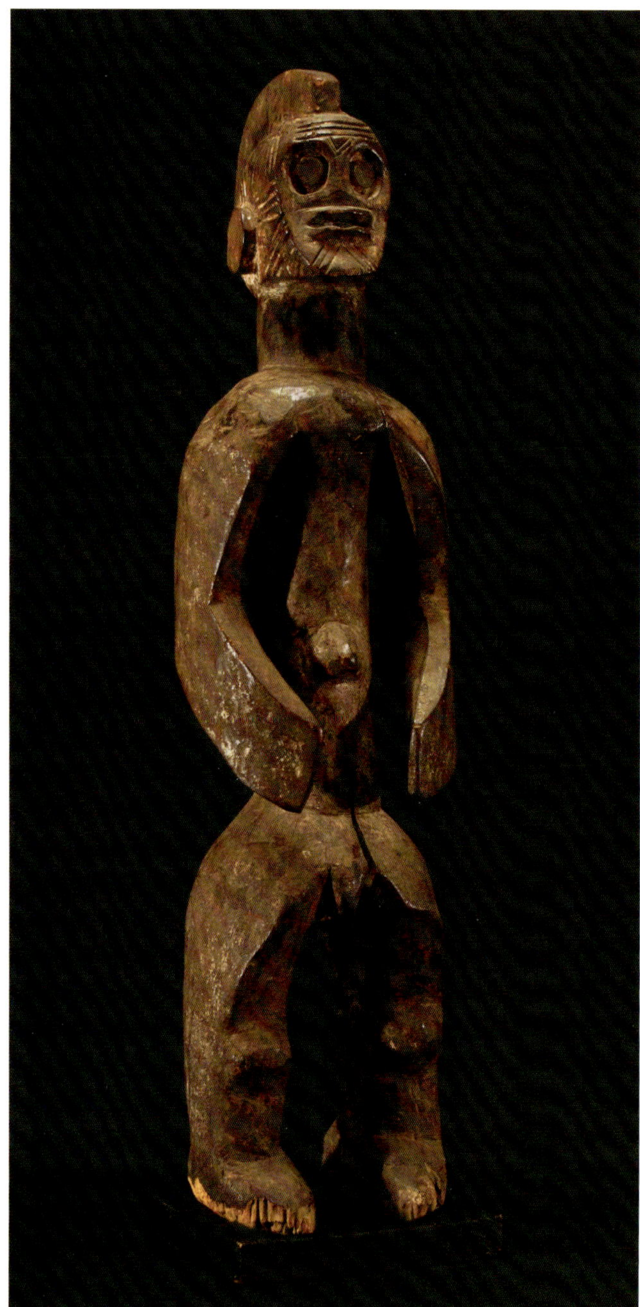

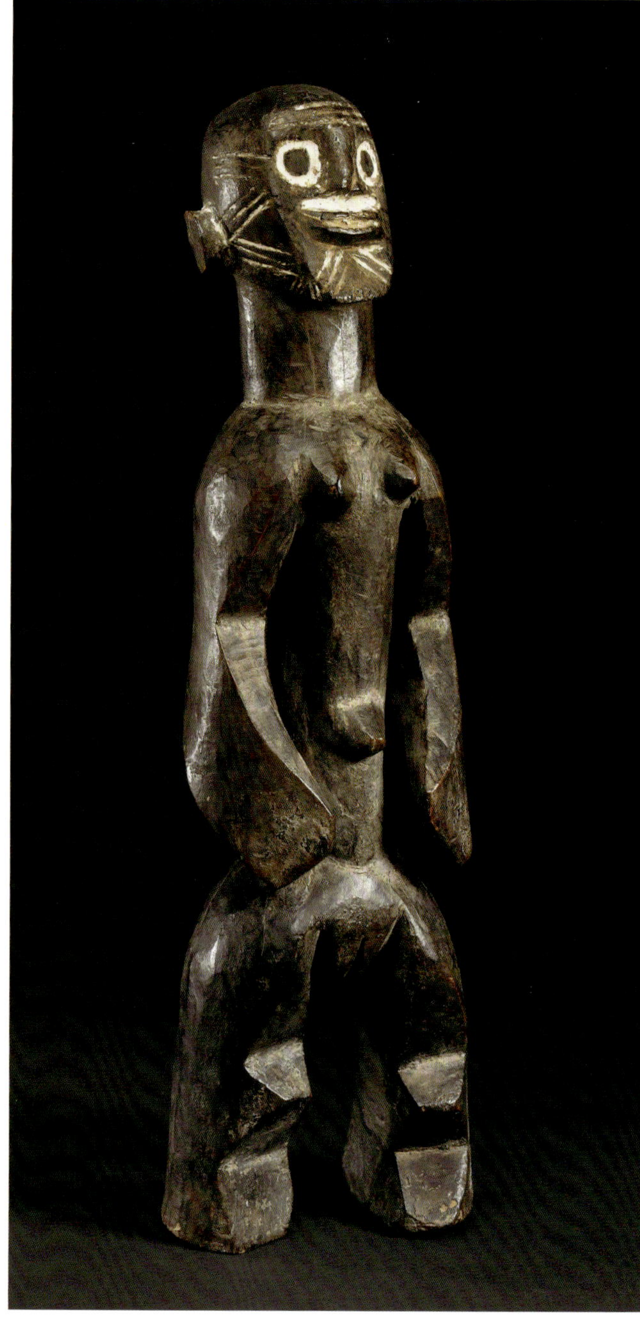

8.38

Male freestanding statue
Mumuye peoples, before 1958
Wood, pigment
H: 57 cm
SIEBER FAMILY COLLECTION
IMAGE: © 2010, MATHERS MUSEUM OF WORLD
CULTURES. PHOTOGRAPH BY
BRIAN KRECIK AND MATTHEW SIEBER.
PROVENANCE: COLLECTED BY ROY SIEBER, 1958

In 1958, twenty-seven years after Lilley
collected a female figure from Binyeri, Roy
Sieber acquired an all but identical male
counterpart to it. This male figure shows wear,
including fading of the white kaolin highlights
around its eyes, consistent with an extended
period of use. That the two figures of this
"pair" are differentiated by gendered features
corresponds more closely to Chamba than
it does to Mumuye conventions. The male
figure may retain remnants of an overall red
ocher coloring (which on occasions whitens
in collected examples). If it is indeed the case
that the male figure was originally red, and
its female "pair" black, this scheme would
correspond to Chamba conventions (as, for
instance, in the matched pair of male and
female figures Lilley collected at the same
time and place).

8.39

Female freestanding statue
Mumuye peoples, before 1921
Wood
H: 48 cm
THE TRUSTEES OF THE BRITISH MUSEUM,
AF1922, 0610.2
IMAGE: © TRUSTEES OF THE BRITISH MUSEUM.
PHOTOGRAPH BY MICHAEL ROW, 2010
PROVENANCE: COLLECTED BY E. S. LILLEY, 1921

This female figure, with a deep black patina
with white highlights, was collected together
with a male with which it had formed a
non-matching pair (fig. 8.40). It was initially
attributed to Chamba, but like the male, it
has subsequently been attributed to Mumuye.
As Philip Fry noticed in his insightful review,
however, the proportions of the stocky figure
are as reminiscent of Chamba as they are of
Mumuye figures.

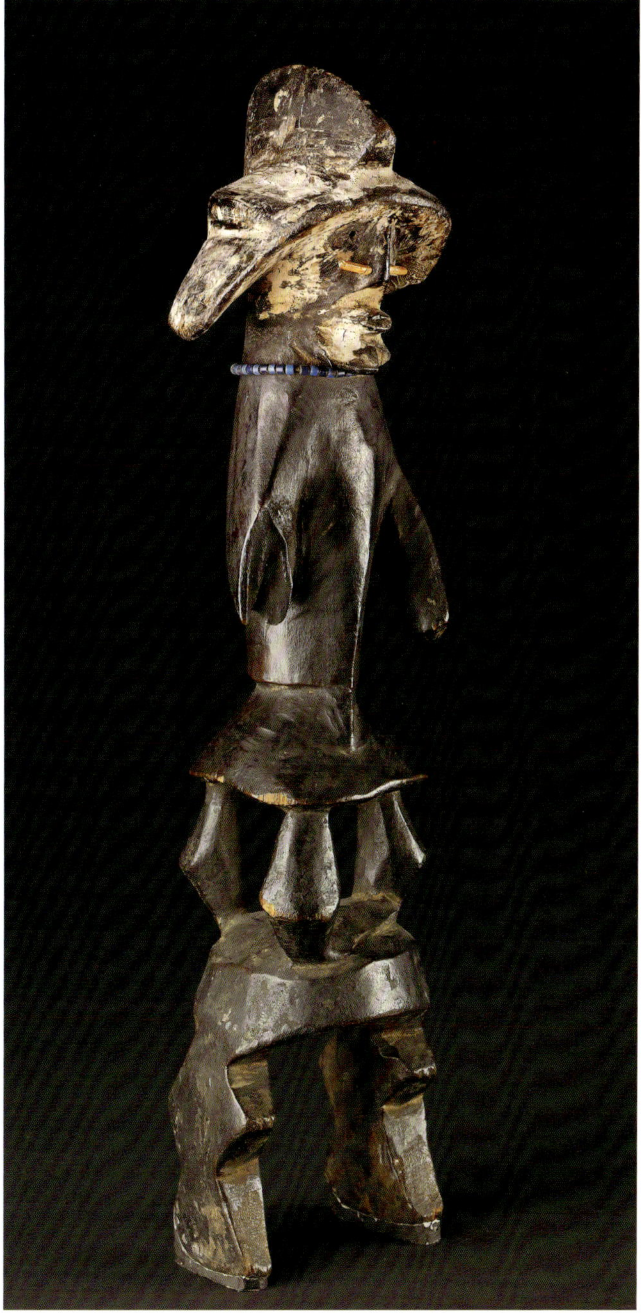

8.40
Small male freestanding statue
Mumuye, before 1921
Wood
H: 47 cm
THE TRUSTEES OF THE BRITISH MUSEUM,
AF1922, 0610.3
IMAGE: © TRUSTEES OF THE BRITISH MUSEUM.
PHOTOGRAPH BY MICHAEL ROW, 2010
PROVENANCE: COLLECTED BY E. S. LILLEY, 1921

This male figure was collected in 1921 by
Assistant District Officer E. S. Lilley from
Binyeri, a Chamba-ruled chiefdom in the
northern Shebshi Mountains, which included
large numbers of Mumuye in its population. It
was accessioned as Chamba but has since been
attributed to Mumuye, which seems appropriate on general grounds of style; however,
nothing quite like it has been collected subsequently. Three small columns of wood separate
the top and bottom masses of the hips. The
figure is slightly skewed, from its lopsided helmet through the central line of the torso, which
leans toward the left arm and continues right
across the hip in what might represent a penis.

feature typical of Chamba volumetric figures rather than of Mumuye figures, suggesting either that the sculptor was not Mumuye or was versed in a non-Mumuye idiom.

The male in this pair of Lilley figures (see fig. 8.40) was the more exceptional,
unlike anything collected since. A small piece with a deep black patina, the head is
surmounted by a crested, conical hat-like protrusion. Its face, whitened like its helmet,
is fully featured, and the nose pierced to accommodate a laterally inserted twig. The
figure's lips protrude almost in a pout, and its chiseled chin seems to end in a goatee;
it wears a necklace of blue and black cylindrical beads. Of the figure's arms, which are
triangular in section, the right is broken, and the left (if intact) short by the standards
of Mumuye figures. Uniquely the hips of the figure, which are solid in all other examples, have been made into openwork by separating their top and bottom masses with
three small pillars that are straight-edged on their inner surface but echo the angles of
the elbows and knees on their outer side. The entire figure has a slight asymmetry or
twist, from its lopsided helmet, to the central line of the torso, which leans toward the
left arm and continues right across the hip in what might represent a penis.

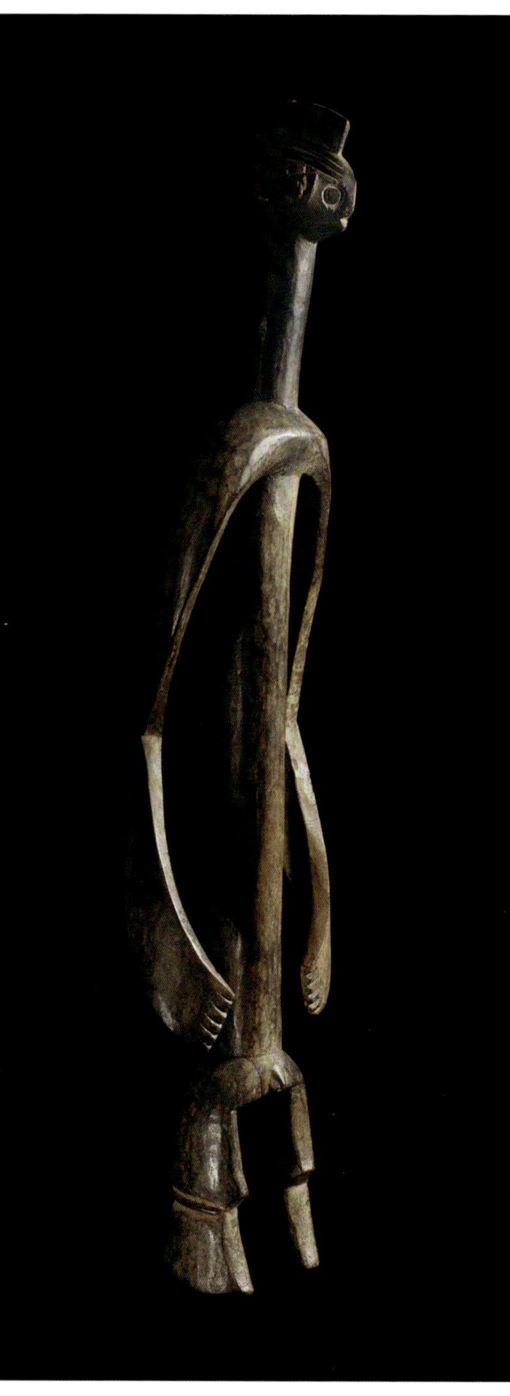

8.41
Freestanding statue
Mumuye peoples, nineteenth to twentieth
century
Wood
H: 100 cm
MUSÉE DU QUAI BRANLY, PARIS, 70.2005.21.3C
IMAGE: © 2010 MUSÉE DU QUAI BRANLY. PHOTO-
GRAPH BY PATRICK GRIES/SCALA, FLORENCE
PROVENANCE: ANNE KERCHACHE

The variety of Mumuye figures—some like
this one willowy with slender elongated torsos
and short legs—enthused early collectors
including Jacques Kerchache.

For about thirty years, these two figures, collected from a Chamba chiefdom and
attributed to Chamba, appear to have been the only potentially Mumuye figure sculptures outside Nigeria. On this account, sculptures resembling the male of the second
pair of Lilley's figures discussed here were initially classified as Chamba in museum
collections. Reattribution of both these pieces to Mumuye has been represented as
a correction of Lilley; however, Lilley's original report provided as exact provenance as
we possess for any Mumuye figures, which, just as he recorded, were collected in a chiefdom ruled by speakers of Chamba. In the case of the bulky female figure that attracted
Henry Moore, it is not even clear that reattribution of the piece improves the record;
the female statue Lilley collected, and its male counterpart collected later by Sieber,
might as well be attributed to Chamba or Verre as to Mumuye. Indeed, in a multiethnic
community such as Binyeri in the 1920s, it is far from clear how the question might be
resolved or even quite what it means. The periodic "corrections" to Lilley reveal the
poverty of trying to fit sculptures into an ethnic grid that was hardly meaningful at the
place and time they were in use. Objects circulated locally and might cross what only
later became ethnic boundaries between proximate people, a finding already remarked of
the local stylistic eddy around Mapeo and reiterated throughout this volume.

Aside from at least one figure of the four that Lilley gave the British Museum,
Mumuye figures are rarely found in collections outside Nigeria before the Civil War,
and the few references to what might be Mumuye figures are not fleshed out without
perseverance. In his essay of 1970, Philip Fry referred to a Mumuye statue belonging to
James Crabtree Esq. that was exhibited in London under the auspices of the Arts Council of Great Britain in 1960. In the catalog of the exhibition, this was one of three figures
then attributed to Chamba (1960, items 308–10). Only one of the three was illustrated:
the female of the British Museum Lilley figures (1960, 308; fig. 8.39), which might as
well be Chamba as Mumuye. This makes it likely that item 309 was the other Lilley
figure in the British Museum (fig. 8.40), leaving item 310 as that owned by Crabtree.
We might have to leave matters there except that a figure with the attribution "formerly
Coll.[ection] of James Crabtree" is illustrated together with the two British Museum
figures in Frank Willett's survey of *African Art* ([1971] 2002, 138, fig. 140, height 45 cm).
Willett writes that he himself took the photographs for which no source is given, so he
presumably took this picture at the 1960 exhibition ([1971] 2002, 268). The same figure
entered the collection of the Metropolitan Museum in 1979 as part of the Rockefeller
Bequest (1979.206.281). Another figure from an unnamed private collection illustrated
before the Civil War remains fugitive. Identified as "probably Chamba," but like the
others showing strong Mumuye conventions, it appears in all three editions of Margaret
Trowell's *African Classical Sculpture* (1954, pl. 1; 1964, pl. v; 1970, pl. v).

The Yale University-Guy Van Rijn Archive of African Art illustrates another
Mumuye figure, altogether slimmer and more elegant, that was once in the Helena
Rubinstein collection, the non-Western elements of which were sold at the Parke-
Bernet Galleries in New York in 1966 (Parke-Bernet Galleries, *African and Oceanic Art:
The Collection of Helena Rubinstein*, parts 1–3, April 21, 1966). As the Van Rijn Archive
notes, the figure was not illustrated in the auction catalog, and we know neither how it
was acquired originally, nor what collection might currently contain it. But the thumb-
nail illustration from the online Archive suggests it to have been a rather willowy,
original, and significant piece most closely resembling the figure donated by Anne
Kerchache to the Musée du quai Branly in 2005 (fig. 8.41).

The record of Mumuye figures in European or American collections before about
1968 is quite remarkably slight. The male figure of the Lilley donations to the British Museum is the only piece in what was later recognized as a core Mumuye style
for which we possess both provenance and its current whereabouts. This is in marked
contrast to the Chamba where, as we have seen, considerable and helpful provenance
can be derived from early examples of figures accessioned by German museums.

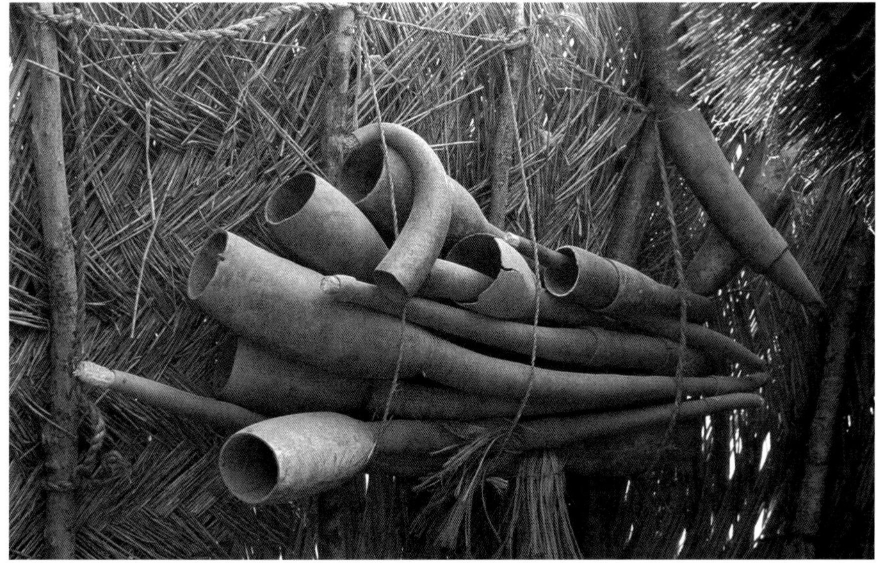

8.42
Calabash horns of different sizes, and hence pitches, are used as musical instruments in the Middle Benue Valley. Those illustrated are from Mumuye, but they are also documented among Jukun, and Chamba horns are similar but curved rather than straight. Calabash horn bands are usually occult instruments tied to particular cults and hidden from the view of noninitiates.

PHOTOGRAPH BY ARNOLD RUBIN, PANTI BELLI, 1971, RUBIN ARCHIVE, FOWLER MUSEUM AT UCLA, NEG. NO. 3112.

Mumuye Figures in Use

By the time Mette Bovin lived among Mumuye in 1964, what was then called Zinna was the center of an administrative district with a Mumuye ruler, although even he had a Hausa title (Sarkin Mumuye, or "Chief of Mumuye") and a Muslim name (Ibrahim Sambo). Meek pictures an earlier ruler of Zinna, attired in the robes popularized by northern Muslims, also holding his British staff of office (1931b, 1: ill. facing p. 447). Like the other ten districts where Mumuye predominated, Zinna fell directly under the Fulani Emir of Muri, who lived in Jalingo, the headquarters of Muri Division. Zing, the current name of Zinna, is according to Bovin a more accurate transcription of a Mumuye name that is said to mean "lion," that is, "a person who fears nothing." In a tradition unchanged between Meek's time and Bovin's, Mumuye living in Zing claimed descent from an ancestor who left Kam to travel north to Yoro. To commemorate this ancestor's long journey, "Yoro" is said to mean "tired." Whether such traditions refer to actual movements is difficult to determine, but purported migrations frequently link places in relations of ritual subordination. It is in this sense that I would interpret the account discussed below that relates how the Mumuye of Zing sought rain from the rainmaker of Yoro.

Like other Middle Benue peoples, Mumuye controlled a wide range of the misfortunes confronting them by means of cults, most of which belonged to men (as, for instance, Jup among Chamba Daka, or Vooma among Chamba Leko; Fardon 1990). These cults were entered through initiation and by payment. In Zing, cults were generically called *vaa*, while in Yoro the term for them was *koko*. In speech, *vaa* most commonly occurred as either a prefix or suffix in compound terms, which served to differentiate the general power that *vaa* connotes. Hence, there are a number of cults including what Meek describes as the two major cults Vaa-Bong (transcribed as "Vabô" by Meek 1931b, 1: 460, ff.*)*, and Vaa-Dosong (Meek's "Vadôsu"), as well as a number of subsidiary cults Vaa-Baka, Sokwan-Baa, Vaa-Songpi, and so on. Vaa-Bong is particularly associated with masquerade (and so I shall discuss it in a later chapter); Vaa-Dosong is associated with the calabash horns (fig. 8.42). As we should anticipate in such a large and varied population, practices differed widely, as did the relative importance and seriousness of the different cults. Meek is clear that any account given should be taken to apply only to a particular place and not generalized to Mumuye as a tribal entity.

The only linguist to have published on Mumuye translated *vaa* as "fetish," but this imprecise term has unfortunate connotations that do not clarify local usage (Shimizu 1983; see Fardon 2007, 94). Whatever its other shortcomings, "cult" encompasses ideas of apparatus, knowledge, procedures, initiation, membership, activities, and effects, all of which are appropriate here. For some, possibly all Mumuye, *vaa* also related to a ritual geography: Mumuye in Zing told Mette Bovin that, "*Vaa* goes out from Yoro at certain times of the year [...] and *vaa* returns to Yoro at other times of the year," tying the annual emanation of cultic power to the origin of the ancestor of the Zing Mumuye themselves. Meek reports that Yoro was not only the rainmaking center for Mumuye, but also for "surrounding tribes," including the Chief of the Jukun of Kona (Meek 1931b, 1: 468–69). Mette Bovin's memoir of her visit to Yoro (chapter 11) is our only firsthand account of the master of rain. Hill-dwelling masters of rain were a regional feature of the Middle and Upper Benue (see Barley 1983 for an account from Dowayo; see also this volume, chapter 17), and it is often the case that the hegemony of a particular rainmaking center was expressed in terms of origin: hence many Chamba chiefdoms traced their origin from the chiefdom called Yeli or Dayela, just as the Mumuye do from Yoro.

The indications we have of cults among Mumuye are consistent with what we know about other societies in the Middle Benue (and beyond). Cults differed in the range of their powers and the extent of their concerns, depending upon their association with greater or lesser degrees of hierarchy. Wherever there was more centralization, a chief and his priests sought to control some of the cults exercising particularly far-reaching powers over his subjects. In uncentralized communities, such powers were diffused among numerous kin groups and the important men—and, to a lesser degree, women—within them. Given the generally decentralized character of Mumuye political and ritual organization, the material culture of cults, including statuary, is likely to have been both widely distributed and largely occulted. When Mette Bovin visited the Master of Thunder on Dangong Mountain, it is notable that only a single statue was brought out to be shown to her, and then briefly and at a distance.

Arnold Rubin seems to suggest that Mumuye were not equally decentralized throughout their range. Among more northerly Mumuye, like those around Zing in the northeast, he tells us that the statues they called *janari*, the same term that Bovin records, lent support to chiefs and elders because they could be approached to assure the well-being of the community (he mentions such collective concerns as protection from drought and epidemic disease, as well as the promotion of crops). This seems to resonate with an observation made by Meek that the Mumuye had melded the native police force with their Vaa-Bong cult, the police being effectively "the attendants and messengers of the cult and the collectors of fines imposed" (Meek 1931b, 1: 362). By contrast, among southern Mumuye where statues were known by a variant name (*jagana* or *lagana*), they were "essentially entrepreneurial" because they allowed people access to divination and healing procedures (Rubin cites problems in childbirth and smallpox as falling under the power of one statue). By implication, southern Mumuye had been less disposed to admit chiefly authority, which seems consistent with Captain R. B. Knight's observation, cited by the Temples, that the title "Panti" (Kpanti) around Yakoko applied to the leader of each extended family, rather than to the leader of a settlement as a whole (Temple and Temple 1922, 292).

Form

Despite earlier misattributions, observers did not find Mumuye statues difficult to identify once Fry pointed to their characteristics. Part of their attraction has been that Mumuye statues are both highly recognizable as such, and yet very different from one another. Incidentally this also makes them potentially easy to fake. All Mumuye statues are columnar in form, although there is a considerable degree of variation in the degree of angularity among them. Most often, Mumuye statues give the viewer an impression of two external surfaces, one of which contains the other creating a space between them (see figs. 8.33–8.35 and 8.43). Henry Moore commented on this in 1951 in relation to

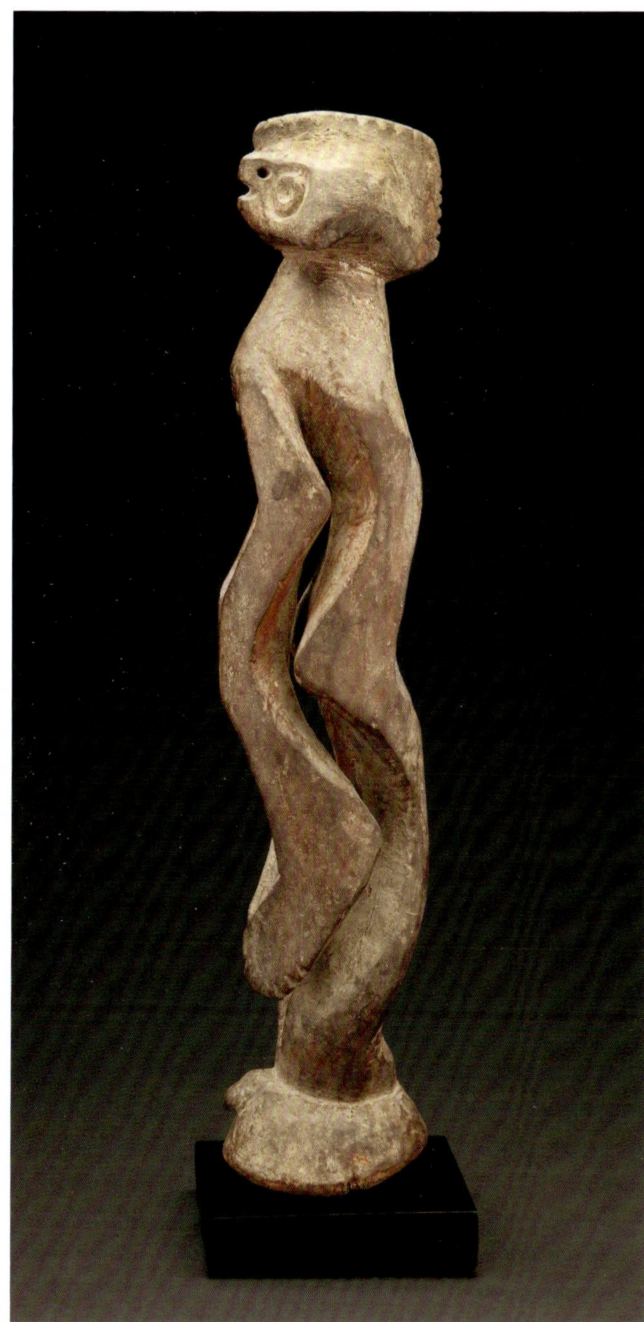
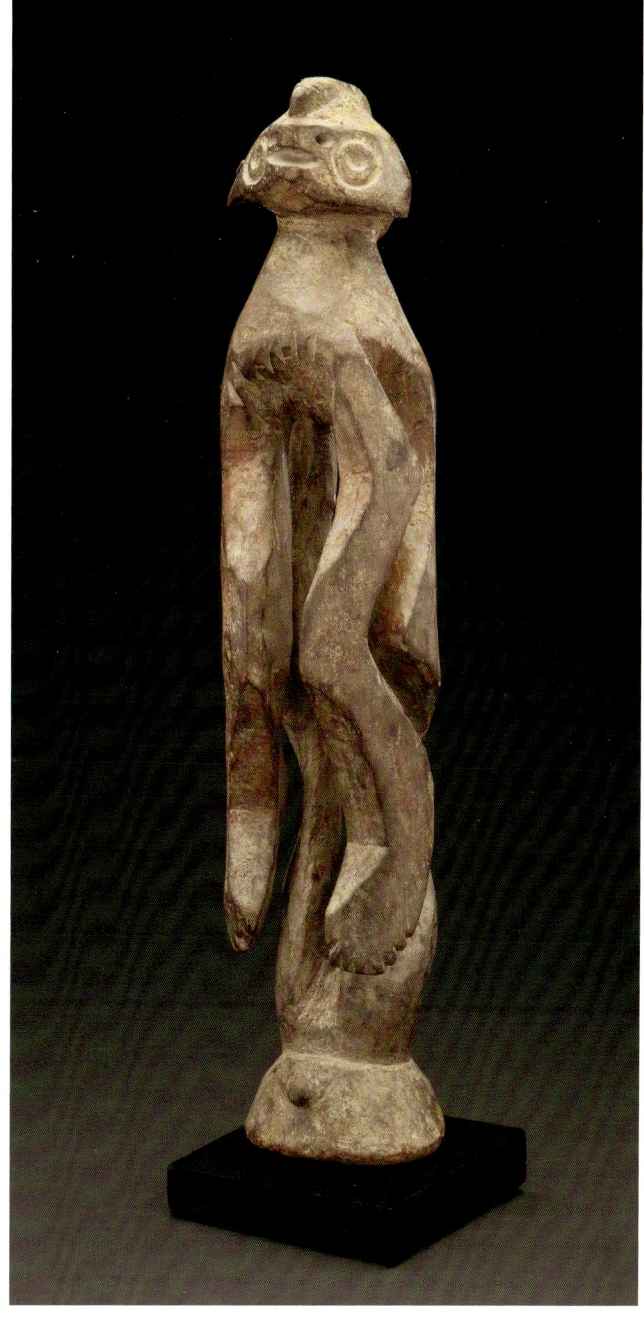

the female of the Lilley figures in the British Museum, which he had sketched on its accession almost thirty years earlier: "[the] carver has managed to make [the figure] 'spatial' by the way in which he has made the arms free and yet enveloping the central form of the body" (1951, 95–96). The outside surface of Mumuye figures is defined by a discontinuous series of flat and curved planes that may alternate and repeat one another (fig. 8.44). Principally, these planes define the arms that hang from the shoulders in the shape of a more or less angular suspended horseshoe, and the legs, which vary greatly in length but are typically straight with notches (as is usual for the Middle Benue), thus contrasting with the flexed arms and perhaps conveying an impression of upper-body movement. Shoulders and hips often echo one another not just in mass but also in shape. The internal space of the statue consists of the torso, the neck (which may be elongated), and the head (though not necessarily the ears and coiffure/head-dress), all of which are rounded. A pronounced navel is almost always apparent, which may be tapered or even pointed; often it protrudes from the internal surface to touch the inside of a virtual external surface suggested by the flexed arms, as if connecting

8.43a,b
Small figure
Mumuye peoples, before 1970
Wood
H: 48 cm
PRIVATE COLLECTION, LOS ANGELES
IMAGE: © 2010 FOWLER MUSEUM AT UCLA.
PHOTOGRAPH BY DON COLE
PROVENANCE: MERTON SIMPSON, NEW YORK

This extraordinary figure is unlike anything documented from fieldwork, being entirely without legs and having a split torso. The original significance of these features, if they were significant, is mysterious. The figure does, however, demonstrate the great latitude for experimentation permitted to Mumuye figure carvers, in this case representing an empty inner space.

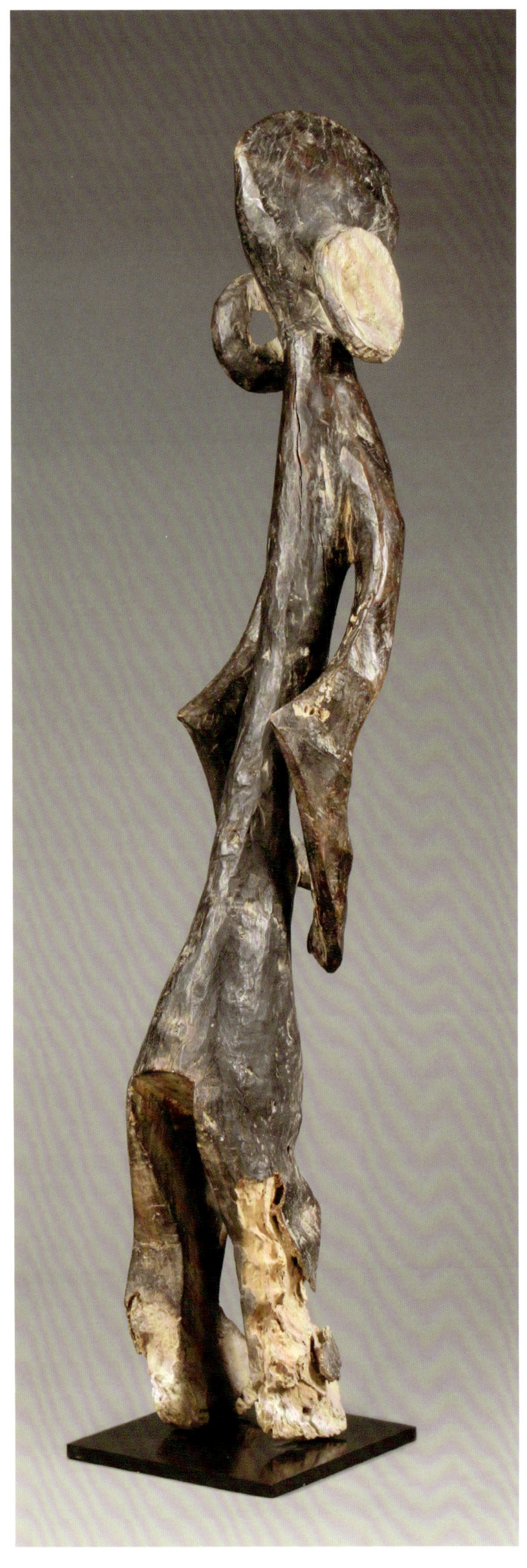
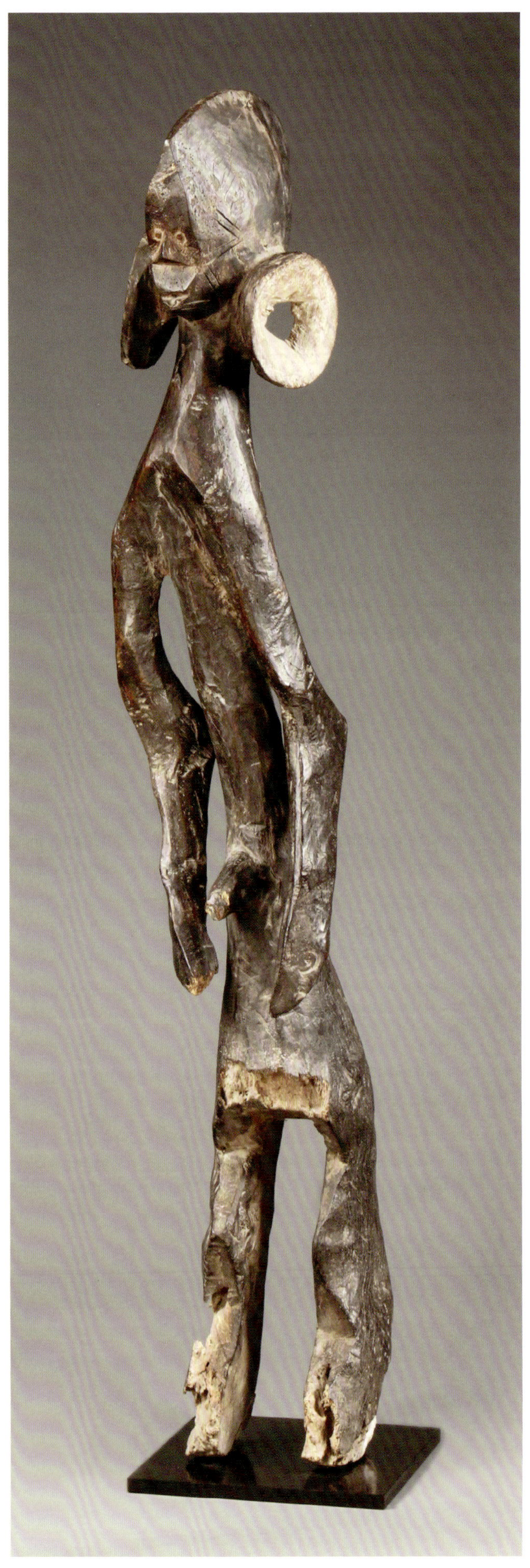

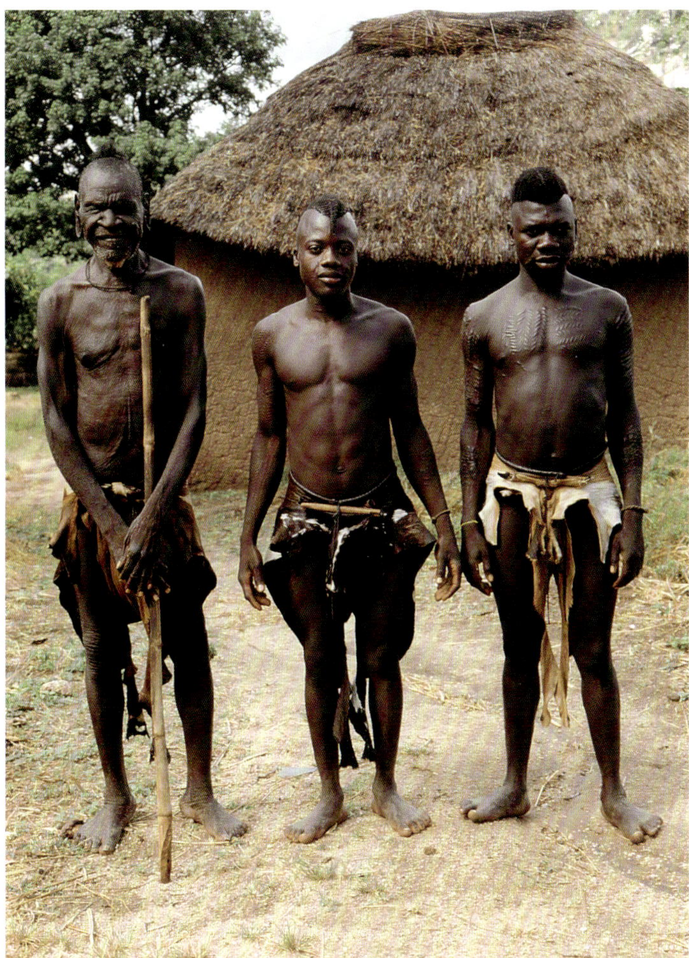

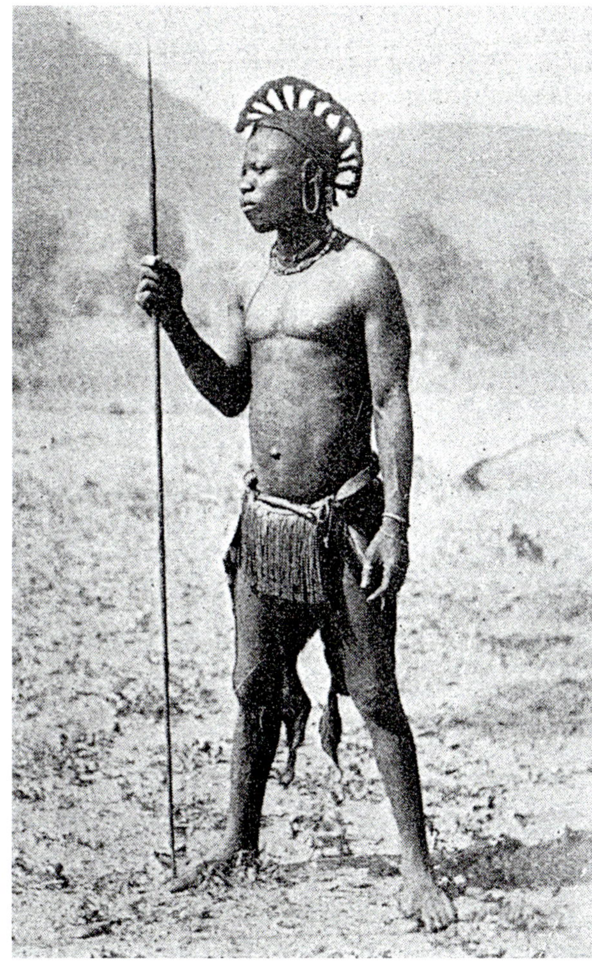

repeats Mette Bovin's comment on another of her photographs, that the woman had removed her discs when attending the market at Zing since she realized they were no longer fashionable. This might have reflected something more coercive than fashion, since the Islamization campaigns carried out in Northern Nigeria after independence, strongly backed by the local emirs, were intensely opposed to what were considered pagan styles of self-presentation, notably nudity. Despite the evidence that both men and women used earplugs, Mumuye informants maintained that statues with large openwork earlobes are to be identified as female (fig. 8.47; see fig. 8.4). Sculpted coiffures, both for men and women, are attested throughout the Benue region in the earlier twentieth century (fig. 8.48). In the Mumuye case, sagittal crests were particularly favored, and they might be ornamented with beads, rings, or metal rods, or built into openwork constructions like the one illustrated in figure 8.49 (note the youth also has extended earlobes).

8.47a,b (OPPOSITE)
Figure
Mumuye peoples, before 1969
Wood
H: 103 cm
COLLECTION OF MR. AND MRS. BRUCE MOORE, CARMEL

IMAGE: COURTESY COLLECTOR. PHOTOGRAPH BY SCOTT MCCUE, 2010

PROVENANCE: COLLECTED BY EDOUARD KLEJMAN, NEAR THE CAMEROON BORDER, 1969; NICHOLAS GESTER, FRANCE; JOHANN LÉVY GALLERY, PARIS

Movement is imparted to this Mumuye figure by its flexing—forward from the waist and back from the neck, as well as from left to right—and through its undulating arms and pointed elbows. The large circular ears, which probably identify the figure as female, are perforated, further accentuating the asymmetry of the form. The head, with scarification and neat features on a relatively flat, ovoid face, is topped with a slight sagittal crest (see fig. 8.45). It was among the earliest of Mumuye figures to leave Nigeria having entered the art market during the Biafran War.

8.48
In Arnold Rubin's 1965 photograph of three Mumuye men, it is the two youths, center and the viewer's right, who have the more intricate hairstyles, which explain the inspiration for the crests on many male statues. The senior man wears a goatee. All three have animal skin loin coverings that have been pulled up between their legs and secured with a stick (as described by Mette Bovin, p. 372). By this date, the costume suggests they are participating in a markedly "traditional" event, since it was no longer everyday wear. All have bodily scarification, which is most elaborate on the youth standing at the right.
PHOTOGRAPH BY ARNOLD RUBIN, PANTISAWA, 1967, RUBIN ARCHIVE, FOWLER MUSEUM AT UCLA, SLIDE NO. A1.10.11.13.

8.49
This image of a Mumuye youth published in 1928 shows the great invention used in the creation of sagittal crests. It is unclear whether his crest is a hat or, more likely, some kind of framework over which his hair has been braided. The youth also has pierced and extended earlobes. "A Mumuye Youth, Nigeria," *Lightbearer*, 1928.

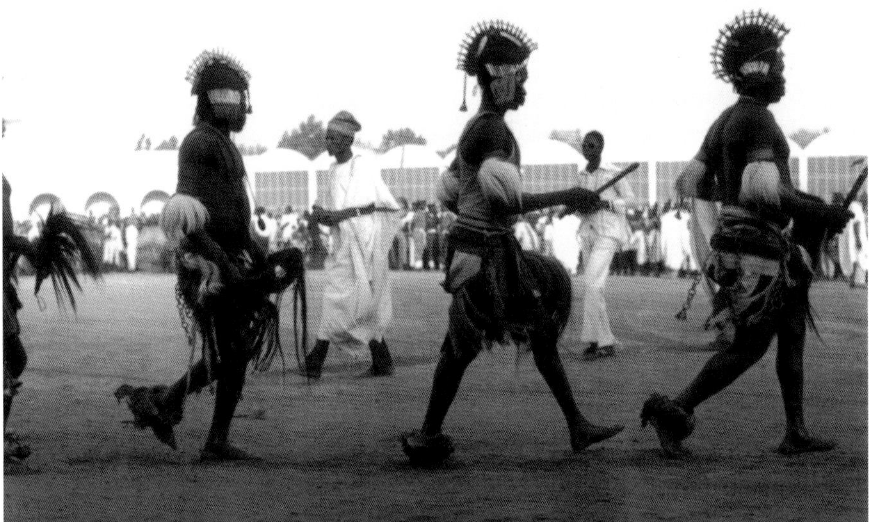

8.50
Mette Bovin's photograph of Mumuye men dancing in 1974 was probably taken at the fourth National Festival of Arts (Nafest), held to select traditional performances for FESTAC in 1977. Note the helmets, which resemble in shape the heads of many male Mumuye wooden figures.
PHOTOGRAPH © METTE BOVIN, 1974.

8.51 (OPPOSITE)
Figure
Mumuye peoples, before 1969
Wood, twine, pigment
H: 160 cm
SEATTLE ART MUSEUM; GIFT OF KATHERINE WHITE AND THE BOEING COMPANY, 81.17.709
IMAGE: © SEATLE ART MUSEUM. PHOTOGRAPH BY ELIZABETH MANN, 2010
PROVENANCE: PURCHASED BY KATHERINE WHITE FROM RODRIGUEZ, 1969

The carver of this extraordinary tall, slender, and flexed figure has radically abstracted its facial features, assimilating its eyes to a round coiffure with a freedom similar to the placement of eyes in the front underside of the headdress of some male figures (see figs. 8.28 and 8.30).

Such crests are difficult to distinguish from helmets worn by Mumuye warriors, which typically had long earflaps (fig. 8.50; see fig. 13.10). The famous statue in the collection of the Fondation Beyeler, discussed above, which was exhibited to acclaim in New York a quarter century ago (W. Rubin 1984, 41; Wick and Denner 2009, no. 2), was likened by the *New York Times* reviewer of the exhibition *Primitivism in Twentieth-Century Art* (1984) to Darth Vader from *Star Wars*, a description that equally fits the Tishman Mumuye statue in the Metropolitan Museum of Modern Art in New York (Brenson 1984; see figs. 8.33, 8.34). These figures are surely hooded, which accounts for the eyes in this and similar pieces being shaded by the crest of their helmet.[17]

The final human ornamentation given to a majority of figures consisted of geometric incisions on their surface that appear to evoke the scarification that especially Mumuye women underwent on their stomachs before marriage (see fig. 11.23). Facial scarification consisted of three sets of "three horizontal rows of small cuts," which were made: on the forehead above the eyes, between the eye and the ear, and on the cheek aligned with the mouth (Temple and Temple 1922, 288). As Fry's sketches of the faces of Mumuye figures attest, while there is not exact correspondence to this schema, many facial markings appear in threes and in more or less the positions described (Fry 1970, 18–19). A figure photographed by Rubin in Pantilapo during 1965 has particularly clear double facial incisions on the upper four sides of an open pentagon (see fig. 8.24). Similar scarification is also to be found on Mumuye vertical masks (see fig. 14.2).

Two further features commonly found in Mumuye statues deserve comment. Many of them are flexed because, or so it seems, the carver has been happy to allow the original shape of the wood at his disposal to be retained in his final work (see fig. 8.47). The fluidity this imparts to the form is reinforced by a feature that Fry argued occurred too often to be accidental: few Mumuye statues are perfectly symmetrical around their central axis when seen from the front. This flexing, however, is far more characteristic of the unprovenanced statues of the early exodus than it is of the statues documented in the field, and it appears hardly at all among the influx of statues to the Jos Museum in the early 1970s. On this, albeit slight evidence, it appears that later Mumuye sculptors lost something of the expressive freedom Europeans and Americans had found in earlier works. The persistence of particular conventions for representing features made the figures recognizably Mumuye, but most lacked the sprightliness conveyed by slim limbs or a flexed torso.

Aside from these more or less shared features, Mumuye statues vary widely but not so widely as to be unrecognizable as such. Philip Fry (1970) and François Neyt

(2006) have developed typologies of the heads and bodies of the statues, and these demonstrate that, however inventive, the set of features that can be combined is not inexhaustibly varied. This does not preclude some highly idiosyncratic examples, which are represented in this exhibition (see. fig. 8.43). Thus far, however, no advance has been made in narrowing the local provenance of these types. One wonders whether it is already too late for a field investigation to make substantial headway in this respect.

In addition to their formal variety, Mumuye statues vary substantially in size. François Neyt has argued that this variation is discontinuous and involves three size ranges: small statues 15–30 cm in height; middle-sized pieces of around 50 cm; and large statues from 90 cm to, exceptionally, 160 cm high (fig. 8.51). One might suppose that the tallest statues were those reported to have been placed in pairs in the open air with their feet buried; Mette Bovin records that these belonged to important people like masters of rain and blacksmiths. Indeed, Bovin does record a male statue around a meter tall standing in the compound of a blacksmith as protection against thieves; however, its female partner was at most a third as high. So it appears that functional pairs of statues were not necessarily matched in size.

This survey may appear disappointingly negative in some of its conclusions, since it remains the case that while we can point toward a variety of uses to which Mumuye put sculpted figures, we have at best tantalizing glimpses of the rituals in which they were addressed. And while we can both identify a number of statues with named carvers thanks to the field record, and attribute at least one group of three statues generally considered masterpieces to the same unnamed carver, the circumstances of the exodus of statues around the end of the 1960s makes more detailed reconstruction of artistic geography from twenty-first-century Nigerian fieldwork highly unlikely. If we are able to extend our knowledge of Mumuye sculpture, it is likely we shall do so by detailed, mass internal comparison of the corpus of examples now in collections in order to extend the salience of the rather modest contextual sources we have to call upon.

JUKUN

Arnold Rubin opened the section of his doctoral thesis (1969) dealing with the then-current understanding of Jukun figure carving, in these terms,

> A small number of rather vague allusions in the literature attest to the existence of a Jukun figure-carving tradition. In terms of the literature, however, Jukun figure carving never emerges as a separate tradition within Jukun art; in contrast to Wukari-area masks, no figures convincingly attributed to the Jukun have been published. [A. Rubin 1969, 78]

Given that Europeans had been visiting the Middle Benue for well over a century, this is remarkable. The record of figurative sculptures from Jukun has grown in the subsequent four decades, but it remains modest compared to that of the eastern neighbors of the Jukun, the Mumuye. I have suggested that the very large numbers of Mumuye statues in American and European collections could be explained by a number of factors, each of which was consequential for others: because Mumuye were relatively numerous and dispersed, and those living on or near mountains had been able to resist outright Fulani domination, the general impact of world religions occurred relatively late; hence carving for historic Mumuye religious purposes continued into the post-independence period in Nigeria; the sweeping impact of world religions, both Northern Nigeria-sponsored Islam and missionary Christianity, was felt just as the Biafran War facilitated large-scale export of artworks via the, more or less open, Cameroon border. Networks of art dealers, predominantly a set of Franco-Cameroonian connections illustrated by Hélène Joubert (see epilogue), built a market for Mumuye art based on their early enthusiasm for the aesthetic and commercial potentials of the strong forms of the figures.

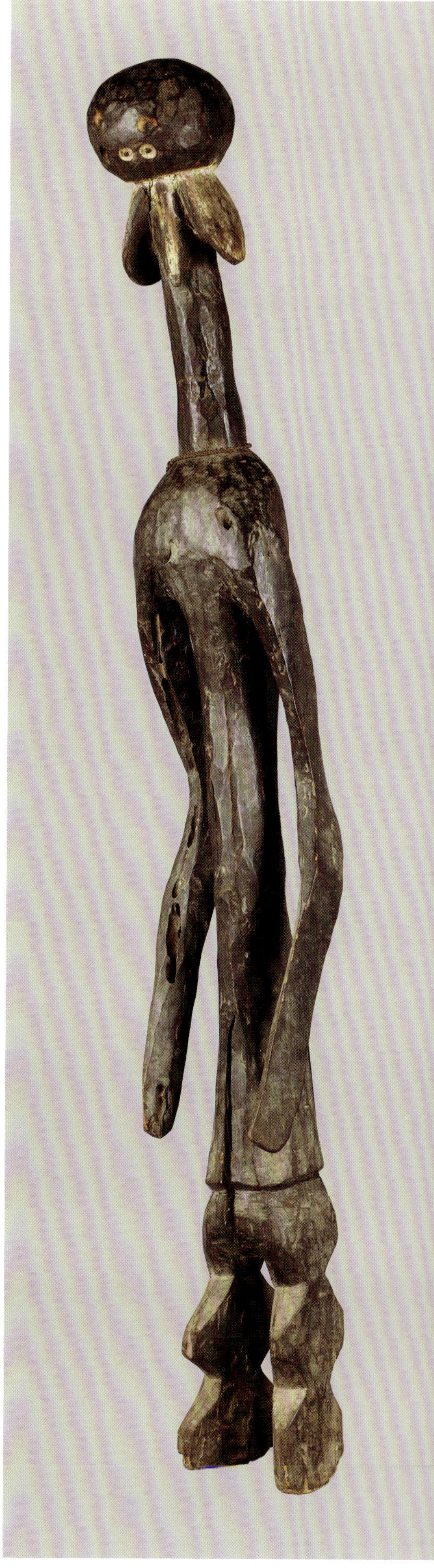

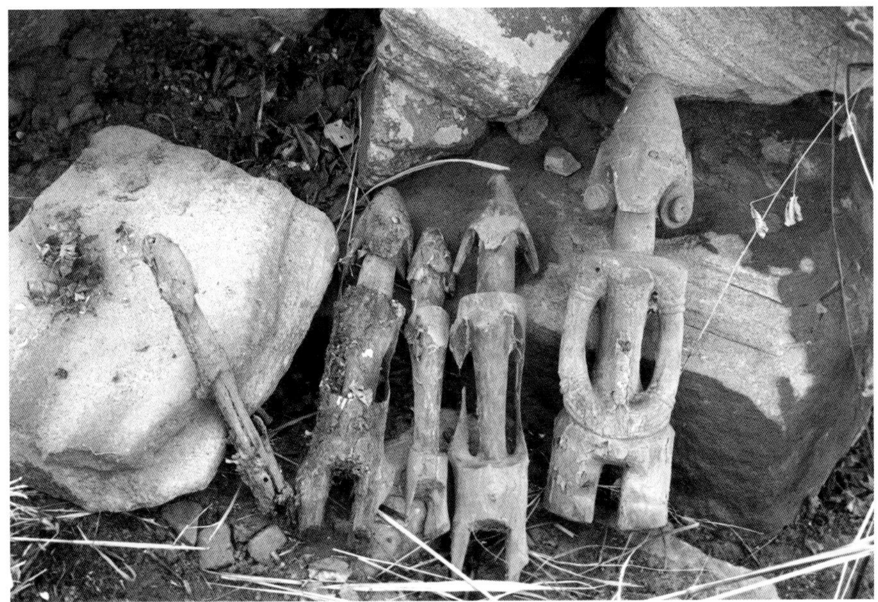

8.52

Arnold Rubin photographed examples of what he defined as the nuclear style of Jukun figure sculpture in Pindiga and Gwana (see p. 276). This photograph shows a group of sculptures belonging to the Akala kindred from a rock shelter near Gwana. The largest figure was named Wipong, and the figures to his right are two wives (Kai and Ayezi) and an "attendant" named Hwai Kai. The large male figure would originally have held an upright spear at its center.

PHOTOGRAPH BY ARNOLD RUBIN, GWANA, JANU-ARY 9, 1966, RUBIN ARCHIVE, FOWLER MUSEUM AT UCLA, NEG. NO. 1532.

8.53 (OPPOSITE)

Female figure (Kai)
Jukun peoples, late nineteenth to early twentieth century or before
Wood

H: 71 cm

JAMES WILLIS TRIBAL ART

IMAGE: © JAMES WILLIS. PHOTOGRAPH BY SCOTT MCCUE, 2010

PROVENANCE: JEAN-MICHEL HUGUENIN, PARIS; GALERIE RENAUD VANUXEM, PARIS

This highly eroded columnar figure is identi-fied in Rubin's field photograph (see fig. 8.52) as Kai, the wife of Wipong.

8.54

Male figure (Wipong)
Jukun peoples, Gwana, late nineteenth to early twentieth century or before
Wood

H: 71 cm

ROBERT T. WALL FAMILY

IMAGE: COURTESY COLLECTOR. PHOTOGRAPH BY DON TUTTLE, 2010

PROVENANCE: COLLECTED IN KARIM (KARIM LAMIDO); JACQUES KERCHACHE, PARIS, ACQUIRED BEFORE 1971

This figure is the same as that photographed by Arnold Rubin in Gwana (see fig. 8.52) and identified as Wipong, which Rubin explains is a personal name rather than a genre. Accord-ing to Rubin, these kinds of figures are likely to represent ancestors, and many of their names appear in lists of past chiefs. Carbon 14 dating of this piece has produced a range of possible dates from the eighteenth to the twentieth century, with a slight bias towards the later dating.

None of these factors really applied to the Jukun. Before the incursions of the Tiv, Chamba, and Fulani, they would have been the predominant people of the plains south of the Benue River, so their nucleated settlements were open to trade, which included the European companies that had established bases on the Benue River. This ceased to be a source of advantage to them, however, when they were confronted by ruthless, mounted adversaries. By the late nineteenth and early twentieth century much of this area was reported to be depopulated, and villages lay in ruins. Chiefs sought accom-modation with the ascendant power, the Fulani, and this involved at least nominal conversion to Islam. Missionary endeavor, notably by the Sudan United Mission, was intensive from an early date, and before the First World War a network of mission centers had established not just churches but also health and educational facilities. Hence, Jukun historic religion was in retreat in many places by the interwar years, and everywhere it was in a contest with world religions.

There may have been rather few Jukun sculptures left to enter export circuits when the Cameroonian route became particularly active beginning in the late 1960s, and Jukun sculptures would have been late entrants to the trade because of the dis-tance of "supply" from the border. In short, the conditions were far from conducive to an outpouring of sculpture on the scale of the Mumuye, and there is in fact remarkably little evidence of figural sculpture being collected even during the colonial period. The situation has, however, changed since Rubin wrote, in part thanks to his own account, and a number of pieces that he documented in the field, or others cognate with them, have subsequently entered European and American collections (figs 8.52–54; see also interleaf E).

Returning to the subject of Jukun sculpture in 1988, almost twenty years later, Arnold Rubin drew upon his earlier work to argue a relationship, albeit not a complete coincidence, between the different dialects and differing material expressions of Jukun speakers. His account transects the Jukun-speaking area with a diagonal slanted from the northwest to the southeast (see fig. 7.2). To the north and east of this line, the predominant form of sculptural expression was statuary, in which we would now feel inclined to include tall vertical masks. To the south and west of the line, the predomi-nant expression was masquerade, dominated by horizontal masks but including other types, some of which performed in concert with horizontal masquerades (see chapter 14). The horizontal masquerades found in the southwest were absent from the north-east; and the vertical masquerades of the northeast were absent from the southwest: the two types were mutually exclusive. Effectively there appeared to be two distinct

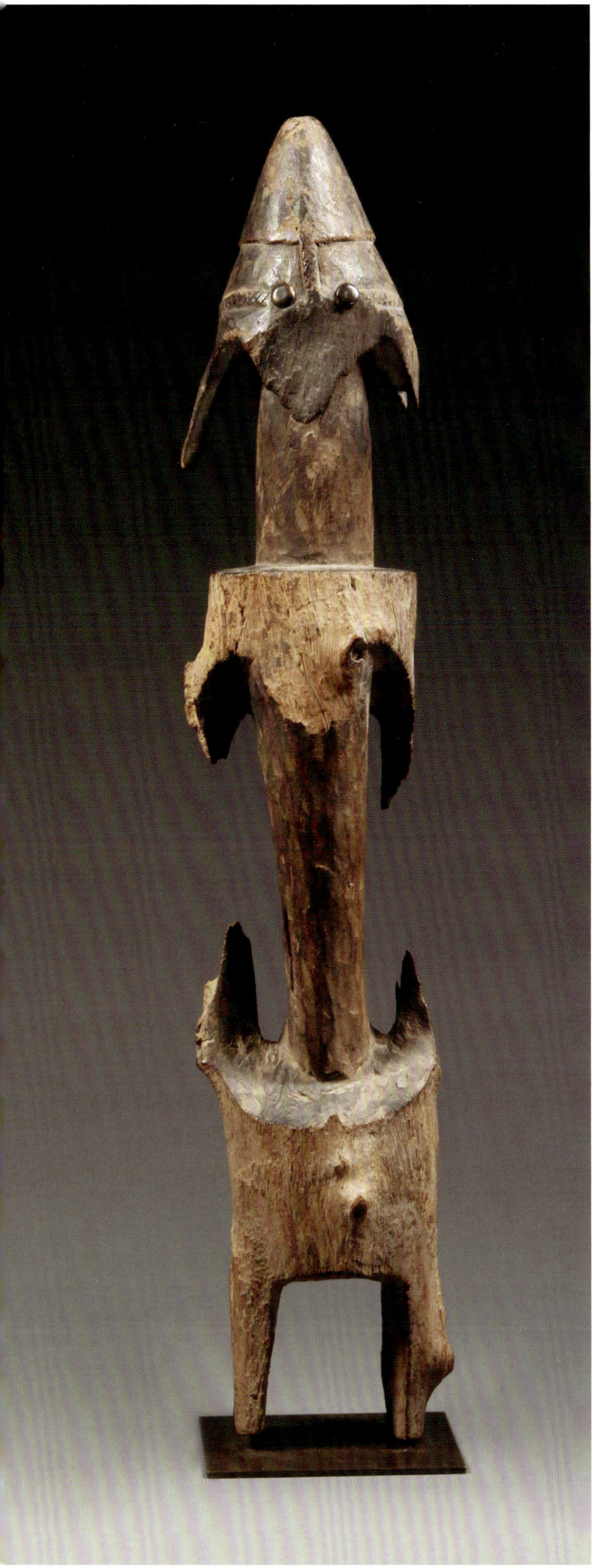

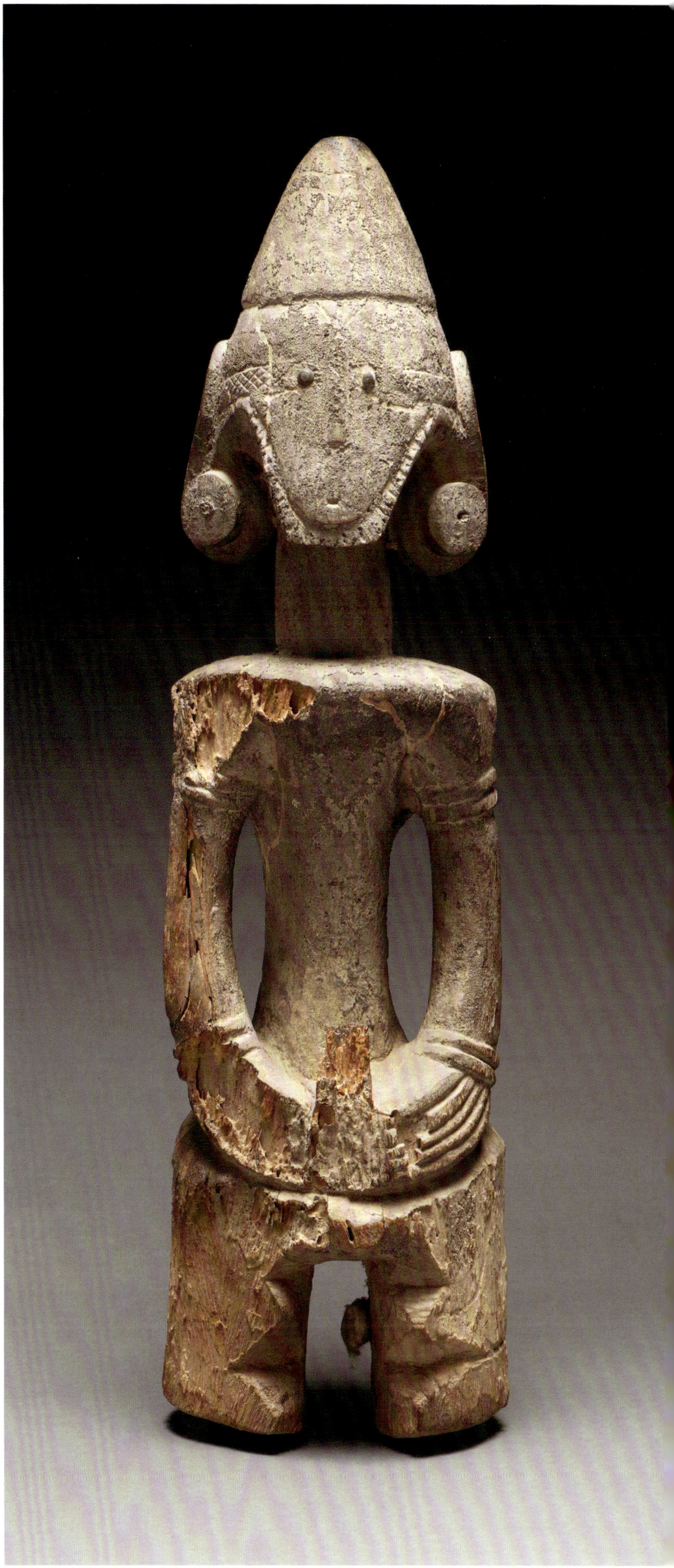

clusters of Jukun artistic expression: the southwestern Jukun typified by masquerade-using cults resembled their non-Jukun neighbors in many respects; certainly they did so more than they resembled the northeastern Jukun. This suggested that material cultural expressions could become shared between neighbors over a relatively short period. Rubin contended, however, that these differences in material culture did not indicate differences in rituals or the conceptions that informed them. Masquerades and statues were used in similar ways to depict ancestral spirits (which, for reasons already explained, I would prefer to annotate as "powers of the dead and the wild"). This variation between the southwest and northeast of Jukun country correlated, according to Rubin, with two phases of Jukun expansion. Whether or not the argument about migration is demonstrable, it supports the contention of this book that artistic variation tends to be regional and not ethnic in character, an observation that is particularly evident in the case of masquerade.

In the section of chapter 10 on Middle Benue masquerades devoted to Jukun, I demonstrate that contrary to first appearances, the masquerades of southwestern Jukun are human-animal fusions that in this respect are formally similar to those of their neighbors, like Mumuye and Chamba south of the Benue, and the Kantana and Kulere (and more obviously Goemai) north of it in the southern escarpments of the Jos Plateau. The wooden elements of tall vertical masquerades among northeastern Jukun resemble masquerades used by the Wurkun and by northern Mumuye (in addition to their horizontal masquerades). Hence, we could say that the different predominant forms of Jukun masquerades conformed to a regional distribution or, to put it the other way around, that the regional distribution of masquerade forms was trans-ethnic.

Rubin's proposal that the Jukun uses of horizontal masks and of statues were mutually exclusive has two aspects. In the northeast, Jukun might use both wooden figures and vertical masks, a pattern similar to Wurkun that does not seem to beg any special explanation. In the southwest, however, Jukun used horizontal masquerades but eschewed figures, which is on the face of it more difficult to explain: craftsmen capable of making wooden masks should also be able to make statues, as they do among Chamba, Mumuye, Mambila, and other neighbors of the southwestern Jukun. One worries whether this apparent absence may be a fabrication of the collecting record, especially given that the reigning Wukari monarch, Aku Uka Ashumanu V, told Rubin that figures had been in use until thirty years prior, that is to say until the mid-1930s (Rubin 1969, 79). Even if it is the case that southwestern Jukun have substituted masks for statues in some contexts, this does not explain why they should have done this in all contexts, which would amount to a positive aversion to iconic representation of human forms as wooden figures. C. K. Meek does not treat the absence of figures as problematic. In his discussion of cults that, he tells us, are usually associated with masquerades, he notes, however, the ubiquity of what he calls "sacred pillars," cone-shaped columns of dried mud, which may support the symbol of a particular cult and which are "characteristic symbols of divinity in all Jukun shrines" (Meek 1931a, 267). We might therefore speculate that these pillars rather than masquerades have taken over the functions of figures as the focus of address and offerings. As Rubin cautioned, however, the literature on Jukun statuary is thin, especially by comparison with that on Jukun masquerade, so there is a likelihood that the present record, rather than past practice, is anomalous.

Rubin surveyed statuary among groups of Jukun speakers both north and south of the Benue River. To the north he documented groups of statues around Wase, Gwana, and Pindiga (see figs 8.52–54; figs. 8.55–8.58); south of the river he recorded figures in Kona, and among the Jibu and Wurbo, of the Taraba River Valley (at Gaji, Gayam, and Wurbon Daudu)—see fig. 8.59, interleaf E. Jibu were much diminished in numbers since many of them had moved together with the Chamba during the nineteenth century to implant themselves among southwestern Jukun speakers

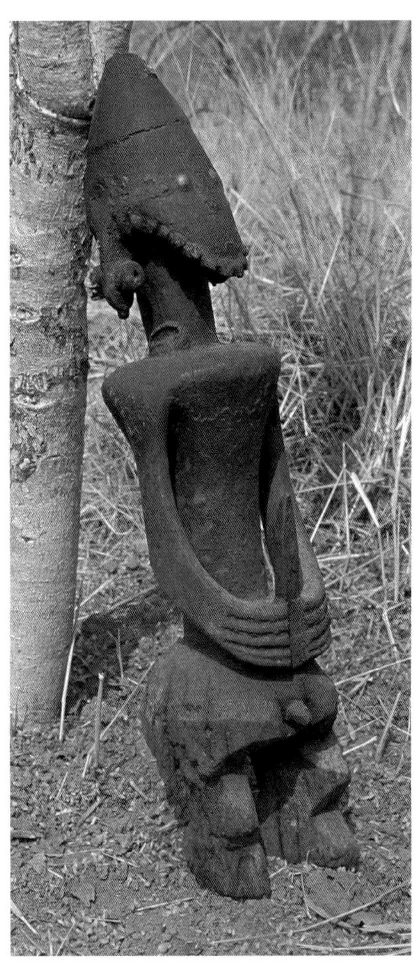

8.55
This figure is also identified by name as Wipong and was photographed in Pindiga where it belonged to a titled official, the Ubandoma Kurku (see fig. 9.10).
PHOTOGRAPH BY ARNOLD RUBIN, NEG. NO. 458.

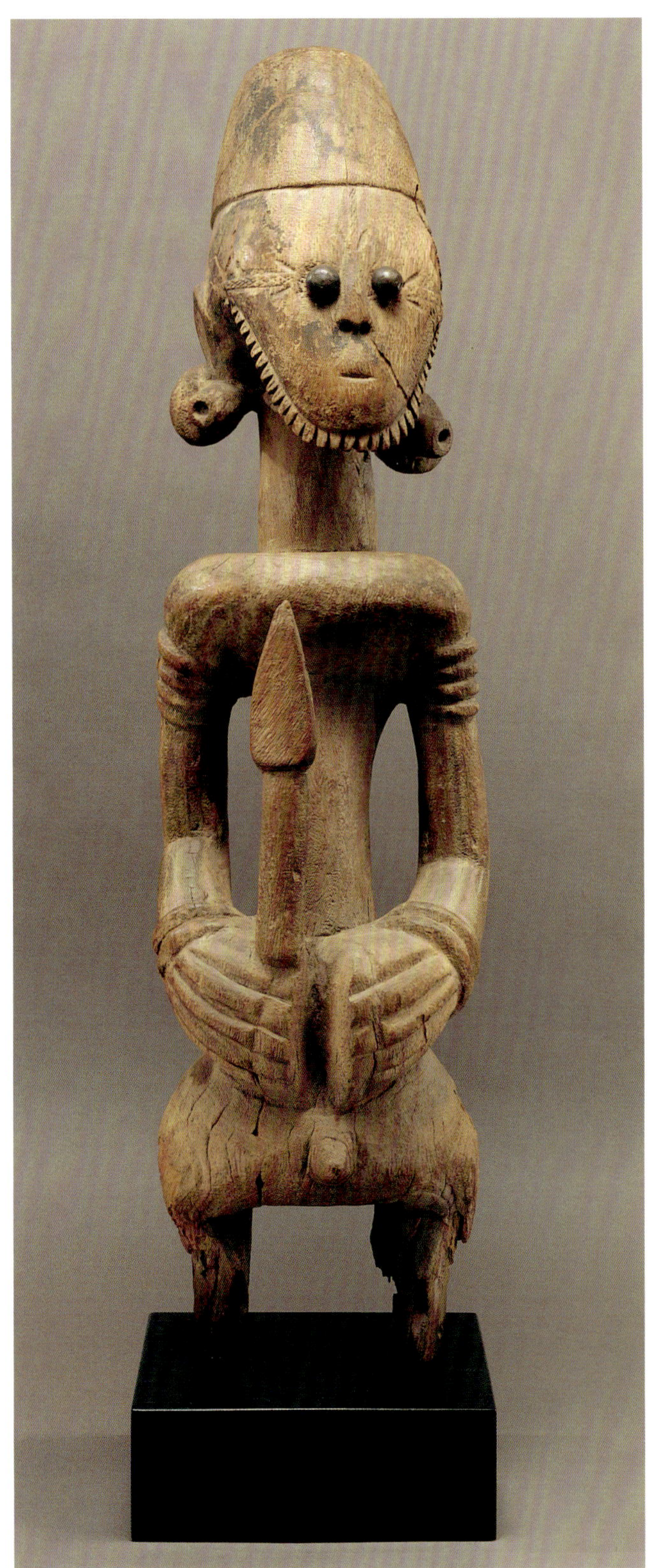

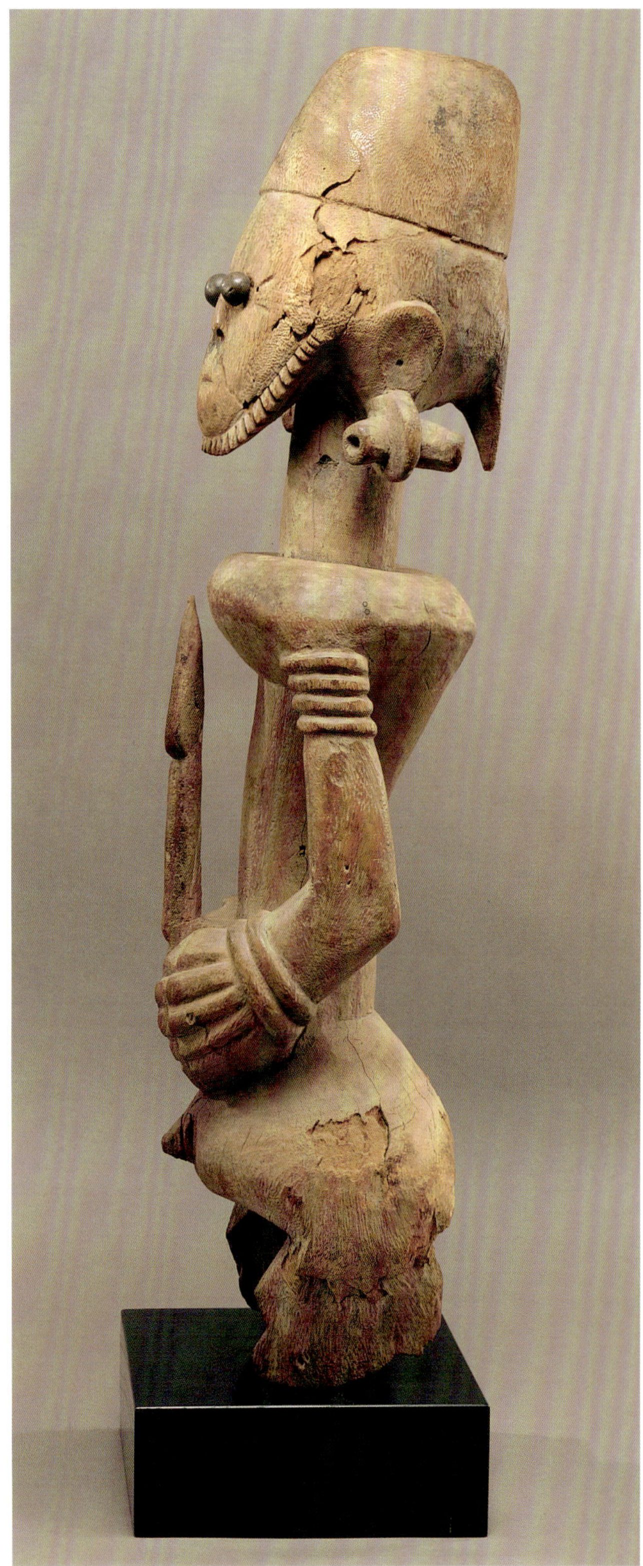

8.56a,b
Male figure
Jukun peoples, Pindiga (?), late nineteenth
to early twentieth century
Wood, metal
H: 74.3 cm
CLYMAN COLLECTION, NEW YORK
IMAGE: COURTESY COLLECTOR. PHOTOGRAPH BY
MAGGIE NIMKIN
PROVENANCE: PACE PRIMITIVE, NEW YORK; JEFFREY
SOREF; DONALD MORRIS GALLERY, NEW YORK, 2005

The upper parts of this figure are unusually
complete. Although its legs are eroded, the
upright leaf-blade spear remains entire. It
is held in the right hand, slightly off-center,
rather than centrally in both hands as seems
more commonly to have been the case. Other
than this, there are close resemblances with
the Pindiga Wipong documented by Rubin
(see figs. 8.52, 8.54), notably in the sculpting
of the ears and ornaments.

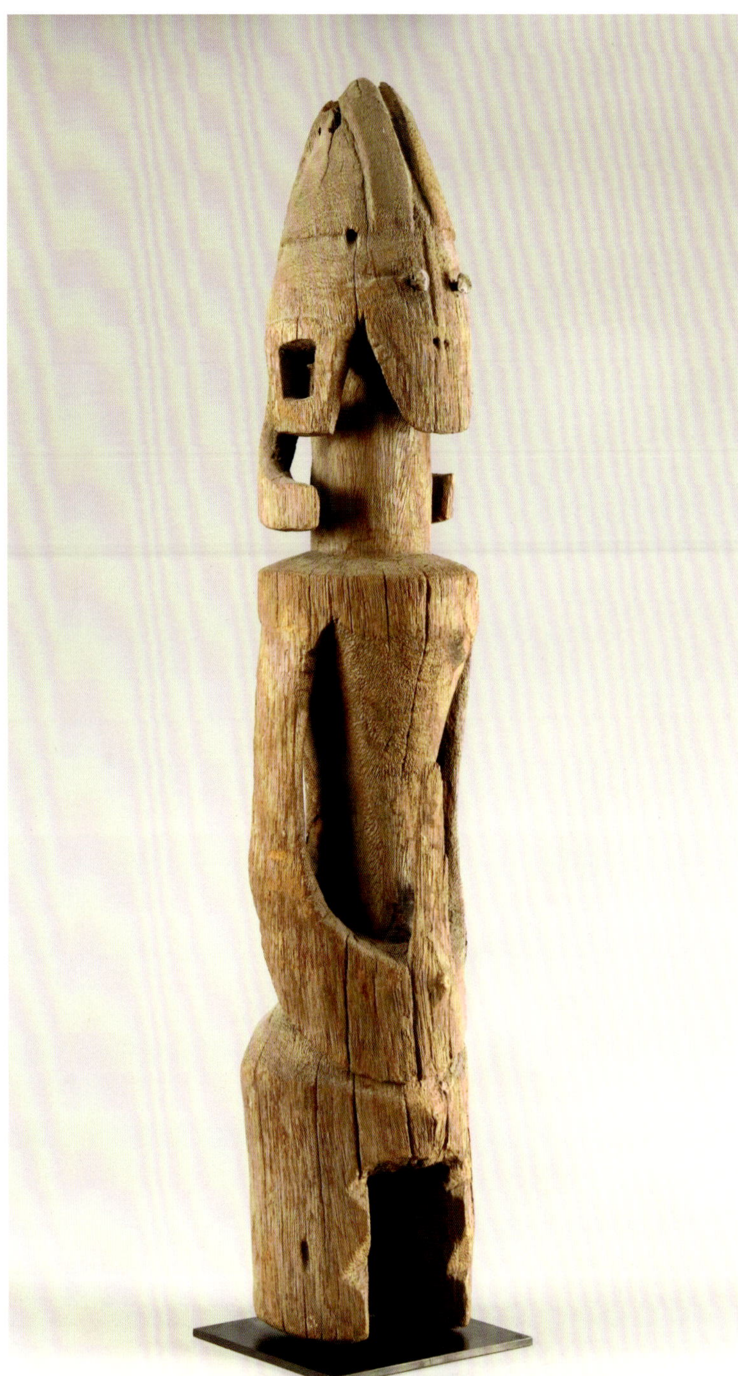

8.57
Male Figure
Jukun peoples, Pindiga (?), late nineteenth
to early twentieth century
Wood
H: 77.47 cm
COLLECTION OF TOBY AND BARRY HECHT
PHOTOGRAPH © 2010 GREG STALEY
PROVENANCE: HÉLÈNE LELOUP, PARIS; ULRICH
VON SCHROEDER

Some of the features of this figure, including
its square, perforated earlobes and dangling
braids, and the two stripes on its cap, are
highly reminiscent of the figure called Akere
photographed in Pindiga by Arnold Rubin
(see fig. 8.58).

around Donga and Takum. Although Rubin saw statues among Jibu, he found their
style highly variable. Generalizing, particularly from thirty statues seen around
Gwana and Pindiga, the northeasternmost Jukun, Rubin defined a "nuclear style" that
most characteristically consisted of husband and wife paired figures, with their lower
bodies wrapped in cloth, the faces of which were subject to particularly intensive
working with facial overhang, dentate beards on male figures, distended and/or ornamented earlobes, facial markings, and white metal eyes (see figs. 8.52–8.54; Rubin
1969, 86; see also this volume, chapter 9).

In some respects this style accorded with Middle Benue conventions familiar
from Chamba, Mumuye, Verre, and Wurkun: opposite-sex statues tending to be paired
with emphasis placed on ornamentation, particularly of the head and face, including
coiffure or cap, modification of earlobes to accommodate ornaments, and scarification.

Like other Middle Benue figures, the northeastern Jukun figures that Rubin saw in the field were both columnar and upright, and like Jukun masquerades generally, but unlike Middle Benue masquerades of the Mumuye or Chamba, Jukun statues often appeared with cloth wrappers provided by the chiefs of the communities they protected. Historically, Jukun were renowned as weavers whose cloths were exported to such distant markets as the Grassfields of Cameroon. Wearing cloth signaled high status, and Rubin follows Meek in emphasizing a close relationship between chiefs and figures, some of which are taken to represent royal ancestors. The cults of "Adom" at Kona, or "Adang" at Gwana seem to be cases in point since the wooden figures who must be propitiated by the king to avert famine and drought were originally a royal couple, and the paraphernalia of the cult includes relics of the right hands of the past kings (Meek 1931a, 269–72; Rubin 1969, 81; a photograph in a report by Meek—taken by O. H. Best in 1926 shows the Gwana ceremony with two carried figures and various other accoutrements, identified in the original annotation [see fig. 14.27]).

In some respects, Jukun figures in Rubin's nuclear style can be distinguished from others from the eastern Middle Benue. The pronounced facial overhang is unusual, and in some examples the symmetry between chin/beard at the front of the face, and coiffure/cap at the back would make the figures appear Janus-faced, were their facial features not confined to the front. This emphasizes what Rubin calls the ithyphallic quality of the male statues. While the arced arms are entirely typical for the region, the way in which the hands meet around the lap area and, in some examples, hold an upright spear are distinctive features. These robust arms, separated from the body almost like jug handles, could be used to carry the figures in procession, as both photographic documentation and the wear patterns on collected examples attest.

The heads of vertical masquerades, at the town of Kona, south of the Benue, called Wunkər and Zənakani (see below), share features of adornment typical of the nuclear style for figures: including metallic eyes, perforated and extended earlobes, and a feather inserted into a sagittal crest (see chapters 9 and 14). According to Dinslage and Storch, Wunkər was in the custody of a clan of slave origin (2000, 64), while an official of the same name belonged to the royal clan. The vertical masks were associated with other cult paraphernalia—including musical instruments consisting of sets of different-sized calabash horns in some cases—in cult organizations that Kona Jukun called *janu*, which were explained to the uninitiated as "ancestors" (for which Kona Jukun share the Wukari term *aku*; Dinslage and Storch 2000, 68), but which initiated men conceived of as dangerous spirits. Cults stored their apparatuses and held their meetings in shrines dotted around the margins of the town, a pattern familiar elsewhere in the Middle Benue. Some cults performed dances with statues (typically held by the arms, in the same way as noted of Gwana royal rituals above; Dinslage and Storch 2000, 107–8).

The use of vertical masquerades, as noted already, is shared by Kona Jukun with their Mumuye and Wurkun neighbors. Although the relationship is at first sight less obvious, I shall argue that there is also a link between Jukun statuary and the Aku masquerades typical of southwestern Jukun, particularly those around Wukari. Here again, the similarity concerns ornamentation of the head: particularly the hair and the pronounced overhang at the chin, which may indicate a beard.

Interleaf E in this volume illustrates a particularly intriguing group of figures that Rubin's fieldwork evidence suggests most probably come from the southeastern corner of his statue-using sector, in the valley of the upper Taraba River and its tributaries, particularly from the people called Wurbo. Although assimilated to the more columnar nuclear style by Rubin, the figures from this region, of which several examples have surfaced since he wrote, appear sufficiently distinctive to justify disengaging them as a distinct group (see figs. E.1, E.2). Wurbo figures share some of the features of ornament and facial overhang typical of the northeastern Jukun nuclear style, but they differ in

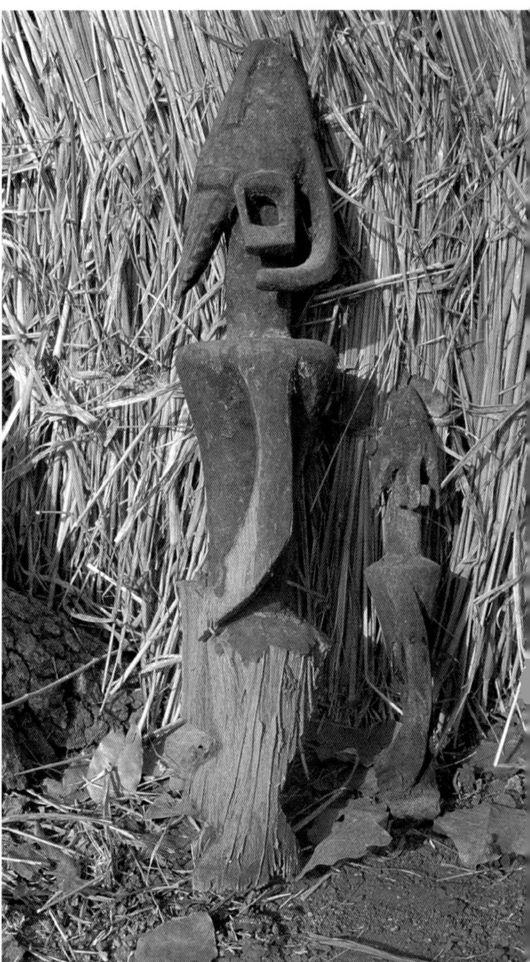

8.58

Arnold Rubin identifies these figures as Akere and his wife Asau, owned by a man identified as Abubakar (a very common name) of Pindiga. The male figure's long beard, hanging braids and openwork ears (similar to some Mumuye figures) make it highly distinctive. The female figure is a more conventional columnar representation, with round earplugs and a head that seems almost Janus-faced in conception with overhangs to the front and rear.

PHOTOGRAPH BY ARNOLD RUBIN, PINDIGA, NOVEMBER 29, 1964, RUBIN ARCHIVE, FOWLER MUSEUM AT UCLA, NEG. NO. 451

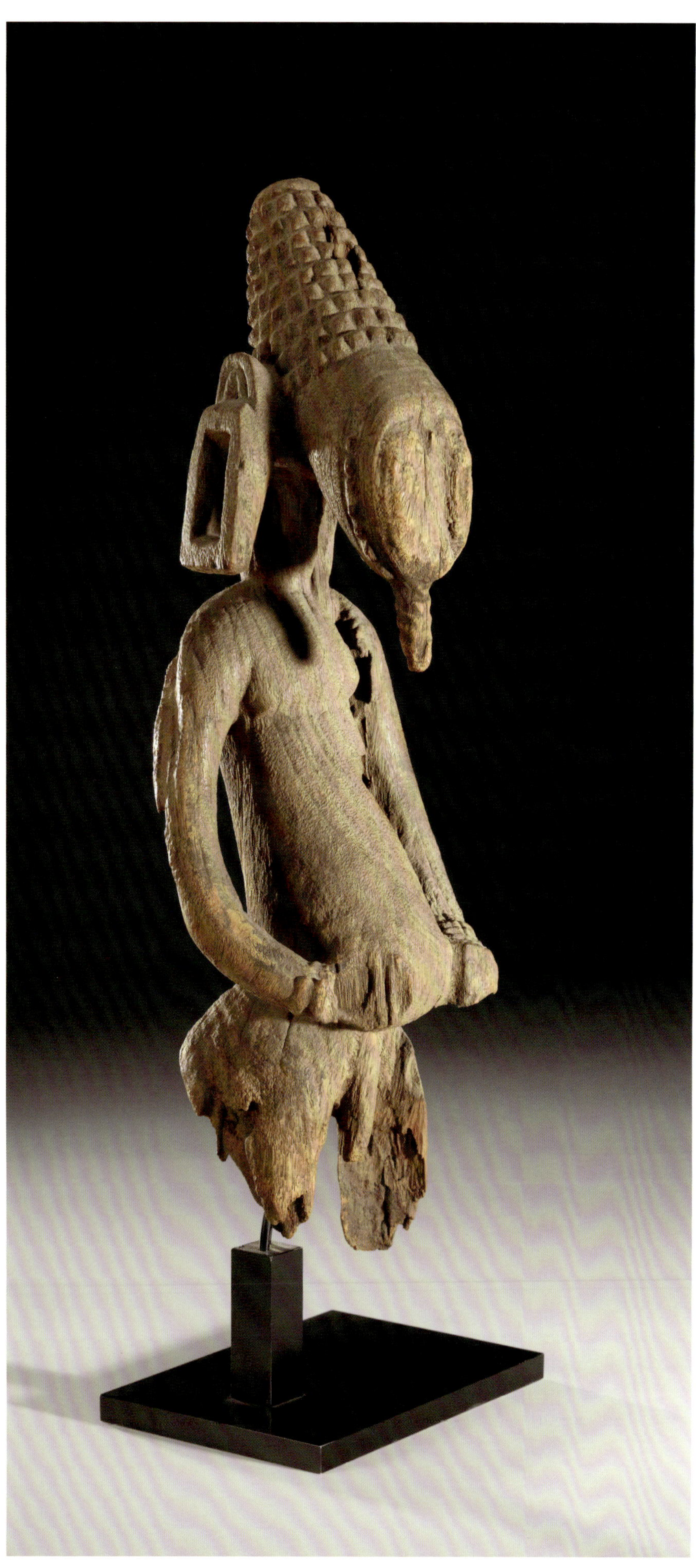

8.59
Figure
Jukun peoples, Gaji village (?), late nineteenth to early twentieth century or before
Wood
H: 62.23 cm

VIRGINIA MUSEUM OF FINE ARTS, RICHMOND; ROBERT AND NANCY NOOTER COLLECTION, ADOLPH D. AND WILKINS C. WILLIAMS FUND, 2005.37

IMAGE: © VIRGINIA MUSEUM OF FINE ARTS. PHOTOGRAPH BY TRAVIS FULLERTON

PROVENANCE: ROBERT AND NANCY NOOTER COLLECTION.

This Jukun figure is very similar to one named Ku, photographed by Rubin in 1965 in the village of Gaji, north of the Benue River (cf. fig. 9.5). Stylistically—with its cantilevered neck, mask-like face, elaborate headdress, and rounded belly—it belongs with the Wurbo figures (discussed in interleaf E), which have been documented south of the Benue River, rather than to the more columnar style of figure sculpture that Rubin defined for northern Jukun.

several respects which are aesthetically startling. The most striking features at first sight are the cantilevered neck, which imparts to the figures an impression of being hunched forward, transforming the overhang of the front facial plane, typical of Jukun figures, by angling the entire head forward from the body, and a distension of the stomach that is entirely unlike Middle Benue columnar statuary (see figs. E.4a,b). This overall configuration is shared by the bulky Jukun male Aku masquerade, the head of which is worn at the front of its body at an angle midway between a horizontal and vertical masquerade. The surface detail of the figures is very finely carved with extensive indications of personal ornament and scarification, including elaborate hats and beards. The torsos of the figures are often elongated, and they stand on relatively short stocky legs, not unlike many Mumuye figures in this respect, although the legs of Wurbo figures were usually covered by cloths. An example of this style of figure, illustrated by Rubin from the Lagos Museum (1969, II, fig. 132) resembles in its overall conformation that of the main figure of the "Yaku Mam" shrine in the village of Gaji in the Upper Taraba Valley, and a further group of three figures from Wurbon Daudu in the same area (fig. 8.59; Rubin 1969, II, figs. 143–46, 147–50; see also this volume, figs. 9.1, 9.2, 9.6). A number of unprovenanced figures similar in style and quality to these has emerged onto the art market subsequent to Rubin's researches and might well come from the same general region. Carbon 14 dates of some antiquity for examples of these are discussed by Berns in this volume (see interleaf E).

WURKUN

The artworks of the people referred to collectively as Wurkun, who live further to the northeast of the most northerly Jukun, are described in detail in Joerg Adelberger's contribution to this volume (see chapter 13). The status of the Wurkun ethnonym, either in the past or present, is complex. It may have been a term that Jukun applied to these neighboring people who nowadays use it of themselves in some contexts (a situation similar to that of the Mumuye described earlier, or indeed of the Chamba). Whatever the differences in origin and language among Wurkun peoples, there are some similarities in Wurkun material culture. A majority of Wurkun figures tend toward a minimalist columnar form (similar to some Chamba examples but more extreme in their abstraction; see fig. 8.8), while their tall vertical masks are more severe and angular versions of those found among the Kona Jukun and some northern Mumuye (see chapter 14). As such, Wurkun fit into the artistic geography of the Middle Benue region as an outlier both in terms of their location and in terms of their aesthetics (see chapter 13). Like their Chamba and Mumuye counterparts, however, Wurkun figures appear to have been highly versatile actors in a variety of settings, including protective and aggressive cults, divination, and broadly ancestral observances.

GOEMAI, MONTOL, KULERE, KANTANA

Moving from the eastern to the western neighbors of the northern Jukun, we encounter a number of peoples living between the Benue River and the broken terrain amid the southern escarpments of the Jos Plateau. These groups are better known for their horizontal fusion masks than they are for figure sculptures.

As we shall see in chapter 10 (pp. 341–42), one type of Goemai masquerade seems to have been heavily influenced by southwestern Jukun conventions, to the extent of copying the male masquerade of the Jukun Aku Maga complex, apparently as a replacement for, or complement to, a preexisting form. Whereas Rubin suggested (as discussed above) that the use of figures and horizontal masquerades had become mutually exclusive among southwestern Jukun, this does not appear to have been the case for Goemai. Roy Sieber published only one of a remarkable series of photographs provided to him by Robin Jagoe (fig. 8.60a) of two statues being carried, with salutes and acclamation, to the vicinity of the graves of the chiefs of Goemai.

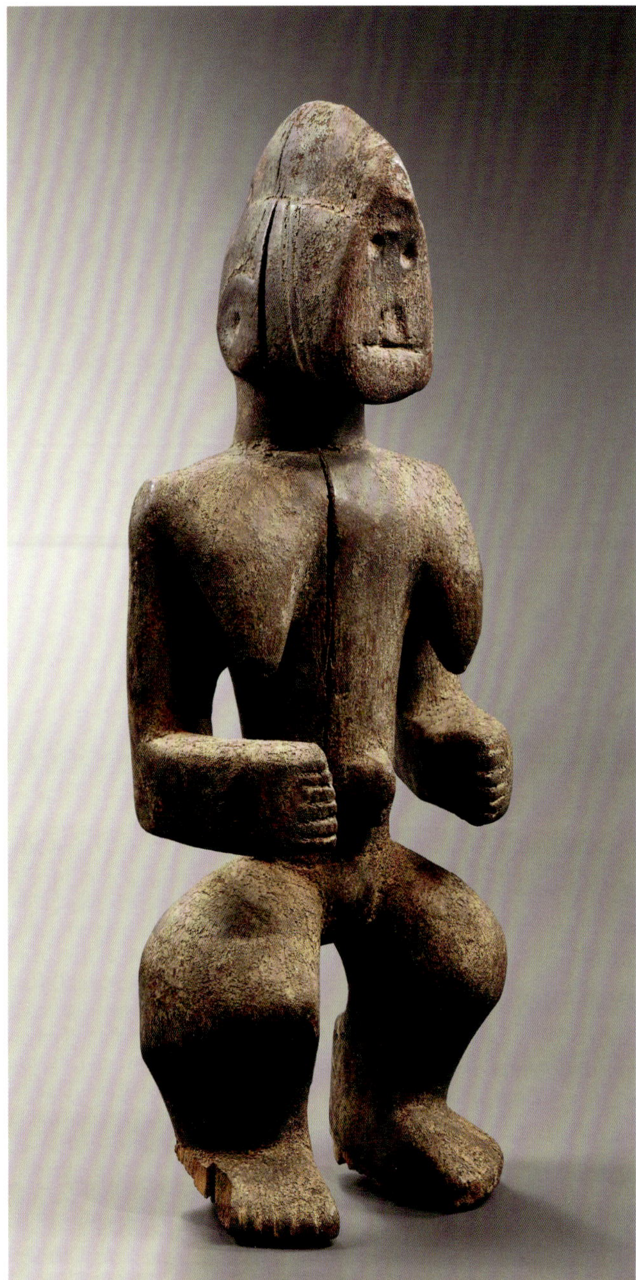

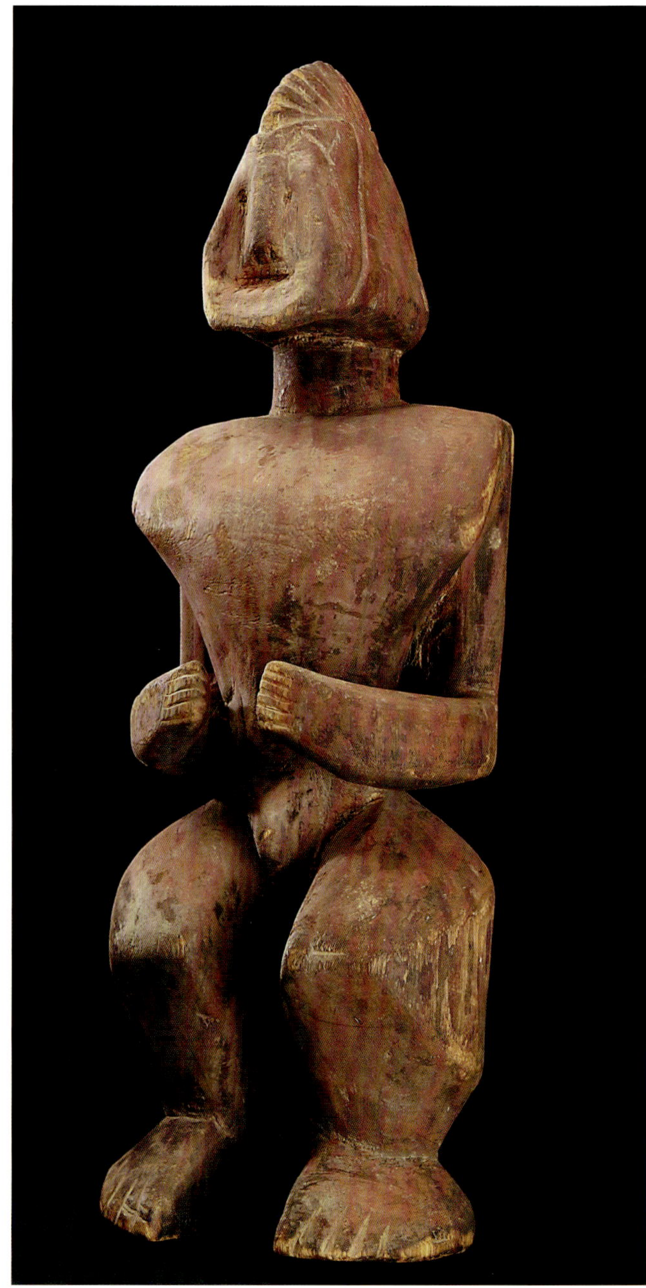

8.61
Female figure
Montol peoples, before 1970
Wood
H: 52
PRIVATE COLLECTION PARIS
IMAGE: COURTESY PRIVATE COLLECTOR. PHOTO-
GRAPH © HUGHES DUBOIS, 2010
PROVENANCE: PURCHASED BETWEEN 1970 AND 1979
BY PRESENT OWNER

This female Montol figure that entered a
private collection in the postcolonial period
is very similar to a male figure that reached
Europe more than a half century earlier (see
fig. 8.62) suggesting it might be by the same
hand, or at least workshop tradition. Unlike the
male, the female is portrayed with earplugs.

8.62
Male figure
Montol peoples, before 1905
Wood
H: 62 cm
MUSEUM DER KULTUREN BASEL, SWITZERLAND,
III 2144
IMAGE: © MUSEUM DER KULTUREN, BASEL, SWIT-
ZERLAND. PHOTOGRAPH BY MARKUS GRUBER, 2006
PROVENANCE: COLLECTED BY HANNS VISCHER,
NIGERIA, 1905

This male figure is carved in the chunkier of
the two styles used in the Komtin cults that
have been considered characteristic of Montol
(cf. fig. 8.1). It was among a group of five
probably collected around 1902 and donated by
the young Hanns (later Sir Hanns) Vischer in
1905 to the Basel Museum für Völkerkunde. An
accession note from the collector, applicable it
seems to all five figures, records they were kept
in small, grass-thatched, round stone houses
("*dodo*," or cult houses, in Hausa), out of sight
of women and children, where they dispensed
justice after libations. In previous times, trophy
skulls decorated the huts (presumably similar to
that illustrated by Kevin Carroll; see fig. 12.16).

can be examined, rather than simply seen in reproduction, ornamentation, patination, and other evidence of use (or neglect) can provide insights into its earlier lifeworld. Information about the subsequent collection and circulation of a figure may narrow its provenance. Considered critically, the quantity of a particular type of object circulating in the artworld (of museums, collections, and auctions) compared to the size of the population that made and used it may tell us something about frequency: does the ratio of, say, figures or masks to population suggest high (like Mumuye figures or Chamba masks) or low (like northeastern Jukun figures) frequency of use?

Leaving formal analysis now, I want to return in conclusion to the fascinating story told by the travels of these objects. Few Middle Benue artworks remain in the contexts for which they were intended. Even those still in Nigeria have gone on arduous journeys. Others have traveled far afield: through the hands of those who made them, sold or gave them, used them in a variety of rituals, removed them from this context (with or without the right to do so, even supposing this right was clear), via "runners," dealers, galleries, auctions, private owners, and public collections. The physical properties of many objects have been altered in the course of this movement (through "restoration" or "cleaning"), and their meanings have also changed. Powers have been gained as well as lost. A figure may have lost its power of speech and action but acquired a market value that may have seemed just as remarkable to its creator. Objects have also acquired new biographies, and as a result of this have entered relations with other objects that they would not have encountered in their original social circles.

All this might make it seem that the first responsibility of the commentator is to position the object for its artworld viewers back into its earlier cultworld context. To strip away accretions. This strikes me as an eminently reasonable request, corresponding to the project of thick ethnographic description. If this is "rescue" ethnography, I do not have a problem with it. To be concerned about the ways things were for an object among the people who called it into being strikes me as a dignity the object is owed. Yet in a world of things and people in motion to disregard the later biographies of objects in order to attend only to the time in their lives when they were "authentic" seems blinkered. We know more about the users who installed these pieces in villas, loft apartments, and museums than we do about the people who stored them in pottery jars within ritual enclosures. The later lives of these objects must be told in terms of movement, marketing, translation, transformation (not to mention copying and misrepresentation), arduous journeys through war-torn countries (colonial Kamerun, Nigeria during the Biafran secession, from Germany to Russia and back for elements of the Berlin collection), and the assumption of elevated statuses as things considered precious on both aesthetic and monetary scales (probably not independently). But the story does not stop there: West Africans are reconnecting with these objects, but in quite different ways ranging from iconoclastic rejection, as traces of heathenism, to reconnection as embodiments of identity within the logical and emotional cathexes of artefactual ethnicity. The biographies of these objects are far from closed, and we may anticipate increasing numbers of voices laying claim to understanding the intentions with which they will be attributed. ●

MARLA C. BERNS

INTERLEAF e

Wurbo Jukun Sculpture from the Taraba and Wase River Valleys

Within the body of figurative shrine sculpture that Arnold Rubin documented in northeastern Jukun communities, the examples he saw along the southern Taraba and northern Wase rivers, tributaries of the Benue, are distinctive enough to be considered a separate subgenre. In his "Memoir" (see chapter 9 of this volume), Rubin described the sculpture from the village of Wurbon Daudu, located along the Taraba River, as representing the "nuclear style" of Jukun figurative carving (see chapter 9, p. 297). Having had the opportunity to see many more examples (now in collections) than Rubin did during his lifetime, we argue here that there was not a single "nuclear" style but rather several substyles that can be identified with particular Jukun towns located north and south of the Benue River.

What we are defining here as the "Wurbo style" (figs. E.1, E.2) differs from the style of Jukun sculpture from the towns of Gwana and Pindiga located to the northeast (see figs. 9.11, 9.12). It is Rubin's pioneering art historical field research of the mid-1960s that allows us to associate particular examples presently in collections with specific places, and there are at least twenty sculptures that we can call Wurbo.[1] This attribution derives from the group of three figures Rubin photographed in the town of Wurbon Daudu (see fig. 9.1) and another three he documented nearby in the village of Gaji (fig. E.3, and see figs. 9.5, 9.6), both located south of the Benue. To the best of our knowledge, three of these six figures are now in private collections (figs. E.4a,b).[2] North of the Benue in the towns of Wase Tofa and Mabo, Rubin documented six additional figures distinguished by their polychromy. Their figurative style is similar enough to include them here as "Wurbo" (figs. E.5a,b, and see fig. 9.15).

According to Rubin's fieldnotes, he spent a total of five days in these Jukun towns in 1964–1965: one in Wase Tofa (December 23, 1964), one in Mabo (December 24, 1964), one in Gaji (October 21, 1965), and two in Wurbon Daudu (October 23–24, 1965). Most of what he learned about the functions and

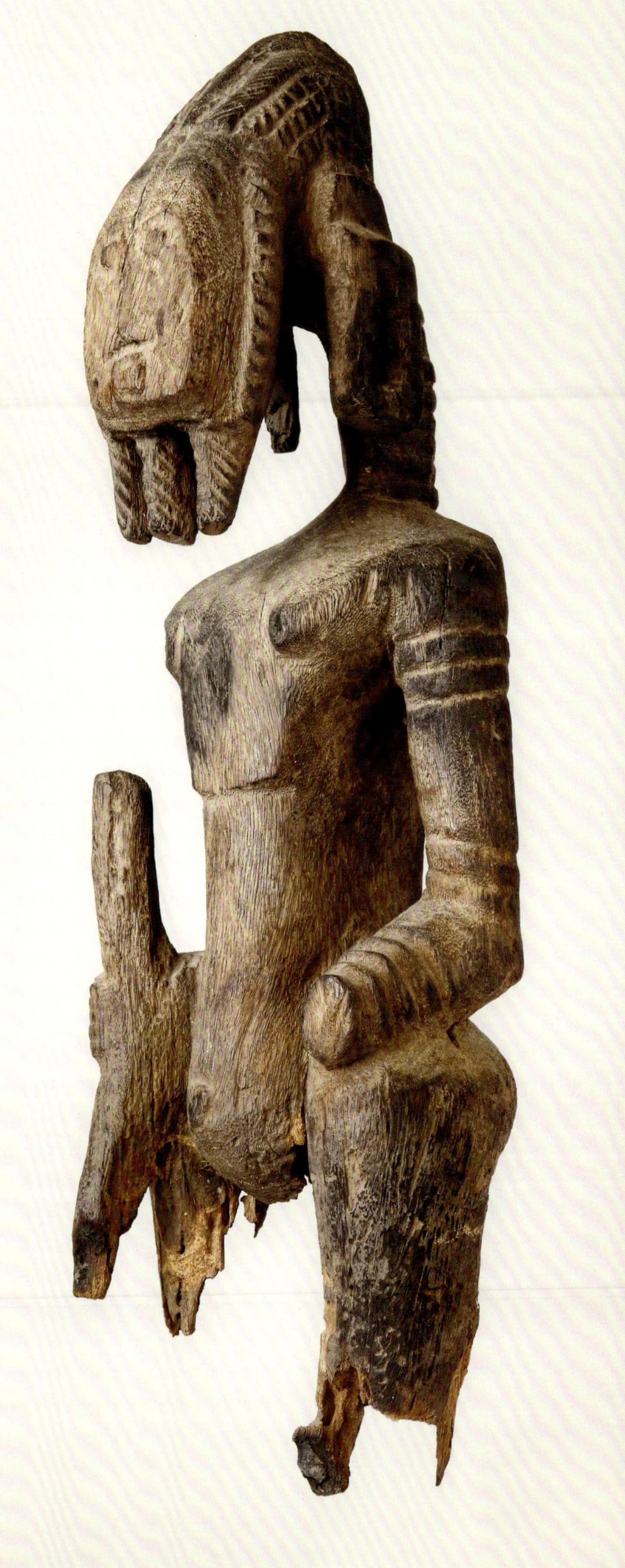

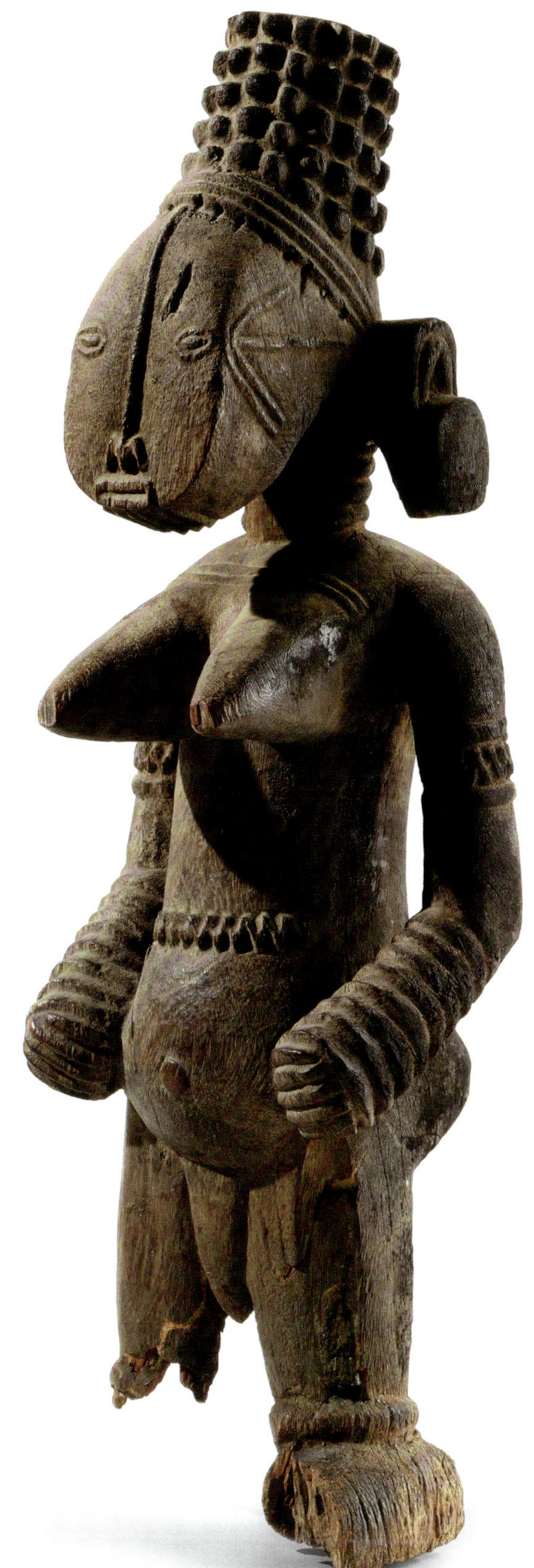

E.1

Standing male figure
Jukun peoples, Wurbon Daudu (?), late nineteenth to early
twentieth century or before
Wood
H: 57.2 cm
PRIVATE COLLECTION, STANFORD
IMAGE: COURTESY PRIVATE COLLECTOR. PHOTOGRAPH BY ROBERT KATO, 2010
PROVENANCE: J. J. KLEJMAN; RENÉE NELSON; ADRIAN SCHLAG

The approach to carving this male figure appears to relate closely to
that used for the female in figure E.2. This is especially apparent in the
elaborate ornamentation of the arms, the rings around the neck, and
the delicacy of its facial features. The blackening of the surface likely
resulted from exposure to heat and smoke, if not to fire directly, at some
point in its history. The same blackening is visible on the left arm and
ear spools of the female in figure E.2, lending additional credibility to
the proposition that these two sculptures (male and female) may have
been enshrined together in Wurbon Daudu (even if we cannot argue that
they were intended as a husband-wife pair).

E.2

Standing female figure
Jukun peoples, Wurbon Daudu (?), late nineteenth to early
twentieth century or before
Wood
H: 59.7 cm
THE MENIL COLLECTION, HOUSTON, 71-05 DJ
IMAGE: © THE MENIL COLLECTION, HOUSTON. PHOTOGRAPH BY HICKEY-
ROBERTSON, 2010
PROVENANCE: EDOUARD KLEJMAN AND JEAN-MICHEL HUGUENIN; J. J. KLEJMAN,
NEW YORK; MENIL FOUNDATION, INC., HOUSTON, 1971

On the basis of its style, this stunning figure is likely from the Taraba
River Valley in the environs of the town of Wurbon Daudu. It is unusual
in the Wurbo corpus because of the fullness of its form, the bracelets on
its lower arms, and the subtle details of its facial and body scarifications.
It recalls maternal sculptures made by peoples living in the Lower Benue
Valley, reminding us of the historical relationship between the Jukun and
those groups.

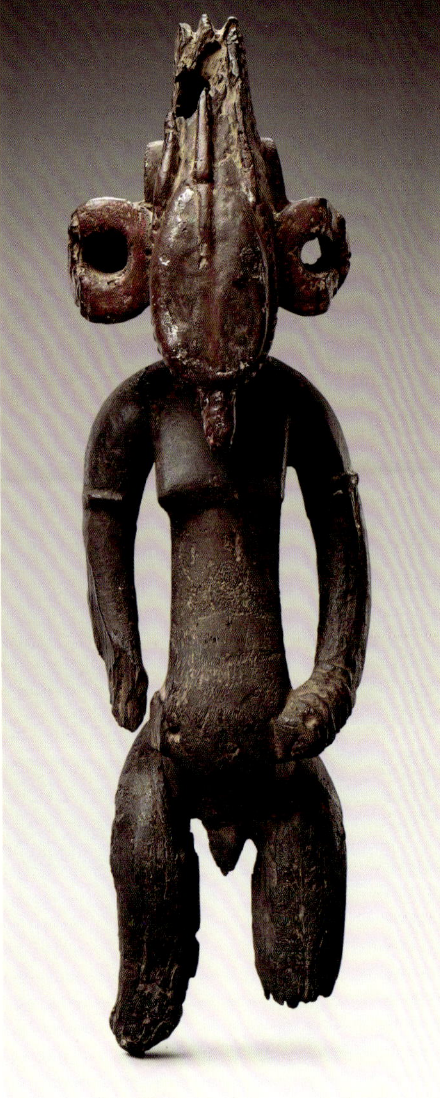

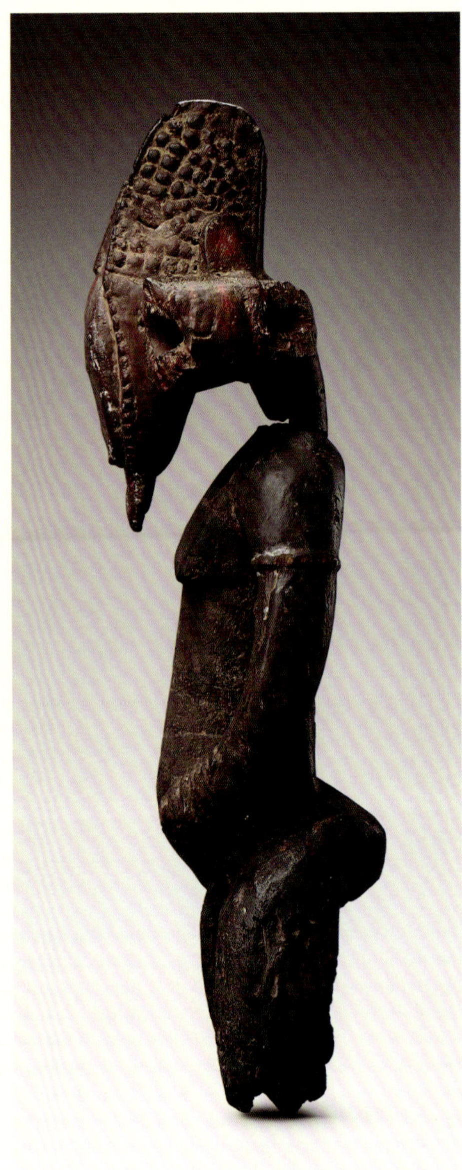

E.3

This wooden figure of Ku, a protective community deity, was enshrined in the village of Gaji in the Taraba River Valley. Ku was kept inside a ceramic bowl and is shown fully dressed, with cloth covering its torso and feathers inserted into a headband around its conical crest. The same sculpture, now in a private collection, is illustrated in figures E.4a,b.

PHOTOGRAPH BY ARNOLD RUBIN, OCTOBER 21, 1965, RUBIN ARCHIVE, FOWLER MUSEUM AT UCLA, NEG. NO.1020.

E.4a,b

Standing male figure (Ku)
Jukun peoples, Gaji village, fifteenth to seventeenth century
Wood, pigment
H: 50 cm

PRIVATE COLLECTION, BRUSSELS, 2008

IMAGE: © COURTESY ARCHIVE OF PRIVATE COLLECTOR

PROVENANCE: OUSMANE (HAUSA DEALER), 1967; PRIVATE COLLECTION, FRANCE; PIERRE DARTEVELLE COLLECTION, BRUSSELS

When Ku was photographed by Arnold Rubin in 1965, none of its body was visible (see fig. E.3, and fig. 9.5). Stripped of its adornments, it is now possible to see that the surface of the figure was blackened and that red pigment (as well as traces of white) was applied to its face, headdress, and large cylindrical earplugs. The probable age of the sculpture suggested by its radiocarbon dating is reflected in its highly fragile state—its head nearly detached and its core completely eaten away by insect infestation.

meanings of these shrine sculptures is included in his "Memoir." In each instance the figures he saw were "dressed" (fig. E.6, and see fig. E.3), and he was told that removing their cloth coverings could cause harm, even death. Rubin noted that the figures he saw in Wurbon Daudu "look pretty crisp" (see fig. E.6), an observation that may have been made in contrast to the three sculptures he had seen just days before in Gaji, where the heads were heavily worn and the bodies fragmentary (see figs. E.4a,b). This interleaf is intended to outline the nuances within this subgenre and suggest the likely longevity of this tradition in the Middle Benue.

All the Wurbo figures are marked by a notable attention to the details of the head and headdress, with the torso, arms, and legs left as rather rudimentary columnar forms arranged mostly in a rigid posture (figs. E.4a,b). The arms are carved away from the body, and the hands in most cases touch the hips, creating a handle-like configuration that makes the sculpture easy to hold by its arms or torso. The angular, jutting buttocks on many examples may have made it easier to wrap the figures

E.5a,b
These two male-female figure pairs from the village of Mabo, north of
the Benue River, are named Mukungudzi and his wife (fig. E.5a, above)
and Kubat and his wife (fig. E.5b). Their style conforms to what we define
here as "Wurbo," but each figure is distinguished by red and white painted
details over a blackened head and torso. The lower extremities were left
unpainted and always kept covered with cloth. Wear patterns on the arms
reveal they were likely carried during performances (see fig. E.9).
PHOTOGRAPH BY ARNOLD RUBIN, MABO VILLAGE, DECEMBER 24, 1964, RUBIN
ARCHIVE, FOWLER MUSEUM AT UCLA, SLIDE NOS. A1.11.13.7, A1.11.13.9.

with cloth. Sometimes a spear or staff is carried in the figure's
right hand, and the arms are ornamented at the wrist, elbow, or
forearm with incisions that may represent bangles (see figs. E.1,
E.7, E.8).

Many of the Wurbo figures are conceived as husband-
wife pairs or in the case of the figures from Wurbon Daudu,
a husband (Asenzo) and his two wives (Ajiku and Agbadu;
Rubin, October 23, 1965). They display an intriguing gender
ambiguity, with males and females wearing beards, and only
one wife, Agbadu (see fig. E.6), carved with breasts. The husband-wife pairs from Mabo reveal other ambiguities. In one
pair, Mukungudzi, the husband, has a "pigtail," or sacramental
lock of hair known to have been worn by Jukun men, but at
the same time has "breasts" that are larger and more conical
than those of his wife (see fig. E.5a, see also fig. E.9). The
same is true of the second Mabo couple, Kubat (see fig. E.5b)
and his wife. Kubat has a topknot and conical breasts, while
his smaller-scale wife (with breasts) has a crested coiffure.
Because both Mabo pairs were dressed with wrappers when
Rubin photographed them, it is impossible to see if they were
carved with primary sexual characteristics. In a similar pair
now in a private collection that lacks any of its cloth coverings, however, the "wife," depicted with a transverse crest,
has breasts, a penis, and even a beard.[3] Rubin's fieldnotes do
not address these inconsistencies, perhaps because he thought
the exaggerated breasts on the husbands referred to the phy-
sique of elder men with sagging pectorals. Other male Wurbo
figures (see figs. E.1, E.8) have clearly indicated circular "nipples," a detail that is absent on Gwana and Pindiga examples.
It also appears that neither the shape of the Wurbo figures'
crests nor their ear ornaments are determined consistently by
gender. There is little doubt that the distinctive style of these
sculptures is intentional, and it may be that their curative
efficacy is enhanced by the ambiguity and/or duality of their
gender references.

Only one known Wurbo sculpture, now in the Menil
collection (see fig. E.2), has unambiguous female features—
sharply protruding conical breasts, a torso swelling at the
stomach, a modesty covering, and forearms laden with bracelets. Such features are reminiscent of Lower Benue maternal
figures (see figs. 2.1, 2.5). This striking carving is also unusual
for the delicate arrow-shaped scarifications on the cheeks and
the raised "cicatrices" around the waist and the upper arms
(see Berns 2008).

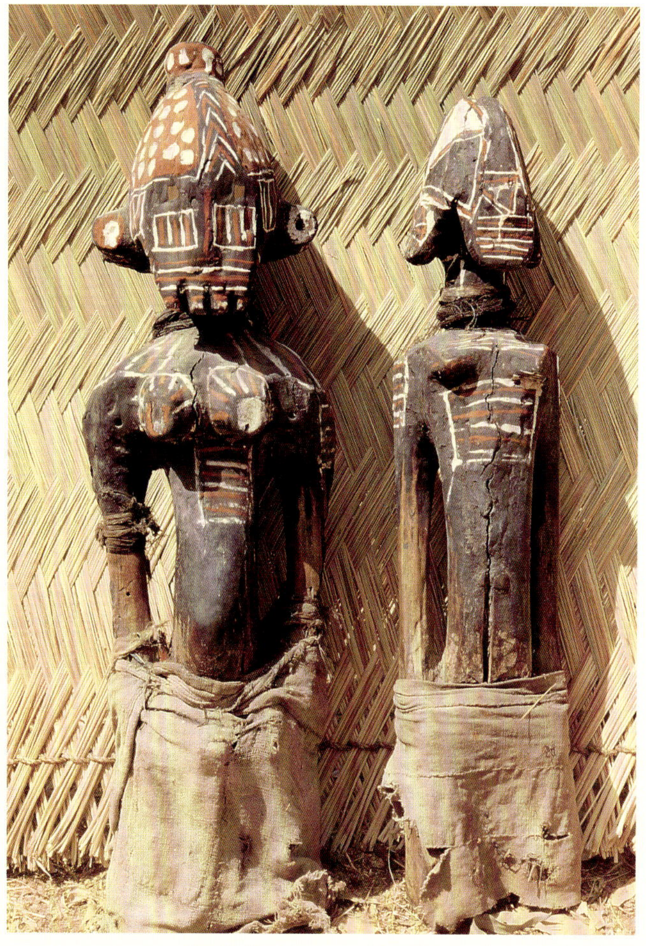

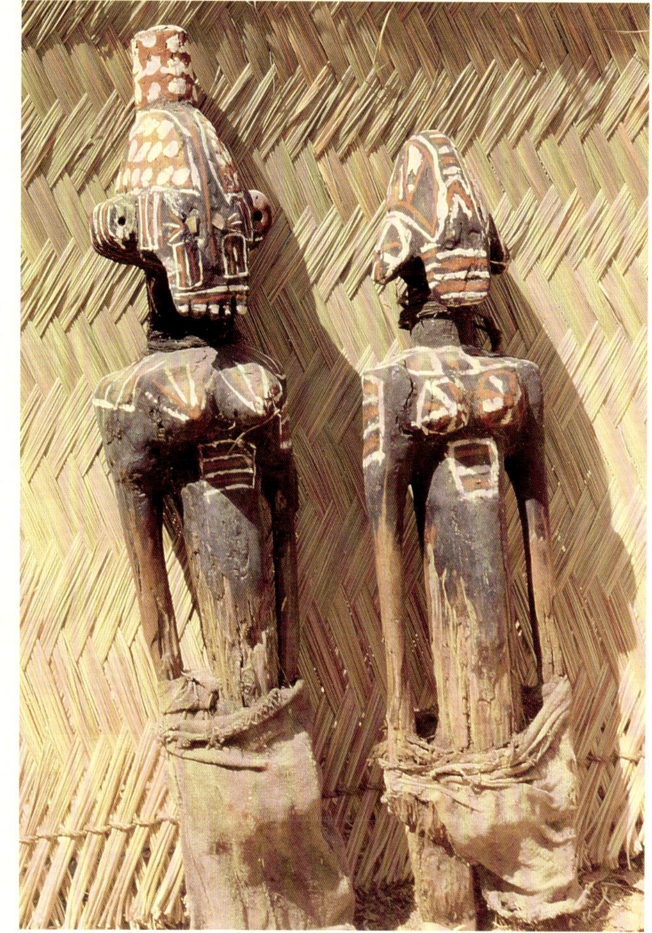

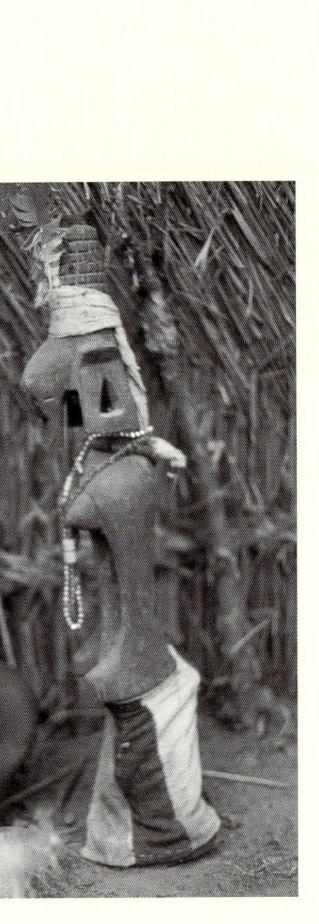

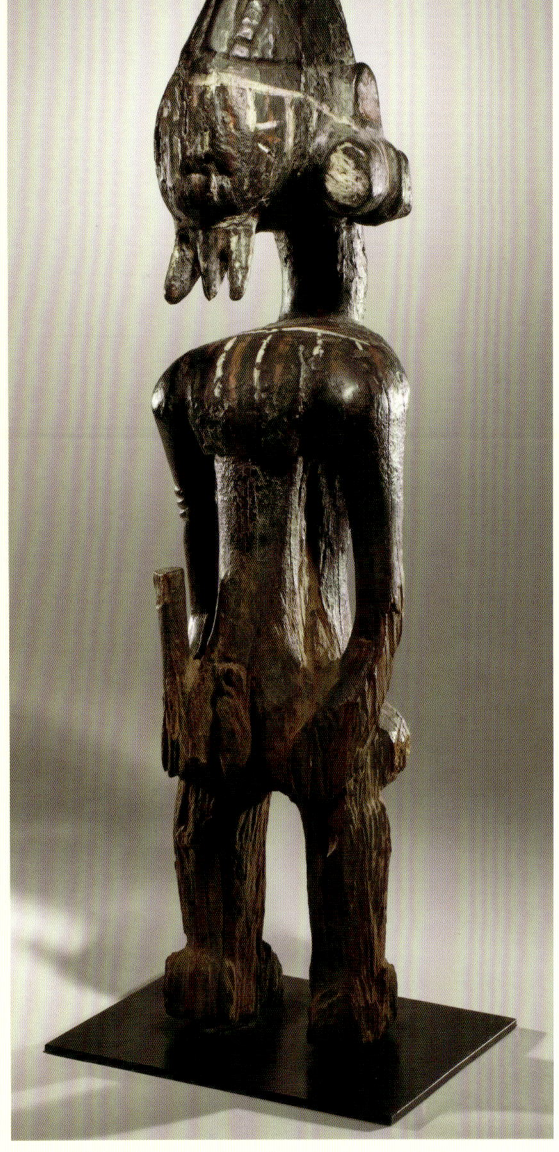

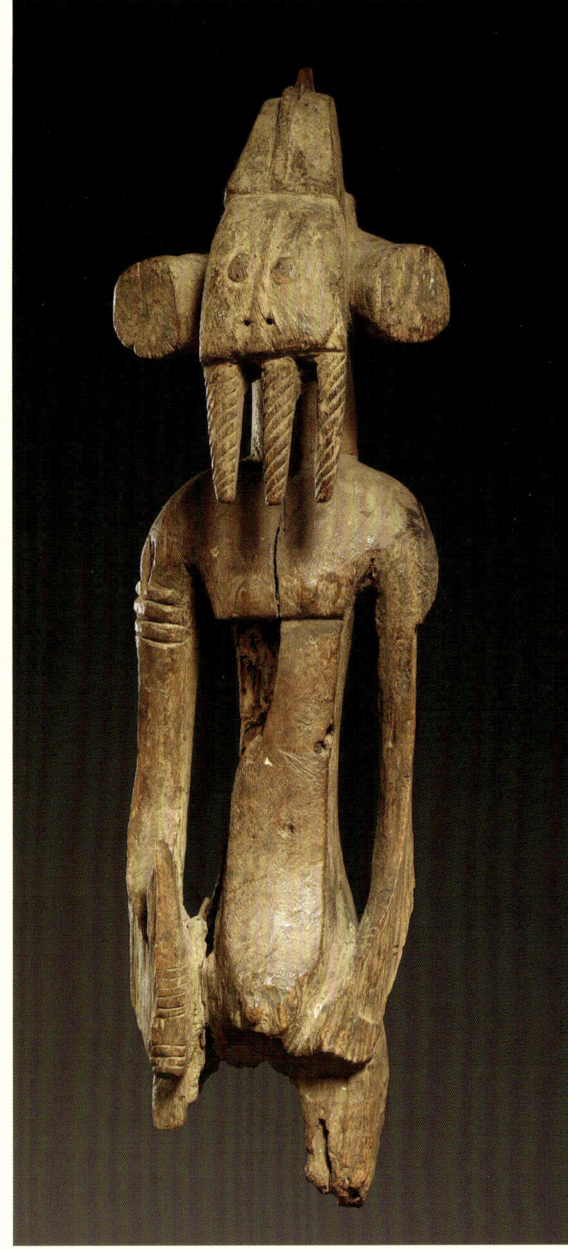

E.6

This side view of Agbadu, the second wife of Asenzo, shows her small pointed breasts, the smooth surface of her upper body and head as well as her straight, upright posture (see fig. 9.1). The large, perforated earlobes and the manner in which the wrapper is bound tightly over the buttocks are easier to read from the profile.

PHOTOGRAPH BY ARNOLD RUBIN, WURBON DAUDU TOWN, OCTOBER 23, 1965, RUBIN ARCHIVE, FOWLER MUSEUM AT UCLA, NEG. NO. 1043.

E.7 (CENTER)

Standing male figure
Jukun peoples, Mabo (?), late nineteenth century or before
Wood, pigment
H: 64.8 cm
PRIVATE COLLECTION
IMAGE: © PRIVATE COLLECTOR. PHOTOGRAPH BY BENJAMIN WATKINS
PROVENANCE: MARC AND DENYSE GINZBERG, NEW YORK, 1984

The linear patterns of red and white pigment on the blackened head and upper body of this sculpture align it more closely with the figures documented from Mabo, north of the Benue River. The worn and heavily repainted surface of this example attests to its long-term use and handling, making it clear as well that its unadorned lower extremities would have been covered in cloth wrappings.

E.8 (RIGHT)

Standing male figure
Jukun peoples, Wurbon Daudu (?), late nineteenth to early twentieth century or before
Wood
H: 61.5 cm
JAMES AND LAURA ROSS, 2001
IMAGE: COURTESY OF LENDER. PHOTOGRAPH © JOHN BIGELOW TAYLOR
PROVENANCE: JOHN KLEJMAN, FAITH AND DORAN WRIGHT, NEW YORK; PACE PRIMITIVE, NEW YORK, 2001

This sculpture conforms to what we are defining here as a "Wurbo" style. Its delicate condition—its lower extremities and body core have been lost to insect infestation—suggests it belonged to an earlier generation of sculptures than those Rubin photographed in Wurbon Daudu in 1965. The striking rectangularity of the face supports the argument being made here that these figures are meant to be understood as wearing a "mask."

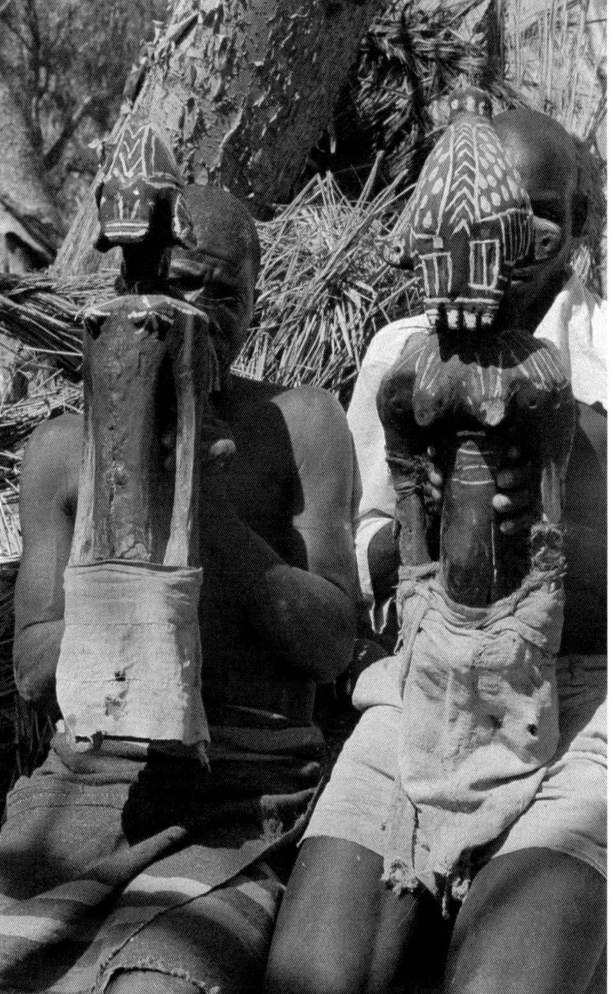

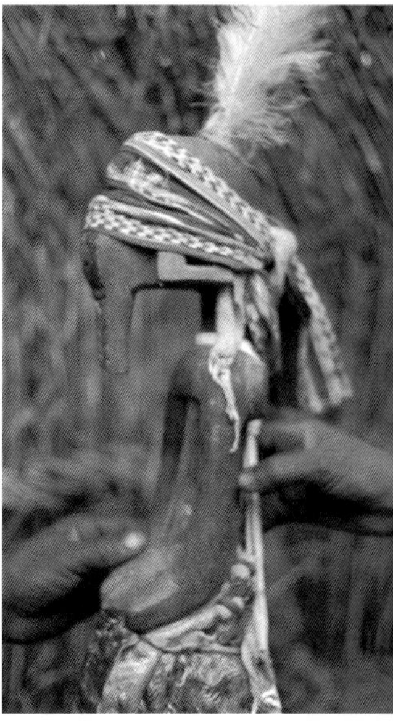

E.9

This photograph shows two Jukun men holding Mukungudzi (right) and his wife by the torso in the manner in which they might have been carried in performance. This image also shows the gender ambiguity of these figures, with the husband's "breasts" larger than those of his wife.

PHOTOGRAPH BY ARNOLD RUBIN, MABO VILLAGE, DECEMBER 24, 1964, RUBIN ARCHIVE, FOWLER MUSEUM AT UCLA, NEG. NO. L-66.

E.10

This profile view of the spirit incarnation, Asenzo, emphasizes the radical cantilever of the head over the chest. The face of Asenzo (see fig. 9.1) also ends in a sharp horizontal line with the tripartite beard projecting straight downward. This unusual treatment suggests that these hybridized Jukun figures have been conceived of as wearing masks associated with traditions documented to the southwest of Wurbon Daudu in the Jukun capital of Wukari.

PHOTOGRAPH BY ARNOLD RUBIN, WURBON DAUDU, OCTOBER 23, 1965, RUBIN ARCHIVE, FOWLER MUSEUM AT UCLA, NEG. NO. 1050.

As previously mentioned, the sculptural focus of these Wurbo Jukun figures is clearly on the head with its highly schematic and nearly featureless face; beard, often in the form of multiple, long plaits; large pierced earlobes framing the sides of the head or huge cylindrical earplugs; and an elaborately carved headdress that is either conical or hemispherical in shape. Despite their striking frontal aspect, which is especially the case with those possessing wide cylindrical earplugs (fig. E.8), it is in profile that the heads best reveal their unusual and highly stylized treatment (fig. E.10). Possessing more than just the "pronounced facial overhang" that Rubin describes, and which distinguishes nearly all Jukun figurative sculpture, the chins of Wurbo examples extend straight forward at right angles from their long narrow necks in a sharp cantilever. The overhanging faces and beards of some are nearly flat, serving as a canvas for the low-relief carving of round eyes (or the insertion of metal plugs), a long linear nose, and a circular or ovoid mouth (or no mouth at all). There are subtle distinctions in the shape of the heads and the details of facial features, beards, and headdresses. For example, the sculptures from Gaji, including the figure of Ku now in a private collection (see figs. E.4a,b), another closely related figure now in the Virginia Museum of Fine Arts (see fig. 8.59), and the figure of Yaku Mam (see fig. 9.6) are all notable for the lack of facial features, the presence of dramatic ear spools or open lobes, and incisions framing the sides of the face and ending in one long plaited beard.

The figures from Mabo (and Wase Tofa) are distinguished by their blackened surfaces, achieved with a pigment made from burnt grasses, over which linear patterns and dots were applied to the head and torso in white and red (see fig. E.5a). Arnold Rubin was told by his Mabo informants that the figures were repainted after every harvest to initiate the new agricultural cycle (Rubin fieldnotes, December 24, 1964). A sculpture in a private collection is also likely to be Mabo based on its polychrome decoration (see fig. E.7). Its rich surface patina, with layers of painted designs confined to the exposed head and upper torso, shows that here, too, the legs would have been covered in cloth.[4]

The curious treatment of the heads on the Wurbo corpus, jutting forward over the vertical axis of the body at a sharp angle, and of their unusually flat, nearly featureless faces deserves further consideration. Their long narrow necks, often curving radically forward and sometimes carved with rings, contribute to the unusual forward thrust of the head (see fig. E.1). Might these figures be intended to be understood as wearing masks? The highly abstract configuration of the Jukun Aku-Wunu mask, worn with its rectangular "snout" tipped down at an angle and with a minimalist approach to the features of the face (see fig. 10.5), could be a model for the distinctively long, flat, and rectangular contour of the faces on most Wurbo figures (see figs E.1, E.2, E.8). On a few, this aspect of the face is so exaggerated, it seems unlikely to be anything *but* a mask (see Yale Univesity-Guy van Rijn Archive of African Art, 0005276-01). At least three other Jukun figures in private collections (fig. E.11) have the same rectangular faces, but their heads are surmounted by curved horns and ears reminiscent of the dwarf forest buffalo or "bushcow." In this they resemble the human-animal fusions characteristic of Jukun Aku-Wunu and other horizontal masking traditions found across the Middle Benue (see chapter 10). The rectangular shape of the face with its upward sweeping horns may indeed reference even more directly the plank form of the Jukun Aku-Ma mask (see figs. 10.12a,b). The distinction Rubin draws between the northeastern Jukun who make figures and the southwestern Jukun who make masks may reside less in the absence of "masks" in the northeast than in an unconventional sculptural rendition of a spirit who is incarnated in the world of the living in a hybridized way.

These Wurbo figures were not only enshrined, where offerings could be made to invoke their assistance but were also very possibly carried during ritual performances, held up by their arms or torso so that they partially obscured the faces and bodies of their carriers (see fig. E.9, see also fig. 14.27). This practice may have functioned as an alternative to a more typical masquerade, where a mask covers the head of the wearer and a fiber or cloth costume conceals his body. As incarnations of spirit principles associated with the healing cult of Mam—said to have originated with the Wurbo Jukun (see chapter 9, 295–97)—they are only partially human in form. During Mam rituals, a healer-diviner was possessed by the spirit and was said to have practiced self-mutilation; the linear patterns on the upper arms of many of these sculptures may represent the resultant scarring (see figs E.1, E.8). The object held in the right hand of some of the male figures may represent the iron spear of Mam, which is the focus of ritual practices at Wurbon Daudu and elsewhere.

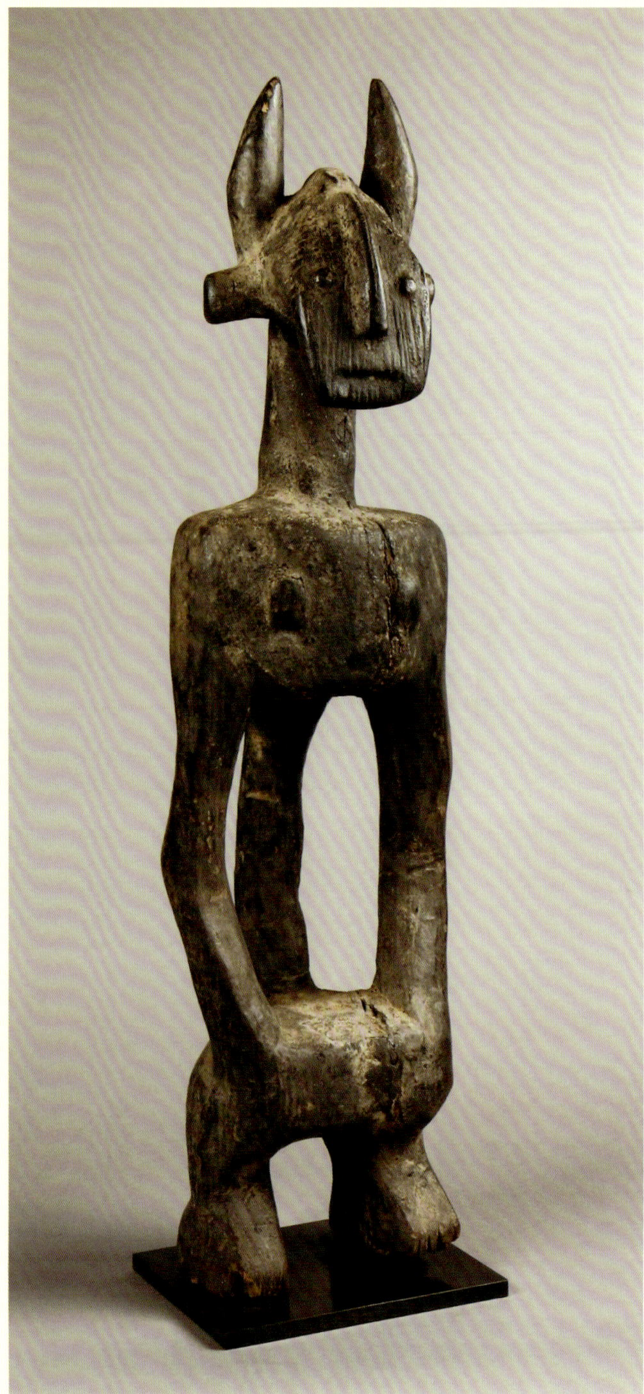

E.11
Standing figure with a buffalo horns
Jukun peoples, early twentieth century
Wood
H: 74 cm
PRIVATE COLLECTION, FRANCE
IMAGE: COURTESY PRIVATE COLLECTOR. PHOTOGRAPH © FRANTZ DUFOUR
PROVENANCE: COLLECTED CIRCA 1980
(NOT IN EXHIBITION)

Only a few Jukun figures in collections combine a human body and face with buffalo or "bushcow" ears and horns. The body of this example is similar to Jukun sculpture documented in Wurbon Daudu (and also in Gwana and Pindiga, north of the Benue River). The figure is carved so its arms form "handles" for carrying (see figs. 14.27–14.29). The rectangular shape of the face and the upward curving horns resemble the Jukun Aku-Ma mask (see figs. 10.12a,b), and it is possible these hybridized figures are conceived as humans wearing animal masks.

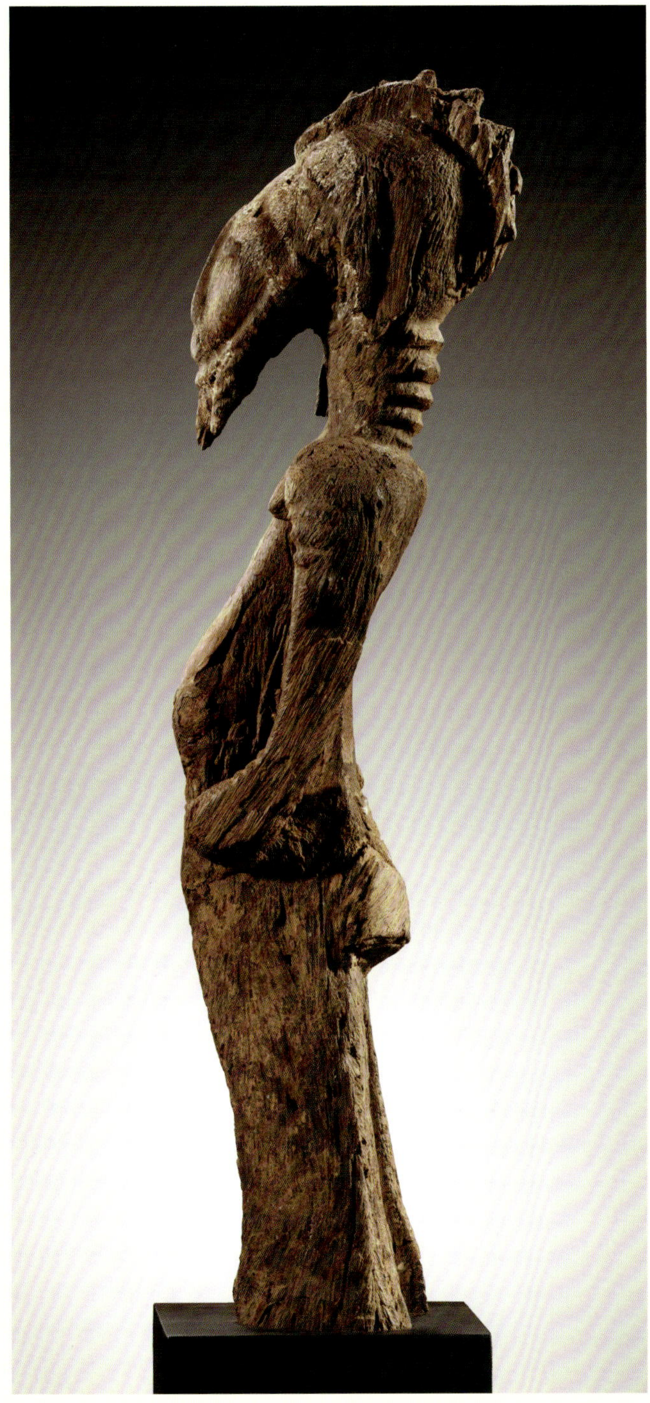

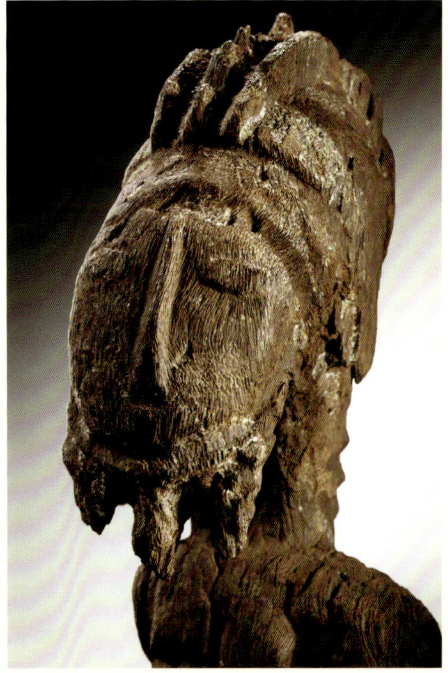

E.12a,b
Standing male figure
Jukun peoples, Wurbon Daudu (?), fifteenth to seventeenth century
Wood
H: 64.5 cm
PRIVATE COLLECTION, FRANCE
IMAGE: COURTESY PRIVATE COLLECTOR. PHOTOGRAPH © STUDIO PHILIPPE
DE FORMANOIR, 2010
PROVENANCE: AKU (CHIEF) OF WUKARI; PIERRE DARTEVELLE, PURCHASED
1966–1967; COLLECTION FRAISSINET, TOULOUSE, FRANCE
(NOT IN EXHIBITION)

This standing male figure has a distinctive stance that deviates from the
more rigid alignment typical of these sculptures. Its sway back creates an
elegant profile, with the backward thrust of the head and the upper curvature of the face, angled sharply over the chest. This is one of two such
sculptures to have been radiocarbon dated. Its possible age is reflected in
its heavily weathered surface. The close-up view of the face (fig. E.12b)
reveals traces of white paint and the minimalism of its features.

A sculpture donated to the British Museum in 1909 by a
Dr. Parsons, who served during the colonial era in the Northern Nigeria Medical Service (see Underwood 1964, fig. 33), is
likely to be the earliest Wurbo figure to enter a collection.[5] The
entire body of this heavily weathered example is intact. This is
unusual in the surviving Wurbo corpus with the exception of
the three figures from Wurbon Daudu, which Rubin felt were
more recently carved (see fig. 9.1), and several others in private
collections (figs. E.12a,b).[6] At least two Wurbo sculptures have
been subjected to carbon 14 testing and dated between the mid-
fifteenth and the seventeenth century.[7] That these pieces could
be more than five hundred years old seems remarkable if not
impossible. Informants from Wurbon Daudu, Gaji, and Mabo
told Rubin that the shrine sculptures he saw had been brought
to their present locations from elsewhere by their forefathers
(with the elders of Mabo naming Kororofa as their ancestral
homeland; Rubin, December 24, 1964).[8] Such relatively small-
scale sculptures could have easily been moved during various
Jukun migrations as a way of securing the ongoing patronage
of powerful tutelary spirits. The fact that the lower extremities of most Wurbo figures are missing or else heavily damaged
by insect infestation, which on many has completely hollowed
the core of their torsos, suggests they were likely enshrined
standing upright on the ground (see figs. E.1, E.8). The convention of wrapping them in cloth surely sustained their ongoing
efficacy despite the ravages of time, and as is evident in the Gaji
example, some were then moved into ceramic bowls to provide
support and protection for their upper bodies and heads against
further infestation (see fig. E.3). Although we are beneficiaries of
Rubin's unparalleled but brief fieldwork on these unusual sculptures, many questions remain unanswered about the meanings of
their highly inventive formal conception and their history of use
and geographical distribution in the Middle Benue. ●

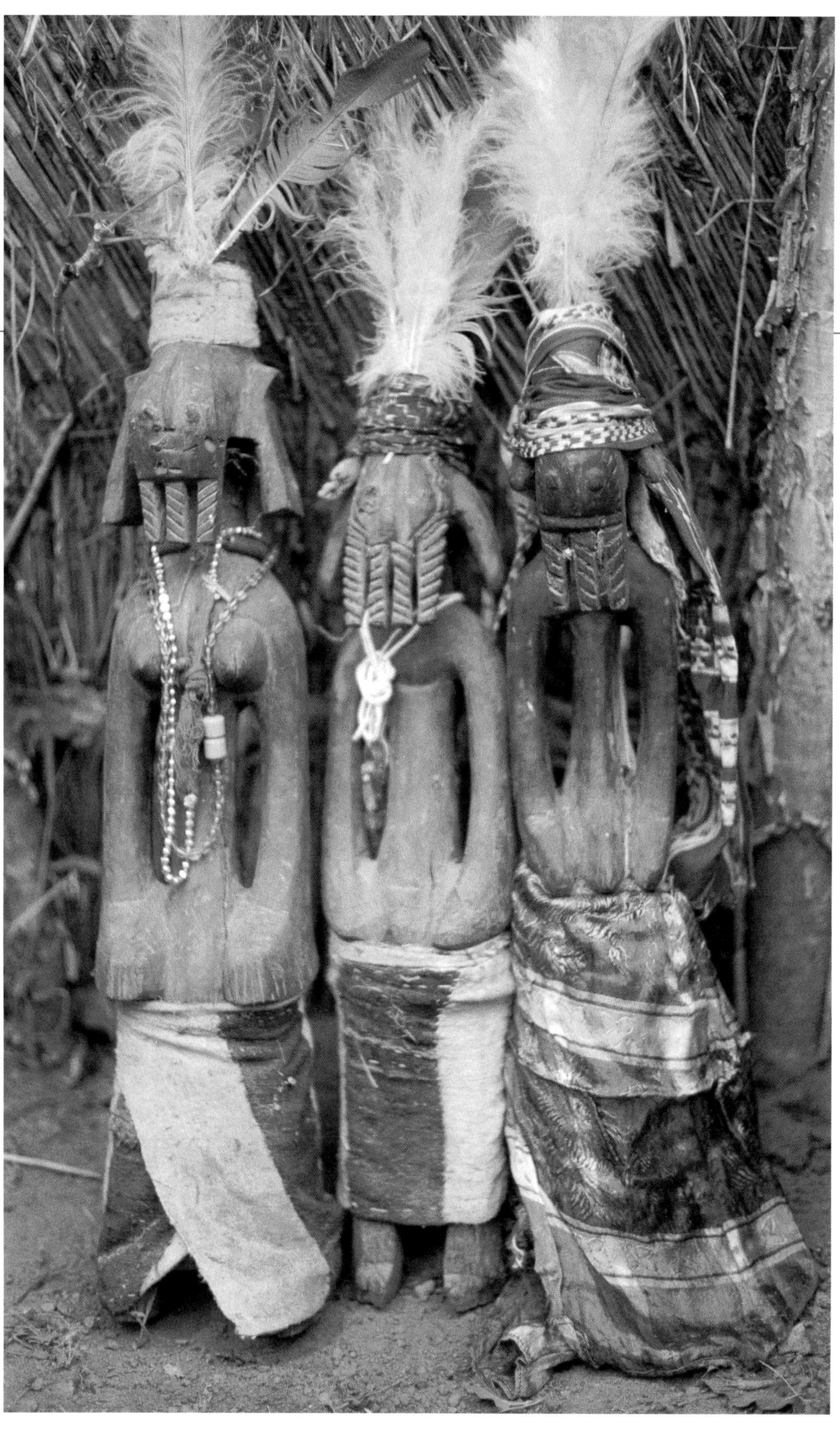

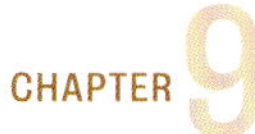

CHAPTER 9

A Memoir: The Jukun of the Middle Benue with a Brief Entry on the Goemai

ARNOLD RUBIN[1]

By the onset of colonization, the valley of the Taraba River, south of the Benue and roughly between the Donga River and the town of Kona, had become a thinly populated cultural backwater. This contrasts with the higher population densities of both the Lower Benue, with its orientation toward the Hausa states, and the Upper Benue, characterized by comparable political, economic, and cultural linkages with Bornu. The contrast, however, might not have been apparent in earlier times. During his travels in the region, C. K. Meek (1931a, 34) reports having seen the ruins of many villages that he concluded had probably been destroyed during the eighteenth and nineteenth centuries. Of these ruined towns, the most extensive was located about twenty miles northeast of Bantaji. The site is identified by Jukun of Wukari (and of most other southwestern towns in this region) as Biepi, the place from which they had dispersed, according to most accounts, late in the eighteenth century.[2]

The classification of Jukunoid languages remains a work in progress. There seems, however, to be broad agreement that the languages of the Kuteb and Yukuben to the southwest around Takum make up one branch of the Jukunoid language grouping and may represent relatively conservative forms of Jukun in terms of Kiyoshi Shimizu's reconstruction of proto-Jukun (1980). Mbembe, on the Nigeria-Cameroon border, makes up one of three subdivisions of Central Jukun, which has led to the hypothesis that Jukun may have expanded from the southeast into the plains below the Benue River. The University of Cologne's current classification distinguishes nine Jukun languages, which largely correspond to areas of Jukun settlement (including Wapan[3] spoken around Wukari and the languages of places such as Takum and Kona, as well as settlements north of the Benue River). Wurbo, the language of widely distributed riverain Jukun, is currently listed with Central Jukun as distinct from both Mbembe and Jukun.

For the most part, Jukun plastic expression can be divided between the artistic genres dominant respectively in the southwest and northeast of their distribution. Carved wooden and fabric masks are the predominant Jukun sculptural mode southwest of a line drawn approximately between the Shemankar and Wase rivers and south of the Benue. To the northeast of this line, anthropomorphic figure sculptures are used in analogous ritual contexts, but they are less well known than the masks: in contrast with the illustrations of Wukari-area masks published in Meek (1931a), only a small number of notices in the literature reveal the existence of this tradition of Jukun figurative sculptures. Thus, delineating the full range and distribution of Jukun sculptural expression casts another pattern across the Middle Benue, apparently reflecting the markedly different historical experiences of the groups involved.

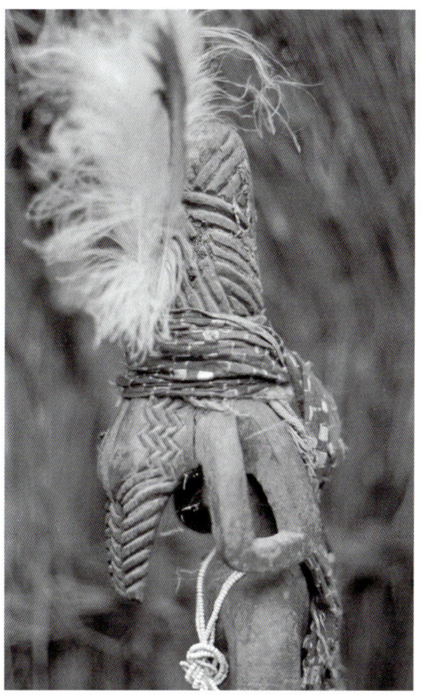

9.2
Detail of Mam's wife, Ajiku (see fig. 9.1).
PHOTOGRAPH BY ARNOLD RUBIN, WURBON DAUDU VILLAGE, OCTOBER 23, 1964, RUBIN ARCHIVE, FOWLER MUSEUM AT UCLA, NEG. NO. 1047.

9.1 (OPPOSITE)
Wooden figures of Mam and his wives—left to right: Agbadu (wife), Ajiku (wife), Asenzo (Mam)—owned by Abubakar.
PHOTOGRAPH BY ARNOLD RUBIN, WURBON DAUDU VILLAGE, OCTOBER 23, 1964, RUBIN ARCHIVE, FOWLER MUSEUM AT UCLA, NEG. NO. 1041.

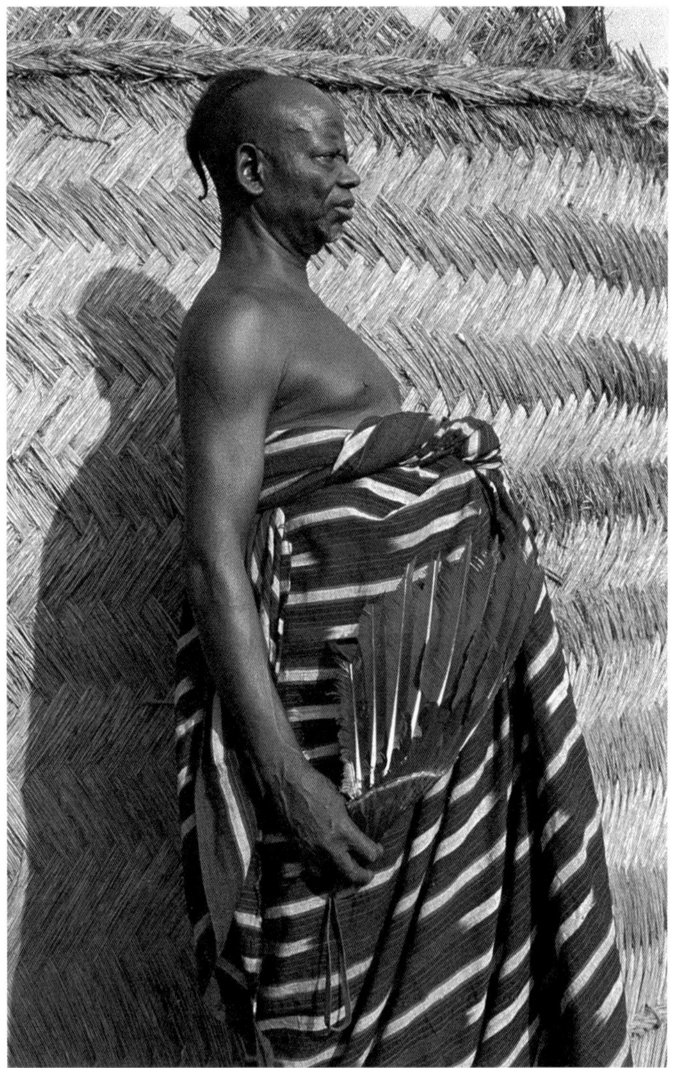

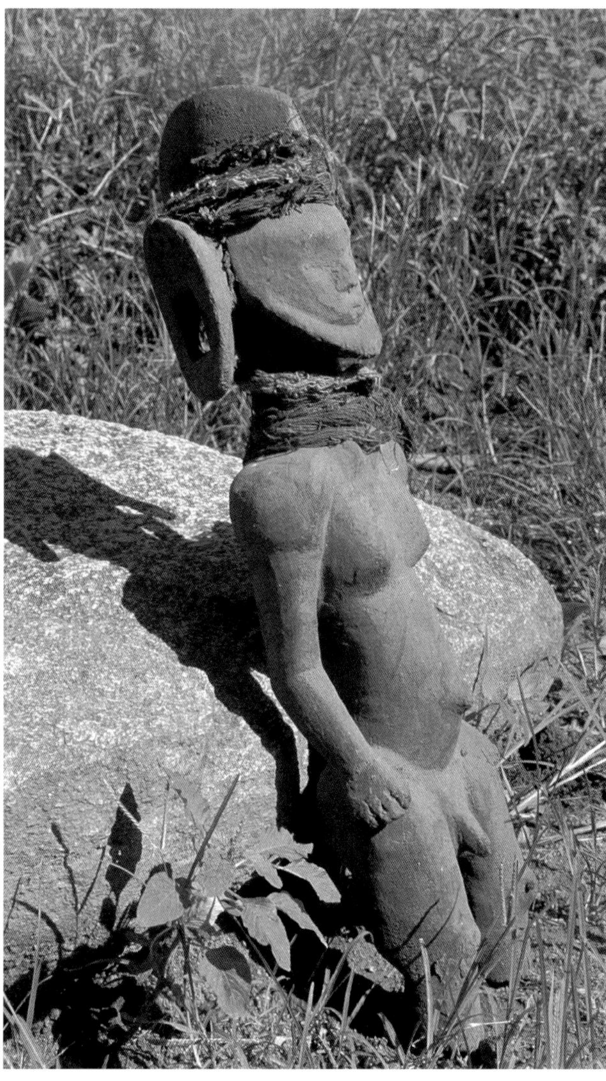

9.3
Plaited lock of hair worn by the Chief of
Tsokundi.
PHOTOGRAPH BY ARNOLD RUBIN, WUKARI VIL-
LAGE, JANUARY 14, 1965, RUBIN ARCHIVE, FOWLER
MUSEUM AT UCLA, NEG. NO. 4.

9.4
Figure of Zaraga, owned by Kibwa Abiyar.
PHOTOGRAPH BY ARNOLD RUBIN, GAYAM
VILLAGE, OCTOBER 22, 1965, RUBIN ARCHIVE,
FOWLER MUSEUM AT UCLA, NEG. NO. 1036.

A notable geological feature of the Middle Benue is the occurrence of salt springs
at Bommanda, near Muri in the northeast and in Kassan Chikki and along the road
between Akwana and Wukari in the southwest. Since the productivity of the springs
was regarded as subject to supernatural sanctions, the apparently very old and region-
wide reputation of the Jukun as religious specialists appears to have supported their
involvement in exploiting these strategic resources. This salt, together with imported
beads and local and imported cloth, was a staple in the network of overland and riverain trade routes, which laced the region, linking the great emporia of the far north
with the kola, ivory, and slave markets of Ogoja and the Cameroon Grassfields. In
the southwest, most of the actual commerce and of the economic specializations upon
which it was based were in the hands of itinerant Hausa traders and craftsmen, both
those deriving from Kano and other metropolitan centers, and the Abakwariga, or
"pagan Hausa," who seem to have been long established in the region. This economic
base seems to have stimulated the emergence of extensive, centralized and stratified
political structures—particularly in the southwest, less so in the northeast—and it
probably contributed to the comparatively high degree of regular and peaceful interaction that apparently prevailed among the peoples of the Middle Benue prior to the
disturbed conditions of the late eighteenth and nineteenth centuries.[4]

A complex network of politico-religious relationships among the divine kings
of the major southwestern city-states, essentially based on reciprocity, cut across
ethnic and linguistic boundaries to a remarkable extent. For the Jukun (and with
ramifications for many of their neighbors), status pyramids from village to district,

culminated in the person and office of the Aku, or king, of Wukari, traditionally regarded as the paramount chief of the Jukun-speaking peoples. By virtue of this primacy, Wukari beliefs and practices have been regarded as paradigmatic by practically all researchers. In fact, most authors have treated the Jukun of Wukari as something of a "mother culture" for the Benue Valley and adjacent areas. A contrary conclusion is suggested by Shimizu's (1971, 39–40) characterization of the Wapan group of dialects as, in linguistic parlance, the "innovation group"—that is, as most changed among the languages of the family to which it belongs. Evidence from history and art prompts suspicions of a similar evolution in the cultural sphere. Thus, the conventional view of the role of the Jukun of Wukari in the history of Northern Nigeria should probably be drastically revised.[5] The Jukun-speaking peoples were not separately enumerated in the 1952 census; Meek's (1931a, 1) proposal that they numbered approximately 25,000 at the time he wrote can be regarded only as the roughest of estimates.[6]

NORTHEASTERN JUKUN

Consideration of the sculpture of the northeastern Jukun can conveniently begin with the Jibu and Wurbo of the Taraba River Valley, even though forms and functions diverge in significant ways from the norms represented by works at Kona, Gwana, Pindiga, and in the Wase area. The Wurbo are a riverain group, primarily engaged in fishing and water transport, living in small villages scattered along the banks of the lower Taraba and much of the Middle Benue, more or less from Lau to Abinsi.[7] The villages of the Jibu are located in the Taraba Valley upstream from the town of Beli, extending as far as Gashaka on the Mambila Plateau. Meek classifies both Wurbo and Jibu as "Jukun subgroups" on the basis of linguistic affinities but otherwise considers their ethnic affiliations to be unclear. For example, no Jibu and only one Wurbo kindred wear the "sacramental plaited hairlock," which appears (for males) to be a central feature of Jukun culture (fig. 9.3; see Meek 1931a, 69; 1931b, 2: 519). On the other hand, according to Meek (1931a, 40), the Jibu and some Wurbo, alone among the Jukun of the present day, "have retained the mother-right principles which formerly governed all Jukun society."

I encountered a few carved wooden images in human form in several Jibu villages near Beli, but they exhibited little in the way of stylistic consistency. At Gayam, a figure called Zaraga represented a spirit invoked in healing procedures. The figure would be installed as a symbolic guardian at the bed of a patient undergoing treatment. A brew of beer was dedicated to the spirit if recovery ensued (fig. 9.4).[8] The Gayam figure was made of heavy, hardwood with a gray, granular patina and festooned with hanks of unwoven local cotton thread. It was characterized by fairly close attention to the anatomical forms of the body and smooth transitions between body parts. Distinctive features included prominent ear loops, an ogival, spatulate beard, and a loaf-shaped sagittal crest. Little more can be said of Jibu sculpture. Meek (1931b, 2: 592) mentions a Jibu masquerade named Gahu, "made entirely of cloth," which was performed in connection with mourning observances, but I saw nothing of the sort during my work in the Beli area.[9]

The town of Bakundi, between Biepi and the Taraba, appears to have been the main Wurbo center until disrupted by the Chamba late in the eighteenth century. Bakundi was conquered by the Fulani of Muri under Burda around 1860. He made it his headquarters for slaving raids into and general control of the southwestern sections of Muri's dominions.[10] Most present-day Wurbo villages trace their origins to Bakundi—among them, Wurbon Daudu on the Taraba downstream from Beli.[11] The Wurbo are associated with the Mam cult throughout the Middle Benue. Meek (1931b, 2: 543) distinguishes an apparently earlier "primary" complex from a "secondary" version of later dissemination that is characterized by violent possession states, sometimes including self-mutilation.[12]

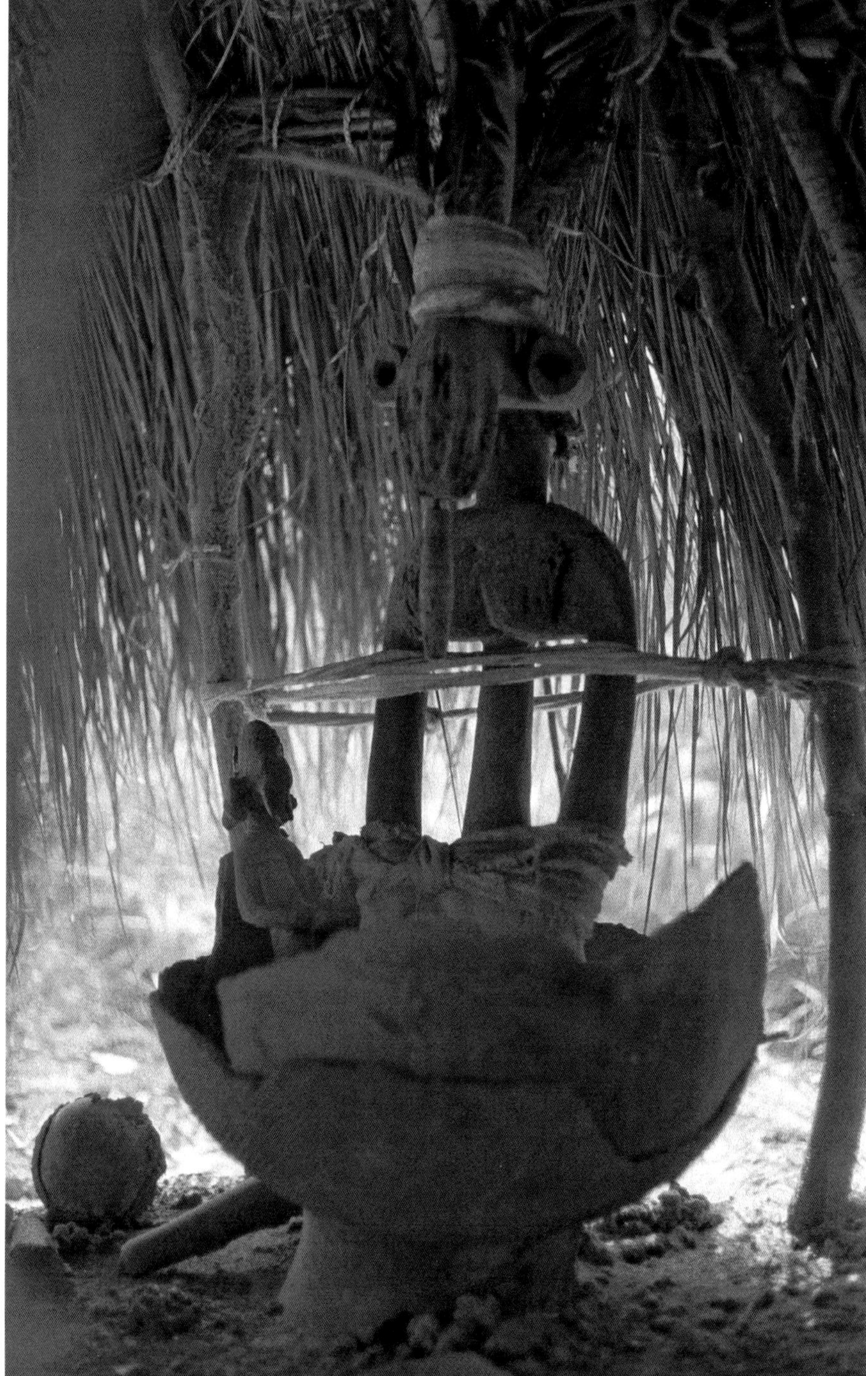

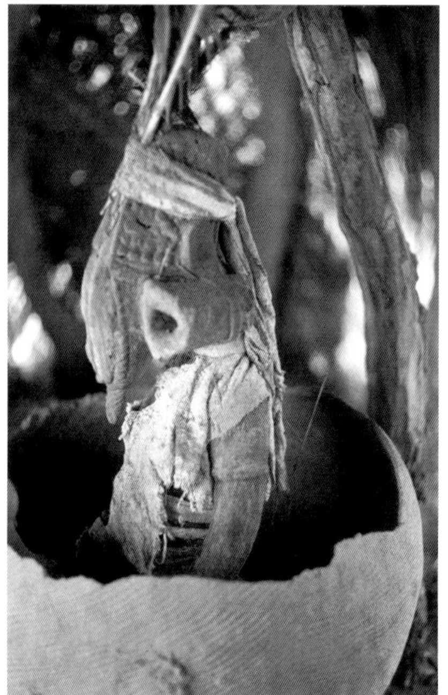

9.5
Shrine of Gar with figure of Ku.
PHOTOGRAPH BY ARNOLD RUBIN, GAJI VILLAGE,
OCTOBER 21, 1965, RUBIN ARCHIVE, FOWLER
MUSEUM AT UCLA, NEG. NO.1022.

9.6
Shrine of Yaku Mam with his child.
PHOTOGRAPH BY ARNOLD RUBIN, GAJI VILLAGE,
OCTOBER 21, 1965, RUBIN ARCHIVE, FOWLER
MUSEUM AT UCLA, NEG. NO. 1026.

At Wurbon Daudu, Mam is instrumental in treating a variety of illnesses (in conjunction with various herbal and other medicines). Possession of the patient or of other devotees by one of the spirits to which the cult is dedicated plays a major role in such curing procedures; most of the men of the town exhibited extensive scarring of their upper arms, attesting to the importance of auto- and mutual-mutilation in the behavioral patterns associated with possession states achieved in the cult. In addition to such "ad hoc" observances on behalf of afflicted individuals, the ceremonies of the cult may also be carried out on behalf of the entire community, usually in the face of some impending disaster such as epidemic disease, crop failure, or war. In addition, every third year, near the end of the dry season, the entire community participates in extensive sacrifices to the tutelary spirits of the cult with a view toward maintaining general well-being.

The focus of the Mam cult at Wurbon Daudu—and everywhere else I encountered it—is "the spear of Mam," a pointed iron rod with branching folded bells at the top and a bunch of feathers fixed at some point along its length.[13] In addition, a group of carved wooden figures in human form (one male, two females) incarnates the spirit principles to which the cult is dedicated and is central to Mam observance. The personal name of the male figure, identified as Mam, is Asenzo; his wives are named Ajiku and Agbadu (fig. 9.1). They exhibit a body of formal conventions so consistent among the Jukun of the northeast, both for images of Mam and for representations of royal ancestors, that they amount to what can be designated a "nuclear style." The following characteristics seem to be recurrent:

Pairs of figures, male and female, designated husband and wife; males frequently ithyphallic; carved of heavy, hardwood; lower body and legs wrapped with cloth; conical, white-metal plugs used to indicate eyes; bands of incised, cross-hatched facial decoration, especially across eyes; pronounced facial overhang; dentate "beard" on male figures; representations of perforated, distended earlobes, either open loops or shown with cylindrical plugs in place; conical "cap" or sagittal crest, often with a feather fixed at top, with carved downward projections representing hair plaits; upper torso in the shape of an inverted cone swelling to the shoulders; pendant, conical breasts for females; long, tapering arms curving forward to meet at hip level; large hands with deep gouges to indicate fingers; legs and feet short and rudimentarily carved.

The three Wurbon Daudu figures are of heavy, hardwood, approximately 46 centimeters in height (see fig. 9.1). They are represented as frontal and standing, with sweeping arms enclosing a comparatively thin torso. Heads are projected forward over chests, and the two female figures (as well as the single male) exhibit what appears to be a three- or four-part plaited beard. Comparatively large spatulate elements with triangular perforations, projecting downward from the sides of the head, were identified as pierced, distended earlobes (fig. 9.2).[14] A loaf-shaped excrescence on top of the head represented the coiffure, and eyes were indicated by small plugs of white metal. White feathers were inserted into a narrow cloth headband, and the figures were heavily ornamented with imported glass and plastic beads. Their lower torsos and legs were covered with wrappers of industrially produced cotton cloth.

Not far away, at the Jukun village of Gaji, between Beli and the road junction at Garba Shegi, I encountered a group of three figures generally similar to those of Wurbon Daudu (figs. 9.5, 9.6).[15] They were preserved in two thatched shelters, supported upright in the hemispherical fragments of large ceramic pots. A single figure standing by itself, called Ku, served a generalized protective function for the entire community (fig. 9.5, see also fig. E.3). It received firstfruits of all crops and a portion of game killed in hunting, and it was prayed to in all crisis situations. In size and general aspect it resembled the Wurbon Daudu figures fairly closely, except that the pierced earlobes were shown with large cylindrical plugs in place, and the "beard" consisted of a rope-like ridge along the jawline with a single downward projection at the point of the chin. The figure was heavily clothed, including a headband into which feathers had been inserted. Metal bits to mark the eyes were not apparent, possibly obscured by accumulated patination.

The other two figures, standing together in a single pot-fragment, were identified as Yaku Mam and his child (see fig. 9.6) The image of Yaku Mam, approximately 76 centimeters tall, was characterized by a more pronounced separation of the elements of head and body from the vertical axis and a marked simplification of the facial features. The second figure, approximately 25.4 centimeters tall, was less expanded in space and had metal eyes and a multipartite beard. Both were shown with large cylindrical earplugs. Their function was described as identical to that of Ku.

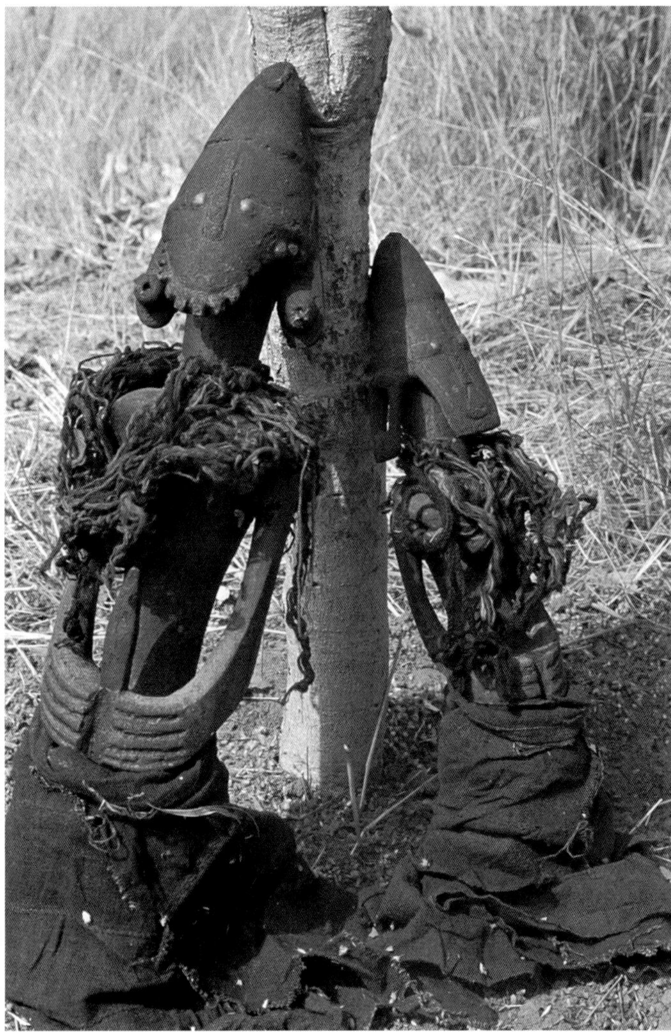

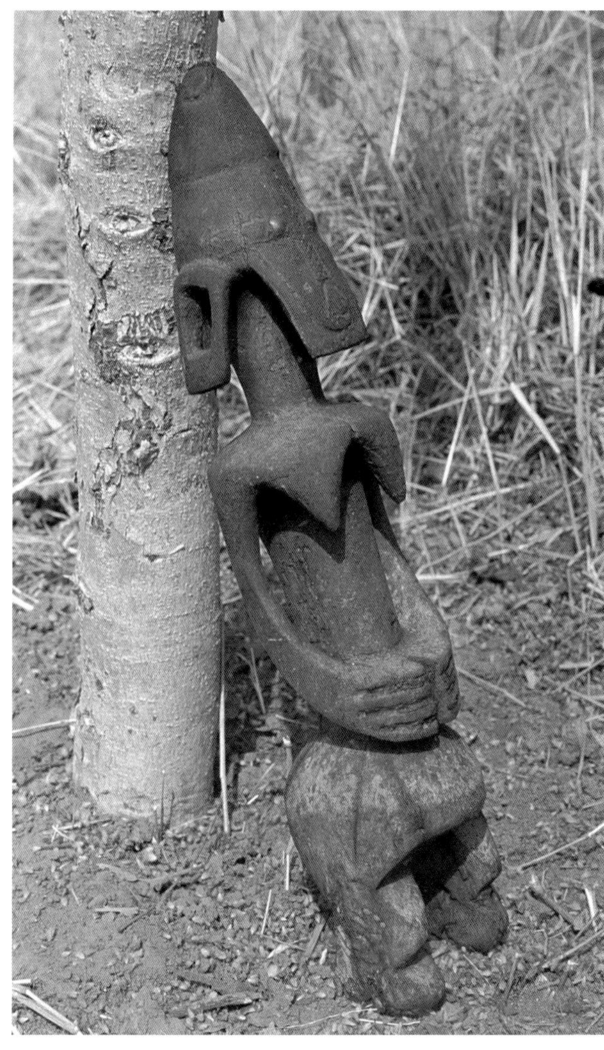

9.10
Carved wooden figures of Wipong (left) and his wife, both wearing cloth.
PHOTOGRAPH BY ARNOLD RUBIN, PINDIGA VILLAGE, APRIL 26, 1965, RUBIN ARCHIVE, FOWLER MUSEUM AT UCLA, NEG. NO. 452.

9.11
Detail of wife of Wipong figure without cloth.
PHOTOGRAPH BY ARNOLD RUBIN, PINDIGA VILLAGE, APRIL 26, 1965, RUBIN ARCHIVE, FOWLER MUSEUM AT UCLA, NEG. NO. 459.

and given new cloth garments (see Meek 1931a, 265ff. regarding the "Kenjo" cult). I was told that white metal bits were used to represent eyes, and both figures had long earplugs and a single plait of hair at the rear; a curved element at each side of the head, described as "horns," may also have represented elements of coiffure. The male figure was not remembered as having been ithyphallic.

As with Kona, a fair amount of information is available for Gwana and Pindiga, although all are less extensively studied than the communities of the southwest. These data indicate substantial if elusive differences between the role of the Jukun chief in the southwest and northeast. Nevertheless, it seems safe to say that the chief's primary responsibility in both areas is for regular and sufficient rains, the fertility of the land, and the security and general well-being of his people. This responsibility is discharged by the living chief in his role as intermediary between his royal ancestors and his people. In the northeast, north of the Benue, carved wooden figures in nuclear style are used to commemorate royal ancestors in addition to their role in Mam observances (figs. 9.10–9.13, and see fig. 8.55). The images represent deceased chiefs, their wives, and attendants, and they serve as the primary means of access to their spirits. Such incarnation is said to be reserved to founding ancestors and their most important successors. The origin of one group of figures at Gwana representing Adang, "a great king of the past," and his wife is traced to their untimely deaths, whereupon "his ghost returned and troubled the land. Droughts came, and famines. So the people in their distress took counsel and made two wooden images, one for the spirit of Adang and the other for that of his wife."[19] Meek (1931a, 159–60) describes in considerable detail the daily service of the cult of Adang at Gwana, whose shrine

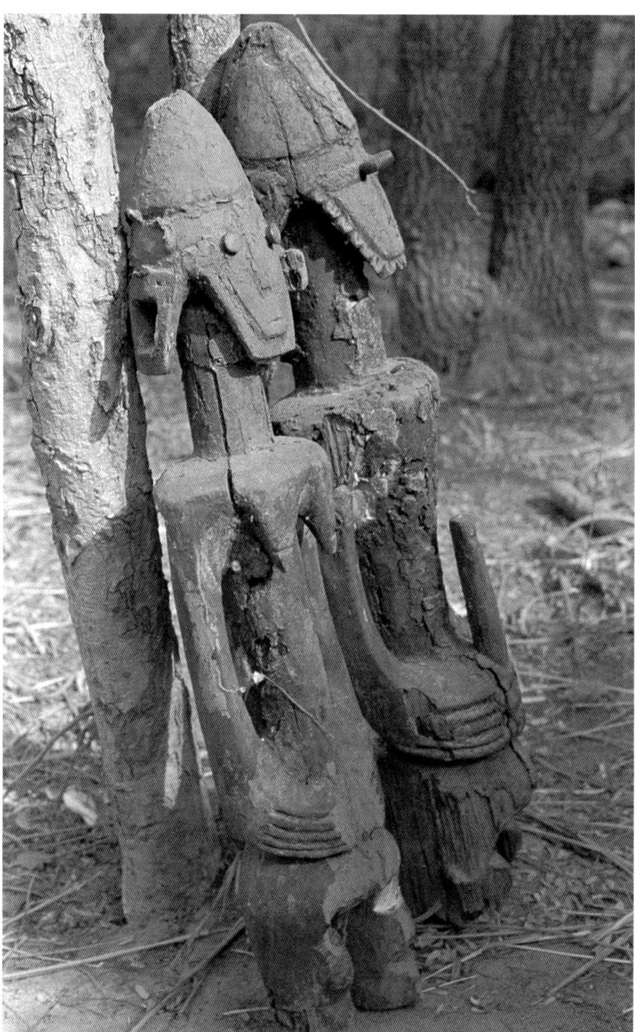

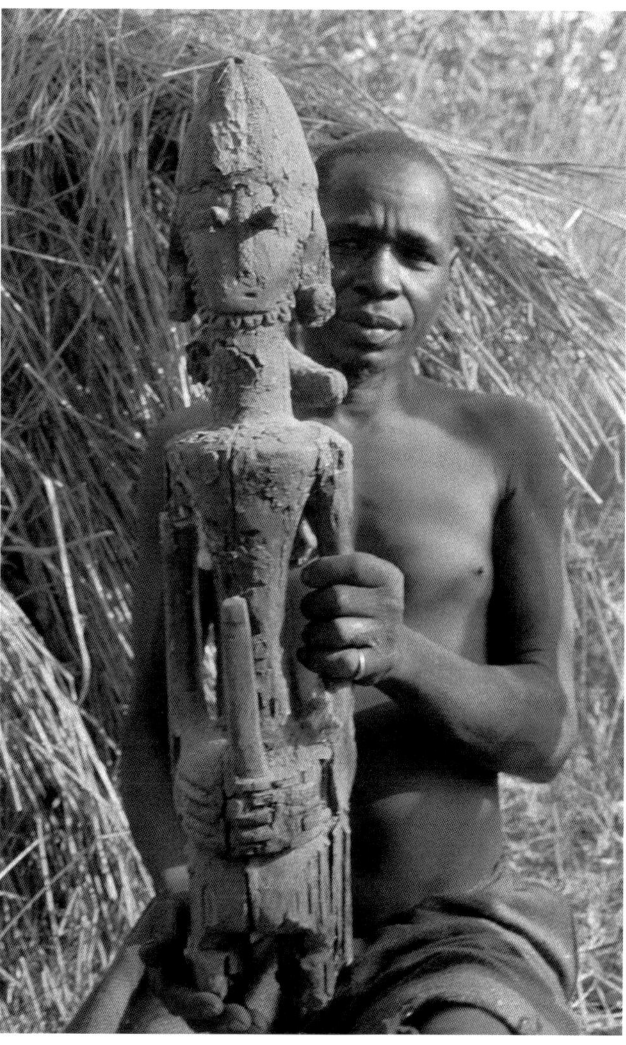

is a replica in miniature of the private enclosure of the chief. It consists of four huts, one of which is the sleeping apartment of the god, one his day apartment, one the hut in which his food is cooked, and the fourth the hut of his wife. Rites, which are the counterpart of those carried out thrice daily for the living chief, are performed by the priest of Adang. At daybreak each morning he and the attendant acolytes proceed to the shrine, take the image of the god from its miniature bed and place it at the threshold of the door of his day apartment. Kneeling before it the priest addresses the god saying, "the chief has sent me to enquire if you have slept well and if all else is well. Grant unto us, we beseech you, health, rain, food and fertility." He pours a libation of beer on the ground in front of the image, and then retires, obliterating his footsteps with a brush. Having washed his hands carefully he and his assistants consume the remnants of the beer. Similar rites are performed at 2 p.m. and at sundown. On the conclusion of the evening ritual the priest addresses the god, saying "have you passed the day well? We are now going to our rest: do you rest well until the morrow." He then deposits the image on the couch of the sleeping apartment.[20]

According to Meek (1931a, 176–77), images of wives and attendants may commemorate human sacrifices offered at the funeral of a chief to provide a retinue for his spirit in the afterlife: "For at Kona it was stated that the chief's favorite wife was strangled with a string and placed in a grave beside the chief, and that a young enclosure-attendant was also killed that the chief might not lack someone to spread his mat for him in Kindo. This was the custom also at Pindiga."

9.12
Carved wooden figures of Mam (right) and his wife Aki.
PHOTOGRAPH BY ARNOLD RUBIN, PINDIGA VILLAGE, APRIL 4, 1965, RUBIN ARCHIVE, FOWLER MUSEUM AT UCLA, NEG. NO. 438.

9.13
Wooden Mam figure with carver and care-taker Abubukar.
PHOTOGRAPH BY ARNOLD RUBIN, PINDIGA VILLAGE, NOVEMBER 29, 1964, RUBIN ARCHIVE, FOWLER MUSEUM AT UCLA, NEG. NO. P44.

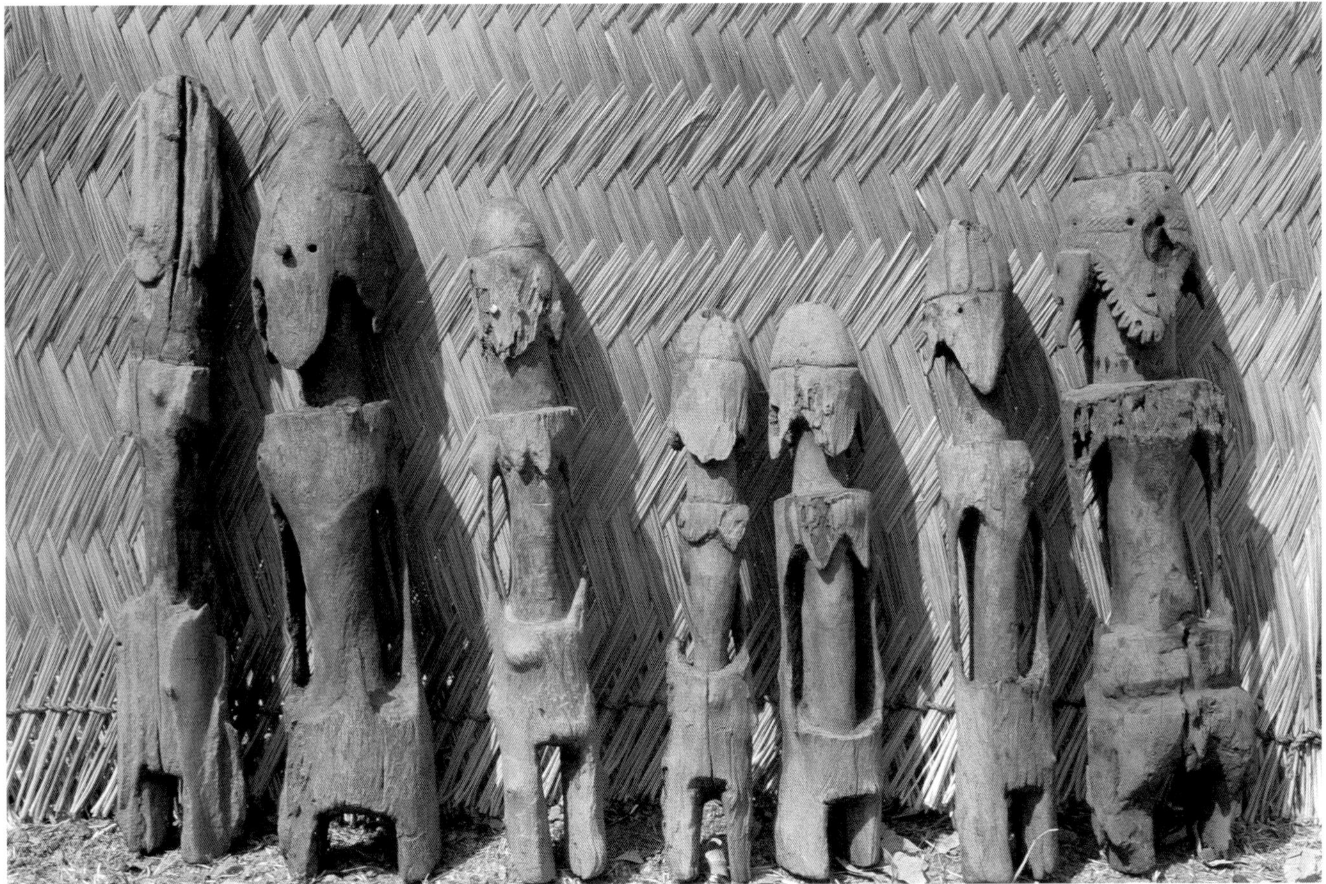

9.14
Group of figures removed from a cave near
Gwana (probably associated with the nearby
deserted Jukun village of Gateri).
PHOTOGRAPH BY ARNOLD RUBIN, JANUARY 9, 1966,
RUBIN ARCHIVE, FOWLER MUSEUM AT UCLA, NEG.
NO. 1647.

In short, the connection of carved images in human form with the chief and chieftainship is very close. Not only do the images represent important former chiefs, they
actually "belong" to the incumbent. The role of officiant or priest is, however, usually
delegated on a hereditary basis to an elder. One or two "sets" of ancestral images typically serve as the religious focus of an entire community, including satellite settlements,
which come together for ceremonies (figs. 9.10, 9.12). An intriguing pattern of shared
names for ancestral images emerges; male figures at Pindiga and Gwana are called
Wipong, for example (see figs. 8.54, 8.55).[21] The names Wunkur and Zinakani were
noted as names of masquerades in Kona; at Gwana, the name Zinkani was given for one
ancestral image and also appears in the list of chiefs I collected there.[22] At Pindiga, the
names Zankar and Nyimkani occur in the list of chiefs. The same names are applied to
a funerary complex for important men, which is also the object of ceremonies at planting time. It does not, however, involve any sculpture.[23]

Consistent patterns of use are reported for these ancestral images. Regular
annual ceremonies, community-wide in scope, take place when the rains are due and
people are preparing to begin farming. Having spent the night at the chief's house,
"on the following morning, the images are carried back in procession to the shrine
where they are adorned with a cloth presented by the chief."[24] Ceremonies also take
place at harvest time, when the images receive offerings of firstfruits (reported at
Kona, Gaji, and Mabo). Special appeals to the figures were also possible on behalf of
individuals (such as barren women) or the entire community in cases of impending
crises such as drought, war, or epidemic.

The group of seven figures that I saw at Pindiga and another group totaling
twenty-three at and near Gwana epitomize what I have called the "nuclear" style of the
northeastern Jukun (fig. 9.14, and see figs. 9.10–9.13).[25] Another figure in the collection
of the Nigerian Museum, Lagos, probably belongs to this corpus, as does a figure collected by Frobenius before 1912 across the Benue from Ibi.[26]

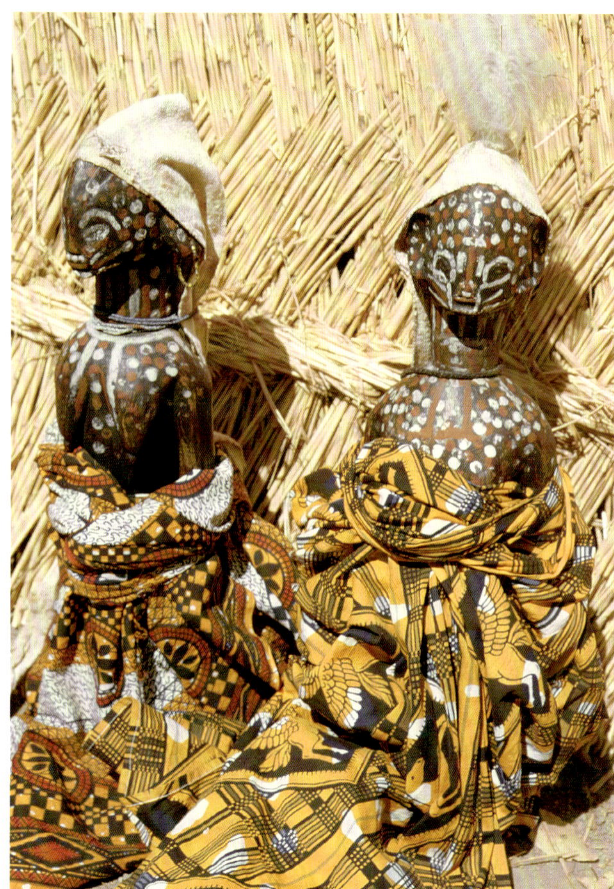

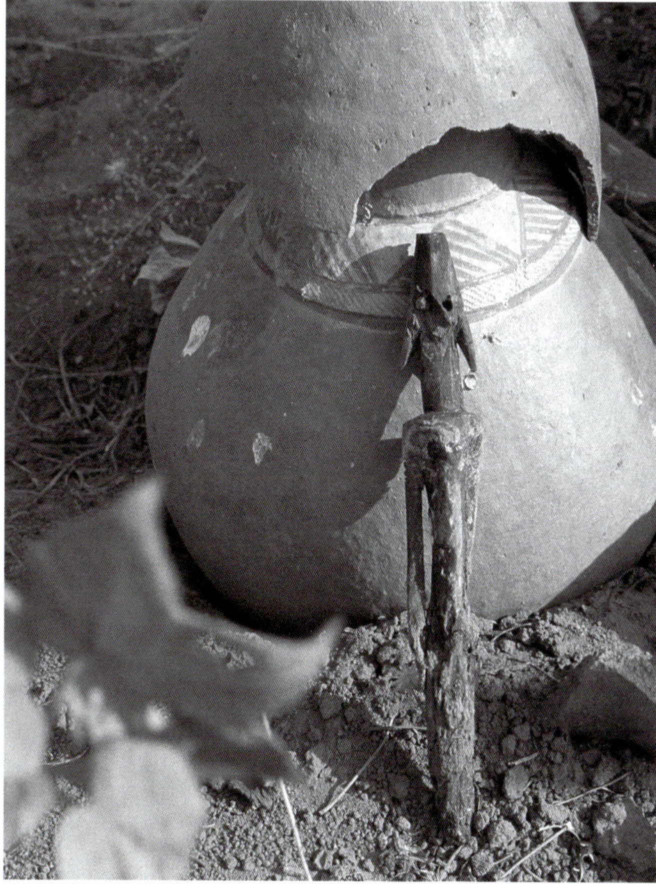

North of the Benue, near Wase, two figures at Wase Tofa and four at Mabo exhibit a distinctive polychromy: strong linear and geometric patterns of red and white set against a black background (fig. 9.15, and see figs. E.5a.b). Otherwise, the Mabo figures conform closely to the canons of the nuclear style, including small flakes of metal (apparently brass in this case) to represent eyes. The Mabo figures were identified as Mukungudzi and Kubat and their wives. In contrast, the Wase Tofa figures of Mam and his wife are, for all practical purposes, outside the conventions of the nuclear style (see fig. 9.15). Despite their name, pierced ears, crests surmounted by feathers, and cloth wrappers, their primary affinities are clearly with the styles of the groups living south of the Jos Plateau (see chapter 12).

In addition to images of deceased kings and figures connected with the cult of Mam, I encountered one additional figurative tradition among the Jukun of the northeast. Represented only by a single, badly weathered male figure seen at Gwana, this tradition, called *ahenbi,* reportedly should involve a pair of figures, male and female, set up in the fields to protect the crops (fig. 9.16). In what might be called a shorthand version of the nuclear style, including metal bits for eyes, pointed plaits of hair, and a long conical abdomen enclosed by curving arms, the figure's most distinctive feature is the conical iron point by means of which it is planted erect in the ground. In this latter respect, and in its function, it closely resembles the field guardians of the nearby Wurkun and more distant Chamba (see fig. 13.5; Palmer 1911, 410; Temple 1919, 177; Meek 1925, 2: 24).

SOUTHWESTERN JUKUN

The last major Jukun migration out of the Taraba River Valley conveyed a substantial population to the north of the Benue into the Kassan Chikki area, southeast of Wase. This movement apparently took place sometime after 1750 and may have been triggered (at least in part) by the earliest Chamba incursions, although prolonged drought and other causes are also mentioned. The migrants apparently included the ruling party

9.15
Polychrome wooden figures of Mam (right) and his wife.
PHOTOGRAPH BY ARNOLD RUBIN, WASE TOFA VILLAGE, DECEMBER 23, 1964, RUBIN ARCHIVE, FOWLER MUSEUM AT UCLA, SLIDE NO. A.11.13.12.

9.16
Carved wooden *ahenbi* figure with metal eyes, owned by Sha'ibu.
PHOTOGRAPH BY ARNOLD RUBIN, GWANA VILLAGE, JANUARY 9, 1966, , RUBIN ARCHIVE, FOWLER MUSEUM AT UCLA, NEG. NO. 1527.

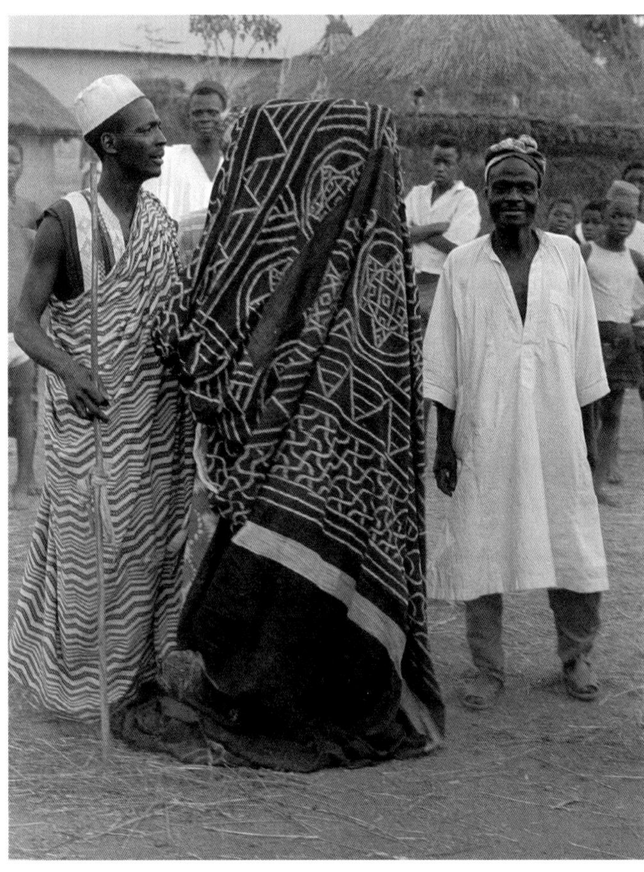

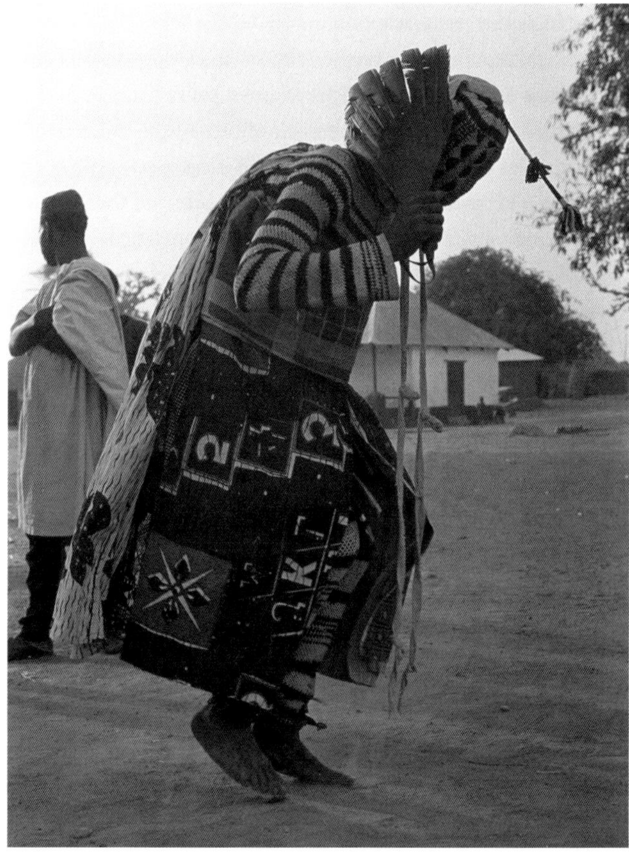

9.17
Ashama masquerade costume owned by
Tohelma.
PHOTOGRAPH BY ARNOLD RUBIN, DONGA VIL-
LAGE, FEBRUARY 8, 1965, RUBIN ARCHIVE, FOWLER
MUSEUM AT UCLA, NEG. NO.189.

9.18
Agashi masquerade costume made of cotton
netting.
PHOTOGRAPH BY ARNOLD RUBIN, WUKARI, MARCH
21, 1965, RUBIN ARCHIVE, FOWLER MUSEUM AT
UCLA, NEG. NO. 403-H.

the present day, no figurative sculpture comparable to that in the northeast is found
among southwestern Jukun.

Abakwariga ancestral masquerades include the Ashama, Agashi, and (according to
most informants) Dodo configurations. They are predominantly constructed of woven
or lightweight, netted fiber materials and appear to be without gender. Wapan masks,
in contrast, involve male-female pairs, with carved wooden males (usually) linked
with constructed fiber females. The Aku-Ma masquerade complex performed by the
Kpan of the Takum-Donga area has come to be accepted as a Wapan mode at Wukari.
More typical of the southwestern Jukun, however, and much more widely distributed,
is the masquerade called Aku-Maga, sometimes associated with a heavy-fiber subordinate called Adashan. (Several other Wapan types will be mentioned later.) A further
distinction between the Wapan and Abakwariga masquerades is that those of the
Abakwariga cannot appear during the annual Muslim fast of Ramadan "because our
ancestors are fasting too."

The Abakwariga Ashama masquerade consists of a tall conical cloth tube with
streamers attached to the peak (fig. 9.17). Examples were seen at Wukari, Donga,
and most of the larger towns with substantial Abakwariga populations south of the
Benue. The masquerader changes the apparent height of the configuration by bending
or straightening his arm. He sings into a mirliton to evoke the voice of the ancestral
spirit that the mask incarnates; in short, the configuration is identical in every respect
to the Iwagu of the Alago, the Alekwa of the Idoma, and other similar Lower Benue
Valley masquerades (see chapter 3).[31]

Agashi consists of a netted cotton costume in the form of a body stocking, which
covers the dancer from the top of his head to his wrists and ankles; a loose mesh
covers his face (fig. 9.18). Patterns are worked out in blue lines and geometric shapes
against a white background. This basic costume is thus identical to forms found among
peoples north of the Middle Benue River (and probably also the Ebira of the Lower
Benue), and will figure prominently in the discussion of Alago masquerades later in

this chapter.[32] The dancer also wears a bulky trade-cloth skirt and bustle, kept in place by a wide band or belt of the same material and a loop of cord, which passes around his neck. He carries a goose-wing fan (of the sort affected by Wukari-area elders), and strings of linked, elongated folded iron bells (or rattles) are fixed at his ankles. Two narrow cloth strips, about four feet long, are fixed at the top of the dancer's head and hang down his back. Two thin sticks, wrapped with brightly colored wool, are attached at the same point. The dance consists of extremely rapid small steps with the upper body held in a fixed position or moving in a slow, languid manner. When two or more Agashi appear together, they dance in turns, each cued by the lead drummer, while the others rest at the perimeter of the dancing area formed by encircling spectators.[33]

In addition to the general life-crisis and psychotherapeutic function shared with other southwestern masquerades, Ashama and Agashi have a special relationship to the Abakwariga women's healing/possession cult known to the Wapan as Jonkpa (spirits, *ajon*, of the Abakpa), and to the Abakwariga themselves as Aljanu (Hausa word for spirit). Each spirit has its own priestess (*kuspa*) and group of followers, usually those who have been "touched" by the spirit with an illness that was successfully cured by the ministrations of the priestess and her coterie. The entire complex is under the tutelage of a male priest/administrator/coordinator chosen from the kindred of the leader of the town's Abakwariga population. Among other responsibilities, this functionary arranges for Agashi and/or Ashama to appear during annual Aljanu festivals and for dances performed to celebrate the successful cure, which also heralds the initiation of a new member of a spirit's retinue.[34]

Dodo masqueraders at Wukari wear face covers consisting of slightly curved sections of calabash, partly encrusted with abrus seeds set in gum or wax (fig. 9.19). The mask is worn with a padded conical cap surmounted by a bunch of feathers, the calabash plaque being held in place by cloth scarves bound above and below a nose modeled of gum or wax. Sprigs of locust-bean leaves are tucked under the top scarf on both sides of the face. The costume consists of a man's cloth gown of standard Hausa *riga* pattern. Thus, the Dodo configuration seems closely to resemble Jankai Dodo of the peoples at the eastern margins of the Jos Plateau. This Jankai is principally involved with male initiation, however, and such practices are found among neither the Abakwariga nor the Wapan of Wukari. On the other hand, the Wukari Dodo masqueraders do not dance, but rather stalk about with stout switches in each hand, threatening children who taunt them. This antagonistic posture of the Wukari Dodo masquerade may thus plausibly be argued to reflect patterns typical of the Jankai complex.

Best known of the Wapan ancestral masquerades, Aku-Maga consists in most instances of a group of two or three masks: the main (male) mask, called Aku Wa'unu [elsewhere in this volume: Aku-Wunu], and one or two females (Aku Wa'uwa [elsewhere in this volume: Aku-Wuwa]). In the towns north of the Benue, a third element may be added: Adashan, identified as "the messenger" or intermediary between the world of the living and that of the spirits (see also Lane 1959). In the majority of cases, the Aku-Maga complex operates according to the general pattern of Jukun ancestral masquerades stipulated earlier. In others, it exhibits a special relationship to the chieftainship. According to Meek (1931a, 274), this relationship is expressed in the widespread belief that the masquerade incarnates the founding ancestor of the royal family:

> The deity represented is vaguely conceived, and in many cases is identified with some local ancestor who is regarded as the tutelary genius of the village. In other cases, the mask appears to represent the plurality of dead chiefs and may be treated by the local chief as the special amulet of himself and his people, daily matutinal offerings of beer being poured into a circular hole in the ground before it. The chief may even regard the mask as embodying his own divine double.

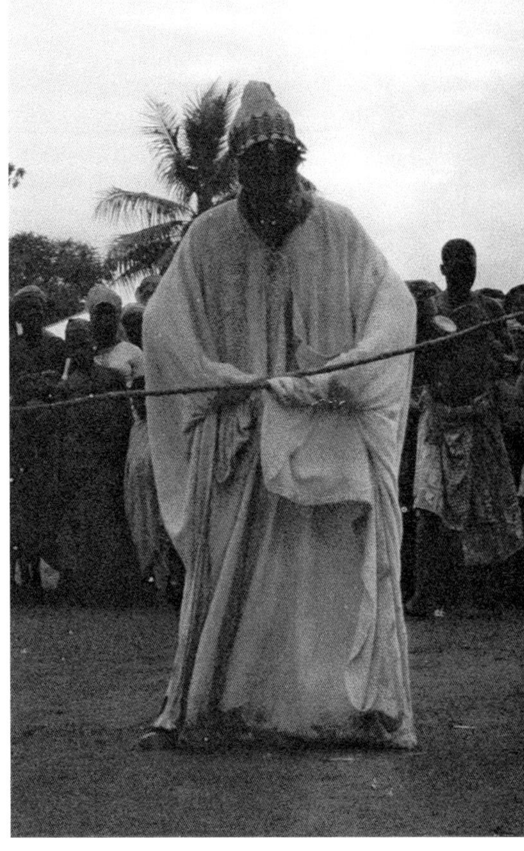

9.19
Dodo masquerade costume with a face cover made of calabash and abrus seeds; owned by Habukuku.
PHOTOGRAPH BY ARNOLD RUBIN, WUKARI, JULY–SEPTEMBER 1965, RUBIN ARCHIVE, FOWLER MUSEUM AT UCLA, NEG. NO. 738B.

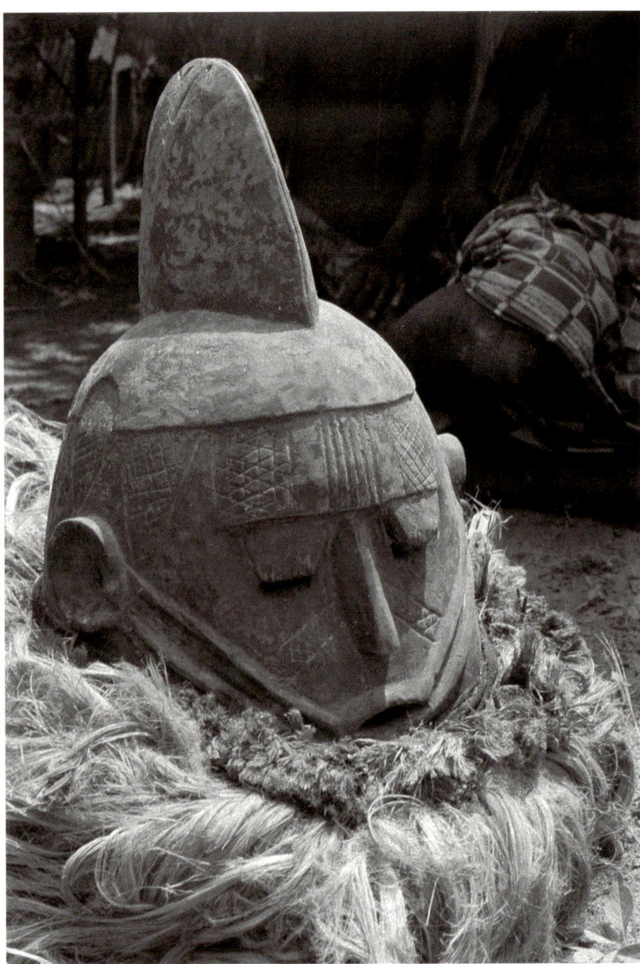

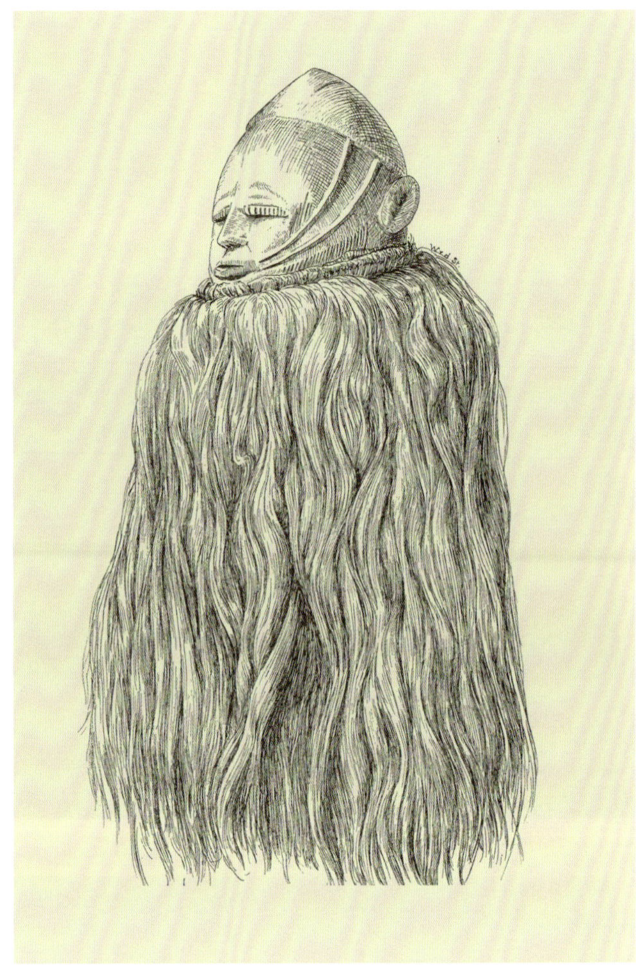

9.25
Wood Aku Wa'uwa (Ashunku) helmet mask
owned by Madaiki Karami Aji.
PHOTOGRAPH BY ARNOLD RUBIN, CHINKAI
VILLAGE, SEPTEMBER 4, 1965, RUBIN ARCHIVE,
FOWLER MUSEUM AT UCLA, NEG. NO. 782.

9.26
Drawing of a Jukun mask collected by Eduard
Flegel, which closely resembles those I photo-
graphed in the field.
REPRODUCED FROM PASSARGE, (1895, 356, ILL. 188).

a loose seam held apart with both hands to provide an opening for vision. A ring of
cotton trade cloth "falls," gathered at the waist by a thick, padded band or belt, and
hangs to mid-thigh, over wide embroidered cotton-cloth trousers of typical Northern Nigerian men's pattern. The masquerader carries a wing-feather fan of the type
customarily used by senior Jukun men. The costume is worn with a helmet mask or
crest representing a human head with facial features and a high sagittal crest, said to
represent an old form of Wukari-area women's coiffure (fig. 9.25). At present, basketry
and wooden versions of this motif exist side by side in some villages of the southwest,
with no agreement among informants as to precedence.[40]

Basketry examples consist of a base in the form of an inverted bowl, made of
hibiscus fiber with palm-rib stiffeners sewn with hibiscus fiber in a coiling technique
(fig. 9.24). The vertical element consists of a rough oval loop made of dried palm-
fronds sewn to the center of this base, which is covered with finely combed hibiscus
fiber sewn in place with chain-stitched ornamental bands of twisted raffia thread.
Loops, coils, and twists representing eyes, ears, nose, and mouth are sewn onto the
base, and usually a small "chignon" is added at the rear of the crest. In use, the facial
portion of the crest seems always to be covered by a cloth band tied around the base
of the vertical element, leaving only the top projecting above.

Wooden Aku Wa'uwa consist of a hollow helmet with human features and prominent sagittal crest (see fig. 9.25). Although eyes were pierced, the diameter of most
examples seemed too small for the mask to have fitted over the wearer's head allowing
the openings to be used for vision. Small holes around the rim, in some cases above a
flange, served for the attachment of costume elements. A prominent feature of most
examples is the heavy and elaborate embellishment of the surface, involving incised
geometric elements and heavy raised ridges running from temples to corners of

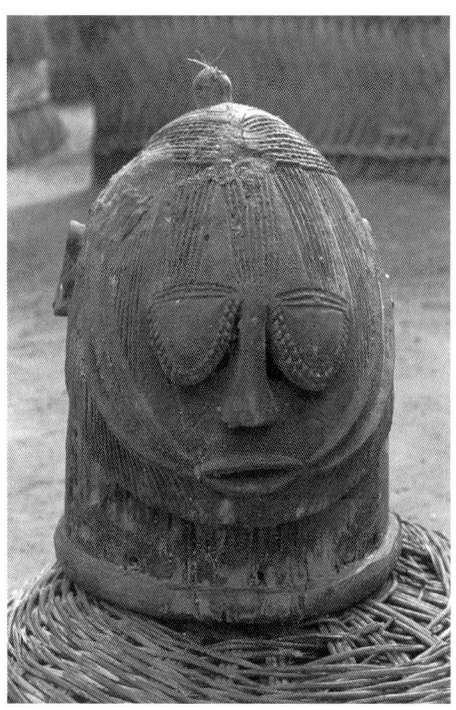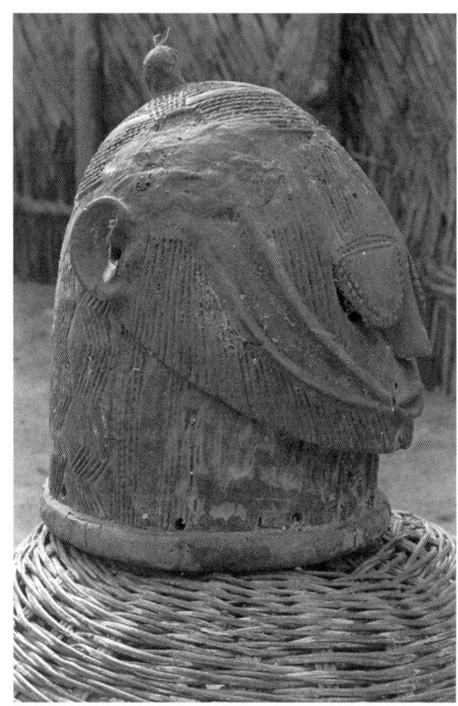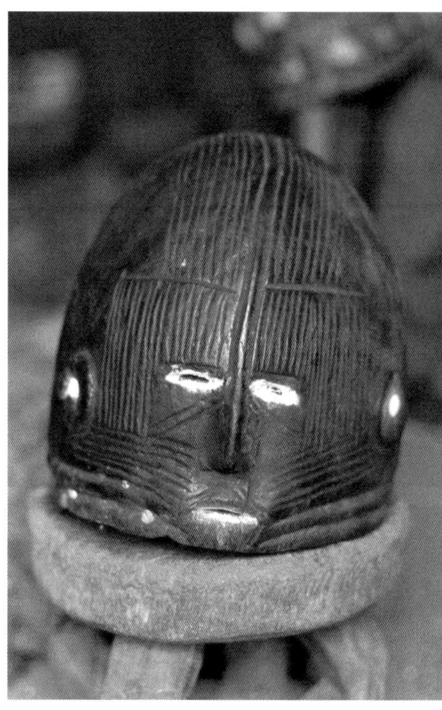

mouth, apparently representing scarification. Where one or more Aku Wa'uwa appear with an Aku Wa'unu, the masquerades dance individually and in turn, each following the cues of the lead drummer. Those masquerades not dancing rest at the edge of the dancing area. The dance of the Aku Wa'uwa consists of a delicate and restrained stepping around, accompanied by a flirting motion of the hips, which rhythmically twitches the cloth bundled at the waist.

The crested wooden helmet or basketry cap of the Aku Wa'uwa closely resembles masks that have been noted as widely distributed in the Lower Benue (see fig. 2.38).[41] In particular, two examples from Idah illustrated by Murray (1949, 88–89) and others from Ibaji in Boston (1960, and see figs. 5.2, 5.6, 5.7, 5.15–17, this volume) strikingly resemble the Jukun helmet collected by Flegel (fig. 9.26) and those I saw in the field. Although the treatment of coiffure varies, a heavy embellishment of surface and distinctive, pouch-like rendering of eyes seem to be shared—characteristics that are also evident in certain Afo masks and figurative sculptures. With only one exception, all the wooden Aku Wa'uwa helmets I encountered were located in towns on or very near the south bank of the Benue: Akwana, Arufu (figs. 9.27a,b, and see figs. 2.38a,b), and Chinkai (see fig. 9.25). The single exception is located at Rafin Kada. The Rafin Kada mask, called Atsinkisha, was made to commemorate the first wife of the founding ancestor of the family to which it belonged (fig. 9.28). Atsi was her given name, Kisha, the Jukun name for the Alago, her origin. When about to die, she announced that the mask that would represent her should be carved rather than of basketry, "since her people were doing it that way."

Meek (1931a, 254ff.) documents in extensive detail the post-burial rites of the Jukun living north of the Benue in Kassan Chikki. These ceremonies involve a precisely structured relationship between the Aku-Maga complex and another

9.27a,b
Two views of carved wooden Aku Washenki (Ayogi) mask.

9.28
Carved wooden Aku Wa'uwa (Atsinkisha) mask owned by Dodo Adi.

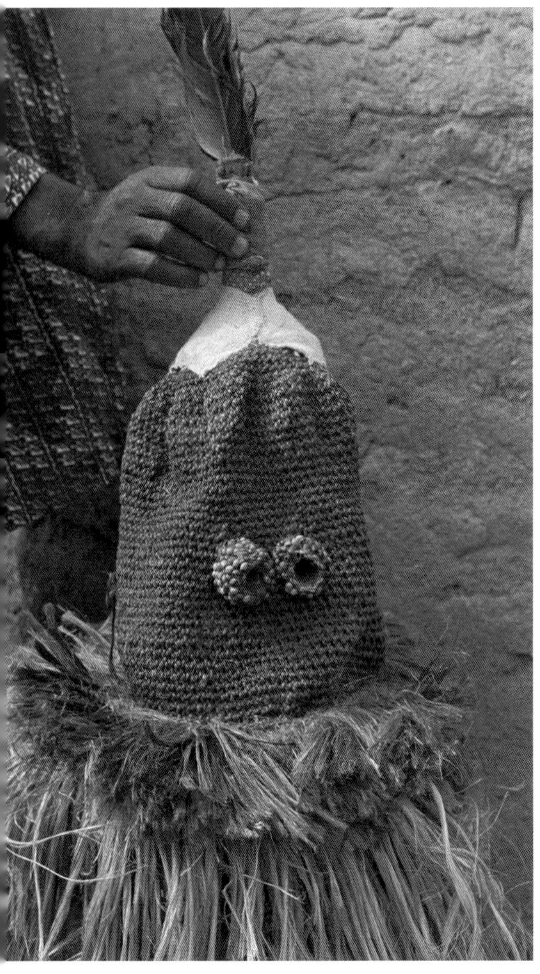

9.29
Adasha mask made of heavy netting, feathers, and stiff fiber ruff.
PHOTOGRAPH BY ARNOLD RUBIN, ARUFU VILLAGE, JANUARY 20, 1965, RUBIN ARCHIVE, FOWLER MUSEUM AT UCLA, NEG. NO. 93.

masquerade, Adasha, which summons the shade (Aku Ahwan) to convey the soul of the deceased to the underworld (fig. 9.29). The configuration consists of a heavy, netted-fiber mask, cylindrical in shape, with projecting abrus-encrusted hollow cylinders representing eyes, a conical peak that incorporates a bunch of feathers, and a stiff fiber ruff at the neck.[42] Several examples of the Adasha configuration were encountered south of the Benue, but they appear to lack the precisely structured mortuary/memorial role encountered in Kassan Chikki. Rather, in the Wukari area, they function as "tutelary deities" with reference to members of the owning kindred in accordance with the general pattern delineated earlier.

Aku Ashenki (the Aku of mourning) performs in connection with funerary rites for prominent people at Akwan, Arufu, and Wukari (Meek 1931a, 276). The mask consists of a wooden or basketry helmet identical to that used for the Aku Wa'uwa masquerade; the basketry example at Wukari was covered with a red cloth sleeve with a line of cowries sewn along the crest. The masquerader arrives at the compound of the bereaved family at the head of a slow and stately procession of elders. There, it is conducted to an overturned mortar outside the entry house, where it sits and sings laments in a call-and-response pattern. Answers are provided by a chorus, who also play rattle-calabashes (like those used to guide the Aku Wa'unu masquerader) and large hemispherical calabashes, which are alternately beaten with the side of the free hand and thumped against the thigh to produce complex rhythmical interludes.

In terms of field experience, I know of only one exception to my earlier statement that all sculpture among the southwestern Jukun takes the form of masks. The exception is a caryatid figure preserved in the village of Gidan Yaku on the south bank of the Benue, a few miles downstream from Ibi (see fig. 2.11). According to Meek (1931a, 281), Gidan Yaku was the principal shrine of an oracular cult called Yaku or Ayo, which involved possession of a medium by a familiar spirit.[43] The image reportedly served as a devotional focus for the medium of the cult. It represents a standing female, with arms raised, holding a flat tray on her head. A cloth wrapper covers her lower body, and she is heavily ornamented with beads and other materials. The surface is black and heavily oiled. A notable feature is the representation of a prominent umbilical hernia which, together with its basic conception and a number of details, closely relates the Gidan Yaku caryatid to a double caryatid collected before 1904 at Wukari (see fig. 2.5).[44] This Wukari double caryatid is generally accepted as belonging to the corpus of "early"-style Afo sculpture, whereas the Gidan Yaku figure might plausibly be associated with "later" Afo style (see chapter 2).[45] On the basis of the analysis presented here, however, both would seem to belong to a larger stylistic corpus of Lower Benue figurative sculptures, which included not only the Afo monuments but also the Idoma Ekwotame documented by Sieber (1961, 9) and related works. Formally, they would also relate to other instances of the caryatid motif that have come to light in the Lower Benue Valley and beyond.[46]

Another figure, reportedly representing an Abakwariga ancestress named Anakatume, is presently in use in Wukari in connection with the Jonkpa cult. I saw it briefly only once, wrapped in cloth in procession. It appeared to be about five feet tall with a hemispherical top, suggesting a caryatid grown huge. The base, however, appeared to be pointed, suggesting affinities with Chamba figures.[47]

GOEMAI

Patterns of social and political organization among the Goemai living northeast of the Shemankar River generally resemble the dispersed settlements and decentralized structures typical of their Montol neighbors. Their arts, according to Sieber (1961), are also similar. For example, the use of carved wooden figures in connection with Kwompten procedures is apparently general among the Goemai; in many cases, the figures involved are obtained from Montol carvers (Sieber 1961, 10; 1974). Temple

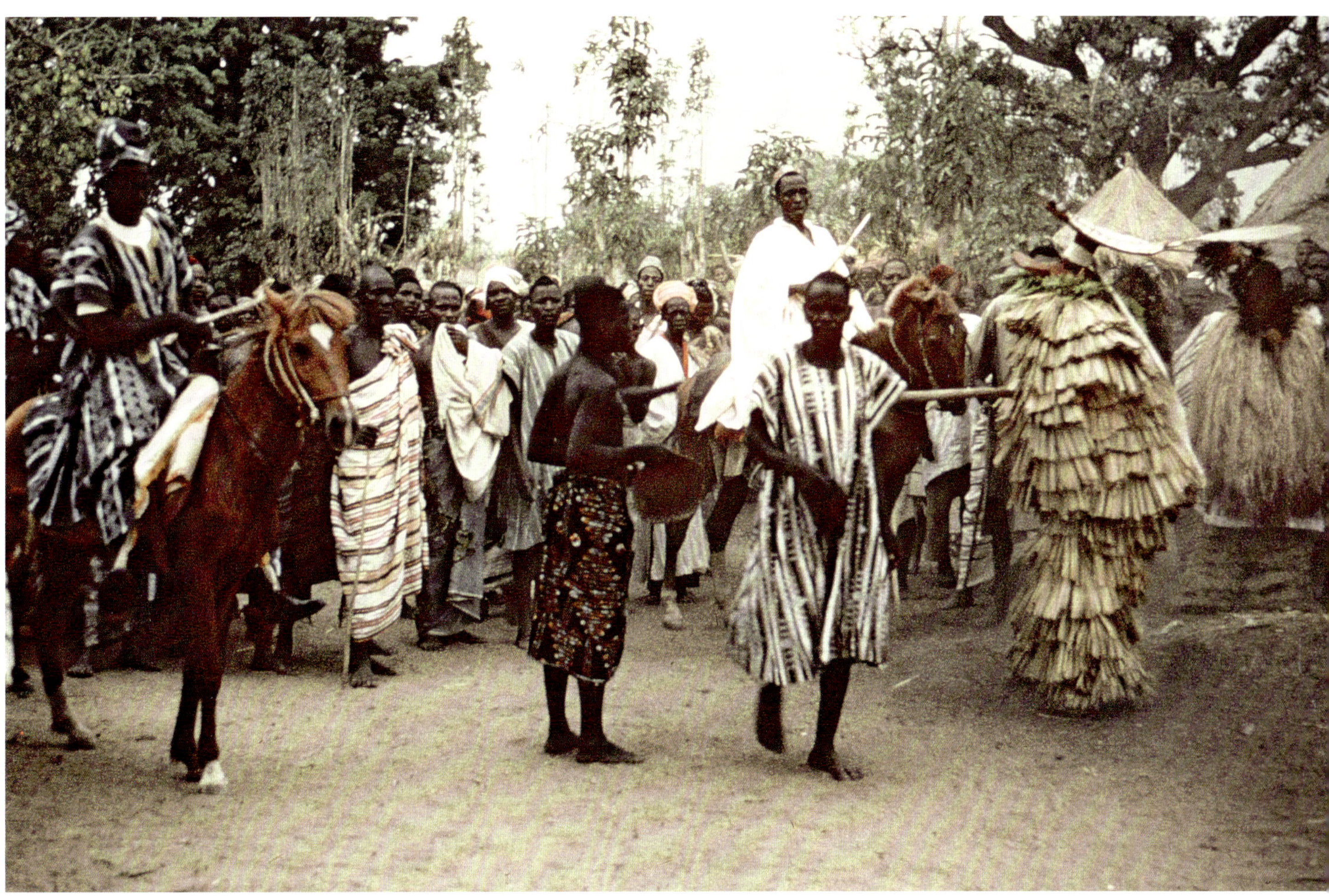

9.30

Mangap performer (far right) in costume composed of stiff vegetable material and accompanied by attendant.

PHOTOGRAPH BY ROBERT NETTING, GOEMAI VILLAGE OF JAK, 1963, RUBIN ARCHIVE, FOWLER MUSEUM AT UCLA, SLIDE. NO. A1.12.11.7.

(1919, 20) mentions a Goemai image of Mat Kerrem, "their tsafi," kept at the royal burial ground. The image in question may be the one illustrated by Sieber (1961, fig. 7), a human figure with the head of Gugwom mask (see figs. 8.60a–c).

Sieber (1961, 26) reports the existence of "a number of fiber masks" among the Goemai but only illustrates one pair, from Mgbo, northeast of the Shemankar. The bulky material and strongly sculptural forms of the masks generally resemble the Montol example he illustrates, though differing somewhat in detail. Dabit, the more important of the pair, is composed of a tube, which covers the face, culminating in a plug on top into which feathers are inserted. Eyes are represented by two abrus-encrusted hollow cylinders. It thus exhibits similarities to the Jukun Adasha configuration. Roy Sieber has shown me photographs of a Goemai masquerade called Begwel, which he witnessed at Shendam and which served as "messenger" for another masquerade.

Southwest of the Shemankar, however, the Goemai towns of Kurgwi, Kwande, and Bakinchiawa (and a few others) exhibit a relatively high degree of political centralization and one particularly distinctive mask type.[48] Sieber (1961, 10) suggests that these towns were "on or near a major north-south trade route that connected them with Ibi and Wukari," a hypothesis corroborated by Fremantle (1922, 59) and amplified to the effect that the route in question also extended to Wase and Bauchi, and to the salt-producing districts of Kassan Chikki.

Although their languages are unrelated, impressive cultural affinities are evident between the Goemai living southwest of the Shemankar, their Alago neighbors to the west, and the Jukun who live interspersed among them (Isichei 1982, 15,19; Agi 1982, 100). These affinities include broad principles of religious belief, details of social and political organization, and conventions of material culture such as the sacramental plaited lock of hair for senior males. Observers interested in the arts have emphasized

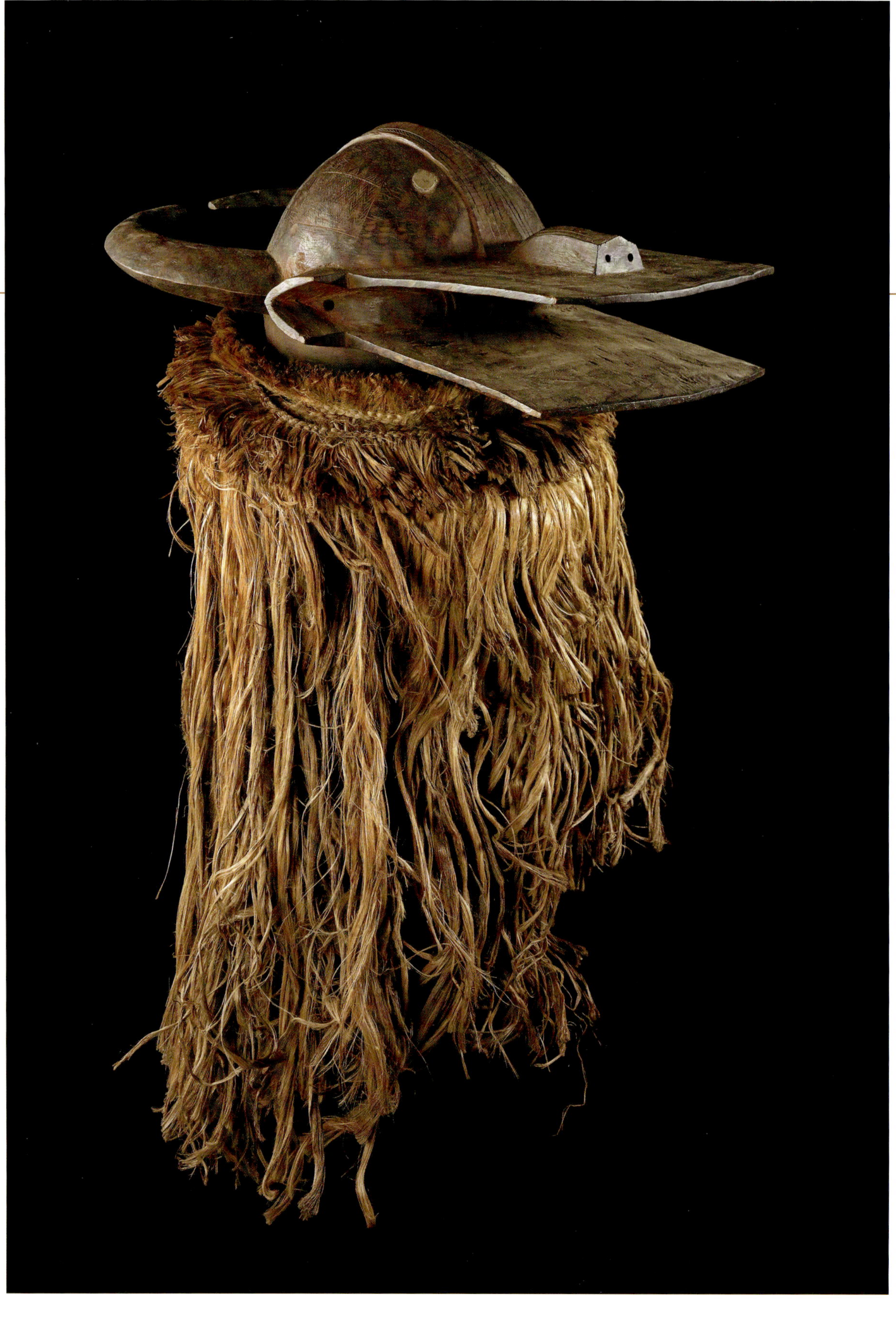

CHAPTER 10

Hybrids: Theranthropic Horizontal Masquerades from the Middle Benue

RICHARD FARDON

Wooden figures from the Middle Benue are, almost without exception, anthropomorphic: they do not necessarily represent humans, but they are human-shaped. On occasion particular figures are reported to have been identified as "ancestors" or past "chiefs," but it is likely that these identities were attributed to them thanks to the way they were used rather than a figure being commissioned specifically to represent, let alone portray, its particular subject. Figurative sculptures were malleable vessels of meaning that might be endowed with the characteristics of human forebears, more distant ancestors, the generic dead of the underworld, or dangerous spirits that took anthropomorphic forms, and in most cases they probably had something of each of these about them. Wooden figures, simply as sculptures, do not seem to have been destined to mean anything specifically, they acquired significance by their presence in assemblages of things and practices during particular moments of propitiation. Chamba, to take an instance for which we have field observations, used identical figures in cults and shrines that differed greatly in purpose, providing us with no evidence that carvers modified the figures they sculpted in the light of their intended use.

Even the apparent exceptions to the rule that Middle Benue figures are anthropomorphic serve to underline that rule. Rare examples combine human bodies with animal heads modeled on horizontal masks (see figs. 8.60a–c, E.11), and so, as noted earlier, by revealing the human inside the costume, they bear a telltale relationship to masquerade (fig. 10.2).[1] This combination of forms that are by convention interpreted as human-like, or "anthropomorphic," with forms that are animal-like or "theriomorphic," can be called "theranthropic." Theranthropism is exceptional in statues but entirely typical of horizontal masquerades,[2] or of masquerade performances that involve horizontal masks in conjunction with others.

On occasion, it helps to distinguish three terms in the course of this discussion: the "mask" (by which I mean most commonly a wooden head, often all that has been acquired in museum collections), the "masquerade" (meaning the mask plus the full costume of the masquerader, although I occasionally use this term more loosely), and the "masquerade performance" (all that the masquerade requires to perform appropriately on those occasions when it is called upon to do so [figs. 10.3, 10.4], which might also require the presence of one or more other masquerades, melodic or rhythmic accompaniments, custodians of the masquerades, and so on). Theranthropism may be a quality of the mask, the masquerade, the masquerade performance, or all of these. It may even be evoked when the masquerade is unseen. Masquerade performances, like many cult performances, are auditory as well as visual phenomena. For noninitiates in

10.1
Masquerade
Chamba Daka peoples, 1921 or before
Wood, metal, fiber
L (of mask): 72 cm
THE TRUSTEES OF THE BRITISH MUSEUM, AF1922,0610.1
IMAGE: © TRUSTEES OF THE BRITISH MUSEUM. PHOTOGRAPH BY MICHAEL ROW, 2010
PROVENANCE: COLLECTED BY CAPTAIN E. S. LILLEY, PRIOR TO 1922, MURI, NIGERIA

This fine example of a western Chamba Daka masquerade, complete with dress, was collected by a British colonial officer, E. S. Lilley in 1921, as part of the same assemblage as the four figures from Binyeri (see figs. 8.39, 8.40). In form it is characteristic of western Chamba Daka masquerades (see fig. 10.37).

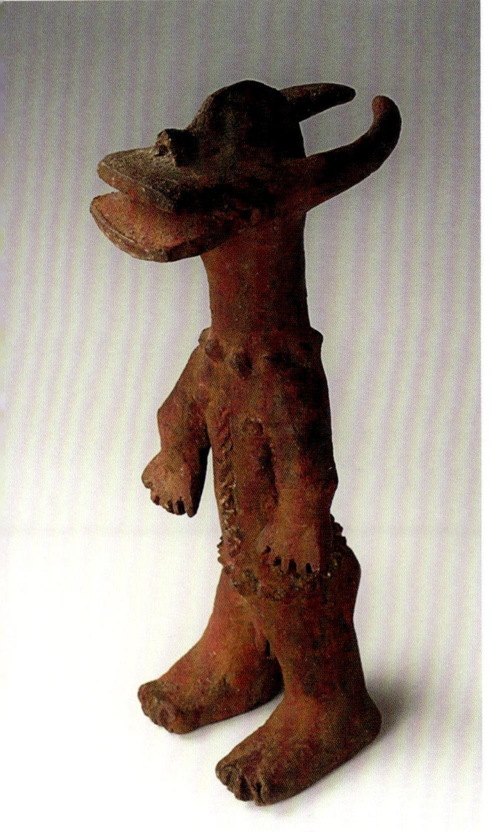

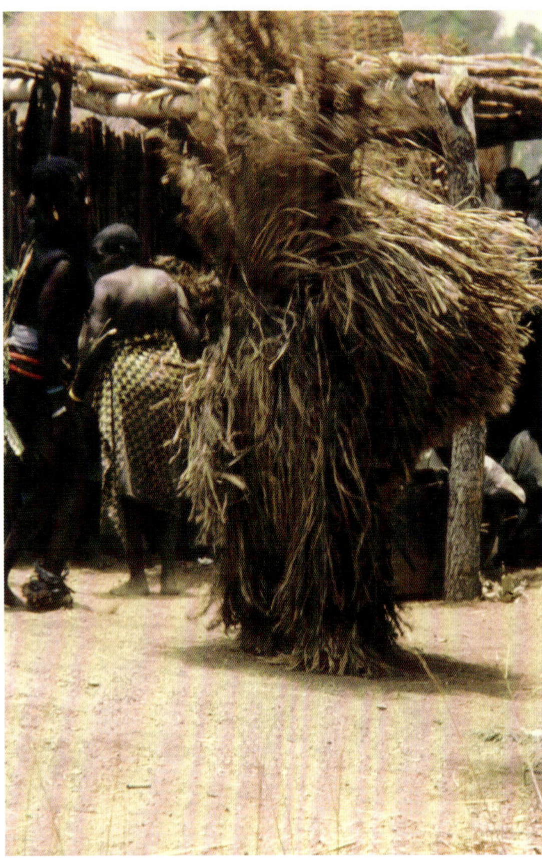

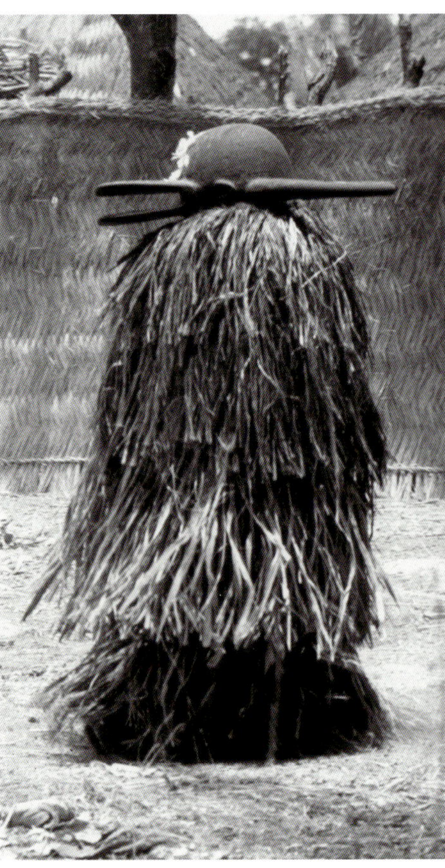

10.2

Male figure with the head of a Chamba mask
Chamba peoples, eighteenth century or later
Ceramic
H: 31 cm
CHRISTOPHE EVERS COLLECTION, BRUSSELS
IMAGE: © CHRISTOPHE EVERS. PHOTOGRAPH BY
DICK BEAULIEUX, 2003
PROVENANCE: PHILIPPE GUIMIOT, CIRCA 1967
(NOT IN EXHIBITION)

Thermoluminescence testing suggests that
this piece could have been made as early as
the eighteenth century. The mask shape, particularly the assimilation of its ears into the
mask's jaws, would suggest an origin among
Chamba Daka speakers, possibly around
Mapeo or Lengdo in the western Alantika
Mountains. The likelihood of the piece coming from this Cameroon-Nigeria border area
is reinforced by our knowledge that it passed
from a "runner" to Philippe Guimiot in
Cameroon as early as 1967.

10.3, 10.4

In 1977 the royal matriclan Gad-Kuna of the
Chamba in Yeli, held their annual "death beer"
to commemorate the deaths of clan members
during the previous year. The masquerade
(generically called Lang-Gbadna in Yeli) of
the royal clan performed with the women past
child-bearing age, but unlike other masquerades attending this occasion, which danced in
pairs, it did not dance with other masquerades
PHOTOGRAPHS BY RICHARD FARDON, YELI,
CAMEROON, JULY 18, 1977.

fact, they may be auditory to the exclusion of visual phenomena. Some masquerades
and cults are associated with percussion on drums or sonorous iron gongs, and cults
emit a variety of more or less uncanny sounds (by swinging bull-roarers, intoning
or blowing into calabash horns, using shrill whistles, or employing voice disguisers).
Because cultic images can be evoked by auditory cues, they are not, in a simple sense,
entirely material or visual manifestations.

Most Middle Benue horizontal masquerades were not just fusions (Fardon 2007)
but also hybrids in the etymological sense of mixing domesticated and wild strains.
The animal and human, as well as the wild and domesticated, components were integrated so that each masquerade belonged to a recognizable named type,[3] which was
both a form of being unlike any other and a composite that could be interpreted, by
those with the knowledge to do so, in terms of a skein of associations among entities
evoked through metonymic—that is, part-whole—relations. Take, for example, the
Chamba mask (discussed in more detail below), it had the horns of a dwarf forest
bushcow or buffalo; but this did not make it a bushcow or buffalo mask (as often
claimed in the literature) because it also had anthropomorphic features modeled on
the same conventions as Chamba figure statuary to depict a human skull, nose, eyes,
and ears, and in some instances, a sagittal crest of hair as well. The theranthropic character of this masquerade is already intrinsic to the form of its wooden mask, although
consideration of its performance and full costume would reinforce this reading. There
are cases, however, when theranthropism does not become apparent simply from
looking at the form of a mask but involves the simultaneous appearance of more than
one masquerade or becomes evident from an entire masquerade performance during
which other accoutrements contribute some elements of the fusion, for instance in
the association of predominantly theriomorphic masks with actual human skulls (see
fig. 12.16; Fardon 2007, 138, 6a). Masquerade performances (like cultic performances
generally) materialized an associational style of religious thought, that is to say, a
concern with the way important properties of the lifeworld connected up. By doing

this, masquerades did not stand in for particular entities other than themselves; rather they exemplified the presuppositions of a worldview—one that was shared in its broad terms in the everyday philosophy of the peoples of the religious ecumene that was the Middle Benue.

THERANTHROPIC HORIZONTAL MASQUERADES

I begin by surveying three masking traditions that readily relate to one another: those of the neighboring Jukun, Mumuye, and Chamba. In so doing, I want also to explore opportunities to compare stylistic differences among the masks of these three peoples with differences existing in their prevailing conventions of figure sculpture. Another very broad distinction becomes useful here. I noted in my introduction to the Middle Benue region (see chapter 7) that two gross general types of masquerade can be distinguished: horizontal masquerades of the kind discussed for the most part in this chapter and vertical masquerades discussed by Marla Berns in chapter 14. In formal terms, horizontal masquerades are predominantly theriomorphic (that is, conventionally animal-shaped), a correlation we might motivate in two ways: either by reference to the elongation of animal compared to human skulls or by the more horizontal posture of animals compared to upright human gait. Vertical wooden masquerades, particularly in the tall form, which is distributed from the northeastern corner of the Jukun and Mumuye and stretches northeastward among the Wurkun, are almost exclusively anthropomorphic, which might be motivated by reference to the upright character of human skulls and human locomotion. This contrast between the animal/horizontal and human/vertical is realized, and mediated, in various ways when we come to look at entire masquerade performances.

Jukun

Southwestern Jukun wooden-headed horizontal masquerades (northeastern Jukun, according to Rubin, either lacked masquerades or had only anthropomorphic vertical masks) took two predominant forms: Aku and Aku-Ma. The first of these, also known as Aku-Maga (where *maga* may refer to the staff it carries) was most common around Wukari and had apparently been copied north of there. Its form was relatively invariant. The second, characterized by extensive formal variation, occurred more frequently in the southwest of Jukun country around Takum, and it resembled other masquerades further to its southwest (see Meek 1931a; Rubin 1969; 1985; 1988; n.d.). The term used for these masquerades, "Aku," was also that used of the dead or ancestors and of some cults (Meek 1931a, xii, 217, 225, 263, 274 n. 1, discussed in Fardon 2007, 123–25). Both the Aku and Aku-Ma masquerades, according to stories of their origin collected by Leo Frobenius—who also photographed them and acquired examples—emerged from the Benue River. The Jukun terms "Aku" and "Aku-Ma" referred both to the, more or less, horizontal male masquerades and to the masquerade performance in which the male masquerade might be accompanied by a female partner, identified in the myths as its "wife": hence, "wife of" Aku or Aku-Ma. Jukun suffixed the terms *-wunu* and *-wuwa* to the mask names respectively to designate their male and female forms (and commonly "female" can be translated as "wife" in such usages; figs. 10.5, 10.6).[4]

> Aku and his wife wanted to leave the Benue River so as to be fed by humans, but they were prevented from doing this by crocodiles. Eventually, Aku prised himself free at the cost of his left arm, which was bitten off by a crocodile. The two masquerades were accommodated and fed by humans, but they caused deaths until they were taken up by everyone to commemorate their deceased fathers and sisters. The masks were also given cloths to wear over their fiber bodies. [Frobenius 1924, 240–42][5]

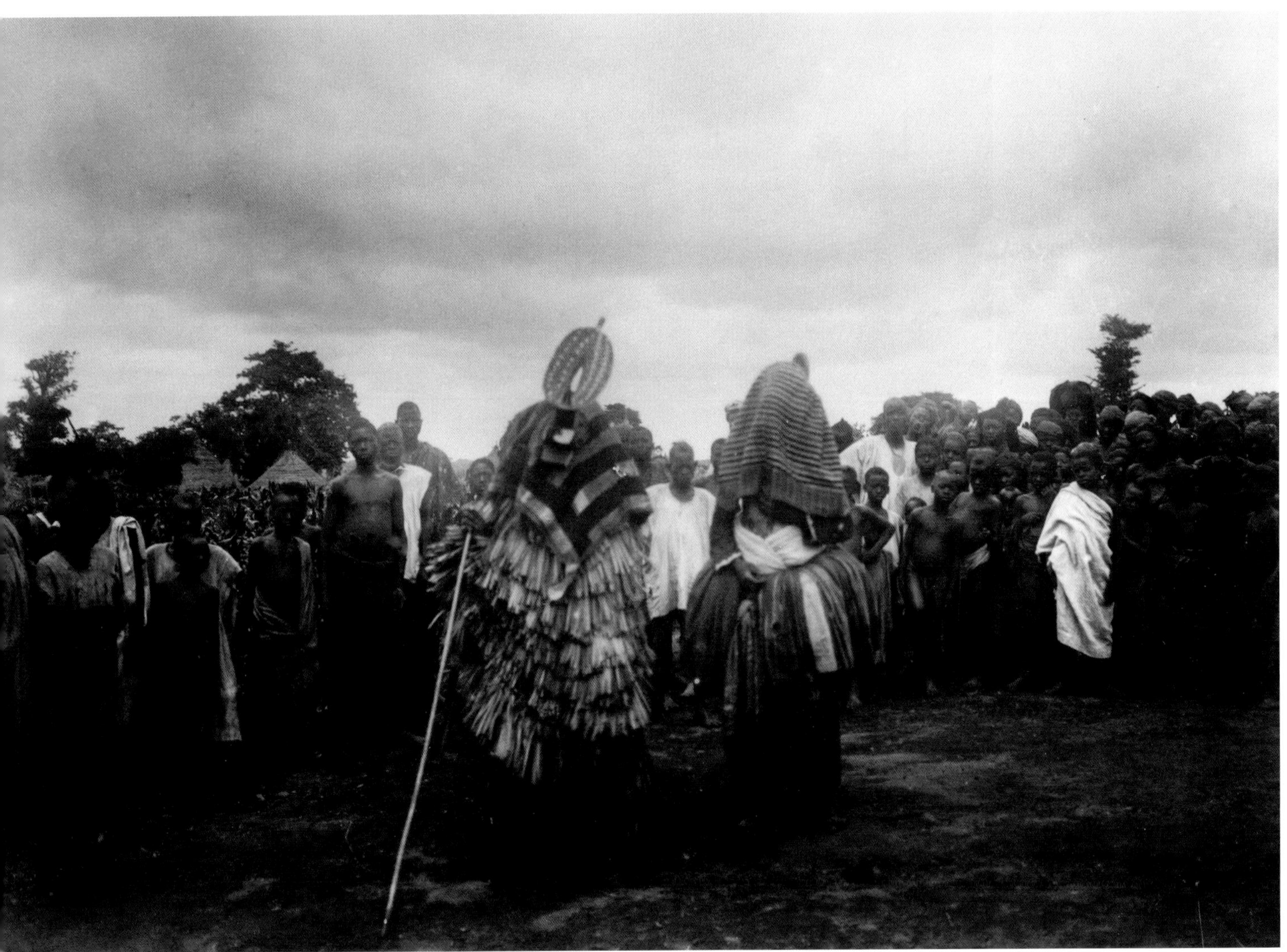

10.5
Leo Frobenius collected several Jukun masks and photographed masquerades in Wukari in 1912. This photograph shows the Aku couple. The one-armed male, Aku-Wunu, wears a checked cloth over his fiber dress; in his right hand he carries a staff. His "wife," Aku-Wuwa, is wholly clad in cloths, and her cap mask is apparent in the picture only as a sagittal crest.
COPYRIGHT: FROBENIUS-INSTITUT, FRANKFURT AM MAIN, NEGATIVE 5763.

The Aku-Ma couple were more reluctant to leave the Benue River.

> Aku-Ma and his wife had fallen from the sky in the forms of a horned man, able to stand on the water, and his long-haired wife, who floated on the water in a calabash she had carried on her descent. On the advice of a diviner, one Jukun man dragged them out of the water by the man's horns and the woman's unruly hair. Like the Aku they caused death among their human hosts until proper arrangements to feed them were arrived at. [Frobenius 1924, 244–46]

The female masks of these couples—Aku-Wuwa and Aku-Ma-Wuwa—were strongly anthropomorphic and ornamented. The wife of Aku was made either in wood or plaited fiber (figs. 10.7, 10.8). In the wooden version, she has elaborate facial scarification (fig. 10.9); both types of female mask sport a prominent sagittal ridge to represent her plaited hairstyle. The wife of Aku-Ma was similar to her Aku female counterpart, but she had a wild profusion of hair rather than braids (figs. 10.10, 10.11). This is an indication, consistent with their stories of origination, that the Aku-Ma couple belong to the wild to a greater degree than do the more refined Aku couple. For instance: Aku-Ma was specifically said in the myth Frobenius collected to have had horns when he dropped from the sky, whereas Aku did not; Aku and his wife desired to leave the water to join humans despite being menaced by crocodiles, but Aku-Ma and his wife had to be dragged by a human to the riverbank; the myths of origination specified that the Aku couple, but not the Aku-Ma couple, were later dressed in cloths.

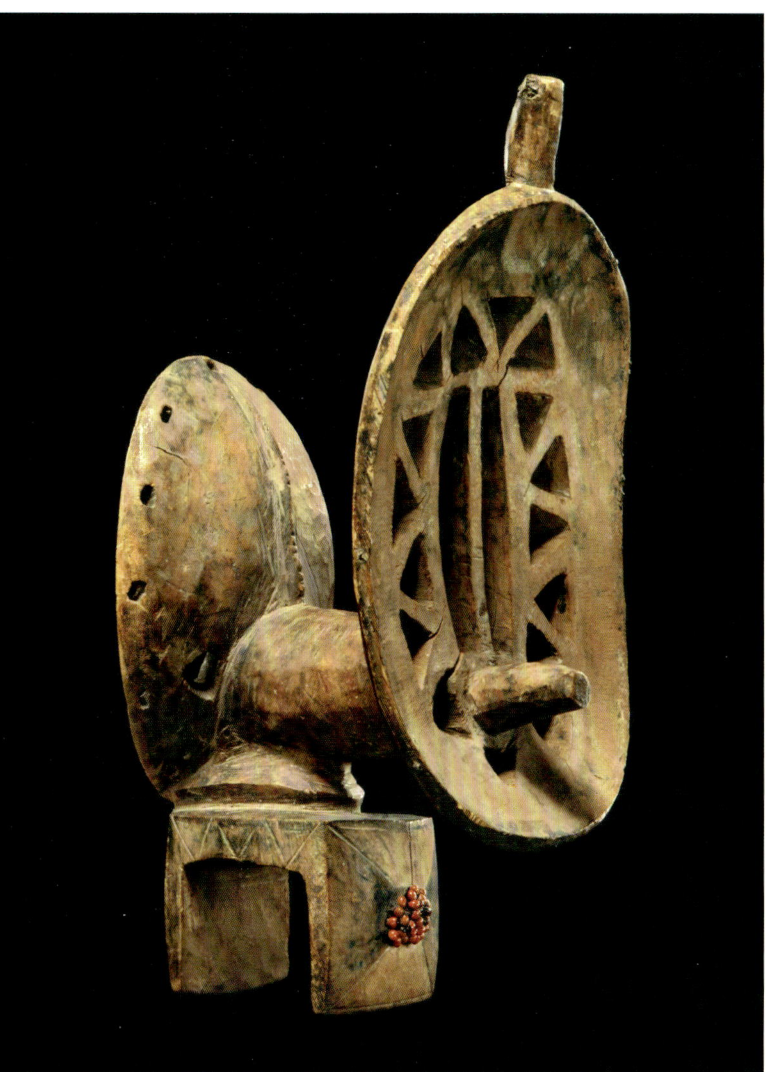

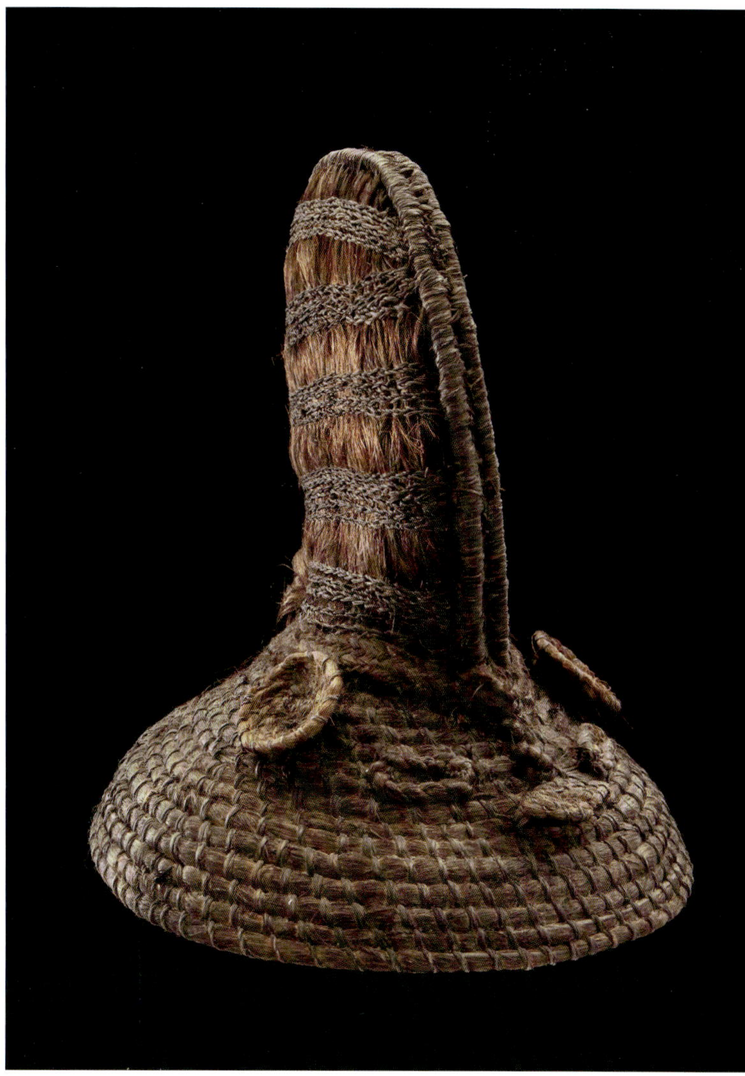

10.6
Male mask (Aku-Wunu)
Jukun peoples, before 1912
Wood, pigment, abrus seeds, resin (?)
L: 55 cm
STAATLICHE MUSEEN ZU BERLIN, ETHNOLOGIS-
CHES MUSEUM, III C29074
IMAGE: © STAATLICHE MUSEEN ZU BERLIN,
PREUSSICHER KULTURBESITZ, ETHNOLOGISCHES
MUSEUM. PHOTOGRAPH BY MARTIN FRANEN, 2010
PHOTOGRAPH BY MARTIN FRANKEN, 2010
PROVENANCE: COLLECTED BY LEO FROBENIUS, 1912

When held vertically (as here), this well-
executed male Aku-Wunu mask becomes an
anthropomorphic face mask with eye holes,
a long nose on its rear face plate, a hair
knot at the top of its front element, and an
overhanging chin studded with abrus seeds.
Held horizontally, the mask transforms
into a theriomorphic image with elliptical
horns punctured by geometric designs and a
gaping mouth. The abrus seeds may become
the beast's nose. In performance, the mask
is angled midway between the vertical and
horizontal to produce a complex theranthropic
fusion of human and animal characteristics.

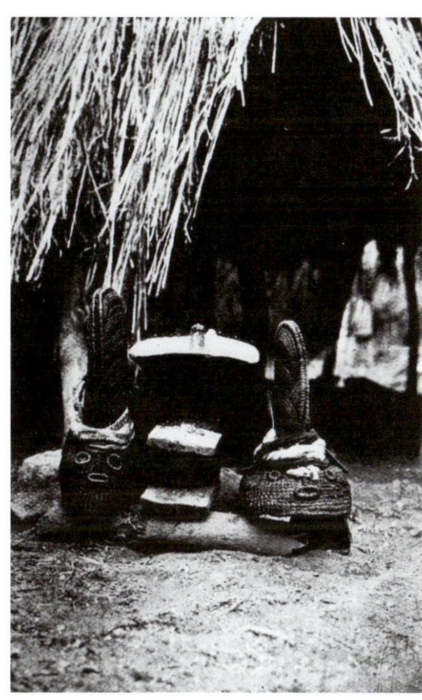

10.7
Female mask (Aku-Wuwa)
Jukun peoples, mid-twentieth century
Fiber
H: 24 cm
FOWLER MUSEUM AT UCLA X86.4734; GIFT OF
ARNOLD RUBIN, 1966
IMAGE: © 2010 FOWLER MUSEUM AT UCLA.
PHOTOGRAPH BY DON COLE
PROVENANCE: COLLECTED BY ARNOLD RUBIN,
NIGERIA

The mask of Aku-Wuwa, the female partner
of the male Aku (see fig. 10.6) is usually made
in basketry. Its neat features and coiffure
contrast markedly with the disheveled hair
of the female Aku-Ma (see figs. 10.10,10.11).

10.8
C. K. Meek's photograph shows the Jukun
male mask Aku-Wunu, made of wood, with
masks of two of his "wives," Aku-Wuwa, made
in their more common fiber form.
REPRODUCED FROM MEEK (1931A, PL. XX, RIGHT,
FACING P. 272).

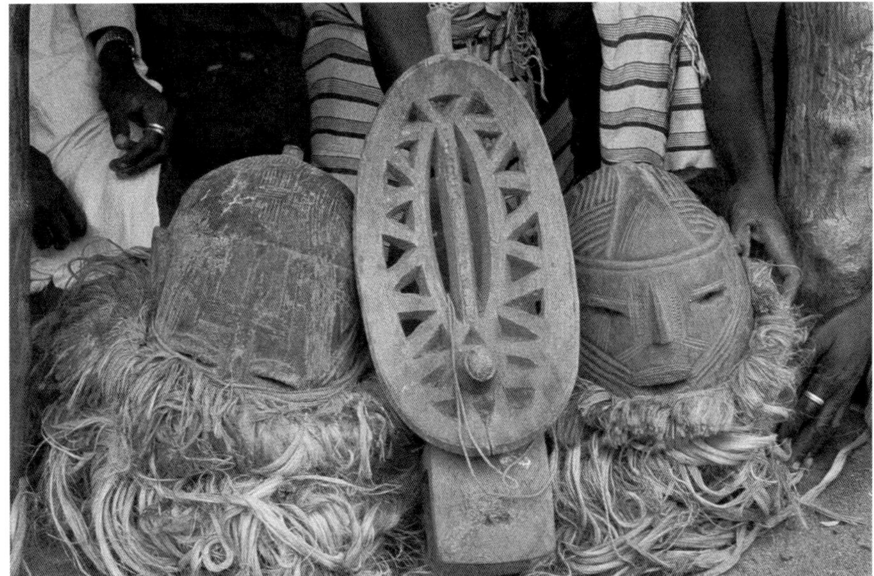

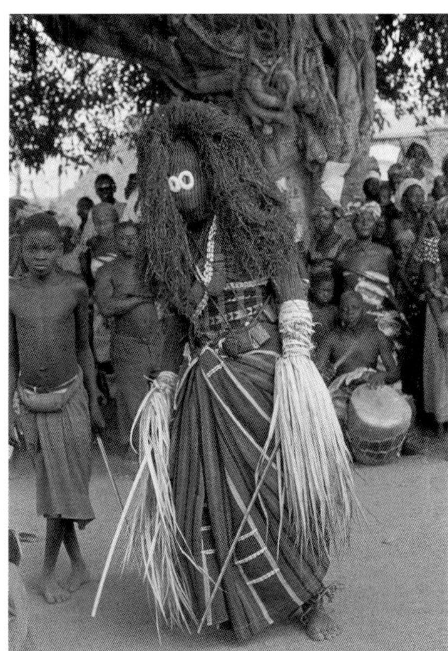

10.9 (ABOVE)

This photograph from the village of Chinkai shows a male Aku mask held at its performing angle (between the vertical and horizontal). In contrast to figure 10.8, the two "wives" on either side of Aku have been executed in wood, but they share the highly cultured appearance of the fiber versions. All three masks had personal names: Asiki (left) and Aku-Achuo (right) for the females; Amboyi for the male. The masks were said to be about twenty years old when photographed.

PHOTOGRAPH BY ARNOLD RUBIN, SEPTEMBER 4, 1965, RUBIN ARCHIVE, FOWLER MUSEUM AT UCLA, NEG. NO. 757.

10.10 (ABOVE RIGHT), 10.11 (RIGHT)

In contrast to the wife of Aku (see figs. 10.7–10.9), the female Aku-Ma mask displays a less-cultivated appearance, including a wild profusion of hair and round staring eyes. There is a prominence of fiber in her dress, sometimes to the exclusion of cloth (as in the masquerade from Kashimbila, right) or with a simple cloth wrapper (as in the example from Wukari, above right).

PHOTOGRAPHS BY ARNOLD RUBIN, KASHIMBILA, NOVEMBER 1965 AND WUKARI, JANUARY OR FEBRUARY 1965, RUBIN ARCHIVE, FOWLER MUSEUM AT UCLA, NEG. NOS. 20, 1347.

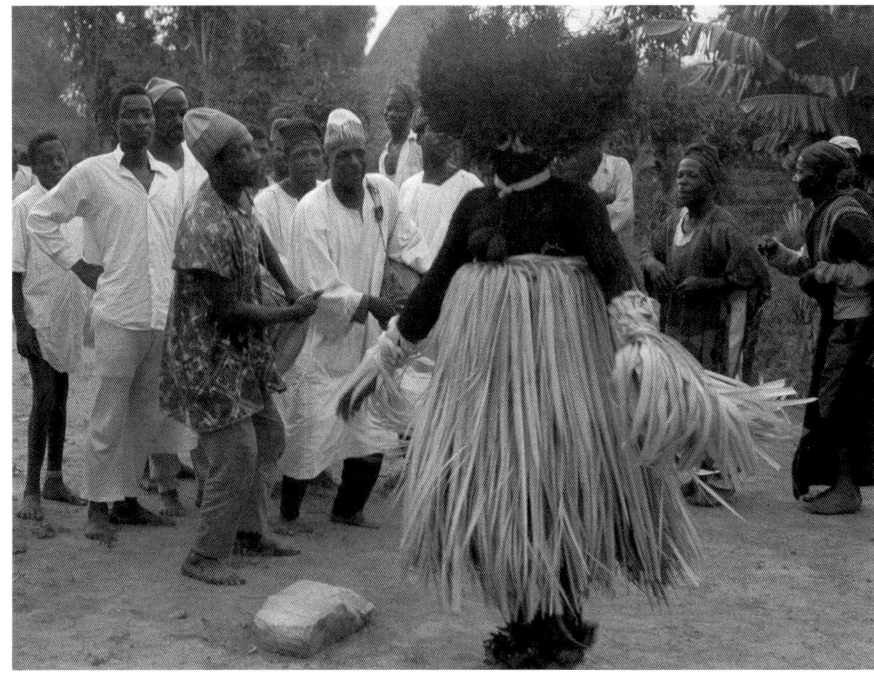

Although, when seen alone the female masks appear anthropomorphic, they never performed alone. For southwestern Jukun, masquerade performance is theranthropic. Both male masks usually had bovine horns (although those of Aku were occluded compared to those of Aku-Ma), hence masquerade performance included both anthropomorphic and theriomorphic elements. Like his wife, Aku-Ma appears to have more of the wild about him than does Aku. The origin myth, as I have noted, identifies Aku-Ma as a horned man. His masks, however, come in a number of forms, only one of which is evidently anthropomorphic. Meek's illustration of this type as sketched by a Jukun artist (fig. 10.13) depicts a plank mask, with some human features, surmounted by horns and worn horizontally (Meek 1931a, 491). Arnold Rubin who documented a Takum workshop producing such masks (1985)—where masks in this genre were named Aluku—explains, however, that the mouth of the mask doubled as a vision port and that the mask was worn at an angle, as would necessarily have been the case if the masquerader were to see through its mouth (figs. 10.12a,b, 10.15). More common forms of Aku-Ma fused the characteristics of a bird, elephant, or crocodile, in the case of a

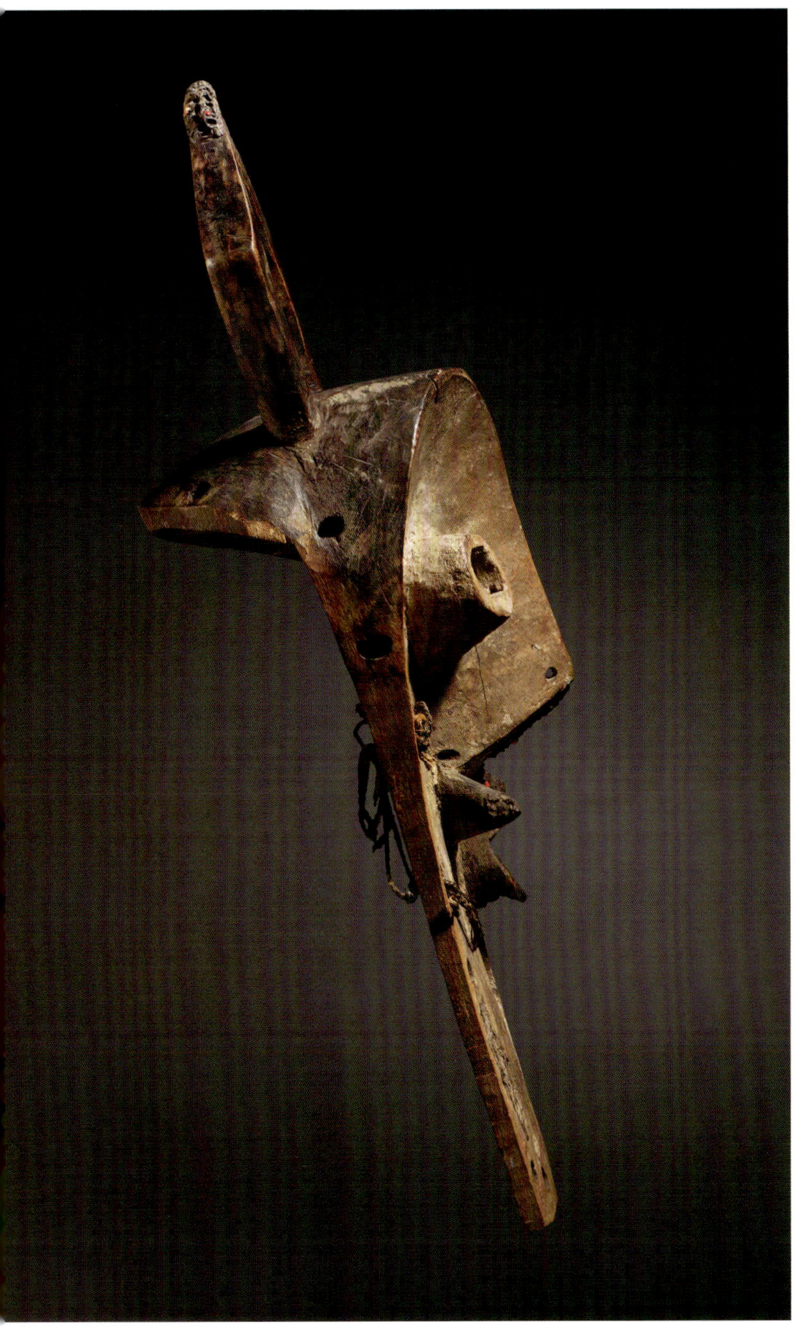

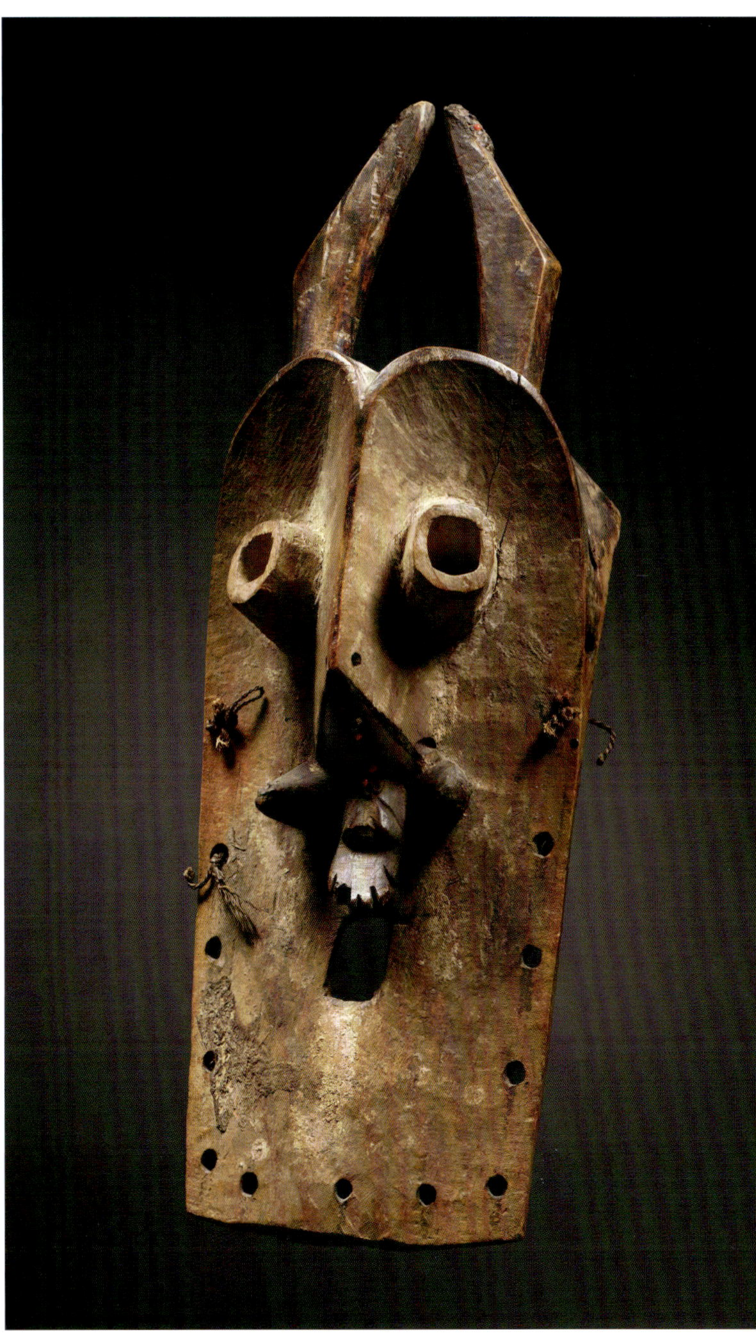

royal mask of Wukari (fig. 10.14) with buffalo horns. Patterns of scarification and hair knots on some such masks might have referenced human features, but theranthropic fusion in Aku-Ma masquerade was more obviously achieved through the pairing of the male and female masks in performance.

Unlike Aku-Ma, the Aku mask was theranthropic in itself: a singularly ingenious fusion, which makes different sense depending whether it is read theriomorphically, as a horizontal mask, or anthropomorphically, as a vertical face mask. Some elements of this design (figs. 10.16, 10.17) were appreciated by Meek (1931a, 273), whose interpretation was later challenged by Erich Herold (1975). My own interpretation draws on these two sources, as well as on Roy Sieber and Arnold Rubin's demonstration of the formal relation between Aku and other buffalo masks, and it reconciles them by suggesting a double reading. In performance, Aku was worn at an angle of about 30 degrees from upright, intermediately between the vertical and horizontal (the predominantly human and predominantly animal), which licenses interpretation in theranthropic terms (see fig. 10.5 and see also chapter 9, p. 309, fig. 9.22). Held vertically,

10.12a,b
Plank mask (Augum or Aluku)
Yukuben or Jukun peoples, mid-twentieth century
Wood, resin/wax, red seeds, raffia, kaolin
H: 72.5 cm
ROBERT T. WALL FAMILY
IMAGE: COURTESY COLLECTOR. PHOTOGRAPH BY DON TUTTLE, 2010
PROVENANCE: COLLECTION BASS, SWEDEN; YANNICK TURENNE, SWITZERLAND

Face masks in this largely anthropomorphic style, although typically augmented by tusks, were made for their own use by the Jukunoid Yukuben, who called them Augum, and made by the Abakwariga, reputedly of Hausa origin, for Jukun living in the town of Takum, who called this type of Aku-Ma mask Aluku.

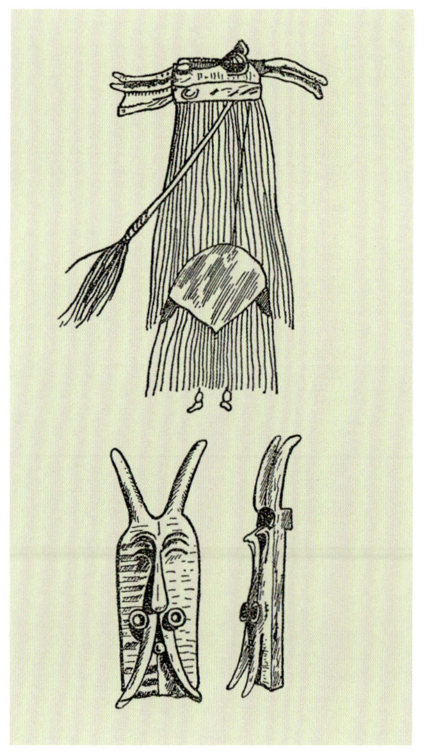

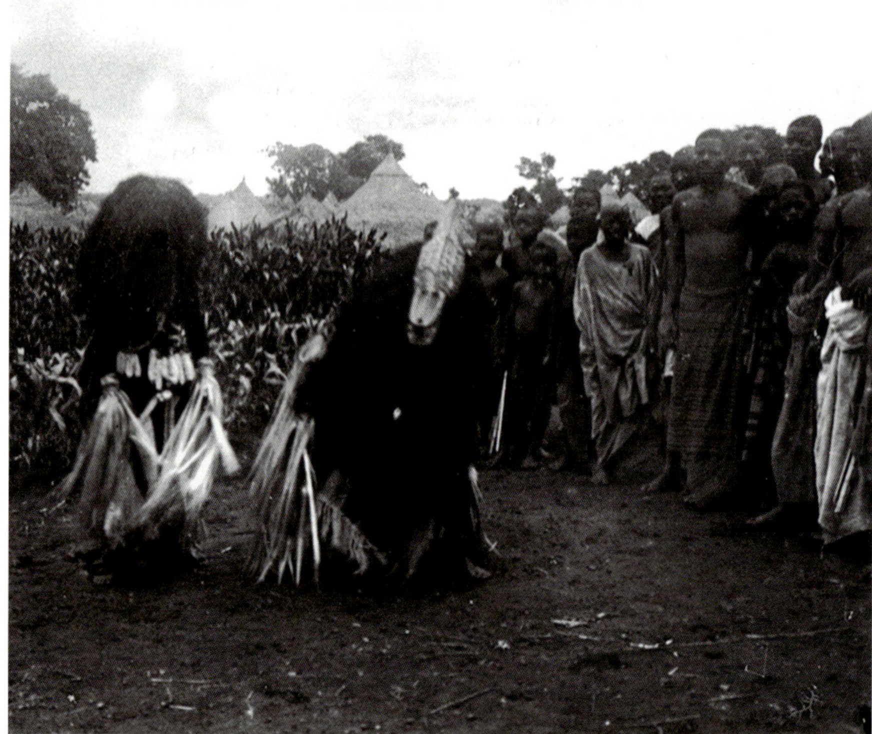

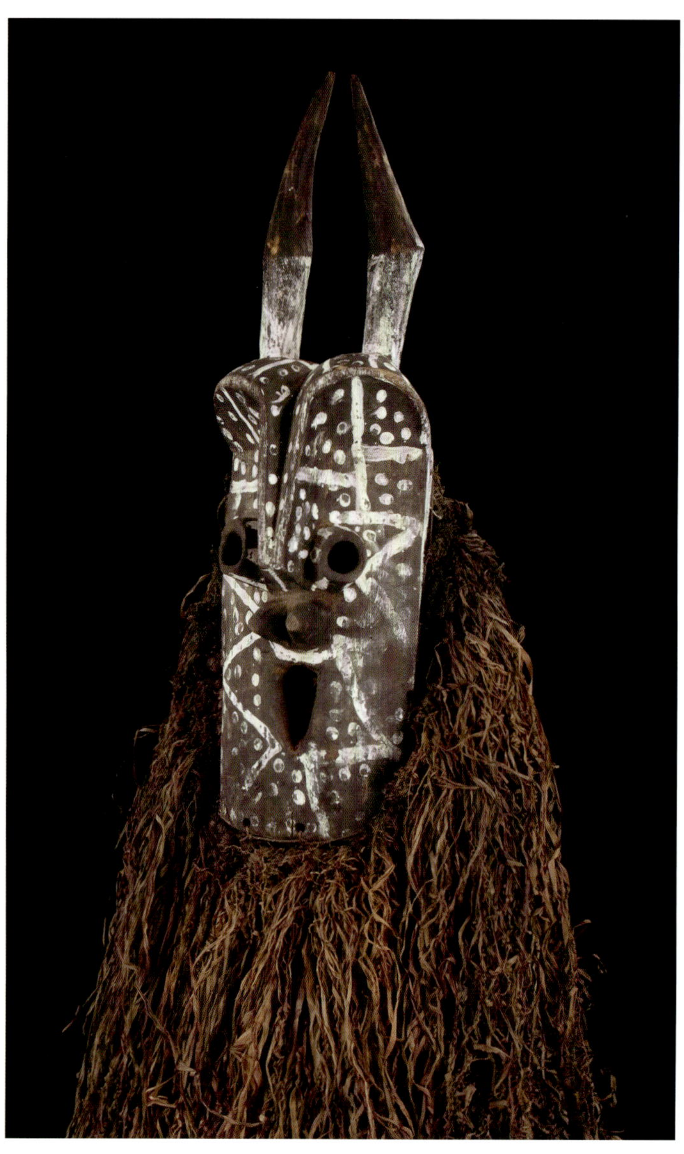

10.13

C. K. Meek (1931a, 491) reproduced "The Costume and Mask of the Genius Akuma, as Depicted by a Jukun Artist." He wrote that sketches by a Jukun artist, presumably including this one, were obtained by H. R. Palmer, Lieutenant-Governor of the Northern Provinces of Nigeria, who had interested himself in the Jukun and the claim that they had been the rulers of ancient Kororofa (Kwararafa).
REPRODUCED FROM MEEK (1931A, 149).

10.14

Leo Frobenius photographed this unusual Aku-Ma crocodile masquerade in Wukari in 1912. The "wife" of the crocodile masquerade is a typically disheveled female Aku-Ma (see fig. 10.10). Arnold Rubin was told that the crocodile mask had been commissioned in 1909 by the king, Aku Agbumanu (1969, 69).
COPYRIGHT: FROBENIUS-INSTITUT, FRANKFURT AM MAIN, NEGATIVE 5751.

10.15

Mask (Aku-Ma)
Takum, mid-twentieth century
Wood, pigment, raffia
H: 72.4 cm
FOWLER MUSEUM AT UCLA X69.76; MUSEUM PURCHASE
IMAGE: © 2010 FOWLER MUSEUM AT UCLA. PHOTOGRAPH BY DON COLE
(NOT IN EXHIBITION)

This Aku-Ma mask of the Aluku type was commissioned by Arnold Rubin in the Sangari compound of Abakwariga carvers in Takum. According to Rubin, the Aluku mask "consists of a horned plank worn tipped down in front at about thirty degrees below horizontal, with arching brows, prominent wedge-shaped nose, tubular eyes, and two points projecting beneath the nose" (1985, 60).

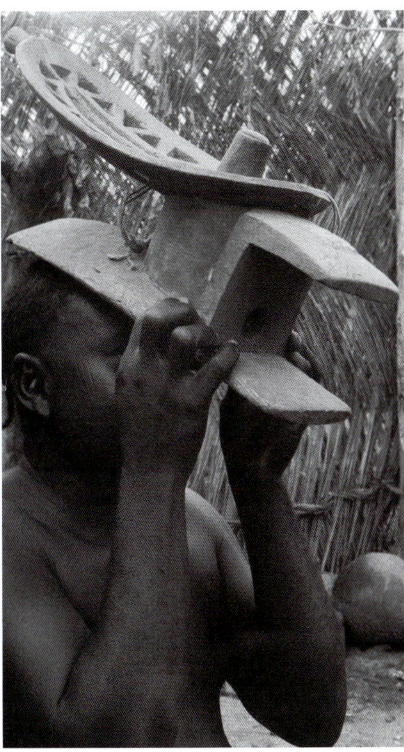

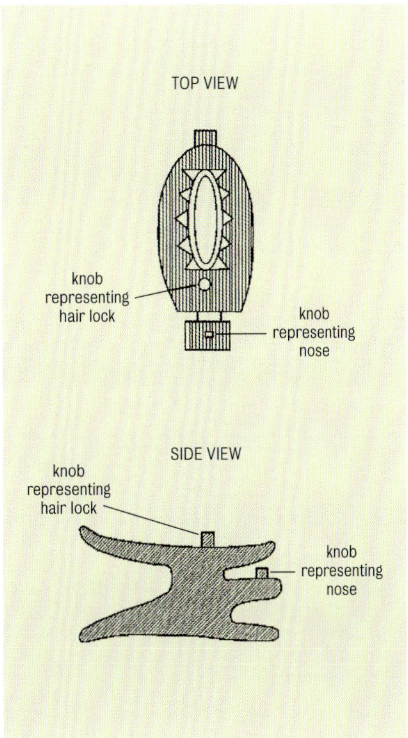

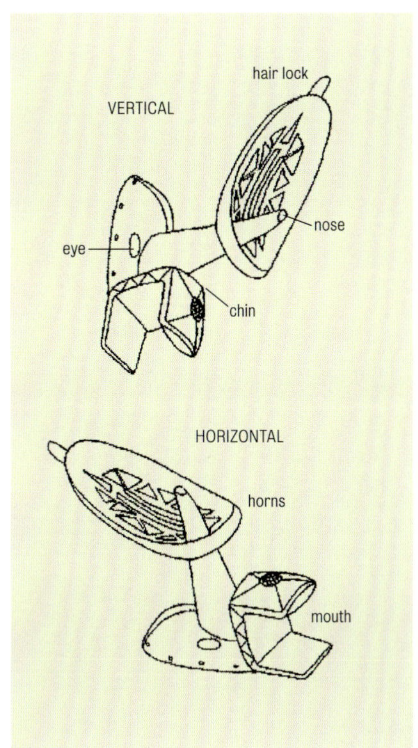

the Aku has human features (fig. 10.18): two eyeholes, a nose (into which the wearer's nose is inserted), a hair knot at the very top of the mask, and a chin with a pronounced overhang (like those of northeastern Jukun statues), which is usually embellished with abrus seeds (perhaps representing the beard). Held horizontally, the same mask's upper surface transforms into a pair buffalo horns (usually meeting at the rear, and sometimes punctured with geometric forms in an ornamental pattern), and a pair of gaping jaws, similar to those of Chamba masks (see fig. 10.18). Remarkably, given that it could serve no practical purpose (unless to hold it during carving), many examples of Aku mask have a hole bored at the back of this animalistic mouth in the position of the spyhole in a Chamba mask. The mask costume is completed with a fiber dress from which only the right arm protrudes holding a stick, recalling that the left arm was severed by a crocodile in the Benue River. The Aku couple wore cloths, the most prestigious and human of coverings, over their fiber bodies.

An apparently unique example of a Jukun monkey or baboon mask was collected by Leo Frobenius in 1912 and accessioned by the Berlin Museum für Völkerkunde (IIIC 29067; Krieger and Kutscher 1960, 31, no. 15, pl. 5). We lack evidence of it in performance, so we do not know whether it danced singly or as a wife to a more horizontal mask. Numerous monkey masks have, however, been collected from Mumuye, where they are definitely conceived as female (fig. 10.20). In both Jukun and Mumuye cases, the monkey mask seems to fit on a continuum between animal and human and between male and female. It is less horizontal than the male animal masks, yet more horizontal than the female human masks: an extrapolation as form of the ambiguous position between animals and humans that monkeys occupy.

Our consideration of Jukun carved figures in a Middle Benue comparison highlighted a couple of specific characteristics. Like most others in this region, a majority of Jukun figures are columnar in form. They are also predominantly male figures with particular emphasis on their beards, expressed as a facial overhang. On occasion, the beard is mirrored by what is presumably the rear extension of a cap. This pronounced facial overhang recurs in the male Aku mask when the animal mouth, seen horizontally, transforms into a chin (often adorned with abrus seeds) once the mask is oriented vertically. In performance the male Aku mask was worn almost as a face mask

The multiple readings that are possible of the male Aku mask derive from its complex form and the way in which it is worn, at an angle of about thirty degrees below the horizontal (a characteristic it shares with the similarly ambiguous Aluku mask, see fig. 10.15). Read vertically, the mask is anthropomorphic; but read horizontally, it becomes theriomorphic; held at an intermediate angle, as in Rubin's photograph, it is betwixt and between, hence theranthropic. The nonfunctional peephole between the jaws of the mask is readily apparent in this photograph.

PHOTOGRAPH BY ARNOLD RUBIN, CHINKAI SEPTEMBER 4, 1965, RUBIN ARCHIVE, FOWLER MUSEUM AT UCLA, NEG. NO. 765.

Meek's diagrammatic representation of Aku-Wunu has confused later writers (1931a, 273), because he failed to distinguish between the human and animal readings of the mask. Hence in his upper diagram of the mask seen vertically, he has labeled the mask's "human" nose as its "hair lock," which should be at the very top of the mask, and its "chin," perhaps with a beard of abrus seeds, as its "nose." Seen horizontally, this human chin indeed becomes the animal's nose, as my revised diagram shows (see fig. 10.18). This colored version of Meek's diagram was found in the Arnold Rubin archive, and its source is unknown.

The readings of the Aku-Wunu mask shift from human to animal depending upon whether it is held as a vertical face mask (similar to Aluku) or as a horizontal cap mask (similar to other Aku-Ma).

DRAWN BY LINDA MILBURN. REPRODUCED FROM FARDON (2007, 109, DIAGRAM 4).

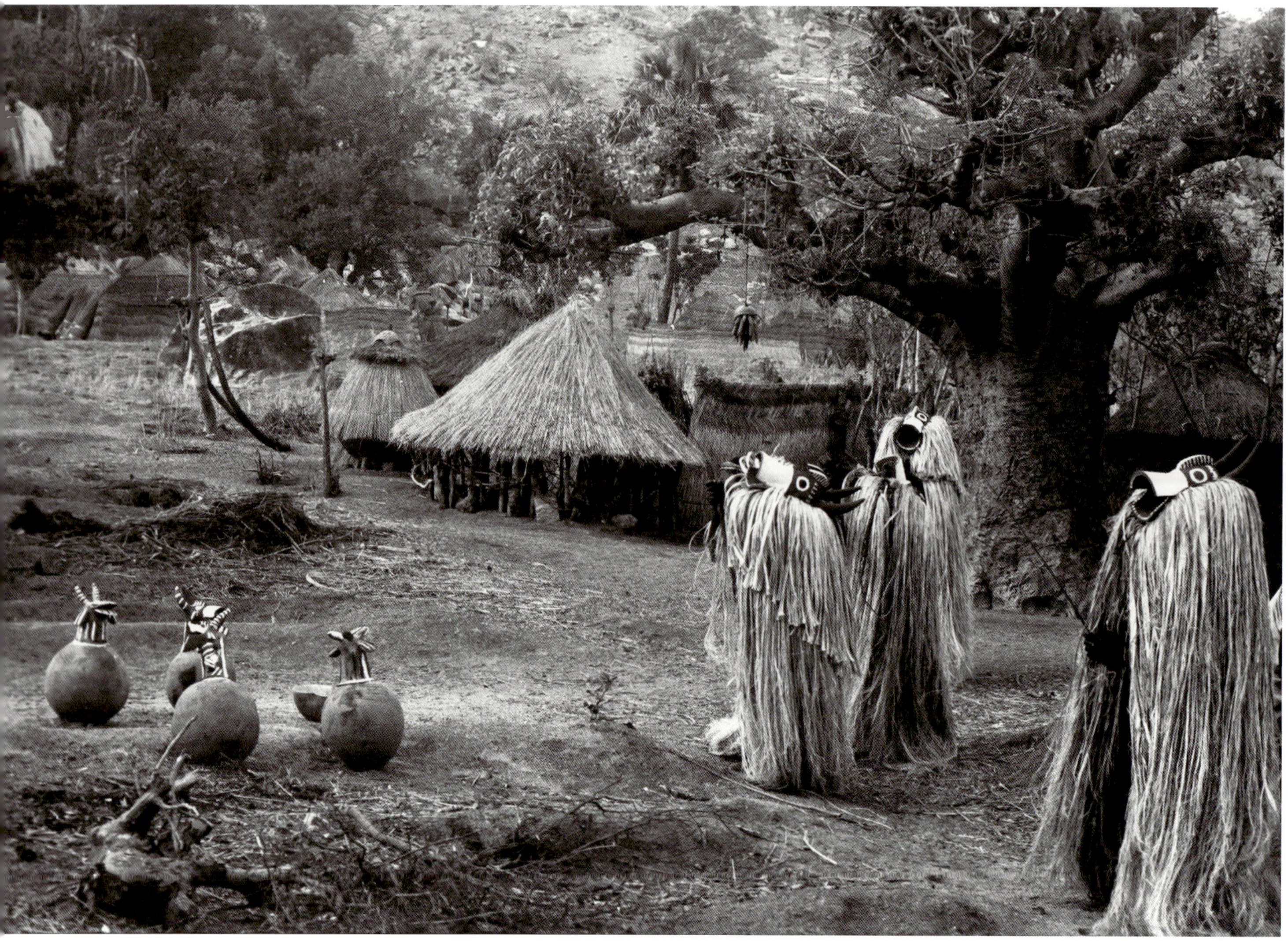

10.19

This photograph shows Mumuye Vaa-Bong masqueraders at the right and bushcow pots at the left. It was taken at a moment when an initiation into the Vaa-Bong cult coincided with a funerary celebration.

PHOTOGRAPH BY ARNOLD RUBIN, PANTISAWA, 1970, RUBIN ARCHIVE, FOWLER MUSEUM AT UCLA, NEG. NO. 2708.

10.20

Monkey mask
Mumuye peoples, twentieth century
Wood, pigment, red ocher (?)
L: 42 cm

FOWLER MUSEUM AT UCLA X91.404; GIFT OF PETER J. KUHN

IMAGE: © 2010 FOWLER MUSEUM AT UCLA. PHOTOGRAPH BY DON COLE

Mumuye monkey masks have been collected or documented in the field in considerable numbers. No example, however, was collected before the end of the colonial period, which might mean that they are a recent innovation. The deep striations on the heads of such masks presumably refer to women's braided hair and are hence an anthropomorphic reference.

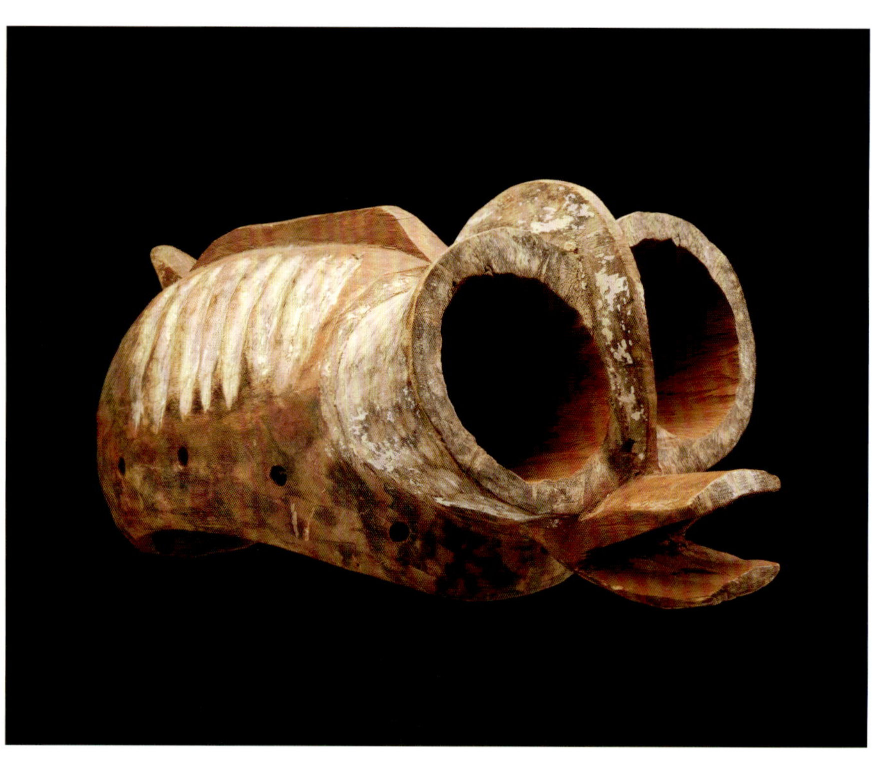

so the "chin" would be more noticeable. This also has the effect of bringing the mask forward from the upright central plane of the masquerade, a performance geometry that is unlike the horizontal masquerades of the Chamba, Mumuye, or Kantana/Kulere, all of which place the wooden mask on top of the masquerader's head (whether as casque, cap, or crown) so that it sits at the center of the masquerade. When the Goemai adopted a version of the Jukun Aku mask as an alternative to their own Gugwom mask, it is fascinating that they "corrected" this anomaly by turning it from a face mask into a substantial cap mask. The off-centeredness found in the Jukun Aku, which is also characteristic of the Aluku variant of Aku-Ma in Takum, as well as the Jukunoid Yukuben face mask (discussed below), is formally identical to the distinctive forward cantilevering of the faces of figures attributed to the Jukun Wurbo, which carbon 14 dating suggests are of some antiquity (see interleaf E). This in turns leads to the speculation that the mutually exclusive distribution of figure sculpture and horizontal masquerade among Jukun, which Arnold Rubin noted in the mid-twentieth century, might not have prevailed at an earlier period.

Jukun masks are well represented in collections, though apparently not as numerous as their Chamba or Mumuye counterparts, which might suggest a more restricted range of uses. The earliest examples are in German collectons: E. R. Flegel collected a well-used mask, locally repaired with an iron rivet, from Wukari in 1880 (Berlin IIIC 16597), and Leo Frobenius made a substantial and varied collection for German museums (for details see Fardon 2007, 105; see also fig. 10.6). Arnold Rubin's fieldwork documented the continuation of a mask carving tradition among southwestern Jukun in detail (1985; n.d.), as well as suggesting in a powerful image the appropriation of masquerade (see fig. 7.8), in particular an Aku-Ma mask, as an instrument used by the Jukun of Wukari to inscribe their claim, literally, to the historically elusive empire of Kororofa (Kwararafa)

Mumuye

In common with Jukun masquerade, Mumuye masquerade is theranthropic in the construction of some individual masks and in its performance (fig. 10.19). The literature suggests that male masquerades may perform either in exclusively male groups (for instance, like a little herd around the initiation of young men, as is shown in a film made by Arnold Rubin and epitomized by Susan Elizabeth Gagliardi in interleaf F) or else together with a "wife" (see Rubin 1988; Herreman 1988; however, Meek 1931b, 1: 461 asserts that the "wife" is invariably present in some form).

Horizontal males have been the most commonly collected of Mumuye masks (fig. 10.21). Large numbers of these came onto the art market after Nigerian independence, thanks in part to a continuing tradition of manufacture (as has also been the case for Mumuye sculpted figures). Three earlier examples can be found in the Pitt Rivers Museum, Oxford, and in the Jos Museum in Nigeria. The most remarkable Mumuye masquerade, speaking both formally and historically, was "captured" in 1907 during a very early military operation against the town of Yakoko (between Jalingo and Yola),[6] and donated in 1913 to the Pitt Rivers Museum by a Miss Kathleen Dillon (fig. 10.24). The accession note claims that the masquerade—consisting of mask and attached costume—was found in a hollow tree on the first occasion that a British expedition was sent to Yakoko. In formal terms, the front element of the mask is typical of Mumuye horizontal masks, however, its rear element resembles a Jukun Aku with horns in oval form carved above (rather than behind) the cap, and a prominent knob, presumably a hair knot, placed at the front of the horns, just as in the case of an Aku. It appears to have been parti-colored in red to the right and black to the left. A second early masquerade in the Pitt Rivers Museum, also said to be from Yakoko, is formally unremarkable, conforming to the style conventions of a majority of Mumuye horizontal masks. It was donated, apparently already broken, to the Museum in 1929 by D. W.

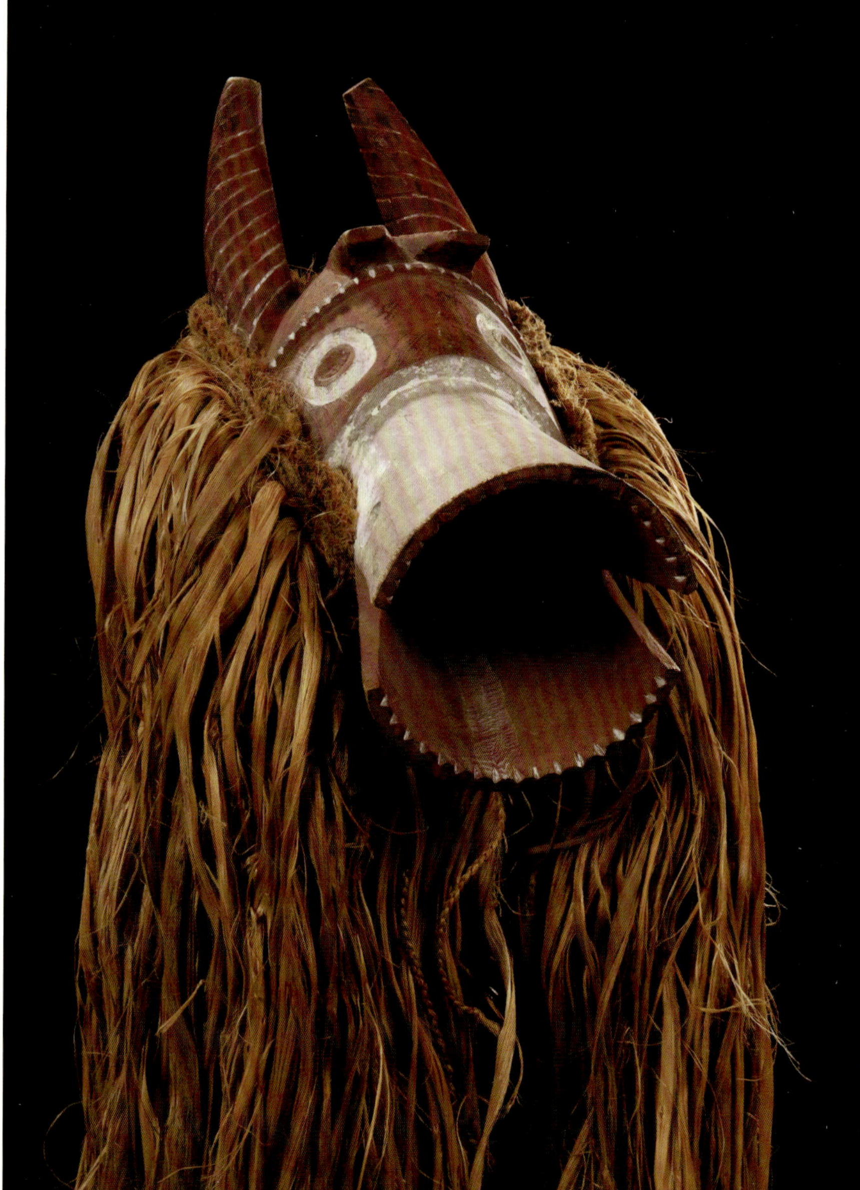

10.21

Horizontal mask
Mumuye peoples, before 1970
Wood, pigment, hibiscus fiber
L: 198 cm

FOWLER MUSEUM AT UCLA X86.2574; GIFT OF
JIM AND JEANNE PIEPER

IMAGE: © 2010 FOWLER MUSEUM AT UCLA.
PHOTOGRAPH BY DON COLE

PROVENANCE: COLLECTED BY ARNOLD RUBIN,
NIGERIA, 1970

This characteristic Mumuye male horizontal
mask, including its full fiber costume, was
collected by Arnold Rubin, who photographed
similar masks in the village of Pantisawa in
1970. Note the striations on the horns of the
mask, as well as on the doubled knots protruding from its forehead, which might represent
braiding. Together with a row of raised lumps
reminiscent of scarification, these features
suggest an addition of human-like decoration
to the predominantly animal subject. Small
lines representing teeth in the mask's flaring
mouth reference animal aggression.

Herdman of the Art Gallery and Museum in Cheltenham, who had acquired it from
a Dr. J. Macfarlane Pollard (1953.9.26). This is a much more crudely carved example
than the earlier Yakoko mask and has conventional horns. So far as I know, the only
other example to enter a collection during the colonial period was acquired by the Jos
Museum in 1955, a "vabon" (Vaa-Bong) mask made by Jabong Zinna (presumably a
compound of a personal and place name, i.e., Jabong from Zinna) on January 1 of that
year. It is a finer example of the same form as the 1929 Pitt Rivers specimen, and it is
unusual only in the asymmetry of its horns, which I will discuss below.

Like other fully horizontal theranthropic masks of the Middle Benue, most obviously those of the Chamba and Kantana/Kulere, Mumuye masks are composed of three
main elements: the mouth, the helmet or cap, and the horns. The way in which each
element is typically handled, however, differs among these three expressions of a similar idea. Mumuye masks have substantial projecting mouth plates, and in this respect
they resemble their Chamba counterparts more than they do Kantana/Kulere. Rather
than the flat parallel plates of Chamba mouths, however, those of Mumuye masks are
rounded. Unlike the Chamba masks, the mouths of Mumuye masks often have teeth
indicated, typically in color rather than by carving (in which they resemble buffalo-
headed pots [figs. 10.22, 10.23, and see figs. 10.19, 10.21] used in the funerary ceremonial

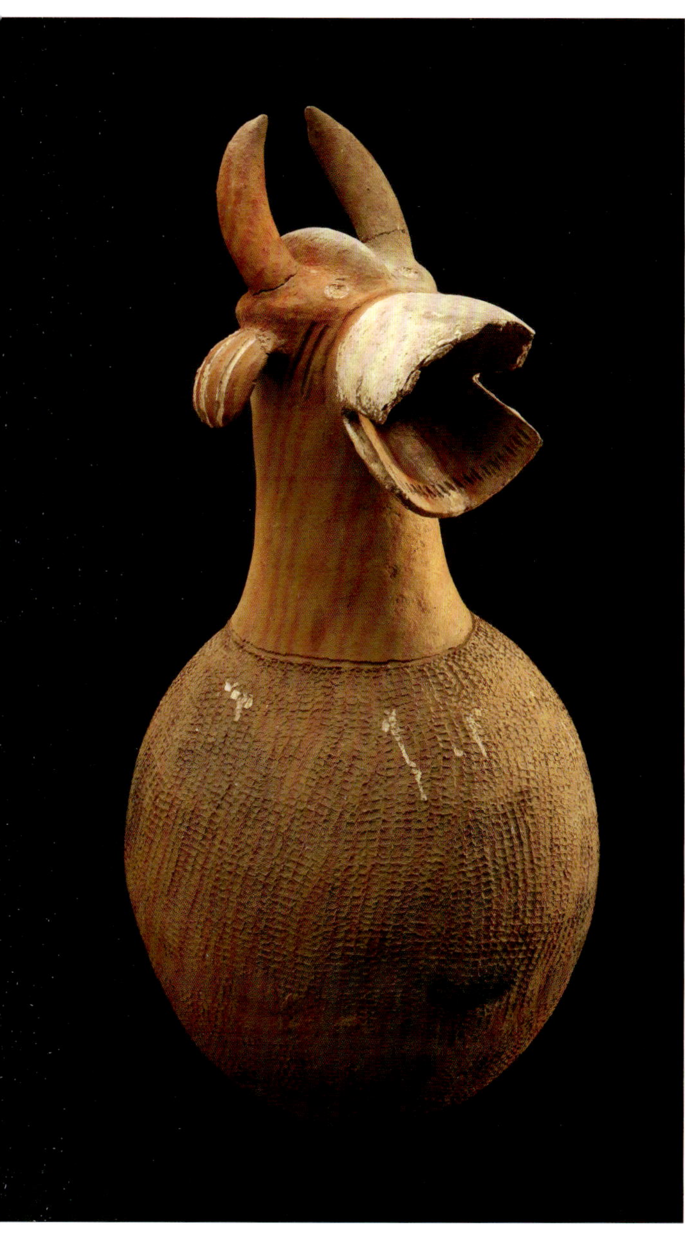

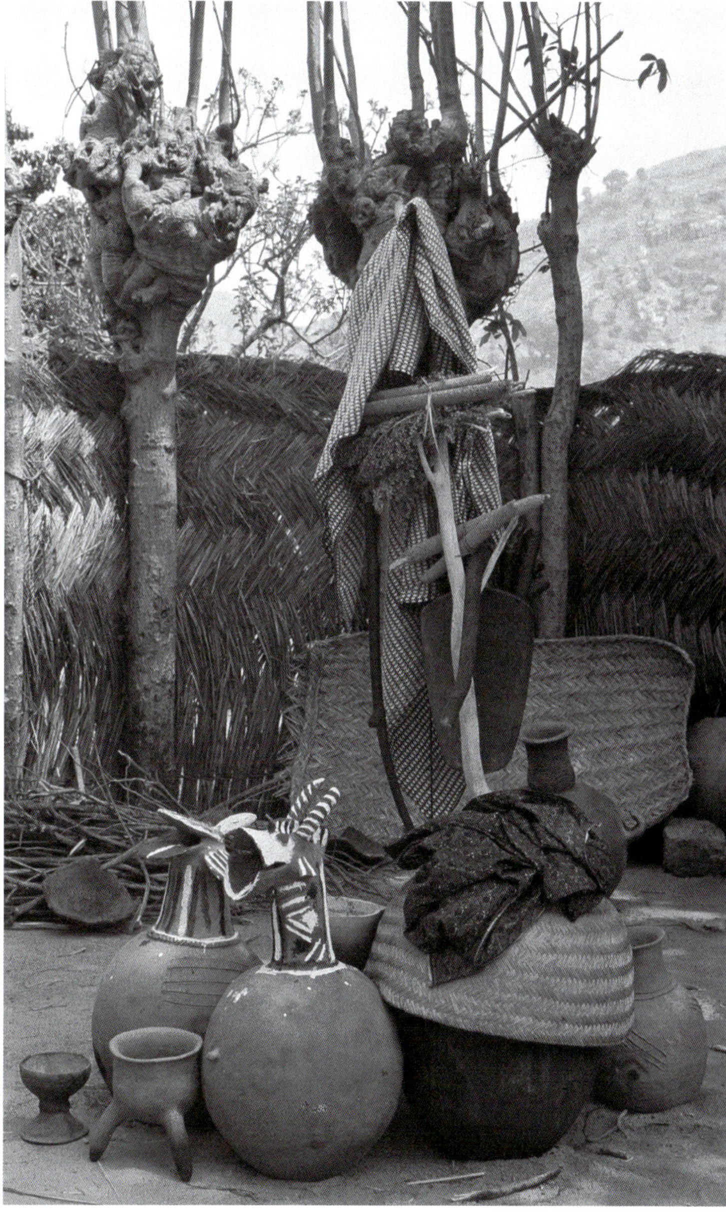

10.22
Pot with the head of a bushcow
Mumuye peoples, before 1970
Earthenware, kaolin, ocher
H: 67 cm
FOWLER MUSEUM AT UCLA X86.4495; GIFT OF
ARNOLD RUBIN
IMAGE: © 2010 FOWLER MUSEUM AT UCLA.
PHOTOGRAPH BY DON COLE
PROVENANCE: COLLECTED BY ARNOLD RUBIN,
NIGERIA, 1970

Arnold Rubin was told in 1965 that a large pot
of this type—the size of a beer jar ornamented
with a buffalo head finial—was made for a
Mumuye man at the time of his initiation;
kept during his lifetime; and smashed in the
funerary rituals held a year or two after his
death. On the basis of witnessing such a ceremony five years later, Rubin wrote a slightly
divergent account, claiming that the pots used
in funerary ritual were commissioned by the
deceased's sister at the time of his death. The
difference in accounts does not preclude symbolic association between the pots of initiation
and of death.

10.23
Mumuye ritual pots often bear striking
resemblance to Mumuye masks (see figs.
10.19, 10.21). This is especially interesting
because women are most frequently associated with ceramic arts among the Mumuye,
and they are proscribed from seeing Vaa-Bong
masquerades (see interleaf F).
PHOTOGRAPH BY ARNOLD RUBIN, ZINNA, NOVEM-
BER 13, 1970, RUBIN ARCHIVE, FOWLER MUSEUM
AT UCLA, NEG. NO. 2863.

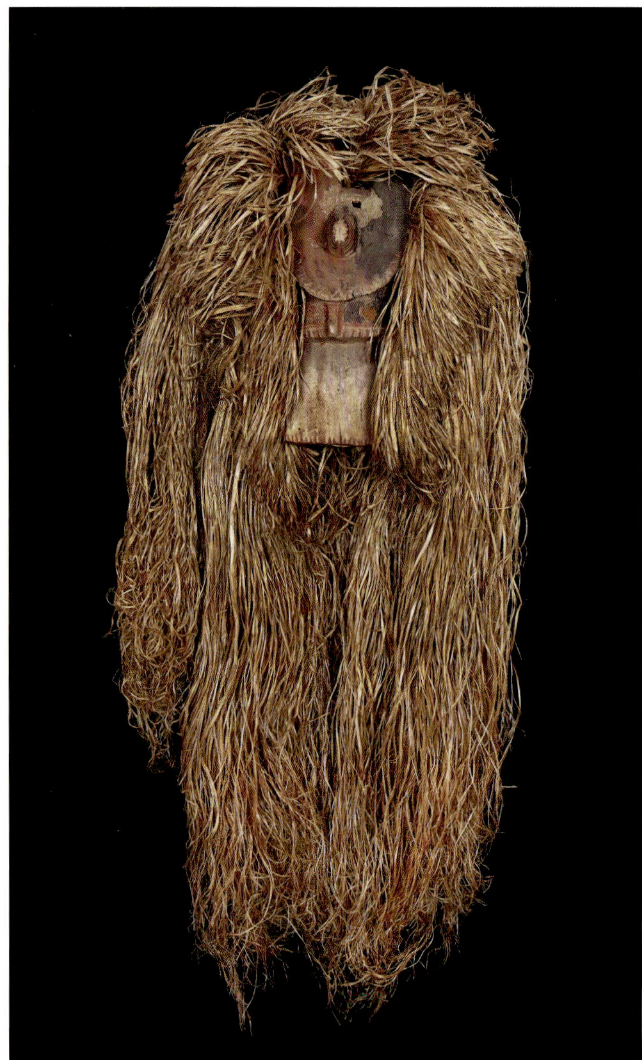

10.24
Masquerade
Mumuye peoples, before 1907
Wood, plant fiber
H: 176 cm
PITT RIVERS MUSEUM, UNIVERSITY OF OXFORD,
1913.39.1
IMAGE: © PITT RIVERS MUSEUM, UNIVERSITY OF
OXFORD
PROVENANCE: CAPTURED DURING BRITISH MILI-
TARY RAID ON YAKOKO, 1907; MISS KATHLEEN
DILLON BEFORE 1913
(NOT IN EXHIBITION)

This Mumuye masquerade, complete with
dress, was the earliest to enter a museum
collection. It has characteristics that are
intermediate between Mumuye and Jukun
horizontal mask forms. Note how its horns are
raised to a horizontal plane above its cap, and
there is a prominent knob at the front where
its horns meet that probably, given its striations, evokes a hair knot. This knob occupies
the same position as it would on a Jukun male
Aku mask, where it would, however, represent
a human nose.

filmed by Arnold Rubin; see Gagliardi, this volume, interleaf F). The horn configurations of Mumuye masks are of at least two kinds: inswept horns—which may even
join at their tips like those of Jukun or Kantana/Kulere—conventionally reference the
bushcow or buffalo in the Middle Benue; upswept, parallel horns contrast with these
and must be assumed to reference creatures with this shape of horn or antler, such
as buck, kob, or antelope, as is also the case for Kantana/Kulere (Jukun and Chamba
masquerades appear to be uninterested in these creatures). The anthropomorphic elements of Mumuye male masks derive not from their overall form but rather from their
embellishments: many have prominent hair knots (fig. 10.25) and/or patterning that
might indicate scarification (fig. 10.26). In this they conform to the regional convention
of indicating humanity through ornamentation, but they differ from Jukun male Aku or
from Chamba masks in that they apparently do not reference human qualities by their
larger form (with respect to the face for Jukun, or to the skull for Chamba).

In addition to performing in male groups, Mumuye horizontal masquerades were
"generally" accompanied by their "wives" (Meek 1931b, 1: 461). These female masquerades took one of two forms. Baboon or monkey masks were not remarked by Meek
but have been documented in the field by Rubin. They lack protruding wooden horns,
and their mouth plates are far shorter than those of their male counterparts (although
Rubin did photograph an example with real bovine horns; see fig. 10.31). Like the Jukun
monkey mask described earlier (p. 325), they are relatively less horizontal than male
masks, and to that extent, they are formally more anthropomorphic in terms of regional
conventions, even without taking into account the human-like characteristics of simians.

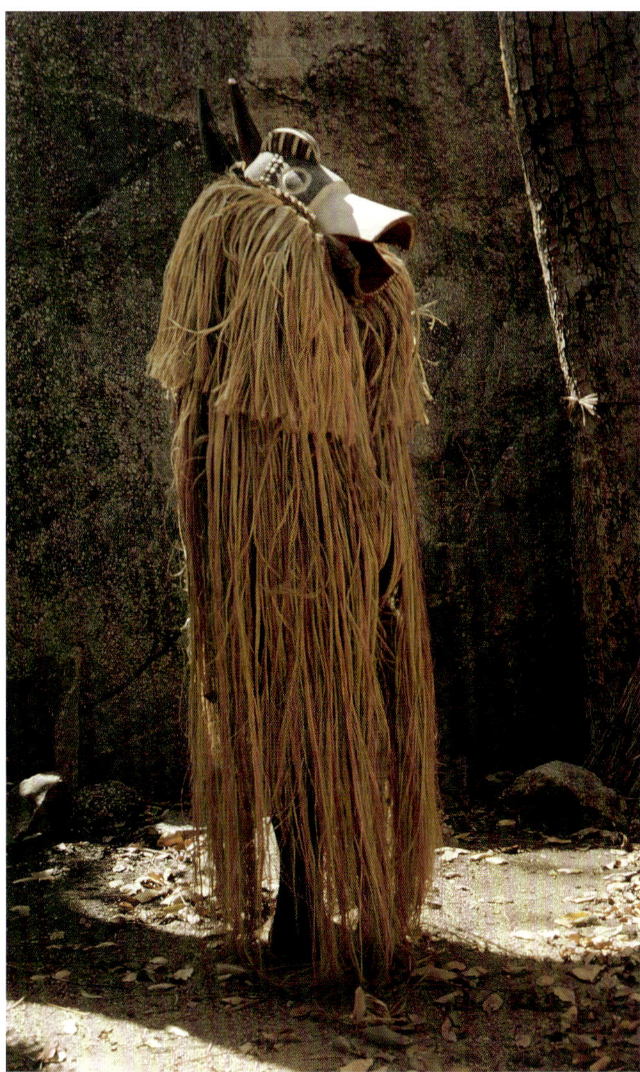

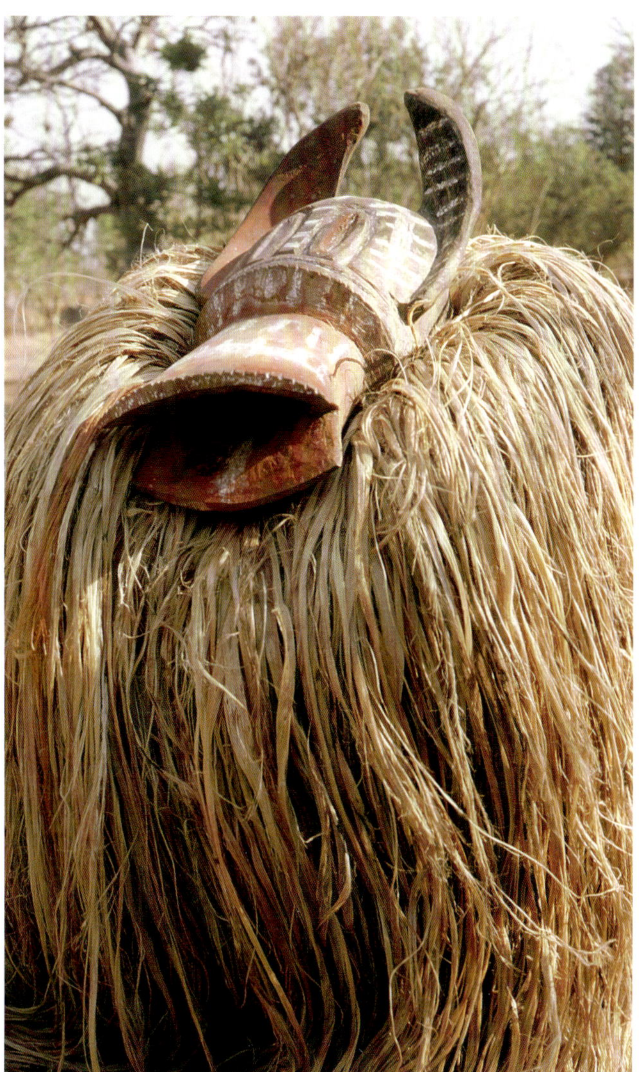

Their anthropomorphic character receives further emphasis from the elaborately carved braids that invariably cover the skulls of examples in collections. As we know already from examining the conventions of their statuary, Mumuye carvers delighted in the sculptural potentials of the malleable features of the human head, notably hair and ears.

The alternative form of the female masquerade that dances with male Mumuye masquerades consists of a fully anthropomorphic, long-necked, vertical mask with a fiber costume. The mask draws its characteristics more directly from Mumuye statuary and might as accurately be seen as an ambulant figure sculpture performing as a masquerade (see fig. 14.10). C. K. Meek illustrates an intriguing instance where this is literally the case: a photograph shows a tall wooden column, featureless except at its top where there is a small head—a headdress symmetrically elongated over both ears—apparently with eyes sculpted into its frontal surface below which a small face with mouth is indicated (see fig. 8.36). Meek labels this as a "Vabô" (Vaa-Bong) symbol, which is erected in the middle of a village as the wife of Vaa-Bong from which the fiber dress of the masquerade is hung. Meek assumes that this is the same dress worn by the male masquerade. While the evidence is slight, it might support the notion that more radical experimentation in Mumuye mask making involved the female to a greater extent than the male forms (see fig. 14.10). The tall vertical masquerade, resembling Meek's pole symbol but fashioned into a functioning mask as Rubin documented, is shared with the Kona Jukun, who are not users of horizontal masks, and with the "Wurkun" to the Mumuye's northeast (see chapter 14). In terms of a stylistic geography, the Mumuye, particularly the more northerly of them, sit at

10.25, 10.26
Arnold Rubin's photographs of Mumuye horizontal masquerades make apparent the variations in design permissible within the basic form and also point out the lightness of the fiber masquerade dress compared to Chamba and Jukun masquerades. This lighter and more revealing masquerade dress may have been considered appropriate because of the complete ban on women witnessing masquerade among the Mumuye.
PHOTOGRAPHS BY ARNOLD RUBIN, ZINNA, RUBIN ARCHIVE, FOWLER MUSEUM AT UCLA, SLIDE NOS. A1.10.17.4, A1.10.17.18.

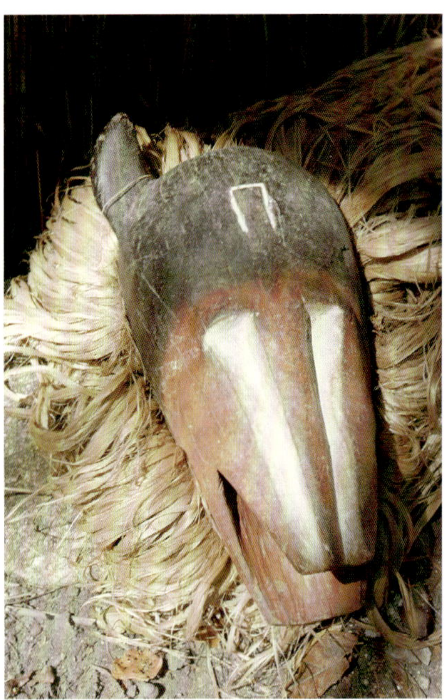

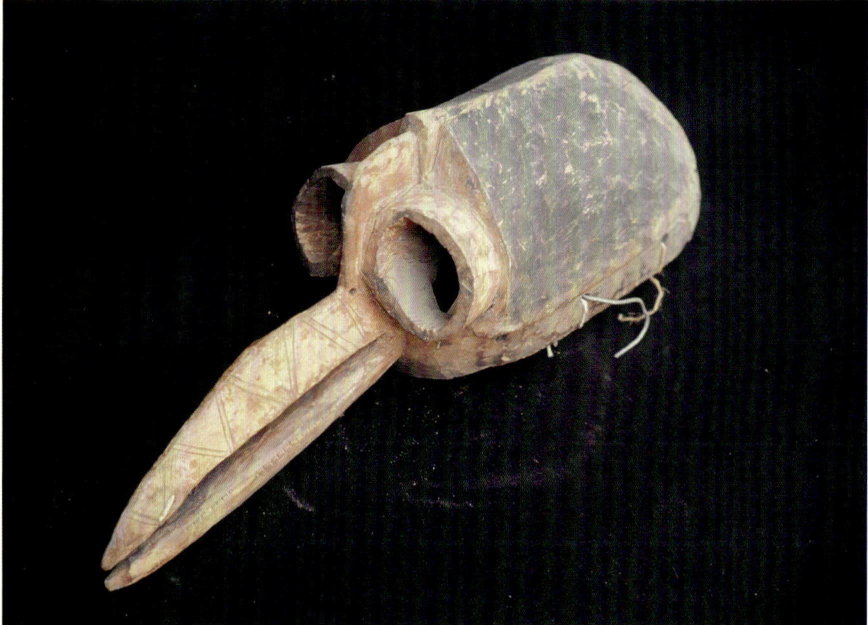

10.27

"Naba" (translated as "old woman") may act as the wife of a horizontal masquerade in the form of a "fish hawk" or "bird of the king-fisher type," as Arnold Rubin noted.

PHOTOGRAPH BY ARNOLD RUBIN, RUBIN ARCHIVE, FOWLER MUSEUM AT UCLA, SLIDE NO. A1.10.17.19.

10.28

Although buffalo, and to a lesser degree monkey, masks predominate among Mumuye horizontal masks, there is evidence from a small number of divergent types for experimentation with images of birds (particularly fish-eating birds), wild pig, dog, and others that defy easy identification.

PHOTOGRAPH BY ARNOLD RUBIN, JOS MUSEUM 72.J.70.6, RUBIN ARCHIVE, FOWLER MUSEUM AT UCLA, SLIDE NO. A1.10.16.6. REPRODUCED COURTESY OF THE NATIONAL COMMISSION FOR MUSEUMS AND MONUMENTS, NIGERIA.

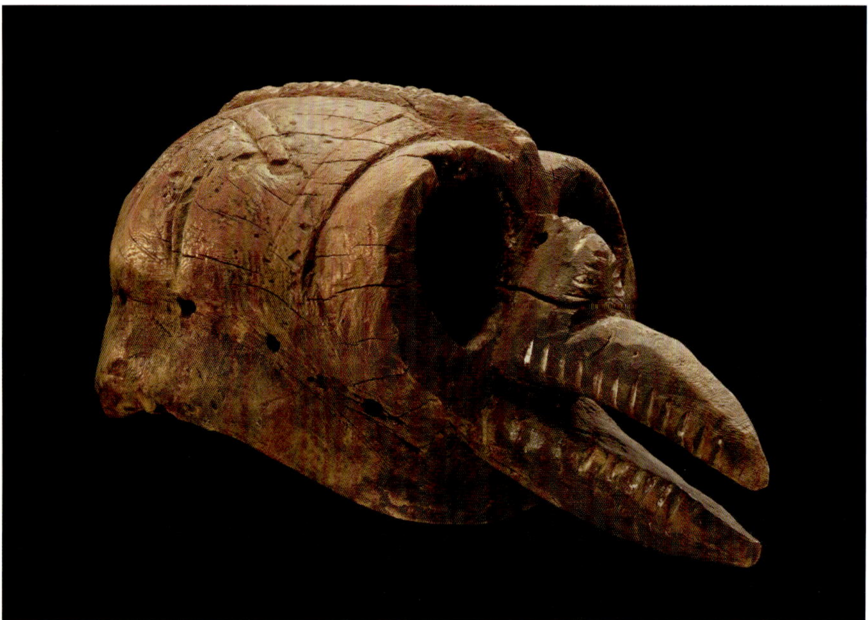

10.29

Bird mask
Mumuye peoples, twentieth century
Wood, pigment
L: 46 cm

FOWLER MUSEUM AT UCLA X91.407: GIFT OF PETER J. KUHN

IMAGE: © 2010 FOWLER MUSEUM AT UCLA. PHOTOGRAPH BY DON COLE

(NOT IN EXHIBITION)

10.30

The interest of these otherwise rudimentary monkey masks lies in the fact that Arnold Rubin was told they might dance with women. It is inviting to speculate that there may be some relationship between the quality of the masks and the latitude allowed to them in performance.

PHOTOGRAPH BY ARNOLD RUBIN, PANTI BELLI, FEBRUARY 17, 1971, RUBIN ARCHIVE, FOWLER MUSEUM AT UCLA, NEG. NO. 3099.

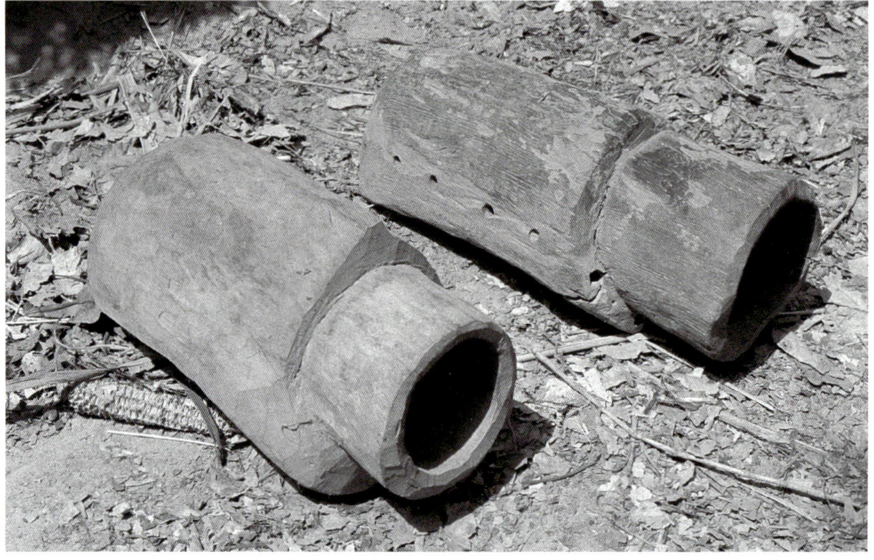

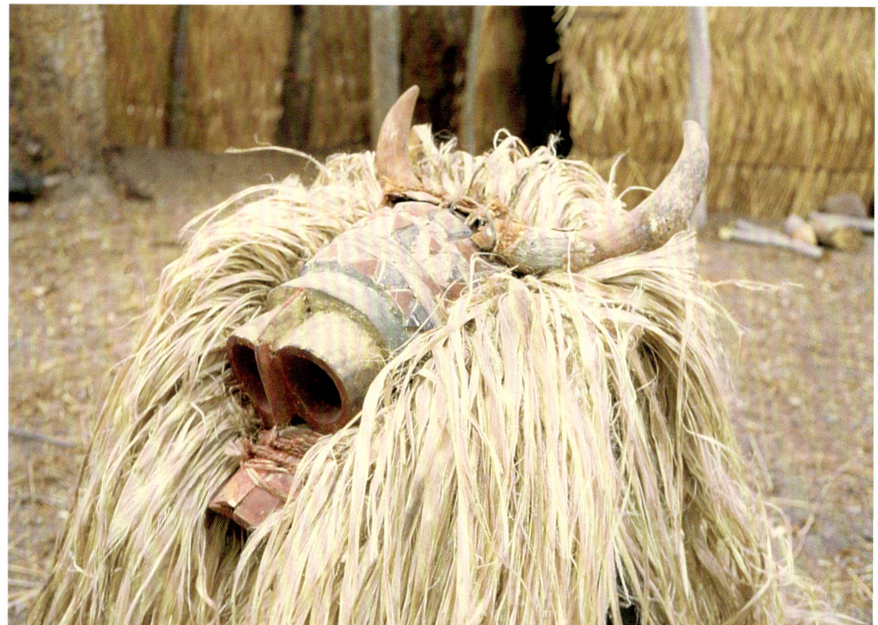

10.31
Rubin photographed this monkey mask among the Yendang, a peripheral Mumuye-like group living to their north, where it was said to have been the work of the Mumuye carver Nyavo (see pp. 250–52). The mask has elaborately cross-hatched cranial decoration to which real cow horns have been attached, and it performed at initiation and the funerals of elders. This hybridization of monkey and buffalo masks has not been documented among Mumuye elsewhere, but it is further evidence for innovation within the conventional terms of Mumuye horizontal masking.
PHOTOGRAPH BY ARNOLD RUBIN, APRIL 20, 1970, RUBIN ARCHIVE, FOWLER MUSEUM AT UCLA, SLIDE NO. A1.10.18.3.

the confluence of traditions of horizontal theranthropic masquerade, explored to their southwest and southeast (notably by speakers of Jukun and Chamba languages), and wooden, vertical anthropomorphic masquerade, explored to their immediate west by Kona Jukun but otherwise typical of the peoples classified together as "Wurkun"/Bikwin to their northeast.

We have evidence that Mumuye masks underwent innovation in the shapes of some unusual (and, in terms of the overall numbers, it has to be added: atypical) specimens in collections, as well as in Arnold Rubin's fieldnote descriptions. For instance, in 1965 Rubin identified a sketch in his fieldnotes as "Naba" (translated as "old woman"), the wife of a buffalo mask in the form of a "fish hawk" (fig. 10.27) or "bird of the kingfisher type" (October 17, 1965, 206–7).[7] The collection of the Jos Museum contains a number of curious masks from the confiscated collection bought by a European in the village of Lankaviri. These include examples in the form of a bird (fig. 10.28), as well as a boar and dog (72J.70.6-8). In each case the basic form is in the shape of an unadorned monkey head differentiated by the distinctive shape of the mouth (fig. 10.29).[8] Rubin documented an extremely rudimentary, featureless, monkey mask (fig. 10.30), which he noted was allowed to dance with women, from Panti Belli, near Jalingo. In Yendang, as noted earlier, Rubin photographed a monkey mask with elaborately cross-hatched cranial decoration to which real cowhorns had been attached. The mask, said to have been carved by Nyavo, performed at initiation and the funerals of elders (fig. 10.31). A small piece of wood appears to have been lashed to the upper surface of its mouth. Another curiosity in the Jos Museum is a Janus-faced bovine mask collected by one of the museum's licensed, presumably Hausa, dealers, Tanko Mohammed (73J.75.2A), from an intermediary in Ganye. We have little interpretative purchase on these masks that would allow us any more specific assumption than that they were the distinctive property of some particular cults. Taken together, this group of oddities demonstrates a willingness to experiment with the parameters of mask making that, for instance, cannot be demonstrated to this degree among Chamba.

Two films shot by Arnold Rubin in April 1970 at the end of dry season in Pantisawa and Zinna are described in this volume by Susan Gagliardi (see interleaf F). Although they depicted events in the same month, their significance would appear different. The Pantisawa meeting takes place at a hillside cult shrine, from which masqueraders periodically descend upon their apparently deserted village (where we

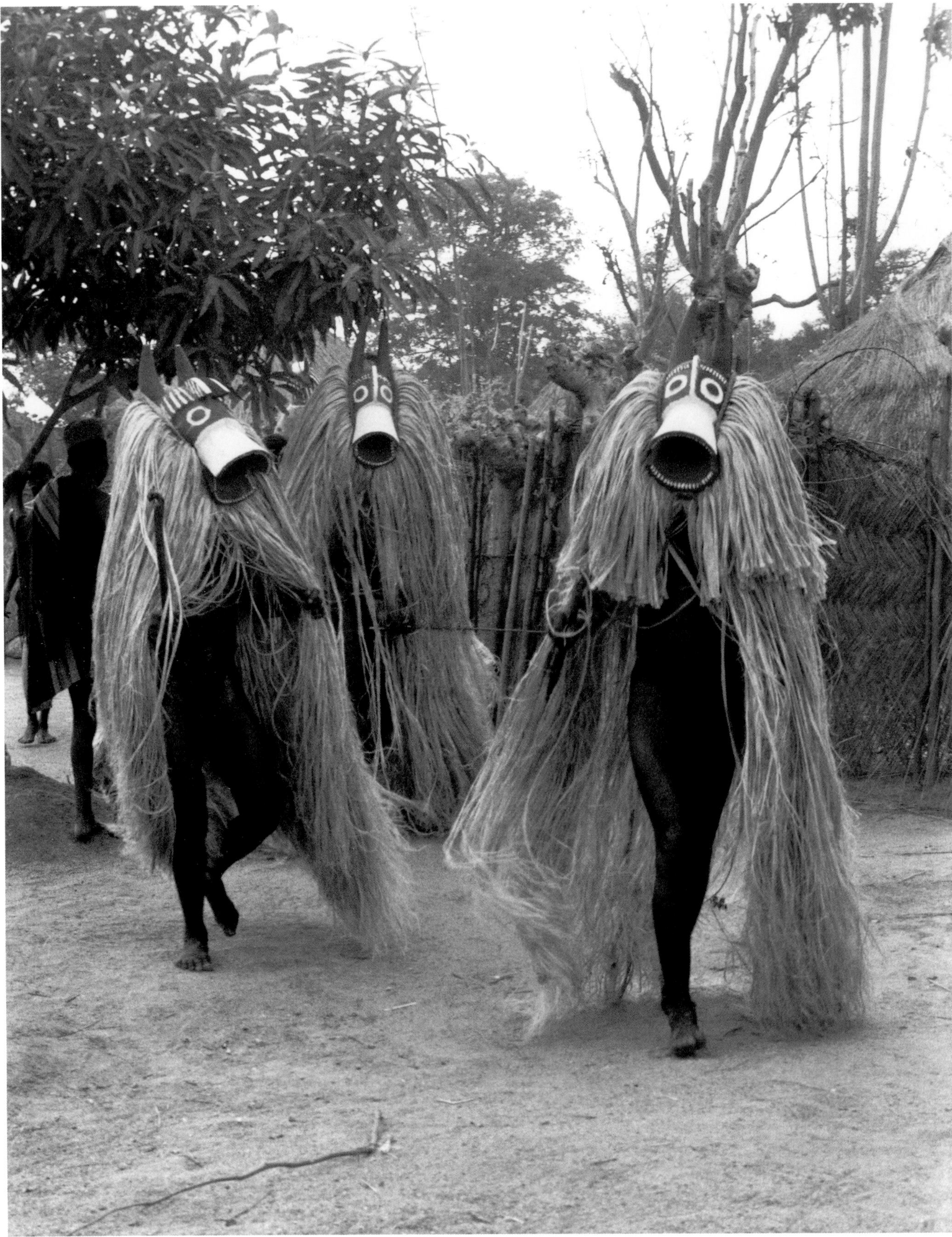

10.32

Adepts of Vaa-Bong participate in a funerary ritual.

PHOTOGRAPH BY ARNOLD RUBIN, PANTISAWA, APRIL 1970, RUBIN ARCHIVE, FOWLER MUSEUM AT UCLA, NEG. NO. 2699.

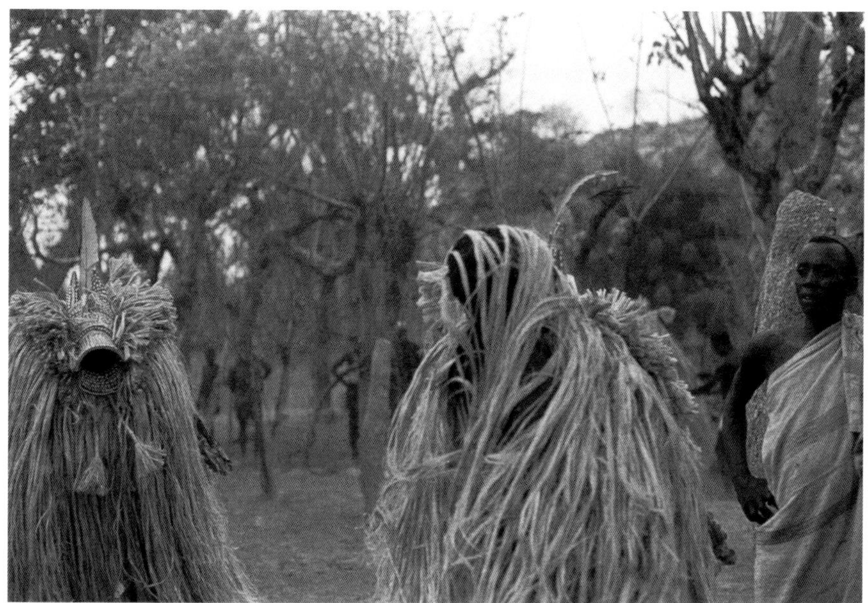

10.33
Initiates witness a masquerader removing his mask head at an initiation event.
PHOTOGRAPH BY, ARNOLD RUBIN, ZINNA, APRIL 21, 1970, RUBIN ARCHIVE, FOWLER MUSEUM AT UCLA, NEG. NO. 2680

may assume women and uninitiated men have concealed themselves). As all sources concur, the uninitiated are endangered by the performance of the masquerade, though there is some equivocation as to whether this is always the case or applies only under certain circumstances. The Pantisawa meeting coincides with a stage of funeral ritual that involves smashing pots associated with the dead either at their gravesides or at crossroads. The symbolism of the occasion associates the person with a pot—in the case of an initiated Mumuye man a pot on the scale of a beer pot. Breaking the pot marks a stage in the distancing of the dead from the living and apparently allows the inheritance of the deceased's property to occur. This kind of ritual, and the association between it and a masquerade that is itself able to evoke the dead, uses a common currency of Middle Benue symbolic action. From Rubin's Pantisawa film it appears that unlike Chamba, whose masquerade costume is meant to conceal the masquerader's body entirely, Mumuye masqueraders might perform wearing their fiber costumes almost like capes, open at the front over naked bodies (fig. 10.32). The Mumuye masquerades thus reveal what Chamba masquerades assiduously conceal: the human inside an animal form. The difference might be explained by the exclusion of uninitiated men and all women from masquerade performance. All Chamba see the masquerade, which is why it is of paramount importance that the masquerader's body be completely covered. Whereas the Mumuye masquerade costume consists of a single layer of fiber attached to the mask and flowing, especially in the Pantisawa film, freely downward, the body of the Chamba masquerader is covered not just by a thick costume attached to the mask but also by a long skirt of fibers worn from the waist and in some cases anklets of fiber designed to conceal the masquerader's feet.

A different play of concealment and revelation of the Mumuye masquerader's body is apparent from the film Rubin shot in Zinna. This is the occasion of the initiation of a young cohort into the cult. The heads of the youths have been shaved, and they are dressed in goatskins drawn between their legs and secured with a stick at the front (see fig. 8.48). This garb appears to be self-consciously anachronistic because, although it corresponds to historical accounts of Mumuye male dress, none of the older men present at the ritual is similarly attired. A matting enclosure has been erected in the initiatory site, and the outset of the performance as filmed finds the neophytes sitting with their backs to the enclosure, inside which initiates put on masquerade costumes that are both thicker and stiffer, and hence more effective as body coverings, than those seen at Pantisawa. As the event plays out, the new initiates are drawn into the dance of the masquerade and witness the adepts remove and replace their costumes and, in one case,

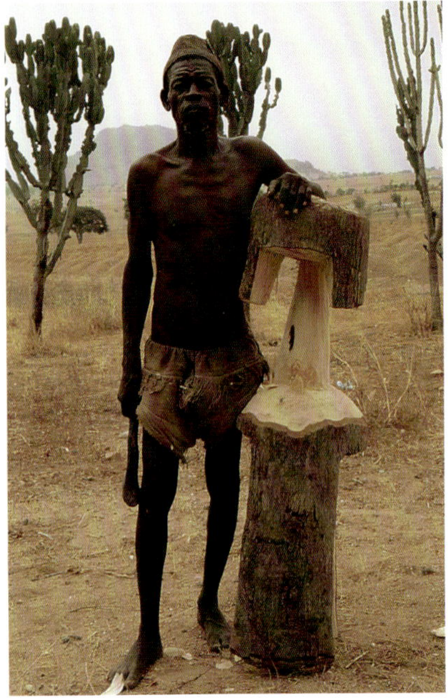

10.34

Lenke was a particularly productive Mumuye
sculptor of Zinna who had learned to carve
from his older brother starting at the age of
ten. By 1970 he had been carving for around
thirty years and traveled to carry out commissions. He estimated he had carved around 150
vertical masks and as many as 500 horizontal
buffalo masks. Lenke was also a weaver but
did not farm (Rubin 1987, 17, fig. 2).
PHOTOGRAPH BY ARNOLD RUBIN, ZINNA, APRIL 8,
1970, RUBIN ARCHIVE, FOWLER MUSEUM AT UCLA,
SLIDE NO. A1.11.2.4.

an adept dancing with the mask supported on his shoulder while his bare head pokes
out through the fiber costume (fig. 10.33). Rubin's documentation notes how groups of
initiates might then commission their own masquerades. Mumuye masquerades appear
to be closely linked to particular cults, especially Vaa-Bong (see Bovin, this volume,
chapter 11), whereas Chamba masquerades have a more free-floating role as markers
of the engagement of their owning clans in rites of passage. This suggests a greater
demand for masks among Mumuye (where each group of initiates possessed them) than
among Chamba (where masks belonged either to clans or in some places, even more
restrictedly, to offices like chiefship). That said, both Chamba and Mumuye masks have
become numerous in the Western artworld and art market.

During his visits to Mumuye settlements (1965, 1970, and 1971), Arnold Rubin
documented around eighty of the masks he was shown. The number of masks in use
was likely to have exceeded this considerably, since Rubin's informants were able
to name around twenty-five carvers of these eighty masks by name, only a few of
whom were credited with more than a single mask in the sample. Had they all been
as productive as the carver Lenke (fig. 10.34), the number of masks would have been
many thousands. Virtually all the masks in Rubin's sample had been carved during the
twentieth century according to the ages he elicited for each piece. What follows is an
extract based on Rubin's fieldnotes:

On April 8, 1970, Arnold Rubin interviewed Lenke,[9] a sculptor and weaver
living in Zing.[10] Lenke had just returned to Zing from the Warri town of Yendang at the time of the interview. Lenke presented himself to Rubin as a prolific artist who had worked for many people in Zing, Yendang, and in several
other places in the region. As he explained to Rubin, he carved in order to
earn money, whether for Mumuye or not. Lenke told Rubin that several men
in his family sculpted: his father, Zuganu, taught Lenke's older brother, Mai
Shera, how to carve. Mai Shera in turn passed the skill onto the ten-year-old
Lenke. At the time of the interview, Lenke said that his own son was not yet
old enough to learn to carve. Lenke indicated to Rubin that he began to carve
on his own just a year after starting to learn, and he had been carving for
some thirty years since then [i.e., from about 1940]. Rubin noted that Lenke
had carved five hundred Vaa-Bong horizontal masks, and a hundred and fifty
Sukuru vertical masks, but just one *janari* standing figure. [Lenke's numbers
presumably reflect his rough recollection of the extent of his corpus.] In an
article, Rubin wrote that Lenke's single attempt at a figure "wasn't appreciated, so he didn't make any more" (Rubin 1987, 11). Rubin inquired specifically about Lenke's masks. With respect to Vaa-Bong masks distinguished
by their long horns, Lenke told Rubin, "we don't have this kind of animal
here." More specifically, the sculptor indicated that despite the form's bovine
mouth and horns, the Vaa-Bong mask was not an image of a bushcow. Lenke
also explained that Vaa-Bong might look similar but function differently with
"each one connected with a different time of year" (Rubin, fieldnotes, 1970,
269). Of the Sukuru vertical mask, Lenke had less to say, just that Sukuru
was the wife of Vaa-Bong and always assumed the same shape. His brother
had imitated an older, heavier version of the Sukuru mask, but Lenke carved
masks that were lighter but still similar in size, hence better.

Lenke was not a successful figure sculptor despite the fact that the vertical masks
that he made in large numbers obviously draw upon Mumuye conventions for representing human beings, notably in their emphasis upon ornamentation of the head by
coiffure or cap and elongation of the earlobes. What of the less obvious relationship
between Mumuye statuary and horizontal masks? Ornamentation of hair knots or

braids (in bovine and monkey masks) is common to both, and most masks and figures share bold eyes outlined as white circles. There is also occasional evidence of asymmetry, which we noted as a feature of older Mumuye figures. As mentioned previously, the earliest Mumuye mask in the Jos Museum, dating from 1955 (55J.74) and described in its accession note as carved by Jabong Zinna—that is Jabong from Zinna, later called Zing, the same place where Lenke lived—has a plain right horn colored red, and a cross-hatched left horn colored black.

Chamba

By contrast with Jukun and Mumuye, the Chamba have only one masquerade.[11] This single genre, however, condenses all the associations made elsewhere in several masquerades. Many of these converge upon the mask (i.e., the wooden head of the masquerade; for a fuller discussion, see Fardon 1990). These masks, according to one story of origin (reduced to its essentials here), were copied by a blacksmith from a tattered buffalo hide.

> A hunter put termites on the hide of a buffalo man who had temporarily discarded it to scrape up salt. Unable to put his skin back on, the buffalo man returned to the bush in human form. The hunter took the skin to the blacksmith so he could copy it. The blacksmith, however, made the error of sculpting human features onto the mask, as well as those of the buffalo.

A very similar story is told about the origins of the bushcow matriclan.

> A hunter saw a beautiful girl abandon her bushcow hide in order to wash. He hid the hide refusing to return it to her when the other buffaloes resumed their shape. She was persuaded to return to his village and marry him on condition he did not reveal her origins. She bore a son and daughter, but one day the hunter revealed his wife's origin, and when he ignored his daughter's warnings, the wife and son impaled him on their horns before returning to the bush. The faithful daughter remained to become ancestress of the bushcow matriclan.

These stories, both of which involve shape-changing bushcows or buffaloes and a human with the outer appearance of an animal, bear a revelatory telltale relationship to the masquerade. As I have argued elsewhere at greater length (Fardon 1990), however, the theranthropic mask has as much to do with the dead as it does with living: in its overall form, the Chamba mask is composed by the superimposition of two shapes, a human skull, at its center, and an animal skull, running from its mouth to its horns (see fig. 10.4). The combination is similar to that in hunting shrines, where the skulls of killed humans (and human-like creatures) are represented by round stones (discarded grinding stones), while the horizontal skulls of other animals are represented by flat stones. Hence the mask fuses a theriomorph (animal shape) and anthropomorph (human shape) in its fundamental form. The masquerade enacts this animal and human character in a passage from the bush to the village, where it performs under the scant control of a human custodian who accompanies it upon a double gong. Its performance completed, it returns to the bush as the place proper to it. The body of the Chamba masquerade is made from overlapping layers of fibers, which entirely cover the performer's body (suspended from the mask itself, from the performer's waist, and in some cases also from his ankles). It is more bulky and enclosed than that of the Mumuye horizontal masquerade, which is almost cape-like; more massive than Jukun masquerades, which have distinct legs and, in the case of the male Aku, an arm extended beyond the costume, or, indeed, than Chamba masquerades in the emigrant communities of Donga and Suntai, which have adapted their masquerade costumes in ways that make them more similar to the Jukun (figs. 10.35, 10.36).

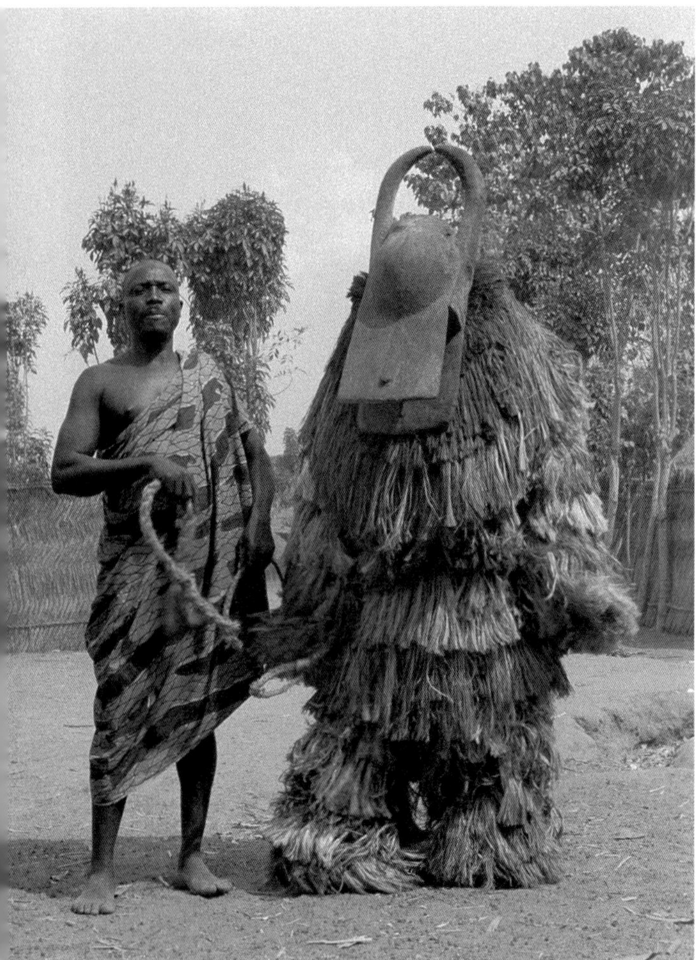

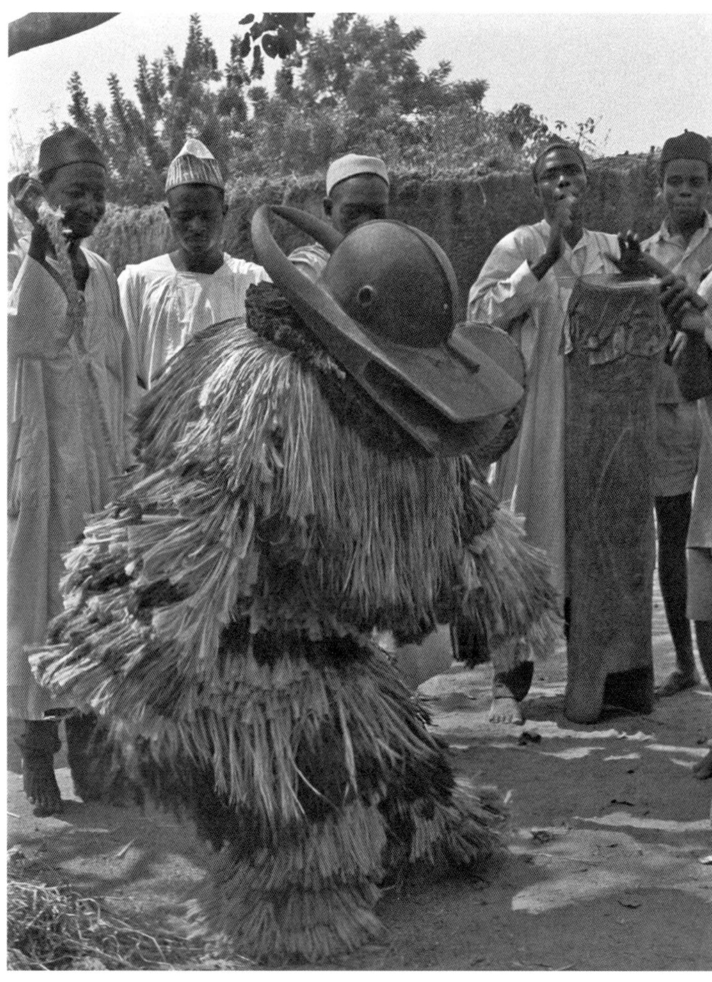

10.35

Arnold Rubin recorded "*kaa*," which means "grandmother" (rather than "mask" or "spirit" as he inferred), as the first part of the personal names of masquerades among the Chamba of the Benue Valley. This masquerade danced at Suntai, where it belonged to the Gara, or chief. It has a particularly large head and a style of dress reminiscent of Jukun masquerades; otherwise, however, it has retained the characteristics typical for Chamba Daka masquerades.

PHOTOGRAPH BY ARNOLD RUBIN; FEBRUARY 9, 1965, RUBIN ARCHIVE, FOWLER MUSEUM AT UCLA, NEG. NO. 199.

10.36

This masquerade belonged to the Gara, or Chief, of Donga, another Chamba-ruled kingdom of the Benue Valley. Whereas the Suntai mask head in figure 10.35 appears to have grown in size relative to those of Chambaland, this Donga example remains similar in scale to Chamba Leko masks. It does, however, have a particularly deep dome, and its ears have been moved out of the horizontal plane connecting mouth and horns.

PHOTOGRAPH BY ARNOLD RUBIN, JANUARY 16, 1965, RUBIN ARCHIVE, FOWLER MUSEUM AT UCLA, NEG. NO. 41.

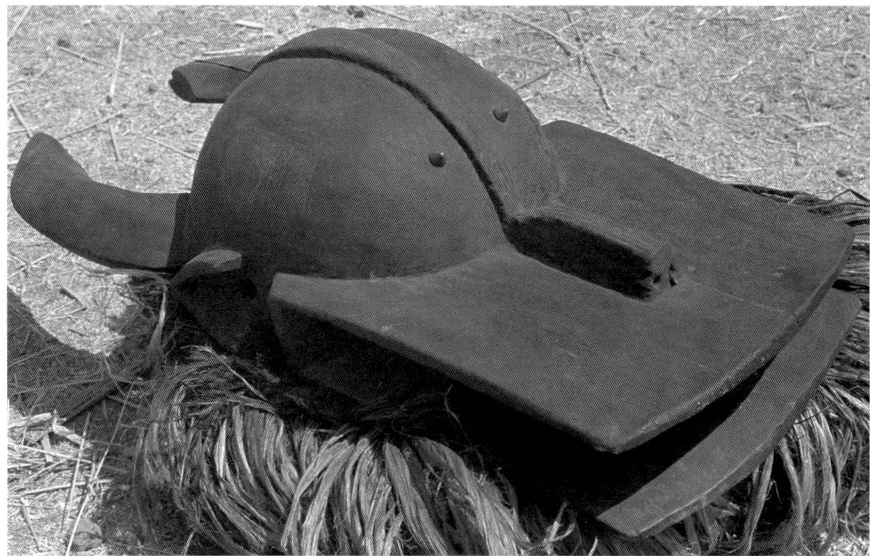

10.37

This masquerade demonstrates continuity in the style of western Chamba Daka masquerades (cf. fig. 10.1). These are characterized by scimitar-shaped horns, decorated sagittal bands, and often metal eyes. They are also considerably larger and flatter in their proportions, than Chamba Leko masks.

PHOTOGRAPH BY ARNOLD RUBIN, DAKKA, MARCH 5, 1965, RUBIN ARCHIVE, FOWLER MUSEUM AT UCLA, NEG. NO. 374.

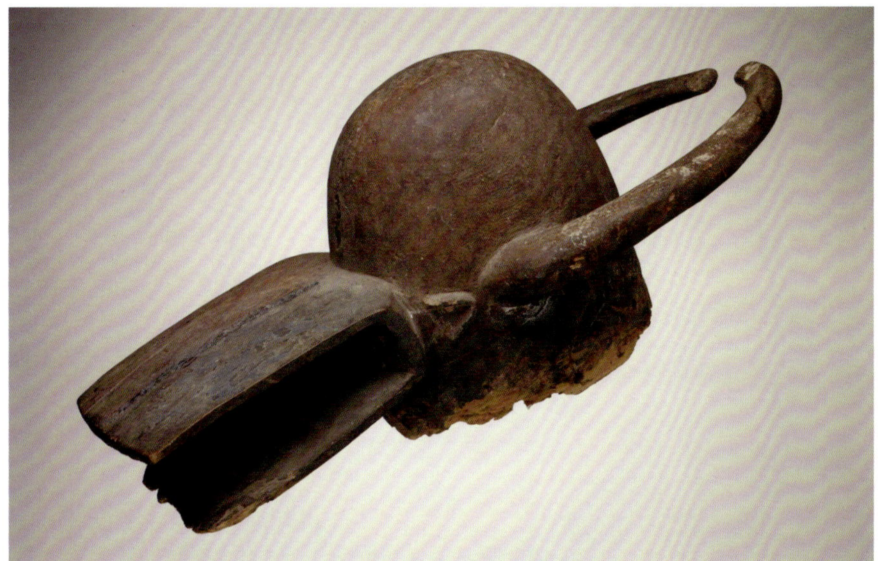

10.38
Mask
Chamba Leko peoples, early to mid-twentieth century (?)
Wood
L: 33 cm
FINE ARTS MUSEUMS OF SAN FRANCISCO; GIFT OF PROFESSOR AND MRS. ERLE LORAN, 76.24.1
IMAGE: © FINE ARTS MUSEUMS OF SAN FRANCISCO. PHOTOGRAPH BY JOSEPH MCDONALD. (NOT IN EXHIBITION)

Eastern Chamba Leko masks are characterized, relative to western Chamba Daka masks, by their accentuated domes and often by an absence of features other than horns, small ears, and a mouth. This example is parti-colored like the masks of the emigrant Chamba of Donga.

Because they are so readily identified and distinguished from other masks of the eastern end of the Middle Benue, not least because they are the only full casque masks that entirely cover the head of their wearer, it is easy to overlook differences among Chamba masks. These differences are indeed relatively minor, but they relate coherently to the larger differences that distinguish Chamba masquerades from those of their western and eastern neighbors. Western Chamba masks (bordering Mumuyoid and Jukunoid speakers) tend to be longer, larger, and flatter than their eastern counterparts. Their facial features—ears, nose, eyes, and particularly sagittal ridge—are much more pronounced than in eastern examples, and many have metal decoration, for instance a nose ornament, or patterns of incisions evoking braids on the sagittal ridge (figs. 10.1, 10.37). The shorter eastern masks have higher domes, shaped much more like human skulls, and they are generally plainer in finish (fig. 10.38). In sum, western Chamba masks appear to be the more theriomorphic; and such anthropomorphic features as they do have reference human features (like hair and scarification) rather than human skulls. This makes them resemble Mumuye masks in ways that eastern Chamba masks do not. For both western Chamba and Mumuye, it seems that the association of human and animal skulls takes place through assemblage (rituals in which skulls and masquerades both feature) rather than through a fusion in a single object (like eastern Chamba masks). Naming practices vary between western Chamba Daka and eastern Chamba Leko and to that extent coincide with differences in form: for Chamba Daka the masquerade is Nam-Gbalang, composed of the noun for animal and an adjective, *gbalang*, which is claimed to evoke its unruly behavior; the most easterly Chamba Leko refer to the mask as Vara, which simply means skull; western Chamba Leko are aware of this usage but call their mask Lang-Gbadna, claiming that *lang* means frightening, and *gbadna* refers to the mask. It seems equally possible that etymologically Gbalang, Lang-Gbadna, and other terms, such as Mangam and Mongop (see below), are semi-homophonous variations on some shared characterization of the oddness of masquerade, perhaps motivated by the repeated two-note phrase on an iron hand gong that accompanies the Chamba masquerade (and some others it appears).

Male and female Chamba masks are formally identical. Masks in the southern part of Chambaland (whether used by Daka- or Leko-speakers) are colored red if they are male and black if they are female. Northern Chamba masks are parti-colored into red and black halves; and it seems by report that all are considered female. The only record of sexual dimorphism in Chamba masks, which is presumably a local innovation, comes from the chiefdom of Gurumpawo, where Phillips Stevens photographed a female, parti-colored mask that he reports differed from its male counterpart by an absence of horns (Stevens 1977). No example of this form has entered a collection to

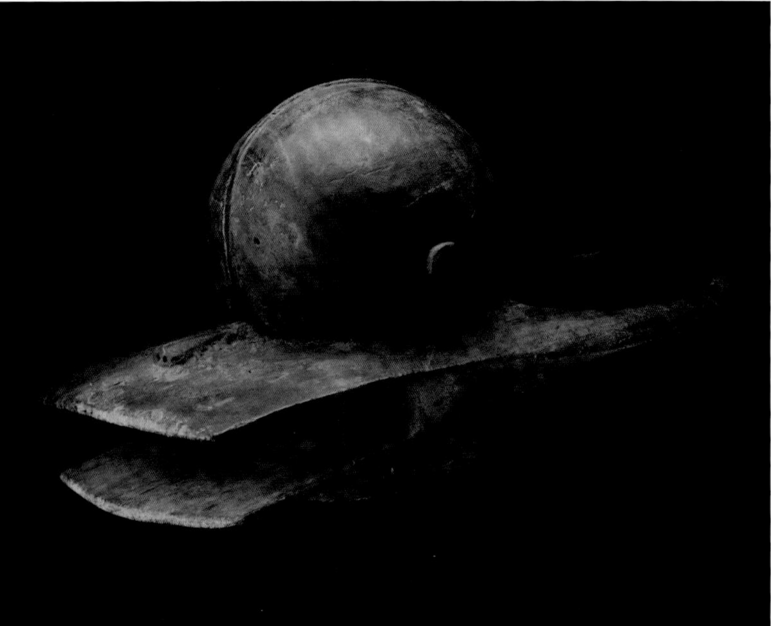

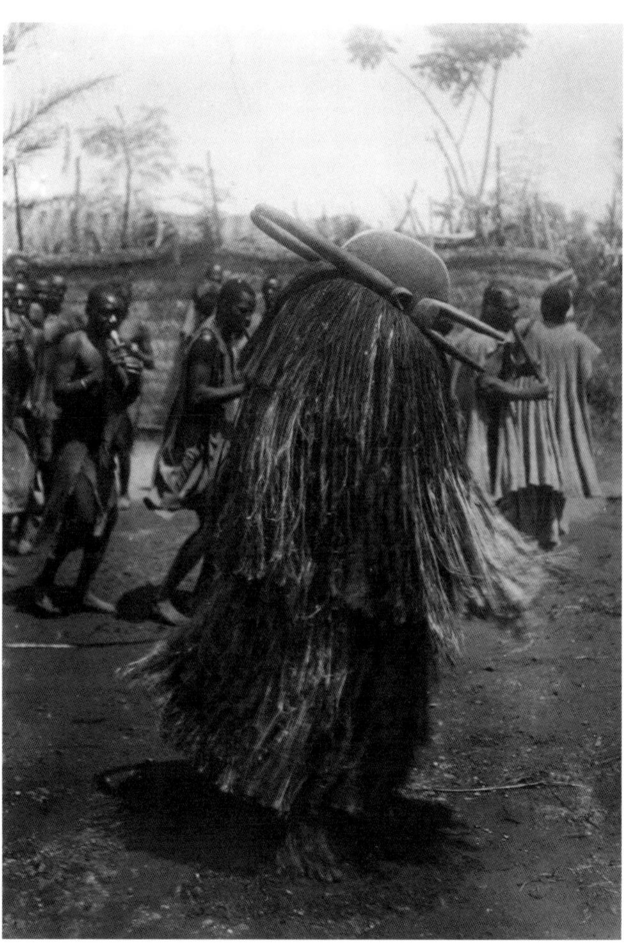

10.39
Mask
Chamba Donga peoples, before 1912
Wood
L: 61 cm
LINDEN-MUSEUM STUTTGART, 83.091
IMAGE: © LINDEN-MUSEUM STUTTGART, STAATLI-
CHES MUSEUM FÜR VOLKERKUNDE. PHOTOGRAPH
BY ANATOL DREYER
PROVENANCE: COLLECTED BY LEO FROBENIUS, 1911
(NOT IN EXHIBITION)

This mask collected by Frobenius from Donga
is strikingly reminiscent of what was probably
its replacement, photographed over half a
century later by Arnold Rubin in 1965 (see
fig. 10.36). This well-executed mask nonetheless has a hole crudely gouged above its
upper mouth plate, which I speculate might
be because the peephole between the mouth
plates failed to align with the wearer's eyes.

10.40
This is one of a series of five photographs
recording Chamba masquerade in September
1911. In the background a band of *lera* (flute)
players circle.
COPYRIGHT: FROBENIUS-INSTITUT, FRANKFURT
AM MAIN, NEGATIVE 5874.

my knowledge, and I had not been aware by report of a similar example elsewhere
until seeing the souvenir publication (fig. 7.9) for the installation of the Paramount
Chief in Ganye as a First-Class Chief in March 2006, which shows a "family" of three
masks performing (male, female, and infant, the latter two definitely lacking horns).

The emigration of nineteenth-century Chamba, who originally left Chambaland
in raiding parties, led them to establish numerous chiefdoms to the southwest and
southeast of their eighteenth-century homelands (see Fardon 2006 for Chamba
emigrants to what is now Cameroon). Only some of these retained a tradition of
Chamba masquerade. Arnold Rubin photographed masquerades in both Donga and
Suntai during his research in 1965 (Rubin 1969) and also filmed the former. The Suntai
masquerade resembles western Chamba masquerades, of which it is a particularly large
example (see fig. 10.35), although its fiber costume, like that in Donga, has adopted
the separated limbs typical of a Jukun masquerade. Most intriguing is the Donga mask
(see fig. 10.36): Rubin's photograph of the mask is virtually identical to an example
collected in the same place by Leo Frobenius in 1912. Now in the Linden-Museum in
Stuttgart, this mask (fig. 10.39) differs in unprecedented ways from typical Chamba
conventions (fig. 10.40). The strict horizontal plane, which unites the mouth, ears, nose,
and horns of figure 10.39, has been allowed to curve; additionally, the cranial dome is
particularly tall. Although beautifully finished, Frobenius's well-used example may not
have been entirely successful in performance. A triangular hole gouged above the upper
mouth plate suggests that the cranial dome was made too deep, with the result that the
wearer's eyes did not align with the peep hole at the back of the mouth. One wonders
whether a skilled Jukun- or Hausa-speaking (Abakwariga) carver was asked to sculpt a
form with which he was unfamiliar. The masquerade photographed by Rubin in figure
10.36 has seemingly resolved this problem—although it resembles Frobenius's example
in other respects—since there is no evidence of a hole above its upper mouth plate.

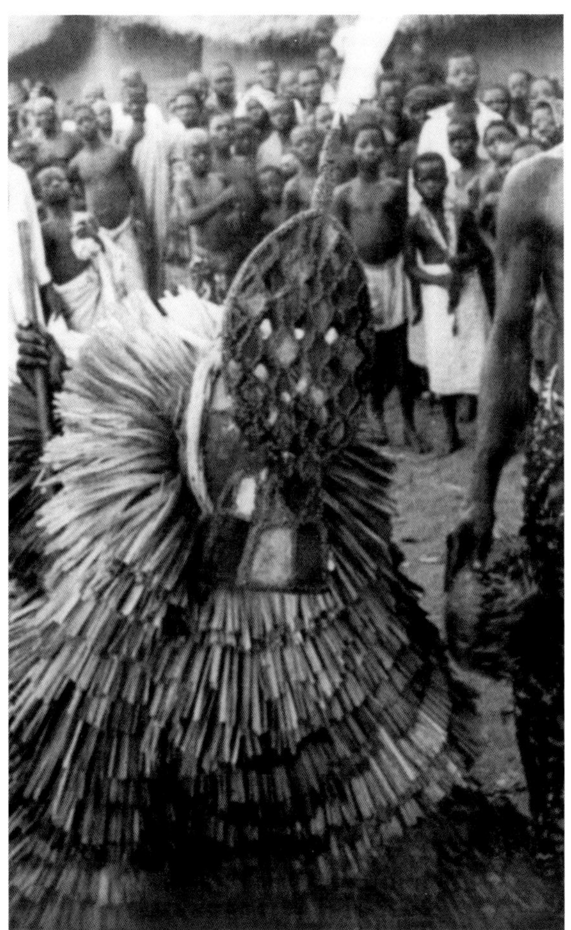

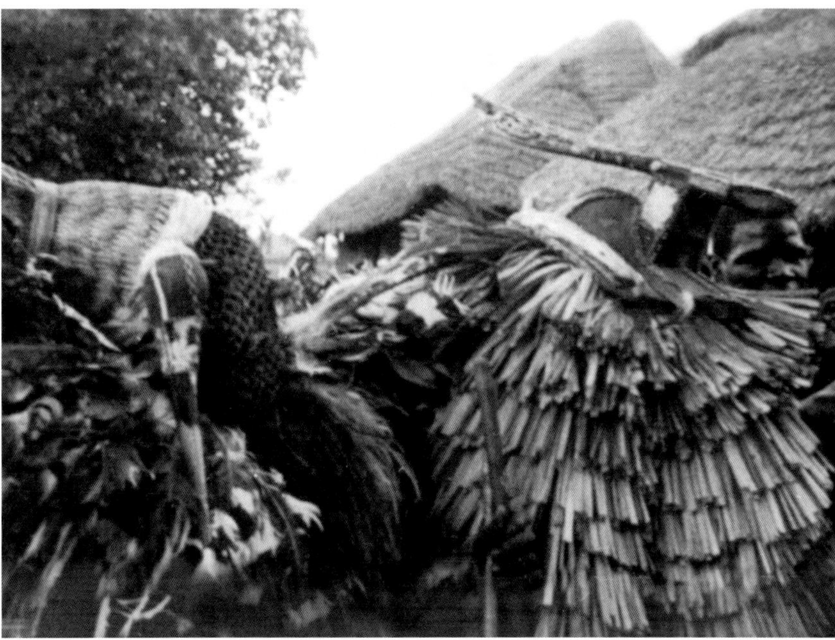

Goemai, Montol, and Sura

Jukun, Mumuye, and Chamba masquerades lend themselves to analysis as a series of formal transformations that work variations on similar concerns. To the north of the Wapan Jukun, the Goemai (or Ankwe as they were known to the Hausa) allow us to observe, or so it seems, not just the formal transformation of a Jukun masquerade but a historical borrowing. The reader may recall that Goemai also resembled northerly Jukun in their manner of performing with figure sculptures in procession (see figs. 8.60a–c, fig. 14.27), so the similarity in their masquerade might be anticipated. Historically, the most plausible inference is that Goemai modified the Jukun male Aku mask while adopting it in place of an earlier horizontal mask, which they shared with their Montol neighbors under the name Gugwom (see fig. 10.46). As we shall see below, the Gugwom mask, replaced by Mongop, was either entirely, or at least predominantly, theriomorphic; however, as Roy Sieber demonstrated from field research carried out a half-century ago, the Jukun-derived Mongop, like the Jukun male Aku, is interpreted by its users in theranthropic terms (figs. 10.41, 10.42; see Sieber 1961; Sieber and Vevers 1974; Sieber and Hecht 2002). In copying the Jukun Aku mask, Goemai carvers moved its upper mouth plate to become part of the same plane as the horns of their Mongop mask and in doing so, weakened the double (horizontal and vertical) motivations that allowed the two readings of the Aku mask. The nose-like projection of the Jukun mask has become almost unrecognizable in the Goemai version, which is also consistent with what had been a face mask for Jukun masqueraders being transformed into a cap mask—rather than covering the masquerader's face, the Goemai mask sits horizontally on the crown of his head (fig. 10.43 and cf. 10.45). The animal features (horns and mouth) remain readily apparent; however, the human characteristics (nose, eyes, hair knot, and overhanging chin) have either disappeared or been repositioned (e.g., the hair knot) so that their significance might easily be lost had it not been

10.41, 10.42
Roy Sieber documented three Mongop masquerades in the Montol villages of Bakinshiawa, Kwande, and Kurgwe. He reports that the first of these, illustrated here (see fig. 10.41), was the most important of the three. It is elaborately carved and decorated with abrus seeds, and it may have been made in the last decade of the nineteenth century. Its costume and staff relate it to the Jukun male Aku, which it probably copies. The architecture of its mask, has, however, been rearranged in some respects. Note how the Mongop mask has a netted partner (see fig. 10.42), which might correspond to the gendered pairings of Jukun masquerades.
PHOTOGRAPHS BY ROY SIEBER, JUNE 18, 1958

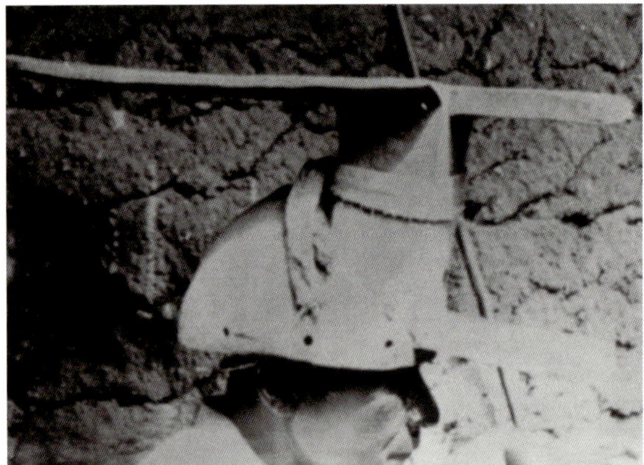

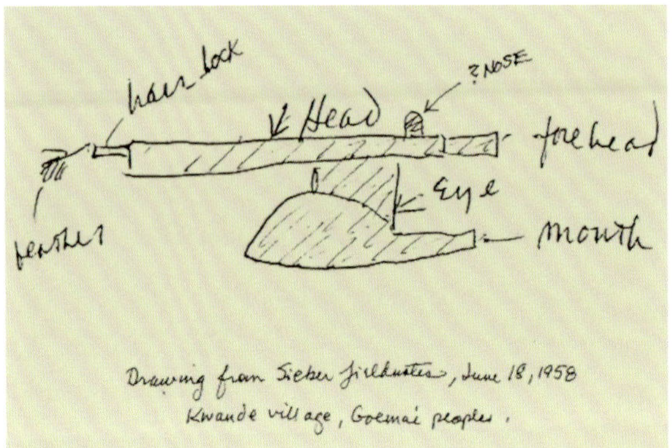

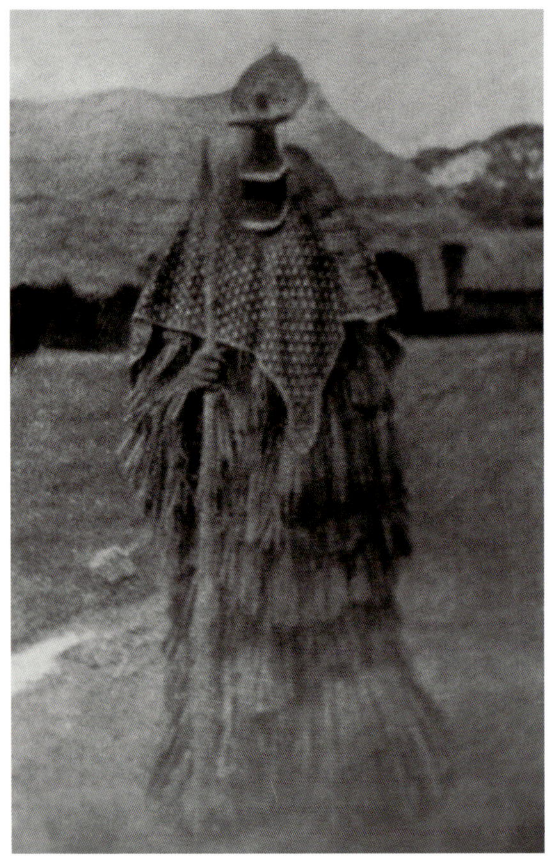

10.43

The Mongop masquerade photographed by Roy Sieber in Kwande is similar in form, although undecorated, when compared to that in Bakinshiawa (figs. 10.41, 10.42). This photograph shows how the mask is worn as a horizontal cap, rather than at an angle of thirty degrees below the horizontal like the Jukun Aku-Wunu (cf. fig. 10.45).

PHOTOGRAPH BY ROY SIEBER, JUNE 18, 1958. REPRODUCED IN SIEBER (1961, 10, FIG. 6).

10.44

Roy Sieber's sketch reveals how the Goemai Mongop mask has reordered its Jukun equivalent, notably by making the upper mouth plate part of the same plane as the horns (cf. fig. 10.18).

© ROY AND SOPHIA SIEBER FAMILY TRUST.

10.45

This photograph by C. K. Meek taken in Wukari shows the Jukun Aku-Wunu mask worn at the typical angle of thirty degrees below horizontal. Meek wrongly labeled this masquerade as "Adashâ."

REPRODUCED FROM MEEK (1931A, PL. XXIII, FACING P. 279).

explained to Sieber (fig. 10.44). This upshot is intriguing because the Goemai may have altered the formal properties of the mask, which sustained the possibility of Jukun reading it in both human and animal terms, yet they nonetheless retained the human and animal interpretation of it. Particularly noteworthy is the identification of an "eye" between the two frontal plates, since this is in the position of the spyhole in horizontal masks, like that of the Chamba, and already otiose functionally in the Jukun Aku. The Goemai Mongop mask, and the earlier of the two Mumuye Yakoko masks in the Pitt Rivers Museum (see fig. 10.20), can be read as different appropriations of the conventions of the Jukun Aku, which does not mean, however plausible it might seem, that we can be entirely sure that this was what historically occurred or that other appropriations were not also at work. Robert Netting's description of Mongop in performance to Arnold Rubin, discussed elsewhere in this volume (chapter 9, pp. 314–15), gives the impression that Mongop has simply assumed the role of the Gugwom masquerade, and it is noticeable that the masquerade does not have the refinements (including use of cloth in the costume) that we know to have been typical of the Aku masquerade.

The Montol, northern neighbors of the Goemai, retained their Gugwom mask because, Sieber noted, they were not under the influence of the Jukun. Two shapes of Gugwom have been documented. One form lacks horns but does have a rear element that could be a hair knot. This mask type's elongated, narrow mouth plates and central cap element are covered with nodules (fig. 10.46) that might reference the crocodile, or else human scarification (Sieber 1961, pls. 9, 31; Wittmer and Arnett 1978, 94 pl. 219). The alternative form of Gugwom combines the straight horns of some kind of antelope with flared mouth plates, which, like Mumuye horizontal masks, have dentition indicated. Both the mouth plates and the cap of the mask are covered in zigzag incisions that might reference anthropomorphic analogies (Wittmer and Arnett 1978, 93, pl. 217). Field documentation of Gugwom is scanty in the extreme: Arnold Rubin (1988) noted the lack of resemblance between the Montol's Gugwom mask (of the first type) and

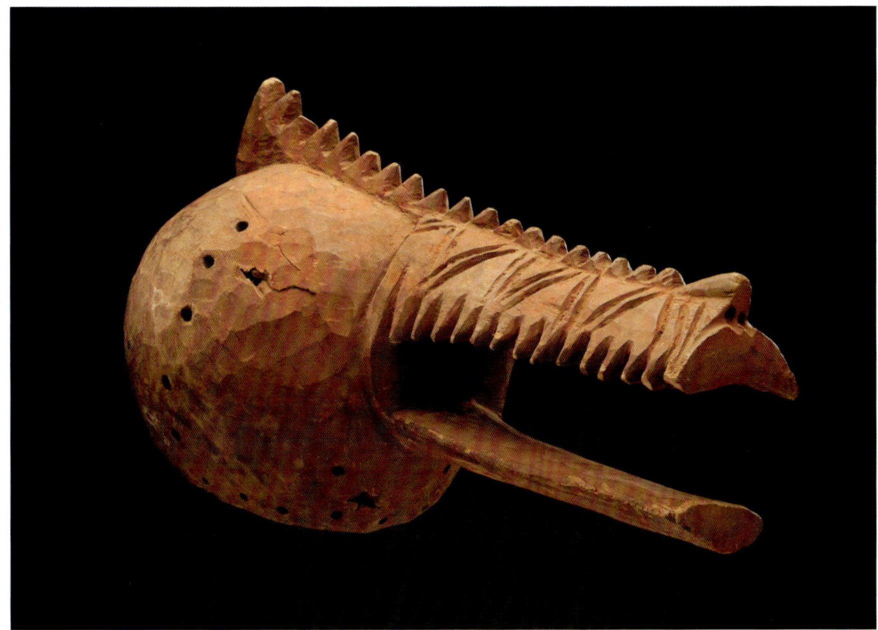

10.46
Horizontal mask (Gugwom)
Montol peoples, mid-twentieth century
Wood, camwood powder or red ocher (?)
L: 62 cm
FOWLER MUSEUM AT UCLA X91.405; GIFT OF
PETER J. KUHN
IMAGE: © 2010 FOWLER MUSEUM AT UCLA.
PHOTOGRAPH BY DON COLE
PROVENANCE: HELEN AND ROBERT KUHN COLLEC-
TION, 1991

This brightly reddened casque mask probably
represents a fusion of human attributes with
those of a crocodile (a creature that was the
subject of an Aku-Ma mask in Wukari photographed by Frobenius, see fig. 10.14). Sieber's
analysis suggests that this kind of horizontal
mask, which was retained by the Montol, had
once also been widespread among Goemai but
had been replaced there by Mongop as a result
of Jukun influence.

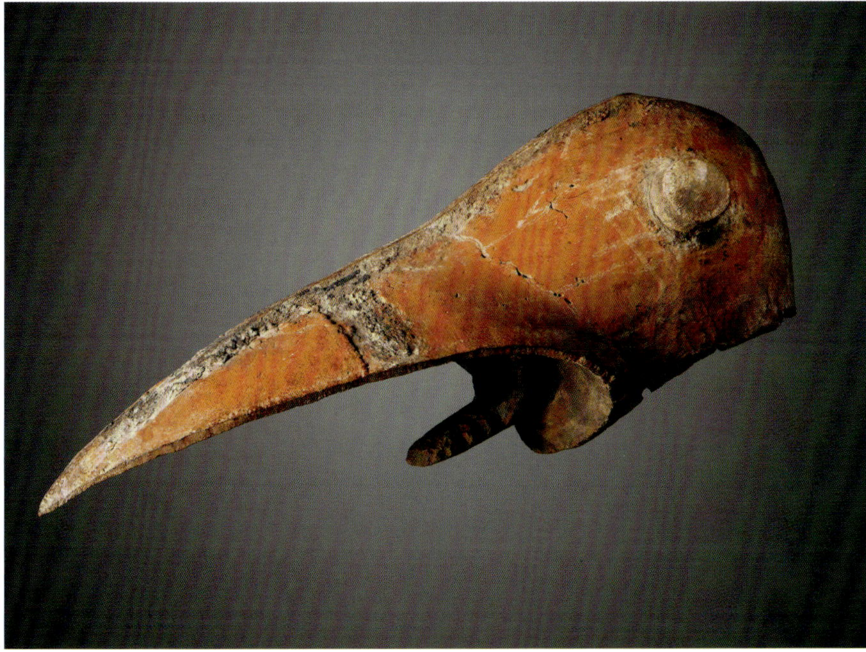

10.47
Horizontal mask (Gugwang)
Sura peoples, early to mid-twentieth century
Wood, pigment, camwood powder
L: 77 cm
MUSÉE DU QUAI BRANLY, PARIS, 70.2002.81
IMAGE: © 2010 MUSÉE DU QUAI BRANLY. PHOTO-
GRAPH BY PATRICK GRIES/SCALA, FLORENCE
PROVENANCE: PRIVATE COLLECTION, PARIS, 1970S;
PRIVATE COLLECTION, MINNEAPOLIS, 1980S

Sura masquerades, represented by this example
in the collection of the Musée du quai Branly
and also by a field photograph (see fig. 10.48),
seem to draw upon regional conventions for
bird-like horizontal masks.

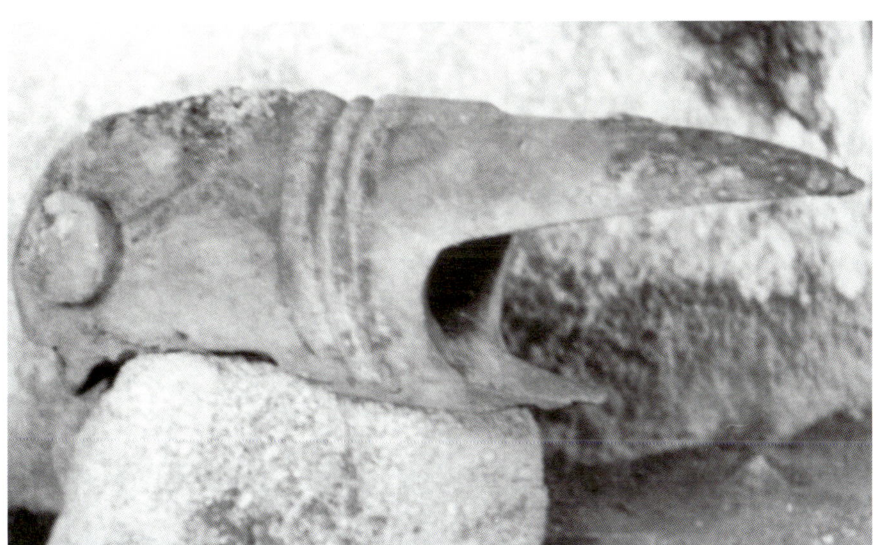

10.48
This Gugwang mask was given the personal
name Shiri and belonged to the Chakfem-
Mushere peoples, who speak a language
closely related to that spoken by the Sura.
The mask was kept in a cave and used in cer-
emonies that took place every four years.
PHOTOGRAPHED NEAR SHENDAM VILLAGE.
REPRODUCED COURTESY OF THE NATIONAL
COMMISSION FOR MUSEUMS AND MONUMENTS,
NIGERIA, NML-PA, NEG. NO. 18.49.3.

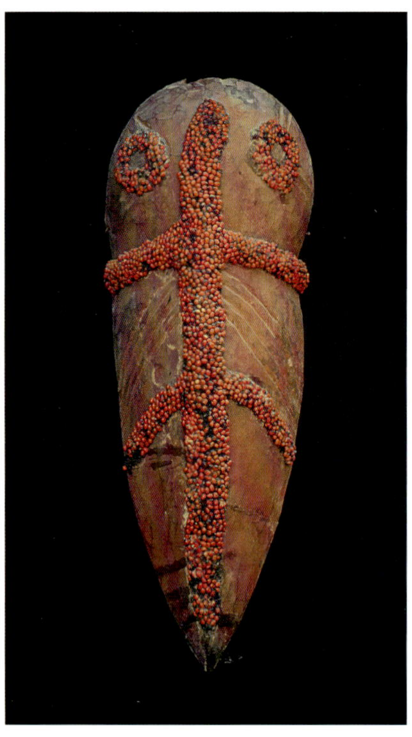

10.49
Given the appearance of this example, Sura masks were probably encrusted with abrus seeds when new.
PHOTOGRAPH BY ROBERT NETTING, JELEM PANSHKIN DIVISION, 1967, JOS MUSEUM, NO. 67.J.28, RUBIN ARCHIVE, FOWLER MUSEUM AT UCLA. REPRODUCED COURTESY OF THE NATIONAL COMMISSION FOR MUSEUMS AND MONUMENTS, NIGERIA.

those of their neighbors, but he was otherwise able only to indicate some of the times at which it was conventional for the mask to appear, notably harvest and chiefly burials.

Under the similar name, "Gugwang," which may be no more than a different transcription of Gugwom, is another striking mask, thoroughly reddened, with a long pointed beak (figs. 10.47, 10.48), reminiscent of some Jukun Aku-Ma in bird-like form, and associated with the Sura (also known as Djibete).[12] Uniquely, this type of "mask," which was around 70 centimeters in length, apparently could have been carried or additionally supported by what looks to be a handle in its beak. In the absence of recorded field observations, it is difficult to imagine quite how this object was used performatively. Both examples shown here have large round eyes and a short lower beak, a deep cap, and what might be attachment holes for a fiber dress around the edge of the cap. The Musee du quai Branly mask shows evidence of patination from use and is missing the red abrus seeds that would have filled the bands across the beak and around the eyes left by the white residue of gum in which they were fixed. A mask of the same type collected when relatively new by Robert Netting in 1967 shows how these masks looked when intact with abrus seeds firmly attached (fig. 10.49).

Jukunoid

Knowing that the Goemai Mongop resembles the masquerade of Wukari-area Jukun, who favor the Aku form, then we might anticipate that the small groups of speakers of Jukunoid languages living to the south of the Jukun around Takum would have masquerades that put us in mind of the Jukun Aku-Ma complex. We would be at least halfway correct.

Jukun Aku-Ma paired a male, predominantly theriomorphic, fusion mask (that added buffalo horns, as well as plausibly anthropomorphic ornamentation to diverse animal references) with an anthropomorphic female mask. Kuteb masquerades achieve something very similar: the male masquerade is a horizontal theriomorphic mask with bovine or bovid horns (fig. 10.50). Striation and ornamentation with abrus seeds, are common and may indicate human referents (fig. 10.51). All this is highly reminiscent of the male Aku-Ma. The female mask, however, is reduced to a small crest worn atop the masquerader's head, which has been concealed under a black balaclava (fig. 10.52).[13] The female mask is hence a minimal marker of a cultivated coiffure and, therefore, more like the female Aku than its counterpart Aku-Ma. The forms of these masks, collected from Yukuben, Kuteb, and some other Jukunoid groups, for all of whom the ethnographic record is thin, show a degree of variation within these terms (fig. 10.53). Worn examples collected during the German colonial period demonstrate that these are not recent innovations (e.g., Kreiger and Kutscher 1960, no. 25, pl. 10; Fagg 1964, no. 56). In addition to the animal forms of mask similar to Aku-Ma documented from the area south and southeast of Takum, there is a version of the distinctive, anthropomorphic plank mask that Rubin tells us was called Aluku by carvers in Takum (fig. 10.54; see also fig. 10.12). Also similar to this is the masquerade called Augum in their own language by Yukuben, four examples of which Rubin photographed in the villages of Lufu and Bete (1969, pls. 80, 81, 82/83, 84/85) along with its "wife" conceived on the same lines as that of the Jukun Aku-Ma (figs. 10.55a–d). Rubin describes the male Augum as a

> plank-shaped face-cover (worn tipped down in front at an angle of about thirty degrees below the horizontal) with tubular eyes, arching brows which merge with the wedge-shaped nose, and a pattern of horizontal stripes. Two more or less prominent points beneath the nose reportedly represent teeth, and from one to three horns may be added.... The mask itself was described as representing a horned, fanged, wild animal, with its painted patterns evoking the spots of the leopard…a composite "fearsome beast of the bush."
> [Rubin 1988, IIID Highlands, 23; see also 1969, 70]

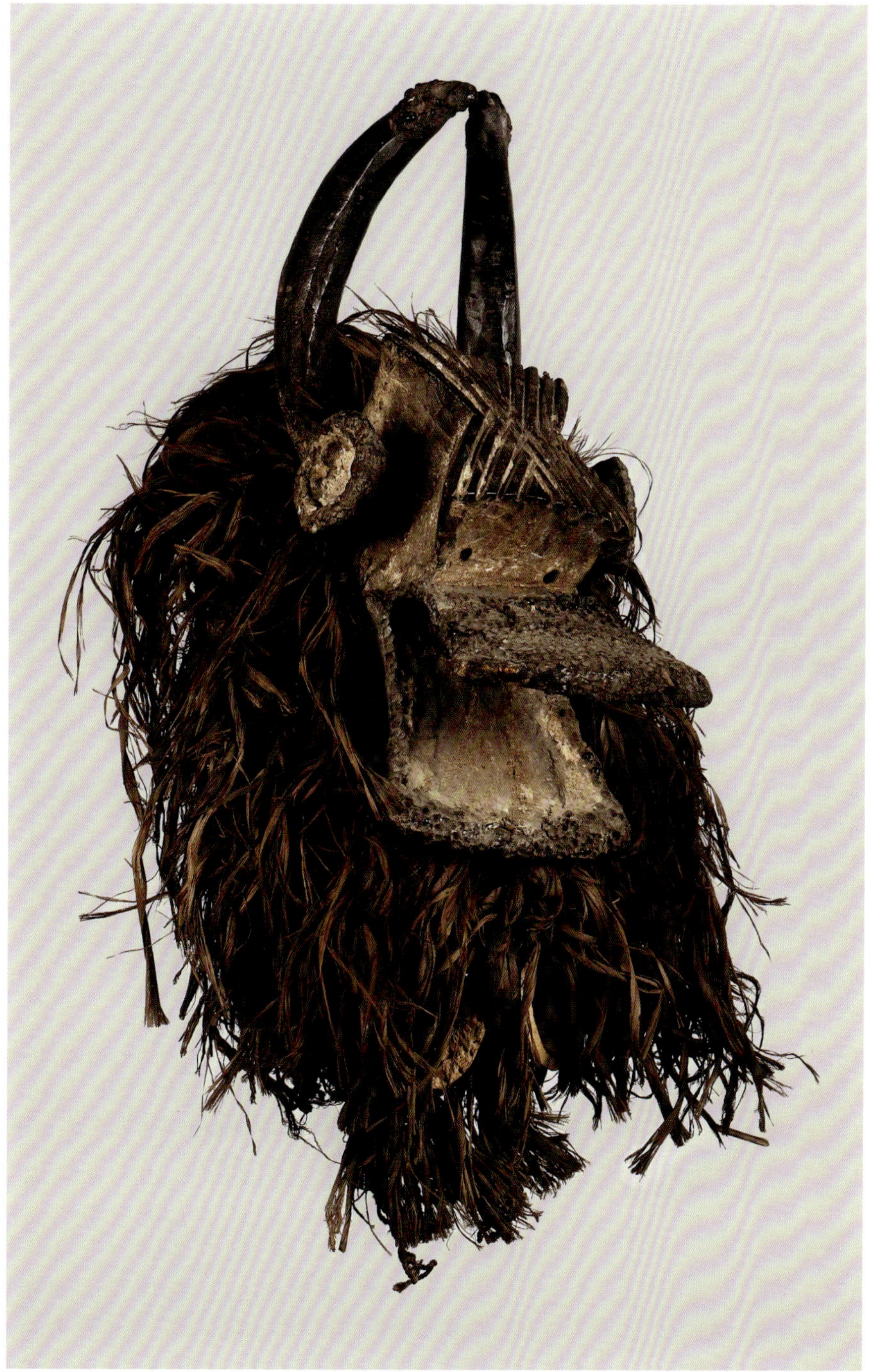

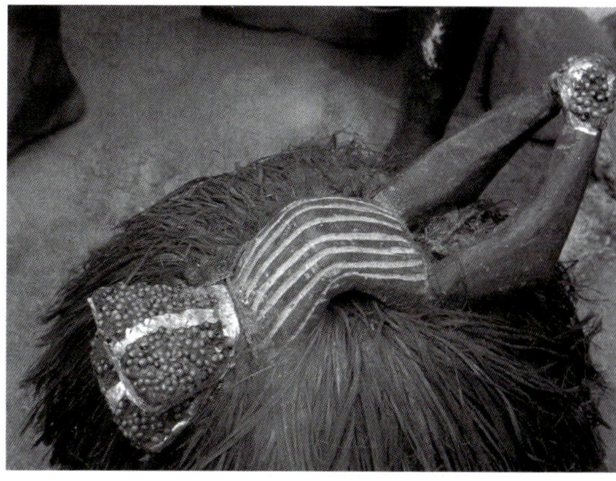

10.51
Arnold Rubin recorded this Kuteb male masquerade in situ. In its handling of mass and line, it differs in only a few respects from collected examples (see fig. 10.50) suggesting a relatively fixed genre.

PHOTOGRAPH BY ARNOLD RUBIN, NOVEMBER 10, 1965, RUBIN ARCHIVE, FOWLER MUSEUM AT UCLA, NEG. NO. 1188.

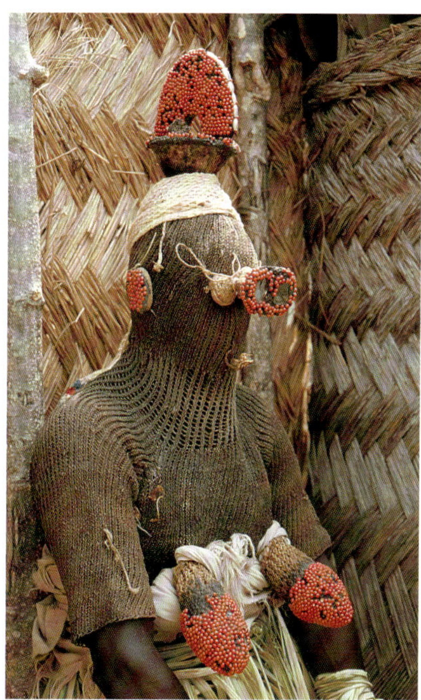

10.52
This example of a female Kuteb masquerade illustrates its similarity to the female Jukun Aku-Wuwa masquerade (see figs. 10.5, 10.7).

PHOTOGRAPH BY ARNOLD RUBIN, TAKUM, JANU-ARY 17, 1965, RUBIN ARCHIVE, FOWLER MUSEUM AT UCLA, SLIDE NO. A.11.7.18.

10.50
Horizontal male mask
Kuteb peoples, early to mid-twentieth century
Wood, fiber
H: 43 cm
ITZIKOVITZ COLLECTION
IMAGE: COURTESY COLLECTOR. PHOTOGRAPH
© BRIGITTE CAVANAGH, 2010
PROVENANCE: JEAN PAUL DELCOURT, ABIDJAN

The Kuteb are speakers of a Jukunoid language living to the south of Takum, so it is not surprising that their horizontal male mask shares features with the Aku-Ma genre of masquerade. Male masks of this kind generally had female counterparts in the form of small wooden crests, which resembled Jukun female Aku masks (see fig. 10.52).

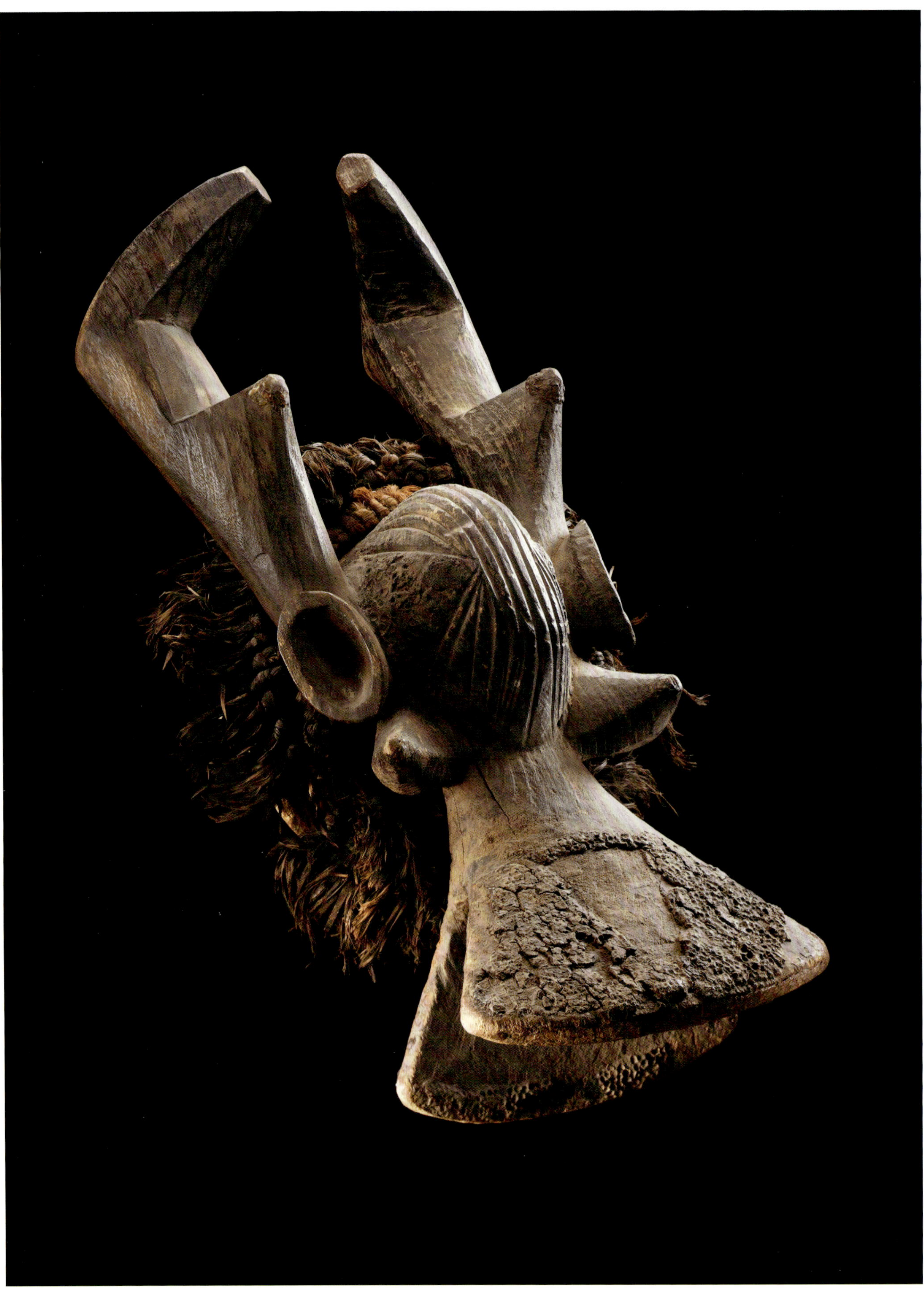

10.53 (OPPOSITE)

Horizontal cap mask
Yukuben peoples (?), early twentieth century
Wood, grayish brown patina, abrus seeds, fiber
L: 63 cm

BARBIER-MUELLER COLLECTION, GENEVA, 1015-22

IMAGE: COURTESY BARBIER-MUELLER MUSEUM,
GENEVA © STUDIO FERRAZZINI BOUCHET PHOTO-
GRAPHIES, 2010

PROVENANCE: GALERIE ROBINS, PARIS; BARBIER-
MUELLER MUSEUM, GENEVA, 1973

Arnold Rubin attributed this extravagant horizontal cap mask to Yukuben (see Schmalenbach
1988, 176). Predominantly theriomorphic, it
has both horns and tusks. Its dome has linear
striations that, to judge by Middle Benue
conventions, might index anthropomorphism.
Rubin's note shows that he was aware that horizontal masks of this kind had been acquired
by early German collectors from Kuteb rather
than Yukuben, yet he did not provide grounds
for his attribution. It is conceivable that some
indication of provenance had been given when
the mask first entered the hands of a dealer.
Rubin remarks the trans-ethnic interaction,
including trade, in what remained a somewhat remote region of the Nigeria-Cameroon
borderland. Hence, Yukuben might use this
mask under the name "Augum," which they
also applied to their plank masks.

10.54

Plank mask, Augum-style
Abakwariga peoples, Takum town, before 1965
Wood, enamel, paint
H: 71 cm

FOWLER MUSEUM AT UCLA X86.4717; GIFT OF
ARNOLD RUBIN

IMAGE: © 2010 FOWLER MUSEUM AT UCLA.
PHOTOGRAPH BY DON COLE

PROVENANCE: COLLECTED BY ARNOLD RUBIN,
NIGERIA, 1965

Arnold Rubin bought this mask in Augum
style from a British colonial officer. It had
apparently been made for a Regional Arts
Festival in Kaduna, rather than for use by
local peoples, which may explain the use of
black and white enamel paints to decorate
it. Rubin speculated that the mask could
have been carved in the Sangari workshop in
Takum. The Sangaris were nominally Muslim
Hausa artisans long-settled among Jukun who
called them Abakwariga. Rubin documented
several types of Aku-Ma masks as well as Aku
carved by the Sangaris.

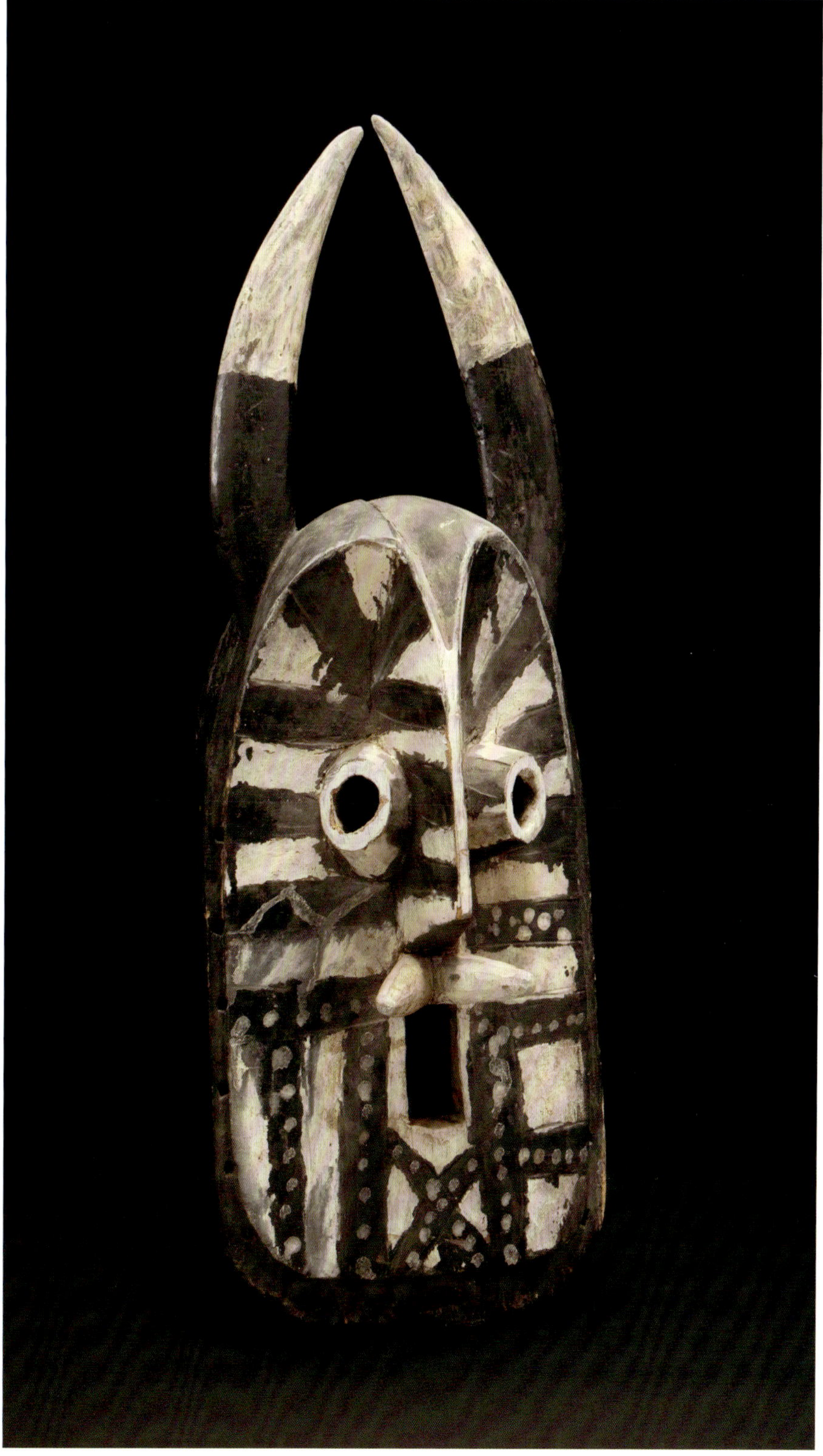

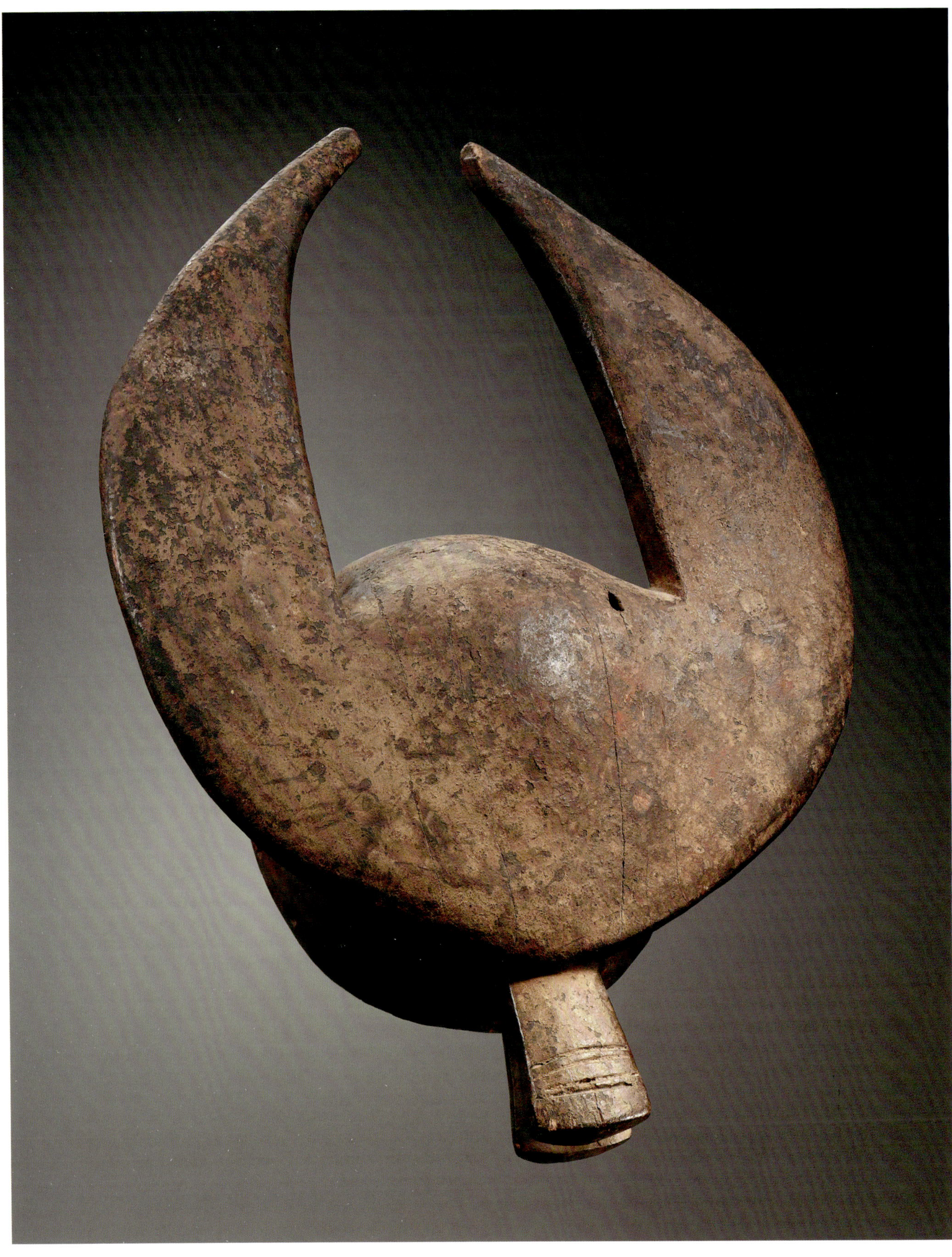

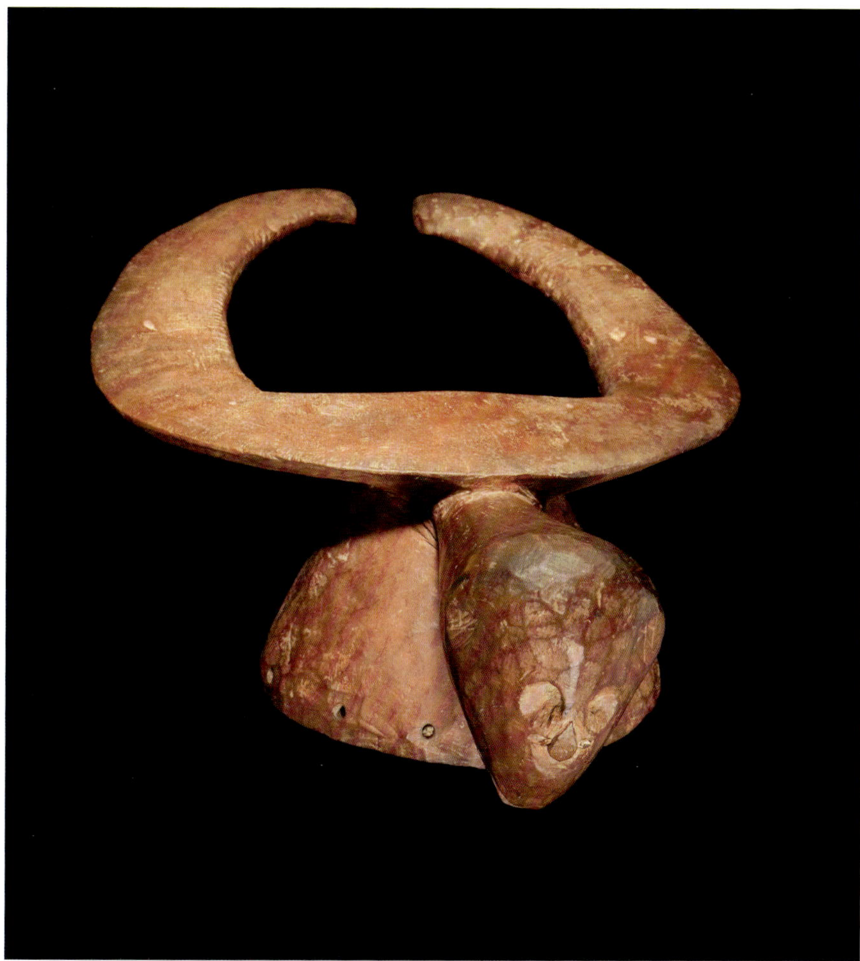

10.58
Mangam mask with human face
Rindre peoples, twentieth century
Wood, ocher
H: 30 cm
COLLECTION OF JILL AND BARRY KITNICK
IMAGE: © 2010 FOWLER MUSEUM AT UCLA.
PHOTOGRAPH BY DON COLE
PROVENANCE: IRWIN HERSEY, NEW YORK

The theranthropic character of the buffalo
Mangam mask is particularly evident in this
example, which has a human face added to its
snout. Masks of this type were documented in
1952 in Rindre villages, suggesting that they
may be a local innovation.

of all the species of buck that might be designated by these terms). As elsewhere in the
region, masks with buffalo referents are easily identified by their rounded horns, here
summarized as clean-lined, flat arcs that are almost circular—in some examples with
tips that meet so as to approximate a pierced disk. In her sampling, Berns estimates
that the horns of up to 80 percent of masks from the region belong to the buffalo rather
than waterbuck or reedbuck conformation (see this volume, interleaf H). In addition to
carved masks, there are, as Rubin notes, examples of Mangam masks made from found
objects, like tree roots, as well as actual skulls.

The scanty ethnographic information accompanying collected examples associates the masquerades comprehensively, but somewhat unspecifically, with the dead,
with the promotion of crop fertility, and with the skulls both of enemies and deceased
relatives. It would be a mistake to try to derive some singular, distinctive reference
from all this. Images of theranthropic fusion are highly suggestive vehicles of power
relevant across any number of contexts. The ethnographic record proposes that such
fusion is multiply evoked: masks themselves may have human features (like a carved
hair knot or miniature anthropomorphic face [fig. 10.58]), and masquerade performances may bring animal skulls (or their formal evocation in masks) into association
with actual human skulls: for instance, those shown as stored on the external shelves
of small huts or granaries in photographs taken by Father Kevin Carroll during the
1950s (see fig. 12.16).

The peoples around Jos were not off well-beaten colonial tracks to the same extent
as those of the eastern Middle Benue, which accounts for their masks entering British
museum collections at a relatively early date. Three masks collected by Olive Temple
(née MacLeod) in 1910–1911 were donated to what is now the World Museum Liverpool
(22.11.24 nos 162/3/4) as part of a larger collection from which the British Museum had

10.57 (OPPOSITE)
"Small" Mangam mask
Kantana/Kulere (?) peoples, early to mid-
twentieth century
Wood
H: 48 cm
PRIVATE COLLECTION, PARIS
IMAGE: COURTESY PRIVATE COLLECTOR.
© PHOTOGRAPH BY HUGHES DUBOIS, 2010
PROVENANCE: PURCHASED IN NIGERIA, 1970

taken a selection. They differ in type: one is in characteristic buffalo shape, another has straight pointed horns, and the third upswept horns flared around their middle section. It is possible that all three were unused, and this is almost certainly so of the mask with straight horns, which lacks the holes around its bottom edges through which to attach it to a masquerade costume. Both buck masks have small features that are probably eyes (identically executed so perhaps by the same hand) and patterned "facial" striations in tripled ridges. The buffalo mask also has what might be eyes, one to each side of a decorated ridge on the upper surface where the horns meet at the front of the mask.

From a similar period are two masks accessioned in the Pitt Rivers Museum (1918: 31 25-26 donated by Hubert Frank Mathews, a colonial officer who is listed as one of the Temples' authorities on the "Mama"; see Temple and Temple [1919] 1922, 267). One of the two belongs to the "buck" genre. It has a domed cap and decorated patterned tripled incisions so similar to those of the two buck masks in the Liverpool collection as to suggest they might be related. Like those masks, it also has an upraised mouth; its horns are tapered and upswept. The other mask in the Pitt Rivers Museum has a relatively unadorned buffalo shape, differing from the Liverpool example in lack of ornament as well as in its upper mouth plate, which is triangular rather than flat in cross section. All of these examples are, or have in the past been, colored a bright red.

As Berns's interleaf demonstrates, these early examples are only a few of numerous Mangam masks in public and private collections with marvelously varied horn configurations, which include examples with two horns aligned one behind the other along the center of the mask the animal referents of which are not evident. Much rarer are plank masks, which put the viewer in mind of a drastically simplified version of the Takum Aluku mask or its Yukuben Augum counterpart (see fig. 12.10), demonstrating the wide distribution of this plank, face mask type in the Middle Benue.

CONCLUSION

I have emphasized the role played by theranthropic masquerade as an image of the fusion of powers, specifically the powers of the dead and the wild. Masquerades may evoke this fusion in themselves, as I have argued is notably the case for eastern Chamba masquerades, which conjoin the shapes of human and animal skulls. Elsewhere, masquerades are only part of a fusion of powers, as seems to be the case in the images of actual human skulls and masquerades from the Kantana and their neighbors. To the east of the Chamba are neighbors who lacked wooden-headed masquerades. The regional concern with the theranthropic fusion of powers does not, however, disappear on this account. During funeral ceremonies among the Dowayo, the corpses of prominent men would be wrapped in layers of cloth and the hides of dwarf cows slaughtered from their herds. The whole bundle, shaped around the corpse seated on the ground with its knees drawn up, eventually took the overall form of the body of the Chamba masquerade. Before its interment, this funeral bundle would be leaned against a tall forked pole in the cattle corral, so as to produce the fusion of a dead human, encased in an animal form, with horns protruding from its head (fig. 10.59). At various points, men might dance wearing the skins of more slaughtered cattle with cattle skulls worn on top of their own heads. Once interred, the wrappings would be removed from the head of the corpse, which was supported by a forked pole that would catch the skull as the body rotted and dropped away—again re-creating the assemblage of human skull with horns (for more detail, see Fardon 2007, based on Barley 1983; Gardi 1965; 1981; 1995). Theranthropic fusion, particularly in its human-bovine manifestation where the outer form of a buffalo encases a living or dead human, was a recurrent and enduring motif in the thought of this region and indeed West Africa more widely. To the degree that men can concretize the powers of the dead and the wild and subject them to control, so they seek to inflect the powers that move their lifeworld.

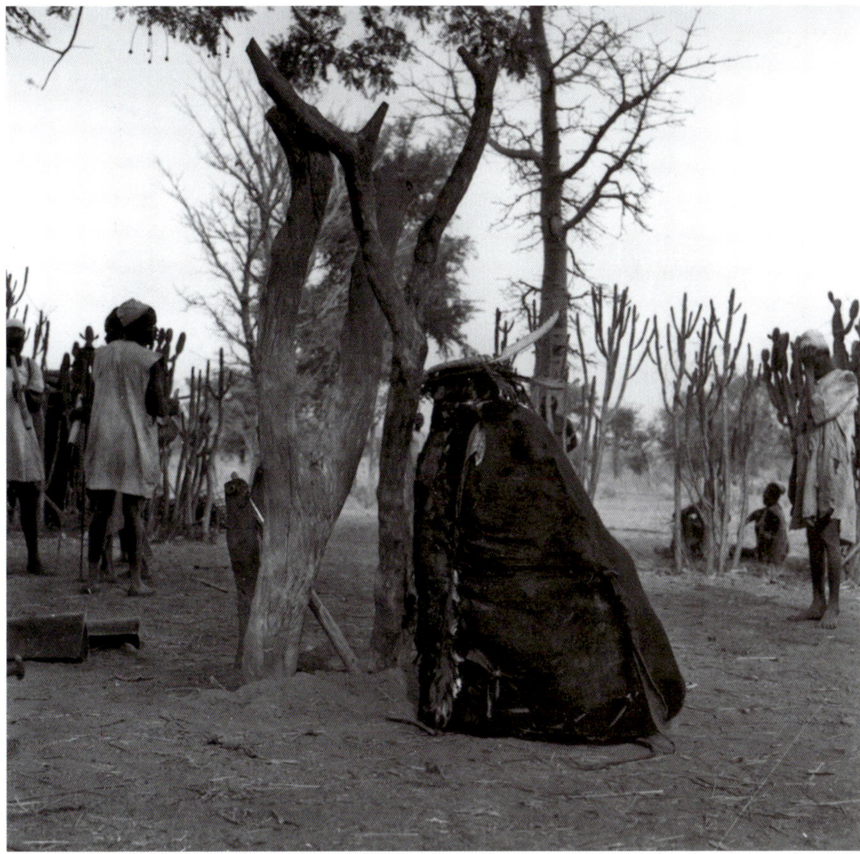

10.59
In formal terms, the bulky body and horns of the Dowayo funeral bundle, which encases a dead human being in the skins of cows, is similar to the Chamba masquerade.
Photograph by René Gardi, 1955, neg. no. 1995. © Bernhardt Gardi.

Like Middle Benue wooden figures, which I described as versatile instruments, Middle Benue masquerades were extremely hard working. Their particular fusion of animal and human traits, however, and the properties and entities these evoke (the potential for violence of the wild, the dead, and the spirits), seem to have suited them particularly for appearance at moments of rupture in the smooth scheme of things: notably at initiation, translation to high office, and death. Masquerades have a conceptual density that seems especially appropriate when human life moves between categorical and existential states of belonging. ●

INTERLEAF 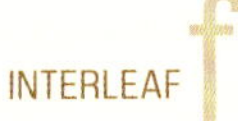

Mining the Rubin Archive: Mid-Twentieth-Century Documentation of Two Mumuye Masquerades

SUSAN ELIZABETH GAGLIARDI

In the late 1960s and early 1970s, people in Mumuye towns danced with and watched Vaa-Bong[1] masqueraders on important occasions such as initiations, funerary ceremonies, and agricultural celebrations. Arnold Rubin's photographs of wooden Vaa-Bong headpieces from Zinna, Pantisawa, and other Mumuye towns south of the Benue River taken during these years bear witness to their great variety.[2] Prominent features of the masks include long horns, circular or ovoid eyes, and wide mouths (see chapter 10, pp. 328–33). Rubin explained "the typical form of a Mumuye mask is that of a honored animal—bush cow or... buffalo—generically called *Va* or *Vabon* [Vaa-Bong]" (1985, 98).[3] The ambiguous term "bush cow" probably refers to the dwarf forest buffalo.[4] Vaa-Bong and variants of it refer to all horned headpieces and mask ensembles maintained in Mumuye towns. Rubin, however, also recorded individualized names with many of the headpieces he documented, including those that he translated into English as "Troublesome,"[5] "Guinea Corn,"[6] "Rat,"[7] "He-Goat,"[8] "Leopard,"[9] "Crazy,"[10] "Brave,"[11] "Pot Mouth,"[12] "Fire,"[13] and "The Wind Can Blow in Any Direction" (cf. 1985; fieldnotes, April 20, 1970, 298).[14] The variety of names that Rubin was offered for individual Vaa-Bong masks likely reflects locally specific concerns and understandings of their owners and caretakers.

Rubin's fieldnotes provide extensive data collected in the region, often from unnamed sources. Together with his still photographs, some of which he arranged into flipbooks, they complement his extraordinary film footage of two very different masquerades witnessed in Zinna and Pantisawa. His images and descriptions of the headpieces, dancing, audience, and timing of the April 1970 masquerade during a period of male initiation in the Mumuye town of Zinna contrasts in significant ways with a performance during the same month that coincided with a pot-smashing funerary ceremony in the nearby Mumuye town of Pantisawa. Although it is regrettable that the technology available at the time limited his ability to capture sounds associated with the performance, Rubin has left remarkable

documentation that provides unparalleled information regarding production, use, and interpretation of the mid-twentieth-century masks and their performances.

A VAA-BONG MASQUERADE AND MULTIDAY INITIATION AT ZINNA

In April of 1970, men and masquerade performers danced together during a daytime performance and multiday initiation event in the Mumuye town of Zinna (fig. F.1). Arnold Rubin attended both the masquerade and initiation festivities. The masqueraders Rubin photographed and filmed in Zinna wore Vaa-Bong headpieces of a type distinct from those he witnessed in Pantisawa (fig. F.2 and cf. fig. F.8). Each masquerader in the footage from the Zinna performance wears a wooden headpiece colored red, speckled with white dots, and adorned with a plume at the back. In his notes, Rubin identifies these feathers as those of an ostrich or other large bird, and he adds that the ostrich feathers would have been bought (April 21, 1970, 305). Inclusion of ostrich feathers in the Vaa-Bong masquerades at Zinna would have indeed been an exceptional novelty, as the birds are not indigenous to the region. The masqueraders also wore hibiscus-fiber coverings that largely obscured their bodies from view.

F.1
Vaa-Bong masqueraders dance in Zinna during a multiday initiation event, during which men danced with the masked performers. In addition to taking still photographs, Arnold Rubin filmed this event.
PHOTOGRAPH BY ARNOLD RUBIN, ZINNA, APRIL 1970, RUBIN ARCHIVE, FOWLER MUSEUM AT UCLA, NEG. NO. 2672.

F.2
Vaa-Bong headpieces photographed in April 1970 in Zinna and Pantisawa resemble each other with their bovine horns and snouts. Dotted surfaces on the headpieces and the performers' full-body coverings, however, distinguish the Zinna masks as seen in these photographs. A feather also extends from the headpiece of each Zinna performer.
PHOTOGRAPH BY ARNOLD RUBIN, ZINNA, APRIL 1970, RUBIN ARCHIVE, FOWLER MUSEUM AT UCLA, SLIDE. NOS. A1.10.19.2, A1.10.18.9.

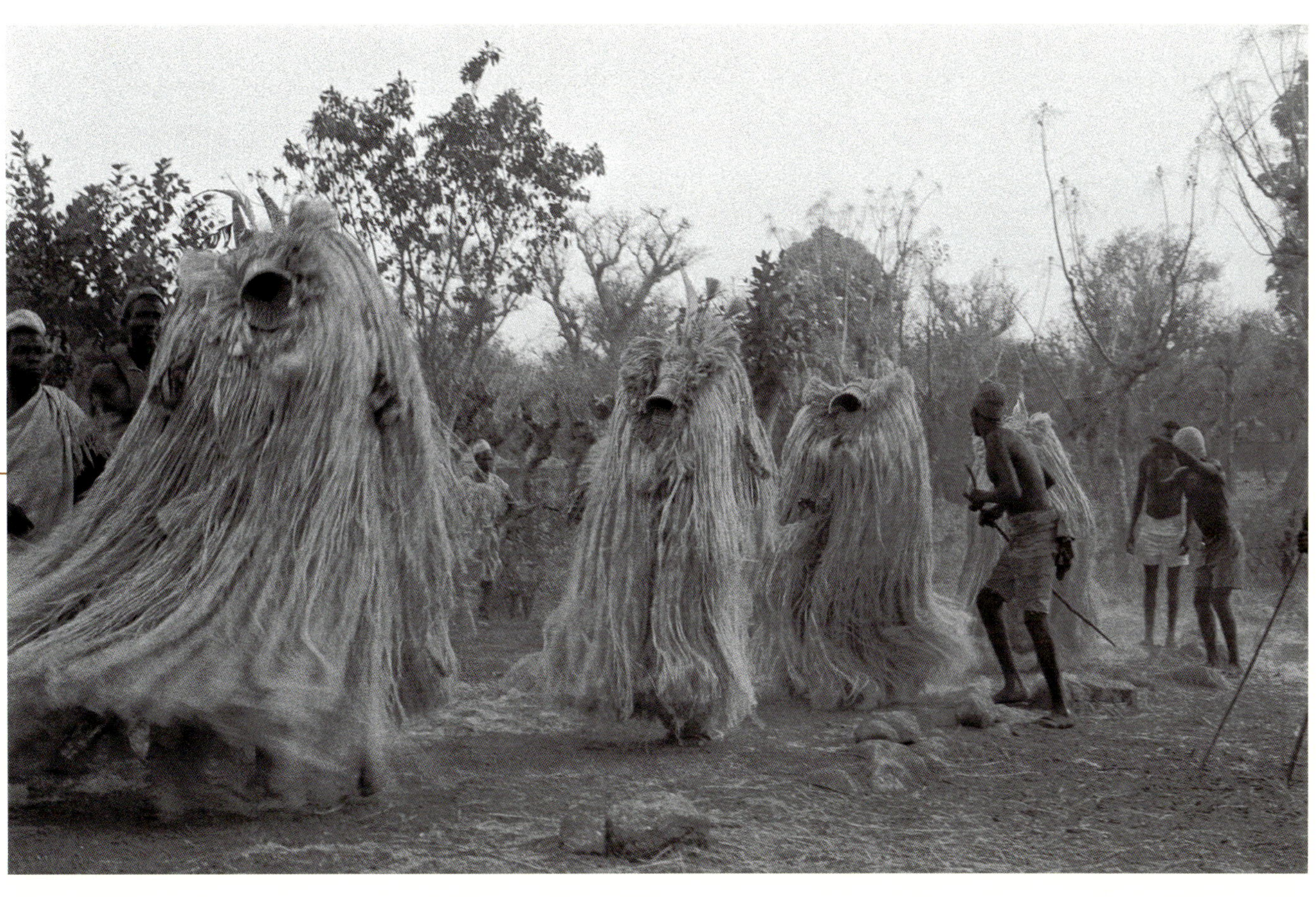

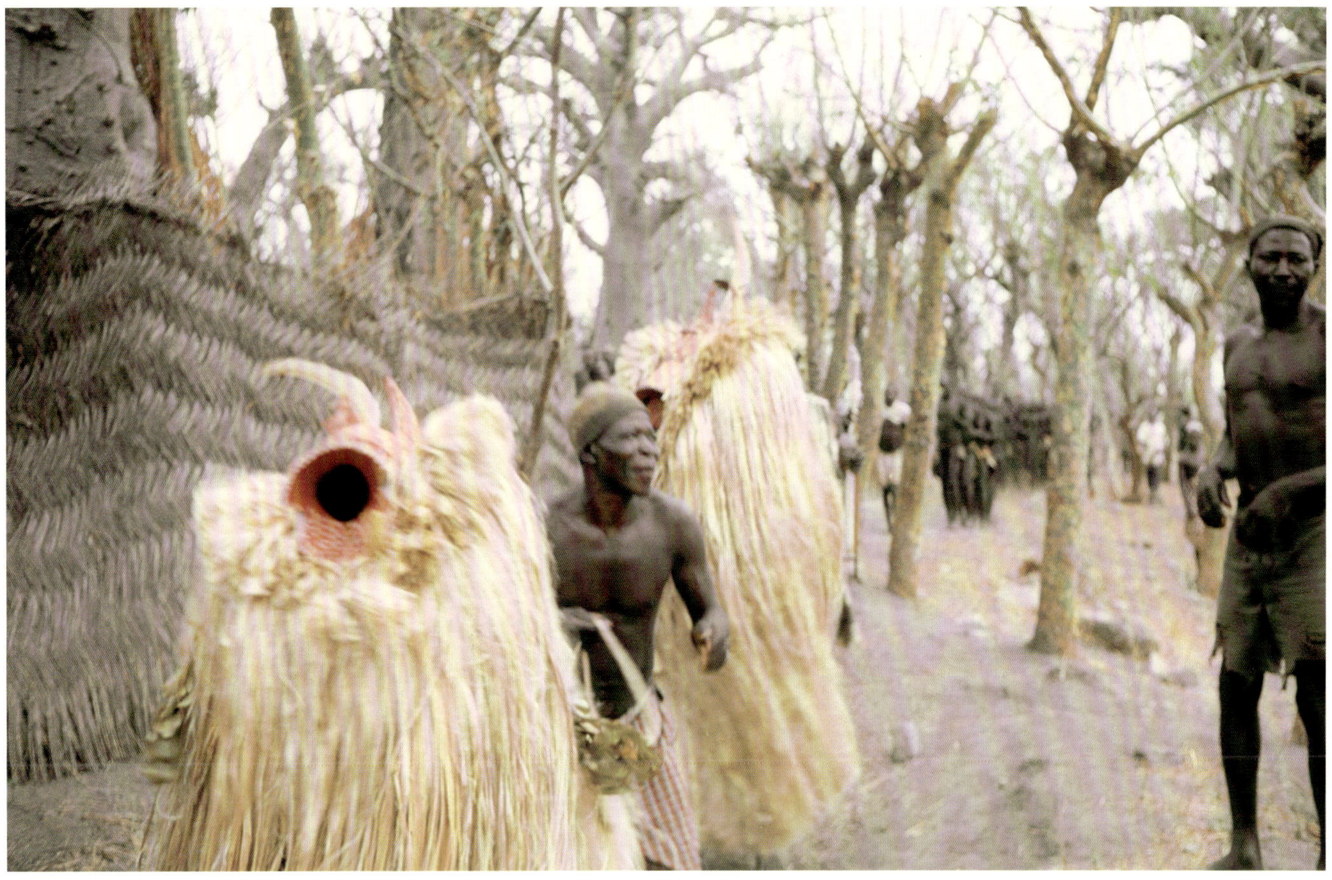

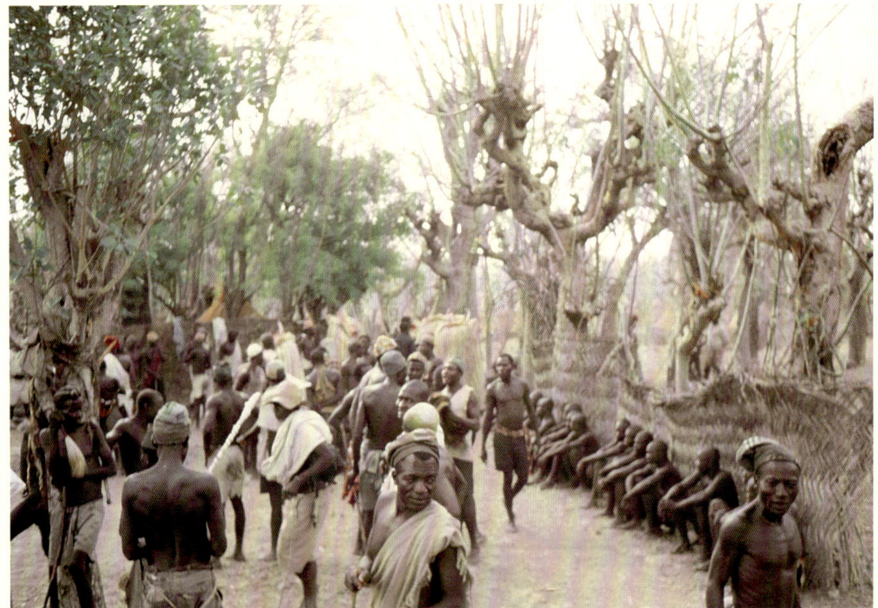

F.3
Initiates, identifiable by their shaven heads, sit in a line during the Zinna performance. Other men mill about, and Vaa-Bong masqueraders are visible in the distance.
PHOTOGRAPH BY ARNOLD RUBIN, ZINNA, APRIL 1970, RUBIN ARCHIVE, FOWLER MUSEUM AT UCLA, SLIDE NO. A1.10.19.3.

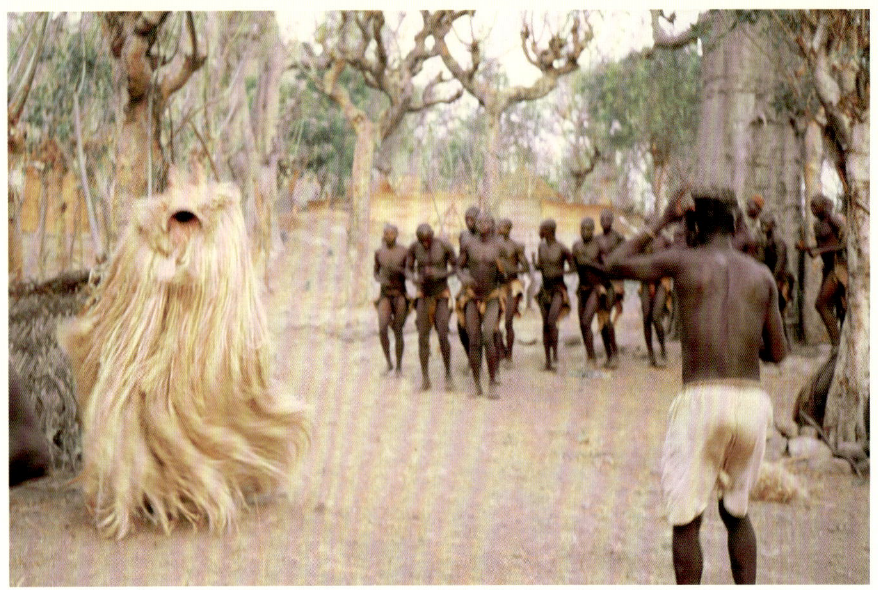

F.4
The male initiates, wearing their characteristic goatskin wraps, stand up and begin to dance behind the masqueraders.
PHOTOGRAPH BY ARNOLD RUBIN, ZINNA, APRIL 1970, RUBIN ARCHIVE, FOWLER MUSEUM AT UCLA, SLIDE NO. A1.10.19.6.

Rubin emphasizes strong connections between male activities and Vaa-Bong masquerades. In his fieldnotes, he links Vaa-Bong performances to agricultural cycles as well as initiation and other male-oriented events including funerary ceremonies, armed conflict, beer making, and the act of men drinking beer together at performances to forge new relationships (fieldnotes, October 10, 1965, 134; October 11, 1965, 136; October 14, 1965, 152; February 16, 1971, 467, 469; see also Rubin 1985, 98–99). He also focuses on the all-male audience in his footage of the Zinna performance. His documentation from Pantisawa shows only men in attendance as well. In certain situations, Vaa-Bong performances may thus have been restricted to men. Rubin's images and writings reinforce the idea that women did not see the masks during the Zinna or Pantisawa events (1985, 98). Yet, elsewhere in his notes Rubin suggests that women may have on occasion seen the masks in certain circumstances (see below).[15]

According to Rubin's notes, young male initiates in the Zinna masquerade audience became "*bona fide* members of [the] community" when they emerged from an initiation (April 21, 1970, 306). Classes of male initiates sometimes chose to commission a single Vaa-Bong mask or a set of masks for themselves. The purpose of the initiation process, however, was not the acquisition of masks. Rather, initiates in each class learned how to work together and persevere in the face of difficulty. Rubin explains that: "Initiates must maintain stoicism [even while] older groups try to break their calm" (April 21, 1970, 306). The reserved demeanor, goatskin wraps, and shaven heads witnessed in a line of seated men at the April 1970 performance appear to have identified these men as initiates and differentiated them from other men in the crowd. At the beginning of Rubin's film footage, the initiate class sits in a line, demurely observing the masks and other actions around them (fig. F.3). Only toward the end of

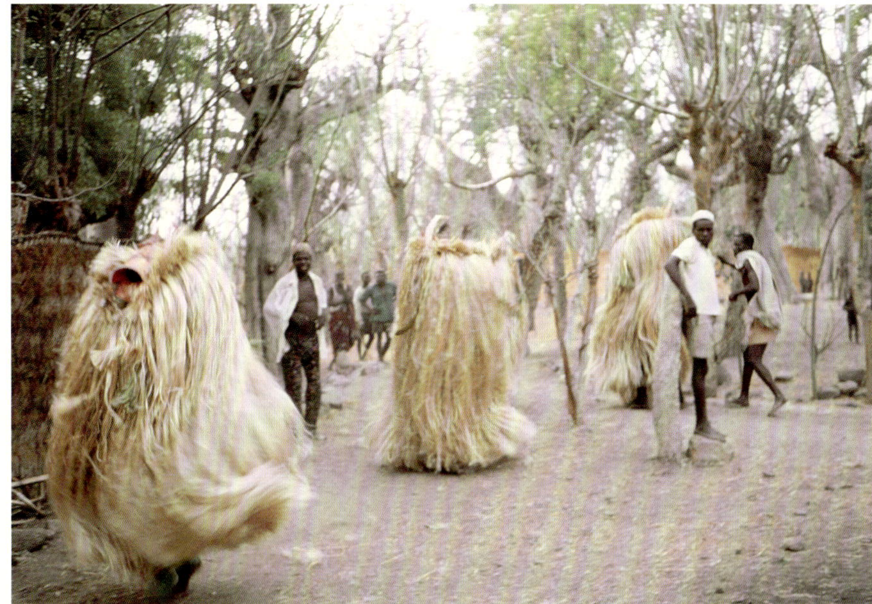

F.5
Masqueraders' hibiscus-fiber full-body coverings shimmer in response to the movements of the performers as they dance.
PHOTOGRAPH BY ARNOLD RUBIN, ZINNA, APRIL 1970, RUBIN ARCHIVE, FOWLER MUSEUM AT UCLA, SLIDE NO. A1.10.18.12.

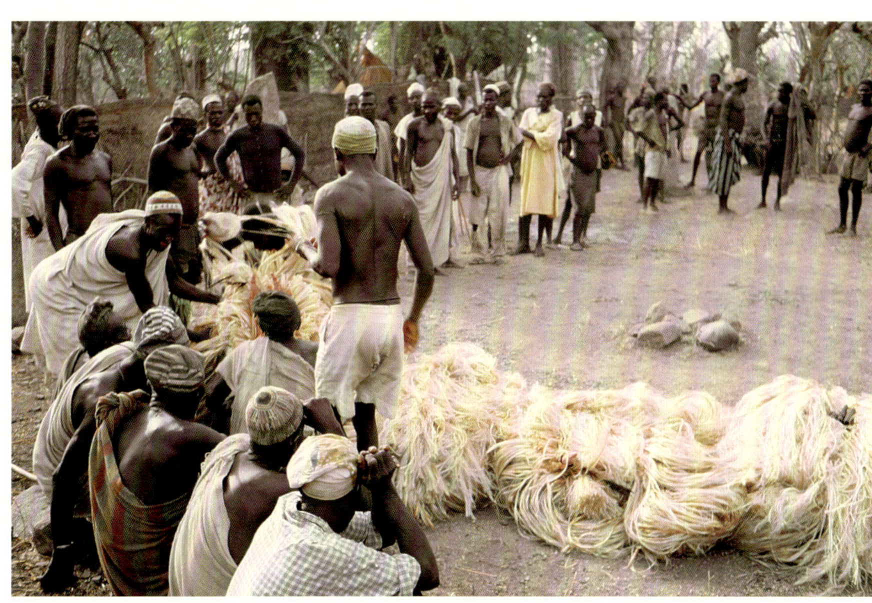

F.6
At one point during the initiation, Vaa-Bong headpieces and fiber coverings rest on the ground before a group of seated men.
PHOTOGRAPH BY ARNOLD RUBIN, ZINNA, APRIL 1970, RUBIN ARCHIVE, FOWLER MUSEUM AT UCLA, SLIDE NO. A1.10.19.5.

the edited footage do the initiates stand and start to dance with the rest of the crowd (fig. F.4).

Rubin portrays an initiation at Zinna that seems to have created distinctions between the new initiates and other men in the crowd, while at the same time having the effect of bringing together members of the new and older initiate classes to foster close cooperation among men in all age groups.[16] Men presumably not part of the initiate class play flutes, spin cotton on bobbins, dance, and otherwise mingle with each other before, during, and after the masquerade dances that Rubin filmed. Thus, the gathering of men, masqueraders, and initiates contributed to the overall experience, one not solely defined by the Vaa-Bong masquerade.

While in the field, Rubin frequently inquired about the inspiration for the masks and more specifically the bovine form of the headpieces. He notes that Vaa-Bong masks represent spirits (October 11, 1965, 136; October 17, 1965, 203) or animals

including buffalos (April 4, 1970, 250; April 8, 1970, 269; April 12, 1970, 279). One person in the Mumuye town of La'ama told Rubin that the spirit assumes the form of a "cow" in a Vaa-Bong mask because "the god [that] created cow is the same as the one [that] created the spirit" (October 11, 1965, 136). After he left the field, Rubin concluded that some Vaa-Bong masks "attained considerable spiritual power" in Mumuye communities (1985, 98) and were considered representations of "male spirits" (1985, 99).

In the course of filming, Rubin paid close attention to the ways in which Vaa-Bong masqueraders entered and moved throughout the performance space. The first masquerader who appears in his Zinna footage enters an already busy outdoor performance arena from behind a straw-mat enclosure. As the performer steps out of the enclosure and into the open space, he quickly adjusts the mask he wears. He then begins to dance, and other Vaa-Bong masqueraders follow him through the enclosure door. The masqueraders position the wooden

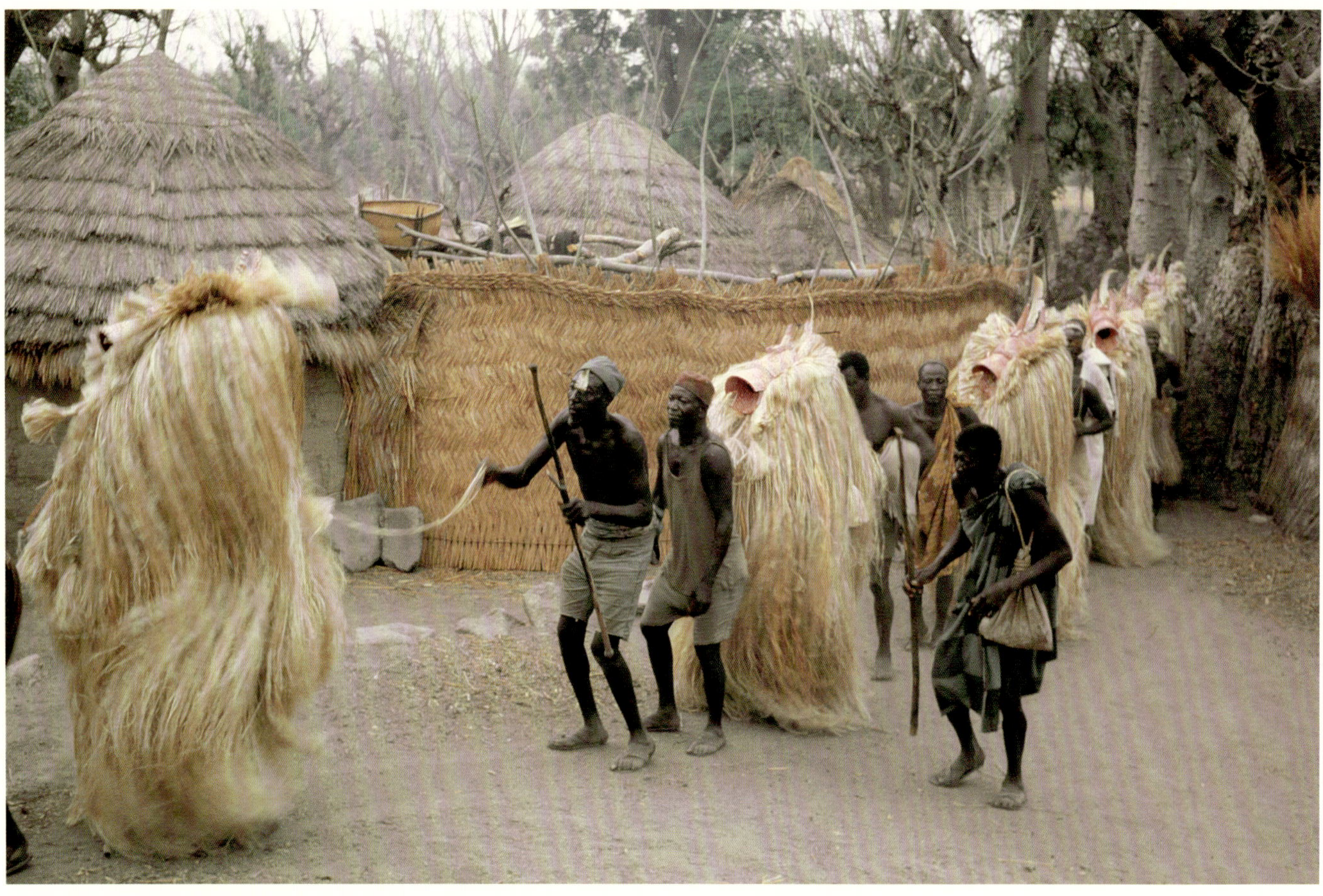

F.7

Performers and men interact with each other during the Vaa-Bong masquerade at Zinna. Rubin notes that the color image was taken on the second day of the performance.

PHOTOGRAPH BY ARNOLD RUBIN, ZINNA, APRIL 1970, RUBIN ARCHIVE, FOWLER MUSEUM AT UCLA, NEG. NO. 2674 (BLACK AND WHITE); SLIDE NO. A1.10.19.1.

headpieces on their heads at a diagonal, presumably so they can better see through the wide-open mouths of the masks. At different moments during the event, masked performers run singly or collectively through the crowd, dance with short steps from side to side, or twirl in full circles as Rubin filmed. Their body-length fiber coverings shake and undulate, accentuating their staccato movements (fig. F.5).

With his lens, Rubin draws attention to the ease with which performers put on and remove their masks before the audience. He captures one moment when empty Vaa-Bong masks rest neatly on the ground in front of a row of seated men (fig. F.6). Other men in the performance arena also sit. An older man near the empty masks lifts a large gourd bowl to his mouth, likely to drink some locally brewed beer. A younger man then walks toward one of the masks, picks it up, and seamlessly places it on his head in front of the crowd. He begins to dance, and another man approaches him to disentangle part of the hibiscus-fiber covering bunched at his back. Several other men in the crowd follow the first masquerader's lead. They each select one of the masks on the ground, place it over the head, and dance. Rubin also focuses on a masquerader who removes the headpiece (see fig. 10.33). The performer pauses for a few

seconds and then continues to dance with the headpiece propped on his shoulder. Rubin's camera focused briefly on the performer's face and his headpiece, both clearly visible to the other men in the crowd.

In the footage, we see frequent interactions between masqueraders and men in the Zinna crowd. One masquerader appears to talk to two men standing next to him just as he obscures his face with a hibiscus-fiber covering. Men not wearing masks at times guide masqueraders. They make gestures or touch the performers (fig. F.7). A few other men in the crowd direct the performance with whips they hold in their hands. Rubin's documentation demonstrates how men and masqueraders in Zinna intersected in many ways to stage a dynamic performance.

In his notes Rubin indicates that the dancing at Zinna continued for three days. Due to technological limitations he faced in 1970, Rubin left us less than twenty minutes of edited footage. As a result, we can recapture fully neither the timing and sequence of the event nor the animating sounds that were part of the crowd's experience. Nevertheless, Rubin provides us with rare images of Vaa-Bong masks in motion as well as insight into the artistry of the masqueraders and performance. He presents clips from initiation-related performances in Zinna that contrast significantly with the Vaa-Bong masquerade he documented in the same month in Pantisawa, another Mumuye town. Comparison of Rubin's images and notes from the two April 1970 events highlights the range of individuals and actions that shape the performance of Vaa-Bong masquerades.

A VAA-BONG MASQUERADE AT PANTISAWA:
READING RUBIN'S "A MUMUYE MASK" (1985)
IN LIGHT OF HIS FIELD DOCUMENTATION

In April 1970, around the time he was also in Zinna, Arnold Rubin filmed and photographed a group of four to six Vaa-Bong masqueraders who descended from a rocky outcrop near the Mumuye town of Pantisawa.[17] Their performance continued in and around the town throughout the day until masqueraders and men shattered ceramic vessels outside the town.[18] A masquerader wearing a more angular and distinctly different headpiece joined the group of masqueraders at the rocky outcrop but is not apparent elsewhere in Rubin's filming of the event (see fig. 10.27).[19] The masks and performance at Pantisawa markedly contrast with what Rubin had recorded in the same month at Zinna. His documentation from these two towns and elsewhere in the region underscores the specificity of masks and performances to individual locales and times. It also offers insights into the gendered reception of Vaa-Bong arts and illuminates shifting and complex roles of the men and women producing them.

As noted above, the Vaa-Bong masks that Rubin photographed in Pantisawa and Zinna share formal similarities including a headpiece with long horns on one end balanced by a long snout on the other. The masks and the masquerade performances also differ. The Pantisawa Vaa-Bong headpieces, for example, are distinguished by bright white pigment covering their cylindrical mouths. The masqueraders also wear hibiscus-fiber coverings that are open in front and display the performers' bodies beneath them (fig. F.8 and see fig. 10.32), unlike the coverings in Zinna that largely conceal the performers' bodies (see fig. F.1).

Rubin's access to the Pantisawa and Zinna events also differed. At Pantisawa, he followed performers from a distance as they processed around the town but offered little information about what happened after they entered the town. In contrast, Rubin appears to have filmed the event at Zinna while moving among lively masqueraders and other audience members. Local exigencies likely contributed to variation in these two and other Mumuye Vaa-Bong masquerade performances. Rubin writes little about the local circumstances surrounding the two events. In an effort consistent with art historical interests at the time, he may have sought to use a single example to describe "all" Mumuye arts rather than elaborate upon differences among them.

In his contribution to Herbert Cole's *I Am Not Myself: The Art of African Masquerade* (1985), a study of the art across the continent, Rubin describes Mumuye masquerades in an essay entitled "A Mumuye Mask." He acknowledges that Mumuye masks were identified by different names in different towns, and he asserts that the "Mumuye are a heterogeneous group of people [who create masks that] serve many and varied purposes" (1985, 98–99). Yet, he provides little additional commentary on the local specificity of Mumuye masks,

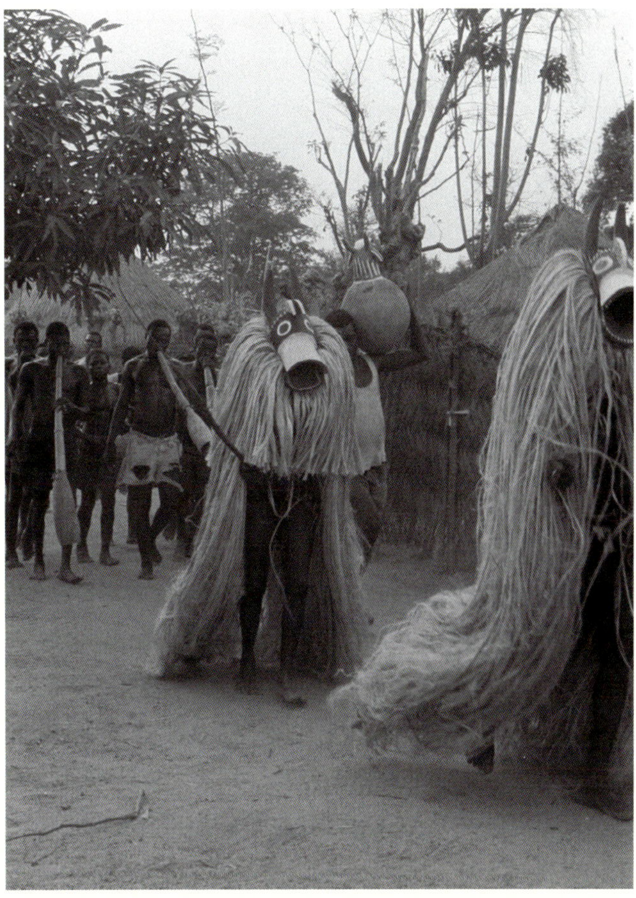

F.8

A masquerader at Pantisawa wears a headpiece with bright white pigment covering its mouth and a hibiscus-fiber body covering that is open in the front.

PHOTOGRAPH BY ARNOLD RUBIN, PANTISAWA, APRIL 1970, RUBIN ARCHIVE, FOWLER MUSEUM AT UCLA, NEG. NO. 2700.

their names, and their performances. He lists occasions when Vaa-Bong masqueraders perform, but he offers scant detail concerning the range of performance possibilities. By describing a single masquerade performance type and presenting it in isolation from the materials in his archive, Rubin offers an essay that suggests that this sole example is representative of characteristics of all Mumuye masquerade performance.

The footage from the two masquerades Rubin witnessed in April 1970, his field photographs, and notes, however, tell a different story and present a more dynamic and varied masquerade form. He indicates the event at Pantisawa took place during an initiation that coincided with a commemorative funerary ceremony, whereas the event at Zinna took place solely in conjunction with a men's initiation (April 21, 1970, 305–7). Rubin's notes do not tell us whether funerary ceremonies similar to that in Pantisawa ever took place at Zinna. He observed other differences as well, for example: "Here [at Pantisawa]: young men drinking, eating meat, vs. Kakulu [Zinna]—only elders" (April 21, 1970, 308). The way people participated in the two events seems to have varied in many ways, yet Rubin did not foreground such differences in the accounts of Mumuye arts he prepared for publication.

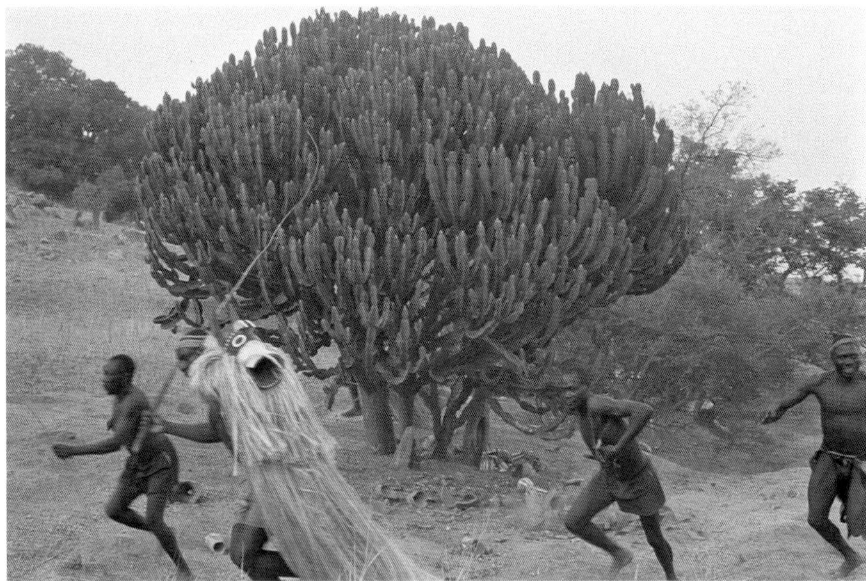

F.9

Men and masqueraders joined in the smashing of pots to commemorate the deceased. Following the pot smashing, the masqueraders removed their masks and ran away from the shattered pots in the company of the other men.

PHOTOGRAPH BY ARNOLD RUBIN, PANTISAWA, APRIL 21, 1970, RUBIN ARCHIVE, FOWLER MUSEUM AT UCLA, NEG. NO. 2715.

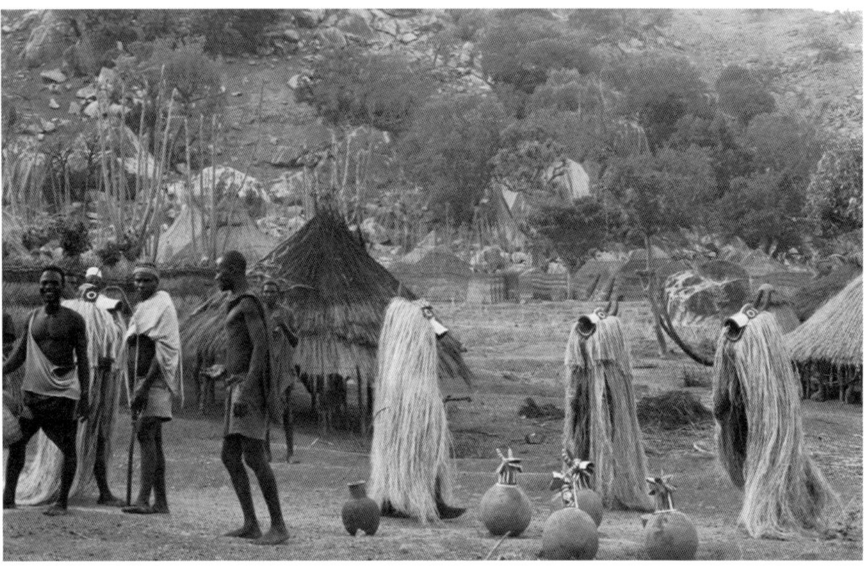

F.10

In Pantisawa in 1970 the relatively rare coincidence of a pot-smashing ceremony with a masquerade performance provided Rubin the opportunity to observe the marked similarities between the forms of the bovine-headed pots and Vaa-Bong headpieces.

PHOTOGRAPH BY ARNOLD RUBIN, PANTISAWA, APRIL 1970, RUBIN ARCHIVE, FOWLER MUSEUM AT UCLA, NEG. NO. 2707.

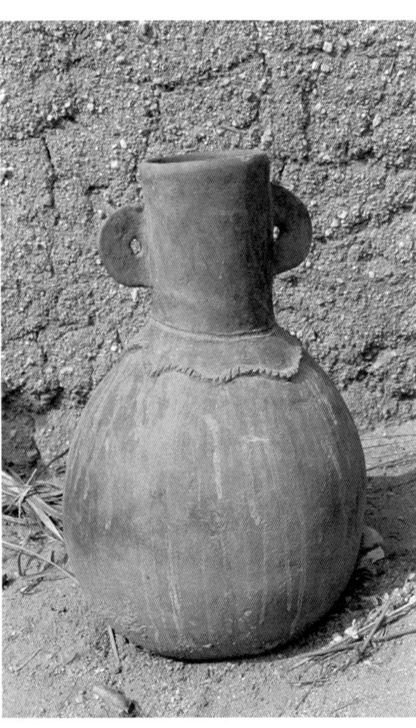

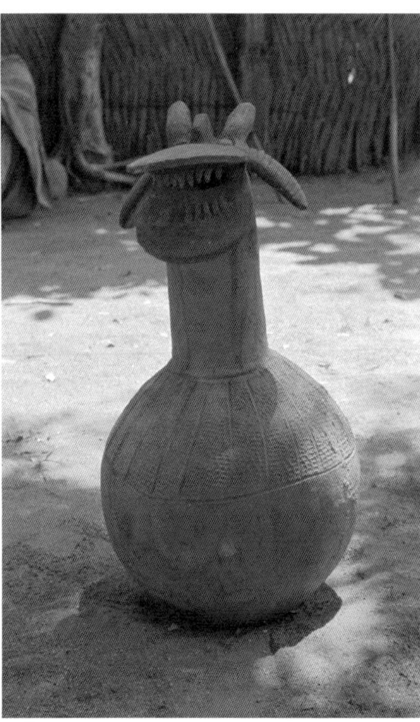

F.11

In contrast to the ceramic bovine heads that topped pots to commemorate deceased men, pots that Rubin referred to as "flap-ear" commemorated deceased women in the community.

PHOTOGRAPH BY ARNOLD RUBIN, PANTISAWA, APRIL 1970, RUBIN ARCHIVE, FOWLER MUSEUM AT UCLA, NEG. NO. 2691

F.12

With respect to the pot illustrated here, Arnold Rubin wrote in his notebook: "These [pots] are made to look like the masks." In the same notebook entry, he wrote that the form "'depends on woman who molds it,'" likely a direct citation from the person he interviewed about the pot. He added that a man would go to a shrine, make a small clay copy of the wooden headpiece, and bring it to the best woman potter in the area as a model. Rubin also noted that the pot belonged to Panti Lapo, the eponymous head of the town of Pantilapo.

PHOTOGRAPH BY ARNOLD RUBIN, PANTISAWA, OCTOBER 19, 1965, RUBIN ARCHIVE, FOWLER MUSEUM AT UCLA, NEG. NO. 1002.

Rubin's essay of 1985 on Mumuye masquerade performances describes an event that he explains "occurs each year (in some places, every two years) when the souls of those who have died during that period are ritually released to the world beyond" (1985, 99). Rubin notes that the ceremony involves breaking pots that are topped with ceramic bovine heads. He explains that the act of shattering the pots "[effected] a final separation of deceased men from the living community" (1985, 99). When the text of the essay is read alongside Rubin's fieldnotes and compared to his film footage, it appears that the account of a single performance type Rubin provided in 1985 is based almost entirely on the one performance Rubin observed at Pantisawa in April 1970. Information he gleaned through interviews in 1965 and 1970 seems to have supplemented his understanding of the event in his focused 1985 essay.

Rubin took the photograph reproduced in his essay of 1985 in Pantisawa in 1970 (see fig. F.8; see Rubin 1985, 99).[20] The correlation between Rubin's essay description and the April 1970 event at Pantisawa also extends to the film record. At the end of the edited film footage from Pantisawa, Rubin includes a series of still images showing masqueraders who remove their headpieces and, in the company of other men, smash ceramic vessels on the ground, just as Rubin describes in the 1985 text.[21] The footage also illustrates that after the masqueraders smash the pots, they run from the site (fig. F.9). Rubin's archive offers images of the pot-smashing ceremony only at Pantisawa, although his notes indicate that such funerary events likely had precedent in the region.[22] He does not specify that pot-smashing events in other Mumuye towns necessarily coincided with masquerade performances.

Rubin had already written many notes about masks and ceramic pots when he encountered the two forms together during the performance of April 1970 at Pantisawa. During an early research trip to the region in 1965, he photographed pots in the Mumuye town of Pantilapo, describing them in some detail and explaining their use in pot-smashing ceremonies. "Everybody who is entitled to see these masks (i.e., sr. men) will have such a pot; [and] on his death, [the] pot [is] broken at a crossroads" (October 19, 1965, 223). Rubin also describes the acquisition of such pots: "After he has seen masks, a man is entitled to have such a pot [i.e., one with a ceramic top similar in form to a wooden mask]; after he has it made, he doesn't do anything with it; it only sits in his compound until he dies. No medicine inside" (October 19, 1965, 223). In 1985, Rubin credits the "deceased man's sister" with the production of the commemorative pot destined for destruction, a statement that seems to correlate directly with his note that "[each of the deceased's] sisters must provide—either make or buy [—] pot w/ [head]" (April 21, 1970, 308). Given that the understanding of Mumuye arts may depend on locally specific contingencies and personalities, Rubin's early notes from different Mumuye towns may or may not directly relate to the pots seen in the April 1970 Pantisawa performance (fig. F.10 and see also figs. F.8, 10.19, 10.22).

While Rubin's essay of 1985 suggests that the commemorative funerary ceremony and masquerade performance happened regularly, his fieldnotes again offer a different view and highlight local specificity. The coincidence of the initiation masquerade and commemorative funerary ceremony that Rubin witnessed in Pantisawa and about which he wrote in 1985 was apparently rare. On October 19, 1965, Rubin wrote that at Pantilapo, a town near Pantisawa, "the breaking of pot (one year after death) indicates end of mourning [and the time when] property [of the deceased can be] claimed by inheritors [and his] wives can remarry" (October 19, 1965, 223). At that time, Rubin referred to musicians who accompanied the person who carried the pot to the place where it was smashed. He did not make specific reference to any masquerade performance that coincided with the pot smashing he related. In his field entry five years later describing the April 1970 event in Pantisawa, Rubin observes: "(pots broken)—*this* year, time coincides [with the masquerade]" (April 21, 1970, 307, emphasis Rubin's; see also April 21, 1970, 310–11). In the same entry Rubin includes a diagram to illustrate a six-year interval between the simultaneous occurrence of the masquerade and pot-smashing ceremony in Pantisawa.

Rubin's essay of 1985 and the film footage from Pantisawa also point to complicated relationships involving gender and Vaa-Bong arts and performances. Men and male masqueraders who gathered outside Pantisawa in April 1970 to break ceramic vessels repeated what Rubin shows women and children doing earlier in his edited footage of that event. In his 1985 description of a Mumuye masquerade, Rubin writes (1985, 99) that "women are barred from [the men's pot-smashing event], yet earlier in the day have conducted an analogous ritual, using a different [plainer] sort of ceramic vessel, for the female dead" (fig. F.11). Some of the men's pots were topped with ceramic bovine heads that resembled Vaa-Bong headpieces worn by male performers.[23] While masqueraders did accompany the men who shattered pots on the ground in Pantisawa, they did not accompany women and children when they did so. Breaking pots in Pantisawa may have reflected attempts to negotiate relationships between the living and the dead. Funerary pot smashing and Rubin's footage of it also highlight possibilities for considering the roles of men and women in the viewing and making of Vaa-Bong arts.

At Pantisawa, production and reception of Vaa-Bong masks and pots reinforce and at times defy divisions between men and women. In Mumuye towns, as in many other communities across Central Nigeria, women, not men, have typically been identified as ceramic specialists. Women thus likely had the expertise necessary to make the pots that men shattered in funerary contexts, including those topped with ceramic bovine heads. According to Rubin's notes from the Mumuye town of Pantilapo (fig. F.12), the "configuration [of the ceramic pot that echoes a local wooden mask form]…'depends on woman who molds it'" (October 19, 1965, 225).[24] Women at times also decorated cermaic bovine-headed pots. Rubin's notes dated April 21,

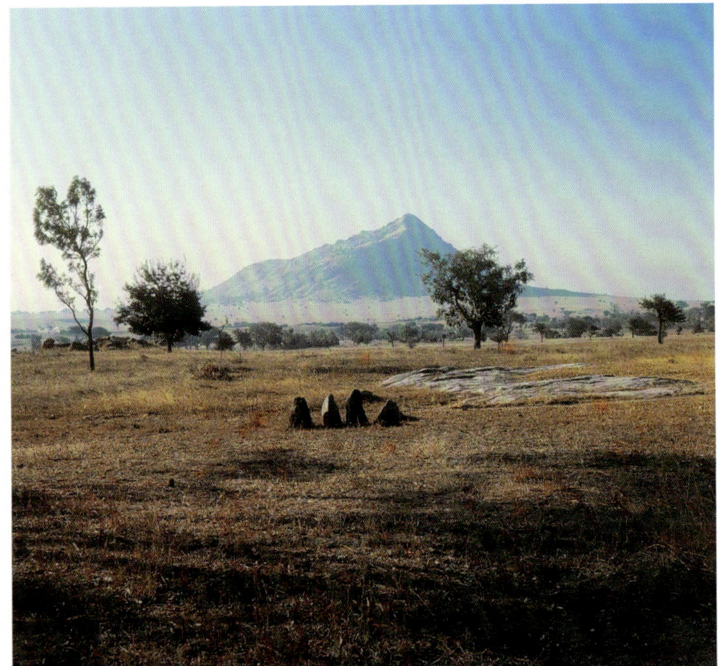

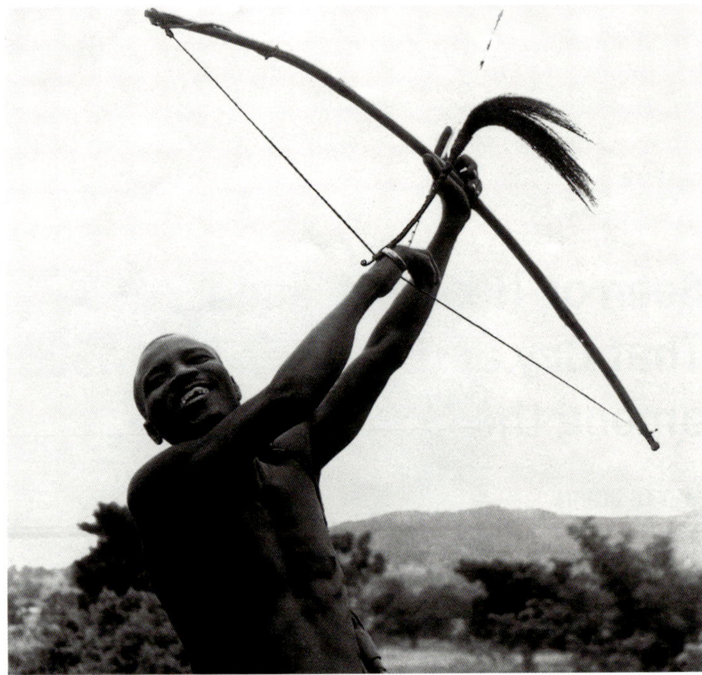

11.2

Grassy plains and four standing stones appear in the foreground of this Mumuye landscape with a mountain looming in the blue horizon. This view was taken from the Zing village area looking toward the southeast.

© PHOTOGRAPH BY METTE BOVIN, AUGUST 1968.

11.3

The Mumuye have always been hunters as well as agriculturalists. This hunter demonstrates his prowess with bow and arrow. Note that he uses a bow puller on his right hand.

© PHOTOGRAPH BY METTE BOVIN, BETWEEN ZING AND JALINGO, LANKAVIRI VALLEY, AUGUST 16, 1964.

LIVELIHOOD: SEASONS AND THE GENDERING OF TASKS

Three general points about Mumuye livelihood are particularly significant for understanding their religious life. The first is that Mumuye were both hunter-gatherers and farmers. The second is that men's and women's work were largely distinct, especially in relation to hunting and gathering. Mumuye men hunted; women gathered roots, fruits, bark, and other natural products. The third, and perhaps most important point, is that the Mumuye year was divided into a rainy season (around May to October) and a dry season (November to April). This distinction, important everywhere in West Africa, was particularly fundamental to the Mumuye, since there were aspects of their social organization that changed with the seasons.

It was during dry season, especially in its final months, that Mumuye men hunted intensively (fig. 11.3). Hunting was carried out collectively, and hunters lived in special huts in the bush. With their weapons (spears, clubs, bows and poisonous arrows, traps, and bird mask decoys), they pursued numerous wild species: from large mammals and birds to monitor lizards and a variety of snakes. The division of labor between men and women was strict. Hunting was entirely men's work, as was making fire, blacksmithing, wood carving (including statues and masks), plaiting, spinning and weaving cotton cloth, leatherwork, and making amulets. Men and boys herded goats and cows, and only they could slaughter animals. Though not all Mumuye families owned cattle, most of them possessed between ten and a hundred goats and also kept chickens (fig.11.4).[1]

Women's lives revolved around keeping the home, gathering firewood and wild foods, carrying water, cooking food, and looking after children. Women and girls also maintained small vegetable plots near their houses. It was the women who made pottery, turned gourds into calabash household utensils, and threaded beads. Most pottery was made in the dry season (fig. 11.5). The range of pottery wares was extensive, and in 1964 I collected nine different types of pots. Although they sought wild resources all year round, it was also in dry season that women gathered most intensively, carrying home wild honey, berries, firewood, fruits, leaves, roots, bark, and grass in huge baskets.

Mumuye, men and women alike, were industrious farmers, although some crops were associated with one sex rather than the other (fig. 11.6). Yam and sorghum were the most important staple foods. Yam planting could begin only after a ceremony held in early September at which the leader of a patriclan symbolically broke the soil using a ritual hoe; this action allowed other clan members to begin work on their fields. At

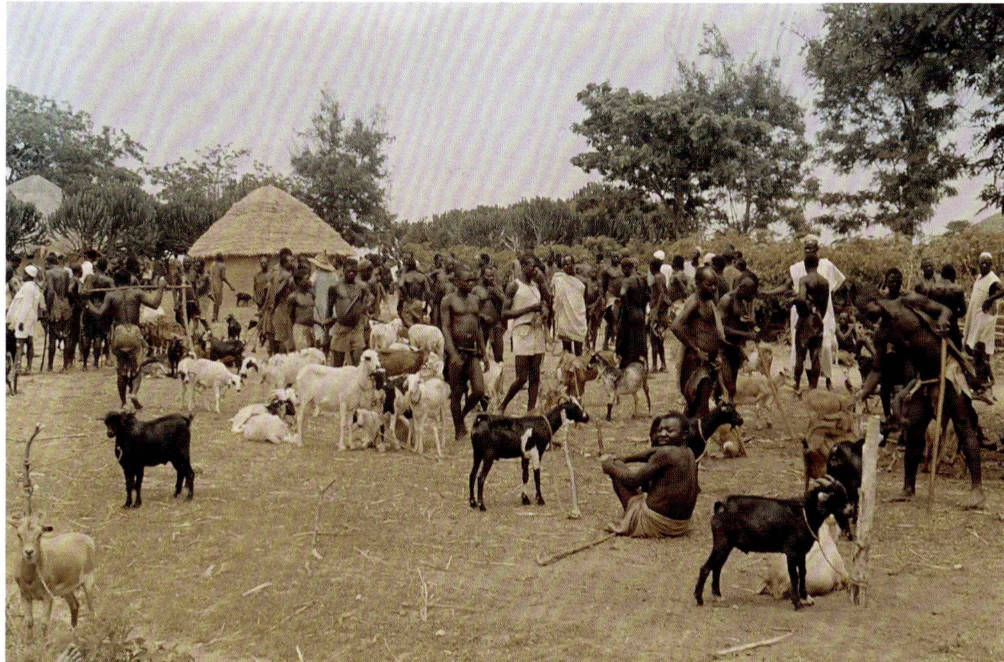

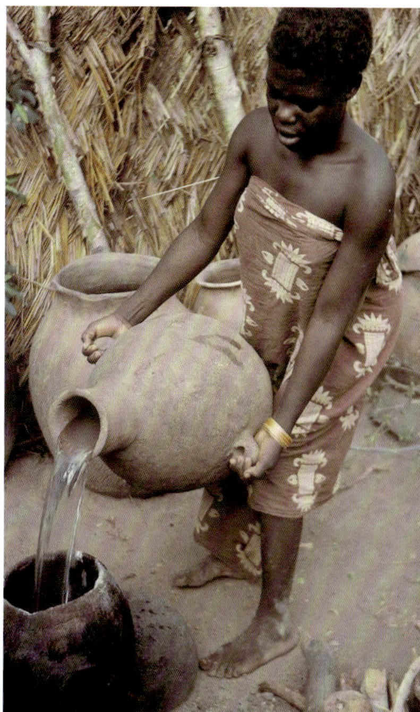

the same time, fields were distributed at a meeting attended by all male household heads. Each Mumuye family cultivated one or several fields in the plain, as well as smaller, narrow fields on the hillsides. On average, families had 1.5 to 2 hectares under cultivation. Most crops were sown in April and harvested in October. During wet season, the growing crops required repeated weeding, when women and men farmed together in fields, often in working parties consisting of fifteen to thirty people. Only women brewed the millet and sorghum beers (*sa*), which were important not just for work parties but for daily life more generally and particularly for any and all rituals. Both men and women were traders, selling agricultural and handicraft products at local weekly markets.

COSMOLOGY AND POWERS

The beliefs I shall describe were still important when I began my research in 1964. Islamization was underway, however, and not only the Sarkin Zinna but also his first minister and judge (known by Hausa titles as the Wazirin Zinna and Alkalin Zinna) were Muslims. Christian missions were also active, run by Roman Catholics as well as a variety of Protestant sects (including Baptists).

When I asked questions about cosmology, Mumuye in Zing told me about Kpanti La, who created the sun (*kpanti* meaning "master"; *la* meaning "sun") and everything else in the world. Shele (the moon) was said to be his wife, and the stars were their children. This account is common to much of the Middle Benue. The name Kpanti La was spoken in prayers and translated for me as "the Almighty, invisible Creator," though this gloss probably owed much to Islamic and Christian understandings. Informants from groups that were hostile to one another nonetheless shared this same word for God. As a Yoro informant confirmed: "We Mumuye believe that the father of the sun (*la*), made earth, sky, and water; but how he did this, no one can explain. We believe that the father of the sun created all people, white, yellow, and black through one man and one woman, but Mumuye are the people first to settle in Yoro."

My informants recalled how power circulated in Zing in precolonial times. The senior elder of one of the clans would wield preponderant influence for three years, after which the elder of another clan came to power. This system of rotation was designed to ensure equality between clans by preventing any of them monopolizing

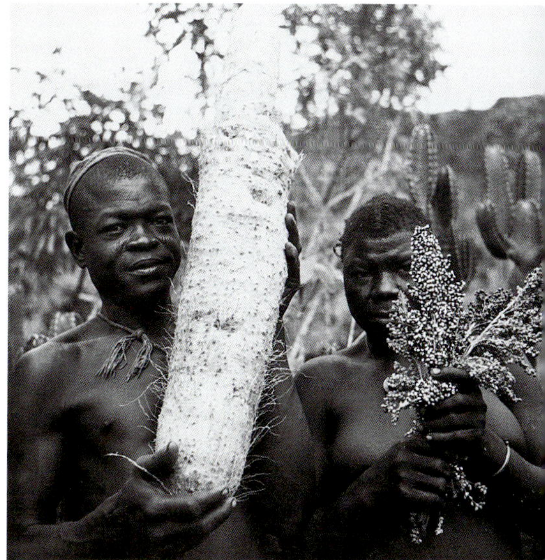

11.4
Goats and other animals are offered for sale in the marketplace at Pantisawa village. Goats are considered to be men's animals.
PHOTOGRAPH BY LUIS DE SANDE, CIRCA 1959.

11.5
Zeshonye, a young Mumuye woman, pours water from one ceramic pot into another. It is beer-brewing time, and sorghum or millet beer (*sa*) is extremely important as it is served at all social occasions.
© PHOTOGRAPH BY METTE BOVIN, DIDANKO VILLAGE, ZING, AUGUST 11, 1965.

11.6
As this married Mumuye couple demonstrates, the yam (left) is considered male, while reddish sorghum is female.
© PHOTOGRAPH BY METTE BOVIN, PANTISAWA MARKET, AUGUST 30, 1964.

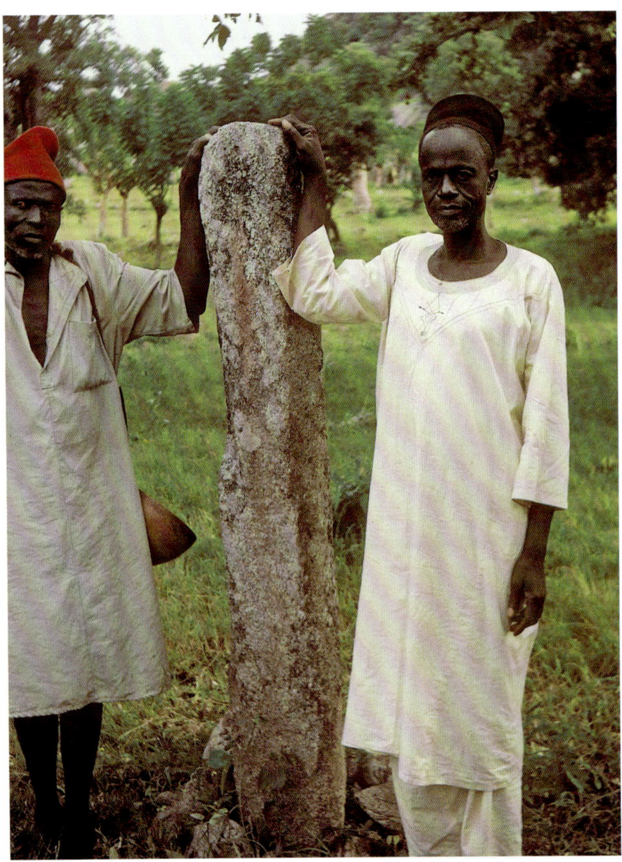

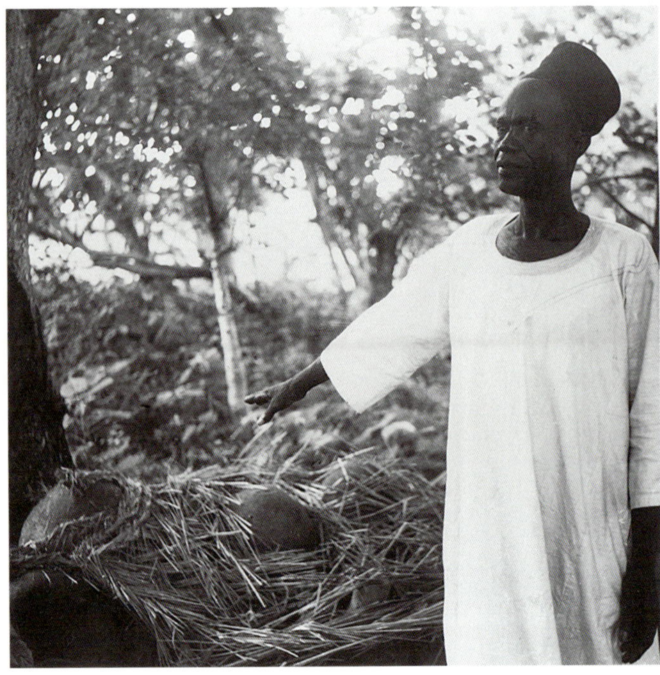

11.7

This stone in the sacred forest of Zing marks the spot where the first ancestor, Shonshina, initially appeared. The monument is thought to be the exact height of Shonshina himself, and the trace of red that runs down the middle of it is probably residue from past sacrifice. To the right of the stone stands Baba Daloba, who was the head of the Shonboro, or senior men's council. He was also the custodian of Shonshina's stone, grave, and sacred drum, as well as of the hunting shrine (all of which were located within meters of each other) within the sacred forest. Jorre Koko, a Shonboro member, stands at the left.

© PHOTOGRAPH BY METTE BOVIN, JULY 21, 1964.

11.8

Baba Daloba (see fig. 11.7) gestures toward the grave of Shonshina, the first ancestor. He reported that the head of Shonshina was placed in a ceramic pot, which had then been covered by broken ceramic fragments and *zanna* mats. Once a year the heads of those who have been buried in this fashion are removed from their pots and an important ritual is performed.

© PHOTOGRAPH BY METTE BOVIN, JULY 21, 1964.

leadership and gaining the opportunity to propel their society toward becoming a chiefdom or kingdom. On the face of it, Zing was a decentralized community.

Nonetheless, there were tendencies toward the centralization of ritual powers outside Zing. In many eyes, the two highest-ranking holders of power were the "Master of Rain" at Yoro and the "Master of Thunder" at Dangong (see below). Yet even these two masters were hardly rulers, for like other Mumuye, they dared not travel outside their villages for fear of murder and decapitation. Mumuye clans once fought one another, taking trophy heads, and the "Masters" had no immunity from these hostilities.

The distinction between seasons complicated questions of power. Rain masters performed rain rituals in wet season, whereas fire masters performed fire and hunting rituals during the dry season. They presided over categories of people of "peace" and "war," as well as mediating between human beings and Kpanti La in their appointed season. Many particular religious functions were carried out by *shon-boro* (elders), a term that included not just the oldest men of each family, lineage, and clan but also their ancestors. Elders held power over women as well as junior men, and they performed sacrifices of chickens, goats, and beer to the spirits of the dead (*sule*), and to the cults (*vaa*).

THE SACRED FOREST OF ZING

Zing people spoke of Yoro as their most powerful ritual center. Closer by, however, they recognized a local sacred forest where their clan ancestor Shonshina (*shon-shina* meaning "man-first") appeared out "of the earth" from Yoro. There I saw the *ta-long*, a stone exactly the height of Shonshina, which stood in the forest to mark the spot where he emerged, and probably still stands there (fig. 11.7). Near Shonshina's stone was his grave (fig. 11.8), and it was said that his skull was kept there in a pot, in accordance with secondary burial customs still practised by Mumuye in the 1960s. The elders responsible for taking care of Shonshina's standing stone and grave gathered regularly in the forest to hold meetings and perform rituals.

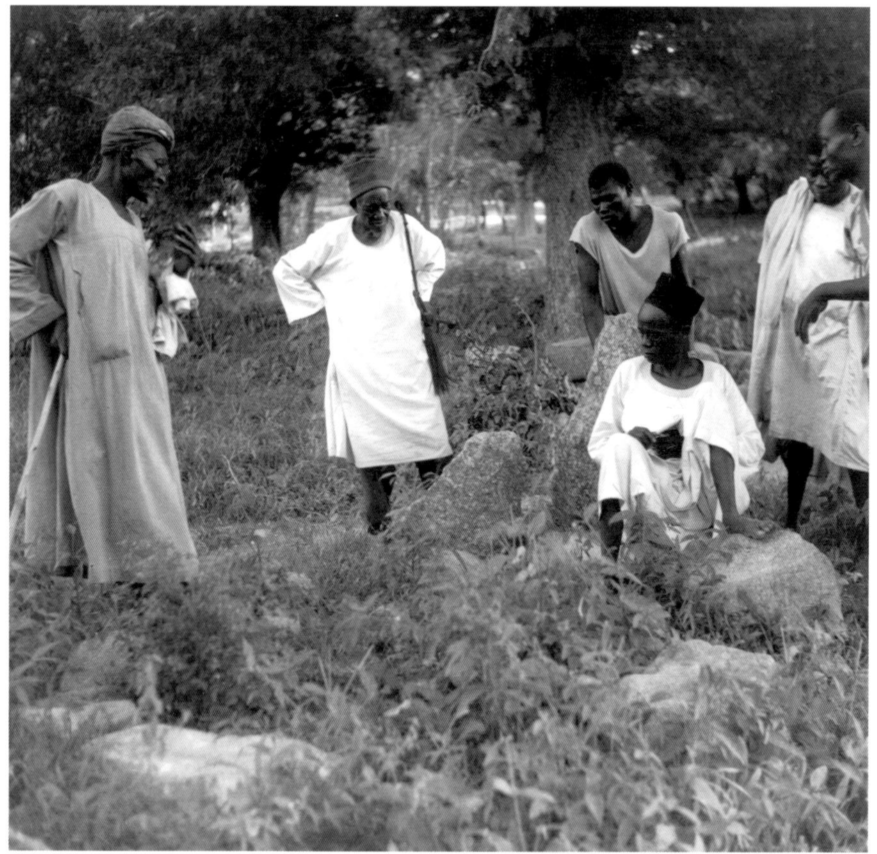

11.9
This circle of old grinding stones served as seating for the Shonboro, or council of senior men, when they met to discuss current issues, to honor their founding ancestor, Shonshina, and to plan for the future of Zing. As the head of the council, Baba Daloba (see figs. 11.7, 11.8) sits on the one stone that has another behind it to serve as a backrest.

© PHOTOGRAPH BY METTE BOVIN, SACRED FOREST OF ZING, AUGUST 21, 1964.

Near his standing stone, a drum belonging to Shonshina was kept in a hut most people were forbidden to enter. The drum's skin was said to have been made of the pelt of a dog-like creature (perhaps a hyena) and extraordinary powers were attributed to it. The senior elder during my sojourn, Daloba (who was addressed by the honorific "Baba," or "father") recalled that when he was nine years old, around the end of the First World War, a British soldier had shot at the drum, but his bullet did it no harm. Then the British soldier tried to set fire to it, but the drum would not burn. "We honor Shonshina's drum, with its wild animal drum skin, like a god," Baba Daloba told me, "because the first man Shonshina prepared it and played it in November, once a year." The drum was still beaten only once a year, during the harvest festival held in November, unless there was some untoward event, such as the death of an important man. Near Shonshina's drum hut was the hunting shrine, discussed below, and by Shonshina's standing stone and the drum hut was a circle of eight old grinding stones, used as seats when the most important elders of Zing met. As he was the senior elder, Baba Daloba sat on two stones, one of which provided him with back rest (fig. 11.9) The seven other elders each occupied one of the remaining flat stones in the circle.

The path through the sacred forest was lined by standing stones called *long-yu* (stone-head), ranging in height between 0.5 and 2.5 meters, of which most were around a meter. Some of the stones were aligned in a row, others apparently unordered. Mumuye claimed no knowledge of how long they had been there. According to my three elderly Zing informants (of whom Baba Daloba was leader), these "headstones" were erected as memorials to decapitated enemies from the Yakoko clan (south of Zing) whose heads were hidden in clay pots in Zing. Unbidden, a pair of men demonstrated how decapitation was carried out: a Yakoko enemy would be thrown to the ground, and the strongest Zing man would hold him with his left hand while cutting his throat with a knife held in the right. Only men took skulls, and they took only the skulls of other men, women's skulls being considered useless. During my fieldwork, people from Zing and Yakoko still feared one another, and no man ever went alone through the other's territory.

village of Kassa. It was the Shon Taka who gave the people of Yoro permission to hunt in the bush, which could be burned only after his own fires had been lit.

Which of the two was the most important was an unresolvable conundrum. Some Mumuye informants claimed that the "Master of Rain" was superior to the "Master of the Bow" because the greatest Rain Master lived on top of the mountain at Yoro, the ritual center of the Mumuye world. Other Mumuye informants retorted that the "Master of Rain" might be the highest ceremonial leader, but he was "a Mumuye man" who, like other Mumuye men, had to undergo the initiation rites of the grades of the various *vaa* societies. On this reasoning, the "Master of Rain," and the many rainmakers (*shon mee*) under him, were subordinate to the "Master of the Bow," the supreme leader of Mumuye society. In practice, each appears to have dominated but only in his own season when his particular powers over life and death were most crucial. So it is necessary to look at each of them in turn. I begin in Zing.

KPANTI MEE "MASTER OF RAIN" AND FERTILITY	KPANTI TAKA "MASTER OF THE BOW" HUNTING AND WARFARE
Rule of succession: the Kpanti Mee himself chooses his successor from among his sons, one of whom is trained and remains separated from the rest of society all his life, The choice is confirmed by a council of the *shon mee*, rainmakers of Mumuye country.	Rule of succession: the Kpanti Taka is chosen from the male members of his patrilineage. The choice will be confirmed by a council of *shon-boro* (elders).
Function of the office: of a purely religious-ceremonial character. No executive political power. The Kpanti Mee is responsible for the complicated rain ceremonies that only rainmakers can perform.	Function of the office: of a political and religious character. The leader in time of war. Also responsible for the *vaa* initiation ceremonies of all young men among Mumuye. Leader during the dry season of the fire ceremony and hunting ceremony.

THE NEW YEAR, WAR, AND THE HUNTING CEREMONY

The fire and hunting ceremony called Belle marked the beginning of the new year for the Mumuye in Zing as elsewhere. It took place every year in mid-January or February. *Shon taka* (the elder of the bow) was the religious leader during that period. He was also the master of fire and hunting, and he controlled smallpox (which he could use to kill people). *Shon taka* decided when the new first fire was to be lit by his son or brother's son. By tradition, *shon taka*'s son started out from Yoro moving to the neighboring village seven days later, then to the next village seven days after that and so on.

By 1964, the Mumuye of Zing no longer waited for a sign from the center at Yoro but instigated their own festival from the hamlet of Zang, where a man climbed the hill in Kakulu and announced to the people that they should make porridge for their dogs and meet him outside. All the men would ready themselves for the signal sounded by a man from Yoro living in Kakulu who blew on the horn, also called *belle*. At this the men would embark on a hunt that lasted four days until the hillsides were burned on the fifth day. During this firing, the women and girls "cried" in memory of their deceased relatives, whether they had died recently or in the distant past. Meals were prepared in every house, and the younger boys and girls ate and drank together in groups. Everyone dressed up in the evening, and elders and young men alike armed themselves with bows and arrows in order to visit their family's skull shrine, where they paid their respects to the bravery of their late grandparents and asked for their blessings. The men responsible prayed for the dead to bless the new year, and all those present offered greetings by touching the shrine with their left hand. Moving to another place away from the skull shrine, they grouped themselves into age-grades, from young boys to elderly men. The women also grouped themselves by age, and as the men passed by them in procession, they praised their sons, brothers, and lovers.

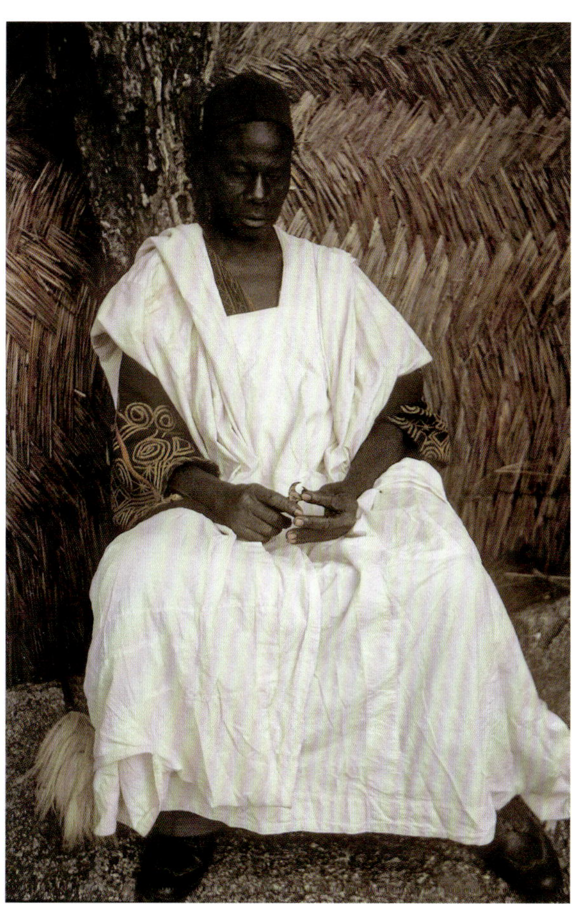

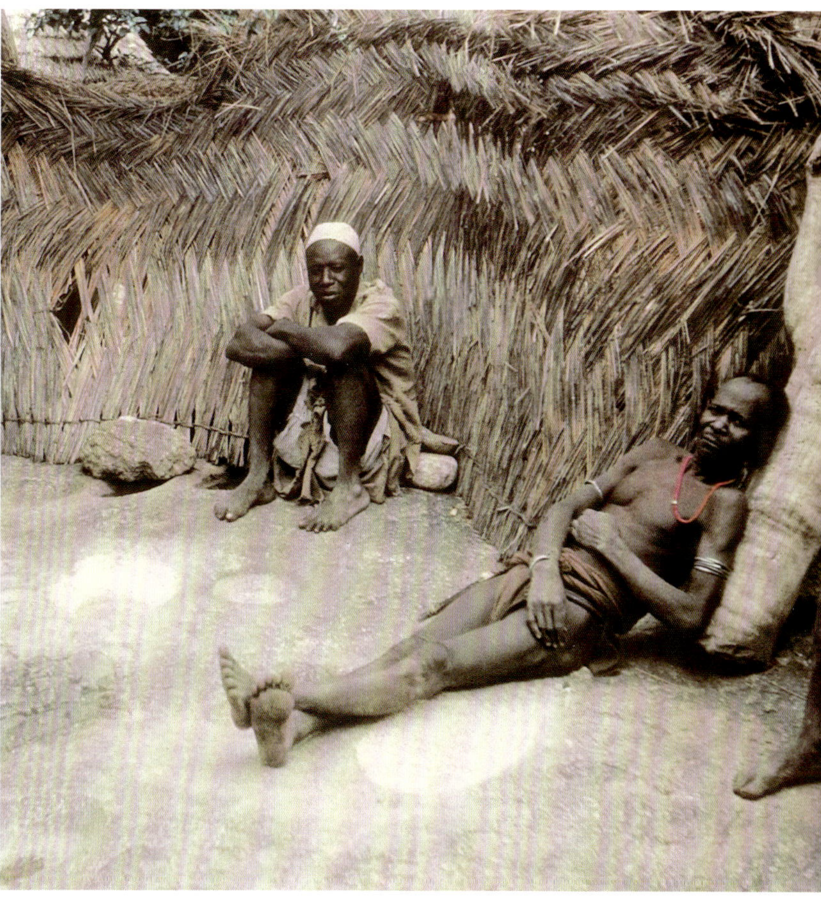

THE RAIN CEREMONY AND THE CHIEF OF THUNDER

As the parched dry season came near its end, people waited eagerly for rain to fall. *Shon taka*'s power waned, and people transferred their attention to *shon mee*, the rainmaker. Should a local *shon mee* be unable to make rain, a meeting must be held; goats, chicken, guinea corn, and so forth collected; and an envoy sent to the greatest Master of Rain, the Kpanti Mee of Yoro on his celebrated mountain. Because the rains had been good, by 1964 two years had passed since Mumuye living in Zing or Yakoko had sent anyone to Yoro.

The Kpanti Mee of Yoro was the original and foremost "Master of Rain" in Mumuyeland; second in rank to him was Kpanti Giriri, the "Master of Thunder"' of Kopo Dangong (Dangong Mountain), near Dingding and Dong, in the high mountains far east of Monkin village. I visited Matakon (figs. 11.13, 11.14), the incumbent Kpanti Giriri, during wet season in August 1964, when I climbed the mountain from the place where we left our horses. From the summit of Kopo Dangong, where Kpanti Giriri lived, was a view to two very characteristically contoured, blue mountains: one was the "male mountain" and the other the "female mountain" (fig. 11.15). Because it rained heavily on these mountains, the lesser rainmakers of the area often consulted the Master of Thunder, bringing him goats, chicken and numerous other gifts. His regalia consisted of iron objects and stones kept in his rain hut. The rain irons represented the flash of lightning in the sky, iron zigzags like the sudden movements of a snake that presage the crash of thunder (figs. 11.16, 11.17). Both "male" and "female" irons, respectively one and two armed, were stuck in the ground inside the rain hut, and the blood of sacrificed animals was smeared on the door as well as the iron and stone objects. I collected examples of iron *jen-lara*, as well as six small stones for rainmaking.

The colonial anthropologist C. K. Meek wrote of the man he called the "Rain Chief," Kpanti Mee, "removing from a large pot the symbol of the cult, which is a piece of iron fashioned like a snake" (Meek 1931b, 1: 467). This account was confirmed

11.13
Matakon was the Kpanti Giriri, the "Master of Thunder" of Kopo Dangong (Dangong Mountain). Here he sits on his throne in the anteroom of his well-guarded compound (see fig. 11.14).
© PHOTOGRAPH BY METTE BOVIN, AUGUST 1, 1964.

11.14
I was received by Matakon, "Master of Thunder" in the anteroom to his compound (see fig. 11.13) after first speaking with his ever-present guards (shown here also in the anteroom). Only Matakon could enter the rain chamber, where his iron implements were kept and where he made sacrifices of chickens, millet beer, and goats to secure rain.
© DETAIL OF PHOTOGRAPH BY METTE BOVIN, AUGUST 1, 1964.

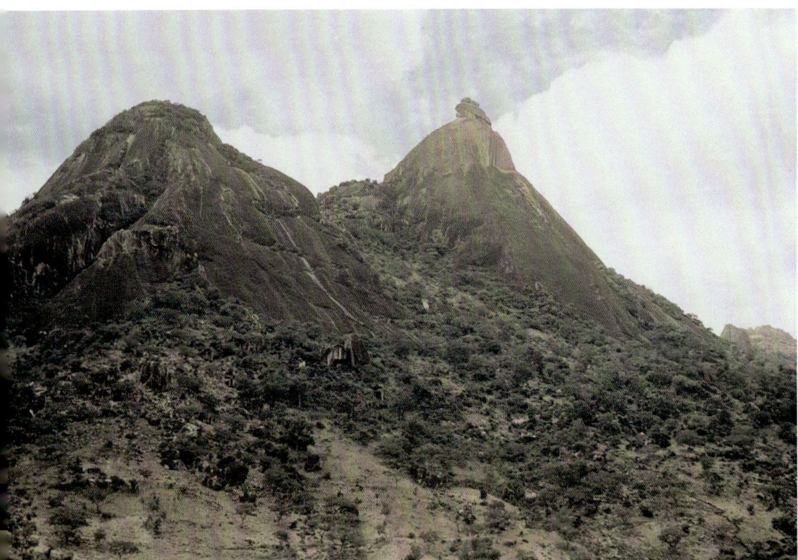

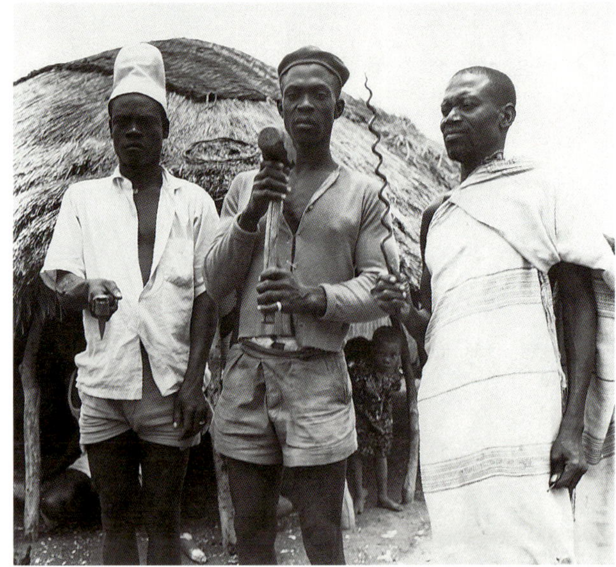

11.15

From his home, Matakon had a view (looking southeast from Dangong Mountain) of the "male" (right) and "female" (left) mountains that the Mumuye regard as a married couple. Their fertile union produces rain.

© PHOTOGRAPH BY METTE BOVIN, BETWEEN MONKIN VILLAGE AND KOPO DANGONG, AUGUST 1, 1964.

11.16

These three Mumuye blacksmiths in Mam village display rain irons. Given that they were just made, the irons were not considered dangerous, and I was able to collect them for the Moesgård Museum in Denmark. Once rain irons enter the hut of the rainmaker, however, they never leave it. The snake-like iron at the far right was considered a "male iron." An iron with two branches was a "female" iron. Together they formed a couple as did the gendered mountains in figure 11.15.

© PHOTOGRAPH BY METTE BOVIN, YAKOKO VILLAGE AREA, AUGUST 8, 1964.

11.17

Rainmaking wand
Mumuye peoples, mid-twentieth century
Iron
H: 58 cm

PRIVATE COLLECTION, LOS ANGELES

IMAGE: © 2010 FOWLER MUSEUM AT UCLA. PHOTOGRAPH BY DON COLE

PROVENANCE: AMYAS NAEGELE COLLECTION, NEW YORK

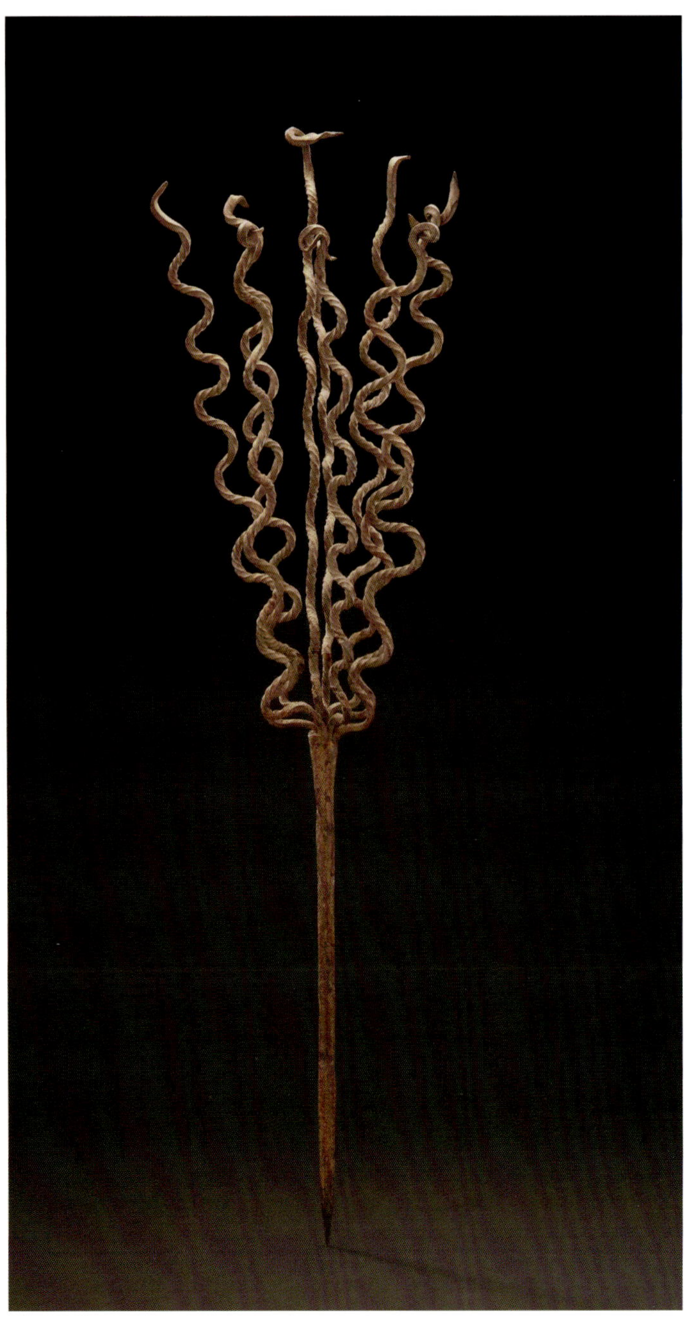

by my informants: the "Master of Thunder" enters the hut alone to eat meat and drink millet beer. Inside the hut, where nobody else may enter, he prays: *Kpanti La, wu jee se mee!* (Master of the Sun [Creator], may you bring us rain!). Then it starts to rain. Lightning and thunder may kill anyone who has offended parents or ancestors. This is why Mumuye feared the "Master of Rain" and "Master of Thunder" and considered them the highest powers in their society.

To control the rain that falls from the sky is also to control the fertility of crops in the earth, and hence the lives not just of human beings but of everything that lives. I sat a whole day at the entrance to Kpanti Giriri's compound with its many huts and his big family inside and politely asked him if I could see the rain objects; but, of course, I could not. Neither was I allowed into the rain hut. When I asked, however, whether I could see a *janari* figure, after some waiting time, a statue was brought out of a hut and was placed on a stone some distance away for a few minutes. I was told it was a *bizin* and held a bow and arrow in its hands. I saw it, and then it was taken back to the hiding place again. While it was out in the open, I heard a whistling in the air; I do not know how it was made, but I heard it. So I am convinced that Mumuye *janari* are not just visible wooden objects, they also perform as auditory phenomena. I thanked Matakon heartily and was allowed to take his picture, and I was also invited to visit part of his compound to greet his wives and take a picture of them. Before my male helper and I began climbing back down the mountain, Matakon gave us precious gifts: two iron bars (like the two bars given by a man for his fiancée) and a *lantang* (burial cloth), and chickens. So, I had what was needed to be married and buried in Mumuye-land, if I so wished. Most trade in the old days involved bartering at the marketplace; iron bars and rolls of burial cloth were used then as special purpose money.

MUMUYE SCULPTURES IN THE ARTWORLD

Although Arnold Rubin and I both carried out researches during the 1960s, our paths did not cross. His contribution and mine to our knowledge of Mumuye arts, their purposes, and meanings do not overlap greatly either. I share his sense that performances connected with the agricultural cycle, particularly planting and harvest rites, were important. Mumuye wooden sculptures and the cults of which they were part, had extremely varied purposes: funerals, peacemaking, warding off epidemics, and punishing social deviants (thieves, disrespectful children, and intractable wives). Rubin's extensive researches covered several observances and objects I never saw. For instance, I did not witness the funerary performance of Vaa-Topo, which involves the breaking of pots (see below). In all likelihood, I was excluded because of my gender (see Bovin 1966). I saw neither the monkey or baboon masks nor the tall vertical masks that Rubin photographed in the field (see figs. 10.31, 10.34). Both types have subsequently appeared on the international market, but I did not even hear about them.

The figures I did see were called *janari* by Mumuye (figs. 11.18, 11.19), a phrase they explicated as "talking figures" ("*ja*" is probably the term for "child," but the sense of "*nari*" is unclear). Large *janari* probably stood in the ground outside a hut or inside a building. Such figures were used to reveal the identity of thieves and other criminals. The juice of a medicinal plant (*gadele* in Hausa) was smeared on the mouth of the statue, which then "talked" to its owner. Blacksmiths, rainmakers, and other important people owned such talking figures, often in male and female pairs. Because the feet and lower legs of the figures were planted in the ground, they gave the impression of being short-legged and without feet. Similar figures served in healing rituals in times of epidemics like smallpox and were probably to be found in many of the secretive cult places that were closed to women.

I had the good fortune to encounter *janari* wooden figures several times in 1964. Musa Dafe, a blacksmith from the little village of Dafe where he lived, sent me wooden figures he had carved through a messenger named Dikko Barau Zinna (see fig. 11.18).

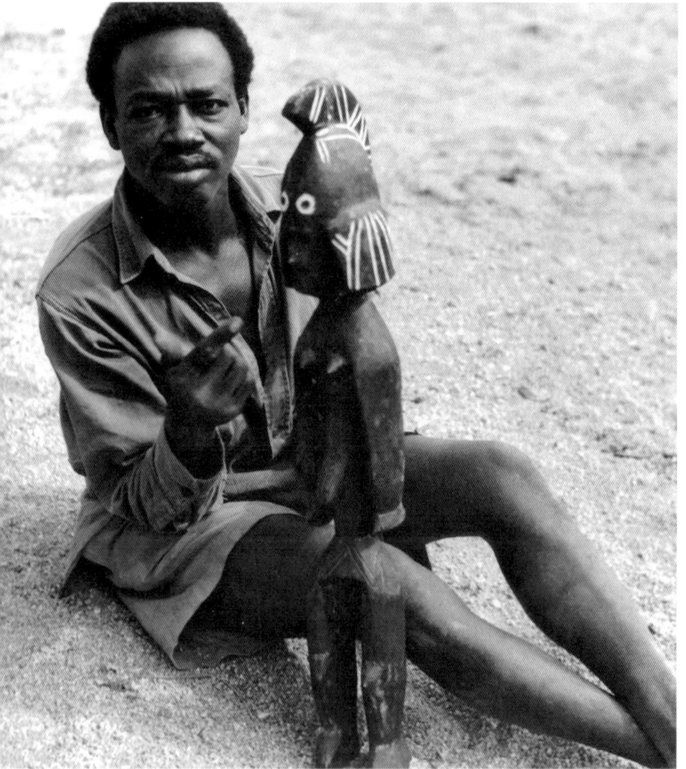

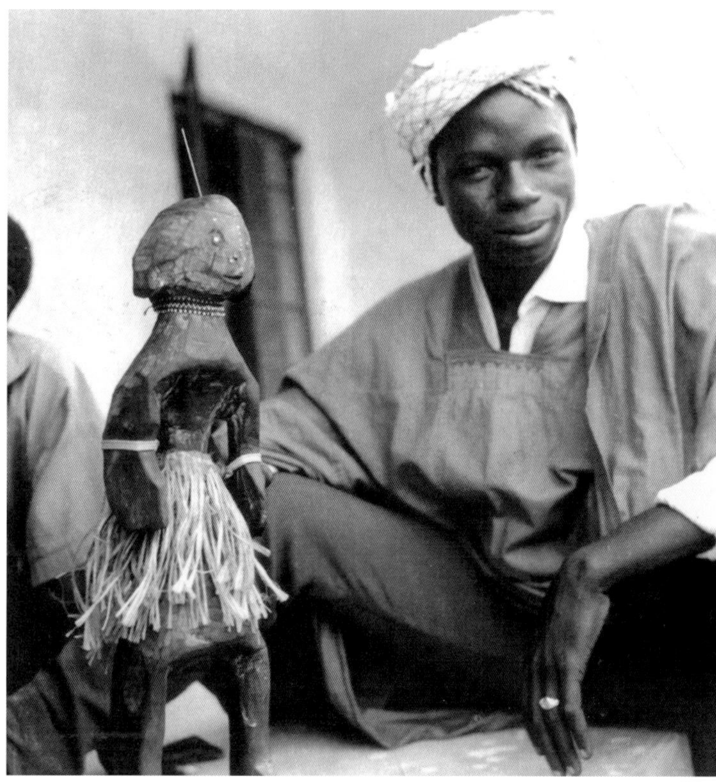

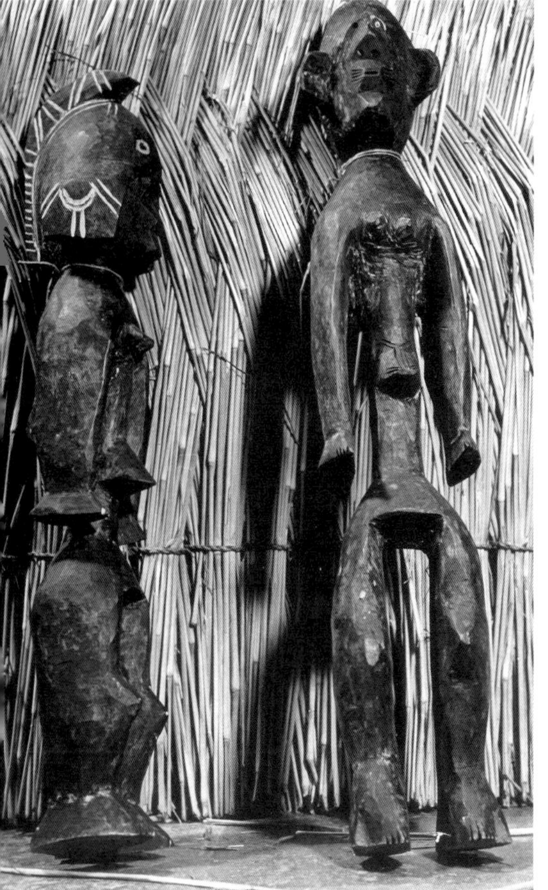

11.18 (ABOVE LEFT)

Dikko Barau Zinna brought this *janari* figure
and three others to me for sale, all of which had
been made by the artist Musa Dafe, who was
an old man at the time. Dikko Barau explained
that female *janari* have long ears because "only
Mumuye women were wearing big wooden earplugs" (see fig. 11.24). He further remarked that
the ears of male *janari* point forward because
"Mumuye men hear better than women."

© PHOTOGRAPH BY METTE BOVIN, DIDANKO
VILLAGE, ZING AREA, AUGUST 11, 1964.

11.19 (ABOVE RIGHT)

Abdullahi Wali of Yoro displays a brown
female *janari* figure, which I was able to
acquire for the Jos Museum. Abdullahi
showed me how the *janari* can talk by placing
a tiny little "snail flute" inside in his nostril.
The flute was made of two circular discs,
each with a central hole, glued together with
a black substance. When Adbullahi exhaled
through the flute, it "talked," or whistled.

© PHOTOGRAPH BY METTE BOVIN, DIDANKO
VILLAGE, ZING, AUGUST 12, 1964.

11.20 (LEFT)

Two black and white *janari* figures, female
and male, form a married couple. They were
photographed against a Nigerian *zanna* mat
at the exhibition I curated for the Moesgård
Museum, Aarhus, Denmark, in 1966 (E.A.
95-270, female; E.A. 95-271, male).

© REPRODUCED COURTESY OF METTE BOVIN.

11.21, 11.22

Figure
Mumuye peoples, late nineteenth to mid-
twentieth century
Wood
H: 127 cm

NATIONAL MUSEUM OF AFRICAN ART, SMITH-
SONIAN INSTITUTION; GIFT OF WALT DISNEY
WORLD CO., A SUBSIDIARY OF THE WALT DISNEY
COMPANY, 2005-6-177

IMAGE: COURTESY NATIONAL MUSEUM OF AFRI-
CAN ART, SMITHSONIAN INSTITUTION.
PHOTOGRAPH BY FRANKO KHOURY, 2010

PROVENANCE: PAUL AND RUTH TISHMAN, NEW
YORK, BEFORE 1970

Figure
Mumuye peoples, early to mid-twentieth
century
Wood, pigment
H: 79 cm

FOWLER MUSEUM AT UCLA X86.1109; ANONYMOUS
GIFT

IMAGE: © 2010 FOWLER MUSEUM AT UCLA.
PHOTOGRAPH BY DON COLE

PROVENANCE: PRIVATE COLLECTION, 1969

These two figures appear to have been
carved by the same hand with similarities
even observable in the adze marks on their
respective surfaces. They resemble a third
figure photographed in the field by Arnold
Rubin (see figs. 8.23a,b) and may also be the
work of the carver Kubwen of Dila. The long
notched legs observable on all three figures
bear intriguing resemblance to a jagged flash
of lightning. It may be that such formal
attributes encapsulate the potential of the
spirits inhabiting the figures to act at the
speed of lightning. Iron rainmaking wands
used by the Mumuye take the same zigzag
form (see figs. 11.16, 11.17).

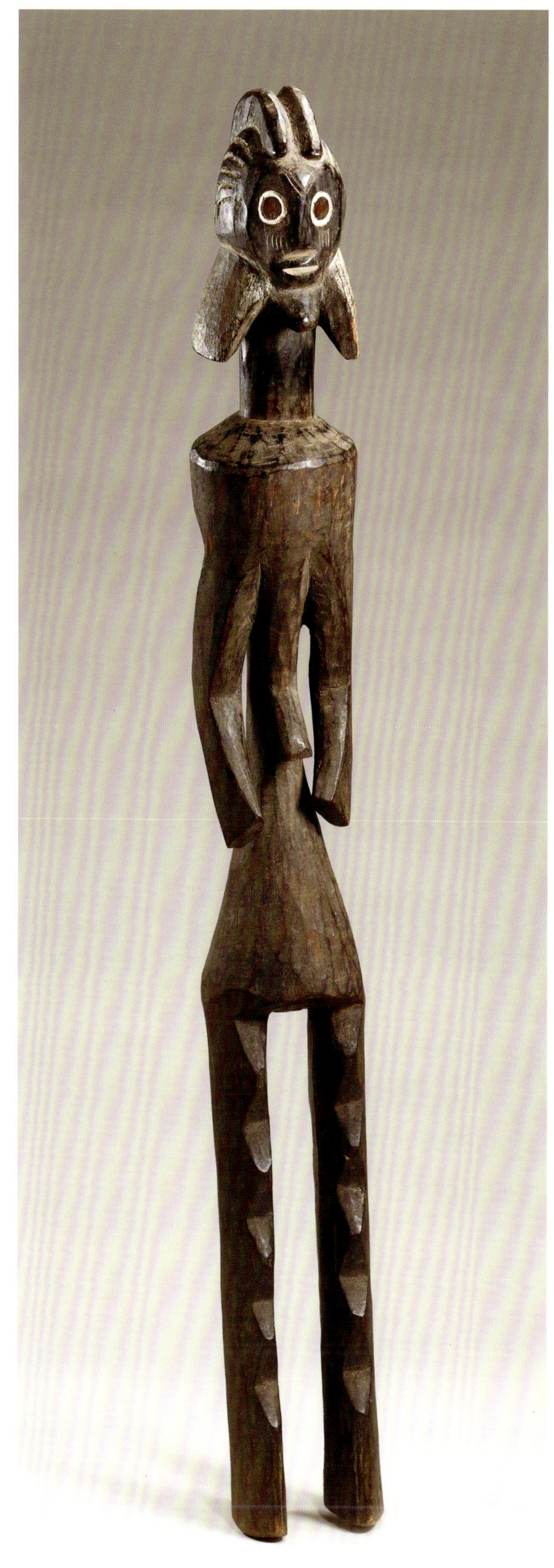

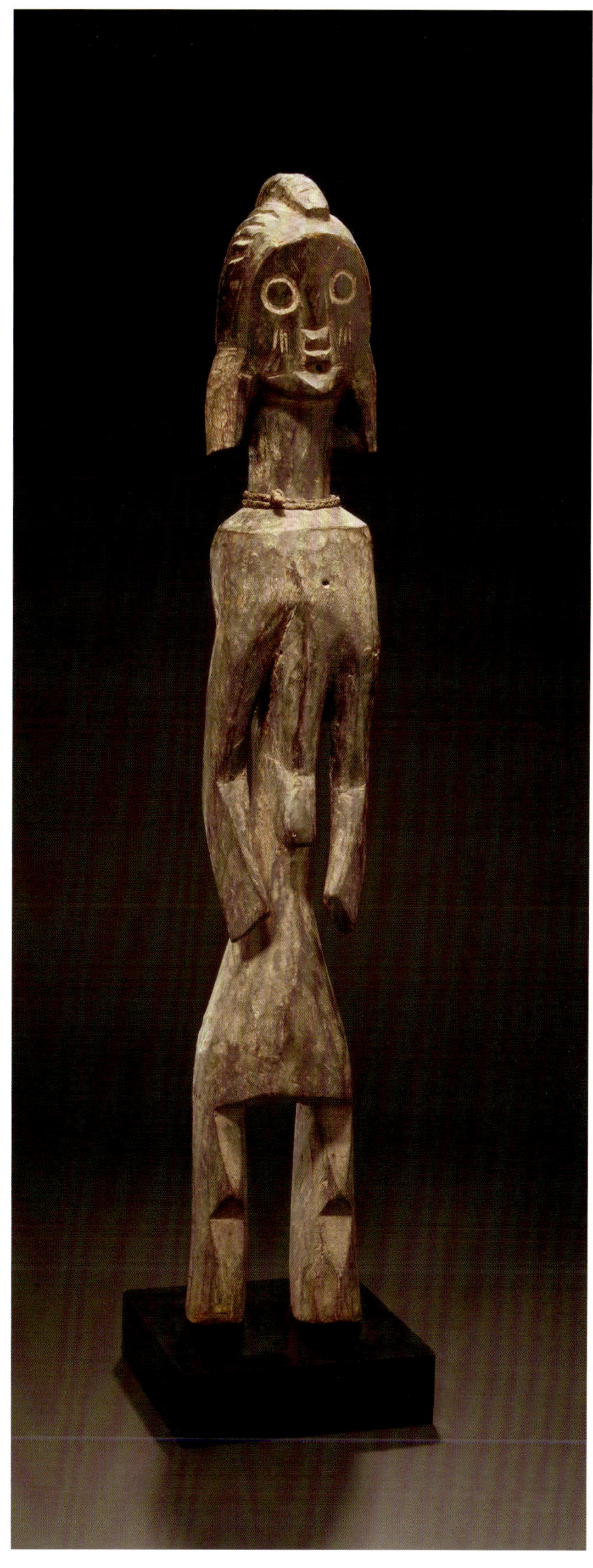

He sold me three *janari* in July 1964. Certain similarities between them readily indicated they were by the same master "hand," despite the different design of the female figure's hairstyle. Many statues I saw *in situ* had been used for a long time and were deteriorating from the feet upward. As a result they had to be stuck ever deeper into the ground. The court in Zinna 1964 used a gendered pair of *janari* that Musa Dafe had carved, very much like the ones I bought for the museum in Denmark. The court couple were a "wife and husband," and they were employed analogously to the sacred texts of Islam and Christianity: Muslims swore on the Quran, Christians on the Bible, and "pagans" by touching the mouth of the *janari* figures (fig. 11.20)

THE ICONOGRAPHY OF MUMUYE FIGURES

Starting with their heads, the element of the anthropomorphic *janari* figures that I first noted was their eyes. These were doubly encircled, which made the figures appear staring and wide-eyed. This might well refer to the seer, a person of extraordinary powers able to see what others cannot, including the truth of accusations. Why the exaggeration of the ears typical of Mumuye figures? Gender and age were pervasively important in the Mumuye world, and they were marked by material objects (such as personal ornaments) considered appropriate to men or women. Mumuye informants were unanimous that statues with large perforated ears were female. Some elderly Mumuye women still wore large, round, wooden earplugs, as did a few men in fact, but by then only in the remotest areas (see fig. 11.24). Extended flaps where ears should appear indicated a male figure, but I incline to believe that these flaps represent the side panels of helmets rather than unperforated earlobes. I had the good fortune to be able to buy a very old Mumuye protective helmet from the time of their wars with the Fulani. It was made from strands of thick, plaited grass sewn together. Because it was clearly an old and well-used example I gave it to the Jos Museum together with the ten objects that seemed the best of those I collected among Mumuye. I kept a photograph of it, and I recognize its form in the heads of some of the most celebrated Mumuye figures in major collections.

Why the very staccato treatment of the body in Mumuye sculpture, full of angles and edges (figs. 11.21, 11.22)? François Neyt refers to Mumuye *janari* as "large dancing figures" (2006, 10). I had never thought of them as dancing, because to me they are standing figures, absolutely still with their feet firmly planted deep into the ground. Dancers do not have unflexed legs, nor is their weight distributed equally on each foot. When I looked at the *janari* in profile, however, I realized at the very least that they are carved to be alert and ready to act, even to fly, to the aid of their owners. Some anthropomorphic figures have zigzag patterns on them, which strike me as resembling the lightning representations of the rainmakers' irons. While such patterns indicate scarification or hairstyle (figs. 11.23–11.25), they seem also to empower the figures. The more general angularity of Mumuye figures could well evoke rapidity and lightning-like effect. From their sharply angled arms to their often notched, stepped legs, Mumuye figures contain an energy akin to that of a lightning strike.

I saw two figures in the open air, in the village of Dankam, northwest of Kassa village. I made some drawings of them, since I could not take photographs. They were a small female figure, about 20–30 centimeters tall, which was very damaged, and a male figure about 90 centimeters to 1 meter tall. The male statue had red paint around his eyes, neck and genitals, the only time I have seen the color red used on a *janari*—they normally had white chalk around their eyes. The two statues were planted firmly in the ground within a stone circle outside the blacksmith's working hut in the back of the compound. Both statues had shortened right legs, apparently the result of termite damage. Inside the stone circle were tall stones and a ceramic pot of brown clay with a big tree on either side. Bracelets of iron or some other metal hung from the branches of the tree. A log outside the stone circle seemed to serve as

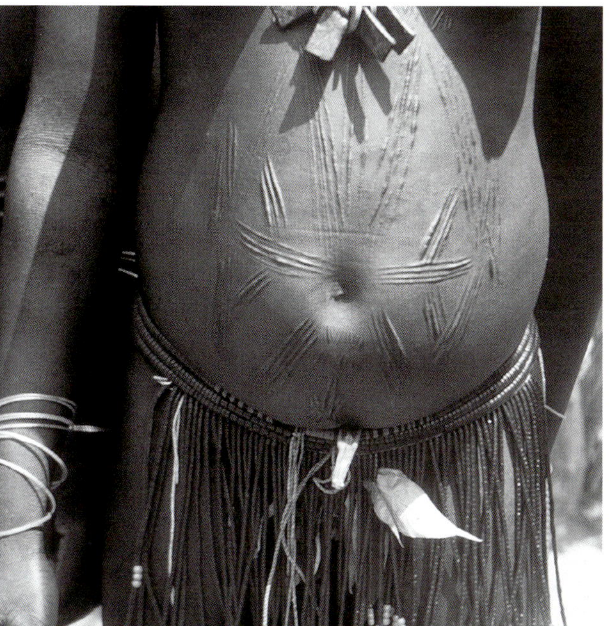

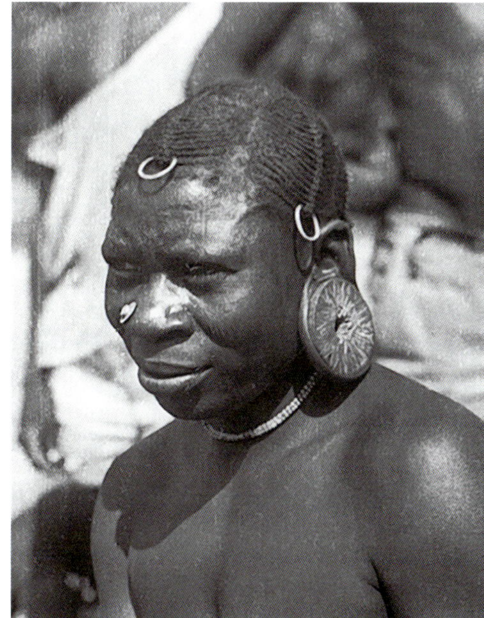

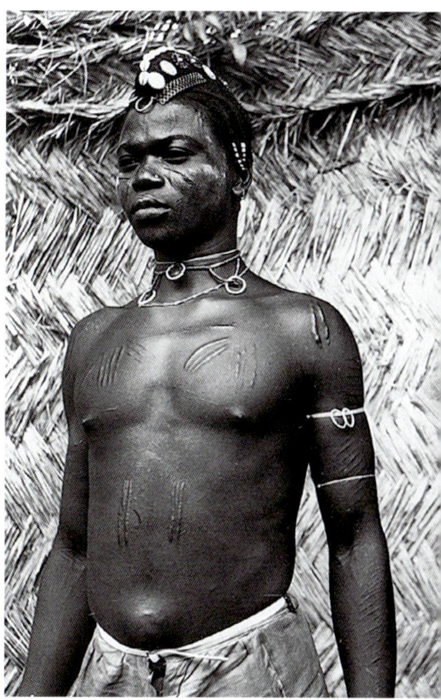

a bench on which people sat during rituals. Informants told me that the statue would tell the blacksmith and his family the identity of any thief who came to the house. Juice from medicinal plants was put into the pot next to the statues, and some of this was daubed on their faces, especially their mouths. The *janari* would then pronounce the name of any thief and even specify which village he came from. I was told that some people kept one or two *janari* inside their hut. These would move around when the occupants were absent and would later tell them everything that had happened while they were away (see fig. 11.1). A *janari* thus may have functioned as a "little policeman" or "detective."

CONCLUSION

Although masks and figures are striking visually, my memory of this fieldwork, now four decades in the past, is just as much of the sounds involved: the tone of horns and pipes, the shouting of the new masquerade at its naming, the rainmaking ceremony at the mountain of Yoro with the clanging of the rain iron shaped like lightning or a snake, which the Kpanti Mee would hit with an iron hammer, producing the sound of thunder and the snake-like flash of lightning. Then there is the "whistling in the air" I heard when shown the *bizin* figure, as well as my informants' assurances that *janari* figures talked. The powers in Mumuye religion were constituted as aural as well as visual manifestations. Moreover they appear highly mobile—literally in the case of the masquerade, but the figures also seem charged with a lightning energy.

The concealment of the visible and the aural qualities of Mumuye art were closely linked. Neither masquerades nor figures were simply wooden objects, placed in particular contexts they acted as fast as lightning. These actions were also manifested dramatically in performances of crying, shouting, whistling, talking, or revealing— lightning fast and thunderously loud. The Mumuye mask hung on a white wall and the figure illuminated brightly in a display case lose their performative contexts, which depend on concealment and revelation and on sound and silence. I hope that this brief memoir will help to restore some of these qualities to our appreciation. ●

11.23
These scarifications appear on the stomach of an unmarried Mumuye girl, radiating outward from the navel like rays of the sun. They are intended to ensure that she bears healthy children. Similar patterns may be observed on female *janari* figures. Before she marries, the girl's scarification program must be completed.
© DETAIL OF PHOTOGRAPH BY METTE BOVIN, ZING VILLAGE, AUGUST 5, 1964.

11.24
A Mumuye woman wears large disk-like wooden earplugs, a stud in her nose, and rings braided into her hair. By this time the custom of wearing earplugs was dying out in many Mumuye villages. This woman had descended from her home on a nearby mountain into the plains to attend the market at Zing.
© DETAIL OF PHOTOGRAPH BY METTE BOVIN, AUGUST 12, 1964.

11.25
A young Mumuye man from the mountains appears in the marketplace at Monkin. He wears a "cockscomb" hairstyle, which is seen on *janari* scuptures, but which was dying out among Mumuye in the plains at this time. The young man has scarification on his face, arms, and chest.
© DETAIL OF PHOTOGRAPH BY METTE BOVIN, AUGUST 8, 1964.

Heavy Metal: The Prestige
of Iron in the Middle Benue

RICHARD FARDON

Metalwork—ironwork in particular—has been the poor relation of Middle Benue art studies.[1] Western conceptions of art
could be expanded to embrace African wooden figures and
masks, and even pots and figures in clay. Metalwork, however,
was more intractable, and within the category, the red metals
of Africa had greater appeal than iron. Works in iron did not
immediately resonate with European high art traditions, nor
was their decay particularly appealing: wood might weather
in attractive fashion; red metals discolored with age; but iron
rusted. Although taste has changed recently, I don't believe
ironworks were much in demand during the heyday of the
trade in exported Middle Benue artworks during and just after
the Nigerian Civil War. This was consequential for my Chamba
fieldwork, and also for this brief account—no more than an
expanded memoir of a subject to which I did not devote close
attention at the time.

My impression in the mid-1970s was of a material culture
in metal substantially more intact on the ground than was
the case for wood. Runners from Cameroon and Nigeria had
stripped cults of wooden figures almost entirely, and only a few
of these had been replaced. The replacement figures were, to
judge by those that would turn up later in American and European collections, inferior both aesthetically and in terms of
workmanship to those lost. Many of them also differed in style
because they had to be sourced from whatever communities
still had carvers, which for Mapeo Chamba often meant Verre.
Although masks were also exported in large numbers, continuing use meant replacements were sought in many instances,
and at least some of those sold show signs of termite or other
damage suggesting that replacement could have been seen as
advantageous. In marked contrast to the fate of wooden objects,
however, examples of virtually every genre of metalwork were
still present, and only a few cults appeared compromised by
losing any of their apparatus in iron or brass (though by report
the paraphernalia of some had been sold).

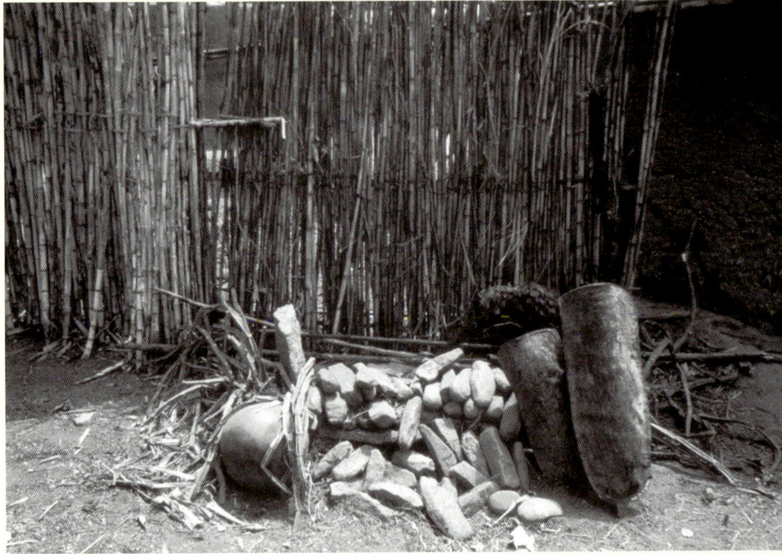

In the impossible event that an account of Chamba material culture had been written by a twentieth-century adept of
the historic religions of the region, the relative importance and
interest attributed to various ritual paraphernalia would have
been quite different from that of the artworld. There would
not be the same preoccupation with wooden carvings. Iron
and brass objects were far more costly than works in wood,
and they necessarily involved the transformative powers of the
smithy. In the eyes of Chamba adepts of cults, metalwork and
medicines were probably the two things most important to
undertaking ritual action. They brought about transformation.
Wooden figures were a convenience for mediation, but losing
them did not make ritual action impossible in the way that
removing metal or medicines would have.

Smiths among Chamba belonged to a small "caste-like"
group in the sense that they lived apart from and did not intermarry with or share food (excepting beer) with other Chamba.
This was entirely typical of the region. Smiths also smelted,

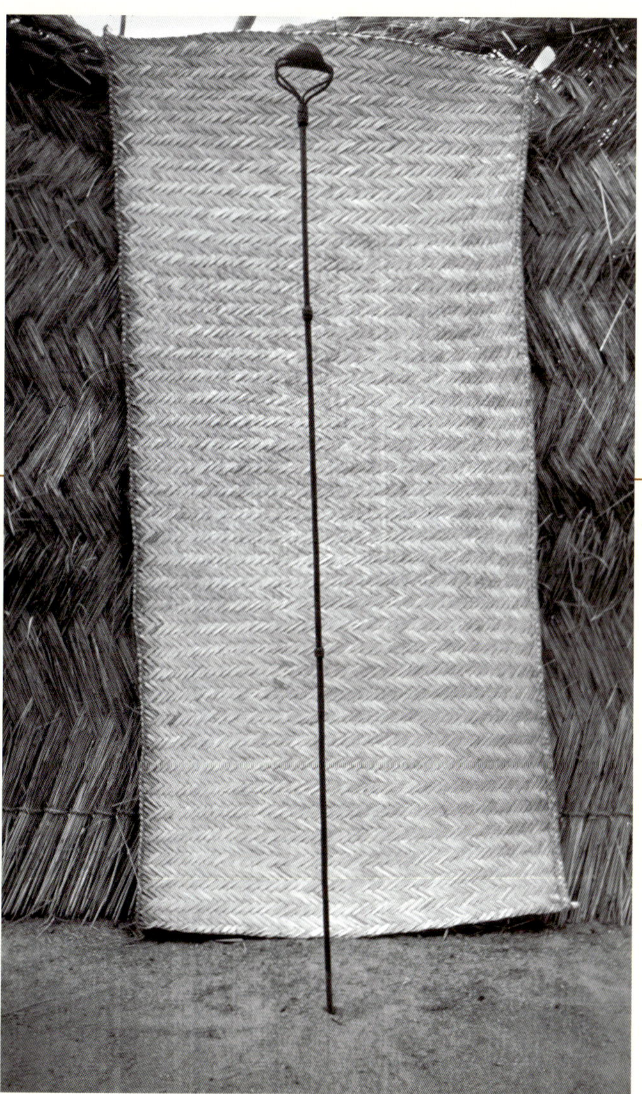

G.1

Oversized iron gongs are found widely in the Benue region and usually formed part of a chief's regalia. This pair has been placed with other objects, including a calabash horn covered in the skin of a civet, alongside the hunting shrine belonging to a chiefly clan.

PHOTOGRAPH BY RICHARD FARDON, TISAYELI, 1977.

G.2a,b

This form of crotal spear is usually called *sɔɔm sakeni* by Chamba Daka, who most commonly associate it with killing. A hunter or warrior who had killed a man or dangerous animal was entitled to shake the spear, taunting those who had not done so and were unable to touch it. The example illustrated is from the Chamba Leko chiefdom of Sapeo, where it formed part of the chiefly regalia.

PHOTOGRAPHS BY RICHARD FARDON, 1976.

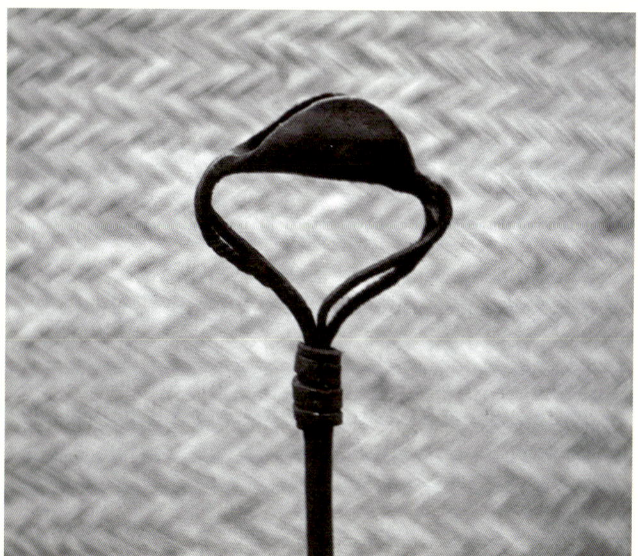

which was not the case everywhere.[2] The attitude of nonsmiths toward the powers of transformation wielded by smiths was ambiguous: without them neither agriculture nor rituals were possible, since they made the apparatuses of both. Despite this, smiths themselves were both feared and mocked: considered both polluted and polluting because of their profession. Nonetheless, where chiefs existed, as Leo Frobenius reports, the chiefs of the smiths were their most essential aides (1913, 249, 289).

Chamba smiths produced a wide range of mundane ironware: heads for spears and arrows, razors, and the blades for hoes, knives, digging sticks, axes, adzes, and sickles were still made in the mid-1970s, and in the past bow pullers and flint irons had also been forged and some were kept as curiosities. Additionally, smiths created a variety of ornaments (rings, bracelets, hairpins, and iron waistbands). Then there were the ceremonial instruments, some sonorous: especially the large pairs of standing gongs that were the prerogative of chiefs (fig.

G.1)[3] and the leg rattles with crotal bells that women wore in sets at public dances, notably at funeral wakes. Finally, there was more or less esoteric equipment: the double hand-gong that announced and accompanied the masquerade; the sickle with a zigzag lightning point (*lama*) that was the insignia of priesthood; circumcision knives, kept in a leopard's paw pouch (Frobenius 1913, facing 272); the crotal spear (figs. G.2a,b)[4] held by killers of men or of dangerous animals (*sɔɔm sakeni*); the small hoe blades, pairs of which were beaten together for percussion in women's cults (*jeem*; illustrated in Fardon 1990, 70; also found among emigrant Chamba in Donga, see Meek 1931b, 1: 347); the outsize, entirely iron hoe of the women cult leaders (*jeem gang*);[5] and the paraphernalia of the men's cults. The last of these included collections of clappers hung on iron rings (fig. G.3); various kinds of cult spears, some adorned with more clappers (fig. G.4), and others resembling lightning or snakes; and the flat metal attachments used to make bullroarers (*langa*), which were capable of causing problems with eyesight.

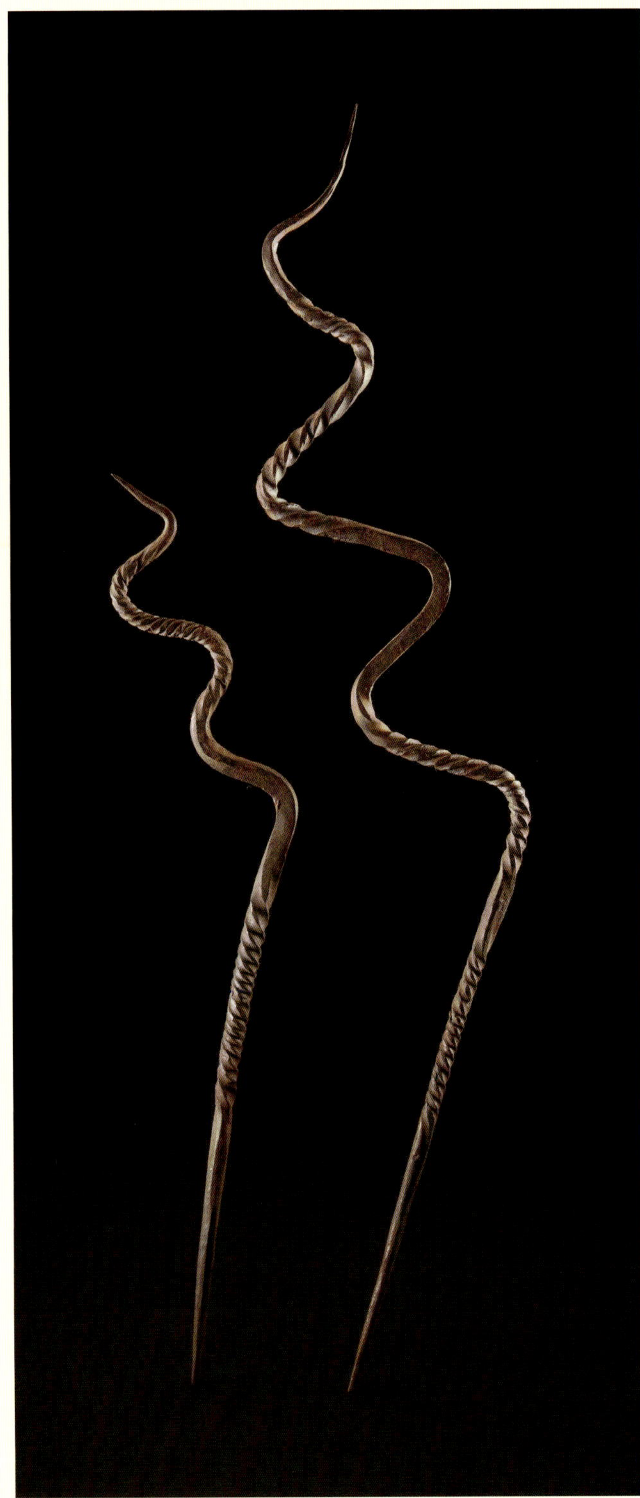

G.9a,b
Rainmaking wands
Mumuye peoples, before 1970
Iron
H (of tallest): 32.3 cm
FOWLER MUSEUM AT UCLA X86.2598, X86.2599; GIFT OF JIM AND JEANNE PIEPER
IMAGE: © 2010 FOWLER MUSEUM AT UCLA. PHOTOGRAPH BY DON COLE
PROVENANCE: COLLECTED BY ARNOLD RUBIN, ZINNA DISTRICT, 1970

Forged iron wands in distinctive zigzag form were part of the ritual
paraphernalia of rainmakers. They represented a flash of lightning or
the sudden strike of a snake, both harbingers of thunder and rain. The
two "snakes" were conceived as a male-female pair with the longer one
being the male.

area: styles of smithing were more similar than were styles of
wood carving, and this probably reflects the special "casted"
status of smiths as a category. For instance, by the mid-1970s
the major families of smiths in the Mapeo area where I lived
were considered Verre, albeit Chamba speakers. I heard that
Chamba Leko smiths had also been more numerous at one
time, but I never learned of smiths whose first language was the
Chamba Daka dialect of Mapeo, and I was not made aware that
anyone considered this situation anomalous.

To the east of Chambaland, it seems probable that Verre
smiths would have produced wares for other Verre similar
to those they created for Mapeo Chamba, and in the west
it appears just as likely that Mumuye smiths would have
produced iron goods for their people similar to those made
for western Chamba speakers of the Nnakenyare dialect of
Chamba Daka. Frobenius's comparative illustrations of some
iron implements suggest as much: for instance, he had his artist
arrange slightly different-shaped iron bullroarers, which are
labeled as ethnic types (Frobenius 1913, 191). A similar analysis could probably be made of other iron goods: for instance,
the clappers of iron rattles attributed to Mumuye hang from
a solid ring, which suggests that it might not have mattered
to Mumuye, as it did to Chamba, whether the clappers could
readily be detached and reattached for ritual purposes. Among
other suggestive objects, likely to be of Mumuye[8] origin, are
clusters of undulating iron rods (fig. G.9, and see figs. 11.16,
11.17) that are probably related to the control of lightning and
rainfall, in one example these are inserted into a pot so that
they stand upright (fig. G.10).

Chamba particularly appreciated and prized a range of
brassware that they claimed not to have been able to produce
for themselves. When I carried out research in the mid-1970s,
I heard accounts from then elderly men of how Verre brass
casters used to be invited to stay in the village for a couple of
weeks. They would be fed handsomely on goats and chicken
and rewarded with such costly prestige goods as gowns in
addition to grain and livestock. In return they would cast *cire
perdu* brass figures, which Chamba used in certain of their
cults. A whole range of brassware was attributed to Verre, and
to a lesser extent Koma, smiths. The cult Karbang was said to
require a small brass statuette of a squatting old woman in its
cult paraphernalia. Father Malachy Cullen includes a sketch of
one in his notes of 1944. I saw only a single example in all the
Karbang cults I attended, but whether this was because there
had never been more or because they had been sold, I do not
know. I have not seen anything in collections or for sale resembling the old woman. One elderly friend told me about a brass
statue he owned (or perhaps had once owned, I was never clear
about this) with which he used to converse. I did not see it, but
I wonder if it looked like the small male figure in the Menil
collection with its hands on its hips, which is reminiscent of a
male figure in clay from the Musée du quai Branly with outstretched arms (see figs. 6.23, 6.24).

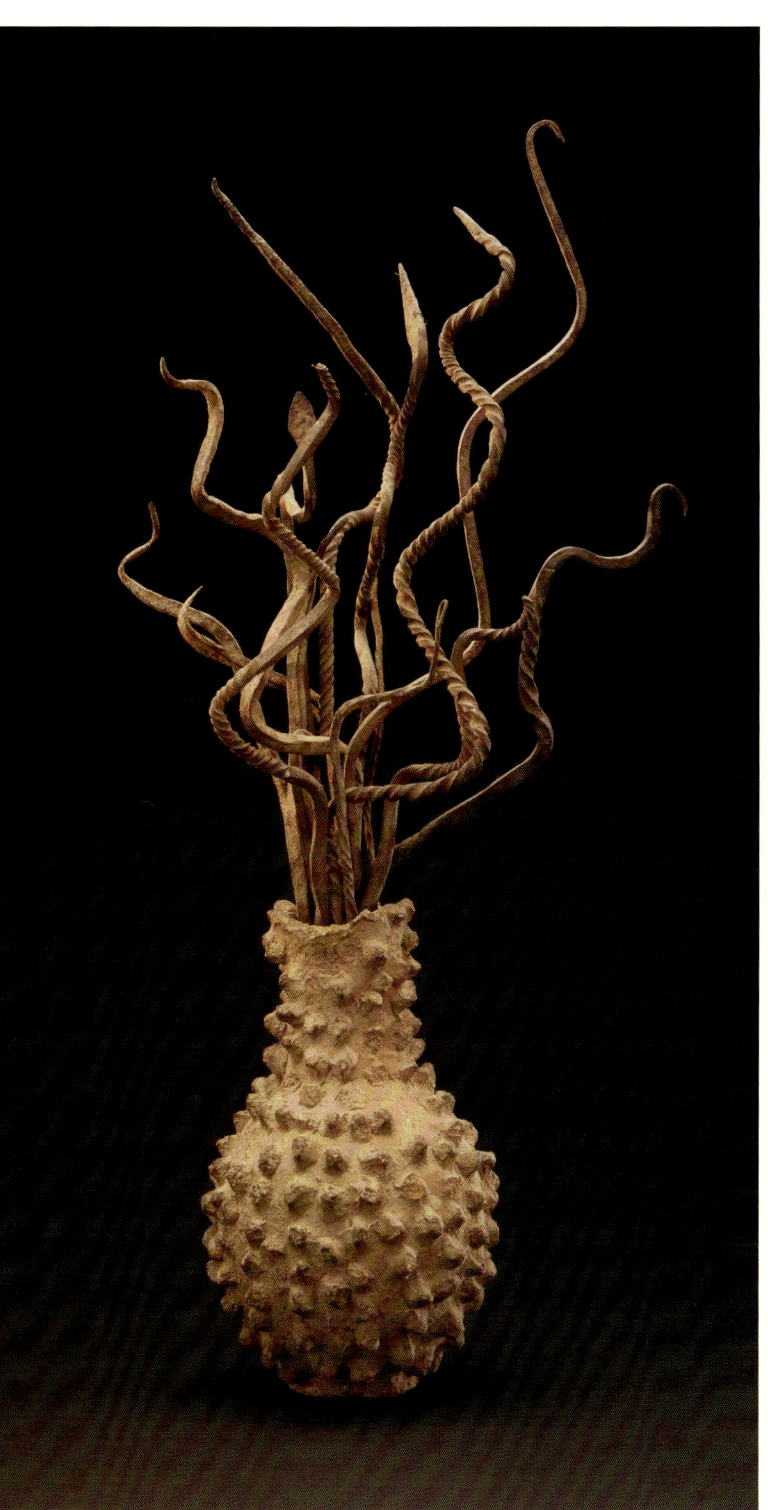

G.10
Vessel with rainmaking wands
Mumuye peoples (?), mid-twentieth century
Ceramic, iron
H: 44.4 cm
FOWLER MUSEUM AT UCLA X2008.32.3; MUSEUM PURCHASE, 2008
IMAGE: © 2010 FOWLER MUSEUM AT UCLA. PHOTOGRAPH BY DON COLE
PROVENANCE: PACE PRIMITIVE, NEW YORK; LEE LORENZ COLLECTION,
NEW YORK; AMYAS NAEGELY COLLECTION, NEW YORK

Given the field documentation of a similar composite bundle of undulating iron rods by Mette Bovin, it is likely that this object is of Mumuye
origin and that its uses were to do with rainmaking. The iron rods appear
to have been impaled into soft clay placed inside the vessel before it was
fired to secure them.

Just as valued as figures were prestigious and expensive
ceremonial hoes in brass. Large decorated bells,[9] small crotal
or pellet bells, leg rattles, and bracelets were less costly but
admired nonetheless. The son of a wealthy man might be ornamented with all these when dancing before his circumcision.
Particularly prized were knives with ornate brass handles and
sheaths; some that I saw in the regalia of Chamba Leko chiefs
(see figs. 6.15, 6.16; see also Wente-Lukas 1977, 227, figs. 303,
304) were apparently old or at least in a very distressed state.
In Chamba Daka these were called *ne yaki* ("man knife" after
the pommel ornamentation with heads, which was a common
device). Circumcision was a time of particular display, and
each boy needed a *tooma*, or crooked stick, with which to dance.
Normally this term referred to the crooked wooden truncheon
that was the insignia of chieftainship, but the *tooma*s of the
circumcision candidates were metal, most commonly a crook
of iron to which old-style, perforated, colonial coins might be
attached to create a rattle. A boy from a rich family might have
one made of brass. Alongside the brass knives, the most prized
object in brass was the two-piece (blade and handle) dancing
hoe, the entire surface of which was elaborately decorated. In
some examples the crook of the handle was worked into the
shape of the head of a horned creature.

These notes, on a topic that was never a main focus of my
fieldwork, are only suggestive. For the most part I have written
only of the Chamba and about their nearest neighbors when I
feel able to extrapolate to them (Verre, Koma, Mumuye). This is
a subject about which there is much more to learn, and we still
await an adequate account of Middle Benue ironworking. ●

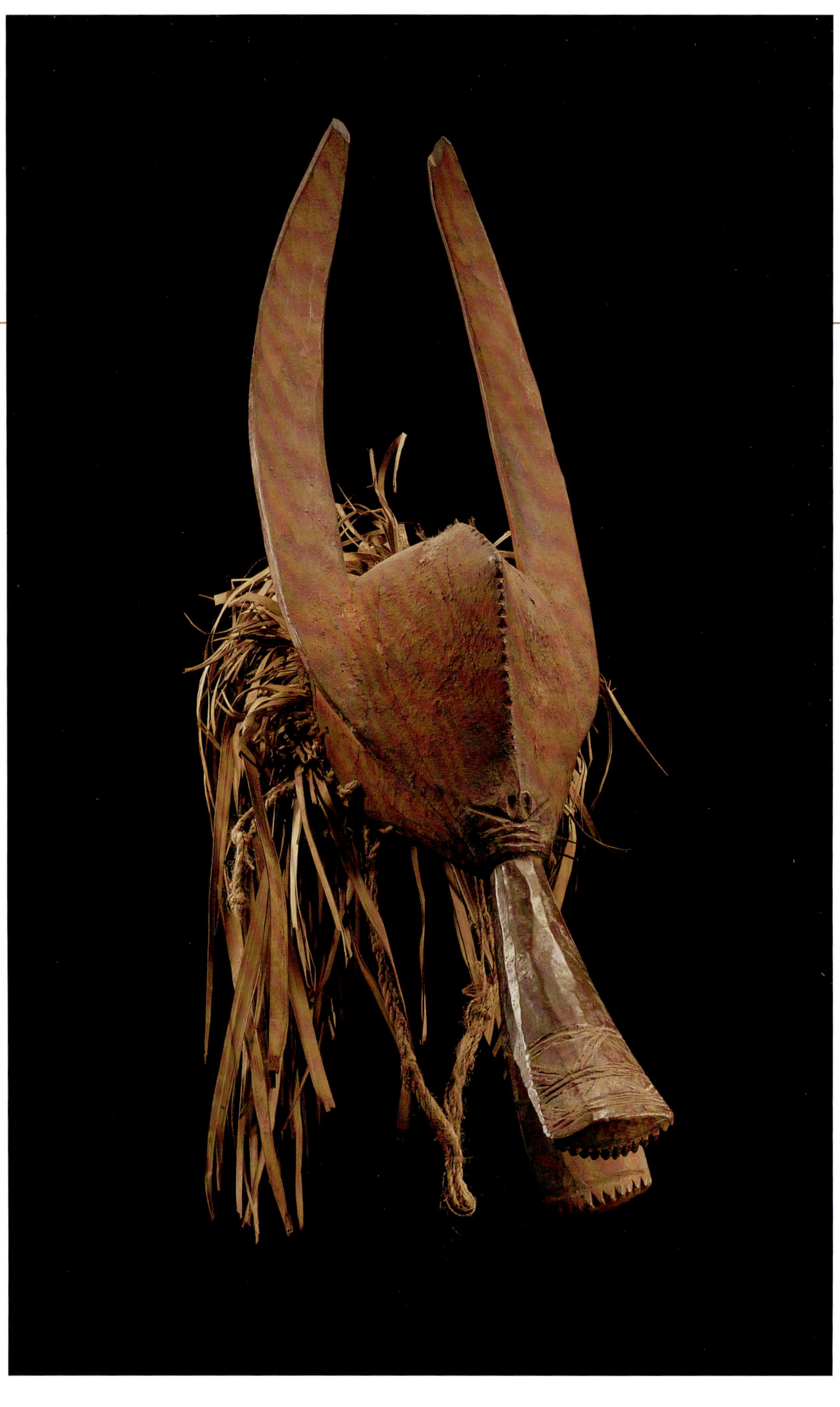

CHAPTER 12

Kantana, Kulere, and Their Neighbors South of the Jos Plateau

BARBARA FRANK[1]

The people living south of the Jos Plateau make up the northernmost extension of the Middle Benue style region as defined for this project. Consisting of a mountain range and its foothills to the north of the Benue River, the environment of the Jos Plateau varies between the hilly, broken terrain of its lowlands and the treeless grassfields of the high plateau. The peoples themselves are also varied, both linguistically and ethnically. Historically, however, they lived for the most part in small, relatively independent villages, and there were continuities in their conceptions of art and religion that must have owed much to the connections that existed between communities and that justify their being treated as a distinguishable element in the Middle Benue mosaic of styles.

Other than for its eastern groups, comparatively little in the way of systematic information has been published on the historic cultures of this region. The main published source of information (apart from linguistic) remains Cecil Ames's compilation from the reports of early colonial officers (1934, 257–82, also 156–62). More recent publications, based on systematic fieldwork, exist for the Kulere in the form of a monograph (Frank 1981), as well as for the Ron (Frank 1974; 1976; 1978; 1983), who do not strictly belong to the subregion on geographical grounds but are included here due to the similarities among their artistic traditions and those of other peoples south of the Jos Plateau.[2] The results of historical research have also been published on the Eggon (Doward 1984; 1987).[3]

The linguistic composition of the area is complex, involving three distinct groups of languages. The bulk of the population speak what linguists have classified as Plateau languages of the Benue-Congo family: the Eggon (formerly Hill Mada), the Mada, the Rindre (Lindiri, Nungu), the Ninzam, and some scattered villages of what is called the "Southwestern sub-group" (Crozier and Blench 1992, 120–21). The Kantana (Mama) are speakers of languages belonging to the Jarawan Bantu group of Bantoid languages (Crozier and Blench 1992, 122). While in the east, the Kulere (Kaleri), the Ron of the Sha village group, and the Ron (Baron, Challa) on the high Plateau speak Chadic languages of the Ron group (Crozier and Blench 1992, 125).[4]

Ethnic composition is just as complex and not always coincident with linguistic difference. Names of broader groups were often invented by foreigners (see, for example, Ames 1934, 257–58, for Eggon; Jungraithmayr 1970, 291, for Kulere, and 230 for Challa), while local peoples might have designated themselves as the inhabitants of particular villages or as descendants of a common ancestor embracing several communities. Despite this, people subsequently adopted these "invented" names to signify groups sharing language, or historical traditions, or cultural similarities. The names

12.1

Mangam mask
Kantana, Kulere peoples (?), early to mid-twentieth century
Wood, ocher, fiber
H: 59 cm
COLLECTION OF LILIANE AND MICHEL DURAND-DESSERT
IMAGE: COURTESY PRIVATE COLLECTOR.
PHOTOGRAPH © HUGHES DUBOIS
PROVENANCE: PRIVATE COLLECTION, PARIS

This "big" Mangam with its shorter forward-curving horns is probably intended to represent a reedbuck. The size of its central crest and the length of its snout are unusual, and it incorporates several humanizing features—a row of delicate incisions bisecting the crown and lines decorating the snout, which recall scarification patterns. This example demonstrates particularly well the practice of rubbing powdery red ocher into the surface of masks. Without specific documentation it is impossible to say whether this Mangam—or others in collections—was made by the Kantana, Kulere, Mada, Rindre, or Ron of Sha.

did not need to capture all potential differences for them to be adopted. Thus, the Chadic-speaking Kulere include as Kulere the inhabitants of three villages in their area who are Plateau speakers. While hill-dwelling Kulere refer to their western neighbors not as Mama or Kantana, but as the "people of the lowland," in which terms they also include other Kulere villages in the lowland. To complicate matters further, peoples in some villages on the borderland between Ron and Kulere have at different times labeled themselves as Kulere, or as Ron, or as people distinct from both (Frank 1978).

The tendency to reinterpret historical traditions in the light of modern conventions is shown by the choice of the name "Kantana" to replace the pejorative designation "Mama" on the basis of traditions of a migration from Kantana in the Bauchi area (Ames 1934, 159). The fact of migration is corroborated by the Jarawan Bantu linguistic affiliation of the restyled Kantana of the Middle Benue. Their complete cultural integration in the region makes it likely, however, that the group of immigrants who settled and introduced their language locally was small. The language affiliation of the Kulere may likewise have changed in consequence of an immigration of Chadic speakers. Traditions of common descent have sometimes led to bonds of friendship; and even among unrelated villages, who may speak different languages, there existed networks of ritual and mundane relationships among what were politically independent communities (see for example Frank 1981, 11, 25–28; 1974, 102–18). The situation in sum is broadly similar to that described by Joerg Adelberger for the Muri Hills in this volume (see chapter 13) or that described by John Picton (see chapter 4) for the Niger-Benue confluence region, so that ethnic labels do not denote distinct material or artistic cultures.

MASQUERADES AND CULTS

A considerable and varied corpus of distinctive sculptures has been documented among these peoples, and many objects clearly deriving from these sculptural traditions have appeared on the international art market in recent decades. The best known of these are carved wooden dance crests or cap masks in the form of highly stylized heads of dwarf forest buffalo, several types of antelope (reedbucks and waterbucks), and other forms, reportedly used in connection with a masquerade called Mangam (figs. 12.1–12.3). Ethnic groups whose names have been linked with these sculptures include the Kantana (identified in the literature primarily as "Mama"), the Mada, Rindre (Nungu), the Kulere, and the Ron of Sha. Although a small number of features might seem to support demarcation of provisional local or ethnic substyles, such an effort would be of little usefulness given the absence of provenance for the majority of masks. Even the large number of examples photographed in the field by Kenneth Murray before 1952 reveals the difficulty of identifying particular styles with specific groups and suggests instead that masks in different styles were able to circulate widely within the region (see interleaf H).[5]

On the basis of his very thorough survey, Murray distinguished three main morphological categories of Mangam masks: waterbuck (antelopes with long backward sweeping horns), reedbuck (antelopes with shorter forward curving horns; see fig. 12.1), and buffalo (with curved horns that nearly meet in a full circle; see figs. 12.2, 12.3, and interleaf H). While the majority of published examples can be encompassed within these three categories, the range of forms is in fact much wider, from "found objects" (such as the skulls of the creatures themselves, or the twisted and gnarled stumps of small trees, with multiple horn-like projections) to horned crests of rather indeterminate—and enigmatic—aspect (fig. 12.4).[6] Most such crests exhibit a powdery red patina, probably ocher, although a few examples with an oily black surface are known (see fig. H.30). Red ocher was widely used as a cosmetic, often with spiritual associations, among peoples of this region.[7] All Mangam variants were worn with a bulky "haystack" costume made from overlapping tiers of palm leaf (fig. 12.5).

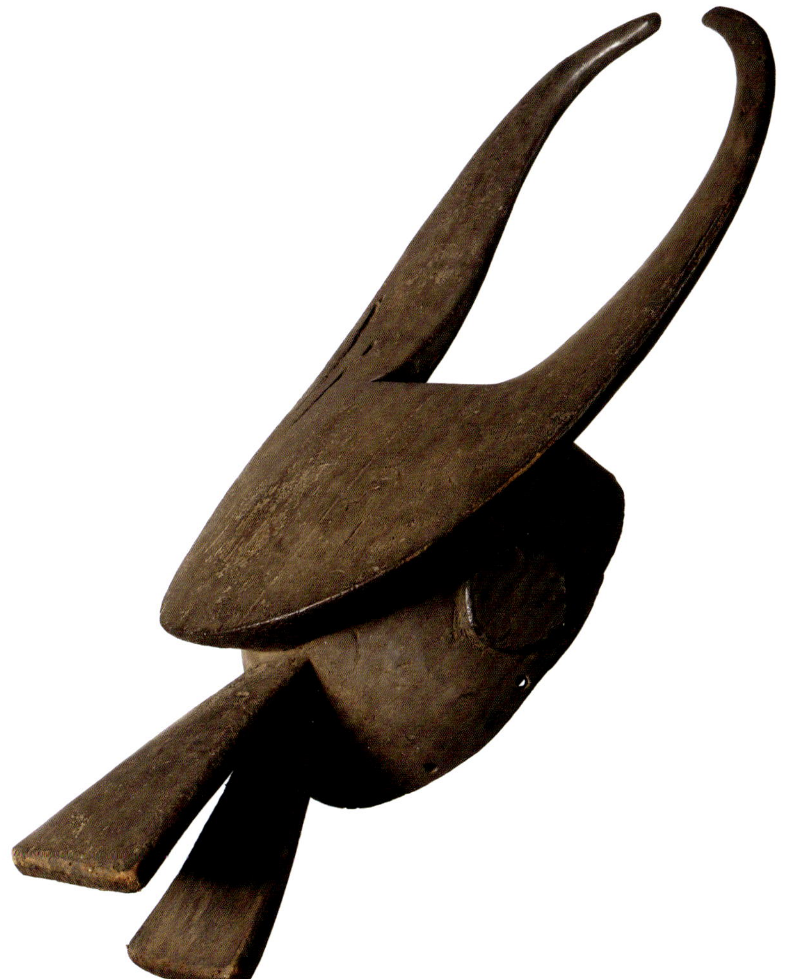

12.2
Mangam mask
Kantana, Kulere peoples (?), early to mid-
twentieth century
Wood
H: 53.5 cm
JAMES AND LAURA ROSS
IMAGE: COURTESY COLLECTOR. PHOTOGRAPH
© 2010 JOHN BIGELOW TAYLOR
PROVENANCE: MICHAEL OLIVIER, NEW YORK

The simple well-balanced elements of this
"small" buffalo Mangam create a strong aesthetic statement. Relatively unadorned except
for what may be circular "eyes" or "ears" at the
sides of the head, this mask has horns whose
complex curvature is particularly graceful.

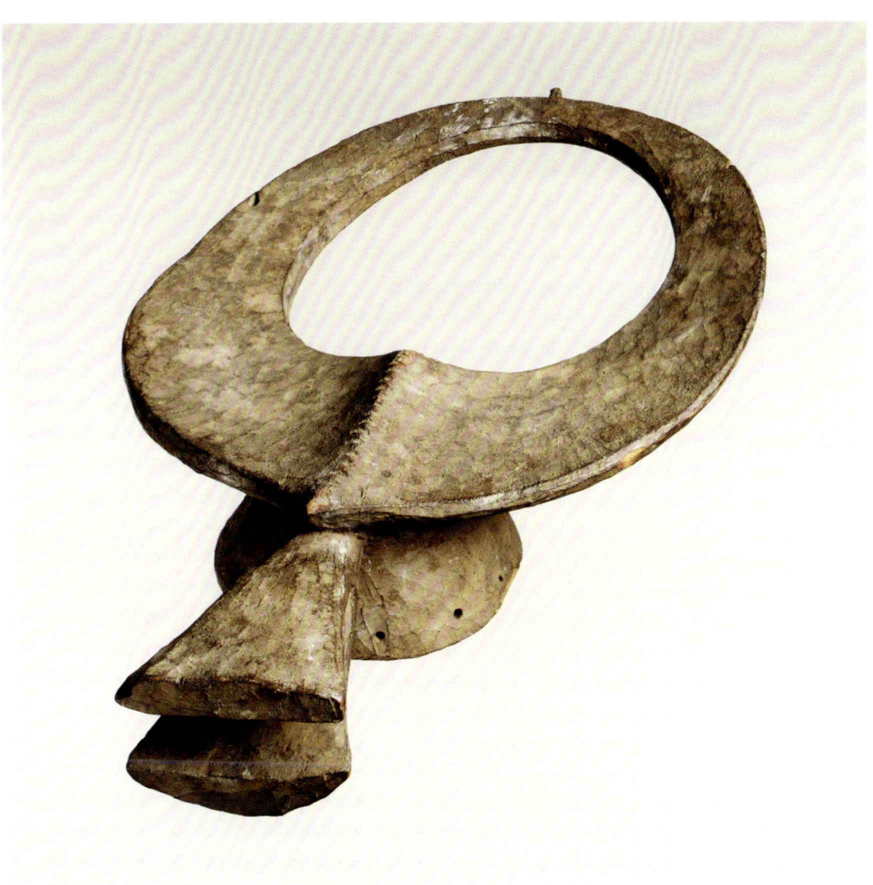

12.3
Mangam mask
Kantana, Kulere peoples (?), early to mid-
twentieth century
Wood, pigment
H: 55 cm
MUSÉE DU QUAI BRANLY, PARIS, 73.1997.4.46
IMAGE: © 2010 MUSÉE DU QUAI BRANLY. PHOTO-
GRAPH BY THIERRY OLLIVIER/MICHEL URTADO/
SCALA, FLORENCE
PROVENANCE: RALPH NASH, LONDON; BARBIER-
MUELLER, GENEVA

The "small" Mangam crests with buffalo horns
carved in a full circle are especially elegant.
Their simple lines and bold geometric shapes
have been extremely attractive to collectors. A
line of incisions added along the center of the
crest suggests a hybrid human-animal identity,
as does the small hair knot indicated where
the horns meet at the rear of the mask.

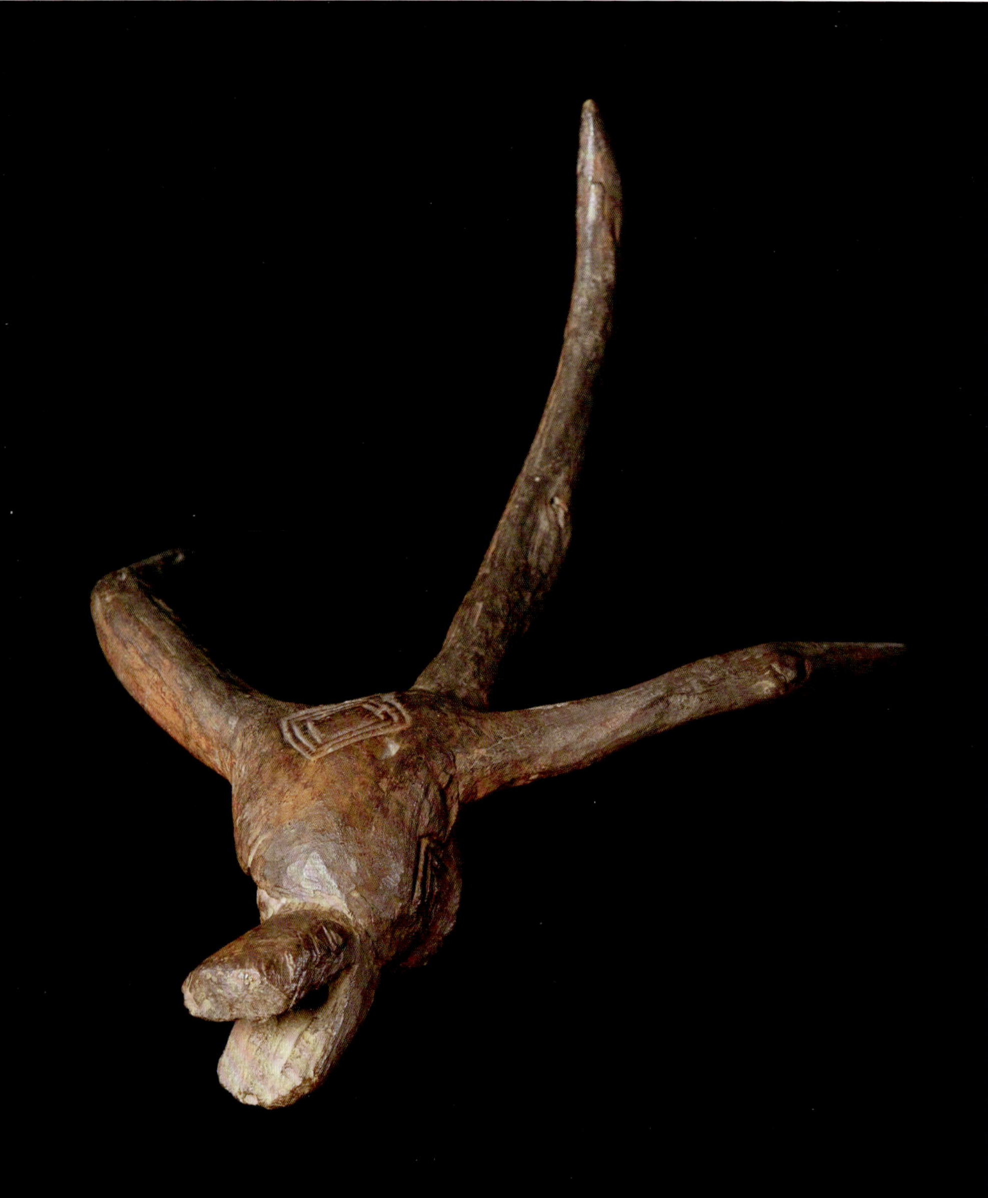

12.4

Mangam mask
Kantana, Kulere peoples (?), early to mid-twentieth century
Wood
H: 48 cm
COLLECTION OF MARK GROUDINE AND CYNTHIA PUTNAM
IMAGE: COURTESY COLLECTOR. PHOTOGRAPH © 2010 ADAM L. WEINTRAUB PHOTOGRAPHY
PROVENANCE: CHARLES RATTON, PARIS; ANDRE SCHOLLER; JAQUIN PECCI; OKRI EDWARDS (?)

Within the Mangam corpus, masks carved to take advantage of the natural formation of tree branches, as with this example, are unusual. The worn and reddened surface of this mask suggests long-term use, as does the near absence of holes for attachment to the fiber costume. The lozenge-shaped incisions at the crown are likely to be references to scarification, as seen on numerous other examples (see fig. 12.6).

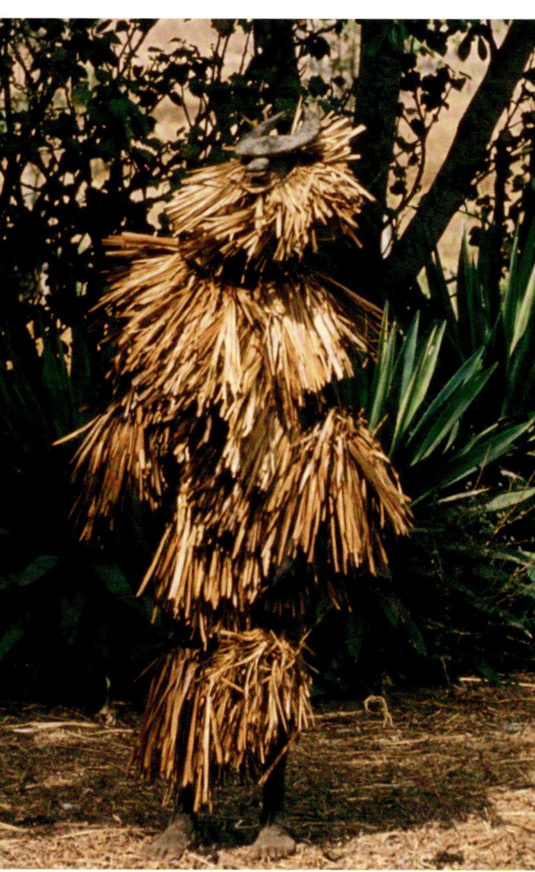

12.5

A wooden mask (representing a dwarf forest buffalo or bushcow; see fig. 12.7) and a dress of overlapping palm leaves complete this Ron Mangam masquerade costume. This masquerader was photographed in the Daffo hamlet of Hottom, which neighbors and is strongly influenced by the Sha.
PHOTOGRAPH BY BARBARA FRANK, 1972.

The importance of the mask types differs according to information given me by members of a small group of western Ron (of the high Plateau group) who intermarry with Sha and so possessed (and carved locally) the Mangam: the antelope head is the "big" (fig. 12.6) and the buffalo the "small" Mangam (fig. 12.7), which in this case also corresponded to the actual size of the carved masks. Murray described Mangam as "a cult whose purpose varies from village to village but which is generally associated with the encouragement of crops" (figs. 12.8, 12.9). He further noted in his report of 1952 that the Rindre of Wamba "believed that the masked figures are the dead people who have emerged from their graves."[8] An otherwise sketchy article on the Kantana (Mama) included in the early ethnographic survey compiled by the Temples (1919, 268–69) also confirms the existence of the Mangam complex and describes that "two men don carved wooden masks, with long horns, in representation of some animal, and fringes of dried grass depending therefrom effectually conceal the countenance of the wearer, who is thought to represent some person or thing long since dead." In accordance with this diversity, the importance of Mangam as compared to other cults (see below) also greatly varies. A description of its overwhelming impact on public life in many of the Kantana villages is given by Ames:

12.6 (TOP RIGHT)

The "big" Mangam, according to Ron informants is the waterbuck, whose horns are long and sweep backward (cf. fig. 12.9). This example also has incisions surrounding the eyes, which likely refer to patterns of facial scarification. Such markings join the human world with that of animals and the wild. Like the "small" Mangam, it is worn with a dress of layered palm leaves.

PHOTOGRAPH BY BARBARA FRANK, RON PEOPLES, DAFFO-HOTTOM, 1972.

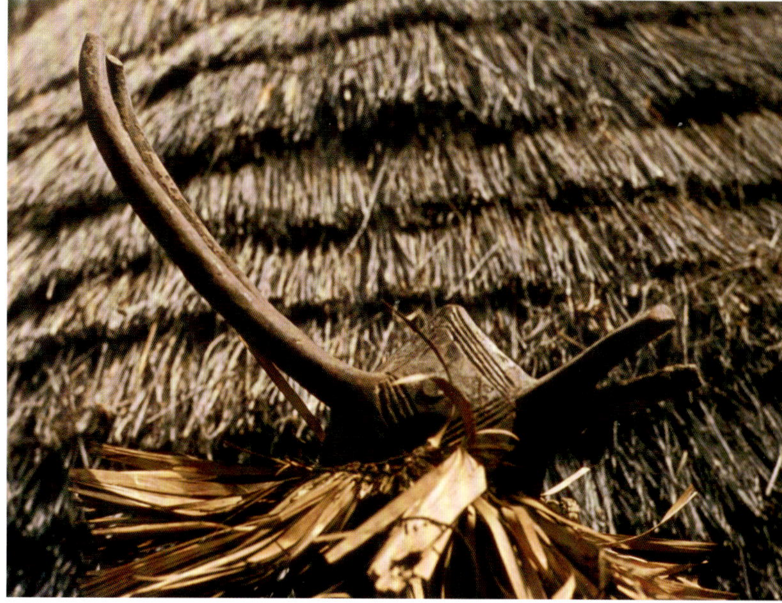

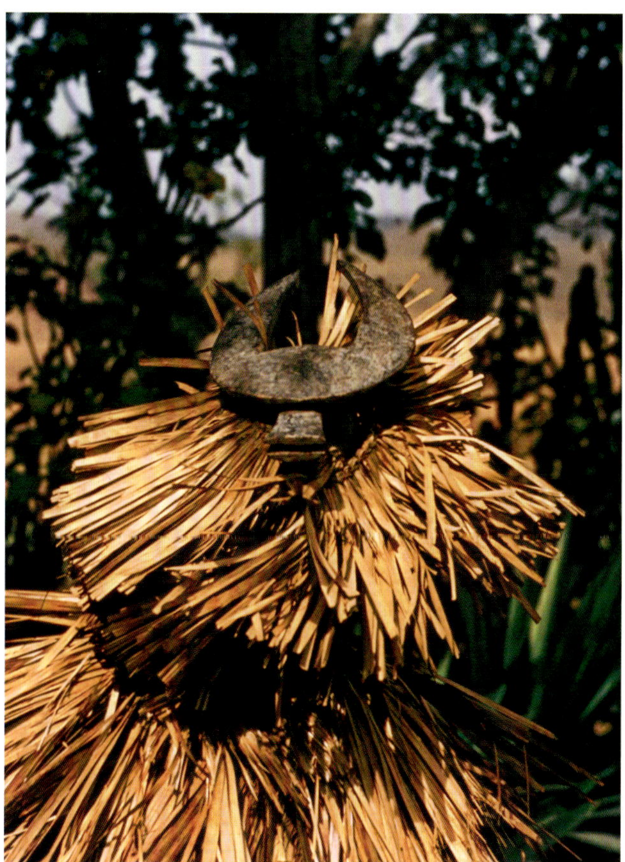

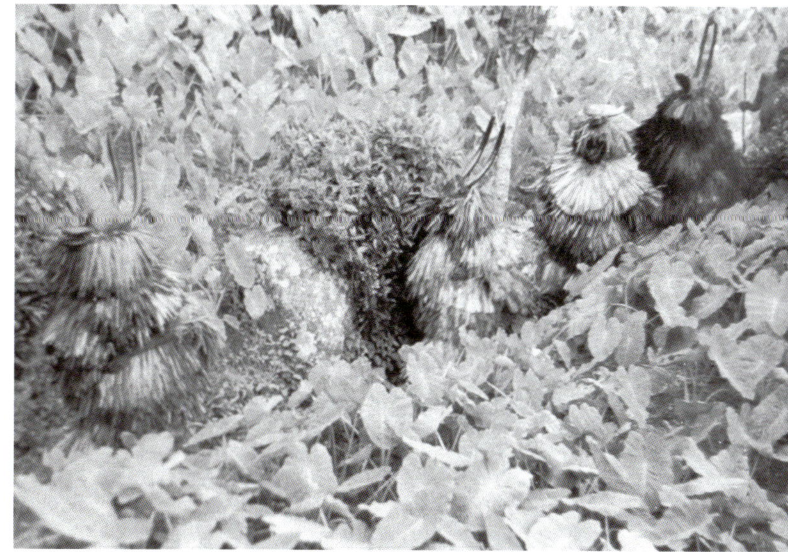

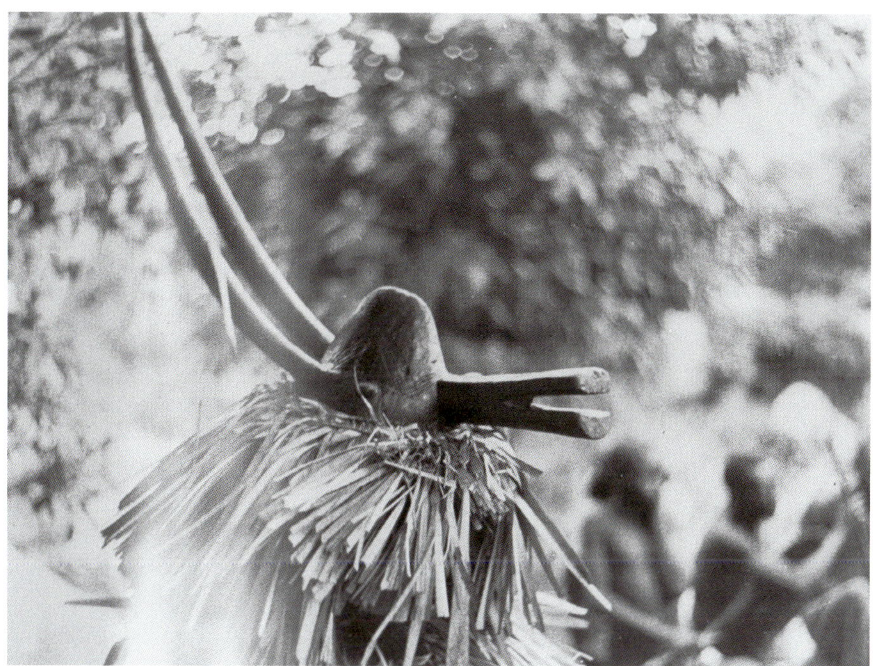

12.7 (CENTER LEFT)

The "small" Mangam masquerader seen in figure 12.5 posed for this picture.

PHOTOGRAPH BY BARBARA FRANK, RON PEOPLES, DAFFO-HOTTOM, 1972.

12.8 (CENTER RIGHT)

A group of Mangam masqueraders pass through a cocoyam field as they progress from one part of Sha village to another.

REPRODUCED COURTESY OF THE NATIONAL COMMISSION FOR MUSEUMS AND MONUMENTS, NIGERIA, NML-PA, 18.9.20.

12.9 (LEFT)

This "big" Mangam masquerade was photographed at Takafili village in 1952. It has the tall horns of the waterbuck and was colored black and rubbed with oil. This mask was given the personal name "Arandong."

REPRODUCED COURTESY OF THE NATIONAL COMMISSION FOR MUSEUMS AND MONUMENTS, NIGERIA, NML-PA, 18.9.19.

> An important social institution of the tribe is one known as Mangam, who may possibly be a supernatural being of which the institution is its natural agent. Although the theoretical aspect of Mangam is curiously indefinite, in practical effect it is a social club and a very exclusive one and yet members of it are alone able to deal with leprosy and skin complaints and sometimes fevers.
>
> Membership is obtained by paying two goats and forty-eight pots of beer and carries rank and honour in the village. It sets up a healthy rivalry in farming amongst the young generation of men so that they can obtain the necessary funds to qualify for election. There are periodical banquets and, whenever a new member is admitted, his entrance fee is consumed by the other members. Each village has its own Mangam with its special meeting-place, but such places have no stone or other sign of religious activity.
>
> In many villages, in fact in all outside the Kwarra [Kantana] group, it is the supreme political body in the village and maintains order and effects arrests of malefactors. In the old days, when it used to pass sentence on offenders, all the elders were as a rule members, and there were men garbed as Dodos [i.e., masquerades] in suitable costumes with which they impressed the general public in obedience to their dictates. [Ames 1934, 273–74]

Ames (1934, 276) reported a similarly high political position of Mangam for the northern villages of the Rindre (Lindiri, Nungu).

Among Kulere, Mangam was not generally of the same importance. In the village of Tof, for example, it was present under the name "Kukom," meaning leprosy, a cult that punished witches and thieves with that dreaded disease. The disease might be healed only by remedies owned by the cult members who enjoyed the cult's protection for themselves and their families as well as their property. The mask was carved locally as part of the cult paraphernalia. It appeared at the illness or death of a member; during feasting after harvest, which was held successively for different cults; at the initiation of a new member into the medical secrets of the cult; or during treatment of a man suffering from leprosy or of a woman having difficult delivery of a child. At these times the masquerader appeared carrying a club in one hand and a metal bell in the other. Strips of palm leaf falling from its costume were carefully collected because they were used as protective amulets (Frank 1981, 157, 177–96, fig. 104). Tof people used to "buy" protective and medical cults from their "owners" in other Kulere or Kantana villages. So it is likely that they once obtained Kukom in similar fashion. One could imagine how Mangam spread in this way from its original centers of importance to places where it was of more marginal significance.

In the Ron-speaking Sha group to the north of the Kulere, information from the village of Mundat shows how Mangam was incorporated as one stage in a hierarchical succession of graded associations (Frank 1976, 133–35). Six grades in the cult hierarchy were presided over by a male and female pair of spiritual beings represented through musical instruments/voice disguisers or masquerades. Initiation into the first two grades was compulsory for all boys. Mangam was the second of the optional stages. Here it was conceived to be a powerful female being who helped villagers secure plentiful crops and human fecundity. Its male pendant was a mirliton, or kazoo-like instrument, made with bamboo and spider's web. The fifth and next stage was called Akirang and was represented by a large male wooden face mask with fiber costume. Akirang's female partner Aja, wore a costume made of netting. Akirang and Mangam are the only wooden mask types to have been reported from the area (figs. 12.10, 12.11). Akirang has also been documented among Kantana (where it is called Ajo; fig. 12.12) and among some Kulere (under the name Asho; fig. 12.13) and may exist elsewhere as yet undocumented.[9] These masks are usually surmounted with a small sagittal crest; a serrated, fin-shaped projection from the chin (parallel to the facial

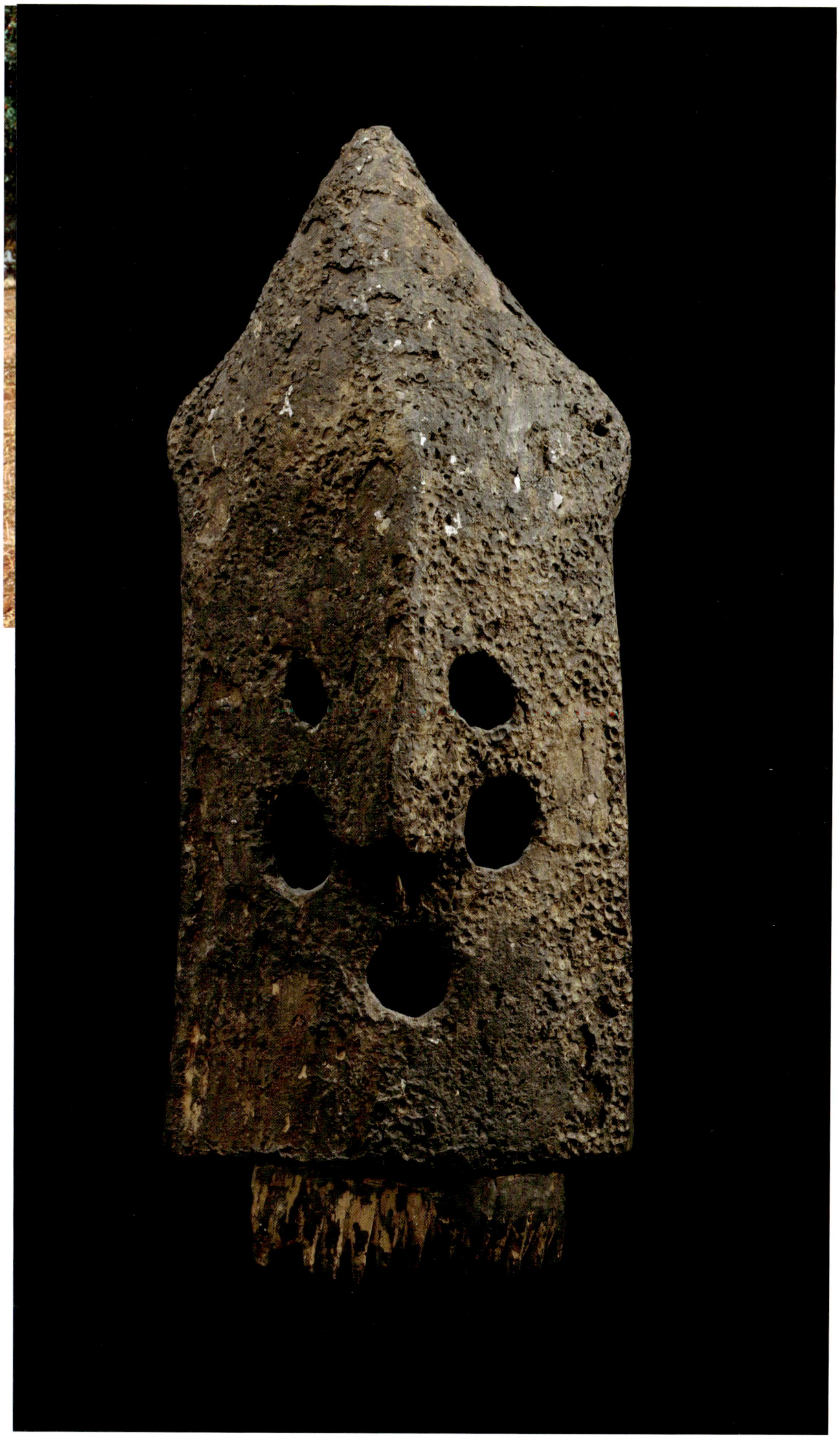

12.10
Mask (Akirang?)
Sha peoples (?), early to mid-twentieth century
Wood, composite material, adhesive
H: 52 cm
PRIVATE COLLECTION, PARIS
IMAGE: © PRIVATE COLLECTOR
PROVENANCE: PURCHASED IN 1970S

Based on its resemblance to figure 12.11, this mask, called Akirang, may have been used by the Ron-speaking Sha in the fifth stage of initiation into a graded ritual association. The double set of eyeholes on this half-helmet mask, which would have been worn over the head, produce a haunting effect. It may be, however, that the second set was carved so that the wearer's own eyes could be properly aligned. The pockmarked surface of the mask indicates where abrus seeds were formerly pressed into gum.

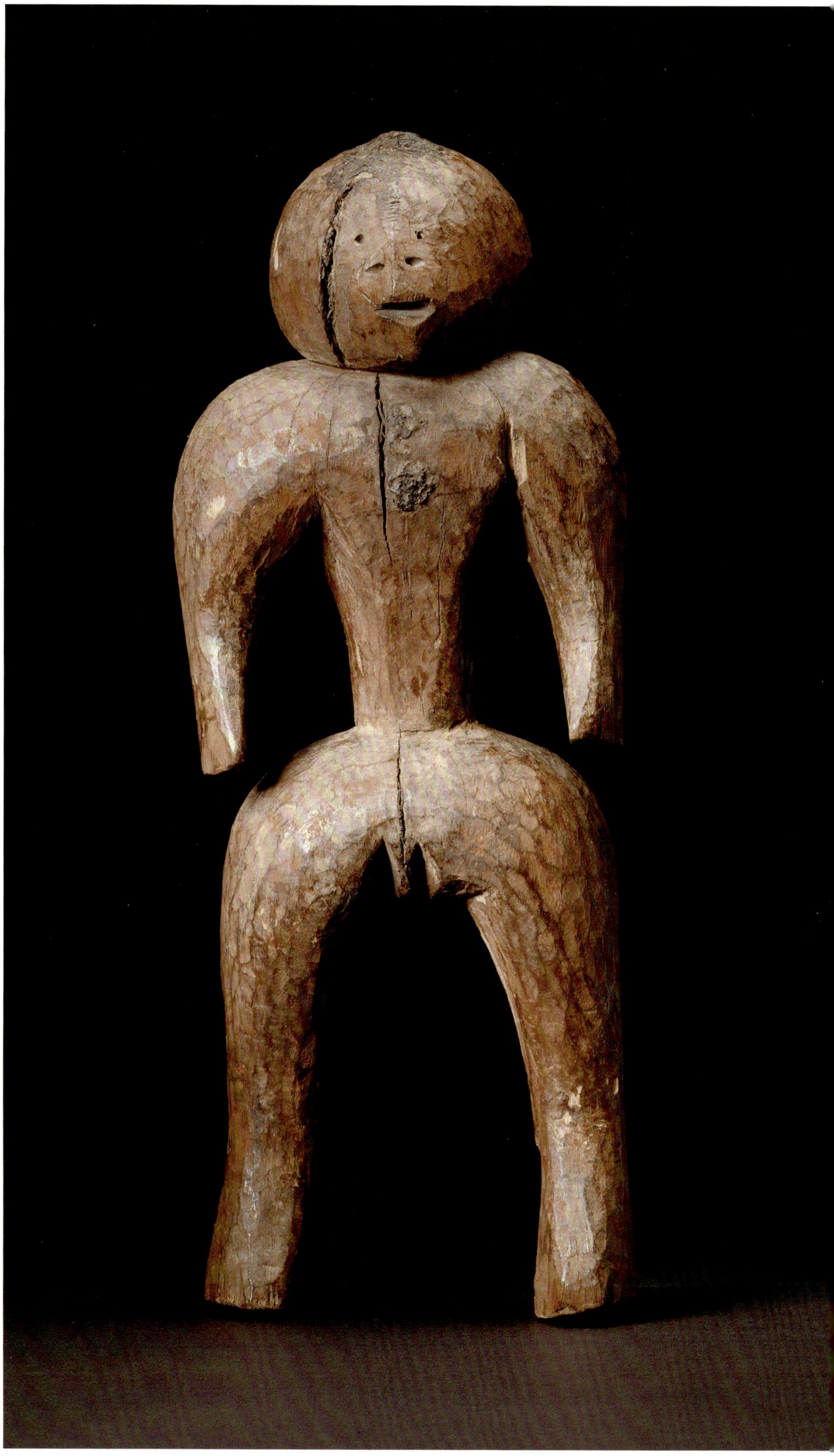

12.19

Female figure
Katana peoples (?), early to mid-twentieth century
Wood, resin, abrus seeds
H: 53 cm

ART INSTITUTE OF CHICAGO; RESTRICTED GIFT OF CLAIRE B. ZEISLER FOUNDATION, 1972.173

IMAGE: © THE ART INSTITUTE OF CHICAGO

PROVENANCE: COLLECTED BY PHILIPPE GUIMIOT; J. J. KLEJMAN, NEW YORK

This small female figure has a kind of toughness, expressed through its broad shoulders, dangling arms, and simple round head with no neck. There is a beautiful balance between the curves of the shoulders/arms and the hips/legs. Covered in the same powdery red ocher as the Mangam crests, this figure also has a residue of gum on the chest and at the top of the head into which abrus seeds would have been pressed. Without documentation, it is impossible to identify who made this figure. Instead, like the masks, it seems that this sculptural genre circulated among a cluster of peoples living south of the Jos Plateau.

12.20

A wooden figure in the Kulere village of Bargesh was called "Shagar" and was dressed with a fiber ruff around its neck. It measured 43 cm in height. Similar figures have been documented with fiber fringe around their hips.

REPRODUCED COURTESY OF THE NATIONAL COMMISSION FOR MUSEUMS AND MONUMENTS, NIGERIA, NML-PA, 12.53.14.

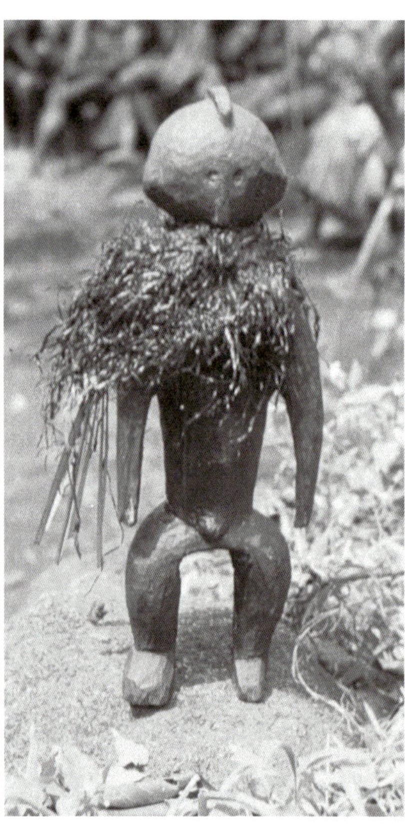

massive, swelling treatment of the upper body with diminutive arms, short, bowed legs, round heads, and schematic facial features (figs. 12.19, 12.20). Such figures typically exhibit the same powdery red patina (similar to most crest masks) and are provided with a short fringe of fiber around the hips.[12] Hardly any information on their use or functions has been reported. An exception is the village of Mundat in the Sha group, where such figures represent different types of masquerade and were shown to initiates in the respective stages of initiation (Frank 1976, 133). They were carved with the attributes of the masquerade in question, like Ajakawa's crest and Akirang's flat, mask face, and they might be adorned with ornaments, such as straws stuck through the nose and ears. Some Kulere figures were used in a cult, Tabalak, concerned with causing and healing skin diseases (Frank 1981, 184, fig. 107). ●

INTERLEAF h

A Myriad of Mangam Masks

MARLA C. BERNS

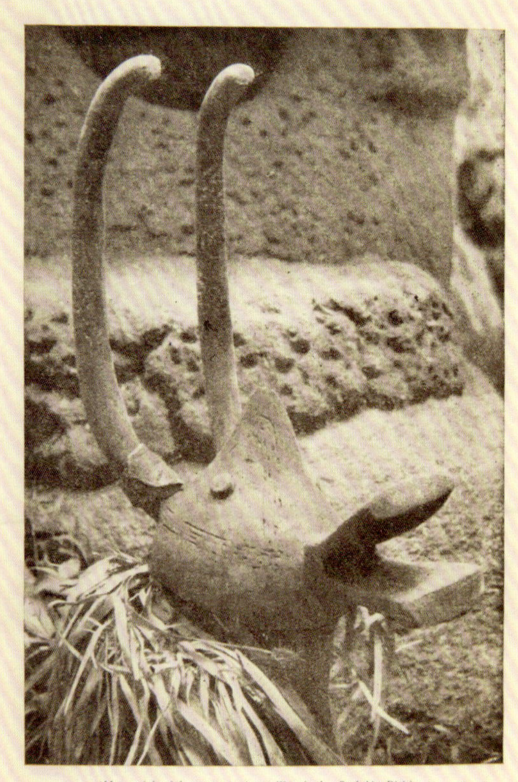
'Mangam' head-dress representing a Waterbuck. Pankshin Division

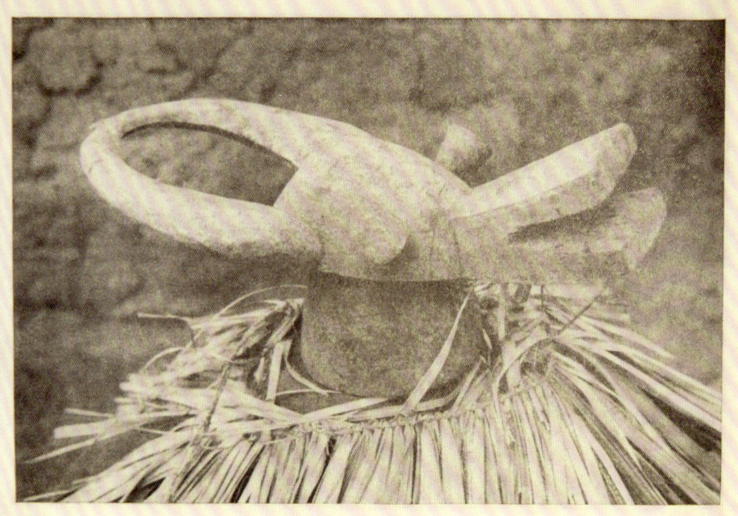
'Mangam' head-dress representing a Reedbuck. Southern Division

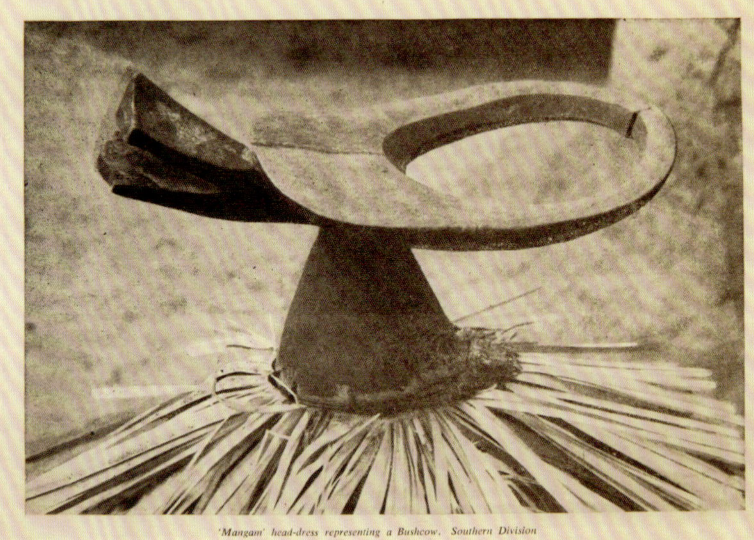
'Mangam' head-dress representing a Bushcow. Southern Division

H.1 (ABOVE)
"'Mangam' head-dress representing a reedbuck. Southern Division."
REPRODUCED FROM MURRAY (1952–1953), COURTESY OF THE NATIONAL
COMMISSION FOR MUSEUMS AND MONUMENTS, NIGERIA.

H.2 (ABOVE RIGHT)
"'Mangam' head-dress representing a waterbuck. Pankshin Division."
This same head crest was later photographed by Christian Duponcheel
and labeled as "Kaleri; Kwariffa village."
REPRODUCED FROM MURRAY (1952–1953), COURTESY OF THE NATIONAL
COMMISSION FOR MUSEUMS AND MONUMENTS, NIGERIA.

H. 3 (RIGHT)
"'Mangam' head-dress representing a bushcow. Southern Division."
REPRODUCED FROM MURRAY (1952–1953), COURTESY OF THE NATIONAL
COMMISSION FOR MUSEUMS AND MONUMENTS, NIGERIA.

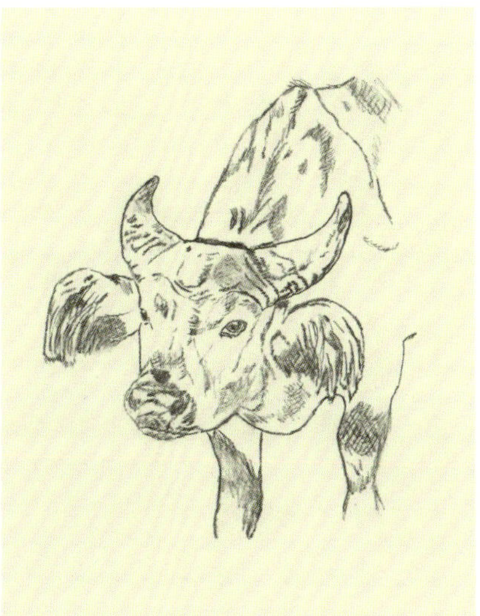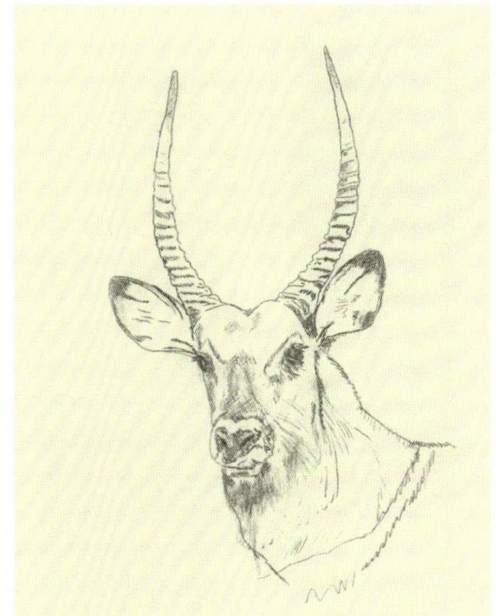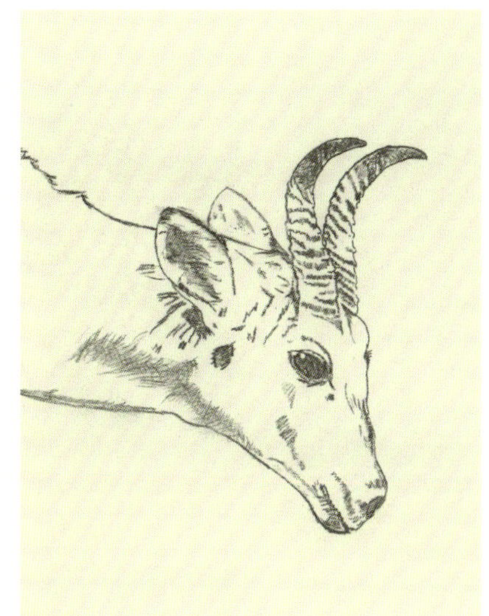

A stunning corpus of nearly 170 wooden crest masks—all photographed in the field—offers another example of the fluidity of artistic production and exchange in the Benue River Valley. In this case among several peoples living in close proximity and located just south of the Jos Plateau: the Kantana, Kulere, Sha, and Rindre, as well as the Mada, Ron of Sha, Bu, and Chesu.[1] As described by Barbara Frank in this volume (see chapter 12), these masks, often collectively identified as Mangam, were worn during events directed at securing agricultural success, promoting healing, and marking rites of passage as a part of a ritual complex called "Mangam."[2] Each Mangam mask consists of a central crest flanked by a snout and horns, a common formula for the construction of horizontal masks in the Benue Valley region and beyond (see chapter 10, this volume; McNaughton 1991). The variety of ways in which the snouts and horns are "arranged" relative to the central crest and the differences in the shapes of the three components are the most striking features of the vast Mangam corpus. The photographic record was carefully analyzed to determine if any correlations could be drawn between the formal characteristics of the masks and either their ethnic group attributions or the towns and villages where they were documented.[3]

Data for this analysis came from two separate photographic archives, and in most cases the photographs were accompanied by identifying information. In the early 1950s, the Antiquities Service of Nigeria under the direction of Kenneth Murray, Surveyor of Antiquities, documented more than 110 Mangam masks in the area south of the Jos Plateau.[4] More than a decade later, over an eleven-month period in 1964–1965, the Belgian art dealer Christian Duponcheel photographed more than 55 Mangam masks in the same area.[5] The extensive innovation evident in the record of photographed masks reinforces the

H.4
Illustration of a bushcow, or dwarf forest buffalo (*Syncerus caffer nanus*).
DRAWING BY SOPHIA LIVSEY. © 2011 FOWLER MUSEUM AT UCLA.

H.5
Illustration of a waterbuck (*Kobus ellipsiprymnus*).
DRAWING BY SOPHIA LIVSEY. © 2011 FOWLER MUSEUM AT UCLA.

H.6
Illustration of a reedbuck (*Redunca redunca*).
DRAWING BY SOPHIA LIVSEY. © 2011 FOWLER MUSEUM AT UCLA.

likelihood of their circulation among the diverse peoples living in proximate towns and villages across the region, an observation made by Frank elsewhere in this volume (see chapter 12, p. 394).

The starting point for this typological study of Mangam masks was the *Annual Report of the Antiquities Service for the Year 1952–1953* (Murray 1952–1953), which identified three key mask genres based on their formal characteristics and their relationship to one of three specific animal references: (1) "the bush cow" (or dwarf forest buffalo, *Syncerus caffer nanus*); (2) the waterbuck (*Kobus ellipsiprymnus*); and (3) the reedbuck (*Redunca redunca*)"[6] (figs. H.1–H.3). Illustrations of each of these animals demonstrate how faithfully the artists who made the masks captured the unique curvature of their horns, a diagnostic element that stands for the creatures themselves (figs. H.4–H.6). Sometimes the distinction between the antelopes is rather difficult to ascertain, but there was an effort to capture the shorter, forward curving horns of the reedbuck versus the long backward-sweeping and upturned horns of the waterbuck. The bushcow masks correspond to what Frank calls the "small" Mangam, and the waterbuck and reedbuck masks to the "big" Mangam. Notably, there were nearly twice as many "small" bushcow masks as "big" antelope masks in the photographic corpus.

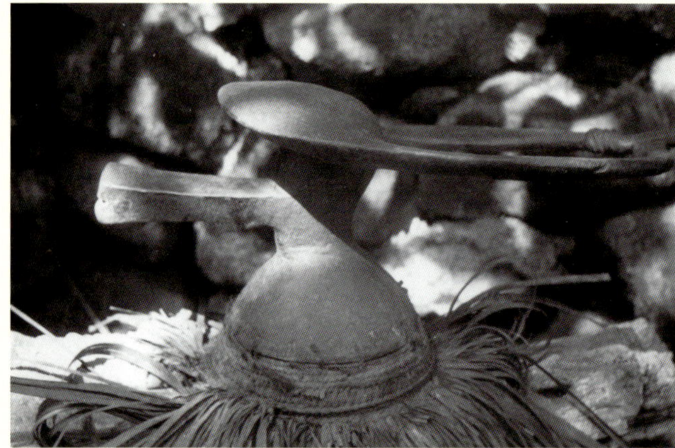

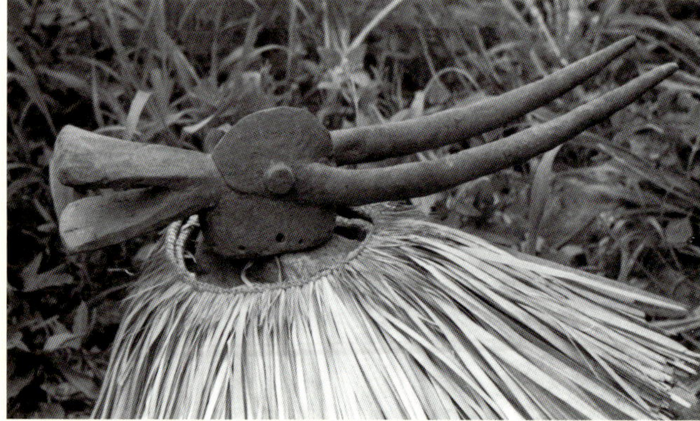

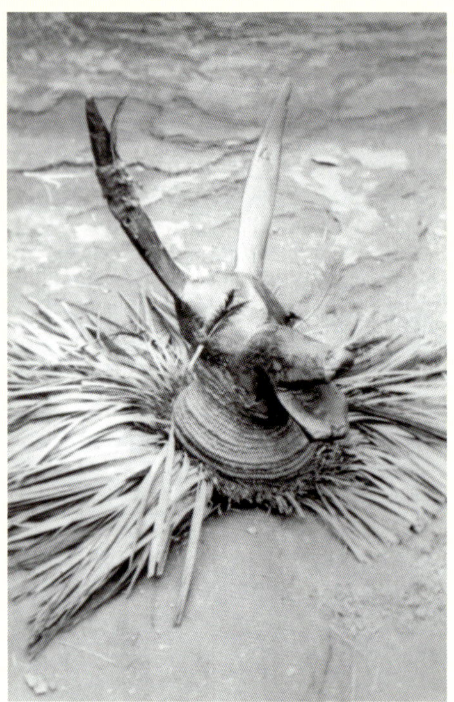

H.7 (ABOVE LEFT)
Mangam mask (called Kusai). Sha peoples. Colored black. L: 52 cm.
Owned by Ashebu at Kwandam Tasha.
PHOTOGRAPH: SHA TOWN, PANKSHIN DISTRICT, PLATEAU PROVINCE, 1952.
REPRODUCED COURTESY OF THE NATIONAL COMMISSION FOR MUSEUMS
AND MONUMENTS, NIGERIA, NML, 18.14.7.

H.8 (LEFT)
Mangam mask (called Arandong). [Sha peoples (?)]. L: 50.8 cm.
PHOTOGRAPH: SHA VILLAGE, 1952.
REPRODUCED COURTESY OF THE NATIONAL COMMISSION FOR MUSEUMS
AND MONUMENTS, NIGERIA, NML, 18.7.7.

H.9 (ABOVE)
Mangam mask. Mama [Kantana] peoples. Colored red. L: 59 cm.
Made before the town's inhabitants were born.
PHOTOGRAPH: KWARRA TOWN, SOUTHERN PLATEAU DISTRICT, PLATEAU
PROVINCE.
REPRODUCED COURTESY OF THE NATIONAL COMMISSION FOR MUSEUMS
AND MONUMENTS, NIGERIA, NML, 18.36.39.

In order to go beyond this general tripartite classification, the photographs were further divided into stylistic subtypes based on formal characteristics. Variety rather than coherence characterizes Mangam mask styles, and artists did not necessarily carve masks to fit a rigid prototype. Rather, they innovated upon the snout-crest-horn model arriving at a dizzying array of combinations, some subtle and others dramatic (figs. H.7–H.9). The small Mangam bushcow masks are a case in point, and artists took liberty in the stylization of the horns, often rendering them in beautiful full circles or nearly complete circles, which have made them especially appealing on the international art market (figs. H.10–H.12; cf. figs. 12.2, 12.3).[7]

Beyond style, the data accompanying each image was analyzed to determine if either location or ethnic group corresponded to particular mask forms. Unfortunately forty-four masks within the corpus were unaccompanied by information specifying ethnic group or location. Nevertheless, the findings (not grounded in statistical analysis) appear to reinforce the observation that Rubin and Frank each made separately, namely that attempts to correlate Mangam mask substyles to specific peoples or locales is "of little usefulness."[8] Neither ethnic group nor location appears to be a determinant of specific Mangam mask types, which circulated fluidly in the area.

Frank suggests that Mangam masks may have spread from "original centers of importance to places where [they were] of more marginal significance," namely from Kulere or Kantana towns to other locales. Of the 127 Mangam masks that had accompanying data, masks attributed to Kulere and Kantana peoples predominate. Masks were often attributed to peoples who called themselves by alternative names, such as Mama and Kwarra for Kantana or Tof for Kulere. Thirty-one masks were attributed to Kulere peoples, and forty-six masks to the Kantana. Three more were attributed to Kulere or Kantana. In addition, twenty-one were attributed to the Rindre (or Wamba), eight to the Ron/Sha, three to the Sha, and one to Chesu. Divorced from specific historical and

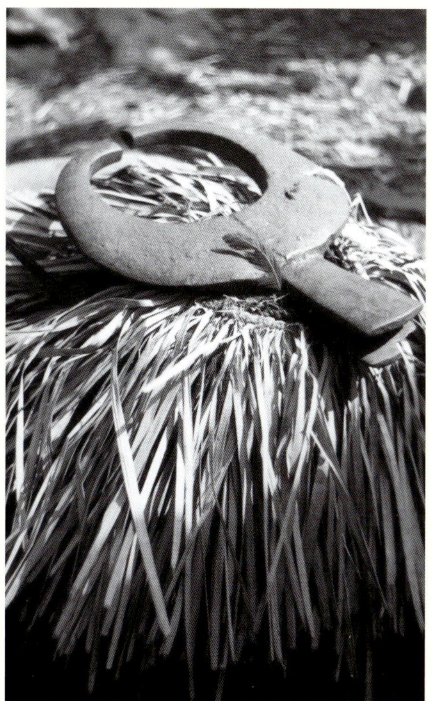

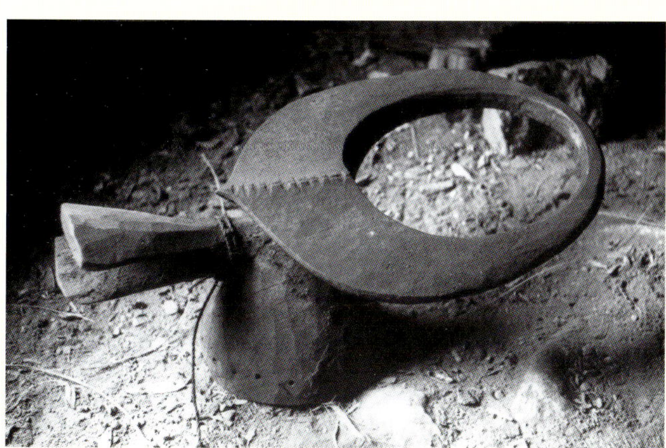

H.10 (LEFT)
"Small" Mangam mask (bushcow). Tof [Kulere] peoples. L. 43.8 cm. Owned by Kabis; carved by his father five years prior.
PHOTOGRAPH: TOF TOWN, PANKSHIN DISTRICT, PLATEAU PROVINCE, 1952.
REPRODUCED COURTESY OF THE NATIONAL COMMISSION FOR MUSEUMS AND MONUMENTS, NIGERIA, NML, 12.56.32.

H.11 (BELOW LEFT)
"Small" Mangam mask (bushcow). Kaleri [Kulere] peoples. L: 48.3 cm.
PHOTOGRAPH: BIRKUL TOWN, PANKSHIN DISTRICT, PLATEAU PROVINCE, 1954.
REPRODUCED COURTESY OF THE NATIONAL COMMISSION FOR MUSEUMS AND MONUMENTS, NIGERIA, NML, 19.96.15.

H.12 (BELOW)
"Small" Mangam mask (bushcow). Kaleri [Kulere] peoples. L: 50.2 cm.
PHOTOGRAPH: RICHA TOWN, PANKSHIN DISTRICT, PLATEAU PROVINCE, 1954.
REPRODUCED COURTESY OF THE NATIONAL COMMISSION FOR MUSEUMS AND MONUMENTS, NIGERIA, NML, 19.92.37.

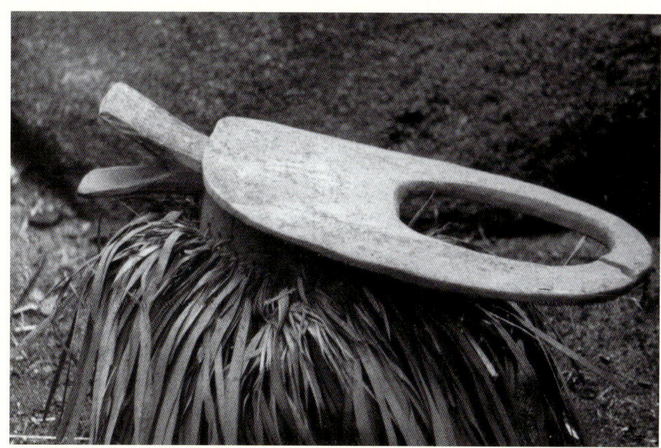

population data or information about the criteria for ethnic group attributions that were used by the Antiquities Service or Duponcheel, the corpus does not provide definitive evidence to confirm unequivocally that Mangam forms originated among Kulere and Kantana peoples and subsequently spread across the region. Nevertheless, data indicate that Mangam masks were concentrated in Kulere and Kantana towns in the mid-twentieth century.

Additional analysis showed that a specific Mangam mask style rarely corresponded to a single town or village, and about twenty-eight locales were included in the survey, presumably those that sponsored masks and Mangam performances.[9] Survey techniques and other factors unknowable from the record may have affected the number of Mangam masks that were shown to surveyors to photograph or otherwise document. We are not considering here categories of information such as a town or village's population, relative wealth, and commitment to Mangam masquerades and their associated ritual complexes, which may or may not be reflected in the number of masks from any given place. Field photographs of the masks in performance, also taken during the Antiquities Service Survey, show that several appeared at once often mixing bushcow and antelope examples (see fig. 12.9).

Fewer than three masks were documented in each of twenty-one of the total named towns. Seven or more were documented in only six named towns: Bargesh (Kulere), Kwarra (Kantana), Richa, Sha, Tof (Kulere), and Wamba (Rindre). In each of these six places, both "big" antelope and "small" bushcow masks were photographed.[10] The most illuminating information emerged from towns where seven or more masks were documented. For example, the archives of Kenneth Murray and Duponcheel include fifteen "small" buffalo and "big" antelope masks in the Kantana town of Kwarra. Two of the "big" antelope Mangam masks appear quite similar to the reedbuck example published in the Antiquities Service report (fig. H.13, see also fig. H.1), but their crowns and horns

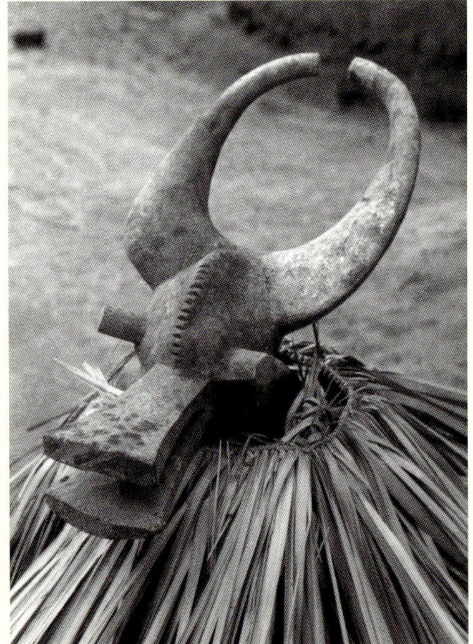

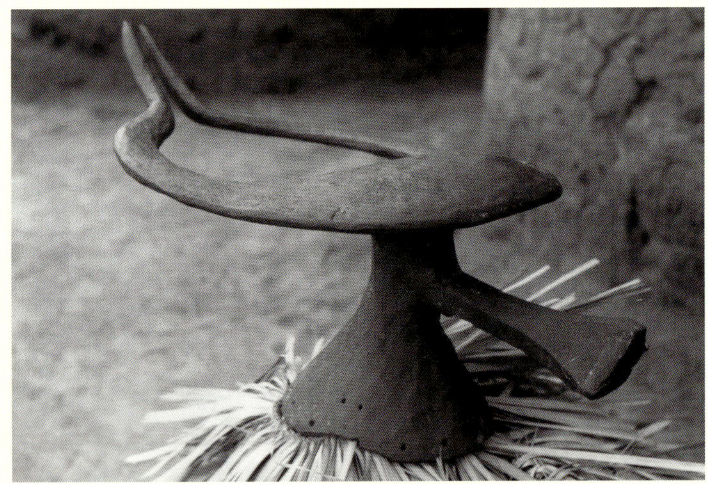

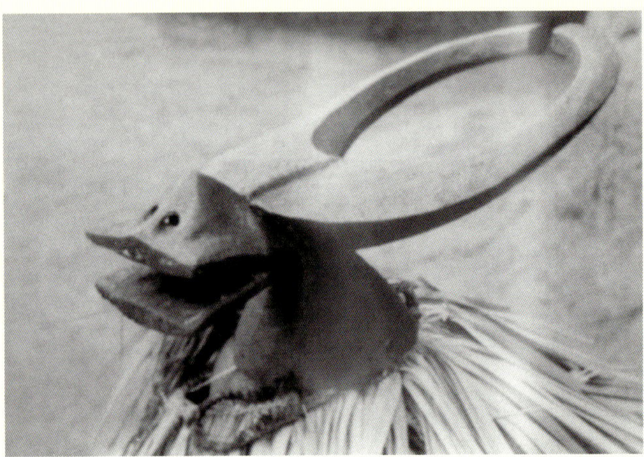

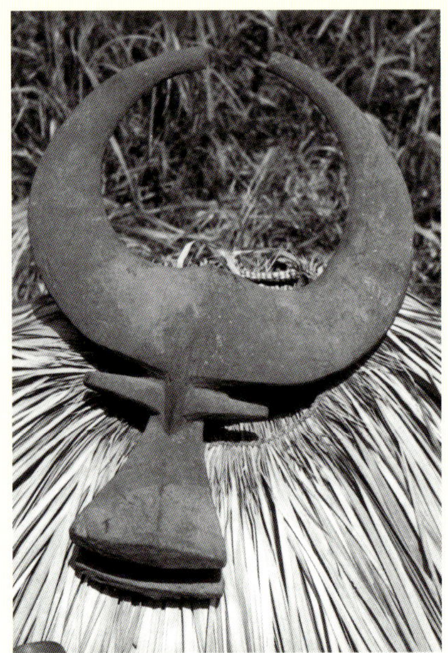

H.13 (TOP LEFT)

"Big" Mangam mask. Mama [Kantana] peoples. Colored red. L: 53.3 cm.

PHOTOGRAPH: KWARRA TOWN, SOUTHERN PLATEAU DISTRICT, PLATEAU PROVINCE, 1952.

REPRODUCED COURTESY OF THE NATIONAL COMMISSION FOR MUSEUMS AND MONUMENTS, NIGERIA, NML, 18.43.5.

H.14 (TOP RIGHT)

"Small" Mangam mask (bushcow). Mama [Kantana] peoples. Colored red. L: 58.4 cm.

PHOTOGRAPH: KWARRA TOWN, SOUTHERN PLATEAU DISTRICT, PLATEAU PROVINCE, 1952.

REPRODUCED COURTESY OF THE NATIONAL COMMISSION FOR MUSEUMS AND MONUMENTS, NIGERIA, NML, 18.45.15.

H.15 (BELOW LEFT)

"Small" Mangam mask (bushcow). Kwarra [Kantana] peoples.

PHOTOGRAPH: KWARRA TOWN, SOUTHERN PLATEAU DISTRICT, PLATEAU PROVINCE, 1952.

REPRODUCED COURTESY OF THE NATIONAL COMMISSION FOR MUSEUMS AND MONUMENTS, NIGERIA, NML, 18.44.12.

H.16 (BELOW RIGHT)

"Small" Mangam mask (bushcow). Kwarra [Kantana] peoples. Kworra wood, colored red. L: 54.6 cm. Carved about twelve years prior.

PHOTOGRAPH: KWARRA TOWN, SOUTHERN PLATEAU DISTRICT, PLATEAU PROVINCE, 1952.

REPRODUCED COURTESY OF THE NATIONAL COMMISSION FOR MUSEUMS AND MONUMENTS, NIGERIA, NML, 18.37.7.

are more gently rounded and incisions were carved along the crests of the head, which may or may not have referred to human scarification markings. Three of the "small" buffalo masks photographed at Kwarra illustrate the breadth of innovation. One is distinguished by a long neck with horns aligned perpendicularly that curve backward into "swallow-tail" tips (fig. H.14). The horns are balanced by a long, slender snout that flares at the lip. Another "small" Mangam has horns that curve backward and outline a heart-shaped void (fig. H.16). The snout ends in a wide flare and "bushcow ears" separate the horns from the snout. The third idiosyncratic Kwarra mask has an unusual snout with an undulating upper lip and two indentations that look like "nostrils," suggesting a more mimetic representation of the animal's head than other masks (fig. H.15). These Kwarra examples are different enough in approach to suggest that several artists were likely to have been responsible for carving them.

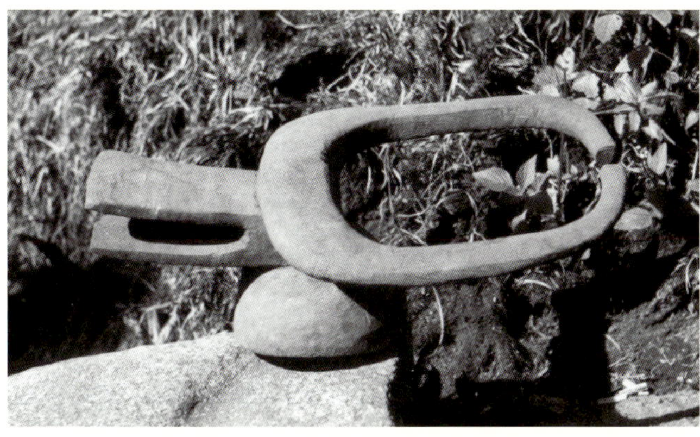

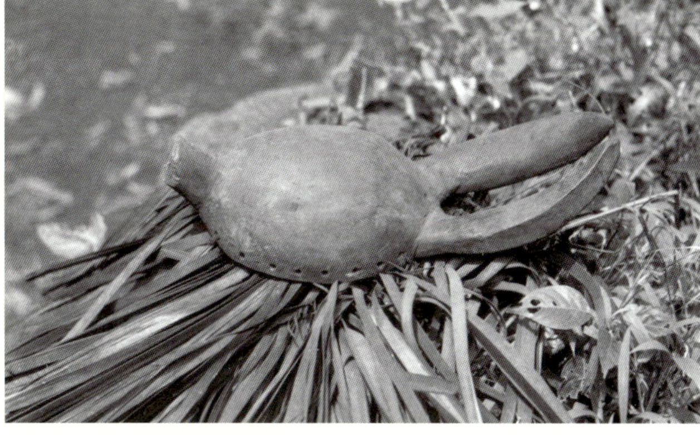

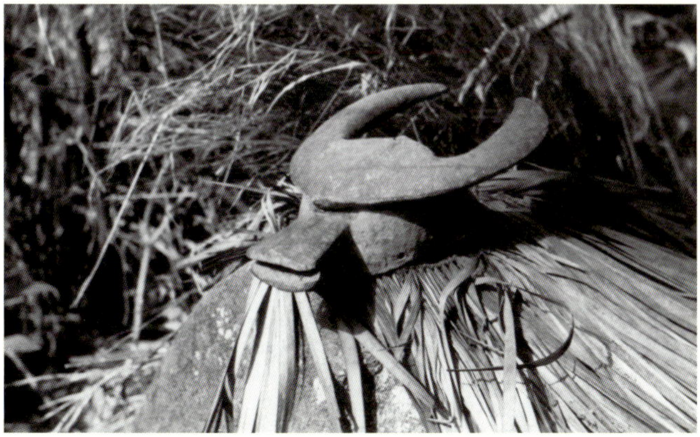

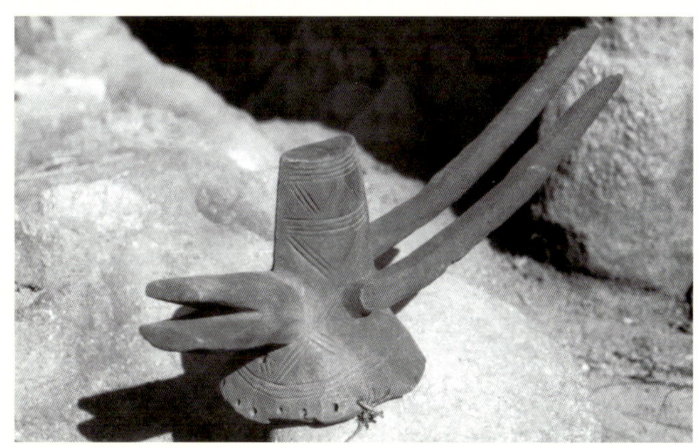

H.17
"Small" Mangam mask (bushcow). Kaleri [Kulere] peoples. L: 38.7 cm.
Owned by Aban; carved by Awoshey of Bargesh twenty years prior.
PHOTOGRAPH: BARGESH TOWN, PANKSHIN DISTRICT, PLATEAU PROVINCE, 1952.
REPRODUCED COURTESY OF THE NATIONAL COMMISSION FOR MUSEUMS AND
MONUMENTS, NIGERIA, NML, 12.49.32.

H.18
"Small" Mangam mask (bushcow). Kaleri [Kulere] peoples. L: 26.7 cm.
Owned by Amusa; carved eight years prior.
PHOTOGRAPH: BARGESH TOWN, PANKSHIN DISTRICT, PLATEAU PROVINCE,
NO DATE.
REPRODUCED COURTESY OF THE NATIONAL COMMISSION FOR MUSEUMS
AND MONUMENTS, NIGERIA, NML, 12.50.34.

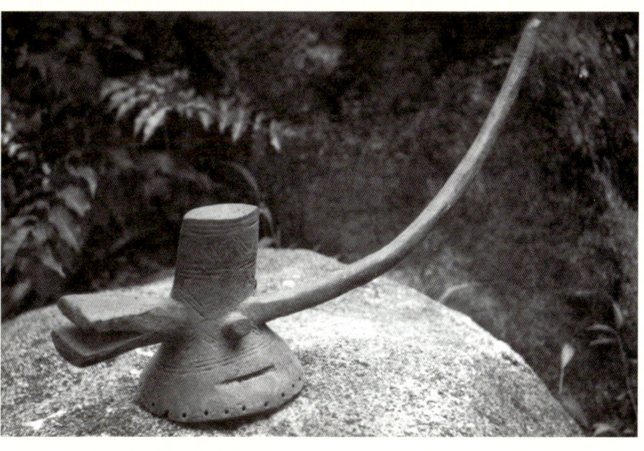

H.19
Mangam mask. Kaleri [Kulere] peoples. L: 34.9 cm.
Owned by Indas; inherited.
PHOTOGRAPH: BARGESH TOWN, PANKSHIN DISTRICT, PLATEAU PROVINCE, 1952.
REPRODUCED COURTESY OF THE NATIONAL COMMISSION FOR MUSEUMS AND
MONUMENTS, NIGERIA, NML, 12.52.7.

H.20
"Big" Mangam mask (antelope). Kaleri [Kulere] peoples. L: 52.1 cm.
PHOTOGRAPH: BARGESH TOWN, PANKSHIN DISTRICT, PLATEAU PROVINCE, 1952.
REPRODUCED COURTESY OF THE NATIONAL COMMISSION FOR MUSEUMS AND
MONUMENTS, NIGERIA, NML, 12.49.28.

H.21
"Big" Mangam mask (antelope). Kaleri [Kulere] peoples. L: 69.9 cm.
Owned by Agbedi, the Wakili [Hausa for "representative"].
PHOTOGRAPH: RICHA TOWN, PANKSHIN DISTRICT, PLATEAU PROVINCE, 1954.
REPRODUCED COURTESY OF THE NATIONAL COMMISSION FOR MUSEUMS AND
MONUMENTS, NIGERIA, NML, 19.94.5.

The diversity of Mangam mask forms in Kwarra was not a singular occurrence. Murray and Duponcheel's archives document a total of fourteen masks from the Kulere town of Bargesh, where both "big" and "small" Mangam masks were represented, ranging from the more commonplace buffalo styles to more distinctive and one-of-a-kind forms. Roughly two-thirds of the Bargesh group were "small" Mangam (figs. H.17, H.18). Several others do not easily fit either the "small" or "big" Mangam categories. For example, one has a short, knob-like snout and an especially rounded crest coupled with the upward curving horns of the reedbuck (fig. H.19). Another rare "big" antelope mask features a columnar crest. A pattern of triangular and linear incisions adorns the crest and continues onto the cap (fig. H.20). The only other example of this substyle was documented in the Kulere town of Richa. It has a single long horn (it is not possible to tell from the photograph if the other had broken off) and rows of linear incisions (fig. H. 21).

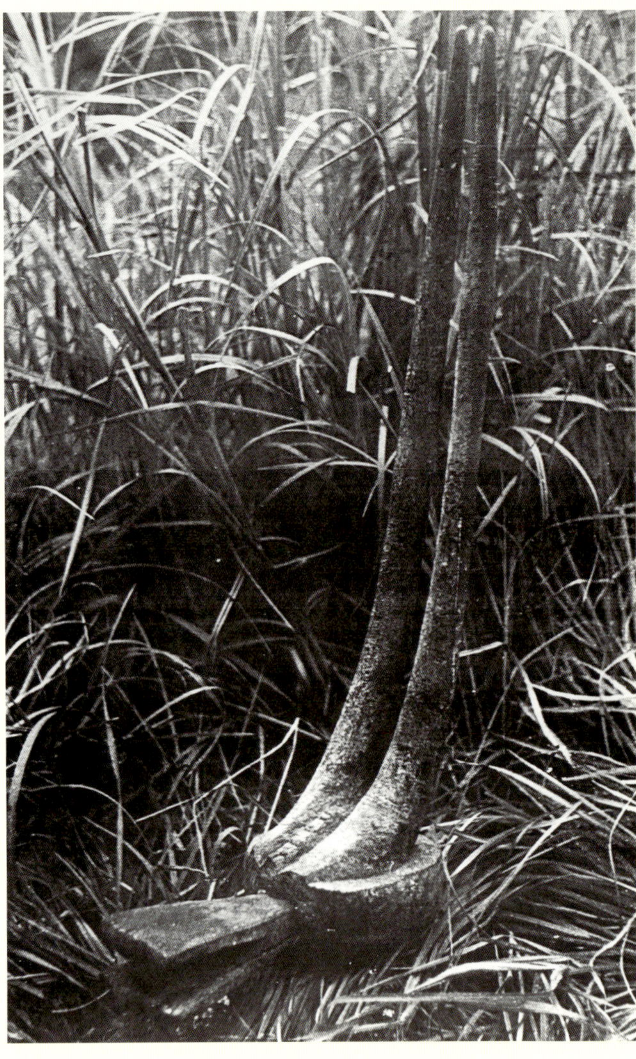

H.27
"Big" Mangam mask. Kantana peoples. L: 66.4 cm.
PHOTOGRAPH BY CHRISTIAN DUPONCHEEL, MANGUR VILLAGE, 1965.

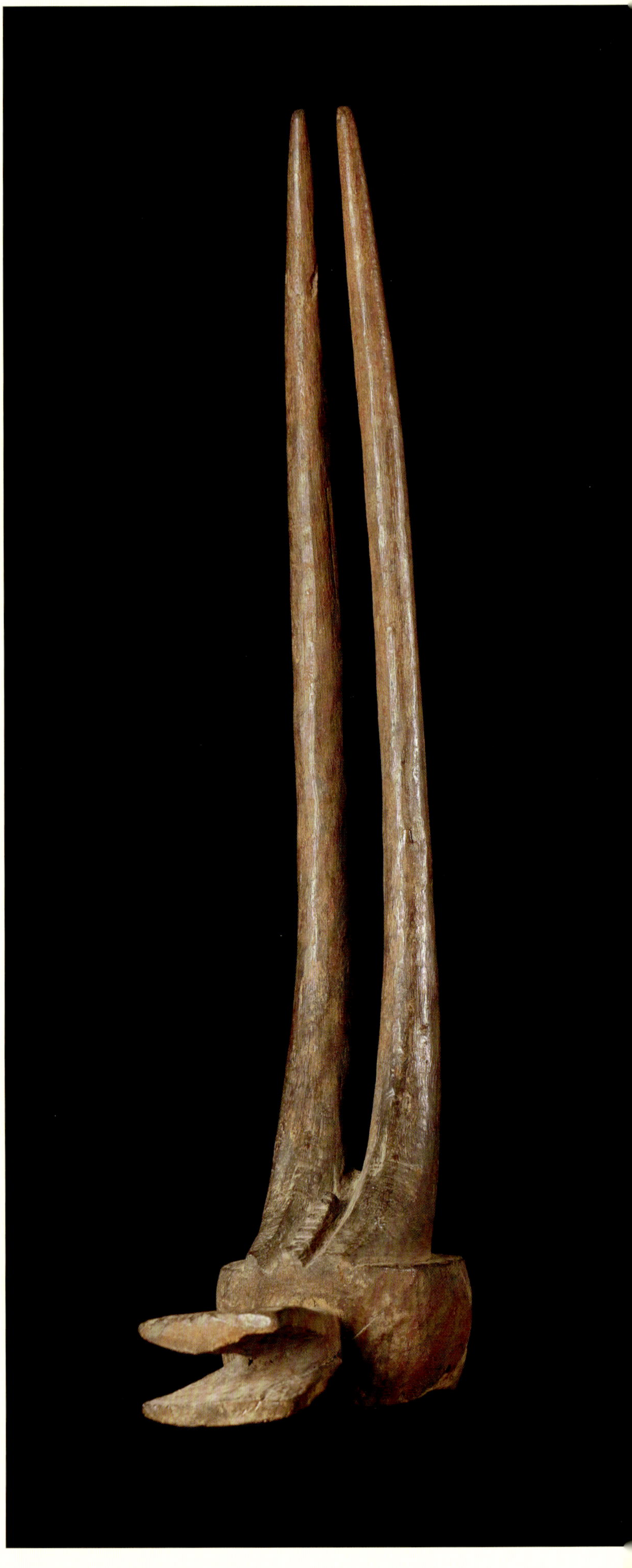

H.28
Crest mask ("big" Mangam)
Kantana peoples, Mangur village, before 1965
Wood
H: 70.1
COLLECTION OF MARK GROUDINE & CYNTHIA PUTNAM
IMAGE: COURTESY COLLECTOR. PHOTOGRAPH © 2010 ADAM L. WEINTRAUB
PROVENANCE: ALAN BRANDT, NEW YORK, 1970S; COLLECTION OF FRIEDA AND
MILTON ROSENTHAL, 1972–2008

This "big" Mangam mask, photographed in situ by Christian Duponcheel
in 1965 (see fig. H.27), has unusually tall straight horns, which emerge
directly out of the crown of the head. The surface has been rubbed with
a red powder and the patina on the horns suggests long term use.

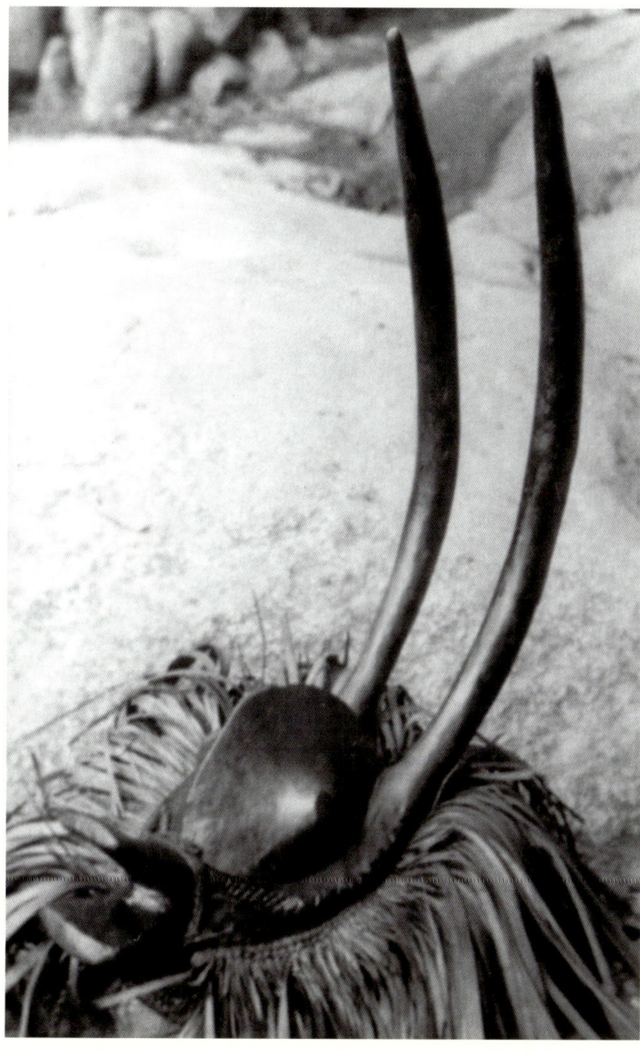

H.29
"Big" Mangam mask (antelope). Ron /Sha peoples. Colored black.
L: 68.6 cm. Named: Arandong.
PHOTOGRAPH: SHA VILLAGE, NO DATE.
REPRODUCED COURTESY OF THE NATIONAL COMMISSION FOR MUSEUMS AND
MONUMENTS, NIGERIA, NML, 18.12.34.

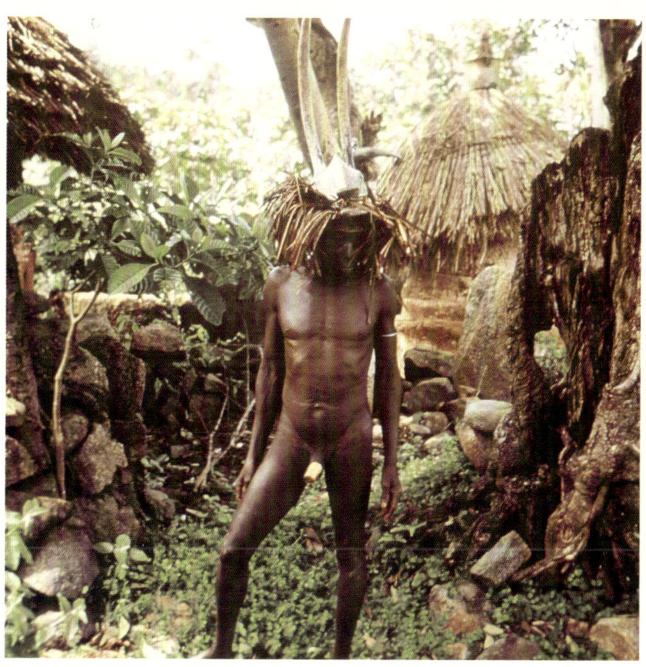

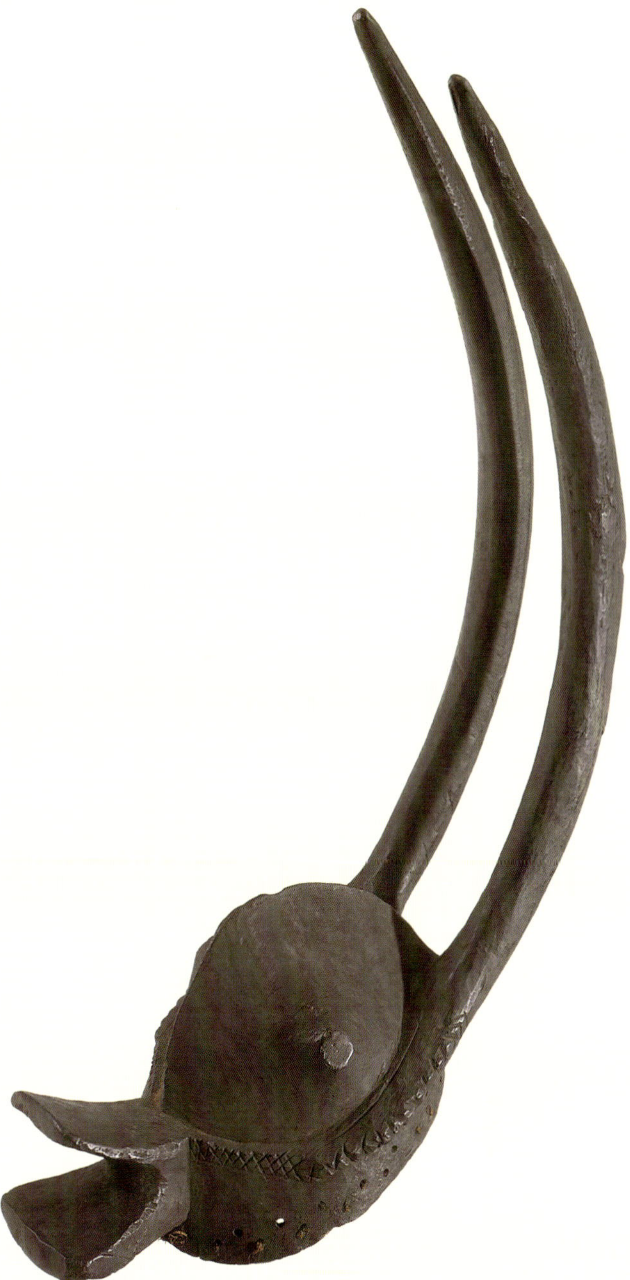

H.30
Crest mask ("big" Mangam)
Ron-speaking Sha peoples, Sha village, before 1952
Wood
H: 65 cm
COLLECTION OF TOBY AND BARRY HECHT
PHOTOGRAPH © 2010 GREG STALEY
PROVENANCE: IBRAHIM KAO

This mask, called Arandong and photographed in situ in 1952 (see fig
H.29), has the long, elegant upward sweeping horns of the waterbuck.
The lines of delicate cross-hatching along the side of its head are likely
to be representations of facial scarification, contributing to its hybrid
human-animal character.

H.31
A man from Sha village wears a "big" Mangam head crest that looks
to be made from the actual skull and horns of a waterbuck. There is an
intriguing relationship between this mask and the one illustrated in
figure H.28.
PHOTOGRAPH BY FRANK MCEWEN, SHA VILLAGE, 1950S–1960S.

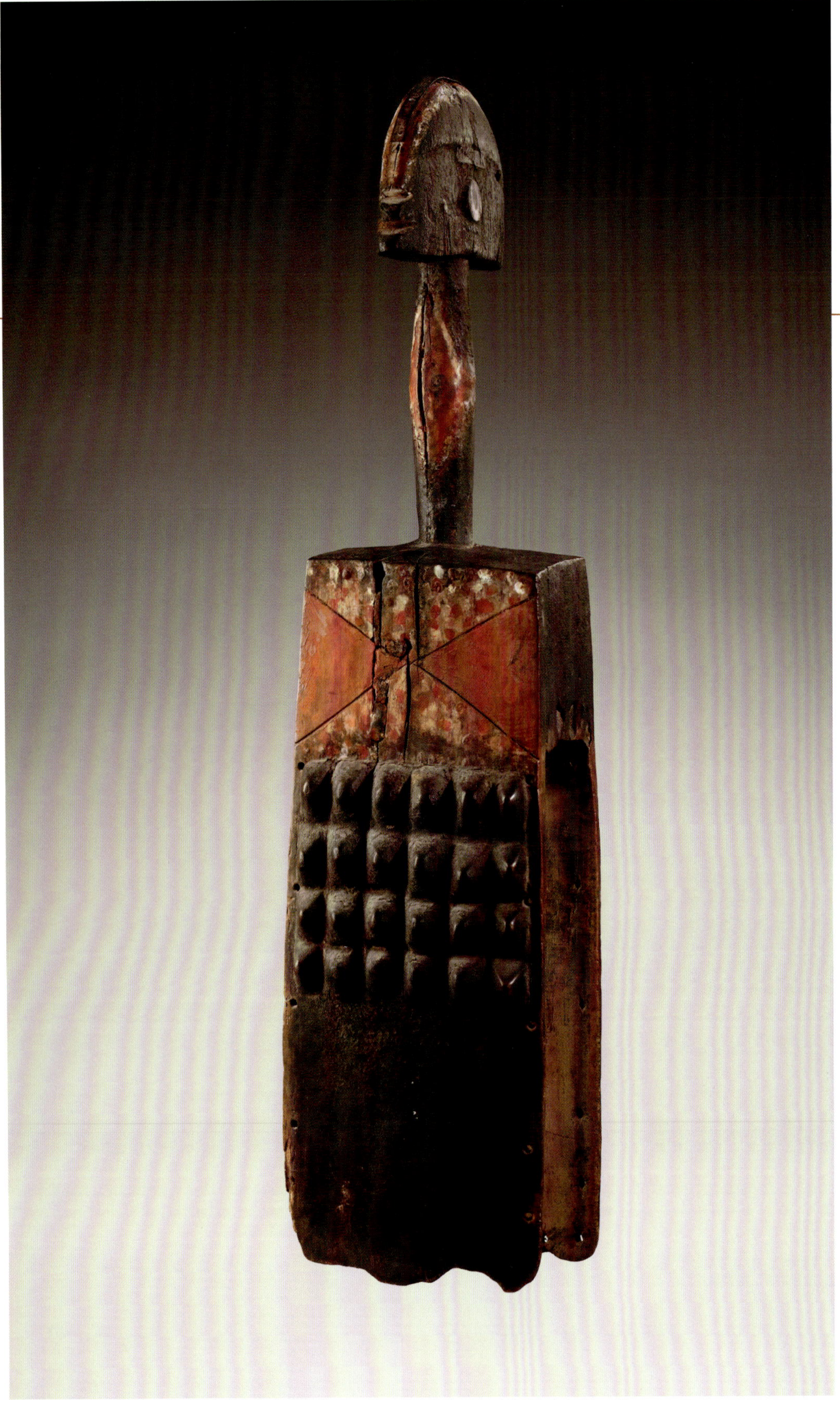

CHAPTER **13**

Embodiments Large and Small:
Sacred Wood Sculpture of the Wurkun

JOERG ADELBERGER

WURKUN AND BIKWIN: PEOPLE OR REGION?

Brief perusal of information on African arts, whether on the Internet or in exhibition and auction catalogs, would give the impression that there existed a "tribe" called Wurkun, particularly acknowledged for producing two types of distinctive wooden objects: small-scale columnar statues and imposing, tall "vertical" masks—often referred to in the literature as "yoke" masks.[1] There is a certain, partial truth to this, but matters are rather more complicated as this chapter will explain. Initially, however, we must address the questions: Who are the Wurkun and Bikwin, and where do they live?

A chain of sandstone mountains, known as the Muri Mountains, runs west to east above the northern bank of the Upper Benue through the Nigerian states of Bauchi, Gombe, Taraba, and Adamawa. The highest peaks of the chain exceed 1,000 meters (fig. 13.2). Around its midpoint, the chain splits into two parallel mountain ranges with a valley between them; the western end of this section joins the Bauchi Plateau, while the eastern end merges into the Longuda Plateau. The hilly character of this land, abetted by partial seasonal flooding along its southern ranges, has rendered it inaccessible; hence it was, and has remained, somewhat marginal both politically and economically. The Muri Mountains are home to numerous, small and diverse ethnolinguistic groups, living predominantly from agriculture (with millet, sorghum, maize, and beans as their staple crops) and keeping cattle and goats in modest numbers (fig. 13.3). The linguistic diversity could hardly be greater: while some groups at the western end of the Muri Mountains speak languages belonging to the Chadic family of the Afro-Asiatic phylum, the remainder speak languages of the entirely different Niger-Congo phylum.[2]

A cluster of these ethnolinguistic groups, living in the western Muri Mountains, has become known as "Wurkun" (for a detailed discussion, see Adelberger 1992). This common designation is Jukun in origin and simply means "people of the hills." Its use predates colonialism. A first written reference to Wurkun occurs in the accounts of members of the Niger-Benue expedition undertaken in 1854 under the command of William Baikie (Crowther 1855, 120). So, we know that by the mid-nineteenth century "Wurkun" already had currency as an umbrella term that externally bestowed an identity wider than that of the local ethnic group. Like other such terms originated by outsiders, it came to be accepted in some contexts by many to whom it was applied. Whether this was also the case by the mid-nineteenth century we have no way of knowing. Nowadays, Piya, Kulung, Kwonci, and Kode, although speakers of largely

Judging from the resemblance of its hemispherical head and minimal features to those of a small *kabalou* figure documented among the Leemak (see fig. 13.26), this vertical mask probably comes from Wurkun or Bikwin groups in the southwestern Muri Mountains. Its weathered surface and the band of metal nailed on the head to keep the wood from splitting further testify to a long history of use (see fig. 13.24). Note the holes along the edges of the support planks where strings of raffia would have been attached to hide the wearer standing underneath the mask. The rows of "bumps" on the front and back panels may represent cicatrization marks, and the swelling in the middle of the neck recalls an Adam's apple.

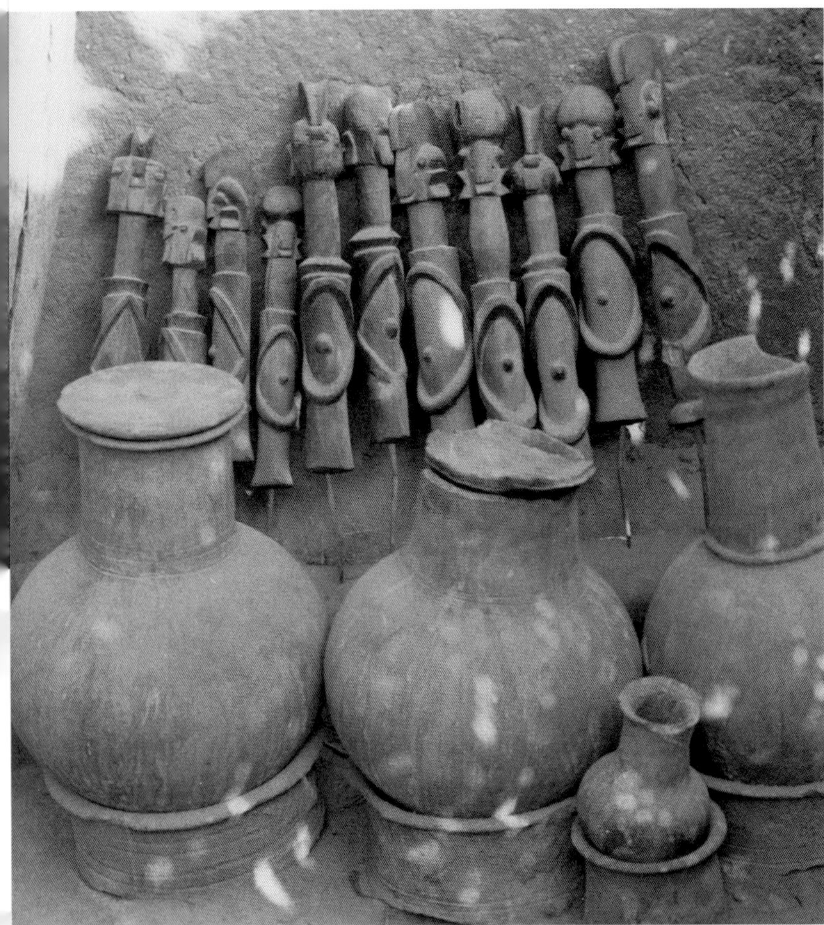

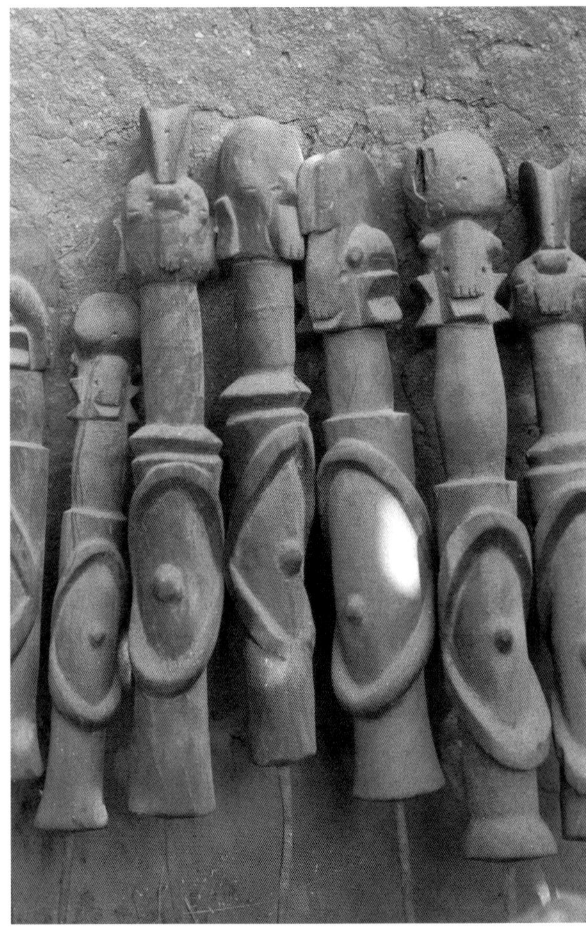

13.4

Taken by Arnold Rubin more than twenty years prior to my own fieldwork, this photograph demonstrates the abundance of columnar spiked figures (*kundul*) that once existed in the Muri Mountains. This collection was found in one compound in Lunga, a Piya village in the northwestern part of the range. The pots in the foreground are associated with offerings made to the *kundul*.

PHOTOGRAPH BY ARNOLD RUBIN, LUNGA, JANU-ARY 10, 1966, RUBIN ARCHIVE, FOWLER MUSEUM AT UCLA, NEG. NO. 1624.

13.5

A close-up of some of the *kundul* seen in figure 13.4 shows that the figures are carved in different sizes with heads and faces that vary greatly. Common to all in this group, however, are lozenge-shaped arms and a protruding umbilicus. Parallel incisions on the upper or lower jaw most probably represent (filed) teeth—a feature most often encountered in the northern Muri Mountains.

PHOTOGRAPH BY ARNOLD RUBIN, LUNGA, JANU-ARY 10, 1966, RUBIN ARCHIVE, FOWLER MUSEUM AT UCLA, NEG. NO. 1626.

Adelberger 2009; Yakubu 1992,147; Hogben and Kirk-Greene 1966, 447–64; Hogben 1967, 239–50). Substantial population movements ensued: it was to escape slave raids by Emir Yakubu of Bauchi that the Piya are said to have migrated from the Gwandum hills in Tangale-Waja area to the south and southwest.[7] Subjected to recurrent attacks by Fulani from Bauchi and Muri, the Nyam who had lived in the western end of the Muri Mountains moved to Gateri (Gwana).[8] The wide distribution of clan names, noted earlier, suggests pervasive processes of migration and reintegration into local communities within the mountains.

In 1923 another of the "world" religions became a proximate presence when the first Christian missionary station was established at Bambur by the Sudan United Mission (SUM). Mission stations followed in Kirim in 1924, and two years later at Filiya (Dong 2000). Other centers of missionary activity were at Kaltungo to the northeast (Harnischfeger 2006) and at Numan to the southeast (Nissen 1968). Conversion to Islam or Christianity had dramatic consequences for the objects symbolizing historically local beliefs, as they were often either burned or otherwise destroyed as an outward signal to mark conversion (see Chappel 1973); if not, they were abandoned, allowed to rot, stolen, sold, or traded to outsiders. I can add a quaint anecdote from my own experience. In Bambur (site of the first SUM station), I met an old man who owned and sacrificed to an exceptionally well-carved pair of statues (*kundul*). I interviewed him, and he allowed me to take photographs of these objects. Some time later I learned that the man had become a Christian and had dumped his *kundul* in his latrine pit (see fig. 13.13).

Before the decline of local beliefs, their embodiments had been ubiquitous (figs. 13.4, 13.5). According to a colonial officer's report on Wurkun District from 1912, "In every village one finds a fetish hut, which is enclosed by a circular zana matting.... The hut is half the size of an ordinary one in which are stored wooden images varying in size from 2 to 4 feet representing male and female figures…. They are carefully preserved and offerings of food are frequently placed before them."[9] Local religious observances were still practiced when I carried out my research a decade and a half ago (1989–1993) but mainly by elderly people; a majority of younger people were attracted either to Islam or to Christianity. Islam in particular had benefited from the political realities of postcolonial Northern Nigeria, where Muslim identity is a precondition for access to many political and economic resources. By now, adherents of the historic religions of the Muri Mountains must have become a very small minority. My brief outline of some basic religious concepts of the two main groups constituting the Wurkun (Piya and Kulung) has to be read against this background.

The Piya and Kulung metaphysical realm is essentially structured by three tiers of powers that occur elsewhere in the Benue region: a now-distant creator god; communal cults concerned with agencies that are at once ancestors and the dead; cults performed by single households or individuals. Specific ideas of the spirit world, and ritual enactments addressed to them, vary from locality to locality, and it is helpful to conceive of the local religion as a fabric consisting of different interpretations of spiritual concepts and ritual performances (Fardon 1990).

At the apex of the spiritual world stands Yamba, the otiose creator god (in Kulung sometimes called Mol). He is not approached directly through rituals. Closer to the sphere of human activities are named spiritual entities (*kindima* in Piya, *basali* in Kulung), associated with collective ancestral spirits or simply the dead. Examples of this category are communal cults like Zugey, Eku and Bongey to which appeals are made for assistance in the face of misfortunes or to secure the well-being of the community or some of its clans. The same powers are used to impose sanctions on the deviant behavior of individuals. The worship of these entities is a matter for men; women have no active part in it and may not even see the cult paraphernalia on pain of paying a fine or in extremis being killed. Even closer to human beings are the spirits addressed by a family or a household, such as the protecting spirits called *waamina* (by Piya) or *purum* (Kulung) or the *kundul*, the latter being represented by distinctive columnar wooden sculptures (fig. 13.6).

While we know that the striking wooden vertical masks collected from Wurkun played a role within the communal cults (see fig. 13.1 and chapter 14), due to the strict secrecy surrounding their performances we cannot say with certainty which of them performed with which cults. I can only go by the accounts of informants, which suggest that vertical masks were only one of several masked cult performances. Three of these communal cults are, or were, concerned with the dead, respectively with adult men, unmarried women and children, and adult women:

1. Zugey or Jugey, considered to be male, is the most powerful of the death cults. The souls of deceased adult males are said to join Zugey. The Kulung relate that Zugey helped them emerge victorious from their confrontations with Fulani Emirate raiders in the nineteenth century. Its masquerade was described to me as being covered with rags, walking on stilts, and probably wearing a mask. Its appearance is accompanied by the sound of a special horn or trumpet.

2. Bongey, considered to be female, is said to be the first wife of Zugey. One Piya informant stated that the cult was brought to the Piya by the Kwonci. The Kulung demurred, however, and claimed Bongey as a local cult. It is associated with the remembrance of the immature dead: unmarried women and children. Its masquerade was described to me as being dressed in raffia and wearing a wooden mask.

3. A third cult, Eku, also considered to be female, is described as the second wife of Zugey. Eku is said to have been adopted from the Jukun of Gwana by the Piya who

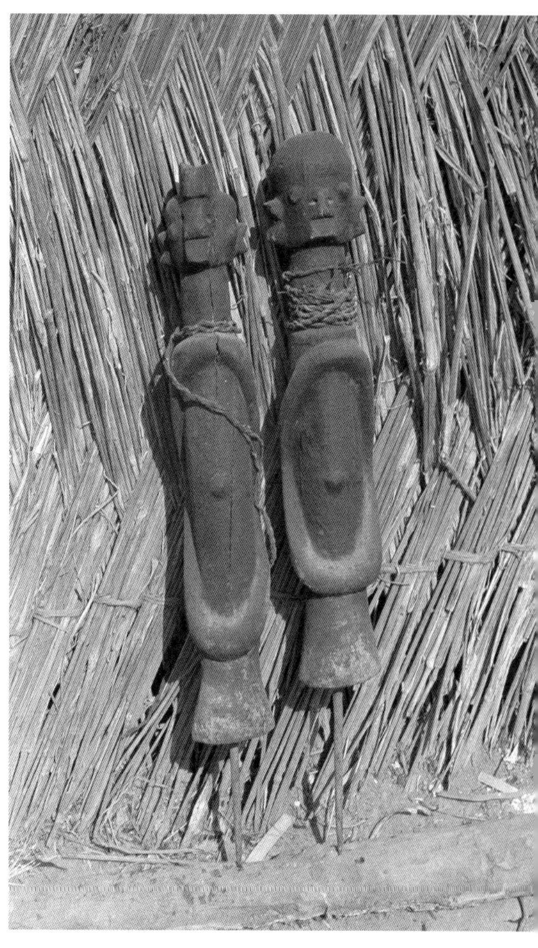

13.6
This typical pair of columnar statues (*kundul*) mounted on spikes was photographed by Arnold Rubin, probably among the Piya. Note the extremely stretched stylized arms and the fiber around the neck, which would have been renewed during an annual ritual.
PHOTOGRAPH BY ARNOLD RUBIN, LALLE VILLAGE, JANUARY 9, 1966, RUBIN ARCHIVE, FOWLER MUSEUM AT UCLA, NEG. NO. 1587.

then gave it to the Kulung. The souls of women go to Eku after death. In a colonial officer's report from 1909, Eku is described briefly, "The deity himself is armed with a long deep-noted-horn horn [*sic*] which he blows at intervals, and makes various remarks. In one case I saw the deity enshrouded with clothes completely, in another he was absolutely naked."[10] The missionary Thekla Kuglin also happened to catch a glimpse of Eku at Bambur, and she describes what she saw more amply:

> They had already draped cloths around Eku so that I shouldn't see it when I came out, as they were sure I would. So I did go out in plain sight, and then it happened—one of the cloths caught on the barbed wire fencing, and I saw Eku. This caused excitement, and all the men huddled together to hide it, so that I should not see what it is. It is a hollowed-out bamboo pole into which the men blow to make the sound which the women believe is Eku. [Kuglin 1941, 44]

The Eku festival is reported to take place after the main crops have been planted around midyear and lasts for three days. It involves groups of men moving through the villages, each accompanying an Eku. Each clan has at least one Eku (cf. Armold 1929; Kuglin 1941). Eku takes precedence as the principal cult among the Tangale, where it is represented by an unchiseled stone about the length of a forearm set into the ground of a sacred grove. There are usually several such sacred groves in Tangale settlements.[11] Marla Berns (personal communication) reported the presence of an Eku sacred grove in a rocky outcropping at Chongom Boh in Tangaleland in the 1980s, which in turn confirms, as per Hall (1994), that every Tangale locality has (or had) its Eku shrine.

Other cults are also associated with masquerades. Particular mention has to be made here of the Jila cult belonging to the Kulung. Like the Kulung Zugey, Jila is considered to be male. It is said to have been adopted from the Leemak. Thanks to Arnold Rubin's reports, Jila (which he calls "Gila") is among the cults that we can almost definitely say used the long-necked vertical masks.[12] According to Meek (1934, 263), "Gila" is a corn spirit or "tutelary genius" connected with agricultural rites. It appears not only at harvest but also around March when there is a rain ritual (Sob-Jila). As a cult, Jila seems to have identical functions to that known as Kodo among most of the Piya. Western sections of the Piya (Peelang and Gaaruma) bordering the Jarawa groups call this masquerade Jiribe, reminiscent of Jila. Kodo and Jiribe masqueraders are reportedly covered by grasses and leaves. Whether Jiribe also is a vertical mask is unclear.

Evidence from elsewhere in the Benue suggests that it is inadvisable to attempt to tie particular masquerades closely to named cults. Masquerades evoked complex and widely ramifying connotations that made their attendance at all kinds of rituals appropriate, particularly if the ceremonies concerned seasonal and life-cycle transitions, at which the masquerades performed as harbingers of transformation (as argued by Fardon for Middle Benue masquerades in this volume). Our only eyewitness reports of vertical masks in performance come from C. W. Guinter, a missionary working under the auspices of the Sudan United Mission and founder of the mission station in Bambur. He published two short accounts in an extremely scarce missionary journal *The Lightbearer* (Guinter 1925; 1926). The more elaborate of the two articles, "Dark Doings at Bambur: A Wurkum Festival," is reproduced in extenso here because it is unique. That said, it also raises numerous problems of interpretation, not only by virtue of its jaundiced tone. We do not know definitely the time of year on which Guinter is reporting (sometime after harvest would be the best guess). What Guinter calls "Boka" (a Hausa term with meanings including healer and soothsayer, but which missionaries frequently interpreted as "spirit masquerader" or "witch doctor") is described as a death cult (like Jila or Zugey) but not under one of the names reported elsewhere.

These are great days in Bambur. On Saturday and Sunday the "Boka" visited the different parts of the town. These are men wearing large wooden masks, and clothed with a loose garment made of grass and fibre. A woman must not see one of these or she will die, or some dreadful calamity befall her. At the first signal the women run for shelter, and remain there until this monster has gone.

Yesterday the elders of the tribe sacrificed to the dead. All night they were busy at the different spirit houses on the hill. All who lost relatives provided beer and fowl or goats for offerings.

To-day [sic] is the greatest day of all. Wurkum from all the surrounding towns have come to the great dance in honour of their principal deity "Basali" [in Kulung, "the ancestors/dead"]. The "Boka" arrive about ten o'clock in the morning and deposit their masks in a row at one side of an open court. The women bring pots of beer by the score until there are several hundred of them lined up side by side on another court. The beating of the drums is the call to dance. No women are allowed. There is dancing and drinking until the participants become so overcome that they lose all sense of decency and propriety. It goes on until about four o'clock in the afternoon. Then the dancing stops, the beer is portioned out and the drinking continues until nearly nightfall. By this time many are much the worse for drink. The "Boka" put on their masks, and after some more dancing by those who are able, they separate and go to the various districts which they represent. What beer remains is portioned out to the various elders, and the women are called to carry it home. Around these beer pots groups assemble, and the drinking and carousing goes on into the night.… After witnessing such a scene as this, one of the young men said to us in all earnestness, "These are our gods." Truly did the Psalmist describe them when he said "All the gods of the heathen are idols." [Guinter 1926, 92–93]

While far from being a sympathetic observer, Guinter gives indications that are sufficient to suggest that a collective festival for the ancestors, lasting two or three days, brought together a regional community represented by the vertical masks. This seems to have been the occasion for a general round of offerings to cults on the hillside outside the village. As the gathering began to disperse, it dissolved into the local beer-drinking groups associated with smaller clan or residential sections.

In his earlier account Guinter (1925) describes largely similar events having taken place around February 1925. On that occasion, about sixteen masqueraders had taken part and the course of events also involved the tall wooden vertical masks being arranged in a row before they were donned again and moved around dancing. The performative sequence suggests that the ritual focus is placed on the mask objects, which are moved around as well as standing still, drawing the attention of the participants to the visual embodiments of the spirits addressed. The placing of the masks on the ground is particularly suggestive, since it indicates that the line between freestanding wooden sculptures, to which I turn next, and walking masks may have been contextual. And it is the case, that the vertical mask shares its elongated character, often the result of a disproportionately long neck, with the most distinctive of smaller Wurkun statuary, which similarly feature extended necks (see, for example, figs. 13.7, 13.8).

EMBODIMENTS: WOOD SCULPTURE

During my research, for reasons noted earlier, I found it difficult to collect information on aspects of historic local religion and ritual. This followed in part because local practitioners felt threatened by Islam and Christianity. C. W. Guinter's reaction to his young interlocutor quoted above is indicative of the disparagement they might

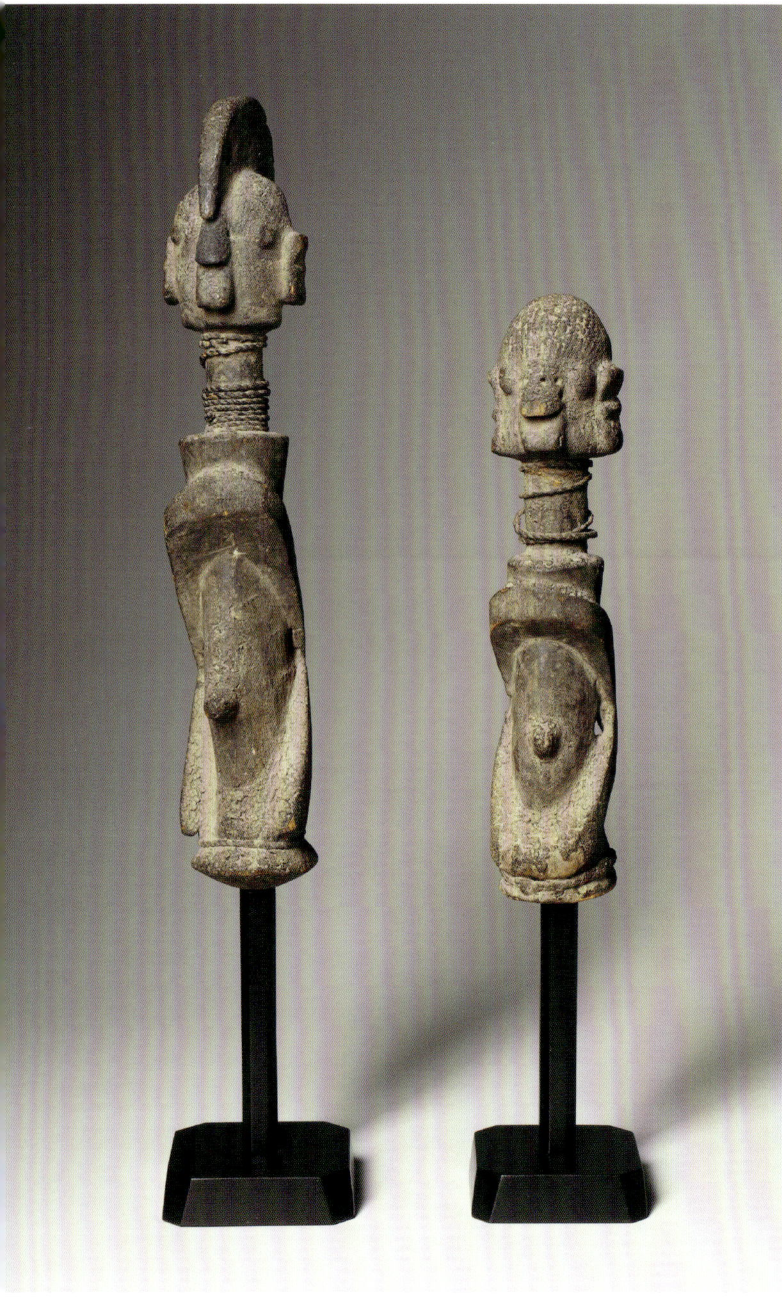

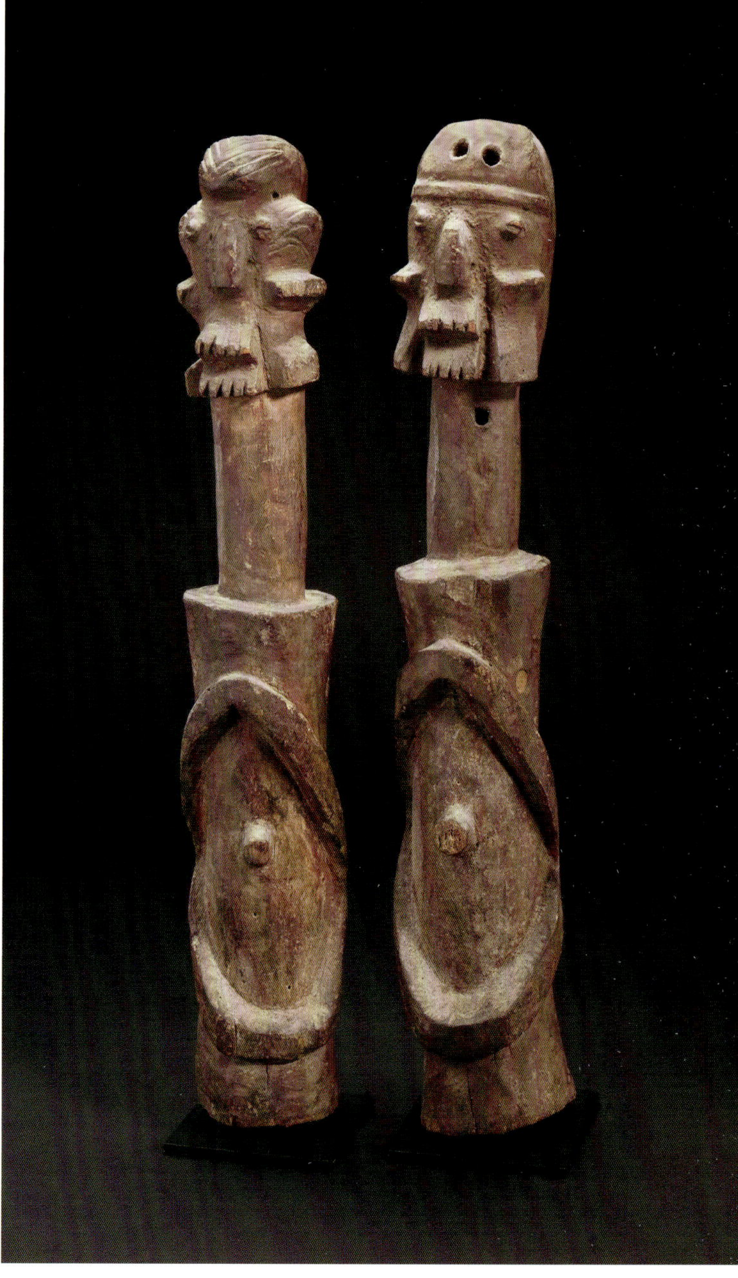

13.7a,b
Male and female figures (*kundul*)
Wurkun peoples, late nineteenth century
Wood, fiber
H (male): 41.2 cm; (female): 31.5 cm
MUSÉE DU QUAI BRANLY, PARIS, 70.2001.3.1,
70.2001.3.2

IMAGE: © 2010 MUSÉE DU QUAI BRANLY. PHOTO-
GRAPH BY PATRICK GRIES/VALÉRIE TORRE/SCALA,
FLORENCE

PROVENANCE: COLLECTED BY PIERRE LEDOUX;
PHILIPPE GUIMIOT, BRUSSELS; COUNT BAUDOIN
DE GRUNNE, BRUSSELS; JACQUES BLANKAERT,
BRUSSELS; BERNARD DE GRUNNE, BRUSSELS

This striking *kundul* pair was collected by
Belgian explorer Pierre LeDoux in the course
of his travels in the Middle Benue region. The
arms are of note because they terminate proximate to each side of the torso, as opposed to
forming the oval shape more characteristic of
pieces from the Muri Mountains.

13.8a,b
Male and female figures (*kundul*)
Wurkun peoples, early to mid-twentieth
century
Wood
H: 55 cm
PRIVATE COLLECTION, LOS ANGELES
IMAGE: © 2010 FOWLER MUSEUM AT UCLA.
PHOTOGRAPH BY DON COLE
PROVENANCE: HARRY FRANKLIN GALLERY,
LOS ANGELES

The abstracted arms of this *kundul* pair form
a symmetrical raised oval with a protruding
umbilicus at its center, a characteristic feature
of Wurkun columnar statuary.

anticipate. But there was, however, another and contrary strand to the reluctance of elderly informants to discuss their local religion with me, although some missionaries and colonial officers could not be refused a view of them from afar. In principle the cults and their associated artifacts had always been secret, hence accessible only to their initiates. Revelations about them ran the risk not only of speaking about what should have remained unspoken but also of referring to ritual paraphernalia that, either in part or in its entirety, no longer existed. From a Kulung informant, I learned that effigies representing the ancestors of different clans, which had been kept in caves in the mountains, had been stolen sometime during the mid-1970s. This theft of ritual items raises difficult ethical questions about how "Wurkun," and other Benue Valley objects entered the African art market during the postcolonial period (see also Schmidt and McIntosh 1996).

These considerations of secrecy applied with greatest force to the most powerful of objects. So shrouded in secrecy were the tall vertical masks, that I never saw one in the Muri Mountains. They were kept in secret places in the hills, accessible only to members of their cult. This strict secrecy frustrated my research. On one occasion, I showed the photocopied image of a vertical mask to an informant who hastily drew me inside his house, afraid of anyone seeing us discussing this arcane topic. I encountered the same attitude throughout the region. Although I was promised several times that I could look briefly at a vertical mask, except for a very small example (of a type discussed below; see fig. 13.26), this never happened. Hence, all the information I have on vertical masks comes from interviews, sometimes prompted by photographs of published examples, such as those reproduced here. Because I was allowed to see sculpted figures, it makes sense to start my survey there.

COLUMNAR FIGURES

Columnar figurative sculptures occur in the western and southern areas of the Muri Mountains, where they are mainly associated with Wurkun groups but are also found among the Pero and other neighboring groups (e.g., Kushi, Burak, and Leemak), and among the Jukun of Gwana (see figs. 13.11, 13.17, 13.23, 8.52).

Most anthropomorphic Wurkun figures reveal distinctive variations of Middle Benue sculptural conventions. Typically, figurative sculptures consist of elongated cylindrical torsos and heads (figs. 13.7a,b, 13.8a,b); they are between 30 and 60 centimeters; and they commonly stand on an iron spike for protection against termites (see figs. 13.4–13.6, 13.12–13.17, 13.21). These types of figures are called *kundul* by the Chadic-speaking groups and *ngunpuro* by the Kulung. Dependent on the context of their use, these designations may change, for example to *jeru* among the Kulung as explained below. Besides generic designations, individual sculptures often have "personal names."[13] Figures commonly occur in male-female pairs: the male figure being distinguished from the female by a crest on its head (fig. 13.9). Contrary to Philip Fry (1970, 23), and consistent with what Mette Bovin argues for Mumuye in this volume, these features atop the heads of male sculptures need not represent coiffures but may be modeled after the variety of helmets or headdresses worn by men on ceremonial occasions, or during dances, or in warfare (fig. 13.10). The figures may further be adorned with plant fibers, a nose peg, or a necklace.

In regional terms, the distinctive features of most examples of Wurkun figurative sculptures include the elongation of the body, lozenge-shaped arms, absence of legs, and the particular method of their iron mounting. The stylization of arms pursues what is a tendency toward abstraction elsewhere in the region to an elegant extreme. Many figures have shoulders, arms, and hands that connect as a single raised ridge forming a diamond or, with the angles of the elbows softened, an oval shape (see fig. 13.5), which encircles the front of the torso (as if a letter "O" had been flattened against the figure's middle). The necks of the figures are elongated and can

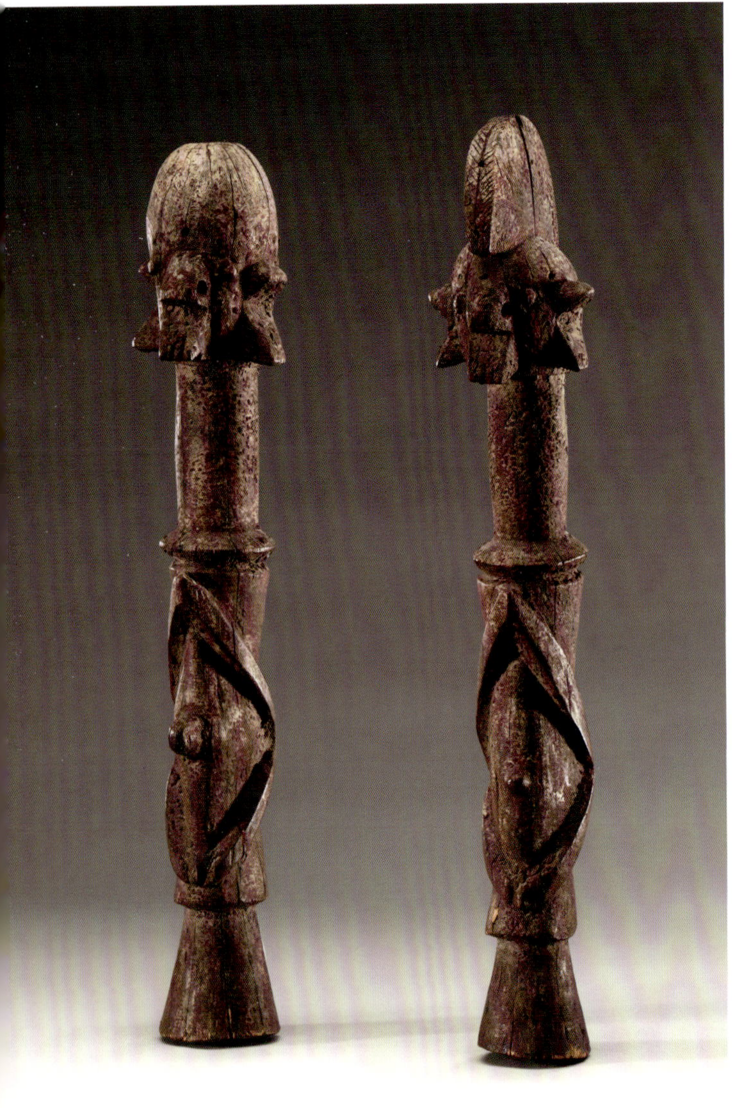

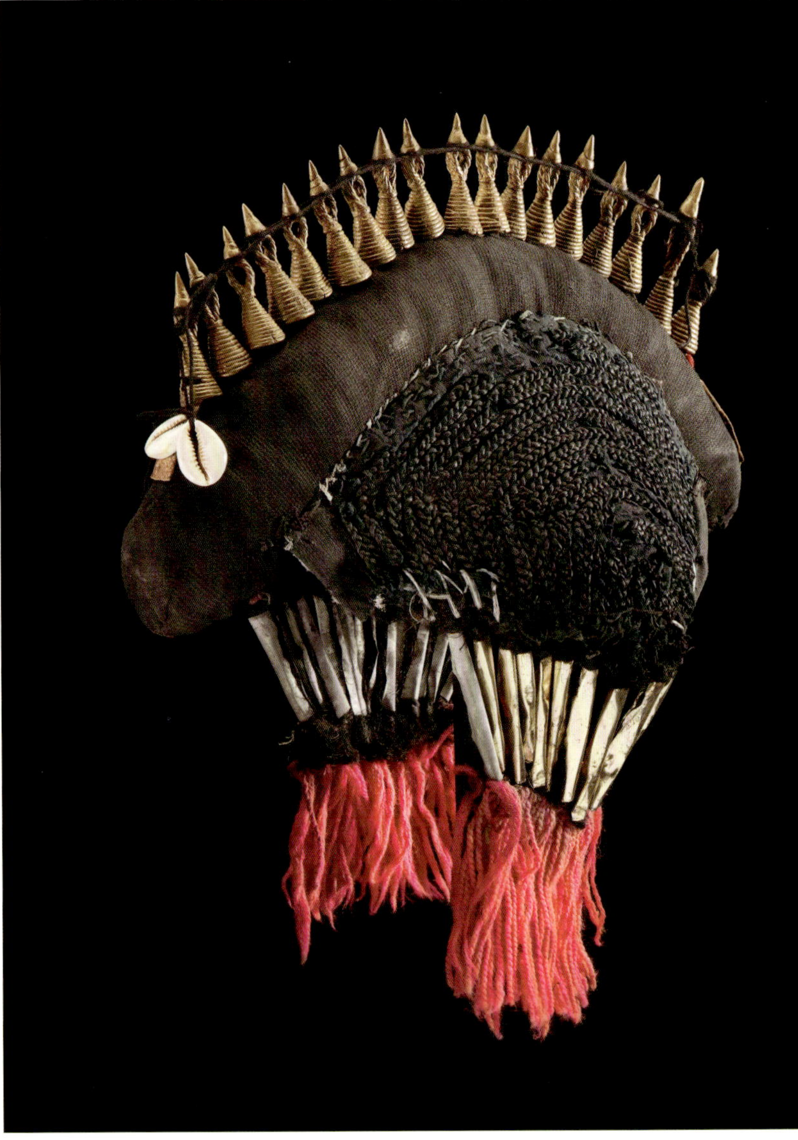

13.9

Male and female figures (*kundul*)
Wurkun peoples, early to mid-twentieth century
Wood
H: 41.55 cm
PRIVATE COLLECTION
IMAGE: COURTESY PRIVATE COLLECTOR. PHOTO-
GRAPH © 2010 STUDIO PHILIPPE DE FORMANOIR
PROVENANCE: LANCE ENTWISTLE; ATLANTIC ART
PARTNERS, NEW YORK

The sagittal crest indicates that the *kundul*
on the viewer's right is the male. The head
is disproportionately large in relation to the
body, and as with the *kundul* in figure 13.7, the
arms terminate without closing the usual oval
shape. The head strongly resembles those of
many vertical masks, thus combining elements
of both types of statuary (see fig. 14.30a,b).

13.10

Dance crest (*needuwe*)
Bangwinji peoples, mid-twentieth century
Wool, metal, cotton, shell
L: 31.75 cm
FOWLER MUSEUM AT UCLA X2010.7.1; MUSEUM
PURCHASE
IMAGE: © 2010 FOWLER MUSEUM AT UCLA.
PHOTOGRAPH BY DON COLE

Dance helmets decorated with cast copper-
alloy clapper bells are worn by male title-holders in ceremonial contexts. They are also worn
by men during age-grade ceremonies and even
by newly married girls when presented to the
spirits for blessings. The high crest and earflaps distinctive to this helmet configuration
are rendered on male figurative sculptures
among the Wurkun and their Mumuye neighbors, who use similar ceremonial headgear.

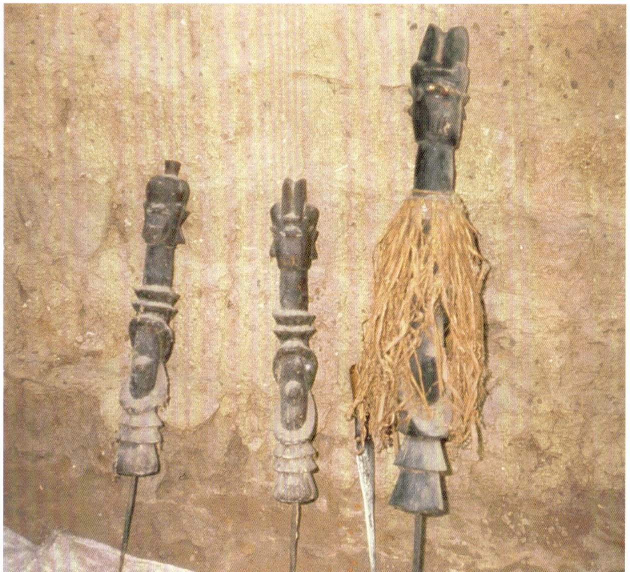

13.11

I was able to document this pair of *kundul* (the female is on the far left) and a *dambang* statue (far right) at the Pero settlement of Gundale. *Dambang* statues, which are regarded as especially powerful, are the property only of traditional priests.

PHOTOGRAPH BY JOERG ADELBERGER, GUNDALE, APRIL 1990.

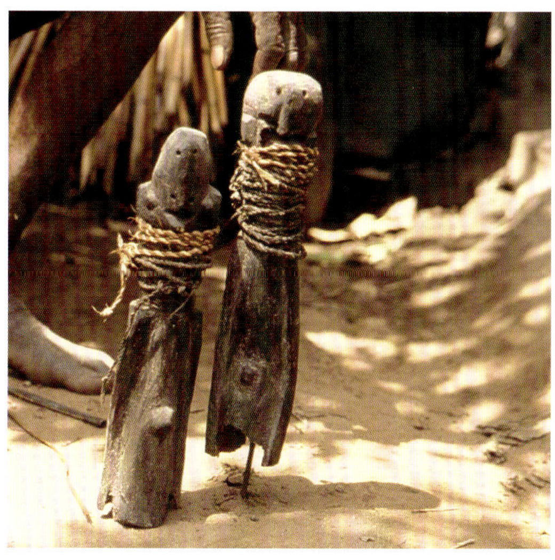

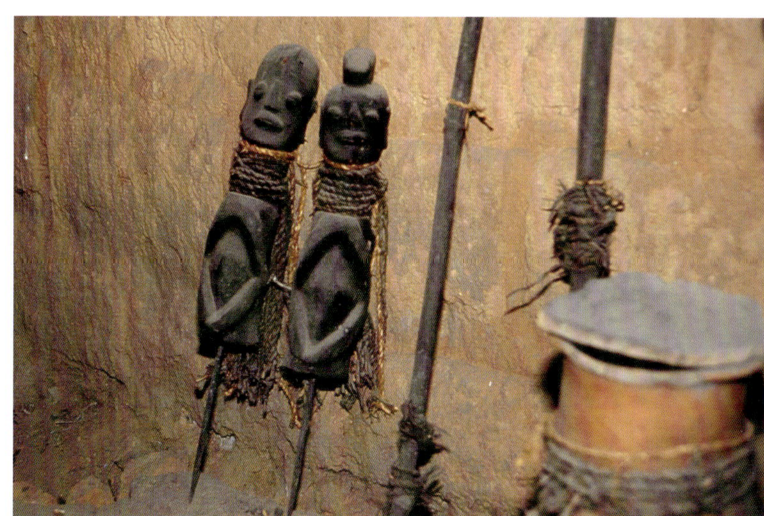

be encircled with fiber (see figs. 13.6, 13.12), a feature reminiscent of Wurkun vertical masks. Legs are entirely absent, unless we take the notched legs typical of many Middle Benue sculptures to be schematically indicated among Wurkun by two carved bands, perhaps representing knees and feet (see fig. 13.11). The absence of feet, like the elongation of the necks and the features crowning the heads of male figures, suggests stylistic continuities between these sculptures and vertical masks. *Kundul* otherwise vary considerably in style, which is strikingly evident in the depictions of their faces, which range from naturalistic to abstract, with outlined ears and/or indications of coiffure and headdress (figs. 13.11–13.17). An attempted mapping of the regional distribution of stylistic variations of *kundul* in the Muri Mountains area did not reveal significant concentrations of substyles in particular localities but rather suggested diverse styles throughout the area. This reinforces our supposition of a high degree of interaction and exchange within this area. Noteworthy exceptions, however, are the *kundul* with facial features executed in a relatively naturalistic style, which are found only in the western Wurkun/Kulung area (see figs. 13.13, 13.14). The parallel incisions on the upper or lower jaw of some figures, most probably representing filed teeth, are another feature that we found only with objects from the northern range of the Muri Mountains, i.e., from Pero and northern Piya peoples (see, for example, fig. 13.5).

Again, these variations are consistent with those found in the sculpture of other Middle Benue peoples. As such, they reflect the distinctive stylistic preferences of

13.12

This worn pair of columnar statues (*ngunpuro*) of the Kulung peoples was still used by an old man when photographed in the late 1990s. Despite the use of spikes, the figures have suffered from termites.

PHOTOGRAPH BY JOERG ADELBERGER, BAMBUR, NOVEMBER 1991.

13.13

These beautiful black-surfaced Kulung *ngunpuro* (columnar figures) provide good examples of the more naturalistic depiction of faces. The pot at the right was used for ritual offerings of millet beer. The fiber cords wound around the necks of the figures would have been added to each year; the shiniest are the most recent. I was later to learn that these statues had been thrown into a latrine pit following their owner's conversion to Christianity.

PHOTOGRAPH BY JOERG ADELBERGER, BAMBUR, NOVEMBER 1991.

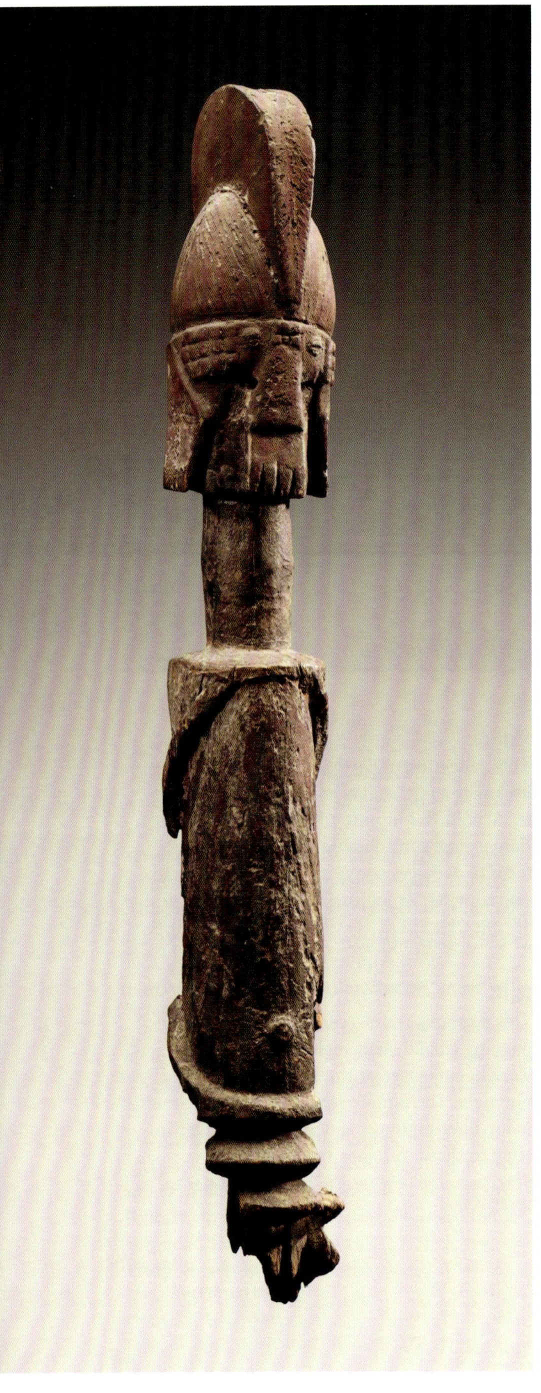

13.19
Male figure (*dambang*)
Wurkun peoples, late nineteenth or early
twentieth century
Wood
H: 66 cm

PRIVATE COLLECTION, BRUSSELS

IMAGE: COURTESY PRIVATE COLLECTOR. PHOTO-
GRAPH 2010 © STUDIO PHILIPPE DE FORMANOIR,
BRUSSELS

PROVENANCE: VON SCHROEDER, ZURICH; GALERIE
RENAUD VANUXEM, PARIS

Dambang statues, the property of traditional
priests, were considered to be especially
powerful. We know this columnar statue is
a *dambang* by virture of its height. Heavy
encrustation on the surface of the figure and
damage to its base, probably the result of
termites, attest to its age.

This is of particular note as anthropomorphic sculptures are used in a variety of
rituals, usually concerned with healing and well-being. For instance, they may be commissioned after a breech birth has taken place (considered inauspicious throughout the
Benue Valley because of the increased risk of mortality for mother and infant) or when
someone has fallen ill, or they may serve as a protective device when a hunter is haunted
by the spirit of an animal he has killed. A *kundul* gains its powers only after appropriate
rituals and sacrifices have been made to give it life. For instance, a person suffering from
disease will visit a healer who may instruct him to procure a pair of these figures as a
component of the treatment. The *kundul* will be sprinkled with the blood of a sacrificed
chicken and with millet beer. A pot may be placed beside the *kundul* to receive regular
beer offerings (see fig. 13.13). Offerings should be repeated annually after harvest, when
the firstfruits of the new crop are sacrificed to the figures. At this time, the *kundul* are
brought out of the house and washed with a solution of water and brown or red clay.
Afterward they are polished with oil made from *guna* seeds (*Cucumis melo*), and they are
fed beer and porridge made from the new millet. This treatment helps explain why the
surfaces of most examples in collections are reddish brown in color with a crusty texture.

Among the Pero too, the *kundul* play an important role in divination associated
with healing rituals (see Faust 1945, 264f), and the pair of figures was kept within the
house of the diviner.[16] Although these figures are key to the diviner's work, the actual
divination process employs an animal skin with the head attached, studded with abrus
seeds and pierced with an iron ring from which two bent-iron bells are hung (Berns
and Hudson 1986, 67). The diviner jiggles the animal vigorously against the edge of
a gourd bowl until he arrives at an answer. Another method involves using two long
sticks and a small clay pot resting on a tall iron spike driven into the ground (fig.
13.20). The sticks are positioned against the pot until the entire thing is balanced, at
which time the diviner reaches his determination; the same process was documented
among the Kushi (Marla Berns, personal communication). The male/female pair of
kundul must be present during the process.

Figures that look similar may be given different names according to their function.[17] In fact, it may be more accurate to think of figures taking their names from their
performative contexts rather than their having fixed names. This becomes apparent
from the *dambang* complex. The spiked figures called *dambang*, which are exclusively in
the possession of a ritual expert (see below), are taller but otherwise stylistically very
similar to *kundul*. Thought more powerful than *kundul* (fig. 13.19), *dambang* are typically
decorated with bast or strings made of palm frond fibers, which are bound around the
neck. Among the Kulung, the *dambang* stand in their own enclosure beside the compound of the priest, shielded from sight by a fence made of grass matting. A spear and
a pot are placed in the shrine (fig. 13.21). The priest uses the *dambang* for divination, in
particular to determine the cause of sickness, for instance where a child is frequently
ill. I was not told the procedures involved in this, but the subsequent treatment may
include the preparation of a pair of protective spiked wooden figures—in this context
they are called *jeru*—which are stuck into the thatched ceiling of the room belonging
to the child's mother. Sacrifices of millet beer and chicken blood made to the *jeru* are
repeated every year after harvest around October. *Dambang*, however, is not simply the
name for the shrine figure: more generally, it is the name of the power, inherited in the
male line, which is a precondition of becoming a *dambang* priest and confers an ability
to heal.[18] *Dambang* is also the name of the festival that is celebrated between March
and April to ensure well-being and a good agricultural season. *Dambang* spirits are
associated with water, and Piya believe that the spirits live in rivers. Faust (1945, 254)
remarks that among the Pero the Dambang festival helps to shorten the usual dry spell
in the rainy season. Here it becomes clear that to argue that a certain kind of sculpted
figure "is" *dambang* would invert the practical logic: it is rather the case that whatever
figures participate in this complex of ideas and practices are *dambang*.

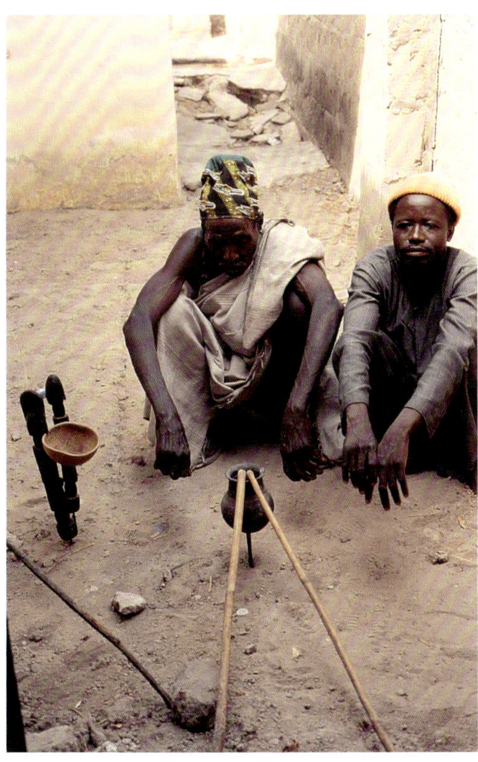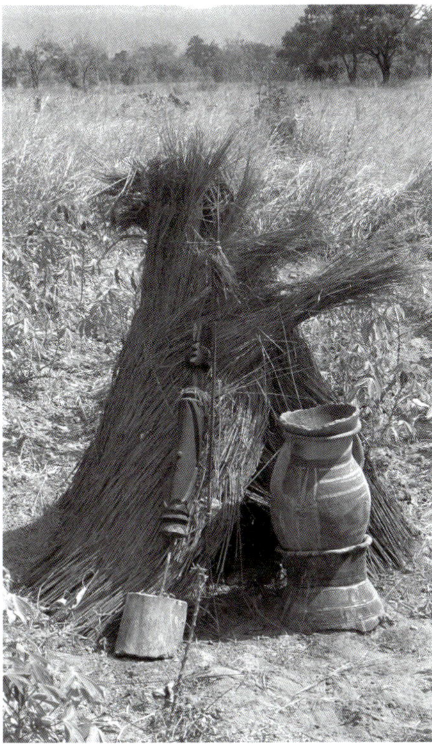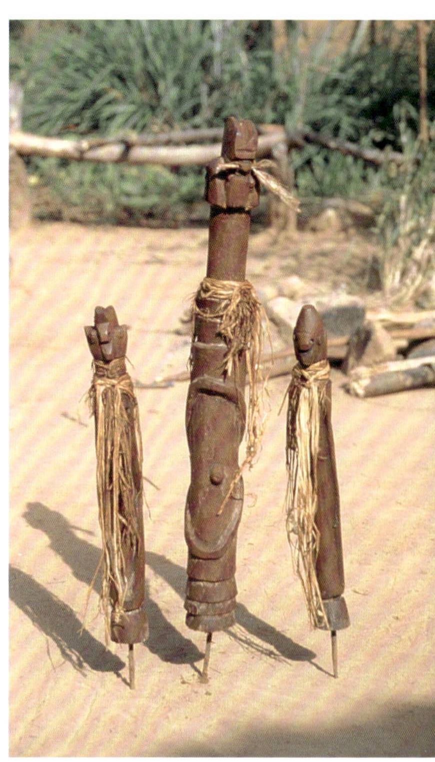

Among the Piya, I documented a set of three figures (fig. 13.22): the largest was identified as a *dambang*, the two smaller as *kundul*. It was explained to me, that the two *kundul* were the "wives" of the *dambang*, and that the *kundul* with the crest was the senior wife. On the occasion of the festival, the *dambang* figure is carried to the dancing place, while his two "wives" stay behind. *Dambang* receives a sacrifice of millet beer and two cockerels (one red, one white) at the dancing place, remains of which are brought back for his "wives." At that time the figures are washed, red ocher is applied, and a new rope made of palm fibers is fixed around their necks.

The *dambang* cult of the Pero differs from that outlined above, suggesting that the term is not tied to an invariant performance. There, *dambang* is associated with a particular tree[19] in a cult that the Pero adopted from neighboring Loo. On the occasion of the *dambang* feast, beer is brought to the cult hut and poured into a pot inside the hut and on the ground (see Faust 1945, 252–56). During the festival, the dancers wear special headdresses which might be made of colored cloth and feathers or consist of a particular cap (called *tayo* in Pero, a helmet of straw coated with resin and decorated with red abrus seeds). The missionary Walter (1928) witnessed a Dambang festival at Gwandum with over 450 costumed male dancers.

The annual Dambang festival among the Pero is the second in a series of festivals with the purpose of ensuring a successful agricultural season. The first in the cycle, which opens the farming season, is called Naaka. These festivals are celebrated by localities in a directional sequence that follows the major migrations of Wurkun groups from northeast to southwest: celebrations start at Filiya, then move to Gundali, Daja, Ameshe, Senge, thence on to the Piya section of Pireego, followed by Pitiko, Mutum Daya, and further afield to the Kwonci and Kode.

In general, spiked figures decorated with grass or fibers and/or feathers are likely to have served in the cult of *dambang* (for instance Rubin 1969, 95; 1973). In addition to these columnar statues with highly abstract human features, however, I also saw more figurative wooden statues that were said to serve the same apotropaic functions as a *kundul*. At Filiya, I collected a Pero figure with such strong resemblance to those used by Mumuye that either copying or import seems likely. Other variant forms are found on the periphery of the Wurkun groups where less-elaborated pairs of figures, reduced

13.20
The *kundul* are present here to assure the success of a divination session. Note the gourd bowl wedged into the mouth of the male *kundul* to receive offerings. The Pero of Filiya perform divintion (*najuli*) using a small clay pot balanced on an iron spike. Two long stalks are then moved until they balance on the lip of the pot, revealing the outcome of the session. The gourd bowl would be filled with sorghum, and some would be rubbed on the *kundul*. This photograph was staged for the benefit of Berns's research.
PHOTOGRAPH BY MARLA C. BERNS, FILIYA, MARCH 1982.

13.21
This *dambang* figure, probably photographed in a Piya village, is shown in front of its shrine enclosure, along with a pot used for offerings and a spear. A spike at the bottom of the *dambang* is fixed to a piece of wood to give it a permanent stand.
PHOTOGRAPH BY ARNOLD RUBIN, LALLE, JANUARY 9, 1966, RUBIN ARCHIVE, FOWLER MUSEUM AT UCLA, NEG. NO. 1583.

13.22
The Piya village priest who owned these three figures explained that the *kundul* to the left and the one to the right of the centrally positioned *dambang* were the *dambang*'s wives. The *kundul* on the viewer's left, which in another context might be regarded as a male figure, was in this case interpreted as the senior wife.
PHOTOGRAPH BY JOERG ADELBERGER, MUTUM DAYA, OCTOBER 1993.

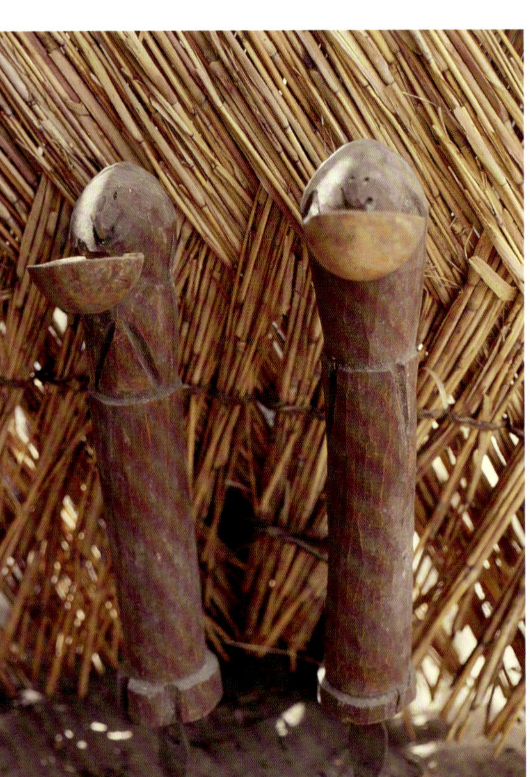

13.23
Much simpler in style than the *kundul* of
the Wurkun are the columnar statues from
ethnic groups located at their periphery, as
these examples from the Burak people in the
northern Muri Mountains demonstrate. This
kundul pair possesses special features: small
calabashes are wedged into their mouths to
receive offerings of sorghum beer, and the
spikes on which they stand are made from
gbaame, a traditional form of iron money.
PHOTOGRAPH BY MARLA C. BERNS, BURAK,
MARCH 1982.

to mere columns of wood with highly schematic heads and faces, serve similar functions.
Marla Berns recorded an interesting stylistic variation among the Burak and the Pero,
where the calabash from which the sculpture is fed is wedged in its mouth (fig. 13.23).

VERTICAL MASKS

As I noted earlier, tall vertical masks, the most striking of Wurkun sculptures, are
surprisingly elusive given their bulk. While *kundul* are associated with rituals performed by households and individual priests, the vertical masks, impersonating the
ancestral spirits of a co-resident descent group or a clan, are associated with collective cults. Like so many artworks from the Benue River Valley, most vertical masks in
private and public collections were acquired without detailed provenance during the
postcolonial period, many in the years immediately following the Biafran War. Hence,
their attributions and uses have remained mysterious, a problem abetted by the strict
secrecy with which they were guarded when in situ. However, the large number that
have been documented in collections and their remarkable scale makes them among
the most impressive sculpture in the Benue River Valley (figs. 13.1, 13.24).

In the Muri Mountains, vertical masks are particularly associated with the Bikwin
groups (the masks are called *nungbwi* in Munga Leelau, *nungbira* in Leemak) and the
Wurkun groups (where there seems to be no general term for them). Literature on the
subject initially attributed vertical masks to the Waja (Leuzinger 1971), but this claim
should be treated cautiously, since the Bangwinji, Dadiya, and Cham, whom I know
firsthand, are closely related to Waja in linguistic and cultural terms and all lack such
masks. Furthermore, the Waja belong to the cultural cluster of peoples at the eastern end of the Muri Mountains, which displays a strong tradition of using figurative
ceramic vessels, similar to those found among Cham-Mwana and Longuda (see Berns,
part 3 of this volume). Nonetheless, oral evidence suggests that at least some Waja
may have used wooden figures in ritual contexts in the past, and the cult artifacts of
the Balanga, a section of the Waja, are said to be related to those of the Jukun (Woodhouse 1924, 112, 196). The diversity of vertical masks in museum and private collections
(see chapter 14) suggests that they derived from several sources that are now difficult
to identify with certainty. Because the Waja attribution was apparently the first to be
published, it became the default attribution for all such objects lacking documented
provenance. The likelihood is that most vertical masks attributed to Waja in fact
came from other parts of a regional distribution that stretched from the Kona Jukun,
through an area of Mumuye, and on to the Wurkun and Bikwin, and possibly the
Waja. In support of this, I was told that the *nungbira* vertical mask found among the
Leemak was brought by the Guma clan, which originates in Mumuye country. As the
records stand, attribution of a vertical mask to particular peoples within its regional
range has to draw upon a small amount of evidence, allied to a degree of inference that
is unwelcome but unavoidable (see chapter 14).

Vertical masks are very substantial wooden objects—between 1 and 2 meters high
and extremely heavy—which are kept hidden in the hills where no outsider is allowed
to see them. They are considered to represent powerful and at times capricious spirits
that cause harm if they are not treated with due caution and respect. Although dangerous, these spirits also guarantee the well-being of the community and keep away
illnesses. Vertical masks are made from wood of certain trees that are believed to be
able "to walk in the night" and are themselves inhabited by a spirit. When cutting a
suitable tree to make a vertical mask, special precautions are taken to prevent the spirit
from escaping: the tree is "speared," and its branches cut.

The festivals in which vertical masks commonly appear recall the one described
by Guinter (see above). They take place twice a year: in June/July in order to ensure
plentiful rains and in December/January once the crop has been harvested to mark
the beginning of a new agricultural cycle. As is commonly the case with Nigerian

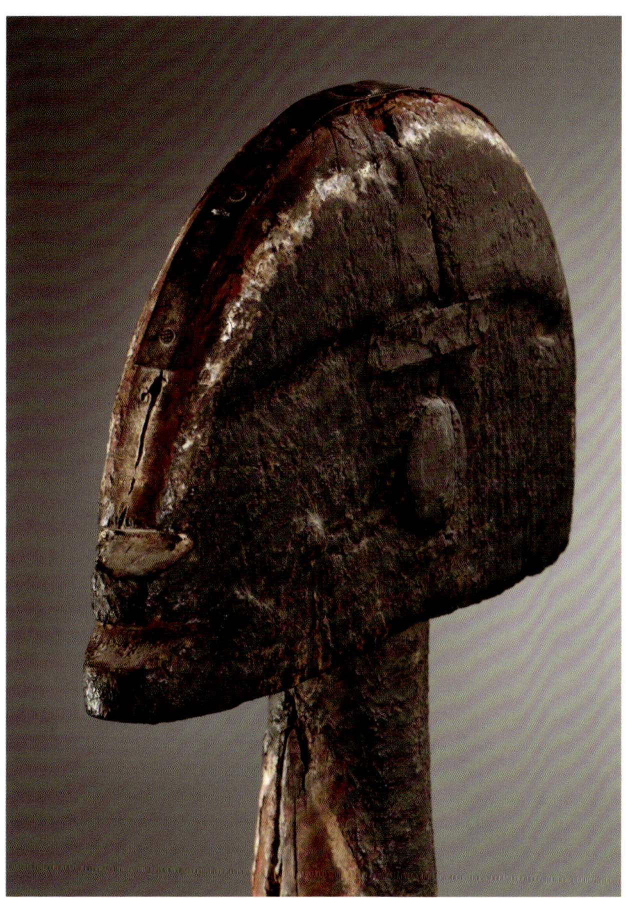

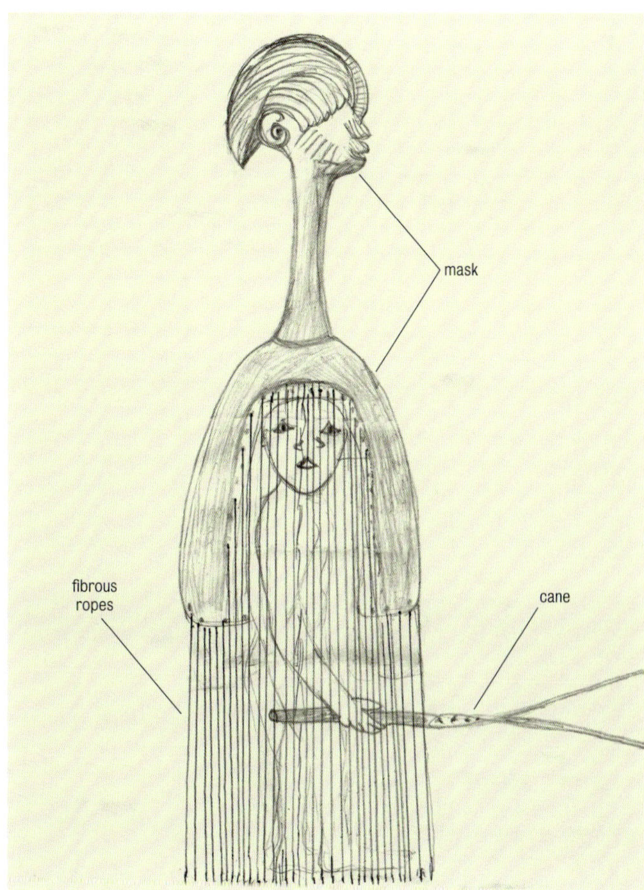

masquerades, the performance cannot be seen by women, who must stay indoors. The men who wear the masks must have observed sexual abstinence for several days.

Quite how these weighty objects were carried remains a matter of conjecture. Such information as I could elicit suggests that the mask, with strings of raffia attached on the U-shaped sides, is carried on top of the head with the face turned sideways. A sketch provided by an informant, who prefers to remain anonymous, gives a good impression of what this involves (fig. 13.25). The masquerader emerges already fully dressed from the shrine enclosure; while moving, he is accompanied by a helper. The masquerader may beat anyone who crosses his path with a cane. Wear patterns on the inside lower portion of the two extensions—evident in many of the examples now in collections— suggest that the wearer, and perhaps his assistants, helped carry the mask from the bottom. To add to the imposing presence of these masqueraders and accompany their no-doubt slow, purposeful movements, ghostly sounds were made by reed flutes.

A more extensive comparative analysis of the style of vertical masks is provided in chapter 14, but here I would particularly like to point out that their elongated necks sometimes feature a swelling, presumably intended to represent an Adam's apple. Taken together with the carved headdresses of many of the masks, this suggests that their male gender is being emphasized. If the masks were worn sideways, as I have sur- mised, then their striking profiles would have been apparent to approaching onlookers. Typically, these tall masks would also have been viewed from below, foreshortening their elongated features. Especially en masse, as Guinter describes them, the vertical masks must have been an intimidating sight, unlike anything else in the visual culture of the peoples of the Muri Mountains.

I noted earlier that formally, vertical masks are as much related to Wurkun statues as they are to other types of masks. This is particularly the case for the small figures, called *kabalou* in Leemak, which are scaled-down, handheld, miniature vertical masks. These seem to serve the functions of both *kundul* and *dambang* elsewhere. They are used in a

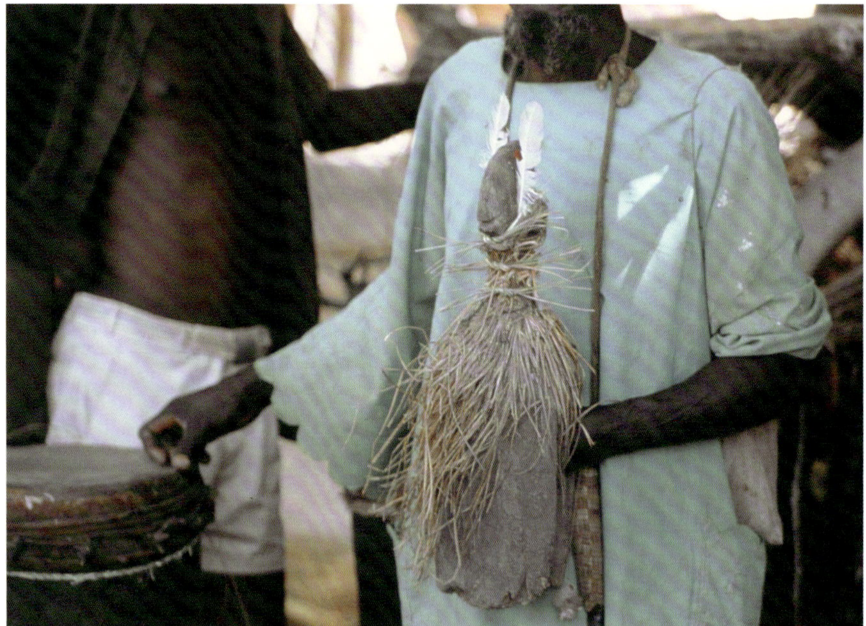

13.26

A traditional priest of the Leemak ethnic group in the southern Muri Mountains shows how a *kabalou*, which resembles a small vertical mask, is carried during ritual performances held to ensure the well-being of the community.

PHOTOGRAPH BY JOERG ADELBERGER, ZOO DUTSE, OCTOBER 1993.

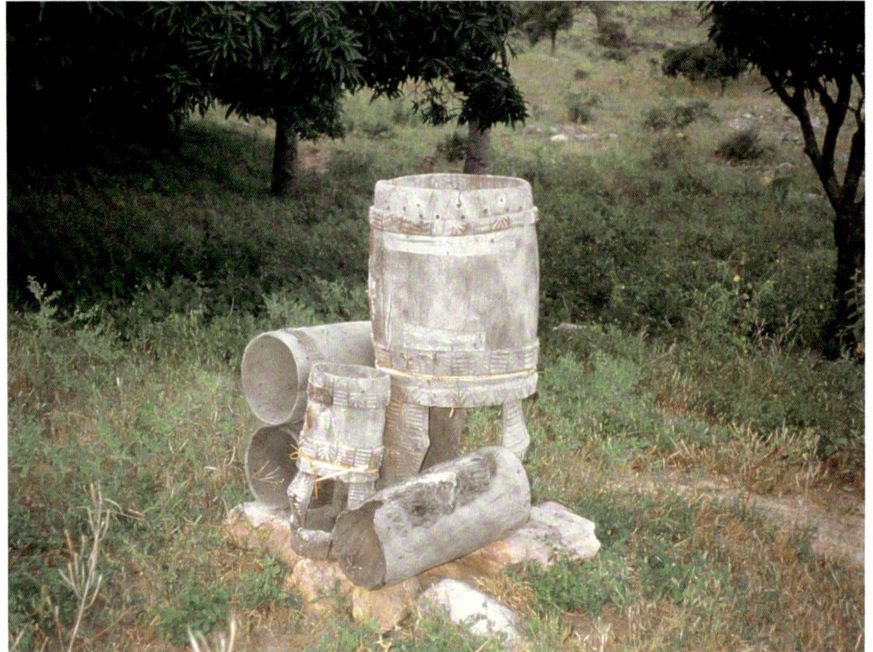

13.27

This complete set of victory drums is from a Kulung community. The smallest, most senior drum, stands on legs like the largest one, which has been repaired with metal bands. This set has three horizontal drums.

PHOTOGRAPH BY JOERG ADELBERGER, BAMBUR, OCTOBER 1990.

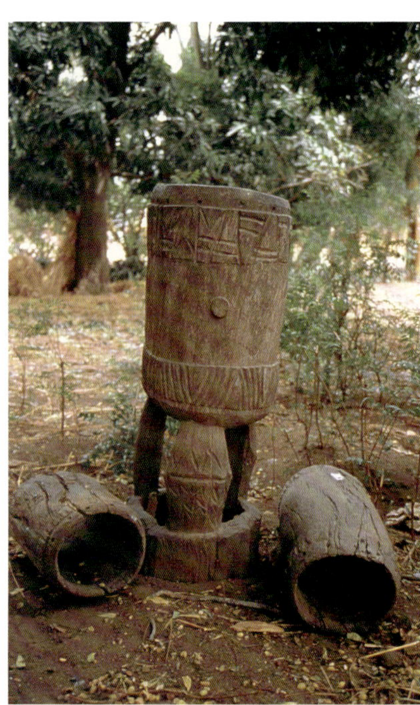

13.28

The carved umbilicus on the large standing drum in this set from a Kulung community suggests anthropomorphism.

PHOTOGRAPH BY JOERG ADELBERGER, BAMBUR, APRIL 1992.

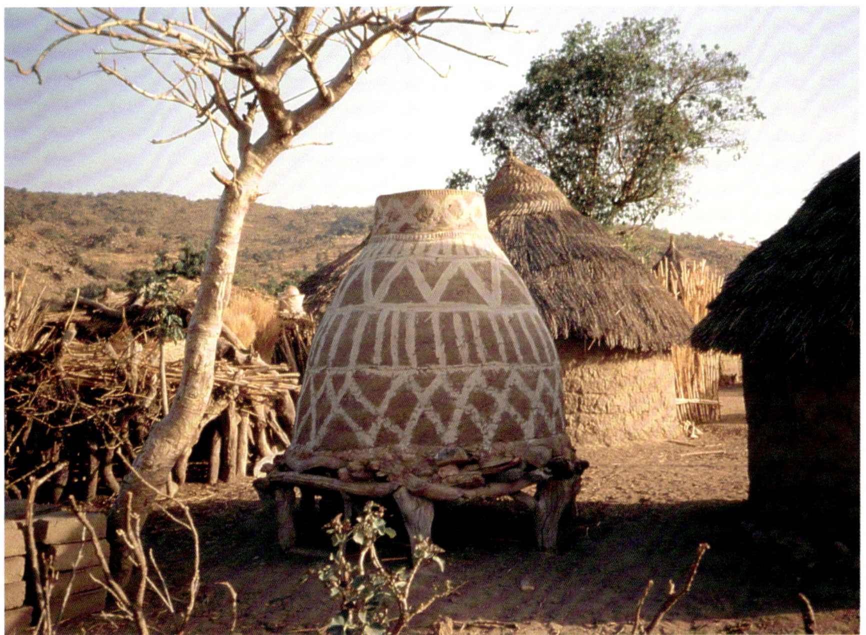

13.29
The decoration typically applied to drums—
geometric patterns with rhomboids, triangles,
and parallel lines—is also used on other meaningful objects, in this case a granary awaiting
a thatched roof and standing on its wooden
platform in a Pero hamlet. A well-filled sorghum bin is a prerequisite for the well-being
of a family group during the period between
harvests.
PHOTOGRAPH BY JOERG ADELBERGER, FILIYA,
APRIL 1990.

variety of ceremonies designed to assure well-being. *Kabalou* receive beer and porridge
made from millet, as well as the sacrifice of a cockerel before harvest begins. Like the
dambang, they may be used in divination to determine the causes of illness (fig. 13.26).
The *kabalou* is carried like a hand puppet, which establishes it at the midpoint of what
might be thought of as a scale of mobility: *kundul* and *dambang* are entirely immobilized
by their spikes being stuck into the ground; vertical masks are mobile, but their size
suggests they are probably less mobile than some of the other Wurkun masks reported by
informants, and Guinter describes them lined up without their wearers, as if they were
immense statues. *Kabalou* combine the scale of statuary with the mobility of masquerade.

DRUMS

The other noteworthy wooden objects are the widely distributed "victory drums," common both to the Wurkun and to the Pero, as well as the Leemak. These usually occur
in sets of four, each set consisting of two horizontal drums, cylindrical and covered
with leather drumskins at both ends, and a large and a small standing drum, each of
which has three feet (fig. 13.27). The horizontal drums are considered junior to the
standing drums. The smaller standing drum is not played and is considered the most
senior. The drum set is played only on special occasions, such as success in hunting
large animals, victory in war, or in some ritual contexts (the use of the set among the
Pero is mentioned by Faust 1945, 98–99). Like the wooden sculptures, the drums are
made by a carver under the instruction of a priest.

Standing drums are found only as parts of sets of victory drums.[20] They have a stylized umbilicus, suggesting anthropomorphism (fig. 13.28). Their standing legs are flexed
at their middle, giving them a triangular shape when seen in profile. Standing drums in
particular are carved with geometric patterns peculiar to the descent group that owns
them (see figs. 13.27, 13.28); I was told that these decorations represent designs from a
once common practice of bodily cicatrization. The building blocks of these decorative
patterns are triangles, lozenges and rectangles, combined in varying sequences. Similar
ornamentation occurs on other wooden objects for everyday use, for example, trowels
used for smoothing mud walls, as well as on stools, which also share the flexed legs of
standing drums. Similar motifs also occur in the decoration of the mud walls of a Pero
granary (fig. 13.29) suggesting the extension of human decorations to other elements
of material culture that we find commonly in the Middle and Upper Benue. ●

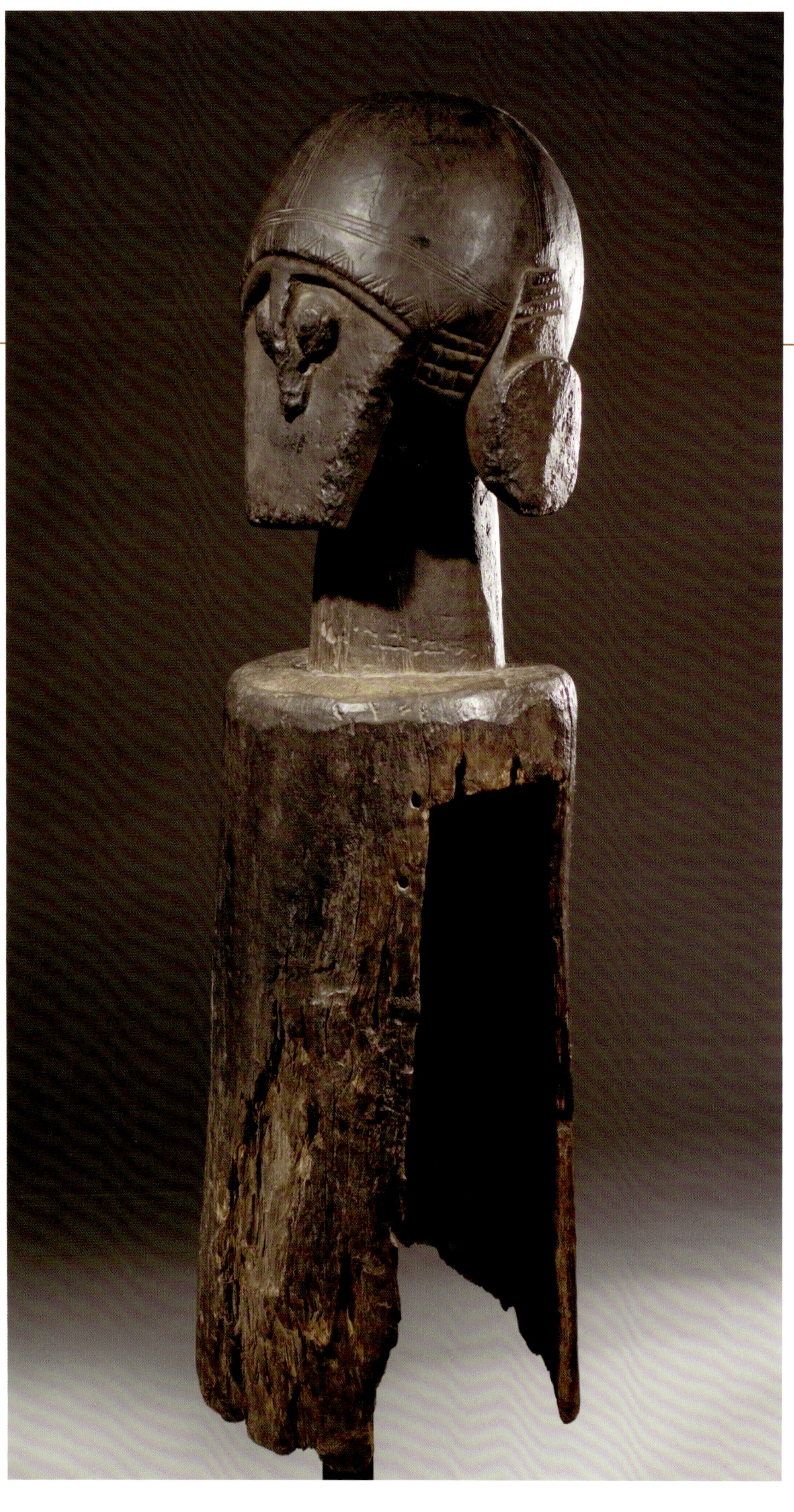

CHAPTER 14

Enigmatic Embodiments: Vertical Masks in Cross-Cultural Perspective

MARLA C. BERNS

One of the most noteworthy outcomes of the collections research associated with this project is the discovery of a large corpus of at least sixty-five highly distinctive vertical masks documented in the field and in museum and private collections. We argue here that these were made by "Wurkun" and "Bikwin," Mumuye, Yendang, and Jukun peoples of the Middle Benue (figs. 14.1–14.4a,b).[1] The masks range from approximately 80 to 160 centimeters in height and all are carved from a single piece of wood. They share a unique configuration, which has been identified in the literature as a "yoke" due to the characteristic inverted U-shaped support. The mask, however, must be worn on top of the head and not on the shoulders, making the categorization "yoke" inaccurate and misleading. Instead, we propose the use of the term "vertical masks" due to their orientation and height. When worn, the heads surmounting the long necks of many examples can tower as much as 61 to 91 centimeters above the height of the wearer.

These masks are among the most imposing sculptures of the entire Benue River Valley region. While they have been known by collectors since the late 1960s, the large number that we have identified in public and private collections, coupled with the degree of stylistic variation among them, makes these masks something of a revelation as a significant genre of Middle Benue artistic expression. The relative paucity of firsthand field observations (nine masks were documented by Arnold Rubin in Kona Jukun and Mumuye villages in 1965 and 1970) and the absence of photographs documenting them in performance also make them among the most enigmatic of Benue artworks.

Vertical masks made by the Mumuye and the Jukun were first illustrated in Arnold Rubin's unpublished doctoral dissertation (1969, pls. 104–10, 174–80). The first three examples to be published, which were not explicitly identified by the term "mask" but as *Kopfplastik*, appeared in Elsy Leuzinger's *Afrikanische Kunstwerke: Kulturen am Niger* (1971). All three were attributed to the Waja people of the Western Gongola Valley, even though they are notably different stylistically (figs. 14.1, 14.5, 14.6).[2] The first of these (fig. 14.5; Leuzinger 1971, fig. 11; see also Eyo 1977, 227), which stands over 130 centimeters tall, was described as a "cult figure with an abstract head" from Waja on the Gongola River. The second mask (fig. 14.6, 88 cm in height), though sharing a similarly shaped support, had a radically different head and face and a highly eroded surface, leading to its description as "*alte expressive Kopfplastik*."[3] The publication of Philip Fry's landmark article of 1970 on Mumuye statuary was probably too close in time to Leuzinger's publication to have allowed the identification of the head of the mask with the distinctive figurative styles of this group (see Stelzig

14.1
Vertical Mask
Jukun peoples, late nineteenth to early twentieth century or before
Wood
H: 114.3 cm

A number of vertical masks like this one closely correspond to the style of Jukun figurative sculpture documented in the villages of Gwana and Pindiga, located north of the Benue River. They share flat rectangular faces with a long bisecting nose, protruding eyes, and large ears with disks. The massive head on this one, especially relative to the length of the planks, lends it a powerful aspect. The relatively narrow straight planks of the support structure, with wear evident at the bottom and sides, show that the mask was supported from below. Its surface patina and evidence of extensive use may also suggest considerable age. See fig. 14.7 for another view of this mask.

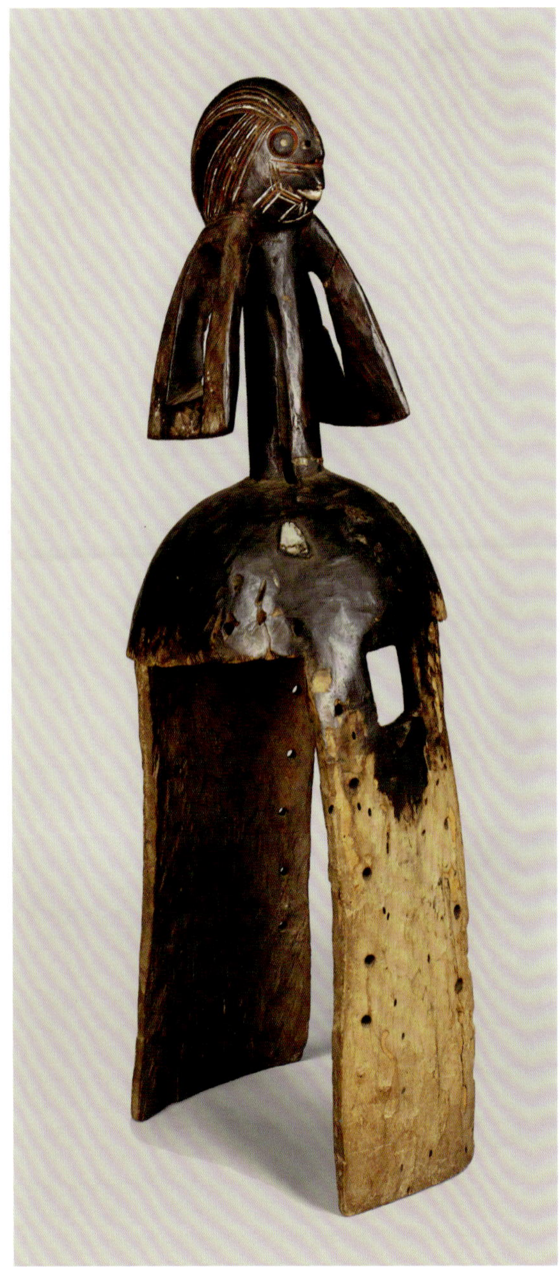

14.2 (ABOVE)

Vertical mask (Sukuru)
Mumuye peoples, mid-twentieth century
Wood, pigment

H: 102.2 cm

SEATTLE ART MUSEUM. GIFT OF KATHERINE
WHITE AND THE BOEING COMPANY, 81.17.708

IMAGE: © SEATTLE ART MUSEUM. PHOTOGRAPH
BY ELIZABETH MANN, 2010

PROVENANCE: GALLERY K, LOS ANGELES, 1975

The heads of Mumuye vertical masks are
easy to recognize given their correspondence
to the heads of Mumuye figurative sculpture.
The exaggerated pierced earlobes are their
most striking feature. This example would
have been worn on top of the masquerader's
head with the porthole in the front plank
allowing the wearer to see. The black pigment
on this mask extends to just below the vision
port, indicating that the lower planks would
have been hidden by a thick hibiscus fiber
cloak. The fiber cloak would also conceal the
masquerader's lower extremities and body.

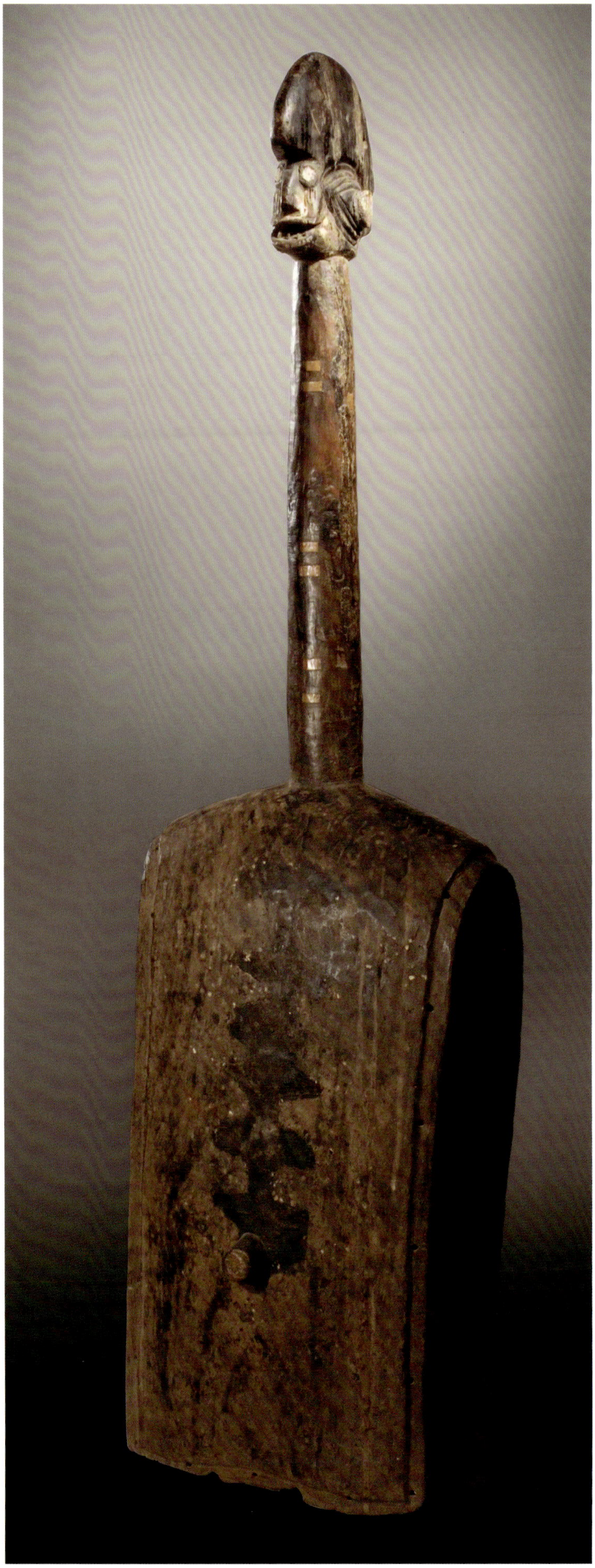

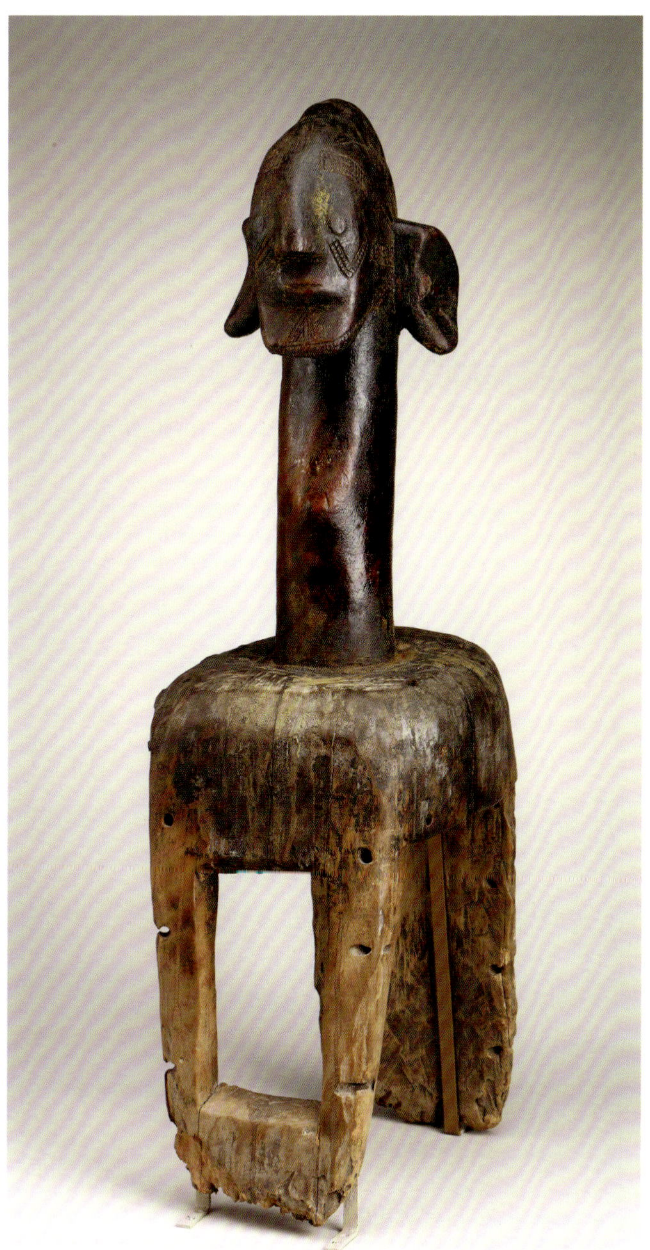

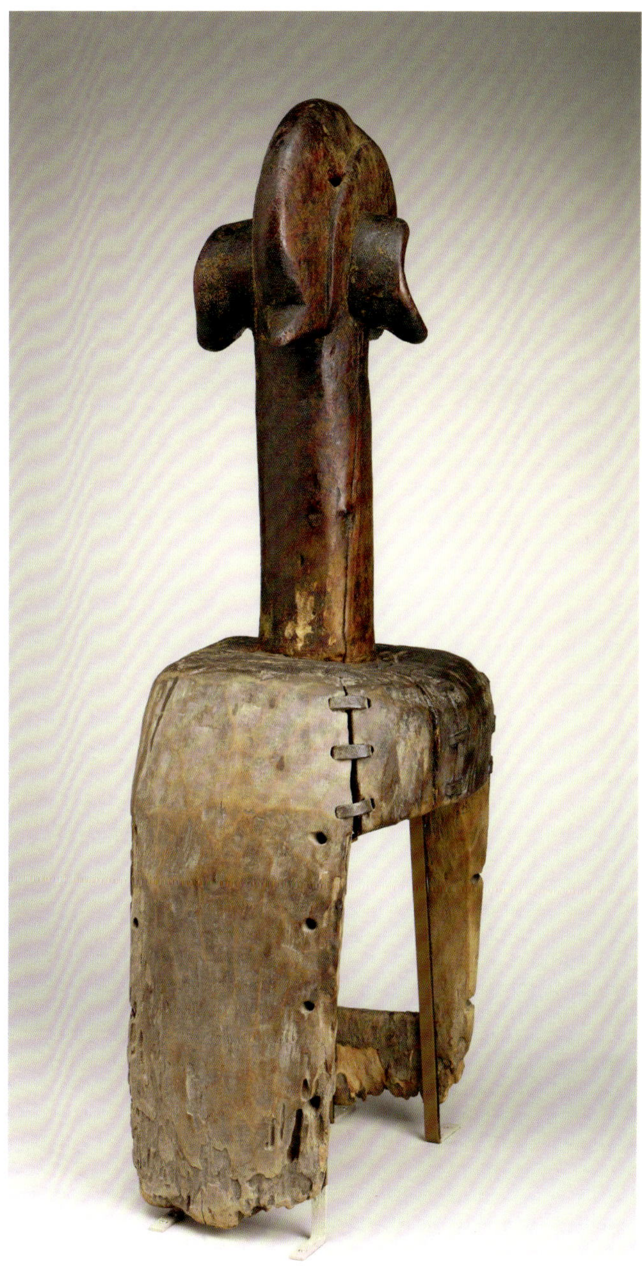

14.3 (OPPOSITE)
Vertical Mask
Wurkun/Bikwin peoples, early to mid-twenti-
eth century
Wood, aluminum, copper, pigment
H: 159.4 cm
PRIVATE COLLECTION
IMAGE: © PRIVATE COLLECTION. PHOTOGRAPH BY
BENJAMIN WATKINS
PROVENANCE: SOTHEBY'S LONDON, JUNE 1992

Many Wurkun/Bikwin vertical masks share
this distinctive configuration: a small narrow
head and elongated neck emerging from a
rather shallow support structure. The planks
are intended to be read as the "body," and the
front plank has a projecting umbilicus. The
narrow space between the planks indicates
that this mask might have been carried rather
than easily worn. See figure 14.34 for a rear
view of this mask.

14.4a (ABOVE LEFT)
Vertical mask (Zənkani)
Jukun peoples, late nineteenth to early twen-
tieth century
Wood, oil
H: 88.9 cm
FINE ARTS MUSEUMS OF SAN FRANCISCO, GIFT OF
THE ERLE LORAN FAMILY COLLECTION, 2008.38.65
IMAGE: © FINE ARTS MUSEUMS OF SAN FRANCISCO.
PHOTOGRAPH BY JOSEPH MCDONALD

This mask, called Zənkani, was field documented by Arnold Rubin in 1965 in the Jukun
village of Kona (see fig. 14.20). Its face, now
missing its foil eyes, has the square jaw/
beard, large trumpet-shaped pierced ears, and
scarification markings associated with Jukun
sculptural styles. The prominent Adam's apple
underscores the male identity of its embodied
spirit. The surface was rubbed with oil reddened with ocher as a ritual anointment.

14.4b (ABOVE)
A rear view of Zənkani (see fig. 14.4a) as it
exists today shows the single pigtail worn by
Jukun men. Also visible are the rows of large
iron staples, which stabilized deep cracks in
the wood and likely allowed it to be used
despite the loss of its lower planks. The powerful role of Zənkani in Kona Jukun ritual life
is mirrored in the efforts to prolong its use.

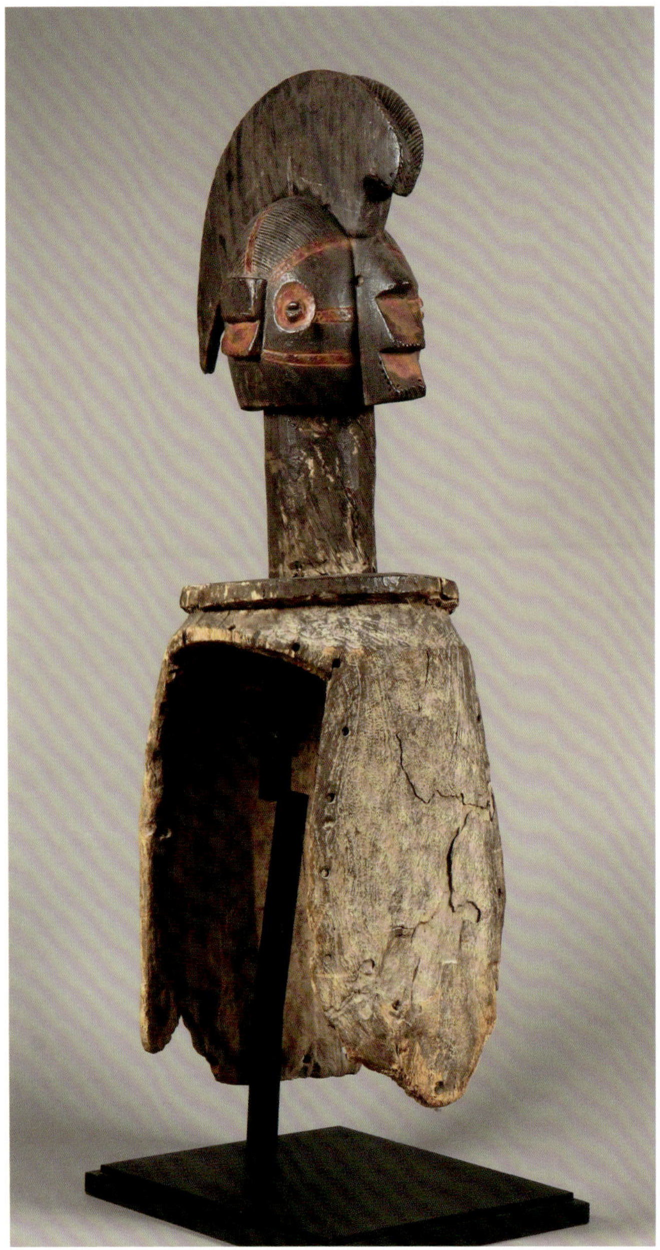

14.5
Vertical mask
Wurkun/Bikwin peoples, late nineteenth
to early twentieth century or before
Wood, pigment
H: 130 cm
PRIVATE COLLECTION, PARIS
IMAGE: COURTESY PRIVATE COLLECTOR.
PHOTOGRAPH © FRANTZ DUFOUR
PROVENANCE: JACQUES KERCHACHE, 1968 (?)
(NOT IN EXHIBITION)

The Wurkun/Bikwin attribution of this mask
is based on the clear correspondence between
the stylization of its face and that observed
on the small-scale healing sculptures made
by the Wurkun, called *kundul* (see fig. 13.9).
Another similar mask, also acquired by Jacques
Kerchache, is illustrated in figure 14.30. Both
examples have support structures of sufficient
size to accommodate a person standing inside
them with his head turned sideways, which
would enable him to see.

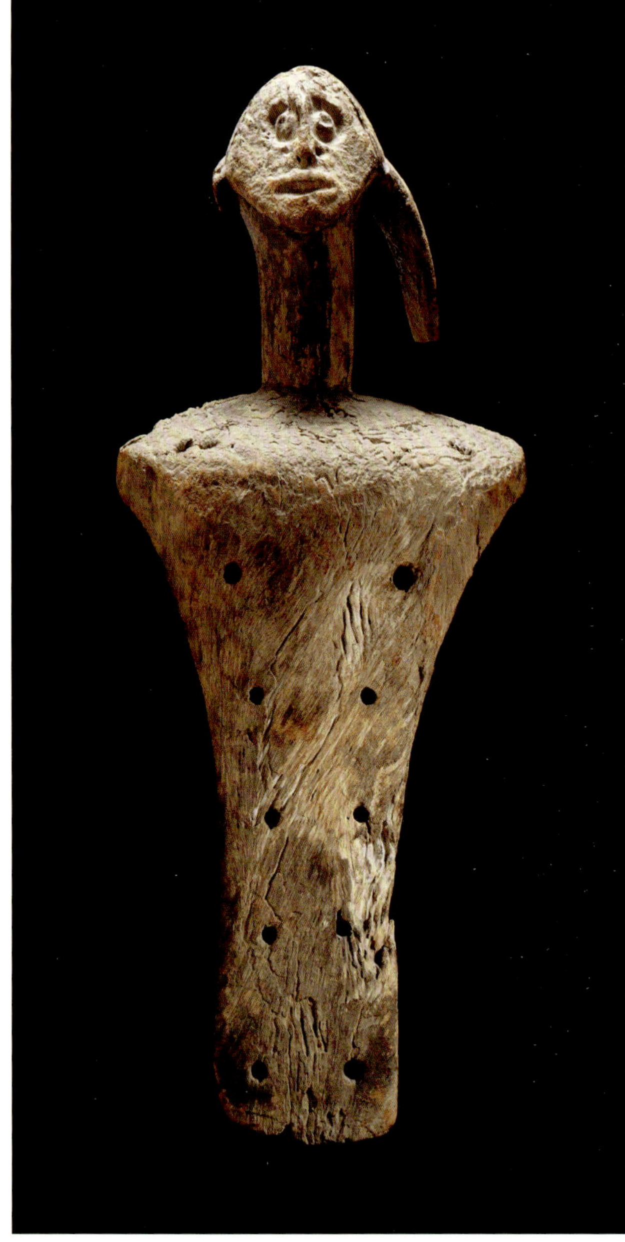

14.6
Vertical mask (Sukuru?)
Mumuye peoples, nineteenth century
or before
Wood
H: 88 cm
PRIVATE COLLECTION
IMAGE: © GALERIE PATRIK FRÖLICH.
PHOTOGRAPH BY HEINZ UNGER, ZURICH
PROVENANCE: JACQUES KERCHACHE; RENÉ
SALANON; GALERIE PATRIK FRÖLICH, ZURICH
(NOT IN EXHIBITION)

Despite its heavily weathered surface, this
haunting mask still retains the distinctive stylistic features associated with other Mumuye
vertical masks (see figs. 14.2, 14.9, 14.10) and
figurative sculpture. The large pierced ears
(one of which is missing) and bold circular
eyes are diagnostic. Not visible in this picture
is the absence of the rear plank support for
the mask.

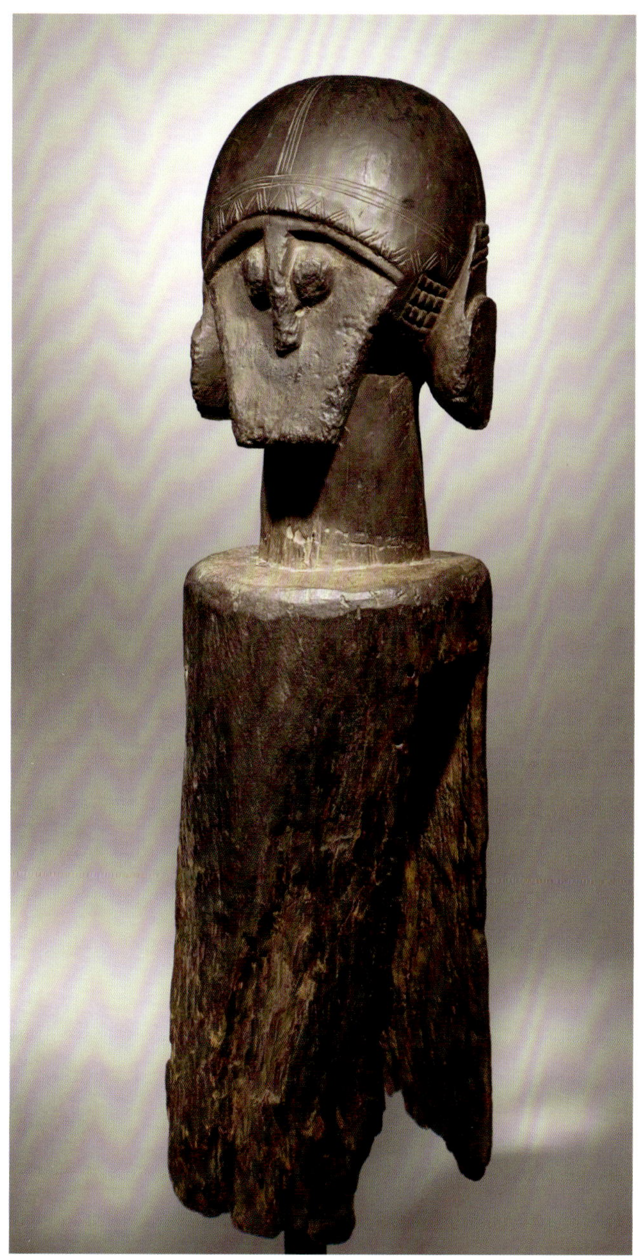

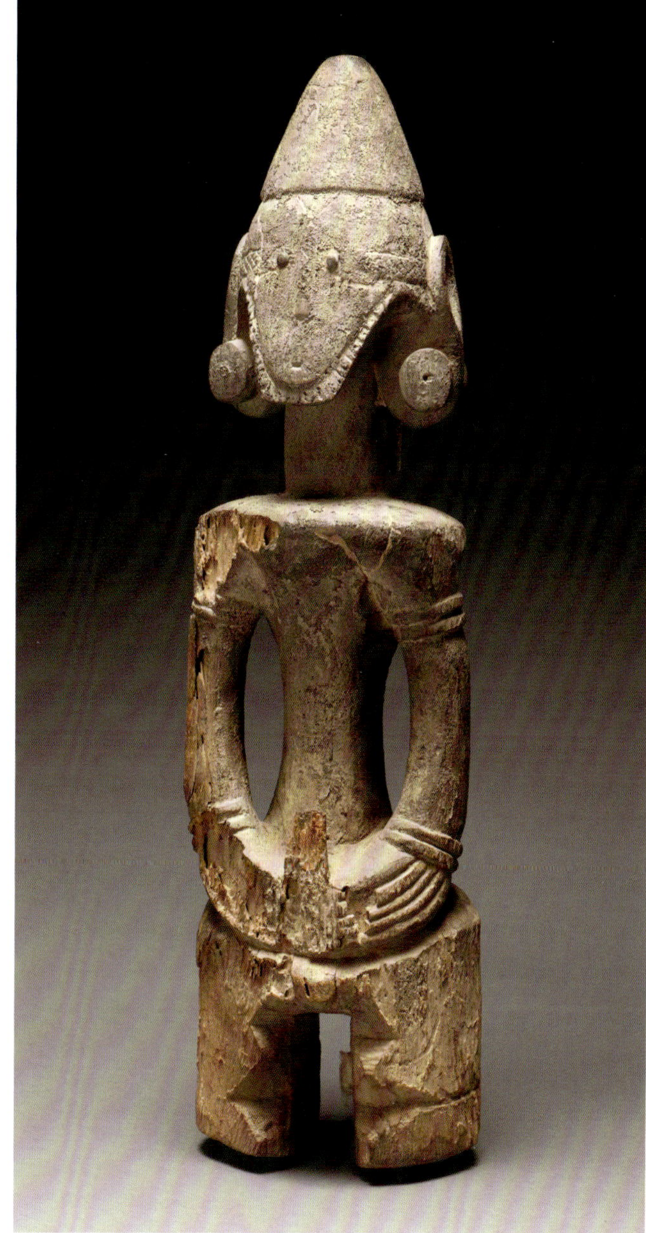

2009). The third was also called "Waja," despite its striking difference from both of the other examples in the book (figs. 14.1, 14.7). This mask was reproduced directly below a standing figure, which was given an attribution of Karim (likely to be short for the town of Karim Lamido), East Nigeria (fig. 14.8).[4] Leuzinger must have seen the intriguing stylistic similarities between these objects, especially in their heads, necks, and shoulders, with the planks of the vertical mask standing in for the rest of the body. At the time of Leuzinger's writing, the contents of Rubin's dissertation of 1969 and his definition of a Jukun style had yet to be widely disseminated. Of interest, Rubin had even photographed the very same standing figure attributed to Karim and reproduced in Leuzinger's book in the Jukun center of Gwana in 1966, and he had illustrated it in his thesis (Rubin, 1969, pls. 123–25; see fig. 8.52).[5] We know that within just a few years, sculptures like these from the Middle Benue began flooding European galleries and auction houses in the wake of the Biafran War.

The "default" attribution of the three emblematic vertical masks in Leuzinger to the "Waja" is not supported by field evidence collected by Rubin, Berns, or Adelberger, each of whom conducted brief periods of research among Waja communities in the 1970s and 1980s (see chapter 13). Instead, the results of these investigations

14.7 (ABOVE LEFT)
See fig. 14.1 for description.

14.8 (ABOVE RIGHT)
Male figure (Wipong)
Jukun peoples, Gwana, late nineteenth
to early twentieth century or before
Wood
H: 71 cm
ROBERT T. WALL FAMILY
IMAGE: COURTESY COLLECTOR. PHOTOGRAPH BY
DON TUTTLE, 2010
PROVENANCE: COLLECTED IN KARIM (KARIM LAMIDO);
JACQUES KERCHACHE, PARIS, ACQUIRED BEFORE 1971

This Jukun shrine figure was documented in 1966 at the hilltop site of Gwana and had the personal name "Wipong" (see figs. 8.52, 8.54). There are clear stylistic similarities between the head and face of this figure and the vertical mask in figure 14.7. This relationship lends weight to the proposition put forth here that the masks may be understood as "walking sculpture."

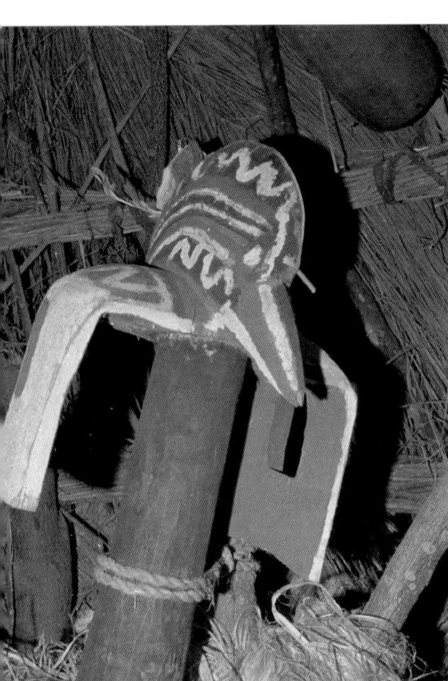

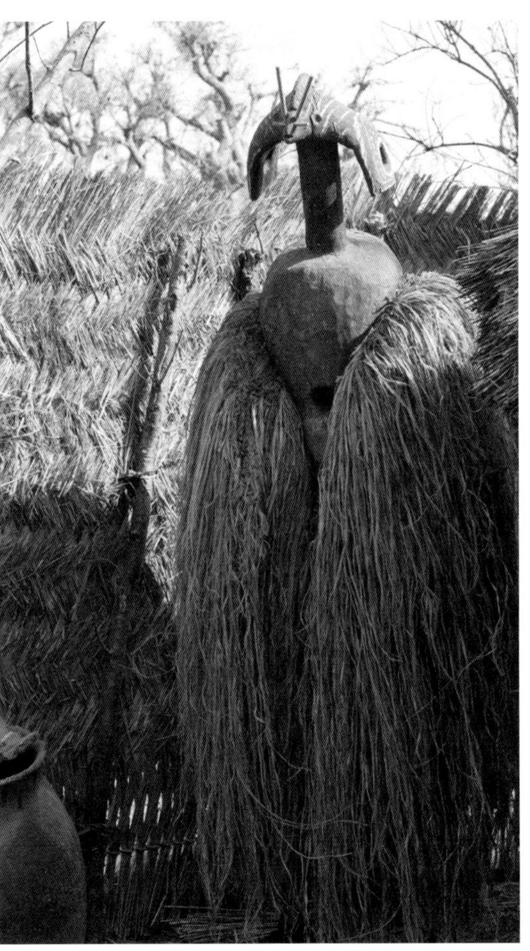

14.9 (LEFT)
This Mumuye Sukuru mask was photographed in its shrine enclosure. It was carved by the artist Lenke's brother, Mai Shera, around 1965. Its face is heavily adorned with painted decoration, and it has the telltale Mumuye earflaps.
PHOTOGRAPH BY ARNOLD RUBIN, APRIL 17, 1970, DIDƏNKO HAMLET, ZINNA, RUBIN ARCHIVE, FOWLER MUSEUM AT UCLA, NEG. NO. 2613.

14.10 (RIGHT)
Mumuye vertical masks had full fiber costumes attached to holes at the sides of the support planks and were often provided with a small central vision port. This mask, called Sukuru (old woman), was carved by the artist Lenke, who came from the Mumuye village of Zinna. The wide pierced "earflaps" are its most distinctive feature. Incised and painted lines reproduce patterns of facial scarification, and pieces of sorghum stalk inserted into the pierced nasal septum and nostrils emulate modes of body decoration favored by Mumuye women.
PHOTOGRAPH BY ARNOLD RUBIN, APRIL 4, 1970, ZINNA, RUBIN ARCHIVE, FOWLER MUSEUM AT UCLA, SLIDE NO. II-258.

demonstrated that the Waja belong to a cluster of related groups who used ceramic sculpture, and not wood, as a focus of ritual activities (see chapter 16). Moreover, it is highly likely that the attribution "Waja," given by runners or traders who sold these masks to Europeans, derived from the name of the broader "Tangale-Waja District" where they were found. The southern border of the district includes the western Muri Mountains where the Wurkun and Bikwin live. The precise locations from which such objects derived were the carefully guarded secrets of runners, and it is doubtful they would be revealed when the works were sold to traders.

This essay will demonstrate that this large corpus of vertical masks is associated with a cluster of related Middle Benue peoples whose historical interaction in the region is reflected in the circulation and shared ritual significance of this spectacular performance genre. All of these groups live in close geographical proximity on both sides of the Benue River. The historical record provides some evidence as to the nature and extent of the relationships among them since at least the nineteenth century. The Jukun, about whom the most is known, established an important religious center south of the Benue River in Kona to which the neighboring Mumuye paid annual tribute (see map, fig. 7.2, p. 216). Jukun influence extended as far east as the Mumuye town of Zinna, present-day Zing (Meek 1931b, 2: 449).[6] The appointment of the chief priest of Zinna was formally confirmed by the Kona Jukun, and the Mumuye assisted the Jukun in resisting Fulani incursions until the Jukun finally succumbed at the end of the nineteenth century (see introduction to this volume). Both groups share the tradition of using vertical masks in ritual contexts, and Rubin documented them in Kona and in Zinna as well as in the Mumuye village of Pantilapo (near Pantisawa); others were photographed in nearby Jukun and Yendang villages. Rubin (1969, 97) speculated that the Jukun versions were likely to have been taken over from non-Jukun people, "probably their Mumuye neighbors."

According to the linguist Kiyoshi Shimizu (1971), who outlined four phases of Jukun expansion corresponding with the three main Jukun language divisions, some of the Kona Jukun moved northward across the Benue River to Pindiga and Gwana, and all three share a closely related Wapan dialect. Two sources date this migration to 1750 (Fremantle 1922, 27; Temple and Temple 1919, 365). Other Kona Jukun moved northward in the aftermath of the destruction of the town of Kona by the Fulani, who were assisted by the French, in 1892 (Dinslage and Storche 2000, 13). This would have put the Jukun in close proximity to the Wurkun and Bikwin groups of the western Muri Mountains. The ethnic designation "Wurkun" is in fact Jukun in origin, meaning "people of the hills" (see chapter 13). Although highly speculative, the pre-jihad histories of the region suggest that Jukun migrants intermarried with groups of Wurkun who themselves arrived in the region from the northeast around the same time (Rubin 1988, c:/bivjh, 20).

The contexts in which these impressive vertical masks were used have been discussed in chapters 8, 9, and 13. Nearly all of the masks were said to have appeared seasonally, especially in conjunction with the annual planting and harvesting of crops, helping to bestow the blessing of agricultural success and community well-being. The Wurkun examples also played a role in ritual performances commemorating the dead, incarnating the ancestors returned to the world of the living.

The similarities between the heads of the vertical masks and the heads of figurative sculpture made by the peoples in question are striking. They become especially marked when concentrating on such diagnostic details as exaggerated ears and prominent dance helmets or crested coiffures. These correlations are a powerful corrective to any assumption that these mask conceptions were the work of a single ethnic group. The shared approach to these highly distinctive configurations is surely a by-product of communication across cultures and among local communities on both sides of the Benue River. Their efficacy may be aligned with their ambiguity, as they are neither true "masks" nor "figurative sculpture," suggesting that their power may be related to the ways in which they disrupt such conventional distinctions. Indeed, our argument here is that these vertical masks are a kind of ambulatory sculpture, a conception that fuses the highly recognizable heads and necks of ritual shrine sculptures with a supporting apparatus that allowed them to be either worn (with the wearer's body hidden inside the support and disguised by grass coverings attached at its sides and bottom) or perhaps carried. Carved of one large log of wood, some examples seem much too narrow to be easily worn by a man or else so heavy as to represent something of a feat for a masquerader to balance on top of his head even while steadying the supports from below. That none of these masks has ever been seen in performance by researchers has added immeasurably to their mystery both formally and functionally. Fortunately, Arnold Rubin's now-precious field documentation gives us a place to begin.

Mumuye vertical masks are perhaps the most easily recognizable given the number and variety of Mumuye figures that have been published over the past forty years (see chapter 8). The masks conform in interesting ways to several figurative styles, and Rubin documented them in three communities. The two masks he photographed in the Mumuye town of Zinna, which were called Sukuru ("old woman"; figs. 14.9, 14.10), represent one major variant. These have small heads and huge pierced ears that extend horizontally like flaps. Their faces have beak-like mouths, raising the question as to whether they are intended to represent a human-avian fusion or just a stylization associated with the genre. Although it seems rather unlikely that a reference to birds would be incorporated into this mask conception, there are Mumuye figures whose faces have features that are handled similarly (see Fry 1970, fig. 14). There are also Mumuye horizontally aligned helmet masks in the form of kingfishers used as a part of the Vaa-Bong complex (see figs. 10.27–10.29). This theranthropism is conventional in Vaa-Bong horizontal masks but exceptional in the case of both vertical masks and figurative sculpture.

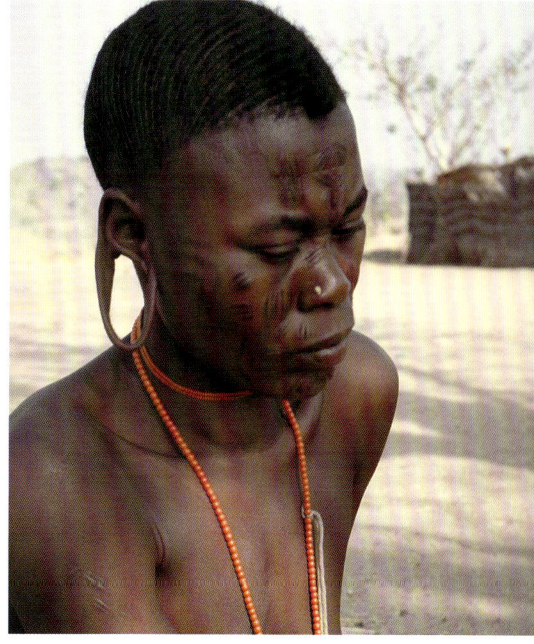

14.11
Arnold Rubin photographed this Mumuye woman in the town of Mika. Her face is covered with complex patterns of scarification, including several recognizable on Mumuye sculpture. Especially notable are the zigzag lines at the sides of the face. She also has long distended earlobes, which are a common feature of Mumuye sculpture.
PHOTOGRAPH BY ARNOLD RUBIN, 1970, RUBIN ARCHIVE, FOWLER MUSEUM AT UCLA, SLIDE NO. A1.10.11.2.

The first Sukuru, which was photographed in 1965 and again in 1970 in the Zang hamlet of Zinna, was said to have been carved by the sculptor Lenke, who was interviewed by Rubin and was recognized for his high output of horizontal and vertical masks (see fig. 14.10; interleaf F, p. 363; chapter 10, pp. 336–37). The Sukuru appeared at funerals of the elderly, in rituals to identify thieves, and in commemorations of the appointment of a new chief, rather than in the context of the agricultural cycle usually associated with this mask genre (Rubin fieldnotes April 4, 1970, 258). It also may have performed alongside a male horizontal "bushcow" mask (Vaa-Bong). The second Sukuru, from the Didənko hamlet, was carved by Lenke's brother, Mai Shera, and performed during harvest festivals (see fig. 14.9). Both of these masks are painted black and have details picked out in red and white pigment. Rubin's fieldnotes (March 4, 1965) identify the meaning of the colors as reported by his informants: black is "to show people that this is to get water [rain] for them"; white is happiness; and red is for beautification. The incised and painted lines reproduce patterns of facial scarification commonly used by Mumuye women and men (see fig. 14.2 and fig. 11.25). Another distinctive form of women's self-decoration was the insertion of a sorghum stalk through a pierced nasal septum. These were also placed vertically in holes pierced through the nostrils, practices reproduced in these Zinna masks (see fig. 8.46; see also Temple and Temple [1919] 1922, 288, 293; Meek 1931b, 1: pl. 44; Fry 1970, fig. 18). Of course the most dramatic feature of Mumuye permanent body ornamentation was the distention of the earlobes created by the insertion of large round disks (fig. 14.11), which when removed, left hanging loops that were translated sculpturally into exaggerated openwork or pierced flaps—a hallmark of the Mumuye figurative carving style (see fig. 14.2 and fig. 8.49). That these masks are called Sukuru (old woman) may refer especially to the exaggerated distention of the lobes associated with advanced age.

Rubin documented another similar mask, said to have come from Zinna, in the Yendang village of Kufuru (fig. 14.12). The Yendang are close linguistic relatives of the Mumuye and live at their northeastern boundary. The mask's owner demonstrated to Rubin how it was worn, resting on the head so that he could look through the small porthole while supporting the lower plank with his hand, a strategy likely to be true of the other Zinna examples. This mask also has large pierced earflaps and a projecting beak-like mouth. as well as the residue of painted decoration.

Other Mumuye vertical masks, distinguished by small heads with large earflaps, are now in collections, including the beautifully proportioned example pictured here from the Brooklyn Museum (fig. 14.13). Its surface is painted black, and the ears, mouth, and eyes are highlighted in red. The wide circular eyes are ringed in white, a convention also typical of Mumuye figures. The small porthole is situated for the wearer's convenience, and it is clear from the small holes along the sides of the unpainted lower surface that it would have been covered by a hibiscus fiber cloak. The lower edges of the planks in figures 14.13 and 14.14 show the kind of wear that indicates they were held to keep the heavy mask stable in performance.

A male and female pair of vertical masks called Vaa-Bong (fig. 14.15), which Rubin photographed in 1965 in the Mumuye village of Pantilapo (near Pantisawa), resembles yet another classic style of Mumuye figurative sculpture (fig. 14.16; see also fig. 8.18).[7] The heads are relatively naturalistic and are carved fully in the round. The faces have long chins and large trumpet-shaped ears as well as distinctive sagittal coiffures. The male mask has a higher crested coiffure and a pronounced Adam's apple. The figure sculpture's head and elongated neck could easily be mistaken for the upper section of a Vaa-Bong mask. Both vertical masks have large rectangular openings in their supports for vision and holes along the edges where grasses would have been attached to conceal the wearers. These Vaa-Bong, which were owned by the Panti Lapo (eponymous leader of Pantilapo) and considered paramount religious sculptures for the community, performed in celebration of the harvest and also every

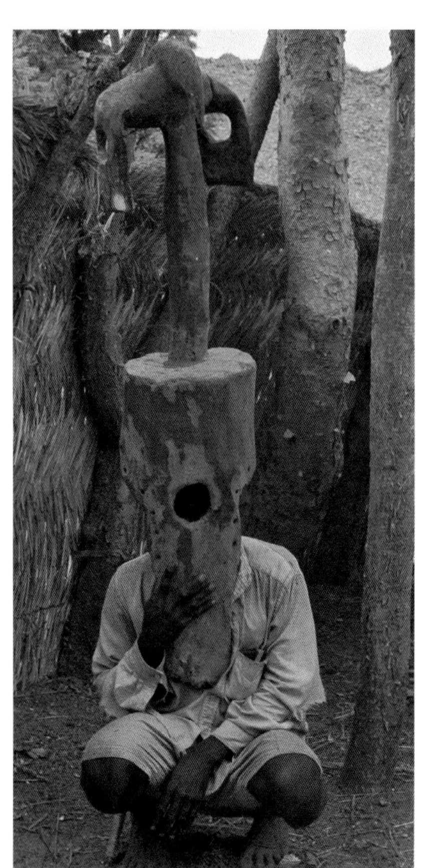

14.12
A man from the Yendang village of Kufuru demonstrates how a vertical mask is worn and stabilized. The Yendang are close linguistic relatives of the Mumuye, and this mask was carved in the Mumuye village of Zinna, according to its owner, Kpeyasha. It has the same wide, pierced ears as other Zinna vertical masks.

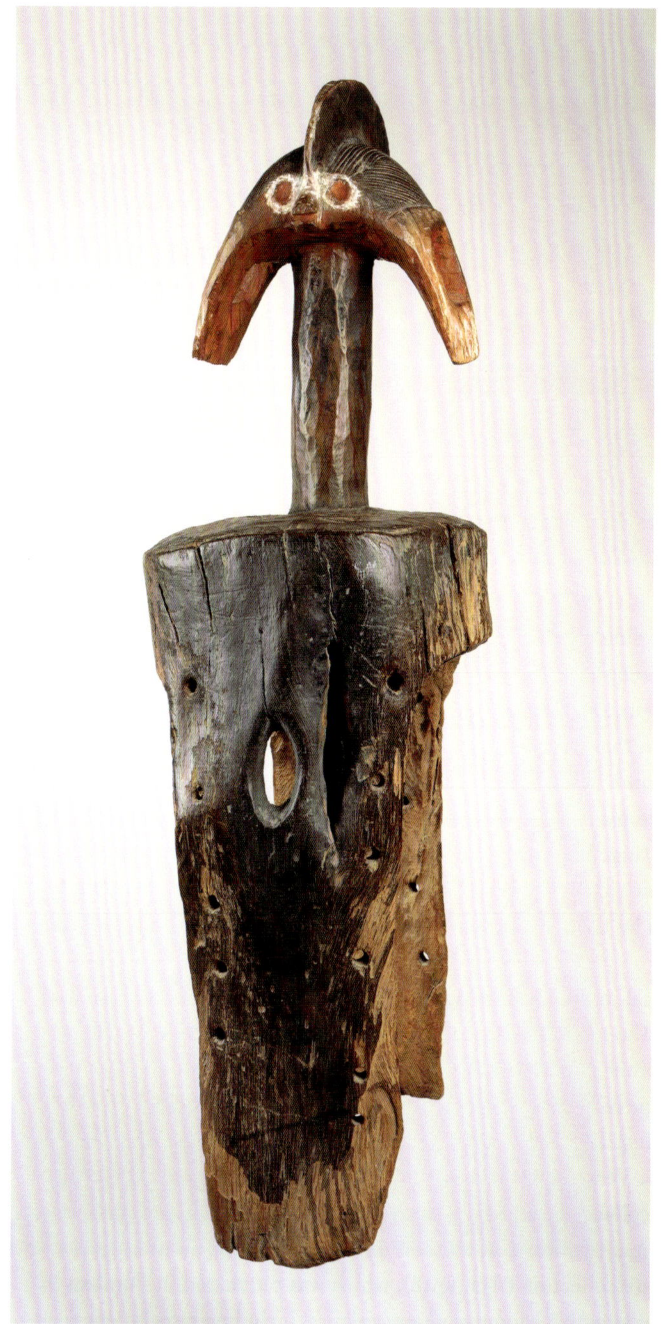

14.13
Vertical mask (Sukuru)
Mumuye peoples, early to mid-twentieth century
Wood, pigment
H: 90.2 cm
BROOKLYN MUSEUM, 2000.72.3; GIFT OF ISRAEL AND MICHAELA SAMUELLY
IMAGE: © BROOKLYN MUSEUM
PROVENANCE: LELOUP COLLECTION; ROBERT AND NANCY NOOTER, EARLY 1980S; WILLIAM WRIGHT, NEW YORK, 1993 OR 1994
(NOT IN EXHIBITION)

This mask shares the stylistic features of other Mumuye Sukuru masks documented in the village of Zinna. The elegant upper curve of the ears, the mask's transverse coiffure, and its close-set circular eyes contribute to making this an especially harmonious example.

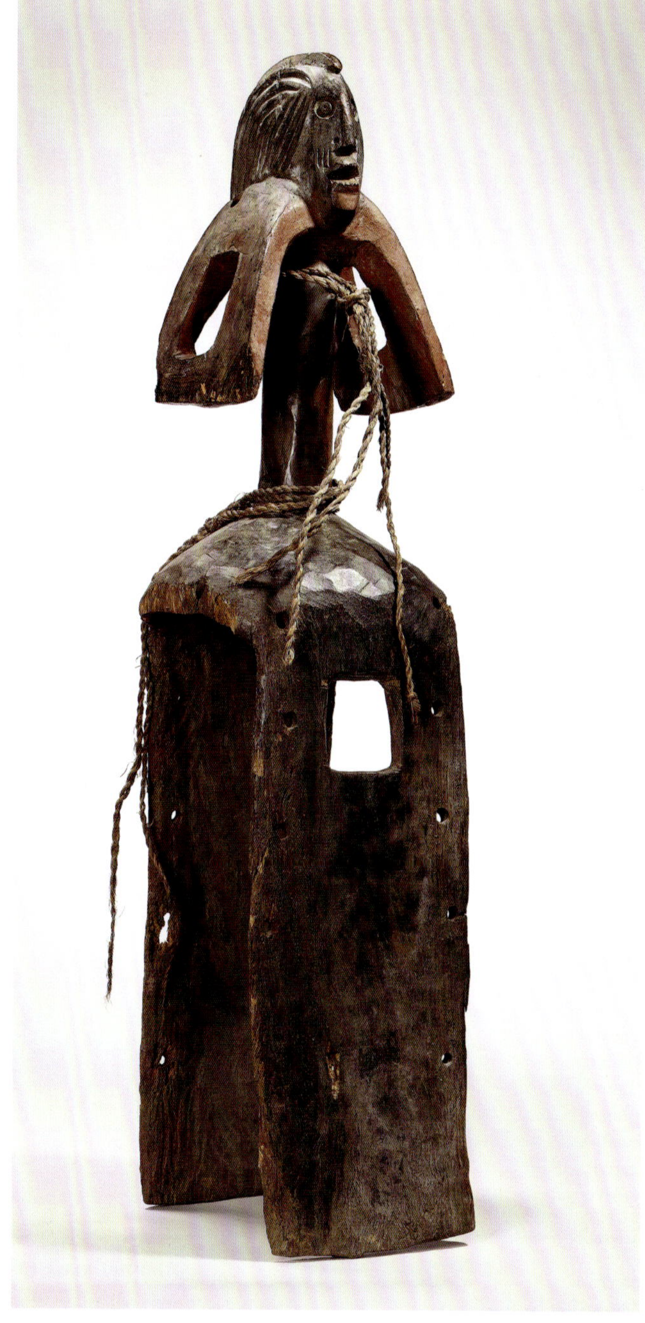

14.14
Vertical mask (Sukuru)
Mumuye peoples, early twentieth century
Wood, plant fibers, pigment
H: 111 cm
MUSÉE DU QUAI BRANLY, PARIS, 73.1997.4.49
IMAGE: © 2010 MUSÉE DU QUAI BRANLY. PHOTOGRAPH CLAUDE GERMAIN/SCALA, FLORENCE
PROVENANCE: COLLECTION BARBIER-MUELLER; FELICIA DIALOSSIN, PARIS

This vertical mask has the exaggerated and pierced earlobes typical of Mumuye examples. Other of its stylistic characteristics—black and red pigment, a porthole for vision—are hallmarks of the genre.

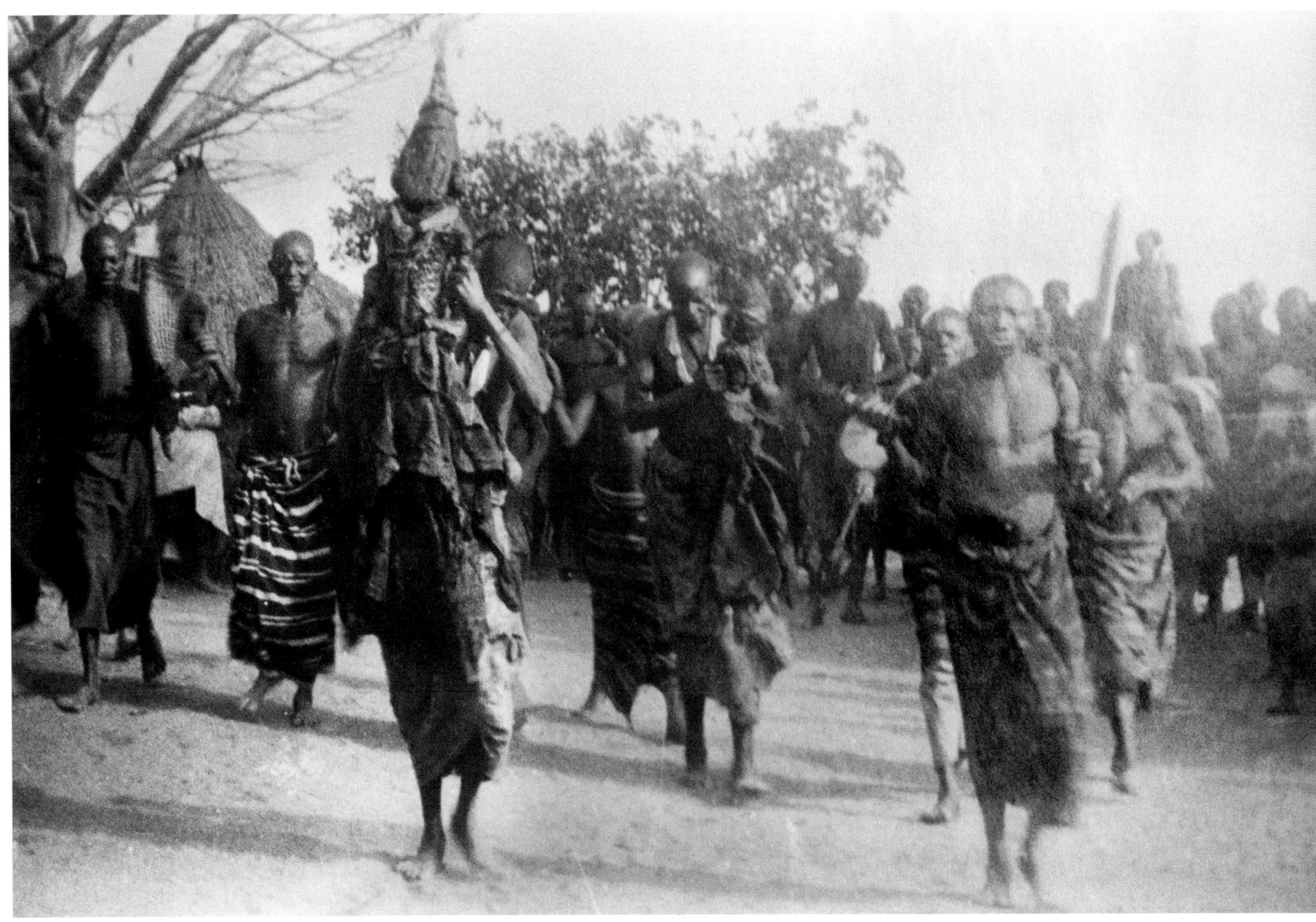

14.27

This rare, previously unpublished, photograph taken in the Jukun town of Gwana in 1926 captures a ritual performance where Adang, a royal ancestor, returns to the community in the form of a wooden figure. It is held by the arms and carried aloft by the man in the front left of the image. Adang's wife, a much smaller figure, is carried by the man in the center. This fascinating photograph shows that the shrine figures were elaborately dressed—wrapped around the waist in cloth just like the ritual leaders who carry them—and adorned with the same necklaces. This image has been digitally enhanced to bring out the complex details of the event and the dress of its participants.

PHOTOGRAPH BY O. H. BEST, GWANA, 1926.

92.5 centimeters tall. Like the sculpture in the O. H. Best photograph, it also has a face that is heavily encrusted with sacrificial materials—or as Meek (1931c) terms it in the text accompanying the photograph, "oil and ashes with which it is smeared from time to time to protect it from weather and insects." It is even possible that the Musée du quai Branly figure, originally acquired by John Klejman probably in the late 1960s, is the one photographed in 1926.[20] The slender arms of the figure are worn just where it would have been held in performance. Indeed, this usage would seem to explain the distinctive style of many Gwana figures Rubin documented in the field—with columnar torsos and mostly straight unflexed arms carved away from the body and attached by the hands at the hips to create handles (see Rubin 1969, pl. 143).[21] Several Jukun half-figures carved without legs that are currently in private collections (fig. 14.29) would seem to have been carved for this same purpose. This strategy is not confined to northern Gwana and Pindiga styles but also to the Jukun shrine sculpture documented in the towns of Wurbon Daudu and Mabo (see fig. E.9). Photographs Rubin took in Mabo show his informants holding such shrine figures up by the arms, and in his fieldnotes he indicates (December 24, 1964) that the "figures [were] danced into town" during rituals that lasted three days. That the lower bodies of all these figures were typically covered with cloth wrappings—and Rubin was told that undressing them was forbidden—may have made articulation of the legs superfluous, explaining why in some cases they were either short and stubby or even nonexistent.[22]

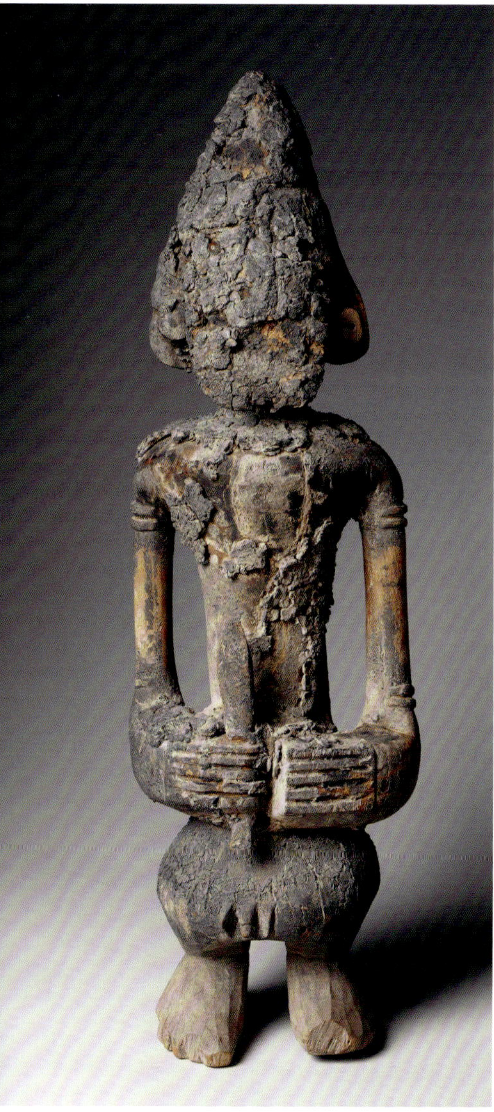

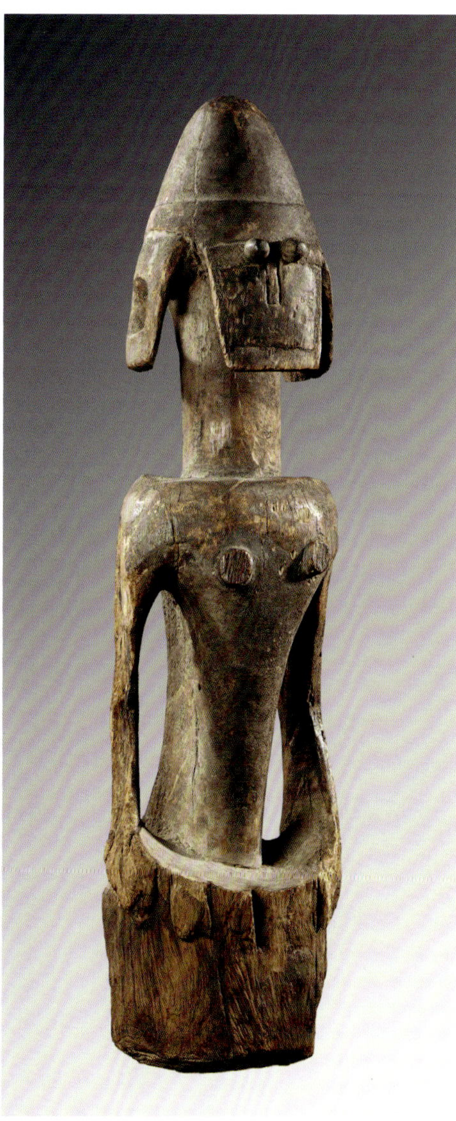

14.28

Male figure (Adang?)
Jukun peoples, Gwana (?), late nineteenth to
early twentieth century or before
Wood, metal, sacrificial material
H: 92.5 cm
MUSÉE DU QUAI BRANLY, PARIS, 73.1997.4.39
IMAGE: © 2010 MUSÉE DU QUAI BRANLY. PHOTO-
GRAPH PATRICK GRIES/SCALA, FLORENCE
PROVENANCE: JOHN KLEJMAN, NEW YORK;
BARBIER-MUELLER COLLECTION
(NOT IN EXHIBITION)

The surface of this Jukun figure is covered with
a thick crust of sacrificial material, resulting
from repeated offerings of animal blood and
beer. Its facial features are completely obscured
and as such it bears an uncanny resemblance
to the head and face on the figure of Adang
being carried in figure 14.27. Both have ears
pierced with cylindrical spools and a pointed
cap. The wear patterns along the handle-like
arms of this sculpture may have resulted from
being held aloft in ritual performance. Like
similar figures from Gwana or Pindiga (see fig.
14.8), it may hold the "spear of Mam," the most
powerful ritual object in the ancestral cult of
which the sculpture is a part.

14.29

Half figure
Jukun peoples, Gwana (?), late nineteenth
century
Wood
H: 63 cm
PRIVATE COLLECTION, BRUSSELS
IMAGE: COURTESY PRIVATE COLLECTOR. PHOTO-
GRAPH © 2010 STUDIO PHILIPPE DE FORMANOIR
PROVENANCE: PHILIPPE GUIMIOT, COLLECTED
IN NIGERIA; BARON FRÉDÉRIC ROLIN & CO.,
NEW YORK
(NOT IN EXHIBITION)

On the basis of its style, this half-figure is
likely to have come from Gwana. Its unique
configuration with a narrow torso and arms
carved as "handles" suggests that it was carried in ritual performance and dressed with
cloth, making the need for legs superfluous.

The tradition of Middle Benue peoples carrying shrine figures in ritual contexts
is further revealed in dramatic photographs of 1957 taken by colonial District Officer Robin Jagoe in a Goemai village, located about 100 miles across the Benue River
north of the Jukun town of Wukari (see figs. 8.60a–c; Sieber 1961, 11). Two men hold
a large wooden figure by the arms. The figure's head takes the form of the long-
nosed Gugwom mask, which was performed near the graves of former chiefs (see fig.
10.46).[23] This idea of carrying sculptural embodiments—in the Gugwom case one that
combines a human figure with a mask head—seems conceptually related to the vertical
mask genre with its emphatic reliance on the distinctive heads of Mumuye and Jukun
figurative styles. The transition from a freestanding figure to a sculptural configuration that could be worn may represent an innovation that allowed a man who might
otherwise carry the figure to be disguised within it. These objects may thereby have
functioned less like conventional masks than as ambulatory sculptures, embodying
powerful spirit forces and allowing the wearer and the spirit to become one.

The largest, most various, and most enigmatic category of vertical masks is the
one we are associating here with the groups identified in this volume as Wurkun
or Bikwin (figs. 14.30a,b, 14.31). Over forty have been identified in collections or
reproduced in publications. Sadly, no actual Wurkun or Bikwin vertical masks were
documented in the field, even though informants remembered and described them and
their uses to Joerg Adelberger during his fieldwork from 1989 to 1993 (see chapter 13).
Following the Leuzinger publication of 1971, gallery advertisements began to appear as

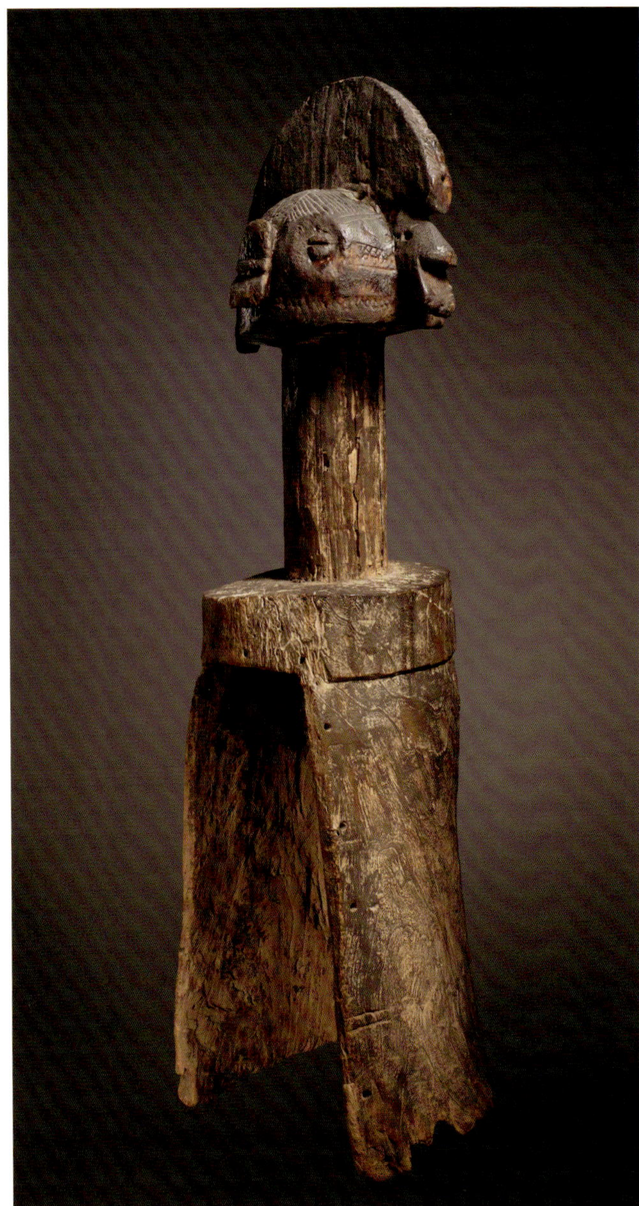
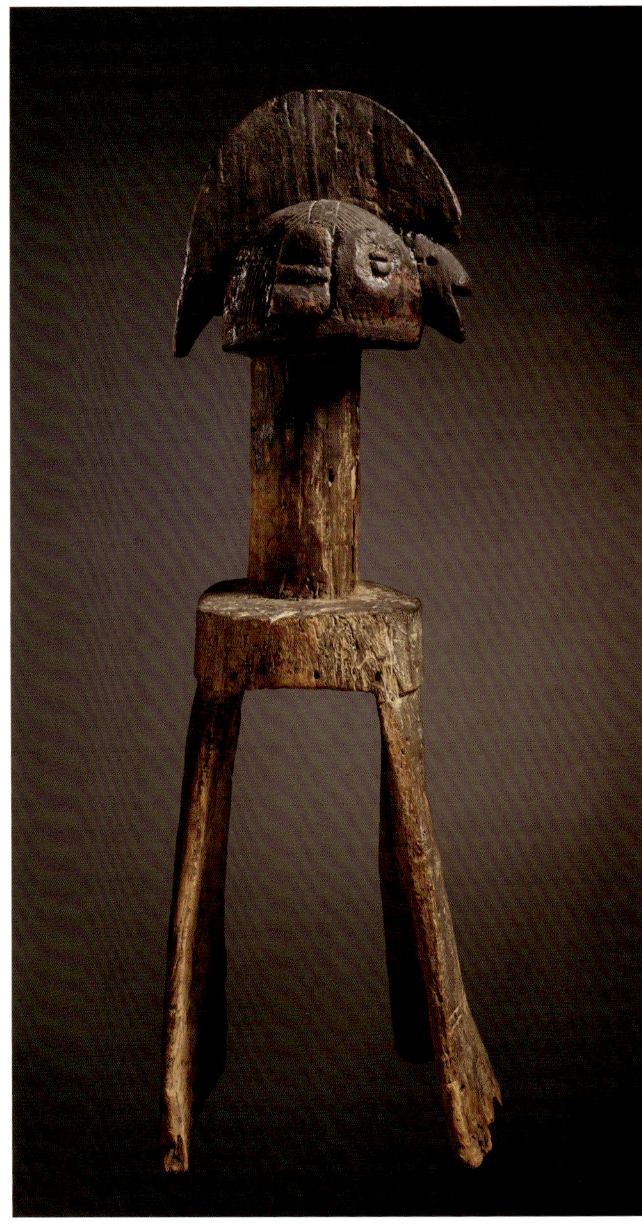

14.30a,b
Vertical mask
Wurkun/Bikwin peoples, late nineteenth to
early twentieth century or before
Wood, palm oil, pigments
H: 129.5 cm
ROBERT T. WALL FAMILY, 2004
IMAGE: COURTESY COLLECTOR. PHOTOGRAPH BY
DON TUTTLE, 2010
PROVENANCE: JACQUES KERCHACHE, LATE 1960S;
WILLIAM RUBIN, NEW YORK, 1982

The powerful stylized head of this paradigmatic "type one" Wurkun/Bikwin vertical
mask recalls the heads—with their high crests
and jagged profiles—on the small columnar
kundul healing sculptures made by the Wurkun
(see fig. 13.7a). The depth and slight torque
of the supporting planks make it possible for
this mask to be worn with the performer's
face turned sideways. The surface of the head,
which is richly anointed with reddened oil,
and the heavily weathered surface of the
planks attest to its probable age and use.

early as 1972 showing these masks, including two in the same issue of the journal *African Arts* (1972, 5, no. 4: 5, 65), one offered by Lance Entwistle and Anthony Plowright
in London and the second by Von Schroeder of Zurich. Others appeared in auction
catalogs in subsequent years and examples in collections began to be published as early
as Karl-Ferdinand Schädler's *African Art in Private German Collections* (1973, 251, no.
354) and Claude Savary's *Sculptures africaines d'un collectionneur de Genève* (1978, 6, fig
2). Although all of them were labeled "Waja," each conforms to one of two distinctive
subgenres of Wurkun/Bikwin vertical mask, with those distinguished by thin, elongated necks and small abstract heads in the majority (see fig. 14.3).

The only eyewitness accounts of vertical masks in performance come from the
missionary C. W. Guinter, who wrote about the Wurkun town of Bambur in 1925
and 1926 (see chapter 13, pp. 422–23). That Guinter (1925) saw as many as sixteen
masqueraders in one memorial rite supports the large numbers of masks identified
in collections and the probability that the ones Guinter saw were of the long-necked
subtype, which Adelberger also considers the most widespread.[24] The Guinter account
(1926, 92–93) does not provide a description of the "large wooden" masks themselves
but provides evidence that they were tall and heavy and only danced by "those who
are able." Adelberger addresses their probable contexts of use and meaning and makes

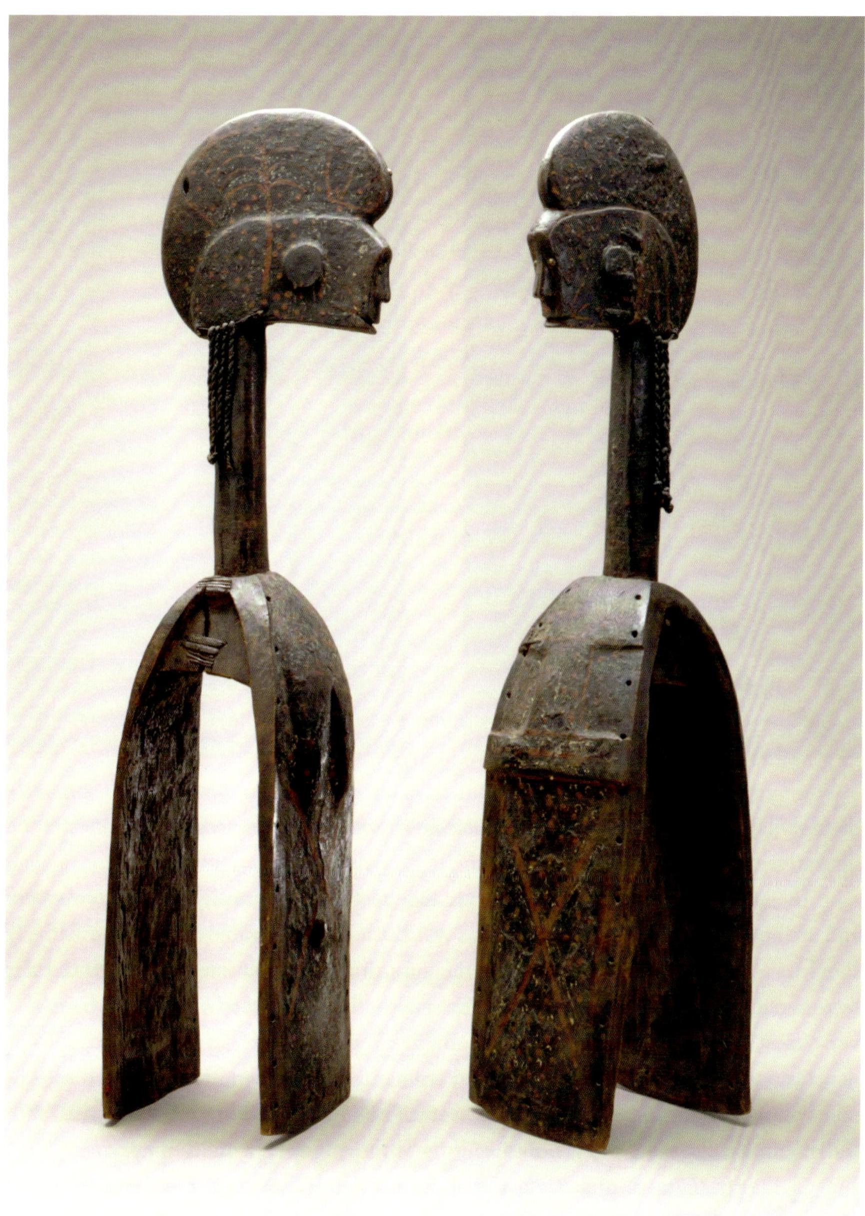

14.31
Vertical mask pair
Wurkun/Bikwin peoples, 1850–1950
Wood, pigment, brass tacks
H (of male): 159 cm; H (of female): 157.5 cm
DETROIT INSTITUTE OF ARTS, 78.41 (MALE), 78.42
(FEMALE); USA/FOUNDERS SOCIETY
PURCHASE/ELEANOR CLAYFORD FUND FOR
AFRICAN ART
IMAGE: © 2004, DETROIT INSTITUTE OF ARTS/THE
BRIDGEMAN ART LIBRARY
PROVENANCE: GASTON DE HAVENON, EARLY 1970S;
BARON FRÉDÉRIC ROLIN & CO., NEW YORK, 1978
(NOT IN EXHIBITION)

These striking masks have the flat narrow
faces and sloping shoulders of "type two"
Wurkun/Bikwin vertical masks. The female
to the left has sculpted breasts, an unusual
feature. The embellishment of the male figure
with red paint is common to the genre as is
the X-formation on the "torso."

a clear case for their stylistic relationship to the small columnar *kundul* and *dambang*
sculptures documented primarily in Wurkun and neighboring Pero communities.
Here, too, as was observed with the Jukun and Mumuye examples, the relationship
to figurative carving styles supports the argument that these "masks" may be better
understood as ambulatory sculptures. Interestingly, *kundul* are conceived as half-figures
without legs (see figs. 13.7–13.9), their bodies ending with a cut-off torso and carved
only with schematic arms as raised ridges surrounding a prominent umbilicus. The
emphasis in *kundul*, as well as in related *dambang* sculptures, is the distinctively carved
head and long neck, which are echoed strongly in vertical masks.

Wurkun vertical masks can be divided into two primary subcategories: those in
the first type (see fig. 14.30a) have large, dome-shaped hemispherical heads (males are
identified by high transverse crests, which female versions lack) and long columnar
necks emerging out of flat-topped supports; and those in the second type (fig. 14.31)
have small narrow heads—some reduced to abstract hemispheres—extremely elongated
necks emerging out of sloping shoulders, and rectangular support planks that are often
wide. There is variation within these two categories, and each is sufficiently different
from the other to suggest that they may have been associated with different peoples
or with different historical sources. The absence of field-documented examples makes

14.35
Standing figure
Wurkun/Bikwin peoples, late nineteenth to
early twentieth century
Wood, metal
H: 95.3 cm
Private Collection
IMAGE: © PRIVATE COLLECTION. PHOTOGRAPH BY
BENJAMIN WATKINS
PROVENANCE: DR. MICHEL GAUD, SAINT TROPEZ;
ALFRED MUELLER, SAINT GRATIEN
(NOT IN EXHIBITION)

This intriguing object seems to combine the
rounded head, neck, and shoulder flange of
a Wurkun/Bikwin vertical mask with a body
made of three narrow, connected poles. The
"arms" are set apart to facilitate the figure
being carried by the torso, where there are
signs of wear. Its use or purpose is unknown,
although it may relate to vertical masks that
were carried rather than worn.

14.36
Standing figure
Wurkun/Bikwin peoples, late nineteenth to
early twentieth century
Wood, metal
H: 99 cm
YALE UNIVERSITY ART GALLERY COLLECTION,
2006.51.552
IMAGE: © YALE UNIVERSITY ART GALLERY
PROVENANCE: PHILIPPE GUIMIOT, BEFORE 1976;
BENENSON COLLECTION, 2004
(NOT IN EXHIBITION)

There is little doubt that this unusual figure
is identical in conception to the only other
known example in a collection (fig. 14.35). It
has the same round head with metal eyes and
schematic features. The attenuated arms on
this example are particularly elegant, and the
surface losses on the central pole would seem
to support the proposition that it was carried
in ritual performance. The lack of a crest may
indicate that it is female.

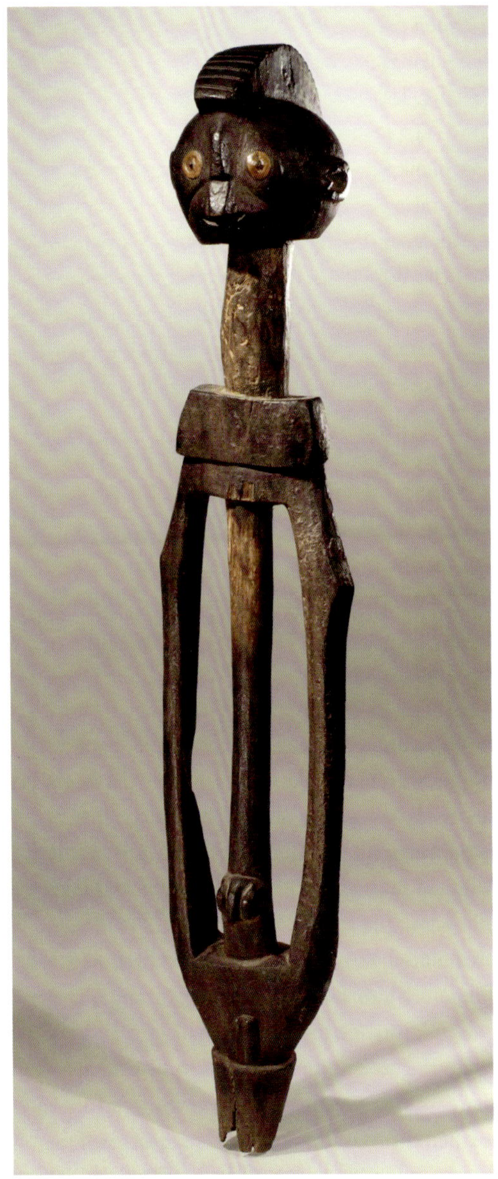

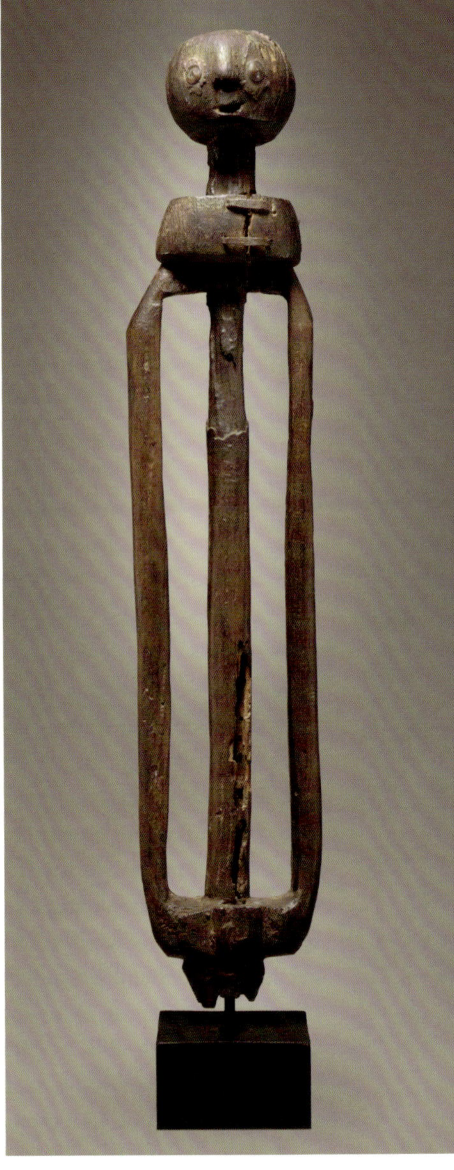

fact that most of the Wurkun/Bikwin masks "read" as powerfully, if not more so, from
the side view may validate the proposition that their wearers moved sideways, confronting viewers with dramatic abstract mask profiles. Indeed, Adelberger's informant wrote:
"When moving, he walks or moves side by side at his left or right hand sides."[25]

It is likely that the weight and awkwardness of these huge objects restricted the
range of movement, and Guinter's report of 1926 indicated that once the performers
entered the town they "would deposit the masks in a row." As a corollary, Adelberger
(p. 432) writes that the masks were made from the wood of certain trees believed able
"to walk in the night." It is not hard to imagine that a group of these towering masks—
lumbering slowly forward or sideways, their heads soaring high over those of the
living—would produce awe associated with their presence as ghostly impersonations.

A group of three related and highly intriguing objects offer additional insights
into the conceptualization of these masks as ambulatory sculpture (figs. 14.35–14.37).[26]
All share the same round head and long neck reminiscent of those on type one
Wurkun vertical masks. Two examples (see figs. 14.35, 14.36) share a unique configuration: their "bodies" are created out of three elongated poles carved in an openwork
pattern, forming a central torso flanked by two arms; the three elements join together
at the base. Figure 14.35 appears to have both male and female genitalia. Lacking legs,
the pointed bases may have been fitted on an iron rod and inserted in the ground, as

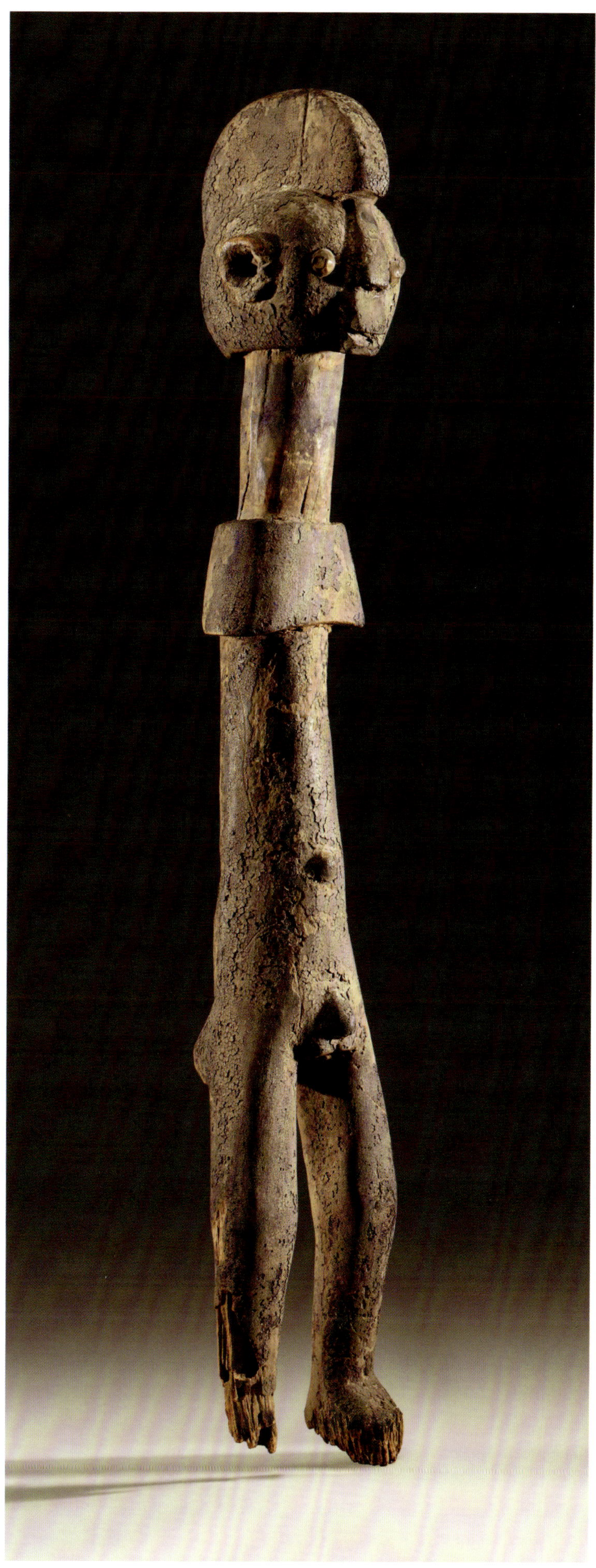

14.37
Standing male figure
Wurkun/Bikwin peoples, late nineteenth
to early twentieth century
Wood
H: 106 cm
PRIVATE COLLECTION, BRUSSELS
IMAGE: COURTESY PRIVATE COLLECTOR. PHOTO-
GRAPH © STUDIO PHILIPPE DE FORMANOIR
PROVENANCE: ULRICH VON SCHROEDER, COL-
LECTED AT THE NIGERIA-CAMEROON BORDER,
EARLY 1970S
(NOT IN EXHIBITION)

There is little doubt that this standing figure
is related to the two openwork sculptures illustrated in figures 14.35, 14.36. Its round head,
neck, and shoulder-flange construction are
evocative of Wurkun/Bikwin vertical masks.
Facial features correspond closely to those on
kundul figures.

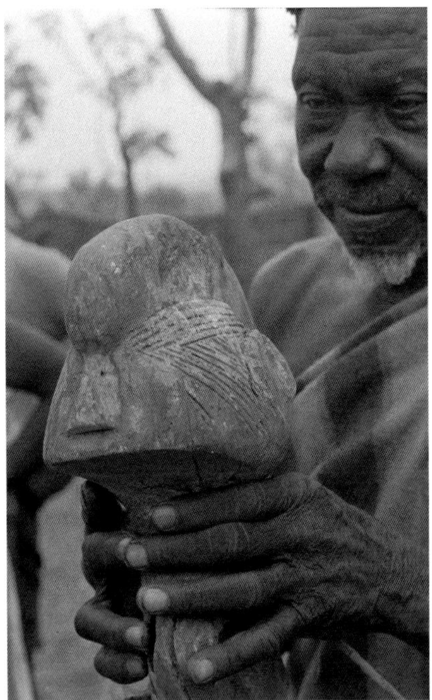

14.38
This fragment of a vertical mask was photographed in the hands of its owner, Kpeyasha, in the Yendang hamlet of Kufuru. The head closely resembles those on Wurkun/Bikwin "type-two" vertical masks, especially given its painted and incised facial decoration. Its owner, however, claimed it had come from the Jukun village of Kona, underscoring the circulation of this mask genre in this part of the Middle Benue.
PHOTOGRAPH BY ARNOLD RUBIN, KUFURU HAMLET, APRIL 20, 1970, RUBIN ARCHIVE, FOWLER MUSEUM AT UCLA, NEG. NO. 2642.

was true of Wurkun *kundul.* That said, the wear patterns on the upper torso and the way the arms are carved away from it (as was true of the Jukun figures illustrated above) suggest that these figures were also likely carried by the torso or the arms, whose formation suggests "handles." The way the necks of the figures emerge from their shoulders, carved as a distinctive flange, is also identical to the shoulder treatment on Wurkun/Bikwin vertical masks. Rope appears to have been bound around the neck of figure 14.35, and it is possible that its spindly torso and arms were covered with cloth when used. Related to these abstract pole figures is a third sculpture, a tall standing male figure without arms but with strikingly similar shoulders, neck, and head (fig. 14.37). It looks intriguingly like a man wearing a vertical mask with his torso and legs exposed. Like other Wurkun masks, the lack of encrustation on the neck suggests it was bound with rope. Although it is impossible to reconstruct how these anomalous pieces functioned given the absence of field evidence, they do support the argument being advanced here that sculptures carried in performance stood in for more conventional mask types documented elsewhere in the Middle Benue.

In contrast, Mumuye (and some Jukun) vertical masks have portholes for ease of vision, and we know from examples photographed in the field that fiber cloaks covered much of the plank supports as well as the sides of the wearer's body. Does this practice suggest that the Mumuye "improved upon" a Wurkun model by making it easier to wear? We can only speculate that the "idea" of this distinctive ambulatory sculpture circulated in this circumscribed sphere of the Middle Benue Valley. Recent scholarship among the Jukun of Kona reveals that masks central to particular ceremonies and ritual practices were "carried around the village," a choice of words that must be a direct translation of what the informants of Dinslage and Storch (2000) described to them. This characterization supports the inferences drawn here that many of these vertical masks were not worn or performed in ways typical of Middle Benue masqerades.

This region of the Middle Benue has had a long history of migrations with populations moving across the Benue in both directions. Adelberger (chapter 13) writes that the Bikwin groups moved to the Muri Mountains from south of the Benue River and that when such migrations occurred powerful ritual objects spread along with them. Groups living along the southern flank of the Muri Mountains include clans of Mumuye origin, which reveals that the Mumuye also moved northward (Adelberger, personal communication, 2010). The various dispersals of the Kona Jukun northward across the Benue, as described above, dated as early as the eighteenth century. It is possible that the Kona Jukun, who possessed considerable religious power locally, took the idea of such a mask with them (if not a mask itself that personified the powerful ancestral spirits on which their survival was believed to depend) when they migrated across the Benue River where they may have encountered Wurkun and Bikwin peoples. Notably, Rubin saw no such masks during his visit of 1965 to the northern Jukun strongholds of Gwana and Pindiga, where the Kona were said to have migrated. What he did find, however, as indicated above, was evidence that carved figures were carried in ritual performance. As detailed here, however, the heads of Gwana Jukun shrine sculptures are nearly identical to those on the group of Jukun vertical masks documented in collections as well as to the mask called Wi'yikune that Rubin photographed in a town north of the Benue. As Rubin's fieldwork led him to conclude, the northeastern Jukun of Gwana, Pindiga, Wurbon Daudu, and Mabo lack the horizontal masks of the Aku Maga complex, which predominate in Jukun communities of the southwest, centered in Wukari. Nonetheless, this does not necessarily mean that these groups lacked "masks," rather that the conception and configuration of their masks may have been different. Jukun vertical masks resemble northeastern Jukun figures more than they do other more typical Jukun masking traditions, and it may be that the vertical mask genre had been more widespread among Jukun communities than Rubin discovered during his fieldwork. The intriguing treatment of the "heads" on figurative sculpture from Wurbon Daudu and Mabo further support the notion that they, too, represented "masked" spirit incarnations (see interleaf E).

The impact of the Fulani on this part of the Middle Benue should not be discounted, and the movements of groups seeking to escape their slave raiding and jihad certainly had a significant impact on the region's cultural history. It is just as likely, however, that the origins of this vertical mask may rest north of the Benue River with the masks, their makers, or even just the conception moving southward to the area occupied by Kona Jukun and neighboring Mumuye communities. Indeed, one head fragment documented by Rubin in the Yendang hamlet of Kufuru looks remarkably like the heads on Wurkun type two masks (fig. 14.38) despite the fact that informants claimed it was brought by a man from Kona "very long ago" (Rubin fieldnotes, April 20, 1970). By locating origins in Kona the objects gain in ritual importance, and the qualification, "long ago," suggests its owners in 1970 could not locate its source in local practice. The head's transverse crest with painted dots as well as its circular ears and linear patterns at the sides of the face are unmistakably "Wurkun" based on the features described here.

In my view, the impressive vertical masks associated with the Wurkun/Bikwin peoples of the Muri Mountains are the most original and idiosyncratic. They are also the most enigmatic, guarded with secrecy and kept hidden in caves, out of the view of colonial officers and, later, ethnographic researchers. If they were so protected and seemingly unknown (except perhaps to resident missionaries), how were so many taken and exported from Nigeria beginning in the late 1960s? What would have occurred to shake loose from their hiding places so many of these huge sacred objects? They were certainly not easily transported across the countryside and must have astonished the first dealers who received them. The argument that the chaos of the Biafran War gave Hausa traders and perhaps other "runners" the "cover" to buy and sell objects with impunity seems insufficient to explain what might have occurred in remote hilltop villages north of the Benue River to precipitate such an exodus. The erroneous attribution of these masks as "Waja" further suggests that when Europeans first encountered them, they had already traveled to more accessible towns away from the remote Wurkun or Bikwin villages in the Muri Mountains. This gave them a mistaken identity, associated with the larger administrative district of which they were a part, Tangale-Waja. There is little doubt that the collection dates for many Middle Benue objects argue in favor of a short but intensive period of collecting starting in the late 1960s, so that by the late 1980s, when Adelberger did his fieldwork, there were few vertical masks still in situ among the Wurkun or Bikwin peoples.[27] The same holds true for Mumuye and Jukun examples, which likewise entered collections after Rubin's field documentation in 1965 and 1970. The pressures of conversion to Christianity or Islam and the abandonment of local religious practices since the early twentieth century (if not before), which intensified in the immediate postcolonial period, surely played a role in the outflow of such objects from this area of northeastern Nigeria. We may never know the full story of these amazing objects, but perhaps it is enough to say that their similarities as a genre point to a dense network of interaction and communication among the neighboring peoples who made and used them, along with a history deep enough to have resulted in considerable local innovation and differentiation. ●

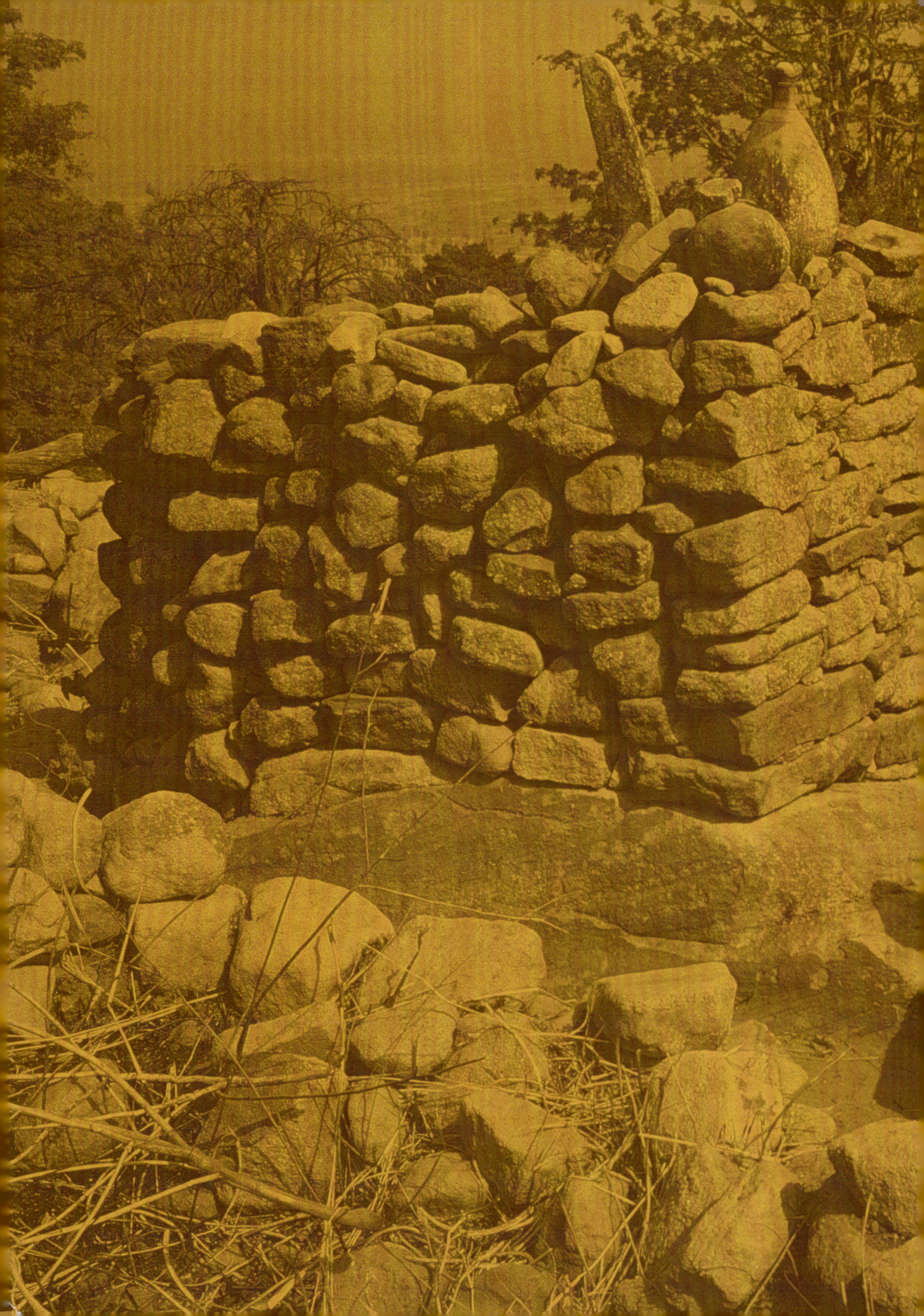

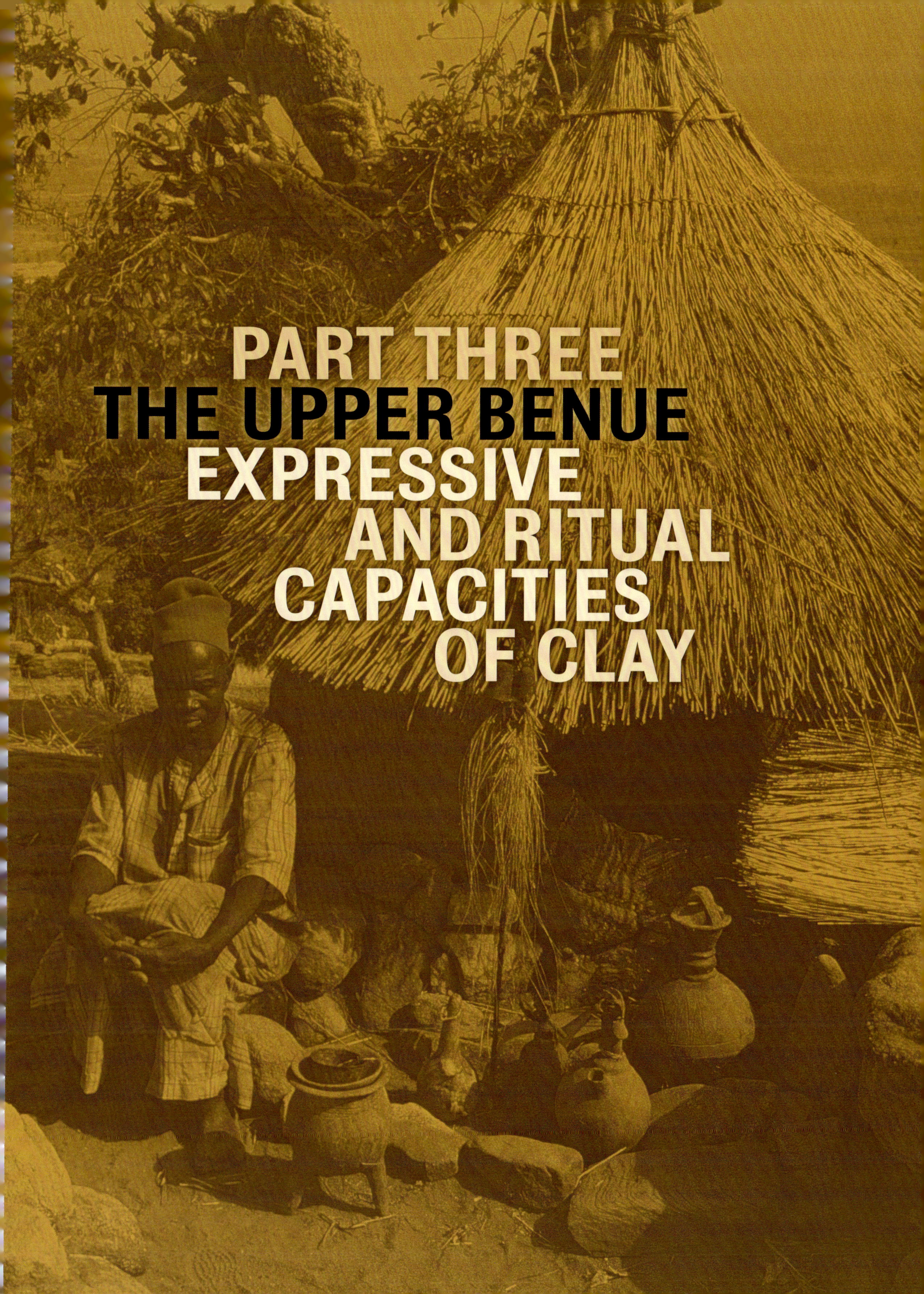

PART THREE
THE UPPER BENUE
EXPRESSIVE
AND RITUAL
CAPACITIES
OF CLAY

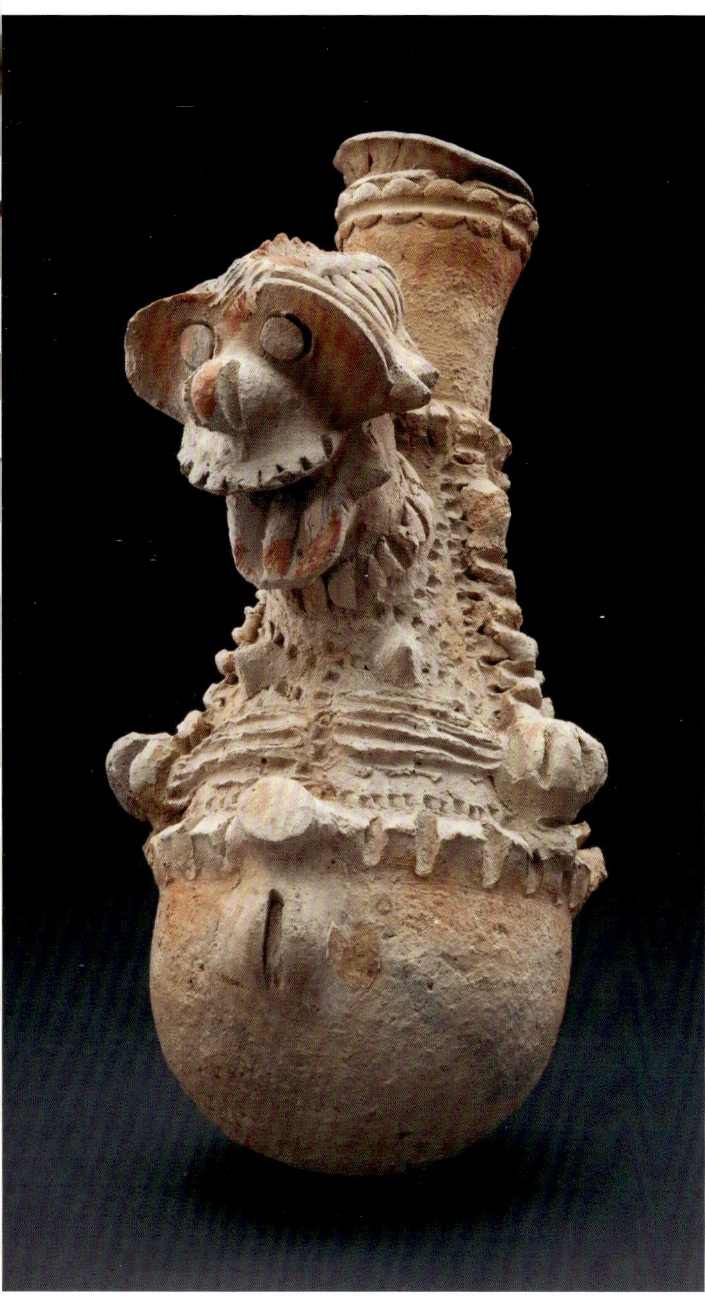

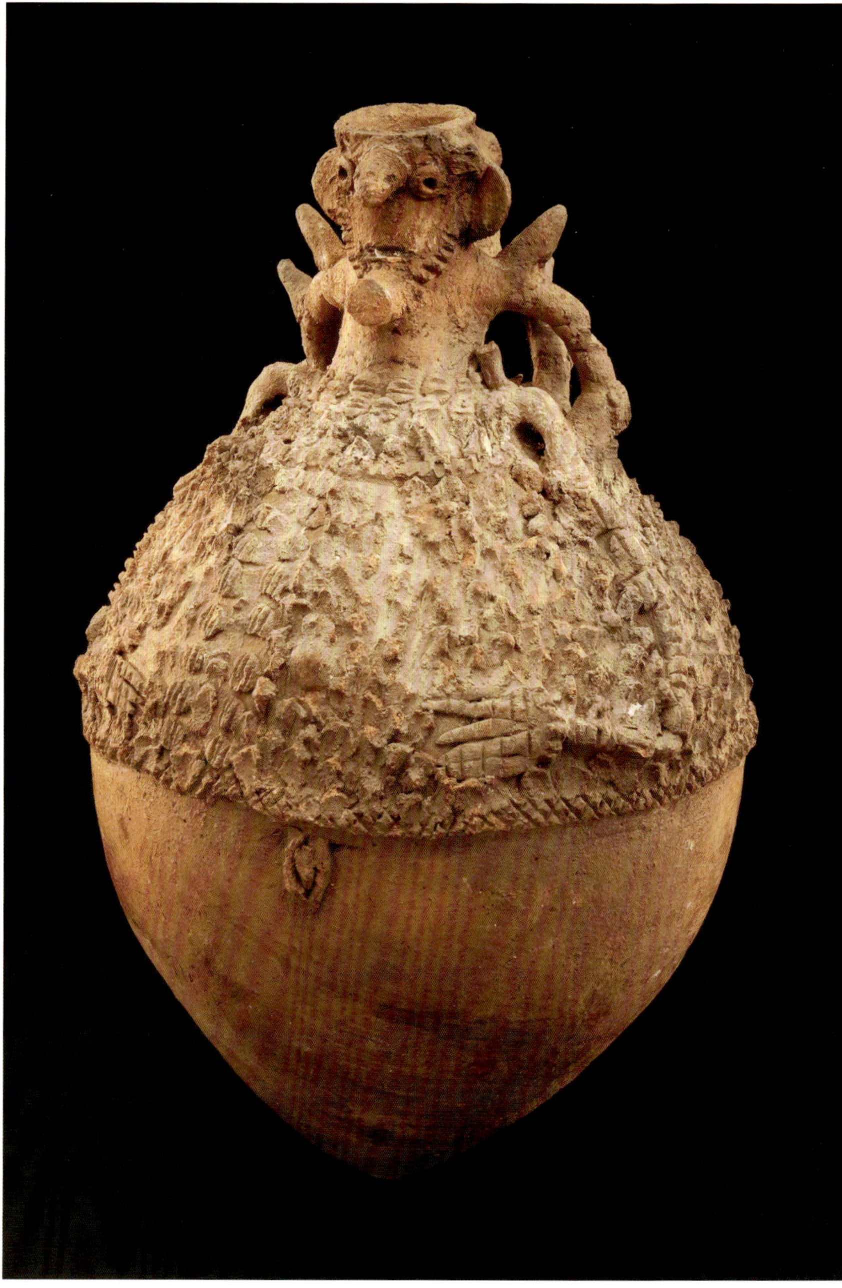

15.5 (ABOVE)
Ngaji (active 1960s–1970s)
Vessel for curing children's diseases
(*jina kwimtiyu*)
Cham-Mwana peoples, Western Gongola
Valley, before 1970
Ceramic, pigment
H: 25.2 cm
FOWLER MUSEUM AT UCLA X86.4690; GIFT OF
ARNOLD RUBIN
IMAGE: © 2010 FOWLER MUSEUM AT UCLA.
PHOTOGRAPH BY DON COLE
PROVENANCE: COLLECTED BY ARNOLD RUBIN, 1970

languages of the Chadic (Afroasiatic) family, which extends eastward into northern Cameroon and beyond to Lake Chad. In the Gongola Valley, speakers of both Western Chadic and Biu-Mandara languages—two of the main branches of Chadic—are represented. The geographical distribution of Chadic speakers suggests that they have migrated to the west and south away from areas of high linguistic consistency (i.e., the Mandara Mountains and the northeastern Nigeria savanna) into the Upper Benue Valley. Speakers of Adamawa (Niger-Congo) languages are concentrated south of the Benue on the Adamawa Plateau. They are a part of a larger linguistic division called Adamawa-Ubangi (Hansford et al. 1976, 181; Crozier and Blench 1992, 123), which stretches eastward from the Benue Valley into Central Africa.

J. A. Ballard proposed a model for tracing the movement of peoples in such linguistically complex areas. Applied to the Lower Gongola, it supports the theory that Chadic groups migrated westward and divided what was likely to have been a continuous distribution of Adamawa speakers. That the Adamawa groups have a higher degree of internal differentiation than the Chadic intervenors, supports the inference that "the divided groups were prior inhabitants of the general area" (1971, 295–96).

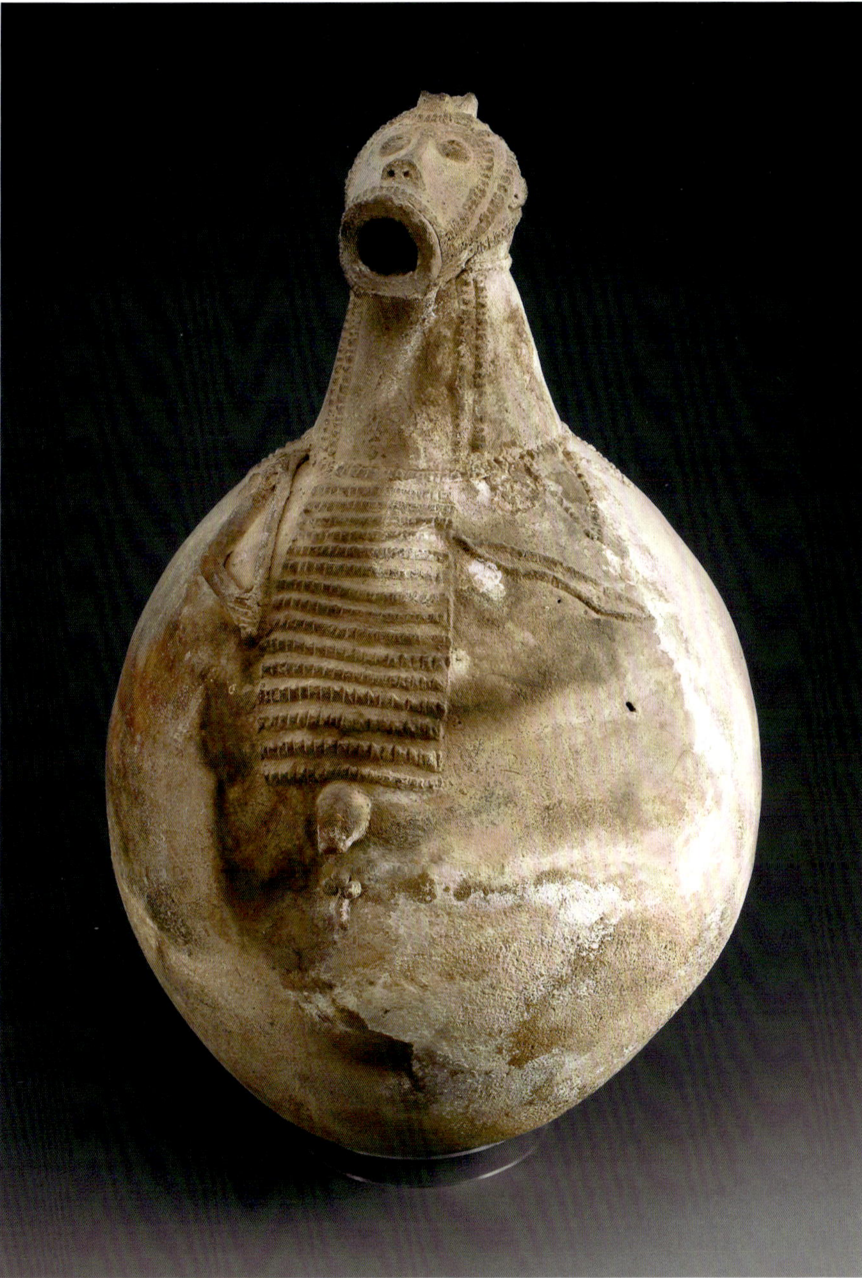

15.6 (OPPOSITE)
Spirit vessel (*changdu*)
Cham-Mwana peoples, Western Gongola
Valley, mid- to late twentieth century
Ceramic
H: 45 cm
FOWLER MUSEUM AT UCLA X2006.18.6; MUSEUM
PURCHASE
IMAGE: © 2010 FOWLER MUSEUM AT UCLA.
PHOTOGRAPH BY DON COLE
PROVENANCE: HAMIDOU MONTOUODORE KPOUMIE,
CAMEROON; AMYAS NAEGELE, NEW YORK
2004–2005

Changdu vessels were used by the Cham-
Mwana for several purposes, including
ensuring a successful rainy season and harvest,
divining illnesses, and protecting hunters from
the avenging ghosts of large game killed in
the hunt. This large anthropomorphized vessel
contrasts with the smaller Cham-Mwana vessels used in healing the sick (see fig. 15.5).

15.7
Spirit vessel (Mbir'thleng'nda)
Ga'anda peoples, Eastern Gongola Valley,
mid-twentieth century
Ceramic
H: 59 cm
KEITH ACHEPOHL COLLECTION
IMAGE: © ART INSTITUTE OF CHICAGO.
PHOTOGRAPH BY ROBERT LIFSON
PROVENANCE: MARTIAL BRONSIN, BRUSSELS;
COLETTE GHYSELS, BRUSSELS, 1999; DOUGLAS
DAWSON, CHICAGO, 2000

This protective deity, carrying an ax over
its right shoulder and a bow on its left, was
kept in a shrine enclosure, which probably
belonged to a Dingai community at the
frontier between the Ga'anda and the 'Bəna
peoples (see fig. 15.9).

Aside from the presence of Chadic-language speakers to the south (Bachama),
east (Dera), and west (Tangale), most of the groups living in the western flank of the
Lower Gongola Valley speak related Northwestern Adamawa languages. They are
classified within a Longuda group, a Waja group (Waja, Tula, Dadiya, Cham-Mwana),
a Jen group, and a Kwa group (Kleinewillinghöfer 1996; Crozier and Blench 1992,
123; Hansford et al. 1976, 181–82). The settlement of the Western-Chadic-speaking
Dera along the fertile floodplains of the Gongola and Hawal Rivers—stretching from
just north of the Gongola's confluence with the Benue and following the course of its
main tributary, the Hawal—is likely to have separated a continuous distribution of
Adamawa speakers across the Upper Benue-Gongola River Valley.

The Ga'anda, 'Bəna, and Yungur live in dispersed communities within the rigorous
terrain of the Eastern Gongola Valley. The Mboi, who speak a language closely related
to Yungur and live just northeast of them, will be discussed in the context of their post-
funerary arts in interleaf I. The Mbula (Jarawan Bantu speakers) and the related Bata
and Bachama (Biu-Mandara Chadic speakers) live south of the Ga'anda Hills and within
the immediate vicinity of the Gongola-Benue confluence.[2] Although they are important

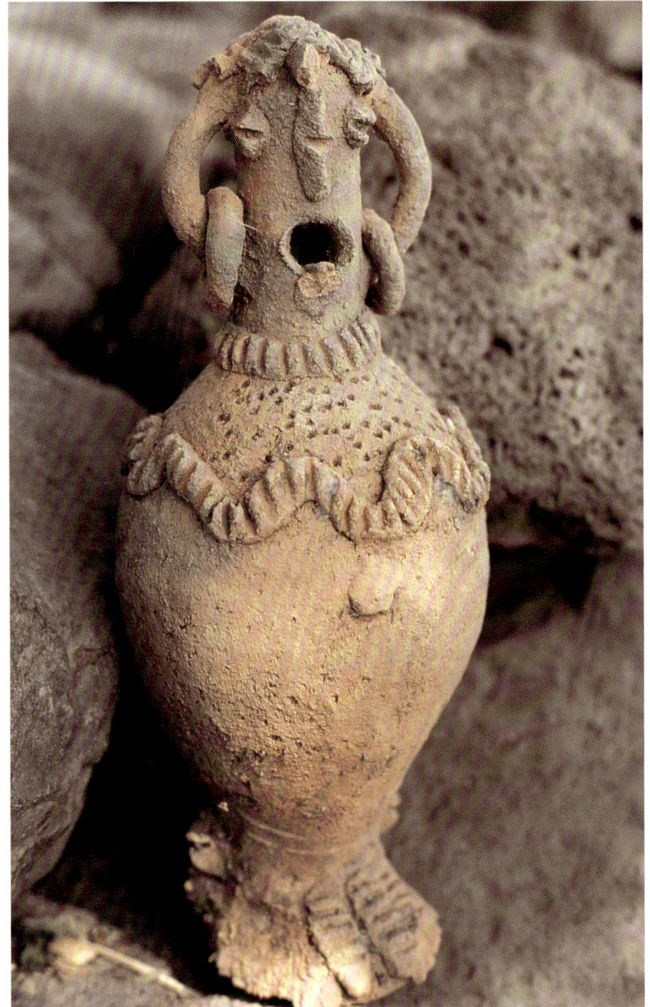

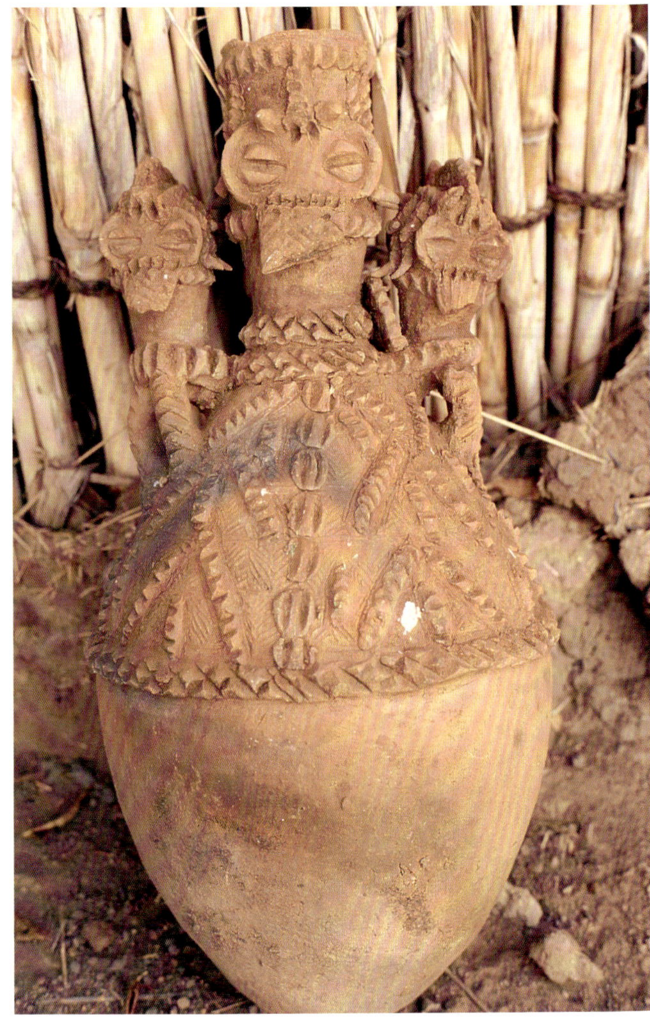

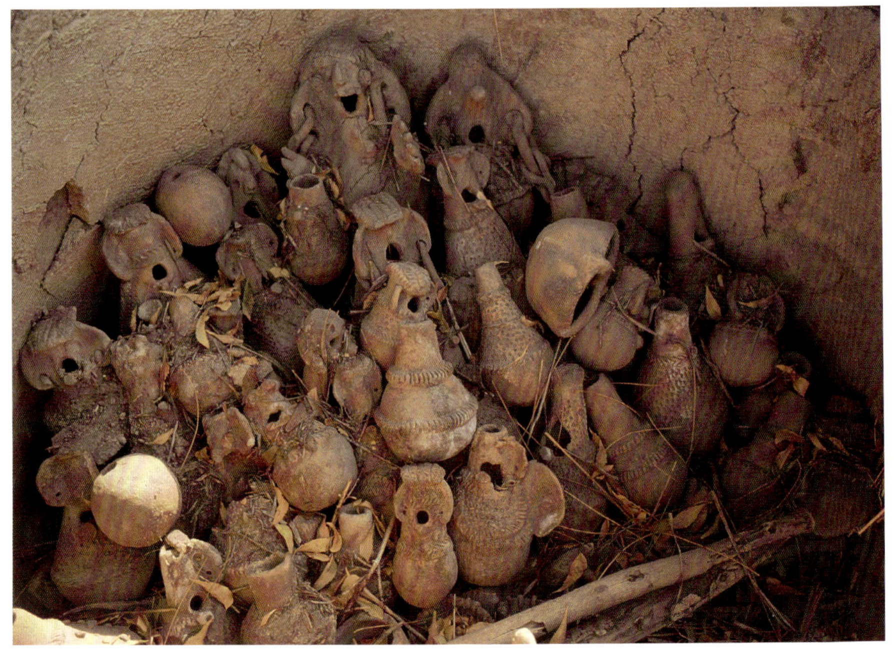

16.5 (ABOVE LEFT)
Longuda *kwandalha* are used for divining and curing illness. This example was 32 centimeters in height.
PHOTOGRAPH BY MARLA C. BERNS, JIU VILLAGE, 1981.

16.6 (ABOVE RIGHT)
This Longuda *sambrawa* (H: 56 cm), a vessel for divining and curing illness, takes the form of a "mother" flanked by her twin "sons." All three are Janus faced, allowing them to seek the sources of disease in all directions.
PHOTOGRAPH BY MARLA C. BERNS, DUKUL VILLAGE, 1981.

16.7 (RIGHT)
The Longuda healing shrine that belonged to the female diviner-artist, Dasumi, who died in 1979, contained this collection of *kwandalha*, which she used for determining causes of illness and then prescribing cures for her patients.
PHOTOGRAPH BY MARLA C. BERNS, GUYUK, 1981.

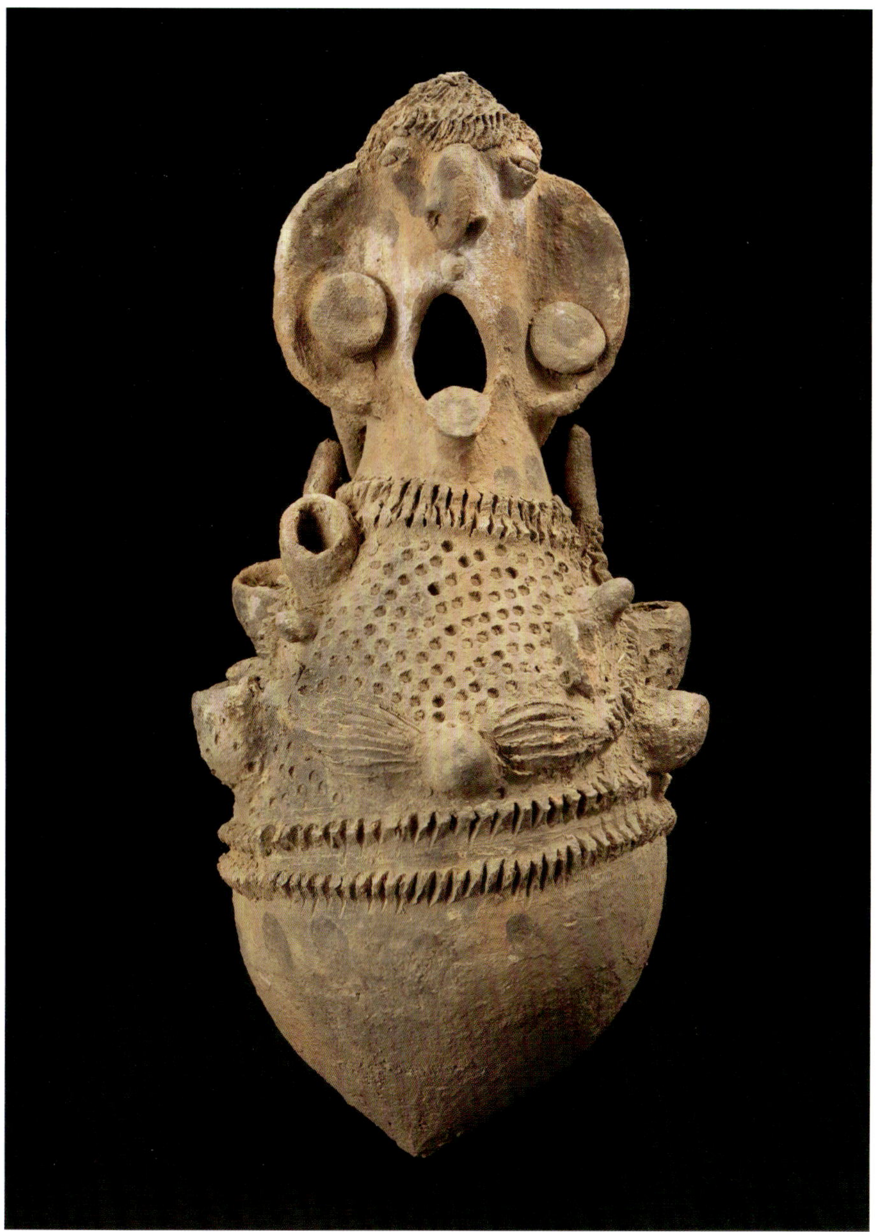

16.8
Healing vessel (*kwandalwa*)
Longuda peoples, late twentieth century
Ceramic
H: 42.5 cm
FOWLER MUSEUM AT UCLA X2008.32.4; MUSEUM
PURCHASE
IMAGE: © 2010 FOWLER MUSEUM AT UCLA.
PHOTOGRAPH BY DON COLE
PROVENANCE: PACE PRIMITIVE, NEW YORK; LEE
LORENZ COLLECTION, NEW YORK; AMYAS NAEGELE
COLLECTION, NEW YORK, 2004

Kwandalha (healing vessels) are still being
made and used by the Longuda, and examples
such as this one have been exported from
Nigeria for sale to dealers and galleries.

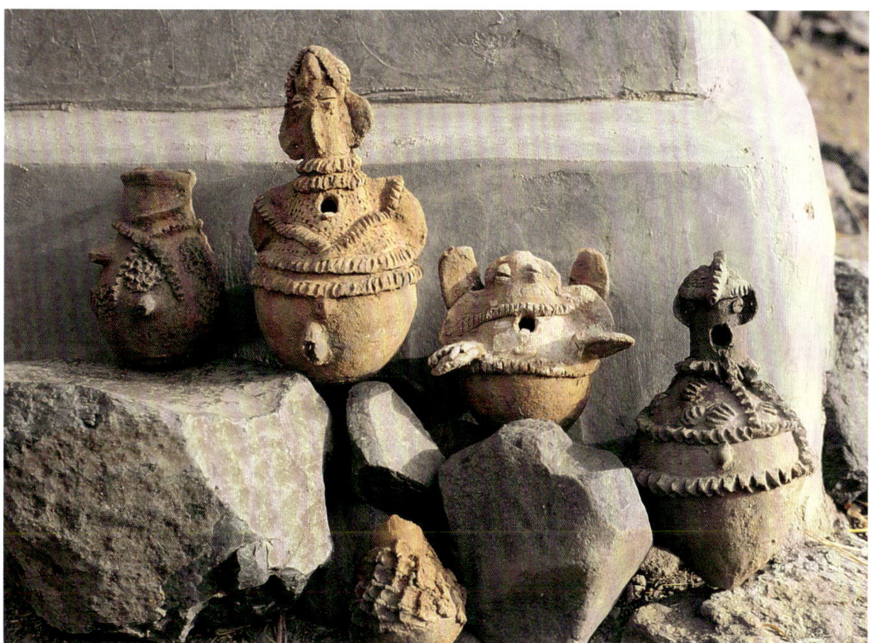

16.9
Longuda *kwandalha* are made for curing
a range of illnesses. Back row (from left to
right), followed by vessel in the foreground:
(1) *kwandal'zwungwa*, for curing madness;
(2) *kwandal'sisuwa*, for curing backaches;
(3) *furi'yalalala*, for curing leprosy;
(4) *kwandal'yinaswaha*, for curing malaria;
(5) *gurguwa*, for curing whooping cough.
PHOTOGRAPH BY MARLA C. BERNS, NYUWAR
VILLAGE, 1982.

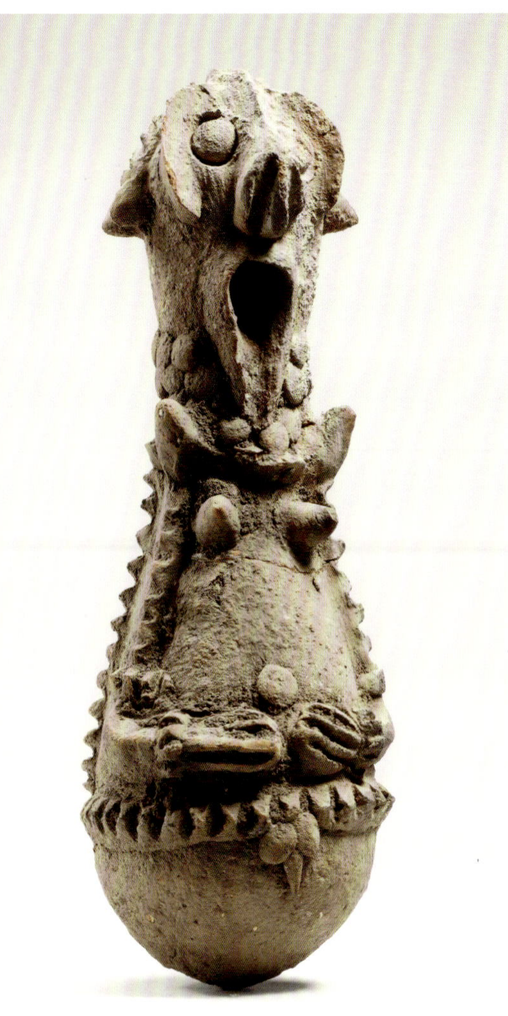

16.10
Healing vessel
Cham-Mwana peoples,
mid- to late twentieth century
Ceramic
H: 24.2 cm
MUSÉE DU QUAI BRANLY, PARIS, 73.1998.12.21
IMAGE: © 2010 MUSÉE DU QUAI BRANLY. PHOTO-
GRAPH BY THIERRY OLLIVIER/MICHEL URTADO/
SCALA, FLORENCE
PROVENANCE: CLAUDE MEUNIER, CAMEROON, LATE
1980S; MUSÉE NATIONAL DES ARTS D'AFRIQUE ET
D'OCÉANIE, 1988

external symptoms of these ailments. Decoration is generally confined to the upper half of the pot's "torso," leaving the base smooth and easier to handle or place upright in the ground. Raised and impressed ridges encircle the vessels, and surfaces are often further ornamented with lumps, spikes, or impressed holes (see fig. 16.8).

Meek (1931b, 2: 352) recorded the following procedure for making and activating these disease-curing vessels:

> [T]he woman takes some soft clay and touches the patient's head and abdomen. It is believed that the disease-producing spirit enters the clay, and the old woman proceeds to fashion the clay into the conventional form of the Towa spirit. The spirits are always given a human form…. When the woman has completed the shaping of the pot she circles it round the patient's head, and then hands it over to him. The owner takes it home, fires it, and deposits it in a shrine close to his house.

A process similar to this one was described to me by informants living in the Longuda village of Nyuwar. A small piece of clay was put on the end of a stalk and circled around the patient to draw the illness into the clay. If the person recovered, a vessel would then be built incorporating the clay on the stalk. The vessel was then fired and kept in a shrine in the event that the symptoms recurred and the vessel was needed again. In the case of a relapse, the pot was washed and air was blown into it through its open mouth to make way for another cure. Figure 16.9 shows five *kwandalha* that I photographed at Nyuwar, each associated with a particular disease. A pot used to cure leprosy (number 3 in fig. 16.9), however, was not kept with them; it was buried in the ground away from the village after it had proven effective in transacting a cure. This demonstrates that the act of transferring the disease from the person to the pot can render the vessel dangerous, and with particularly debilitating afflictions, more stringent measures were required to protect the living from the spirits capable of inflicting pain, suffering, and disfigurement (see fig. 16.4).

The Cham and Mwana, who live west of the Longuda Plateau, also make pots for curing disease. The modern town of Cham lies in a valley that divides the two parallel ridges of rolling, rocky hills where the hamlets of the Cham (on the northern ridge around Fitilai) and of the Mwana (to the south) were once exclusively situated. The Cham-Mwana, however, were dispersed southward, due in part to pressure from the neighboring Waja in the late nineteenth century. Although some people still live there, the hills around Fitilai are dotted with abandoned settlements that reveal the former importance of defensive positions and the preference for structures built of drystone masonry.[7] The people who identify themselves as Cham or Mwana appear to do so largely because of different kinship ties, but from the perspective of language, the two groups are synonymous and have been classified within the "Waja" group of Northwestern Adamawa languages (Kleinewillinghöfer 1996, 87–88). Their arts and culture are also the same, and for ease of discussion they will be treated here as the Cham-Mwana.[8]

Although very little ethnographic data has been published on the Cham-Mwana, their ceramic healing vessels are relatively well documented (fig. 16.10; see also fig. 15.5). They are broadly similar in form and function to Longuda *kwandalha*, and diviners use them to diagnose diseases and prescribe cures in a similar fashion. Whereas both Longuda women and men could model healing pots, only men did so among the Cham-Mwana. In the past, male healer-sculptors specialized in one illness and served a broad community; this skill was passed along patrilineally. By the 1980s, however, healers had begun to produce multiple types of pots, a change that probably had to do with the relocation of hillside hamlets to centralized villages in the valley. It is remarkable that this traditional method of curing had not been superseded by modern medicine by the early 1990s when it was observed by Joerg Adelberger (personal communication, 2010).[9]

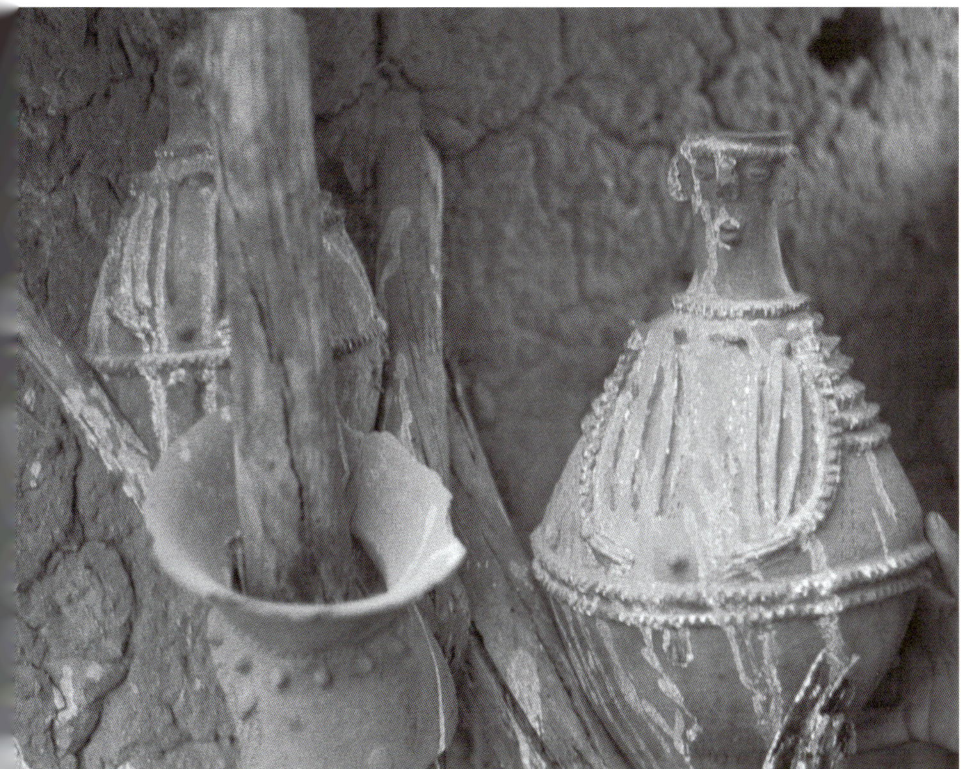

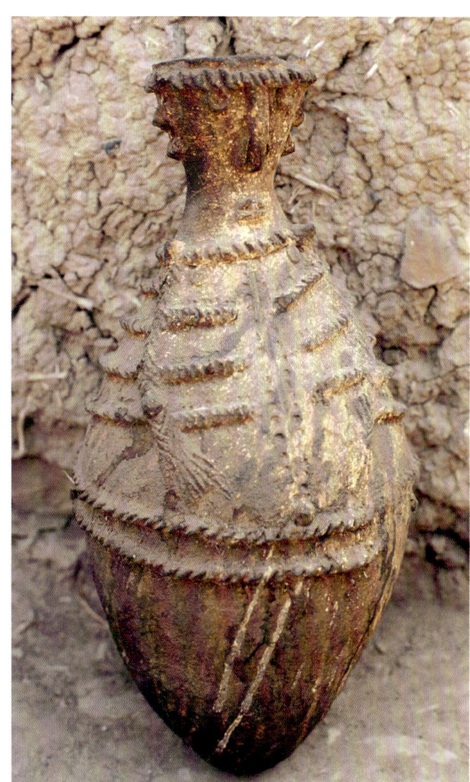

Two British colonial officers, Jack Leggett (aka Jonathan Slye) and John Hare, worked in the Tangale-Waja District in the 1950s and 1960s and documented healing practices associated with the Cham-Mwana.[10] Their accounts describe a diviner who lived in a compound separate from the rest of the village and determined the cause of a patient's illness by consulting a male or female terra-cotta vessel (depending on the sex of the patient), which was conceived of as an oracular device.[11] According to Hare,

> When the diviner receives his answer from the pot, he advises the person who has consulted him to go to a particular draftsman who has the skills to make the pot which will suit his or her need. The petitioner then does this and on payment of an agreed fee the pot is built. This payment was formerly made in either chickens or tobacco but in recent years this payment has been made in cash. The newly-built pot is then taken to the diviner who invests it with "magical" power. This is usually done by an incantation accompanied by the spilling of a cock's blood, but in certain rare cases water from a certain pool is used. [Hare 1983, 8–9]

Hare identifies the divination vessels as *changdu*, which are distinguished within the corpus of small Cham-Mwana healing pots by their larger size, shape, and sculptural details.[12] He notes that these pots could also be used as "household protectors" (1983, 17). The female oracular vessel (fig. 16.1) published in Hare's collection (1983; now in the Indiana University Art Museum) was earlier photographed in Cham Town by Arnold Rubin in 1970, where it was installed alongside its male counterpart (fig.16.11). These ovoid pots (H: approximately 40–45 cm) have slightly carinated bodies with two long flanking arms and projecting facial features modeled near the "mouth" of the vessel. Breasts, navel, and genitalia are modeled in relief along with raised and impressed ridges demarcating the waist and ornamenting the torso and the back. Whereas this decoration resembles that observed on Longuda *kwandalha*, there is a restraint and control in its application that differs from the more vigorous approach of most Longuda wares.

16.11 (ABOVE LEFT)
This photograph of a *changdu* shrine in Cham Town shows the vessel photographed in figure 16.1 and its male counterpart. The residue of white paste from brewing sorghum beer is visible splashed on the surfaces of the vessels, a part of their activation during healing rituals.
PHOTOGRAPH BY ARNOLD RUBIN, CHAM TOWN, MARCH 1970, RUBIN ARCHIVE, FOWLER MUSEUM AT UCLA, NEG. NO. 2304.

16.12
This Cham-Mwana oracular vessel (*changdu*) is used in rituals to protect hunters and also to chase away ghosts seen in dreams.
PHOTOGRAPHED BY MARLA C. BERNS, CHAM TOWN, 1982.

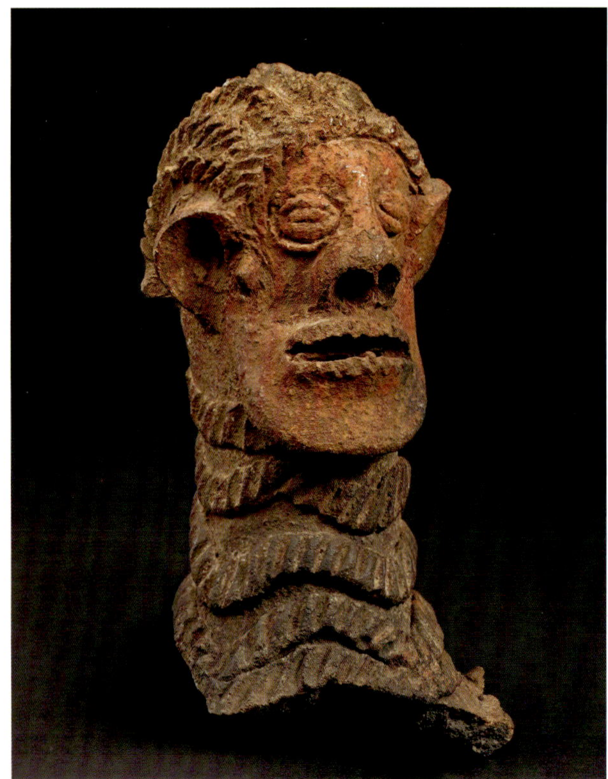

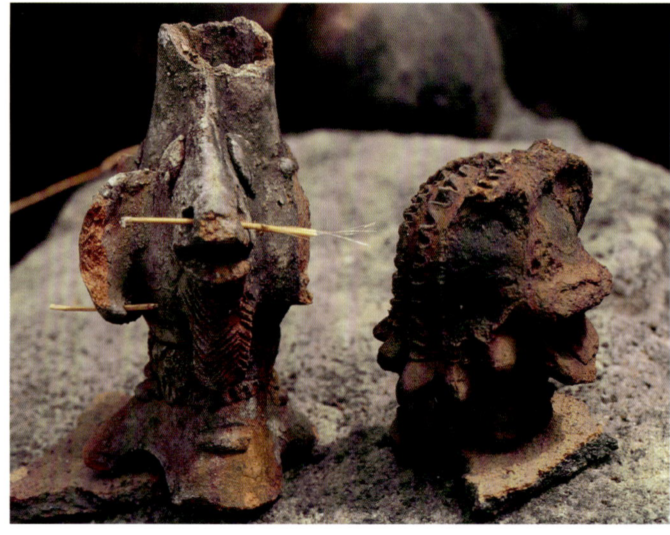

16.13
Head fragment
Cham-Mwana or Longuda peoples (?),
before 1913
Ceramic
H: 16 cm
THE TRUSTEES OF THE BRITISH MUSEUM, AF1913,
1013.47
IMAGE: © TRUSTEES OF THE BRITISH MUSEUM,
PHOTOGRAPH BY MICHAEL ROW, 2010
PROVENANCE: COLLECTED BY C. L. TEMPLE AND
O. TEMPLE BEFORE 1913

Given the style of figurative vessels documented in the field, it seems possible that this
head fragment once belonged to a *changdu* or
a Longuda *kwandalwa*. When acquired this
piece was attributed to the Waja.

16.14
These two *changdu* head fragments were photographed at the abandoned hillside site of
Fi where the Mwana had once lived. A group
of large vessels was kept high in the rocky
landscape along with several small healing
pots and these two heads. Said to have been
used to protect hunters, the head on the left
is male and the one on the right, female. Note
the elaborate plaited coiffure of the female,
which resembles that of figures 16.13 and 15.8.
PHOTOGRAPH BY MARLA C. BERNS, FI, 1982.

According to my informants, *changdu* were "spirit pots," connected with bringing
rain, fostering good crops, punishing thieves, and protecting hunters (see fig. 15.6).
I photographed an example in Cham Town in 1982 very similar to the one at Indiana
(fig. 16.12). The *changdu* would be filled with water the night before men set off for a
hunt. In the morning they would drink the water and wash their eyes with it. This was
intended to ensure success in the hunt and to protect the hunters from the avenging
ghosts of previously killed game; such "ghosts" were seen in dreams, and by washing
the eyes, such images would be cleansed away.[13]

There is a striking stylistic disparity between the relatively few extant *changdu* and
the rest of the Cham-Mwana corpus. Out of 153 pots that Slye was shown from across
the Cham-Mwana territory, only two were identified to him as being oracular (1969, 501).
Even if he did not provide the name for it, the one of these that he illustrated is of the
changdu type shown here. The form and function of *changdu* align them with vessels used
for similar purposes by the neighbors of the Cham-Mwana, the Dadiya, Tula, and Jen.
There are also intriguing stylistic similarities to figurative vessels documented among
the western 'Bǝna, who live just across the Gongola River around the town of Gureshi.

Two heads broken from their vessel "torsos" in the British Museum—donated by
Mr. and Mrs. C. L. Temple in 1913 (fig. 16.13; and see also fig. 15.8)—are said to be from
the Upper Benue region (Fagg 1962, fig. 132). William Fagg, who was keeper of the
museum's collections from 1955 to 1974, identified these sculptures as "Waja." They are,
however, more likely to be early versions of Cham-Mwana *changdu* or Longuda *kwandalha*, based on their raised surface decoration and physiognomic details, particularly the
way their eyes, noses, and plaited coiffures have been rendered.[14] Ceramic heads that I
photographed at an abandoned Cham-Mwana hillside shrine (fig. 16.14) reveal the similarity. Without their bodies and their distinctive surface treatment, however, it is difficult to determine their provenance precisely. Nevertheless, as will be shown below, their
resemblance to ceramic vessels extant among the Waja is less likely, and it may be that
Fagg confused the people called "Waja" with the Tangale-Waja District in which these
western Gongola groups lived during the colonial period, even though he also wrote that
"Similar charms are made by the Longuda and others nearby" (1963, fig. 132).

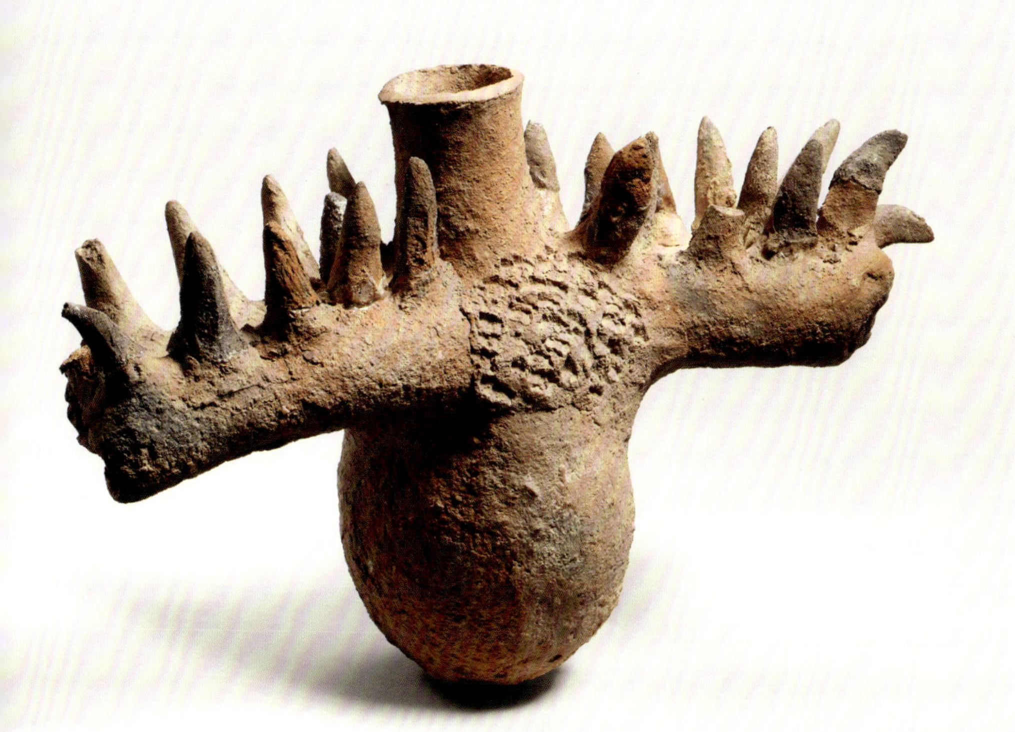

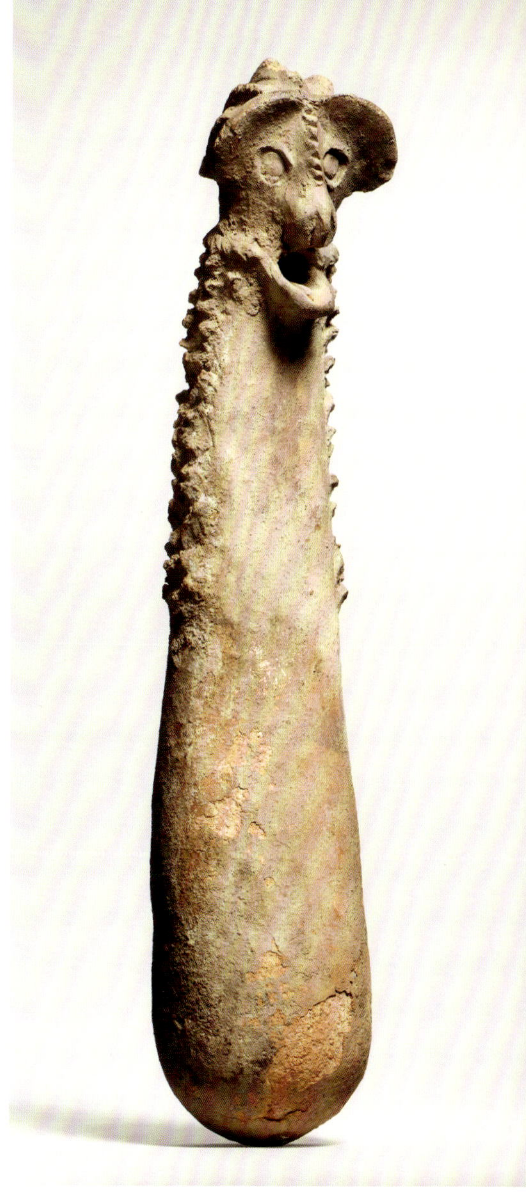

16.15
Vessel to cure backache (*kulok-kulok*)
Cham-Mwana peoples,
mid- to late twentieth century
Ceramic
W: 28.5 cm
MUSÉE DU QUAI BRANLY, PARIS, 73.1998.12.4
IMAGE: © 2010 MUSÉE DU QUAI BRANLY. PHOTO-
GRAPH BY THIERRY OLLIVIER/MICHEL URTADO/
SCALA, FLORENCE
PROVENANCE: CLAUDE MEUNIER, CAMEROON, LATE
1980S; MUSÉE NATIONAL DES ARTS D'AFRIQUE ET
D'OCÉANIE, 1988

16.16
Vessel to cure vomiting (*gando*)
Cham-Mwana peoples,
mid- to late twentieth century
Ceramic
H: 35.8 cm
MUSÉE DU QUAI BRANLY, PARIS, 73.1998.12.3
IMAGE: © 2010 MUSÉE DU QUAI BRANLY. PHOTO-
GRAPH BY THIERRY OLLIVIER/MICHEL URTADO/
SCALA, FLORENCE
PROVENANCE: CLAUDE MEUNIER, CAMEROON, LATE
1980S; MUSÉE NATIONAL DES ARTS D'AFRIQUE ET
D'OCÉANIE, 1988

Cham Mwana healing vessels are remarkable for their extreme variety, as their formal details are mimetic of the disease symptoms they are intended to cure. Most are relatively small (H: 20–35 cm) and rendered in anthropomorphic form with highly expressive faces (usually with open mouths and circular punched eyes) and vigorous surface treatment (with raised and impressed ridges and projecting lumps or spikes; see fig. 16.10). The large corpus of published examples and the number photographed in the field make it possible to correlate particular vessels with specific diseases and to identify the most common types. Unfortunately, however, certain discrepancies in field data make it impossible to propose a definitive classification of all pot types with corresponding names and illnesses.

To begin with, Hare (1983) calls these pots generically "*itinate*," a term that is not found elsewhere in the literature and was not given to Rubin or to me by informants. Hare identifies sixteen different types of Cham-Mwana healing vessels. I, coincidentally, recorded sixteen pot types as well, but only five of these two sets of sixteen share the same name and associated illness. Moreover, only three of these five share the same name and stylistic features: (1) *gando*, an elongated narrow vessel with a wide-open mouth for curing vomiting (fig. 16.16); (2) *sujang*, a stirrup-spout variety for curing bronchial disorders (fig. 16.17); and (3) *kulok-kulok* (or *tsen-tsenle*) a vessel with two or more horizontally projecting tubes covered in spikes for curing backaches (fig. 16.15).[15] Even one of the most idiosyncratic types, built with a blind-spout in the form of an open-mouthed head emerging at a diagonal from the side of the pot (rather than the front or "neck" of the vessel), is named differently: *ni bare* by Hare (1983, figs. 19–20) and *jina bitibiyu* by Rubin (fig. 16.18). Slye (1977, fig. 3) also illustrates one of this type, and all of them seem to have been used by women to cure illnesses or discomfort associated with pregnancy or to protect the fetus.

The great majority of Cham-Mwana healing vessels were indeed made to protect pregnant women, mothers, and children. One of the most common, used for shielding infants from disease, is called *jibar bweyiliyu* (Hare's *jiniang tarwe* and Rubin's *jina bitibiyu*) and is modeled as a woman with a baby on her back. There is a fair amount of leeway in the execution of details on these pots, and three examples photographed in

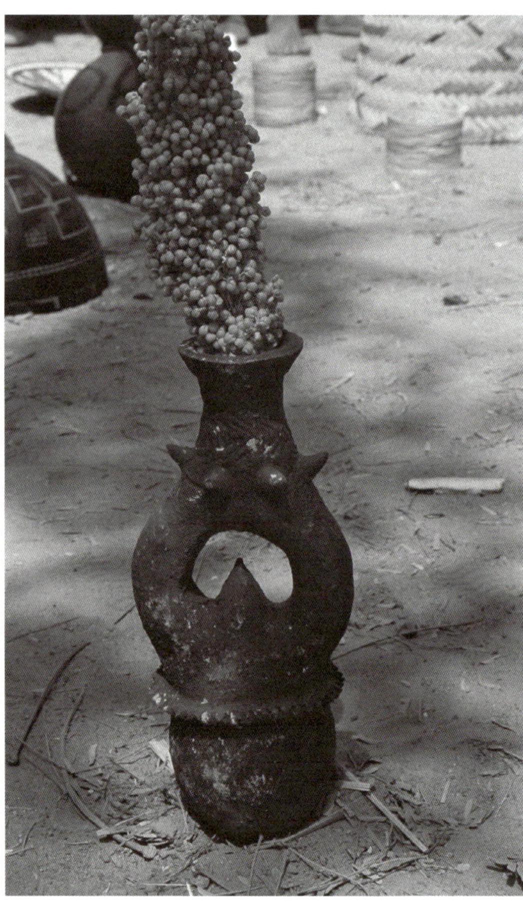

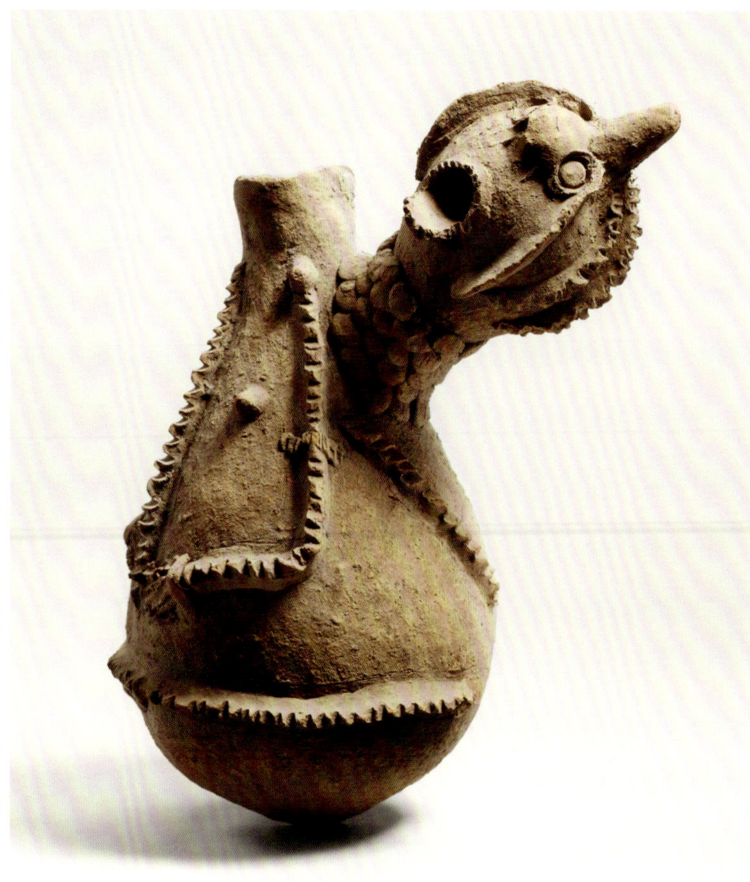

16.17
The Cham-Mwana *sujang* vessel is used for curing chronic bronchial disorders. According to Rubin's fieldnotes (see the entry for March 3, 1970), this example was made by the chief of Mwana Town, Ndere.
PHOTOGRAPH BY ARNOLD RUBIN, MWANA TOWN, MARCH 1970, RUBIN ARCHIVE, FOWLER MUSEUM AT UCLA, NEG. NO. 2270.

16.18
Vessel to protect a pregnant woman and her fetus (*jina bitibiyu*)
Cham-Mwana peoples, twentieth century
Ceramic
H: 26 cm
MUSÉE DU QUAI BRANLY, PARIS, 73.1998.12.6
IMAGE: © 2010 MUSÉE DU QUAI BRANLY. PHOTO-GRAPH BY THIERRY OLLIVIER/MICHEL URTADO/SCALA, FLORENCE
PROVENANCE: CLAUDE MEUNIER, CAMEROON, LATE 1980S; MUSÉE NATIONAL DES ARTS D'AFRIQUE ET D'OCÉANIE, 1988

the field by Rubin in the 1970s—all made by the artist-diviner Ngaji to cure children's diseases and called *jina kwimtiyu*—were each distinctive (see fig. 15.5). Such vessels could be passed from generation to generation, and some mothers kept several in their rooms to protect more than one child at a time (Hare 1983, 20).

Whereas most Cham-Mwana vessels are anthropomorphized and modeled to imitate particular disease symptoms, others depict animals, fowl, or fish. Slye (1969, 503) documented a vessel whose decorative elements included a reference to the beak of a predatory bird. He learned that the vessel had been made to protect the owner's chickens, which had been ravaged by hawks. Thus, ceramic devices were also deployed to protect and "keep well" the resources on which communities depended for survival.

While some of these ceramics were kept and "reactivated" with animal blood or beer, in most circumstances, once a vessel had helped effect a cure for a particular disease, it was discarded or even hidden in the rocky hillside. Slye (1969, 496–97) describes the number of ritual ceramics he found "undisturbed" in hillside locations where Cham-Mwana communities were once situated. They were hidden in rock shelters, caves, or the hollows of large trees, and sometimes they were buried in the ground. The belief that the disease or the disease-causing spirit is ritually transferred from the person to the pot, as described above for the Longuda, renders it potentially harmful; informants have even claimed that the pots were carried on large sherds to avoid physical contact. Moreover, building and firing a new vessel is clearly a vital part of the healing process, and each afflicted person would need his or her own ceramic therapy.

As I have written elsewhere, the disease-causing spirit enters the clay in its raw "uncooked" state, and health is conferred after the vessel is transformed by fire (see Berns 2000, 62–63). Clay serves both materially and symbolically as an agent of change. The malleability of wet clay gives healers the capacity to give shape to the ineffable, and just as the fire transforms the pot, so too, is the disease contained and controlled. The pot functions as the agent of a cure and the embodiment of the disease, making the particularities of its form a mechanism for drawing the symptoms away from the person into the vessel. That most Longuda and Cham-Mwana pots have some human reference, however stylized and abstract, reinforces the belief that the forces determining health and well-being are more accessible when rendered in recognizable terms. Other examples, such as the *kulok-kulok* used for curing backaches, are rendered in a form that dramatically captures the pain that the particular disease engenders—in this case with rows of sharp, pointed "vertebrae"—in an effort to draw it away (see fig. 16.15). The visualizations of illness in these vessels are portraits of both their physical and even psychological manifestations. The elongation of the body on vessels used to cure vomiting (*gando*; see fig. 16.16) captures the sharp upward force of regurgitation. The pot for curing chronic coughs (*sujang*), has an unusual stirrup spout, the shape of which echoes the bronchial tree.[16] The characteristic wide-open mouths provide an obvious point of entry for the disease-causing spirit. The vessel's interior becomes the spirit's prison; and its surface, an insulating barrier. While specific programs of decoration attract these spirits through their verisimilitude, they also function apotropaically for those who handle and ultimately dispose of them (see David et al. 1988, 377).

The need to remove potentially harmful vessels to neutral locales not only accounts for their profusion around old Cham-Mwana settlements but also explains why so many have found their way into public and private collections.[17] The formal and functional similarities of Longuda and Cham-Mwana vessels make distinguishing between some of them—especially those that have been more recently found and have entered the art market and collections—difficult. For example, all the pots Hare (1983) identifies as Longuda, are, based on my research, more likely to be Cham-Mwana. The proximity of these peoples and the likelihood of their historical interactions (both friendly and hostile), especially over the last century, have blurred the boundaries between them. Nevertheless, upon close evaluation, as this survey establishes, it is possible to distinguish what is sculpturally typical of the Cham-Mwana and of the Longuda.

The Waja are western neighbors of the Longuda and were formerly dispersed in hillside communities within seventeen "districts."[18] Their descent from these Muri Mountain locations to the northern plains in the mid-twentieth century put them into close contact with the Jera and Tera.[19] This has had a strong impact on traditional patterns of religious observance and political organization, resulting in widespread conversion to Islam and a centralization of authority with secular chiefs positioned in each village. The chief of the town of Talasse is commonly acknowledged as the paramount Waja leader.

In the past, the Waja, like their Longuda neighbors, depended upon the intercession of powerful spirit priests to maintain community well-being.[20] An important festival of community renewal, called Gwiyandi, rotated among Waja communities every seven years and appears to have provided some ethnic consolidation. Also uniting the dispersed Waja groups was the pacification of spirits (*guti*; sing.: *guto*) associated with disease, using a procedure largely identical to the one described above for the Longuda *kwandalha*. Male healers diagnosed diseases and were responsible for modeling clay pots, also called *guti*, to effect a cure. These vessels were kept in shrines maintained by healer-sculptors. The remains of one such shrine in the abandoned Talasse hamlet of I'Yemberi show how these vessels differ stylistically from those of the Longuda (fig. 16.19). Faces are modeled on the "neck" of the vessel, near its mouth opening, and features are individually applied, creating a more restrained expression than seen on Longuda wares. The bodies have narrow arms flanking a round torso impressed with controlled geometric patterns.

Tiny *guti* vessels (H: 5–15 cm) serve as personal amulets and take various forms depending on the disease being treated (fig. 16.20). *Bapuro*, which feature spiky projections, are used for curing skin disease; *baduwi* have simple raised ridges and help relieve small children of stomachaches.[21] Several photographed in the village of Dela Waja are strikingly like the Cham-Mwana vessels described above, including one

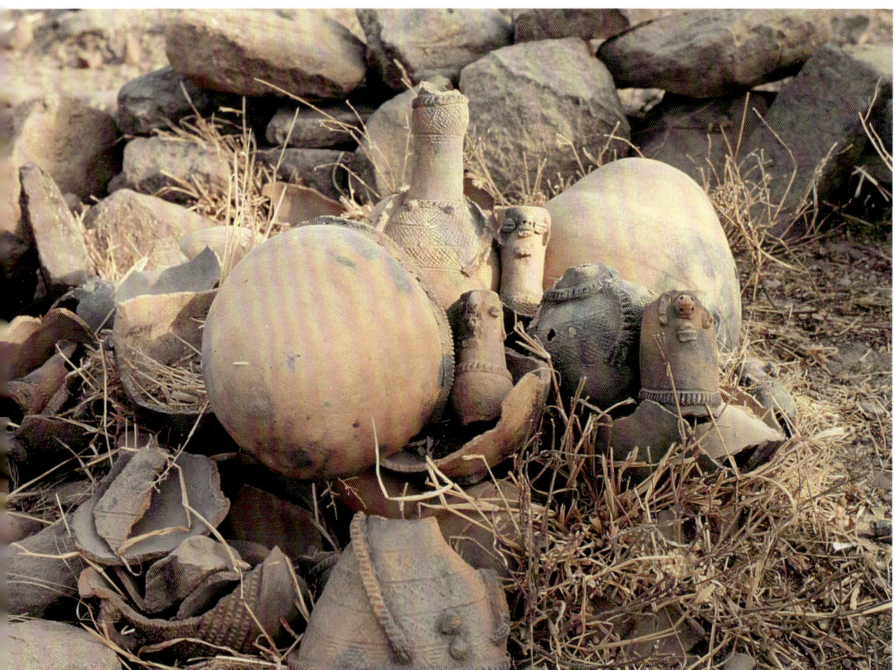

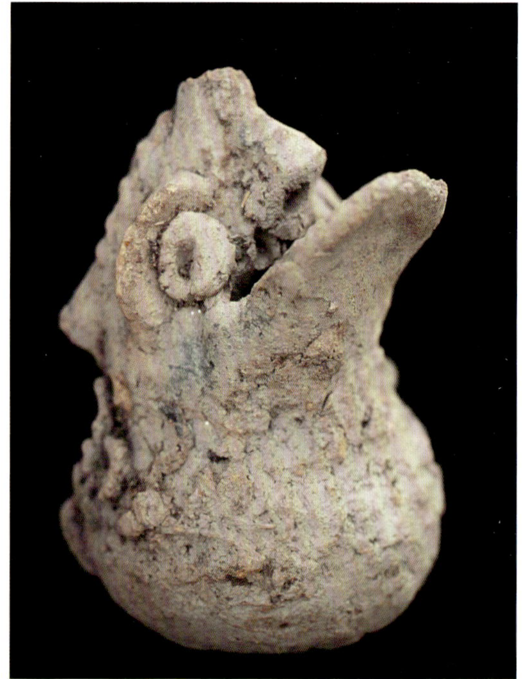

16.19
These Waja healing vessels (*guti*) found at the abandoned site of I'Yemberi would have been enshrined for use by a healer who had also likely made them.
PHOTOGRAPH BY MARLA C. BERNS, OLD TALASSE, 1982.

16.20
This small Waja *guti* vessel was intended for healing skin diseases.
PHOTOGRAPH BY MARLA C. BERNS, GALENGU VILLAGE, 1982.

16.21
The middle Waja healing vessel (*guti*) in this group, which has a baby on its back, and the one to its right are both used to cure fever in children. These examples are very similar to those made by the Cham-Mwana for curing children's diseases (*jina kwimtiyu*). The vessel to the left, *nyingnandi*, was used to cure dizziness.
PHOTOGRAPH BY MARLA C. BERNS, DELA WAJA, 1982.

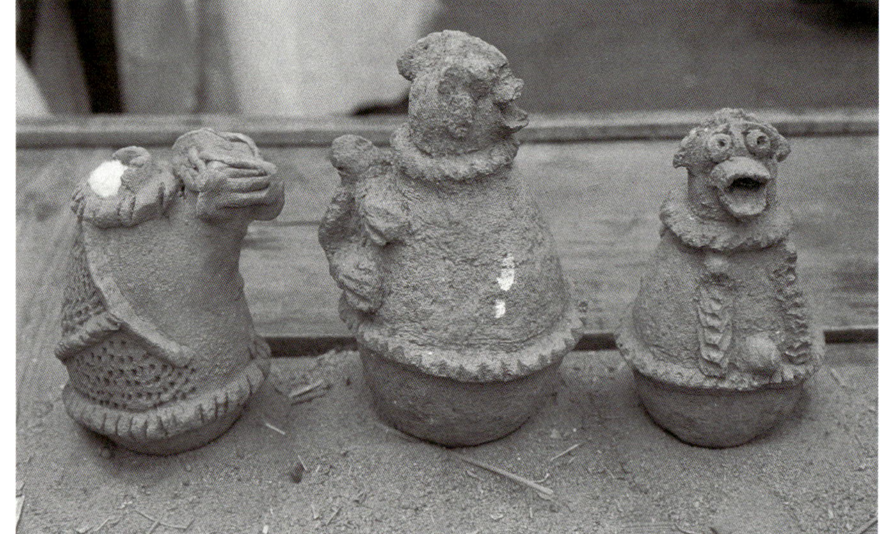

16.22
Tula houses hug the northern plateau of the Muri Mountains and look out over the adjoining western plains. Such hillside communities provided a strong defensive position, and the elaborate stone terraces for farming are visible in the upland terrain across the valley.
PHOTOGRAPH BY MARLA C. BERNS, 1982.

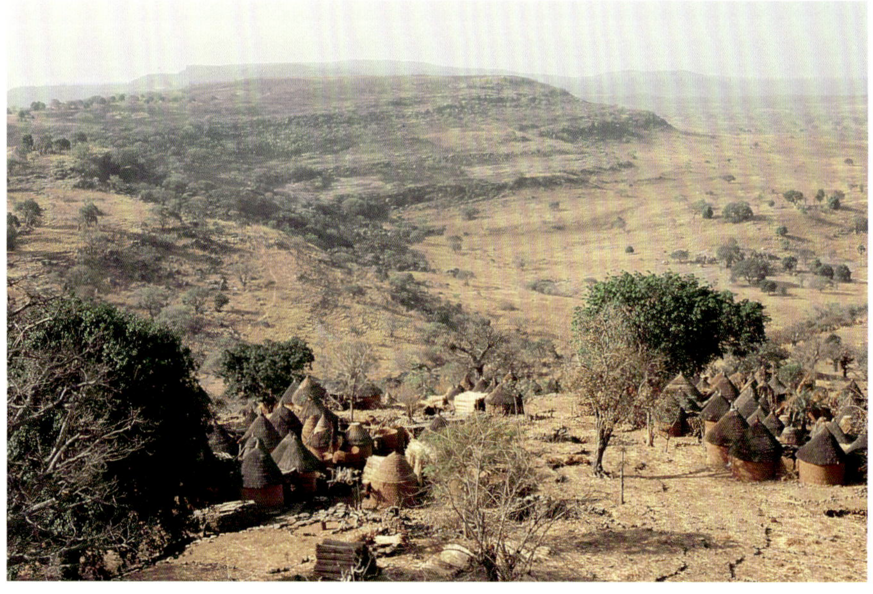

example with a baby on its back used to cure children's fevers (fig. 16.21). A healer takes the tiny pot and circles it over the patient's head while reciting specific incantations, afterward the patient takes the *guti* home and sleeps with it until cured. The vessels are then removed from the house of the patient, as is done elsewhere, and deposited under a granary. At one abandoned household site in Talasse, I saw eight tiny *guti* within a granary's foundation stones.

The Waja are perhaps best known in the literature for the dramatic tall vertical masks that have been attributed to them (see Leuzinger 1971). Arnold Rubin, however, saw no evidence of wood sculpture on his visit to Galengu in 1970, and similarly I saw none on my visits to five Waja villages in 1981. Further, we were not told about any masks or associated ancestral worship. This supports the argument made by Adelberger in this volume (see p. 432) that the masks identified as "Waja" in the literature were most likely made by the cluster of Wurkun and Bikwin groups living to the southwest in the Muri Mountains. The Wurkun also use small columnar wood sculptures (*kundul*) as opposed to ceramics in determining and healing illnesses. The strong resemblances between the faces on *kundul* and the vertical masks also argue powerfully in favor of their coming from the same place. I think it unlikely that the monumental masks now in collections were made or used by the Waja even if none of them has been documented in situ in the Muri Mountain area. It is likely that here, too, confusion arose between the people called "Waja" and the Tangale-Waja District in which these groups lived in the colonial and immediate postcolonial era.

TULA, DADIYA, JEN, AND KWA

The Tula live on and at the base of a rugged plateau situated in the northern range of the Muri Mountains (fig. 16.22). Two of their three main villages, Tula Wange and Tula Baule, are at the crest of the plateau with unobstructed views of the Kaltungo Hills far to the west. The third, Tula Yiri, is located on the plains below. The three villages were formerly independent and had strong local identities; Tula Wange serves as the administrative center today. In the precolonial period, there was considerable internecine warfare between the Tula and their Tangale (Kaltungo), Waja, Dadiya, and Cham-Mwana neighbors.[22] The Tula had a strong defensive position high in the rocky landscape, and their households were still built in tight clusters with granaries sandwiched between in 1982. Structures, as elsewhere in the region, were joined by low stone walls that created narrow passageways and helped prevent erosion. The hillsides had to be elaborately terraced to permit farming. Even the open plains around Tula Yiri suffered from poor farmland, and sorghum (guinea corn) was planted in raised sandy rows.

The most distinctive feature of Tula villages is the presence of ritual precincts constructed entirely with drystone walls (see figs. 16.3, 16.23, 16.24). Each patrilineal kindred group had its own precinct, which suggests the degree of decentralization common to Tula communities in the past. Ritual centers photographed in 1982 typically consisted of a *seh*, a high rectangular wall with a low shelf along the front for displaying important objects, and a *kwer*, a high circular "throne" for chiefs or priests to sit on and to display ceramic vessels (see fig. 16.3). These stone structures are points of contact among the living, their ancestors, and other spirit forces. The objects kept on them help priests facilitate interaction with these forces on behalf of their families. Missionary activity among the Tula from the early twentieth century resulted in widespread conversion to Christianity, and only a few such precincts were still used for religious worship in the 1980s.

The most important activity to take place in these precincts was the harvest thanksgiving called Kuram and held each December. In figure 16.3 large pots called *kur* are kept on top of the *kwer* throne for storing seeds of the newly harvested sorghum crop that will be planted the following spring. When the first heads of the sorghum plants begin to show, the ritual priest climbs on top of the *kwer* to beseech

16.26
Sule (active 1970s–1980s)
Healing vessel (*beji*)
Tula peoples, twentieth century
Ceramic
H: 25 cm
FOWLER MUSEUM AT UCLA, X86.2577; GIFT OF JIM
AND JEANNE PIEPER
PROVENANCE: COLLECTED BY ARNOLD RUBIN,
TULA WANGE, 1970

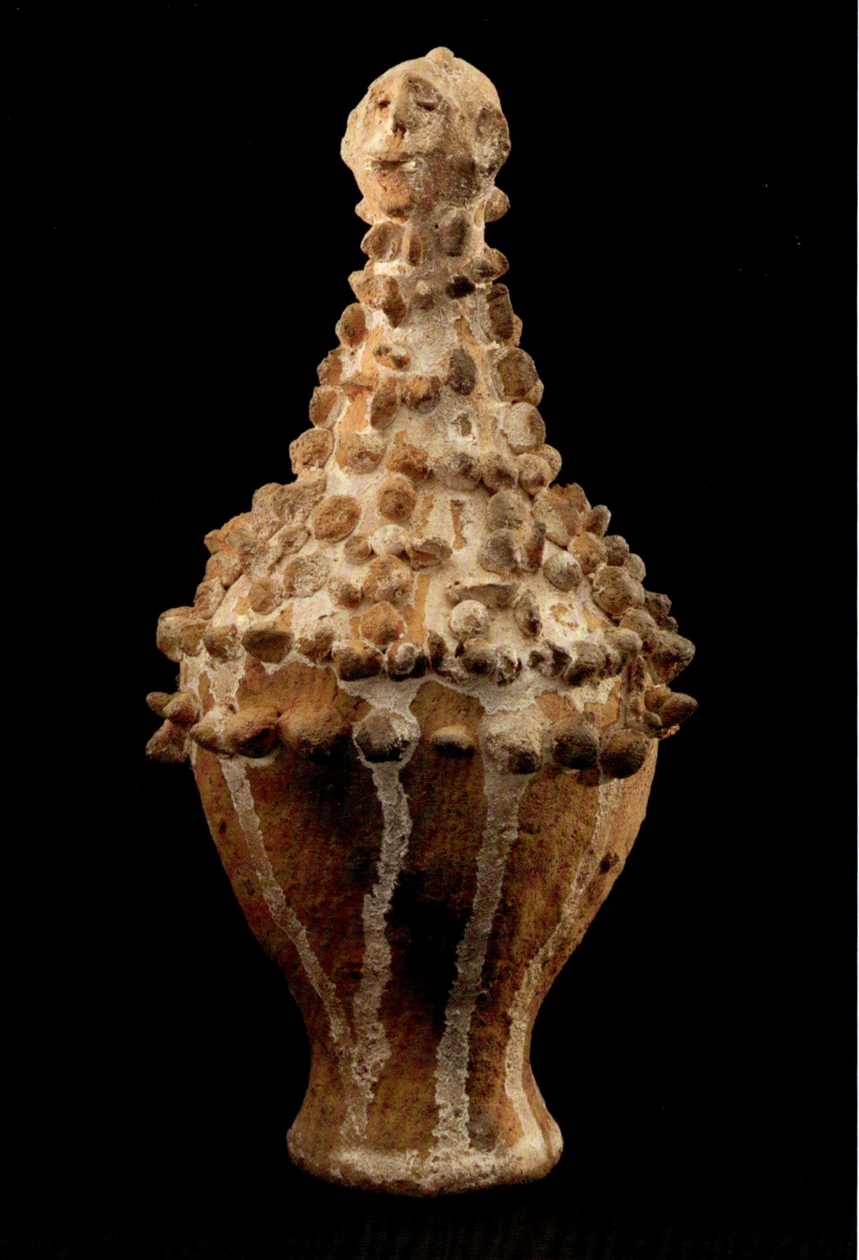

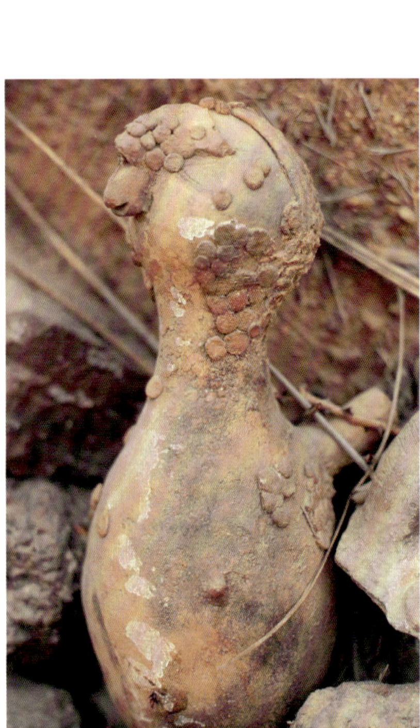

16.27
Covered with flat pellets, which signal an
association with healing skin diseases, this
beji vessel was enshrined on the *seh* belonging
to the Bwem hamlet of Tula Wange. It was
also used in rituals to mark the end of the
agricultural cycle.
PHOTOGRAPH BY MARLA C. BERNS, 1982.

16.28
The artist Sule of Swelebo hamlet in Tula
Wange stands in front of his family's *seh* and
carries one of the *beji* healing vessels he created (see also fig. 16.26). Note the multiple
spouts and small head surmounting the vessel,
which is covered with the "bumps" referring
to the skin diseases such pots were intended
to cure.
PHOTOGRAPH BY MARLA C. BERNS, 1982.

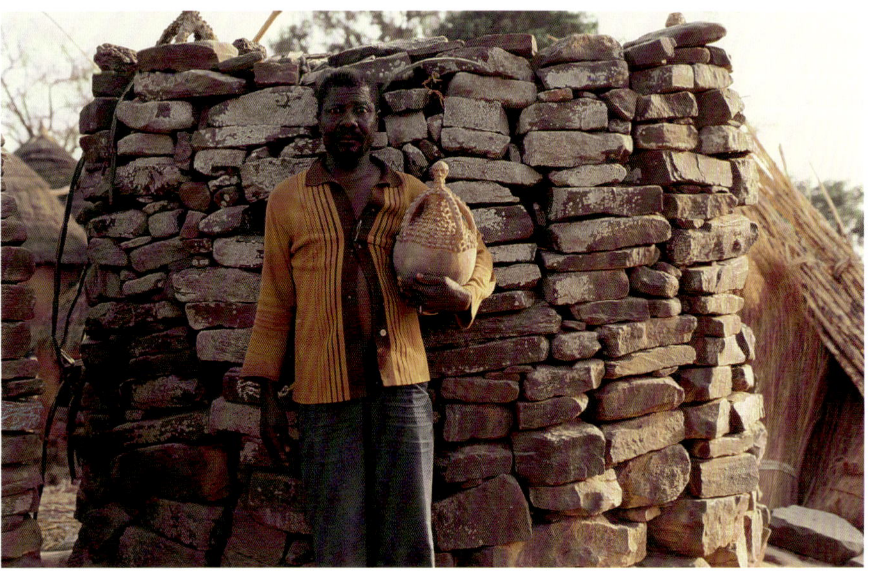

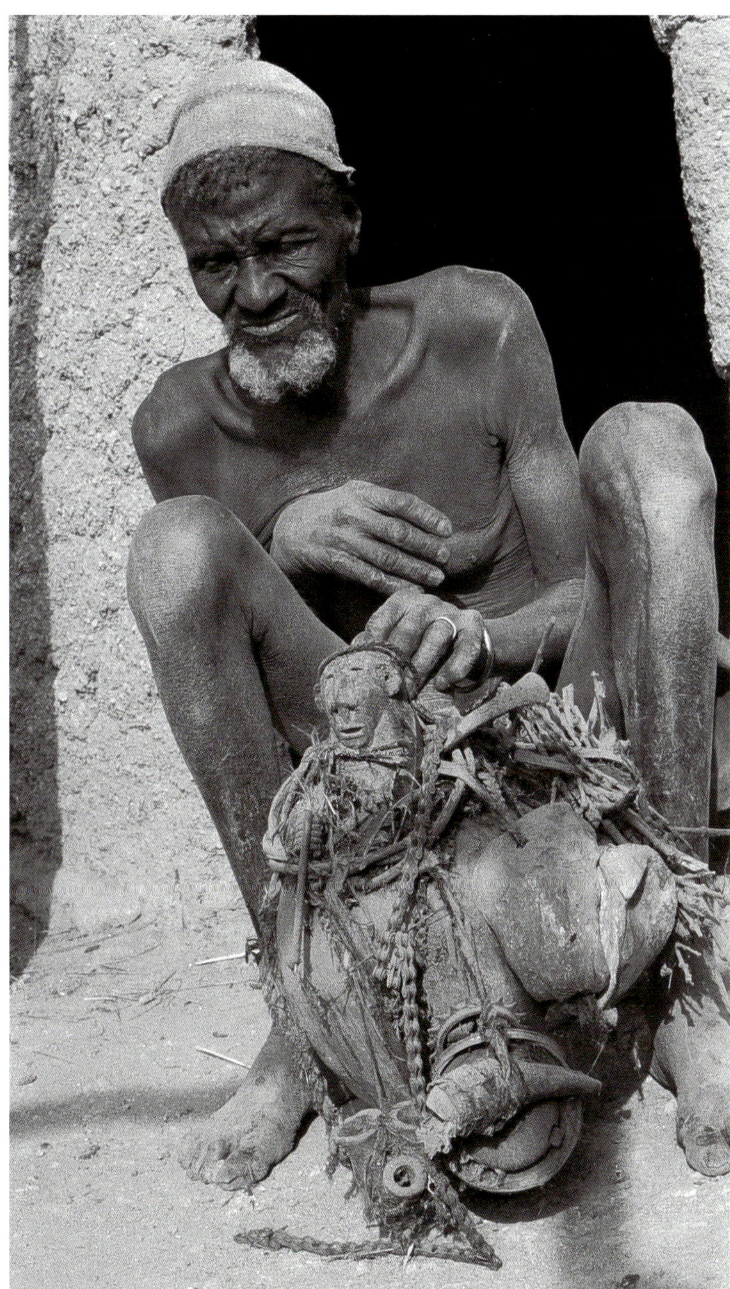

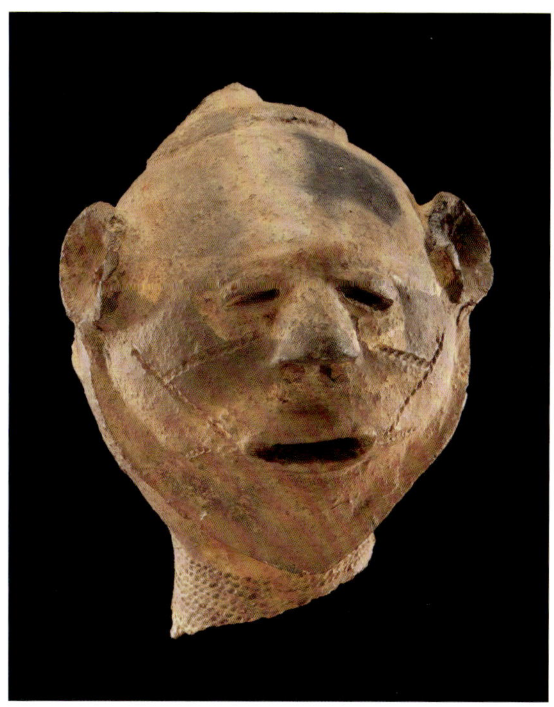

to protect the Tangale of the town of Biliri (fig. 16.29). Its custodian, named Lakədi, inherited the vessel from his grandfather and was obligated by his father to make offerings to it at least twice a year, once after the harvest and once when the new crops were planted, to secure its beneficence. The spirit vessel could also cure sickness and bring wealth. Rubin's sketch of the ovoid pot shows that the head is a blind spout with the actual working spout located at the back in a configuration identical to that of the Tula *beji*. Its body is obscured by the accumulations of materials, each adding to the spirit's power and authority; the bicycle chain, for example, is a "bridle" for the spirit's horse, and the ax blade belongs to the spirit. Nothing like this was documented elsewhere, and the Tangale of Biliri told Rubin that it was "the only one." This vessel must have accrued power based on its singularity and mystery. Its custodian had no idea who had made it. He knew only that it represented the spirit of his grandfather.[26] Judging by the age of Lakədi in the photograph with his sculpture in 1970, it could date to the late nineteenth century. As will be detailed below, this type of vessel is also reminiscent of figurative ceramics enshrined by the Dadiya and Jen. Examples of the latter were collected as early as 1894.[27]

16.29
A protective power sculpture is displayed by Lakədi, its custodian, in Biliri Town, Tangale. It consists of a range of materials added to a ceramic vessel identical to a Tula *beji*. The additions empower and activate the vessel.
PHOTOGRAPH BY ARNOLD RUBIN, FEBRUARY 1970, RUBIN ARCHIVE, FOWLER MUSEUM AT UCLA, NEG. NO. 2260.

16.30
Head fragment (*beji*)
Tula peoples, before 1970
Ceramic
H: 14.5 cm
FOWLER MUSEUM AT UCLA X86.4691; GIFT OF ARNOLD RUBIN
IMAGE: © 2010 FOWLER MUSEUM AT UCLA. PHOTOGRAPH BY DON COLE
PROVENANCE: COLLECTED BY ARNOLD RUBIN, TULA WANGE, 1970

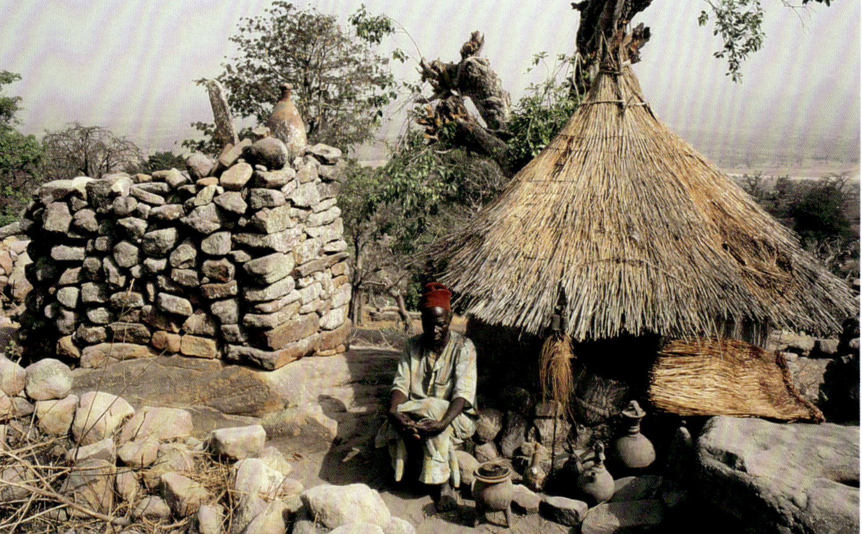

16.31

The shrine custodian sits in front of the Kan Mam (house of Mam)—where all of the displayed ritual paraphernalia was ordinarily kept—in the ritual precinct belonging to the Lokwilla hamlet, Dadiya Hill. To the left is the drystone wall (*tanyal*) where the spirits are invoked. The sprouted guinea corn splashed on the wall's surface to activate the spirits is visible.

PHOTOGRAPH BY MARLA C. BERNS, 1982.

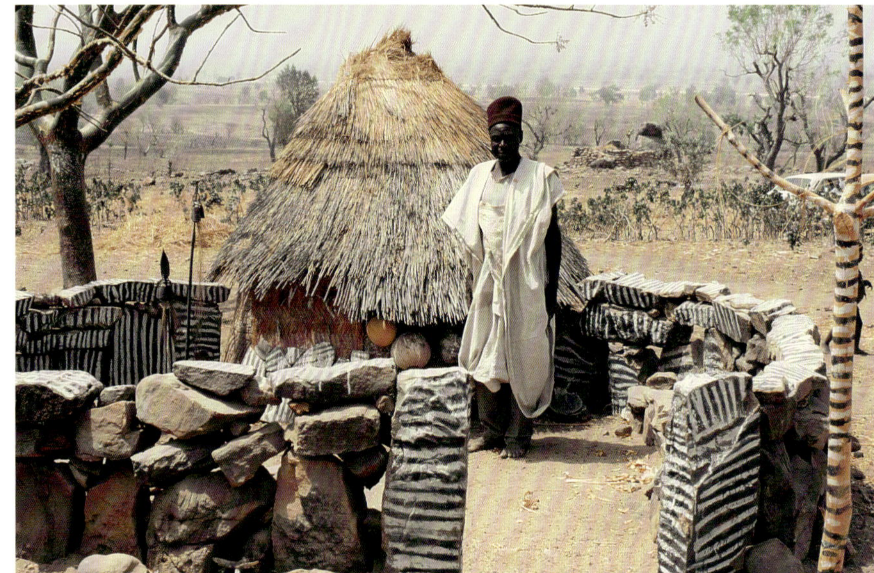

16.32

The stone wall surrounding the Kan Mam ritual enclosure in Jalingo hamlet, Dadiya, was painted in alternating stripes as an offering to local spirit protectors. To the left of the shrine's custodian and the structure, note the spears of Mam (*swe mam*).

PHOTOGRAPH BY MARLA C. BERNS, 1982.

16.33

One nearly complete *magula* (with broken arms) and one head fragment inside a Dadiya Kan Mam reveal surfaces ritually painted with guinea-corn paste mixed with water. According to Arnold Rubin's fieldnotes, the artist who made these vessels was named Bebuli.

PHOTOGRAPH BY ARNOLD RUBIN, DADIYA TOWN, MARCH 1970, RUBIN ARCHIVE, FOWLER MUSEUM AT UCLA, NEG. NO. 2312.

16.34

This *magula* vessel belonged to the Loteni hamlet, Dadiya Dutse.

PHOTOGRAPH BY MARLA C. BERNS, 1982.

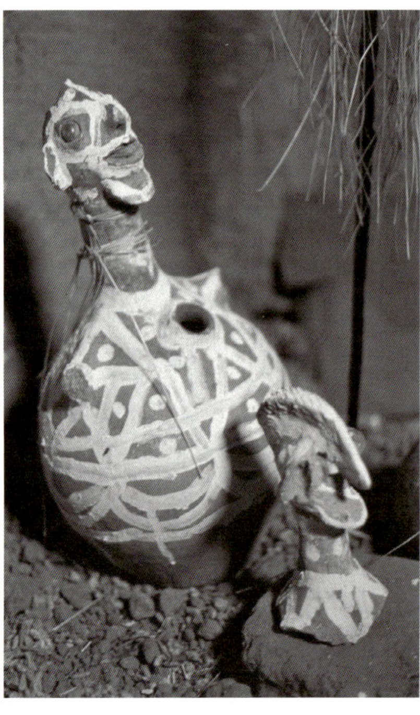

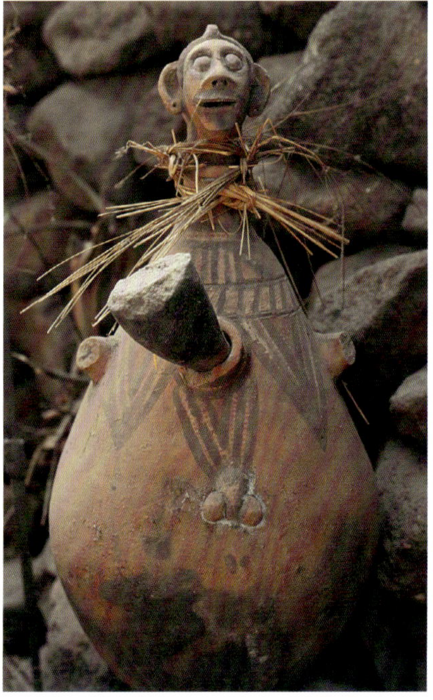

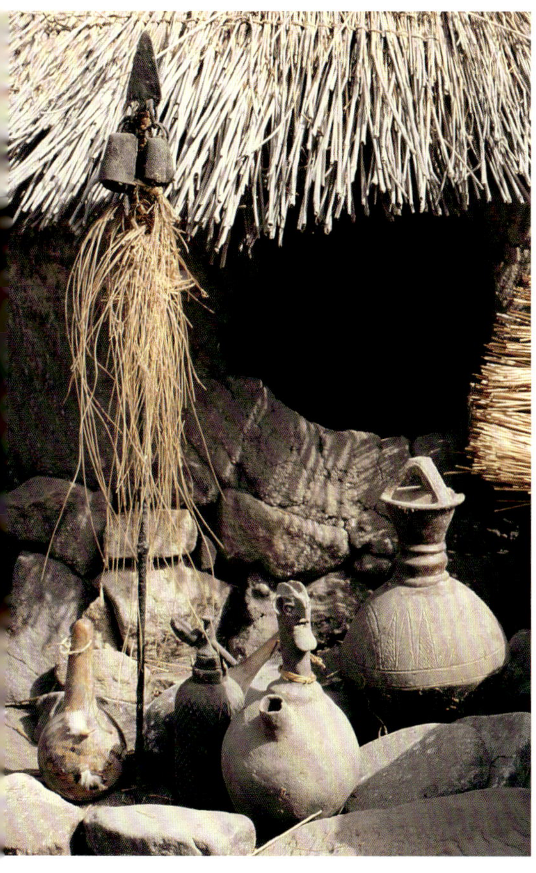

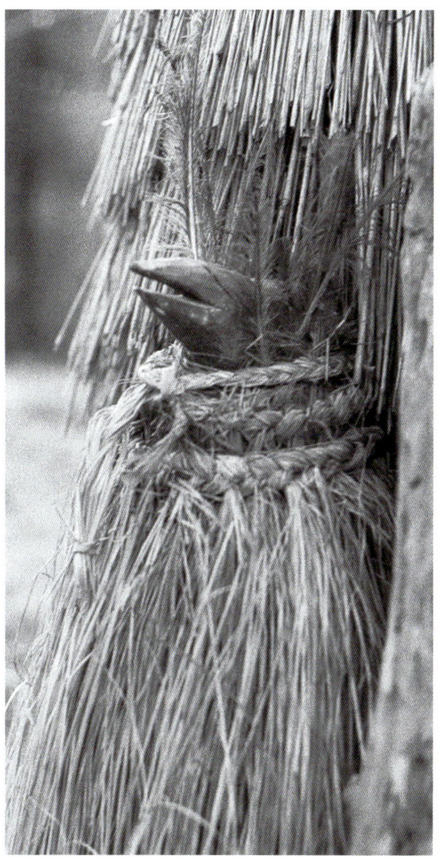

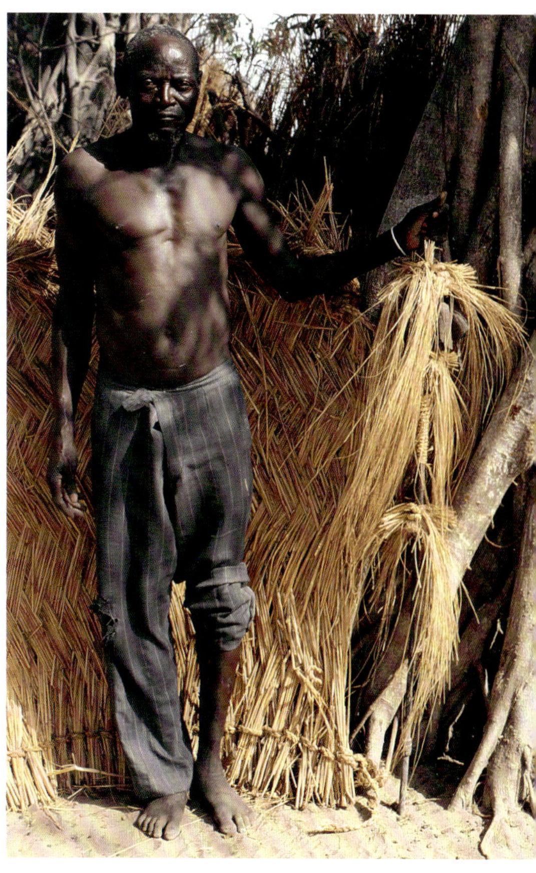

The Dadiya live within the southern chain of the Muri Mountains, south of the Tula, east of the Wurkun and Bikwin groups, and north of the Jen and Kwa.[28] Dadiya Dutse (Dadiya Hill) is the largest community in the foothills, situated below the area where protected Dadiya hamlets formerly had broad views of the northern plains. Though many hillside settlements are now abandoned, several survived in 1982 to reveal that houses were constructed of mud and, while densely packed, were surrounded by drystone walls to protect and separate compounds as well as form narrow internal passageways. As was true among the Tula, each hamlet had its own ritual precinct, dominated by a high drystone wall (*tanyal*) and a shrine enclosure, Kan Mam (house of Mam), built of mud with a thatched roof (fig. 16.31).

Mam is the most important spirit principle identified by the Dadiya.[29] Ritual priests contact Mam with the aid of several sacred objects, including ceramic vessels, a gourd rattle (*kwal mam*), and an iron spear with large bent-iron clapper bells and grasses tied around the top (*swe mam*)—all of which are kept inside the Kan Mam (fig. 16.35). A festival, also called Mam, is held twice a year: once at the close of the dry season to pray for plentiful rain and once after the first harvest to show thanks, a pattern that is consistent within the region. The pots kept inside the Kan Mam are removed and filled with beer, which is later consumed by ritual priests and male elders. As was done by the Tula, ground-sprouted guinea corn used to make the beer is mixed with water and "painted" over the drystone wall, sometimes in tight linear patterns, functioning as a ritual offering or spiritual activation (fig. 16.32). Several types of vessel are kept in the shrine (see fig. 16.35): a tripod cooking pot (*talinan*); a large ovoid pot with an everted mouth and lid (*whel*); and a figurative vessel with a blind spout in the form of a fully modeled human head (*magula*). The contents of one Kan Mam photographed by Rubin in 1970 in Dadiya Town (fig. 16.33) show that the *magula* vessels are ritually painted, as were the Tula *beji*.

The figurative *magula* also closely resembles the Tula *beji* in basic shape and in the relative naturalism of the modeled heads. Although the four examples I documented

16.35
This detail of figure 16.31 highlights the contents of the Lokwilla family's Kan Mam. From left to right are the items used in healing rituals: a gourd rattle (*kwal mam*); an iron spear (*swe mam)*; an old siphon bottle for holding sesame oil; the figurative *magula* for holding beer; and another beer vessel (*whel*).
PHOTOGRAPH BY MARLA C. BERNS, DADIYA DUTSE, 1982.

16.36
The carved wooden head of an incarnation of Kue, the Jen protective deity, is just visible peering over its grass-encased body. This figure belonged to the Veh-Wambu family.
PHOTOGRAPH BY ARNOLD RUBIN, APRIL 1970, RUBIN ARCHIVE, FOWLER MUSEUM AT UCLA, NEG. NO. 2586.

16.37
Samamba, the chief (*kulong*) of the Veh-Faga family, holds the tall iron spear (*bi*) festooned with grasses that is used in oath-taking ceremonies among the Jen.
PHOTOGRAPH BY MARLA C. BERNS, JEN, 1982.

in three Dadiya ritual precincts are each different, there are similarities in physiognomic details (figs. 16.34, 16.35). All have flaring ears, circular punched eyes, and slightly open, horizontal mouths; some have beards and others have a single or double sagittal crest. Surface detail is typically minimal, except for the *magula* from the Loteni hamlet, which has black, red, and white slip decoration, as well as arms that would have projected from the body, a pattern that correlates strongly with Jen pottery conventions (see fig. 16.34; cf. Jen, fig. 16.40).

Dadiya *magula* are incorporated into healing rites enacted at the Kan Mam by priest-healers. They are filled with beer, which is consumed by priests and their families. Sacrificial offerings of chicken blood are also poured over the pots as well as the other ritual paraphernalia used to divine illnesses and their cures. Determining the cause of an illness involves shaking the gourd rattle kept inside the shrine. The most important healing medium, however, is the iron spear (*swe mam*), which is circled over the patient's head in what one healer claimed was a symbolic act of "killing" the spirits causing disease. As was true of related healing procedures practiced by the Cham-Mwana and Longuda, small pots could also be circled over a patient's head and then taken home overnight to help draw away the disease. Additionally, the healing process involved applying sesame oil with a chicken feather to the patient's chest. In the shrine shown in figure 16.35 an old metal siphon bottle was used to contain the sesame oil. The figurative *magula* provides a point of contact between ritual specialists and the forces they seek to influence for the benefit of an individual supplicant or for the good of the community during seasonal rites. It is clear that the efficacy of these appeals is enhanced by the presence of *magula* vessels with their intentionally humanized form.

The Jen live along the Benue floodplain, and their more accessible location brought them to the attention of European explorers and colonial officers in the late nineteenth and early twentieth centuries, resulting in brief ethnographic accounts and notices in the literature (see Meek 1931b, 2: 519–36; Passarge 1895, 20). Although their history remains unclear, several accounts (including one I collected in 1982) indicate that the Jen were forced down the Benue from the Numan area at the Benue-Gongola confluence during the period of Fulani expansion in the early nineteenth century (Meek 1931b, 2: 519; Kirk-Greene 1969, 2). The Jen also claim to have lived even further up the Benue River and report having been pushed westward by the Yungur. Their figurative shrine sculpture fits within the shared distribution of vessels outlined here, but aspects of form and decoration also offer intriguing parallels to the portrait *wiiso* made by the Yungur (see below, chapter 18).

The riverain situation of the Jen means that their material culture differs from the hill peoples heretofore described. Hamlets are dispersed along the floodplain, and large refuse mounds suggest long-term occupation. Hamlet heads (*kulong*) formerly had authority over local religious and judicial matters. One chief priest, the *yifa nwaka*, had power over all the *kulong* and supervised the most important sacred and ritual activities.

According to Meek (1931b, 2: 520), the Jen believe in a supreme deity named Fi, who is associated with the sun. A secondary deity is called Ma or Mə and is regarded as the servant of Fi and the creator of all living things. Meek considers Jen religion to be an offshoot of that of the Jukun, who believe in a secondary deity called Ama or Ma.[30] The spirit principles with the most direct impact on the lives of the Jen are Kwiyeh, who are responsible for health and prosperity and are maintained by the *yifa nwaka* priest. Although informants told me about Kwiyeh, physical manifestations of them were shrouded in secrecy. They were said to come out at the beginning of the hunting season "covered in grass" and visible only to Jen men. Meek (1931b, 2: 524) referred to Kwiyeh as "Kue" and described them collectively as "tutelary genii" and "executive officers" of Ma. He also wrote that chief among the Kue was Kue Akwa, who appeared during the dry season and again after the crops were harvested "clothed in a costume of hibiscus fibre" and wearing "a hornless mask surmounted with the feathers of a stork."

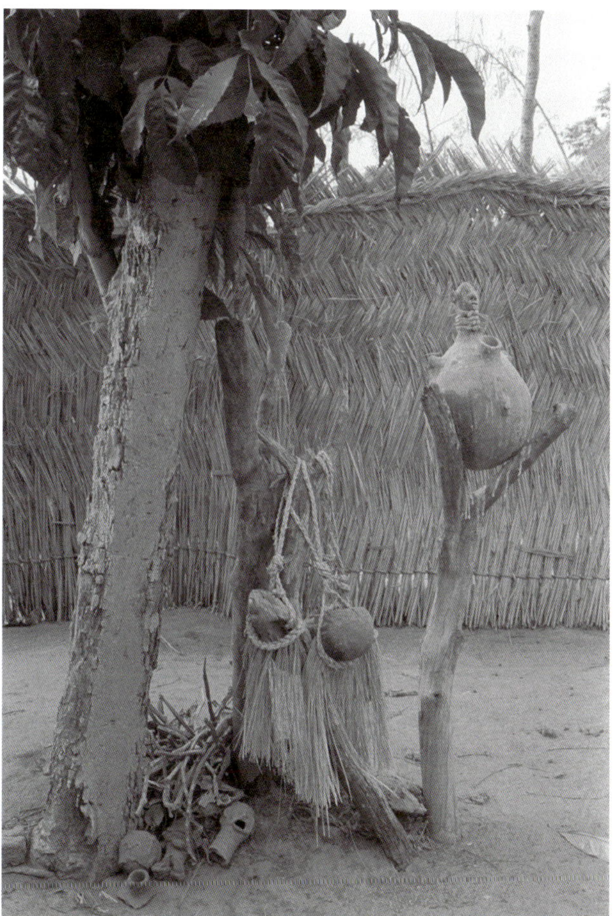

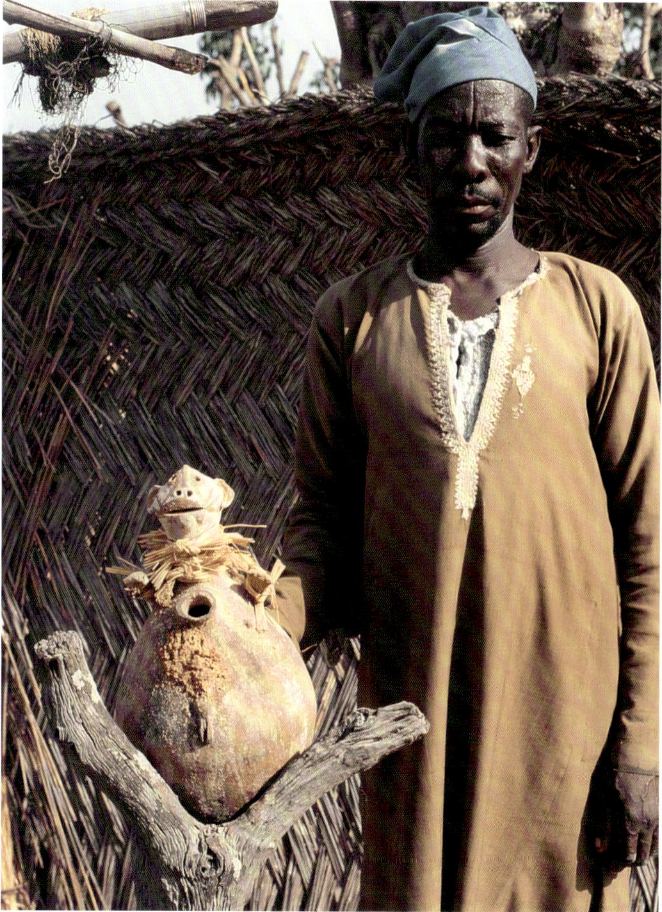

Arnold Rubin documented Kwiyeh/Kue among two different Jen clans.[31] His field notes describe Kue in one instance as having feathers crowning a straw cone and being used to heal the sick or punish thieves. In the second instance, he photographed a representation of Kue leaning against a thatched enclosure, standing about 1.5 meters tall with a carved wooden, bird-like head with a beak and a body completely encased in a straw cloak (fig. 16.36). While the form underneath the cloak is completely obscured, this Kue has feathers surrounding the head as noted by Meek. It may be that Rubin and Meek are referring to the same thing. In both their accounts Kue's appearance is related to ensuring crop fertility and hunting success, yet it also functions as an agent of social control. It is difficult to situate this anomalous spirit embodiment, but it is intriguing to consider how it may relate to the dramatic vertical masks with their wooden heads and grass coverings that are worn by the neighboring Wurkun, Gwana Jukun, Kona Jukun, and Mumuye for similar purposes (see chapter 14).[32]

The Jen also maintain a shrine dedicated to Ma, where individuals would go to settle disputes. I documented one such shrine in 1982, maintained by the chief of the Veh-Faga family and situated in an area within the household bounded by woven mats and containing a central fig tree (*Ficus Thonningii*). Oaths were sworn on a tall iron spear (*bi*) with suspended bent-iron clapper bells.[33] The spear was tied at intervals with knotted dried grasses (fig. 16.37). The oath-swearing ceremony was performed in the presence of the chief of Ma and involved ingesting the leaves of the fig tree. The deities Fi and Ma decided the fate of the oath taker, and it was believed that good or evil would befall the supplicant depending on whether he told the truth. This Jen practice is related in name and function to the Dadiya cult of Mam, where an identical iron spear with bent iron bells is also the central object (see figure 16.35). The pervasiveness of healing, oath taking, or possession cults in the Middle and Upper Benue that use the names Ma, Mə, Mam—or some cognate thereof—and that incorporate similar iron

16.38
This view of the Jen shrine precinct maintained by the Veh-Nwakwemmeh family shows its *kuchan* in a forked tree. Also visible in this photograph of 1970 are the wooden trophy heads suspended from another branch and the fragments of old *kuchan* at the base of the tree. When I photographed the same shrine in 1982, the main *kuchan* (now in the Jos Museum collection) had been replaced with another and the trophy heads had deteriorated. See also figure 16.42.
PHOTOGRAPH BY ARNOLD RUBIN, JEN, 1970, RUBIN ARCHIVE, FOWLER MUSEUM AT UCLA, NEG. NO. 2591.

16.39
The custodian (*kulong*) of the Veh-No family stands with its female *kuchan*. The grasses wrapped around the neck of the vessel are the same as those that would have been wrapped around the head of a victim killed during warfare in the past. Visible on the surface of the *kuchan* are traces of an offering made from the same sprouted sorghum used in making the beer kept inside the vessel and offered to the protective spirits of the hunt.
PHOTOGRAPH BY MARLA C. BERNS, 1982.

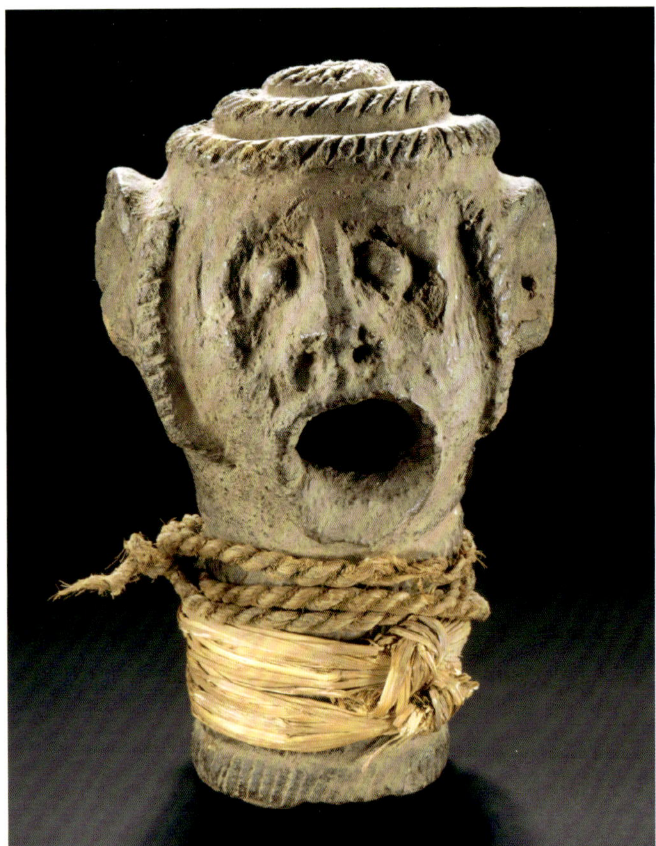

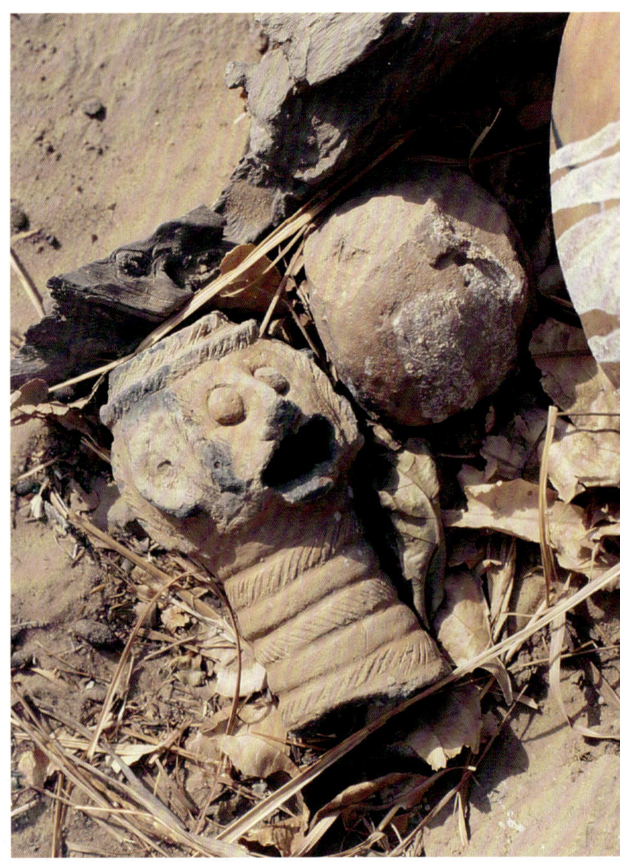

16.41

Head fragment from a vessel (*kuchan*)
Jen peoples, before 1912
Ceramic, pigment, fiber rope
H: 14 cm
STAATLICHE MUSEEN ZU BERLIN, ETHNOLOGIS-
CHES MUSEUM, III C 29323
IMAGE: © STAATLICHE MUSEEN ZU BERLIN,
PREUSSISCHER KULTURBESITZ, ETHNOLO-
GISCHES MUSEUM. PHOTOGRAPH BY MARTIN
FRANKEN, 2010
PROVENANCE: COLLECTED BY LEO FROBENIUS, 1912

This head shares the distinctive spiral coiffure
seen in figures 15.1 and 16.42, as well as the
rope and grass binding observed around the
necks of many examples photographed in the
field in 1970 and 1982.

16.42

This head fragment from a *kuchan* was located
at the base of the Veh-Nwakwemmeh shrine.
Note the resemblance between this head (also
photographed in situ by Arnold Rubin in
1970) and the one collected by Leo Frobenius
in 1912 (see figs. 16.38 and 16.41).
PHOTOGRAPH BY MARLA C. BERNS, JEN, 1982.

spirits associated with these ceramic heads could cause the miscreant to fall ill. Not to
be overlooked in the physical appearance of the enshrined *kuchan* (whole or fragmentary) are the grasses tied around their necks (see figs. 16.38, 16.39, 16.41). The same
strategy was evident in the grasses tied around the top of iron spears (see figs. 16.35
and 16.37) and around the *ku* trophy heads (said to have been completely wrapped with
grasses). The plaited grass or rope still visible on the one early twentieth-century head
fragment may be an explanation for the consistent decoration of the necks of figurative
vessels with linear patterns. Does the rope or grass provide another type of insulating
barrier? How does the use of fiber on these vessels or spears resemble the "protective"
and concealing fiber cloaks worn by masqueraders elsewhere or the fiber that appears
around the neck of a *kundul* or of a Wurkun vertical mask (see figs. 13.12, 13.13, 14.33).

The use of anthropomorphic vessels in rituals associated with protecting hunters or warriors is common to the region and was described above for the Cham-
Mwana, Tula, and Dadiya. These more expressively modeled Jen vessels differ from
the restrained Tula *beji*, although both are relatively naturalistic compared to the
exuberance of other western Gongola Valley ceramics (cf. figs. 16.8–16.10). There are
intriguing stylistic parallels that can be drawn among the documented examples of Jen
kuchan, Dadiya *magula*, and Cham-Mwana *changdu* (illustrated in Slye 1977, 23; cf. figs.
16.1, 16.13, 16.14). Certain approaches to rendering the faces of these vessels, especially
the deeply punched eyes and almost animal-like facial shape with their cup-like ears
are common across the three genres. It is possible that many of these pots were produced by specialists living in one place who supplied examples to various neighboring
groups, who in turn incorporated them into local shrines. Support of this hypothesis
can be found in the Jen claim that their *kuchan* were made by Lotsu-Piri and Kwa
specialists, who live northeast of them in the Muri Mountains (fig. 16.43).[38] When a
kuchan breaks, the Jen generally commission a replacement from a Kwa sculptor. The
Dadiya live just northwest of the Kwa, which may explain why their few surviving
magula so closely resemble Jen and Kwa examples (cf. fig. 16.34).[39]

The Kwa themselves use the same anthropomorphic vessels that they make for the Jen, but they call them *bogi*. They are used in rituals associated with warfare and hunting (fig. 16.44).[40] Like the *kuchan*, *bogi* are made for men who have killed an enemy during battle and are used in rites to protect them from avenging spirits of the dead. Beer poured into the *bogi* is consumed by the Kwa victor once a year for the rest of his life. The Kwa also made trophy heads out of clay to represent those killed in battle. *Bogi* have been used to protect hunters since the colonial period. Although only a few survived in 1982, a woman name Bilau was said to have produced the vessels for Kwa and Jen clients.

SUMMARY

Throughout the western Gongola Valley ceramics are a focus of ritual life, operating both on behalf of communities and individuals. The geographical proximity and linguistic affinities among Northwestern Adamawa-speaking groups help explain the broad similarities in the figurative ceramics made by the Longuda, Cham-Mwana, Waja, Tula, Dadiya, Jen, and Kwa for healing and protection. At the most essential level, the insistence that these figurative works be vessels is crucial to their presumed efficacy as containers of spirits or as agents of ritual transactions. There is a distinct shift between the healing vessels made by the Longuda, Cham-Mwana, and Waja and the vessels for protecting hunters and warriors found mostly among the Tula, Dadiya, Jen, and Kwa. The roughly modeled, highly extroverted, small-scale pots made to transfer the spirits responsible for specific diseases have an immediacy that reflects their use in the private sphere. Their surfaces describe—sometimes literally—the essence of diseases and their symptoms, enhancing their capacity to attract the offending spirits. Wide-open mouths offer easy and direct access for them. Bulahay informant Kodje Dadai explained to Nicholas David, Judith Sterner, and Kodzo Gavua (1988, 377) that "Decoration is like prayer," describing the surfaces of the "god" pot Zhikele, used for protection among the Bulahay and Mafa peoples of the Mandara Mountains to the east of the lower Gongola Valley. This elegant characterization seems equally apt for vessels of the Cham-Mwana, who produce such a diverse and specialized vocabulary of healing ceramics. Discarded across the rocky terrain of the Muri Mountains, Cham-Mwana figurative pots map the incidence of disease, describe associated symptoms, and celebrate successful containment. In other instances, such ceramics are kept protected in shrines, like the one that belonged to the Longuda healer Dasumi, whose large accumulation of vessels marked her successful work on behalf of a community of patients (see fig. 16.7).

How very different are the larger-scale, relatively restrained, and carefully executed tutelary vessels that serve entire communities among the Tula, Dadiya, Jen, and Kwa. Rather than being secreted within a healer's shrine, these very public vessels serve as sentries during the dry season, displayed against the drystone walls of community-based ritual precincts or highly visible in forked tree branches. As containers they hold the beer used to secure a direct connection between those who seek and those who confer positive intervention. Their anthropomorphism functions to encourage the transfer of power between spirits and the people who negotiate its risks. The efficacy of the vessels is announced in the visible traces of their activation left on the surfaces of the pots themselves, their stone backdrops, and the bodies of those seeking protection. Such decorative transformations demarcate the charged spaces of ritual at the same time that they provide protection from its dangers. The power that inheres within these vessels, which accumulates over time, is not dispersed if the pot breaks. Thus broken shards and intact heads are kept and carefully preserved on shrines. Such fragments embody genealogies of intervention and contain in their very fabric traces of repeated spiritual activation and deployment. The haunting fragments that were collected early in the twentieth century are evidence of their historical importance and of the likelihood that such figurative ceramics have been embedded in the cultural beliefs and practices of communities across the western Gongola Valley for much longer. ●

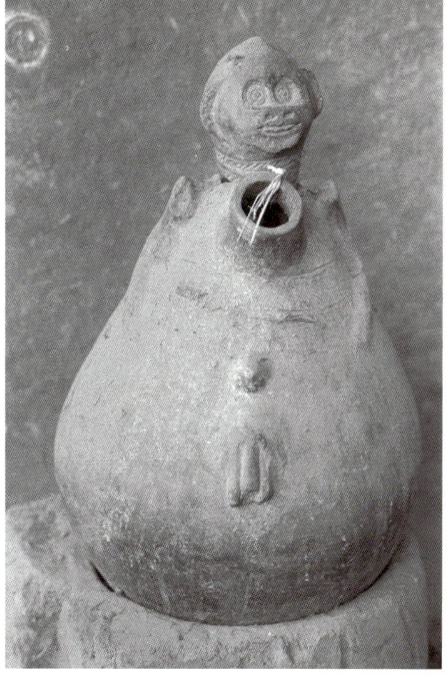

16.43
This female *kuchan* was said to have been acquired from a Lotsu-Piri sculptor. The Lotsu-Piri live north of the Kwa in the Muri Mountains.
PHOTOGRAPH BY ARNOLD RUBIN, JEN, APRIL 1970, RUBIN ARCHIVE, FOWLER MUSEUM AT UCLA, NEG. NO. 2590.

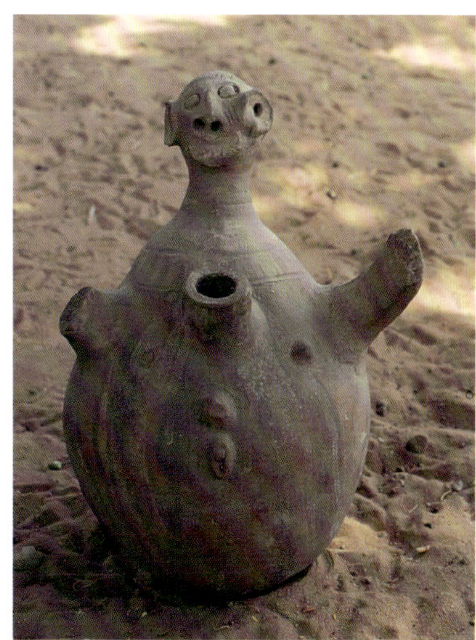

16.44
Bogi vessels made by the Kwa were used in the same way as the Jen *kuchan*.
PHOTOGRAPH BY MARLA C. BERNS, KWA, 1982.

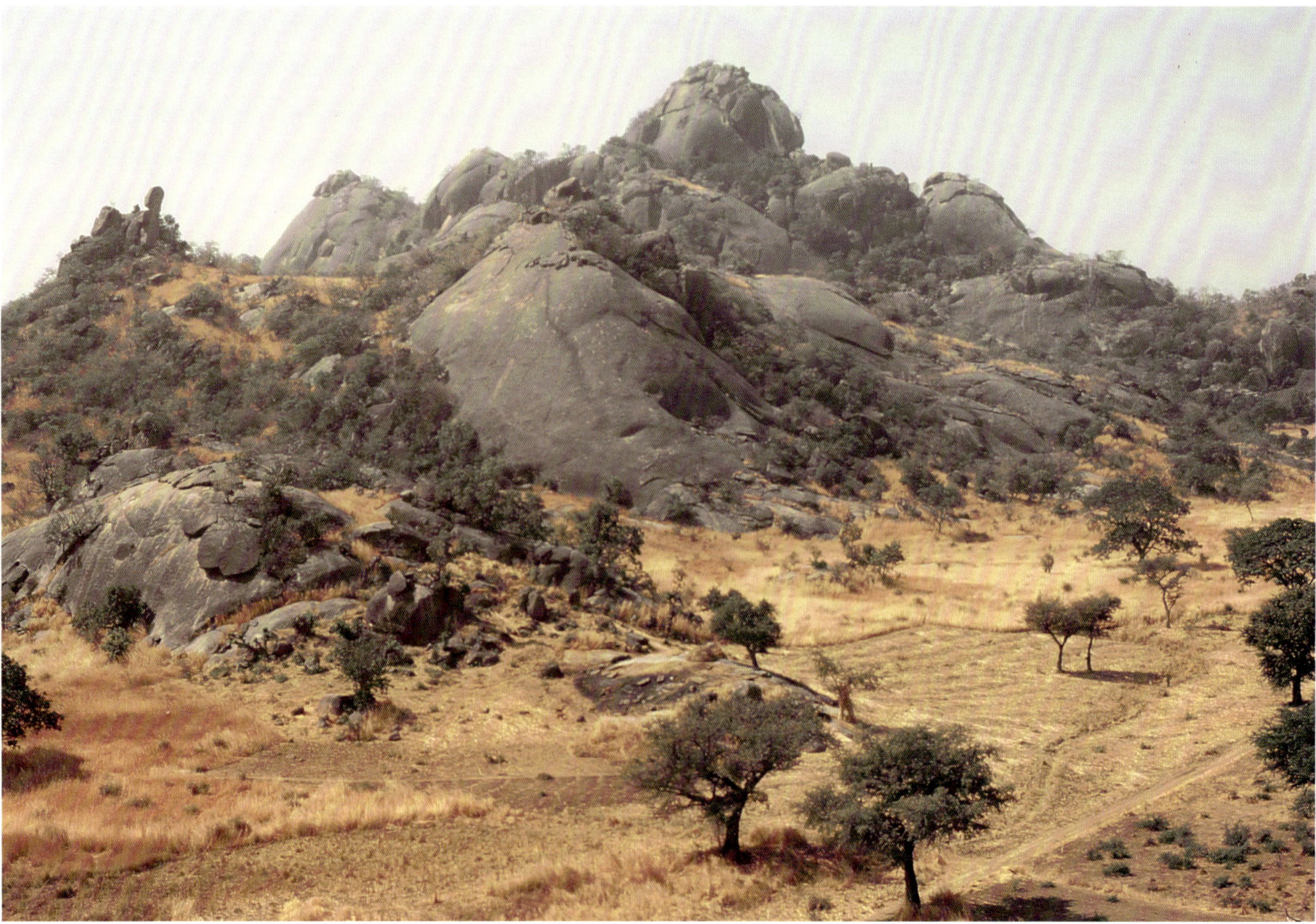

17.2

This view opens on Hurchetera—the dramatic granite hills in the Ga'anda district of Gabun—where the family of the same name once lived.
PHOTOGRAPH BY MARLA C. BERNS, 1980.

'Bəna, and Yungur, which have been observed since the early twentieth century (see Meek 1931b, 2: chaps. 13, 14).

Historical source materials on Ga'anda Hill groups from the precolonial period are minimal. Accounts begin with reports of Fulani attacks on the "Lala tribes" by Modibbo Adama from his base of operations in the town of Song (Kirk-Greene 1969, 132). The nickname "Lala" was evidently coined by the Fulani for the so-called "pagan" groups inhabiting the region. Colonial officer G. W. Webster explained that the word meant "naked" or "an old calabash broken into many parts," referring derogatorily to the scattered and "unclothed" populations living in this hilly, inaccessible region.[3] Records show that Adama (after whom the Adamawa Emirate and ultimately Adamawa State were named) "made little impression and once suffered defeat with a considerable loss in men and cattle" (Kirk-Greene 1969, 132). The Ga'anda, in particular, note their resistance to Fulani attempts at subjugation, recounting specifically the defeat in 1899 of Adama's successor, Zubeiru, whose slave-raiding zeal was legendary.[4] Military success contributed in part to the reputation of the Ga'anda across the region, augmenting their considerable authority as rainmakers—with power vested especially in the rain priest situated in the sacred precinct at Makwar Mountain. Even though the British ruled through the Fulani during the colonial era, Ga'anda Hills groups sustained a strong degree of politico-religious autonomy and maintained long-held traditional practices until at least the late 1980s.[5]

Characteristic of the Ga'anda, 'Bəna, and Yungur was the use of ceramic vessels to focus, contain, or facilitate contact with ancestral and tutelary spirits. Like their Adamawa-speaking relatives across the Gongola River to the west, each of these groups also incorporated vessels in rituals oriented toward healing diseases. Extensive fieldwork allowed for the documentation of pottery shrines belonging to many families and communities, resulting in a large corpus of examples and the ability to map their

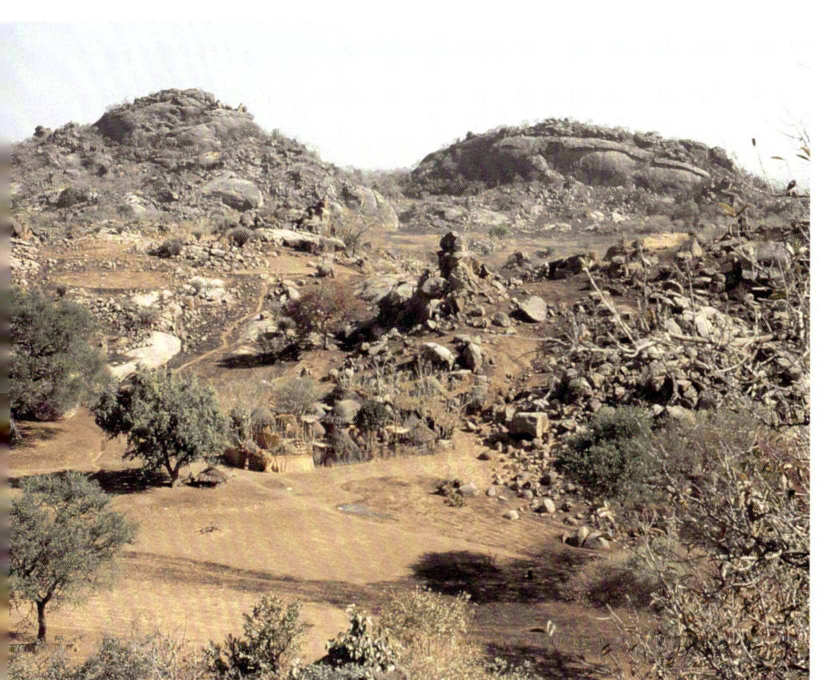

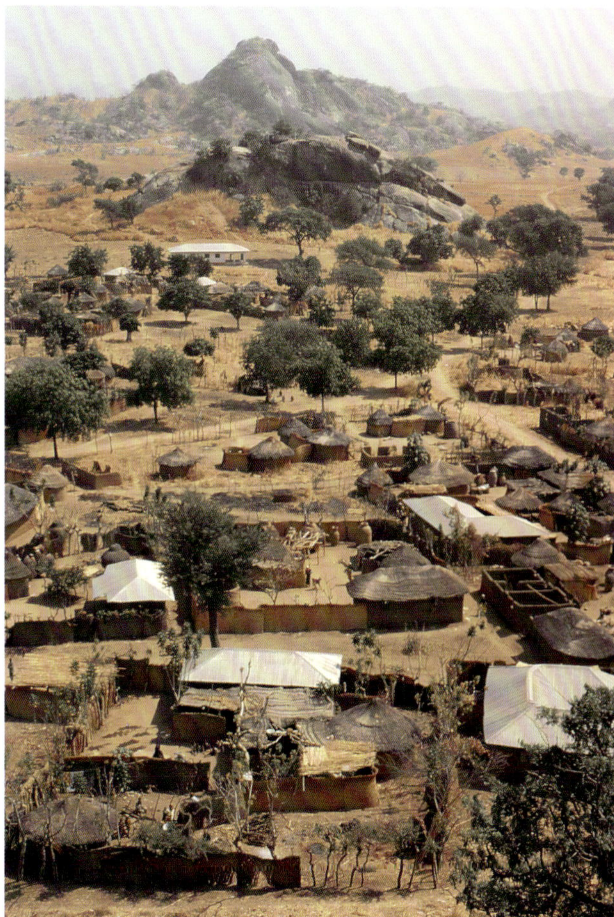

distributions and interpret the ways in which they unmask the dynamics of local history. Evidence from visual culture supported the degree and extent of intergroup relationships that language alone could not reveal.[6]

My most intensive research in the eastern Gongola Valley was conducted among the Ga'anda, who are dispersed over approximately 250 square kilometers. Since colonial reorganization, they have lived in more centralized villages and towns in the plains, as opposed to the hilly outposts where they previously dwelled and where family shrines were still extant in the 1980s (fig. 17.4).[7] Ga'anda Town is the administrative center with other large communities to the southwest around the town of Boga, to the northwest in Gabun, and to the west around Dingai, where Ga'anda hamlets are closely interspersed with those of the 'Bəna. All of these locations are near granite hills and outcroppings where families previously lived. These remote hill sites continued to house most pottery shrines, which were not moved, and ritual leaders made pilgrimages to them for the purpose of transacting annual religious activities. The state of repair of the shrines varied considerably from site to site, but in general most lacked the enclosures that once fully protected their contents from view and from harm (see fig. 17.7).

My research from 1980 to 1982 showed that a significant portion of the Ga'anda population continued to maintain what could be called a "traditional" way of life and set of beliefs despite the presence of the Lutheran Church of Christ, Nigeria, and a Muslim mosque. The requirement that girls undergo the permanent alteration of their bodies through an elaborate sequence of cicatrization in order to qualify for marriage had been outlawed in 1978 by the local government authority even though most women still displayed the subtle raised patterns that proclaimed their identity and socialization (see fig. 17.33).[8] Marriage also involved ritual negotiations with protective spirit forces, which sanctioned such alliances and promoted the future fertility of women. Such tutelary spirits still governed the health and prosperity of Ga'anda communities and

17.3
Makwar Hill, the most important Ga'anda ritual precinct is situated in the distance at the far right in this view of the rocky terrain surrounding Ga'anda Town.
PHOTOGRAPH BY MARLA C. BERNS, 1980.

17.4
The rocky outcropping of Hurgabun appears in the middle distance and the hills of Hurchetera beyond in this view of Gabun. In 1980, the town of Gabun was a mixture of traditional compounds with round mud structures, joined by woven-grass walls, and newer rectangular mud-brick houses roofed in corrugated metal. The rectangular building painted white in the distance was the local school.
PHOTOGRAPH BY MARLA C. BERNS, 1980.

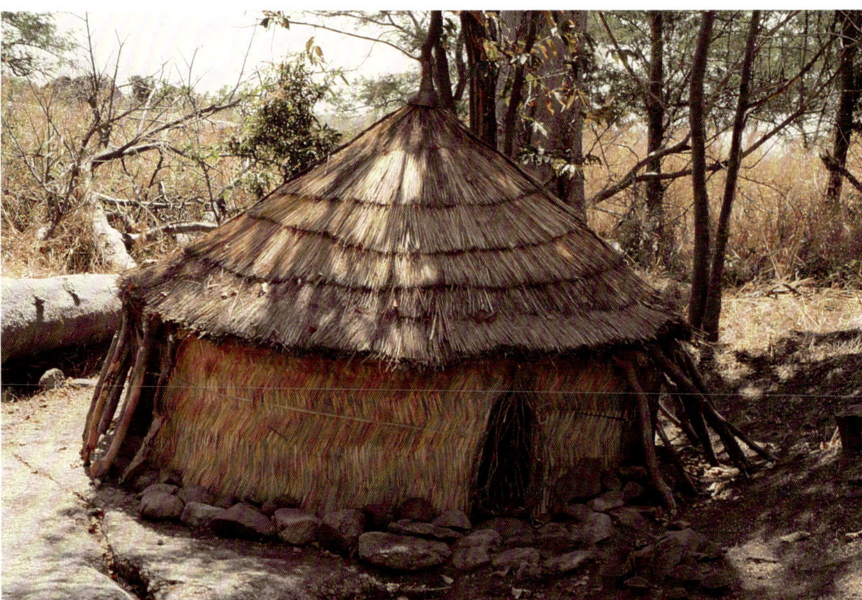

17.5

This structure for housing Ga'anda sacred vessels (*kətənbucha*) is located in the ritual precinct at Makwar Hill. New woven-grass walls had been added in November 1980 in preparation for the annual Ho'mbata harvest festival. This particular shrine was still being maintained in 2010 and was considered the most important repository of protective spirit vessels in the Ga'anda region.

PHOTOGRAPH BY MARLA C. BERNS, 1980.

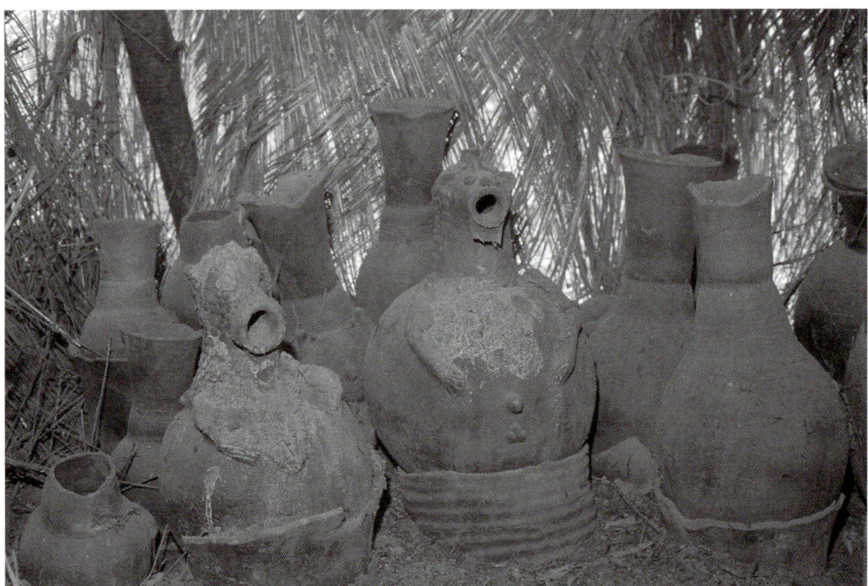

17.6

Inside the *kətənbucha* kept by the Ga'anda living in the hamlet of Kwanda near Dingai, two Mbir'thleng'nda are surrounded by *sambarcha* vessels, each containing the spirit of an ancestor. The chipped and beer-splashed surfaces of the Mbir'thleng'nda testify to their long history of use.

PHOTOGRAPH BY MARLA C. BERNS, 1981.

were propitiated annually by priests whose lineages had long maintained dominance in religious affairs. It is in the context of such activities that the Ga'anda example provides especially cogent information about the production and use of ceramic vessels, since changes to these ritual procedures had been relatively recent and modest in the early 1980s (though conversions to Christianity and Islam continued to increase). A full explication of Ga'anda ceramic arts and their meanings is not possible within the scope of this essay, and the text that follows will emphasize the two spirit beings the Ga'anda consider the most significant and accessible via their ceramic representations—Mbir'thleng'nda and Ngum-Ngumi.

The Ga'anda recognize the supreme spiritual authority of Farta, creator of the earth, sky, and all living things (Hammandikko and Berns 1980, 8). Farta is never worshipped or approached directly; instead, this remote and omnipotent force is contacted by means of a pantheon of lesser spirit intermediaries.[9] Because these lesser spirits are considered accessible to people and capable of being influenced, ritual priests, known as Kuturcha (sing.: Kutira), enlist their positive intervention through prescribed procedures and ceremonies. Of all the Kuturcha, the Ga'anda priest from the Gudban family holds the highest position of religious authority, his rank based on control of 'Yera, the

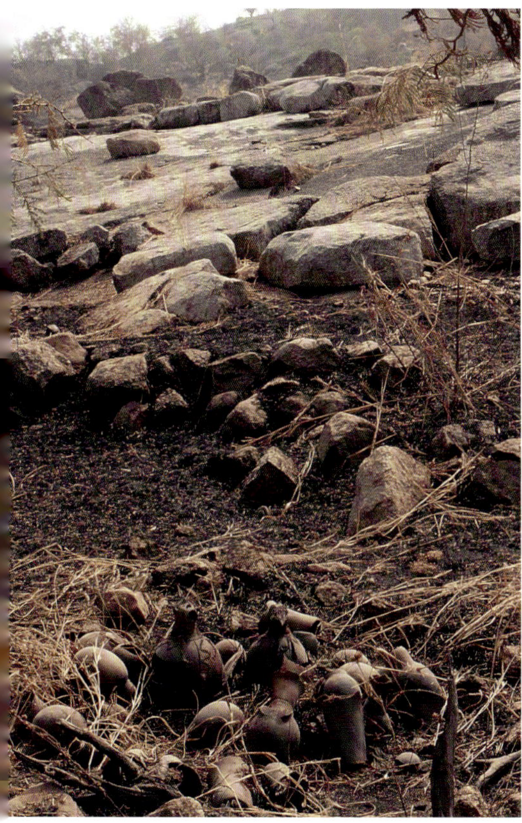
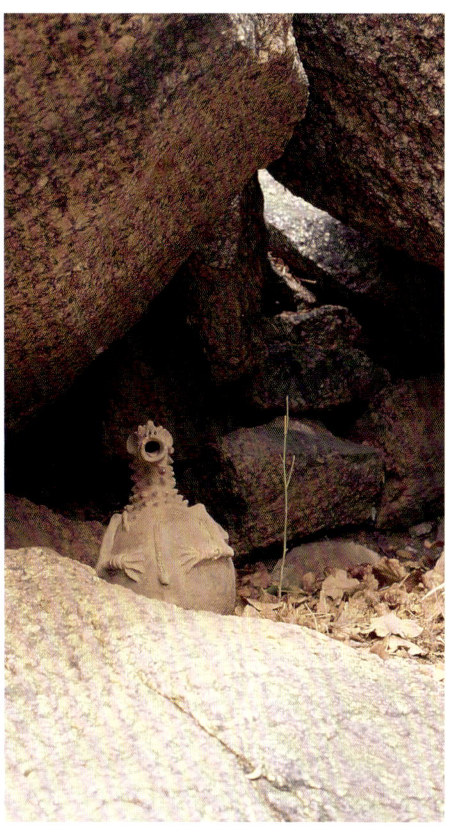
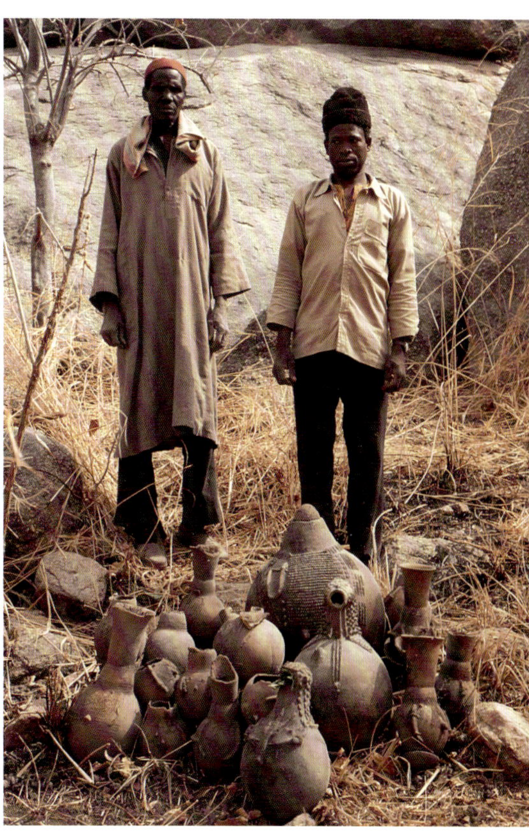

spirit force associated with rainfall. The rain priest's reputation and religious authority extended as far west as the Dera chiefdom of Shani, located on the Gongola River.[10]

The Gudban Kutira oversees the most important Ga'anda religious precinct at Makwar, called *hurdəfta* (wooded grove), where rainmaking and other regular propitiatory activities take place. The ceramic vessels that objectify Ga'anda tutelary spirits (and agents of Farta) are kept in *kətənbucha* (houses for pots) erected within the sacred grove (fig. 17.5). The Gudban *hurdəfta* is not the only such sacred site, and most individual hamlets maintain *kətənbucha*, where rituals are enacted and where most of the same tutelary spirits are enshrined. The distribution of shrine enclosures mirrors the dispersed settlement of the Ga'anda across the hilly terrain. This is because the physical proximity of these shrines to the communities they are entreated to protect is critical to their efficacy. Everywhere, the year begins and ends with Ho'mbata, the harvest festival of thanksgiving held in November when all the tutelary forces enshrined in *hurdəfta* precincts or *kətənbucha* shrines are thanked for their past favors and asked to renew their support (see below).

The *kətənbucha* documented across the Ga'anda region invariably consist of at least one vessel named Mbir'thleng'nda (see fig. 17.1), which is surrounded by a number of long-necked containers for ancestral spirits (fig. 17.6), called *sambarcha* (sing.: *shembera*) or *thləf'ncha* (sing.: *thləf'nda*). Mbir'thleng'nda is regarded as the most influential and approachable manifestation of Farta and the spirit best able to protect and sustain the health and prosperity of the Ga'anda. The preeminent religious authority and accessibility of Mbir'thleng'nda are objectified by the vessel's central placement, directly facing the entrance to a shrine (see figs. 17.6, 17.14b). By 1980 most such shrines had been left to deteriorate in their remote locations, exposed to the damage caused by transhumant Fulani herders and brush fires (fig. 17.7). Even when left unprotected by shrine enclosures, however, most such vessel accumulations retained their strict structural configuration with Mbir'thleng'nda occupying the central position. Other Mbir'thleng'nda pots had been rescued and relocated to rock clefts overlooking households below or adjacent (fig. 17.8), and some were even placed under family granaries for protection.

17.7
The abandoned *kətənbucha* of the Kapurta hamlet of Boga is situated in rocky hills and is some distance from the more accessible location to which the Kapurta moved circa 1970. In the foreground, the vestiges of the circular shrine are just visible surrounding the overturned and mostly broken *sambarcha* and two Mbir'thleng'nda. When Ga'anda families relocated, they did not take their sacred vessels with them, choosing instead to leave them in historic sites such as this one.
PHOTOGRAPH BY MARLA C. BERNS, 1980.

17.8
A Ga'anda Mbir'thleng'nda is situated high in the shelter of a rocky outcropping overlooking the hamlet of Chijera.
PHOTOGRAPH BY MARLA C. BERNS, 1981.

17.9
The contents of the *kətənbucha* maintained by the Pumta family of Pitel hamlet, Ga'anda/Dingai, are displayed before the two shrine custodians. Two Mbir'thleng'nda are at the center of the vessel accumulation with a Ngum-Ngumi (called Yinifarihi by this Dingai subgroup) behind. Surrounding these vessels are *sambarcha* and a larger *lekleke* at the far left.
PHOTOGRAPH BY MARLA C. BERNS, 1980.

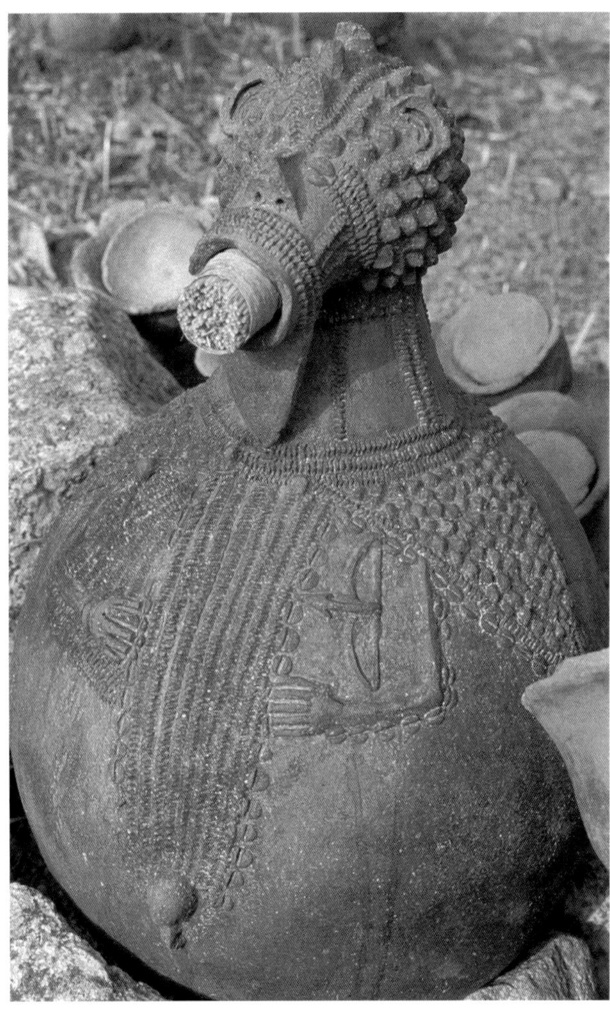

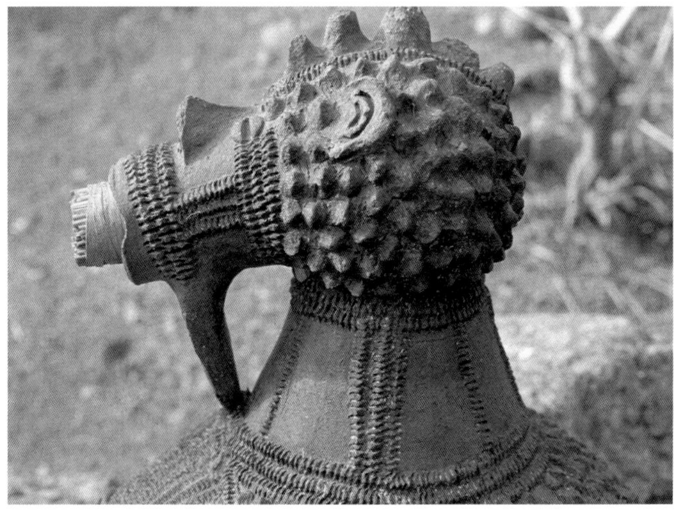

17.10
This Mbir'thleng'nda was kept in the *kətənbucha* within the *hurdəfta* precinct on Makwar Hill. The decoration of the surface is very finely executed, and the anatomical and iconographical details are modeled with precision. The bundle of straw in the mouth of the figure is meant to contain its own power and to prevent other uninvited and potentially negative forces from entering. No longer enshrined at Makwar and most likely stolen, this vessel has been replaced with another example that is much less finely modeled.
PHOTOGRAPH BY MARLA C. BERNS, 1980.

17.11
A detail of the head of figure 17.10 emphasizes the carefully executed raised decoration, as well as the coiffure of hair tufts along the crest of the head (*topro*), a style worn by initiated men.

I collected many stories about Mbir'thleng'nda's dual nature—the power of the spirit to have both a positive and negative impact on the destiny of Ga'anda individuals and communities. As David et al. (1988, 372) have cogently argued, the power associated with such cosmic forces is ambivalent—it is neither good nor bad in itself but always inherently dangerous. In recognition of this unpredictability, culture has provided mechanisms for the control and manipulation of such forces for positive ends. In the case of Mbir'thleng'nda, the spirit's ubiquity in shrines, where there are sometimes multiple representations present (fig. 17.9; see also Berns 1989, fig. 15), underscores the likelihood that the Ga'anda regard it as powerful insurance against the forces threatening survival. Furthermore, they used the iconography of Mbir'thleng'nda vessels to convey information about the spirit's meanings, roles, and potentiality to act.

I mapped over fifty-two Mbir'thleng'nda vessels across the Ga'anda region, and the deity's ceramic identity can be immediately distinguished within the corpus of sacred and ritual wares. The vessels range widely in size (H: 20–75 cm) and in detail, with no two being identical. Nearly all, however, have the same kind of profile and approach to surface decoration dominated by two diagnostic features: a round head with a projecting tubular "mouth" and appliqué pellets or nodes covering the head and neck, often extending to the shoulder in a triangular pattern (fig. 17.10). Mbir'thleng'nda's mouth serves as the vessel's spout and is aligned perpendicularly to the head, creating a striking cantilevered effect (fig. 17.11). A beard-like flange often joins the mouth to the pot's shoulder, a convention that may have originated to support the weight of the projecting mouth. Regardless of its functional necessity, the beard appears to maintain the integrity of the sculptural program and helps construct the male aspect of the spirit's identity.

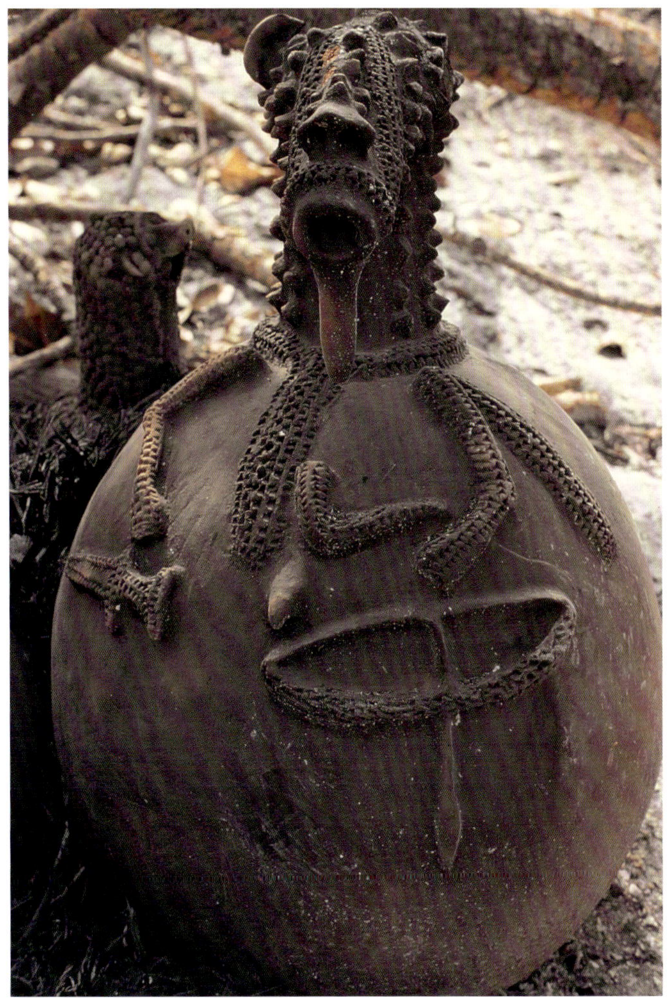

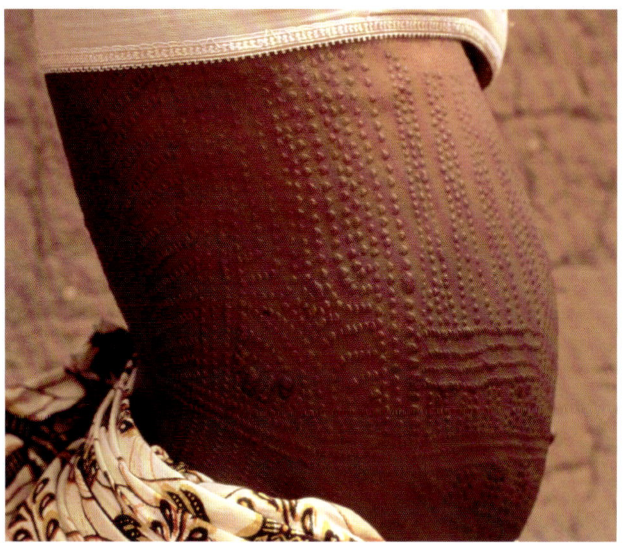

The deity's accessibility is made manifest through its essential human attributes. Mbir'thleng'nda has a face modeled on top of the projecting mouth, including coffee-bean eyes, a sharply keeled nose, and large cup- or disk-shaped ears modeled further back on the head. Mbir'thleng'nda always has arms and sometimes other anatomical features—nipples, a projecting umbilicus, and genitalia, usually male (fig. 17.10). His maleness is further indicated by a row of knobs along the sagittal plane of the head emulating the "comb," or hair tufts (*topro*), worn by men upon completing initiation (see fig. 17.11). Often tools, weapons, or other male attributes are modeled in relief, such as an ax over the right shoulder, a hoe over the left shoulder, a bow and arrow on the left side, or a dagger near the right hand (see figs. 17.10, 15.7). Sometimes these male tools are pronounced, amplifying the deity's male aspect, as seen in the Mbir'thleng'nda enshrined at Kwitpe (fig. 17.12). Most vessels, however, simultaneously have a female aspect, depicted through the raised decoration on the vessel's body, emulating in clay the pattern of cicatrices worked on a woman's torso as part of the elaborate program of Ga'anda body modification, called Thleta, which all girls must undergo before they can marry (cf. fig.17.10 and fig. 17.13). The decoration of Mbir'thleng'nda vessels thus refers to key male and female aspects of the Ga'anda social order, defining the spirit's power and authority in the same human terms—terms that signal conformity to and control over social roles and expectations.

Perhaps the most striking human capacity referenced in these vessels is the ability to modify and transform the skin's surface purposefully and permanently in order to communicate social messages and life passages. Likewise, other changes to human skin can be dramatic visual markers of temporary imbalance or disease, and through the rendering of Mbir'thleng'nda's "skin," the Ga'anda can project a similar mutability

17.12
This striking Mbir'thleng'nda enshrined by the Kwitpe family in the Kwanda hamlet of Ga'anda/Dingai is covered with iconographic emblems of the deity's male aspect. These include bow, arrow, quiver, smoking pipe, and dagger. This example is relatively large at 74 centimeters in height.
PHOTOGRAPH BY MARLA C. BERNS, 1980.

17.13
The cicatrization incisions on the torso of a 'Bəna woman heal as a pattern of raised bumps that are similar to the texture worked on the surfaces of Mbir'thleng'nda vessels. The same texture is present on the skin of Ga'anda women who have undergone scarification.
PHOTOGRAPH BY MARLA C. BERNS, RIJI, 1981.

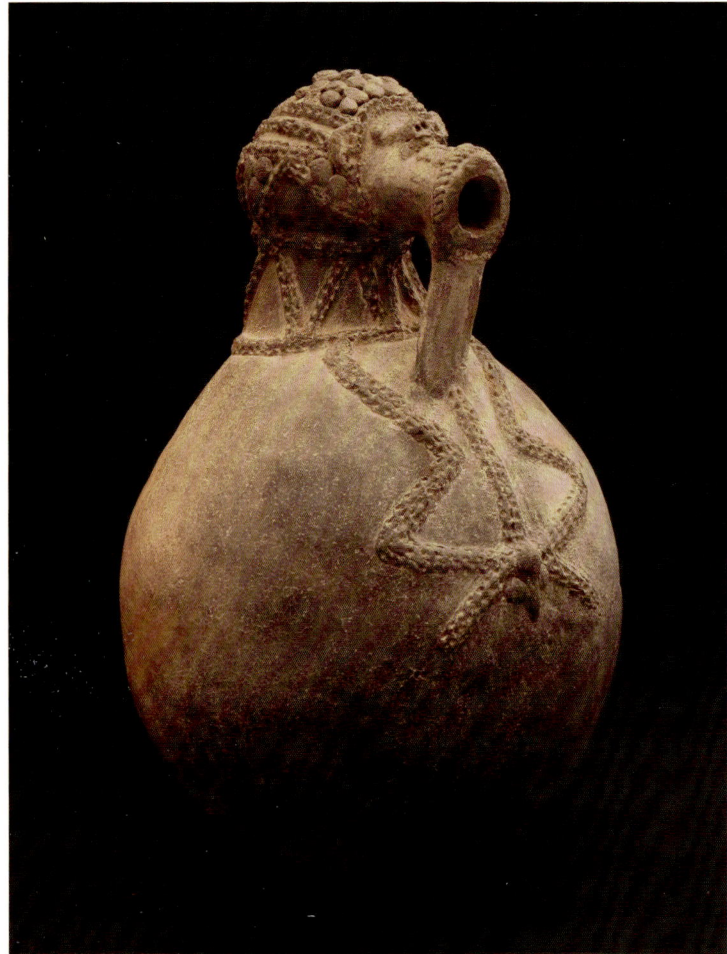

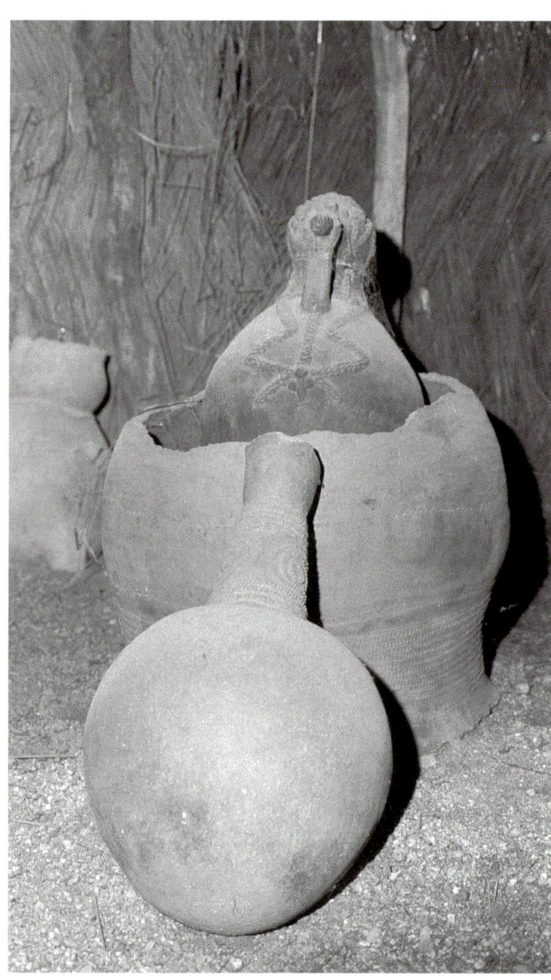

17.14a
Spirit vessel (Mbir'thleng'nda)
Ga'anda peoples, Gabun, Hurgabun family,
before 1980
Ceramic
H: 38 cm
FOWLER MUSEUM AT UCLA X2008.32.1; MUSEUM
PURCHASE
IMAGE: © 2010 FOWLER MUSEUM AT UCLA.
PHOTOGRAPH BY DON COLE
PROVENANCE: HAMIDOU MONTOUODORE KPOUMIE,
CAMEROON; AMYAS NAEGELE, NEW YORK, 2001;
MARSHALL MOUNT, NEW JERSEY; AMYAS NAEGELE
COLLECTION, NEW YORK, 2005

This Mbir'thleng'nda is unusual for its wavy
"arms," surrounding the raised central ridge of
"scarifications" (njoxtimeta), as well as for the
absence of any applied iconographic elements.
It exemplifies the variability of the deity's
representation, which is likely due to the idiosyncratic approach of the artist who made it.

17.14b
The small Mbir'thleng'nda in figure 17.14a was
formerly enshrined in the kətənbucha of the
Hurgabun family in Gabun. Elders who showed
me the shrine in 1980 said that Mbir'thleng'nda
would warn the Hurgabun chief if anything
bad was to happen and when someone died.
Elevated in a large, broken, and overturned
storage vessel, it squarely faces the entrance of
the shrine. Leaning against the storage vessel is
the ceramic culture hero, Ngum-Ngumi.
PHOTOGRAPH BY MARLA C. BERNS, 1981.

onto the spirit's own personality. The elaborate decoration of Mbir'thleng'nda with
appliqué pellets, nodes, or spikes, as well as patterns of impressed ridges, is often the
vessel's most striking physical aspect (see 17.1). Such excrescences are a common convention for distinguishing ritual from utilitarian wares or in this case for marking
a vessel as a repository for something powerful and potentially dangerous.[11]

What can we read in the pattern of raised decoration on Mbir'thleng'nda's head
and neck? The bumpy texture may be the sculptural equivalent to the rows of raised
"dots" resulting from cicatrization incisions (see fig. 17.13). Despite this textural
verisimilitude, however, their concentrated application over the head and neck suggests they may be communicating something else. The application of rounds of clay
may have a literal meaning since the deity is known to inflict certain skin diseases as
punishment for disobeying its maxims. The Ga'anda claim, for example, that visible
changes in the skin mean a person was "touched" by Mbir'thleng'nda. Ringworm, for
one, is characterized by the formation of ring-shaped discolored patches covered with
scales or small raised blisters. More lethal is smallpox with its raised round pustules,
which leave depressed depigmented scars in its survivors. Although specific data
about the Ga'anda Hills region is not available, it is known that smallpox epidemics
swept through areas of Northern Nigeria decimating populations. Thus, on the one
hand, the raised nodes on Mbir'thleng'nda may objectify the kinds of diseases the
spirit could inflict on social offenders and remind those who served the deity of its
conditional tutelage. On the other hand appeals could be made for Mbir'thleng'nda's
protection against the devastation of the very same debilitating diseases with their
prominent visual traces.

The pattern of nodules on the vessels is particularly characteristic, because it is
almost always framed at the shoulder by a raised zigzag border (see figs. 17.15a,b, 17.1).

This geometric shape and its repetition may refer to the distinctive cast-brass pendants (*tiltil*) lashed onto a strip of reddened goatskin that are worn by girls across the chest when they celebrate the completion of Thleta scarifications (see Berns 1988, 65). The mud frieze that distinguishes a new bride's compound also takes the form of a row of triangles. The consistent use of triangles or lozenges to signal physical and social transformations suggests that their incorporation on Mbir'thleng'nda symbolizes the spirit's commitment to supporting the Ga'anda social order. Most Mbir'thleng'nda vessels have several vertical rows of "inscriptions" down the center of their torsos, which may reproduce another key Thleta design element called *njoxtimeta* (see figs. 17.10, 17.15a). The raised ridges of clay, extending from the neck to the navel, are inscribed with closely placed incisions made with a stalk or a gourd fragment. This emulates the central column of cicatrices on a young girl, which can remain visible for years until her family can marshal sufficient resources to complete the final stage of Thleta (see Berns 1988, 74). This same vertical column is prominently worked on other Ga'anda spirit pots, which are likewise scarified to reveal their humanity and their enculturation. It is clear that just as people have the unique ability to permanently transform the surface of their skin to signify shifts in identity, spirits draw upon these paradigms as well in order to define their roles and capacities.

Mbir'thleng'nda's most prominent identity is shaped by such references to its human aspects. The vessel's ceramic details allude to the various guises the deity is known to assume—a male elder (with a beard), a brave warrior (with weapons), or a young girl (with scarifications). Such avatars of Mbir'thleng'nda appear in dreams, and diviners or ritual specialists are called upon to interpret their mostly inauspicious messages.[12] By this means, the power of Mbir'thleng'nda becomes even more credible, and specialists have used the potentiality of a "tangible" presence as a formidable device for social control. In fact, the spirit is even credited with a protean capacity to manifest in forms other than a pot. In keeping with Mbir'thleng'nda's dual nature, the deity's intervention in human guise has been used to explain certain extraordinary events in Ga'anda history, among them the resounding defeat of the Fulani in 1899, as reported by Hammandikko:

> The spiritual force associated with Mbir'thleng'nda responded to every misfortune that occurred in the Ga'anda region. But only the chief and his four assistants knew the secret force of Mbir'thleng'nda. For example, when the Fulani threatened to invade the Ga'anda area in their search for slaves, the Chief, Timshani, was concerned because he didn't have time to warn his people, who were working on their farms. When the Fulani were in sight, Mbir'thleng'nda split into three sections, each of which became a "person," and the three people moved toward a hill called Kwanda, the direction from which the Fulani were approaching. While the Fulani were surveying the landscape, they detected the three "people" gathered together one mile away and decided they were in a position to capture them as slaves. In the meantime, people from all the surrounding villages responded to the call of Timshani and gathered at a village north of Ga'anda Town called Barni, where a group of Roba lived. Mbir'thleng'nda's intention was to divert the Fulani so that the Ga'anda could prepare themselves to overtake the Fulani by surprise. Once the Ga'anda were in control, the three "people" became one and resumed their form as Mbir'thleng'nda.[13] [Hammandikko and Berns 1980, 5–6]

In Ga'anda memory, this momentous victory was due to the shrewdness of Chief Timshani and his capacity to activate Mbir'thleng'nda's assistance and capacity to transform into not one but three "people." By crediting the deity in this way, the Ga'anda have strengthened their conviction that the spirit acts as their primary champion. Mbir'thleng'nda's power has also been enlisted to protect against crises, such as epidemics (as previously noted) or whirlwinds and other natural threats caused by other spirits or forces as punishment for social deviance. Figure 17.15a was said to insulate the people of the Hurwire hamlet (Finguela family) living near the village of Chohita against the devastation of Shuuta, the force that "disciplines evil people" and "moves across the sky like a whirlwind," unleashing powerful winds and laying waste to whatever lies in its path (see Hammandikko and Berns 1980, 9). The placement of the Mbir'thleng'nda vessel in a rock cleft (fig. 17.15b) not only gave the spirit a vantage point but also protected it from harm. Seeing it so situated also served to warn the unauthorized of potential danger. Although the vessel was photographed in situ by Rubin in 1970 and again by me in 1980, its remote location did not ultimately protect it from being removed and exported from Nigeria and entering the Barbier Mueller collection in 2002, after having been purchased in Paris (see Berns 2008, 440–41).

The second spirit vessel frequently represented in Ga'anda *kɔtɔnbucha* is Ngum-Ngumi, the culture hero conceived of as a pot that, moving on its own volition, led the Ga'anda in their migration from the "east" (fig. 17.16 and see fig. 17.9).[14] This spirit pioneer "stopped" at the impressive isolated granite mountain called Makwar, signaling to the Ga'anda where to establish their first settlement. It was in the sacred grove of Makwar that the most powerful ritual precinct was created and Ngum-Ngumi was enshrined (see fig. 17.5). Ngum-Ngumi is replicated in various shrine contexts across the Ga'anda Hills, which would seem to be a way of legitimizing the dispersals and resettlements of Ga'anda families from Makwar. Unlike Mbir'thleng'nda, whose physical placement and imposing presence dominates most pottery shrines, Ngum-Ngumi can be striking in its absence and is often said to be hidden under boulders or buried in the ground with a coterie of spirit "brethren" serving as intermediaries—most of which are recognizable by virtue of shared iconographic elements. At the ritual precinct of Makwar, however, Ngum-Ngumi was never removed from the *kɔtɔnbucha* and was offered annual libations of beer through his ceramic surrogates (see fig. 17.29). In some Ga'anda locations, vessels that evidenced the same diagnostic motifs and meanings as Ngum-Ngumi were called by different names, such as Yinifarihi or Komalamne (fig. 17.17). All of them shared the historical distinction of having led their families to their present locations.

I photographed twenty-two Ngum-Ngumi vessels in shrines across the Ga'anda region. Two different ceramic representations of Ngum-Ngumi were documented: the first and rarer of the two, is a spherical pot with a long straight narrow neck decorated with circular motifs (see figs. 17.14b, 17.16); and the second, is a large spherical vessel with a distinctive funnel-shaped mouth and a "body" covered with elaborate surface decoration and iconographic details (see figs. 17.9, 17.19). By conforming to a recognizable program of decoration, each Ga'anda community can acknowledge its historical debt to Ngum-Ngumi and provide a shared mechanism by which tribute can be offered to Makwar where Ngum-Ngumi first officially "stopped."

Like Mbir'thleng'nda, Ngum-Ngumi is humanized with arms, breasts, navel, and frequently male genitalia. Facial features, however, are never rendered on Ngum-Ngumi. Male tools and weapons, like those seen on Mbir'thleng'nda, are rendered on the left and right sides of the pot (figs. 17.18a,b). The number and arrangement of motifs varies from vessel to vessel, appearing both on Ngum-Ngumi and its surrogates, but the following elements are typically represented: (1) an ax (*wurta*) gripped in the right hand; (2) a bow (*riya*) and sometimes a quiver (*kwecheta*) modeled on the left side of the torso; (3) a dagger (*thluuta*) at the lower right side located approximately at waist level; and (4) brass bracelets (*shiding'nda*) worn on either arm. One motif informants could not identify, which was always included in Ngum-Ngumi iconography and sometimes reproduced more than once, is a small circle filled with a cluster of raised nodes (see figs. 17.18a,b). Because all of the other motifs depict tools or weapons, it is

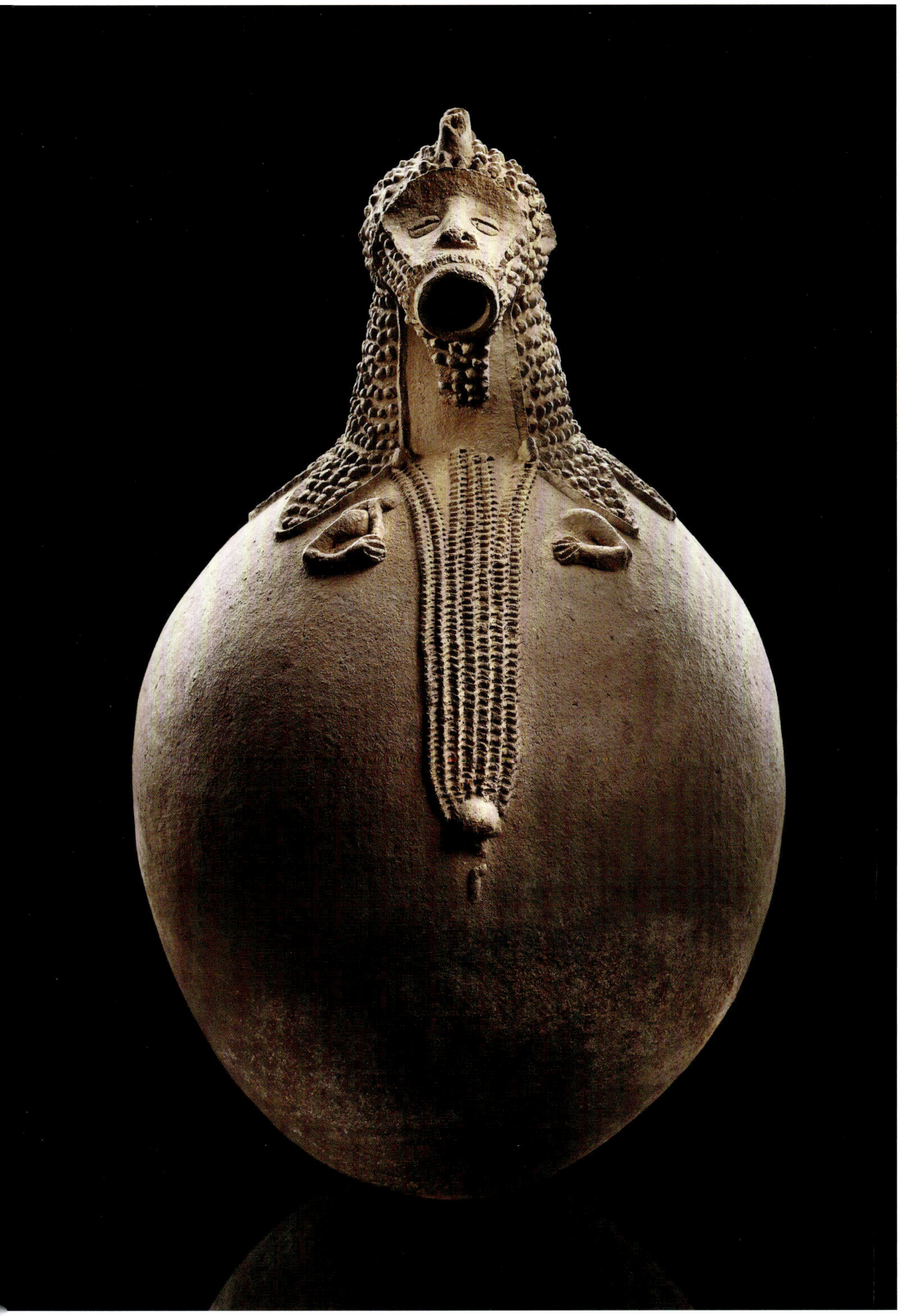

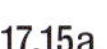

17.15a
Spirit vessel (Mbir'thleng'nda)
Ga'anda peoples, Dingai, Chohita village,
Hurwire hamlet, Finguela family, before 1970
Ceramic
H: 60 cm
BARBIER-MUELLER MUSEUM, GENEVA, 1015-160
IMAGE: COURTESY BARBIER-MUELLER MUSEUM,
GENEVA. PHOTOGRAPH © STUDIO FERRAZZINI
BOUCHET
PROVENANCE: GALERIE L'ACCROSONGE, PARIS, 2002

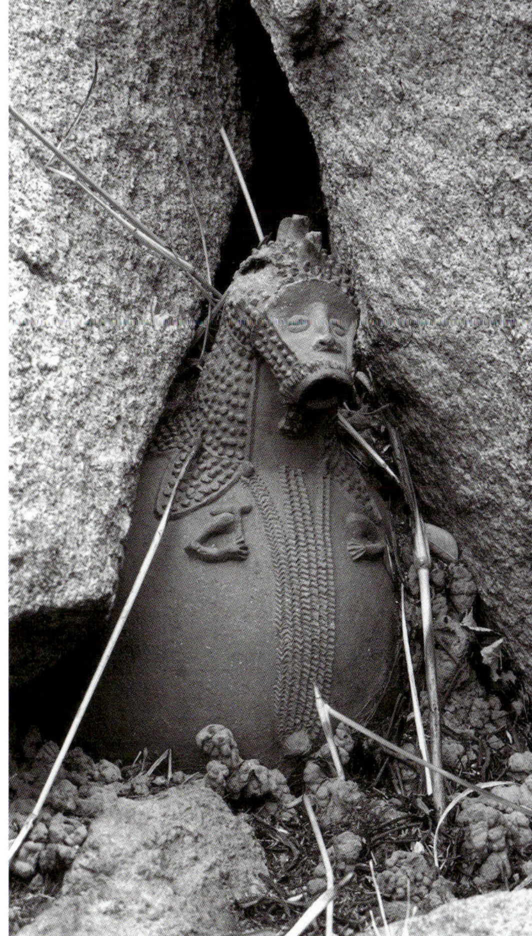

17.15b
The Mbir'thleng'nda in figure 17.15a was
photographed in situ above the hamlet of
Hurwire by Arnold Rubin in March 1970.
The same vessel was still situated within this
rock cleft in 1980 when it was photographed
again by Berns.

PHOTOGRAPH BY ARNOLD RUBIN, 1970.

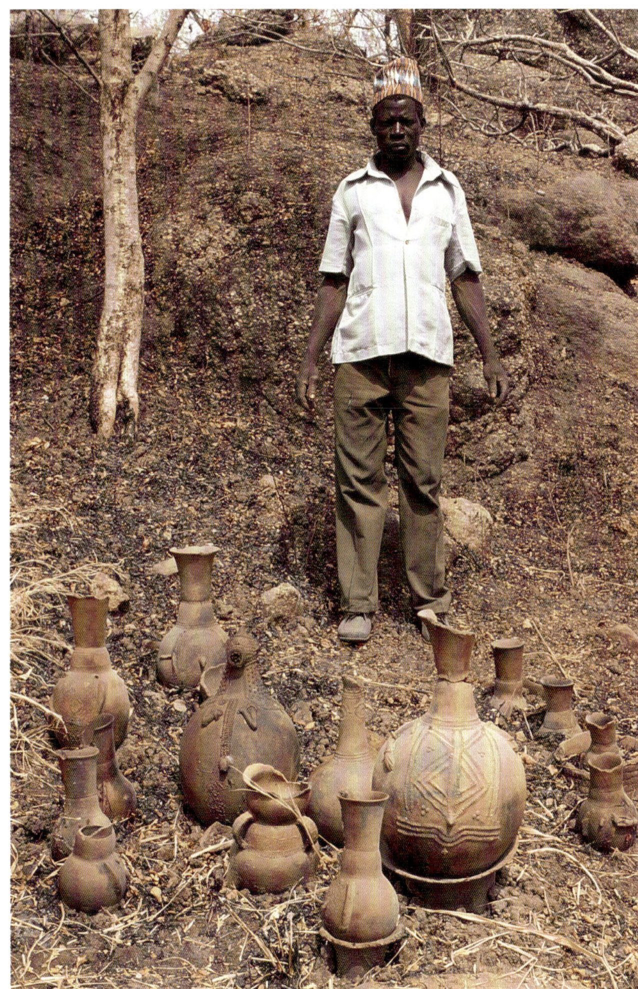

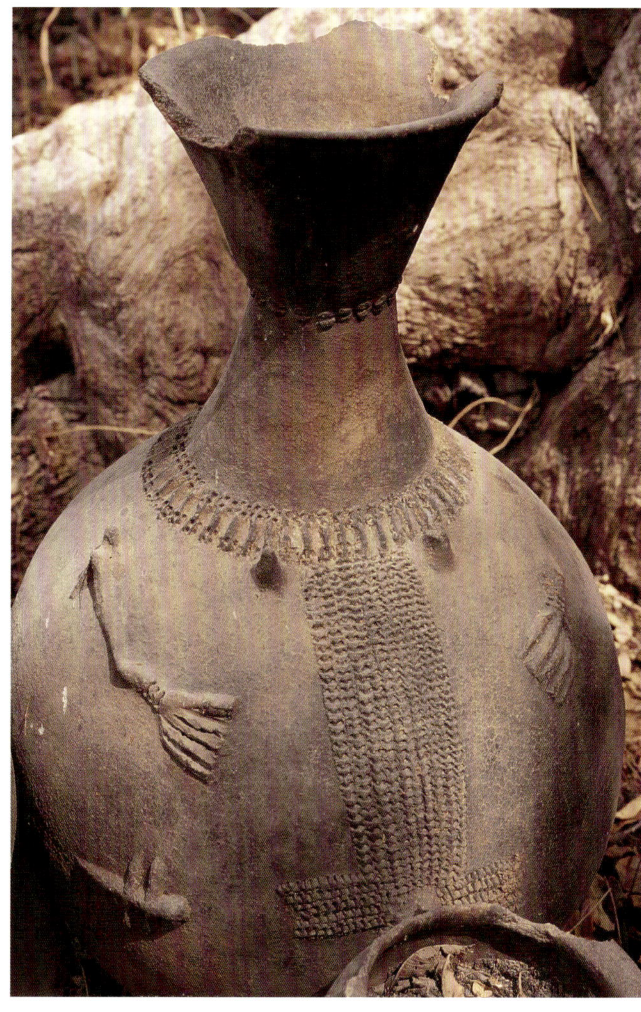

17.16
This abandoned *kətənbucha* belonged to the Darkəsar family of Pitel hamlet, Ga'anda/ Dingai. This accumulation of spirit vessels, located high in the hills above Pitel, retains its formation despite the absence of an enclosure. To the right of Mbir'thleng'nda is the long narrow-necked vessel representing Ngum-Ngumi with a large *lekleke* beer vessel to its right. They are surrounded by a circular formation of smaller *sambarcha* and larger *thləf'ncha*, which would have lined the perimeter of the shrine enclosure. The shrine's custodian stands behind the vessels.
PHOTOGRAPH BY MARLA C. BERNS, 1980.

17.17
Among the Ga'anda of Dingai, the culture hero Ngum-Ngumi is sometimes given the name Yinifarihi. This Yinifarihi vessel, enshrined by the Kandihata family of Chohita village, has the diagnostic "bib" of texture down the torso and other iconographic elements, such as the dagger on its right side.
PHOTOGRAPH BY MARLA C. BERNS, 1981.

logical to assume that this rather signature emblem would be thematically consistent. It may be a representation of a circular shield with the kind of embossed nodes that are typical of those made of thick hide seen elsewhere in the region (see fig. 16.24).[15] All of these features refer to social and economic responsibilities associated with the roles of Ga'anda men. On Ngum-Ngumi, these attributes enhance the spirit's capacity to protect and defend local Ga'anda communities in the same way.

On most examples, the dominant decorative element is a "bib" of raised and impressed ridges down the vessel's torso, a reference to Thleta, as also seen in depictions of Mbir'thleng'nda. In some examples, such as the Ngum-Ngumi vessel enshrined in Chohita (see fig. 17.15a), the raised ridges emulate the previously mentioned *njoxtimeta* motif also observed on many Mbir'thleng'nda. On most vessels, however, it is not the pattern of cicatrices that matter as much as the process used to achieve them. Ridges of clay are applied to the surface and then impressed with the edge of a broken piece of calabash in a method parallel to the way that human skin is lifted with a small hook and then cut across with a razor during cicatrization (fig. 17.19). Through its permanent "scarification," Ngum-Ngumi signals an irreversible association with the Ga'anda people. Allusions to Thleta do not necessarily identify Ngum-Ngumi as female, but they reveal that the spirit's responsibility to the Ga'anda requires changes in its "skin" that are the same as those undergone by girls to signify their commitment to perpetuating the social order.

Despite a certain degree of sculptural variation, the essential and diagnostic features of Ngum-Ngumi are the same everywhere the culture hero has "stopped" in the process of Ga'anda migrations and population dispersals. When I recently sent photographs of one example with especially clear iconography (see fig 17.18a,b) and

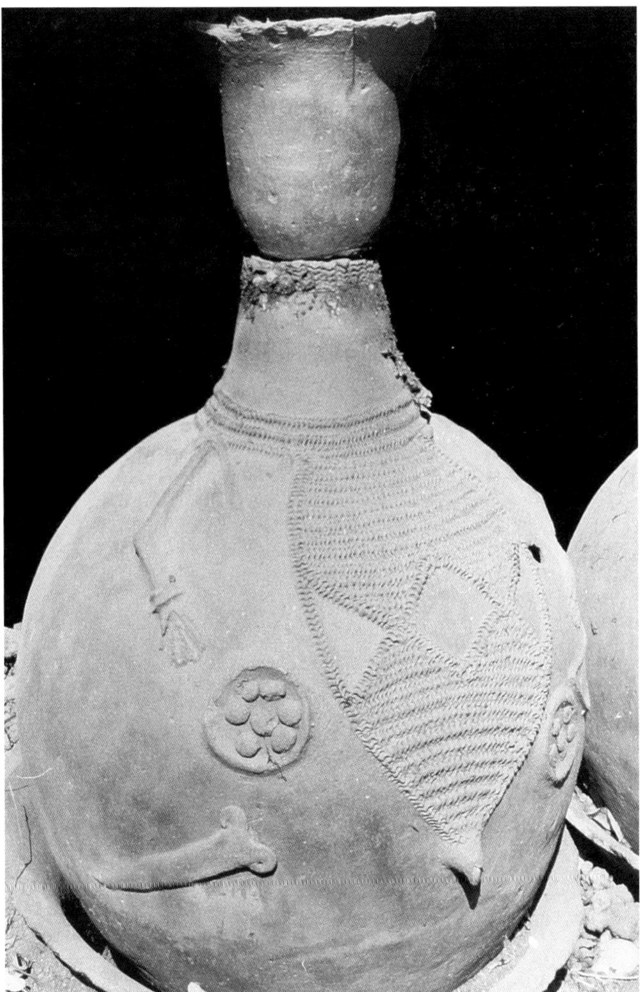 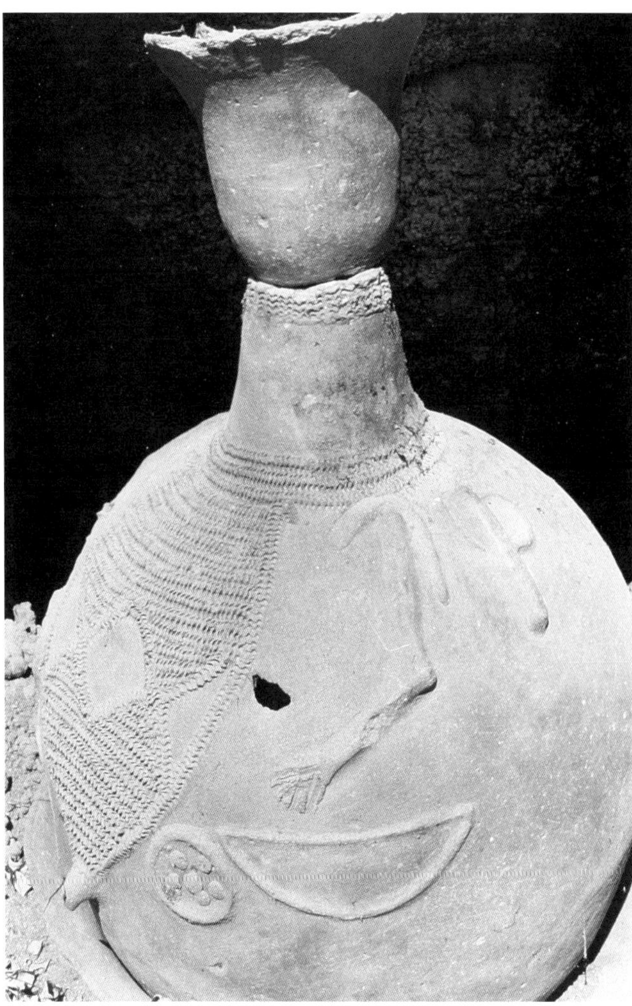

requested that Gudban elders in Ga'anda Town interpret the decorative elements again, they were still unable to explain the circular motif. They did confirm my explanation of the other more obvious weapons and tools, however, as well as identifying the texture running down the center of the "torso" as Thleta scarifications.[16] The most fascinating aspect of their response to the photographs, however, was their disbelief that a "Ngum-Ngumi" was located anywhere but the *hurdəfta* grove at Makwar since that is where it stopped, and it "was not supposed to move" (Benson Ali, personal communication, November 16, 2009). Even though the specific image I sent was of a vessel that functioned as an intermediary of Ngum-Ngumi—a *'butə'shita* (a vessel for holding the ritual beer offered to spirit pots and shared with custodians; see also p. 523)—I found it remarkable that these elders claimed to be unaware of additional replications of the renowned Ngum-Ngumi spirit pot at Makwar.

Of the corpus of twenty-two Ngum-Ngumi vessels that I documented in the field, by far the most numerous and elaborately decorated are the thirteen dispersed across the Boga Hills, especially those belonging to the Wetu family (fig. 17.20 and see fig. 17.19). The Wetu family examples typically have crisp corrugations defining a central "bib," often flanked on the left by three vertically aligned blocks of the same texture and on the right by one long vertical block as well as a ridge worked around the base of the neck. Four nodes often appear just to the right of the bib and on the left are three or more framing rows of what look to be "beaded" strands. These bibs are cut away at the bottom to leave room for a herniated navel and male genitalia. On several "Wetu" examples, three rather than one set of navels and male genitalia are depicted, obviously enhancing this masculine principle (see fig. 17.20). The numbers three and four have definite gender connotations in Ga'anda ritual life, with actions repeated

17.18a,b
This vessel served as an intermediary of Ngum-Ngumi and was enshrined at Tiyir'wira in the Tumbar hamlet of Ga'anda. On the vessel's left side (17.18b) are a large bow, quiver, hoe, and circle with inset "bumps," and on the right side (17.18a) are an ax, dagger, and circle with inset "bumps." The central torso has an elaborate pattern of raised and impressed ridges with large lozenges that refer to women's scarification motifs.
PHOTOGRAPHS BY MARLA C. BERNS, 1981.

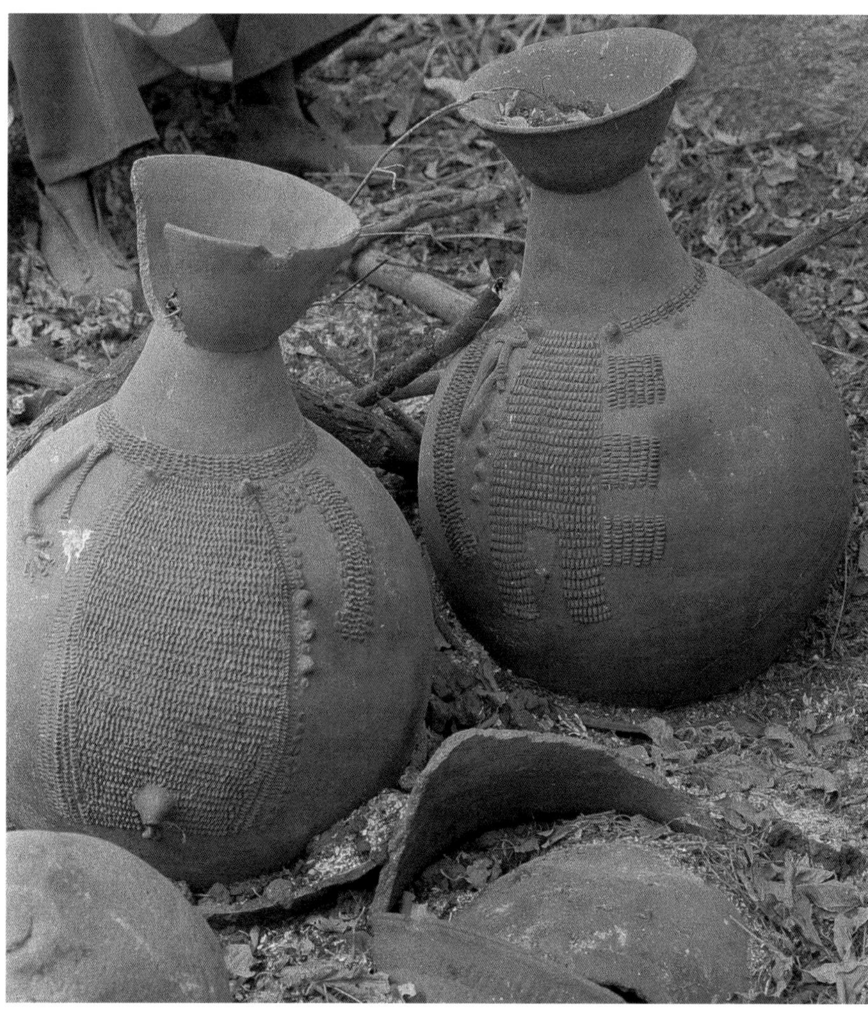

17.19
Two Ngum-Ngumi vessels were enshrined by the Wetu family of the Boga district. Their torsos reveal the crisp corrugations that emulate the texture of raised cicatrices on the skin of Ga'anda women.
PHOTOGRAPH BY MARLA C. BERNS, 1981.

three times for men and four times for women.[17] Even the curious alignment of three blocks of corrugations on the left side of Ngum-Ngumi may symbolically refer to the same male principle, while the four protruding nodes may be the female corollary.

Given the emphasis on male weapons reproduced on these vessels, another explanation can be proposed for the enigmatic composition of raised "waffle" decoration on the "Wetu" variants (see fig. 17.20). The contour of the central panel, as well as its highly regular and grid-like texture, may describe chain mail armor. Chain mail shirts, originally of sixteenth- or seventeenth-century Mameluke manufacture, were worn by Fulani and Kanuri cavalrymen (Bravmann 1983, 54). Examples of this armor still survive in museum collections, and illustrations show that the distinctive rectangular opening at the lower hem creates a broken contour closely resembling the main panel of Ngum-Ngumi corrugations (fig. 17.21a). On the chain mail the opening must have allowed for the shirt to hang free on either side of the saddle's pommel.[18] It may also be the regularity of ridge-riveted chain mail (fig. 17.21b) that inspired the laboriously worked grid across Ngum-Ngumi's torso. It is possible that such garments found their way to the Ga'anda through contact with the Fulani or other northern invaders. Rubin (1974, 168) documented two chain mail hauberks from the armory of the Emir of Biu and another fragment was recorded in Walama, a town about 45 kilometers west of Ga'anda.[19] The relative rarity and prestige value of these hauberks, as well as their association with skilled warriors and powerful foreign intruders, may have made them an appropriate martial attribute for Ngum-Ngumi, enhancing the deity's magical powers and potential to protect and defend the Ga'anda.

Yet another possibility is that Ngum-Ngumi's iconography depicts the way in which the body of a deceased male elder is publicly displayed in full martial panoply.

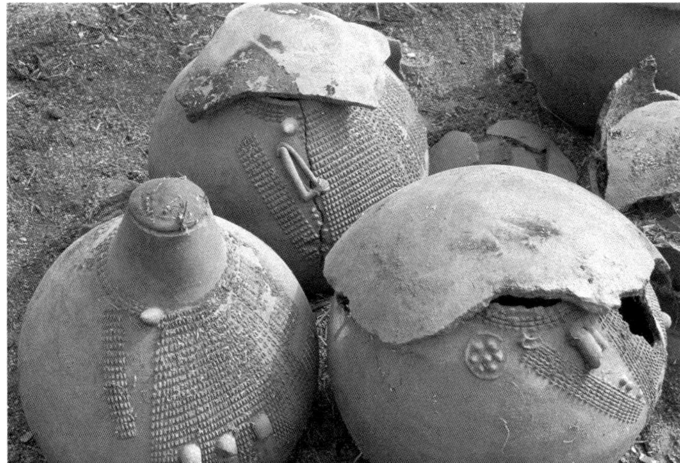

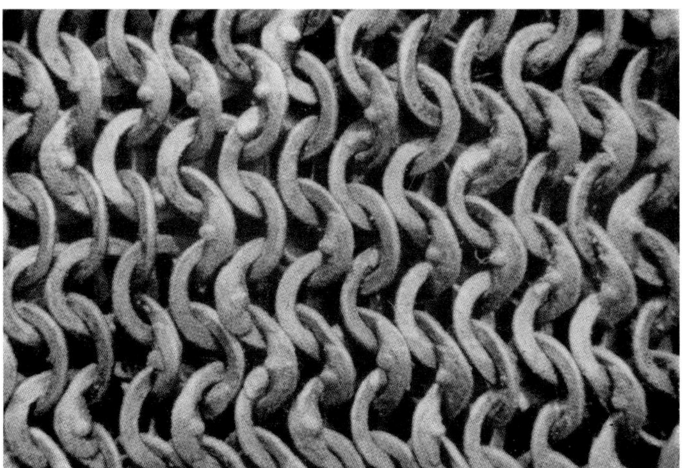

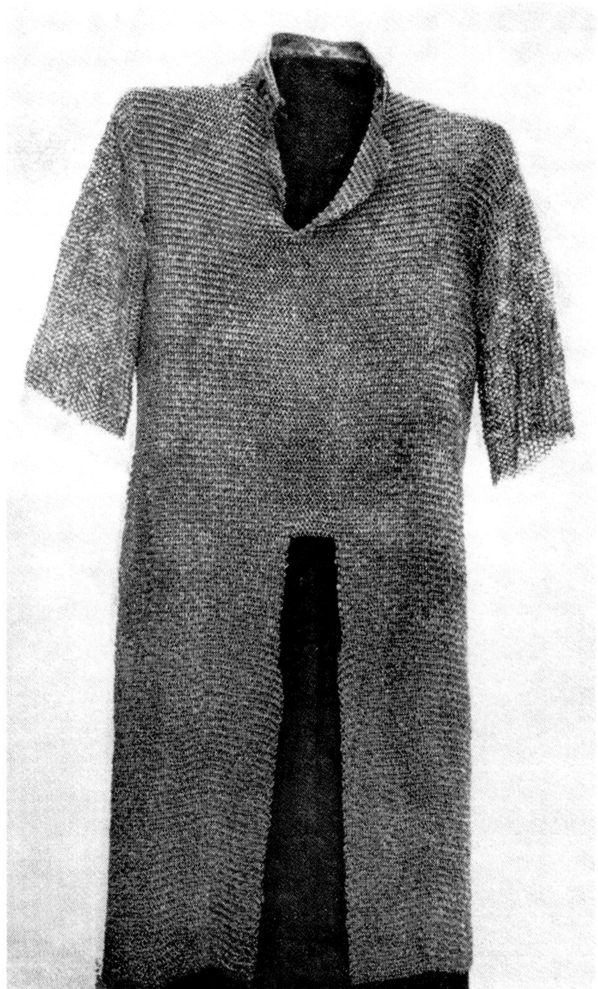

The deceased is positioned with an ax over the right shoulder, a quiver and bow over the left, and a dagger strapped around the waist. Even the inclusion of chain mail armor on this occasion would be thematically consistent. Given this context, the circular emblem depicted on Ngum-Ngumi might represent a gourd filled with grains of sorghum thrown on the corpse by his relatives (Meek 1931b, 2: 377). Of note, instead of the conventional dagger modeled on most Ngum-Ngumi vessels, some Wetu examples include a representation of the distinctive cast-brass *thluti kuturcha* (knife of chiefs) with its five humanoid heads, which was also displayed on the bodies of deceased chiefs at their funerals (figs. 17.22, 17.23).

The tools, ornaments, and insignia of rank displayed on Ngum-Ngumi align the spirit's authority and identity with that of living Ga'anda chiefs. It seems uncontroversial to suggest that a founding ancestor would sustain historical ties with descendants, particularly those belonging to ruling lineages. That Ngum-Ngumi is conceived as a perambulating vessel is in itself significant. As a container, it can hold and focus the spirit's "essence," and at the same time, purposeful manipulation of the pot's decorated exterior defines Ngum-Ngumi's nature and potentiality. Both Ngum-Ngumi and Mbir'thleng'nda communicate essential messages about cosmology, social organization, and "legitimations of the existing order" (Vansina 1984, 210). The identity of both spirits may be linked explicitly to the roles of men; yet, the permanent alterations of their surfaces refer to the dramatic physical transformations that only women make in their commitment to Ga'anda society. What women most dramatically symbolize in terms of social perpetuation, Ngum-Ngumi as a "founding hero" and Mbir'thleng'nda as the most powerful community "protector" represent for Ga'anda historicity and continuity. It may be the very gender ambiguity of these ceramic representations that helps

17.20
These three Ngum-Ngumi intermediaries were enshrined by the Wetu family of Boga. The example on the lower left shows an emphasized male aspect with three sets of navels and genitalia.
PHOTOGRAPH BY MARLA C. BERNS, 1981.

17.21a
This chain mail shirt of European manufacture, which forms part of the collection of the Jos Museum, Nigeria (54/33/4), displays the same wedge-shaped opening as the bib of corrugated texture on the torso of Ngum-Ngumi. A row of crosses on the rivets around the open flaps of this hauberk have suggested that it was originally of Western European Christian manufacture (Bivar 1964, 36–37).
PHOTOGRAPH FROM BIVAR (1964, FIG. 20), REPRODUCED COURTESY OF THE NATIONAL COMMISSION FOR MUSEUMS AND MONUMENTS, NIGERIA.

17.21b
A detail of the ridge-riveted chain mail in figure 17.21a highlights the extremely regular texture, which is not unlike the careful impressions made on Ngum-Ngumi's "bib."
PHOTOGRAPH FROM BIVAR (1964, FIG. 21), REPRODUCED COURTESY OF THE NATIONAL COMMISSION FOR MUSEUMS AND MONUMENTS, NIGERIA.

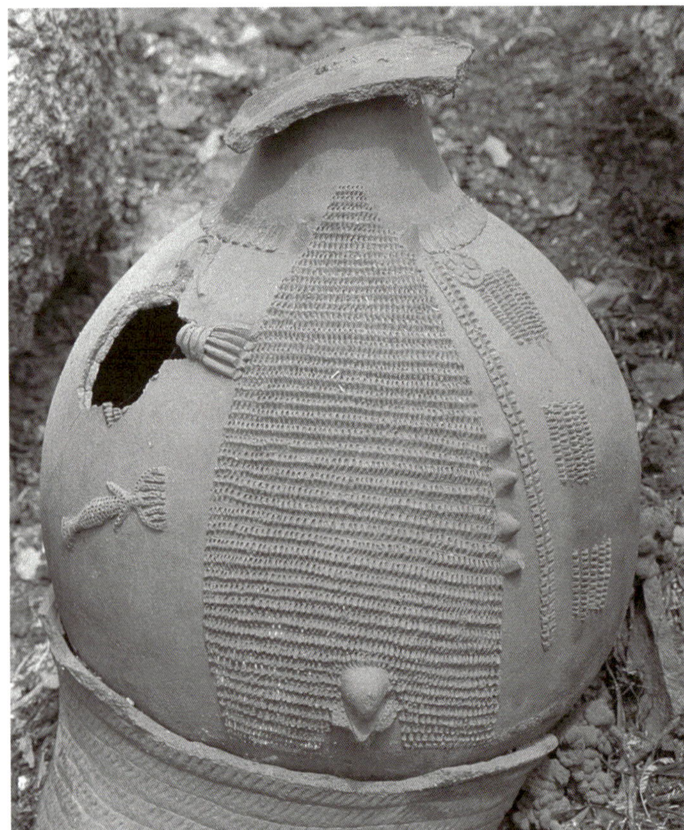

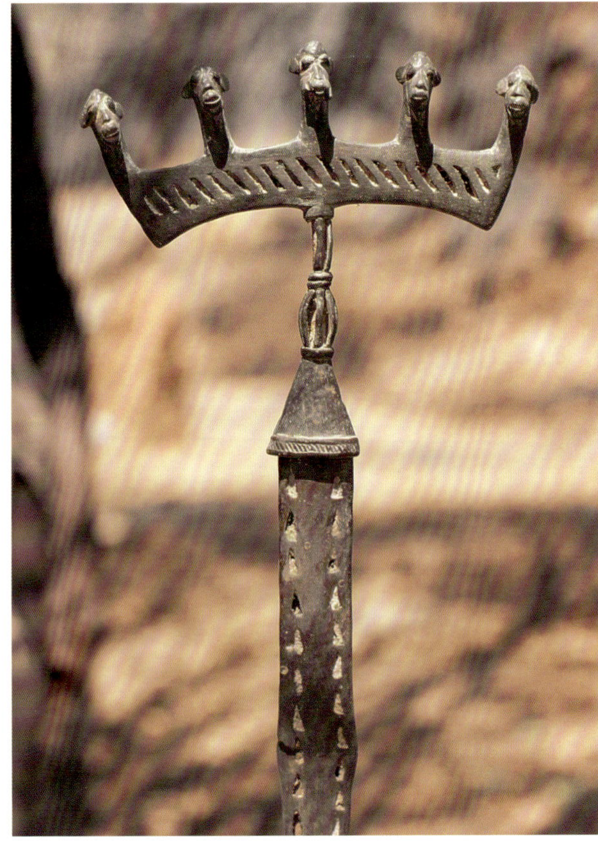

17.22

An Ngum-Ngumi sits at the site of Hurung-uthla belonging to the Wetu family of Boga. It includes a representation of the cast-brass *thluti kuturcha* (knife of chiefs), illustrated in figure 17.23. This vessel was purchased by Douglas Dawson in 2001 and is now in a private collection.

PHOTOGRAPH BY MARLA C. BERNS, 1981.

17.23

A Ga'anda knife of chiefs (*thluti kuturcha*), made of cast copper alloy, features five heads on the crossbar. These represent the chief (in the center) flanked by his four assistants. This example belonged to the Wurafur family of Gabun and was said to have been brought to Gabun from Baagira, a place located near the Mandara Mountains on the Nigeria-Camer-oon border. An elder wore it strapped around the waist during male initiation rituals. The knife is 36.5 centimeters in length.

PHOTOGRAPH BY MARLA C. BERNS, 1981.

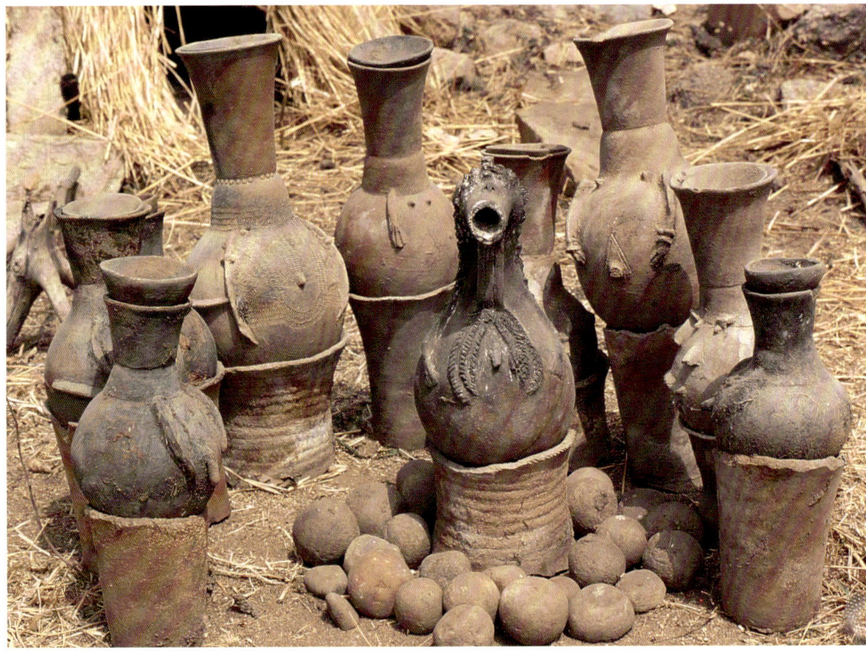

17.24

Displayed are the contents of the *kətənbucha* maintained by the Kanpita family in the Chohita village of Ga'anda/Dingai. Mbir'thleng'nda is surrounded by *sambarcha* and one large *lekleke* (third from the left). All the vessels are raised off the ground in broken pottery necks, and the round grinding stones signal Mbir'thleng'nda's power.

PHOTOGRAPH BY MARLA C. BERNS, 1980.

to empower them and to elevate them to the status of key spiritual guardians of the Ga'anda people.

Surrounding the centrally situated Mbir'thleng'nda and Ngum-Ngumi pots in *kətənbucha* are several other categories of ritual and sacred vessels, which further illuminate the Ga'anda cosmos. Some are *lekleke*, large distinctive beer pots with profiles that duplicate Ga'anda water jars (*'butə'yema*; or, "pots for the water") and have highly decorated surfaces (see fig. 17.16; see also Berns 1989a, 56, fig. 15). They are used to pour the beer shared by ritual specialists and community elders during renewal ceremonies and funerals. *Lekleke* have arms flanking the torso, small breasts, and a herniated umbilicus, the basic elements of anthropomorphization evident on other Ga'anda spirit pots. Similarly, their torsos are decorated with raised or impressed decoration recalling female cicatrization patterns. The most frequently rendered motifs from Thleta are the parallel lines that underscore the navel in a semi-circle and continue to the edge of the torso (*kun'kanwannjinda*) and the rows of lozenges framed by vertical lines that appear at the sides of the body (*kwardata*).[20]

Whereas each shrine might have one *lekleke* and one *busarta*, a three- or four-legged pot used by ritual leaders to cook any animal meat sacrificed and offered to the deities, the largest number of vessels encircling the perimeters of these shrines and clustering around Mbir'thleng'nda and Ngum-Ngumi are the previously mentioned *thləf'ncha* (sing.: *thləf'nda*) or *sambarcha* (sing.: *shembera*), used to contain the spirits of ancestors (fig. 17.24). A *thləf'nda* closely resembles a *lekleke* and thus has a contour similar to the Ga'anda water jar, but with an especially elegant and elongated segmented neck with flaring mouth (fig. 17.25). Like *lekleke*, *thləf'ncha* are distinguished by elaborate designs that emulate the patterns of Thleta, but they do not typically have arms. It is sometimes difficult to tell the difference between a *lekleke* and a *thləf'nda*, and the custodians who showed me shrines were not consistent in their identifications. *Sambarcha* are smaller versions of *thləf'ncha* but differ from them and *lekleke* in that they have far more rudimentary surface decoration and their anthropomorphic references are limited to small excrecences suggesting breasts, a large herniated navel, and sometimes arms flanking the torso (fig. 17.26). Reference to Thleta is usually a simple incised chevron over the navel, the first cuts made when a young girl initiates the six progressive stages of the scarification program (see fig. 17.16; see also Berns 1988). Informants were also not always consistent in distinguishing *sambarcha* from *thləf'ncha* on the basis of these stylistic distinctions, reflecting an interchangeability in their "naming" as well as their respective ancestral meanings.

When Ga'anda men and women die, it is believed that their spirits do not immediately depart the world of the living. Instead, they reside for a period of a year in a *thləf'nda* with a red gourd bowl covering its "mouth." This is kept elevated in a forked branch in the deceased's former sleeping room (fig. 17.27).[21] Because the Ga'anda view death as a liberation of a soul, which might prove dangerous to the living, the spirit of the departed must be confined and protected in a *thləf'nda*, which also provides an avenue for it to be tended and honored by the living. The pot is rubbed with oil to enrich its surface luster, filled with beer whenever the family has an occasion to brew it, and the sleeping room in which it is placed is swept clean with fires lit in it during the cool harmattan season. The relationship between the living and the deceased continues as if the family member were still alive. The humanity of the *thləf'nda* is objectified in the elaborate scarification markings inscribed on its torso, regardless of whether the deceased was male or female. The distinctively blackened *thləf'nda* is irreversibly marked in order to "civilize" the potentially harmful and unpredictable spirit.

In most cases, however, the relationship fostered between the Ga'anda and their immediate ancestors via the *thləf'nda* vessel is only temporary. It terminates abruptly with a second funeral ceremony one year later, which is known as Foxta (smashing). At that time the *thləf'nda* is held by the neck and broken against the rocky outcroppings

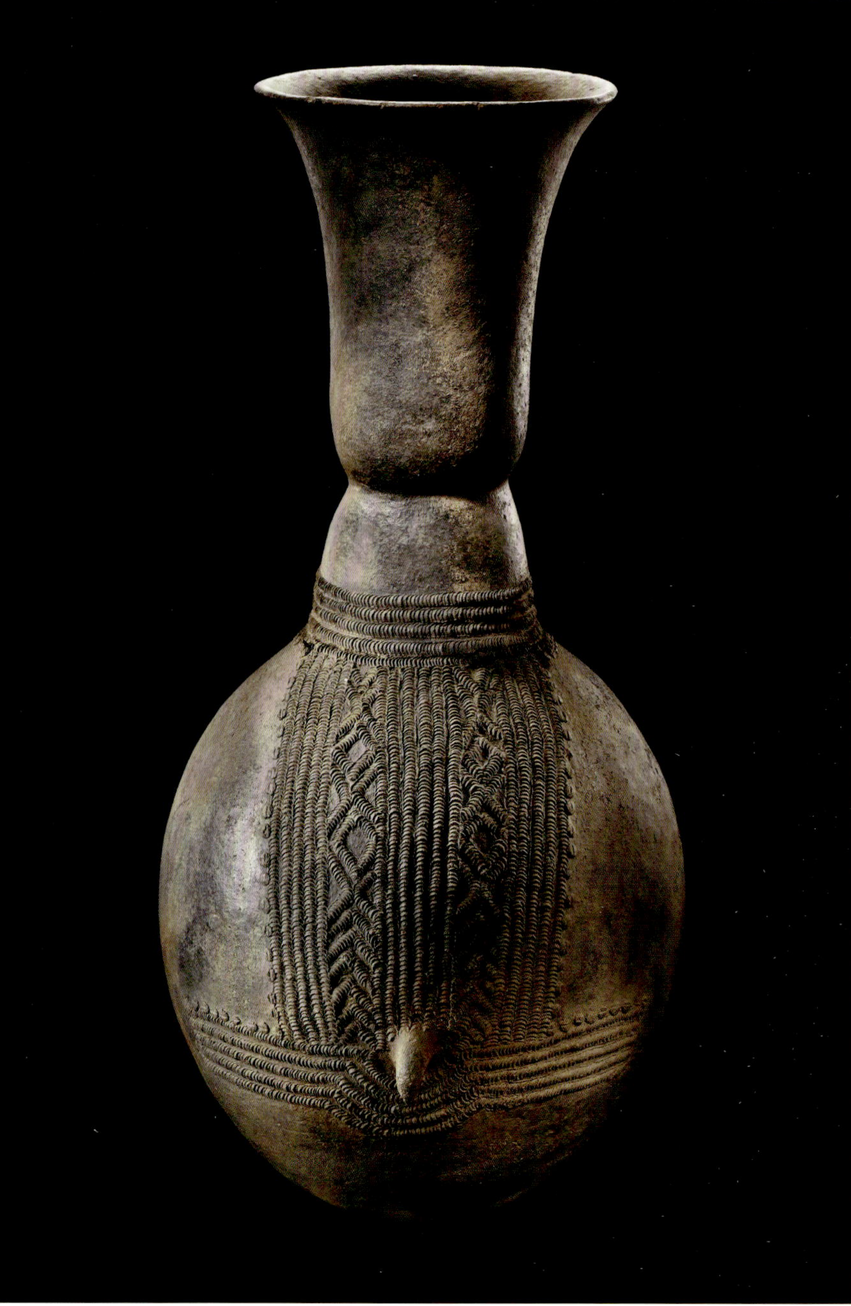

17.25
Ancestor vessel (*thləf 'nda*)
Ga'anda peoples, late twentieth century
Ceramic
H: 53 cm
BARBIER-MUELLER MUSEUM, GENEVA, 1015-162
IMAGE: COURTESY BARBIER-MUELLER MUSEUM,
GENEVA. PHOTOGRAPH © STUDIO FERRAZZINI
BOUCHET
PROVENANCE: UNKNOWN (PER BARBIER-MUELLER
MUSEUM)

The torso of this vessel, which was built to
contain the spirit of a man or woman who
died, is densely covered with impressed
decoration emulating the designs worked
on a woman's torso as part of Thleta.

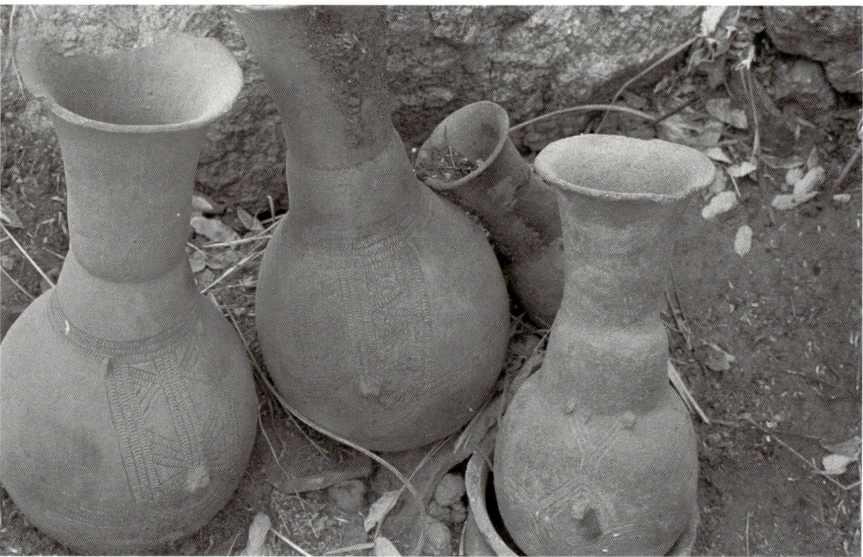

17.26
Maintained in the abandoned *kətənbucha* of
the Tamsata hamlet of Ga'anda Town were two
thləf 'ncha (left) and one *shembera*. This grouping reveals the stylistic differences between
the two categories of ancestral vessels.
PHOTOGRAPH BY MARLA C. BERNS, 1980.

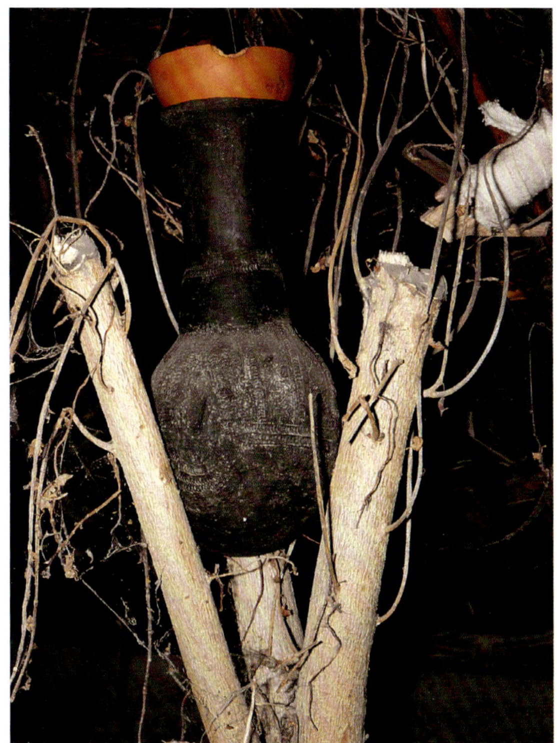

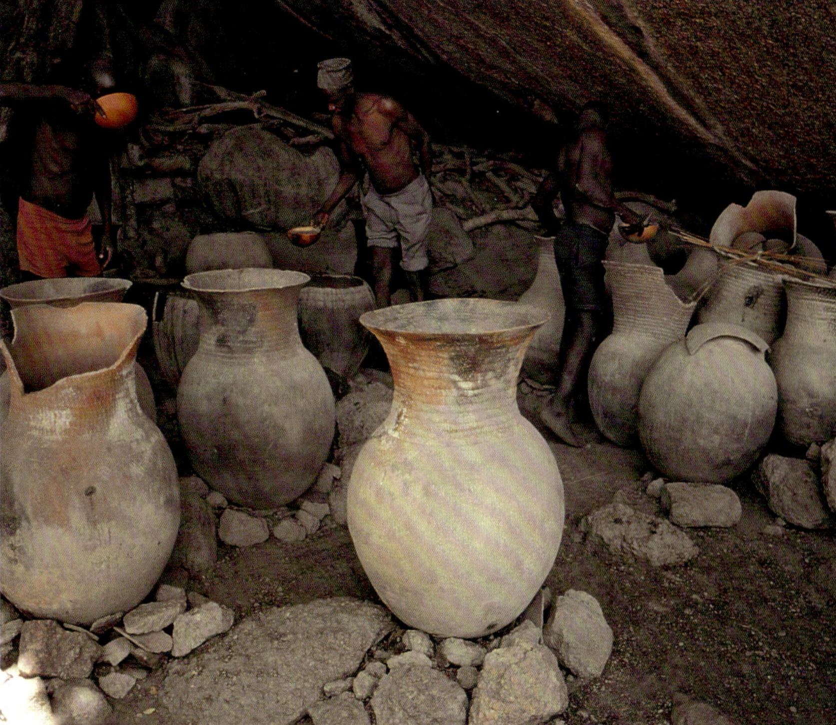

of a designated site in order to sever ties with the living at last and to send the ancestral spirit to the afterlife through this bold iconoclastic gesture. Not every ancestral spirit is banished in this way, however, as certain of them require special attention. The painstakingly decorated *thlǝf'ncha* that take their places in Ga'anda pottery shrines along with *sambarcha* are used to house the spirits of those ancestors considered to have been troublesome during life and thus in need of a longer period of supplication, generally seven years (see figs. 17.26, 17.16). If a diviner determined that an illness or misfortune was due to the interference of a recently departed relative, he recommended that a *shembera* be built to neutralize the wayward spirit. *Sambarcha* and *thlǝf'ncha* accumulate in family pottery shrines, where their proximity to Mbir'thleng'nda and Ngum-Ngumi is essential to their restraint. In most shrines, the ancestral vessels surround Mbir'thleng'nda in a highly orderly arrangement, often elevated in broken pot necks (see fig. 17.24). Elders and shrine custodians can propitiate them together at annual festivals in a single act of protecting the living from harm. Unlike their neighbors in the Ga'anda Hills, the Ga'anda view the presence of ancestral spirits, as well as their involvement in the affairs of the living, as potentially threatening. The extra years of supplication they receive reduce the risk of troublesome intervention.

Ho'mbata is the primary annual occasion for the Ga'anda to renew the *kǝtǝnbucha* and make offerings to the tutelary spirits who preside there. Ho'mbata occurs in November after the harvest and includes a series of rituals performed by priests and custodians within the local precincts where the sacred shrines are located. Pots lead lives like people: their houses need repair, their bodies need washing, and their appetites need satiation. In 1980 I documented the enactment of Ho'mbata at the ritual precinct on Makwar Mountain, maintained by the Gudban family (fig. 17.28). As indicated earlier, this is the most important ritual site for the Ga'anda—the place where Ngum-Ngumi stopped and where the Gudban rainmaking priest and his assistants do their work. Ho'mbata is also the time to celebrate the rainmaker's success or to chastise him for his failings (Hammandikko and Berns 1980, 11, 14).

Ho'mbata began with the repair of the *kǝtǝnbucha* at Makwar (see fig. 17.5), undertaken by the four ritual custodians of the precinct who served the Kutira, or chief, of

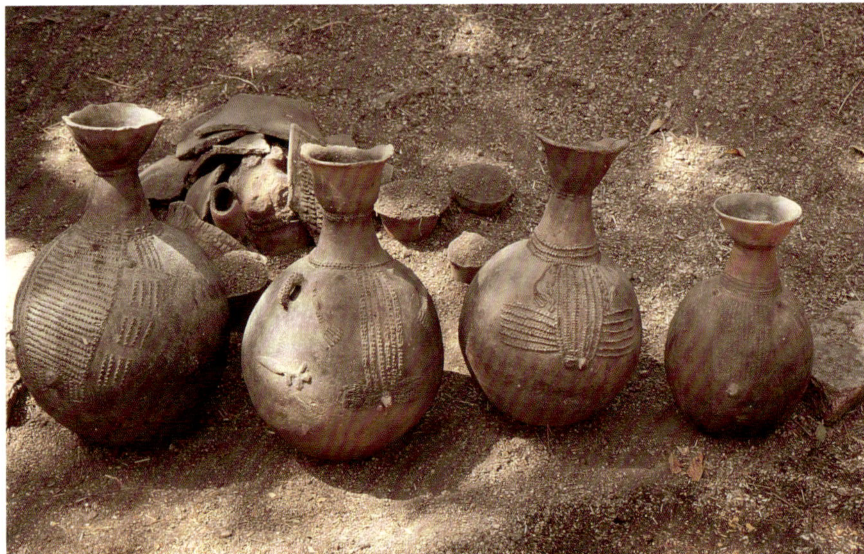

17.29
These three *'butə'shita* and one *'butəkwefa* (far right) were removed from the Makwar *kətənbucha* during Ho'mbata, so that they could be filled with beer. The *'butə'shita* are intermediaries of Ngum-Ngumi and are decorated in a manner similar to the ceramic culture hero.
PHOTOGRAPH BY MARLA C. BERNS, 1980.

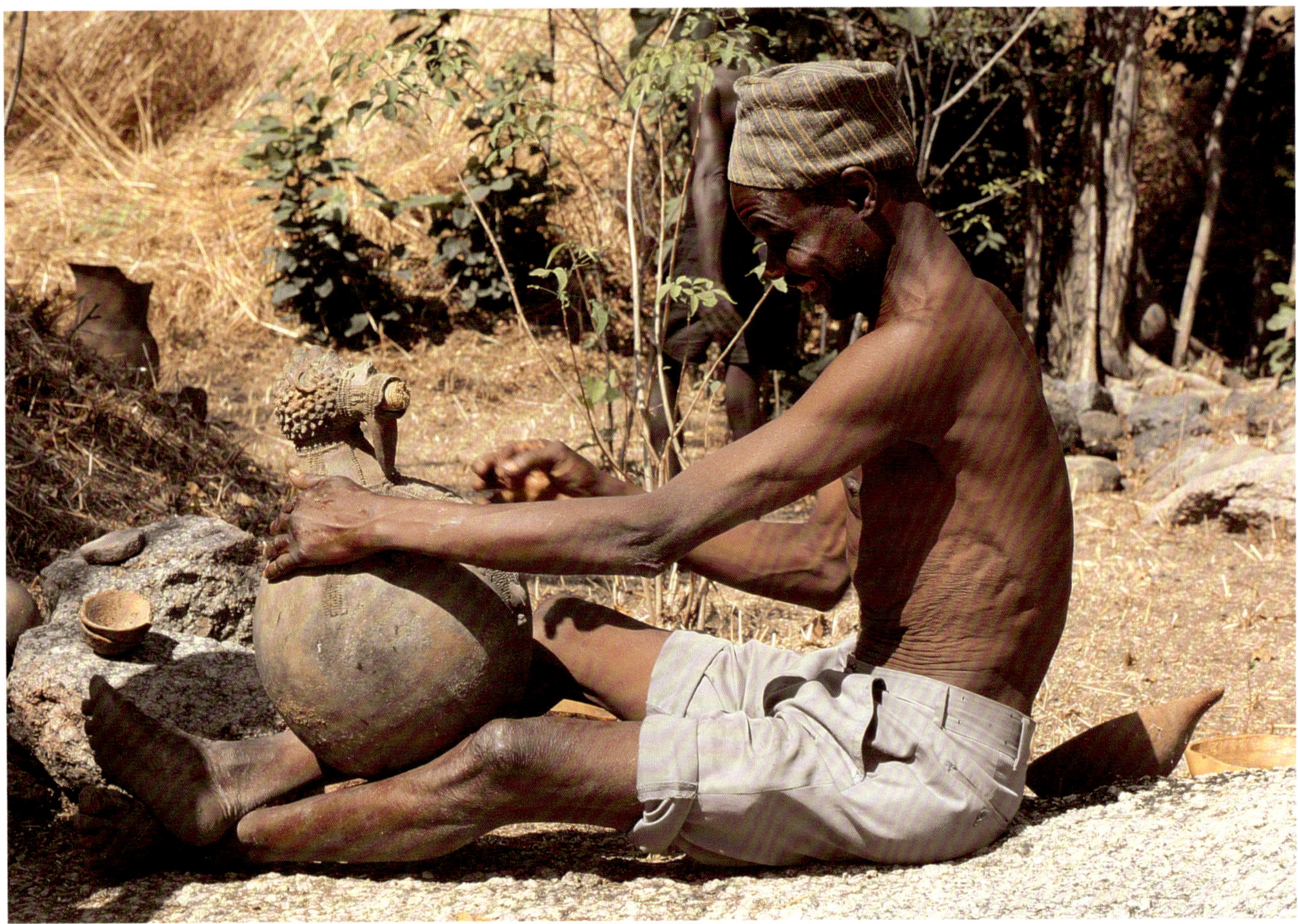

17.30
The ritual custodian, Ngət'hilengchawa Mammadu Sherpələm, prepares to wash Mbir'thleng'nda. The vessel was removed from the Makwar *kətənbucha* during Ho'mbata.
PHOTOGRAPH BY MARLA C. BERNS, 1980.

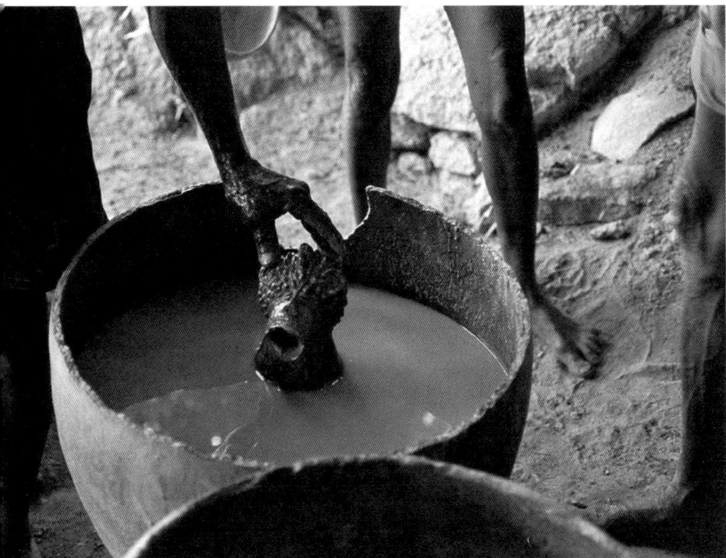

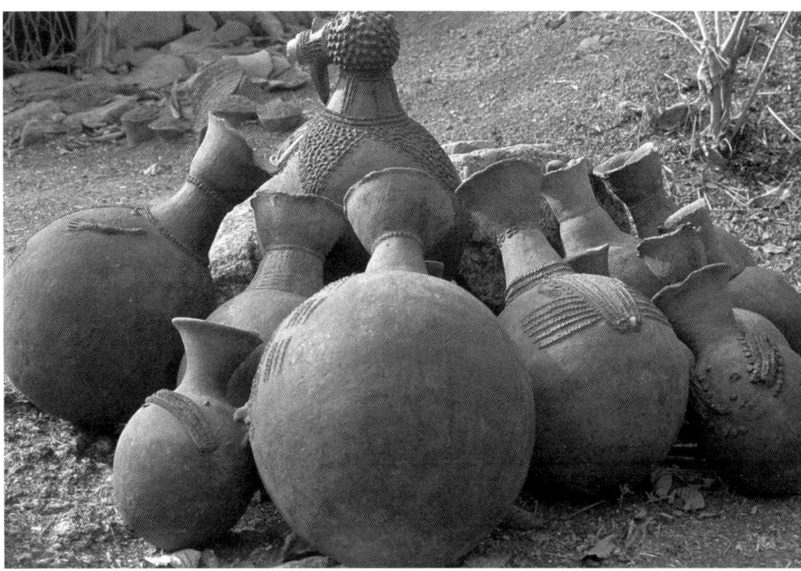

Gudban. The structure was given new woven-grass walls. Nearby, within Makwar's impressive rock shelter, the large vessels were permanently kept that were used to brew the special sorghum beer, called *yamnda*, which would be offered to all of the spirit vessels within the *kətənbucha* and shared a day later by its ritual priests and other male elders (see fig. 17.28).[22] On the first day of Ho'mbata the custodians removed all of the pots in the shrine for washing, including Mbir'thleng'nda, three of Ngum-Ngumi's intermediaries known as *'butə'shita* (fig. 17.29), one *'butəkwefa* (pot for the Kwefa festival), and ten *thləf'ncha* (or *sambarcha*). Ngum-Ngumi remained inside the shrine during the festivities. The washing of Mbir'thleng'nda was particularly notable, and it began with Ngət'hilengchawa Mammadu Sherpələm, one of the vessel's custodians, holding it between his legs (fig. 17.30). I was struck by the intimacy with which he engaged Mbir'thleng'nda—face to face—with no evidence of concern about physical contact with the vessel itself. After the washing, Mbir'thleng'nda's "stomach" was emptied of the twenty-five small polished stones kept inside it, and they were counted. If all twenty-five are present, it is a sign that the spirit has renewed its tutelage for another year. These stones seem to embody the permanence and immutability of Mbir'thleng'nda's power. If a vessel breaks, its replacement is activated by transferring the stones from its old to its new body. That the Mbir'thleng'nda in collections seem not to have stones within them may indicate that the pots were desacralized before being exported.

All of the washed vessels were then filled with the special libation, *yamnda*, poured directly into their funnel-shaped mouths, except for Mbir'thleng'nda who drank beer in an astonishing way: the entire vessel was submerged in a wide ceramic bowl filled with *yamnda* so that the spirit could "drink" its fill (fig. 17.31). After drinking, Mbir'thleng'nda's mouth was closed with a "plug" of tightly bound grass to prevent the intrusion of any harmful forces (fig. 17.32). Consuming this potent brew nourished and reactivated the capacity for positive intervention of Mbir'thleng'nda and Ngum-Ngumi, who was offered the beer through the *'butə'shita* intermediaries (see figs. 17.29, 17.32), modeled in its image. At the same time, offerings made to the *thləf'ncha* placated the spirits of deceased members of the Gudban clan considered potentially dangerous to their descendants.

The vessels were all returned to the *kətənbucha* for twenty-four hours after which time the custodians and male elders of the Gudban family returned to the shrine to remove them and drink the *yamnda* kept inside them. The contents of Mbir'thleng'nda are always consumed first followed by the three *'butə'shita* and then the *thləf'ncha*. The same evening, new Ga'anda brides who had completed the program of Thleta

17.31
Mbir'thleng'nda "drinks" ritual beer (*yamnda*) by being fully submerged in a large pot of it as a part of Ho'mbata.
PHOTOGRAPH BY MARLA C. BERNS, 1980.

17.32
After the beer in all the spirit vessels was consumed during Ho'mbata, the vessels were aligned in this formation prior to being returned to the Makwar *kətənbucha*. Mbir'thleng'nda retains the same central position in this formation as it does inside the shrine.
PHOTOGRAPH BY MARLA C. BERNS, 1980.

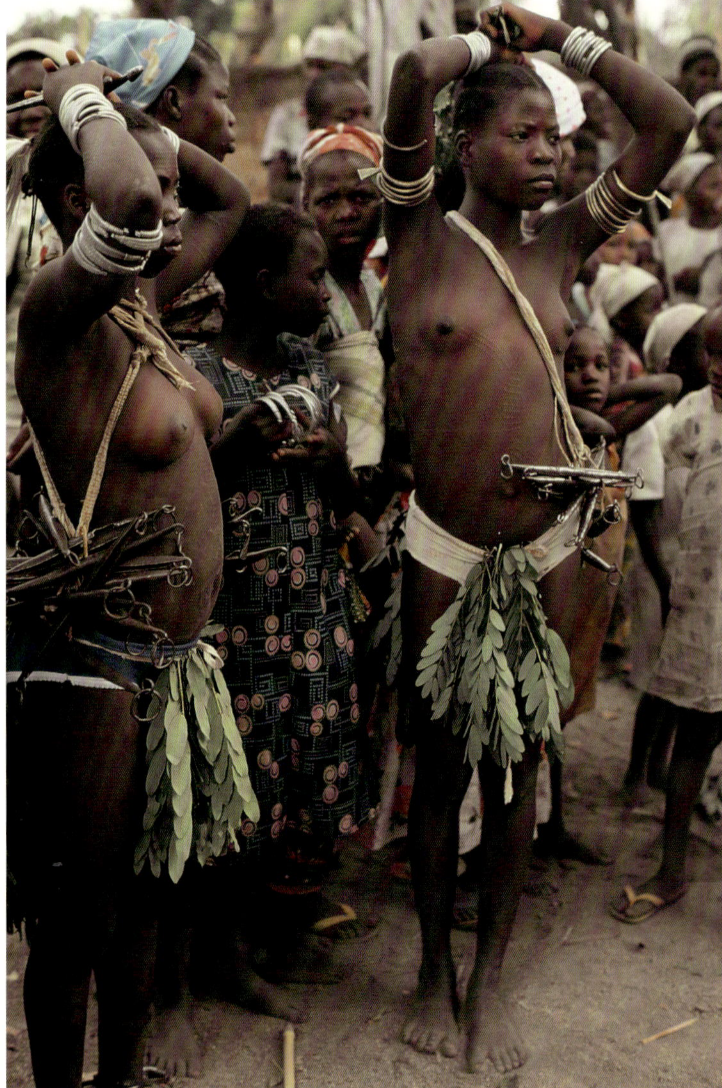

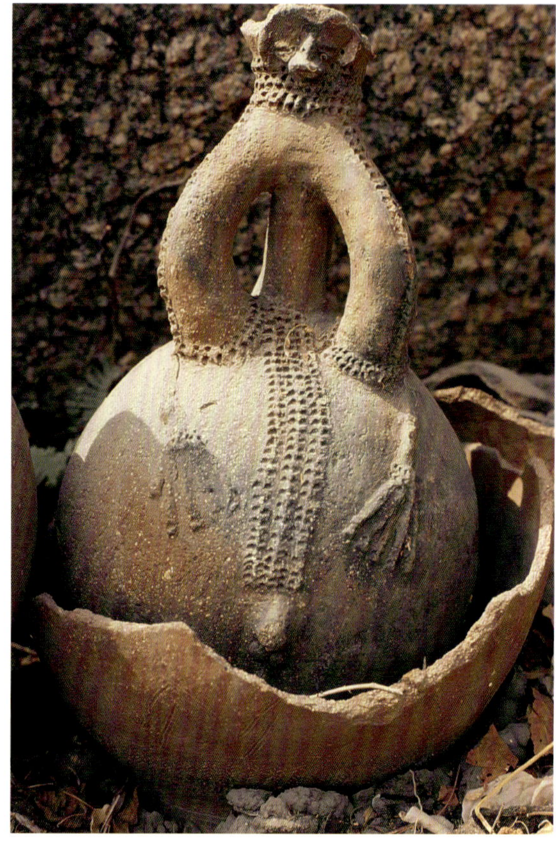

17.33

New Ga'anda brides (*perra*) were presented to the community during the Ho'mbata festivities held in November 1980 in Ga'anda Town. Because Thleta had been proscribed in 1978 by local government authorities, these two young women had not completed their scarification programs; however, the key torso motif, *njoxtimeta*, is just visible.

PHOTOGRAPH BY MARLA C. BERNS, 1980.

17.34

This *'bahanda* vessel used for relieving frustration, worry, or anger was kept by the Tang'ah family in Boga. It was 46 centimeters in height. Said to be female, it prominently displays the *njoxtimeta* scarification markings that appear down the center of a woman's torso. Young girls were brought to this vessel to ask for protection and strength during the strenuous program of Thleta scarifications.

PHOTOGRAPH BY MARLA C. BERNS, 1980.

scarifications were led to the ritual precinct to participate in this sacred act of drinking beer. By this means, the ritual leaders responsible for community welfare and new brides soon to have children literally consume the beer imbued with the spirits' presence and potency. It is telling that after the beer was consumed and the sacred rituals at Ho'mbata completed, all the now-empty spirit vessels were aligned around Mbir'thleng'nda in what appeared to be a gesture acknowledging its authority and centrality (fig. 17.32). All the vessels were then replaced in the *kətənbucha* until the following year's festival. Three days of public festivities and dancing followed, which took place in Ga'anda Town below Makwar Mountain. The new Ga'anda brides (*perra*) played a prominent role, their rite of passage communicated via their permanently altered bodies, which were highlighted with the red ritual cosmetic, *məsa'ta,* and a prescribed set of ornaments (fig. 17.33; see Berns 1988, 66–67, fig. 11).

Such social transitions have their conceptual parallel in the essential transformation that occurs when clay vessels are fired to become ceramic. As instruments of social thought (Barley 1994), they provide a model for explaining other life experiences by serving as a powerful idiom for change. The permanent shift from clay to ceramic can be likened to the irreversible changes people make as they are socialized from childhood to adulthood, passages that are expressed in the highly recognizable vocabulary of scarification motifs. The use of ceramic to incarnate the presence of powerful spirits is a reminder that the involvement of these forces remains as fluid and changeable as the human condition itself. Thus, it is easy to see why a vessel might serve as an economical vehicle both for containing and locating the spirits who have a tangible presence in people's lives. Furthermore, the essential plasticity of clay means that the spirit vessels can be made to look like the people they serve and ultimately protect. The particularly rigorous ways in which Ga'anda artists model their most important tutelary deities is surely a mechanism by which they hope to control the unpredictabilities inherent in their lives.

In addition to the spirit vessels described above, pots are also used by the Ga'anda for healing illnesses, continuing the practice documented across the Western Gongola. Among the Ga'anda, illnesses are either physical disorders, such as constipation or skin rashes, or take the form of psychological distress, such as frustration or anger.[23] Diseases of any kind are equated with some manner of spiritual interference caus-ing an imbalance, and specific named forces are identified with particular symptoms. Diviners or healers can determine the spirits responsible for causing diseases and then prescribe appropriate remedies. Healers often advise that a vessel be made through which the disease-causing spirit is appeased.

The most sculpturally distinctive and ritually important healing pot is called *'bahanda* (troublemaker). This pot was typically the exclusive property of ritual chiefs (Kuturcha) or clan elders and was kept for the relief of frustration or anger (fig. 17.34). Although people who suffered these emotions could appeal to *'bahanda* for help, its most important purpose was to restore the mental equilibrium of ritual leaders who had important sacred responsibilities. *'Bahanda* vessels were not made each time these symptoms occurred; rather, enshrined examples were approached by chiefs whenever they felt imbalanced by the "heat" of anger. White, ground-sprouted sorghum mixed with water (*chikta*) was sprayed over the vessel and then dabbed on the patient's tem-ples, shoulders, and abdomen to directly transfer the "cooling" effect of this activated substance.[24] The association of *'bahanda* with coolness and composure is reinforced by the fact that in the past, before men left for battle, they would undergo the same procedure. Similarly, before young girls underwent the final and most grueling stage of scarification, they would be presented to *'bahanda* to ease their fears.

The distinguishing sculptural feature of a *'bahanda* is a tripod spout substituting for the neck.[25] The three narrow channels join to form a single mouth and may repre-sent the vessel's "neck" and "arms." Three of the examples I documented show that the pot's mouth has a face modeled with distinct features—eyes, nose, mouth, and ears. As with other Ga'anda spirit vessels, *'bahanda's* torso has arms with hands, an umbilicus, and in this example, male genitalia. The raised and impressed ridge down the center of the vessel reproduces *njoxtimeta*. Thus, *'bahanda* combines male and female references in much the same way as they are depicted on Mbir'thleng'nda and Ngum-Ngumi.

Ga'anda domestic pottery and most ritual wares were made by women special-ists (*thleten'buuca*, or "makers of pots"). I documented several notable women potters living in various Ga'anda subsections—Ga'anda, Boga, Jebre, and Jaromboyi—and observed a striking consistency in their method of building vessels using coiling and in their highly meticulous and painstaking approach to decoration using split stalks, gourd chips, rope roulette, and blades of dried grass. In the hamlet of Jaromboyi, I photographed and filmed one of these women, Ndinuwa, producing a *lekleke* with the assistance of her husband, Mamuda. She built and decorated the pot, and Mamuda added the arms in an intriguing demonstration of collaboration, which I did not witness anywhere else. Despite my efforts, I was not able in over seven months of fieldwork to observe a man (or a woman) making a sacred vessel like Mbir'thleng'nda. Ga'anda elders claimed that only certain older men were responsible for modeling the most sacred Ga'anda wares. I have argued elsewhere that I find this claim to be questionable and that instead it is more likely that older women made most of the elaborately modeled Mbir'thleng'nda, Ngum-Ngumi, *lekleke,* and *thlɔf'ncha*.[26] The great variety among Mbir'thleng'nda vessels, for example, and the numbers of them kept by

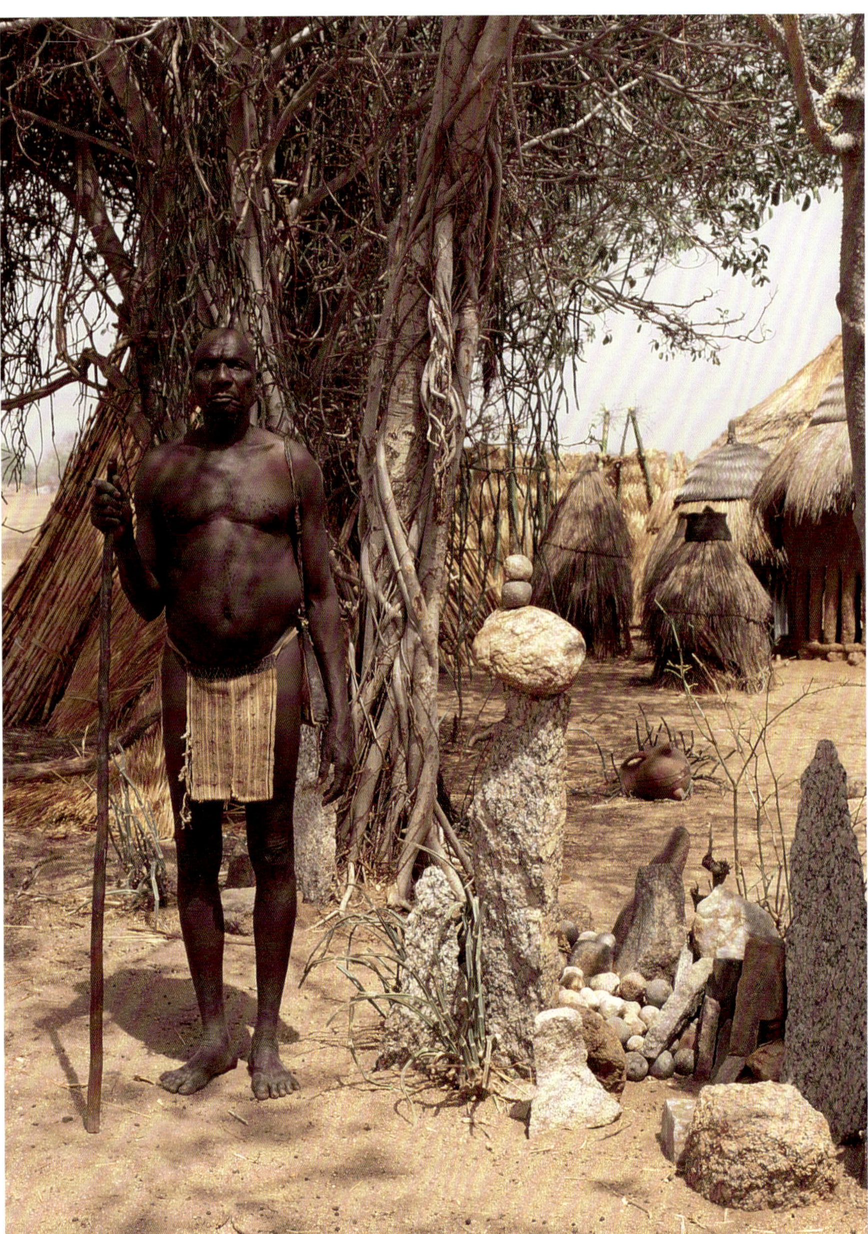

17.35a

This stone assemblage was situated at the entry to the compound of Pumtahuka Waziri Boga, the ritual chief (Kutira) of the Pum'ah family. The Waziri (Hausa: "chief") wears a handwoven cotton apron (*wanfiicha*) and carries a forked wooden staff, both insignia of his office. The stones have various meanings, and the tall hewn slab at the far right attracts spirits who protect the household. The round stones are divinatory, and should the Waziri hear one fall, it foretold an unexpected event affecting him or his family.

PHOTOGRAPH BY MARLA C. BERNS, 1981.

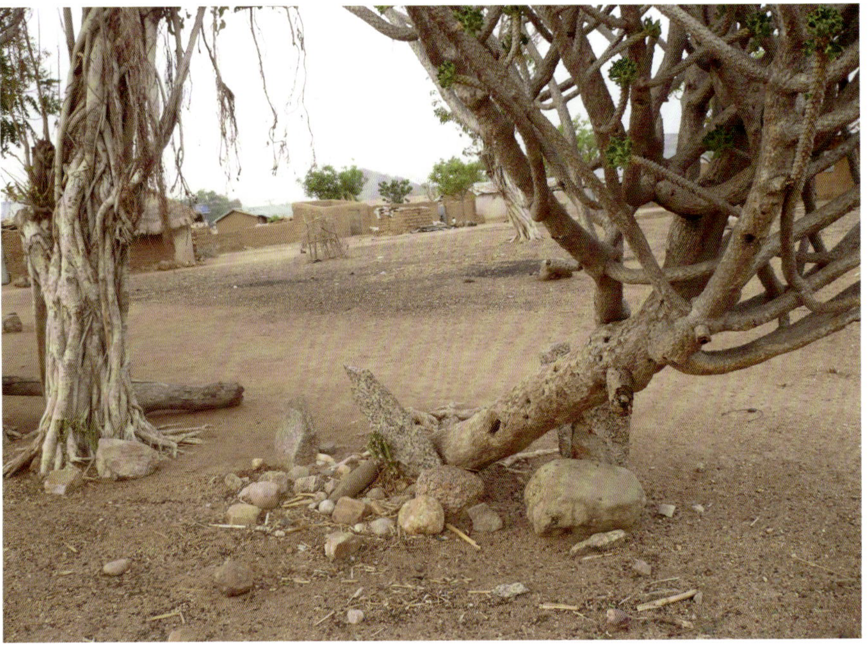

17.35b

This site seen in figure 17.35a was again photographed by Benson Ali in 2010. At that time only the slab to the far right and a few spheres survived from the original carefully orchestrated accumulation, signaling the death of the Waziri and the demise of his power and shrine. In fact, his entire household is now gone from the site, and it appears to have burned to the ground.

PHOTOGRAPH BY BENSON ALI, 2010.

families across all of the Ga'anda subsections, reveal the hands of many artists, sometimes more than one within a single shrine. The regularity and precision of the Wetu (Boga) variation of Ngum-Ngumi and its concentration in this locality (where more than ten examples were photographed) suggests that one female specialist or a specialist workshop may have produced them all (as well as others documented in neighboring 'Bəna hamlets; see figs. 18.8–18.10).

It should be noted that in many shrine contexts, stone is used to reinforce the power of clay to attract and situate powerful spirit forces, providing an even more durable mode of physical representation. Stone, as has been remarked, is both abundantly available and morphologically diverse in the Ga'anda region. Assemblages of stones at the entrances to sacred groves, the compounds of ritual priests, or in front of *kətənbucha* were used to denote the presence of powerful and potentially dangerous forces and to warn off intruders (fig. 17.35a,b and see fig. 17.24). Distinctive combinations of upright stone slabs and precariously perched stone spheres effected striking and unmistakable visual statements, especially when situated within the rocky landscape. The Ga'anda who showed me these places disclaimed responsibility for having shaped these stone slabs. Within the massive geological formations of the landscape, they were interpreted as "messages" about where to establish points of contact with spirit forces.

The critical role of stone in communicating spiritual favor was also illustrated in the way the small, polished stones kept inside Mbir'thleng'nda verified the spirit's continued tutelage. Although such small polished stones or larger spherical stones were pervasive ritual markers, hunting shrines, called *sambal*, are dotted across the Ga'anda landscape and consist primarily of upright monoliths, clustered in tight groupings and often assembled around a hidden core of stone spheres (fig. 17.36). Their main purpose was to display the large game killed during the hunt as a way of acknowledging the skill of the hunter and the favor of spirits who facilitated success. The most dangerous and feared of all wild animals is the leopard, and the killing of this dangerous carnivore was considered an especially auspicious sign of skill, bravery, and spiritual favor. When the leopard's body was displayed, a stone sphere was wedged inside the animal's mouth to imbue the stone with the animals' potency.

As was true across the western Gongola Valley, annual hunting rites took place at these stone shrines, and activating substances, such as blood or red hematite mixed with oil (*məsa'ta*), were applied to a hunter's body to transfer the protective forces that had been invested in the stone. Bows and arrows were also dipped directly into these ingredients once a year, and before every hunt, they were left overnight in front of the stones to gain further power. Thus, the spiritual basis for a hunter's skill was the accumulated energy invested in the stone by his most-prized quarry. ●

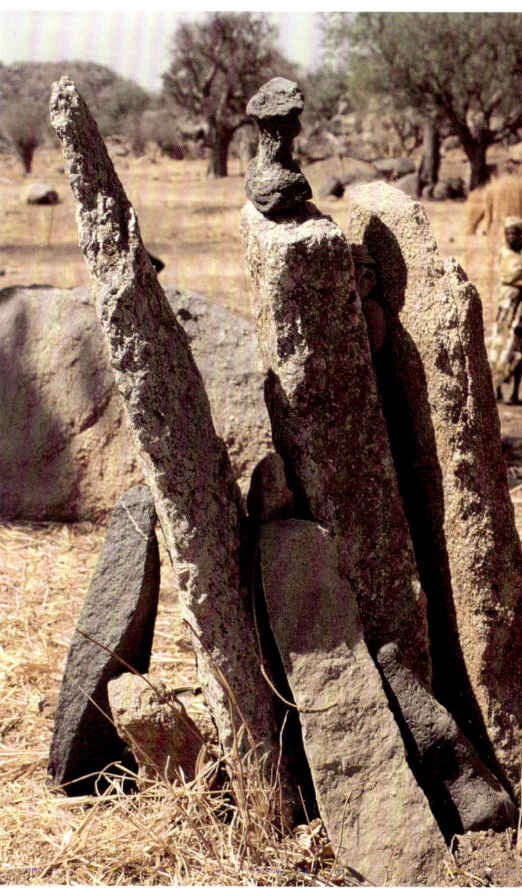

17.36
This *sambal* hunting shrine was kept by the Gudban family of Ga'anda Town. The bows and quivers of hunters would be placed here the night before the hunt, and any large game killed would ultimately be displayed in front of the stone accumulation.
PHOTOGRAPH BY MARLA C. BERNS, 1980.

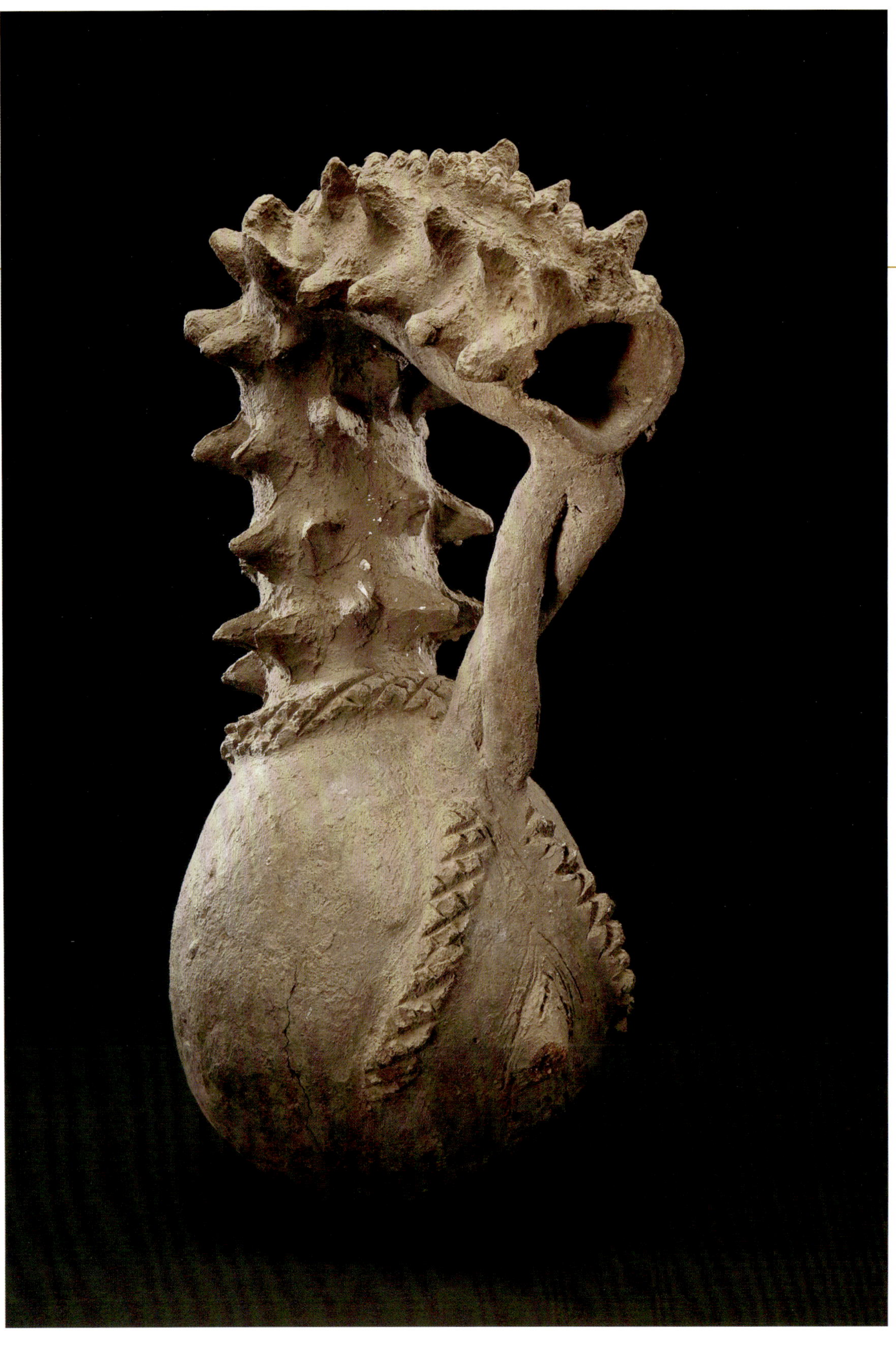

CHAPTER 18

Containing Power: Identities in Clay in the Eastern Gongola Valley, the ʻBəna, Yungur, and Dera

MARLA C. BERNS

ʻBƏNA

The ʻBəna live immediately west of the Ga'anda and their villages extend to the Gongola River just north of the town of Shellen (see map, fig. 15.2, p. 466). The members of two linguistic divisions of ʻBəna speakers, called Dingai and Roba, live in a cluster of villages about 20 kilometers west and southwest of Ga'anda Town. Members of another, called Yang, are concentrated further north, and those belonging to a fourth are centered in the village of Gureshi, the furthest west.[1] The close geographical proximity of the Ga'anda and ʻBəna is reflected in the many points of similarity in their social organization, spirit veneration, and material culture. For example, they share traditions of full-body scarification for girls (Sā) and septennial initiation ordeals for boys (Xono). The intensive historical interaction and exchange between these two groups is most evident among the ʻBəna living between the villages of Dingai and Riji, near the ʻBəna-Ga'anda border. The spirit vessels within shrines maintained by these communities reveal striking correspondences in their conception and objectification to those of the Ga'anda.[2] Despite the differences in languages spoken and the names given to various spirit representations, these shrines bear witness to the level of communication that must have characterized local relationships among geographically proximate communities.[3]

Like the Ga'anda, the ʻBəna formerly lived in villages located near major rock formations. By the mid-twentieth century, most of their remote and scattered communities had relocated to the more accessible plains. Communities are united under local priests (Gubo) who traditionally held secular and sacred authority. A Gubo carries a long iron staff (*keda*) forged in one piece, which is elaborately ornamented along the shaft with a succession of hammered designs and iron loops or jangling pods attached at two or more points. The primary responsibility of ʻBəna priests is to maintain community shrine complexes, called *xidwiisa* ("houses of *wiisa*"; in Yang and Gureshi dialect, *xidwiija*), which accommodate ceramic vessels (*wiisa*) containing the ancestral spirits (also called *wiisa*) of important male elders and chiefs (fig. 18.2). The vessels are renewed and propitiated at yearly pre-planting rituals, called Wiisho, to enlist the assistance of ancestors in maintaining community health and well-being.

Wiisa spirit vessels are generally built with the same contours as ʻBəna domestic wares, as was true of Ga'anda spirit pots. ʻBəna pottery is distinguished by an all-over surface pattern that emulates the initial coiling process; a thick rope or cord may have been used to achieve this characteristic yet unusual surface effect (figs. 18.2, 18.3).[4] There are two types of *wiisa* made by most ʻBəna groups. One is small and made as a repository for the spirit of a deceased family member; it would be kept in a sleeping

18.1

Musa Rabkabaw (active 1950s–1970s)
Spirit vessel (Ngwarkandangra)
ʻBəna peoples, Riji village, circa 1955
Ceramic
H: 30.9 cm
FOWLER MUSEUM AT UCLA X86.4693; GIFT OF ARNOLD RUBIN
IMAGE: © 2010 FOWLER MUSEUM AT UCLA. PHOTOGRAPH BY DON COLE
PROVENANCE: COLLECTED BY ARNOLD RUBIN IN 1970

The twisted beard on this example is unusual and may be an innovation by the artist who created this vessel.

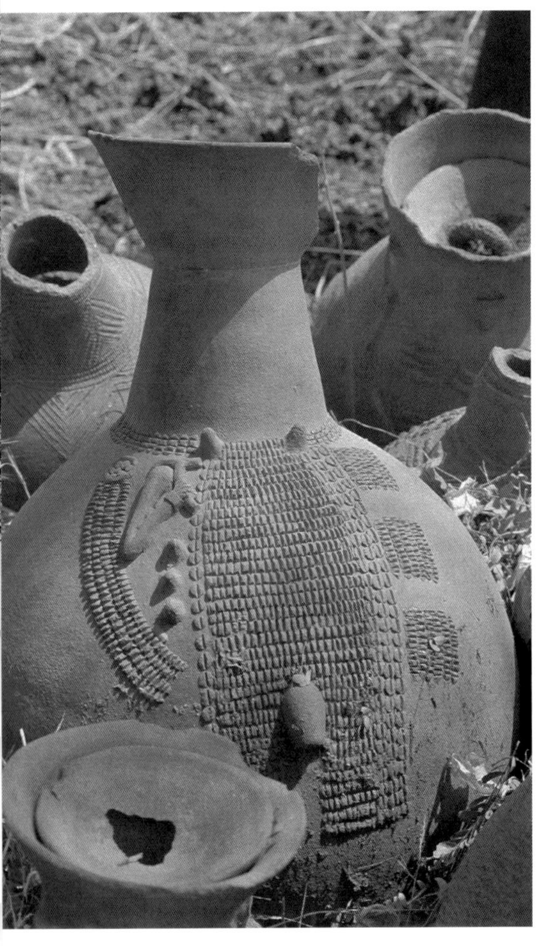

18.8
A *wiisa* vessel from the shrine on Hatta Hill
is virtually indistinguishable from the Ngum-
Ngumi vessels made by the Wetu family of
the Boga Ga'anda.
PHOTOGRAPH BY MARLA C. BERNS, 1981.

The Hatta shrine is decidedly atypical in the variety and number of its contents, especially in comparison with other 'Bəna Roba *xidwiisa*, including one shrine maintained by another Roba family called Hotta (see fig. 18.2). Now disconnected from the family who lived proximate to them, these vessels may once have been enshrined in multiple locations on Hatta Hill, providing a single focus for rituals and propitiation. The majority of the twenty-five vessels currently in the Hatta shrine are identical to types of Ga'anda sacred, ritual, and even domestic wares (including the highly decorated water jar, *'butə'yema*). Although my 'Bəna informants called them all *wiisa*, the inclusion of so many Ga'anda-like wares raises intriguing questions about the nature of interaction between the Ga'anda and their 'Bəna neighbors. Does the composition of this shrine argue for the assimilation of Ga'anda material symbols by 'Bəna ritual leaders, based perhaps on the reputed power and efficacy of these symbols? Or, did 'Bəna speakers move into remote hillside communities once occupied by the Ga'anda? Or, did Ga'anda specialist potters perhaps produce particular vessel types, like the Wetu Ngum-Ngumi, for a broad market, again based on their reputed effectiveness? Although it may not be possible to reconstruct the kinds of negotiations transacted by Ga'anda and 'Bəna ritual leaders, it should not be forgotten that the largest vessel placed at the center of this shrine is unambiguously "'Bəna" based on its diagnostic surface decoration and the impossibility of confusing its "skin" with the uniform smoothness of Ga'anda wares.

To address these intriguing historical questions and to test what the ceramic evidence could unmask about local history, it was necessary to vist the area of Dingai, the western frontier of Ga'anda and 'Bəna occupation in the 1980s, where such patterns of interaction were the most intensive. The Ga'anda-speaking hamlets in the area were located mostly to the north of those that were 'Bəna-speaking. The Dingai Ga'anda said they could not understand the 'Bəna language, although the 'Bəna spoke Ga'anda. This bilingualism may be a useful indicator of the direction of the flow of ideas and objects or the nature of power relations in the Ga'anda Hills, where the Ga'anda rainmaker was regarded as the highest religious authority in the land. The material evidence certainly suggests that the 'Bəna were heavily "Ga'andaized."[6] This is further supported by the historical claims made by Dingai 'Bəna groups that a pot led them to the locations they now occupy, having migrated from the southern 'Bəna area. The name given this perambulating spirit vessel is Komalamne, and all the examples of vessels so-named are identical to the Wetu versions of Ngum-Ngumi (fig. 18.9). I photographed the vessel illustrated in figure 18.9 in 1981 in a protected rock shelter high in the hills above the hamlet of Ngwatkame (fig. 18.10), where the people settled after having followed Komalamne there.

The largest Dingai 'Bəna shrine was maintained by the Tontomra clan, the chief priests for the Dingai (see fig. 15.9). Protected only by its conical roof armature (minus the thatching), I was able to view its crowded contents in 1981, when it was filled with ten large (H: approximately 60 cm) and four small (H: 40 cm) "sons of Komalamne." In the center was the largest Komalamne (H: 90 cm) around which all the other vessels were tightly clustered. This was the largest agglomeration of "Wetu" vessels that I documented across the Ga'anda Hills. All of them revealed a remarkable level of standardization. The idea that Komalamne was served by his "sons" or intermediaries is a notion consistent with that held by the Ga'anda about Ngum-Ngumi, especially among the Wetu family of Boga and the Gudban family of Makwar (cf. figs. 17.20, 17.29). Also included in this shrine were a number of Ga'anda *thlef'ncha*, called by the 'Bəna name *wiisa*. Their purpose here was to provide a means for neutralizing the potentially negative influence of the ancestors, a conceptualization more aligned with Ga'anda cosmology than with that of the 'Bəna.

In front of the central Komalamne was a vessel easily recognizable as a Ga'anda Mbir'thleng'nda but called by the 'Bəna name Ngwarkandangra. Like its Ga'anda corollary, this spirit pot was ascribed a tutelary function. This meticulously decorated example, however, notably lacked the spikes and nodes characteristic of most

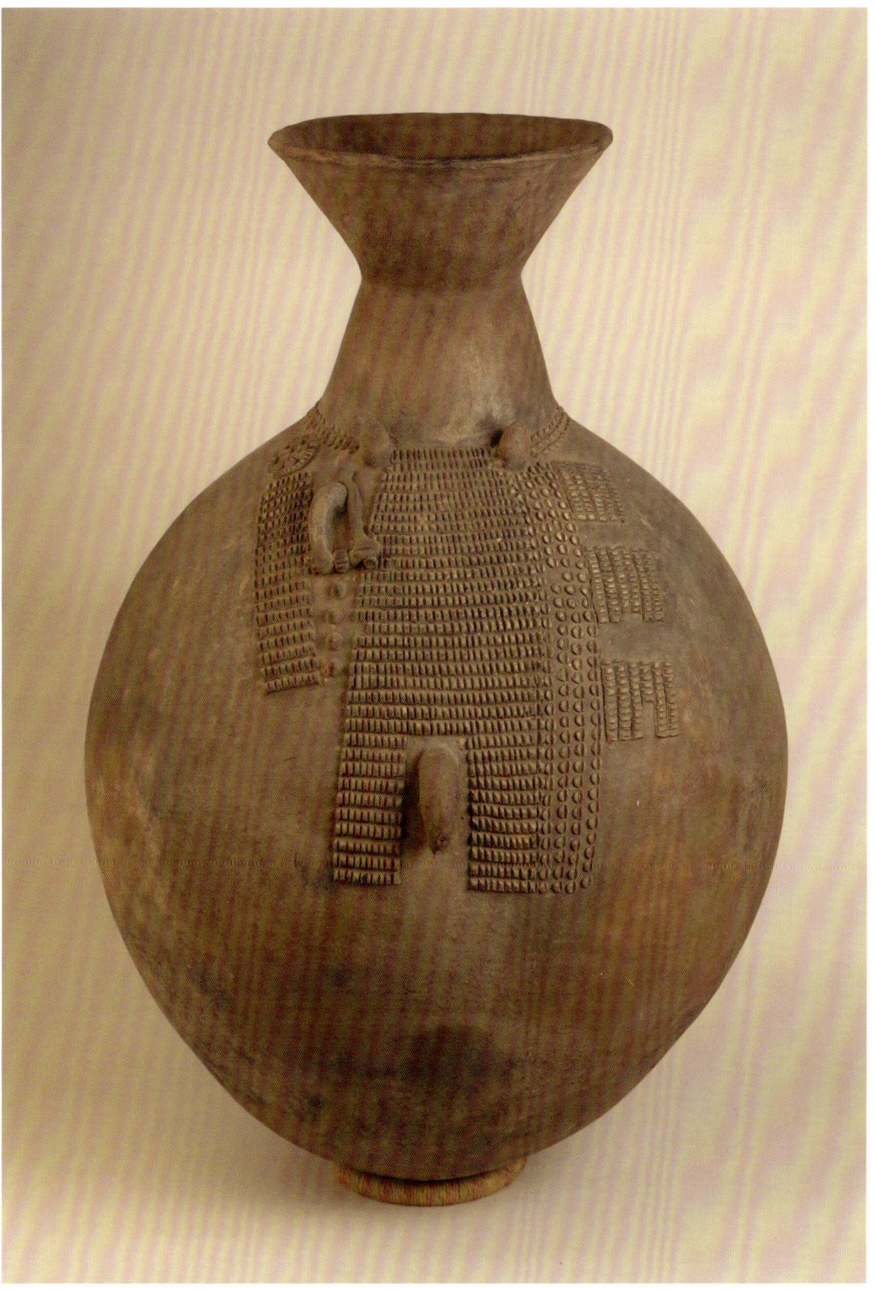

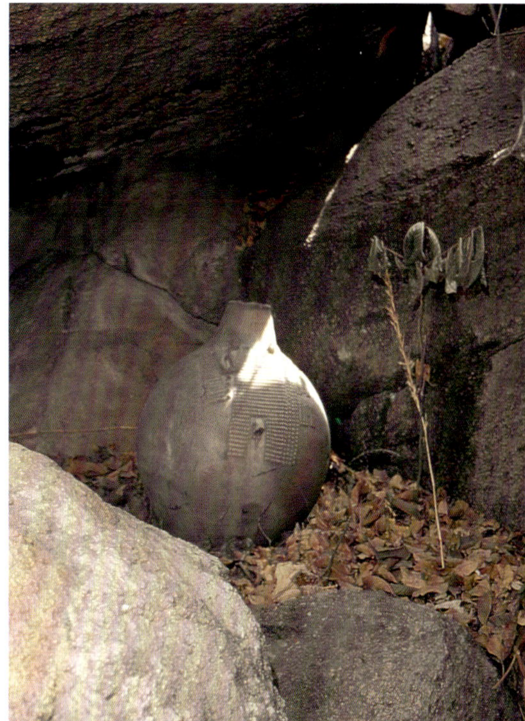

18.9
Spirit vessel (Komalamne)
'Bəna Dingai peoples, Ngwatkame hamlet,
twentieth century
Ceramic
H: 72. 5 cm
COLLECTION OF BILL AND GALE SIMMONS
PHOTOGRAPH © 2010 ALDO MAURO
PROVENANCE: HAMIDOU MONTOUODORE KPOUMIE,
CAMEROON

Komalamne is the name of the spirit vessel
the Ngwatkame followed to reach the hilltop
location adjacent to the rock shelter where
they once lived and where this vessel was formerly enshrined (see fig. 18.10). Ngwatkame is
a 'Bəna Dingai name for the conceptually and
stylistically identical Ga'anda Ngum-Ngumi.
The in situ view of this vessel in figure 18.10
shows that its "mouth" has been rebuilt, a
repair likely done by a local artist who used
the same clay body and knew the correct angle
at which to evert the rim.

18.10
The culture hero Komalamne was kept in this
rock shelter hidden high in the hills above
Ngwatkame hamlet, 'Bəna Dingai, before
being exported from Nigeria prior to 2000.
PHOTOGRAPH BY MARLA C. BERNS, 1981.

Mbirhlen'nda (see fig. 17.10). Instead, the same crisp corrugations seen on Komalamne
appeared to have been grafted onto its surface, suggesting that it was likely produced
by the same hand or by the same workshop as the other vessels in the shrine. The
contents of this impressive accumulation mirror the types and disposition of vessels
enshrined by the Ga'anda, and significantly, they have the same roles and purposes.
Pottery shrines in other Dingai 'Bəna communities reveal the same correspondences,
and in some, such as figure 18.11, the only way to distinguish whether it belonged to
a Ga'anda or a 'Bəna family was the presence of punch marks covering the surfaces
of the small *wiisa*. When this group of vessels was compared with those in a Ga'anda
Dingai shrine (fig. 17.16), one key difference was the absence of highly decorated
lekleke and other Ga'anda ritual wares, which is typical of Bəna accumulations.

The name Ngwarkandangra is also given to a class of vessels found across the entire
'Bəna area that were primarily used for curing skin ailments.[7] With their dramatically
cantilevered tubular mouths and pattern of clay spikes or bumps over the head and neck
(and sometimes body), they unmistakably recall Mbir'thleng'nda (figs. 18.1, 18.12–18.13,
and cf. fig. 17.10). Physiognomic details on Ngwarkandangra tend to be minimal, and

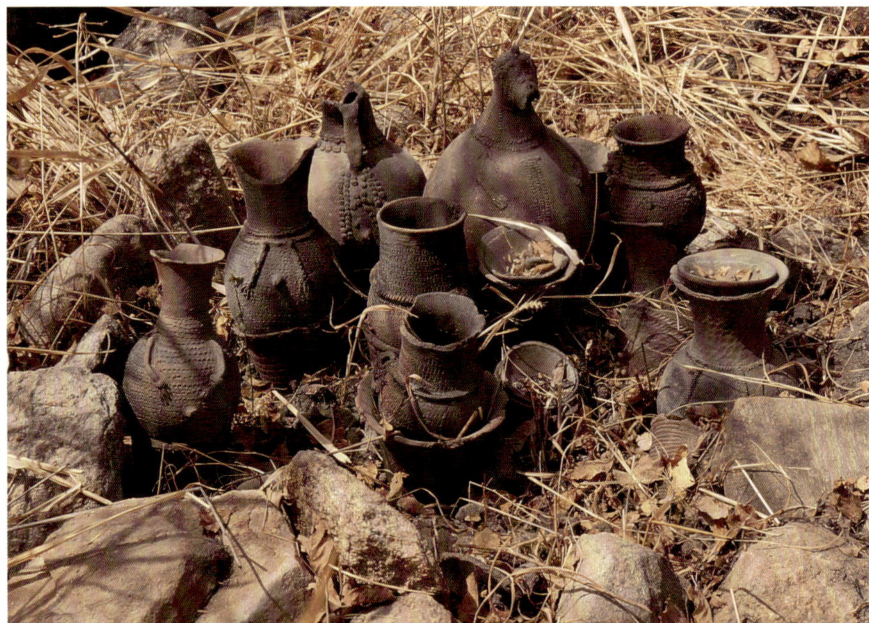

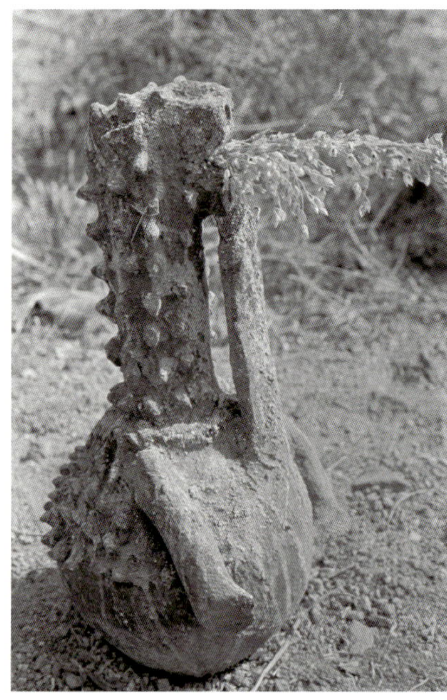

18.11

This *xidwiisa* belongs to the Kokoroko family of 'Bəna Dingai. It is distinguished by the presence of two Mbir'thleng'nda surrounded by the ancestral *wiisa*. The Kokoroko used the Ga'anda name Mbir'thleng'nda for these smooth-surfaced spirit pots, but their ancestral vessels were decorated with the all-over patterning typical of 'Bəna wares.

PHOTOGRAPH BY MARLA C. BERNS, 1981.

18.12

This small 'Bəna Ngwarkandangra vessel (H: 28 cm) was identified as female and was used not only to cure illnesses but also to ensure a good sorghum crop, as evidenced by the stalk of sorghum in its mouth. The plank-like extension of the chin, parallel to the neck, evokes the cantilevered "hook" shape of the wooden funerary effigies (*kwanda*) made by the 'Bəna (see fig. 1.6).

PHOTOGRAPH BY MARLA C. BERNS, DU'A HAMLET, 1981.

18.13

Spirit vessel (Ngwarkandangra)
'Bəna peoples, late twentieth century
Ceramic

H: 39.2 cm

FOWLER MUSEUM AT UCLA X2008.32.2; MUSEUM PURCHASE

IMAGE: © 2010 FOWLER MUSEUM AT UCLA.
PHOTOGRAPH BY DON COLE

PROVENANCE: HAMIDOU MONTOUODORE KPOUMIE, CAMEROON; AMYAS NAEGELE, NEW YORK, 2004

This Ngwarkandangra has the elongated neck and plank-like beard support typical of 'Bəna healing vessels. The latter differ from the beards observed on Ga'anda Mbir'thleng'nda. Also distinctive to these 'Bəna vessels is the minimal decoration on the torso, which is limited to projecting breasts and a schematic reference to the scarifications worked over a woman's navel.

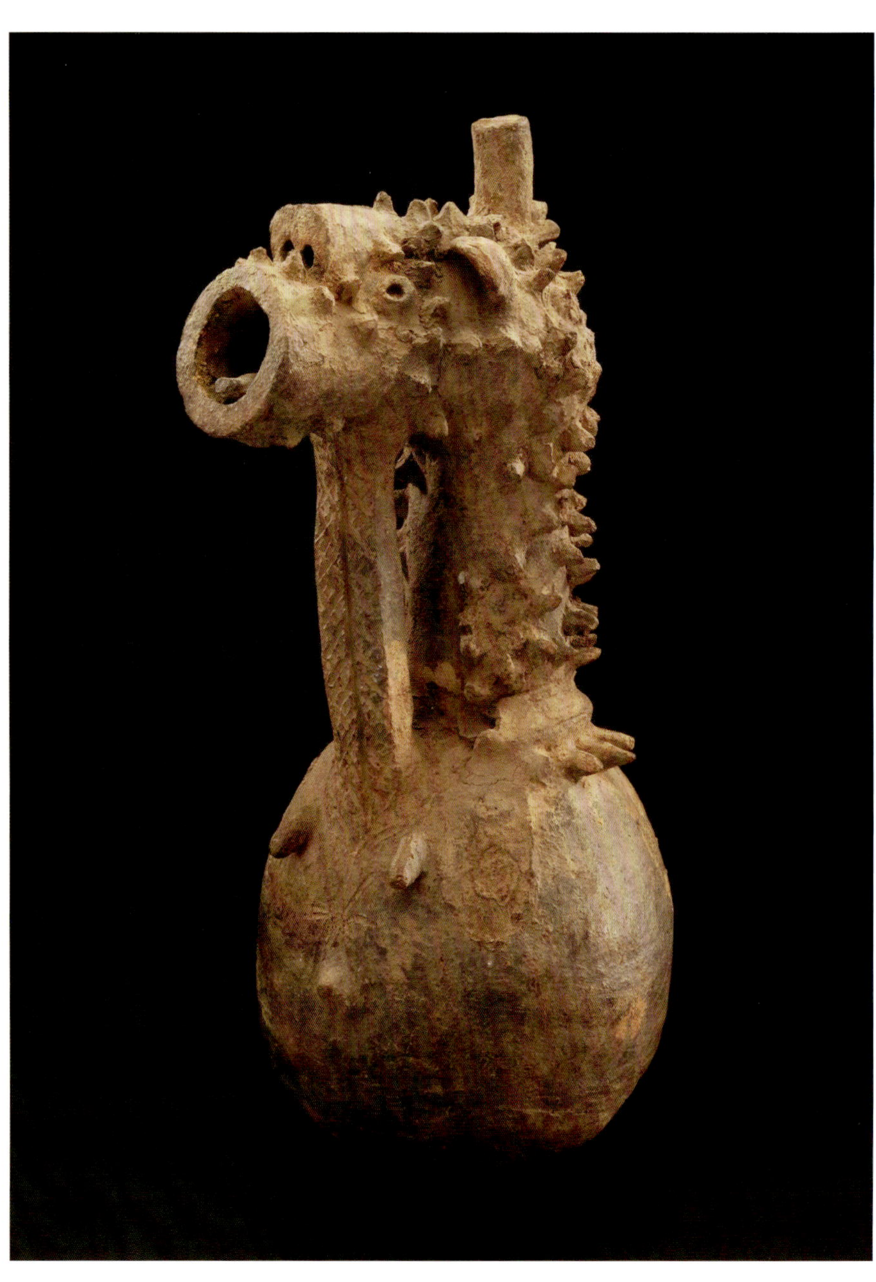

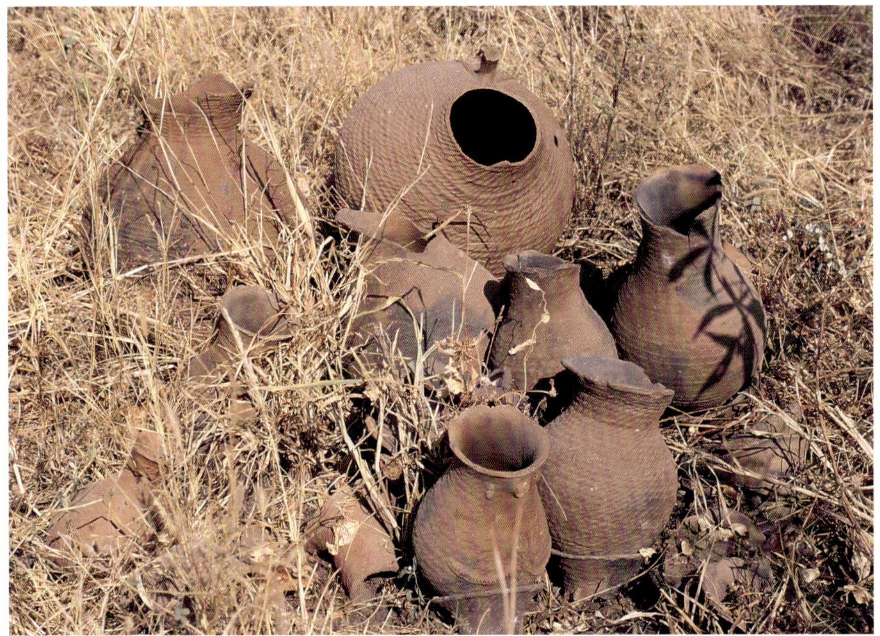

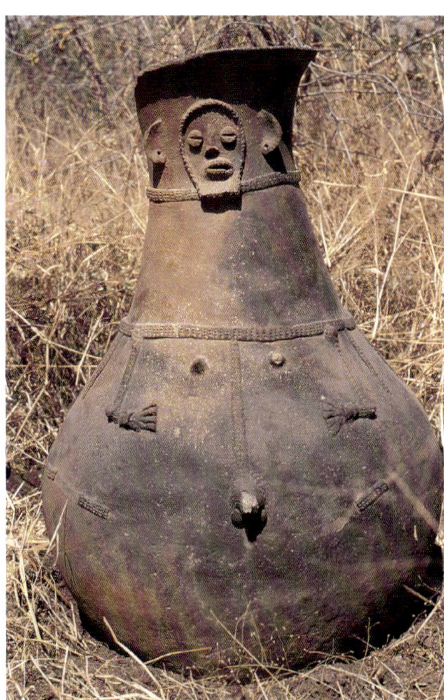

many examples were modeled with a simple sagittal ridge sometimes terminating in a pair of large nostrils positioned over the open mouth (see fig. 18.13). Because the head and neck are often large (and heavy) relative to the pot's "body," a "beard" was often added to support the weight. Sometimes the gender of the vessel is clearly indicated.

Even though some Ngwarkandangra resemble Ga'anda Mbir'thleng'nda in their size, profile, and proportions, most are rendered with an elongated neck and a clear emphasis on an exaggerated, spiky texture that describes the visible symptoms of the skin afflictions they are made to exorcise (see figs. 18.1, 18.12). The approach to surface decoration is very different from the meticulousness of Mbir'thleng'nda's decoration and complex iconography. Nevertheless, they both share a projecting tubular mouth and a bumpy surface texture that suggest that one is likely to have derived from the other. That Mbir'thleng'nda punishes Ga'anda social offenders with skin diseases suggests that the correlation is conceptual as well as formal. Not enough evidence exists to prove which was the prototype; however, it would seem more likely that the sculpturally complex and rigorous Ga'anda version developed out of a Ngwarkandangra model. That a particular set of ideas and objects circulated in the Ga'anda Hills among geographically proximate and linguistically distinct communities is clear from the ceramic evidence presented here. Yet, looking beyond the Ga'anda Hills to the kinds of vessels made to cure specific diseases by other Adamawa-speaking groups living west of the Gongola River and related to the 'Bəna—Longuda, Cham-Mwana, or Tula—shows that the kind of vigorous treatment of surface decoration evident on Ngwarkandangra is widespread and may have provided the model for the more refined Mbir'thleng'nda.

It may be in fact that Mbir'thleng'nda depended on a 'Bəna model. To demonstrate that the dynamics of interaction were unlikely to be unidirectional, however, the appearance of the highly uniform and diagnostic Ngum-Ngumi vessels in 'Bəna sacred shrines argues in favor of their dissemination from a workshop located among the Wetu Boga, who live east of Dingai. Although we cannot confirm the origins of the idea of a perambulating ceramic culture hero, Ngum-Ngumi's profile and precisely modeled surface, like Mbir'thleng'nda's distinctive decoration, have direct formal correspondences with other categories of Ga'anda ceramics if not other categories of Ga'anda visual culture. The presence of Ga'anda vessels in 'Bəna shrines reveals that the frontier between these two groups was highly porous, and by virtue of their ascribed power and efficacy, Ngum-Ngumi vessels crossed ethnolinguistic boundaries acquiring new names while retaining aspects of their initial identity and meaning.

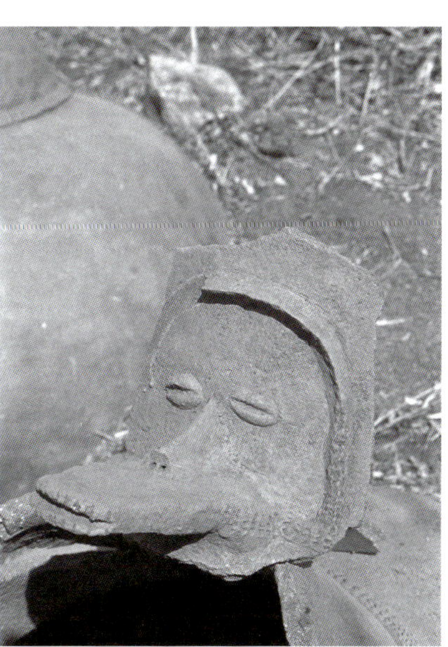

18.14
This *wiija* shrine, located in the old site of Gureshi in western 'Bəna, contains vessels that have the same rope-like texture as *wiisa* documented in 'Bəna communities located to the east (see figs. 18.2, 18.5).
PHOTOGRAPH BY MARLA C. BERNS, 1981.

18.15
This vessel (*gontime*) was used to contain beer offered to the ancestors at annual pre-planting festivals maintained by the 'Bəna Gureshi. The face rendered on the vessel's "neck" is similar to other 'Bəna *wiisa* (see fig. 18.7) even though the flange around the face is unusual.
PHOTOGRAPH BY MARLA C. BERNS, OLD GURESHI, 1981.

18.16
This broken head from a 'Bəna Gureshi *gontime* has an unusual projecting mouth.
PHOTOGRAPH BY MARLA C. BERNS, OLD GURESHI, 1981.

Among the westernmost 'Bəna who live around the town of Gureshi, no vessels were documented resembling the Komalamne or Ngwarkandangra that are distinctive of the Roba or Dingai 'Bəna. Small *wiisa* vessels were, however, used to contain the spirits of family ancestors from whom blessings of health and well-being were sought. The form and surface decoration of these are the same as those photographed among Roba and Yang groups (fig. 18.14). Distinctive to the Gureshi, however, were very large figurative vessels, called *gontime* (H: 75–85 cm), which were filled with beer offered to the spirits of ancestors during annual pre-planting festivals (fig. 18.15). They are modeled with faces, arms, breasts, navels, and genitalia. The handling of the facial features with coffee-bean eyes, a keeled nose, and a prominent and projecting mouth, is reminiscent of the faces on figurative vessels enshrined at Hatta (cf. fig. 18.6). The use of raised and scored ridges of clay is also a consistent strategy for outlining the vessel's arms and decorating its broad burnished surface. Two other *gontime*, though broken, also have faces framed by a flange with sharply projecting mouths (fig. 18.16). It is intriguing to compare the faces on these 'Bəna vessels with those on certain Mbir'thleng'nda (see fig. 17.15a) as well as *'bahanda* (see fig. 17.34) healing pots, as all share the same approach to rendering features. These correspondences further support the likely movement and amalgamation of ideas westward across the Ga'anda Hills. Looking south to the Yungur, similar conventions persist in their ancestral vessels, which are among the most diverse and elaborate in the Gongola River Valley.

YUNGUR

The Yungur live in an area dominated by parallel rows of granite hills and are dispersed over about 500 square kilometers of the eastern Lower Gongola Valley (fig. 18.17). Their communities are concentrated in three main localities—Diterra, Waltandi, and Suktu. The town of Dumne near Diterra is the Yungur administrative center. Distinctive to this rugged area is the valley formed by the eastward-flowing Loko River, which joins the Kilengi River before emptying into the Benue. This river valley provides a rich, loamy soil for farming and must have been attractive to settlers. It served historically as a conduit into the upland zone but also provided access for Fulani slave raiders, who from their headquarters in the town of Song were known to have launched attacks on the Yungur working on their farms (Meek 1931b, 2: 437). Early colonial reports described Yungur hamlets situated high in the rocky slopes and surrounded by barriers of thorn hedges with individual compounds further fortified by cactus hedges and narrow entryways blocked by low stone walls (Wilkinson 1923, 25). Defending the Yungur against intruders, these measures also served to protect shrine precincts situated within the perimeters of hamlets. Centers of spiritual power remained high in rocky citadels, and in 1981 many were still in use in remote locations.

Each Yungur locality was governed by a chief or Gubo (pl.: Gubsa), whose primary obligation as elsewhere was to maintain the religious associations (formerly referred to in the literature as "cults") upon which survival depended. Because his duties were primarily sacred, secular matters were delegated to his deputies, called Pagubsa. Settlement within each locality was organized around patrilineal families, the leaders of which were called Ed Handa. The governing councils of Yungur centers consisted of Pagubsa, Ed Handa, and the Gubo, who served as the titular head. This politico-ritual hierarchy provided the structure and rationale for the complex system of shrines (*xidwiiso*, or "rooms for *wiiso*") dispersed across the Yungur area. These housed ceramic vessels called *wiiso*, containing the spirits of deceased male Yungur leaders or men belonging to families eligible to have produced leaders (*amwapa*). Every hamlet had one or more *xidwiiso* (fig. 18.18), and many such shrines were still filled with a stunning variety of *wiiso* vessels in 1981.

The most elaborate system of political organization evolved in Diterra, where as many as sixteen hamlets were grouped under one Gubo.[8] In fact, the Diterra Gubo

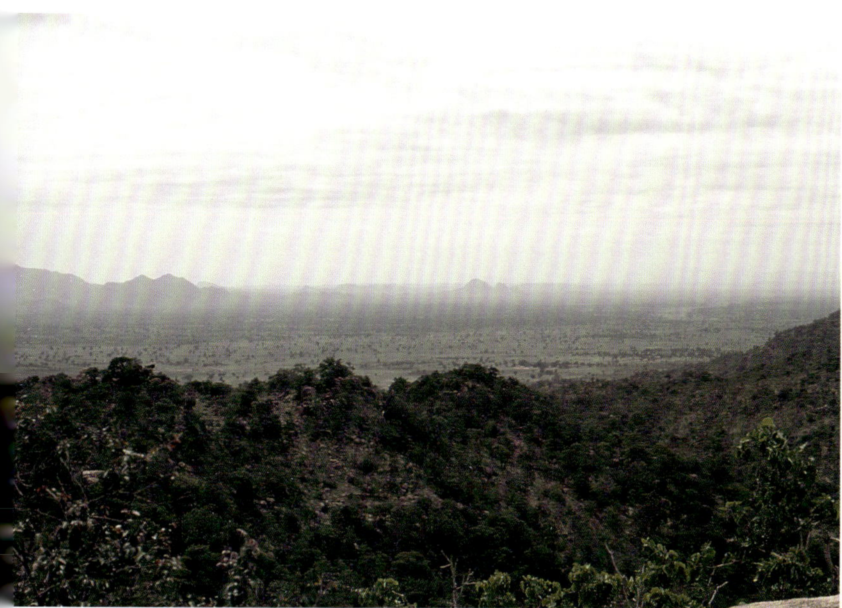

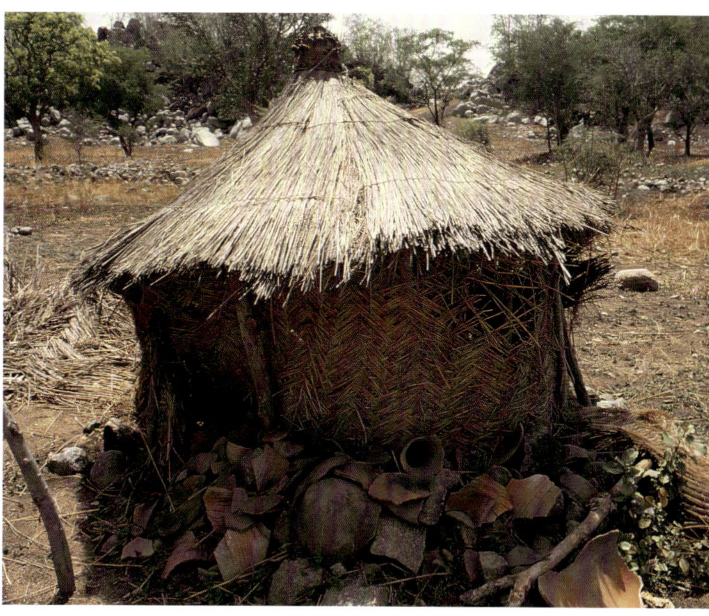

was nominally regarded as the spiritual head of all the Yungur, and he was responsible for maintaining the largest and most powerful precinct with nine discrete shrine enclosures.[9] Two of these shrines housed the vessels for spirits of deceased chiefs and two for spirits of members of chiefly lineages who did not attain the status of high office (*amwapa*), along with several others for the most important sacred paraphernalia brought by the Yungur from their mythic homeland, Mukan.

Through the spirits of their chiefly ancestors, the main creator god, Leura (or Ed Gunda), was asked to bring prosperity or to rid the community of misfortune. The power of such *wiiso* spirits is based on the belief that when the elderly die, especially chiefs, their spirits go to the realm of Leura as a reward for good character (Nissen 1968, 148). Their closeness to Leura makes them appropriate conduits through which the living can directly appeal for health and prosperity. The enshrined *wiiso* vessels objectify these ancestral forces and provide a focus for ritual offerings at key moments during the year.

Wiiso shrines are renewed at Mam Nsara, the annual harvest festival held in October-November, and again at Mama, the pre-planting festival held in April.[10] Mama was the more important of the two events and was the time when Gubo and Ed Handa made special appeals to ancestral spirits for sufficient rainfall and agricultural fertility. As elsewhere, beer brewed from sorghum and sprouted with rainwater was central to renewal ceremonies. The beer was offered to the *wiiso* in gourd bowls and splashed over the pots. After three days, it was shared with living leaders to reinforce bonds of affiliation across successive generations and to secure the beneficent intervention of the ancestors. One or more domestic animals were also sacrificed, and blood was sprinkled on the sacred objects kept inside the *xidwiiso* shrines (figs. 18.19).

Offerings made to past Gubo and other ritual leaders who served or were eligible to have done so were meant to appease the spirits considered responsible should rain be inadequate or other calamities strike. In this event, living leaders convened in specially demarcated areas that functioned as oracles, where the names of *amwapa* were called out until there was a sign indicating which one was responsible. The *wiiso* corresponding to the forebear in question was then removed from the shrine and offered more beer in an effort to reverse the situation. These practices reveal that the Yungur believe *wiiso* vessels and the forces they embody to be the ancestors, made physically present in the lives of their descendants. With proper treatment the *wiiso* offered a crucial avenue for asserting control over the conditions necessary for human survival. The ongoing authority of Yungur leaders rested on successful negotiations with their immediate and distant ancestors.

18.17
From the rock outcropping of Kərim northeast of the town of Song, the Yungur Hills are visible. The valley formed by the Loko River may be seen in the distance.
PHOTOGRAPH BY MARLA C. BERNS, 1981.

18.18
The sacred pottery shrine (*xidwiiso*) kept in the Yungur district of Waltandi has woven-grass walls and a thatched roof. It resembles local domestic architecture but is distinguished from it by the broken pottery surrounding the walls and a ceramic roof finial (*bwela*). The *bwela* (pl.: *bwelta*) is elaborately modeled with projecting decorative elements, including clusters of stylized human figures (see Berns 1990, 59–60).
PHOTOGRAPH BY MARLA C. BERNS, 1981.

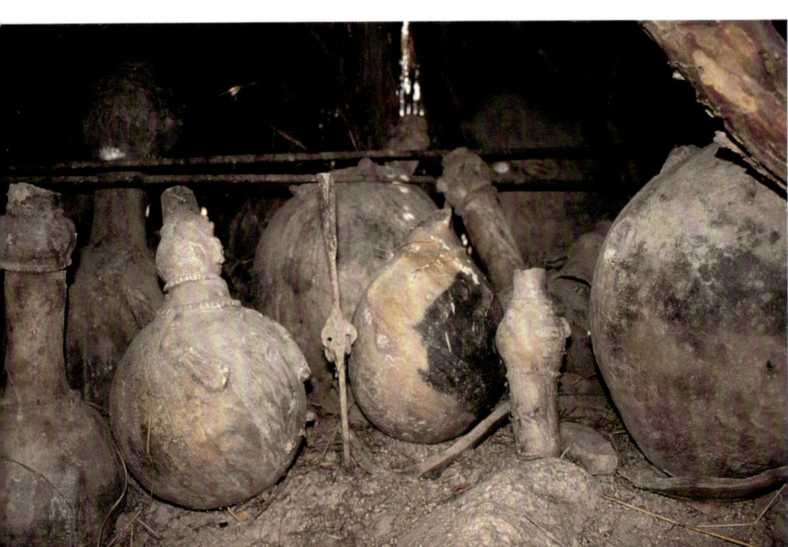

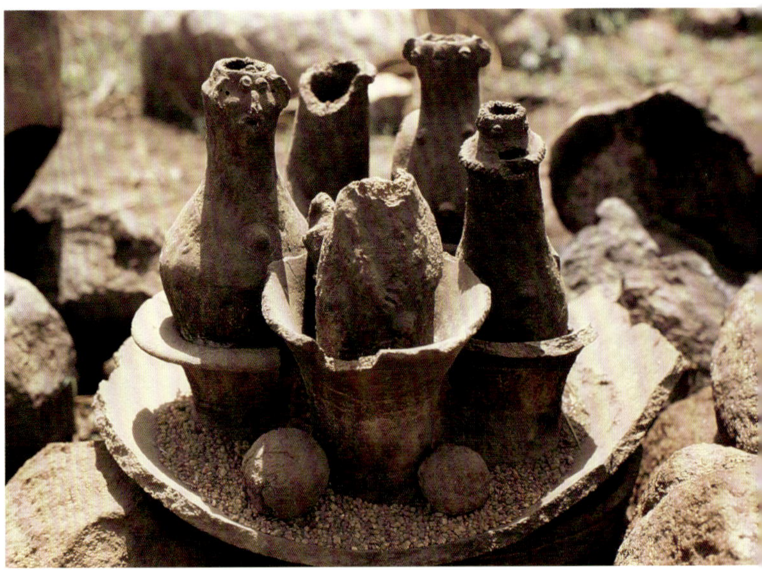

18.19

Within the second of the nine *xidwiiso* maintained by the Yungur of Diterra, the *wiiso* vessels contain the spirits of *amwapa*, men who were eligible for, but did not attain, chiefly status. Traces of beer and blood offerings splashed onto the vessels' surfaces during annual harvest festivals are still visible. Several of the *wiiso* have notably elongated necks and small heads. The iron spears kept in the shrine were formerly used by Yungur chiefs in battle.

PHOTOGRAPH BY MARLA C. BERNS, 1981.

18.20

This cluster of small Yungur *wiiso* (H: 15–17 cm) was kept by the Vorro family, Gumba hamlet, Waltandi district. Even at this small scale each of the vessels is individualized to contain the spirit of an Ed Handa who died. Each of the five represented here was remembered by name: Umbelandan, Ownbwelowandania, Bwota, Owbwota, and Bwansareh.

PHOTOGRAPH BY MARLA C. BERNS, 1981.

That *wiiso* represent specific individuals is revealed in their striking variety. With the exception of one category (see below), I found no two to be identical. I have argued elsewhere that Yungur *wiiso* can be considered "portraits" not because they capture personal likenesses but because their stylistic traits are manipulated to establish Yungur identity and to express differences between lineages and localities.[11] In 1981 I had the opportunity to document several hundred *wiiso* extant in shrines in Diterra, Suktu, and Waltandi. It is easiest to classify them by size (they range from 10 cm to 95 cm in height) and to note the ways that examples drawn from family-based shrines share common stylistic features, just as the members of the family share genetically based physiognomic resemblances (fig. 18.20 and see fig. 18.19). Individuation is expressed through the handling of certain sculptural elements: size and profile of the vessel, the alignment of arms on the torso, the location of the face along the "neck" of the pot, the arrangement of features on the facial plane, and the elaboration of signifiers of Yungur social identity, such as body scarification, chipped teeth, ear piercing, and coiffure. Yungur *wiiso* stand out among the other ceramic traditions by virtue of their degree of anthropomorphization and the ways in which their iconography intensifies the fundamental linkages between pots and people, as well as people and spirits. *Wiiso* communicate essential ideas about social, cultural, or historical identities through the purposeful manipulation of form and detail.

This is nowhere more emphatic than in the one exceptional category of *wiiso* that is remarkable for its near-exact duplication in several Yungur locations, as well as its large size and the degree of realism in the modeling of its head and face. The most imposing example of this type was situated at the entry to the Diterra sacred precinct, half-buried in the ground, and given the name Tentire (fig. 18.21). When viewed from the side, the curvature of the cheeks, forehead, and back of the head of this vessel reveal an interest in anatomical structure that is absent in most *wiiso* (see fig. 1.3). Also distinctive is the beard, which follows the jawline and projects over the face in a triangular shape (as opposed to the more frequent rectangular flange on smaller examples), and a tall crest or coiffure opening into a spout. Compared to the highly exaggerated physiognomy of other *wiiso*, the facial features tend to be quite restrained: the eyes are conceived as raised slits, the nose is a keeled triangle, the mouth is open slightly to expose small chipped teeth, and the ears are perforated disks. The chiefly status of the spirit that this vessel contains is communicated by the curved staff modeled over the left arm or on the torso, a reference to the bent iron staff (*salawa*) carried by a Gubo during the Mama festival. Despite possessing this emblem of male authority, Diterra elders told me that Tentire was female and that her male counterpart, Tire, was buried

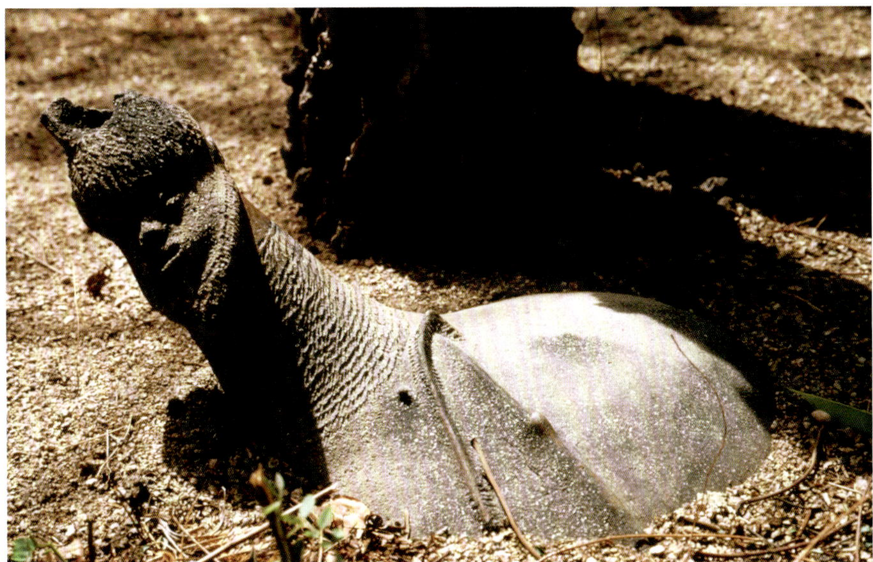

18.21
A large *wiiso* serves as a sentry for the sacred precinct of Diterra and is named Tentire. The staff over the left shoulder of the vessel represents the bent iron staff (*salawa*) that the Yungur chief (Gubo) carried during rainmaking rites.
PHOTOGRAPH BY MARLA C. BERNS, 1981.

nearby and covered with an overturned pot in an effort to protect the living from his "troublesome character."

Vessels identical to this *wiiso* were enshrined in at least three of the nine *xidwiiso* within the Diterra shrine district. In one (fig. 18.22), situated in a rocky site overlooking the valley below, two of these monumental *wiiso* (H: 95 cm) were enshrined along with a long-necked iron vessel. Informants claimed that this *wiiso* type (as well as the iron vessel) originated in the Mandara Mountains along the Nigeria-Cameroon border, from which it was brought to Mukan, the ancestral homeland of the Yungur (as well as their northern 'Bəna relatives). The Yungur say that Mukan is "somewhere in the Ga'anda Hills," but its location could not be precisely identified. These vessels embody the power and the presence of Mukan ancestral chiefs who first established spiritual ties with the forces governing Yungur survival. Their inclusion in these shrines legitimizes the religious authority of their descendants and their ties to this mythic homeland. They also serve as mnemonic devices reminding present-day Yungur leaders of their legacy and responsibility to affirm and maintain the social order. Although no scientific dating has been accomplished, it is possible that some of these "Mukan" *wiiso* are quite old (see interleaf 1), suggested by their worn or eroded surfaces, especially visible on the Tentire sentry and on one of the preserved and broken "heads" (fig. 18.23).

A closely related example (fig. 18.24), also said to have come from Mukan via the Mandaras, was kept within the most important of the pottery shrines, called the *xidwiisoguno* (major room for *wiiso*), which was also located in the rocky outcroppings on Diterra hill (fig. 18.25). The *wiiso* in this shrine were approached before all the others, and the shrine's contents included fragments of broken pots along with this single large "Mukan" *wiiso*, photographed in 1981 leaning at the back. It entered the collection of the Barbier Mueller Museum in 2000, having been purchased in the United States, and it is impossible to reconstruct the terms under which this commanding and historically significant vessel was exported from Nigeria. Like the other spirit pots now in collections, it is likely that several factors are responsible, including the intensification of pressures to abandon local religious practices in favor of the world religions. Its removal has afforded the opportunity to study its details more carefully and to posit that it may be a prototype for the others illustrated here. The head and face resemble those on the other Mukan *wiiso* described above but some of the surface decoration is distinctive, especially the treatment of the neck and the decoration on the torso and forehead. The thick applied ornamentation of the neck may be a more explicit rendition of the heavy woven cord that seems to be suggested in the impressed patterns around the necks of the others.

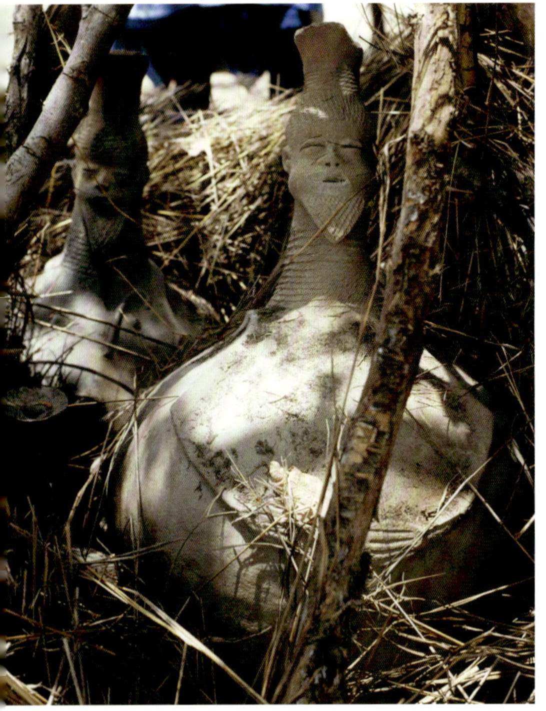

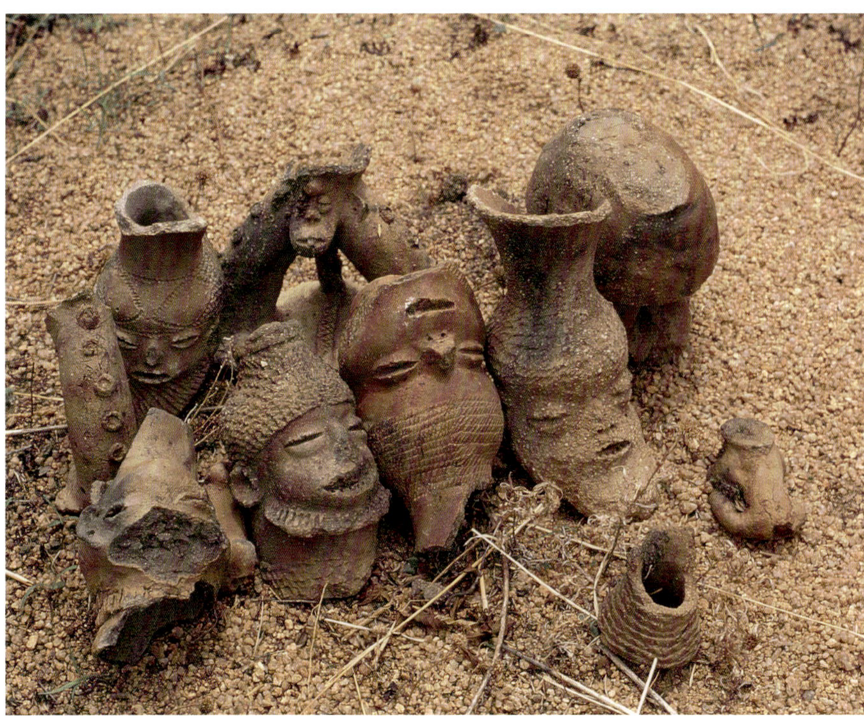

18.22
Two "Mukan" *wiiso* representing chiefs (Gubsa) who have died were enshrined in the fourth *xidwiiso* in Diterra. A staff of office (*salawa*) is visible on the left shoulder of the vessel at the back. The *wiiso* in the foreground is 95 centimeters in height. Included in this shrine is a long-necked iron vessel, which like the *wiiso*, was said to have come from the ancestral homeland, Mukan.
PHOTOGRAPH BY MARLA C. BERNS, 1981.

18.23
These *wiiso* head fragments can be classified as "Mukan" variants. The one at the far right is nearly identical to the *wiiso* illustrated in figures 18.21 and 18.22; its eroded surface suggests that it may be of considerable age.
PHOTOGRAPH BY MARLA C. BERNS, 1981.

Very striking is the bold decoration of the torso with a series of nested chevrons bisected by a central line ending at the umbilicus. This reproduces in clay the designs that appear on a Yungur woman's torso that are called *kele* and are executed as part of the nine-stage program of facial and body scarification called Sā (fig. 18.26; see Chappel 1977, 206, fig. 222). As was true among the Ga'anda and 'Bəna, all girls must undergo this complex sequence of markings, which signals their commitment to maintaining the prescribed social order, before they can marry. Yungur scarification designs draw from a common vocabulary of motifs seen on the bodies of their northern neighbors with chevrons and lozenges predominating. Among the Yungur, however, the spatial alignment of cicatrices differs. Broader expanses of skin are left uncut so that the raised patterns that result stand out more crisply. This is especially true of the chevrons worked down the center of the torso, accomplished by several parallel lines of closely placed cuts, which are rendered dramatically on the "skin" of this Mukan *wiiso* as impressions made with the edge of a gourd chip. The bold triangle on the vessel's forehead is also likely a quotation from the line of triangles worked across a woman's forehead. Again, the essential linkage between pots and people and between people and their ancestors is expressed through the most permanent and visible markers of enculturation. As is true across the Ga'anda Hills, pots share the process of irreversible transformation with people—with scarification as the ultimate visual and tactile signifier of commitment to social perpetuation. The nature and degree of interaction among the peoples living in the Eastern Gongola Valley is surely revealed in the "reservoir" of symbols from which they have commonly drawn to produce meaningful visual signifiers.[12] These Mukan *wiiso* are powerful symbols of belonging and are able to communicate much about the social lives and histories of their makers.[13]

The same type of chiefly *wiiso* was also documented in Waltandi, located just west of Diterra, where its inclusion served to legitimize the spiritual authority of this Yungur subsection. In the Vorro Hills, where the Waltandi were said to have first settled, I photographed a very large accumulation of *wiiso* (fig. 18.27). Most were heads broken from their bodies, but two complete, if damaged, vessels remained. Waltandi informants said that these two pots, plus the broken head and neck of another, traveled to Vorro on their own volition; one of them is easily identifiable as of the "Mukan" type. These "first" arrivals were discovered in a nearby rock shelter by the ancestors of

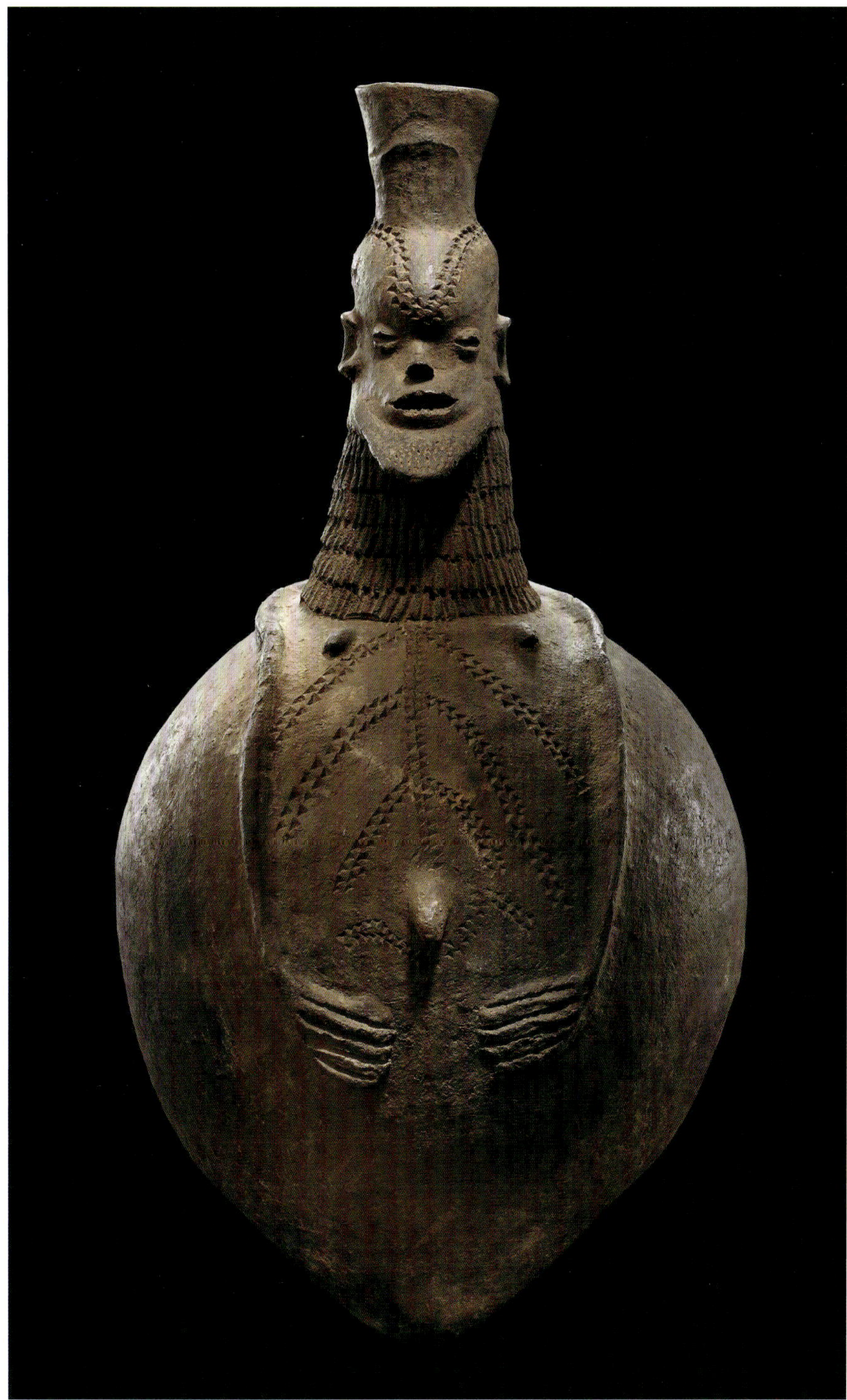

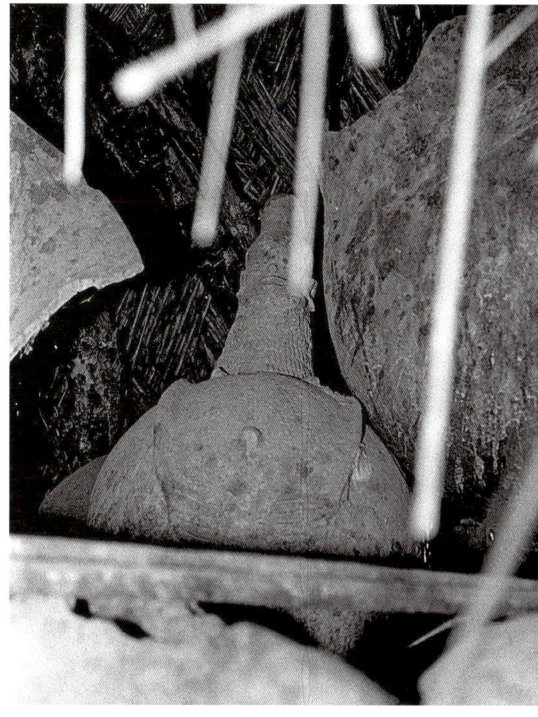

18.24
Ancestor vessel (*wiiso*)
Yungur peoples, Diterra district, early to mid-twentieth century
Ceramic
H: 58 cm
BARBIER-MUELLER MUSEUM, GENEVA, 1015-115
IMAGE: COURTESY BARBIER-MUELLER MUSEUM, GENEVA. PHOTOGRAPH © STUDIO FERRAZZINI BOUCHET
PROVENANCE: NORWOOD GALLERY, AUSTIN ART CONSORTIUM, AUSTIN, 2000

This commanding *wiiso* was formerly kept in the most important of the nine shrines (*xidwiisoguno*) maintained in the sacred precinct of Diterra. It resembles the other "Mukan" examples but is highly distinctive for the ribbed texture of the neck and the finely articulated torso scarifications, which emulate those executed on Yungur women's torsos (see fig. 18.26). For a profile view of this vessel, see figure 1.13.

18.25
The *xidwiisoguno* shrine, located high in the rocky site of Diterra, at one time contained the vessel illustrated in figure 18.24, which is lying down on its back in the center of the photograph. The *wiiso* in this shrine were approached before those in the other *xidwiiso* in the Diterra ritual precinct.
PHOTOGRAPH BY MARLA C. BERNS, 1981.

the present-day Waltandi who made them the focus of yearly pre-planting and harvest rites. A view of the accumulation from behind (fig. 18.29) shows the rocky hillside that offers these pots protection. The two largest examples have blind spouts at the back allowing the heads to be modeled completely in the round. The tight rows of plaits over the top of the head or the spiral patterns encircling it represent hairstyles restricted to Yungur men of high rank.

Most of the broken heads at this site were collected from abandoned shrines or rock shelters dotted over the Vorro Hills to provide a single focus for their propitiation. This is a remarkable group of fragments with some of the most finely modeled of all the examples documented. As is true across the Lower Gongola Valley, power resides in the heads of these vessels, whose individualized features sustain associations with the specific ancestors they are meant to represent. Their accumulation

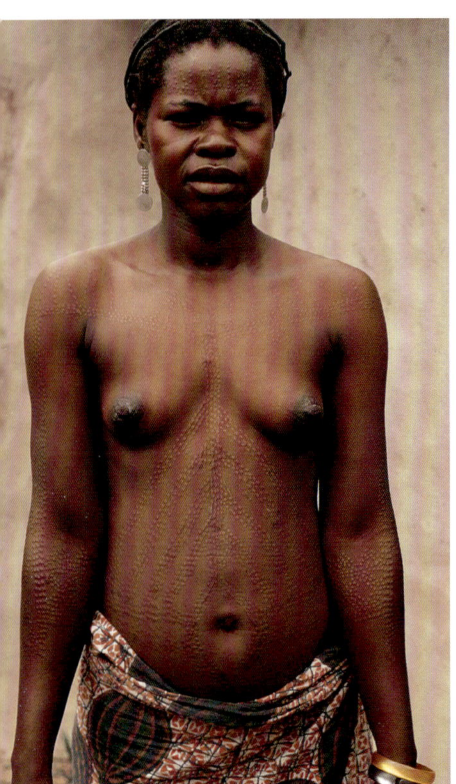

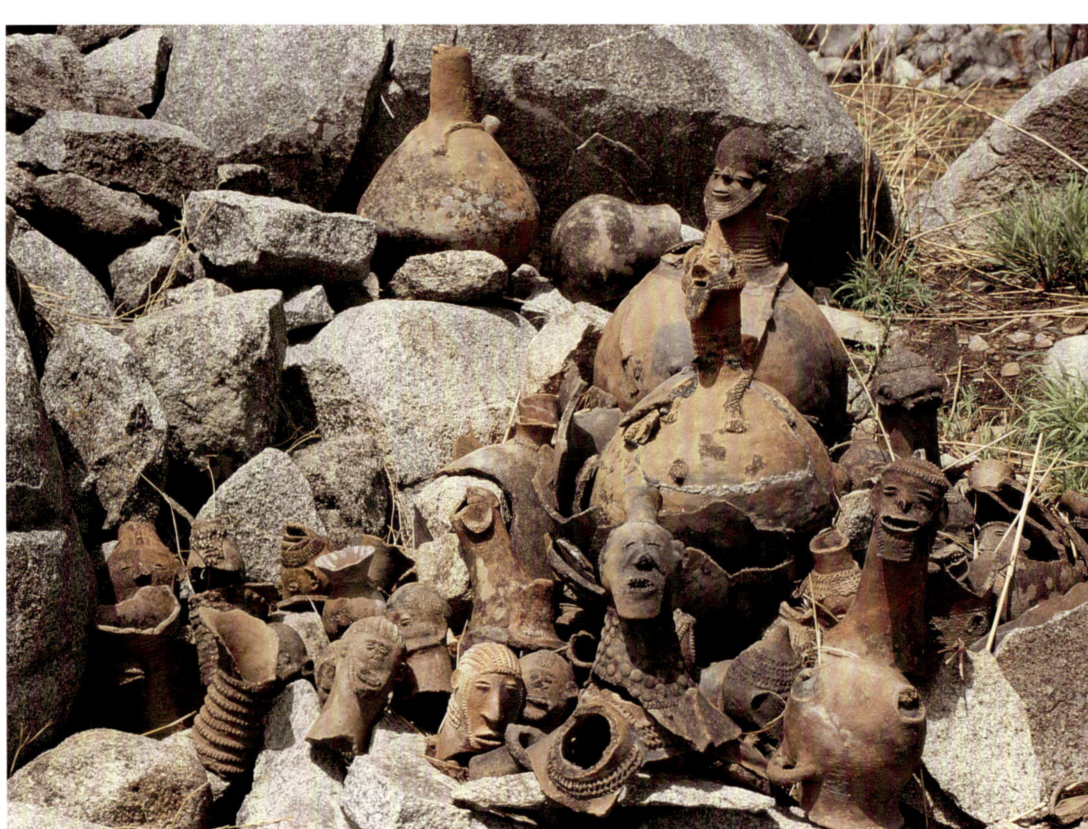

18.26

This Yungur woman displays the prominent torso scarifications called *kele*, which are sometimes depicted on the bodies of *wiiso*. She also has a row of triangles (*tura*) across her forehead.

PHOTOGRAPH BY MARLA C. BERNS, 1981.

18.27

All of the Yungur *wiiso* vessels in this large accumulation at the site of Pəle'wo in the Vorro Hills were said to have come to the location on their own volition. The *wiiso* belong to the Vorro family of Waltandi, and the first to arrive was the large intact vessel on the right at the back, which has the conventional features of the "Mukan" variety. His "wife" is present as a head fragment, her neck covered with flat pellets, directly below him in the foreground. She was, however, replaced with the second intact vessel that is situated between them.

PHOTOGRAPH BY MARLA C. BERNS, 1981.

dramatically shows that no two heads are exactly alike, supporting my contention that they are individual "portraits" despite commonalities in their stylized faces, elaborate coiffures, and raised texture around the neck. Many of these heads also have the chipped teeth and pierced ears that underscore Yungur identity and enculturation.

Two other shrines at Diterra contain vessels that further demonstrate the marked stylistic diversity of the *wiiso* corpus. One large and expressively modeled example containing the spirit of an *amwapa* has a spherical body with long dangling arms ringed with bracelets and ending in expressive hands (fig. 18.28). It also has a staff of office on the right shoulder, and its mouth is filled with chipped teeth. The face resembles those of the Mukan variety but lacks the attempt at realism.

An interior view of a second Diterra shrine for *amwapa* shows how *wiiso* accumulate and differ stylisically, some executed with very long narrow necks ending in large spherical heads; others, with round faces modeled near the "mouth" of the vessel (see fig. 18.19). Another Diterra clan, the Bera Kumla, maintained a shrine with very similar types of *wiiso*, mostly broken but showing even more clearly the elongated necks topped with heads of different sizes framed by raised ridges of decoration. The faces have familiar features—coffee-bean eyes, keeled noses, slit-like mouths with chipped teeth, cup-shaped pierced ears, and small rectangular beards.

There are many *wiiso* that range from 25 to 40 centimeters in height enshrined across the Yungur landscape. The ones found in Suktu (fig. 18.30) exemplify the variety in the expressive modeling of facial features that can exist within one shrine context. Individualized portraits, however, have a beard, chipped teeth, pierced ears, and an elaborately plaited coiffure, recalling the actual appearance of ranking Yungur men. The bodies of some *wiiso*, however, also bear the female scarification design that initiates Sā, a lozenge framing a girl's navel (*detkale*). Details of other *wiiso* in this size category likewise capture the dramatic extroversion and differentiation of these ancestral representations (see fig. 15.11).

The smallest *wiiso* (H: 10–20 cm) are found principally at Waltandi where they represent deceased Ed Handa village heads (fig. 18.31, and see fig. 18.20). These small

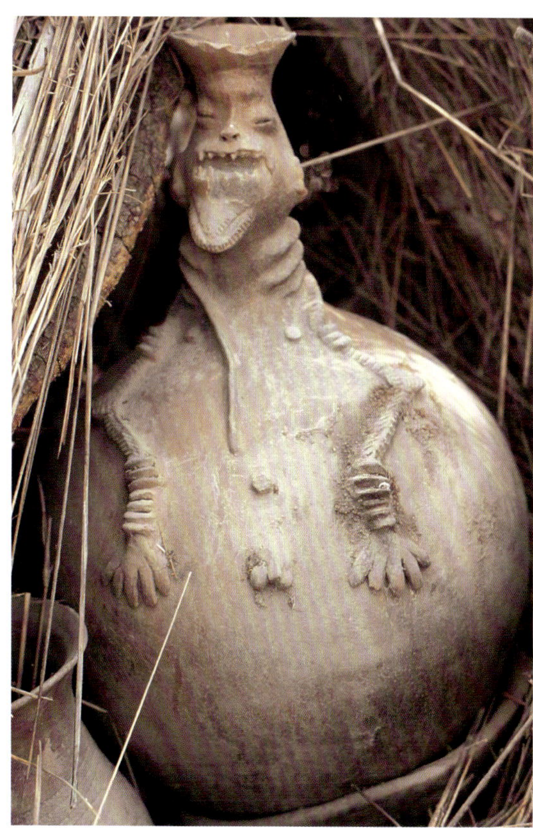

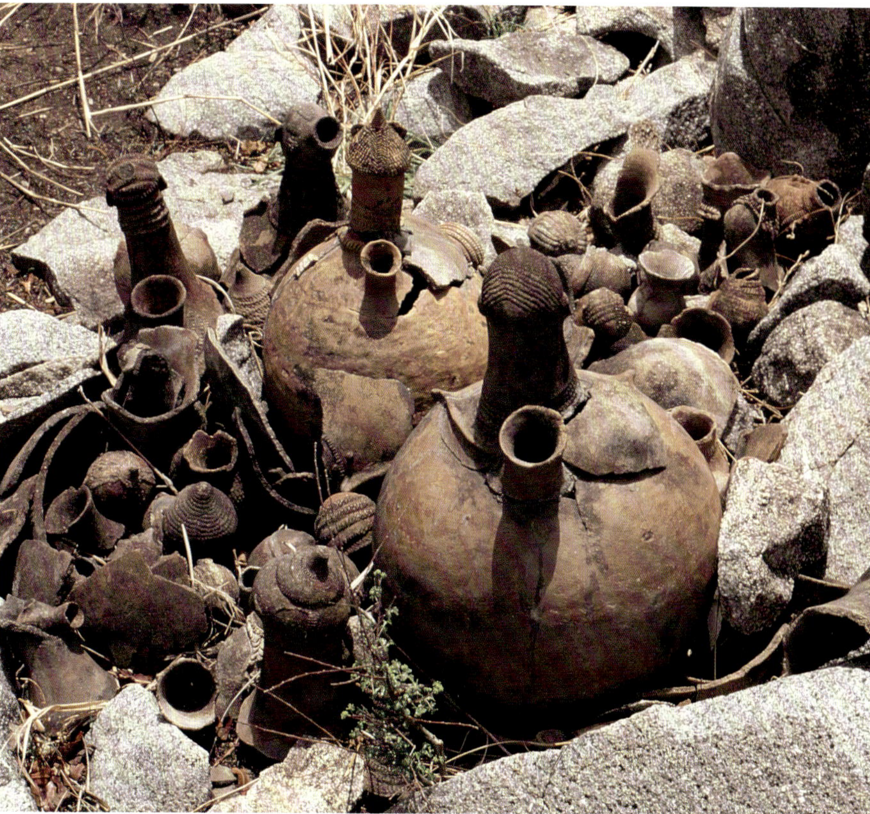

clusters of vessels, elevated on broken pot "necks," were covered by large overturned storage vessels, and kept within the perimeter of local hamlets. These small *wiiso* have very simple contours and rudimentary facial features modeled on the "neck" of the pot near its "mouth." Yet, even at this small scale, each *wiiso* is differentiated to represent an individual ancestor.

There is little doubt that the diversity within the *wiiso* corpus is due in part to the number of older women potters who make the vessels for their own extended families. Although informants varied as to whether men or women made the *wiiso*—with those in Diterra saying they were made by male ritual specialists—I would argue that here, as elsewhere, the primacy of women as potters and producers of domestic and ritual wares makes them more likely to be the artists of *wiiso* than men.[14] Indeed, producing *wiiso* is perceived as a creative act much like giving birth, and Leura, the creator god, "the potter, the fashioner of men and all living things," is said to "make" new life from the spirits contained in *wiiso*.[15]

Although the Yungur believe their ancestors are directly involved in maintaining the good health of their descendants, there are also other spirit forces responsible for causing and curing specific diseases. As with the 'Bana, ceramic vessels are the focus of healing procedures and are the repositories into which spirits of illnesses are transferred and contained. Vessels of this sort mostly take the form of small, roughly modeled pots, called *warsa*. Some have pointed nodules or other raised features that describe the symptoms they are meant to cure. No vessel with a cantilevered head like that of Ngwarkandangra, however, was documented among the Yungur, suggesting that this distinctive sculptural tradition is confined to the northern and western areas of the Ga'anda Hills.

How can the stylistic and conceptual parallels among the ceramic vessels made by the Ga'anda, 'Bana, and Yungur help untangle the historical links between them? One clue may lie in the consistent reference to the sacred ancestral homeland of Mukan by the 'Bana and the Yungur (including the closely related Mboi, Handa, and Libbo groups). The Yungur locate Mukan somewhere in the northern Song District of the Ga'anda Hills. The 'Bana locate it in the same general area around the town of Jangara,

18.28
This *wiiso* contains the spirit of an *amwap*a, a man who was eligible for but did not achieve chiefly status. It is an especially notable example, covered with many emblems of male status, including a staff around the neck, teeth chipped to points, and many bracelets. It was enshrined in the third *xidwiiso* in the Diterra precinct, which was reserved for the ancestral spirits of *amwapa*.
PHOTOGRAPH BY MARLA C. BERNS, 1981.

8.29
The rear view of the shrine at Pale'wo in the Vorro Hills (see fig. 18.27) shows how the *wiiso* were nestled within the rocky terrain to provide some sanctuary. Seeing the vessels from behind reveals the use of blind spouts on the two intact "Mukan" *wiiso*, an innovation not seen elsewhere, which allowed the artist to impart an added naturalism to their heads.
PHOTOGRAPH BY MARLA C. BERNS, 1981.

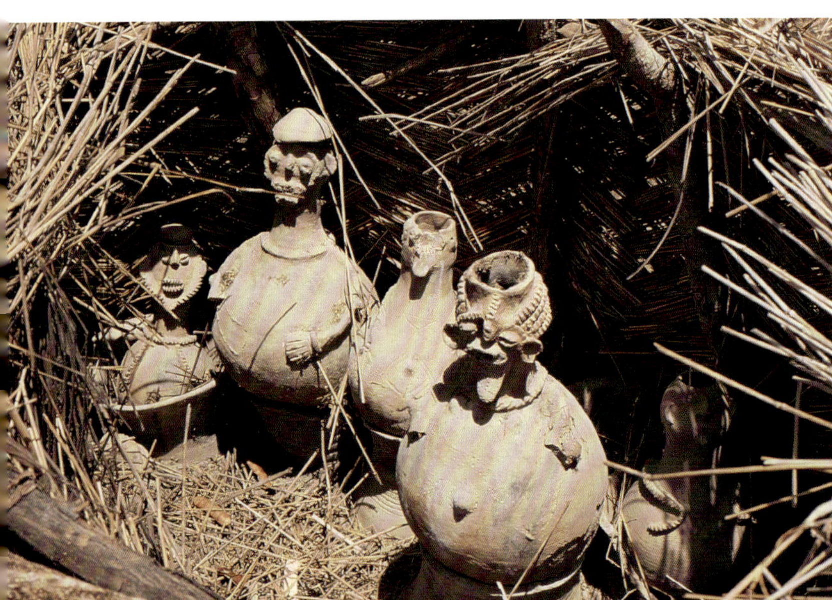

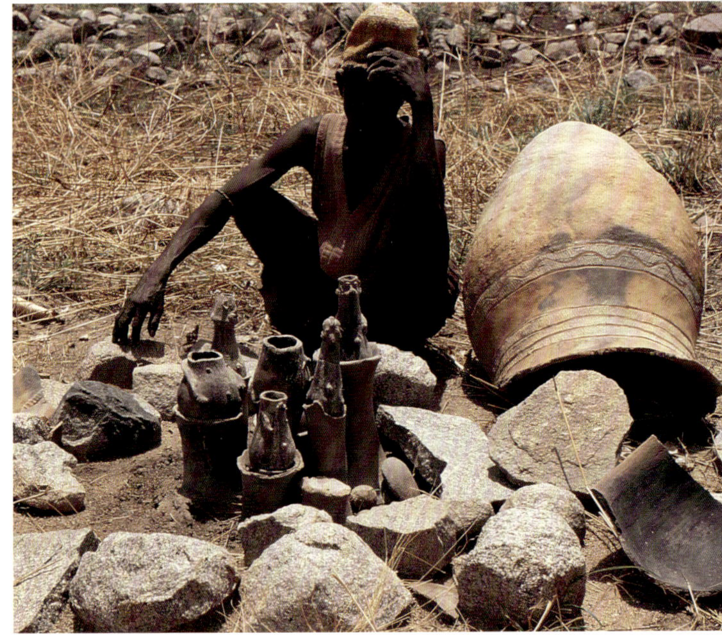

18.30
These four *wiiso* vessels were kept in one of three *xidwiiso* maintained by the Yungur of the Suktu district, and each contains the spirit of an *amwapa*. Their differentiation as specific "portraits" is striking, achieved through the handling of sculptural details.
PHOTOGRAPH BY MARLA C. BERNS, 1981.

18.31
These small *wiiso* were kept by the Gwarizata family of the Waltandi Yungur, and each contains the spirit of an *amwapa*. Next to the shrine's custodian is the large storage vessel (*to*) that is used to conceal and protect the *wiiso*.
PHOTOGRAPH BY MARLA C. BERNS, 1981.

about 19 kilometers southeast of Riji near the village of Jaromboyi, which is occupied both by 'Bəna and Ga'anda speakers.[16] I have speculated that Mukan may be the Ga'anda sacred site of Makwar, a dramatic isolated mountain in Ga'anda Town where the Gudban rainmaker conducts annual rites to ensure rainfall and agricultural fertility.[17] Both the 'Bəna and the Yungur acknowledge the Ga'anda rainmaker to be the most powerful religious authority in the region.[18] It is possible that the Adamawa word "Mukan" has been Ga'andaized, undergoing a Chadic language "sound shift" to become "Makwar."[19] Even if the Mukan Hill remembered by related Adamawa speakers is situated elsewhere, naming the site of their key religious precinct Makwar suggests that the Ga'anda may have linked their authority to a legitimizing myth integral to the history of the region. By this means, the Ga'anda justified their use of Makwar's vast rock shelter and adjacent areas as the locale in which to maintain their most powerful religious symbols and to transact rituals that affected the entire region. Looking closely at the large storage pots kept in the Makwar rock shelter to prepare the beer used during annual Ho'mbata rituals (see fig. 17.28), intriguing formal correspondences with the storage pots made by the Yungur soon appear. Both share the same profile and have wide necks elaborately decorated with tight encircling lines. Yungur potters achieve this grooved effect by leaving visible very fine coils of clay. The Ga'anda typically achieve theirs with tight rows of split-stalk or gourd-chip impressions (see fig. 17.25). The large vessels set up at the front of the shelter, as well as those grouped to the side, could as easily be considered Yungur as Ga'anda, based on contemporary examples. When I photographed the Makwar shelter for the first time in 1978, the elderly ritual specialists who took me there explained that the vessels "discarded" to the side represented "chiefs who have died." It is tantalizing to imagine that these large and impressive pots may have been in this shelter before the Ga'anda arrived.

Contributing to the possibility that ancestors of the Yungur once lived in the northern Ga'anda Hills is an anomalous shrine complex in the vicinity of Gabun, the northernmost Ga'anda settlement area situated amidst some of the most spectacular hill formations in the region (see fig. 17.3). This shrine is located in a rocky citadel called Kanpelam (meaning, "in the shade of Pelam rock") and was photographed in 1970 by Arnold Rubin and again by me in 1980 (fig. 18.33). It consists of an accumulation of small figurative ceramic vessels (H: approximately 30–40 cm), solid clay figurines, stone balls, and broken sherds and heads. Rubin was told that the contents of the shrine were called *dexaa'nafca* (lit., "idols of people"), and I was told they were *sambarcha*, both

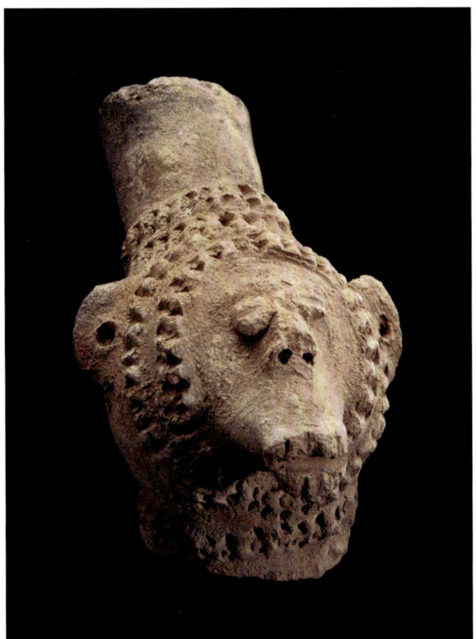

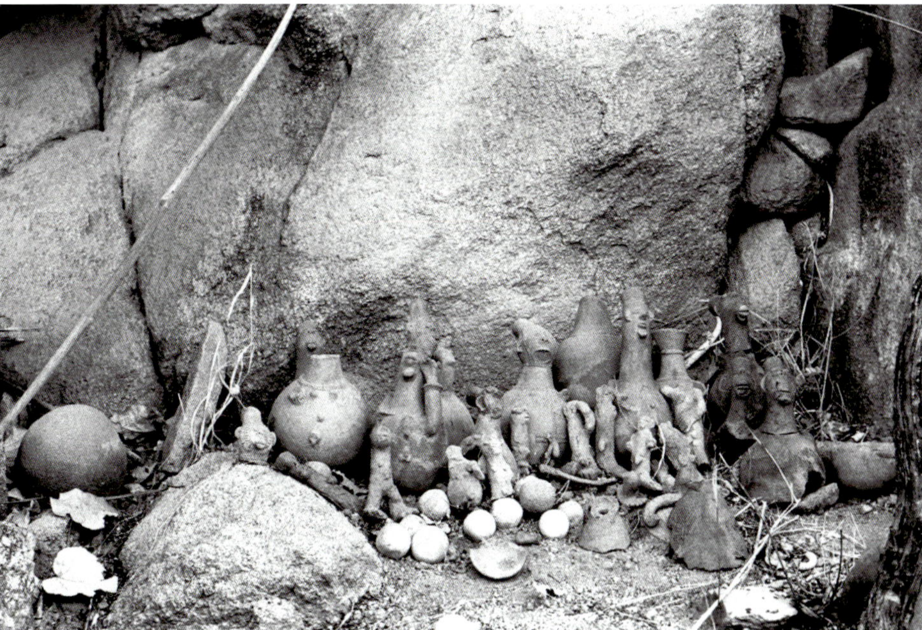

terms referring to their function as repositories of ancestral spirits. They were venerated in the same way as other *sambarcha* kept in Ga'anda pottery shrines.

The heads on Kanpelam vessels have facial features recalling those on Yungur *wiiso*—coffee-bean eyes, keeled noses, projecting lips, cup-shaped pierced ears, and flange-like beards (figs. 18.32, 18.35). Several also have chevron motifs worked over the navel to evoke female scarification. One even resembles the "Mukan" *wiiso* with its relatively restrained features and textured spout. Several are modeled with one or two arms raised to the face, almost as if cupping the hands to call out in (see fig. 18.33).[20] This animated gesture is rare on such vessels.

Some also have a head that tilts sharply backward with a projecting mouth, so that the facial features are aligned on a nearly horizontal plane (figs. 18.34, 18.35). It is tantalizing to consider whether this sculptural convention had any impact on the conceptualization of the distinctive cantilevered head of Mbir'thleng'nda, with its facial features also aligned on top of the vessel's "mouth" and sometimes confined within a ridged flange (see figs. 17.15a,b).

The contents of the shrine at Kanpelam suggest that they may have been originally made by someone other than the Ga'anda. The solid figurines recall the figures adorning ceramic finials (*bwelta*) that distinguish the houses of Yungur Gubo and Ed Handa as well as *xidwiiso* (fig. 18.36 and see fig. 18.18). They are elaborate constructions incorporating clusters of stylized figurines modeled onto globular bases and lashed to the top of a pointed thatched roof. The *bwelta* figurines are basically columnar supports for highly expressive and stylized faces, and as accumulations they represent the "people" a Gubo or other Yungur leader was meant to protect. Chappel (1977, 205) wrote that the hills above Diterra were littered with the remains of these finials. Each year at Mama, they were splashed with beer along with the ancestral *wiiso*. When they broke, the pieces were kept because even as fragments they contained the essence of the leaders who lived in the houses they once adorned. It is possible that the figurines gathered at Kanpelam served a similar ritual purpose and were asked, along with the spirits of ancestors invested in the associated *sambarcha,* for blessings of well-being.

It would be impossible to prove that the Kanpelam vessels were left by a long-departed population related to the present-day Yungur, although it seems inarguable that they more closely resemble the figurative *wiiso* of the 'Bəna or Yungur than of the Ga'anda pots. The historical relationship between the Ga'anda/Gabun and Yungur can be supported by another bit of material evidence. In the group of broken *wiiso*

18.32

Head fragment (*shembera*)
Ga'anda peoples, Gabun district,
Kanpelam Hill, before 1970
Ceramic
H: 12.2 cm
FOWLER MUSEUM AT UCLA X86.4685; GIFT
OF ARNOLD RUBIN
IMAGE: © 2010 FOWLER MUSEUM AT UCLA.
PHOTOGRAPH BY DON COLE
PROVENANCE: COLLECTED BY ARNOLD RUBIN, 1970

Arnold Rubin collected these two head fragments from the Kanpelam shrine when he visited it in 1970. At the same time, he collected another head, one broken hand, and a fragmentary vessel, which were deposited in the Jos Museum, Nigeria.

18.33

The shrine at Kanpelam Hill in the Ga'anda district of Gabun includes a large number of *sambarcha* ancestor vessels, which are rendered with features more closely aligned to the portrait vessels of the Yungur or 'Bəna than to those of the Ga'anda. One vessel near the left side of the photo has its hand raised to its face as if to call out.
PHOTOGRAPH BY ARNOLD RUBIN, 1970, NEG. NO. 2532.

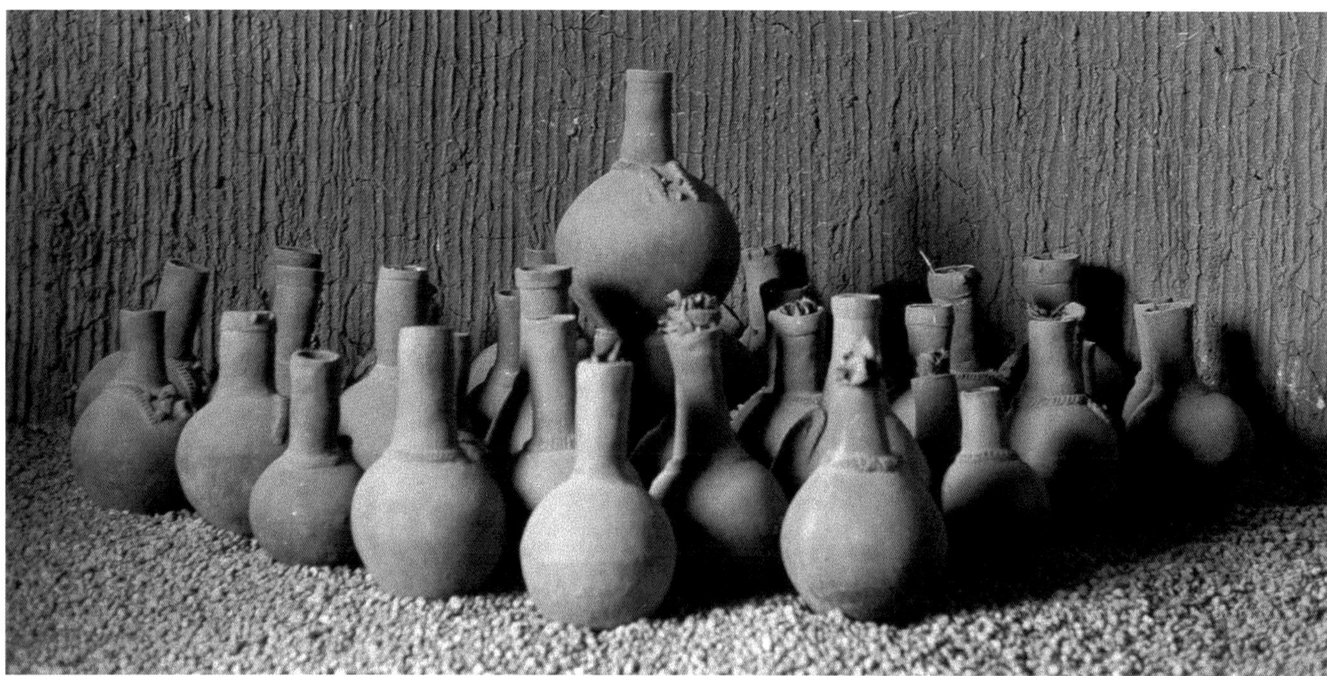

18.37
This memorial shrine, located in the compound of the Dera chief of Shani Town, consists of long-necked vessels called *muywuyo*, which contain the spirits of deceased ancestors of the Shani chief.
PHOTOGRAPH BY ARNOLD RUBIN, 1970, NEG. NO. 2207.

Shani is 40 kilometers west of Ga'anda Town on the west bank of the Hawal. Ga'anda historical traditions claim that they migrated from the "east" with the Gabun and the Dera, the latter having continued westward beyond Makwar in search of water for their cattle (Hammandikko and Berns 1980, 1). Oral traditions collected in Shani reinforce this story (Nissen 1968, 90), as do accounts collected from the Dera of Shellen. All of these stories point to a chain of alliances associated with the importance of rainmaking that stretched across the Gongola-Hawal Valley (see Berns 1986, 361–64). The paramount Ga'anda rain chief was selected from the Gudban family, and the chief of Shani had to confirm the choice. The Shani chief was then required to send certain insignia of office along with seven cows, three of which were distributed to communities en route as tribute for their role in relaying information relative to the new rain chief's selection across the rugged Ga'anda Hills. The high price paid by the Shani attests to their debt to the Gudban rain priest and to his powerful shrine at Makwar.[25] Hence, the Dera like the 'Bǝna and Yungur regarded the Ga'anda rain priest as the highest authority in the land and ultimately responsible for regional agricultural survival.

Although the classification of languages would seem to refute direct ties between the Western-Chadic-speaking Dera and the Biu-Mandara-speaking Ga'anda, these accounts are evidence that an actual network of communication and contact must have existed to link the various groups living across the Lower Gongola—a dynamic of interaction not limited by ethnolinguistic boundaries. The vestiges of a ceramic tradition existed by which the Dera venerated royal ancestral spirits, providing material support for their eastward orientation. The forms and functions of these sacred vessels are closest to those of the 'Bǝna, their most proximate neighbors. Ancestor vessels were offered the firstfruits of the harvest during Menwara or Menjoli. They were also propitiated at a biennial "all souls" festival called Menwuyo. In 1970 Arnold Rubin documented a major memorial shrine located in the compound of the Shani chief where over twenty "long-necked" pots were grouped around a central elevated vessel containing the spirit of the most recently deceased chief (fig. 18.37). Anthropomorphic references are highly schematic with arms wrapping around the "neck" of the pot and small nodes representing breasts and a navel. This shrine was no longer in existence when I visited Shani in 1980.

Dera vessels enshrined in Shellen and known as *bilima mǝra* have arms made of raised and impressed ridges of clay and projecting facial features modeled at the end of the elongated, segmented neck (fig. 18.38). These pots were given regular offerings

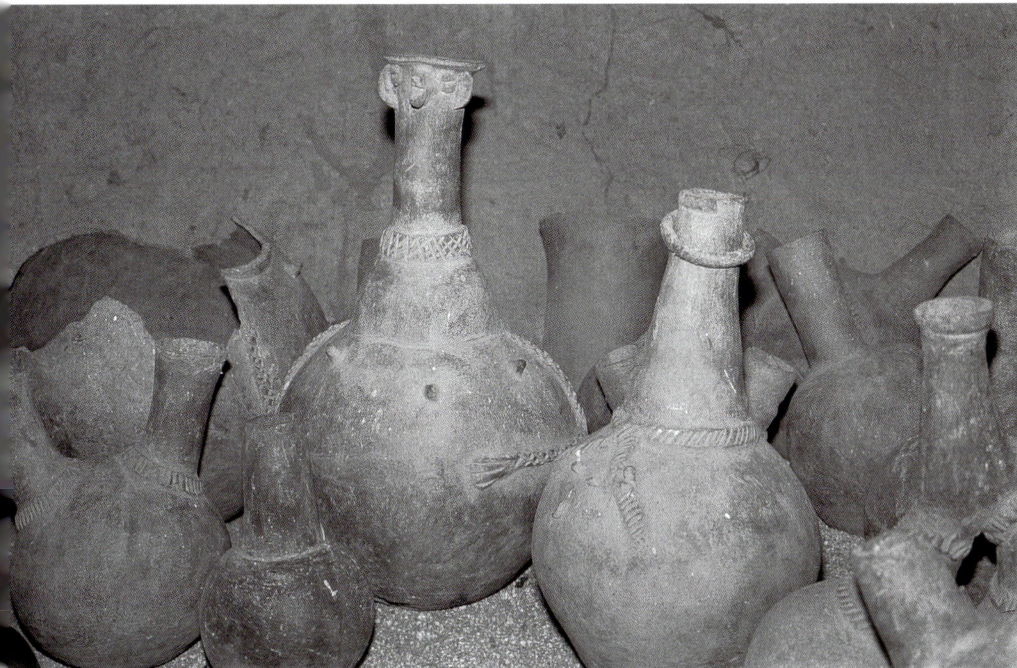

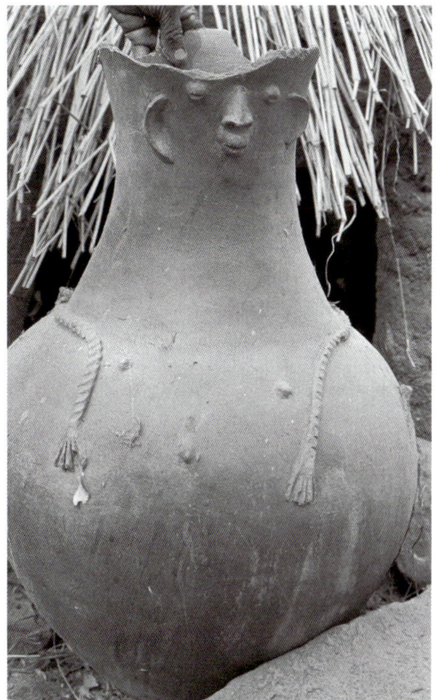

Dera vessels called *bilima mɔra* were enshrined in the town of Shellen and were given beer offerings to secure the well-being of the community. The tallest pot in the center is the most powerful; its form is reminiscent of some long-necked Yungur *wiiso* (see fig. 18.19).
PHOTOGRAPH BY MARLA C. BERNS, 1981.

This Dera vessel (*kanimen*; H: 74 cm) was kept in a shrine in the town of Kiri. These shrines held ritual objects associated with past warfare, and the *kanimen* contained beer consumed by chiefs before they went to war. Since the colonial period, however, such vessels have been used to propitiate ancestors.
PHOTOGRAPH BY MARLA C. BERNS, 1981.

of beer to secure the help of the ancestors with crop fertility and community well-being. These and others (*kanimen*), which were kept by the Kiri Dera on the graves of ancestors, most closely recall the *gontime* vessels documented in the western ʿBɔna town of Gurɔshi (cf. figs 18.15, 18.16). There is a striking similarity in the modeling of facial features (fig. 18.39), and both types of vessel were intended to contain the beer offered to the ancestors as opposed to housing the spirits. Like the *gontime*, *kanimen* echo the style of the portrait *wiisa* in the ʿBɔna shrine at Hatta (cf. fig. 18.7). The ceramic arts made by the riverain Dera serve as the frontier of Eastern Gongola Valley traditions.

CONCLUSION

Mapping the ritual and sacred vessels made within the Western and Eastern Gongola Valley reveals the manner in which objects and ideas circulate, as well as how they come to embody local strategies for social perpetuation and survival. These objects symbolize the centrality of change to the human condition, and their forms and meanings communicate the ways people manage the dynamism of their worlds. The ceramics of the Western Gongola, mostly focused around healing, capture the immediacy and specificity of responding to disease, whether affecting the health of an individual or an entire community. The tradition of making anthropomorphic vessels to help neutralize the negative potential of avenging spirits, whether of game killed in the hunt or enemies killed in battle, reveals the same impulse to insulate against danger and disequilibrium. Communication across cultures is surely reflected in the shared symbolic vocabulary from which artists and healers drew to create individual and sometimes innovative material responses.

Across the Eastern Gongola, vessels were made to contain the spirits of deceased ancestors, and the purposeful linkages between the ways pots and people look helped negotiate enduring relationships between the living and the dead. The striking expressive variety of vessels functioning as ancestral "portraits" helped construct the complex genealogies of chiefs and elders to whom individual prayers were offered. This strategy differs from the one underlying the representation of powerful tutelary and legitimizing ceramic deities, where consistencies in their elaborate decoration and meticulous execution created mnemonic devices for collective history as well as mechanisms for the living to assert control. Here, too, artists seemed to have drawn from a shared pool of iconographic motifs that could be adapted, transformed, and remixed. ●

Vestiges in Wood:
Ancestor Sculptures of
the Eastern Gongola Valley

MARLA C. BERNS

Starting in 1968, at least eight nearly life-size male sculptures from northeastern Nigeria entered collections in Europe and the United States (fig. 1.1).[1] The best-preserved example is in the Menil Collection, Houston (fig. 1.2; see Berns 2008), purchased in 1972 from the J. J. Klejman Gallery in New York. By 1975 five related figures were known, and all were given the attribution "Mboye" (Mboi), the name of a people who live in the Eastern Gongola River Valley (see map, fig 15.2, p. 466).[2]

Notes accompanying the Menil sculpture stated that it had come from the "region of Bauchi, the village of Djemeta or Jemeta," finding its way to New York via Cameroon, where it was collected by Edouard Klejman in 1971.[3] It is possible that the sculpture entered Cameroon via the town of Jimeta, which is just north of Yola on the Benue River, a long distance from the town of Bauchi but south of the rugged mountainous zone where the Mboi have lived since at least the twentieth century. The Mboi are one of a cluster of geographically proximate peoples who speak Northwestern Adamawa languages classified within the 'Bəna-Mboi (=Yungur) group and share a number of cultural practices (Kleinewillinghöfer 1996, 82; Crozier and Blench 1992, 123). Even though it is unclear why these impressive figures were specifically identified as Mboi, evidence collected in the field suggests it is plausible that they came from the Eastern Gongola Valley where the Mboi, Yungur ('Bəna Yungur), and the 'Bəna live.[4]

This small but stunning corpus of male sculptures is anomalous in the Upper Benue region where ceramic vessels predominate as an artistic medium and as a focus of ritual activity (fig. 1.3). The source of the "Mboye" attribution is unexplained, and no information about the use of these wood figures was collected in the field. Moreover, standing wooden figures of this size and scale, carved with powerful and highly muscular male bodies, are unlike anything else documented across the entire Benue River Valley (fig. 1.4 and see fig 1.2). They are notable for their broad shoulders and chests, long

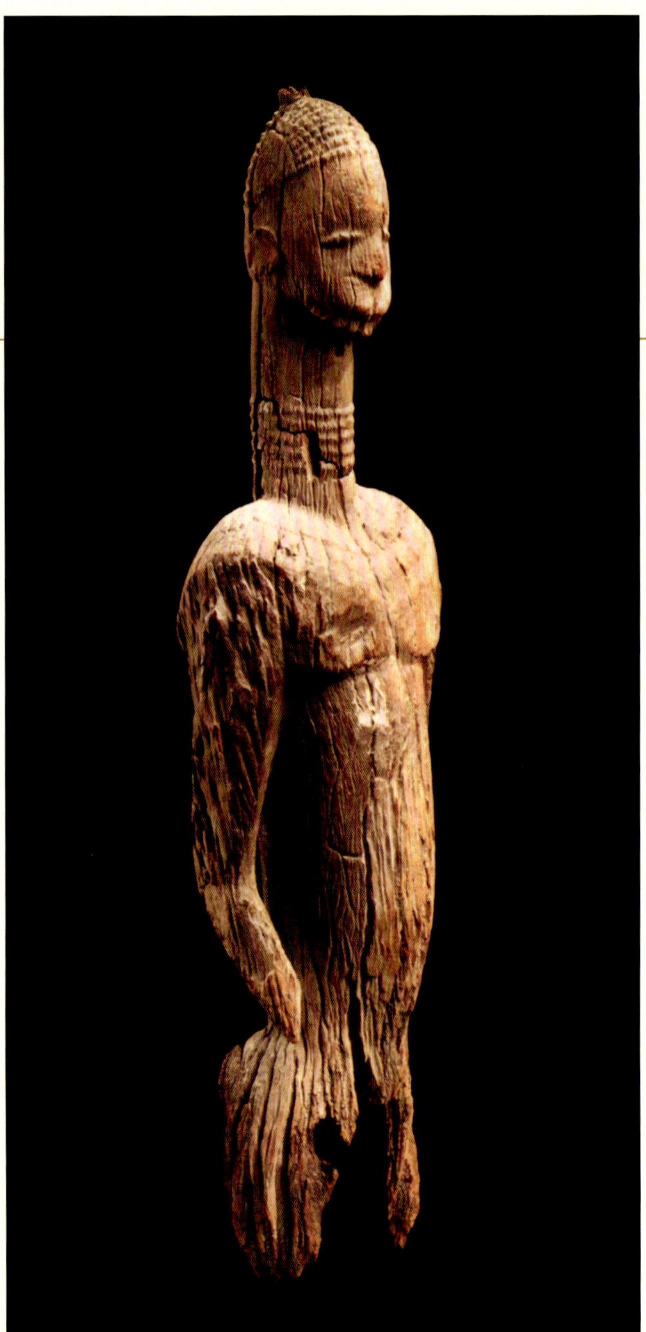

I.1
Male figure
Yungur/Mboi/'Bəna peoples, Eastern Gongola Valley,
fourteenth to sixteenth century
Wood
H: 110 cm
PRIVATE COLLECTION, FRANCE
PHOTOGRAPH COURTESY ARCHIVE GALERIE, BERNARD DE GRUNNE
PROVENANCE: PHILLIPE GUIMIOT, 1968; BERNARD DE GRUNNE, 1971
(NOT IN EXHIBITION)

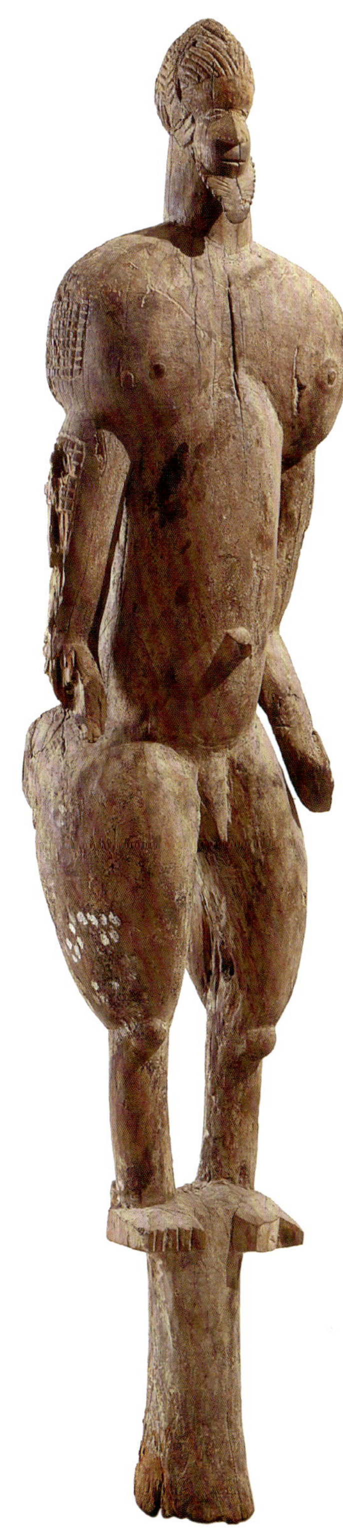

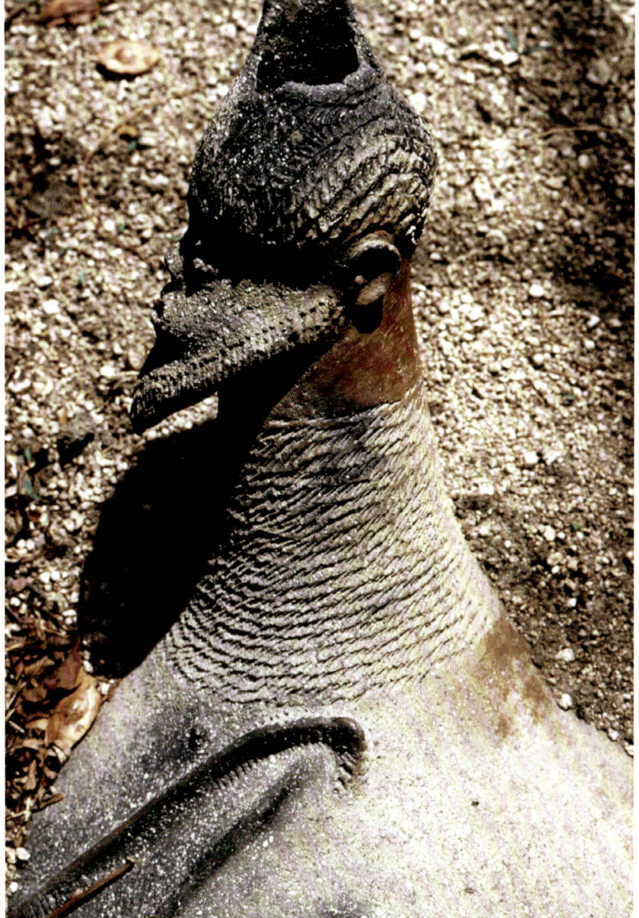

I.2

Male figure

Yungur/Mboi/'Bəna peoples, Eastern Gongola Valley,
fourteenth to sixteenth century

Wood, traces of red iron oxide

H: 176.5 cm

THE MENIL COLLECTION, HOUSTON, Y301

IMAGE: © THE MENIL COLLECTION, HOUSTON. PHOTOGRAPH BY HICKEY-
ROBERTSON, HOUSTON

PROVENANCE: EDOUARD KLEJMAN, 1971; J. J. KLEJMAN, NEW YORK, 1972; JOHN AND
DOMINIQUE DE MENIL, HOUSTON, 1973; MENIL FOUNDATION, HOUSTON, 1998

I.3

The Yungur ceramic *wiiso*, called Tentire, was situated at the entry to the
ritual precinct of Diterra (see fig. 18.21).

PHOTOGRAPH BY MARLA C. BERNS, 1981.

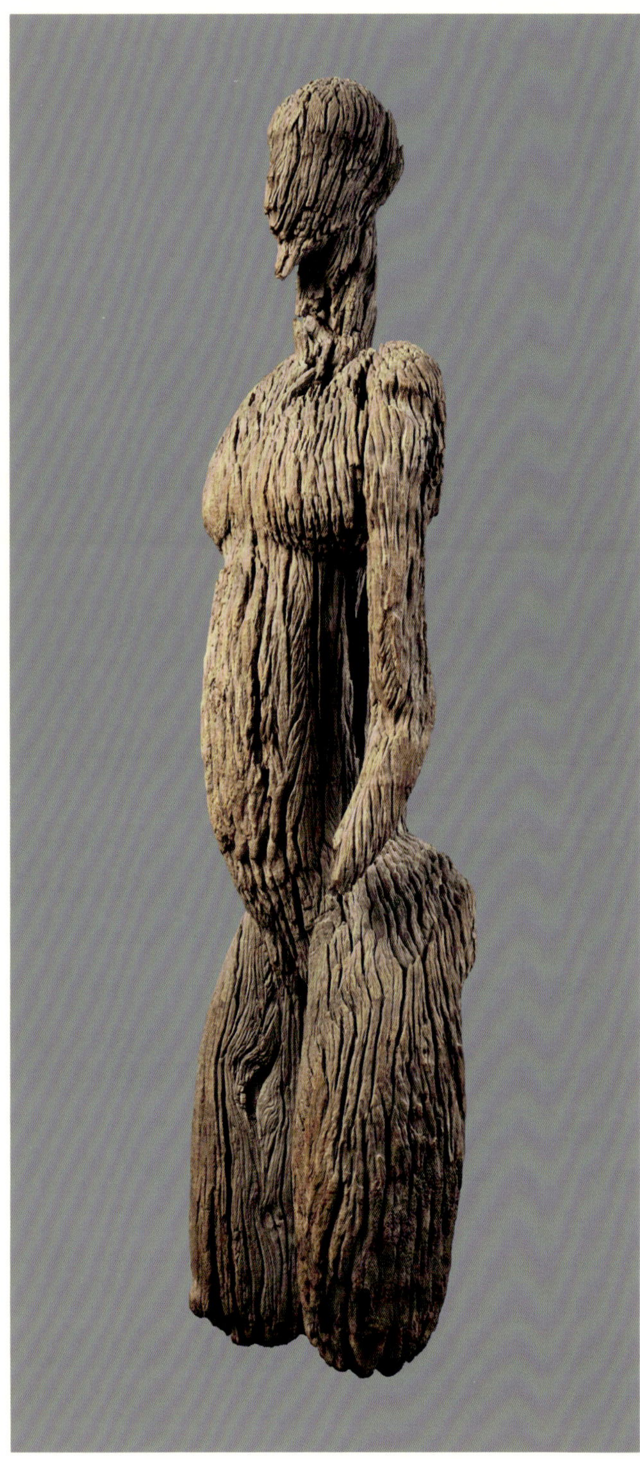

I.4
Male figure
Yungur/Mboi/ˈBəna peoples, Eastern Gongola Valley,
nineteenth century or before
Wood
H: 110 cm
PRIVATE COLLECTION, PARIS 1976
IMAGE: COURTESY PRIVATE COLLECTOR. PHOTOGRAPH © BRIGITTE
CAVANAUGH, 2010
PROVENANCE: ALAIN DUFOUR, CIRCA 1970; LUCIEN VAN DE VELDE, ANTWERP;
LOED VAN BUSSEL, AMSTERDAM; PRIVATE COLLECTION, PARIS

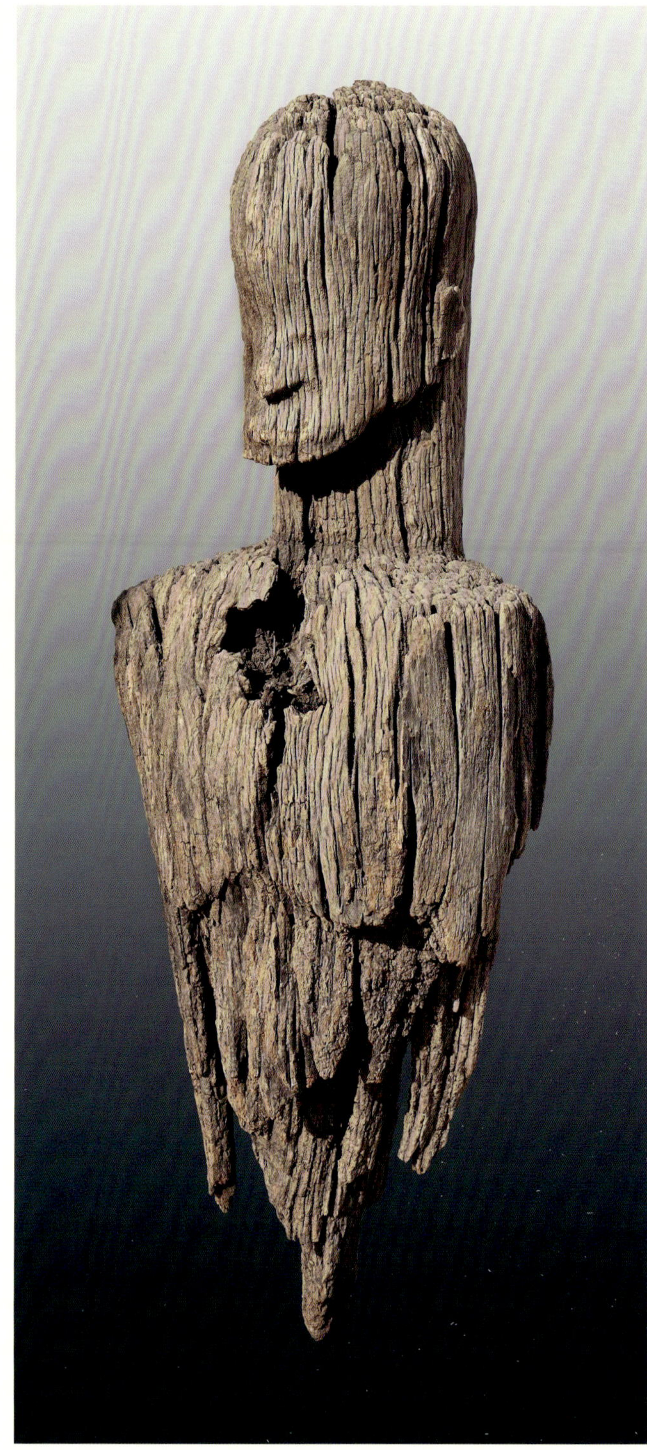

I.5
Male figure
Yungur/Mboi/ˈBəna peoples, Eastern Gongola Valley,
nineteenth century or before
Wood
H: 90 cm
ITZIKOVITZ COLLECTION, PARIS
IMAGE: COURTESY COLLECTOR. PHOTOGRAPH © BRIGITTE CAVANAUGH, 2010
PROVENANCE: PURCHASED IN PARIS, 1970
(NOT IN EXHIBITION)

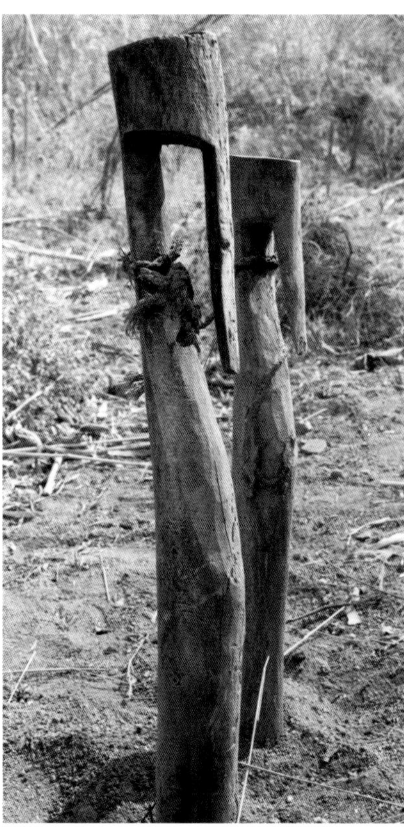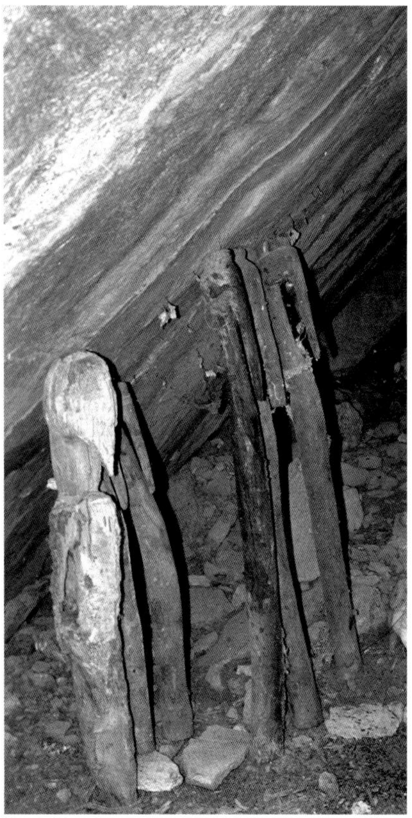

I.6
The long overhanging chins or beards on these Two 'Bəna wooden funerary effigies (*kwanda*), bear an uncanny resemblance to 'Bəna Ngwar-kandangra healing vessels, which likewise have long plank-like beards that extend the length of the neck (see fig. 18.12). The figure in the foreground is male and 85 centimeters in height; the one in the background is female and 72 centimeters in height.
PHOTOGRAPH BY MARLA C. BERNS, DU'A HAMLET, 1981.

I.7
Six *kwanda* funerary effigies are kept inside the rock shelter at the old ritual site of Hotta, located near the 'Bəna town of Fotta. The wooden figure in the foreground (90 cm in height) was made to commemorate the chief of Hotta, and though eroded, it appears to have arms and a face with a pointed beard. The floor of the shelter is littered with half-buried pots and sherds.
PHOTOGRAPH BY MARLA C. BERNS, 1981.

torsos, well-developed thighs, arms hanging loosely at their sides, and male genitalia. Relatively small heads rest on thick elongated necks, and most show a tightly fitting cap or a coiffure with a circular pattern of plaited hair; two of the examples have a topknot (see figs. 1.1, 1.14). Where visible, they each sport a beard, disk-shaped ears, and relatively schematic facial features. The sculptures exude a sense of restraint and introversion that seems even more haunting and pronounced in those that are highly eroded and fragmentary (fig. 1.5).

Although the Mboi, Yungur, and 'Bəna shared the regional emphasis on ceramic vessels as containers for ancestral spirits, they also incorporated carved wooden effigies of the dead in post-burial funeral rites held to honor and secure the blessings of the departed spirits. In 1980–1981, I documented a number of extant examples, most of which took the form of highly schematic cylindrical figures, carved from a single log, with long cantilevered and overhanging faces or beards (fig. 1.6). The practice of incorporating wood sculpture in memorial rites offers one explanation for the original purpose of the large standing figurative sculptures now in museum and private collections. Even more tantalizing support for the Eastern Gongola Valley attribution of these rare and imposing figures, however, comes from a group of stylistically related figurative ceramic vessels enshrined by the Yungur as permanent repositories for the ancestral spirits of deceased chiefs (see fig. 1.3; see also chapter 18, this volume).

Elders whom I interviewed during the course of fieldwork in 'Bəna, Yungur, and Mboi villages explained that men and women who had reached old age were honored after death at post-burial rites held at the beginning of each rainy season to celebrate their transition to the realm of the ancestors. The rites preceded planting so that the new ancestral spirits could help ensure a bountiful harvest. Their presence was made visible through the display of wooden effigies, which when not in use were kept in caves to be employed in successive memorial rites (fig. 1.7). The continuity among the generations was emphasized by drawing on the accumulative investment of ancestral energies in these wood sculptures over time.

British colonial anthropologist C. K. Meek (1931b, 2: 439–40), while working among the Yungur of Pirra, collected the most complete description of post-burial rites for deceased chiefs.[5] Meek related that during March, before the planting season began, a wooden effigy of the dead chief was made by the "chief elect." The figure was carved with "head, eyes, nose, body and legs," and the figure was dressed in a cap, gown, and sandals. It was erected in a public space where it was saluted by community members and given gifts of sorghum (guinea corn). Each person threw sorghum grains over the effigy so that by the end of the day it was "half-buried in corn." A maternal relative then returned the sculpture to a cave in the hills. Meek explained that celebrating the chiefly ancestor in this way was important because the dead chief had performed the annual rites for securing a successful harvest the March before, making the new crops "his." He must therefore still preside even if he had died before their harvest. As Meek relates, the "fiction must therefore be maintained that he is still present with his people," embodied in sculptural form until his successor assumed responsibility for the rites the following March. Throwing

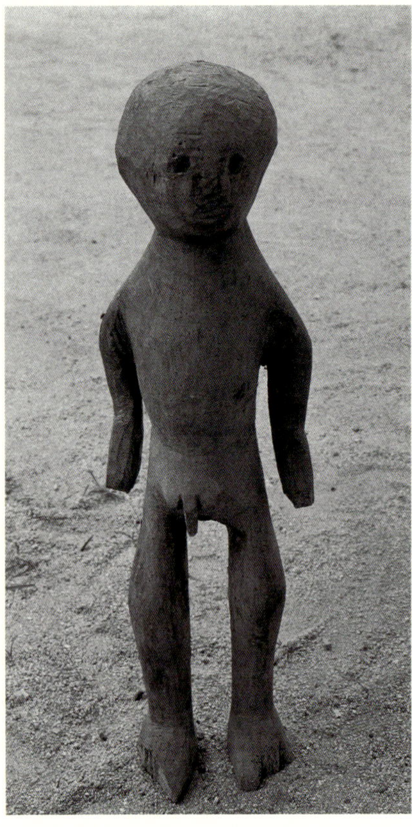

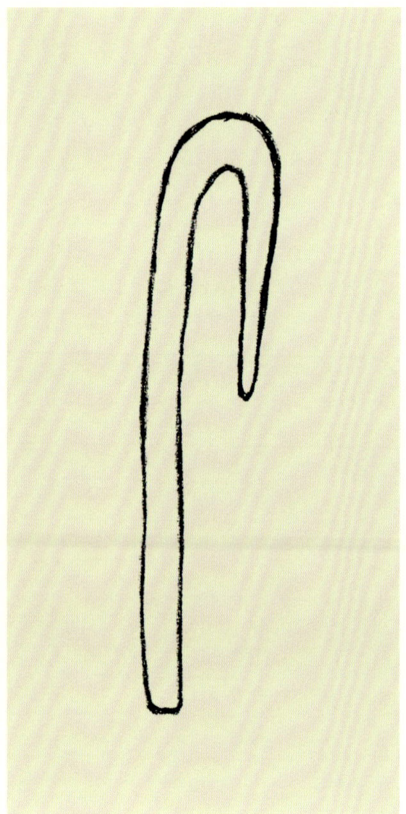

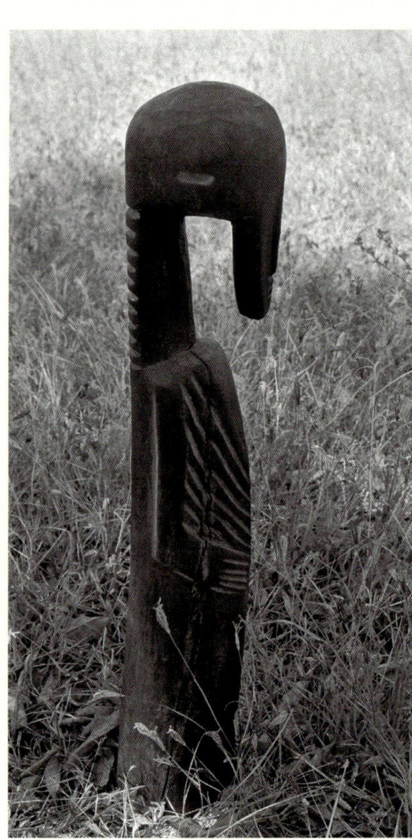

sorghum over the effigy showed that the harvest was indeed his and conferred upon him the food he needed for the afterlife.

It is easy to imagine the nearly life-size sculptures shown here being dressed and displayed to represent departed chiefs in the manner described by Meek.[6] The plinth surviving on the Menil figure provides strong support for the contention that it was inserted in the ground for public display. Leon Siroto (1976, 11–12, fig. c) concluded that this sculpture was likely used as an effigy of an "earth priest," as per the description provided by Meek.[7] Yet, nothing I documented in the field in the 1980s comes close to the monumentality or anatomical articulation of these male sculptures. I photographed the last-surviving *kpanda*, or wood memorial figure, in the Yungur community of Dirma, a rudimentary human form carved to represent a deceased chief or village head (fig. 1.8). At 54 centimeters, it is less than half the height of the large versions in collections, but the *kpanda's* stance and hanging arms present an intriguing, while tenuous, echo. According to the chiefs of Dirma (one of four main Yungur centers of occupation), the eldest son of the deceased carved the *kpanda*.[8] *Kpanda* were also made as representations of non-chiefly male or female elders who died, and these were carried during post-burial rites and displayed in front of the houses of the deceased (see Meek 1931b, 2: 440–41). A simplified "hooked" form was used for these effigies (fig. 1.9).

I documented the largest number of surviving wooden memorial figures in six different 'Bəna-speaking communities located to the north of Dirma in the Ga'anda Hills, where they were called *kwanda*. Carved in pairs, they were the property of extended families and were reused until another set of carvings

1.8
This Yungur *kpanda* figure (54 cm in height) was carved to memorialize a deceased chief or village head.
PHOTOGRAPH BY MARLA C. BERNS, DIRMA HAMLET, DITERRA DISTRICT, 1981.

1.9
This sketch shows a Yungur effigy figure that would have been carried during post-burial rites of a non-chiefly male or female elder.
DRAWING AFTER MEEK (1931B, 2: 441).

1.10
Shown outside the cave near the town of Gureshi where it was stored, this 'Bəna *kwanda* (68 cm in height) would have been held horizontally and danced during funerals.
PHOTOGRAPH BY MARLA C. BERNS, 1981.

was made as a supplement or replacement (see fig. 1.6). Most had a simple narrow cylindrical form with a long, plank-like overhanging "face," and they ranged in height between 75 and 85 centimeters. During memorials, these *kwanda* were usually rubbed with red oil and then danced; they were held horizontally as a corpse would be carried. A single *kwanda*, which I photographed in the western 'Bəna village of Gureshi, was used in the same manner but had a blackened surface, a rounder profile, and was carved with incisions demarcating facial features and arms resting on its stomach, as well as linear striations across its chest and back of the neck (fig. 1.10). Meek (1931b, 2: 440) reported that the 'Bəna, like the Yungur, also threw sorghum seeds over these images to provide food for the afterlife.

Custodians of the ancient ritual site of Hotta, located near the 'Bəna town of Fotta, showed me a rock shelter with eight *kwanda*—one pair at the entry marking the site (fig. 1.11) and

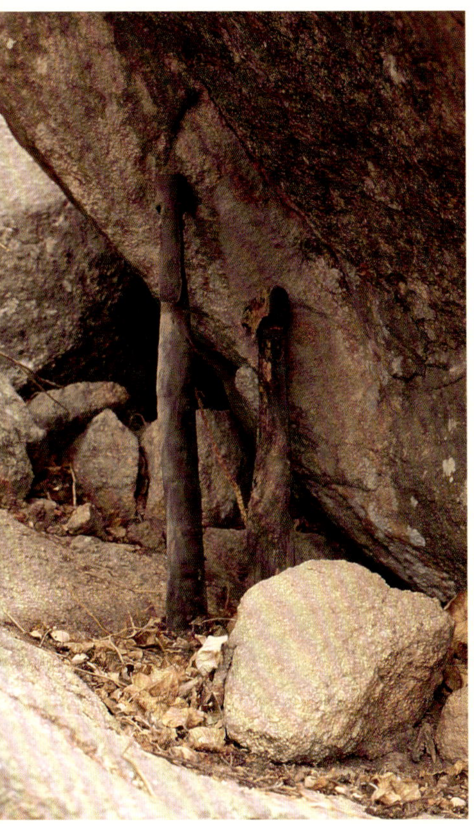

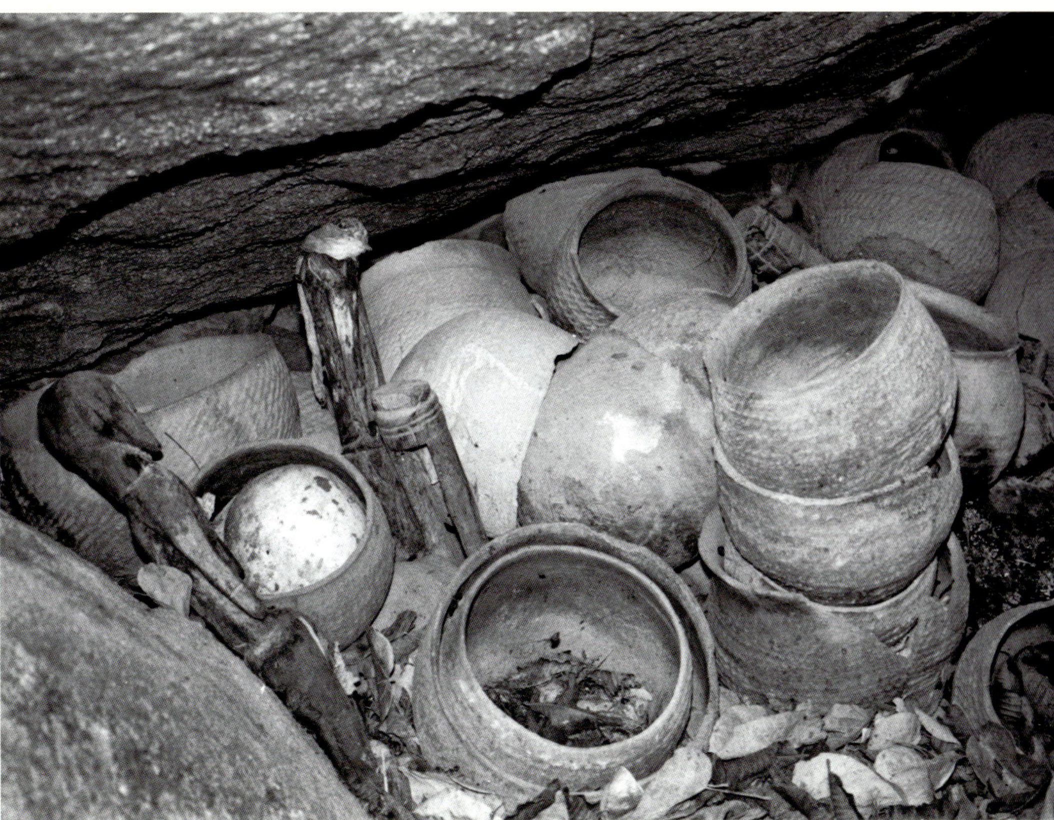

two pairs and two individual figures inside (see fig. I.7).[9] The floor of the interior was littered with potsherds and half-buried pots, suggesting that it had long been used as a site for ritual activities. The *kwanda* in the foreground of figure I.7 was said to commemorate the memory of the local chief. Although it was badly damaged by termites and its sculptural details obscured as a result, the figure may once have had a face, beard, and arms.

The Mboi, most commonly named in the literature as the makers of the Eastern Gongola Valley wooden sculptures, live near an impressive cluster of steep-sided granite massifs, situated northeast of the Yungur. In 1981 I visited their former hilltop occupation site, which was protected by a five-foot tall drystone wall.[10] The Mboi held second funeral ceremonies where all deceased male or female elders, whether chiefs or commoners, were represented by wooden effigies, called *kpaniya*.[11] The preserved skulls of chiefs (exhumed two years after death) along with their *kpaniya* were kept in the sacred site of Gwen Avele located high in the hills. When I photographed this rock shelter in 1981, there were three or possibly four *kpaniya* surrounded by a large number of vessels (*torketa*) in which the skulls of deceased chiefs (and their sons) were kept (fig. I.12).[12] The relatively small figure in the foreground with its schematically carved arms and legs and a head with an overhanging chin or beard, resembles the *kwanda* at Fotta (see fig. I.7) as well as the *kpanda* from Dirma (see fig. I.8).

The evidence I collected in the field provides little support for assigning the large wood sculptures that have come to light uniquely to the Mboi. Nevertheless, the tradition of using wood figures, however rudimentary, to celebrate the

I.11

These two *kwanda* were kept at the entry of the ʻBəna rock shelter at Hotta.
PHOTOGRAPH BY MARLA C. BERNS, 1981.

I.12

The skulls of deceased chiefs or their sons were kept in ceramic pots inside the Mboi rock shelter at Gwen Avele. Along with the pots are several wooden effigies (*kpaniya*), brought out at second funeral festivals. The small figure in the foreground is carved with an overhanging chin as well as arms and legs unlike the more rudimentary pole figures typical of most ʻBəna *kwanda*.
PHOTOGRAPH BY MARLA C. BERNS, 1981.

dead at post-burial ceremonies, does support the inference that the sculptures in collections may have come from the Eastern Gongola Valley. Sacred precincts were formerly located high in rocky citadels where caves and shelters were found. The life-size figures no doubt experienced a lengthy period of sanctuary in these protected sites, and their highly eroded condition and insect-eaten extremities attest to their probable age. Radiocarbon dating of the Menil figure in 1972 produced the dates of 1470 +/- 90 CE and dating of the ex-de Grunne figure (fig. I.1) in 1994 produced the dates of 1440 +/- 55 CE.[13]

The remarkably preserved Menil example has traces of red iron oxide on its surface (Portell 1988), which may relate to the twentieth-century ʻBəna practice of rubbing the *kwanda* with red oil when it was displayed. Throughout the Eastern Gongola Valley (including the Gaʼanda Hills), I documented instances where social and sacred transformations were marked by anointing the body with ground red hematite mixed with

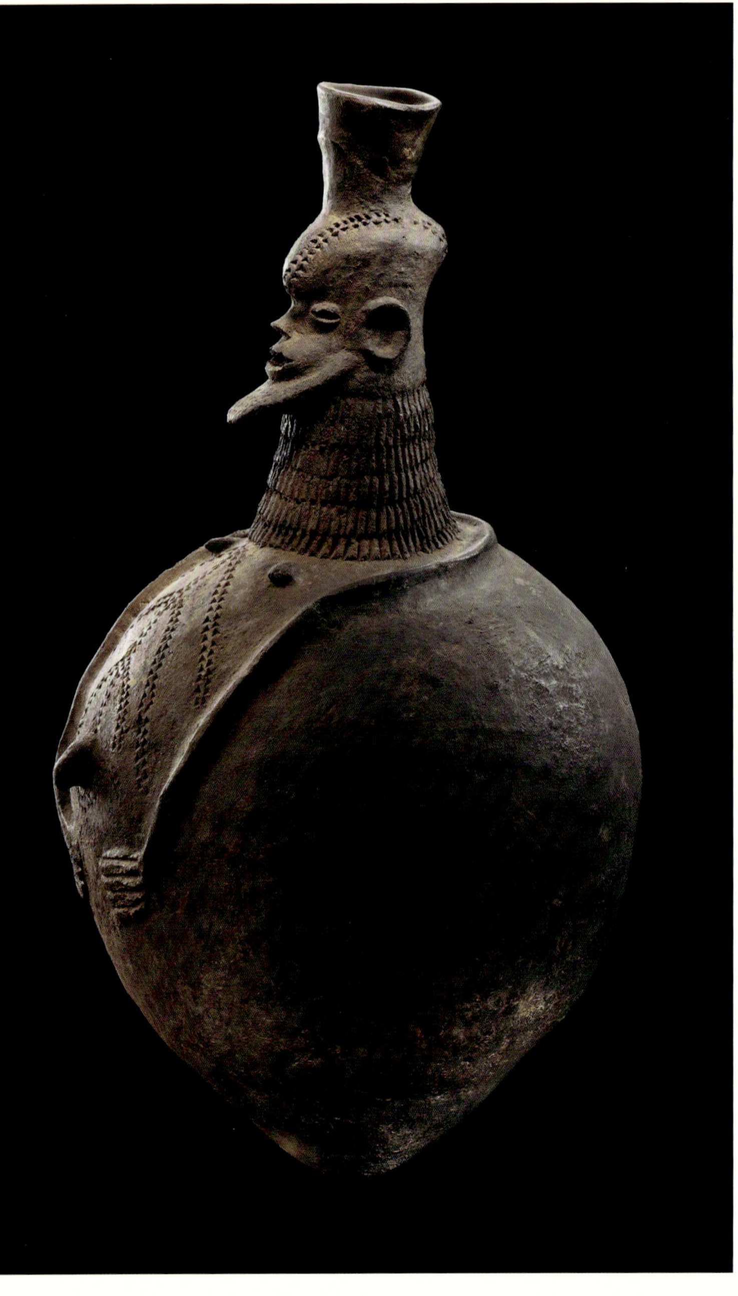

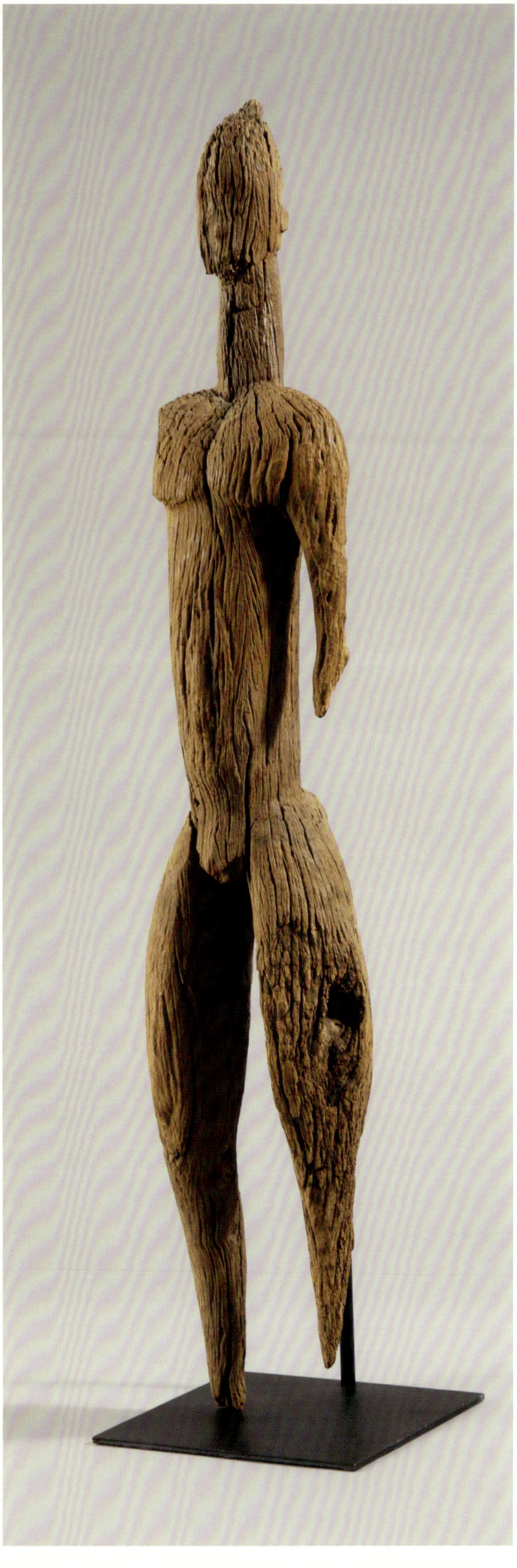

I.13
Ancestor vessel (*wiiso*)
Yungur/Mboi/'Bəna peoples, Diterra district,
twentieth century or before
Ceramic
H: 58 cm
BARBIER-MUELLER MUSEUM, GENEVA, 1015-115
IMAGE: COURTESY BARBIER-MUELLER MUSEUM, GENEVA. PHOTOGRAPH
© STUDIO FERRAZZINI BOUCHET
PROVENANCE: NORWOOD GALLERY, AUSTIN ART CONSORTIUM, AUSTIN, 2000

See figure 18.29 for a frontal view of this vessel.

I.14
Male Figure
Yungur/Mboi/'Bəna peoples, Eastern Gongola Valley,
nineteenth century or before
Wood
H: 133 cm
MUSEUM FOR AFRICAN ART, NEW YORK, 2001.1.1
IMAGE: MUSEUM FOR AFRICAN ART. PHOTOGRAPH BY JERRY L. THOMPSON, 2010
PROVENANCE: JACQUES KERCHACHE PARIS; ARMAN COLLECTION, NEW YORK

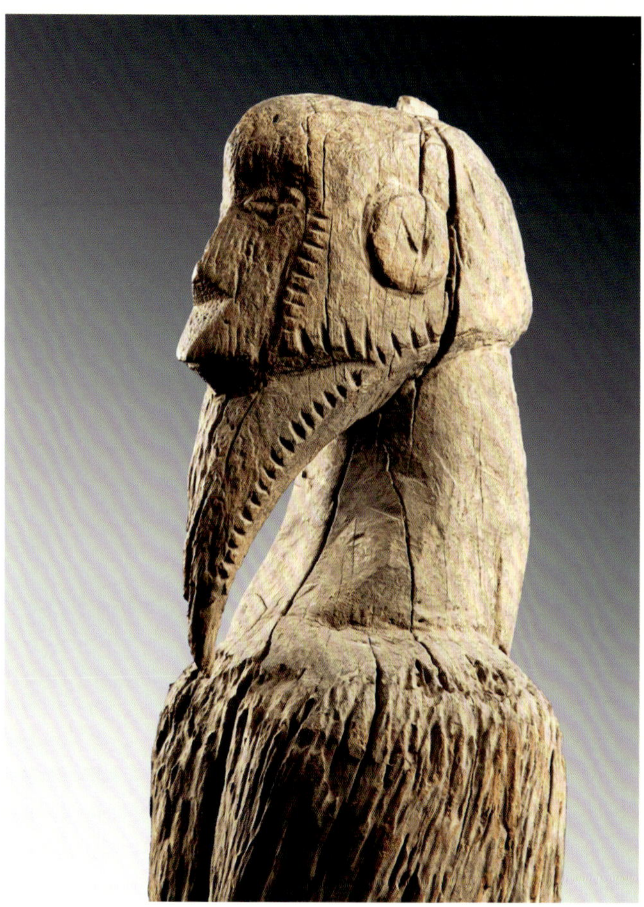

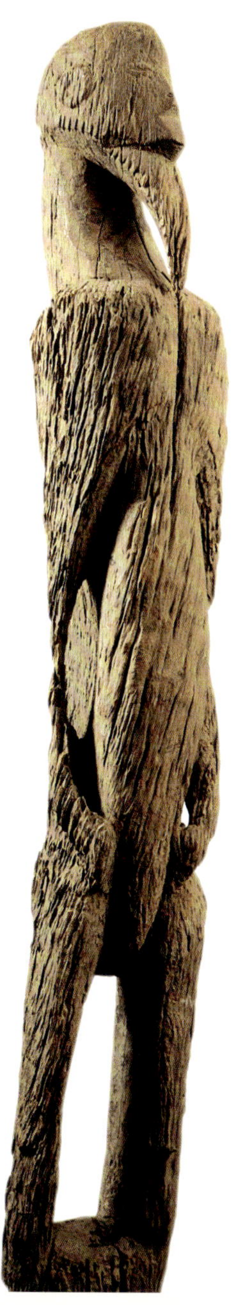

I.15a
Note the relationship between this profile view of the carved wooden head of figure I.15b and that of the ceramic *wiiso* in figures I.13 and I.3.

I.15b
Male Figure
Yungur/Mboi/'Bəna peoples, Eastern Gongola Valley,
pre-twentieth century (?)
Wood
H: 144 cm
IMAGE: PHOTOGRAPH BY JEAN VIVIER, 2004
COLLECTION OF MARIE-FRANCE ET JEAN VIVIER, 2003
PROVENANCE: MARTIAL BRONSIN, 2002
(NOT IN EXHIBITION)

oil, especially in the context of initiations. It is not surprising, therefore, that an effigy of a dead chief would be similarly treated and activated with this same ritual cosmetic. Moreover, the grid of incisions visible on the right shoulder and upper arm of the Menil sculpture may refer to the cicatrizations inscribed on a boy's shoulders during initiation among the Mboi and 'Bəna, signifying prowess in hunting and the transition to manhood.[14]

Despite the parallels that can be drawn between the wood sculptures in collections and regional mortuary practices in the Eastern Gongola Valley, another compelling stylistic and conceptual corollary survives in the ceramic vessels (*wiiso*) made by the Yungur to contain the spirits of chiefs who have died (see chapter 18, this volume). The necks and heads of the sculptures are strikingly similar to a particular type of *wiiso* that the Yungur

associate with their sacred homeland, "Mukan." Examples of this *wiiso* type were enshrined in the ritual precincts of Diterra and Waltandi (see figs. 18.27, 18.21; see p. 538 above). I was told, as was Meek (1931b, 2: 434) more than fifty years earlier, that Mukan or "Mokan" was located "somewhere in the Ga'anda Hills."[15] The many Yungur *wiiso* I photographed in the field are notable for their great variety, yet this Mukan type is distinctive for its uniformity (see fig. 1.3 and fig. 18.24). The contours of its face, especially in profile (fig. 1.13), and the specific features, particularly the disk-shaped perforated ears, slit-like eyes and mouth, as well as the pointed beard with inscribed edges, are very similar to those on the wooden sculptures (fig. 1.14; see also fig. 1.1). These chiefly *wiiso* also share with the sculptures an incised rounded "cap" or coiffure, which depicts a style formerly restricted to men of high rank. The unusually thick

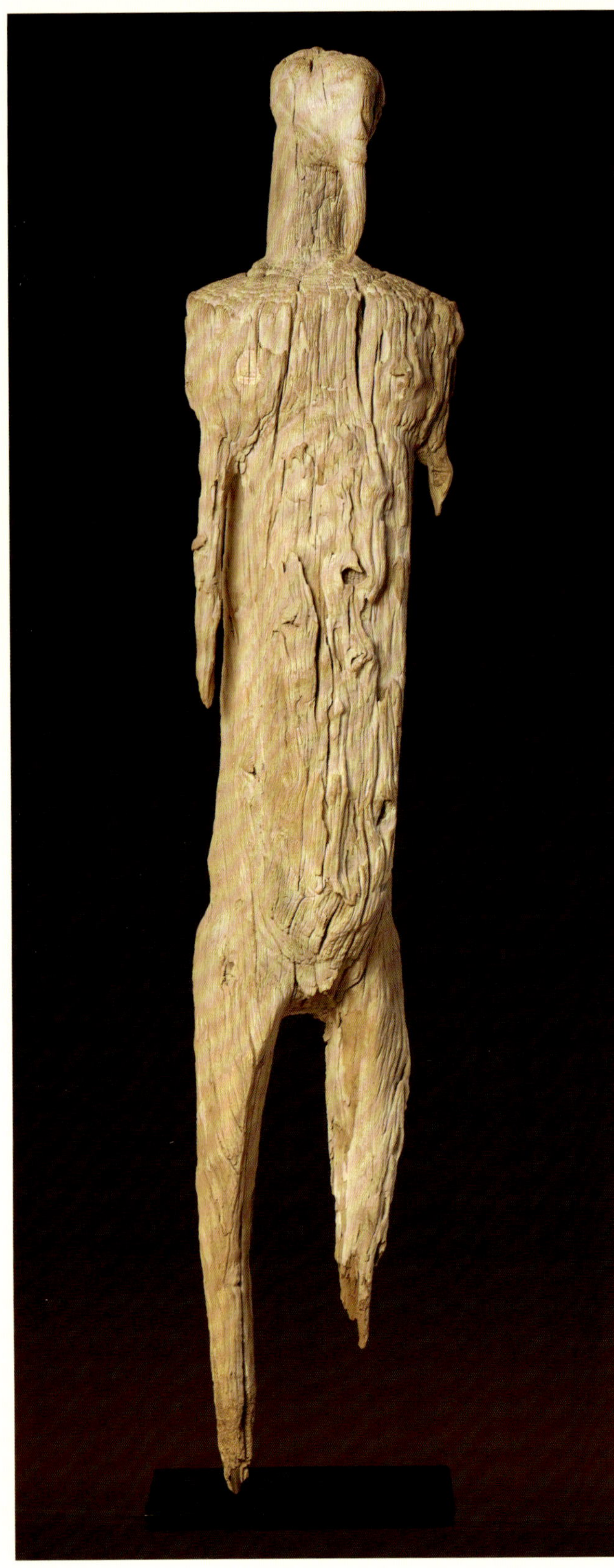

1.16
Male Figure
Yungur/Mboi/'Bəna peoples, Eastern Gongola Valley,
pre-twentieth century
Wood
H: 150 cm
PRIVATE COLLECTION, PARIS
IMAGE: COURTESY PRIVATE COLLECTION AND JOHANN LÉVY GALLERY
PROVENANCE: PHILLIPE GUIMIOT, LATE 1960S; RENE SALANON
(NOT IN EXHIBITION)

and elongated necks, as well as the impressions encircling them, strongly suggest that the heads of the wooden figures may have relied on a ceramic model (rather than the reverse). The downcast or even closed eyes (rendered as raised slits on the *wiiso*) may mean that these figures are actually powerful evocations of the "dead," returning to the realm of the living.

The ceramic *wiiso* associated with Mukan are considered representations of originating chiefly ancestors, whose presence in shrines historically legitimizes the authority of chiefs who followed them, binding them all to the work of securing the well-being of their descendants. It is plausible that the same visual formula would survive on wooden embodiments of what may have been the same chiefly ancestors who likewise "returned" to bestow their beneficence. And, these large wooden sculptures may have derived from the same historical source (real or imagined) ascribed to the ceramic *wiiso*—the sacred site of Mukan.

At least three other nearly life-size figurative sculptures exist in private collections—also said to be Mboi, no doubt based on their stylistic affinities to the other published examples (figs. 1.15–1.17). Yet, they are different enough from the standing male figures described above to be classified as a separate subgenre. In shape they more closely resemble the individual logs from which they were carved. Their arms appear in relief hugging the body or hanging close to their sides, and in the case of figure 1.17 the legs are barely defined. Most distinctive, especially when viewed from the side, are the long pointed beards, arching over the chest. This exaggerated feature recalls the sharply overhanging "chins" of the 'Bəna *kwanda* (see fig. 1.6) and the triangular "chins" evident on the eroded figures kept in the cave at Hotta and the Gwen Avele in Mboi (see figs. 1.7, 1.12). The faces of this subgroup have the same slit-like eyes, wedge-shaped noses, and circular ears as those carved on the more fully articulated standing sculptures with the same affinities to the Yungur vessels (see fig. 1.15a). They, too, were likely inserted into the ground for display. The extremely worn and eroded surface of figure 1.17, the facial features of which are nearly invisible, attests to its probable age and makes it possible that both types of wooden figure existed simultaneously. Notably, figure 1.16 was exported to Europe by Phillipe Guimiot in the late 1960s along with figure 1.1. By contrast, figures 1.15 and 1.17 were both collected in Cameroon in 2002 by the Belgian dealer Martial Bronsin and sold to their present owners in 2003. Bronsin attributes them to the Ga'anda region (Barry Hecht, personal communication, 2009), which is just east of Fotta and the area occupied by the 'Bəna, strengthening the argument offered here that "Mboye" is too narrow and unsubstantiated an attribution. That these two sculptures were still in Nigeria at the beginning of the twenty-first century is surprising but not impossible given the likelihood that such funerary effigies were secreted in inaccessible caves or rock shelters (see fig. 1.12).

The known corpus of at least eleven Eastern Gongola Valley wooden sculptures may constitute the only remnant of a now-abandoned memorial tradition.[16] Both wooden effigies and anthropomorphic ceramic vessels were the focus of rituals aimed at making contact between the living and the dead, but the vessels have proved the more enduring and individualized representations.[17] It is possible that clay eventually took precedence and that wooden figures once played a more prominent role in the veneration of chiefly ancestors than they did by the 1980s. Although modeling clay and carving wood are very different processes (one fundamentally additive and the other subtractive; one associated with women and the other with men), there are obvious similarities in the surface decoration of each, especially the textures worked around the neck, at the edge of the beard, and over the top of the head (see fig. I.1).

The available evidence does not allow us to firmly ascribe a specific ethnic attribution to these robust wood sculptures, anomalies not only in the Upper Benue but also across the entire Benue River Valley. The mid-twentieth-century ceramic evidence aligns these figures stylistically most closely with the Yungur, yet they are likely to have had a broader historical significance across the region, especially if they are as old as the dating of the Menil example suggests. In the past, the inhabitants of the Eastern Gongola Valley had far more localized identities than they do today, and the people who came to be called "Yungur," "'Bəna," or "Mboi" in the colonial era had formerly lived within lineage-based communities. Even if each maintained its own shrines and ritual centers, they seem to have shared a reservoir of cultural practices and material symbols that were by-products of the communication and circulation of ideas among them.[18]

Most of the sculptures featured here had entered collections by the mid-1970s, suggesting that they may have left Nigeria around the same time, never to be replaced or reproduced. Other sculptures kept in caves, such as the equally large and impressive vertical masks associated with the Wurkun and Bikwin groups in the Western Gongola Valley (see chapter 14, this volume), were also collected around the same period, in the aftermath of the Biafran War (1967–1970). While it may be too simplistic to blame the chaos of the postwar period for the intensive collecting of sculpture from the Middle and Upper Benue regions at this time, it is lamentable that these enigmatic works exited Nigeria before they could be studied in situ. As has been argued throughout this volume, it is better to associate these impressive works with the cluster of related Northwestern-Adamawa-speaking "Yungur group" peoples of the Eastern Gongola Valley who may have long shared similar material and symbolic strategies for remembering and honoring their deceased chiefs, whether in wood or in clay. ●

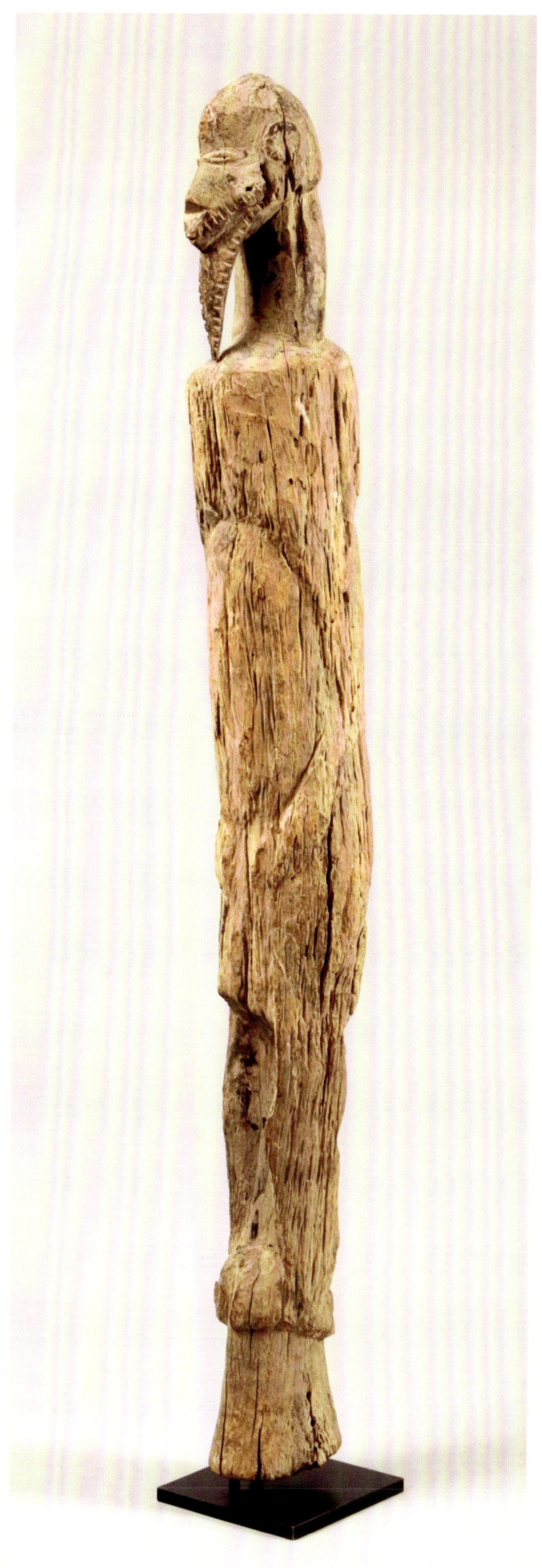

I.17
Male Figure
Yungur/Mboi/'Bəna peoples, Eastern Gongola Valley, pre-twentieth century (?)
Wood
H: 150 cm
COLLECTION OF TOBY AND BARRY HECHT
PHOTOGRAPH © GREG STALEY, 2010
PROVENANCE: MARTIAL BRONSIN, 2002
(NOT IN EXHIBITION)

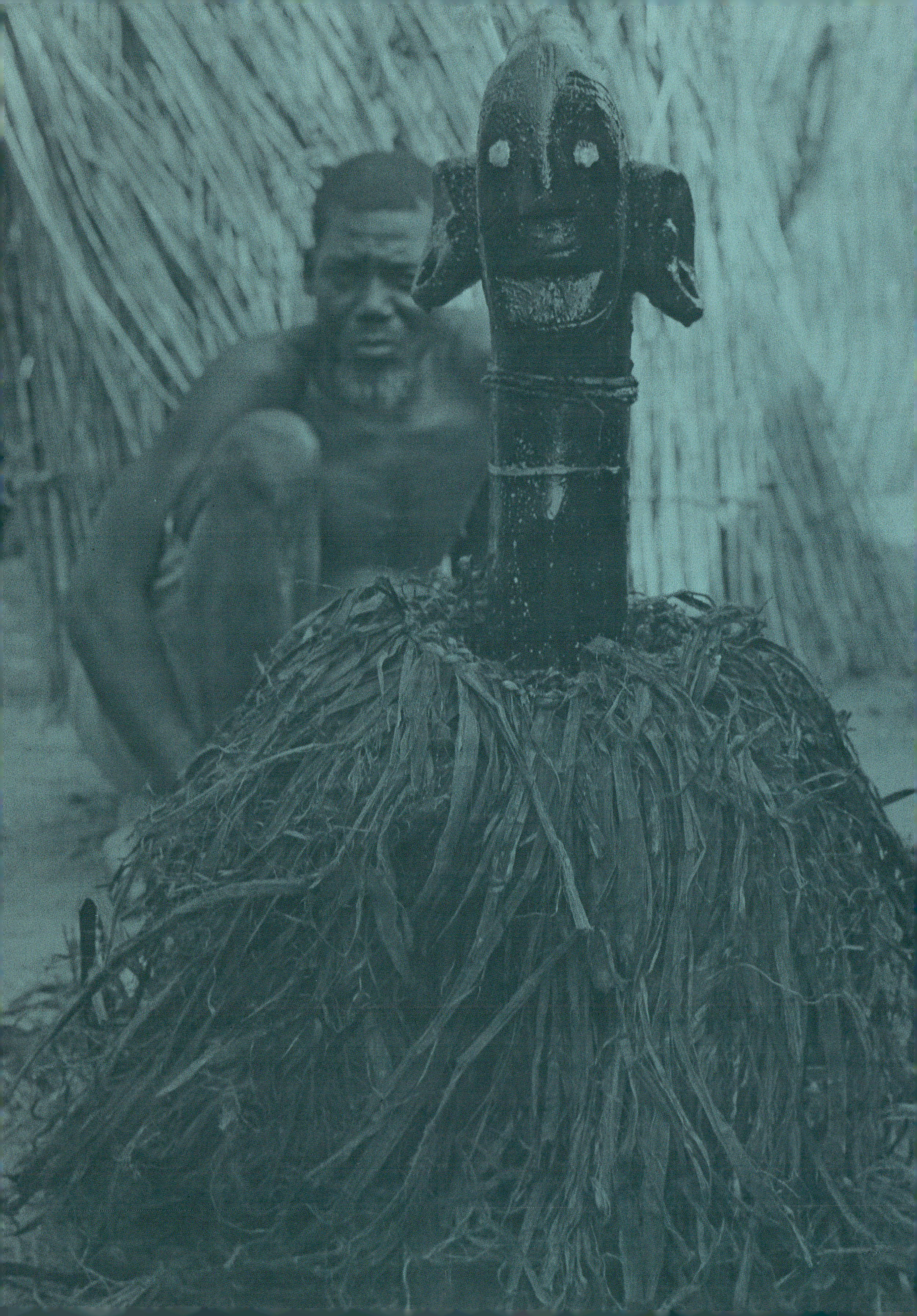

Epilogue—Making the Market for Benue Arts: Notes on the French Connection

HÉLÈNE JOUBERT   Translated by Richard Fardon

It was in Paris starting in 1965, and to a lesser degree Brussels, that a market for artworks from the Benue River Valley was created, eventually spreading to other locales in Europe and to the United States. This brief account is based in part upon interviews that I conducted in late 2009 with dealer/collectors who were instrumental in developing this international market. As such, it is a highly anecdotal history of that time and its protagonists, and one to which some may take exception. It is undertaken, however, in an attempt to record in brief the situation and the perspectives of those who were instrumental to introducing these artworks to the world.

PARIS AS A CLEARINGHOUSE FOR AFRICAN ART

At the beginning of the 1960s, few objects from the region of the Benue Valley could be found on permanent display in European public institutions or in private collections[1] or even illustrated in published sources. Exhibitions rarely touched on the region,[2] and as a consequence its arts were little known. A well-rehearsed set of predominantly national labels had long been used to designate the arts of sub-Saharan Africa (Mali, Côte d'Ivoire, Gabon, the two Congos). These were considered the "classical" styles of African art, and they represented the tastes of several generations of enthusiasts, which had in turn structured the Paris art market over several decades. Nigeria was known largely for the arts of the Kingdom of Benin, which had reached the European market after 1897 but had little presence in French collections, public or private.

By 1950 a network of African traders—initially Senegalese[3] and later Malian (beginning in the 1960s)—had formed and was bringing artworks originating in Côte d'Ivoire and Mali, as well as West Africa more generally, directly to Paris for sale. Between 1960 and 1970, almost all objects passed through Paris, while trade via Brussels in West African objects was slight. In those years the Bamako traders of Mali, who had already prospected their own country for salable works of art, turned toward Cameroon. They either took the initiative of visiting Parisian dealers or, as in case of the more professional among them—including Mamadou Sylla, chief of the Bamako antiquaries; Ahmadou Coulibaly; Mamadou Diaow; El Hadj Gouro Sow; and Diongassy Almamy—waited for the Parisians to come to see them in their hotel rooms where objects were displayed and deals concluded.

The generation of great Parisian dealers in African art, like Charles Ratton (who was advised by the British art historian William Fagg on Nigerian objects), René Rasmussen, and Pierre Vérité, who were considered the "mandarins" of the profession, did not travel to Africa. Instead, African objects arrived in Paris by different channels, via African dealers who might be of Dioula or Hausa ethnicity, collectors of various stripes, or even researchers. The specialist galleries of the time were run by Robert Duperrier (an associate of Rasmussen), Felicia Dialossin (of Argiles), Maurice Nicaud, André Level, Olivier Le Corneur and Jean Roudillon (of Galerie Le Courneur-Roudillon), and then Marcel Schanté (of the Reine Margot). The older and more established among them had enriched the collections of the Musée de l'Homme or the Musée de la France d'Outre-Mer between 1940 and 1960, and eventually they would also contribute to the collection of the new Musée des Arts africains et océaniens, established in 1960 at the dawn of African independence.

In a noteworthy departure from established practice, Hélène and Henri Kamer, who had established their gallery on the boulevard Raspail, began to travel to Africa and collect in the field starting in 1956.[4] With the opening in 1960 of a gallery on Madison Avenue in New York—in association with the publicist Alan Brandt who had begun by working for Julius Carlebach—the Kamers came to play an important role in the formation of the great American collections of African art.[5] In 1964, while her husband and Pierre Langlois went to Ethiopia, Hélène recalls that she decided to travel alone to Nigeria, and left for Lagos and Benin City. As her trip was designed to familiarize herself with the arts of the region, she visited museums but collected no objects. In 1968 Hélène Kamer began to operate independently. She opened the Galerie Kamer on the quai Malaquais in Paris and soon came to occupy a place in the hierarchy of great dealers, alongside Rasmussen and Duperrier. This standing guaranteed her first choice of newly arrived stock.

Following suit, other suppliers and dealers, some of them already familiar with Africa, began to travel to collect objects. Of note, however, they rarely sought objects at the source but received them instead from local runners in the service of African antiquaries. On occasion dealers temporarily worked together in order to increase the likelihood of making a profit through sharing contacts and dividing the costs and risks of the trip. Once returned, they sometimes provisioned other dealers who were better established, whether Parisians (like Rasmussen and Duperrier), Europeans (like Erich Storrer in Zurich),[6] or Americans, who had frequented French art circles since the late 1950s.

It should be remembered that at the end of the 1950s, the American gallery scene was itself dominated by European immigrants who had arrived during the Second World War and specialized in various fields. Julius Carlebach, an immigrant of German origin familiar with what were then called "primitive arts," became close to the Surrealists in New York.[7] John Klejman, an antiquary from Poland and a specialist in porcelain, became interested in these arts with the opening of New York's Museum of Primitive Art in 1954, founded by Nelson A. Rockefeller, and developed links with the Parisian art market though his agent, M. Kozlowski. Mathias Komor, a dealer of wide reputation from Hungary, whose uncles were antiquaries in Peking specializing in Asian arts, extended his interest to African art with purchases from Hélène Leloup (Hélène Kamer had by this time married Philippe Leloup, changing the name of their gallery to Galerie Leloup) and Pierre Langlois. In the mid-1950s, Aaron Furman, who until then had favored Mexican and pre-Columbian art, began to develop professional interests in the broader field of "primitive arts," and he ran his gallery in New York relying on his ability to spot pieces of artistic merit rather than on a specialist knowledge of the field.

The market for primitive art was comparatively little developed in the United Kingdom. Alongside the major dealers like John Hewett—one of the principal suppliers to Robert and Lisa Sainsbury—who soon turned his attention to other fields, a new generation of dealers interested in these arts emerged only at the end of the 1970s, the principal representatives of which were Anthony Plowright, who dealt particularly in rare books and the arts of Oceania, Indonesia, and Africa, and Bobbie and Lance Entwistle with whom Plowright was for a time associated. Despite Britain being the former colonial power, objects from Nigeria did not particularly pass via London during this time. Earlier, however, British colonial officers had brought important collections of objects from Nigeria to the British Museum, the Horniman Museum, the Pitt Rivers Museum, and the Liverpool Museum.

BENUE ARTS AND THE PROBLEM OF ATTRIBUTION

Acquiring artworks indirectly through runners posed problems with regard to their attribution, and this was certainly the case with the little-documented arts of the Benue River Valley. Those involved in the "promotion" of a repertoire of new forms recall that, despite the lack of knowledge about their history, it was necessary to label objects in order to classify them. An object without a definite identity and locality was difficult to value, and putting objects into a discursive framework was an essential part of any sales strategy. Hence dealers were keen to come by information that would allow them to place an object in its cultural ensemble and to locate it on a map, if only to improve the manner in which objects were presented to their new admirers.

To further complicate matters, local African suppliers, however close they might have come to the "source" of their objects, tended to be intentionally imprecise in their statements to dealers so as to safeguard their privileged access. Even today, Western dealers claim it remains difficult for them to find firsthand information sufficient to trace an object back to its village of origin. Back then, however, dealers were working with secondhand or even more remote scraps of information that might be more or less accurate. They therefore combined some grasp of the general area from which objects came with a perusal of the scant published literature. Thus it was that during the early years of a developing market, the arts of the Benue remained little understood.

For players in the Francophone art market, insights were restricted to references published in general surveys on African art (such as Elisofon and Fagg 1958, illustrated with 405 photographs) and to exhibition catalogs of limited circulation published in English or German. By virtue of assembling a corpus of works, Roy Sieber's slim volume *The Sculpture of Northern Nigeria* (1961) served as an important, if modest, point of departure and reflection on this new field. The publication in French of William Fagg's *Merveilles de l'art nigérian* in 1963 illustrated fifteen objects from the Benue (Fagg 1963).

The first exhibition to display an important body of works from the Benue was not held until 1970. It took place in the Kunsthaus in Zurich from October 31, 1970, to January 17, 1971, and was organized by Elsy Leuzinger in collaboration with Jacques Kerchache and Philippe Guimiot (see below). The exhibition catalog achieved major significance, not least because of its abundant reproductions of collected objects (Leuzinger 1971; [1972] 1976, 1977). In 1977, more than a decade after publication of Fagg's book on Nigeria, Ekpo Eyo's *Two Thousand Years of Nigerian Art* illustrated the Benue region with a series of sixteen objects. The small number of objects published in these few works was used to delineate an ethno-geography of artifacts that had persisted since 1958. In 1978, the catalog of the William Arnett collection, *The Three Rivers of Nigeria*, produced with editorial assistance from Roy Sieber, brought together objects from central and southeastern Nigeria according to the geography of the three principal waterways, the Niger, Benue, and Cross rivers. François Neyt's *The Arts of the Benue to the Roots of Tradition: Nigeria* (1985) was a synthesis of works, mostly from the Lower Benue region, and popularized the phrase "Arts of the Benue." It was heavily relied upon by French and English readers, largely because of its illustrations of important objects in collections.[8]

THE PRINCIPAL EUROPEAN PLAYERS IN THE MARKETING OF BENUE VALLEY ARTS

The dealers with whom I spoke in late 2009 likened the introduction of objects from the Benue to a "bolt of lightning" striking Paris and overturning long-held views of African art. The powerful sculptural styles of many of these works was new to the Parisian audience, as was their striking yet comparatively unrefined aesthetic, the application of pigment, and their acquired patina. This group of dealers, especially those who were just starting out in the early 1960s, reacted as though they had discovered a veritable El Dorado of aesthetic surprises, which had an additional advantage in that the objects, being relatively unknown, were affordable. Contributing to the thrill of discovery was the excitement of being able to style themselves pioneers of a "new" artistic frontier. Most of these dealers developed their commercial activities in tandem with building collections, sometimes secretly, which reflected their particular interests.

Jean-Michel Huguenin was one of the few dealers to have traveled to Nigeria before the attempted Biafran secession and Nigerian Civil War (1967–1970). Earlier, in 1961 he opened the Galerie Majestic in Paris on the rue Guénégaud. Huguenin had by that time spent ten years in the French Sudan (now Mali) where he recalls initially becoming familiar with the field of primitive arts. In 1963–1964 he was in Cameroon, based in the Bamum capital, Fumban, when objects from Nigeria began to cross the border, and in 1968 he organized the first exhibition of Mumuye statues at his Parisian gallery.[9] The exhibition was a sensation among a then-small group of avid collectors, and it would also inspire a seminal essay of lasting import by Philip Fry (1970), which is discussed by Richard Fardon in chapter 8 of this volume.

Hundreds of Mumuye sculptures arrived on the heels of the first consignment, attracting attention from collectors, dealers, and researchers. Jacques Kerchache was seduced by the allure of their sculptural form and acted as an intermediary in bringing these pieces to public view. It was not long before Mumuye figures assumed a primary position among the arts of the Benue River Valley in terms of financial value and aesthetic appreciation thanks in large part to their promotion and valuation by the galleries. Huguenin indicates that he retains in his personal collection some of the objects that had especially captivated him at this early date.

Edouard Klejman recounts how he had agreed to the suggestion of Julius Carlebach, owner of a New York gallery, that he accompany him to Mali in 1962 to seek artworks on Carlebach's account and that of Joseph Maes. Together with Jean-Michel Huguenin, Klejman subsequently turned his attention toward Cameroon, which remained the main source of Nigerian objects until the 1980s. Klejman was particularly attracted to Expressionist art and developed a taste for what he calls the "unexpected" (*inattendu*). As well as furnishing objects to French dealers, he became a supplier to several major American dealers (Merton Simpson, as well as his unrelated namesake, John Klejman of New York), while retaining his booth at the Puces de Clignancourt.

Max Itzikovitz, a dentist by profession, began collecting in Côte d'Ivoire in 1963. He opened the Galerie Maya (soon renamed Maya'n) on the rue Mazarine in Paris in 1964, in part to house his already important collection. Having sold pieces to major collectors, such as René Salanon and those close to him (including Rasmussen and Duperrier), he ceased commercial activity in 1972. He has remained a major collector still interested in Africa but also Oceania and most recently Asia. Fascinated by African polychrome objects, initially collected exclusively from Côte d'Ivoire, Itzikovitz was also attracted to the encrusted patinas of some Nigerian sculptures (see fig. 10.50). He sees himself as an adventurous collector, open to unusual objects whose offbeat invention and rhythm make them less accessible to European collectors than those considered the great classics of African art.

After having worked in the mining industry in Kota country in Gabon between 1958 and 1963—where under the guidance of Dr. Jean-Claude Andrault he gained an appreciation for African antiquities—Philippe Guimiot recounts that he left his post as Director of Administration. He did so to enter the field and collect objects that he has described as "tenacious witnesses" to "the relationship between men and the forces surrounding them." In 1965, Guimiot set up in Cameroon to pursue the art trade. Resident in Fumban, capital of the chiefdom of Bamum, on the edge of the Grassfields—and living in the home of Mamadou Yende, one of the most important and knowledgeable of local traders—Guimiot profited from access to a network of Bamum runners that he sent to Nigeria. Moving later to Douala, he opened the Galerie Africa, which became an obligatory port of call for Western dealers, including Jacques Kerchache. Meeting Kerchache proved a decisive moment for Guimiot, as from that point on he had a backer whose finances allowed him the first choice of available objects that came to him via runners. Between 1965 and 1970, extraordinary objects left Cameroon: first from the Bamileke chiefdoms[10] and then from Nigeria.[11] Returning to Brussels, Guimiot ultimately broke with Kerchache. He traveled to Nigeria again in 1973–1974 to collect Urhobo statues from the Niger Delta region. Other relationships turned Guimiot's attention toward India and Indonesia until the late 1980s when he resumed traveling to Africa.

In 1964, when Claudie Lebas and her husband, Alain, were still students, they became interested in African objects and began to collect them at public sales and from galleries. In 1969, they undertook a journey of more than a month to West Africa, focusing particularly on Dogon country. These experiences preceded their encounter with Nigerian objects, particularly those from the Igbo and Mumuye, which were flowing into the market in Paris. Between 1973 and 1975, the couple traveled regularly to Fumban, and this experience inspired Claudie to become a professional dealer. In 1982 she opened the Galerie l'Accrosonge (which only closed its doors in 2009) and devoted herself solely to Africa from 1984 to 1985. By the late 1980s the couple had followed the center of marketing from Cotonou to Lomé.

In 1965, Alain Dufour was working for Air France when he began to make trips to Africa and to collect objects there. He undertook his national conscription as a *coopérant* in the Dakar Museum between 1967 and 1968 and became a full-time African art dealer in 1974. Dufour maintained something of a distance from Parisian circles by establishing himself in Saint-Maur and opening a summer gallery in Ramatuelle. From the outset, he assembled a personal collection with the intention of including the best examples from all the areas he knew, particularly the Benue region of Nigeria. As he explained to me, "force, refinement, and emotional power" were the criteria for choosing the pieces he decided to retain in his own collection.

Asher Eskenazy was attracted early to the trade in primitive arts. He had acquired a knowledge of art history by obtaining the qualifications required to become a guide to the permanent and temporary displays in French national museums, and as a pupil of Jean Guiart at the Musée de l'Homme. Eskenazy confesses to an eclectic range of interests from natural history to archaeology via ethnography. Moving from gallery to gallery, he also worked collaboratively with Loed Van Bussel particularly dealing with German collections, both public and private, of objects from Oceania, which were coming onto the market at the time. After meeting Roy Sieber (to whom he sold an album of postcards from Central Africa), Ezkenazy read and was inspired by the American art historian's publications on Nigeria. He then took an unusual step among his contemporaries, who, as described above, worked through intermediaries: he made a field trip to Africa together with the London dealer Pierce Morris. Their motives were both commercial and research oriented. During two months in 1972 they traveled from Lagos to Idoma country documenting objects still in use, which people did not wish to sell, as well as buying others that were for sale.

Samir Borro's family lived in Côte d'Ivoire and supported him when he embarked upon a career as an art dealer. He recalled for me first coming into contact with African art objects at the gallery of Madame Dervain in Abidjan, the city in which he would open his own gallery in 1968. There he became part of a local network of dealers and collectors including Jean-Paul Delcourt and André Blandin. He met Jacques Kerchache around 1963–1964. Borro became interested in the Nigerian objects being brought by traders to Cotonou starting the late 1960s, and over several decades he assembled a collection of objects from Côte d'Ivoire and Nigeria. He became an important intermediary in the Abidjan art trade due to his specialist knowledge of Ivorian objects, and he dealt with French and Belgian, as well as American, dealers, including Alan Brandt, Merton Simpson, Bryce Holcombe, and the Swiss Paolo Morigi. In 1978 he opened a gallery on rue Bonaparte in Paris, and he then entered the American market between 1980 and 1984 with his gallery "Pokou" on Madison Avenue. This last venture, however, did not bring him the commercial success that he had anticipated. Borro fell back on his Ivorian base once more before the troubles there during the 1990s propelled him to leave for Brussels.

Pierre Dartevelle, who had established himself as a dealer in Brussels in 1966–1967, headed to Cameroon in 1967–1968 in the footsteps of French dealers such as Huguenin, Klejman, and Guimiot, with whom he collaborated on occasion. Although resident in Fumban, he recalls accompanying a runner as far as Jalingo in Nigeria in 1968. During the preceding years so many objects had come across the border from this area that Cameroon had become a hot spot for the art market. By 1970, however, the volume of trade had begun to diminish, and so Dartevelle turned his attention toward the Belgian Congo.

Beginning in 1968, Martial Bronsin, who had been a general antiquary in Brussels, developed a specialist interest in Cameroon and Nigeria. A close friend of Christian Duponcheel—who had already made an important nine-month journey through Nigeria carrying out basic research (the results of which have never been published; see interleaf H)—Bronsin concentrated on the Benue and northern regions of Nigeria, which particularly interested him. Attracted by original and rare works of art, he defines himself as an object seeker (*chercheur d'objet*) and has kept only what pleased him from Nigeria. Although always partly based in Douala, he realized that while the volume of objects coming via Fumban was much diminished, the market remained viable because there was little competition.

Being the first to see a particular type of object appear on the market brought with it considerable excitement, as did the selection of some truly remarkable works of art, which could attest to a discerning eye. The first objects to arrive in Cameroon were from areas closest to its frontier with Nigeria and made by such peoples as Mumuye, Mambila, and Ejagham, and the last to arrive were the furthest removed (the Koro peoples of the western Plateau). Waves of objects succeeded one another rapidly between 1965 and 1970, having originated with the following peoples: Igbo, Mumuye, Mambila, Eket, Ogoni, Ejagham, Ibibio, Oron, Montol, Verre, Chamba, Mama (Kantana/Kulere etc.), Mboi, Jukun, Tiv, Idoma, Igala, Afo, Bassa Nge, and Koro.

THE PARTICIPATION OF AFRICANS IN FORMATION OF THE ART MARKET

European dealers in the arts of the Benue benefited from a number of unforeseeable circumstances—many of them tragic in nature—that promoted the flow of objects into their hands. These included political instability, religious conversion, the retreat of traditional religions, the loss by particular groups or individuals of social prestige, the lack of a sense of the historical or ancestral value of material culture, the desire to acquire signs of modernity, and so on. African runners drew upon their knowledge of local trends and developments to time their entry into territories just as objects were being desacralized.

Even in cases where objects were not initially for sale, it did not mean they remained so. Some of the interviewees mentioned that suspicion and fear surrounded access to particular ritual wares by local people. Initially, therefore, it was very difficult to acquire such objects as their owners feared retribution. As Jean-Michel Huguenin was to find in the Cameroonian Cross River area, and Edouard Klejman around Mamfe, however, once it became known that the first to dare to sell such objects were not beset with misfortunes, the willingness to part with them became more general. The Biafran War gave rise to yet another set of circumstances. Muslim Hausa soldiers in the army of the Federal Republic looted and destroyed sanctuaries in Igbo country (and elsewhere) in the course of reprisals. They then organized traffic in ritual objects, which they considered "pagan," often bulking them for transport over the Cameroon border.[12]

It is noteworthy that Nigerians hardly featured in the establishment of art market networks beyond the local level. They acted primarily as runners who assumed the risks involved in bringing objects either to a particular point, such as the town of Jalingo, where they met up with their Cameroonian counterparts, or else crossing just over the Nigeria-Cameroon border to meet them at Mamfe. Some Nigerian traders, however, did make direct contact with the European market and occasionally traveled to Paris, or more regularly to Zurich, and above all to the United States.

The market established at Fumban at the beginning of the 1960s was a legacy of German and French colonial heritage, which had encouraged the development of a state-sponsored *artisanat* selling new craft products as souvenirs largely intended for European residents and visitors. Alhaji Mama, Alhaji Salifou Mbekom, and Amadou Yende, all of whom were considered highly skilled sculptors, ultimately broke with this colonial vestige to create a locally controlled *artisanat*. Artists and dealers in sculpture, they expanded into the trade in African traditional arts. Working in a highly organized manner with trusted agents, they handled objects from Cameroon as well as from Nigeria in numbers that are difficult to estimate. The Président of the Association de l'Artisanat et des Antiquaires, Alhaji Mumie, made regular trips to Paris. The titled sculptor of the Sultan of Fumban was also a trader in traditional arts, and his younger brother, Alhaji Idrissou, made a career as an art dealer in the United States.

Later on, with the growing development of the art market in West Africa and its concomitant decline in Cameroon, Nigerian objects began to pass via Cotonou in Benin and Lomé in Togo, which has remained a hub for trade in Nigerian antiquities, including those from Nok. There, other great families of traders would eventually take over, gradually becoming familiar with the objects and developing a network of runners. Noteworthy among these were Alhaji Abdou Inoua and his brother Amuda Al Madani, as well as Ousmane Abdoulaye.

These African traders, who were predominantly Hausa, had the advantage of being able to send out runners who spoke Hausa, which was widely used as a lingua franca across West Africa. This facilitated transactions through barter, especially in secondhand products (notably clothing). All of these factors contributed to the general affordability of Nigerian objects. This in turn diversified the landscape of collectors in Europe (essentially Belgian, French, and German) with a more modest class of emerging collectors, among them artists and teachers. Some pieces, however, were costly before they left Africa, not least because an object might pass quickly through several hands before export with a profit being realized at each stage. This chain of transactions served further to obscure questions of original provenance, frustrating the inquiries of subsequent researchers.

CONCLUSION

From the interviews that I conducted, I gained the impression that the passion of Europeans involved in the trade in Benue Valley artworks was genuine, as was a generally held conviction that this interest was a way to protect objects from destruction and disappearance. This was a moment when the availability of objects within cultural groups undergoing drastic change was matched by an external desire to acquire them. The coincidence of these two factors accelerated the movement of objects. Looking at the other side of the equation, attributing motives to those who decided to abandon elements of their patrimony, whether personal or communal, is risky. Historical, social, political, and cultural, as well as personal, factors have to be taken into account, and the evidence that would allow such reconstruction at this remove in time is largely wanting.

It is an uncomfortable conclusion to reach that the postcolonial development of a network of weakly regulated local markets led to the preservation and then conservation of most of the finest examples of Benue Valley art not in the Nigerian National Museums but in the private collections and museums of Europe and the United States. Whatever the circumstances that initially gave rise to it, it was the market network that brought these artworks to wider attention and aroused interest in them; the network, and its commercial significance, grew alongside the development of this interest. The purpose of this account has not been to judge this complex outcome but simply to contribute toward an understanding of the history that led to it.

Notes to the Text

Introduction (Berns and Fardon)

1. Arnold Rubin completed a draft manuscript for *Sculpture of the Benue River Valley* in 1988. Although we have drawn on his essays for information and insights, this volume has been rethought by its editors and reduced organizationally in ways that are discussed later in this introduction. The ideas incorporated in the essays written by our co-editor, Sidney Littlefield Kasfir, have been used here as have those of other contributing authors.

2. Defining which speech forms are languages (rather than dialects) and which local identities are to count as ethnicities (rather than clans or settlements) is necessarily contentious, so readers are advised to treat these figures, and others like them, as indicative rather than definitive. But in round terms two hundred would be about half of the ethnolinguistic groups in Nigeria.

3. While historians have generally accepted the existence of an entity called Kwararafa or Kona (Apá), which is noted in both the Kano and Bornu Chronicles, they have understood it in very different ways. For instance, Sargent (1999) sees the Jukun Kingdom as a successor state to Kwararafa, rather than its remnant as H. R. Palmer had done (see his preface to Meek 1931a). Social anthropologists, such as John Boston, conscious of the potential contemporary uses of "traditions," have been more skeptical about the historicity of oral accounts of Kwararafa (see Kasfir, this volume, ch. 1, 41–42). The record of artworks cannot easily be related to these discussions.

4. The distinction between "runners" and "dealers," which we report here concerns two stages of the commerce: at this time most typically—but not invariably—undertaken by Africans with villagers in the first instance, and by Europeans with non-Africans, including proprietors of galleries, in the second. Not all arrangements conformed to this reported model, which itself changed over time.

5. Kasfir reports that there were instances where dealers would pay for replacement objects among the Idoma, something that neither Berns nor Fardon witnessed in the field.

6. See also Jegede (1996) for a detailed discussion of cultural property issues relating to Nigeria, especially the trade in illicit antiquities and its ramifications. He also addresses failed practices on the part of Nigerian authorities and accredited agents (pp. 130–31) as well as the role of local communities in disposing of or trying to protect their own cultural property (pp. 134–45). Although his arguments focus on events in Southern Nigeria as well as archaeological rather than ethnographic objects, relevant to our discussion here is his observation that "poverty and disinterest become strong reasons for the disposal or removal of cultural property or for becoming an accessory to its disappearance" (p. 134).

7. One of the sculptures from Gwana was published as early as 1971 in Leuzinger. When Rubin returned to Gwana in 1971, all the sculptures he photographed there in 1966 were gone (see Rubin, this volume, chapter 9, n. 20). In his field notebook of January–February 1971, he includes on its final pages a declaration of theft, which he presumably wanted the Jukun chief of Gwana (Jeji) to certify. It is unclear whether Rubin ever pursued the matter but it is worth reproducing the text here:

   Dated this eighth day of February, Nineteen Seventy-one at Gwana, Wurkun District, Muri Division, Adamawa Province, Northeastern State, Nigeria.

   This is to certify that during the month of September (Dawa [sorghum] Harvest Time) person or persons unknown entered certain shrines at Gwana and removed religious carvings still in use by the people of Gwana without let or permission. This theft involved the following objects:

   Adong, "The Strong One," male figure; Kai, female figure, his wife; Wipong, male figure and two wives; Hwai Kai, male figure and two wives. One brass crown of bi-conical shape.

   Two figures photographed by Rubin in the nearby village of Pindiga are now in the National Museum, Lagos (*Guide to the Nigerian Museum, Lagos*, n.d., 37).

Chapter 1 (Kasfir)

1. John Boston (1969) has written a detailed account of the oral traditions of Igala kingship and its Benin, Yoruba, and Jukun (Apá) connections.

2. In the 1920s an indigenous distinction was still drawn between Akpoto and Idoma, the latter meaning those with a tradition of having come from Apá. This kind of status difference would suggest Akpoto were the autochthones to the region, the true "owners of the land." But conversely, Brooke (1922, 5), a colonial district officer, claimed that "Okpoto" was a disparaging term used by the Igala and Igbo to refer to the "offshoots of Idoma, Igara (Igala), and Apa (Jukun) who intermingled and settled there"—in other words, what we would call "immigrants" today. This explanation seems slightly more plausible, in the absence of an Akpoto/Okpoto language but also points up the complex cultural mixing that has gone into modern Idoma ethnicity and equally into Idoma aesthetic practice.

3. There are numerous examples but the Akweya of Akpa District stand out, since much of the Idoma sculpture in collections is actually the work of Akweya-Idoma artists.

4. In the 1950s these included ethnographers Laura and Paul Bohannan (Tiv), Robert Gelton Armstrong (Idoma), John Boston (Igala), and Elsy Leuzinger and Jolantha Tschudi (Afo). In 1958, Roy Sieber conducted a brief field survey of Igala, Idoma, Montol, and Goemai masks and figure sculpture. After Nigeria's political independence in 1960, Peace Corps volunteers and other young ethnographers collected for the Jos and Lagos Museums. John Picton and Perkins Foss worked for the National Museum Lagos. In what was by then called Benue-Plateau State, Anita Glaze collected and documented Idoma sculpture for the Jos Museum, as did Anna Craven with Afo works.

5. The Kano Chronicle, which lists the kings of Kano and the events associated with their reigns from 1000 CE onward, indicates that Kororofa was an important state by the fourteenth century. It attacked Kano some time between 1582 and 1618, again between 1652 and 1660, and finally in 1671. Bornu records of a similar nature indicate that Kororofa besieged Bornu between 1645 and 1684. The only reference to any of these military campaigns that Meek found among the Jukun in the 1920s was an account of the chief of Pindinga's alleged attack on Kano in the fifteenth century (Meek 1931a, 29). While an extremely valuable source for historians, the Hausa and Kanuri traditions themselves are not unimpeachable. The Kano Chronicle was not written down until the late nineteenth century, and as Meek sardonically remarked (1931a, 24), "Any imaginative Muslim who can write is capable of manufacturing history for the benefit of the unlettered."

6. The other migrations, for which Erim (1981, 140) collected two hundred and ninety-five separate accounts from 1,065 informants, may be real, or modern political constructions, or a combination of both. However they are construed, Idoma-speaking people were displaced, for various political and environmental reasons and settled further westward in the Benue Valley.

7. British military forces took Kano against fierce opposition in March 1903 and Sokoto in July of the same year. The earliest military patrols south of the Benue River were in 1908–1910.

8. The first European expedition to attempt to explore the Benue (then known as the Tchadda) was by MacGregor Laird and R. A. K. Oldfield (1837) and was undertaken in 1833 in an attempt to open up the Niger and Benue region to British trade in ivory. The second, and more successful, European expedition to the Lower Benue took place aboard the *Pleiad* in 1854, with the same intention of establishing ivory trading stations. Also on board was Reverend Samuel Ajayi Crowther who collected informants' accounts of the languages spoken and who eventually set up a Church of England Christian mission at Lokoja on the west side of the Niger-Benue confluence. The *Pleiad* expedition resulted in three separate published accounts: Crowther (1855), William Baikie (1856), and T. J. Hutchison (1855), providing substantial information on Doma Kingdom. Adolphe Burdo (1880) undertook an exploratory voyage up the Niger in 1878 and then continued by foot through Akpoto counry along the south bank of the Benue. Burdo, a member of the Belgian Geographical Society, was sponsored by the British Government through diplomatic ties. The great nineteenth-century German explorers Heinrich Barth (1850–1855) and Gustav Nachtigal (1869) never came far enough south to see the Benue but reported stories about Kororofa from Bornu and other places on their travels through the West African sahel.

Chapter 2 (Kasfir)

1. Idoma ancestral shrines did not contain figures, but many other shrines did, especially those relating to the fertility of crops.

2. Although often described as stools, most of these Benue caryatid figures hold up a winnowing tray. The examples I have seen are born aloft during processions and not used to sit on.

3. Biamegh can refer to the ceremony in which a newly deceased person's skull is added to the family group's ancestral relics such as *imborivungu*. It can also refer to the ceremony initiating a new group member into the select cadre of those allowed to look at the relics. The latter ceremony involved the elaborate construction of clay figures upon clay platforms, including one image of the deceased alive and another lying dead (Downes 1933, 58–64). It is equally tempting to compare these to Mbari houses in neighboring Igbo country or grave memorials in the Cross River region, though much more documentation would be needed. Later, in the 1950s, puppets came to play an important role in Kwaghir performances, though the ones I have seen were carved from wood (see fig. A.20) or made from papier-mâché.

4. Twenty years after Sieber and Fagg added Afo and Idoma sculpture to the canon, Father François Neyt made his own brief field trip to the Benue which resulted in his privately published book *Arts of the Benue: To the Roots of Tradition* (1985). In it he popularized the idea of Ekotame as a genre of figure, rather than the singular hybrid object it actually was. The result has been the misnaming of several maternity figures as Ekotame, particularly in European collections.

5. There was considerable exchange across the Benue between Afo and Agatu settlements, with Agatu villages on both banks. Agatu District was recorded as a post-jihad refugee enclave in the early colonial reports. It was subsequently Idoma-ized by a combination

of northern Idoma influence and British incorporation of it into Idoma Division.

6. By this I mean a prescribed set of artifacts, foods, and medicines; a priesthood; devotees; songs and enactments; shrines and performance rules; as well as a generally followed, though unwritten, cultural script incorporating beliefs.

7. According to Sieber (1961, 12), similar ceramic pieces are also in the Jos Museum (including a maternity by Azume) and have also been linked to the Jukun center of Wukari. A terra-cotta seated female figure is in the collection of the Musée du quai Branly in Paris (ex-Barbier Mueller collection; Martin, Féau, and Joubert 1997, fig. 292), but it does not look to be by the hand of Azume.

8. The figure in the Jos Museum was photographed in 1952 in the course of survey work carried out by the Department of Antiquities in 1952–1953. Sieber illustrated the head of this same sculpture in his catalog of 1961 (as figure 28 and on the cover).

9. H. R. Palmer, in his *Sudanese Memoirs* (1928), propounded a theory of divine kingship with a vaguely "Eastern" origin, exemplified by the Jukun King, as the major civilizing influence in the Benue Valley. By this yardstick, the Jukun as well as the Alago, Idoma proper, and Igala, who also embrace divine (sacred) kingship, were responsible for its spread southward to the Nri, Edo, and Yoruba.

10. A group interview with the Osana (king) of Keana and fifteen of his councilors in February 1989 yielded the statement that Jukun was senior, Igala second, and Alago/Idoma third in order of dominance prior to the breakup of the federation.

11. Sargent (1988, 25) states that the first Jukun to rule Kororofa was Ata Agba Adi Kenjo between 1610 and 1640. For several centuries before that it was "dominated by Abakwariga (non-Muslim Hausa) and Greater Doma in a shared political relationship."

12. For example, during my fieldwork in Idoma Nokwu in 1986 and 1989, everyone insisted that they (despite the fact that their kingdom appears on a map made by Leo Africanus and that they have an even longer kinglist than Igala) also migrated initially to present-day Igalaland but later left and returned to Doma.

13. This "husband and wife" pairing was suggested to me by the Och'Akpa himself, who averred that the husband might have been gradually dropped or "lost" (March 3, 1986). While not a watertight explanation, it does have resonance with the important role women played in conferring recognition on social manhood.

14. The Idoma word for leopard is *eje*, not *ekpe*.

15. The notion of "the enormous" was carried through in the initiation ceremony for new members, when each was required to bring, and then consume, huge quantities of food and drink: twenty yams and four pots of millet beer. (Needless to say, very few people could do this, so fines were usually imposed.) In addition participants had to smoke a specially made, very large clay pipe full of tobacco (interview with Agida, Head of the Itrokwu society, Otobi, 1978).

16. According to the District Head, both Akpnmobe masks were stolen from Akpa District in 1988, though by the time I learned of it in 1989, replacements had been carved by Omaga Ido and Inogwu Odaba. In 2009 I saw the Otobi Akpnmobe by Oba in a private collection in Paris.

17. The stool is large and cylindrical and probably hollow. It is of the type used by the Akweya to store (and conceal) important ritual objects and is kept in the inner sanctum of the clan head's compound.

Interleaf A (Kasfir)

1. See Marcel Griaule (1965). Over the course of thirty-three interviews, Ogotemmeli, a Dogon elder, laid out an extremely complex and detailed cosmology of Dogon belief that has since been viewed by some scholars as a "key" to unlocking the meaning of Dogon art and culture, and by others with considerable skepticism (Van Beek 1991).

2. The Jos Museum lists two separate artists in its collection, Oba of Otobi and Oba of Ochobo, but it is clear from the style and technique that they are one and the same person.

3. General Jack Gowon was the head of Nigeria's Military Government from 1966 to 1975, and as a native son of Plateau State, he was very popular in the Benue region.

4. Messenger (1973, 119) describes a "Marmee Water" performance in Annang puppet plays. Aba claimed to have seen a similar one in Mbausu, Tivland.

Chapter 3 (Kasfir et al.)

Kasfir:

1. This appearance of multiple ancestral masquerades does not occur in Ebira (John Picton, personal communication).

2. To avoid confusion, I have not included the contemporary Nupe ancestral belief complex Gugu, which is derived from Egungun and practised by Yoruba settlers in Nupe (Nadel 1954, 274). Gugu appears to be a reintroduction—a case of feedback in an altered form, if one accepts the hypothesis that Egungun originally derived from Nupe (Henry Drewal, personal communication, August 7, 1979). The Nupe Elo masquerade also derives some of its form, but not its meaning, from Egungun prototypes.

3. Alago is also the Hausa term for the Idoma north of the Benue in Doma and Keana

kingdoms, among the former, I shall argue, the mask originated.

4. The current label for the remnants of this group is "Egbira" (Picton, personal communication) to differentiate them from the Okene Ebira across the Niger, though both were founded from Idah at different times and speak dialects of the same language. Kwotto or Kwotto-Gara was their Hausa name, purportedly derived from Okpoto-Igara (Igala). See Paula Brown (1970, 55).

5. An ethnoscape is a landscape of group identity and interaction. See Appadurai (1996, 48).

6. Alekwu refers to an ancestral spirit, while Alekwuogboogba refers to a spirit who no longer has living sons to raise him up (i.e., to venerate him). Alekwuafia is the risen spirit in the form of a masquerade.

7. Erim O. Erim ("History of the Idoma," 60), following C. K. Meek's interviews of 1925 with Idoma elders, identifies Otiya as an old Doma settlement on the north bank of the Benue, but A. Paul Anyebe, an Idoma judge and local historian, interprets it as synonymous with modern-day Otukpo, the largest town in Idomaland (personal communication, May 1978).

8. A village in northern Idoma near the Idoma-Igala border.

9. Importantly, this prototype has two parts: an ancestral incarnation appearing in its burial shroud. In the many versions described here by other authors, the textile varies considerably from place to place and so does the infrastructure used to elongate it.

10. North of the Benue, all Doma lineages venerate Alekwu, ancestral spirits, but only the Ashama lineage there (who are Doma, not Abakwariga) has the Iwagu masquerade (Kasfir fieldnotes, 1989).

11. Greenberg (1946) described ancestral beliefs among the non-Muslim Hausa near Kano, who were known as Maguzawa.

12. Published initially in Italian with the title *Della descrittione dell'Africa et delle cose notabili cheiui sono, per Giovan Lioni Africano* in 1550 but written before 1526.

13. Doma had an official kinglist of forty-one rulers at the time of my first visit in 1986, thirty-nine of whom were undisputed.

14. See Adamu (1978, 40–41). Prior to woven textiles, barkcloth and vegetable or palm fibers were used in masquerade costumes, as elsewhere in Africa.

15. I am using Erim's (1981) distinction here between ethnically homogeneous Idoma polities as "chiefdoms" and heterogeneous, highly centralized Idoma polities with royal and nonroyal clans, subclans, and lineages as "states."

16. Armstrong points out however that the Agila and Igumale dialects of Idoma are quite distinct from Igala so this shouldn't be taken too literally (Armstrong 1955, 121).

17. Yoruba and Edo apparently also purchased their red *ododo* cloth for use in masquerades and ceremonial garments there (Henry Drewal, Paula Girshick Ben Amos, personal communications). John Picton's account of the use of red hospital blanket material in Ebira dates to the colonial period, while the Yangedde market was precolonial, though the ultimate source of the *ododo* cloth traded at Yangedde was also likely to be external, either Portuguese or, less likely, trans-Saharan.

18. Part of a sacred king's installation is a period of seclusion during which his funeral is celebrated, so ritually speaking, he is already dead when he assumes office.

19. The material on the Igala Egwu Afia that appears here originally formed part of the late John Boston's essay on Igala art, which appears as chapter 5 of this volume.

Picton:

20. For information about continuing resistance to proscription and the revival of masquerade after some twenty years, I reiterate my thanks to Elishe Renne, Constanze Weise, and Adinoyi-Ojo Onukaba. The references will be found in chapter 4 of this volume.

21. Regarding Abakwariga and Abakpariga, "kpa/kwa" is a systematic sound shift between Hausa and other languages; while *riga* is the Hausa word for the wide-sleeved gown.

Weise:

22. Field and archival research for this paper was supported with an International Fieldwork Fellowship from the UCLA International Institute in 2009; a Hoxie Bonus Fund Grant from the UCLA History Department; a Mellon Pre-Dissertation Fellowship from the Institute of Historical Research at the University of London in 2008; a UCLA Mellon Pre-Dissertation Fellowship in 2008; a DAAD Research Exchange Fellowship in 2002; a Peter Dornier Foundation Travel Grant in 2000; a DFG (German Research Foundation) Fellowship of the Graduiertenkolleg "Religion und Normativität" at Ruprecht-Karls University Heidelberg (Germany) in 2000. I would like to thank Dierk Lange, Jan Assmann, Till Foerster, Christopher Ehret, and Andrew Apter who supported different stages of my research with advice and patience. I further would like to express gratitude to Anna Towlson, Assistant Archivist at the Library of the London School of Economics and Political Science, who greatly assisted me with accessing Siegfried Nadel's fieldnotes and photographs; the staff of the Frobenius Institute Frankfurt, who supported my research concerning the Frobenius fieldnotes; and the staff of the Nigerian National Archives in Kaduna. My field research in Nigeria would not have been possible without the support and supervision of Dr. Abiodun Adediran, Obafemi Awolowo University, Ile-Ife; the late Dr. Aliyu Idrees,

University of Abuja; and the late Dr. Philip Shea, Bayero University Kano. I am also grateful to my host families in Nigeria without whose support I would not have been able to connect to consultants and local sites. In 2000 I stayed with the family of Mr. Mohammed Ndanusa in Bida. In 2009 the former Commissioner for Agriculture of Kogi State, Major Adesina Albert Soje and his family, in particular his daughter Khadiza Aliyu Lami Soje, generously hosted me in Lokoja. Last but not least I have to give my highest appreciation to my consultants the late Maji Dodo of Kusogi and the Nomba of Bassaland, as well as to my research assistants J. B. Adams and Dauda Abdulrahman for the Bida region and Adesina Moses Akefo, Adesina Oseka Matthew, and Musa Akogun for the Lokoja and Bassa Nge areas.

23. Another, less common name for the Bassa Nge is Nupe Tako. This term, however, is more frequently used by linguists to denote the Nupe dialect that the Bassa Nge speak.

24. At the first appearance of a Nupe word, the spelling with diacritical marks is also provided, usually within parentheses. Words for which no spelling with diacritical marks is provided should have a mid-tone, which is unmarked.

25. Apart from the Bassa Nge, other known Nupe diaspora groups live in Abeokuta, Ibadan, and in Lagos. See Kohnert (2007, 67, n. 57).

26. As to whether the Ndako Gboya belong to the genre of ancestral masquerades, see below.

27. The word "*ndako*" in Nupe may mean (1) father, (2) ancestor, or (3) smallpox. Cf. Banfield (1914, 354). "*Gboya*" contains the verb root "*gbo*," which means "to be large or big" (Banfield 1914, 197).

28. Nadel ([1954] 1970, 189); also personal communication from the Alagba of Ejigbo, June 12, 2000.

29. See the entry in Nadel's field diary for September 14, 1936, in Patigi. Nadel fieldwork diaries, edited by Roger Blench, 236 (unpublished).

30. The commonly assumed date for this event is set by most scholars in the sixteenth century, but there are actually no dates available for this time period. Cf. Obayemi (1978); Frobenius (1912, 1: 376–78).

31. Constanze Weise, fieldnotes, Kusogi, May 16, 2000.

32. Constanze Weise, fieldnotes, Kusogi, May 15, 2000.

33. Constanze Weise fieldnotes, Kusogi, May 15, 2000; Gboloko, June 28, 2009.

34. Known cult centers are Lade, Tankpafu, Gbado, Zambufu, Kusogi near Bida, and Kusogi near Patigi in Cekpan. The prohibition of the cult occurred in Tankpafu. In Kusogi in Cekpan the Ndako Gboya lodge had stopped the performance because most of its cult members had converted to Islam and considered these "pagan" rituals incompatible with their new religion.

35. The prohibition particularly affected Bida Emirate. See Nadel (1935c, 442).

36. Mr. Derwar, A.D.O. in the Colonial Service of Northern Nigeria, wrote in a memo on "witchcraft" to the Resident, Niger Province: "In practice, if not always in theory, 'black' and 'white' magic are inextricably mingled in primitive philosophy and… religion and magic (including 'black magic' or witchcraft) are similarly associated. Any attempt, therefore, to interfere with or destroy witchcraft…must certainly interfere with and might altogether destroy the religion into the fabric of which they are so closely woven" (Derwar, "Notes on Witchcraft in Its Relations to Adminstrative Problems," National Archives, Kaduna [NAK], MINIPROF, M 1228, 1934), cited in Kohnert [2007, 57, n.]).

37. Frobenius published these accounts in German (1924; 1925). My reading of his fieldnotes did not reveal any references to the Nupe original versions. Frobenius's fieldnotes are archived at the Frobenius Institute at the Johann Wolfgang Goethe-University, Frankfurt am Main, Germany.

38. Nadel qualified the cult as a secret society, although he admitted that "the *ndako gboya* represent something between the organization of a kinship group in which a secret knowledge and practice is vested and a 'society' proper, a voluntary association that is, of which (theoretically) everybody can become a member. Yet like the 'real' secret societies the *ndako gboya* is secret only in so far as its inner organization and its esoteric proceedings are concerned. The society as such is well known and even recognized as such officially" (Nadel 1935c, 435).

39. Constanze Weise, fieldnotes, 2000.

40. See my description of the initiation into the cult (Weise 2003, 282–86). Nadel did not observe the initiation, but it was described to him. There are nevertheless many resemblances in his description to what I observed sixty-five years later. Cf. Nadel (1935a, 143, 129–32; 1935c, 8, 4, 423–47; 1937, 91–130).

41. Weise, fieldnotes, Kusogi, May 6 and 15, 2000. For the description of the initiation see Weise (2003, 280–86). Judith Perani considers the Ndako Gboya to be ancestral as well. See Perani and Wolff (1999, 42).

42. Nadel ([1954] 1970, 189). To my knowledge Crowther and Taylor ([1859] 1968, 215) made the first written reference to Gunnuku. The men who would be able to dance the masquerade would be the boys who were initiated during the annual Gunnu festival. Weise (2003, 284).

43. Recordings from the initation, Weise, fieldnotes, Kusogi, May 6 and 15, 2000; Weise (2003, 285).

Willis:

44. Adedeji (1969) builds on traditions that Johnson documents. It is unclear whether the Iyamode was a member of this group of women. See also Babayemi (1980a, 19–20). It was the Iyamode's job to call out the royal masquerade from its sacred resting place during the subsequent annual festivals in Oyo and communicate the desires of Oranyan to Shango. Together, these women performed the rituals for this royal masquerade, the precursor to Egungun.

45. Deji Kosebinu et al. (2000, 24–25). I was able to confirm this in 2005 during an interview with Chief Joseph Olusegun, Atokun of Otta, Ijana ward, Otta.

46. A number of scholars (i.e., Johnson, Law, and Babayemi) believe that Shango was not a historical figure, which suggests that either someone else performed the tasks attributed to Shango or that beginning either during the pre-imperial or imperial period of Oyo history, devotees of Shango and Egungun collaborated to uphold the power and status of the monarchy of Oyo and of their own ritual communities. The anthropologist Eva Meyerowitz collected a tradition that identified the Iyamode as an unmarried, celibate priestess who lived after Shango held the status of royal deity at Oyo, since she was reported prone to frequent possessions by his spirit. This tradition allows the reader to infer that the first custodians of Egungun were Shango devotees, a collaborative endeavor or relationship that persists from the era of Oyo imperialism up to present date in many communities where both Shango and Egungun exist. Babayemi (1980b, 21) Meyerowitz (1946, 30).

47. According to an early tradition from the Yoruba town of Ile-Ife, the first Egungun emerged here in the form of a society known as Eluyare. The Igbo people, today found mostly in eastern Nigeria, are thought to have been the indigenous inhabitants of Ile-Ife, and the Yoruba people, led by Odudua and his followers, migrated to Ile-Ife and upon their arrival displaced the Igbo inhabitants. In retaliation for their expulsion, the Igbo created a masquerade society known as Eluyare, which used masks made of raffia to attack Odudua's group. Eluyare is thought to have been the precursor of Egungun. See Babayemi (1980b, 40).

48. Adedeji cites traditions contained within lineage and Egungun oriki and Odu Oworinse and the Odu Oworin Meji from Odu Ifa corpus and interprets them as reflecting the cooperation of Nupe and Oyo people in creating the Egungun society (1969, 78–97).

Borgatti:

49. Fieldwork in Nigeria was initially undertaken between 1971 and 1974 under the auspices of the Federal Department of Antiquities and partially funded by the UCLA Patent Fund, The Ralph Altman Memorial Fund, and an NDEA Title VI grant awarded through the African Studies Center at UCLA; in 1979 under the auspices of the Institute of African Studies at the University of Ibadan and partially funded by an ACLS-SSRC grant; and in 2002–2003 under the auspices of the University of Benin and funded through a Fulbright-Hays teaching and research grant.

50. With specific reference to Okpella and neighboring peoples, Isah Afegbua in his history of Okpella notes a Yoruba invasion of 1817 that produced changes in settlement patterns in western Okpella and sparked a "unilateral" movement eastward by the Oteku subclan (Afegbua 2003, 27, 49 [referencing the *Ilorin Gazetteer* 1911]) and another Nupe invasion in 1860 (p. 27). According to colonial intelligence reports, both Okpella and Ososo (Akoko-Edo) suffered attacks from Yoruba raiders in 1875 (Spottiswode 1941, 13). By 1877, Ososo had fallen under the control of the Islamized Nupe; Okpella (Ogute) capitulated during the 1880s (Walker 1915, 6). See also Bradbury (1957, 101–2 [Ekperi and the three Ibies] and 110–13 [Northwest Edo]). Michael Mason discusses the turmoil in this region in his article "The Jihad in the South: An Outline of the Nineteenth Century Nupe Hegemony in North-Eastern Yorubaland and Afenmai," *Journal of the Historical Society of Nigeria* 2 (June 1970): 193–209. With regard to Yoruba warfare in the nineteenth century, see "Yorubaland in the Nineteenth Century" by J. F. Ade Ajayi and S. A. Akintoye in Obaro Ikime's *Groundwork of Nigerian History* (Ibadan, Nigeria: Heinemann Educational Books, 1980, 280–302), particularly the sections that focus on the ramifications of the realignment of forces in western Yorubaland in eastern Yorubaland (289–93).

51. For example, in Etsako alone, Okpenada, one of Ekperi's seventeen villages (this scattering a result of the Nupe invasions) maintains a shrine called Okhailopokhai, meaning "a warrior will not enter the house of another warrior." The name refers to the efficacy of the cult's power materials (*ikhumi*) in protecting the village from Nupe slave raiders. Although the cult originated in the late nineteenth century in response to the Nupe problem, it continues to function as a focus for village worship (Borgatti 1976c, 60). Avianwu and Weppa-Wano maintain marriage institutions in which the children of wives acquired with little dowry belong to the matrilineage. These were children often used as slave tribute to the conquering Nupe in the nineteenth century (Borgatti, fieldnotes, Avianwu-Fugar, February 4, 1972; Nwalutu, 2004, 12–15). Finally, there is the history of Okpella's Olimi festival, born out of contact with other people and a need to strengthen ties with the land and ancestors during the reconstruction period after the nineteenth-century dislocation of population (Borgatti 1976a).

52. According to elders in Okpekpe (North Ibie), four kindreds—Imiekpe, Imidah, Imiukpe, and Imiebe—celebrate New Year (Aga) with food for the dead at a central community shine (*elimejo*). Later in the year, their sponsored masquerades named Atada Imiukpe, Igaga Imiekpe, Ogiaga Imiekpe, Balogun Imidah, and Agia Imiebe come out (fieldnotes, May 24, 1972). During my brief visits to Okpekpe and other North Ibie communities in 1972, I tended to focus on pottery, since this was one of the two Edo North pottery centers making large storage pots, Oja in Akoko-Edo being the other, and my trips were restricted because of the difficulty of access. The North Ibie still lived on the hilltops, and the dirt roads leading to their communities were steep, deeply rutted, and generally poorly maintained. I never actually saw the masquerades that they described as being something like the extendable masquerade known locally as the Igala-derived wonder dance (*ogumogu*) that is illustrated in Borgatti (2003, 40, fig.1). In retrospect, I surmise that these masquerades resemble the tall ghosts documented in Okpella, Ekperi, and Weppa where I did see them, and as they are illustrated in this essay.

53. Examples photographed in Weppa-Wano communities Iviukhue (slides 72.11.2-9); Emokwheme (slides 72.11.21-24); Aiygiere (72.09.2) and the Ekperi community of Okpenada (72.21.4). References in fieldnotes derive from interviews in the Weppa-Wano communities of Agenebode (February 7, 1972); Iviebua-Igbagba (March 15, 1972); Aigyere (March 15, 1972); Iviukhua (March 27, 1972); Emokhwemhe (March 28, 1972); and the Ekperi communities of Okpenada (February 5, 1972); Ugbekpe (May 31, 1972); Azukhala (November 20, 1972 and November 3, 2003). Omese from Weppa-Iviukhua is published in Borgatti (1979c, 4).

54. Information about shrine sanctuary names is tabulated in Borgatti (1979a, table 2, 576–77). Like Okpella's Ilukpekpe and Iyabana, Igala's Abule is a night society embodying the collective authority of the dead with the corresponding power to curse

in the name of the land (Boston 1968, 155–56, 225). Ilukpekpe and Abule use cognate terms for their forest sanctuaries, *okula* and *an'okula*, a term in Igala denoting the grave sanctuary for the nonroyal ancestral shrines (Boston 1968, 130).

55. Carol Ann Lorenz (1995, 361–66; 368–85) discusses the masquerade society, its performance, functions particularly with regard to social control and political order, the extent of its distribution, and its antiquity in Ishan.

56. A note on administrative terminology: Edo North is generally coterminous with Edo-speaking areas north of Benin in the past designated as Kukuruku or Afenmai plus Ishan. Until 1915 Okpella (also spelled Upila, Ukpila, Okphela) was considered part of the Northern Region for administrative purposes, but in 1915, Kukuruku Division was created, under the jurisdiction of the Western region, and Okpella transferred into it. Kukuruku Division incorporated much of what became divided among Etsako, Owan (Ivbiosakon), and Akoko-Edo local government areas. Its headquarters were located at Fugar (Avianwu) in 1915 and later moved to Auchi in 1921 where they remained until 1958. In 1958, the provincial system of government was replaced by a system of local government based on divisions, districts, and urban councils. At this time, Kukuruku and Ishan were amalgamated into Afenmai Division with headquarters at Ubiaja (Ishan). After 1966, when the twelve-state system was introduced in Nigeria, Afenmai was subdivided into four administrative units: Etsako, Owan (Ivbiosakon), Akoko-Edo, and Ishan divisions. The Etsako divisional headquarters were relocated to Auchi. The creation of seven new states in Nigeria in 1976 did not affect this area, although the divisions became referred to as local government areas. In 1991, a number of local government areas were added. Etsako, the area of concern to us, was divided into two groups (subsequently three) with Okpella, North Ibie, and Weppa-Wano grouped together in Etsako East with its center at Agenebode; Etsako Central incorporating Avianwu and Ekperi with its center at Fugar, and Etsako West incorporating Uzairue, Auchi, and Aviele with its center at Auchi. The ethnic designations follow Bradbury (1957, 100). Various maps in local publications show some additions. This information derives from various sources, including Ojior (2001, maps); Nwalutu (2004, 2); Borgatti (1976a, 49). Etsako East Local Government Area is part of Edo State, one of Nigeria's thirty-six states. It was formed in 1991 when its predecessor, Bendel State, was divided into two states, Edo and Delta respectively. "Bendel" was simply a 1976 renaming of the existing Midwestern region that had been put into place in 1963 (Edo State Official Website http://www.edostate.gov.ng/history.php, accessed October 5, 2009) and represented a differentiation of this area from the largely Yoruba-speaking Western region.

57. The story of Okpella's migration from Benin has numerous versions, but all generally agree on Benin origins and the presence of earlier immigrants and autochthonous peoples. The Okhu who live in western Okpella are thought to have arrived earlier than the Okpella. See Borgatti (1976a, 64–67) where a history has been reconstructed from those collected and variations cited in footnotes. See also Borgatti (1979a, 579–86) and Afegbua (2003, 23, 57–60).

58. The late Chief T. I. Enamudu, Erhame of Oteku, remarked on the Ighiafodio of Awuyemi and the Ekphema of Afokpella (inteview, 1972, tape 5, side ii: 200–53, Ethnomusicology Archive, UCLA). Another account notes the presence of the Ekphema as well as another group, the Utobis, at Iddo (Audu 1972). Afegbua refers to the people of the Ighiafodio Lake area in western Okpella (2003, 23, 49–50),who claim to be autochthonous or at least to have been already there when the Okhu people arrived. He also writes of the Ekphema (pp. 67–68) and the Utobis (pp. 74–75) in eastern Okpella.

59. The discussion with respect to the Ekperi from Borgatti (2003, 42–43) follows (including citations in that article): "At the time of Ekperi's departure from Benin, Benin and Idah were engaged in open warfare, and both kingdoms record the settlement of fringe areas in the aftermath of conflict (Boston 1962:380–81; Dike 1976:6/2–5). The prevalence of night societies and title systems like those of the Igala and Igbo suggests that a local population inhabiting the area prior to the sixteenth century absorbed Igala influence (Eboreime 1978:2; see also Borgatti 1976c, 1979c, 1989). Peacetime activities resulted in even greater cross-cultural communication among the peoples living along the Niger, for the river served as a major highway to the coast. The Igala capital at Idah faces the northern Edo settlement of Agenebode (Uwepa-Uwano) on the opposite bank, and what is now the Ekperi area is said to mark a point on the border between Edo and Igala authority prior to the Idah war of 1515 (Eboreime 1978: 2). Furthermore, the Igala were a nautical people who regularly traveled downriver to trade. Elizabeth Isichei notes that they stayed away from home for long periods of time, living in large covered houseboats or in temporary housing. From this it was but a short step to permanent settlements. Indeed, a whole chain of Niger Igbo towns claim Igala origins, as Ossomari does, or like Illah, have quarters that trace descent from Igala. Both of those communities use masquerades that retain Igala as a spoken language (Isichei 1976:54-55)."

60. Oteku scattered to eight sites—Ogiriga, Obedu, Ukhomi Unyo (from which the early name of Afokpella, Kominio or Komunion, was taken), Eguasha, Ukpano, Akporaobe, Eseldumi, and Idedeowa—under Nupe pressure, coalescing into three umbrella Oteku communities after the pax Britannica—Ogiriga (from Ogiriga refugees), Afokpella from Ukhomi Unyo, Akporaobe, and Eseldumi, and Iddo made up of refugees from Obedu, Eguasha, and Ukpano who relocated to Idedeowa. See Borgatti (1976a, 66, nn. 37, 38).

61. See Borgatti (1976a, 68–75). This was confirmed on October 19, 2003, in conversations with Iyeluwa's Itilimi (Father of Masquerades and "festival" head), as documented in my fieldnotes: "Anything else I should know for the record? Ogiriga is the oldest Olimi festival, followed by Iyeluwa. Ogiriga and Iyeluwa are the same. Iyeluwa moved from Ogiriga to this place c. 1932. When they moved, did they bring msq. or make their own? When they came out, they still went to Ogiriga for festival. Once they became more populous, the ones who had Olimi began to do their own in Iyeluwa."

62. In Okpella, people have a variety of ideas about the power of this cloth. In Ogute (western Okpella) it was said that the real (commemorative) Omeshe (as opposed to Aja) has special cloth called *ebe* made by Ebira as part of its costume. The weaver

doesn't look at it after it is incorporated into such a costume on pain of death. Someone else must remove it from the loom when it is finished (fieldnotes, August 24, 1972). In Iddo (eastern Okpella), the cloth is also said to come from Ebira and serve as a powerful charm capable of protecting a house against thieves. Youths cannot weave this cloth. It is believed to be made by old women in the sacred state of nudity; moreover, these elderly weavers die when the cloth is finished, hence its power (fieldnotes, May 11, 1973). The cloth, used by the Ebira in their own tall ghosts masquerades, actually comes from the Bunu Yoruba where it serves as shroud cloth and is part of the funerary display for wealthy and important men. One of five categories of the cloth, a single strip like that used in the older Okpella commemorative masks, is actually called *ebe* and was woven on the day of the funeral (Renne 1995, 110–113).

63. These are descriptions of Omeshe solicited as part of a survey on aesthetic preference carried out in Okpella in 1979. The numbers in subsequent notes refer to the respondent/questionnaire number. These are rough transliterations without phonetic or diacritical marks. This data has been archived as a dataverse, though not yet public, with the Murray Archive at Harvard University.

64. I am indebted to Margaret Thompson Drewal (performance studies specialist) and ethnomusicologist Robert Witmer for viewing and listening to films and music in order to help me appropriately describe both movement and sound.

65. Praise given to the Alukpekpe by the Otaru of Afokpella, March 14, 1974 (tape 7, side II: 078–083).

66. 018: The playing of Omeshe is like the movement of the wind. The beating is hard. (*Abola o omeshe o ro le abi okiki olitsu a ra kpeli Ekpeli oa tuekilighi na le.*)

67. 102: I like it when Omeshe is dancing like a "circling wind" (dust devil). (*I no omeshe oa bola abo okiki-olitsa ora ti mhe elue.*)

68. 169: Omeshe has no eyes, hands, or feet. When it dances, it jumps upward. (*Omeshe oa zi kpalo. Oa zo we ali obo. Okhagbishimi oa fiala idane*). 250: Omeshe is just a thing on the ground with no legs, hands or head that can be seen. (*Omeshe onu liabie emi no la eka we agia me, awe, abo, ali ukhomi ogoli.*)

69. 063: When Omeshe comes to the playing ground, it is like a cloth carried by the wind; when dancing, it is like a wild animal. (*Ini Omeshe obale olele o li abie ode na ru khasi ni apiapia o re. O kha bie ishimi o li abi elami*). 132: [I like the way] Omeshe does not fall down [when it dances]. (*I dede noa ya de.*) Similar sentiments were expressed by respondents 283 and 376.

70. For Ilukpekpe songs that celebrate its power and goodness, see Borgatti (1976a, 134–41).

Chapter 4 (Picton)

1. That paper has field illustrations of most of the things mentioned here, as well as linguistic maps of the region.

2. In so doing, I have followed Bravmann (1973), Kasfir (1984), and Vansina (1984), as well as Nadel (1942).

3. Fardon (1995, 5) contrasts three ways of understanding the questions we are trying to answer, and his discussion of the categories "local" and "global" in the last paragraph on page 5 points us toward a way through.

4. In my use of the word "thing," I follow the fourth-century African philosopher-theologian Saint Augustine, who wrote "All teaching is teaching of either things or signs," and while some things are just things, others "are at the same time signs of other things. There are other signs whose whole function consists in signifying. Words, for example.... So every sign is also a thing, since what is not a thing does not exist. But it is not true that every thing is also a sign" (Green 1997, 8–9).

5. There are some aspects of African visual practice, in particular the modernist developments beginning with the inception of photography, that simply do not respond to ethnic classifications. Indeed, photography is the obvious example: the technology is international, but the subject matter and usage of any given photograph is necessarily determined (at least in part) by local circumstances. It is an effective paradigmatic example of what can happen in the engagements between local and global. Two examples from 1960s Ebira come to mind. The first of these was the increasingly popular display of photographs of deceased elders in Ebira funerary processions (see Picton 2002; also p. 121, this volume, fig. 3.33), perhaps assuming the role of other forms of commemorative display, including Ekuoba, which were no longer being made. The second example involved the way that some night singers, Eku'rahu, had had themselves photographed, not as they would perform at night in the presence of men with their faces uncovered, but always wearing a cloth hood to prevent women recognizing them (see p. 117, fig. 3.28). Yet photography was not unique in the coming together of forms and practices of wider distribution with local elements. Most of the forms and practices discussed in this essay embody this kind of dialectic. What matters, what makes the "coming together" distinctive, is not the general principle but the particularities of its manifestations in this or that locality.

6. I would not have known about the mediating role of Ebira in this regard were it not that toward the end of 1965 K. C. Murray recommended that I move on from the Yoruba-speaking region in my work for the Nigerian Government Department of Antiquities, and as I had already visited some of the villages around Kabba in the Yoruba extreme northeast, he suggested moving toward the confluence and that I base myself in Okene, the administrative center of what was then the Igbirra Division within the government of Northern Nigeria. Thereafter I was in and out of Ebira many times through the years that followed. In 1968 I was joined by Susan Picton, who surveyed Akoko-Edo, as well as the region around Dekina in northern Igala, including the so-called "Bassa Nge" (in Nupe, "we are not Bassa"; Gunn and Conant 1960, 72) and the Bassa Komo (or Ukuomu, the "true Bassa"). Also in the late 1960s, John Boston had published his Igala research; Eva Krapf-Askari had researched the Owe communities centered on Kabba; Mike Mason was following up nineteenth-century Nupe history; Phillips Stevens documented Nupe sculpture; and Arnold Rubin had initiated his survey of Jukun and Benue Valley material culture. After Susan and

I left the employment of the Nigerian government in 1970, Jean Borgatti researched Okpella (also spelled Ukpila), an Etsako-speaking (Edo-related) community adjacent to Akoko-Edo, Sidney Kasfir researched Idoma, and Elisha Renne, Abinu (or Bunu), a "Yoruba" people east of Kabba. Apart from Ebira, Akoko-Edo, Bassa Nge, and Bassa Komo, where the account presented here is dependent on Susan's and my field research, the sources on which this essay depends are given in the references listed at the end of the book; and I have thus chosen not to pepper the text in the usual academic manner.

7. Indeed, I was told that the boundary between the lands controlled by Kabba (in Yoruba) and by Ososo (in Akoko-Edo) originally ran through the present site of Okene market (John Omoluabi, personal communication, 1982).

8. Modern standard Yoruba is the language used in Akoko-Edo primary education, given the diversity of "little" languages.

9. Why Aworo is classed as "Yoruba," while Igala is not, is almost certainly a political question.

10. The most accurate map of the various Yoruba peoples is still that in Forde (1951).

11. See Constanze Weise on Nupe and the late John Boston on Igala, both in this volume, as well as Boston (1968).

12. To be more precise, the timing of the festivals was determined by means of a calendar of moons and markets that was understood by one particular group of elders and a source of mystery to everyone else. Every Eku'rahu and Ekuecici (see below), however, had to apply to the Native Authority for a license to perform.

13. Many thanks to Elisha Renne for sending me press cuttings from Nigeria about how masked performers had gone out in performance in spite of the ban, been arrested in costume, and made to undress in public before the magistrate!

14. The political complications I experienced in Ebira in the 1960s were the outcome of British colonial rule within a now-independent nation-state in which Ebira personnel were to be found in many leading positions. Though Europeans were not seen in Ebira until 1903, Christian missionaries, colonial personnel, and European traders had been active along the Niger and Benue rivers since the middle of the nineteenth century, and they were known about in Ebira as the region came under British colonial rule. In due course, British misunderstanding of Ebira political realities would have a profound effect upon local institutions and upon a local understanding of those institutions.

15. Mason (1970a; 1970b), quoted by Isichei (1983, 213). See also Jimada (2005).

16. The structures and systems of Edo chiefly authority can be interpreted as a grandiose development of the age-grade/title-taking system common to all Edo-related peoples.

17. "It had become a means of establishing and representing a common identity among a diverse population that included people of Jukun, Idoma, Nupe, Ebira, Edo, Akpoto (the indigenous basis of Igala) and Igbo descent" (Picton 1990, 60). See also Boston's apposite comment (1968, 10): "The fact that traditions of Jukun, Yoruba and Benin origin can exist in the same corpus of legends shows that the king list [i.e., in Igala] is not bound by the conventions of sequence that occur in a linear time scale." I shall return to this problem below.

18. The research on which this essay is based began in the 1960s, and from place to place these patterns may well have been amended within a postcolonial legal environment, especially when and where land has become personal (rather than lineage) property and thereby subject to sale and purchase.

19. I was puzzled by the examples I had collected in the late 1960s, until Ted Celenko told me how they were made on the basis of his research in the Egbira region north of the confluence. In a letter with accompanying photographs that he wrote to William Fagg (dated March 1, 1977), Celenko describes the smiths as Egbira, and the tools shown in the photographs, taken at a village northwest of Umaisha, indeed suggest that the smiths were not Uneme—especially due to the absence of a very distinctive form of Uneme hammer found throughout Ebira and Akoko-Edo. The brassed-iron pipes Celenko shows being made, together with the circular thatched form of the smithy, could, however, suggest that the smiths were, if not Uneme, at least Uneme-related or influenced. Of course, given my antipathy to ethnicity as the all-purpose paradigm, one might wonder why I am so bothered by this. The answer is that southwest of the confluence, the Ebira/Uneme difference had continuing social value throughout the period of my research, and an Uneme ethnicity continued to have constraints on what a man or woman might do. Lastly, in regard to metalworking, just to add to the confusion, there are reports of (non-Uneme) brass casting at Kabba and at Koton Karifi. Moreover, although Igu (Koton Karifi) and Opanda had a reputation for metalworking, there is almost no material evidence to support this reputation.

20. Willett (2002, 190–91) quotes from a discussion I had with an Ebira elder regarding a "Bassa Nge" mask.

21. He invented for himself the title, Atta of Igbirra, and proved himself an extraordinary modernizing innovator, ensuring that everyone had access to clean piped water, planting tree-lined avenues, building the local prison and the hospital, constructing the out-of-town cemetery, and encouraging school education and the progress of Islam. Nevertheless, his reign was controversial and in 1954 he was ousted by rival political elements.

22. Elisha Renne (1995, ch. 6) gives the full and authoritative description of these cloths and the processes of their weaving. Prior to the availability of red woolen hospital blankets in the colonial period, she cites other possible sources available indirectly, and at great cost, via coastal and, possibly, trans-Saharan trade. By the late fifteenth century, a woven, felted, red woolen cloth obtained from Portuguese trade had already been incorporated into Benin City court ceremonial (Renne 1995, 220–21, n. 8). See Kasfir's discussion of *ododo* cloth, this volume (see chapter 3, p. 111).

23. The Ebira verb "*ci*", meaning "to come down" (whether from a tree, a hill, or a motor vehicle), also has the figurative significance of coming down to someone's house to enjoy the hospitality offered therein.

24. These included Ekuahete (mask of stamping feet), which heralded the opening of the feast, while clearing the community's public spaces of witchcraft; Ekuoba, the walking shrouds; Akatakpa, supposedly women slaves in the world of the dead, who also sang at Ekueci; and Owuna, the precise form and nature of which remains unclear as it was no longer performed by the 1960s. Little by way of costuming was worn by these mask categories, as women were shut indoors for the night.

25. The first person to gather musicians and singers together, performing from house to house during Ekueci was Itemirege, and in the 1920s, even as an old white-haired man, he was still performing.

26. See my discussion elsewhere in this publication: "Ebira Masquerade and its Histories" (pp. 115–23).

27. As I recall, he made this statement in a seminar at UCLA during my term there in 1987.

28. I am also grateful to William Rea for referring me to Peel (1989) when I was drafting my paper of 1994 on the Yoruba artist.

29. Post-1897 Benin is another example of cultural reinvention in the face of colonial rule, to judge from Charles Gore's work (2007). Indeed, in Benin City cultural reinvention is a continuing necessity.

30. See Ruth Watson (2003).

31. See Michael Echeruo (1977).

Chapter 5 (Boston)

1. John Boston was originally commissioned to write this essay by Arnold Rubin, and it was submitted to Rubin during his lifetime. Professor Boston died in 2001, and we are very grateful to his widow, Sally Boston, for providing permission to print this essay and reproduce the field photographs that illustrate it. Special thanks are also due to Kathi Jenkins for helping to locate Profeesor Boston's original field photographs and having them digitized. The images by Professor Boston that appear here were selected by him when he submitted his essay. Sidney Kasfir has edited the essay and moved a section of it to chapter 3 (pp. 113–14) so that it could illuminate the mapping of ancestral masquerades in the Lower Benue.—Eds.

2. Others include Uloko, Agama, Atododo, Okiti, and Echogwu.

Chapter 6 (Neaher)

1. Copper alloy refers to a metal composed primarily of copper, zinc, and other elements, including tin, silicon, and lead. Brass can contain up to 40 percent zinc, and its color is often distinctly yellow. Bronze is associated with correspondingly greater quantities of lead or tin, and coloration can vary. For a variety of reasons, the literature on sub-Saharan African metal arts has often employed these terms interchangeably. Over recent decades scientific analyses revealing the precise composition of Ife, Benin, and Igbo-Ukwu "bronzes" has opened up new directions in determining their respective histories. With few exceptions, however, the varied corpus of Benue copper-alloy artworks has yet to be subjected to similar examination.

2. Thanks to the Ata's generosity, I was able to examine eight staffs and other items, although no photographs were permitted. Chike Dike discusses the *okute* briefly and includes a black and white photograph of fourteen examples. It is difficult, however, to ascertain much detail. He terms them "Benin" heads (Dike 1984, 70; also 1987), yet their small scale and original interpretation seem to distance them from a Bini model.

3. See Mockler-Ferryman (1892, 383); Wilson-Haffenden (1927, 381ff.); Phillip Allison (1974). Also see objects in the National Museum, Lagos, 61.1.163 and 147a.

4. This piece was acquired for the Indianapolis Museum of Art by its long-term curator of African art, Theodore Celenko, who did fieldwork among the Egbira of the Niger-Benue confluence zone in the 1970s. Other related examples are in the British Museum (AF1954, 23.1121) and the World Museum Liverpool (22.11.24).

5. For example, Kenneth Murray, who purchased a cast pipe-bowl from a smith in 1944, now in the collection of the National Museum, Lagos (84.297.22); Temple (1919, 144), Jos 66.J.61.133 (pipe bowl); Kasfir (1979, appendix); W. Fagg (1963, pl. 142); Armstrong (1955,137); Schädler (1997, 264, no. 515); and Nadel (1942, 259–69); World Museum Liverpool, headdress, no number.

6. Rubin also photographed an ax of this type among the regalia of the Chamba chief at Kashimbila (see Rubin 1973, pl. XXIVc). It has an unusual flared blade.

7. Several are in the Pitt Rivers Museum, including one collected by G. I. Jones and donated in 1931 (VIII.492) and a second donated by H. Balfour in 1930 (VIII.402).

8. For voice disguisers see Downes (1933, 52); Abraham (1931); Rubin (1982, 44–45). For other areas with voice disguisers see Pitt Rivers Museum (H. Balfour), 1939, no. 445, from Onitsha, and the 453, 454, 455 from Aguleri, Onitsha, and Boki.

9. Records published in 1916 observe "men…skilled in metal…and some clever weavers" (Judd 1916, 53). Nearly contemporaneously, Temple comments on the quantity of brass ornaments worn by Tiv men and women, and while he claims the principal industries involved textile manufacture, he also cites work in iron and brass as locally produced (1919, 300–301). The British District Officer C. C. Feasey (1927) contributes specific information on brass figures collected among the Mbatiav clan and their method of manufacture. He describes the lost-wax process, which involved the use of "wild rubber" for modeling. A few years later euphorbia latex (a milky sap produced by a variety of savanna shrubs) was identified as the modeling material, resulting in "extremely fine braid work" (Pitt Rivers Museum, 1933.29.4). Latex was also documented for the creation of a fine figurated ring made by a named metalsmith from a Nanev clan hamlet (National Museum, Lagos, 54.11.38). The middle of the twentieth century offers short, yet significant, evidence of a local tradition. Brass pipes were purchased from a "large manufacturing and distributing center" in northern Tiv country (Abraham 1940, 38), and other clans were said to be responsible for making snuff holders, including examples in the shape of a figure-eight with extremely delicate braid work (National Museum, Lagos, 54.LL.33 and 54.11.36). Philip Allison claims that an individual, Autse of Mbagua, made snuff takers (1974), further affirming the existence of Tiv production.

10. A second wand is in the collection of the Musée du quai Branly (A96-1-10); see Martin et al. (1997, fig. 28).

11. Sieber and Hecht (2002, b) refer to it as a "staff head."

12. In the mid-nineteenth century, Hutchinson described the Fulani (Filatahs) as a mixture of Akpa and Hausa (1855, 110). Meek, whose travels along the Upper Benue resulted in an important body of work, refers to Hausa-speaking groups who were captured by the Jukun at the turn of the nineteenth century and were assigned to "quarters at the present site of Wukari," becoming known as Abakwariga (1931, 40). In the remembered past, Igbo smiths in Awka who worked at the Niger-Benue confluence, and who occasionally went eastward in search of new work orbits, commented on the presence of "abawa" as far east as Garoua on the Nigeria-Cameroon border (Malcolm 1921, 39; Neaher 1975).

13. Tremearne (1912, 194, 290–91). The Hausa hoe, distinctive in shape, was much in demand across the Benue Valley. Some of my informants remembered the Hausa engaged in casting; sometimes they commented on rivalries with the Hausa. On the other hand, one smith was taken in by a Hausa smith and given temporary lodgings, saying that "all smiths are brothers" (Neaher 1975).

14. In an unpublished paper for the Menil Collection (Menil Archives, n.d.), Leon Siroto expands on Fagg and Rubin's hypothesis by suggesting that Hausa "higher attainments" may account for the more sophisticated bronze casting found along the Benue. He adopts the Abakwariga thesis, postulating a "Middle Benue figure-and-weapon metal style" to account for items like the Tiv axes, some of the Verre daggers, and the finer human figures discussed in this essay. For Siroto, these represent vestiges of a "pre-Islamic sculptural tradition(s) of the Hausa," prevalent before prohibitions on figurative imagery took effect. From there, his argument continues, formal concepts and technology were transmitted to others, resulting in pallid echoes of the originating tradition. Siroto feels the absence of evidence from other indigenous groups "leaves us with no better explanation of the figure-and-weapon style than the Abakwariga presence." Shain's research (2005) suggests Abakwariga metalsmithing may have been a response to their displacement by the Hausa newcomers in the salt and long-distance trade, which they had formerly dominated, making their engagement in pre-Fulani metalworking questionable. Siroto also overlooks major developments in southeastern Nigeria, even as a complementary source of figurative bronze casting. The massive numbers of objects found throughout southeast Nigeria and the formidable historic record of the Igbo-Ukwu bronzes pose problems for his interpretation.

15. Frobenius (1912, 639) referred to a Yola dagger, various examples of which may be found in the Jos Museum collection, e.g., Jos 66.J11.534, 577, 618, 619; Meek (1931a, facing 134); Islamic type collected by Frobenius, Berlin IIIC 28151ab; Chad semicircular pommel, Jos Museum, 73.J.38.58.

16. Kandert's survey (1990) of eastern Nigerian and western Cameroon nonferrous metal arts gives a general overview, mainly based on secondary sources.

17. From an initial survey, however, Verre cast works seem to be clearly separable from those of western Cameroon.

18. The Dera also made cast gauntlets (*boli*) that were worn by young men in pre-marriage ceremonies where iron-bladed dance axes were struck against the gauntlets during performances (see Berns 1986, 354, fig. 154).

19. Fleming and Nicklin (1982, 57). Also, Nicklin (1982, 47, 50); Peek and Nicklin (2002, 53, 58); Neaher (1976a); Van Dyke (2008, 61–65).

Interleaf C (Neaher)

1. The study of smaller, less-spectacular objects in Nigerian art history owes its inspiration to the pioneering approach of Arnold Rubin, who served as one of the author's advisers during her doctoral research. He believed that "students of African art have tended to disregard literally tons of other works in brass and bronze; bracelets, rings" plus "…knife-handles and scabbards, pipes, bells, boxes and amulets" (1973, 221). It is hoped that this study reflects the value of following the trail of humble items in the search for bigger truths.

2. The term "Egbira" refers here to Egbira-speaking peoples who lived principally north of the Niger-Benue confluence. The density and overlapping configurations of groups at the confluence are fully explicated in Picton's chapter 4 in this volume.

Chapter 8 (Fardon)

1. Elsewhere in this book, what I occasionally call anthropomorphic statues are referred to as figurative sculptures. I would find it confusing to abandon entirely the terminology used in two previous books, since I need a way to speak of wooden statues composed of two anthropomorphic figures. By wooden sculpture I understand here both masks and statues. Anthropomorphic statuary has a human shape, though this does not mean humans are represented by it, as I have already noted that spirits are also considered to take human-like form, even if that form is deformed or anomalous in some respects. Statues are made up of one or more human-like figures. Very occasionally examples of figures with animal attributes have entered collections; however, all of these seem to evoke a human-shaped body with the head of a mask rather an animal.

2. The earliest collected example of a Wurkun figure would appear to be that acquired by Olive MacLeod (later Temple), apparently in unused condition, in 1910 during her ascent of the Niger and Benue in company with the Talbots. This piece is now in the collection of the World Museum Liverpool where it is on permanent display (accessioned 22.11.24, item 275). Judging from her published account, it is likely that Olive MacLeod bought the statue from a marketplace or trader in Ibi or Lokoja (MacLeod 1912). The figure is strongly columnar, with a rounded, possibly ithyphallic head, and is set upon a metal spike.

3. Whitman published an account of Christian missionization in which he described spirits "inferior" to the supreme being who "may be represented by a stone or a bit of broken pot placed to mark the boundary of a field, or a stick with a carved head set up in a garden or compound as a supposed protection against thieves. Finding some of these carved sticks one day near a broken-down hut I wanted them carried to the house, but no pagan boy would touch them, in fear that the spirit represented by the sticks would surely inflict disease, or even death, upon him. Finally some Christian

lads, whose faith had emancipated them from this terrible fear, came along, and the fetishes were carried in for safe keeping" (no original date or pagination, *Christ or the Fetishes: The Story of Christian Work among the Jukun of Northern Nigeria*, London: SUM). These statues were likely the pair that Whitman donated to the Commercial Museum.

4. The whereabouts of one of the male statues was unknown to us when we wrote our account (see Fardon and Stelzig 2005, fig. 1e), but its head and torso, now without the one leg it retained, have surfaced in the collection of Bernard de Grunne.

5. A second entire forked statue has been proposed for inclusion in the corpus of Soompa's works since Christine Stelzig and I published our catalog of them in 2005. It may well be genuine, though I have seen it only in photograph and have no information on its collection history. If genuine, it would be the only example of a male figure with hair crest worn transversely (that is from ear to ear) rather than sagittally (from front to back). There is also photographic evidence for a single-figure fragment that could well come from a sculpture of this kind (which is listed in our 2005 volume).

6. These include: two collected by Glauning in the same areas as his double-figure statues (Berlin III C 17618 from Lengdo near Mapeo, now lost; III C 19025 from Yeli); an example collected by Rothe from the chiefdom of Gurumpawo (Dresden 240-67); a pair of figures in the Museum für Völkerkunde in Leipzig before World War Two (Leipzig 23217-8) illustrated by Arriens in his drawing of *Heilige Figuren der Tschamba*, in Frobenius (1913, 2 right, 3 left); a piece collected as far south as Gashaka purported to be Chamba (Vienna).

7. Two figures (66.J.11.709; 66.J.11.720) were accessioned from the same source in 1966 to judge by their accession numbers. A third was accessioned in 1973 (73.J.59.3A).

8. A further group of four figures in the Jos collection (74.J.41,194-6 & 200) attributed to Chamba are more likely to be Verre to judge by their proportions (Fardon and Stelzig 2005, 77, figs. 14 a–d).

9. Rosalind Krauss's essay on Alberto Giacometti is illustrated with a Mumuye figure. It is unlikely, however, that his participation in the circle and discussions around Michel Leiris would have exposed Giacometti to Mumuye sculptures in Paris at an early date (Krauss in W. Rubin 1984, 2: 531). A direct influence on Henry Moore, about whom more below, is demonstrable from the evidence of his sketchbooks and writings of 1922–1924 (Alan G. Wilkinson in W. Rubin 1984, 2: 597). A recent exhibition has revisited the theme of African art and European modernism (Wick and Denner 2009).

10. See the Yale University-Guy van Rijn Archive of African Art database.

11. Even this underestimate is three times greater than the (also under-) estimated numbers of Chamba still living in the Nigerian part of their homelands by the same source (Temple and Temple 1922, 79).

12. I am grateful for personal communications from Hélène Leloup, which recall these events with slight differences. She notes that Jean-Michel Huguenin and Edouard Klejman had collected their pieces in Cameroon together in 1968. Their initial exhibition in November of that year consisted of fourteen, not eighteen, pieces, of which she and her then husband Henri Kamer acquired nine, the best of which were taken for sale to their New York gallery. J. J. Klejman's first exhibition in New York was not, as she recalls, a great success because of the prices asked for these hitherto unknown pieces. Huguenin and Edouard Klejman returned to Cameroon in 1969 to collect further examples (personal communications, September 24, October 6, 2009). Eleven Mumuye figures, ten bought by the seller in 1970, of which four were acquired from Huguenin and Klejman, reentered the market in 2008 with the sale of the Parat collection (*Artcurial*, June 10, 2008).

13. In December 2003, the late Christian Duponcheel described in detail to the author and Christine Stelzig the evacuation of a large art collection from Nigeria during the Biafran War by lorry and finally by headloading across the Cameroon border, made possible with the assistance of the Fulani chiefs of the border towns of Toungo and Koncha. On the Nigerian side of the border, the attraction of commerce in antiquities was enhanced for local Muslim chiefs by the campaign against heathenism waged from the top down in independent Northern Nigeria. Dinslage and Storch (2000, 13, 163, 228) recount the death in disgrace of the last chief of Kona, ostracized by his own people for turning his back on their traditions and selling cult objects. His behavior was not unique. Arnold Rubin recorded in his fieldnotes for April 6, 1970, that the Village Head of Zo had sold masks to people who came with a "licence" that had been shown to the Emir of Muri.

14. I am indebted to Susan Gagliardi for her careful review of Arnold Rubin's original Mumuye fieldnotes held at the Fowler Museum. Although accession ledgers in the Jos Museum recorded acquisitions from Rubin in 1970, I could not find the records that would have corresponded to the earlier period of his research. We can tell when Rubin collected a piece from the field because he usually augmented his field photograph with a later image (as indicated in my tables). In the records of his 1970s fieldwork, Rubin allocated distinct number series to photographs of collected objects, and he distinguished those acquired by the Jos Museum (which helps to match these pieces with the Jos accession ledgers, which could be found for this but not the earlier period of Rubin's fieldwork). Collected wooden figures (WF) and wooden masks (WM) were identified ordinally (hence, WF1, WF2…. WM1, WM2 and so on) in Rubin's photographic catalog.

15. Fry claims Nyavo lived in Pantilapo (1970, 27), but Rubin's fieldnotes place Nyavo in Pantisawa. The two villages are not distant from one another, respectively to the west and southwest of the town of Jalingo. I have not seen the original letter to Jacqueline Fry, so cannot explain where the slippage in attribution occurred.

16. Because of the move of the British Museum ethnographic collection from the Museum of Mankind underway at that time, this pair was not available for viewing when Christine Stelzig and I completed our 2005 account of Chamba statuary. Hence the pair is wrongly described there, following the museum's accession record, as two female figures, which on inspection is evidently not the case (Fardon and Stelzig 2005, 135).

17. The review by Michael Brenson on 28 October 1984 was accessed at http://www.nytimes.com/1984/10/28/arts/gallery-view-discovering-the-heart-of-modernism.html; Christine Stelzig (2009) refutes any direct influence on George Lucas. Lucas also

Interleaf F (Gagliardi)

I offer my appreciation to Marla Berns for inviting me to work closely with the archive of the late Arnold Rubin. I never met Arnold Rubin in person, but his fascinating field data have left me with a partial image of who he was. I am grateful to Z. S. Strother who taught a graduate seminar at UCLA during the spring quarter of 2005 that significantly changed how I think about masquerade and thus how I have understood Arnold Rubin's film footage from Zinna and Pantisawa. She generously commented on earlier versions of this text. I likewise thank readers, including Gassia Armenian, Marla Berns, Richard Fardon, Marcia Gagliardi, Chris Higa, and Lynne Kostman, who offered their comments on earlier versions of this text. Edited clips of Arnold Rubin's film footage of masquerades at Zinna and Pantisawa used in the *Central Nigeria Unmasked* exhibition may be seen at www.fowler.ucla.edu.

1. Terms used to refer to the "Vaa-Bong" masks and masquerade performances vary. For example, Meek refers to "*Va-bô*" (1931a). Rubin uses "*Vabon*" (1985, 98–99), "*vabô*" (n.d. edited film footage), and "*Va*" (1985, 98–99; 1988). In his unpublished exhibition manuscript, Rubin explains different use of the terms to refer to the masks and perhaps associations that sponsor the masks. Rubin uses "*Va*" in the 1988 text and explains: "In several compounds around Monkin and Zing, at La'ama and near Jalingo, the type was called *Va*; at Lama, the name was given as *Va*, or *Vabon* for emphasis."

2. Arnold Rubin used different spellings to refer to Mumuye towns he visited. In a 1985 publication, he refers to the *Va* or *Vabo* masquerade in the town of "Pantisawa." In the unpublished manuscript prepared in conjunction with the exhibition of Benue River arts that he was designing, he refers to "Zing" and "Sawaa" and explains that the two towns had previously been identified as "Zinna" and "Pantisawa" (1988).

3. Richard Fardon writes: "No Chamba with any claim to know what he or she was talking about ever told me that their mask represented a bushcow *tout court*" (Fardon 2007, 35). He suggests that the term originated with researchers rather than with people who invented and created the masks. Arnold Rubin uses the term "bushcow" in his notes and publications. For example, in an entry dated October 17, 1965, Rubin explains that a Vaa-Bong mask at Pantisawa "represents bush cow—just as acceptable as cow" (October 17, 1965, 207). Previously in the same entry Rubin refers to the same mask as a "buffalo" (October 17, 1965, 206). Unfortunately Rubin's notes do not indicate if he himself perpetuated use of "bush cow" or if the people in Mumuye towns to whom he talked in the 1960s and early 1970s used the term.

4. See Fardon (2007, 38). The dwarf forest buffalo (*Syncerus caffer nanus*) is an animal typically found in the forests of West and Central Africa.

5. April 20, 1970, 299; see also Data Card associated with neg. no. 2632.

6. February 19, 1971, 485; see also Data Card associated with neg. no. 3143–3144.

7. April 13, 1970, 282; see also Data Card associated with neg. no. 2608.

8. April 13, 1970, 282; see also Data Card associated with neg. no. 2606–2607.

9. In reviewing Rubin's fieldnotes of 1964–1966 and 1969–1971, I have not found a specific reference to "Leopard" or "The Wind Can Blow Any Direction" as individual names for Vaa-Bong masks. It is therefore possible that he obtained this information later.

10. April 20, 1970, 304; see also Data Card associated with neg. no. 2664–2665.

11. April 13, 1970, 282; see also Data Card associated with neg. no. 2609–2610; cf. February 19, 1971, 485.

12. April 13, 1970, 283; see also Data Card associated with neg. no. 2611–2612.

13. February 16, 1971, 468.

14. Rubin publishes a similar list of names in *I Am Not Myself: The Art of African Masquerade*, edited by Herbert M. Cole (1985, 98). Other names he recorded and translated into English include: "Brave Person" (April 20, 1970, 300; see also Data Card associated with neg. no. 2629), "Foreigner" (April 20, 1970, 303; see also Data Card associated with 2662–2663), "Fulani" (April 20, 1970, 304; see also Data Card associated with neg. no. 2666), "Slave" (April 24, 1970, 314; see also Data Card associated with neg. no. 2719), "Talkative" (April 24, 1970, 316; see also Data Card associated with neg. no. 2719D), "When Something Falls into a Well, Difficult to Remove" (April 20, 1970, 303; see also Data Card associated with neg. no. 2658).

15. Mette Bovin likewise notes that women were not allowed to see the masks, at least not on certain occasions (see chapter 11, 375–79).

16. Arnold Rubin's fieldnotes indicate that there were six age groups in Zinna and that each age group was represented by a Vaa-Bong mask. He explains that the first and third age groups were responsible for the initiation of the new group. The second and fourth groups did not participate in the ceremonies. The elders comprised the fifth and sixth age groups, and they, too, presumably did not attend the initiation events (April 21, 1970, 305).

17. Rubin (1985, 99) refers to "four to six maskers" in a description of Vaa-Bong performances that corresponds closely to his documentation of the April 1970 event at Pantisawa.

18. Rubin does not specify the duration of the event. In his notes describing the event, he writes: "This AM—masks dressed, pntd. / proper dancing this PM, tomorrow" (April 21, 1970, 307). He thereby suggests that performers prepared in the morning for a dance that started in the afternoon or evening and continued until the next day.

19. In his fieldnotes describing the April 1970 performance at Pantisawa, Rubin does not identify the angular headpiece as a particular form. On October 17, 1965, he photographed a similar headpiece in Pantisawa. He tentatively described it in his notes as a "fish-hawk," "bird of a kingfisher type," and "Naba = 'old woman.'" Rubin also considered it "a beautiful piece" and questioned why a horn was included on the fish hawk form (October 17, 1965, 206–7). In his unpublished manuscript for this exhibition, Rubin refers to the different, yet formally similar headpiece seen in the April 1970 Pantisawa performance as a "kingfisher" or "*Naban*." He therefore seems to have considered the classificatory information he obtained in 1965 relevant to the identification of the mask he filmed at Pantisawa (cf. Rubin 1988).

20. In the 1985 publication, the caption to Rubin's photograph reads: "Two *Vabon* maskers with trumpets and an attendant carrying a memorial ceramic pot; Pantisawa, Nigeria. Photo: Arnold Rubin, 1969." However, the field notebooks in Arnold Rubin's extant archive provide no indication that Rubin visited Pantisawa in 1969. Furthermore, the film negative of the image reproduced in the 1985 publication is cataloged alongside Rubin's other images from the April 1970 performance.

21. It is not clear what, if anything, the pots contained. The previously mentioned October 19, 1965, notes from Pantilapo specify that there was "no medicine inside" the pots when they were smashed and that there was nothing inside the pots that would harm people present when the pots were smashed (October 19, 1965, 223).

22. In his unpublished exhibition manuscript, Rubin identifies Saawa (or Pantisawa) and Lapo as two towns that commemorated deceased elders with bovine-headed ceramic pots (1988).

23. Rubin refers to the top of the pot as the "bush cow finial" (1985, 99).

24. Pots were topped with ceramic heads that echoed different mask forms, including Vaa-Bong headpieces.

25. Rubin's notes suggest that the pots topped by ceramic bovine heads may not have been ubiquitous in Mumuye towns at the time. For example, during his April 19, 1970, interview with Alkali in Zinna, Rubin asked if there were such pots in Zinna given that there were pots in Pantisawa. When Alkali responded that there were different pots in Zinna, including pots used for making rain, Rubin asked if ceramic heads topped the Zinna pots. Alkali told Rubin that pots topped by ceramic bovine heads were not the type found in Zinna (April 19, 1970, 292).

26. In his notes Rubin does not qualify the groups of women who would have been allowed to see Vaa-Bong masks.

27. Despite the large number of wooden headpieces they said they had produced, Rubin curiously documented only one that he attributed to Lenke and another he attributed to an artist named Mangare. He attributed none of them to Madaowre. The discrepancy may reflect several different factors. Artists may have carved Vaa-Bong headpieces for patrons in Mumuye towns for generations, and thus some of the artists may not have been alive when Rubin was in the region. Some people may not have remembered the names of the artists who carved certain headpieces. In addition, Rubin noted that some of the original patrons were deceased or otherwise unavailable at the time of his interviews.

28. Rubin's notes indicate that the pots' tops were fashioned after the headpieces that women could not see rather than the reverse (October 19, 1965, 225–26). Rubin writes in his notes that pots were made to look like masks "to show that men [had] attained age & stature to see masks; when pot taken to be broken, mask goes in front" (19 October 1965, 226).

29. Rubin's notes also include information about the pigment that Meku used. He described the black pigment as the product of burnt groundnuts and the red a product of dried earth from the riverbed (21 April 1970, 309). He wrote that the white pigment was a whitewash but had previously come from the "excreta of lizard" (April 21, 1970, 309). Rubin notes that the same colors were used on the masks, further reinforcing the connection between the pots and Vaa-Bong masks.

Chapter 11 (Bovin)

I am extremely grateful to Richard Fardon for his heroic efforts in helping me to get this essay into publishable form. I would also like to express thanks to my Mumuye friends and informants for all that they contributed to my fieldwork during my two stays in 1964 and 1968. My appreciation goes as well to Poul Kjaerum, the head of the Archaeology Department at the Moesgård Museum, for letting me use his fabulous Rolleiflex camera in Mumuyeland in 1964.

1. Luis de Sande, a Spanish Catholic priest resident in Zing in 1964 generously gave me the photograph that appears here as figure 11.4, as well as others that he had taken prior to my arrival. He was also instrumental in helping me transport Mumuye objects that I had collected for the Moesgård Museum in Cophenhagen from Zing all the way to the Jos Museum.

Interleaf G (Fardon)

1. Although there have been surveys (notably within Wente-Lukas 1977 for northern Cameroon and Nigeria), publication of the results of intensive research has been exceptional. Arnold Rubin's articles "Bronzes of the Middle Benue" (1973) and "Notes on Regalia in Biu Division, Northeast Nigeria" (1974) focus respectively on archaeological finds among the Jukun and on the ironwork in the chief's treasury in Biu District, which belongs to the Upper Benue in terms of the organization of this volume and the exhibition that accompanies it. A brief notice on Verre brass casting by Timothy Chappel appeared in Jean-Hubert Martin et al. (1997, 223–24).

2. I was told (both in Mapeo and in Yeli) that tribute in the form of worn-out hoes had once been paid by Mapeo to Yeli to avert drought and locust infestation. The Mapeo version claimed the hoes were used to block the hole from which locusts would otherwise issue; the more prosaic Yeli account was that the iron was reused by their smiths. Iron was valuable and worn items were always reforged.

3. I saw examples of these in several Chamba Leko chiefdoms, as well as in Tisayeli, Mapeo (see fig. G.1; also published in Fardon 1990, 164).

4. A similar spear, along with an outsize all-iron hoe, formed part of the insignia of Nyaa Gangwu (lit., "Mother Chief-Woman"), the woman head of the chiefdom of Sugu, and in this context, it was called *wuru sɔɔm* (dead/ancestor spear). These spears were known to Chamba Leko by a variety of terms, including *yaa dinga* (horse spear). Post-menopausal women danced with the royal spear in the Chamba Leko chiefdom of Yeli during the annual funerary rites of the royal clan. Spears and spear washing (*ding sugnbia*) were of great significance in emigrant Chamba conquest kingdoms in ways I have tried to reconstruct elsewhere (Fardon 2006, 120–25).

5. These flat-bladed straight hoes were described to me as the earliest type of hoe used by Chamba before the introduction of wooden-handled hoes hafted at a right angle. I was further told that these were used in a sitting position. This was an account I

disbelieved before actually coming across an elderly woman using one while seated.

6. Frobenius's claim regarding the cult rattles illustrated by his artist B. Bauschte (see fig. G.5) is that some of them had degenerated into mere belt amulets. These kinds of ornaments were used to deck out circumcision candidates particularly. They also seem similar to the clappers of the mysterious iron-shafted "spear of Mam," which more resembles a fighting stick without a blade or point, photographed by Meek (1931a, facing 277), discussed here by Marla Berns (interleaf E, p. 290).

7. I also saw a *lama* in the form of a throwing knife, which had been imported. Frobenius illustrates another throwing knife (different in shape) in the insignia of the Chamba Daka chief of Kiri (1913, 242, *Heiliges Gerät der Dakka "Kirri" Königs* by Carl Arriens). Throwing knives strayed on occasion into the Middle Benue but were apparently not made there (Westerdijk 1988).

8. Composite wavy iron rods, similar to this example, though less complex, were collected by Mette Bovin in Yakoko in 1964 and have been accessioned by the Moesgård Museum, University of Aarhus, Denmark (E.A. 95-210; E.A. 95-158). Similar examples, presumably attributed to Mumuye by those who sold them, appear on dealers' Web sites, typically misidentified as money or currency.

9. One such large brass bell with a clapper, collected by Olive MacLeod in 1910, is in the collection of the World Museum Liverpool (22.11.24, no. 24), where it is described as "worn by big man's horse" and attributed to Bachama. It is similar to a brass bell with iron clapper illustrated in Wente-Lukas (1977, 247, fig. 332).

Chapter 12 (Frank)

1. A first shorter essay on this region was written by Arnold Rubin (1988). Barbara Frank (1936–2004) followed his concept of treating art objects—not ethnic groups—in context. She incorporated, with alterations, Rubin's general passages on the area, descriptions of objects, and references, and among them especially, the ones relating to Rubin's research in museums. After Frank's death, Richard Fardon and Marla Berns edited her draft manuscript, added citations, and inserted her field slides as well as other suitable images from Rubin's fieldwork and reproductions of objects selected for the exhibition. We are grateful to Dr. Hermann Forkl, Curator, Africa Department, Linden Museum, Stuttgart, for locating and sending the field photographs that Frank had identified for her chapter, and to Barbara Frank's sister, Dr. Elisabeth Zindler-Frank for granting us permission to publish this version of the essay.—Eds.

2. Fieldwork by Frank was carried out in 1971–1973 among the Ron and in 1973–1975 among the Kulere. The author was an associate member of the Institute of African Studies of the University of Ibadan. Funding for her research was provided by the Deutsche Forschungsgemeinschaft (German Research Council). She wished to make the following acknowledgments: "Nigerian authorities and many individual people in Nigeria and Germany helped me. I want to mention three of them in particular: Andrew Awadeng Azzuwut and Ishaya Adagi, who were most helpful during my research among the Kulere, and Hermann Jungraithmayr, who gave me invaluable advice for my first sojourn in Africa. I wish to thank again all the institutions and persons for their help. In 1986 I paid a visit to the area of my former research and obtained an impression of the present conditions there."—Eds.

3. Some additional information on different groups is contained in the mimeographed collection of interview texts: J.O.H.L.T. (1981).

4. Meek (1925, 2: 190, table 12) gave the Kantana population as 8,111, that of the Kulere as 6,500, and of the Mada as 51,936; Murdock (1959, 92) provided a figure of "about 15,000" for the Kantana and Kulere, "about 100,000" for the Mada and most of the remaining peoples of the Jos Plateau as defined here. Dorward (1987, 201) estimated the Eggon as 60–80,000. See Frank (1978) for a review of local history and ethnography on the eastern border of this area; also Isichei (1982, 13). Regarding the ethnic complexity of the region, see Frank (1976). For a definition of the culture area under consideration here, see Frank (1981, 243–44).

5. The Photographic Archive of the Nigerian Museum, Lagos, contains records of the large number of masks documented by Murray. Among other things, he found that the Kantana (Mama) carved many masks for their neighbors; Murray (1952–1953, 12). [See Berns (this volume, interleaf H).]

6. For illustrations, see, e.g., Fagg (1963, pl. 137; 1960, nos. 317–22; 1980: 98–99); B. Fagg (1965, no.116); Leuzinger (1972, N6, N27); Carroll (1966, 158, pl. 20); Smith (1961, pl. 4a); Frank (1981, pl. 104); Drewal (1977, nos. 49, 50). Regarding the use of skulls and other types of "found objects," Frank McEwen photographed a man of Sha village wearing an actual antelope skull as a Mangam headdress; a fringe of palm leaves attached to the base of the skull (as for wooden examples) supports this identification, see also Mohr (1960, 118–19). The style of Sha masks seems to be distinctive, characterized by thin and attenuated forms; their version of the buffalo crest typically exhibits "swallow-tail" horn tips; see, e.g., Fagg (1969, 126, no.151).

7. See Fievet (1959, 228, 233); Temple (1919, 268); Tremearne (1912, 150, 165); Gunn (1956, 30); Frank (1981, 136; 1974, 123).

8. Murray (1952–1953, 12); cf. Tremearne (1912, 187, pl.12, fig. 2, no.18), where an antelope crest from the Nadu is described as a "hunter's disguise." See also Photographic Archive, National Museum, Lagos, 18.12.38; 18.22.18; 18.22.19; 18.23.25.

9. For example, Photographic Archive, National Museum, Lagos, 18.18.30 Pierre Harter; Aguya (1985, 224) states for the Kulere of Marhai, "Aso was the one placed in the farm to oversee the crops," which suggests a function similar to Munja in Tof.

10. For Rindre (Nungu), see Temple (1922, 317) and Ames (1934, 269); for Mada, see (Ames 1934, 266); for Eggon, see Dorward (1984, 85); for Kantana (Mama) of Kwara, which seem to have many similarities to Tof, see Ames (1934, 273, 274); see also J.O.H.L.T. (1981) for various groups, and Aguya (1985, 208f., 224) for other Kulere villages; for a comparison of the eastern groups, see Frank (1976, 142, 143).

11. For example, Photographic Archive, National Museum, Lagos, 12.65.19; 17.14.22; 18.9.17; 18.10.21; 18.35.32; 18.35.33; see also Fievet (1959, 234). Similar costumes were photographed by Fagg (1980, 20) at Nok village. Rubin also mentions netted fiber

masks emphasizing heavy, sculptural forms. He is probably referring to costumes of the Ajakawa/black Munja type.

12. Tremearne (1912, 167). Neiers (1979, 38); Photographic Archive, National Museum, Lagos, 12.53.14; 18.34.25; Fagg (1960, pl. 31b, nos.323, 324; 1969, 59, no.52); J. Fry (1972, no. 16).

Interleaf H (Berns)

1. These photographs are housed in the Photographic Archives of the National Museum, Lagos (NML), a division of the National Commission for Museums and Monuments, formerly the Nigerian Antiquities Service (and after that the Federal Department of Antiquities). Another group of photographs was taken by Christian Duponcheel and is in the possession of his family in Belgium. With one exception, only images from the Nigerian archive are reproduced here and many taken by Duponcheel are of the same masks as those in the NML. In Barbara Frank's essay in this volume (chapter 12), she provides considerable detail about the ethnic and linguistic diversity of the peoples living in the region south of the Jos Plateau where the masks were field documented and where she did extensive fieldwork among the Kulere.

2. The name "Mangam" is used in the *Annual Report of the Antiquities Service for the Year 1952–1953* (Murray 1952–1953, 11, n. 59). See also Frank, chapter 12. In Barry Hecht's (Sieber and Hecht 2002, 56) discussion of a Mangam mask in his collection (see fig. H.30 in this interleaf), he also notes that among the Kantana these masks were worn in performances belonging to the Udawaru society, drawing on information published in Leuzinger (1977, 210) and communicated to him by Duponcheel in 1993.

3. I would like to acknowledge the contributions of Susan Elizabeth Gagliardi in the careful analysis of the entire corpus and in the drafting of this essay. Although the conclusions are mine, the research benefited greatly from her collaboration.

4. Arnold Rubin thoroughly photographed the documentation of the Antiquities Service held at the National Museum in Lagos during the field research he conducted in 1964–1965. It is Rubin's photographs, and his notes concerning them, that are reproduced here, courtesy of the National Commission for Museums and Monuments, Nigeria.

5. I would like to gratefully acknowledge Barry Hecht for providing a full set of photocopies of Duponcheel's photographs, which he received from Duponcheel in the early 1990s. Hecht was also kind enough to provide copies of his records of Kenneth Murray's photographs so that we could do a thorough check of the corpus and note the duplication of masks photographed by both Murray and Duponcheel. See also Sieber and Hecht (2002, 56).

6. Footnotes 58 and 59 from the *Annual Report of the Antiquities Service for the Year 1952-1953*, which detail the region surveyed and the purpose of the study, are quoted here in full: "58. A fairly extensive but rapid survey was made of the arts and crafts of peoples in the vicinity of Jos. The following places were visited: Daffo, Kwarrifa, Sha, Amper, Bargesh, Mushere, Panyam and Tof in Pankshin Division, Fiskan Mata in Jos Division, Arun, Chesu, Kwarra, Waiyo and Wulko in Southern Plateau Division, Gwade in Jemma Division, Baltap, Gerkawa, Kurgwi, Kwande, Peshiep, Shendam and Wase in Shendam Division and Dajim and Bununu in Bauchi. / 59. Study was made of the purpose and distribution of head-dresses worn in ceremonies, particularly those usually called '*Mangam*' which are used chiefly in Southern Plateau Division in connection with a cult whose purpose varies from village to village but which is generally associated with the encouragement of the crops and the '*acha*' grain plant in particular. Villages visited were fairly thoroughly explored for these carvings and all head-dresses seen were listed and photographed. Three main types of '*Mangam*' head-dresses exist and represent different types of horned animals: the bush-cow, the water-buck and reed-buck. It would seem that each type has its own kind of expression which, on account of its consistency among the carvings of its kind, suggests the existence of a professional skill in the carvers." See also Fardon (2007, 38) on "bushcow," the vernacular name for the dwarf forest buffalo.

7. The landmark exhibition *African Negro Art*, held at the Museum of Modern Art, New York, in 1935, included one forest buffalo Mangam mask (Sweeney 1935, fig. 306), which was then in the collection of Charles Ratton, Paris (now in the Musée Dapper, Paris). Its curving horns nearly meet at the top, and this elegant abstraction resonates with the work of early twentieth-century artists and the tastes of their collectors.

8. Rubin (1988, III.B.2, 12); Frank, chapter 12, this volume, p. 394.

9. We have not been able to identify all the named villages and towns on available maps and therefore cannot verify all of the locations listed in the archives of the NML and Duponcheel.

10. The archives of the NML and Duponcheel suggest that only "big" (antelope) Mangam masks were found in some towns and "small" (buffalo) Mangam masks in others. The small sample sizes of masks in towns with only either "big" antelope or "small" buffalo masks, however, make it difficult to conclude that each town only ever commissioned either "big" antelope or "small" buffalo masks.

11. Olive Macleod, who later became Olive Temple, field collected three Mangam masks in 1910–1911. They are now in the World Museum Liverpool (22.11.24, nos. 162, 163, 164). Two masks were also accessioned into the Pitt Rivers Museum around the same time (1918: 31. 25-26), donated by Hubert Frank Mathews (see Fardon, chapter 10, 351–52).

12. In Frank's essay (chapter 12), she describes the mud relief decoration on granaries and other structures meant to hold cult paraphernalia (see figs. 12.15–12.18). This decoration includes both artistic representations of as well as the actual over-modeling of the skulls themselves. The fluid shifting between the real and the represented may be conceptually similar in the Mangam masquerade tradition.

Chapter 13 (Adelberger)

My thanks are due to Marla Berns for the invitation to contribute to this project and for stimulating discussions; to Richard Fardon for his inspiring comments and indefatigable efforts to improve my text; to Ulrich Kleinewillinghöfer and Mohammed

Sanda Soro for sharing their knowledge on Waja; to Sule Yerima for keeping up communication and providing me with invaluable information on various aspects of local rituals; to Gassia Armenian for procuring copies of several articles from *Lightbearer*; and to Lynne Kostman for knowledgeable editing. Field research was undertaken within the framework of the research project SFB 268 "Cultural Development and Language History in the Environment of the West African Savannah" funded by the German Research Foundation DFG.

1. In the literature, these have been referred to as "yoke masks" or "shoulder masks," based upon the U-shape of the base. This U-shape, however, functions only as a support for the often-elongated neck and head components of the mask. In the cases under discussion, the wearer most probably stood sideways within the U-shaped arch (see fig. 13.25). As there is no true "yoke," we will use the term "vertical mask" throughout the present volume.—Eds.

2. Speakers of Chadic languages (Pero, Piya, Kwonci, Kushi, Kode, and Nyam) belonging to the Bole-Tangale group of Western Chadic are all located in the western parts of the Muri Mountains. Southeast of the mountains are the Bachama who speak a Central Chadic language. The Niger-Congo languages are more diverse: in the eastern parts of the mountains three separate subgroups (Waja, Bikwin, and Kwa) of Northwestern Adamawa languages of the Niger-Congo phylum are to be found, and Kulung in the southwest is a Jarawan Bantu language, which is classified in the Benue-Congo branch of Niger-Congo (Adelberger and Kleinewillinghöfer 1992, 47; see also Crozier and Blench 1992).

3. An overview of the various groups of the Muri Mountains with emphasis on their traditions of origin can be found in Adelberger (1994).

4. Bikwin as a linguistic category was introduced by Ulrich Kleinewillinghöfer (Adelberger and Kleinewillinghöfer 1992; Kleinewillinghöfer 1996)

5. According to Meek (1934, 263), this happened some time in the 1910s; the cult symbol among the Kulung is an iron rod decorated with bells and feathers. However, in an early missionary's report (Guinter 1924, 101), a pair of wooden images is mentioned as having a role in the cult: "A little way off stood two little wooden images, representing male and female. Before these the dancers would fall in supplication for the power of the spirit to come upon them." The cult is widely distributed in the Middle und Upper Benue and in some other instances associated with carved wooden figures (Rubin, chapter 9, pp. 95–97).

6. A more recent study of Tangale religion is Laudarji (1994).

7. Gazetteer of Adamawa Province (1936, 99), Nigerian National Archives, Kaduna (NAK) Yola Prof K.5/SII.

8. "Incidents and Customs of the Kulung of Wurkum District, Adamawa Province, Nigeria, by Ira E. McBride," International African Institute, London (IAI), cons. 2 box 2(4), McBride.

9. See the report compiled by T. H. Haughton (1912): "Muri Province: Wurkum Pagan District, Assessment Report: Wurkum 'A' and 'B' Districts." Nigerian National Archives, Kaduna, Min. of Local Govt. –4377/1912.

10. "Wurkum Patrol 1909: Report on Wurkum Patrol 1909 by K. V. Elphinstone," Nigerian National Archives, Kaduna, SNP 7–5093/1907. See also Haughton (1912), which draws on the information from the earlier report.

11. Hall (1994, 116f). Hall, who worked for sixteen years as a missionary in Kaltungo, reports that there were no wooden sculptures for ritual purposes among Tangale (cf. Hall 1994, 112–113).

12. Arnold Rubin (unpublished MS, n.p.) reports that "Near Mutum Daya [where the settlement areas of Kulung, Piya and Kwonci merge], I heard about (but did not see) male-female pairs of masks, called *Gila*, apparently yoke-shaped with long necks." Unfortunately, we have no more information on this aspect of a male-female duality in vertical masks, but Fardon (following Rubin) notes the occurrence of gendered pairs of vertical masks among Mumuye some distance to the southwest (2007, 95, 100).

13. The practice of giving ritual objects a "personal name" is also recorded for Chamba and Mumuye (Fardon 2007, 44 n. 2, 94).

14. Similar figurines on iron rods are reported from Chamba, Jukun, Mambila, and possibly, but less likely, among the Waja (see Evers 2003, 41, fig. 38; Fry 1970, 9–10; Drewal 1977, 53; Sieber and Vevers 1974; Schwartz 1972, fig. 40 for Mambila). Among the Mambila, however, the rods are made of wood (David Zeitlyn, personal communication).

15. Following this logic, the dumping of *kundul* into a latrine pit, after the conversion of their owner, mentioned earlier in this essay, would be a culturally acceptable way to return them to the realm of the spirits. Allowing *kundul* to wear away as a result of exposure to the elements (see fig. 13.13) would be equally acceptable.

16. Marla Berns documented the use of *kundul* (*kwandul*) by diviners in the Pero towns of Filiya, Gwandum, and Gundale in 1982 (personal communication, 2008). The diviner was called an *amkundul* (one who masters the *kundul*), which suggests the centrality of these figures to divination process.

17. Arnold Rubin (unpublished manuscript, n.p.) Arnold Rubin spent several days among the Wurkun living between Filiya and Bambur in 1966 and 1971.

18. When Arnold Rubin carried out research in the 1960s, he was told that spiked *dambang* figures were placed as field guardians to protect crops. Twenty years later I did not observe this practice, which, if it survived at all, must have been carried out on a much-reduced scale. Apart from any change in belief in the interim, it seems likely that demand from the African art market would have made protective devices themselves vulnerable to theft. The sheer number of *kundul* that Arnold Rubin was still able to document in one settlement bears witness to a drastic decline in the local use of these figures within the last twenty years (see fig. 13.4).

19. The *dambang* tree was identified to me as *cediya* (Hausa for *Ficus thonningii*). Faust (1945, 253) calls it *banyam* (*banyan* tree, or *Ficus benghalensis*; however, this particular subspecies does not grow in Northern Nigeria. I am grateful to Roger Blench for this information).

20. Similar drums, often with four or more legs, can be found among other ethnic groups in the Middle Belt, for example among the Icen/Etkwyan of southern Taraba State (Roger Blench, personal communication). Their occurrence as part of a drum set is peculiar for the Muri Mountains.

Chapter 14 (Berns)

1. See Adelberger, Rubin, and Fardon in this volume for references to these masks among these Middle Benue peoples. I have personally seen thirty-two in museum and private collections. The total count of masks derives from the nine examples documented in the field, the thirty-two I have seen, and those available on the Yale University-Guy Van Rijn Archive of African Art, hosted by the Yale University Art Gallery. Additional examples came to our attention via a call posted on H-Net List for African Expressive Culture. Despite the high numbers, this total is by no means exhaustive, and it is likely that more examples exist in private collections that are as yet unknown to us.

2. All three pieces were in the collection of Jacques Kerchache, who bought them shortly after they were exported from Nigeria. Figure 14.1 came to Kerchache from Phillipe Guimiot, who acquired it in Nigeria or Cameroon.

3. This mask, now in a private Belgian collection and included in an exhibition at the Beyeler Foundation in Basel (Wick and Denner 2009), is missing the back plank of the support, not evident in the photograph in Leuzinger (1971). Views from other angles reveal fascinating aspects of this object, which will be discussed below.

4. Karim Lamido is an administrative center for Taraba State north of the Benue, and it is the home of the Como-Karim (or Karimjo), a Jukunoid-speaking group. This sculpture was in the collection of Jacques Kerchache until 2004, when it was purchased by its present owner. In 2004 it was radiocarbon dated by Alliance Science Art, Francine Maurer. The bracketed dates after calibration are: AD 1673–1778 (40.5%); AD 1800–1942 (57.2%); AD 1945–1951 (2.3%). C14 dating is acknowledged to be the most ambiguous for objects less than three hundred years old. On the basis of its style and condition, it seems likely that this sculpture dates at least to the late nineteenth century.

5. At the time of his visit, Rubin noted that the mountaintop center of Gwana was in decline and in the process of being deserted. This likely would have left the more than fifteen sculptures he saw and photographed there, which were otherwise kept in rock shelters, vulnerable to theft. Indeed, not just one but two of these sculptures are included in this volume (see figs. 8.52–8.54). See also Rubin this volume, chapter 9, note 20.

6. Adelberger (personal communication, 2010) collected an oral account from the Munga Leelau people (Bikwin group), who live in the vicinity of Karim Lamido, claiming that the ritual tribute they paid to Kona was formerly given to Gwana, the Jukun center north of the Muri Mountains. It may have been the pressures on Gwana by the Fulani emirates that redirected the Leelau to Kona.

7. A close-up of this figure from Pantisawa photographed by Rubin in 1965 was used by Fry (1970, 8) to attribute an as yet unidentified style of carving to the Mumuye, as represented in two famous pieces—one in the British Museum and the other in the Musée de l'Homme (see fig. 8.17).

8. Rubin's informants also identified two small wood figures (*jagana*) as the children of Vaa-Bong (fig. 8.24). They added that the "masks" of the cult of which they were a part wished to have children just like their human counterparts.

9. Another pair was documented by this author in a private Belgian collection.

10. The caption to this mask fragment indicates that it was carbon 14 dated to the fifteenth century. While these dates must be treated with skepticism, given the challenges associated with this dating technology, other sculptures from the Middle Benue have also been tested and show similarly early dates.

11. The spellings of the names of these masks and information concerning their use are published in Dinslage and Storch (2000). The authors did research among the Kona Jukun subgroup called the Jibe in the late 1990s. I am grateful to Joerg Adelberger for bringing this publication to my attention. It provides important ethnographic information about the use of these masks as well as Kona Jukun religious beliefs and practices, which supplement Rubin's much briefer field survey work in Kona in 1965. It is also intriguing that the same word *wunkər* is the title given to a member of the royal clan who lives where the male members of this clan are buried and who takes charge of religious activities in the absence of the Jibe sacred king (p. 87). Not surprisingly, where Rubin was shown the vertical masks described and illustrated here, the two women authors were not allowed to enter the complex cluster of shrines still maintained in Kona or to see their contents, which are taboo to women. Their descriptions are thus based solely on verbal accounts from informants. It is remarkable that such Jibe practices were still maintained by traditional clan elders in the late 1990s, even if the authors feared that the pressures of modernity would ultimately discourage young people from sustaining them (p. 221).

12. This mask was in the collection of Erle Loran, who acquired it in 1973 (see Loran, Seligman, et al. 1974, 51, fig. 51), before being donated to the Fine Arts Museums of San Francisco, de Young Museum.

13. Another closely related mask of this type was published in Loudmer (1991, lot 86).

14. Although Dinslage and Storch call these objects "gourds," this is probably due to the fact that they could not see the shrine interiors. It is most likely that these "gourds" took the form of trumpets or horns (long tubular gourds), which are used across the Middle Benue in ritual contexts (Richard Fardon, personal communication, 2010). For an illustration of Mumuye gourd trumpets (*vadoso*) stored inside a room in the town of Pantibelli taken by Arnold Rubin 1971, see Berns and Hudson (1986, 73; fig. 41; see also this volume, fig. 8.42).

15. It may be that Rubin, who was not a linguist (where the work of Dinslage and Storch was directly involved in the preservation of the Jibe language), transcribed the name of these figures incorrectly (Asando instead of Asanu)

16. Such spears, called *saw mam*, are associated with the cult of Mam, which is widespread

in the region, and described in Dinslage and Storch (2000, 72) as having come from the Wurbo Jukun (see also Rubin and Fardon this volume). I documented the same type of spear, called *swe mam*, among the Dadiya and the Jen, who live across the Benue from the Kona Jukun (see Berns this volume).

17. A fourth example of this Jukun variant was published by Marie-Louise Bastin (1984, 223, no. 221).

18. Rubin (1969, 17, n. 8) writes that "There were apparently no distinctively Jukun patterns of scarification," which seems to be clearly contradicted by the markings present on the faces of Jukun figurative sculpture and vertical masks. Perhaps by the time Rubin did his fieldwork such facial markings were no longer in vogue, but their legacy is retained in these sculptures. See also Kasfir, chapter 2.

19. This unpublished manuscript written by Meek (1931c) is titled "Illustration to Notes on Jukons of Gwana," and it identifies each of the nine performers in the foreground of the picture and describes the enclosure in the background where the "sacrifice" itself took place, presumably in honor of Adang. My thanks go to Joerg Adelberger for bringing this document to my attention (NAK SNP 17-K2441, vol. IV). Meek (1931a, 159–60; 271–72) describes the shrine maintained for Adang, which replicated the private enclosure of a Gwana chief, as a place for priests to supplicate Adang daily as a way to appease his broken heart over the murder of his wife: "two wooden images, one for the spirit of Adang and another for that of his wife" were kept in the shrine. It is likely that these same two figures were carried in the photograph taken by Best. See also Rubin, chapter 9, note 20.

20. Arnold Rubin's field notebook of 1971 indicates that when he returned to Gwana his informants told him that a figure called Adang had been taken without permission (see introduction to this volume, n. 7).

21. Adang and his wife would seem to be a corollary to the couple called Wipong and his wife, illustrated in Rubin (1969, pls 123–25; see also this volume, fig. 9.10), where the female is much smaller than the male and where the male has the same distinctive ear treatment as evident on the Musée du quai Branly example with double "bangles" at the upper arm and wrist.

22. Rubin's fieldnotes (December 24, 1964) indicate that when the figures were danced in Mabo, women could see them and even pray to them for children, but they could not see their "bare legs," providing further evidence for the lower bodies of these figures being wrapped with cloth. Certain of the Wurbon Daudu and Mabo figures were carved with rather long straight legs, but the fact that they were not exposed likely explains why other Jukun figures had minimal legs or none at all.

23. The Goemai people, who live about 60 miles north of the Benue River near its tributary the Shemankar River and about 100 miles from the Jukun center at Wukari, had contact with the Jukun. This is most evident in their primary masking tradition, called Mongop, which is closely related to the Jukun Aku Maga (Sieber 1961, 10–11; see also this volume, chapter 10).

24. Adelberger took photocopies of published pieces to the field in 1990–1993 in order to elicit information about them from his informants. His efforts to align certain substyles with particular Wurkun or Bikwin groups was hampered by the limited corpus of reproductions he had assembled as well as the difficulty of securing information about objects treated as highly secret. Therefore, it is difficult to know whether the numbers of masks in this substyle are the most widespread or simply those that were collected most successfully.

25. Adelberger's Wurkun informant has requested anonymity.

26. For figure 14.35, see also Bastin (1984, 223, fig. 222); for figure 14.36, see Vogel and Thompson (1990, fig. 87); and for figure 14.37, see Crédit Communal de Belgique (1977, no. 59).

27. Adelberger (chapter 13) was never allowed to see these masks, said to be hidden in the hills. His informants also indicated that such masks were "stolen sometime in the mid-1970s, mostly by Cameroonians." Even though Adelberger surmised that new versions had been made as replacements, his restriction from ever seeing them means that there is no way to prove how many were or are in existence, still hidden in the Muri Mountains.

Chapter 15 (Berns)

1. Survey field research was conducted among other groups not mentioned here; this essay focuses on the groups whose ceramic arts are the most distinctive and numerous or are represented in the accompanying exhibition. For information on other related peoples, see Berns (1986; 2000).

2. The Mbula are a Jarawan Bantu (Benue-Congo) group whose linguistic relatives are clustered considerably to the west in the hills south of Bauchi. The Bata and Bachama speak dialects of the same Chadic language classified within a different subgrouping from the Ga'anda. The geographical distribution of related Bata-speakers suggests that the Bata moved southward and then westward into the Upper Benue from the vicinity of Mubi. The Ga'anda also trace their origins to the same area of the Mandara Mountains as that from which Bata-speakers are thought to have dispersed.

3. See David et al. (1988) for a discussion of vessels with appliqué pellets and Bickford Berzock (2005, 73–74).

4. Rubin (1974, 161) considered the area around Biu to have been a primary "gateway" between Borno and the Upper Benue Valley.

5. Descriptions of navigation along the Benue can be found in Baikie (1856); Flegel (1890); and Passarge (1895).

6. Most of the reports of colonial officers have been collated and filed in provincial notebooks, which today are kept in the National Archives, Kaduna, Nigeria (NAK). Henceforth, such reports will be identified by their authors and dates of submission; if known, NAK file numbers are cross-referenced in the bibliography.

7. See, for example, the following documents in the collection of the National Archives, Kaduna, Nigeria (NAK): G2.Q; G2.S; J.18.

8. Other churches active in the region, such as ECWA (Evangelical Church of West Africa, formerly SIM, Sudan Interior Mission) and CEM (Christian Brethren Mission) did not produce such systematic or comprehensive texts, but several useful novels and articles describing circumscribed areas, peoples, and topics have been published.

9. See Western Gongola section, pp. 483–84, below for more on these collections.

10. I have been communicating via e-mail with Solomon Boga Valdon, Benson Ali, Felix Ndukwadan Theman, and Polycarp Ayuba Chifartawa since January 2008.

11. I would like to thank the young Ga'anda men who are struggling to document Ga'anda history and culture before their traditional religious practices and the objects that support them disappear for sharing their thoughts with me via e-mail. It has been an invaluable way to learn about the current situation and the attitudes of some Ga'anda elders and youth. See *Topics in the History of Ga'anda* by Ayuba Chifartawa (2009).

12. Felix Theman (personal communication, August 12, 2009) explained that the Mbir'thleng'nda at Makwar had been stolen and that it had been rebuilt by an elderly woman potter. He also said that the Ngum-Ngumi had been hidden for safe keeping, which supports the claim that this vessel is central to the Ga'anda legitimizing mythology. In a video interview between Theman and current Ga'anda religious leaders responsible for the religious precinct at Makwar, I could see that the Mbir'thleng'nda removed from the shrine was not the one that I photographed in 1981 (see introduction, figs. 5–7; see also fig. 17.10). I am very grateful to Theman, Ali, and Chifartawa for arranging this interview in April 2010 and for agreeing to allow us to share excerpts from it in this volume (pp. 31–32).

13. The use of the term "symbolic reservoir" is drawn from Sterner (1992) who proposed that the peoples of the Mandara Mountains have drawn on a shared body of "symbols, beliefs, values, and ideas" in the decoration of sacred vessels. The concept of a "symbolic reservoir" comes from McIntosh (1989, 79) in reference to Middle Niger terra-cottas.

Chapter 16 (Berns)

1. Meek (1931b, 2: pls. 28–30) amply illustrates Longuda stone shrines and "sitting out places."

2. My research on the Longuda was carried out October–November 1981. Eight hill villages were studied in addition to Guyuk. See also Meek (1931b, 2: 331–68) and Nissen (1968, 161–65).

3. See Berns and Hudson (1986, 162) and Meek (1931b, 2: 357–59).

4. Nissen (1968,163–64) claims the Longuda had family shrines to ancestral spirits that were housed in vessels called "Kwandalmarwa." My informants denied the use of ceramic pots in ancestor worship or that ancestors were involved in the well-being of their descendants. Instead, Kwandalmarwa were identified in 1981 as specific *kwandalha* for curing "swollen feet or thighs." Nissen (1968, 164) does concur that the Longuda made pots into which "the spirit causing the disease would move."

5. *Sambrawa* were also identified by informants as pots used to cure madness. Jehann Teilhet was given this explanation in 1968 by the healer Dasumi (Teilhet, personal communication, 1988).

6. The late art historian Jehann Teilhet worked with Dasumi in 1968 and commissioned several vessels, which were deposited in the Jos Museum. I am grateful to Teilhet for sharing her fieldnotes and photographs. Her work among the Longuda was carried out under the auspices of the Federal Department of Antiquities. See also Teilhet (1997–1978) and Fagg (1977, 32).

7. The unpublished notes of C. D. Bala on "Old Cham Settlements" (Zaria Archaeology Paper 3) describe these hillside homesteads and the drystone structures within them. Bala did fieldwork in the area in 1974–1975. Paper 4 deals with Cham terra-cotta figurines. My work in Cham-Mwana villages in 1982 confirmed the importance of drystone masonry as well as the number of ceramic vessels abandoned in the rocky hillsides.

8. Kleinewillinghöfer (1996, 88) divides the Cham into three sections: Mwana/Mona (Bwilim), Kindiyo (Dijim), and Looja (Jalabe or Jalaa). Adelberger (personal communication, 2010) goes on to explain that Bwilim, Dijim, and Jalaa are the designations of the peoples themselves; Mwana, Kindiyo, and Looja are regionalized terms referring to their main settlements. Jalaa claim to have originally come from a settlement (Baalabe or Kwa Dutse) in the Muri Mountains south of their present area, where they had lived together with the Kwa. They were the first settlers in the area of the Cham. The Kindiyo and Mwana originally came from Jingum near Shani, migrating via Nyuwar to Fitilai/Kuntur and thence to their present area. It was only at Fitilai that they divided into Mwana and Kindiyo. They were dispersed from Fitilai by the Waja in the late nineteenth century.

Notes made by District Officer S. W. Walker in 1929 relate the following: "Two villages: Kindiyo in Waja District and Mwana in East Tangale District. 3–4 miles SE of Kulane is old site Kwem with remains of many stone walls and tombs. Kindiyo say they came from Fitilai on the southern edge of the Plateau (called by Waja Kuntur). Older people say they can still remember being driven out by Waja to whom they were no match for the Wajas bows and arrows. Mwana tend to acknowledge Sarkin Dadiya. Their ceremonies (rain ceremony) revolve around Fitilai" (National Archives, Kaduna, NAK SNP 17-9150, Cham Tribe, Ethnological Notes on).

9. It is unclear whether or not ceramic vessels are still used for healing among the Cham-Mwana. The fact that such vessels are still being brought out of Nigeria by traders suggests that these traditions continue to have local relevance and/or that there is a presumed market for such lively works of art, which are well represented in museum collections (see notes 10, 17, below).

10. See Jonathan Slye, the name under which Legget published (1969, 499–502; 1977, 23), and Hare (1983, 8–9). Each made a substantial collection of diverse examples. Leggett's was auctioned at Christie's in 1978 and is now in the British Museum, and Hare's collection was dispersed, with eleven pieces sold through Christie's in 1984 (June 26, 1984, auction catalog), and a selection of examples in the University of Indiana Art Museum. Pearlstone (1973) deals with one Mwana pot type (*sujang*) in a discussion

that argues for the independent invention of the stirrup-spouted vessel in Africa.

11. I documented among both Cham and Mwana clans another divination procedure for identifying diseases, called *divilin*. I witnessed the diagnosis of a hernia by the healer Gumba Bekuto of the Kwaser clan of Mwana. The male patient entered the diviner's drystone shrine and sat on a stone "chair" to the left of the entry. The diviner began by grinding the bark of the desert date tree (*Balanites aegyptiaca*) into a powder. This powder was then added to water kept in a pot within the shrine, and the mixture was stirred into foam, which was then poured into a gourd bowl. The foam was rubbed on the parts of the patient's body where symptoms were felt. Other objects may also be introduced into the foam to ritually activate them and assist in the diagnosis. Once a decision was reached, a patient was sent to the appropriate healer-sculptor to produce the vessel for transferring the disease. The clay used for making the pot could be activated by circling it over the patient's head three times, a procedure common to the Longuda and other Western Gongola groups.

12. Slye (1969, 499) describes a similarly styled vessel as oracular and illustrates another stylistically similar *changdu* (Slye 1977, fig. 1). I saw a very similar example in Cham Town in 1982, fig. 16.12. All are female. The *changdu* Slye identifies as male and illustrates (1977, fig. 2) is very different stylistically, resembling nothing else published or seen in the field among the Cham-Mwana. Instead it is clearly related to Jen anthropomorphic vessels; see pp. 496–98 below.

13. Arnold Rubin, who did fieldwork in Cham and Mwana villages in March 1970, also noted that the *changdu* vessels were used to confer success in hunting and to chase away hostile spirits.

14. In *Nigerian Images* (1963, pl. 132), Fagg writes that this terra-cotta bust (1913.10-13.48) was "probably a charm against sickness, collected before 1913 in the upper Benue Valley. Examples from the Waja tribe are in the Jos Museum, though similar charms are made by the Longuda and others nearby."

15. The British Museum has a vessel for curing backache in its collection (1913.10-13.10) from "Northern Nigeria." William Fagg also called this vessel "Waja," supporting the argument made here that he confused all the ceramics collected in Tangale-Waja District with the Waja people. This distinctive pot type is undoubtedly Cham-Mwana.

16. Pearlstone (1973, 484), drawing on Arnold Rubin's 1970 fieldnotes, writes that his Mwana informant said that the vessel had two necks and one mouth because one branch "goes to the stomach and the other to the lungs." The Cham-Mwana believed that bad coughs were caused by the chaff from sorghum plants. A stalk of sorghum was circled around the chest of the sufferer three times in a gesture linking the cure directly with its cause. Hare (1983, 24) illustrates another "*sukjang*" and writes that it was activated by being "filled with water from a pool which it is believed has magical powers."

17. There are large collections of Cham-Mwana vessels in the British Museum (former Leggett collection), the Musée du quai Branly, and the Jos Museum (National Commission for Museums and Monuments, Nigeria). The earliest collected example is in the Museum of Mankind (1913.10-13.10), identified as "Northern Nigeria." Catalog notes by William Fagg describe the pot as "Waja of S.E. Bauchi." Based on what we now know about this tradition, this pot is clearly a Cham-Mwana *tsen-tsenle* with long, toothed tubular projections used to cure backaches.

18. These districts were identified in an unpublished oral history collected in November 1978 from the chief of Talasse, Alhaji Muhammadu Garba. He repeated the same information to me in February 1981.

19. In *The Essential Gourd*, I situated the Waja within the Gongola-Hawal geographical region. This decision was based on the close parallels between Waja, Tera, and Dera gourd decoration as well as their programs of facial scarification and domestic pottery decoration (see Berns and Hudson 1986, 152–56). For the purposes of this survey, the Waja are located within the western Gongola Valley, which accords more closely to their linguistic relationship to other Northwestern Adamawa speakers in this region and their production of ritual pottery for use in healing.

20. The Waja claim to have migrated to this area of the Gongola-Benue with the Longuda. While this claim is controversial, the Waja did, at some point in the past, occupy the sacred homeland of the Longuda, a hill named Wanda. Although the site is abandoned today, my informants indicated that the Waja moved there after the Longuda had left (or were driven out). Evidence of small Waja healing vessels in abandoned households confirms this claim.

21. Woodhouse (1924, 113, 120) describes various methods for healing diseases and the use of "small pots." He also mentions unaccountable illnesses as sometime being due to "*guto*."

22. I conducted research in all three Tula villages in March 1982. Oral traditions were collected from elders in each and refer to warfare between the Tula and neighboring groups.

23. In the abandoned hamlet of Ronga-Fi in the hills where the Mwana formerly lived, a drystone wall very similar to a *seh* was still standing in 1982. Called a *chin*, this site was likewise used for displaying game from a hunt. Additionally, a solution made with ground red hematite is poured on the *chin* stones during rituals to facilitate contact with spirit forces.

24. Although my informants did not specify this, Rubin's fieldnotes indicate that the beer in these pots was not only consumed by elders but was offered to the ancestors during Kuram.

25. Unpublished fieldnotes, Arnold Rubin, dated February 26, 1970, 136–37.

26. On Biliri Hill, above the plains where Biliri town had been relocated, I saw the remains of shrine complexes, called Yekku, which included overturned vessels surrounded by piles of stones. The shrines were used to appeal for rain, and beer was poured on the pots. As was true of the Tula, ritual precincts were defined by a combination of stone and ceramic, although I did not see any figurative ceramics in the various Tangale communities that I visited other than the anomalous sculpture described here.

27. See below, pp. 498 and note 35.

28. According to Adelberger (personal communication, 2010), Dadiya claim to have migrated from the east, first having settled at Teeba in the Longuda area before arriving at Dogon Dutse, a mountain just to the north of the Muri Mountains chain, and from there they moved south to their present area. See Adelberger (this volume) for a lengthy discussion of the linguistic and ethnic complexity of the western Muri Mountains (pp. 417–19). I conducted field research in the region in 1982, primarily among the Dadiya and the Jen, who will be discussed below. One day's work was done in Burak Village, where I documented wooden divination figurines related to the better-known Wurkun *kundul* (see Berns and Hudson 1986, 67, fig. 34; see chapter 13, this volume).

29. A possession cult named Mam is widely distributed in the Middle Benue area, and Meek (1931b, 2: 521) suggests that it has derived from the Wurbo subgroup of the Jukun. Meek's Jukun-centric viewpoint, articulated in *A Sudanese Kingdom* (1931a), should be treated with discretion, but it is noteworthy that so many groups use a cognate of this word (Ma, Mə, Ama, or Mahn) for particular spirits associated with second sight or with healing or taking an oath. Adelberger in this volume also notes that the Kulung have an arm-slashing cult, called Mam Gabra, which was adopted from the Wurbo Jukun. The Yungur festival of Mama is certainly conceptually related to the Dadiya festival called Mam.

30. The identification of supreme deities with the sun is common to many African cultures as is a secondary deity who is the creator of all things. Meek (1931b, 2: 520) describes the Jen deity Ma as having fashioned "all living things as a potter fashions a pot," a metaphor often encountered in creation stories. That Meek identifies Ma or Mə as male seems surprising since it is almost always women who are the potters and closely associated with the earth. Curiously, Meek goes on to say that if Ma "is careless or in a capricious mood he fashions men in ugly guise."

31. Unpublished fieldnotes dated April 6, 1970, p. 263.

32. Rubin feels Meek's description of the Kue Akwa masquerade suggests affinities with the "yoke" masks of the Mumuye, Jukun, and Wurkun of the Middle Benue. Although Rubin was told about Kue in 1970, he never saw them in performance, although they were apparently still in use. Rubin indicated to me that they "had reportedly been hidden 'in the bush' two years earlier due to concern over widespread theft and expropriation of important sculptures in the area" (personal communication, 1987).

33. Arnold Rubin documented the same shrine to Mam during his 1970 fieldwork (see unpublished fieldnotes, April 6, 1970, 262).

34. Although Meek does not refer to the *kuchan* or to the *ku* (possibly because he visited the Jen during the rainy season when these objects were not on display), he does claim the Jen believed that an enemy killed in war could seek rebirth through the wife of his slayer (1931b, 2: 526–27). If this enemy spirit saw his killer as "evil," however, he could refuse to be reborn and instead pursue his killer and "cause his strength to waste away."

35. Another Frobenius example is in the Museum für Volkerkunde, Hamburg. Two additional *kuchan* are in the Jos Museum, Nigeria. One of the two was collected by Arnold Rubin in the Dadiya town of Bambam, and though it was identical to a Jen vessel, it was called by the Dadiya name, *magula*.

36. Curiously Meek does not mention the *kuchan* vessels in his discussion of the Jen. He (1931b, 2: 521) does identify the Jen god of war and hunting as Umwa and explains, "He is the patron of hunting, and it is said that if any dangerous animal is struck by a spear, it is Umwa who takes away the animal's 'heart,' i.e., its life." The name of this deity was never mentioned to me during my work among the Jen.

37. The large lozenges down the center of the torso radiating out from the umbilicus, as well as the dotted lines, relate to the kinds of designs documented among eastern Gongola groups who still practiced full-body scarification in the early 1980s. See below, chapters 17 and 18.

38. The Jen call the makers of the *kuchan* the Piri (also known as the Tsobo or Lotsu-Piri and classified within the "Waja Group"; see Crozier and Blench 1992, 123). Rubin was told a Piri man was responsible for the Jen pots in 1970. When I worked with the Jen in 1982, I discovered they were referring to a subsection of the Kwa.

39. The valley of the Bolere River served as a highway in a north-south direction within the Muri Mountains. The Tunga-Dadiya are an offshoot of the Dadiya, having moved southward where they live among Kwa and Tsobo neighbors (Joerg Adelberger, personal communication, 2010). A very similar vessel collected by Arnold Rubin in 1970 among the Dadiya is in the Jos Museum collection and may be by the same hand as the *bogi* that I photographed in the Kwa hamlet of Gyakan.

40. Very little is written about the Kwa in the literature. They speak a Northwestern Adamawa language classified within the Kwa group (Crozier and Blench 1992, 123). I spent only one day working in the village of Gyakan where I was shown several shrines. Consistent with regional traditions, the Kwa maintain healing shrines (*nata*) with ceramic vessels as the primary means of access to offending spirits of disease. Called *gafara* (which may be related to the Kulung Mam Gabra), these pots are covered with neat rows of raised nodes. On the day I was there, the Gyakan Kwa also held their annual pre-planting rite called Nangau, the central activity of which is a possession dance. Three women and one man emerged from a hut, coaxed by drumming and possessed by the spirit Kawo, who is called upon to help ensure a successful harvest. This Kwa ritual may be related to the Jen masquerade involving Kwiyeh, who also appears in pre-planting rites.

Chapter 17 (Berns)

1. The full spectrum of arts produced and used by the peoples of the Ga'anda Hills include decorated gourds, elaborate body scarifications, forged iron regalia, cast-brass ornaments, and architectural monuments. For a fuller treatment of these arts, see Berns (1986).

2. One Ga'anda account was compiled by Musa Wawu na Hammandikko in 1971 as part of the *History of Ga'anda*, and a draft in Hausa was sent to Arnold Rubin. It was then edited and translated into a published history by this author (Hammandikko

and Berns 1980). I collected other oral accounts from 1980 to 1981 among numerous Ga'anda families and subgroups, which mostly indicated origins to the east in the Fali area north of the town of Mubi. See also Polycarp Ayuba Chifartawa *Topics in History of Ga'anda* (2009). That the Ga'anda speak a Biu-Mandara Chadic language supports an eastern origin, but we do not know when their ancestors moved westward to their present location. The tendency to look eastward for origins seems to reflect the impact of Islam and the importance of linking local histories with the direction of Mecca and Medina. There is little doubt that such accounts were often colored by local preoccupations with self-serving historical legacies, especially in the context of economic, social, religious, and political change in Nigeria.

3. Webster's account appears in Temple and Temple ([1919] 1965, 255). Despite the imprecision of the word "Lala" when used to encompass both the Ga'anda and 'Bɔna speakers, it is still employed as a designation for the several "Yungur group" languages in Hansford et al. (1976, 118) and in the second edition of Crozier and Blench (1992, 123). In the *Gazetteer of Yola Province*, compiled by C. O. Migeod ([1927] 1972) from material collected by two colonial officers (S. H. P. Vereker and Captain E. A. Brackenbury), "Lala" is defined as the "name applied to a number of clans, of which the principal are Gudban, Kabun (Gabun), Dingai, Robba, and Bina" (p. 29), which conforms to the general tendency in the colonial literature to consider the Ga'anda and 'Bɔna as a single "tribe." Curiously, in this account the authors claim that the "origin of the Lala tribe is shrouded in mystery but several hundred years ago they adopted the Jukon 'tsafi' [Hausa for 'spirit'] and acted as an intermediary between Wukari and Biu." It is surprising to imagine connections across this wide a geographical area, and many of the observations and interpretations in the *Gazetteer* are fraught with misunderstandings and misrepresentations.

4. See Meek (1931b, 2: 437), Kirk-Greene (1969, 63), Nissen (1968, 216), and Migeod ([1927] 1972, 2: 29). Hammandikko and Berns (1980, 6) report the Ga'anda version of this event.

5. For a discussion of the current situation among the Ga'anda, see chapter 15, pp. 472–73.

6. See Berns (1989a, 48–51) for a more detailed explanation of the role of language in reconstructing history and its importance as evidence alongside other patterns of relatedness in oral traditions, ethnography, archaeology, and art production.

7. I spent over seven months among the Ga'anda, surveying many dispersed communities in the four centers of Ga'anda, Gabun, Boga, and Dingai and interviewing elders. Most of them still maintained family shrines, which were almost all still located in the hills where people lived until sometime in the mid-twentieth century. Walks to these shrines often took between one and two hours over rugged terrain starting from the more accessible locations reachable by car.

8. See Berns (1988) for a full explication of Ga'anda scarification.

9. Farta is identified as having a dual nature: he rewards obedience with the promise of health and well-being while punishing those who transgress with eternal suffering in the afterlife (Pan). The spirits who comprise the Ga'anda pantheon are likewise neither strictly benevolent or malevolent. Some manifest kind and constructive qualities, and others are evil and dangerous; the former can be provoked to malevolence, and the latter can be controlled through supplication and appeasement. Thus, the Ga'anda cosmology encompasses avenues by which the living can control their own fortunes.

10. See Berns (1986, 193–95). Migeod ([1927] 1972, 29) writes that the disparate clans of the "Lala" acknowledge the authority of the Chief of Ga'anda, head of the Gudban clan, who is "keeper of the great Juju."

11. Wente-Lukas (1977, 40, ills. 32–34) writes that in the Mandara region most sacred vessels are distinguished by raised decoration, which typically includes covering large areas of their surfaces with "wart-like" knobs. The examples she illustrates have textures very closely related to those identified with Mbir'thleng'nda.

12. One Ga'anda man, who had converted to Christianity, showed me the Mbir'thleng'nda shrine belonging to the Tamsata family (Ga'anda) in 1980. After this visit, he said that he was plagued by the spirit's image in dreams. He interpreted this as punishment by Mbir'thleng'nda for having had the temerity to assume the role of the spirit's custodian and show me the shrine in light of his conversion to Christianity.

13. The original translation of the Hausa manuscript into English in the published account has been slightly modified and condensed for the present essay.

14. For more details on Ga'anda history and migrations, as reported by Ga'anda elders, see Berns (1986,184–90); see also Hammandikko and Berns (1980. 1–2). See as well note 2 (above).

15. I did not document a circular shield of this type in a Ga'anda village. It is logical to presume that shields were used to deflect arrows or spears in the context of local warfare. Hunters would have continued to use bows, arrows, and quivers after colonial pacification, but shields likely would have become unnecessary. One informant I asked about this circular motif suggested it was an iron thumb ring used by hunters to draw a bowstring. Such iron rings are forged as tight spirals, which does suggest a circular format; however, the descriptive accuracy of the other relief emblems on these vessels makes such a schematic rendition seem doubtful.

16. My correspondent, Benson T. Ali (American University of Nigeria, Library) showed the photographs to Musa Wawu na Hammandikko (my research assistant during the period of my fieldwork) and several other elders associated with the ritual precinct at Makwar during the week of November 7–15, 2009. I am in regular e-mail contact with Mr. Ali and his colleagues Polycarp Ayuba Chifartawa and Felix Theman.

17. The use of the numbers "3" and "4" to represent male and female principles respectively may have derived from a desire to reach the total of "7," a number with strong ritual connotations. Most key events, such as Sabta and Kwefa, are reenacted septennially. Other community festivities, including Ho'mbata, last for seven days.

18. Bravmann (1983, 54, fig. 38) includes an illustration of a chain mail shirt now in the Royal Ontario Museum, Toronto (961-141-50). Several chain mail shirts are illustrated in Bivar (1964) and are in the Jos Museum collection. They clearly show the rectangular-shaped "cut-out" at the lower hem.

19. A "cavalryman with shirt and cap of chainmail" was photographed by Leo Frobenius (1913, facing 608) among the Chamba, who live southwest of the Benue-Gongola confluence (see map, fig. 7.2).

20. The use of these motifs to decorate Ga'anda ancestral pots, whether male or female, is discussed in detail in Berns (1988).

21. For a longer discussion of Ga'anda ideas about death and its management by the living, see Berns (1986, 69–70, 126–134).

22. *Yamnda* is a powerful ritual infusion made from the previous year's sorghum grains sprouted with rainwater, also kept from the previous season, and fermented in a special spirit-charged ceramic pot called a *'butɔthler'chikta* (pot for sprouting). This pot is not kept in the rock shelter at Makwar but on a rock slope in Ga'anda Town, which in 1980 was adjacent to the Lutheran Church of Christ, Nigeria (LCCN) mission station (established by the Sudan United Mission, Denmark). See Berns (1986,140–41).

23. Ga'anda healer/diviners recommended a range of special pots be made to cure adult illnesses, including: *'butɔs'inda* (pots for argumentativeness), *pingira* (pots for madness), *wan'depa'ta* (pots for constipation), *ferchataha* (pots for skin rashes), and *'butɔkaraha* (pots for stiff neck). Children's diseases were also treated with ceramic vessels, such as *dikawa* (pots for hair loss), *'butɔmenmandi* (pots for dizziness), and *mo'deta* (pots for eye illness). Such pots are rarely used today, having been superseded by the modern medical care available to the Ga'anda both in local clinics and in large town hospitals. See also Berns (2000, 64–65, 76).

24. The Ga'anda *'bahanda* may be what Meek (1931b, 2: 375) described as a "soul safe" into which a Ga'anda man could transfer his "spirit double": "It is a common practice, therefore, for a young man who has set up a home of his own, to ask a friend to make a pot for him in order that he may deposit his soul in the pot. The young man lies down on the ground and the potter sits beside him shaping the clay into what is supposed to be a likeness of the subject. Ears, eyes, mouth and nose are indicated, and the shoulders and arms are represented by excrescences raised across the body of the pot, which is supposed to represent the heart, i.e. the life. There are no legs. When the pot has been fired, the owner deposits it in some secret place in the bush, generally in a small cave…. If the owner feels ill he goes to his secret pottery symbol, smears it with red oil, takes a wisp of straw and transfers some of the oil to his left and right temple, his left and right shoulder and to the abdomen. This causes his 'soul' or 'heart' as they say, to resume its former vigour."

    Although I was not offered the explanation documented by Meek, I did see several *'bahanda* abandoned in hillside locations where Meek claims "soul pots" were deposited.

25. Vessels with a tripod-spout configuration are common across the Upper Benue Valley where they are used for various healing purposes. One version made by the Cham-Mwana is called *sujang* and was used to cure a chronic cough (see Pearlstone 1973). Among the Kwanta subgroup of the Ga'anda, a judicial spirit named Fingdehata (red spirit presence) was invoked to identify and punish thieves. The spirit was served by its "children," represented by stirrup-spouted vessels, which have pellets worked over their shoulders (see Berns 2000, 55–56, fig. 3). Notably, the guilty are punished by unremitting diarrhea until they confess. To effect a cure the thief has ground red hematite mixed with oil dabbed on his or her forehead, navel, back, and shoulders, in much the same way Meek (1931a) described "soul safes" (see note 24, above).

26. Issues of gender and the production of ceramics are addressed in "Art, History and Gender: Women and Clay in West Africa" (Berns 1993). In recent e-mail exchanges with several young Ga'anda men about the ongoing use and status of spirit pots, I was told by Felix Theman (July 28, 2009) that older women are the ones who build the vessels and that "even the recent one [made as a replacement for a Mbir'thleng'nda that was 'stolen'] was built by an elderly woman" (see introduction, fig. 5).

Chapter 18 (Berns)

1. 'Bɔna is a Northwestern Adamawa language (formerly Adamawa-Eastern) classified in the 'Bɔna-Mboi (=Yungur) group (Kleinewillinghöfer 1996, 82). The 'Bɔna discussed in this section are divided into four subgroups according to geographical location: 'Bɔna (Lala) of Bodwai, 'Bɔna (Lala) of Yang, Roba, and Dingai. The 'Bɔna Yungur are a separate subgroup but are called Yungur here for ease of discussion. Meek (1931b, 2: 434–80) has a chapter on "The Yungur-Speaking Peoples," where he identified subgroups that largely conform to subsequent linguistic divisions but also claimed that most Yungur speakers referred to themselves as "Binna." I should also note that because Meek compressed his discussion of these related groups into one chapter, the clear ethnographic and art historical distinctions between the northern 'Bɔna and the southern Yungur were often lost.

2. This section of chapter 18 focuses primarily on ceramic arts made by the 'Bɔna. For more information on other 'Bɔna arts as well as details of their social organization, see Berns (1986, chap. 7).

3. In my article "Ceramic Clues: Art History in the Gongola Valley" (1989a), I provided a detailed analysis of the historical relationships between the Ga'anda and the 'Bɔna, drawing on their ceramic arts, as well as language, oral traditions, and other categories of visual evidence.

4. Although I documented a woman potter in the 'Bɔna town of Teno making a small cooking pot and leaving the coiling impressions visible on the exterior, the linear patterns on the larger wares seem too dense to have been made with the fingers. It may be that thick cord was impressed into the clay, wrapped around a flexible stick or less likely, that the vessel was wrapped entirely with cord to impress the all-over patterns (Nicolas David and Judy Sterner, personal communication, 2009).

5. In my detailed 1990 analysis, "Pots as People: Yungur Ancestral Portraits," I argue that Yungur ancestor pots, *wiiso*, can be considered portraits largely due to the likenesses that are established between the way Yungur people actually look and the way pots are decorated and due to the fact that with one exception, no two *wiiso* are identical.

6. For a more detailed argument about the nature and extent of Ga'anda and 'Bɔna interactions and their historical implications, see Berns (1989a, 54–56).

References Cited

Abimbola, Wande
2001   "The Bag of Wisdom: Osun and the Origins of Ifa Divination." In *Osun across the Waters: A Yoruba Goddess in Africa and the Americas*, edited by J. Murphy and Mei-Mei Sanford, 141–54. Bloomington: Indiana University Press.

Abiodun, Rowland
1989   "Woman in Yoruba Religious Images." *African Languages and Cultures* 2, no. 1: 1–18.
2001   "Hidden Power: Osun, the Seventeenth Odu." In *Osun across the Waters: A Yoruba Goddess in Africa and the Americas*, edited by J. Murphy and Mei-Mei Sanford, 10–33. Bloomington: Indiana University Press.

Abraham, Roy Clive
1931   "Mba Tsav Secret Society, Tiv." Ethnographic Document 241.
1933   *The Tiv People*. Lagos: Government of Nigeria.
1935   *The Principles of Idoma*. London: Crown Agents for the Colonies.
1940   *The Tiv People*. 2nd ed. London: Crown Agents.
1951   *The Idoma Language*. London: University of London Press.
1967   *The Idoma Language*. 2nd ed. London: University of London Press.

Adamu, Mahdi
1978   *The Hausa Factor in West African History*. Zaria, Nigeria: Ahmadu Bello University Press.

Ade Ajayi, J. F., and S. A. Akintoye
1980   "Yorubaland in the Nineteenth Century." In *Groundwork of Nigerian History*, edited by Obaro Ikime, 280–302. Ibadan, Nigeria: Heinemann.

Adedeji, Joel
1969   "The Alarinjo Theatre: The Study of a Yoruba Theatrical Art from Its Earliest Beginnings to the Present Times." Ph.D. diss., University of Ibadan.

Adefuye, Ade
1982   "The Alago Kingdoms: A Political History." In *Studies in the History of Plateau State*, edited by Elizabeth Isichei, 108–22. London: Macmillan.

Adelberger, Joerg
1992   "The Problem of 'Wurkun': New Evidence for the Clarification of an Enigma in Northern Nigerian Ethnography and Linguistics." *African Languages and Cultures* 5: 1–9.
1994   "Bevölkerungsbewegungen und interethnische Beziehungen im Gebiet der Muri Berge: Eine vorläufige Darstellung." In *Mitteilungen des Sonderforschungsbereichs 268: Burkina Faso und Nordostnigeria*, edited by Herrman Jungraithmayr and Gudrun Miehe, 11–29. Westafrikanische Studien 1. Cologne: Rüdiger Köppe.
1995   "Zum Verhältnis von Sprache, Ethnizität und Kultur in den Muri-Bergen Nordost-Nigerias." In *Sprachkulturelle und historische Forschungen in Afrika. Beiträge zum 11. Afrikanistentag*, edited by Axel Fleisch and Dirk Otten, 13–27. Köln, September 19–21, 1994. Cologne: Rüdiger Köppe.
2009   "Maxims and Mountaineers: The Colonial Subjugation of the Peoples of the Muri Mountains and the Adjacent Regions in Northern Nigeria." *Afrikanistikonline*. <http://www.afrikanistik-online.de/archiv/2009/1910/>.

Adelberger, Joerg, Karsten Brunk, and Ulrich Kleinewillinghöfer
1993   "Natural Environment and Settlement in Chonge District, Eastern Muri Mountains, Northeastern Nigeria: An Interdisciplinary Case Study." In *Proceedings, International Symposium—SFB 268—Frankfurt/Main, 16.12.–19.12.1992*. Berichte des Sonderforschungsbereichs 268: Kulturentwicklung und Sprachgeschichte im Naturraum Westafrikanische Savanne 2: 13–42. Frankfurt: SFB.

Adelberger, Joerg, and Ulrich Kleinewillinghöfer
1992   "The Muri Mountains of North-Eastern Nigeria—An Outline of the Ethnographic and Linguistic Situation." *The Nigerian Field* 57, nos. 1–2: 35–48.
2009   "A Kulung Dictionary." Unpublished manuscript.

Adelberger, Joerg, and Anne Storch
2009   "The Jukun of Kona, the Emir of Muri and the French Adventurer: An Oral Tradition Recounting Louis Mizon's Attack on Kona in 1892." *Afrikanistik Online*. <http://www.afrikanistik-online.de/archiv/2008/1573>.

Afegbua, Isah
2003   *Okpella: Origins, Communities, and Neighbors 1400–2000*. Awuyemi, Okpella, Nigeria: Centre for Development and Documentation (Etsako Affairs Directorate).

Agi, John Ola
1982   "The Goemai and Their Neighbors: An Historical Analysis." In *Studies in the History of Plateau State*, edited by Elizabeth Isichei, 98–107. London: Macmillan.

Aguya, Pius Arege
1985   "The History of the Kulere People from Early Times to Circa 1960." Unpublished manuscript for the Department of History, University of Jos, Nigeria.

Akinwumi, Olayemi
1998   "The Abakwariga and the Economic Transformation of the Jukun Kingdom of Wukari, c. 1650–1900." *Nordic Journal of African Studies* 7, no. 1: 93–102.

Alagoa, E. J.
1980   "The Masquerade in Nigerian History and Culture: Keynote Address." In *The Masquerade in Nigerian History and Culture*, edited by Nwanna Nzewunwa, 268–84. Port Harcourt, Nigeria: University of Port Harcourt.

Allen, W., and T. H. R. Thomson
1848   *A Narrative of the Expedition to the River Niger in 1841*. 2 vols. London: Bentley.

Allison, Philip
1968   *African Stone Sculpture*. London: Humphries.

Ames, Cecil
1934   *Gazetteer of the Plateau Province, Nigeria*, edited by H. Hale Middleton. Jos, Nigeria: N.p.

Anyebe, A. P.
N.d.   "Alekwu in Idoma Religion." Unpublished manuscript.

Appadurai, Arjun, ed.
1986   *The Social Life of Things: Commodities in Cultural Perspective*. Cambridge: Cambridge University Press.
1996   *Modernity at Large: Cultural Dimensions of Globalization*. Public World, vol. 1. Minneapolis: University of Minnesota press.

Armold, J. J.
1929   "The Feast of Ukoo." *The Lightbearer* 25, no. 4: 83–84.

Armstrong, Robert G.
1955   "The Igala" and "The Idoma-Speaking Peoples." In *Peoples of the Niger-Benue Confluence*, edited by Daryll Forde, 77–90, 91–114. Ethnographic Survey of Africa, Western Africa, part 10. London. International African Institute.

Artcurial
2008   Press release. June 10. <http://www.artcurial.com/pdf/presse/2008/r1473_en.pdf>.

Audu, Anidu
1972   Unpublished manuscript.

Babayemi, S. O.
1980a   *Egungun among the Oyo Yoruba*. Ibadan, Nigeria: Board.
1980b   *The Fall and Rise of Oyo, c. 1706–1905: A Study in the Traditional Culture of an African Polity*. Lagos: Lichfield Nigeria.

Baikie, William B.
1856   *Narrative of an Exploring Voyage up the Rivers Kwóra and Bínue (Commonly Known as the Niger and Tsadda) in 1854*. London: J. Murray.

Bala, C. D.
N.d.   "Old Cham Settlements." *Zaria Archaeology Papers*, no. 3 (cyclostyled).

Ballard, J. A.
1971   "Historical Inferences from the Linguistic Geography of the Nigerian Middle Belt." *Africa* 41: 295–96.

Banfield, A. W.
1914   *Dictionary of the Nupe Language*. Shonga, Nigeria: Niger Press.

Barber, Karin
1991   *I Could Speak until Tomorrow: Oriki, Women and the Past in a Yoruba Town*. Washington, D.C.: Smithsonian Institution Press.

Barley, Nigel
1983   *Symbolic Structures: An Exploration of the Culture of the Dowayos*. Cambridge: Cambridge University Press.
1984   "Placing the West African Potter. " In *Earthenware in Asia and Africa,* edited by John Picton, 93–105. London: Percival David Foundation of Chinese Art, University of London School of Oriental and African Studies.
1994   *Smashing Pots: Feats of Clay from Africa*. London: British Museum.
2008   "African Pottery or the Firing of the Imagination." In *African Terra Cottas: A Millenary Heritage in the Barbier-Mueller Museum Collections*, edited by Floriane Morin and B. Wastiau, 18–23. Geneva: Musée Barbier-Mueller.

Barth, Heinrich
[1857–1859] 1965   *Travels and Discoveries in North and Central Africa…1849–1588*. 5 vols. London: F. Cass.

Bascom, William R.
1944   "The Sociological Role of the Yoruba Cult-Group." *Memoirs of the American Anthropological Association* 46 (1, part 2): 1–75.

Bassing, Allen
1973   "Grave Monuments of the Dakakari." *African Arts* 6, no. 4: 36–39.

Bastin, Marie-Louise
1984   *Introduction aux arts d'Afrique noire*. Arnouville-lès-Gonesse: Arts d'Afrique Noire.

Baudrillard, Jean
1983   *Simulations*. New York: Semiotext(e).

Beacham, C. Gordon
1928   *New Frontiers in the Central Sudan*. Toronto: Evangelical Publishers.

Beek, Walter E. A. van
1991   "Dogon Restudied: A Field Evaluation of the Work of Marcel Griaule." *Current Anthropology* 32: 139–67.

Beier, Ulli.
1956   "The Egungun Cult." *Nigeria Magazine* no. 51: 380–92.
1964   "The Agbegijo Masquerades." *Nigeria Magazine* no. 82: 188–99.

Berns, Marla C.
1986   "Art and History in the Lower Gongola Valley, Northeastern Nigeria." Ph.D. diss., University of California, Los Angeles.
1988   "Ga'anda Scarification: A Model for Art and Identity. " In *Marks of Civilization: Artistic Transformation of the Human Body*, edited by Arnold Rubin, 57–76. Los Angeles: Museum of Cultural History, University of California, Los Angeles.
1989a   "Ceramic Clues: Art History in the Gongola Valley." *African Arts* 22, no. 2: 48–59, 102–3.
1989b   "Art, History, and Gender: Who Made the Nok Terracottas?" Paper presented at the Annual Meeting of the African Studies Association, Atlanta.
1990   "Pots as People: Yungur Ancestral Portraits." *African Arts* 23, no. 3: 50–60, 102.
1993   "Art, History, and Gender: Women and Clay in West Africa." *The African Archaeological Review* 11: 133–53.
2000   "Containing Power: Ceramics and Ritual Practice in Northeastern Nigeria." In *Clay and Fire: Pottery in Africa*, edited by Christopher D. Roy, 53–76. Iowa Studies in African Art: The Stanley Conferences at the University of Iowa 4. Iowa City: University of Iowa, School of Art and Art History.
2008a   "Male Figure/Mboi-Yungur and Female Figure/Jukun." In *African Art from the Menil Collection*, edited by Kristina Van Dyke, 146–47. New Haven: Yale University Press.
2008b   "Man." In *African Art from the Menil Collection*, edited by Kristina Van Dyke, 142–43. New Haven: Yale University Press.

Berns, Marla C., and Barbara Rubin Hudson
1986   *The Essential Gourd: Art and History in Northeastern Nigeria*. Museum of Cultural History Monograph Series 28. Los Angeles: Museum of Cultural History, University of California, Los Angeles.

Bickford Berzock, Kathleen
2005   *For Hearth and Altar: African Ceramics from the Keith Achepohl Collection*. Chicago: The Art Institute of Chicago and Yale University Press.

Bivar, A. D. H.
1964   *Nigerian Panoply: Arms and Armour of the Northern Region*. Lagos: Department of Antiquities, Federal Republic of Nigeria.

Bohannan, Laura, and Paul Bohannan
1953   *The Tiv of Central Nigeria*. London: International African Institute.
1956   "Beauty and Scarification amongst the Tiv." *Man* 56, no. 129: 117–121.
1968   *Tiv Economy*. Evanston: Northwestern University Press.

Bohannan, Paul
1954   "The Migration and Expansion of the Tiv." *Africa* 24, no. 1: 2–16.
1954   *Tiv Farm and Settlement*. London: Her Majesty's Stationery Office.
1966   *African Outline: A General Introduction*. Harmondsworth: Penguin.

Borgatti, Jean
1976a   "The Festival as Art Event—Form and Iconography: Olimi Festival in Okpella Clan, Etsako Division, Midwest State, Nigeria." Ph.D. diss., University of California, Los Angeles.
1976b   "Okpella Masking Traditions." *African Arts* 9, no. 4: 24–33.
1976c   "Songs of Ritual License from Midwestern Nigeria." *Alcheringa: Ethnopoetics*, n.s. 2, no. 1: 60–71, record insert, ill.
1979a   "Art and History in West Africa: Two Case Studies." In *The Visual Arts*, edited by J. Cordwell, 567–92. World Anthropology Series. The Hague: Mouton.
1979b   "Dead Mothers of Okpella." *African Arts* 12, no. 4: 48–57.
1979c   *From the Hands of Lawrence Ajanaku*. Museum of Cultural History Pamphlet Series, vol. 1, no. 6. Los Angeles: Museum of Cultural History, University of California, Los Angeles.
1980   "Levels of Reality: Portraiture in African Art." Working Papers, no 36. Boston: African Studies Center.
1982   "Age Grades, Masquerades, and Leadership among the Nothern Edo." *African Arts* 16, no. 1: 36–51.
1989   "Atsu Atsogwa: Art and Morality among the Northern Edo of Okpella, Nigeria." In *Man Does Not Go Naked: Textilien und Handwerk aus afrikanischen und anderen Landern,* edited by Beate Engelbrecht and Bernhard Gardi, 175–95. Basel: Ethnologisches Seminar der Universitat und Museum fur Völkerkunde.
2003   "The Otsa Festival of the Ekperi: Igbo Age-Grade Masquerades on the West Bank of the Niger?" *African Arts* 36, no. 4: 40–57.

Borgatti, Jean, and Richard Brilliant
1990   *Likeness and Beyond: Portraits from Africa and the World*, New York: Center for African Art.

Boston, John S.
1960   "Some Northern Igbo Masquerades." *Journal of the Royal Anthropological Institute* 90: 54–65.
1962   "Notes on the Origin of Igala Kingship." *Journal of the Historical Society of Nigeria* 2: 373–83.
1968   *The Igala Kingdom*. Ibadan, Nigeria: Oxford University Press.
1969   "Oral Tradition and the Igala." *Journal of African History* 10, no. 1: 29–43.
1977   *Ikenga Figures amongst the North-West Igbo and the Igala*. Lagos, Nigeria: Federal Department of Antiquities.

Bovin, Mette
1966   "The Significance of the Sex of the Field Worker for Insights into the Male and Female Worlds." *Ethnos* 31: 24–27.

Boyle, C. V
1915   "The Lala People and Their Customs." *Journal of the African Society* 15, no. 57 (Oct.): 54–69.

Bradbury, R. E.
1957   *The Benin Kingdom and the Edo-Speaking Peoples of South-Western Nigeria*. London: International African Institute.
[1957] 1970   *The Benin Kingdom and the Edo-Speaking Peoples of Southern Nigeria*. London: International African Institute.
1973   *Benin Studies*. London: Oxford University Press.

Bravmann, René
1973   *Open Frontiers: The Mobility of Art in Black Africa*. Seattle: University of Washington Press.
1983   *African Islam*. Washington D.C.: Smithsonian Institution.

Brenson, Michael
1984   "Discovering the Heart of Modernism." *New York Times (October 28)*. <http://www.nytimes.com/1984/10/28/arts/gallery-view-discovering-the-heart-of-modernism.html>.

Brierly, T. G.
1954   "Wurkum District, Report by Mr. T. G. Brierly, A.D.O." Nigerian National Archives, Kaduna, Yola Prof—5640.

Brincard, Marie-Thérèse
1982   *The Art of Metal in Africa*. New York: African-American Institute.

Brooke, N. J.
1922   "Ethnological Report on the Okpoto and Egedde Peoples of Okwoga Division of Munshi Province." Nigerian National Archives, Kaduna, Agency mark K.2012, vol. 1.

Brown, Paula
1970   "The Igbira." In *Peoples of the Niger-Benue Confluence*, edited by Daryll Forde, Paula Brown, and Robert G. Armstrong. Ethnographic Survey of Africa, West Africa. London: International Africa Institute.

Burdo, Adolphe
1880   *Niger et Bénué voyage dans l'Afrique centrale*. Paris: E. Plon.

Byng-Hall, F. F. W.
1908   "Notes on the Bassa Komo Tribe." *Journal of the Royal African Society* 8, no. 29:13–20.

Carroll, Kevin
1966   *Yoruba Religious Carving: Pagan and Christian Sculpture in Nigeria and Dahomey*. New York: Frederick A. Praeger.

Chappel, T. J. H.
1973   "The Death of a Cult in Northern Nigeria." *African Arts* 6, no. 4: 70–74, 96.
1977   *Decorated Gourds in North-Eastern Nigeria*. London: Ethnographica.
1982   "On Twin Figures from West Africa." *African Arts* 15, no. 4: 79.
1997   "Les Verre." In *Arts du Nigéria: Collection du Musée des Arts d'Afrique et d'Océanie, 22 avril-18 août 1997*, edited by Jean Hubert Martin, Etienne Féau, and Hélène Joubert, 223–24. Paris: Réunion des Musées Nationaux.

Chifartawa, Polycarp Ayuba
2009   *Topics in History of Ga'anda*. Vol 1. Yola, Nigeria: Paraclete.

Christie's
1984   Auction Catalogue, June 26.

Clifford, G. M.
1936   "Resident's Summary of Intelligence Report by D. H. F. Macbride, A.D.O." Nigerian National Archives, Kaduna, G2.0 [1935–39].

Cole, Herbert M.
1970   *African Arts of Transformation*. Santa Barbara: Regents of the University of California.
1982   *Mbari: Art and Life among the Owerri Igbo*. Bloomington: Indiana University Press.
1985   *I Am Not Myself: The Art of African Masquerade*. Los Angeles: Museum of Cultural History, University of California, Los Angeles.

Cole, Herbert M., and Chike C. Aniakor
1984   *Igbo Arts: Community and Cosmos*. Los Angeles: Museum of Cultural History, University of California, Los Angeles.

Coppens, Martien
197(?)   *Sculpturen van Noord-oost Nigeria: Bauchi, Waja, Wurkum*. Eindhoven: M. Coppens.

Crédit Communal de Belgique
1977   *Arts premiers d'Afrique noire: Exposition Studio 44 du 5 mars au 17 avril, 1977*. Brussels: Centre Culturel de Crédit Communal de Belgique.

Crowder, Michael
1960   "End of an Empire." *Nigeria* 64 (March): 56–71.

Crowther, Samuel
1855   *Journal of an Expedition up the Niger and Tshadda Rivers Undertaken by MacGregor Laird in Connection with the British Government in 1854*. London: Church Missionary House.
[1855] 1970   *Journal of an Expedition up the Niger and Tshadda Rivers*. 2nd ed. with introduction by J. F. Ade Ajayi. London: Cass.

Crowther, Samuel, and John Christopher Taylor
[1859] 1968   *The Gospel on the Banks of the Niger: Journals and Notices of the Native Missionaries Accompanying the Niger Expedition of 1857–1859*. Reprint of first edition. Colonial History Series. London: Dawsons.

Crozier, D. H., and R. M. Blench
1992   *An Index of Nigerian Languages*. 2nd ed. Ilorin, Nigeria: Abuja, Federal Capital Territory, Language Development Centre, Nigerian Educational Research and Development Council, Department of Linguistics and Nigerian Languages, University of Ilorin.

Cullen, Malachy
1944   "Notes on Mapeo Chambas, Origin, Custom, Juju." Unpublished manuscript. Mission House, Mapeo; subsequently moved to archives in Yola.

David, Nicholas, Judy Sterner, and Kodzo Gavua
1988   "Why Pots Are Decorated." *Current Anthropology* 29, no. 3: 365–89.

Denham, Dixon, Hugh Clapperton, and Walter Oudney
1826   *Narrative of Travels and Discoveries in Northern and Central Africa, 1822, 1823, 1824*. London: John Murray.

Dike, P. Chike
1976   "Igala Kingship: Symbolism and Ritual." Draft of Ph.D. diss., University of Nigeria, Nsukka.
1984   "Some Items of Igala Regalia." *African Arts* 17, no. 2: 70–71, 92.
1985   "Regalia Divinity and State in Igala." *African Arts* 20, no. 3: 75–78.

Dinslage, Sabine, and Anne Storch
2000   *Magic and Gender: A Thesaurus of the Jibe of Kona (Northeastern Nigeria)*. Westafrikanische Studien, Franfurter Beitrage zur Sprach- und Kulturgeschichte 21. Cologne: Rüdiger Köppe.

Dong, Peter Marubitoba, et al.
2000   *The History of the United Methodist Church in Nigeria*. Nashville: Abingdon Press.

Dorward, David
1984   "Ritual Warfare and the Colonial Conquest of the Eggon." *History in Africa* 11: 83–98.
1987   "The Impact of Colonialism on a Nigerian Hill-Farming Society: A Case Study of Innovation Among the Eggon." *International Journal of African Historical Studies* 20, no. 2: 201–24.

Downes, Rupert Major
1933   *The Tiv Tribe*. Kaduna, Nigeria: Government Printer.
1971   *Tiv Religion*. Ibadan, Nigeria: Ibadan University Press.

Drewal, Henry John
1977   *Traditional Art of the Nigerian Peoples: The Milton D. Ratner Family Collection*. Washington, D.C.: Museum of African Art.
1988   "Interpretation, Invention, and Re-presentation in the Worship of Mami Wata." In *Performance in Contemporary African Arts*, edited by R. Stone, 101–39. Bloomington: African Studies Program, Indiana University.
2008   *Mami Wata: Arts for Water Spirits in Africa and Its Disaporas*. Los Angeles: Fowler Museum at UCLA.

Drewal, Margaret Thompson, and Henry John Drewal
1978   More Powerful than Each Other: An Egbado Classification of Egungun. *African Arts* 11, no. 3: 28–39, 99.

Eboreime, J.
1978   "Okpe Title, Ukpi Drum and Traditional Political Authority in Avianwu Clan in Etsako Local Government Area of the Bendel State of Nigeria." Research Report for the Federal Department of Antiquities, Nigeria.

Echeruo, M. J. C.
1977   *Victorian Lagos*. London: Macmillan.

Elisofon, Eliot, and William B. Fagg
1958   *The Sculpture of Africa: 405 Photographs*. New York: Praeger.

Ellis, Stephen
1999   *The Mask of Anarchy: The Destruction of Liberia and the Religious Dimension of an African Civil War*. New York: New York University Press.

Elphinstone, K. V.
1909   "Wurkum Patrol 1909: Report on Wurkum Patrol 1909 by K. V. Elphinstone." Nigerian National Archives, Kaduna, SNP 7—5093/1907.

Erim, Erim O.
1977a   "Leopards, Civet Cats, Birds, and History: The Idoma Case." Paper presented at the Canadian Association of African Studies 7th Conference, Sherbrooke, Quebec.
1977b   "A Pre-Colonial History of the Idoma of Central Nigeria." Ph.D. diss., Dalhousie University.
1981   *The Idoma Nationality, 1600–1900*. Enugu, Nigeria: Fourth Dimension.

Evers, Christophe
2003   *Art of the Upper Benue River*. Brussels: Arsmundi.

Eyo, Ekpo
1977   *Two Thousand Years of Nigerian Art*. Lagos, Nigeria: Federal Department of Antiquities.

Fagg, Bernard
1948   "A Note on the Nok." Nigeria: The National Museum, Lagos.
1977   *Nok Terracottas*. Lagos, Nigeria: Ethnographica for the National Museum.

Fagg, William
1958   *The Sculpture of Africa*. London: Thames and Hudson.
1960   *Nigerian Tribal Art*. London: The Arts Council of Great Britain.
1963a   *Nigerian Images*. New York: Praeger.
1963b   *Merveilles de l'art nigerian*. Paris: Editions du Chène.
1964   Afrique: *Cent tribus—cent chefs d'oeuvres: Musée des Arts Décoratifs, Palais du Louvre-Pavillon de Marsan, 28 octobre–30 novembre*. Paris: Congrès pour la Liberté de la Culture.
1965   *Tribes and Forms in African Art*. New York: Tudor.
1966   "The Niger Basin Tribes." In *African Tribal Sculptures*, vol. 1. New York: Tudor.
1969   *African Sculpture*. Washington, D.C.: International Exhibitions Foundation.
1980   *Masques d'Afrique dans les collections du Musée Barbier-Müller*. Geneva: Editions Fernand Nathan.

Falola, Toyin
2009   *Colonialism and Violence in Nigeria*. Bloomington: Indiana University Press.

Fardon, Richard
1984   "Sisters, Wives, Wards and Daughters: A Transformational Analysis of the Political Organization of the Tiv and Their Neighbours—Part 1: The Tiv." *Africa* 54, no. 4: 2–21, 88.
1988   *Raiders and Refugees*. Washington, D.C.: Smithsonian Institution.
1990   *Between God, the Dead, and the Wild: Chamba Interpretations of Ritual and Religion*. Edinburgh: Edinburgh University Press.
1995   "Introduction: Counterworks." In *Counterworks: Managing the Diversity of Knowledge*, edited by Richard Fardon, 1–22. London: Routledge.
2006   *Lela in Bali: History through Ceremony in Cameroon*. Oxford: Berghahn, Cameroon Studies.
2007   *Fusions—Masquerades and Thought Style East of the Niger-Benue Confluence, West Africa*. London: Saffron.

Fardon, Richard, and Christine Stelzig
2005   *Column to Volume: Formal Innovation in Chamba Statuary*. London: Saffron.

Faust, Arthur J.
1945   "The Religious Conceptions of the Pero People." Ph.D. diss., Hartford Seminary.

Feasey, C. C.
1927   "Tiv (Munshi) Juju." Ethnographic Document 253. British Museum, London.

Fiévet, J. M.
1959   *White Piccaninny: Adventures of a Mother and Child in West Africa* [L'enfant blanc de l'Afrique noir]. Translated by Alan Houghton Brodrick. London: Jarrolds.

Fischer, W. B.
1972   Populations of the Middle East and North Africa: A Geographical Approach. New York: Africana.

Flegel, Eduard
1890   *Vom Niger-Benue: Briefe aus Africa*. Leipzig: W. Friedrich.

Fleming, S. J., and Nicklin, K. W.
1982   "Analysis of Two Bronzes from a Nigerian Asunaja Shrine." *MASCA Journal*. University Museum, University of Pennsylvania, Archaeometallurgy Supplement 2, vol. 2: 53–57.

Forde, Daryll
1951   *The Yoruba-Speaking Peoples of South-Western Nigeria*. London: International African Institute.

Forde, Daryll, Paula Brown, and Robert G. Armstrong
1955   *Peoples of the Niger-Benue Confluence*. London: International African Institute.

Frank, Barbara
1974   "Handwerk und Handelsbeziehungen im Ron-Gebiet (Benue-Plateau-Staat, Nigeria)." *Tribus: Jahrbuch des Linden-Museums* 23: 91–130.
1976   "Initiation, Verdienstfeste und Kultbünde bei den Ron und Kulere (Benue-Plateau Staat, Nigeria)." *Paideuma* 22: 123–50.
1978   "Historical Traditions of the Ron." *African Marburgensia* 11, no. 1: 19–42.
1981   *Die Kulere. Bauern in Mittelnigeria*. Wiesbaden: Franz Steiner.
1983   *Menschenbilder früher Gesellschaften*, edited by Klaus E. Müller, 205–21. Frankfurt: Campus.
1995   "Permitted and Prohibited Wealth: Commodity-Possessing Spirits, Economic Morals, and the Goddess Mami Wata in West Africa." *Ethnology* 34, no. 4: 331–46.
2004   "Gendered Ritual Dualism in a Patrilineal Society: Opposition and Complementarity in Kulere Fertility Cults." *Africa* 74, no 2: 217–40.

Fremantle, John Morton
1922   *Gazetteer of Muri Province*. London.

Frobenius, Leo
1912–1913   *Und Afrika sprach: Wissenschaftlich erweiterte Ausgabe des Berichts über den Verlauf der dritten Reise-Periode der Deutschen Inner-Afrikanischen Forschungs-Expedition in den Jahren 1910 bis 1912*. 3 vols. Berlin: Vita.
1913   *Voice of Africa: Being an Account of Travels of the German Inner African Exploration in the Years 1910–1912*. 2 vols. London: Hutchinson.
1924   *Dämonen des Sudan*. Atlantis—Volksmärchen und Volksdichtungen Afrika, vol. 7. Jena: Eugen Diederichs.
1924   *Aus dem Zentral-Sudan*. Atlantis—Volkserzählungen und Volksdichtungen, vol. 9. Jena: Eugen Diederichs.
1925   *Dichten und Denken im Sudan, Atlantis*, vol. 5. Jena: Eugen Diederichs.
[1925] 1987   *Peuples et sociétés traditionelles du Nord-Cameroun* [Dichten und Denken im Sudan]. Translated by Eldridge Mohammadou. Stuttgart: Franz Steiner.

Fry, Jacqueline
1972   *African Art from Canadian Collections*. Winnepeg: Winnepeg Art Gallery.

Fry, Philip
1970   "Essai sur la statuaire mumuye." *Objets et mondes* 10, no. 1: 3–28.

Gardi, René
1965   "Über den Totenkult bei den Doayo in Nordkamerun. Beobachtungen und Tagebuchnotizen." In *Festschrift Alfred Bühler*, edited by Carl A. Schmitz and Robert Wildhaber, 117–26. Basler Beiträge zur Geographie und Ethnologie, Ethnologische Reihe 2. Basel: Pharos.
1981   *Alantika. Vergessenes Bergland in Nordkamerun. Bericht über zwei Reisen im Abstand von fünfundzwanzig Jahren*. Bern: Eigenverlag.
1995   *Momente des Alltags: Fotodokumente aus Nordkamerun 1950–85 (Tschadsee, Mandara, Alantika)*. Basel: Museum of Ethnology and Swiss Museum of European Folklife.

Gazetteer of Adamawa Province
1936   Nigerian National Archives, Kaduna, Yola Prof K.5/SII.

Geary, Christraud M., and Stéphanie Xatart
2007   *Material Journeys: Collecting African and Oceanic Art, 1945–2000. Selections from the Geneviève McMillan Collection*. Boston: Museum of Fine Arts.

Gilliland, Dean S.
1986   *African Religion Meets Islam: Religious Change in Northern Nigeria*. Lanham: University Press of America.

Gillon, Werner
[1979] 1980   *Collecting African Art*. 2nd ed. New York: Rizzoli International.
1984   *A Short History of African Art*. Harmondsworth: Penguin.

Gore, Charles
2007   *Art, Performance and Ritual in Benin City*. International African Library 37. Edinburgh: Edinburgh University Press.

Green, R. P. H.
1997   *Saint Augustine: On Christian Teaching*. Oxford: Oxford University Press.

Greenberg, Joseph.
1946   *The Influence of Islam on a Sudanese Religion*. New York: J. J. Augustin.

Griaule, Marcel
1965   *Conversations with Ogotemmeli: An Introduction to Dogon Religious Ideas*. London: Oxford University Press.

Grunne, Bernard de
2001   "Une main de maître mumuye de l'est du Nigeria." In Bernard de Grunne, *Masterhands: Afrikaanse beeldhouwers in de kijker*, 83–90. Brussels: BBL Cultuurcentrum.

Guimiot, Philippe, ed.
1975   *Sculptures africaines: Nouveau regard sur un heritage*. Brussels: P. Guimiot.

Guinter, C. W
1924   "A Cutting Dance." *The Lightbearer* 20, no. 6: 101.
1925   "Savage Africa: Extract from a Letter from Rev. C. W. Guinter, Bambur, Nigeria." *The Lightbearer* 21, no.1: 3–4, 7.
1926   "Dark Doings at Bambur: A Wurkum Festival." *The Lightbearer* 22, no. 5: 92–93.

Gunn, Harold D., and F. P. Conant
1960   *Peoples of the Middle Niger Region, Northern Nigeria*. London: International African Institute.
1966   *Peoples of the Plateau Area of Northern Nigeria*. Ethnographic Survey of Africa: Western Africa (part 7). London: International African Institute.

Guralnik, David, ed.
1978   *Webster's New World Dictionary of the American Language*. Prentice Hall.

Habi, Yakubu H.
2006   *The People Called Bassa-Nge*. Zaria, Nigeria: Tamaza.

Hall, John S.
1994   *Religion, Myth, and Magic in Tangale*. Edited by Herrmann Jungraithmayr and Joerg Adelberger. Westafrikanische Studien: Frankfurter Beiträge zur Sprach- und Kulturgeschichte 5. Cologne: Rüdiger Köppe.

Hammandikko, Musa Wawu na, and Marla C. Berns
1980   *History of Ga'anda/Tarihin Ga'anda*. Edited and transcribed by Marla C. Berns. Occasional Paper 21. Los Angeles: African Studies Center, University of Los Angeles.

Hansford, Keir, John Bendor-Samuel, and Ronald Stanford
1976   *An Index of Nigerian Languages*. Studies in Nigerian Languages 5. Accra North, Ghana: Summer Institute of Linguistics.

Hare, John N.
1983   *Itinate and Kwandalowa: Ritual Pottery of the Cham, Mwana, and Longuda Peoples of Nigeria*. Ethnographic Arts and Culture Series 5. London: Ethnographica.

Harley, George W.
1950   "Masks as Agents of Social Control in Northeast Liberia." *Papers of the Peabody Museum of American Archeology and Ethnology* 32, no. 2: 1–43.

Harnischfeger, Johannes
2006   "'Man-Eaters under New Management': Christliche Mission bei den Tangale in Nigeria." *Zeitschrift für Mission* 4: 388–433.

Harter, Pierre
1973   "Les pipes ceremonielles de l'ouest camerounais." *Arts d'Afrique noir* 8: 18–43.

Haughton, T. H.
1912   "Muri Province: Wurkum Pagan District, Assessment Report: Wurkum 'A' and 'B' Districts." Nigerian National Archives, Kaduna, Min. of Local Govt.—4377/1912.

Henderson, Richard N.
1972   *The King in Every Man: Evolutionary Trends in Onitsha Ibo Society and Culture*. New Haven: Yale University Press.

Herold, Erich
1975   "Zur Ikonographie der 'Aku-Onu' Masken (Jukun, Nigeria)." *Abhandlungen und Berichte des Staatlichen Museums für Völkerkunde Dresden* 34: 77–93.

Herreman, Frank
1988   "La masque de bovidé chez les Mumuye (Nord-Est du Nigéria)." In *Anthropologie de l'art: Formes et significations*, vol. 1, edited by Louis Perrois. Paris: Laboratoire d'Archéologie Tropicale et d'Anthropologie Historique, ORSTOM.

Hogben, Sidney J.
1967   *An Introduction to the History of the Islamic States of Northern Nigeria*. Ibadan, Nigeria: Oxford University Press.

Hogben, Sidney J., and Anthony H. M. Kirk-Greene
1966   *The Emirates of Northern Nigeria: A Preliminary Survey of Their Historical Traditions*. London: Oxford University Press.

Husaini, Alhaji Isa
1986   *The History and Culture of the Egbira (Ebira)*. Lokoja, Nigeria: Oowu.

Hutchinson, Thomas J.
1855   *Narrative of the Niger, Tshadda, and Binue Exploration, Including a Report on the Position and Prospects of Trade up Those Rivers, with Remarks on the Malaria and Fevers of Western Africa*. London: Longman, Brown, Green, and Longmans.

Ibrahim, Yakubu A.
2000   *Ebira Tao, Lessons from History (1): The Need for a Strong Central Organization in Ebiraland*. Zaria, Nigeria: Mumanrak.

Idrees, Aliyu Alhaji
1998   *Political Change and Continuity in Nupeland : Decline and Regeneration of Edegi Ruling Dynasty of Nupeland 1805–1945*. Ibadan, Nigeria: Caltop.

Isichei, Elizabeth
1976   *A History of the Ibo People*. New York: St. Martin's Press.
1982   *Studies in the History of Plateau State, Nigeria*. London: Macmillan.
1983   *A History of Nigeria*. London: Longman.

Jaggar, P. L.
1973   "Kano City Blacksmiths: Precolonial Distribution, Structure and Organization." *Savanna* 2, no. 2: 11–26.

J. Camp Associates, Ltd., and Arman
1980   *Fragments of the Sublime, March 18–April 5, 1980*. New York: J. Camp Associates, Ltd.

Jedrej, M. C.
1980   "Structural Aspects of a West African Secret Society." *Ethnologische Zeitschrift Zürich* 1: 133–41.

Jeffreys, M. D. W.
1962   "Traditional Sources prior to 1890 for the Grassfield Bali of Northwestern Cameroons." *Afrika und Ubersee* 46, nos. 1–2: 169–98, 296–313.
1968   "Awka Bronze Bells." *Anthropological Journal of Canada* 6, no. 3: 24–27.

Jegede, Dele
1996   "Nigerian Art as Endangered Species." In *Plundering Africa's Past*, edited by Peter R. Schmidt and Roderick J. McIntosh, 125–42. Bloomington: Indiana University Press.

Jell-Bahlsen, Sabine
1982   *Divine Earth—Divine Water*. Film. New York: Ogbuide Corp.

Jimada, Idris Sha'aba
2005   *The Nupe and the Origins and Evolution of the Yoruba, c. 1275–1897*. Zaria, Nigeria: The Abdullahi Smith Centre for Historical Research.

Johnson, Samuel
1921   *History of the Yoruba: From the Earliest Times to the Beginning of the British Protectorate*. Lagos: C.M.S.

Jones, G. I.
1984   *The Art of Eastern Nigeria*. Cambridge: Cambridge University Press.

J.O.H.L.T.
1981   "Two Early Rains." *Jos Oral History and Literature Texts*. Jos, Nigeria, University of Jos.

Jouve, Marie-Laure, ed.
2008   *Fragments du vivant: Sculptures africaines dans la collection Liliane et Michel Duran-Dessert*. Milan: Five Continents.

Judd, A. S.
1916   "Notes on the Munshi Tribe and Language." *Journal of the African Society* 16 (1916/17): 52–61, 143–48.

Jungraithmayr, Herrmann
1970   *Die Ron-Sprachen: Tschadohamitische Studien in Nordnigerien*. Glückstadt: J. J. Augustin.

Kandert, Josef
1990   "Tradition of Metal-Casting in Eastern Nigeria and West Cameroon between 1840 and 1940." *Annals of the Naprstek Museum* [Prague], no.17: 7–110.

Kasfir, Sidney Littlefield
1979   *The Visual Arts of the Idoma of Central Nigeria*. London: University of London.
1980   "Patronage and Maconde Carvers." *African Arts* 13, no. 3: 67–70, 91–92.
1981   "Afo and Afo-Related Entries." In *For Spirits and Kings: African Art from the Paul and Ruth Tishman Collection*, edited by Susan Mullin Vogel and Jerry L. Thompson, 152–53, 163–64. New York: Metropolitan Museum of Art.
1982   "Anjenu: Sculpture for Idoma Water Spirits." *African Arts* 15, no. 4: 47–51, 91–92.
1984   "One Tribe, One Style? Paradigms in the Historiography of African Art." *History in Africa* 11: 63–93.
1985   "Art in History, History in Art: The Idoma Alekwuafia Masquerade as Historical Evidence." *Working Papers*, no. 103. Boston University, African Studies Center.
1986   "The Mask of Aja." *African Arts* 19, no. 2: 83–84.
1987   "Apprentices and Entrepreneurs: The Workshop and Style Uniformity in Sub-Saharan Africa." In *Iowa Studies in African Art*, edited by Christopher D. Roy, vol. 2. Iowa City: University of Iowa.
1988   "Celebrating Male Aggression: The Idoma Oglinye Masquerade." In *West African Mask and Cultural Systems*. Edited by Sidney Littlefield Kasfir, 85–108. Tervuren, Belgium: Musée Royal de l'Afrique Centrale.
1989   "Remembering Ojiji: Portrait of an Idoma Artist." *African Arts* 22, no. 4: 44–51, 86–87.
1999   *Contemporary African Art*. London: Thames and Hudson.
2000   "Artists' Reputations: Negotiating Power through Distance and Ambiguity." *African Arts* 33, no. 1: 70–77, 96.
2007   *African Art and the Colonial Encounter*. Bloomington: Indiana University Press.

Kasfir, Sidney Littlefield, ed.
1988   *West African Masks and Cultural Systems*. Tervuren; Musée Royal de l'Afrique Centrale.

Kerchache, Jacques
1975   "Les arts premiers de l'est nigérien." *Connaissance des arts* 285: 66–73.

Kerchache, Jacques, J. H. Martin, and A. Nicolas
1997   *African Faces, African Figures: The Arman Collection*. New York: Museum for African Art.

Kerchache, Jacques, Jean-Louis Paudrat, and Lucien Stéphan
[1988] 1993   *Art of Africa*. New York: Harry N. Abrams.
1989   *Die Kunst des schwarzen Afrika*. Freiburg: Herder.

Kirk-Greene, A. H. M.
1957 "Von Uechtritz's Expedition to Adamawa, 1893." *Journal of the Historical Society of Nigeria.* 1, no. 2 (Dec.): 86–98.
1969 *Adamawa Past and Present: An Historical Approach to the Development of a Northern Cameroons Province.* Reprint ed. London: Dawsons; London: Oxford University Press, 1958.
1972 *Gazetteers of the Northern Provinces of Nigeria.* 4 vols. London: Frank Cass.

Kleinewillinghöfer, Ulrich
1991 *Die Sprache der Waja (nyan wiyau).* Europäische Hochschulschriften Reihe 21—Linguistik 108. Frankfurt: P. Lang.
1996 "Die nordwestlichen Adamawa-Sprachen—Eine Übersicht." In *Afrikanische Sprachen zwischen Gestern und Morgen,* edited by Uwe Seibert, 80–103. Frankfurter Afrikanistische Blätter 8. Cologne: Rüdiger Koppe.

Kohnert, Dirk
2007 "On the Articulation of Witchcraft and Modes of Production among the Nupe, Northern Nigeria." In *Hexenglauben im modernen Afrika: Hexen, Hexenverfolgung und magische Vorstellungswelten,* edited by Burghart Schmidt and Rolf Schulte, 64-94. Hamburg: DOBU, Wiss. Verl. Dokumentation

Kopytoff, Igor
1986 "The Cultural Biography of Things: Commoditization as Process." In *The Social Life of Things: Commodities in Cultural Perspective,* edited by Appadurai, Arjun, 64–94. Cambridge: Cambridge University Press.
1987 *The African Frontier: The Reproduction of Traditional African Societies.* Bloomington: Indiana University Press.

Kosebinu, Deji, et al.
2000 "Millennium Egungun Festival in Ota Awori: Special Program Brochure." Ota, Nigeria: Bisrak Communications.

Kotalla, Ralf Laboratory
1987 Certificate of Authentication, Thermoluminescent Analysis of Copper Alloy Female, Haigerloch-Weildorf.

Kramer, Fritz
1993 *The Red Fez: Art and Spirit Possession in Africa.* London: Verso.

Krapf-Askari, E.
1965 "The Social Organisation of the Owe." *African Notes* 2: 9–12.
1966 "Brass Objects from the Owe Yoruba." *Odu* 3: 82–87.

Kren, Alfred
2010 *Out of Africa: An Important Selection of Historic African Ceramics and Textiles from Private Collections in Europe and Texas. Dallas:* Pollock Gallery.

Krieger, Kurt
1965 *Westafrikanische Plastik,* vol 1. Berlin: Veröffentlichungen des Museums für Völkerkunde, Neue Folge 7.
1969 *Westafrikanische Plastik,* vol 2. Berlin: Museum für Völkerkunde.

Krieger, Kurt, and G. Kutscher
1960 *Westafrikanische Masken.* Berlin: Museum für Völkerkunde.

Kuglin, Thekla
1941 "Eku at Bambur." *The Lightbearer* 37, no. 3: 43–44.

Laird, MacGregor, and R. A. K. Oldfield
1837 *Narrative of an Expedition into the Interior of Africa, by the River Niger, in the Steam-Vessels Quorra and Alburkah, in 1832, 1833, and 1834.* London: Richard Bentley.

Lander, Richard
[1832] 1837 *Journal of an Expedition to Explore the Course and Termination of the Niger.* 2 vols. New York: Harper and Brothers.

Lane, Michael G. M.
1959 "The Aku-Ahwa and Aku-Maga Post-Burial Rites of the Jukun Peoples of Northern Nigeria." *African Music Society Journal* 2: 29–32.

Last, Murray
1967 *The Sokoto Caliphate.* London: Longmans.

Laudarji, Isaac Babandudu
1994 "Ritual as Quest for Well-Being in the Religious Universe of the Tangale People of Nigeria." Ph.D. diss., Northwestern University.

Law, Robin.
1995 "'Legitimate' Trade and Gender Relations in Yorubaland and Dahomey." In *From Slave Trade to "Legitimate" Commerce: The Commercial Transition in Nineteenth-Century West Africa,* edited by Robin Law, 195–214. Cambridge: Cambridge University Press.

Le Soir
1973 "Au coeur d'un monde inconnu…dans une maison de Wezembeek." *Le Soir* (March 1).

Leith-Ross, Sylvia
1970 *Nigerian Pottery.* Ibadan, Nigeria: Ibadan University Press for the Department of Antiquities.

Leuzinger, Elsy
1960 *Africa: The Art of the Negro Peoples.* New York: McGraw-Hill.
1966 "Die Schnitzkunst im Leben der Afo von Nord-Nigeria." *Geographica Helvetica* 21, no. 4: 152–61.
1971 *Afrikanische Kunstwerke, Kulturen am Niger: Handbuch zur Ausstellung.* Recklinghausen: Bongers.
1972 *Die Kunst von Schwarz-Afrika.* Recklinghausen: Bongers.
[1972] 1976 *Die Kunst von Schwarz-Afrika.* Recklinghausen: Bongers.
1977 *The Art of Black Africa.* Translated by R. A. Wilson. London: Studio Vista.

Lewis, M. Paul, ed.
2009 "Ivbie North-Okpela-Arhe—A Subdialect." In *Ethnologue: Languages of the World.* 16th ed. Dallas: SIL International. Online version. <http://www.ethnologue.com>. Accessed October 3, 2009.

Lilley, E. S.
1921 "Historical and Ethnographical Notes on the Chamba People of Dakka." Nigerian National Archives, Kaduna, J8 The Chamba: Collected Historical and Anthropological Papers: 1921–38.
1922 Ethnological Document No 226. London: British Museum. (Part copy: sections 52 to end of Lilley 1921).

Loran, Erle, T. K. Seligman, J. P. Dwyer, and E. B. Dwyer
1974 *African and Ancient Mexican Art: The Loran Collection.* San Francisco: M. H. de Young Memorial Museum.

Lorenz, Carol Ann
1995 "Ishan Sculpture: Nigerian Art at a Crossroads of Culture." Ph.D. Diss., Columbia University.

Loudmer, Guy
1988 *Arts primitifs.* Paris-Drouot, December 7, lot 86.
1991 *Arts primitifs.* Paris-Drouot, June 30, lot 170.

MacBride, D. H. F.
1936 "Intelligence Report." Nigerian National Archives, Kaduna, G2.0 [1935–39].

MacLeod, Olive
1912 *Chiefs and Cities of Central Africa: Across Lake Chad by Way of the British, French, and German Territories.* Edinburgh: William Blackwood and Sons.

Macleod, T. M.
1925 "Report on the Western Areas of Okwoga." Nigerian National Archives, Kaduna.

Magid, Alvin
1976 *Men in the Middle: Leadership and Role Conflict in a Nigerian Society.* Manchester: Manchester University Press.

Malcolm, L. W. G.
1921 "A Note on Brass-Casting in the Central Cameroon." *Man* 32, no. 1: 1–4.

Martin, Jean Hubert, Etienne Féau, and Hélène Joubert, eds.
1997 *Arts du Nigéria: Collection du Musée des Arts d'Afrique et d'Océanie: 22 avril-18 août.* Paris: Réunion des Musées Nationaux.

Mason, M.
1970a "The Jihad in the South: An Outline of the Nineteenth-Century Nupe Hegemony in North-Eastern Yorubaland and Afenmai." *Journal of the Historical Society of Nigeria* 2: 193–209.
1970b "The Nupe Kingdom in the Nineteenth Century: a Political History." Ph.D. diss., University of Birmingham.
1981 *The Foundations of the Bida Kingdom.* Zaria, Nigeria: Ahmadu Bello University Press.

Maxwell, John Lowry
1953 *Half a Century of Grace: A Jubilee History of the Sudan United Mission.* London.
1981 *The Foundations of the Bida kingdom.* Zaria, Nigeria: Ahmadu Bello University Press.

McBride, Ira E.
1927 "Incidents and Customs of the Kulung of Wurkum District, Adamawa Province, Nigeria, by Ira E. Mc Bride. " International African Institute Archive, London, Cons. 2 Box 2(4).

McIntosh, Roderick J.
1989 "Middle Niger Terracottas before the Symplegades Gateway." *African Arts* 22, no. 2: 74–83.

McNaughton, Patrick R.
1991 "Is There History in Horizontal Masks? A Preliminary Response to the Dilemma of Form." *African Arts* 24, no. 2: 40–53, 88–90.

Shaw, Thurstan
1968 "Radiocarbon Dates." *West African Archaeological Newsletter* 9: 73.
1978 *Nigeria: Its Archaeology and Early History*. London: Thames and Hudson.

Shields, Francine
1997 *Palm Oil and Power: Women in an Era of Economic and Social Transition in Nineteenth Century Yorubaland* (South-western Nigeria). Stirling: University of Stirling.

Shimizu, Kiyoshi
1971 "Comparative Jukunoid: An Introductory Survey." Ph.D. diss., University of Ibadan.
1983 *The Zong Dialect of Mumuye: A Descriptive Grammar; with a Mumuye-English and an English-Mumuye Index*. Hamburg: Helmut Buske.

Sieber, Roy
1961 *Sculpture of Northern Nigeria*. New York: Museum of Primitive Art.
1974 "Figure Carvings Used in Healing Contexts among the Goemai and Montol of Northern Nigeria." Paper presented at the symposium "The Role of Three-Dimensional Art Forms in West African Healing Systems," American Anthropological Association annual meeting, Mexico City, November 19–24.

Sieber, Roy, and Barry Hecht
2002 "Eastern Nigerian art from the Toby and Barry Hecht Collection," *African Arts* 35, no. 1: 56–77, 95–96.

Sieber, Roy, and Tony Vevers
1974 *Interaction: The Art Styles of the Benue River Valley and East Nigeria*. Lafayette: Purdue University.

Sieber, Roy, and Roslyn Adele Walker
1987 *African Art in the Cycle of Life*. Washington, D.C.: Smithsonian Institution.

Siroto, Leon
1976 *African Spirit Images and Identities*. New York: Pace Primitive and Ancient Art.
N.d. Unpublished manuscript. Fort Worth, Texas: Menil Collection.

Slye, Jonathan
1969 "Pagan Ju-Ju Ceramics in the Northern States." *Nigeria Magazine* (Sept.-Nov.), no. 102: 496–515.
1977 "Mwona Figurines." *African Arts* 10, no. 4: 23.

Smith, John
1968 *Colonial Cadet in Nigeria*. Durham: Duke University Press.

Smith, Marian W.
1961 *The Artist in Tribal Society: Proceedings of a Symposium Held at the Royal Anthropological Institute*. New York: Free Press of Glencoe.

Sotheby's
1991 *The Kuhn Collection of African Art*. November 20, lot 37.
2010 *A New York Collection*. Paris, November 30.

Spottiswode, H.
1941 "Ososo Intelligence Report" (KD 656). Nigerian National Archives, Ibadan.

Starkweather, Frank
1968 *Traditional Igbo Art: 1966, an Exhibition of Wood Sculpture Carved in 1965–66*. Ann Arbor: University of Michigan Museum of Art.

Stelzig, Christine
2009 "Art of the Mumuye." In *Visual Encounters: Africa, Oceania, and Modern Art,* edited by Oliver Wick and Antje Denner, section 8, 1–13. Basel, Switzerland: Fondation Beyeler.

Sterner, Judy
1992 "Sacred Pots and 'Symbolic Reservoirs' in the Mandara Highlands of Northern Cameroon." In *An African Commitment: Papers in Honour of Peter Lewis Shinnie*, edited by Judy Sterner and Nicholas David, 172–79. Calgary: University of Calgary Press.

Stevens, Phillips, Jr.
1966 "Nupe Woodcarving." *Nigeria Magazine* 88: 21–35.
1973 "The Nupe *Elo* Masquerade." *African Arts* 6, no. 4: 40–43.
1976 "The Danubi Ancestral Shrine." *African Arts* 10, no 1: 30–37, 98.
1977 "A Propos: The Danubi Ancestral Shrine," *African Arts* 10, no. 2: 90.

Strybol, Jan
1998 *Peuplement, habitat et structures agraires au sud de la Bénoué: Le cas du pays mumuye*. Paris: Peeters.

Sweeney, James Johnson
1935 *African Negro Art*. New York: The Museum of Modern Art.

Sydow, Eckart von
1954 *Afrikanische Plastik*, edited by Gerdt Kutscher. Berlin: Gebr Mann.

Talbot, P. Amaury
1926 *Peoples of Southern Nigeria*. 4 vols. London: Oxford University Press.

Tamuno, T. N.
1965 "Peoples of the Niger-Benue Confluence." *A Thousand Years of West African History*, edited by J. F. Ade Ajayi and Ian Espie, 201–11. Ibadan, Nigeria: University Press.

Teilhet, Jehann
1977–1978 "The Equivocal Role of Women Artists in Non-Literate Cultures." *Heresies* 1, no. 4 (winter): 96–102.

Temple, Charles, and Olive Temple
1919 *Notes on the Tribes, Provinces, Emirates, and States of the Northern Provinces of Nigeria*. Cape Town: Argus Printing.
[1919] 1922 *Notes on the Tribes, Provinces, Emirates and States of the Northern Provinces of Nigeria*. 2nd ed. Lagos: C.M.S. Bookshop.
[1919] 1965 *Notes on the Tribes, Provinces, Emirates and States of the Northern Provinces of Nigeria*. 3rd ed. Lagos: London: Frank Cass.

Thompson, Robert Farris.
1974 *African Art in Motion: Icon and Act in the Collection of Katharine Coryton White*. Los Angeles: University of California, Los Angeles.

Thompson, Jerry L., and Susan Vogel
1990 *Closeup: Lessons in the Art of Seeing African Sculpture from an American Collection and the Horstmann Collection*. New York: The Center for African Arts.

Tremearne, A. J. N.
1912 *The Tailed Head-Hunters of Nigeria*. London: Seeley.
1914 *The Ban of the Bori: Demons and Demon-Dancing in West and North Africa*. London: Heath, Cranton and Ouseley Ltd.

Trowell, Margaret
1954 *African Classical Sculpture*. London: Faber and Faber.
1964 *African Classical Sculpture*. 2nd ed. London: Faber and Faber.
1970 *African Classical Sculpture*. 3rd ed. London: Faber.

Tschudi, Jolantha
1956 *Les peintures ruepestres du Tassili-n-Ajjer*. Neuchatel: La Baconnière.
1970 "The Social Life of the Afo, Hill Country of Nasarawa, Nigeria." *African Notes* 6, no. 1: 87–99.

Ukpabi, S. C.
1971 "Nsukka before the Establishment of the British Administration." *Journal of Yoruba and Related Studies* 6: 101–10.

Underwood, Leon
1947 *Figures in Wood of West Africa*. London: Tiranti.
1964 *Figures in Wood of West Africa*. London: Tiranti.

Unomah, A. Chukwudi
1982a "The Gwandara Settlements of Lafia to 1900." *Studies in the History of Plateau State*, edited by Elizabeth Isichei, 123–35. London: Macmillan.
1982b "The Lowlands Salt Industry." *Studies in the History of Plateau State*, edited by Elizabeth Isichei, 151–78. London: Macmillan.

Van Dyke, Kristina
2008 "Anthropomorphic and Zoomorphic Sculptures." In *African Art from the Menil Collection*, edited by Kristina Van Dyke, 140–41. Houston: Menil Foundation.

Van Dyke, Kristina, ed.
2008 *African Art from the Menil Collection*. New Haven: Yale University Press.

Vansina, Jan
1965 *Oral Tradition: A Study in Historical Methodology*. London: Routledge and Keegan Paul.
1984 *Art History in Africa*. London: Longman.
1985 *Oral Tradition as History*. London: James Currey.

Verger, Pierre
1965 "Grandeur et décadence du culte de Iyami Osoronga: Ma mère la sorcière chez les Yoruba." *Journal de la Société des Africanistes* 35 no. 1: 201–19.

Vogel, Susan, and Jerry L. Thompson
1981 For Spirits and Kings: African Art from the Paul and Ruth Tishman Collection. New York: Metropolitan Museum of Art.

von Sydow, Eckart
1954 *Afrikanische Plastik*. Berlin: Gebr. Mann.

Walker, J. C.
1915   "Assessment Report on Kukuruku Dst., Kabba Division, Ilorin Province" (cso 26/03100). Nigerian National Archives, Ibadan.

Walter, V. E.
1928   "The Pero Dumbung." *The Lightbearer* 24, no. 5: 98–100.

Watson, Ruth
2003   *Civil Disorder Is the Disease of Ibadan.* Oxford: James Currey.

Webster, J. B.
1975   "Chiefs and Chronology: Jukun Colonies in the Benue Valley." Paper presented at the African Studies Conference, York University, Toronto, Ontario, February 17–19.

Weise, Constanze
2003   "Kingship and the Mediators of the Past: Oral Traditions and Ritual in Nupeland, Nigeria." In *Sources and Methods in African History: Spoken, Written, Unearthed*, edited by Toyin Falola and Christian Jennings, 268–94. Rochester: University of Rochester Press.

Wente-Lukas, Renate
1977   *Die materielle Kultur der nicht-islamischen Ethnien von Nordkamerun und Nordostnigeria.* Studien zur Kulturkunde 43. Wiesbaden: F. Steiner.

Weston, Bonnie E.
1984   "Northeastern Region." In *Igbo Arts: Community and Cosmos,* edited by Herbert M. Cole and Chike C. Aniakor, 145–62. Los Angeles: Museum of Cultural History, University of California, Los Angeles.

Westerdijk, Peter
1988   "The African Throwing Knife: A Style Analysis." Ph.D. diss., University of Utrecht.

Whitford, John
[1877] 1967   *Trading Life in Western and Central Africa.* 2nd ed., facsimile reprint. New York: Barnes and Noble.

C. L. Whitman
N.d.   *Christ or the Fetishes: The Story of Christian Work among the Jukun of Northern Nigeria.* London: SUM.

Wick, Oliver, and Antje Denner, eds.
2009   *Visual Encounters: Africa, Oceania, and Modern Art.* Basel: Beyeler Museum.

Wilkinson, H.
1923   "Notes on the Yungur Tribe." Nigerian National Archives, Kaduna, J.17 [1912–1928: 17–38].

Willett, Frank
[1971] 2002   *African Art.* New ed. London: Thames and Hudson.

Wilson-Haffenden, James Rhodes
1927   "Ethnological Notes on the Kwottos of Toto (Panda) District, Keffi Division Benue Province, Northern Nigeria." *Journal of the Royal African Society* 26 (part 1), no. 104: 368–79; 27 (part 2), no. 106: 24–46.
1930   *The Red Men of Nigeria: An Account of a Lengthy Residence among the Fulani, or "Red Men," and Other Pagan Tribes of Central Nigeria, with a Description of their Headhunting, Pastoral, and Other Customs, Habits, and Religion.* London: Seeley.

Wittmer, Marcilene K., and William Arnett
1978   *Three Rivers of Nigeria.* Atlanta: High Museum of Art.

Woodhouse, C. A.
1924   "Some Account of the Inhabitants of the Waja District of Bauchi Province, Nigeria." *Journal of the African Society* 23, no. 1: 110–21; no. 2: 194–207.

Yakubu, A. M.
1992   "Violence and the Acquisition of Slaves in the Bauchi Emirate, 1805–1900." In *Warfare and Diplomacy in Precolonial Nigeria: Essays in Honor of Robert Smith*, edited by Toyin Falola and Robin Law, 145–56. Madison: University of Wisconsin-Madison.

Index

Contributors

Joerg Adelberger, an independent scholar, has carried out extensive field research among the peoples of the Muri Mountains in the Middle Benue region. In addition to his focus on the culture, oral history, and art of these groups, he has done considerable linguistic research. Adelberger has published his findings in numerous scholarly journals and is co-author with John S. Hall and Herrmann Jungraithmayr of *Religion, Myth, and Magic in Tangale* (1994).

Gassia Armenian holds the position of Curatorial and Research Associate at the Fowler Museum at UCLA. As such, she plays a prominent role in collections research and in the planning and organization of museum exhibitions. She has also been involved in the preparation and translation of manuscripts, as well as photographic research and permissions gathering, for many Fowler Museum publications.

Marla C. Berns has primarily concentrated her research on the arts of northeastern Nigeria, where she conducted fieldwork in the early 1980s. She has given specific attention to ceramic sculpture and other women's arts. Her publications, all accompanying exhibitions, include: *The Essential Gourd: Art and History in Northeastern Nigeria* (1986); *"Dear Robert, I'll See you at the Crossroads": A Project by Renée Stout* (1995); *Ceramic Gestures: New Vessels by Magdalene Odundo* (1995); and *Paul Tuttle Designs* (2001). Since 2001, Berns has held the position of Shirley & Ralph Shapiro Director at the Fowler Museum at UCLA.

Jean Borgatti has dedicated much of her research to African masquerades and photo and film documentation of Nigerian masquerade performances involving textiles. She has curated and co-curated related exhibitions and has published numerous essays and articles. Borgatti is the author with Richard Brilliant of *Likeness and Beyond: Portraits from Africa and the World* (1990). She has held the position of visiting professor at institutions in the United States and Africa.

John Boston (1930–2001) conducted field research in Igalaland under the auspices of the Nigerian Institute of Social and Economic Research, eventually becoming the acknowledged expert on the Igala peoples. His book *The Igala Kingdom* (1968) remains an important resource. He was a professor of anthropology at the University of Hull in the United Kingdom.

Mette Bovin carried out her field research in Mumuyeland in 1964 and 1968. She has long been intrigued with the correlation of the agricultural practices of various ethnic groups to their social values. Her essays have appeared in numerous scholarly journals and exhibition catalogs. Most recently, she has worked among nomadic peoples in West Africa as reflected by her book *Nomads Who Cultivate Beauty: Wodaabe Dances and Visual Arts in Niger* (2001).

Richard Fardon is Professor of West African Anthropology at the School of Oriental and African Studies, University of London. He has undertaken research in and about Nigeria and Cameroon since the mid-1970s. He is the author or editor of numerous books on anthropological theory, as well as on the Chamba peoples and their neighbors: *Raiders and Refugees: Trends in Chamba Political Development, 1750–1950* (1988); *Between God, the Dead and the Wild: Chamba Interpretations of Religions and Ritual* (1990); *Column to Volume: Formal Innovation in Chamba Statuary* (with Christine Stelzig, 2005); *Lela in Bali: History through Ceremony in Cameroon* (2006); and *Fusions: Masquerades and Thought-Style East of the Niger-Benue Confluence, West Africa* (2007).

Barbara Frank (1936–2004) was a leading scholar of the Kulere peoples of the Nigerian Middle Belt, performing fieldwork in the 1970s and 1980s. Her publications include *Die Kulere: Bauern in Mittelnigeria* (1981) and *Die Andere Moderne Afrikas: Kunst aus den Sammlungen des Linden-Museums Stuttgart* (with Hermann Forkl, 2004). She was a professor at the Ludwig-Maximilians-Universität München, Institut für Völkerkunde und Afrikanistik.

Susan Elizabeth Gagliardi is an assistant professor of art history in the Art Department of The City College of The City University of New York. In 2010 she completed her dissertation on the arts and patronage of power associations in western Burkina Faso, based on nearly twenty months of field research. Gagliardi also spent fifteen months in Ghana, conducting research in Birifor- and Lobi-speaking communities. She has published essays on arts from Ghana, Burkina Faso, Côte d'Ivoire, and Mali.

Hélène Joubert is the Curator for African Collections at the Musée du quai Branly, Paris. Her research focuses upon African textile weaving and dyeing, as well as the history of private and museum collections in Africa, Europe, and the United States. She has contributed to numerous museum catalogs, and over the past five years, she has worked on a number of documentary film projects, including *Les ibeji Yoruba* (2007) and *Osun Osogbo, la forêt et l'art sacré des Yoruba* (2008).

Sidney Littlefield Kasfir is a recognized expert on the visual arts of the Idoma peoples. While continuing to focus on Idoma arts throughout her career, she has also written more widely about Africa. Her publications include *West African Masks and Cultural Systems* (editor and contributor, 1988), *Contemporary African Art* (2000), and *African Art and the Colonial Encounter: Inventing a Global Community* (2007). Kasfir was the Faculty Curator of African art at the Michael C. Carlos Museum in Atlanta from 1998 to 2006 and since that time has held the position of Professor of African Art History at Emory University, where she has taught since 1989.

Nancy Neaher Maas is an independent scholar and artist who taught at the university level for many years. She carried out her fieldwork in West Africa specializing in metal arts and local metallurgical workshops, particularly along the Benue River Valley. This culminated in her dissertation on "Bronzes of Southern Nigeria and Igbo Metalsmithing Traditions." She has published her research in a number of scholarly essays.

John Picton is Emeritus Professor of African Art at the School of Oriental and African Studies, University of London. He taught there from 1979 to 2003, having previously worked for the British Museum, 1970–1979, and the Nigerian government's Department of Antiquities (now the National Commission for Museums and Monuments), 1961–1970. His many publications include the seminal study *African Textiles: Looms, Weaving, and Design* (with John Mack, 1979).

Susan Picton served as an ethnographer for the Nigerian Museum Service in the 1960s, where she assumed the multiple roles of curator, educator, and field researcher. Her field research permitted her to spend time in the Dekina region of Nigeria, where she had the unique opportunity to meet the artist Umale, whose work she photographed and documented in the field.

Arnold Rubin (1937–1988) carried out field research in the Benue Valley from 1964 to 1966 and from 1969 to 1971. He made two additional trips to the region in the 1980s. A fuller description of his research in the Benue River Valley—primarily on the Jukun peoples—will be found in the preface to this volume. Rubin pursued a variety of scholarly interests during his tragically short career. His publications include *African Accumulative Sculpture* (1974); *Marks of Civilization: Artistic Transformations of the Human Body* (1988); and *Art as Technology: The Arts of Africa, Oceania, Native America, Southern California* (with Zena Pearlstone, 1989).

Constanze Weise, a doctoral candidate in the Department of History at UCLA, is currently completing her dissertation "Ritual Sovereignty and Governance in the Niger-Benue Confluence: A Political, Social, and Cultural history of the Nupe, Igala, and Northern Yoruba People in Central Nigeria," based on nearly eighteen months of field research in the region. She has published essays on the history and arts of the Nupe.

John C. Willis is an assistant professor of African history at Carleton College in Northfield, Minnesota. In 2008, he completed his dissertation on the history and politics of masquerades in the Yoruba town of Otta, Nigeria, based on nineteen months of field research. His current research challenges some of the prevailing assumptions about the relationship between women and masquerades in West Africa.

Fowler Museum at UCLA

Marla C. Berns, *Shirley & Ralph Shapiro Director*
David Blair, *Deputy Director*

Stacey Ravel Abarbanel, *Director of External Affairs*
Patricia Rieff Anawalt, *Director, Center for the Study of Regional Dress*
Gassia Armenian, *Curatorial and Research Associate*
Manuel Baltodano, *Operations Supervisor/Technical Coodinator*
Sam Bartels, *Technical Support Consultant*
Danny Brauer, *Director of Publications*
Sebastian M. Clough, *Director of Exhibitions*
Don Cole, *Museum Photographer*
Christian de Brer, *Assistant Conservator*
Pablo Dominguez, *Financial Services Coordinator*
Bridget DuLong, *Events Manager*
Luis Figueroa, *Weekend Operations Supervisor*
Susan Gordon, *Director of Development*
Gina Hall, *Manager of School and Family Services*
Roy W. Hamilton, *Senior Curator/Curator of Asian and Pacific Collections*
Jo Q. Hill, *Director of Conservation*
Isabella Kelly-Ramirez, *Collections Manager*
Lynne Kostman, *Managing Editor*
Stella Krieger, *Store Manager*
Lori LaVelle, *Membership Coordinator*
Jennifer Leitch, *Development Coordinator*
Sophia Livsey, *Executive Assistant*
Ben Mitchell, *Exhibitions Production Supervisor*
Sheryl Nakano, *Project Registrar*
Patrick A. Polk, *Curator of Latin American and Caribbean Popular Arts*
Bonnie Poon, *Manager of Public Programs*
Betsy D. Quick, *Director of Education and Curatorial Affairs*
Rachel Raynor, *Director of Registration and Collections Management*
Gemma Rodrigues, *Curator of African Arts*
Roberto Salazar, *Human Resources Coordinator*
Barbara Belle Sloan, *Associate Director, Center for the Study of Regional Dress*
Agnes Stauber, *Digital Media Analyst*
Wendy Teeter, *Curator of Archaeology*
Emry Thomas, *Facilities Supervisor*

CENTRAL NIGERIA UNMASKED: ARTS OF THE BENUE RIVER VALLEY

Lynne Kostman, *Managing Editor*
Danny Brauer, *Designer and Production Manager*
Don Cole, *Photographer*
Gassia Armenian and Sophia Livsey, *Editorial Assistants*
Jenna Kush, Joe Bodwin, Scott Kepford, *Cartographers*

Printed in Hong Kong by Great Wall Printing Company, Limited.

COVER: See fig. 10.19, p. 326.
PAGE 1: See fig. See fig. 8.60a, p. 280.
PAGE 3: See fig. 5.1, p. 164.
PAGE 5: Arnold Rubin points toward the Benue River.
PHOTOGRAPH BY ZENA PEARLSTONE, 1987.
PAGES 34-35: See fig. 2.28, p. 66.
PAGES 212-13: See fig. 9.20, p. 308.
PAGES 462-63: See fig. 16.31, p. 494.
PAGE 560: See fig. 9.9, p. 299.
PAGE 608: See fig. F.8, p. 359.

Library of Congress Cataloging-in-Publication Data

Central Nigeria unmasked : arts of the Benue River valley / edited by
Marla C. Berns, Richard Fardon, and Sidney Littlefield Kasfir ; with
contributions by Joerg Adelberger ... [et al.].
   p. cm.
"... accompanies an exhibition that opened at the Fowler Museum in
February 2011 and will travel to venues in Washington, D.C., Stanford,
and Paris"--Preface.
   Includes bibliographical references.
   ISBN 978-0-9778344-5-7 (soft cover) — ISBN 978-0-9778344-6-4 (hard
cover)
1. Art, Nigerian--Benue River Valley (Cameroon and Nigeria)—Exhibitions. 2. Art, Nigerian--Nigeria, Northern—Exhibitions. 3. Masks--Be-
nue River Valley (Cameroon and Nigeria)—Exhibitions. 4. Benue River
Valley (Cameroon and Nigeria)—Social life and customs—Exhibitions.
I. Berns, Marla. II. Fardon, Richard. III. Kasfir, Sidney Littlefield. IV.
Adelberger, Joerg. V. Fowler Museum at UCLA.
   N7399.N52B4758 2011
   709.6695--dc22

2011017579

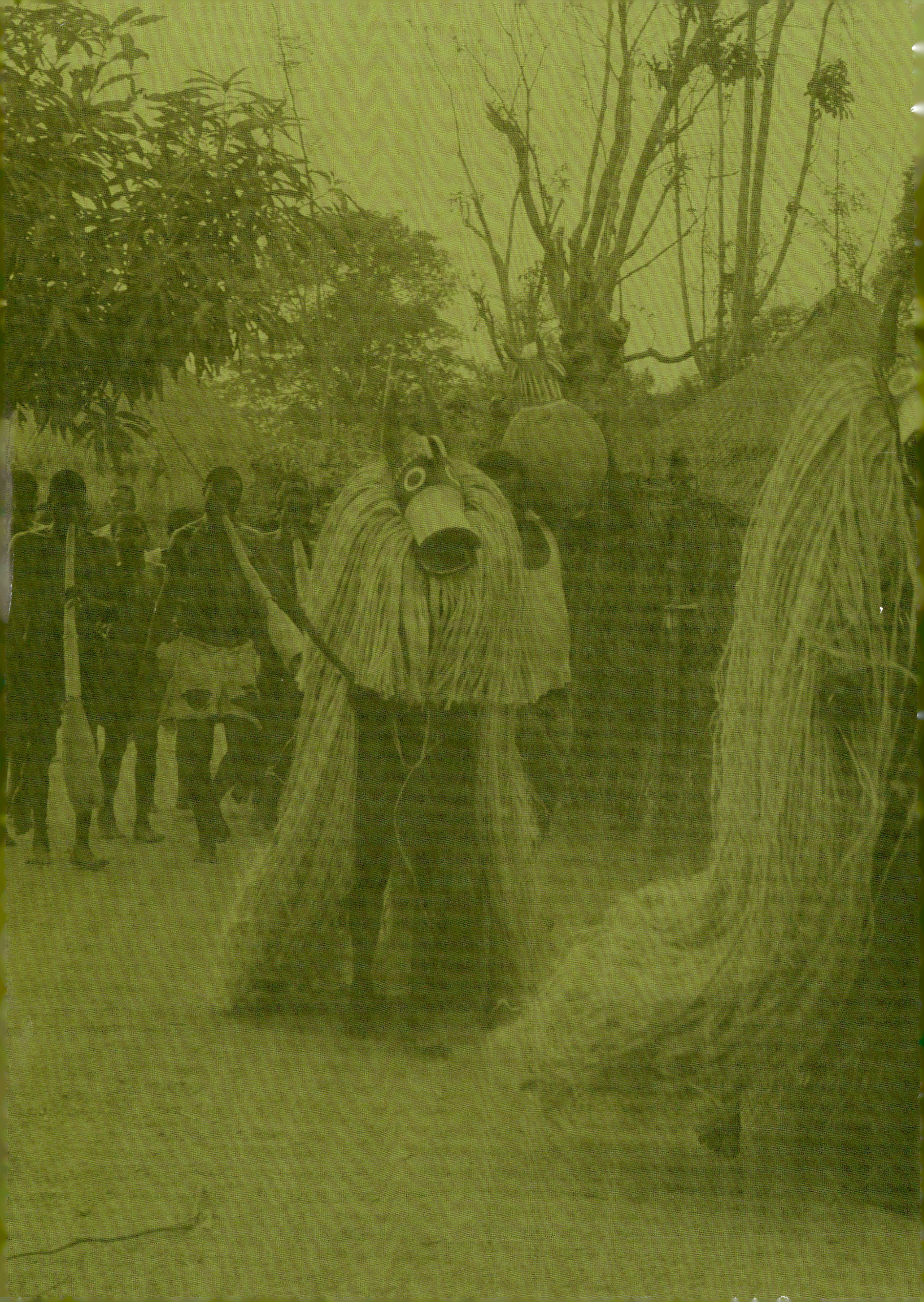